Business Law
PRINCIPLES AND CASES

Business Law
PRINCIPLES AND CASES

HAROLD F. LUSK, S.J.D.
Indiana University Foundation

CHARLES M. HEWITT, J.D., D.B.A.
Visiting Distinguished Professor
The University of Georgia

JOHN D. DONNELL, J.D., D.B.A.
Indiana University

A. JAMES BARNES, J.D.

1974   Third U.C.C. Edition

RICHARD D. IRWIN, INC.   Homewood, Illinois   60430
IRWIN-DORSEY INTERNATIONAL   London, England   WC2H 9NJ
IRWIN-DORSEY LIMITED   Georgetown, Ontario   L7G 4B3

Third U.C.C. Edition

First Printing, May 1974

Second Printing, September 1974

ISBN 0-256-01577-5
Library of Congress Catalog Card No. 74–75087

Printed in the United States of America

Preface

The authors have in this edition sought to preserve the basic strengths of a textbook which have given it increasing sales through 10 editions. We have at the same time considerably broadened its scope. We believe, on the basis of our own research[1] and our knowledge of the concerns of people in business, that familiarity with the antitrust laws, the Federal Trade Commission Act and the securities laws are as important to the business man or business woman as knowledge of the law of contracts or Article 2 of the Uniform Commercial Code. It is, in our opinion, a mistake to argue whether it is better to concentrate on government regulation of business or on the legal topics traditionally viewed as commercial law. A business manager, whether the business be large or small, needs some knowledge of both, as well as some understanding of tort law to be aware of important risks, and perhaps some of the opportunities, facing his business operations.

So in this edition we have not only again expanded our treatment of torts but also have added a chapter dealing with some of the constitutional issues underlying government regulation of business and a chapter on regulation of business through the security laws. We have also added a chapter on the law dealing with environmental problems. This promises to be an area of growing concern to businessmen as pollution problems and shortages in energy compound the complexity of the vital policy decisions which ultimately must be resolved in the courts.

Again, we have continued the policy of replacing most of the older cases with current ones, but we have not hesitated to keep a few of the older ones which we thought were unusually effective for teaching purposes. With only

---

[1] John D. Donnell, "The Businessman and the Business Law Curriculum," 6 *Amer. Business Law Journal* 451 (1968). See also Carruth, "The 'Legal Explosion' Has Left Business Shell-Shocked," *Fortune,* April 1973, pp. 65 *et seq.*

a few exceptions, we have tried to limit ourselves to cases involving business relations and have looked for cases with fact situations that should add depth and breadth to the business student's understanding of actual business operations. Some of the cases were chosen primarily as useful vehicles for discussion or for suggesting possible trends in the law rather than being statements of the decisions of a majority of courts. The latter is the function of the textual material.

The problem cases at the end of each chapter are based upon decided cases except for a few questions related to introductory material. These cases are selected to supplement the cases in the chapters and sometimes to illustrate viewpoints different than those represented by the cases in the text. We recommend their use to give the student experience in analyzing legal fact situations and in developing a general understanding of the possible legal ramifications involved in diverse business situations.

The workbook first offered with the last edition has been well received. Professors Phillip J. Scaletta of Purdue University and Thomas W. Dunfee of Ohio State University have thoroughly revised it for use with this edition.

We appreciate the many suggestions we have received from teachers using the last edition, including those who received and responded to our rather detailed questionnaire. We are especially indebted to Howard Lansinger, recently retired from East Tennessee State University, and to Dugald Hudson and his colleagues at Georgia State University who gave us very detailed criticisms and suggestions on the last edition. Also, we wish to express special thanks to David Reitzel of Mankato State College and Clyde Carter of the University of North Carolina, both of whom read nearly the entire manuscript for this edition. However, frequently suggestions were inconsistent, and we made the final decisions, so the responsibility for errors of any kind is our own.

We also wish to express appreciation to our research assistants, Phillip Scaletta, Jr., Robert L. Wood, Robert Lauritzson, Robert Hunt, David Cornwell, John Settle, and Charles King; to our secretaries, Roberta Aubin and Kay Fauth; and to our teaching colleagues, all of whom have made substantial contributions to this edition.

Most credit, however, is due Harold F. Lusk, who not only launched the book and created its structure and format, but who continues to serve as an inspiration to the present authors. After preparing two revisions, we appreciate more than ever the magnitude of the task he and his wife Vera performed.

Professor Hewitt gratefully acknowledges the opportunity afforded him by Dean William C. Flewellen of the University of Georgia and Dean Schuyler F. Otteson of Indiana University to concentrate on research and writing during the past academic year as a Visiting Distinguished Professor at the School of Business, University of Georgia.

We recommend that students keep this text for their personal libraries. They will probably find a number of occasions to refer to it for both their personal and business affairs.

April 1974

CHARLES M. HEWITT, JR.
JOHN D. DONNELL
A. JAMES BARNES

Contents

Part II
TORTS

Crimes: *Introduction. Nature of Crime. Relationship Involved. Scope of Criminal Law. Essentials of a Crime. Capacity to Commit a Crime. Fraudulent Acts. Forgery. Decisions Protecting the Accused.* Torts: *Introduction. Elements of Torts. Nature of Torts.* Interference with Personal Rights: *Assault and Battery. False Imprisonment. Defamation. Malicious Prosecution and Abuse of Process. Right of Privacy. Infliction of Mental Distress.* Rights of Property: *Nature of Property Rights. Trespass to Land. Trespass to Personal Property. Conversion. Deceit (Fraud).* Business Torts: *Economic Relations.*

Negligence: *Nature of Negligence. Standards of Conduct. Special Duties Imposed by Law. Proximate Cause. Defenses. Last Clear Chance. Res Ipsa Loquitur.* Strict Liability: *Nature of Strict Liability.* Nuisance: *Nature of Nuisance.*

Part III
CONTRACTS

Nature of Contract: *Basis of Contract. Evolution of the Contract.* Changing Role of Contracts: *Role at Turn of Century. Contracts after 1900.* Classification of Contracts: *Formal and Informal or Simple. Unilateral and Bilateral. Valid, Unenforceable, Voidable, Void. Executed and Executory. Express and Implied.* Quasi Contracts: *Historical Development. Measure of Damages. Basis for Recovery.* The Uniform Commercial Code: *Purpose of the Code. Scope of the Code.*

Introduction: *Nature of Offer. Form of Offer. Intent. Certainty of Terms. Omission of Terms. Usage of Trade. Preliminary Negotiations. Advertisements. Rewards. Bids. Auctions.* Terms Included in Offers: *Tags, Tickets, Folders, Etc.* Termination of Offer: *Duration of Offer. Provisions in Offer. Lapse of Time. Revocation. Communication of Revocation. Revocation of Offer to Public. Revocation of Offer for Unilateral Contracts. Rejection. Inquiry regarding Terms. Death or Insanity. Destruction of Subject Matter. Intervening Illegality.* Changes under the Uniform Commercial Code: *The Offer.*

The Acceptance: *Requirements for Acceptance. Offer in Unilateral Contract. Offer in Bilateral Contract. When a Writing Is Anticipated. Silence as Acceptance. Intention to Accept.* Communication of Acceptance: *Requirements for Communication. When Acceptance Is Communicated. Authorized Means of Communication. When Acceptance Is by a Means Not Authorized.* Changes under the U.C.C.

Introduction: *Nature of Real Consent.* Misrepresentation and Fraud: *Misrepresentation. Fraud.* Duress and Undue Influence: *General Nature. Duress. Undue Influence.* Mistake:

Nature of Mistake. Mistake Resulting from Ambiguity. Mistake as to Material Fact. Mutual Mistake. Unilateral Mistake. Mistakes in Drafting Writing. Mistakes of Law.

9. Consideration   165

History and Function of Consideration: *Historical Development.* Detriment or Benefit: *Analysis of Test. Legal Detriment. Legal Benefit.* Preexisting Obligation: *Nature of Preexisting Obligation. Criminal and Tortious Acts. Holder of an Office. Public Officers. Contractual Obligations. Exceptions. New Contract.* Debt, Compromise, and Composition: *Liquidated Debt. Compromise (Accord and Satisfaction). Composition.* Forbearance to Sue: *Right to Bring Suit. Valid Claims and Reasonable Claims.* Bargain and Exchange: *The Bargain. Adequacy of Consideration. Nominal Consideration.* Past Consideration: *Nature of Past Consideration. Implied Promises to Compensate.* Consideration in Bilateral Contracts: *Mutual Obligation. Illusory Promise. Right to Cancel Contract.* When Consideration Unnecessary: *Promise Inducing Substantial Action. Charitable Subscriptions. Business Promises. Debts Barred by Statute of Limitations. Debts Discharged in Bankruptcy. Promise to Perform a Conditional Duty.* Consideration under the Uniform Commercial Code: *In General.*

10. Capacity of Parties   192

Introduction: *Capacity. Parties to Contract. Presumption as to Capacity.* Infants' Contracts: *Theory of Infants' Incapacity. Period of Infancy. Emancipation. General Rule. Business Contracts. Infant Partner.* Necessaries: *Liability for Necessaries. Nature of Necessaries.* Disaffirmance of Contract: *Right to Disaffirm. Time of Disaffirmance. Return of Consideration. Infants' Rights on Disaffirmance. Misrepresentation of Age.* Ratification: *Nature of Ratification. Requirements for Ratification. Effect of Ratification.* Infants' Tort Liability: *Nature of Liability.* Insane and Drunken Persons: *Nature of Liability. Test of Insanity. Effect of Adjudication of Insanity. Necessaries. Disaffirmance of Contract. Ratification of Contract.* Married Women's Contracts: *Contractual Capacity at Common Law. Married Women's Statutes.*

11. Illegality   208

Introduction: *Nature of Illegality. Classification. Presumption.* Bargains in Violation of Positive Law: *Scope of Positive Law. Bargain to Commit a Crime. Bargain to Commit a Tort.* Bargains Made Illegal by Statutes: *Types of Statutes Wagering Statutes. Stock and Commodity Market Transactions. Statutes Declaring Bargains Void. Regulatory Statutes. Revenue-Raising Statutes.* Public Policy: *General Concept. Bargains Injurious to Public Service. Bargains to Influence Fiduciaries. Bargains Relieving from Liability for Negligence. Bargains in Restraint of Trade. Miscellaneous Illegal Bargains.* Effect of Illegality: *General Rule. Ignorance of Fact or Special Regulation. Rights of Protected Parties. Knowledge of Illegal Use. Divisible Contracts. Rescission before Performance of Illegal Act.* Unenforceable Contracts and the Uniform Commercial Code: *Unconscionability.*

12. Writing   239

Statute of Frauds: *Introduction. Provisions of Statute of Frauds. Interpretation of Statute of Frauds. Scope of the Statute of Frauds.* Collateral Contracts: *Nature of Collateral Contracts. Original Contracts.* Interest in Land: *Scope of Provision.* Not to Be Performed within One Year: *Scope of Provision. Computing Time. Contracts to Extend Time of Performance. An Indefinite Time Stated.* The Writing: *Nature of Writing Required. Content of the Memorandum. The Signing. Oral Variation of Contract.* Effect of Failure to Comply:

General Effect. Rights of Parties to Oral Contract. Sale of Goods and the Code: *The Memorandum. Part Payment or Part Delivery. Admissions in Pleadings or Court. Specially Manufactured Goods. Effect of Noncompliance.* Interpretation: *Necessity for Interpretation. Basic Standards of Interpretation. Rules of Interpretation. Usage.* Parol Evidence: *Scope and Purpose of Parol Evidence Rule. Admissible Parol Evidence. Subsequent Contracts. Partial Writings. Ambiguous Contracts.*

13. Rights of Third Parties   270

Assignment of Contracts: *Introduction. Contracts Not Assignable. Contracts Which Are Assignable. The Delegation of Duties.* Rights Acquired by Assignee: *General Rule. Notice of Assignment. Successive Assignments. Assignment of Wages.* Assignor's Liability to Assignee: *Implied Warranties. General Liability.* Third-Party Beneficiary: *Classes of Third-Party Beneficiary Contracts. Donee Beneficiaries. Creditor Beneficiaries. Incidental Beneficiaries. Municipal or Governmental Contracts.* Assignment under the Uniform Commercial Code: *Scope of Application. Assignment.*

14. Performance and Remedies   287

Conditions: *Introduction. Nature of Conditions. Creation of Conditions. Independent Promises.* Architects' and Engineers' Certificates: *Requirement of Certificate. When Failure to Produce Certificate Is Excused.* Performance and Breach: *Duty of Performance. Complete or Satisfactory Performance. Substantial Performance. Material Breach. Prevention of Performance. Time Is of the Essence. Performance to Personal Satisfaction. Good Faith Performance under the U.C.C.* Impossibility of Performance: *Nature of Impossibility. Illness or Death of Promisor. Performance Declared Illegal. Destruction of Subject Matter. Commercial Frustration.* Discharge: *Nature of Discharge. Discharge by Agreement. Waiver. Discharge by Alteration. Discharge by Statute of Limitations. Uniform Commercial Code.* Franchises: *Termination of Franchises.* Nature of Remedies: *Objective in Granting Remedy. Enforcement of Remedy. Uniform Commercial Code.* Classification of Damages: *Introduction. Mitigation of Damages. Liquidated Damages. Nominal Damages.* Equitable Remedies: *Specific Performance. Injunction.*

Part IV
AGENCY

15. Creation of Relation and Authority   321

Introduction: *Background. Nature of the Relation. Scope. Master and Servant. Principal and Agent. General and Special Agents. Franchising and Other Relationships. Independent Contractor.* Creation of Relation: *Requirement to Create Agency. Statutory Requirement.* Capacity of Parties: *Infants and Insane Persons as Principals. Unincorporated Associations as Principals. Capacity to Act as Agent. Business Organizations as Principals.* Authority to Bind Principal: *Authorization. Express Authority. Implied Authority. Apparent Authority.* Ratification: *Nature of Ratification. Requirements for Ratification. What Acts May Be Ratified. Effect of Ratification. Ratification Must Be Entire.*

16. Relation of Principal and Third Person   340

Disclosed or Partially Disclosed Principal: *Liability of Agent of Disclosed Principal. Liability of Agent of Partially Disclosed Principal. Execution of Writings.* Undisclosed Principal:

Nature of Relation. Rights of the Third Person. Scope of Liability of Undisclosed Principal. Rights of Undisclosed Principal. Liability on Special Transactions: *Basis of Liability. Liability for Agent's Representations. Liability for Agent's Warranties. Liability for Payment to Agent. Liability for Credit Contracted by Agent. Liability on Negotiable Instruments.* Notice to or Knowledge of Agent: *Effect of Notice to Agent. Knowledge of Agent. Limitations on the Rule.* Liability for Acts of Subagents: *Appointments of Subagents. Liability of Principal for Acts of Subagents.* Liability for Torts and Crimes: *Agents Who Are Employees. Scope of Employment. Liability for Torts of Professional Agent. Liability for Deceit of Agent. Intentional Torts. Tort Liability Is Joint and Several. Crimes.*

Part V.
PARTNERSHIPS

Possession of Partnership Property. Creditors of Individual Partner. Management of Business and Compensation: *Voice in Management. Right to Compensation. Profits and Losses.* Fiduciary Duties: *Loyalty and Good Faith. Duty in Transacting Partnership Business. Books of Partnership. Disclosure of Information. Duty to Account.*

25. Operating the Corporate Business 505

Corporate Powers: *Sources of Powers. Limitations in Articles of Incorporation. The* Ultra Vires *Doctrine. Liability under the Doctrine.* Management of the Corporation: *Authority.* Directors: *Duties and Powers of Directors. Practices of Boards of Directors. Powers and Rights of Director as Individual. Number and Qualifications of Directors. Election of Directors. Removal of Directors. Directors' Meetings. Committees of the Board. Compensation of Directors.* Officers and Employees: *Officers of the Corporation. Statutory Liabilities of Officers. Employees of the Corporation.* Fiduciary Duties of Directors, Officers, and Others: *General. Acting within Authority. Due Care and Diligence. Loyalty and Good Faith. Transactions with the Corporation. Usurpation of a Corporate Opportunity. Transactions in the Corporation's Stock. Oppression of Minority Shareholders. Federal Securities Laws. Other Statutory Liabilities of Directors. Defense of Good Faith.* Liability for Torts and Crimes: *Torts. Crimes.*

26. Shareholders' Rights and Liabilities 539

Shareholders' Meetings: *Exercise of Shareholder Functions. Annual Meetings. Special Meetings. Notice of Meetings. Quorum. Conduct of the Meeting. Shareholder Proposals and Right to Speak.* Voting Rights: *Shareholders Entitled to Vote. Cumulative Voting. Proxy Voting. Voting Trust.* Dividends: *Introduction. Types of Dividends. Funds Available for Dividends. Tests of Validity of Dividend Payments. Directors' Discretion in Payment of Dividends. Dividend Payment on Preferred Stock. Stock Dividends and Stock Splits. Distributions. Dividend Declaration. Effect of Transfer on Right to Dividend.* Inspection of Books and Records: *Common Law Right to Inspect. Statutory Inspection Rights.* Preemptive Rights: *General. Application of Preemptive Rights. Preemptive Rights under the Model Act.* Extraordinary Corporate Transactions: *Introduction. Procedure for Amending Articles. Other Extraordinary Transactions. Appraisal Rights.* Shareholders' Actions: *Shareholders' Individual Actions. Shareholder Class Action Suits. Shareholders' Derivative Actions. Reimbursement in Class and Derivative Actions. Minority Shareholder Suits. Dissolution at Suit of a Minority Shareholder.* Shareholder Liability: *Shareholder Liability on Shares. Shareholder Liability on Illegal Dividends and Distributions. Shareholder Liability for Corporate Debts. Duties of Controlling Shareholders.*

27. Securities Regulation 577

Introduction: *Background and Objectives. What Is a Security? Exemptions. Private Offerings.* Requirements of Issuers: *Registration under the 1933 Act. Registration under the 1934 Act. The Prospectus. Periodic Reports. Proxy Statements and Annual Reports.* Requirements of Directors, Officers, and Others: *Reports of Stock Transactions. "Short-Swing Profits."* Tender Offers. Antifraud Provisions: *Introduction. Antifraud Provisions of 1933 Act. Antifraud Provisions of 1934 Act.* Liabilities and Penalties: *Civil Liabilities. Criminal Sanctions.* State Securities Legislation: *Purpose and History. Types of Statutes.*

28. Foreign Corporations 615

Rights of Foreign Corporations: *Introduction. The Model Act.* "Doing Business": *Introduction. Subjecting Foreign Corporations to Suit. Taxing Foreign Corporations. Admission of a Foreign Corporation. Penalty for Failure to Obtain Permission.*

Part VII
PROPERTY

Nature and Classification: *Nature of Property. Possession. Real and Personal Property. Tangible and Intangible Property. Public and Private Property.* Acquisition of Personal Property: *Production or Purchase. Taking Possession. Gift. Lost Property. Confusion. Accession.* Nature and Creation of Bailment: *Essential Elements. Creation of Relation. Custody of Servant or Agent.* Rights and Liabilities of Parties: *Bailee's Duty of Care. Alteration of Liability by Contract. Bailee's Duty to Return Property. Bailee's Right to Compensation. Bailor's Liability for Defects in Bailed Property.* Special Bailment Situations: *Bailment of Fungible Goods. Safe-Deposit Boxes. Involuntary Bailments. Common Carrier. Innkeepers.*

Fixtures: *Nature of Fixture. Express Agreement. Mode of Attachment. Use with Real Property. Additions by Owner. Additions by Tenants.* Rights and Interests in Real Property: *Fee Simple. Life Estate. Leasehold. Easements. Licenses.* Co-ownership of Real Property: *Nature of Co-ownership. Tenancy in Common. Joint Tenancy. Tenancy by the Entirety. Community Property. Tenancy in Partnership. Condominium Ownership. Cooperative Ownership.* Acquisition of Real Property: *Origin of Title to Real Property. Acquisition by Purchase. Acquisition by Gift. Acquisition by Adverse Possession. Acquisition by Tax Sale. Acquisition by Will or Descent.* Transfer by Sale: *Steps in a Sale. Real Estate Brokers. Contract for Sale. Financing the Purchase. Transfer by Deed. Quitclaim and Warranty Deeds. Form and Execution of Deed. Recording Deeds. Warranties in the Sale of a House.* Disposition on Death of Owner: *Statutes of Descent and Distribution. Right of Disposition by Will. Execution of Will. Limitations on Disposition by Will. Revocation of Will.* Public Controls on the Use of Land: *Nuisance Control. Zoning and Subdivision Ordinances. Eminent Domain.*

Leases: *Landlord-Tenant Relationship. Nature of Lease. Execution of Lease. Rights, Duties, and Liabilities of the Landlord. Rights and Duties of the Tenant. Termination of the Lease.*

Introduction: *Historical Perspective. The Environmental Protection Agency. The National Environmental Policy Act.* Air Pollution: *Introduction. 1970 Clean Air Act. Automobile Pollution. Pollution from Other Sources.* Water Pollution: *Introduction. Federal Legislation. Clean Waters Act of 1972. Citizen Suits. Ocean Dumping.* Pesticides and Toxic Substances: *Introduction. Federal Pesticide Legislation. Suspension and Cancellation. Toxic Substances.* Noise Pollution and Radiation Control: *Noise Control Act of 1972. Radiation Control.*

Part VIII
SALES

Introduction: *Nature of Sales and the Law of Sales. Uniform Commercial Code—Sales.* Terms of the Contract: *General Terms. Delivery and Payment Terms.* Title: *Introduction.*

Provisions for Passing of Title. Rights of Third Parties: *Introduction. Creditor's Rights. Transfer of Voidable Title. Buyer in Ordinary Course of Business.* Risks: *Introduction. Explicit Agreements. Identification and Insurable Interest. Risks of Loss—General Rules.* Sales on Trial: *Sale on Approval. Sale or Return. Sale on Consignment or on Memorandum.* Bulk Transfers.

34. Warranty and Product Liability 740

Nature of Warranties: *Representations. Warranties—General.* Express Warranties: *Nature of Express Warranty. Creating an Express Warranty.* Warranty of Title: *Nature of Warranty of Title. Scope of Warranty of Title.* Implied Warranties: *Nature of Implied Warranty. Implied Warranty of Merchantability. Implied Warranty of Fitness for Particular Purpose.* Exclusions, Modification, or Conflict of Warranties: *Common-Law Rule. Exclusions or Modifications. Conflict of Warranties.* Who Benefits from Warranty: *General Rule. Demise of the Privity Doctrine. Uniform Commercial Code.* Product Liability: *Negligence. Strict Liability.*

35. Performance 767

Introduction: *General Rules. Course of Dealing and Usage of Trade. Modification, Rescission, and Waiver. Assignment and Delegation. Cooperation Respecting Performance.* Delivery: *General Rules. Seller's Duties of Delivery.* Inspection and Payment: *Buyer's Right of Inspection. Payment.* Acceptance; Revocation; Rejection: *What Constitutes Acceptance. Effect of Acceptance. Revocation of Acceptance. Buyer's Rights on Improper Delivery. Manner of Rejection and Duties after Rejection. Failure to Particularize.* Assurance, Repudiation, Breach, and Excuse: *Assurance. Anticipatory Repudiation. Excuse.*

36. Remedies for Breach 783

Seller's Remedies: *Recovery of Purchase Price. Recovery of Damages for Breach. Resale as Measure of Damages. Seller's Remedies on Discovery of Buyer's Insolvency. Seller's Right to Stop Delivery.* Buyers' Remedies: *Right to Recover Goods. Buyer's Right to Damages for Nondelivery. Damages for Defective Goods.* General Rules: *Buyer and Seller Agreements as to Damages. Proof of Market Price. Statute of Limitations.*

Part IX
COMMERCIAL PAPER

37. Negotiable Instruments 801

Background: *Historical Background. Uniform Commercial Code—Commercial Paper.* Forms of Commercial Money: *Nature of Commercial Paper. Draft. Check. Certificate of Deposit. Promissory Note.* Benefits of Negotiability: *Rights of Assignee of Contract. Rights Acquired by Negotiation.* Formal Requirements for Negotiability: *Basic Requirements. Importance of Form. Language of Negotiable Instrument.* In Writing and Signed: *Writing. Signing.* Unconditional Promise or Order: *Requirement of Promise or Order. Promise or Order Must Be Unconditional. Express Conditions. Special Provisions of the Code.* Sum Certain in Money: *Sum Certain. Payable in Money.* Payable on Demand or at Definite Time: *Payable on Demand. Definite Time.* Payable to Order or Bearer: *Necessity of Words of Negotiability. Payable to Order. Payable to Bearer.* Special Terms: *Additional Terms and Omissions. Ambiguous Terms.*

Part I

The American Legal System

chapter 1

The Nature of Law
and Its Development

A Society of Laws. A shaft of black diorite unearthed in 1901 is the first great monument to man's continuing search for justice. It records the code of Babylon's King Hammurabi . . . a list of crimes and penalties demanding, in essence, an eye for an eye and a tooth for a tooth. Five centuries later, the Mosaic Code still echoed this harsh doctrine. But by the Sixth Century A.D. Justinian's Code was shifting the emphasis from punishment to due process, ruling that a man was innocent until proved guilty. In 1215, England's nobles forced King John to sign the Magna Carta, which recognized such basic rights as that to a fair trial. Over the centuries the law continued to grow, adapting to the changing needs of society as it progressed, from the Napoleonic Code of 1804, which legalized the reforms of the French Revolution, to the civil rights decisions of today's U.S. Supreme Court. The search for justice still goes on, attempting to fulfill the promise made by Hammurabi 4,000 years ago: "The oppressed . . . shall read the writing . . . and he shall find his right."[1]

Concepts of Law

Defining Law. Ancient as the concept is, it is most difficult to develop a useful and meaningful definition of law. Legal scholars and other "experts" are not in agreement, particularly if the effort goes beyond a relatively simple dictionary definition.

At this point it may be more helpful to the student who is studying law for the first time merely to point out some erroneous ideas as to what law is. A police officer is part of "the law" but neither he nor the courts completely encompass what is meant by this term. Although a statute passed by a legislature may properly be called a law, statutes are only a small part of the law. Nor is law just a system of rules of conduct and the methods used for their enforcement. Indeed, it is more accurate to conceive of a law as a process by

---

[1] S. N. Kramer, *Cradle of Civilization* (New York: Time, Inc., 1967), p. 170.

which numerous functions needed by society are carried out than as a body of rules. Law may also be viewed as a system of many interacting parts of which rules are only one aspect.

It is suggested that instead of seeking a definition of law to learn at this point, the student read the introductory chapters of this textbook with the objective of learning as much as possible about law in general so that he or she can gain a better understanding of the text and cases which follow.

Legal Philosophy. From time immemorial men have discussed the nature of law, its sources and its functions, as well as that even more illusive concept, "justice." Writings are available by the thousands, including statements from the great philosophers of the ages such as Plato, Aristotle, and St. Thomas Aquinas, down to John Dewey of recent times. Others can be quoted from legal scholars and legal philosophers such as Cicero and Papinian of Rome, Henry de Bracton and Sir Edward Coke of England, Friedrich von Savigny and Rudolf von Jhering of Germany and the late Roscoe Pound of the United States. Until one has gained some familiarity with the materials of the law and more particularly some appreciation of the difficulties judges face as they deal with specific fact situations and seek to justify their decisions in specific disputes, a discussion of legal theories may be relatively meaningless. On the other hand, some general notion of the concepts of the law expounded by some of the great legal thinkers who have helped to shape our law is likely to be useful to the student as he or she reads a case and seeks to understand the judge's opinion.

Pound distinguishes and briefly outlines 12 different concepts of law in his *Introduction to the Philosophy of Law.*[2] However, there are four basic concepts, some encompassing several of those identified by Pound, which reappear most frequently in the writings of philosophers and scholars as well as entering into the thinking of judges as they decide specific disputes.

Law as What Is Right. The first of these concepts is that law is "what is right" in a moral sense, whether the notion of right is derived directly from a divine source or from the nature of man. This concept suggests that laws may be bad because they are inconsistent with properly reasoned deductions from God's revealed will or man's inherent nature and that improvement of the law, and therefore of the society of men, may come from better reasoning and/or new revelations. Critics of this view question the existence of any fixed code of right and wrong. They also question the ability of any person to set out such a code, because as anthropologist Ruth Benedict says, "No man ever looks at the world with pristine eyes. He sees it edited by a definite set of customs and ways of thinking."[3]

---

[2] Roscoe Pound, *Introduction to the Philosophy of Law* (New Haven, Conn.: Yale University Press, 1922), pp. 26–30, paperback edition.

[3] Ruth Benedict, *Patterns of Culture* (Boston: Houghton Mifflin Co., Mentor Books, 1934), p. 18.

Law as Custom.   Another concept is that law is a historical accretion, developed over ages from the traditions and customs of a society, which reflects the peculiar nature of the people interacting with a particular environment. Some of the thinkers emphasizing this concept of law have visualized legal development as the unfolding of some basic idea. For example, Sir Henry Maine noted that under the rigid class hierarchy system that characterized feudalism nearly all legal rights and duties that a person had depended upon his position in the hierarchy—or his status. The feudal structure was shattered by the expansion of trade and industry which involved the use of contract. This led to his famous generalization that the history of law is the progress from status to contract.

Law as Command.   A third basic concept of the law is that it is a body of rules which are essentially the commands of a political entity, backed by sanctions imposed by that entity. Under this view it is the will of the ruler or the ruling group rather than reason or morality which shapes and defines the law, and the influence of group character and tradition is minimized.

Law as Social Planning.   A fourth concept of law emphasizes its purpose rather than its source and views law as a means of social control which seeks to balance conflicting claims and values of the society and its various elements. Pound, the leader of the group called the sociological school of jurists, says:

Sociological jurists seek to enable and to compel lawmaking, whether legislative or judicial or administrative, and also the development, interpretation, and application of legal precepts, to take more complete and intelligent account of the social facts upon which law must proceed and to which it is to be applied. . . . (They) insist that we must look at law functionally. We must inquire how it operates, since the life of law is in its application and enforcement.[4]

Schools of Jurisprudence.   Although, of course, students of the law differ in the emphasis which they give to these four general concepts, the outstanding thinkers are frequently classified as belonging to a group which can be identified according to which of these concepts seems uppermost in their thinking. The metaphysical or natural law theory adherents stress the concept of law as "what is right." The historical group stresses the second concept, custom and tradition; the analytical group or positivists stress the third or imperative theory; and the sociological school is the name given to those holding the fourth concept. As Roscoe Pound points out, these differences stem from concentration on different processes or phenomena which are lumped together as law. The precepts or rules are the focus of the analytical school. The technique of the law or the way judges find a basis for their decisions, which tends to be particularly tradition bound and slow to change, is the central focus of the historical school. The metaphysical or natural law schools concentrate primarily on the ideal element of the law, that is, what the law ought to be.

---

[4] Roscoe Pound, *Jurisprudence* (St. Paul, Minn.: West Publishing Co., 1959), 1:350–52.

As has been indicated, the sociological school focuses on the balancing and compromising of interest in society to achieve social ends.

Many legal scholars are convinced that no theory or group of theories can adequately describe law. Some, often called the realists, prefer to focus on law as a process. For example, Llewellyn says:[5]

Actual disputes call for someone to do something about them. First, so that there may be peace . . . and secondly, so that the dispute may really be put to rest. . . . This doing of something about disputes, this doing of it reasonably, is the business of the law. And the people who have the doing in charge, whether they be judges or sheriffs or clerks or jailers or lawyers, are officials of the law. *What these officials do about disputes is, to my mind, the law itself.*

Still other writers attempt to define law in terms of the function it performs.

Summary

Writings of many great men have discussed the nature of law. Four major concepts can be identified. They are: (1) law is what is right, (2) law is custom, (3) law is the command of the ruler, and (4) law is an attempt at social planning.

Functions and Limits of Law

Changing Functions through Time. If law cannot be adequately defined by theory, can it at least be described in terms of the major functions law has performed for society? Roscoe Pound traced the development of law from ancient to modern times.[6] He concluded that in terms of major functions performed, the law has evolved through four stages.

In the first stage, found in primitive societies, the major function of law is to keep the peace. In more advanced societies, represented by Greek and Roman law and also by the law of medieval England where landholding was the major interest, the prime function of law tends to shift to maintenance of the status quo. Pound characterizes this stage as, "An idea of justice as a device to . . . keep each man in his appointed groove and thus prevent friction with his fellows." The third stage was a product of the Age of Enlightenment, the appeal of reason against authority. The change in legal theory to the view that justice is a device to secure a maximum of individual self-assertion, especially through freedom of contract, followed similar thinking in religion, philosophy, politics, and economics and came as the emphasis in economic activity shifted from agriculture to trade and manufacture. Finally, the fourth and current stage emphasizes social justice. This is the stage that Pound himself helped to usher in.

---

[5] K. N. Llewellyn, *The Bramble Bush* (New York: Oceana Publications, Inc., 1960), p. 12.

[6] Roscoe Pound, "Liberty of Contract," 18 *Yale Law Journal* 454 (1909).

The law today still performs the earlier functions, but also others. Eight of the functions performed by modern law will be discussed briefly. The list that follows is not all-inclusive; others could be added. Note that some of these functions are in inherent conflict with others, as, for example, the maximizing of individual self-assertion is frequently inconsistent with the promotion of social justice.

Peace Keeping. One of the important functions of modern legal systems is keeping of the peace. Disruptions of the equilibrium in highly interdependent modern societies tend to spread and tend to penalize innocent nonparticipants. In addition, rising standards of education tend to militate against self-help and any form of unjustifiable injurious conduct by any members of society. Criminal law and tort law seek to maintain the peace and to punish or penalize those who disturb the social order. Tort law also seeks to provide reimbursement for the members of society who suffer losses due to the dangerous or unreasonable conduct of others.

Influence and Enforce Standards of Conduct. Although legal standards often differ from moral standards, the law frequently influences or shapes the social consensus concerning standards of morality. Price-fixing agreements by businessmen, for example, were neither criminal nor immoral until after the passage of the Sherman Act in 1890. The failure of the National Prohibition experiment, however, would seem to indicate that there are limits on the power of law to shape and influence the moral standards of society.

The law sets standards as to what constitutes reasonable or acceptable performance of legal duties. For business this has meant that as more careful or efficient processes have been developed these improved processes tend to establish new higher legal standards for judging business conduct. Thus the modern businessman must exercise a great deal more care in making, advertising, and distributing his product than did his counterpart of the last century.

Maintenance of the Status Quo. Cohen gave an example of law functioning to maintain the status quo when he analyzed the British law of real property:

. . . back of the complicated law of settlement, fee-tails, copyhold estates, of the heir-at-law, of the postponement of women, and other feudal incidents, there was a great and well founded fear that by simplifying and modernizing the real property law of England the land might become more marketable. Once land becomes fully marketable it can no longer be counted on to remain in the hands of the landed aristocratic families; and this means the destinies of the British Empire. For if American experience has demonstrated anything, it is that the continued leadership by great familes cannot be as well founded on a money as on a land economy. The same kind of talent which enables Jay Gould to acquire dominion over certain railroads enables Mr. Harriman to take it away from his sons. From the point of view of an established land economy, a money economy thus seems a state of perpetual war instead of a social order where son succeeds father. . . .[7]

---

[7] Morris R. Cohen, "Property and Sovereignty," 13 *Cornell Law Quar.* 8, 10 (1927).

Rapidly changing modern law affords few clear examples of this status quo function.[8]

Facilitate Orderly Change.   A more important function of modern law is to facilitate orderly change in order to meet the changing needs of a dynamic society. American law paradoxically functions so as to preserve both stability in the law and yet to permit and facilitate change. Indeed, Whitehead states that, "The art of progress is to preserve order amidst change, and to preserve change amidst order."[9] Justice Holmes once stated that, "Every important principle is in fact at bottom the result of views of public policy." Subsequent chapters will disclose how the courts have initiated policy changes in many vital areas. These court-made changes have been especially important in antitrust, product liability, and other areas of vital concern to businessmen.

Maximum Individual Self-Assertion.   Although the concept of political democracy goes back to the Greeks, the ideas of individual freedom in terms of a minimum of external restraints was formalized into economic theory and had maximum impact on the law during the 19th century. Ideas of personal freedom of thought, dress, and private activity have had greater impact in the last half of this century, perhaps in response to the greater concentration of a growing population. Freedom for the individuals in society, however, must always be defined in relative terms. The total absence of restrictions means anarchy where no rights are recognized or protected by law. In legal terms absolute rights cannot exist because legal rights cannot be defined except in terms of the corresponding legal duties imposed upon others.

In absolute terms a businessman's "right" to run his factory on his own land as he pleases could become the duty of society to accept foul odors, loud noises, and perhaps even physical damage to property. The absolute right to strike could mean the legal duty of society to tolerate the stoppage of essential public services.

Facilitate Planning and the Realization of Reasonable Expectations.
In a modern industrial society businessmen must, within limits, be able to plan ahead. This involves not only a basis for predicting the risks and consequences of alternative courses of action, but, also, some means for planning and seeing that reasonable expectations are realized. Tort law, insurance law, sales law, contract law, and other areas provide a basic legal framework to facilitate both the prediction of risks and the effectuation of economic plans.

Promotion of Social Justice.   Since the turn of the century the emphasis has shifted toward the positive use of governmental powers as a means of affording all citizens equal access to the benefits of our economic and political life. Congress has passed legislation establishing a social security system, welfare for the poor, and medical payments for the old. Statutes requiring business-

---

[8] Zoning laws represent attempts to protect the status quo interests of property owners.

[9] A. N. Whitehead, *Process and Reality* (New York: The Macmillian Co., 1929), p. 515.

men to give equal opportunities for service and in employment have sought to overcome historical patterns of discrimination. Courts too have tended more and more to protect the disadvantaged. The U.S. Supreme Court decisions requiring school desegregation and the furnishing of legal counsel to impoverished persons accused of crime are examples of such efforts which tend to make the legal system operate more nearly in accord with our creed of equal justice for all.

Provision of Compromise Solutions. In a special sense American law usually functions so as to avoid extremes which, according to Aristotle, is the true path to justice. Freund summarizes this when he says of the U.S. Supreme Court:

By avoiding absolutes, by testing general maxims against concrete particulars, by deciding only in the context of specific controversies, by accommodating between polar principles, by holding itself open to reconsideration of dogma, the Court at its best provided a symbol of reconciliation. Perhaps it is this blend of idealism and pragmatism that constitutes, in the end, the most notable characteristic of the judicial process.[10]

Limits on the Law. Although legal rules have been created concerning most aspects of our vital relationships, there are definite limits not only as to what law can do but also limits as to what the law will try to do. Some of these limits are imposed by the Constitution. Other limits have been self-imposed by the courts. The courts generally will refuse to deal with trifling or insignificant matters. Considerations of public expense and the prestige of the court system probably are behind this policy. In addition, the courts have evolved various hands-off policies in certain areas of the law such as certain types of internal family disputes, political questions, and social insults or affronts. The Supreme Court in its reapportionment cases recently reversed its long-standing policy of keeping hands off reapportionment and other "political" questions.[11]

Historically, American courts have refused to answer hypothetical questions or to give advisory opinions by the requirement that there must be a bona fide case or controversy before the court. By refusing to address themselves to hypothetical or feigned questions the courts both avoid unseen pitfalls and preserve maximum flexibility for the real controversies that may eventually arise.

For similar reasons American courts will not address themselves to moot issues. An issue becomes moot if later events render any decision by the court meaningless in regard to a specific case. Assume that a businessman files suit to have an action by an administrative agency enjoined and while this suit is pending the agency is abolished and its orders are negated by an act of Congress. The question of the action by the agency would then become moot.

---

[10] Paul A. Freund, "The Supreme Court," Harold J. Berman (ed.), *Talks on American Law* (New York: Random House, Inc., Vintage Books edition, 1961), pp. 83–84.

[11] The leading case is *Baker v. Carr,* 396 U.S. 186 (1962).

In a democracy, at least, there is another important limitation on the law. If any particular legal rule which specifies conduct is to have its intended effect, at least the great majority of those persons affected by it must believe the rule to be reasonable and fair or at least be willing to follow it voluntarily. Even authoritarian regimes find it difficult to enforce rules which are generally perceived to be unnecessary and unjust by those to whom they apply.

Summary

The main functions of modern law include: peace keeping; influencing and enforcing standards of conduct; maintaining the status quo; facilitating orderly change; providing for maximum individual self-assertion; facilitating planning and the realization of reasonable expectations; promotion of social justice; and the provision of compromise solutions.

The Constitution limits the application of law. Other limits have been self-imposed by the courts themselves, such as refusal to deal with insignificant matters, hypothetical questions and moot issues. Rules of conduct which are not accepted as reasonable and fair by most people affected are likely to be difficult to enforce.

Sources of American Law

English Common Law.   The English legal system was developed by the Normans after their conquest in 1066. The body of law known as the "common law" developed in the two or three centuries following the Conquest. It acquired its name from the desire of William the Conqueror and his successors to unite England under their rule. One device to accomplish this was to replace the varying bodies of custom or law of each locality with a uniform or "common" system administered by the king's personal followers in his name.

This body of rules called the common law grew from the decisions of judges in settling actual disputes, the judges following the determinations of their predecessors and fellow judges in similar situations. Very early, a strong legal profession grew up in England, and legal apprentices (later law students) began to compile records of the decisions in the royal courts. These earlier decisions or precedents were then used by lawyers to support their clients' petitions for relief and by judges to justify their decisions. Thus, the rule of *stare decisis*—a Latin phrase meaning to "let the decision stand"—developed, and once a court had decided a dispute, it would decide later cases which were similar in the same way.

Equity.   The law of equity and the Court of Chancery grew out of the Norman Kings' Council as did the common law. Under the Normans the chancellor was the most powerful executive officer of the king and the chief law member of the King's Council. He not only issued writs which permitted an aggrieved person to bring an action in a common-law court, but he himself, as a personal representative of the king, heard pleas which the common-law courts were unable to handle. Procedure, too, at least in the earlier period, was more flexible in chancery. So a separate body of law, equity, with a separate court, the Court of Chancery, gradually developed. Equity had precedence over the common law because its decrees applied to the person of the defendant and disobedience to a decree was a contempt of court.

The remedies in equity were also more flexible. While a judgment of a law court was limited to money damages or recovery of property, courts of equity, for example, would grant an injunction (a decree forbidding the defendant to do some act, even a prohibition against pursuing a cause of action in a common-law court), specific performance (ordering the defendant to perform his con-tract), reformation (rewriting a contract or instrument to conform to the actual intent of the parties), partition (to divide disputed property). It might be said that the common-law courts emphasized form, while the chancery courts were more interested in the merits of the case and the justice of the decision. Another distinction was that juries were not used in equity.

The Law Merchant. Even before the Middle Ages trading cities existed throughout Europe and the merchants and traders established their own courts and developed a set of rules which were international in origin and application governing trade and commerce. These courts existed outside of established systems of courts. It was in these courts that our law of sales of goods, negotia-ble instruments and other commercial law developed. It was not until the 18th century that the law merchant and the merchants' courts were absorbed into the common law.

Adoption of English Law by the United States. Although English law also included royal decrees and later statutes enacted by Parliament, the deci-sions rendered through the centuries by the law courts and by the merchants' courts constituted the bulk of English law. It was this body of law and the English legal system which came to this continent with the first English settlers and its use became solidified during the colonial period of English rule. There-fore, despite the American Revolution and the anti-British feelings of the time, the newly independent states remained in the English legal tradition, and the judges in the new nation continued to look for guidance to the decisions of English judges.

A single English legal writer, William Blackstone, probably had the greatest influence on American law. His *Commentaries on the Laws of England,* written in the years from 1755 to 1765, is believed to have sold as many copies in America as in England, a thousand sets selling at £10 each, having been imported by colonists before 1771.[12] Since most lawyers were trained by a kind of apprenticeship system in which they "read law" with a practicing attorney,

---

[12] Charles M. Haar, preface to William Blackstone, *Commentaries on the Laws of England: Of Public Wrongs* (Boston: Beacon Press, 1962), p. xxii.

this four-volume work came to serve as the leading legal textbook. In fact, it was used in law schools too until the end of the 19th century.

However, a number of lawyers also read treatises based upon the French civil law and Roman law. Through them, concepts from these bodies of law once again influenced the common law as it developed in America to serve the needs of a society rather different from that of England.

As additional states were admitted to the Union, they, too, except for Louisiana, adopted the English legal system. Louisiana, as a French colony, had previously adopted and it continues to base its law upon the French civil law which culminated in the Code Napoléon, which, in turn, had its roots in the Justinian Code of Rome. Roman law also has influenced the law of California and Texas through their Spanish heritage (Spain's law also is based upon Roman law).

Some states have codified, that is, enacted as statutes, large parts of the common law. Most commonly this includes the criminal law. The legislature may, while compiling and systematizing, intentionally change certain rules of the common law, and subsequent legislatures may more or less frequently make additional changes.

Although some states established separate courts of chancery, in most of the states the same judges sat, often at separate periods, both as law judges and chancellors. Some states, such as Delaware and New Jersey, continue to maintain courts of chancery, but in most states the distinction between law and equity has been all but eliminated in the federal courts and those of most states.

Summary

The newly organized states of the United States adopted the English legal system and generally followed English common law and the law merchant insofar as they were applicable to American conditions. The English equity law tradition was also adopted although most states did not establish separate courts of chancery. However, Louisiana adopted the French civil law system, and the law of Texas and California has also been influenced by the civil law which is based upon Roman law.

Sources of Current Law in the United States

Fifty-one Legal Systems. Basic to an understanding of the American legal system is appreciation of the fact that there are 51 different systems. In addition to the federal court system there are 50 different state court systems each, for the most part, applying its own body of law. A brief description of the federal court system and of a typical state court system appear near the end of this chapter. Presented first is an outline of the sources of the body of law of each jurisdiction.

Constitutions.   A constitution, federal or state, is the basic source of law for the jurisdiction. Constitutions not only specify the structure of the government and outline the powers of its principal officers and subdivisions, but they also allocate power between levels of government—between federal and state in the United States Constitution and between state and local governmental bodies in state constitutions. In addition, constitutions contain limitations upon governmental power which proscribe certain governmental actions and certain kinds of laws. The best known example of such proscriptions is the Bill of Rights of the United States Constitution.

The federal Constitution is written in broad and general language. Some of the state constitutions are much more detailed and specific, with the result that they have been amended much more frequently than the federal Constitution. The latter has only 26 amendments, the first 10 of which were adopted immediately following ratification of the basic document. Since the federal Constitution is the supreme law within the United States, any provision of a state constitution which conflicts with the federal document is of no force and effect; likewise, a state or federal statute conflicting with the Constitution is unenforceable.

Treaties.   According to the United States Constitution, treaties made by the President with heads of foreign governments that have been ratified by the Senate are "the Supreme Law of the Land." Although there has been considerable debate concerning the wisdom of the Founders in drafting this section and as to its proper interpretation, it has not had a very great impact upon our domestic law. Nevertheless, treaties have not infrequently been the basis for holding either a state or federal statute inoperative.

Statutes.   The major responsibility for changing the law of a jurisdiction belongs to the legislature. It can see a need for rules governing a new situation—for example, the dangers of radiation—and enact or "pass" a statute or "law" to prohibit or control certain uses of radioactive materials. The legislature can establish a new agency of government to administer the statute, or it can abolish an existing government agency. The legislature can repeal an outdated or unsatisfactory statute, and it can also change the common or judge-made law by superseding it with a statute which changes the rule. For example, a number of state legislatures have recently established "no fault" plans for providing damages to those injured in automobile accidents, a system which supersedes, at least in part, the centuries old common-law tort liability system.

One of the major advantages of the legislative process as compared to the common-law method of law development is the opportunity for all interested persons and groups to be heard. In the development of legal rules through the settlement of disputes in court, only the disputants and their lawyers are permitted to try to influence the judge, although occasionally the judge may permit other interested parties to file a legal argument or "brief" as an *amicus curiae,* or friend of the court, in cases likely to have an impact much broader than the parties to the lawsuit. A second advantage is that the legislators are always directly elected by the people and are more likely to be responsive to the public will. Also a broader range of viewpoints than among judges is likely to emerge in the election of legislative representatives.

Ordinances.   State governments have many subsidiary units to which the state, by statute, delegates certain functions. Some of these, such as water or school districts, have rather specific and limited functions. Others, such as counties, municipalities, and townships, exercise a number of governmental functions. Legislative enactments of municipalities are called ordinances, and this term is sometimes applied also to such enactments of other political subdivisions. Ordinances are enforceable provided they do not exceed the legislative power conferred by the state legislature upon the subordinate legislative body nor violate constitutions of the state or federal governments.

Administrative Regulations.   Although included as part of the executive branch of government, administrative agencies such as the Federal Trade Commission and the Securities and Exchange Commission and the state commerce or utility commissions also contribute to the body of law of their respective jurisdictions. Indeed, in 1952 Justice Jackson asserted,

The rule of administrative bodies probably has been the most significant legal trend of the last century and perhaps more values today are affected by their decisions than by those of all the courts, review of administrative decisions apart.[13]

Starting with the predecessor to the Veterans Administration in 1789, the number and size of the administrative agencies established by acts of Congress have increased steadily.

The federal agencies with which businessmen are most frequently involved other than those mentioned above include the National Labor Relations Board, the Environmental Protection Agency, and the one upon which most of the others have been modeled—the Interstate Commerce Commission, which was established in 1887. They have not only the power to issue regulations which have the force of law but also the power to initiate proceedings under those regulations (and also usually under certain statutes), to investigate, prosecute and make a decision or adjudicate the matter. In deciding cases the administrative agency also may establish new rules. However, in most cases the agency must go into the courts to enforce its orders.

This concentration of functions—legislative, prosecutive, and adjudicative—in a single agency has been much criticized. However, the advantages of specialization and consequent expertise, of continuous rather than case-

---

[13] *FTC v. Ruberoid Co.,* 343 U.S. 470, 487 (1952).

by-case development of policy through rule making and adjudication, and of the simpler procedures generally followed are claimed to outweigh the risks of abuse of the powers granted. The Administrative Procedures Act of 1946 was enacted to require the agencies to keep these functions separate within the agency, to follow fair procedures, and to afford better protection of the rights of persons appearing before them.

Executive Orders.   The President, governor, or mayor may also make law if, as is frequently the case, he or she is delegated the right by the legislative body to issue executive orders to effectuate the purposes of a statute or ordinance. For example, the President has issued a number of executive orders implementing various federal civil rights acts. These have accomplished such things as racially integrating the armed services and forbidding the federal government from purchasing from firms that discriminate on the basis of race.

Summary

There are 50 state legal systems as well as a federal system. The law which they apply is derived from a number of sources. The fundamental law is the constitution of the jurisdiction, state or federal, and the United States Constitution, which supercedes all state constitutions and other sources of law. Under the Constitution treaties with foreign nations are also the "Law of the Land."

The English common law serves as a basis for the law of each jurisdiction but a major part of the law is statutory. The major role in changing the law is that of the legislature, and it has advantages over the common-law method of law development in that it provides a means for all interested parties to make their interests known to the legislators, who being popularly elected, may be more responsive to the public will and have a wider range of viewpoints than judges.

Subsidiary governmental units, such as cities and counties, have such powers as are granted by the state legislature. Their ordinances have the force of law if enacted within the granted powers. Administrative regulations, decisions of administrative bodies, and official orders by executive officers such as the President or a governor also may become part of the law.

The Courts as Lawmakers

Deciding Controversies.   The traditional and principal function of the courts is to interpret the law and apply it in settling disputes either between the government and a person, as, for example, when there is a charge of a crime or where a governmental agency seeks to enforce a statute or its own regulation, or between two persons. However, the courts have a good deal more power than is generally appreciated.

American courts today continue the tradition of the early common-law courts of England. When there is a dispute between two persons, it is the function of the appropriate court, when asked to resolve it, to apply the applicable law to decide whether the petitioning party (plaintiff) is entitled to what he claims, such as money damages for some injury to his person or property he has suffered as a result of the activities of the other person (defendant). There may be one or more statutes or, possibly, even governmental agency regulations which apply. If so, it or they will be applied, but frequently, however, there are none. Such a state of affairs would not permit the court to abdicate its function. It still must decide the controversy, and it then relies upon the previous decisions of the appellate courts in the same state in similar situations. It uses the rule of conduct developed in the earlier case—the precedent—to decide the present controversy.

If the controversy involves a new situation, the court's job is more difficult. For example, the old common-law rule that a landowner owned the space under his land to the center of the earth and above it to the heavens served well enough to resolve disputes between landowners and power companies seeking to string wires to serve their customers. It did not, however, appear to be satisfactory when the landowner complained of airplanes flying overhead, and the courts modified the old rule so as to balance society's interest in developing the new invention and the interest of the individual landowner. Even the modified rule was later subject to revision in a case against one who used an airplane to attempt to cause precipitation through chemical seeding of clouds over the plaintiff's land.[14] In these new situations courts cannot await legislative action. A decision must be made, and in rendering it the court makes new law.

Interpreting Enacted Law. Even when there is a pertinent statute the court cannot always go to the statute books and find a clear answer as to whether the plaintiff or the defendant is right. It is very difficult and frequently impossible to draft a statute that is not ambiguous when applied to a specific controversy. Legislators may intentionally enact a statute that uses broad and general terms because they feel incapable of foreseeing the variety of situations to which they might later like to see it applied. The Sherman Act, discussed in Chapter 46, is a prime example of this kind of statute. In addition, draftsmen and promotors of legislation may also choose to use rather unspecific or unclear wording because they think it more likely that the bill will be passed in that form than if it is made more specific. In addition, it should be pointed out that even when people seek to be precise and specific, their words are frequently susceptible to more than one meaning, especially when applied to an unforeseen situation.

Courts in the final analysis, therefore, determine what the law is even where

---

[14] See *Southwest Weather Research v. Rounsaville*, 320 S.W.2d 211 (Ct. Civ. App. Tex. 1959).

a legislature has spoken. This observation is also true of administrative (agency) regulations and even of constitutions. As Justice Charles Evans Hughes once said of the United States Constitution and the Supreme Court, "The Constitution is what the Judges say it is."

Judicial Review. The federal courts have another power, one which does not appear in the Constitution but which was exercised by Chief Justice John Marshall in 1803 in the famous case of *Marbury v. Madison.* It is called the power of judicial review and under it the courts have claimed successfully the right to declare that an act by either of the other two branches of government is unconstitutional and, therefore, unenforceable. The Supreme Court has on a number of occasions declared regulations of the administrative agencies and acts of Congress unconstitutional. It has also held acts of governmental officials unconstitutional, and in a few cases has held an act of the President to be unconstitutional. State laws and actions by state officials may also be found to conflict with the United States Constitution. It is this power of judicial review, now well established and accepted even though not always popular in particular cases,[15] which leads commentators to say that the judiciary is the first among the three equal branches of government. State courts also exercise the power of judicial review.

Limits on Courts. The power of judicial review, however, does not give judges free reign to indulge their biases and predilections. First, judges in all but the court of final resort, state or federal (and it is the United States Supreme Court when a matter of interpretation of the federal Constitution is involved), may be overruled by a higher court upon appeal. Secondly, there is self-restraint. Judges are expected to base their decisions on precedents under the doctrine of *stare decisis,* thus maintaining continuity and a considerable amount of consistency in "judge-made law." Although a court—even a trial court —may refuse to follow a precedent which seems clearly applicable, this is a very rare occurrence. If it is a trial court, the decision is quite certain to be appealed, and if it is the highest appellate court, it will feel bound to justify its action in terms of new conditions or a previous error. Thirdly, appeal courts generally publish opinions in which they carefully explain the rationale leading to their decision. Fourthly, appellate judges sit in groups of from three to nine or more, depending upon the court. Biases are, therefore, likely to be cancelled out to a greater or lesser extent depending upon the similarity of backgrounds of the judges. A fifth restraint is that in many states some or all judges are elected. However, the federal judiciary is appointed for life and in a number

---

[15] Much of the major legislation of the New Deal was declared unconstitutional by the Supreme Court in the mid-1930s. As a result, President Roosevelt proposed that Congress increase the number of justices so that he could appoint enough new justices to gain majority votes upholding his legislative program. The "court packing" proposal was dropped when two of the justices began in 1937 to vote to uphold similar legislation.

of states the judges are appointed, and if they stand for election at all, it is infrequently and the voters can only remove. Under this system, if a judge is defeated his successor is appointed.

Summary

The courts not only continue to make law as the English courts did by deciding disputes but they determine the meaning of constitutions, statutes, and administrative regulations. They also have the power of judicial review which permits them to declare unconstitutional federal and state statutes, regulations of government agencies and even the acts of governmental officials, including the President.

There are a number of restraints on the freedom of judges to decide cases as they might wish, varying for different courts. They include: (1) right of appeal (except in the highest court); (2) tradition and their oath of office; (3) necessity of appeal courts to publish a written opinion; (4) multiple judge courts on appeal; and (5) need to be reelected.

How Judges Find the Law

Trial Judges. The trial judge is bound to apply the law of the jurisdiction, and if there is a jury he must instruct it properly as to what the law is. There may be an applicable provision of the state or federal Constitution or a statute which will clearly apply and decide the case once the facts are determined. Where their applicability is uncertain or their meaning ambiguous, the courts have, over the years, developed a number of rules for interpreting documents. However, there is often considerable opportunity for disagreement. In such a situation, the attorneys will each argue for (and submit proposed instructions if there is a jury) the interpretation that is most favorable to their particular clients. The judge must then determine, perhaps making his own independent study, what he believes to be the correct interpretation and so instruct the jury. If there is no applicable statute or constitutional provision, then the attorneys, and ultimately the judge, must determine the law from earlier decided cases, as described above. Indeed, prior cases decided by appeals courts of the jurisdiction will also be looked to for an authoritative interpretation of a statute or constitution provision.

Appeal Courts. The function of appeal courts is to correct errors of law made by inferior courts and, particularly for the supreme court or whatever the highest court of the jurisdiction is called, to declare authoritatively what the law is. The supreme court has all of the difficulties of interpreting the law that the trial court has, and its role is much more important because it has the final word, subject only to a change by the legislature or overruling by the court in a later case.

Much has been written on how judges, especially appeals court judges, decide cases. Obviously, it is not a mechanical process, and all judges do not approach the task in the same way. Indeed, it can be a highly creative process and much of it is intuitive. Some understanding of the process should be helpful to anyone reading the cases in this text or trying to understand a news account of a recent decision of the United States Supreme Court.

The first step in deciding a case in which there is no applicable statute, since our courts operate under the doctrine of *stare decisis,* is to find precedents, that is, decisions of the court in cases involving substantially the same facts. Since it is seldom that the facts will be precisely the same, there is room for some discretion and even imagination in selecting the facts of the present case which are fundamental to the decision and thus in determining what kinds of cases offer precedents upon which the judge may rely. A celebrated example is Justice Benjamin N. Cardozo's opinion in *Buick v. McPherson.*[16] Instead of following the decision in a case involving a stage coach upon which Buick was confidently relying, Cardozo in his opinion argued persuasively that decisions in cases involving a poison and a coffee urn were more appropriate precedents. As Edward H. Levi says, "The problem for the law is: when will it be just to treat different cases as though they were the same?"[17] The second step is to abstract from these precedents a rule which states the law as it has developed through those cases. The third and final step then is to apply this rule to the present case in order to find either for or against the plaintiff.

Judges are required under the doctrine of *stare decisis* to consider precedents within the same jurisdiction, but they may choose to "distinguish" (that is, find they don't apply because the present case differs in some material fact) the case or, in the case of the highest appeals court, even overrule them. They may or may not follow a precedent from another jurisdiction, according to whether the judges find the reasoning in the opinion persuasive.

Summary

The task of the trial judge in applying or instructing the jury as to the law of the jurisdiction is frequently difficult whether he is applying a statutory or constitutional provision or finding precedents among earlier decided cases. Even statutes can be ambiguous and their applicability uncertain.

The same difficulty inheres in the task of the appeals court. There the judges tend to follow a three-step process: (1) select as precedents cases which have involved similar facts; (2) determine from them a rule of law which would explain how they were decided; and (3) apply that rule to the present case. The process is not a mechanical one but can involve great creativity on the part of the judge in determining what facts to emphasize in seeking similar cases as precedents.

---

[16] 111 N.E. 1050 (N.Y. 1916).

[17] *An Introduction to Legal Reasoning* (Chicago: University of Chicago Press, 1948), p. 3.

Federal Court System

Jurisdiction.   No court has authority to hear every sort of dispute that might be brought to it. Some are specialized as to subject matter; for example, a probate court deals only with property left by deceased persons. Every court serves only some geographic area; citizens of California cannot bring a dispute arising in California to a Nevada court, nor can a dispute involving Canadians arising in Canada be appealed to the United States Supreme Court. Minor state courts may have their authority to hear cases—their jurisdiction—limited to disputes of less than some sum of money, such as $1000.

Article III of the Constitution establishes the Supreme Court and leaves to Congress the duty of establishing such additional courts as it feels are desirable. Under this article federal courts may hear cases arising under the Constitution, federal statutes and treaties, admiralty cases, controversies to which the United States is a party or between states or between a state and citizens of another state. Also, the federal courts have jurisdiction to hear cases between citizens of different states. Thus, most of the case load of the federal courts falls into two categories of cases: those involving a federal question and those involving diversity of citizenship. Cases involving federal statutes, including crimes defined by federal law, and claiming violation of rights granted by the Constitution are federal questions. Diversity of citizenship exists when one of the parties on one side of the suit is from a different state from any of the parties on the opposing side. For this purpose a corporation is treated as a citizen of the state of its incorporation or of the state in which it has its principal or general office if that is a different state. Congress has restricted the federal courts in civil (noncriminal) cases involving either a federal question or diversity of citizenship to those in which the amount in controversy exceeds $10,000 exclusive of interest and costs.

Federal courts have exclusive jurisdiction over patents, copyrights, bankruptcy, crimes defined by federal law, and a few other matters. They have concurrent jurisdiction with the state courts over the broad area of general civil actions involving diversity of citizenship, that is, a plaintiff can choose either the federal or a state court. If he chooses a state court the defendant may have the case removed to the federal court if the jurisdictional amount ($10,000) is involved.

District Court.   With a few exceptions the district court is the court of original jurisdiction in the federal system. It is here that suits are started, and it is here that issues of fact are determined. There is at least one United States District Court for each state and the more populated states have two or more districts. There may be one or more judges assigned to a district depending upon the case load.

Court of Appeals.   There are 11 United States Courts of Appeal, one serving the District of Columbia alone because so many cases involving the federal government arise there. Ordinarily appeals from United States District Courts are taken to the court of appeals for the region in which the district court is located. The court of appeals also has jurisdiction to review directly certain orders of administrative agencies such as the Securities and Exchange Commission and the Federal Trade Commission. Courts of appeal hear most cases in panels of three judges but some matters may be heard *en banc,* that is, by all of the judges of that circuit. The number of judges in each circuit varies according to the workload—from three to 15 at the present time.

The function of a court of appeals is to review the work of the district court. To be granted an appeal, a party who is discontented with the judgment of the trial court, the appellant, must allege that an error of law was made during the course of the trial. Such an error might be an erroneous ruling on a motion or an incorrect statement of the law made in an instruction to the jury. The court of appeals reviews the record of the case, reads the briefs, hears the arguments of the attorneys for the parties to the suit, and decides the issues raised on the appeal. If no material error has been committed, the judgment of the district court will be affirmed. If material error has been committed, the court of appeals may grant a judgment for the appellant, thus disposing of the case; or it may set aside the judgment of the lower court and send the case back for retrial, that is, the case is reversed and remanded. In some instances, the judgment of the lower court may be affirmed in part and reversed in part. If the case is an equity case, the court of appeals may modify the decree of the trial court, may set it aside and order a new trial, or may affirm it.

Supreme Court.   Whether a case decided by a federal court may be reviewed by the Supreme Court is determined by statute and the Court's own rules. There are two procedures by which review is obtainable—by appeal and by writ of certiorari. The latter is entirely discretionary with the court, and review is granted usually to resolve conflicts between prior decisions of different courts of appeal or in questions of legal importance to the nation. Even where a party is entitled to appeal, the Court may grant a motion to affirm a case coming from a federal court or a motion to dismiss a state court case without a hearing.

Review may be had on appeal from a court of appeals of cases where that court has held a state statute to be unconstitutional or in conflict with laws (or treaties) of the United States. Review of the court of appeals' decision may be had by writ of certiorari in other criminal and civil cases. Also, a court of appeals may certify a case to the Supreme Court when it desires instructions. In such a situation the Court may give instructions or decide the entire case. Where a matter is required to be heard by a three-judge district court, appeal may be taken directly to the Supreme Court. Such courts are required, for example, to hear actions seeking to enjoin enforcement of a federal or state statute on the ground the statute is unconstitutional. The federal government may also request such a court to hear an enforcement action brought under the Sherman Act.

The Supreme Court may also review on appeal a final judgment of the highest court in a state when the state court has decided a case on the ground that a federal statute or treaty is invalid or when the state court has held a state statute valid despite the claim of the losing party that the statute is in conflict with the Constitution or laws of the United States. The Supreme Court may also take cases from the highest state court by writ of certiorari where a right is claimed under the Constitution or where the validity of a federal statute is in question.

Original jurisdiction is given to the Supreme Court in cases affecting ambassadors and consuls of foreign countries and where a state is sued by another state.

Special Courts.   The federal court system also includes several special courts. The Court of Claims is established to hear claims against the United States, although district courts may also hear such cases. There is also a Customs Court to hear controversies over the imposition of duties on imported goods and a Court of Customs and Patent Appeals, which hears appeals from the customs courts and appeals from the Patent Office involving patents and trademarks. Bankruptcy proceedings are heard by the district courts.

Administrative Agencies.   In addition, there are numerous quasi-judicial bodies within the government agencies. Usually, the governing body of the agency acts as the final point of appeal within the agency. This is true for the Interstate Commerce Commission (ICC), the National Labor Relations Board (NLRB), the Securities and Exchange Commission (SEC), the Federal Trade Commission (FTC), and several others. The Tax Court is also an administrative court within the Department of the Treasury.

Summary

The Constitution establishes and gives specific jurisdiction to the Supreme Court but leaves to Congress the jurisdiction and organization of lower courts. In the federal system the district court is the trial court. When a dissatisfied party claims the trial court made an error of law, he or she may take an appeal to the court of appeals, although under certain circumstances appeal may be taken directly to the Supreme Court. The function of an appeals court is to correct errors of law. Cases can go to the Supreme Court either on appeal or a writ of certiorari. Even where a party is entitled to an appeal under the statutes defining the jurisdiction of the Supreme Court, the Court may refuse to grant a hearing and may decide the case on motion. It has full discretion as to whether to grant a writ of certiorari. The Supreme Court is granted original jurisdiction by the Constitution in certain cases, such as suits of one state against another.

State Courts

Jurisdiction.   The states have general jurisdiction over controversies arising between the citizens of the state. They have jurisdiction over all controversies involving the title to land, other than federally owned land, which is within their borders, and they have jurisdiction over all crimes committed within the state, except crimes against the federal government. The various courts of the state system have whatever jurisdiction is conferred on them by the constitution and statutes of the state. The names of the various courts and the way they are organized varies widely between the different states but the following brief description will provide a general understanding of their nature.

Inferior Courts.   A very large volume of cases involving minor violations of criminal statutes and civil controversies involving relatively small amounts of money are handled in courts which keep no transcript of the testimony and proceedings, that is, they are not courts of record. Such courts may be called a justice of the peace (j.p.) court in rural areas or municipal court in towns and cities. The judicial officer may not be a trained lawyer. Some cities have a small claims court where the claimant may argue his own case and procedure is informal. If an appeal is taken, there must be a trial *de novo;* that is, since there is no record there will be a new trial in a court of record.

Trial Courts.   State courts of record having jurisdiction to hear criminal and civil cases without limit as to penalty or amount of damages, are usually called circuit, superior, district or county courts. Their geographic jurisdiction is often a county. In the more populous states, and areas within those states, special courts are often established to handle particular types of cases, such as domestic relations courts, probate courts and juvenile courts.

State Appeals Courts.   In most states there is only one court having general appellate jurisdiction, usually called the supreme court. Some states have two appellate courts. Where there are two courts, the intermediate court is usually called the court of appeals. It may be provided that certain cases can be appealed from the intermediate court to the supreme court and that some types of cases may be appealed to the highest court directly from the trial court. New York's nomenclature is confusing since there the highest court is called the court of appeals and the intermediate court is the supreme court, one division of which also serves as a trial court.

Summary

The court systems of the states vary considerably but include inferior courts such as those of justices of the peace and municipal courts. Trial courts of general jurisdiction are often called circuit or county courts. Some states have two levels of appeals courts, others only one. Where there are two tiers it may be provided that appeals in certain types of cases may be taken directly to the highest court, usually called the supreme court.

Procedure

The Adversary System. Disputes are settled by courts under what is known as the adversary system. In this system the judge's role is viewed not only as unbiased but also as essentially passive.

It is up to the party who claims to have been injured or otherwise wronged to prove in court both that the facts he relies upon actually occurred and that the law entitles him to a recovery. The other party seeks to disprove one or both of these claims. It is the lawyer's job to present his client's version of the facts, to convince the judge (or jury if one is used) that they are true and to undermine confidence in the other party's allegations to the extent they are inconsistent. Each lawyer seeks to persuade the judge that his interpretation of the law applicable to the case is the correct one, and he proposes jury instructions which state the law in the light most favorable to his client's case. If there is no jury the lawyer seeks to present the judge with a line of reasoning which, if accepted, will result in a decision favoring the lawyer's client. It is believed that this competition between counsel in presenting their competing versions of the facts and conceptions of the law will result in the judge, or jury, sorting out the true facts and the judge finding the soundest view of the law. Proponents believe that the principal advantage of the adversary system rests in the fact that it limits the role and power of judges. The facts and issues are developed by the competing parties and the system makes it more difficult for a judge to control the outcome of the case.

However, the judge does not have to be entirely passive. He is responsible for the correct application of the law and he may ignore the legal reasoning of both of the opposing attorneys and base his rulings and decisions wholly on his own study of the law. Also, he may ask questions of witnesses and suggest types of evidence he would like to have presented. In certain types of disputes, especially in domestic relations matters, judges assume much more of the initiative and may even change character completely and engage in attempts at mediation.

The Functions of Procedure. There is a large body of law which establishes the rules and standards for determining disputes in the courts. Much of this law is complex and technical. However, knowledge of some of the basic principles of the law of procedure is necessary if the student is to understand the reports of cases included in this text and for a businessman if he is to be able to cooperate effectively with his lawyer when he becomes a party to a legal controversy.

The law of procedure varies in different jurisdictions and in different types of cases. For example, the procedure followed in a criminal case is somewhat different from that applicable to a civil case. Equity, probate, and admiralty cases have still different rules. Since businessmen are most frequently involved in civil cases only civil procedure will be discussed.

Summons, Complaint, and Answer.   When suit is brought against a person, he or she is entitled to notice of the suit and must be given an opportunity to defend. In most jurisdictions the issuing and serving of a summons is the first step taken in the starting of a civil lawsuit. The summons notifies the defendant that suit has been started against him by the named plaintiff. The form of the summons in general use states briefly the nature of the suit and the time within which the defendant must enter his appearance, which can be done through an attorney.

The rules relative to the service of the summons vary widely. At common law and generally in civil law cases the summons is served on the defendant personally by the sheriff or one of his deputies within the territorial limits of the court's jurisdiction. For instance, a summons issued out of a circuit or district court having jurisdiction over a county would have to be served on the defendant within the boundaries of that county. In some states the summons may be left at the defendant's residence or place of business; and in a few states, service may be made by mail. Other rules relative to service apply in cases such as divorce suits or suits to quiet title to land.

In order that the defendant may know the claims of the plaintiff and be prepared to defend against those claims, the plaintiff is required to file a complaint (also called a declaration or a petition). Under the rules generally in force, the plaintiff's complaint must state in separate, numbered paragraphs the plaintiff's claim in full. Any matter omitted from the complaint is not a part of the plaintiff's case; and evidence, in the case of trial, is not admissible to prove material facts not stated in the complaint. The complaint will also state the remedy requested by the plaintiff. In a civil law case the remedy requested is usually a stated sum of money as damages. It is of the utmost importance that the plaintiff state all the facts of his case to his attorney, since the omission of material facts from the complaint may be fatal to the plaintiff's case.

If the defendant wishes to defend, he or she must, within the permitted time, file an answer. It answers the plaintiff's complaint paragraph by paragraph, either admitting or denying the matters stated in the paragraph or neither admitting nor denying the matters stated but leaving the plaintiff to his proof. The defendant may, in addition, state an affirmative defense to the plaintiff's case. For example, suppose the plaintiff bases his suit on a contract. The defendant may admit the contract but set up, by way of affirmative defense, facts which, if established, would prove that the defendant was induced to enter into the contract by fraudulent representations made by the plaintiff and therefore is not bound by the contract.

If the defendant sets up an affirmative defense, he must state the facts of the defense in the same form as that required of the plaintiff in his complaint, and the plaintiff must make an answer (called a reply) to the defendant's statements in the same form as that required in the defendant's answer to the plaintiff's complaint. Likewise, a counter claim may be made by the defendant.

The complaint and answer (called "pleadings") serve a twofold purpose: they inform the parties of their relative claims, fulfilling the constitutional requirement of "notice," and they form the basis for the trial of the case. Only those points which are matters in dispute or issues in the case will be considered on the trial of the case. Points which are not stated in the pleadings and points admitted in the pleadings are not issues in the case, and no evidence will be admitted to prove such points. If a material point has been omitted from the pleadings, the trial judge may, after proper motion has been made, permit an amendment of the pleadings and allow the omitted matter to be added.

Demurrer.   If a defendant's attorney, upon reading the complaint, believes that the plaintiff could not recover even if the alleged facts are true, he will file a demurrer (often called a motion to dismiss) instead of an answer. Such a response necessitates a hearing and a determination by the judge as to whether the complaint states a cause of action. The judge may permit amendment of the complaint, but if it remains insufficient, the case is dismissed without further proceedings.

Discovery and Pretrial Hearing.   The trend in legal procedure has been away from legal technicalities toward simplification, greater flexibility, and emphasis upon the merits of the case. One important development with this purpose is "discovery procedure." In civil cases (suits between private parties) rules of procedure adopted by the federal courts and by many of the states in the last few decades give the parties access to the facts upon which the other party relies. This permits a lawyer, in the presence of the opposing lawyer, to interrogate the other party's witnesses under oath prior to trial and to obtain copies of pertinent documents and other data. In an injury case the defendant would be permitted to have a physician of his choice examine the plaintiff and to have copies of such potentially pertinent evidence as x rays and photographs. The pretrial interrogations, called depositions, may be used to impeach the testimony of the witness at the trial, if there should be discrepancies. Either party may make use of depositions to bring into the trial testimony from a person who cannot be present in person.

Another recent procedural device of great importance is the pretrial conference during which the opposing attorneys are required to sit down with the judge to try to get agreement, a "stipulation," on as many of the pertinent facts as possible so that the time required to establish legal proof of them through witnesses in court may be eliminated. Also, the judge will encourage the parties to try to settle the case by coming to an agreement disposing of the dispute so that it need not go to trial. Both efforts are directed at clearing the increasingly congested calendars of most courts so as to shorten the time between the filing of the pleadings (the complaint and answer) of the parties and the conclusion of the trial. Simplification of pleading procedure serves the same purpose as well as putting more emphasis on merit than form.

Trial of Case. When the pleadings are complete and the issues determined, the case will be set for trial. The parties will decide whether or not they wish a trial by jury, unless the case is to be tried in equity, in which case a jury, as a general rule, will not be used. If a jury is desired, it must then be selected and sworn in, after which the attorneys will usually make statements to it, outlining the claims their clients make in regard to the controversy. The witnesses for the plaintiff will then be sworn, examined, and cross-examined. When all the evidence of the plaintiff has been presented, his attorney will so indicate, and the attorney for the defendant will take charge.

At this point the defendant's attorney may make a motion asking the judge to direct a judgment for the defendant. If the judge decides that the plaintiff has offered no evidence which would justify the granting of the remedy requested, he will grant the motion, and the trial will end at this point. However, if the judge feels that the plaintiff has offered any evidence which would support a judgment, he will deny the motion, and the trial will continue.

The defendant's witnesses will then be sworn and examined on direct examination by the defendant's attorney and cross-examined by the plaintiff's attorney. When all the testimony of the witnesses has been heard, the case is ready to be presented to the jury. At this point in the trial, either the defendant's attorney or the plaintiff's attorney, or both, may make a motion for a directed verdict. If both attorneys make motions for a directed verdict, the case will not, under the rules of procedure generally followed, be presented to the jury but will be decided by the judge. If only one motion for a directed verdict is made, the judge will deny the motion unless he feels that no credible evidence has been offered which would justify the jury in finding for the other party. If no motion for a directed verdict is made, or if such motion is made and denied, the case will be presented to the jury for its consideration.

The attorneys will sum up the case and give their arguments to the jury, after which the judge will instruct the jury as to the law which applies in the case. In his instructions the judge must not, under the laws of most states, comment on the weight of the evidence or credibility of the witnesses; he must confine himself to expounding the rules of law which the jury should apply in reaching its verdict.

Where the amount of the plaintiff's loss is in dispute, the jury not only finds for one of the parties but if it finds for the plaintiff, its verdict will state the amount of the recovery. The attorney for the losing party may make a motion for a judgment notwithstanding the verdict. If the judge finds no competent evidence to support the verdict, or decides that the law requires the opposite result, he will grant the motion; otherwise it will be denied.

If the verdict is not set aside, the judge will enter a judgment based on the verdict. The defeated party may make a motion for a new trial. This gives the trial judge an opportunity to correct material errors which may have been made during the trial; however, such motions are usually denied. If the unsuccessful party thinks a material error was committed during the trial, he may appeal the case.

If there is no jury, the judge is the finder of facts. Upon appeal, his findings of fact, as in the case of those of a jury, are accepted as correct unless the appeal court finds no competent evidence supporting a finding of fact.

Procedure in Administrative Agencies. The procedure followed in administrative agencies is more informal than that followed in the courts. In general, the members of the agency investigate suspected and reported violations of the regulatory law over which agency has jurisdiction. If the members of the agency decide that there has been a violation, the accused will be prosecuted. The hearing is held before the members of the agency, who are invested with quasi-judicial powers, and who will impose sanctions if the accused is found guilty. The accused does have the right to appeal to the courts; but under the terms of the act creating the agency, this right is limited. In general, no appeal is allowed if the decision involves only the discretionary powers of the persons rendering the decision. However, the court will, as a general rule, hear and determine an appeal if it is based on the ground that the person making the decision acted capriciously or was guilty of discrimination, or that the subject matter of the case was not within the scope of the powers vested in the agency.

Summary

American courts operate under what is known as the adversary system. The determination of liability (or guilt or innocence in criminal cases) is made through a contest in which the attorney for each party tries to persuade the jury (or judge if he is the trier of fact) what are the true facts and the judge what the appropriate rules of law are. The law of procedure provides a complex body of rules by which this contest is conducted.

In a noncriminal case the suit begins with the serving of a summons on the defendant which requires him to appear in court on or before a certain time. A complaint stating the plaintiff's claim must also be given to him. The defendant must serve an "answer" on the plaintiff. The purpose of these documents, called the pleadings, is to inform the parties of the relative claims and the trial is limited to those claims.

A demurrer filed by the defendant's attorney may result in dismissal of the case without trial. Through "discovery" procedure either party may get information to help him prepare his case. A pretrial hearing may be held by the judge to try to shorten the trial or eliminate it by settlement.

On the trial of a case, the plaintiff's witnesses are sworn and examined first, then the defendant's witnesses are sworn and they testify. Rebuttal witnesses may testify but no new facts can be introduced on rebuttal. When all the witnesses have been heard, the lawyers argue the case, the judge charges the jury, and it then deliberates the case in secret and brings in a verdict. The judgment is entered by the judge. The judge has the power to set a verdict aside on proper motion provided no credible evidence has been offered which supports the verdict.

Arbitration

Nature and Advantages.   Arbitration is a method of settling disputes which is available as an alternative to the court system. The parties to the dispute select a person or persons who may or may not have been trained in the law, to hear and determine the dispute. Most disputes arising under labor contracts, many involving exports and imports, and a small proportion of other commercial contracts are resolved by arbitration.

Frequently, the parties have agreed as part of the contract into which they have entered to submit any dispute arising out of the contract to arbitration. Procedure in arbitration is usually more informal than in a court and technical rules of evidence are not applied. However, frequently the arbitrator will render a written award.

The principal advantages claimed for arbitration are: (1) disposition of the dispute is usually much quicker—perhaps days instead of months or even years; (2) an arbitrator may be chosen who has considerable familiarity with the technical background of the dispute; (3) since procedure tends to be informal the parties need not employ lawyers to represent them (although they frequently do); and (4) the time required of executives to be witnesses and other costs are likely to be much less than in a trial.

Questions

1.   How would you briefly explain the nature and functions of law in America to a visitor from Peking?
2.   Why is the concept of law as merely a set of rules inadequate?
3.   What are the principal differences between the common law and statutes as sources of law in the United States?
4.   What are the principal characteristics of the adversary system of judicial determination?
5.   To what extent does the doctrine of *stare decisis* make the decision in a lawsuit predictable?

chapter 2

Flexibility and Growth in the Law

Introduction

Law Is Dynamic. The courts, not just the legislatures, serve an important function in keeping the law in tune with the beliefs and felt needs of the times. Chapter 1 discussed the tendency for the principal functions of the legal system to change over time and how the common law permits change despite its usual adherence to the doctrine of *stare decisis.* This chapter will provide a specific example of this process. Here the focus will be on the changing meanings of the Commerce and Due Process clauses of the United States Constitution as they have been interpreted by the courts, and especially the Supreme Court, in dealing with attempts by the Congress and the state legislatures to regulate business.

Demand for Government Regulation. As the Industrial Revolution was completed in America near the end of the 19th Century and as the power of businessmen grew, some of their practices came to be viewed as undesirable and demands for regulation became insistent. Railroads, in particular, were heavily criticized for discriminatory rates and policies. There was also a strong trend towards concentration of economic power in all kinds of processing and manufacturing industries through agreements to divide territories, to fix prices, and to combine huge aggregations of capital through the trust device or by corporate mergers. Federal legislation was enacted to deal with these evils, first the Interstate Commerce Act in 1887 and then the Sherman Antitrust Act in 1890.[1]

Constitutional Challenges of Government Regulation. In the period prior to World War II, businessmen frequently turned to the courts to resist limitations upon their freedom of action imposed by statutes seeking to regulate

---

[1] Treated in Chapter 46.

30

their activities. Their lawyers raised constitutional issues, claiming either that the United States Constitution does not grant power to the Congress to enact such a regulatory measure, or that a prohibition in the Constitution prevents either the Congress or the state legislature from passing such legislation.[2]

These constitutional challenges were founded upon the basic concept of constitutional government. A constitutional government is one that is limited in its powers.[3] It cannot violate or take away certain rights retained by its citizens or, in the case of our federal government, rights retained by the states.[4] In addition, the Constitution and certain of the amendments, especially the first eight, set forth certain specific prohibitions or limits on the exercise of governmental power by the federal government. Therefore, Congressional legislation must both be authorized by the Constitution and not prohibited by it. By interpretation of the Supreme Court, the Fourteenth Amendment has been held not only to impose upon the states the prohibitions contained in that amendment but also those contained in the first eight amendments.

Insofar as regulation of business today is concerned, the most important power granted to the federal government by the Constitution is the Commerce Power, found in Article I, sec. 8, par. 3. The Due Process Clauses of the Fifth and Fourteenth Amendments have been used most frequently in the past to challenge government efforts to regulate business.

Summary

In the American system of constitutional government the federal government has only those powers delegated to it by the states through that document. The power that is most important to business is the Commerce Clause. The powers given are limited, however, by specific prohibitions in the Constitution. The most important of these in the past have been the Due Process Clauses of the Fifth and Fourteenth Amendments.

The Commerce Clause

Interstate versus Intrastate Commerce.   In the earliest Supreme Court case involving the Commerce Clause, *Gibbons v. Ogden,*[5] Chief Justice Marshall refused to follow the argument of Daniel Webster, Gibbons' attorney, that the

---

[2] Another common basis for resisting government actions affecting businessmen was that the agency or official has not been properly authorized to take the action complained of.

[3] Some governments having documents called constitutions are not constitutional governments in this sense.

[4] The Tenth Amendment declares that the federal government has no power not delegated to it by the states through the Constitution. The Ninth Amendment declares that the enumeration of certain rights belonging to the United States "shall not be construed to deny or disparage others retained by the people."

[5] 9 Wheat. 1 (1824).

federal government should be given exclusive power over commerce and held that regulation of commerce wholly within a state is reserved solely to that state by the Constitution. Thus, for many years the courts viewed mining, processing, manufacturing, and retail sales as inherently intrastate activities.

By this view the federal power to regulate commerce extends only to commerce between the states and with foreign nations, not to commerce which is wholly contained within a single state and which does not affect commerce between states. This was held clearly to extend to regulation of transportation industries such as railroads, trucking companies, and airlines, and it also applies to telephone companies and TV stations whose signals cross state lines. Likewise, users of the mails such as correspondence schools have also been considered to be engaged in interstate commerce. Generally it has been held that interstate commerce in goods begins when they are delivered to an interstate carrier (or a connecting carrier) and that they remain in interstate commerce during temporary interruptions or transfers to another means of carriage and even after they arrive at their destination while they remain unsold in their original packages.

"To Regulate." Once an activity is found to be interstate commerce, the power of Congress to legislate with respect to it is very broad. The power to regulate was early recognized as the power to prohibit so that, unlike the use of the Tax Power to regulate, there are essentially no inherent limits on the Commerce Power. Indeed, it has been used to give, in effect, the federal government the "police power" that it was not otherwise given by the Constitution. The police power in a constitutional sense is the power of a government to promote the health, safety, and general welfare of the people. Although the Preamble of the Constitution states that one of the objects of the federal government is "to promote the general welfare," under the doctrine of delegated powers some specific power must be found elsewhere in the Constitution to validate any particular piece of legislation. Therefore, there was considerable doubt as to the constitutionality of the early use of the Commerce Clause to regulate or prohibit something deemed harmful to the general welfare.

Trends in Court Decisions. In 1895 Congress passed a law prohibiting transportation of lottery tickets into a state from another state or foreign country. This was upheld by the Supreme Court in a 5 to 4 vote in the Lottery Case.[6] Later the Food and Drug Act of 1906 was upheld on its authority.

However, when Congress passed the Federal Child Labor Act of 1916, which prohibited transportation in interstate commerce of products of factories and mines where children under age of 14 had been permitted to work more than 8 hours a day or 6 days a week, the Court declared the Act unconstitutional by a 5 to 4 vote in *Hammer v. Dagenhart.*[7] The majority opinion said that the

[6] *Champion v. Ames,* 188 U.S. 321 (1903).
[7] 247 U.S. 251 (1918).

power over mining and manufacturing within the states was left solely to the states under the Tenth Amendment, and the Commerce Power could not be used to oust the states from the exercise of their powers. However, later, without overruling *Dagenhart,* the Court upheld the power of Congress to use the Commerce Power to prohibit interstate commerce in stolen automobiles and in kidnapped persons.

In *Schecter Poultry Corp. v. United States*[8] the Court declared unconstitutional the National Industrial Recovery Act, which was the Roosevelt administration's major attack on the Great Depression of the 30s. The Act fixed wages and hours in almost all industries in the country and also sought to regulate what were considered unfair trade practices. Although the poultry corporation purchased some of its live poultry outside New York State, the effect of the Code applied to it under the Act was only to control the hours and wages it paid its workers in its plant in Brooklyn and its sales practices within the state. The Court held that the live poultry had come to a permanent rest within the state so that what happened to it thereafter was purely intrastate commerce.

Several other parts of the New Deal legislation enacted in the early 1930s were found to be unconstitutional by the Supreme Court, but in 1937 in a landmark decision the Court upheld the National Labor Relations Act when applied to labor organizing within an individual plant as a valid exercise of the Commerce Power. In this case, *NLRB v. Jones & Laughlin Corp.,*[9] Chief Justice Hughes emphasized the widespread operations of this large corporation, saying that the effect of unfair labor practices upon interstate commerce would be more than indirect and remote. However, on the same day the Court also upheld the application of the Act to two small companies.

Extent of Commerce Power Today. Once the Commerce Power came to be interpreted as applying to activities such as manufacturing, which had previously been viewed as inherently local and intrastate, it was difficult to draw a sharp new boundary upon the reach of the Commerce Clause. In our highly interdependent economy, few activities do not affect interstate commerce, and federal power to regulate under the clause has been interpreted to extend even to the raising of grain for consumption on the farm.[10] Thus most economic activity is within the reach of federal regulation under the Commerce Power today, and it is used generally for other kinds of police power regulation.

For example, the Commerce Clause was the basis for the Civil Rights Act of 1964. When application of the Act to a downtown motel which refused to rent rooms to blacks was questioned in *Heart of Atlanta Motel v. United States,* the Court upheld it saying, "It is said that the operation of the motel here is of a purely local character. But assuming this to be true, 'if it is interstate

[8] 295 U.S. 495 (1935).
[9] 301 U.S. 1 (1937).
[10] *Wickard v. Filburn,* 317 U.S. 111 (1942).

commerce that feels the pinch it does not matter how local the operations that applies the squeeze.' "[11]

Summary

In an early case the Supreme Court interpreted the Commerce Clause to give to the federal government broad power to regulate interstate commerce but to the states sole power to regulate commerce entirely within their boundaries. Mining and manufacturing were considered to be activities which could not be reached by federal legislation. Beginning in 1937, the Court broadened its interpretation and now even local activities such as farming and motel-keeping are subject to federal regulation under the Commerce Clause if their operation affects, even indirectly, interstate commerce.

Wickard v. Filburn

317 U.S. 111 (U.S. Sup. Ct. 1942)

Filburn (plaintiff) a farmer, sought an injunction against Wickard (defendant), who was Secretary of Agriculture, to enjoin enforcement of a penalty against Filburn. The District Court held for Filburn, and the case was appealed to the Supreme Court. Reversed.

The Agricultural Adjustment Act of 1938 was passed by Congress in an effort to stabilize agricultural production so as to give farmers reasonable minimum prices. The scheme for wheat involved an annual proclamation by the Secretary of Agriculture of a national acreage allotment which was apportioned to the states and eventually to individual farms. Filburn was a small farmer who kept dairy cattle and chickens and raised a small acreage of winter wheat, some of which was sold but much was used on the farm as livestock feed and for family use. His quota for 1941 was established at 11.1 acres. However, he sowed and harvested 23 acres. For this he was assessed a penalty of $117.11.

MR. JUSTICE JACKSON.   Filburn says that this is a regulation of production and consumption of wheat. Such activities are, he urges, beyond the reach of Congressional power under the Commerce Clause, since they are local in character, and their effects upon interstate commerce are at most "indirect."

*   *   *   *   *

The Court's recognition of the relevance of the economic effects in the application of the Commerce Clause . . . has made the mechanical application of legal formulas no longer feasible. Once an economic measure of the reach of the power granted to Congress in the Commerce Clause is accepted, questions of federal power cannot be decided simply by finding the activity in question to be "production" nor can consideration of its economic effects be foreclosed by calling them "indirect. . . ."

---

[11] 379 U.S. 241 (1964).

Whether the subject of the regulation in question was "production," "consumption," or "marketing" is, therefore, not material for purposes of deciding the question of federal power before us. That an activity is of local character may help in a doubtful case to determine whether Congress intended to reach it. The same consideration might help in determining whether in the absence of Congressional action it would be permissible for the state to exert its power on the subject matter, even though in so doing it to some degree affected interstate commerce. But even if Filburn's activity be local and though it may not be regarded as commerce, it may still, whatever its nature, be reached by Congress if it exerts a substantial economic effect on interstate commerce and this irrespective of whether such effect is what might at some earlier time have been defined as "direct" or "indirect."

* * * * *

The effect of consumption of homegrown wheat on interstate commerce is due to the fact that it constitutes the most variable factor in the disappearance of the wheat crop. Consumption on the farm where grown appears to vary in an amount greater than 20 percent of average production. . . .

. . . One of the primary purposes of the act in question was to increase the market price of wheat and to that end limit the volume thereof that could affect the market. It can hardly be denied that a factor of such volume and variability as home-consumed wheat would have a substantial influence on price and market conditions.

Rasmussen v. American Dairy Ass'n

472 F.2d 517 (9th Cir. 1972)

This was a suit by Rasmussen (plaintiff) against the American Dairy Association and others (defendants) seeking recovery for violation of the Sherman Act. The district court dismissed the suit as being beyond the reach of the Sherman Act because interstate commerce was not involved. Reversed and remanded.

Rasmussen was in the fluid milk business in the Phoenix, Arizona, area. In 1965 he introduced a "filled milk" product called "Go." He purchased the dried milk and other ingredients outside of Arizona and mixed them with water at his plant near Phoenix. Dairy Association and the other defendants determined in 1966 to drive "Go" and the other filled milk products out of the Arizona market. To accomplish this they (1) sought to get the Central Arizona Milk Marketing Order amended to reclassify "Go" and other similar products as "Class I" milk, which would increase costs sufficiently to eliminate sales; (2) sponsored legislation to eliminate filled milk from the Arizona market; (3) engaged in a widespread false advertising campaign disparaging "Go" and other filled milk products; and (4) caused the Arizona Dairy Commissioner to issue regulations restricting the labeling, display, and sale of "Go" and other filled milk products.

Dairy Association's principal defense was that the production and sale of "Go" was conducted wholly within Arizona, and, therefore, the Sherman Act did not apply since it could not reach beyond the power of Congress to regulate business that was granted in the Commerce Clause of the Constitution.

BROWNING, CIRCUIT JUDGE. "That Congress (in passing the Sherman Act) wanted to go to the utmost extent of its Constitutional power in restraining trust and monopoly agreements . . . admits of little, if any, doubt. The purpose was to use that power to make of ours, so far as Congress could under our dual system, a competitive business economy." (*United States v. South-Eastern Underwriters Ass'n*) The reach of the Sherman Act is "as inclusive as the constitutional limits of Congress' power to regulate commerce." [Report of the Attorney General's National Committee to Study the Antitrust Laws 62 (1955).] As judicial construction of the commerce clause has expanded over the years to reflect changing evaluations of the necessary scope of the federal commerce power, so too has the reach of the Sherman Act.

In short, the conduct of the defendants is within the jurisdictional reach of the Sherman Act if Congress can prohibit that conduct under the commerce clause.

*   *   *   *   *

The "necessary and proper" standard is met if the regulated conduct has a "substantial economic effect" upon interstate commerce. As the Court said in *Wickard v. Filburn* (1942):

(E)ven if . . . (the) activity be local and though it may not be regarded as commerce, it may still, whatever its nature, be reached by Congress if it exerts a substantial economic effect on interstate commerce, and this irrespective of whether such effect is what might at some earlier time have been defined as "direct" or "indirect."

Or as the Court said in *Heart of Atlanta Motel v. United States,* (1964):

(T)he determinative test of the exercise of power by the Congress under the Commerce Clause is simply whether the activity sought to be regulated is "commerce which concerns more States than one" and has a real and substantial relation to the national interest.

*   *   *   *   *

We turn to whether the complaint, read in the light of the stipulated facts, alleges conduct having a sufficient impact upon interstate commerce in the ingredients of "Go" to bring it within the regulatory power of Congress under the commerce clause, as manifested in the Sherman Act. We hold that it does.

. . . Although local water is the major ingredient of "Go" by volume and weight, in economic terms "Go" consists almost wholly of the ingredients that move in interstate commerce. The fact that those ingredients are not combined until they reach plaintiff's Arizona plant is not enough to interrupt the practical continuity of the movement.

Even if "Go" is not actually "in commerce," however, the relationship between defendants' conduct in suppressing the sale of "Go" and a restraint upon interstate commerce in "Go's" ingredients is, in a realistic business sense, close and substantial. If defendants are successful in preventing the sale of "Go" and other Arizona-made filled milk products in the State of Arizona, those products cannot be sold at all. The quantitative effect on the overall interstate flow of dried milk and other ingredients is not alleged. But it is the nature of the effect that is important: to whatever extent, it is certain that the flow of "Go's" ingredients into Arizona *will* be diminished by an anticompetitive restraint imposed on a product substantially composed of those ingredients. And the states in which those ingredients originate are powerless to protect their commerce against this diminution. Such an "effect" is "substantial" for the purpose of the commerce clause; it has a "real and substantial relationship to the national interest" in a competitive economy as expressed in the Sherman Act.

State Regulation

Power and Limitations.   The original states forming the United States were considered sovereign and, therefore, the federal government has only those powers delegated to it. There is, therefore, no limit on the police power of state governments, including their power to regulate business, except those given up through the Constitution and the limitations in the constitution of the particular state. The most important constitutional limitation is in the Fourteenth Amendment which applies to action by a state or any of its agencies including local governments. Another limitation is that since the Constitution gives the power to regulate interstate commerce to the Congress, state action which obstructs or interferes with such commerce will be void under Article VI, sec. 2, The Supremacy Clause.

State versus Federal Power over Interstate Commerce.   To what extent federal power over interstate commerce is exclusive has been the subject of many Supreme Court opinions, and Chief Justice Marshall early explored this problem in *Gibbons v. Ogden*. Subsequently, the Court has shifted ground from time to time. Some decisions have held state statutes void because the Court found that Congress had enacted legislation on the same general subject as to the state statute under attack, and by so doing it ousted the state from jurisdiction although the state and federal statutes did not actually conflict. During the height of laissez-faire thinking on the Court, it was quick to find that a state statute imposed an unconstitutional "burden" on interstate commerce. Today a state act would have to impede rather clearly the free flow of interstate commerce or discriminate in favor of local businessmen before the Court would be likely to invalidate it. Not all federal statutes, however, intend to exercise the regulatory power of Congress to the full extent permitted by the Constitution.

Summary

States have full authority to regulate business except to the extent their own constitution and the federal Constitution limit their "police powers." The Commerce Clause of the Constitution has been interpreted as a prohibition of state regulation which obstructs or interferes with the free flow of interstate commerce. Although earlier the Supreme Court was quick to find unconstitutional burdens on interstate commerce, it tends not to do so today unless there is clear interference or discrimination against it.

Other Constitutional Restraints on Regulation of Business

The Due Process Amendments. The Fifth and Fourteenth Amendments to the United States Constitution (the Fifth applying to activities of the federal government and the Fourteenth to those of the states) have been the source of the greatest volume of constitutional litigation. During the last two decades they were used as the basis of a widespread attack on the practices of police officers in dealing with suspected criminals which resulted in recognition of a new set of specific rights. These rights were interpreted by the Supreme Court as being implied in the phrase, "nor be deprived of life, liberty, or property, without due process of law," contained in the Fifth Amendment and appearing in essentially the same form in the Fourteenth. However, from near the end of the 19th century until 1937 they were used by the Court primarily to invalidate both federal and state efforts to regulate business.

Substantive Due Process. The original meaning of due process referred to those procedures *due* at common law when the government accused, tried, and imprisoned a person for a crime. It was also applied to the procedures used in affecting other rights, such as, for example, taking an individual's property for a public purpose such as a highway. Essentially, it required procedures considered to be fair. This is what legal scholars call "procedural due process."

The constitutionality of regulatory legislation was attacked, however, not on the ground that the procedures followed in enacting or enforcing the statute were unfair but rather that the statute itself was an arbitrary and unreasonable exercise of legislative power. This is known as "substantive due process." As a noted constitutional authority and critic of substantive due process declared in 1938:

> Today the clause is chiefly important as a restriction upon the substantive content of legislation, and what it means is, in effect, the *approval of the Supreme Court.* The phraseology of judicial decisions is, of course, hardly so outspoken as this. What the Court says is, that legislation must not be "arbitrary" or "unreasonable"; but what this means, is that legislation must not be *unreasonable* to the Court's way of thinking.[12]

An early effort by the Illinois state legislature that fixed minimum charges for storing grain in elevators, which had been challenged as taking property without due process, was upheld by the Supreme Court.[13] However, soon thereafter the Court became heavily influenced by the laissez-faire economic philosophy and began to respond favorably to legal arguments that freedom of contract was included within the term *liberty* written into the Fifth and Fourteenth Amendments.[14] It was not until 1937 that this long line of cases based upon substantive due process arguments was overruled.[15]

---

[12] Edward S. Corwin, *Court over Constitution* (Princeton: Princeton University Press, 1938), pp. 107–8.

[13] *Munn v. Illinois,* 94 U.S. 113 (1877).

[14] See discussion in Chapter 5.

[15] *West Coast Hotel Co. v. Parrish,* 300 U.S. 379 (1937).

Other Restraints. The clause which immediately follows the Due Process Clause of the Fourteenth Amendment, the Equal Protection Clause, has generally been interpreted in business regulation cases as overlapping it in large measure. However, it has been separately relied upon occasionally by the Court to strike down discriminatory state regulation. There is no Equal Protection Clause in the Fifth Amendment.

Restraints Today. The Court is no longer a battleground for economic ideologies. No major act of Congress regulating business has been successfully challenged on constitutional grounds since World War II, and the states are permitted very broad regulatory powers in the economic sphere. Today litigation is most apt to occur where federal and state regulation does or may conflict, with the effect of hindering the free flow of interstate commerce.

Summary

The acceptance by the Supreme Court of the concept of substantive due process permitted it to declare federal regulatory statutes invalid under the Fifth Amendment and state statutes unconstitutional under the Fourteenth Amendment if it thought them unreasonable. After 1937 the Court discontinued invalidating economic regulation under the Due Process Clauses, and today there is little restraint on either level of government in this field except where their regulations do or may conflict.

Burbank v. Lockheed Air Terminal, Inc.

411 U.S. 624 (U.S. Sup. Ct. 1973)

Suit brought by Lockheed Air Terminal (plaintiff) against the City of Burbank, California (defendant), seeking an injunction against enforcement of an ordinance adopted by the Burbank City Council. Burbank appealed from the judgment for Lockheed, and this was affirmed by the court of appeals. Affirmed.

The ordinance prohibited "pure jet" aircraft from taking off from the Hollywood-Burbank Airport between 11:00 P.M. of one day and 7:00 A.M. the next day and made it unlawful for the operator of the airport to allow such a takeoff. Lockheed was the airport operator. The only regularly scheduled flight affected by the ordinance was an intrastate flight on Pacific Southwest Airlines departing for San Diego every Sunday night at 11:30 P.M. The district court found the ordinance unconstitutional on both Supremacy Clause and Commerce Clause grounds because the Federal Aviation Act of 1958 gave the FAA broad authority to regulate the use of airspace and the Noise Control Act of 1972 obligated the FAA and EPA to develop a comprehensive scheme of federal control of the aircraft noise problem.

MR. JUSTICE DOUGLAS. There is to be sure no express provision of preemption in the 1972 Act. That, however, is not decisive. It is the pervasive nature of the scheme of federal regulation of aircraft noise that leads us to conclude that there is preemption.

*   *   *   *   *

Our prior cases on preemption are not precise guidelines in the present controversy, for each case turns on the peculiarities and special features of the federal regulatory scheme in question. Control of noise is, of course, deep seated in the police power of the States. Yet the pervasive control vested in EPA and in FAA under the 1972 Act seems to us to leave no room for local curfews or other local controls. What the ultimate remedy for aircraft noise which plagues many communities and tens of thousands of people is not known. The procedures under the 1972 Act are underway. In addition, the Administrator has imposed a variety of regulations relating to takeoff and landing procedures and runway preferences. The Federal Aviation Act requires a delicate balance between safety and efficiency, and the protection of persons on the ground. Any regulations adopted by the Administrator to control noise pollution must be consistent with the "highest degree of safety." The interdependence of these factors requires a uniform and exclusive system of federal regulation if the congressional objectives underlying the Federal Aviation Act are to be fulfilled.

If we were to uphold the Burbank ordinance and a significant number of municipalities followed suit, it is obvious that fractionalized control of the timing of takeoffs and landings would severely limit the flexibility of the FAA in controlling air traffic flow. The difficulties of scheduling flights to avoid congestion and the concomitant decrease in safety would be compounded. In 1960 the FAA rejected a proposed restriction on jet operations at the Los Angeles airport between 10:00 P.M. and 7:00 A.M. because such restrictions could "create critically serious problems to all air transportation patterns."

Problem Cases

1. Huron Cement Company operated several ships used to transport cement from its mill to distributing plants located in various states bordering the Great Lakes. Two of the ships had hand-fired marine boilers which had to be fired and cleaned periodically while the ships were in port to load or unload. During the cleaning, the smoke emitted from the boiler stacks exceeded the standards allowable under the Detroit Smoke Abatement Code. Structural alterations were required for the ships to comply with the Code. The ships, including their boilers, had been licensed for operation in interstate commerce under federal regulation.

    Detroit instituted criminal proceedings against Huron Cement, and Huron brought an action to enjoin further prosecution of the case and otherwise enforcing the Code against its ships except where excessive smoke emission was caused by improper use of the boilers. Is enforcement of the Code either (1) in conflict with the federal regulation or (2) a burden on interstate commerce?

2. Dade County, Florida, enacted an ordinance prohibiting advertising signs within 200 feet of any expressway and regulating the nature of signs within 600 feet. It permitted nonconforming signs to remain for five years. Elliott Advertising Company and other owners of billboards brought a class action contending the ordinance was invalid as violation of the Due Process Clause of the Fourteenth Amendment because it had no substantial relation to the public health, safety, or welfare. Is the ordinance unconstitutional?

3. Polar Creamery Company was a large processor and distributor of fluid milk located in Pensacola, Florida. It had been purchasing approximately 30 percent of its raw milk from

Florida producers and the remainder from producers and brokers in other states. Its Florida producers could not meet Polar's requirements. In addition, the out-of-state milk was purchased at an average lower cost than the Florida produced milk. The Florida Milk Commission, acting under Florida's Milk Control Act, established a minimum price for fluid milk purchased from the Pensacola milk production area and, in effect, required distributors, including Polar, to purchase all the fluid milk offered by Pensacola area producers at the high price. The effect on Polar would be to raise substantially its average cost of milk and to reduce its out-of-state purchases. Congress had granted authority to the Secretary of Agriculture to establish marketing regulations on milk but had declared that they could not exclude milk from any production area.

Polar challenged the validity of the regulations as imposing an undue burden on interstate commerce. Are the regulations unconstitutional?

4. Illinois enacted a statute requiring contoured mudguards on the rear wheels of trucks operated within the state while nearby states required straight mud flaps. Although passage of the statute had been urged as a safety measure, the trial court found no safety advantage and held that the contoured mudguards created a safety hazard because they tended to cause a buildup of heat in the brakedrum and were more likely to fall off on the highway. It also held that the requirement would seriously interfere with the common practice of interchanging trailers between carriers. Navajo Freight Lines and other truckers sought a declaratory judgment challenging the constitutionality of the statute.

Should the trial court's finding that the statute is an unconstitutional burden on interstate commerce be affirmed?

5. Griggs and other black employees of Duke Power Company brought an action alleging that Duke's use of the Wonderlick Personnel Test, purporting to measure general intelligence, and the Bennett Mechanical Aptitude Test was a violation of the Civil Rights Act of 1964. Scores approximating the national median for high school graduates on these tests were required for transfer of any employee from the labor department to the other four operating departments of Duke. Prior to the effective date of the Act, Duke had openly discriminated against blacks, hiring them only in the labor department, where the highest paying job was below the lowest paying job of the operating departments. White employees hired prior to the use of the tests performed satisfactorily and received promotions in the operating departments.

Does the Commerce Clause give Congress power to prohibit discrimination in private employment and if so, does this use of the tests discriminate against blacks?

Part II

Torts

chapter 3

Crimes and Intentional Torts

Crimes

Introduction. The criminal law area includes not only law designed to punish conduct harmful to the interests of society; but also, law designed to give maximum protection to the innocent. In order for a crime to be committed there must be a preexisting law which defines the prohibited conduct in terms which a reasonable person can understand. Various parts of criminal law apply to the detection, apprehension, prosecution, and subsequent punishment of criminal law offenders.

Nature of Crime. A crime may be defined to be any act done by an individual which is considered a wrong by society and for the commission of which the law has provided that the wrongdoer shall make satisfaction to the public. The term *wrong* as used in its popular sense includes violation of moral or ethical standards, failure to perform social duties imposed by the group of which the individual is a member, and many other acts. However, under the legal definition of crime, such conduct is not necessarily classed as criminal. It is not criminal unless it is condemned by law and unless the wrongdoer is subject to punishment imposed by the state, in which case the state will bring an action in its own name against the wrongdoer. One of the difficult problems confronting society is where to draw the line between that conduct which is so socially undesirable that it should be punished as criminal and that conduct which should be merely treated as a breach of a social duty with only civil liability, or perhaps with no legal liability at all being imposed. Which conduct will be held to be criminal and punishable as such will depend on the values and attitudes of the particular society at a given time.

The fact that the definition of criminal conduct changes over time should not be taken to preclude the existence of a large degree of historical continuity in the criminal law area. Almost all societies have considered treason, murder, theft, and certain sex offenses as crimes; however, the nature and severity of the penalty imposed for the commission of these crimes has varied from country to country and from time to time. At one time in England, and in some countries today, any expression of disagreement with the policies of the rulers of the country was treason; and in England prior to the reform of the criminal law, the death penalty was imposed as punishment for substantially all crimes. During the early colonial period here in America, blasphemy and witchcraft were punished as crimes.

In the common law serious crimes involving moral turpitude, such as arson, rape, and murder, were classed as felonies. Today the term *felony* has no definite meaning except where it has been defined by statute. Generally, however, felonies are punishable by confinement in penitentiaries for substantial periods of time. Misdemeanors are lesser crimes, such as traffic offenses, breaches of the peace, and petty larceny; these generally are punishable by fines or by limited periods of confinement in city or county jails.

Relationship Involved. In the area of criminal law the relationship involved is that of the individual and the society of which he or she is a member. Society is represented by the organized government, and in the event the individual is accused of criminal conduct, the action brought against him or her will be brought by the state.

In the United States, criminal law is recognized as a separate division of the law. The rules of procedure followed in the trial of criminal cases differ in important respects from those followed in the trial of civil cases. For example, in criminal cases the accused is presumed to be innocent, and his or her guilt must be proven by the state beyond a reasonable doubt.

This presumption of innocence and other principles of our criminal law[1] are grounded on the belief that our criminal law system should function so as to give maximum protection to the rights of innocent people charged with crimes even if this results in fewer guilty people being apprehended and punished.

If the verdict of the jury in a criminal case is "not guilty," the state cannot appeal, but the accused can always appeal as a matter of right. All criminal cases are brought in the name of the state, as, for instance, *State v. John Brown,* or *United States v. John Brown* in the event the crime is punishable by the federal government.

In civil cases the action is brought by one individual in the society against another. There is no question of guilt involved. The only consideration is whether one party has invaded the rights of another under circumstances which justify the state in using its power to protect the rights of the injured party.

---

[1] The exclusionary evidence rule affords another important illustration of our policy to protect our citizens from oppressive acts by the agents of public authority. Under this rule evidence illegally obtained cannot be offered in evidence against the accused.

There is no presumption in favor of either party; and the party plaintiff must prove by a preponderance of the evidence—not beyond a reasonable doubt— that the defendant did wrongfully invade his or her (the plaintiff's) rights and that the plaintiff was injured thereby. The plaintiff must establish his or her right to the remedy asked. The remedy granted will be in the nature of compensation to the plaintiff, not as punishment of the defendant, except punitive damages are allowed in some types of tort cases.

CIVIL CASE

Scope of Criminal Law. It is the function of the legislature to define the criminal act and to state the punishment to be imposed on those guilty of the commission of such act. It is the function of the court to determine whether or not the accused is guilty and, if so, to impose the penalty set out in the criminal statute. In performing this function, the court must interpret the criminal statute, determine its scope, and decide whether or not the crime of which the party is accused comes within the provisions of the statute. It is the function of the prosecutor to investigate the case, prepare the indictment, and present the facts to the court.

Essentials of a Crime. At common law, two elements were considered essential to criminal liability: the criminal act accompanied by criminal intent (*mens rea*). Today, as a general rule, those acts which are declared to be crimes will be defined by the criminal statutes. Establishing the fact that a criminal act has been committed is, in most criminal cases, a relatively simple matter. Also, the identity of the person or persons who are guilty of performing the criminal act may be established with a reasonable degree of certainty by direct evidence. However, the accompanying criminal intent cannot be established by direct evidence. Intent is a state of mind.

We require the proof of criminal intent as a means of distinguishing between inevitable accident, for which those involved should not be held criminally liable, and willful conduct, in which case those involved should be held responsible. No means has as yet been devised whereby we can prove the state of a person's mind at any given time; consequently, intent is not a question of the state of the actor's mind at the time he acted.

Intent is established through the use of legal standards, and the standard applied is that of the "ordinary man." That is, what would one be justified in assuming that an ordinary man would have intended if he had been in the position of the accused and had acted as the accused did? If one voluntarily does a criminal act, he will be held to have intended the natural and probable consequences of his act.

Capacity to Commit a Crime. With the exception of certain exempt classes, all persons are held to be responsible for their criminal conduct. In general, infants of tender years and persons who are insane or intoxicated are not held to be criminally liable, because they do not have mental capacity to entertain the criminal intent which is an essential element of crime. However, self-induced intoxication offers only limited protection against punishment.

In regard to infants the common law concept of an infant's liability for crime has been replaced by a new theory. The age at which a person is considered an infant under the criminal law is, in many states, 16 or 17 years. Juvenile courts have been established in almost every state, new administrative procedures have been set up, and new methods of dealing with juveniles have been adopted. The prevailing philosophy is that a child is not a criminal and that it is the duty of society to guide an erring child in his conduct and to help him develop into a desirable citizen.

There are many stages of insanity. The generally accepted rule is that if the person committing the criminal act was, at the time the act was committed, incapable of distinguishing right from wrong, he or she cannot be held criminally liable for his or her conduct. In some states the courts have held that if the criminal act was done under an irresistible impulse, the person committing the act will not be criminally liable. If the accused, after the commission of the criminal act, becomes insane and, as a result of this insanity, is incapable of aiding in the conduct of his or her trial, the prosecution will be postponed or dismissed. If a person becomes insane after conviction but before sentence, he will not be sentenced again until he has regained sanity. As a general rule, the insane person who has committed a crime will be confined in a mental hospital.

Fraudulent Acts.   Many of the crimes against business involve some type of fraudulent conduct. In some states, it is a crime for an officer of a bank knowingly to overdraw his or her account with the bank without the written consent of the board of directors; and in some states, it is a crime for a banker or broker to receive deposits while insolvent. In substantially all states, it is a crime to obtain property by fraudulent pretenses, to issue fraudulent checks, to make false credit statements, to make false statements in advertisements, and to convey property for the purpose of defrauding one's creditors. The giving of short weights or measures is generally declared to be a criminal act.

Forgery.   The crime of forgery pertains to the making of false writings. In general, the definition of the crime is sufficiently broad to include the false and fraudulent making or alteration of any writing which, if genuine, would, or on its face might, have some legal effect upon the rights of others. Forgery is usually thought of as the signing of another's name to negotiable instruments, but the crime is much broader than this. It includes counterfeiting, changing trademarks, falsifying public records, and altering wills, deeds, leases, or any other legal document. In fact, it includes all falsification of or tampering with any document of any kind or nature which is of legal significance.

Decisions Protecting the Accused.   Justice Holmes expressed a basic philosophy of the American criminal law system when he said: ". . . and for my part I think it less evil that some criminals should escape than that the

Government should play an ignoble part." In a series of decisions, the U.S. Supreme Court clarified and expanded the constitutional guarantees of people, particularly of poor people, accused of crimes.

Some of the recent landmark decisions established the following principles:

1. A suspect charged with a federal crime must be taken before a magistrate without "unnecessary delay" or any confession obtained will not be admissible.
2. Illegally obtained evidence may not be admitted in either federal or state courts.
3. Any indigent person charged with a crime the punishment for which may involve a prison sentence has a right to be represented by court appointed counsel.
4. The Fifth Amendment protection against self-incrimination applies to both state and federal criminal proceedings.
5. When police questioning begins to focus on the accused for accusatory rather than for investigative purposes, the accused must be permitted to consult with counsel.
6. The police must advise the accused of his right to remain silent and his right to counsel prior to any questioning.
7. An indigent defendant cannot be confined beyond the maximum sentence specified by statute because of inability to pay the monetary portion of the sentence.
8. Capital punishment statutes which permit room for caprice, whim, and discrimination are unconstitutional as representing cruel and unusual punishment prohibited under the Eighth Amendment.
9. A state prison regulation which permits indigent prisoners to have only a very limited access to law books was found to be unconstitutional on the ground that it denied such prisoners reasonable access to the courts.[2]

In addition to providing more rights for those accused of crimes, the Supreme Court in recent years has declared unconstitutional many types of criminal statutes of long standing. Examples include various vagrancy, obscenity, and antidemonstration statutes stricken for vagueness, or overbreadth on due process and/or First Amendment grounds; and abortion statutes stricken as being violative of due process.[3]

---

[2] These principles were established in the following cases: *Mallory v. United States,* 354 U.S. 449 (1948); *Mapp v. Ohio,* 367 U.S. 643 (1961); *Gideon v. Wainwright,* 372 U.S. 335 (1963); *Malloy v. Hogan,* 378 U.S. 1 (1964); *Escobedo v. Illinois,* 378 U.S. 478 (1964); *Miranda v. Arizona,* 384 U.S. 436 (1966); *Williams v. Illinois,* 399 U.S. 235 (1970); *Furman v. Georgia,* 408 U.S. 238 (1972); and *Younger v. Gilmore,* 404 U.S. 15 (1971).

[3] The *Coates* case in the text is an example of the former group while *Roe v. Wade,* 410 U.S. 113 (1973) is an abortion decision.

Summary

A crime is a wrong forbidden by law which is subject to punishment by the state and which the state prosecutes in its own name. Not all wrongs are punishable as crimes. What conduct will be held to be criminal and punishable will depend on the attitude of society at a given time. Many acts are declared to be criminal today which were unknown or were not so declared 50 or 75 years ago.

With the exception of certain exempt classes, all persons are held responsible for their criminal conduct. Infants, insane persons, and others who do not have the mental capacity to entertain a criminal intent cannot be held criminally liable.

Our policy is to afford a maximum degree of protection to the rights of those accused of crimes. Recent Supreme Court decisions have expanded these rights.

Coates v. City of Cincinnati

402 U.S. 611 (1971)

Coates, a student, was involved with others in a demonstration. They were arrested and convicted and took an appeal to the U.S. Supreme Court. Held, reversed for Coates and the other defendants.

MR. JUSTICE STEWART.   A Cincinnati, Ohio, ordinance makes it a criminal offense for "three or more persons to assemble . . . on any of the sidewalks . . . and there conduct themselves in a manner annoying to persons passing by. . . ." The issue before us is whether this ordinance is unconstitutional on its face.

The defendants were convicted of violating the ordinance, and the convictions were ultimately affirmed by a closely divided vote in the Supreme Court of Ohio, upholding the constitutional validity of the ordinance. Throughout this litigation it has been the defendant's position that the ordinance on its face violates the First and Fourteenth Amendments of the Constitution.

In rejecting this claim and affirming the convictions the Ohio Supreme Court did not give the ordinance any construction at variance with the apparent plain import of its language. The court simply stated:

> The ordinance prohibits "conduct . . . annoying to persons passing by." The word "annoying" is a widely used and well understood word; it is not necessary to guess its meaning. "Annoying" is the present participle of the transitive verb "annoy" which means to trouble, to vex, to impede, to incommode, to provoke, to harass or to irritate.
>
> We conclude, as did the Supreme Court of the United States in *Cameron v. Johnson* . . . in which the issue of the vagueness of a statute was presented, that the ordinance clearly and precisely delineates its reach in words of common understanding. It is a "precise and narrowly drawn regulatory statute [ordinance] evincing a legislative judgment that certain specific conduct be . . . proscribed."

Beyond this, the only construction put upon the ordinance by the state court was its unexplained conclusion that "the standard of conduct which it specifies is not dependent upon each complainant's sensitivity." But the court did not indicate upon whose sensitivity a violation does depend—the sensitivity of the judge or the jury, the sensitivity of the arresting officer, or the sensitivity of a hypothetical reasonable man.

We are thus relegated, at best, to the words of the ordinance itself. If three or more people meet together on a sidewalk or street corner, they must conduct themselves so as not to annoy any police officer or other person who should happen to pass by. In our opinion this ordinance is unconstitutionally vague because it subjects the exercise of the right of assembly to an unascertainable standard, and unconstitutionally broad because it authorizes the punishment of constitutionally protected conduct.

Conduct that annoys some people does not annoy others. Thus, the ordinance is vague not in the sense that it requires a person to conform his conduct to an imprecise but comprehensible normative standard, but rather in the sense that no standard of conduct is specified at all. As a result, "men of common intelligence must necessarily guess at its meaning." . . .

It is said that the ordinance is broad enough to encompass many types of conduct clearly within the city's constitutional power to prohibit. And so, indeed, it is. The city is free to prevent people from blocking sidewalks, obstructing traffic, littering streets, committing assaults, or engaging in countless other forms of antisocial conduct. It can do so through the enactment and enforcement of ordinances directed with reasonable specificity toward the conduct to be prohibited. . . . It cannot constitutionally do so through the enactment and enforcement of an ordinance whose violation may entirely depend upon whether or not a policeman is annoyed.

But the vice of the ordinance lies not alone in its violation of the due process standard of vagueness. The ordinance also violates the constitutional right of free assembly and association. Our decisions establish that mere public intolerance or animosity cannot be the basis for abridgment of these constitutional freedoms. . . . The First and Fourteenth Amendments do not permit a State to make criminal the exercise of the right of assembly simply because its exercise may be "annoying" to some people. If this were not the rule, the right of the people to gather in public places for social or political purposes would be continually subject to summary suspension through the good-faith enforcement of a prohibition against annoying conduct. And such a prohibition, in addition, contains an obvious invitation to discriminatory enforcement against those whose association together is "annoying" because their ideas, their lifestyle, or their physical appearance is resented by the majority of their fellow citizens.

The ordinance before us makes a crime out of what under the Constitution cannot be a crime. It is aimed directly at activity protected by the Constitution. We need not lament that we do not have before us the details of the conduct found to be annoying. It is the ordinance on its face that sets the standard of conduct and warns against transgression. The details of the offense could no more serve to validate this ordinance than could the details of an offense charged under an ordinance suspending unconditionally the right of assembly and free speech.

Torts

Introduction. Under the Anglo-Saxon law, no distinction was made between crime, tort, and breach of contract; the present-day distinction came later. But even today, there is an overlap which points to their common origin, and one and the same act may be a crime, tort, or breach of contract. The first distinction to be recognized was that made between the act of crime and the other two acts: tort and breach of contract. At a somewhat later time the distinction between the act of tort and that of breach of contract was recognized. In the United States today the relation between crime and tort is closer than that between tort and breach of contract. The same act may be both a crime and a tort. The fact that a person has been convicted of the crime and punished by the state in no way relieves him or her from his or her liability in tort to the person injured by his wrongful conduct.

Under the early English law an individual's right to a remedy was based on the concept of right and wrong, and unless a person was guilty of wrongful conduct, he was not subject to punishment or to the imposition of a penalty. At an early date the breach of the king's peace was the basis for wrongful conduct, and the penalties for such conduct were imposed by the king for his benefit. The next step in the development of the law was the recognition of the individual's right to redress for his personal injuries. This gave rise to the concept of legal duty.

The basis of a person's liability in tort is his breach of a duty owed to a fellow member of society. In the development of the law of torts the courts at first recognized the duty of a person to refrain from an intentional aggression on another. At a somewhat later time, they began to recognize the duty of a person when engaged in a course of conduct to act with due care with respect to consequences which might reasonably be anticipated. As society developed, personal contacts increased, and the duties owed by members of society increased accordingly. Today the area of tort law is developing rapidly. Every new scientific invention has its impact on society and may give rise to new duties the breach of which will give rise to a remedy in tort.

For the most part the law of torts is based on concepts of legal standards of conduct. Each member in society is under a legal duty, in his daily activities, to follow a course of conduct which does not fall below the social standards recognized in the community. If a person, without any legal defense or justification, harms or interferes with the legally recognized interests of others as a result of conduct falling below recognized social standards, such person will be held liable. The interests protected from unjustifiable interference include those related to physical integrity, freedom of movement, peace of mind, privacy, freedom of thought and action, and the acquisition of property and services essential to material well-being.

The protection of these and other interests inevitably involves a balancing process for public policy and the law. If the law protects physical integrity to an extreme, societal interests in freedom of movement may be unduly burdened with legal risks. If the law protects peace of mind, privacy, and interests in a good reputation to an extreme, freedom of speech and freedom of press might be unduly restrained.[4]

Prosser lists the following factors as worthy of special mention in determining whether or not given conduct causing harm to others may result in liability under tort law: (1) the moral aspect of the defendant's conduct; (2) the convenience of administration if liability is attached; (3) the defendant's capacity to bear the loss; (4) the preventative or deterrent benefits to be derived from imposing liability; and (5) the motive or purpose underlying the defendant's conduct.[5] If a particular type of conduct causes harm to others and one or more of these factors suggests logical reasons for holding persons engaged in such conduct liable, it is likely that the conduct will be classed as tortious.

Elements of Torts. A tort is a breach of a duty, other than a duty created by contract, for which the wrongdoer is liable in damages to the injured party. The concept of duty shifts with social developments. In general, culpable conduct which causes injury to another person is an essential element of tort liability. Under some circumstances, failure to act may be a tort, but the law usually does not impose liability on a person who fails to play the part of the Good Samaritan. Base ingratitude, cruel refusal of kindness, and discourtesy are not the basis of tort liability. One of the objectives of our society is to assure to each individual in society the greatest degree of freedom consistent with a like degree of freedom for others. Our law of torts aids materially in the accomplishment of this objective.

Nature of Torts. In general, torts may be classified as intentional tortious conduct, negligence, and strict liability. Intentional torts may be subdivided into intentional interference with the person and intentional interference with property rights.

Summary

The basis of a person's liability in tort is breach of a duty owed to a fellow member of society which breach causes harm to such member. For the most part the law of torts is based on standards of conduct. If a person fails to maintain the accepted standard of conduct and, as a result of such failure, another is injured, such person will be required to answer for the resulting damage unless he or she can establish a legal justification for the harm inflicted. Torts may be classified as intentional breaches of duty and nonintentional

---

[4] For a detailed discussion of the role of tort law in balancing conflicting societal interests, see William L. Prosser, *Law of Torts,* 4th ed. (St. Paul, Minn.: West Publishing Co., 1972), p. 15.

[5] Ibid., p. 16.

breaches. Intentional breaches may be further subdivided into intentional interference with the person and intentional interference with property. The nonintentional torts are negligence and strict liability.

Interference with Personal Rights

Assault and Battery. An assault is the intentional act of putting another person in immediate apprehension for his or her physical safety. Actual physical contact is not an element of an assault, and neither is fear. For example, if Addison threatens Berry and shoots at Berry but misses him, Addison is liable to Berry in tort. Berry has not been physically injured and he may not have been frightened, but he was apprehensive that he would be injured.

Battery is the intentional touching of another without justification or without the consent of that person. This does not mean that a tort results every time one person touches another. In our everyday activities, especially in crowded cities, there are many physical contacts between persons which are not torts, since such contacts cannot be classed as intentional interference with the person of another.

False Imprisonment. False imprisonment is the intentional confining of another for an appreciable time within limits fixed by the one causing the confinement. Unless the one confined knows that he or she is confined and has not consented to it, the act is not false imprisonment. Suppose a private detective mistakenly thinks a customer in a store is a shoplifter and, over the protests of the customer, locks him in the manager's office until the manager returns from lunch about an hour later. In such a case the customer, if not guilty, has a right of action against the store owner for false imprisonment.

Defamation. Closely related to the protection of the person's body is the protection of the person's reputation and good name. The twin torts of libel and slander are based on defamation. A distinction is made between libel and slander, in that libel is written defamation whereas slander is oral defamation.

In both libel and slander the basis of the tort is the publication of statements which hold a person up to hatred, contempt, or ridicule. By publication is meant that the defamatory statements must have been made to one other than the defamed party. If you accuse a person to his face or write him a personal letter, these acts do not constitute publishing your statements. From a legal standpoint, statements made by a husband or wife to his or her spouse are not considered published. The courts have generally held that the dictation of a letter to a stenographer or the communication of statements by one corporate officer to another is publication, although a minority of courts do not so hold. If defamatory statements are made to the defamed person and overheard by another, the courts have held that this constitutes publication. A person who repeats or republishes defamatory statements is liable even though he gives the source of his statements.

Truth is a complete defense to a defamation suit. In addition, false statements may be either absolutely privileged or conditionally privileged. Statements made by congressmen on the floor of Congress, official papers filed in court proceedings, statements made by judges or attorneys during a trial are examples where absolute privilege usually attaches. Reports made between corporate officials concerning matters pertinent to their jobs and credit bureau reports may be qualifiedly or conditionally privileged.

Now false and defamatory statements made about public figures, or on any matter of public or general interest, are privileged if made without malice.[6] Conditional privileges may be lost if the defendant's conduct is malicious or he or she abuses the privilege in some way. In order to show malice the plaintiff must prove that the defendant had either actual knowledge of falsity, or a reckless disregard for the truth. Negligence in collecting or publishing the information does not defeat the privilege.

Malicious Prosecution and Abuse of Process. Tort cases involving malicious prosecution are closely related to cases involving abuse of civil process. In the former, the defendant "maliciously" instigates criminal proceedings against the plaintiff and the proceedings are later terminated in the plaintiff's favor. In the latter, the defendant employs civil proceedings to harass or injure the plaintiff.

The presence of probable cause (grounds for reasonable suspicion) usually will excuse the defendant from liability in a malicious prosecution suit because of the broad public interest in encouraging people to report suspected criminal conduct. The plaintiff must prove both the absence of probable cause and the presence of malice on the part of the defendant. Malice means that the defendant acted with an improper motive. The bringing of a lawsuit for ulterior motives, such as to ruin the defendant financially rather than for the relief asked in the complaint of the plaintiff, may constitute abuse of process even if the suit is successful. In abuse of process suits the courts are balancing the interests of society in permitting wide use of civil process against the interests of people who are unduly harassed by persons with improper motives.

Right of Privacy. A recent development in this area of the law is the granting of a remedy for the invasion of privacy. The boundaries in this area are not definitely determined, but the law is primarily concerned with the protection of a mental interest, such as freedom from mental anguish resulting from the invasion of one's privacy. The cases granting relief have involved: the use, without permission, of a picture of a person for advertising purposes; intrusion upon a person's physical solitude, such as by wire-tapping; the public

---

[6] *New York Times v. Sullivan,* 376 U.S. 254 (1964) was the seminal case aimed at encouraging more public discussion of matters of legitimate public concern.

disclosure of private facts; and, the giving of publicity which places a person in a false light in the public eye. A person who is currently in the public eye does not have the right of privacy in matters published concerning him if such matters would be classed as news.

Infliction of Mental Distress.   Historically, the courts have been hesitant to grant redress for alleged mental injuries for fear of opening the floodgates to fictitious claims. Modern medical science has established the fact that traumatic experiences involving strong emotions such as rage, shock, fright, or shame can induce physical changes which can be detected. As a result, modern courts are more receptive to claims involving claimed mental injuries of various types. The courts try to contain this new type of liability by imposing requirements that the conduct causing the distress must be "outrageous" and the resulting physical injury must be of a substantial and serious nature.

Summary

The safety of the person is important to any society, and the wrongful interference with the person is a tort. Assault is the intentional act of putting a person in apprehension of physical injury. Battery is the intentional act of touching another without the consent of that person and without justification. False imprisonment is the intentional act of confining another for an appreciable time within limits fixed by the one causing the confinement.

Closely associated to these are the torts of libel, slander, malicious prosecution, and the invasion of the right of privacy. Libel and slander are the defamation of character or good name. Libel is written, and slander is spoken. The basis of both libel and slander is the publication of false statements which hold one up to hatred, contempt, or ridicule. Invasion of privacy involves using a person's picture for advertising without his consent, unwarranted publicity, and other similar acts which cause a person mental anguish. The intentional infliction of emotional distress may create tort liability where there is outrageous misconduct. The trend in tort law is for the courts to recognize an increasing variety of new torts thus making the law more sensitive to various types of harms.

Southwest Drug Stores of Mississippi, Inc. v. Garner

195 So.2d 837 (Sup. Ct. Miss. 1967)

Mrs. Garner (plaintiff) sued Southwest Drug Stores of Mississippi, Inc. (defendant), for damages for false imprisonment and slander. The jury returned a verdict for Mrs. Garner for $8,000. Southwest appealed. Affirmed.

Mrs. Garner and her sister stopped at Southwest Drug Store in the Gardiner Shopping Center in Laurel. They went into the drugstore, leaving her father, who was ill, in the car in the parking lot in front of the drugstore.

While Mrs. Garner was at the cosmetic counter looking at soap, Ratcliff, the store manager, approached her and asked if he could help her. She told him she wanted a bar of soap, and he said he would have one of the ladies wait on her. With the assistance of the saleslady Mrs. Garner found the soap, and with the saleslady went to the cashier and paid for it. She received a sales ticket and the soap was placed in a small paper bag.

Mrs. Garner's sister continued to shop, since she also wanted some soap. Mrs. Garner told her that she would go to the car to see about their father and would take some of the sister's packages with her. She walked out of the store, and before she reached the car Ratcliff hurried after her, calling in a loud voice to stop.

She testified that he said to her in a rude and loud manner, "Hey, wait there. . . . You stop there, I want to see what you got in that little bag. You stole a bar of soap." Mrs. Garner said further, "And I looked at him, I said, 'You mean you're accusing me of stealing this soap.' I pulled the soap out. He says, 'Yes, you stole the soap, and let's prove it, let's go back.'"

Mrs. Garner said a number of people were close by and heard the words, but that she did not know any of them. Ratcliff did not put a hand on her or her belongings, but he did demand that she return to the store.

When they got back in the store Mrs. Garner asked the cashier if she had bought the soap, and the cashier told her that she had paid for the soap. She told the cashier that Ratcliff was accusing her of stealing the soap. She then began to cry and was embarrassed. . . . Mrs. Garner said the incident made her sick and she had to go to the family doctor twice.

INZER, JUSTICE.   Southwest Drug urges that the lower court erred in not granting a requested peremptory instruction. They argue that the proof shows a qualified privilege existed and it was not exceeded; that Ratcliff investigated what he believed to be a case of shoplifting upon probable cause in a reasonable manner, and therefore under the laws of Mississippi such an investigation was privileged and no action was maintainable thereon. The statute relied upon is Mississippi Code Annotated section 2374–04 (Supp. 1964), which reads as follows:

If any person shall commit or attempt to commit the offense of shoplifting, as defined herein, or if any person shall wilfully conceal upon his person or otherwise any unpurchased goods, wares or merchandise held or owned by any store or mercantile establishment, the merchant or any employee thereof or any peace or police officer, acting in good faith and upon probable cause based upon reasonable grounds therefor, may question such person, in a reasonable manner for the purpose of ascertaining whether or not such person is guilty of shoplifting as defined herein. Such questioning of a person by a merchant, merchant's employee or peace or police officer shall not render such merchant, merchant's employee or peace or police officer civilly liable for slander, false arrest, false imprisonment, malicious prosecution, unlawful detention or otherwise in any case where such merchant, merchant's employee, or peace or police officer acts in good faith and upon reasonable grounds to believe that the person questioned is committing or attempting to commit the crime of shoplifting as defined in this act.

* * * * *

Southwest argues that Ratcliff had observed Mrs. Garner and believed by her actions that she was committing an act of shoplifting; that her actions gave him probable cause to investigate, and that he acted in good faith and upon an occasion of privilege in carrying out his duties to protect his employer's property.

Although the occasion was one of qualified privilege, the privilege was lost by the manner in which it was exercised. Mrs. Garner testified, and the jury found that she was wrongfully accused of stealing in a rude and loud voice in the presence of other people outside the place of business. Granting that Ratcliff had reason to believe that Mrs. Garner had put a bar of soap in her purse and left the store without paying for it, and that he had probable cause to make inquiry, still he was careless and negligent in his method of ascertaining whether Mrs. Garner had paid for the soap.

Hood v. Dun & Bradstreet

486 F2d 25 (5th Cir. 1973)

Action by David Hood (plaintiff) a building contractor, against Dun and Bradstreet (defendant) for damages for having published libelous statements in a financial report. Hood appealed after the district court granted a summary judgment to Dun & Bradstreet. Reversed and remanded.

On October 11, 1968, D. & B. prepared a credit report on David Hood and distributed the report to eleven subscribers. Included in this report were three statements which read as follows:

*   *   *   *   *

(1) As a matter of interest, David P. Hood has always declined financial information other than to say that sales are in excess of $100,000 and that net worth is in excess of $3,000. These two estimates were submitted in July 1967.

(2) Public records reveal suit #248479 filed June 10, 1968, for $103, *Whittock Dobbs Inc. v.* subjects. Also suit #238558 filed Apr 3, 1968, *Westron Corp v.* subject.

(3) Although complete details are not available, working capital appears limited at times with some trade, slowness noted.

D. & B. acknowledges that the two law suits reportedly filed against the plaintiff were actually filed against another individual named David Hood. D. & B. does not dispute the falsity of the additional statements in the report.

INGRAHAM, CIRCUIT JUDGE.   D. & B.'s . . . contention in regard to privilege is that credit reporting agencies should be afforded a conditional privilege based on Georgia law. To determine the validity of this contention it is necessary for us to examine case authority, statutory enactments, and the underlying principles of the conditional privilege itself.

Initially, we point out that the great majority of jurisdictions, with the exception of Georgia and Idaho, confronting this issue has held that the credit reporting agency is entitled to a conditional privilege. Georgia presently has a statute that delineates the conditional privilege and provides as follows:

Privileged communications. The following are deemed privileged communications:
1.   Statements made bona fide in the performance of a public duty.
2.   Similar statements in the performance of a private duty; either legal or moral.
3.   Statements made with the bona fide intent, on the part of the speaker, to protect his own interest in a matter where it is concerned.

. . . In construing an identical statute, the Georgia Supreme Court reasoned in *Johnson v. The Bradstreet Co.* (1886), that a credit report concerning the plaintiff in that case was false and therefore immoral. Since immoral contracts were void, there was no duty, legal or moral, and consequently the credit reporting was not included within the provisions of the conditional privilege statute. . . .

The fundamental reason for allowing credit reporting agencies to claim the conditional privilege . . . was predicated upon the idea that if no privilege existed, the reporting agencies would be driven out of business by the cost of defamation suits.

We find at least two reasons why a Georgia court would adhere to its earlier supreme court decisions.

First, this case demonstrates that in one of the states that has refused to grant the privilege, credit reporting agencies exist and are thriving on the credit reporting business. . . . We find that D. & B. is not the only credit reporting agency doing a thriving business in Georgia, but there are at least twenty others, one of which is Retail Credit Co., one of the largest such organizations in the United States.

A second reason for our decision is that in recent years there has been an apparent shift in emphasis from the protection of the credit reporting agency to the protection of the individual or business enterprise being investigated. The growth in consumer protection in regard to credit reporting is obvious from legislation such as the Fair Credit Reporting Act (FCRA) 15 U.S.C.A. §§ 1681–1681t (Supp. 1971). Pursuant to the FCRA, the credit agency must disclose to the consumer the substance and sources of information upon its demand, the consumer has a right to correct and explain information contained in the report, and it may limit access to those who have a "legitimate business need." Furthermore, the Act does not preclude an action at common law except where information that would give rise to a cause of action is obtained by the complainant pursuant to the provisions of the Act.

In an action for libel under Georgia law, the plaintiff must specifically allege, and prove special damages where the defamatory statement is not libel per se. . . .

Plaintiff specifically alleges two grounds upon which he might prove special damages. First, in *Bradstreet Co. v. Oswald* (1894), the Georgia Supreme Court categorized as special damages the pecuniary expense incurred by the plaintiff in removing from customers' minds the effect of false statements made in a credit report. Accordingly, plaintiff's complaint specifically alleges that he suffered special damages of incurring pecuniary loss in terms of total hours expended in removing from the minds of certain business associates the harmful effect of the false statements.

Second, plaintiff asserts that the flow in his business has decreased without any specific reference to customers or construction projects. The requirement of special damages is also satisfied where "the plaintiff can, under the circumstances, only know that the flow of his business as a whole is diminished, and it would be impossible to point to any specific customers or orders which have been lost. . . ."

Jones v. Walsh

222 A.2d 830 (Sup. Ct. N.H. 1966)

Dolores Jones (plaintiff) sued John Walsh (defendant) for damages for slander and defendant Walsh appealed from an adverse ruling. Affirmed.

LAMPRON, JUSTICE. Jones' declaration reads in part as follows: "On or about Friday, May 22, 1964, at Exeter . . . at Tula's Restaurant . . . owned and operated by Walsh, Walsh did injure the character and good name of Jones who was at that time a waitress in the employ of Walsh and by his acts caused it to be believed that Jones was guilty of the crime of embezzlement in that in the course of a certain conversation, which Walsh had with Jones in the presence of a number of people in a crowded restaurant, falsely and maliciously accused Jones of embezzlement as follows to wit:

"You are not ringing the cash up in the cash register." Jones replied, "Are you accusing me of stealing?" Walsh replied, "Well, you're not ringing in the cash."

If one falsely and without a privilege to do so publishes spoken words which imputes to another conduct constituting a criminal offense chargeable by indictment or information either at common law or by statute and of such a kind as to be characterized as morally reprehensible, he is liable to the person to whom such wrong doing is imputed without proof of special damage. A charge of the commission of embezzlement constitutes such a slander *per se.*

It is not necessary that the words used charge Jones with such a crime in a technical or direct manner. "A mere insinuation . . . the putting of words in the form of a question . . . a mere expression of opinion or of a suspicion or belief may be actionable." The test is whether the words used taken in the sense in which they are reasonably understood under the circumstances by persons familiar with the language used are capable of the defamatory construction of accusing Jones with a criminal offense of the type previously described.

We are of the opinion that hearers of common and reasonable understanding could ascribe such a meaning to Walsh's words. Whether they did under the circumstances of this case is a question to be decided as a fact.

"Not all slander, however, is actionable. Some spoken defamation may fall within a class which the law terms privileged, and for which no damages may be recovered." Walsh suggests in his brief that, having a legitimate interest in the receipts of his business, he "cannot be liable because the statements were made on a conditionally privileged occasion and nothing appears in the writ and declaration to indicate that the occasion was abused."

It is true that "an occasion is conditionally privileged when the circumstances induce a correct or reasonable belief that (*a*) facts exist which affect a sufficiently important interest of the publisher, and (*b*) the recipient's knowledge of the defamatory matter will be of service in the lawful protection of the interest." *Restatement, Torts,* s. 594. However, to come within that privilege "the defamatory communication must be made to a person whose knowledge of the defamatory matter because of his social or legal duty or his interest thereto is likely to prove useful in the protection of that interest." Furthermore such a "privilege may be so far abused by an unnecessary and excessive publication that the immunity is lost."

Nevada Credit Rating Bureau, Inc. v. Williams

503 P.2d 9 (Sup. Ct. Nev. 1972)

Williams (plaintiff) won a judgment of $3,002 compensatory damages jointly and severally against defendants, Nevada Credit Rating Bureau (Nevada Credit) and Aden, and punitive damages of $1,500 against Nevada Credit and $250 against Aden for abuse of process. Defendants appealed. Held affirmed.

Williams was in the mining business and owned excavation equipment. In 1961, Williams met Aden who offered to purchase bulldozer rails Williams needed and to let Williams repay him by doing some excavation work. Williams finally accepted this offer and became indebted to Aden in the amount of $4,287.03 for the rails as well as for miscellaneous advances for operating expenses and repairs to other equipment. Aden later contacted Nevada Credit about collecting the amount owed Aden by Williams and Nevada Credit took an assignment of Aden's claim for the purpose of bringing suit. On November 20, 1961, Nevada Credit brought suit against Williams seeking recovery of $4,395.07, plus interest, costs and attorney's fees. On this same date, Nevada Credit authorized an attachment of Williams' equipment and appointed Aden as its agent to accompany the deputy sheriff to Williams' property to execute the writ. Aden instructed the deputy sheriff to attach all of Williams' equipment, including his housetrailer. The deputy served Williams with a copy of the writ, inventoried the equipment and placed sheriff's seals on most major pieces. . . . The deputy sheriff instructed Williams that he was not to move or touch any of his equipment. All of Williams' equipment which the trial court found to have a reasonable value of over $30,000 was attached to secure the alleged debt amounting to less than $5,000. In February of 1966 Williams brought an action for wrongful attachment and/or malicious prosecution.

BATJER, JUSTICE.   Here the trial court awarded damages for abuse of process based primarily upon the facts that the attachment was far in excess of that necessary to secure the debt, and was used in an attempt to pressure Williams into paying the claim. The defendants assert that the damages were improperly awarded because there was no adequate showing of the necessary elements of malice and want of probable cause. Although malice and want of probable cause are necessary elements for recovery in an action for wrongful attachment and malicious prosecution they are not essential to recovery for abuse of process. The two fundamental elements that constitute the basis of the tort of abuse of process are (1) an ulterior purpose and (2) a willful act in the use of the process not proper in the regular conduct of the proceeding. The action for abuse of process hinges on the misuse of regularly issued process, in contrast to malicious prosecution which rests upon the wrongful issuance of process.

Although the property was divisible, it was attached in its entirety. . . . Efforts to release parts of the property were summarily rejected while defendants possessed full knowledge of the devastating effect of the attachment upon Williams' business. These actions of the defendants in willful disregard of the right of Williams to use his property (subject only to a reasonable attachment) gave the trial court adequate grounds of concluding that the purpose of the attachment was to pressure payment rather than to secure a debt; that the attachment, in an amount so much greater than the alleged debt was a misapplication of process; and that the inability of Williams to continue to use his equipment caused damages for which he should be compensated.

Dietemann v. Time, Inc.

449 F.2d 245 (9th Cir. 1971)

Dietemann (plaintiff) sued Time, Inc., (defendant) for damages for invasion of his privacy. Time, Inc., appealed from a verdict of $1,000 for Dietemann. Affirmed.

Dietemann, a disabled veteran with little education, was engaged in the practice of healing with clay, minerals, and herbs.

. . . The November 1, 1963, edition of *Life* carried an article entitled "Crackdown on Quackery." The article depicted Dietemann as a quack and included two pictures of him. One picture was taken at Dietemann's home on September 20, 1963, previous to his arrest on a charge of practicing medicine without a license, and the other taken at the time of his arrest.

Two employees of *Life,* Metcalf and Ray, had entered into an arrangement with the District Attorney's Office of Los Angeles county whereby utilizing a ruse to gain entry, they would visit Dietemann and obtain facts and pictures concerning his activities.

Metcalf told Dietemann that she had a lump in her breast. Dietemann concluded that she had eaten some rancid butter 11 years, 9 months, and 7 days prior to that time. . . . The conversation between Metcalf and Dietemann was transmitted by radio transmitter hidden in Metcalf's purse to a tape recorder in a parked automobile occupied by another *Life* employee, Miner, of the District Attorney's Office, and Leake, an investigator of the State Department of Public Health. While the recorded conversation was not quoted in the article in *Life,* it was mentioned that *Life* correspondent Bride was making notes of what was being received via the radio transmitter, and such information was at least referred to in the article.

Dietemann, although a journeyman plumber, claims to be a scientist. He had no listings and his home had no sign of any kind. He did not advertise nor did he have a telephone. He made no charges when he attempted to diagnose or to prescribe herbs and minerals. He did accept contributions.

HUFSTEDLER, CIRCUIT JUDGE.   The appeal presents . . . [these] issues: (1) Under California law, is a cause of action for invasion of privacy established upon proof that *Life's* employees, by subterfuge, gained entrance to the office portion of Dietemann's home wherein they photographed him and electronically recorded and transmitted to third persons his conversation without his consent as a result of which he suffered emotional distress? (2) Does the First Amendment insulate Time, Inc., from liability for invasion of privacy because Life, Inc.'s employees did those acts for the purpose of gathering material for a magazine story and a story was thereafter published utilizing some of the material thus gathered?

In jurisdictions other than California in which a common-law tort for invasion of privacy is recognized, it has been consistently held that surreptitious electronic recording of a plaintiff's conversation causing him emotional distress is actionable. Despite some variations in the description and the labels applied to the tort, there is agreement that publication is not a necessary element of the tort, that the existence of a technical trespass is immaterial, and that proof of special damages is not required. [*Nader v. General Motors Corp.* (1970) and other cases].

. . . [W]e have little difficulty in concluding that clandestine photography of Dietemann in his den and the recordation and transmission of his conversation without his consent resulting in his emotional distress warrants recovery for invasion of privacy in California.

The most recent expression is found in *Briscoe v. Reader's Digest Ass'n,* a privacy action based upon the publication of an article disclosing plaintiff's conviction of a felony 11 years earlier. The court equated the growing acceptance of the right of privacy with ". . . the increasing capability of . . . electronic devices with their capacity to destroy an individual's anonymity, intrude upon his most intimate activities, and expose his most personal characteristics to public gaze."

Men fear exposure not only to those closest to them; much of the outrage underlying the asserted right to privacy is a reaction to exposure to persons known only through business or other secondary relationships. The claim is not so much one of total secrecy as it is of the right to *define* one's circle of intimacy—to choose who shall see beneath the quotidian mask. Loss of control over which "face" one puts on may result in literal loss of self-identity and is humiliating beneath the gaze of those whose curiosity treats a human being as an object.

Concurrently with the development of privacy law, California had decided a series of cases according plaintiffs relief from unreasonable penetrations of their mental tranquility based upon the tort of intentional infliction of emotional distress. Although these cases are not direct authority in the privacy area, they are indicative of the trend of California law to protect interests analogous to those asserted by plaintiff in this case.

Time, Inc. claims that the First Amendment immunizes it from liability for invading Dietemann's den with a hidden camera and its concealed electronic instruments because its employees were gathering news and its instrumentalities "are indispensable tools of investigative reporting." We agree that newsgathering is an integral part of news dissemination. We strongly disagree, however, that the hidden mechanical contrivances are "indispensable tools" of newsgathering. . . . The First Amendment has never been construed to accord newsmen immunity from torts or crimes committed during the course of newsgathering. The First Amendment is not a license to trespass, to steal, or to intrude by electronic means into the precincts of another's home or office. It does not become such a license simply because the person subjected to the intrusion is reasonably suspected of committing a crime.

No interest protected by the First Amendment is adversely affected by permitting damages for intrusion to be enhanced by the fact of later publication of the information that the publisher improperly acquired. Assessing damages for the additional emotional distress suffered by a plaintiff when the wrongfully acquired data are purveyed to the multitude chills intrusive acts. It does not chill freedom of expression guaranteed by the First Amendment. . . .

Rights of Property

Nature of Property Rights.   Property and property rights are of such importance to society that they are protected against unwarranted interference by others. In cases of tortious interference with property rights, any action brought to recover damages, as a general rule, is brought by the party in possession rather than by the owner. However, an action for trespass may be brought by the owner of land which is leased to another if the nature of the trespass is such that it results in damage to the owner's reversionary interests. The recognized torts against property are trespass to land, trespass to personal property, and conversion.

Trespass to Land.   Any entry by a person onto the land in the possession of another, or the causing of anything to enter onto the land of another, or the remaining on the land or the permitting of anything to remain on the land in the possession of another is a trespass to that land unless permission is given or unless the entry is privileged. Actual pecuniary harm to the land is not an essential element of the tort. The interference with the right of possession is sufficient injury on which to base a suit. If no harm is done, only nominal damages can be recovered.

Walking across land in the possession of another, throwing water against a building in the possession of another, shooting across land in possession of another, or damming a stream and thus causing the water to back up on land in possession of another are trespasses to land. In fact, any interference with land in possession of another may be a trespass whether it is of short or long duration and whether or not pecuniary harm results. If no harm is done, it is a technical interference with the property rights of the possessor.

The early cases laid down the rule that the right to land extended from the center of the earth to the heavens. This rule has been modified since the advent of aircraft. Today the temporary invasion of the air space over the land by aircraft is privileged, provided it is done in a reasonable manner and in conformity with legislative requirements. The operation of aircraft, at the present time, is considered an extrahazardous activity; and if anything is dropped from an aircraft, or if a forced landing is made, the aviator is liable for any actual harm which results. The trend in the law is to impose greater duties on landowners to keep their premises in a reasonably safe condition even where trespassers are concerned.

Trespass to Personal Property.   Any intentional intermeddling with personal property which is in the possession of another is a trespass if the intermeddling does harm to the property or deprives the possessor of the use of the property for an appreciable time unless it is privileged or is done with the consent of the possessor. Suppose Adams moves an automobile a few feet to enable him to park his own automobile. He is not liable for trespass. However, if, as a joke, Adams moves the automobile around the corner, and the owner, although he uses reasonable diligence, cannot find it for some time, say an hour or more, Adams is liable for trespass. As a general rule, if one intermeddles with the personal property of another and the property is harmed in no way, no trespass has been committed. However, if the property is personal to the owner, say, for instance, an undergarment, and the owner refuses to use the property after the intermeddling, a trespass has been committed even though the property has not been damaged physically.

Conversion.   A conversion is an unlawful dominion over, or the unlawful appropriation of, the personal property of another. A conversion takes place when a distinct act of dominion is wrongfully exerted over another's personal property in denial of, or inconsistent with, his ownership or rights therein. Generally, the gist of a conversion is the wrongful deprivation of a person's personal property to the possession of which he is entitled. If a person unlawfully takes goods from the possession of another, he is guilty of conversion even though he mistakenly thought he was entitled to the possession of the goods. If a person wrongfully sells, pledges, mortgages, leases, or uses the goods of another, that person is guilty of conversion. A person is guilty of conversion if he wrongfully, even though by mistake, delivers goods of one person to another who is not entitled to the possession of the goods. In the case of a conversion of goods the owner, or the one entitled to the possession of the goods, is entitled to recover the reasonable value of the goods from the one guilty of the conversion.

Deceit (Fraud).   The tort of deceit, included in the broader term "fraud," is based on injury resulting from a misrepresentation of a material fact, knowingly made with intent to deceive, which is justifiably relied on to the injury of the defrauded party.[7] The keystone of the tort is misrepresentation of a material fact; but misrepresentation is also the basis for equitable relief in fraud cases, and it also plays a major role in quasi contract and restitution cases. There is no clear line of demarcation between these fields. A misrepresentation may be the basis for the rescission of a contract, relief in equity, recovery in quasi contract, or the remedy of restitution in law; but as a general rule,

---

[7] Fraud as it relates to contracts is discussed extensively in Chapter 8.

misrepresentation standing alone cannot be the basis for recovery of damages in tort.

Five elements are considered as essential to a recovery in deceit. There must be (1) misrepresentation of a material fact, (2) knowingly made or made in disregard of the truth of the representation, (3) with the intent to induce action, (4) justifiably relied on, and (5) injury must result. The misrepresentation must be of an existing or past fact. A statement of opinion or a prediction of future events generally cannot be the basis of the tort of deceit. The person making the statement must know that it is false or must know that he does not have sufficient information to make a positive statement. An honest mistake of fact is not actionable. Intent is tested objectively, and a person is held to have intended the usual and normal results of his acts. If the party to whom the statement is made knows it is false or under the circumstances should know that it is false, he cannot recover in deceit. The relation of the parties and their experience and intelligence will be considered in determining whether a person has justifiably relied on a false representation. If no injury has resulted from the false representation, there can be no recovery in tort.

Summary

The torts for interfering with property rights are trespass to land, trespass to personal property, and conversion. Any wrongful interference with the possession of land is a trespass. Likewise, wrongful intermeddling with the possession of personal property is a trespass. Conversion is, basically, such a serious interference with a person's right to control or to dispose of personal property that the party who interferes is generally required to pay full value for the property and take title to it. Deceit is based on misrepresentation of a material fact knowingly made with the intent to mislead, justifiably relied on to one's injury. Through deceit one gains a wrongful economic advantage of another.

Franc v. Pennsylvania RR

225 A.2d 528 (Sup. Ct. Penn. 1967)

This was an action to recover damages for personal injuries brought by Franc (plaintiff) against the Pennsylvania Railroad (defendant). Franc was severely injured when she fell through a gap in the planking on a single track railroad bridge. The gap was covered by snow and had been in the bridge for about three weeks. The bridge was the private property of the railroad although the public had used it to cross the creek for many years. Franc sued and the trial court gave a judgment notwithstanding the jury verdict to Pennsylvania Railroad. Franc appealed. Reversed and the jury verdict for Franc reinstated.

MUSMANNO, JUSTICE.   The duty of the railroad company in situations such as the one here outlined is spelled out in the *Restatement of Torts,* Sec. 335:

A possessor of land who knows, or from facts within his knowledge should know, that trespassers constantly intrude upon a limited area thereof, is subject to liability for bodily harm caused to them by an artificial condition, thereon, if (a) the condition (i) is one which the possessor has created or (ii) is, to his knowledge, likely to cause death or serious bodily harm to such trespasser and (iii) is of such a nature that he has reason to believe that such trespassers will not discover it; and (b) the possessor has failed to exercise reasonable care to warn such trespassers of the condition and the risk involved therein.

Comment (c):

. . . If, however, the condition, though obvious to adult trespasser, is such as not to disclose to him that there is a risk on its full extent, the possessor is under a duty to warn the trespasser of the risk and its extent.

Comment (f):

. . . On the other hand, he (the possessor) is not entitled to assume that the trespassers will discover conditions which are unusual to land of the character upon which the trespasser intrudes, or which are due to carelessness in the maintenance of those conditions which are necessary to the use of the land. . . .

As above stated, the railroad company knew or should have known of the defect in the floor of the bridge and it is clear that it failed to exercise reasonable care to warn users of the bridge of the condition and the risk involved in crossing the bridge. It displayed no signs on or near the structure, warning civilians away, nor did railroad employees inform civilians to keep off the bridge. On the contrary, the railroad employees joined with the civilians in the march across the missing-plank bridge.

Justices Roberts and Eagen agree that the result is correct but "without reliance on *Restatement 2d, Torts,* Section 335."

Dissent. "The majority opinion . . . invokes Section 335 of the *Restatement of Torts* to delineate the duty of the railroad in this situation, even if the plaintiff be considered a trespasser. Not only has Section 335 not been adopted by this court, but it is contrary to the long recognized rule in this Commonwealth, that is, that a plaintiff who is a trespasser can recover only if the defendant is guilty of wanton or wilful misconduct."

Business Torts

Economic Relations.   The modern courts recognize interference with economic relations as a tort, but the boundaries of this field have not been definitely determined. The determination of the rights of the parties requires a fine balance between free competition which is the life of trade, the encouragement of individual initiative, and the general social welfare. The law relating to business torts is discussed in Chapter 45.

Problem Cases

1. Seligman and Latz operated a beauty salon in Rich's department store which Grant visited to have her hair combed. She received a bill for $1.50 for the service and discovered she only had $1.29 in her possession. Grant testified that it was about 11:45 A.M. when she informed her cashier of her predicament. The cashier told her to "Have a seat" and she sat down. About 15 minutes later she got up and asked the cashier if she could look for a girl friend who was supposed to meet her there, to which the cashier replied, "Yes, leave your pocketbook up here and go ahead," or words to the same effect. She left her purse, searched through the store unsuccessfully, and returned to the area of the beauty salon. When she went to the desk the cashier asked her, "Did you find (or look for) your girl friend?" She answered, "I didn't find her," and the cashier replied, "Well, have a seat," and she again sat down. Other conversation took place, and Grant informed the cashier that she did not have a charge account and also told her where she worked. On previous occasions Grant had observed that no one was continuously out front where customers waited, but on this occasion whenever the cashier left the area she would ask another employee to come out front. Grant was allowed to use the telephone to call a friend, who eventually came with enough money to pay the bill, and they left about 1:10 P.M. Grant sued Seligman and Latz for damages for false imprisonment. Should Grant's complaint be dismissed?

2. Conway's husband used a credit card issued by Signal Oil & Gas Company. Conway had never used the credit card, but she had paid for some of the charges with checks written by her. When the bill became delinquent, Signal wrote Conway's employer accusing her of being past due on her account and seeking the aid of the employer in collecting such indebtedness. Conway sued for libel and invasion of privacy. Signal contended that they had a privilege as a creditor which barred Conway's action. Is this a good defense?

3. Gray, a patient with severe back trouble, signed a hospital "consent form" for an operation. Gray was not informed of the dangerous risks (a 20 percent chance of paralysis) involved in the operation. Although done without negligence, the operation resulted in paralyses of both legs. Gray sued the doctor for damages for battery and the doctor set up the consent form which purported to waive all of Gray's rights to sue. Is this a good defense?

4. At a public hearing on Supry's application for a variance, Bolduc, an owner of adjoining property, appeared before the zoning board and spoke in opposition to the application. Her testimony, given under oath, was recorded, transcribed, and made a part of the record. After the zoning board denied the application, Supry filed suit against Bolduc, alleging that Bolduc had slandered him at the public hearing. Bolduc claimed that her remarks concerning Supry were made during a judicial or quasi-judicial proceeding and were therefore absolutely privileged. Under the circumstances of this case, does the privilege of absolute immunity attach?

5. While conducting an investigation of McCormick's business dealings with the City of Philadelphia, Spector, the district attorney, held a press conference in which he outlined the nature of his inquiry. In a suit filed by McCormick charging libel and slander, Spector's defense was that since he made the statements in the exercise of his duties and in relation to matters pending in the district attorney's office, they were protected by the absolute immunity accorded his official position. Is this a good defense?

6. While shopping in a local A&P grocery store, Paul was accosted by the assistant manager, Parker, who believed him to be a shoplifter. Calling him a "thief," Parker frisked Paul in

the presence of other patrons. When sued by Parker for slander, A&P's defense was that none of the other customers knew Parker or knew who he was. Is this a good defense?

7. *Life* published an article, complete with pictures, depicting the lifestyles of young Americans, living in caves in the village of Matala on the Island of Crete—one of whom was Goldman. The author of the article had interviewed Goldman on three different occasions for a total of four to five hours. In these sessions Goldman had knowingly posed for photographs, some of which later appeared in *Life* along with the article. In a subsequent suit, based on an invasion of privacy, Goldman alleged that the article portrayed him in a "false light," thus injuring his reputation. Anticipating a defense premised on *New York Times v. Sullivan,* Goldman took the position that only concrete, specific events could constitute the basis of a story entitled to the protection of newsworthiness. Is this a valid contention?

8. On a radio talk-show, Gerhart, the announcer, falsely stated that his wife had been overcharged by Matus, a snowplower, for clearing their driveway of snow, and that "people like that shouldn't be in business." Matus sued Gerhart for defamation, and in his defense Gerhart stated that Matus was involved in an event of public concern and thus these communications were privileged. Is this a good defense?

9. An article appeared in the *Tribune* calling Farnsworth, an osteopath, a "quack." Dr. Farnsworth claims she was libeled by the newspaper's statement. In its defense the *Tribune* argued that Farnsworth should be considered a public figure who must show malice to recover, because medical quackery is an area of general public concern. Does this defense have merit?

10. Mark Peth and Mary Peth were engaged in the collection business and were employed by Dr. Lydic to collect a $197 debt that Joan Housh owed Dr. Lydic.

    The Peths called Housh on the telephone many times in the course of a day with regard to this collection and called her at her place of employment three times within 15 minutes on March 19, 1954. As a result, her employer told her on March 19, 1954, that unless this collection is "straightened up" on or before March 23, 1954, that Housh would be discharged from her employment.

    The Peths also called the Supervisor of Music of the Dayton Public Schools and called the Housh's landlord regarding the collection claiming that she did not pay her bills and inquiring as to her earnings. Two weeks prior to filing her suit, the Peths called Housh at her place of residence eight or nine times a day dunning her for this collection, giving her notices and warnings and called her as late as 11:45 P.M. Housh sued the Peths claiming that their conduct constituted an invasion of her right of privacy. Is Housh entitled to damages?

11. Allied held a mortgage on Medlin's home. Allied, erroneously believing Medlin was in default on his mortgage payments, sent two default notices to Medlin and to the F.H.A. They also made abusive telephone calls to Medlin. Medlin sued to recover damages for mental anguish and emotional disturbance. Allied argued that its negligence in billing could not be the basis for recovery under these facts. Is Allied correct?

12. Biggans had been purchasing supplies from Hajoca Corporation for a considerable period of time. In August 1947, Hajoca hired a private detective agency because it believed its inventory had been disappearing unaccountably. An employee of Hajoca of 40 years' standing was observed by the detectives delivering goods to Biggans without recording them. When informed of this behavior, the corporate officers conferred with the firm's

general counsel who further consulted another attorney. They did not tell the lawyers that company practice with respect to such records had been so lax over an appreciable period of time that specific instructions to correct the practice were issued during this same month nor that Biggans was a substantial and well respected contractor. It also appeared that the company officers had made no check with supervisors in the warehouse to determine what the actual practices were. Hajoca had criminal charges brought against Biggans. Biggans was acquitted and he immediately brought a malicious prosecution action and was awarded a judgment for $15,000 damages. Should this decision be reversed on appeal?

13. Heuer agreed to sell and Wiese agreed to buy for $600 a clover crop then standing on Heuer's field. Heuer was to cut the crop when directed by Wiese. Heuer cut the crop on July 31, 1971. After Heuer had cut the crop, he notified Wiese by letter to remove the crop by August 10, 1971. Wiese failed to remove the crop by August 10, 1971, and a week later Heuer took possession of the cut crop and with a chopper cut the crop up on his field. On September 25, 1971, Heuer brought suit againt Wiese to recover the unpaid balance of the purchase price of the crop and Wiese filed a counterclaim for damages for the conversion of the crop by Heuer. Can Heuer recover the balance of the purchase price?

chapter 4

Negligence and Strict Liability

Negligence

Nature of Negligence. In the law of torts, negligence occupies a position midway between intentional tort and strict liability. Each person in society should be given the maximum freedom of action consistent with the like freedom of other persons. If a person is given freedom to act, he or she is legally bound to give due consideration to the rights and welfare of other members of society and to exercise such a degree of self-control that his or her acts are not injurious to others. Each member of society owes a duty to refrain from following a course of action which will result in harm to another.

To recover damages for negligence, a person must establish that (1) the defendant has been guilty of negligent conduct toward the plaintiff and (2) that plaintiff has suffered an injury as a result of such conduct. Negligence without resulting injury is not actionable.

Standards of Conduct. The presence or absence of negligence is determined by applying standards of conduct to the facts of the case. The standard which has been adopted is the conduct of a reasonable man of ordinary prudence under the same or similar circumstances. This standard is flexible and serves as a measuring stick in the infinite variety of situations arising in the negligence cases. It also satisfies the requirement that a standard be external and objective and that, as far as possible, it be the same for all persons. The standard is one which must be applied by the jury, or by the court in the absence of a jury. Since negligence is based on conduct, the court, in applying the standard, attempts to put itself in the place of the actor and to pose the following questions: "Did the actor, in the light of the existing conditions, act like a reasonable man of ordinary prudence? Should he, as a reasonable and prudent man, have foreseen the danger of harm and prevented it?"

71

(handwritten margin note: foreseeable risk negligence)

Ignorance, honest mistakes, and physical defects of a person do not relieve a person from his or her responsibility to persons whom he or she has injured. Under the law of negligence, each member of society is required to act in such a manner that he does not create unreasonable risks which endanger the person or property of others. To have negligence, there must be a recognizable risk, and the conduct of the person causing the injury must be unreasonable in relation to the foreseeable risk. That is, his personal conduct must be below the accepted standard, which is the conduct of a reasonable and prudent person under the circumstances.

Special Duties Imposed by Law.   Special duties of care may be imposed by statutes. The wording of the statute and the intent of the legislature controls in such circumstances. This is treated subsequently as a form of strict liability.

Special duties of care may be created by the relationship between the parties. Common carriers, with a few exceptions, are absolute insurers of goods being shipped, and innkeepers at common law were held strictly accountable for any loss or damage to the personal effects of guests.

Under the doctrine of *respondeat superior* employers have a form of strict liability for the harm caused by agents or employees acting in the line and scope of authority. The trend is to impose greater duties of care on landowners—even where trespassers are concerned. These and other forms of special duties are discussed in subsequent chapters.

Proximate Cause.   When a person has acted affecting others, it may be impossible to trace to the ultimate end all the consequences of the act. Therefore, it is necessary to place a limit on a person's responsibility for the results of his or her acts. Early in the development of the law of negligence the court adopted the rule that a person would not be held liable unless his or her act was the "proximate cause" of the injury. The choice of language was unfortunate because it connotes proximity in time and place. Some courts have held that the person is not liable unless the harm is the natural and probable consequence of his act or unless the resulting harm is foreseeable. Other courts have held that the act must have been a substantial factor in producing the harm. In all but a limited number of cases the question of "proximate cause" will be a question of fact for the jury; or for the judge in the absence of a jury, to solve by the application of good common sense to the facts of each case.

(handwritten margin note: contributory neg. assumption of risk)

Defenses.   There are two principal defenses to a tort action for damages for negligence, namely, assumption of risk and contributory negligence. A person may, either by express agreement or by his conduct, enter into a relation with another which involves danger to himself. He may indicate his willingness to assume the risks of the known or foreseeable dangers, thereby relieving the other party from any legal responsibility for injuries.

In many cases, no express agreement to assume risks exists, but the assumption of the risks is implied from the conduct of the parties and from the surrounding circumstances. By voluntarily entering into a relationship which involves obvious danger, it may be taken as an assumption of the risks of the situation and relieve the other party from legal responsibility. If a person goes to a ball game, he or she may have assumed the risk of being hit by a ball. On the other hand, the ball park management may have installed defective netting on the backstop thus creating an unreasonable risk of being hit. If the person had no knowledge of this risk the defense would not be available. Ordinarily, a person will be held to have assumed only those risks which are known or which are foreseeable.

Each person in society is required to exercise a reasonable degree of caution and to look out for himself. If one does not exercise a reasonable degree of caution and this failure combined with the negligence of another results in an injury, neither party can recover damages from the other. Each party has been negligent, and their combined negligence has caused the injury. If either party sues in tort for damages for negligence, the other party can set up "contributory negligence," which would be a complete defense under the rule followed in most, but not all, states.

The trend is to narrow the scope of defenses and immunities in negligence cases. A growing number of states now allow plaintiffs guilty of contributory negligence to recover based on the doctrine of comparative negligence. The jury is instructed to determine the extent each party was at fault. If the jury finds the plaintiff suffered $6,000 in damages and was 20 percent at fault for the accident, the plaintiff is allowed to recover $4,800. Common law immunities such as those for state and municipal governmental activities, charitable institutions, and intra-family litigation seem to be gradually disappearing in nearly all jurisdictions.

Last Clear Chance. This doctrine applies where a plaintiff through initial negligence exposes himself to a risk of harm but then is helpless to avoid the harm, and the defendant has a last clear chance to avoid the harm but fails to do so. Under these circumstances the plaintiff is allowed to recover in spite of the fact that his or her initial negligence was a contributing cause. Prosser suggests that the "last clear chance" doctrine is more a matter of dissatisfaction with the defense of contributory negligence than anything else.[1]

Res Ipsa Loquitur. The injured plaintiff normally has the sometimes difficult burden of proving how and when the defendant was negligent. The so-called *res ipsa* doctrine permits a plaintiff to establish a prima facie case of negligence simply by showing that: (*a*) the event which injured him would not ordinarily occur in the absence of negligence, and (*b*) the defendant was in

---

[1] William L. Prosser, *Handbook of the Law of Torts,* 4th ed. (St. Paul, Minn.: West Publishing Co., 1972), p. 428.

exclusive charge or control of the instrumentalities causing the harm. The Latin words *res ipsa loquitur* translated mean "the thing speaks for itself" and where the doctrine is held to apply the defendant must defend himself against the prima facie case thus made or run the risk of having a judgment rendered against him.

Summary

Liability for negligence is based on a breach of duty to refrain from following a course of action which will result in foreseeable harm to another. The standard of conduct in determining a person's duty to fellow members of society is the conduct of a reasonable man of ordinary prudence under the same or similar circumstances. There is no liability for mere negligent conduct. To have liability, there must be injury resulting from negligent conduct.

The courts have attempted to limit the scope of a person's liability for his negligent conduct. One theory for the limitation of liability is the theory of "proximate cause," that is, the injury must be the direct result of the negligent act.

The principal defenses to liability for negligence are (1) assumption of risk, and (2) contributory negligence. The *last clear chance* doctrine permits an injured plaintiff to recover under some circumstances even though he was guilty of contributory negligence.

The doctrine *res ipsa loquitur* in effect shifts the burden of proof from the plaintiff to the defendant. The defendant must rebut the prima facie case the plaintiff makes when the plaintiff proves his injury falls under circumstances where the doctrine applies.

Special affirmative duties of care may be created by the existence of economic relationships or may be created by statute. The trend in tort law is towards the imposition of greater duties of care in virtually all areas of the law.

Enos v. W. T. Grant Co.

294 A.2d 201 (Sup. Ct. R.I. 1972)

On November 23, Mrs. Enos (plaintiff) and her daughter and daughter-in-law were shopping in Grant's (defendant) department store. The store was more crowded than usual and the patrons included both adults and children. While ascending the stairway leading from the basement to the ground floor, Mrs. Enos was bumped by a 10 to 12 year-old girl who was running up the stairs. As a result she lost her balance and fell to the floor. Mrs. Enos sued Grant and appealed from a judgment in favor of Grant. Affirmed.

JOSLIN, JUSTICE.   Turning from the procedural question to the substantive issues we advert generally to the obligations of a storekeeper who holds his premises open to the members of the public and invites them to enter thereon hoping that they will inspect and purchase his wares. That invitation does not make him an insurer of the safety of those who accept his invitation. Neither does it impose upon him the duty of anticipating and protecting those invitees against the unlikely or the improbable.

He does, however, owe them the duty of exercising reasonable care to protect them against physical harm caused by the acts of third persons, if he either knew, or in the exercise of due care should have known, that the third person was likely to conduct himself in a manner that would endanger his customers' safety and, if, notwithstanding that knowledge, he failed to take reasonable measures to protect his customers against that harm.

When we apply these rules to the facts before us we find that the obvious weakness in Mrs. Enos' case is the lack of any evidence which even remotely suggests that Grant either knew, or had reason to know, that it was likely that a 10 to 12 year-old child would run up the stairs and either negligently or intentionally bump into a customer and cause her to lose her balance and fall. Mrs Enos' attempts to fill this testimonial void by stressing that she was injured during the Christmas shopping season when Grant's store was more than usually crowded with both adults and children. Those special conditions, she argues, justify the drawing of an inference that Grant should reasonably have anticipated the conduct which in fact resulted in her injury. Under our law, however, the fact that it was the Christmas shopping season when a department store is likely to be more than usually crowded, *without something more,* would not necessarily put an ordinary prudent shopkeeper on notice that his customers were likely to be harmed unless he instituted safety precautions to protect them while using a stairway in his premises.

In this case, . . . there is an evidentiary deficiency with respect to the foreseeability of what happened. That gap could have been filled, for example, by a past history of similar instances taking place when the defendant-store was more than usually crowded or by evidence that during past Christmas seasons unruly and boisterous children had been observed on the premises. Without that or similar proof, to hold that the customer here was entitled to have her case submitted to a jury would be tantamount to saying that Grant was duty bound to guard against not only what is likely to happen, but also against the unlikely or slightly probable event. Sound judgment forbids us to go that far.

Jiffy Markets, Inc. v. Vogel

340 F.2d 495 (8th Cir. 1965)

This was an action brought by Vogel (plaintiff) who received extensive lacerations as the result of walking into and through a large glass panel which formed the front of the building in which Jiffy Markets, Inc. (defendant) operated a supermarket. Vogel sued Jiffy and won a judgment in the federal district court and Jiffy appealed. Affirmed.

MATTHES, CIRCUIT JUDGE.   There were no signs or markings of any kind on the glass panels on the night of the litigated occurrence and the glass was spotlessly clean.

Vogel stopped his automobile with the front facing the vending machine. He turned off the lights, got out of the automobile 18 or 20 feet from the front of the store and proceeded toward the building intending to enter the store and make a purchase. From the testimony, the jury was warranted in finding that as Vogel approached the store he was walking at a normal gait and with his head up; that although he was looking ahead, he did not see the glass or its bordering metal frame and saw no reflections from lights or identifying marks of any kind on the glass. He did not realize until he crashed through the glass that what he thought was the entrance to the store was, in fact, a solid plate-glass panel.

Inasmuch as the litigated incident occurred in the State of Kansas, we look to the law of that state for ascertainment of the duty imposed on the proprietor of a business establishment toward his patron or business invitee. Both parties cite and rely upon *Little v. Butner* (1960). That case teaches that the business proprietor is under a duty to use care to keep in a reasonably safe condition the premises where guests or customers may be expected to come and go; if there is a dangerous place on the premises, the proprietor must safeguard those who come lawfully thereon by warning them of the condition and risk involved: "The true ground of liability is his *superior knowledge* over that of business invitees of the dangerous condition and his failure to give warning of the risk . . . however, he is not an insurer against all accidents which may befall them upon the premises."

Jiffy contends that under all of the evidence favorable to Vogel and giving to Vogel the benefit of all reasonable inferences, it conclusively appears that Jiffy did not breach any duty toward Vogel; that Jiffy was not guilty of any actionable negligence, and the issue of liability should not have been presented to the jury. To support this contention, Jiffy invokes and presses upon us the "superior knowledge" test enunciated in *Little*. It insists (a) that the evidence clearly showed that the glass panels constituted an accepted method of construction, and the presence of the glass was clearly observable to a person in the exercise of ordinary care for his own safety; (b) that there was no duty on the part of Jiffy to warn Vogel of the claimed hazardous condition (glass panels) because the evidence conclusively established that the condition was apparent and would have been seen by Vogel if he had been giving reasonable attention to the surrounding physical conditions.

We are not so persuaded. To be sure, transparent plate glass is recognized as suitable and safe material for use in construction of buildings, indeed, it is common knowledge that such glass is used rather extensively in commercial buildings. However, it seems to us that the number of reported cases, involving personal injuries from bodily contact with transparent glass doors and walls is some indication that with the advantages that may be derived from such construction are concomitant risks which the proprietor must assume. Of course, whether the proprietor is responsible to a patron who comes in contact with a glass door or wall and sustains injuries, depends on the facts and circumstances surrounding the incident judged in light of the controlling legal standards. . . . The jury was not required to speculate as to the dangerous and unsafe condition created by the glass front. There was evidence to that effect. A former employee of Jiffy testified that during a period of eight months he observed four or five persons come in contact with the glass front and "bounce off." A safety engineer testified it was a hazardous arrangement, and detailed the methods that could have been employed to correct the lack of visibility of the glass.

Without further discussion, we conclude and hold that there was substantial evidence from which the jury could find: (1) that the glass front constituted a dangerous and unsafe condition; (2) that Vogel was exercising ordinary care for his own safety; (3) that there was a duty on the part of Jiffy to warn its patrons of the condition and (4) that Jiffy breached its duty. . . .

Scott v. John H. Hampshire, Inc.

227 A.2d 751 (Ct. App. Md. 1967)

This was an action brought by Scott (plaintiff) against John H. Hampshire, Inc. (defendant) for injuries sustained when Scott was hit by a chain. Judgment for Hampshire Company and Scott appealed. Reversed and remanded.

On the date of the accident, Scott was working for a contractor in the construction of a regional library. He noticed that a piece of chain attached to a steel cable for the purpose of lengthening it was being used as a choker in the unloading of steel from a truck with a crane. Concerned about what he had observed, Scott came down from the building to warn nearby workmen of the dangerous situation. When the supervisor was informed that the use of the chain to unload steel was dangerous and that someone was likely to get hurt, the supervisor and crew ignored his warning. As the steel was moved ahead, the chain broke and struck Scott on his head and about his body while he was standing about 20 feet away. Hampshire, who was the roofing contractor, was the owner of the steel.

When Hampshire Company moved for a directed verdict at the close of the case for Scott, the trial judge, assuming the existence of primary negligence, ruled that Scott had assumed the risk and was therefore guilty of contributing to the accident.

HORREN, JUDGE. There is a difference between an assumed risk and contributory negligence in that an assumed risk implies an intentional exposure to a known danger whereas contributory negligence is the doing or failure to do something which directly contributes to the injury sustained. The distinction between the two is often difficult to draw and, as is the case here, is often without importance. So regardless of whether the defense was contributory negligence or assumption of risk, neither defense is applicable in this case where the conduct of Hampshire Company appears to have created such a situation as to justify if not to compel Scott to undergo the risk of being injured in order to warn others and avert their harm.

This court, in recognizing the principle that it is commendable to save life, has consistently held that a person who endeavors to avert the consequences of the negligence of another person, by an act which is dangerous but not reckless, is not precluded from recovering damages for injury suffered as a consequence of having interposed. In *Marney* it was said that the "law had so high a regard for human life that it will not impute negligence to an effort to preserve it, unless made under such circumstances as to constitute rashness."

Hughes v. Moore

197 S.E.2d 214 (Sup. Ct. Va. 1973)

Moore (plaintiff) brought this action to recover for personal injuries sustained as a consequence of fright and shock caused when an automobile driven by Hughes (defendant) crashed into the front porch of her home. Moore won a verdict for $12,000 and Hughes appealed. Affirmed.

Hughes was operating his automobile along a highway in Virginia. He ran the car off the road, struck an automobile parked in the driveway of Moore's home, and crashed into the house which was set back approximately 35 feet from the highway. The skid marks from the highway to Moore's home measured 285 feet.

Moore was standing in a doorway of her house between the kitchen and living room, looking through a picture window, when she heard a noise and saw the headlights of Hughes' car shining into her living room. The car crashed into the front porch of the house, and after the initial collision the car moved back and forth against the porch several times. Moore said that she "froze in her tracks" and screamed. Immediately thereafter she became weak and felt as if her legs were going to fold under her. She became very nervous, could not sleep that night, and had pains in her chest and arms as the result of the collision. Although she received no physical injury from without, she could not breast-feed her three-month-old baby for lack of milk, and her menstrual period started.

Moore consulted her doctor and finally a psychiatrist diagnosed her condition as "anxiety reaction, with phobia and hysteria." He testified that she was experiencing physical pain in her body from the emotional disturbance and that her condition presented a serious mental problem. The pain was real and "not imaginary."

I'Ansor, Justice.   An analysis of the early cases holding that there can be no recovery for mental or emotional disturbance and consequent physical injuries resulting from negligence unaccompanied by contemporaneous physical injuries to the person indicates that there were three basic arguments supporting the rule: (1) medical science's difficulty in proving causation between the claimed damages and the alleged fright; (2) the fear of fraudulent or exaggerated claims; and (3) concern that the absence of such a rule would precipitate a flood of litigation.

A rapidly increasing majority of courts have repudiated or not followed the "impact rule" for the reasons that the early difficulty in tracing a resulting injury back through fright had been minimized by the advance of medical science; that the possibility of fraud should not prevent those with legitimate claims from proving their cases; and that courts should not shirk their duty merely because of the possibility of an increase in litigation, which has not proved to be a fact.

Many eminent scholars have considered the rule and are virtually unanimous in condemning it as unjust and contrary to experience and logic. Our research reveals that a total of 35 jurisdictions have considered the rule. Of these at least 25 have either completely rejected it or abandoned it as being unsound. Since 1929 every jurisdiction which has considered the issue, except the Supreme Court of Washington . . . has either abandoned the rule or refused to adopt it.

We adhere to the view that where conduct is merely negligent, not willful, wanton, or vindictive, and physical impact is lacking, there can be no recovery for emotional disturbance alone. We hold, however, that where the claim is for emotional disturbance *and* physical injury resulting therefrom, there may be recovery for negligent conduct, notwithstanding the lack of physical impact, provided the injured party properly pleads and proves by clear and convincing evidence that his physical injury was the natural result of fright or shock proximately caused by the defendant's negligence. In other words, there may be recovery in such a case if, but only if, there is shown a clear and unbroken chain of causal connection between the negligent act, the emotional disturbance, and the physical injury.

The rule, of course, is subject to familiar limitations. A defendant's standard of conduct is generally measured by the reaction to be expected of a normal person. Absent specific knowledge by a defendant of a plaintiff's unusual sensitivity, there should be no recovery for mental or emotional disturbance and consequent physical injury to a hypersensitive person where a normal individual would not be affected under the circumstances.

Under the rule adopted today we are not saying that a plaintiff, in an action for negligence, may recover damages for physical injuries resulting from fright or shock caused by witnessing injury to another, allegedly occasioned by the negligence of a defendant toward a third person, or caused by seeing the resulting injury to a third person after it has been inflicted through defendant's negligence.

In the case at bar, there was evidence that Moore suffered physical injuries which were the natural result of the fright and shock proximately caused by Hughes' tortious conduct.

Strict Liability

Nature of Strict Liability.   Under some circumstances a person is held liable for the results of his acts without reference to the question of negligence. In such a situation the actor is an "insurer" of those who may be injured by his acts. These cases involve a situation in which the undertaking is hazardous and harm is foreseeable even though the greatest of precaution is taken, yet the undertaking is of sufficient social benefit that it will be permitted. The actor is permitted to proceed but is required to assume all the risks of the undertaking. The keeping of wild or vicious animals, spraying crops from aircraft, blasting, and trespassing of domestic animals are examples of situations in which strict liability has been imposed. In addition, many legal authorities have noted a trend in the cases to expand the application of the doctrine of strict liability.[2] In recent years, for example, strict liability has become the majority

---

[2] In 1914 Roscoe Pound wrote: "There is a strong and growing tendency, where there is blame on neither side, to ask, in view of the exigencies of social justice, who can best bear the loss and hence to shift the loss by creating liability where there has been no fault." "The End of Law as Developed in Legal Rules and Doctrines," 27 *Harv. L. Rev.* 195 (1914).

rule concerning sales of defective products where such defects expose purchasers to unreasonable risks. In a growing number of jurisdictions strict liability is being applied to the leasing of goods, to sales of services, and even to the sale of new houses.

Conduct in violation of a statute can amount to negligence *per se* which means no actual negligence needs to be proved. The injured person can recover under this doctrine only if such person is a member of the class that the legislation seeks to protect; and, the type of harm suffered is the type contemplated in the statute. It should be noted that contributory negligence is not a defense to an action based on strict liability although some forms of assumption of risk may provide a defense. The expansion of strict liability in the product liability area is covered in detail in Chapter 34.

Summary

Cases of strict liability may involve situations in which the undertaking is hazardous and harm is foreseeable yet the undertaking is of sufficient social benefit so as to make outright prohibition of such conduct not feasible. The full risk of injury is placed upon the person engaged in this type of conduct. The modern trend is to expand strict liability on the basis of social policy criteria. Strict liability in the form of negligence *per se* may be created by statute. Contributory negligence is not a defense to actions based on strict liability.

Shone Coca-Cola Bottling Co. v. Dolinski

420 P.2d 855 (Sup. Ct. Nev. 1966)

Dolinski (plaintiff) brought this action for damages against Coca-Cola Bottling Company (defendant) claiming that he suffered physical and mental distress when he partially consumed the contents of a bottle of "Squirt" containing a decomposed mouse. Coca-Cola appealed from a verdict of $2,500 in favor of Dolinski. Affirmed.

THOMPSON, JUSTICE. We affirm the verdict and judgment since, in our view, public policy demands that one who places upon the market a bottled beverage in a condition dangerous for use must be held strictly liable to the ultimate user for injuries resulting from such use, although the seller has exercised all reasonable care, and the user has not entered into a contractual relation with him. Perhaps the supporting policy reasons are best expressed by William L. Prosser in his article, "The Fall of the Citadel," (1966): "The public interest in human safety requires the maximum possible protection for the user of the product, and those best able to afford it are the suppliers of the chattel. By placing their goods upon the market, the suppliers represent to the public that they are suitable and safe for use; and by packaging, advertising, and otherwise, they do everything they can to induce that belief. The middleman is no more than a conduit, a mere mechanical device, through which the thing is to reach the ultimate user. The supplier has invited and solicited the use; and when it leads to disaster, he should not be permitted to avoid the responsibility by saying that he made no contract with the consumer, or that he used all reasonable care."

In *Escola v. Coca Cola Bottling Co.* (1944), Justice Traynor, in a concurring opinion, wrote: "Even if there is no negligence, however, public policy demands that responsibility be fixed wherever it will most effectively reduce the hazards to life and health inherent in defective products that reach the market." That point of view ultimately became the philosophy of the full court in *Greenman v. Yuba Power Products, Inc.* (1962). There Justice Traynor wrote: "The purpose of such liability is to insure that the cost of injuries resulting from defective products are borne by the manufacturer that put such products on the market rather than by the injured persons who are powerless to protect themselves."

We believe that the quoted expressions of policy are sound as applied to the manufacturer and distributor of a bottled beverage. Indeed, 18 states have judiciously accepted strict liability, without negligence and without privity, as to manufacturers of all types of products; and six more have done so by statute. Though the appellant suggests that only the legislature may declare the policy of Nevada on this subject, the weight of case authority is contra. As indicated, most states approving the doctrine of strict liability have done so by court declaration.

Our acceptance of strict tort liability against the manufacturer and distributor of a bottled beverage does not mean that the plaintiff is relieved of the burden of proving a case. He must still establish that his injury was caused by a defect in the product, and that such defect existed when the product left the hands of the defendant. The concept of strict liability does not prove causation, nor does it trace cause to the defendant.

General Electric Co. v. Bush

498 P.2d 366 (Sup. Ct. Nev. 1972)

Bush (plaintiff) was injured while assisting in the reassembly of a giant vehicle specially designed for use in open-pit mining. Bush sued and was awarded $3 million damages, his wife $500,000 for loss of consortium, and their three children $50,000 each for loss of their father's companionship. Westinghouse and General Electric (defendants) appealed. Affirmed except as to award to the children.

The vehicle was a Haulpak, a truck type that has as one of its major component parts a heavy electrical control cabinet which consists of a metal box weighing about 1,130 pounds and which contains a variety of electrical components such as switches, relays, and the like. This cabinet had to be lifted onto the truck bed by eyebolts mounted on the cabinets.

No rigging diagram or warning was given by any of the manufacturers. The rigging crew was experienced and professional. A test lift was performed safely, then the cabinet was raised 8 to 12 inches into approximate position above the truck's fender where the cabinet remained suspended for about 20 minutes.

While the crew was aligning the cabinet with the fender and aligning both with the frame one eyebolt broke. This allowed the cabinet to drop at that end and slide down the fender toward the rear of the truck. Bush, who was under the suspended cabinet tending to his duties, was struck on the head and his skull was crushed. His injuries are such that he will live, but he has neither mental nor physical capacities.

ZENOFF, CHIEF JUSTICE.   The principal defense was that the bolt failed, not because it was defective in material or design, but because the workmen's rigging was not in accordance with the custom and practice to keep the angle at 45 degrees or above. They also sought to assert Bush's contributory negligence and assumption of risk.

The evidence showed that the rigging was in accordance with usage and custom in the trade. Had the companies required a different rigging, such as vertical lifts using a spreader bar which the companies claimed should have been done, suitable instructions or warnings to that effect would have been appropriate. Without them the riggers were free to use the accepted method they felt proper.

We have heretofore held that a defective product is dangerous if it fails to perform in the manner reasonably to be expected in the light of its nature and intended function. Beyond that a product being defective gives rise to strict tort liability even though faultlessly made if it was unreasonably dangerous for the manufacturer or supplier to place that product in the hands of a user without giving suitable and adequate warnings concerning the safe and proper manner in which to use it.

The doctrine of strict liability for an injury caused by a defective product applies even though the supplier has exercised all possible care in the preparation and sale of his product. When classifying these riggers as "professionals" that term is used in the sense of their knowledge and experience in their particular skill, which is a highly variable factor as compared to the true sense of "professional" applied to doctors, lawyers, engineers, and the like. Warning need not be given against dangers which are generally known, but the hazard here was not one generally known to these workmen. Nothing in their work experience could have forewarned them of the defective bolt or that a vertical lift was the only safe method of lifting this cabinet.

Under strict liability the manufacturer is entitled to assume that his product will not be subjected to abnormal and unintended uses, and consequently no liability follows an injury resulting from an abnormal or unintended use. But here, the eyebolts were being used for lifting as intended by a procedure that was approved by custom and usage in the trade. There was no misuse or abuse.

The defendants point out that this action was prosecuted on three theories (a) that the eyebolt was defective (b) that the design of the lifting provision for the cabinet was defective, and (c) that the design was defective only in the sense that General Electric did not furnish a warning as to the proper use of the product. If the third theory was accepted by the jury, defendants claim it sounds in negligence and that therefore they were entitled to defense instructions on contributory negligence and assumption of risk. All three theories give rise to strict tort liability to which ordinary contributory negligence and assumption of risk are not defenses.

The question of the wife's right to recover for the loss of her husband's society has not been heretofore decided by this court. An aging doctrine based upon the danger that she was seeking a double recovery and that the loss of such things as companionship and society were too indirect to measure in terms of money discouraged her compensation. As time went on, however, the doctrine that the wife of an injured spouse has a right of action developed.

In 1968, the New York court shifted from the old to the new and ruled that the consortium action on behalf of the wife although based upon the wife's right of support from her husband, more importantly, recognizes instead that consortium covers a variety of other intangible interests which the wife has in the welfare of her husband. These are described as "love, companionship, affection, society, sexual relations, solace and more."

In all respects the serious harm that the sadness, shock, and anguish of seeing a spouse suffering from all kinds of physical injury, in addition to her complete inability to ever again bear children by her husband is fundamentally injury that the wife suffers separate and distinctly apart from the question of support.

As an additional safeguard against the danger of double recovery we require that she will have her cause of action only if joined for trial with the husband's own action against the same defendant.

Are the children of a father injured by the negligent acts of third persons entitled to maintain independent actions to recover damages for their loss of consortium with their father the same as their mother? Only one court has recognized their cause of action. Substantial differences exist in the consideration of the childrens' claim as against that of their mother, all of which have compelled the overwhelming weight of authorities to be against an action for the children.

We are satisfied to await legislative action, if any, on this issue.

Brockett v. Kitchen Boyd Motor Co.

100 Cal. Rpt. 752 (Cal. Ct. App. 1972)

The Brocketts (plaintiffs) brought this action against Kitchen Boyd Motor Company (defendant) after having an automobile collision with Jimmie Huff, an intoxicated minor who was an employee of Boyd's. The Brocketts appealed from a trial court adverse decision. Reversed.

The Brocketts were injured when the automobile in which they were riding was struck by a Thunderbird driven by Jimmie Huff, an intoxicated minor of the age of 19, who was an employee of Boyd Motor Company. Huff became intoxicated at his employer's Christmas party where he was served copious amounts of liquor, and placed in his automobile and directed to drive home. Section 25658 of a state statute made it a misdemeanor to sell, furnish, or give alcoholic beverages to a minor.

GARGANO, ASSOCIATE JUDGE. The common-law rule, immunizing the furnisher of liquor from civil liability, has been picturesquely described as a "back-eddy running counter to the mainstream of modern tort doctrine." In some states the rule has been partially eliminated by statutes, known as "Dram Shop Acts"; these statutes impose liability on vendors of intoxicating beverages for injuries caused by the intoxication of persons to whom the beverages are sold. In other states, the specious reasoning of the common law has been modified by judicial fiat; liability is imposed when, in contravention of a statute, liquor is sold to intoxicated persons or to a minor.

In June 1971, the California Supreme Court unmasked the common law fiction; it declared that the real question to be decided in each case is one not of probable cause but rather whether the defendant is guilty of a breach of duty to the injured party. The high court, in *Vesely v. Sager,* said:

A duty of care, and the attendant standard of conduct required of a reasonable man, may of course be found in a legislative enactment which does not provide for civil liability. In this state a presumption of negligence arises from the violation of a statute which was enacted to protect a class of persons of which the plaintiff is a member against the type of harm which the plaintiff suffered as a result of the violation of the statute. The Legislature has recently codified this presumption with the adoption of Evidence Code section 669: "The failure of a person to exercise due care is presumed if: (1) He violated a statute, ordinance, or regulation of a public entity; (2) The violation proximately caused death or injury to person or property; (3) The death or injury resulted from an occurrence of the nature which the statute, ordinance, or regulation was designed to prevent; and (4) The person suffering the death or the injury to this person or property was one of the class of persons for whose protection the statute, ordinance, or regulation was adopted."

In the instant case a duty of care is imposed upon defendant Sager by Business and Professions Code section 25602, which provides: "Every person who sells, furnishes, gives, or causes to be sold, furnished, or given away, any alcoholic beverage to any habitual or common drunkard or to any obviously intoxicated person is guilty of a misdemeanor." This provision was enacted as part of the Alcoholic Beverage Control Act of 1935 and was adopted for the purpose of protecting members of the general public from injuries to person and damage to property resulting from the excessive use of intoxicating liquor.

Boyd Motor Company points out that the Supreme Court narrowed the perimeter of the *Vesely* decision to commercial vendors; the court did not "decide whether a noncommercial furnisher of alcoholic beverages may be subject to civil liability under section 25602 or whether a person who is served alcoholic beverages in violation of the statute may recover for injuries suffered as a result of that violation." Nevertheless, the rationale of the *Vesely* decision charts the course to be followed in this state. We consider the problem presented in this appeal with this premise in mind.

Defendant suggests that if we lift the common law immunity of noncommercial suppliers of alcohol, we will subject every social host to civil liability for injuries caused by intoxicated guests and will soon flood the courts with a myriad of perplexing problems. Following are a few examples: How is an unsophisticated social host to determine when a guest has reached his alcoholic tolerance; to what extent is a host to supervise social activities; is a host required to ignore social convention by refusing to serve a guest a drink because he merely suspects the guest may be intoxicated?

We do not reach the broad question as to whether a host at a social gathering is subject to liability under section 25602 for injuries caused by intoxicated guests. Section 25658 is directed to a special class; it pertains to young people who because of their tender years and inexperience are unable to cope with the imbibing of alcoholic beverages. Under this section a person's duty is unequivocal; it requires no expertise to perform; it involves no exercise of judgment, nor is one faced with undue difficulties because of traditional niceties or convention or compulsion.

It is suggested that the extension of the *Vesely* rationale to furnishers of alcoholic beverages to minors imposes almost absolute liability on vendors and on every parent who keeps intoxicating liquor in the home. As we have stated, the scope of this decision is limited to the facts as alleged in plaintiffs' complaint, that the minor's intoxication was induced by his employer as the result of a Christmas party where the employer did *knowingly make available* to the minor copious amounts of intoxicating beverage with knowledge that the minor was going to drive a vehicle upon the public highways.

Nuisance

Nature of Nuisance.   Nuisances may be divided into private and public. A private nuisance is created when a landowner's use or enjoyment of his land is lessened substantially due to unjustifiable conduct on the part of another. The conduct creating the nuisance may be either intentional or negligent. In a few situations liability may be imposed due to the extra-hazardous activity of the defendant even though neither intent nor negligence are present. The fact that the conduct or use of land by a neighbor hinders an owner from putting his land to a special or "delicate use" does not mean the owner hindered can enjoin the conduct. Thus, where one owner operated a race track with the use of floodlights at night, and the adjacent owner operated an open-air movie, it was held that the latter could not prevent the former from using the flood-lights.[4] With increasing population and urbanization, nuisance litigation is increasing. The new law protecting the environment is discussed in Chapter 32.

Sundowner, Inc. v. King

509 P.2d 785 (Sup. Ct. Idaho 1973)

King (defendant) appealed from a trial court order which directed him to remove part of a sign which amounted to a spite fence used against Sundowner (plaintiff). Affirmed.

In 1966 Bushnell sold a motel to King, and then built another motel, the Desert Inn, on property immediately adjoining that sold to King.

King thereafter brought an action against Bushnell based on alleged misrepresentations by Bushnell in the 1966 sale of the motel property. In 1968 King built a large structure, variously described as a fence or sign, some 16 inches from the boundary line between the King and Bushnell properties. The structure was 85 feet in length and

---

[4] *Amphitheaters, Inc. v. Portland Meadows,* 198 P.2d 847 (1948). A public nuisance is an act or omission causing damage or inconvenience to the public such as: blocking a public highway or operating a house of prostitution.

18 feet in height. It was raised 2 feet off the ground and was 2 feet from the Desert Inn building. It paralleled the entire northwest side of the Desert Inn building, obscuring approximately 80 percent of the Desert Inn building and restricting the passage of light and air to its rooms. It cost $6,500 to erect.

Bushnell brought suit seeking damages and injunctive relief compelling the removal of the structure. The trial court ordered the structure reduced to a maximum height of 6 feet.

SHEPARD, JUSTICE.   Under the so-called English rule, followed by most 19th century American courts, the erection and maintenance of a spite fence was not an actionable wrong. These older cases were founded on the premise that a property owner has an absolute right to use his property in any manner he desires.

Under the modern American rule, however, one may not erect a structure for the sole purpose of annoying his neighbor. Many courts hold that a spite fence which serves no useful purpose may give rise to an action for both injunctive relief and damages.

In *Burke v. Smith* a property owner built two 11 foot fences blocking the light and air to his neighbors windows. The fences served no useful purpose to their owner and were erected solely because of his malice toward his neighbor. Justice Morse . . . concluded:

But it must be remembered that no man has a legal right to make a malicious use of his property, not for any benefit or advantage to himself, but for the avowed purpose of damaging his neighbor. To hold otherwise would make the law a convenient engine, in cases like the present, to injure and destroy the peace and comfort, and to damage the property, of one's neighbor for no other than a wicked purpose, which in itself is, or ought to be, unlawful. The right to do this cannot, in an enlightened country, exist, either in the use of property, or in any way or manner. There is no doubt in my mind that these uncouth screens or "obscurers" as they are named in the record, are a nuisance, and were erected without right, and for a malicious purpose. What right has the defendant, in the light of the just and beneficent principles of equity, to shut out God's free air and sunlight from the windows of his neighbor, not for any benefit or advantage to himself, or profit to his land, but simply to gratify his own wicked malice against his neighbor? None whatever. The wanton infliction of damage can never be a right. It is a wrong, and a violation of right, and is not without remedy. The right to breathe the air, and to enjoy the sunshine, is a natural one; and no man can pollute the atmosphere, or shut out the light of heaven, for no better reason than that the situation of his property is such that he is given the opportunity of so doing, and wishes to gratify his spite and malice towards his neighbor.

We agree both with the philosophy expressed in the *Burke* opinion and with that of other jurisdictions following what we feel is the better-reasoned approach. We hold that no property owner has the right to erect and maintain an otherwise useless structure for the sole purpose of injuring his neighbor.

Our decision today is not entirely in harmony with *White v. Bernhart* (1925). *White* held that an owner could not be enjoined from maintaining a dilapidated house as a nuisance, even though the house diminished the value of neighboring property. *White* is clearly distinguishable from the case at bar. Rather than a fence, it involved a dwelling house which was not maliciously erected. The rule announced herein is applicable only to structures which serve no useful purpose and are erected for the sole purpose of injuring adjoining property owners. There is dictum in *White* which suggests that a structure may only be enjoined when it is a nuisance per se. Such language is inconsistent with our decision today and it is hereby disapproved. . . .

Problem Cases

1. Mick had been a customer of Krogers for several years. During this period Krogers had maintained a carry-out service for its customers. One particular day Mick was informed that no one was available to help her take groceries to her car. She then lifted a 30-pound bag, carried it outside, and fell stepping off the sidewalk onto the parking lot pavement. She sued Kroger for the resulting injuries and won a jury verdict for $4,000. A lower appellate court sustained judgment on the theory that a jury could find that Kroger's duty of reasonable care included assisting customers in carrying large packages of groceries. Should the judgment be sustained by the state supreme court?

2. At 2:30 A.M. Hone stopped his tractor-trailer truck in the right-hand lane on Munson Avenue, a four-lane street designated as a state trunk-line highway, in order to ascertain whether the rear lights were functioning properly. The point where he stopped was posted "No Parking at Any Time" pursuant to orders issued by the State Highway Department. Bensinger, riding a motorcycle, collided with the rear of the truck causing injuries which resulted in his death. Bensinger's family sued Hone, alleging that he was negligent as a matter of law in parking his vehicle on the highway in violation of the Michigan traffic code. The statutes referred to in the complaint provide in part that no person shall park a vehicle, except when necessary to avoid conflict with other traffic, or in compliance with the law or the directions of a police officer or traffic control device, such as an automatic signal light . . . . "at any place where official signs prohibit stopping." On appeal, should the ruling by the trial court that there was no proof of negligence on Hone's part be upheld?

3. Mrs. D'Ambra suffered mental anguish when she witnessed her four-year-old son being run over by a truck. She sued the negligent driver for damages for mental anguish. In his defense he stated that her presence at the scene of the accident was unforeseeable and therefore he was not liable. Is this a good defense?

4. Driving home from a company Christmas party, Wolf struck and severely injured Halvorson. Alleging that the accident was caused by the condition of Wolf, who was so intoxicated that he was incapable of operating an automobile, Halvorson sued Wolf's employer, Boiler, for damages. Halvorson alleged that Boiler was liable because he furnished intoxicants to Wolf, knowing he was intoxicated and unable to properly operate a motor vehicle; and knowing that he had had his driver's license revoked as a result of a prior accident. Halvorson also alleged that Boiler allowed Wolf to continue to consume liquor with knowledge that he was an alcoholic, and then permitted him to drive away from the party in his automobile. Should Boiler's motion to dismiss for failure to set forth a cause of action be granted?

5. The Mayrath Company supplies retailers with farm elevator parts, including protective shields for assembly to customer's order. Should the Mayrath Company be held liable for injuries suffered by Willeford because of an unshielded elevator assembled by the retailer?

6. In a common negligence action brought on behalf of her eight-year-old son for prenatal brain injuries incurred when Mrs. Womack was involved in an automobile accident during her fourth month of pregnancy, the district court denied recovery on the grounds that the fetus has no legal rights as a person under the present law. Should the verdict be sustained?

7. Stupka was injured while riding in a cab owned by Peoples Cab. The facts showed that the accident was clearly the fault of the driver of the other car. In a later court action, Stupka sued the Peoples Cab for not obtaining the identity of the driver of the private vehicle that hit the cab. Does Stupka have a cause of action against the Peoples Cab?

8. While on the premises of Griffeth Brothers Tire Company having his automobile repaired, Boggs fell and sustained injury, by reason of a step-down between the yard and office area. Boggs sued Griffeth Brothers, alleging injury due to the failure of Griffeth Brothers to exercise ordinary care in keeping the premises and approaches safe. Boggs introduced evidence showing two step-downs, each being approximately six inches and that there were no warning signs. Furthermore, Boggs alleged that decals plastered on the glass door of entry interfered with the vision of one opening the door and that the colors of the floors inside the office and on the steps blended into each other. The trial court directed a verdict for Griffeth Brothers, stating that the evidence did not show any defect in the condition of the premises which would be sufficient to make Griffeth Brothers liable to Boggs for whatever injuries he had sustained. On appeal, should Boggs be granted a trial on the merits of his negligence suit?

9. Goforth invited Wells into his home and as Wells was entering, he slipped on an ice patch on the porch. Wells sued Goforth for injuries received in the fall and as a defense, Goforth stated that an icy porch is not an extra-hazardous condition and a failure to warn of the condition is not active negligence. Who wins and why?

10. Jackson suffered a heart attack while at work and under no unusual strain, but he had been out for several days with chest pains he believed to be a bad cold. The lower court held that he was not able to recover under Workmen's Compensation, because there was no evidence of any "unusual strain" offered to prove that the heart attack was an accidental injury arising out of the course of his employment. Can Jackson win an appeal?

11. Mrs. Metcalf was injured by a stampede caused by sidewalk shoppers scattering to avoid being struck by glass that was pushed out of a third-story apartment window by a trespassing nine-year-old child. Mrs. Metcalf sued the landlord for failure to inspect the defective window. Glasgow, landlord, argued in his defense that he was not responsible for the acts of a trespasser and could not have reasonably foreseen or anticipated the injury. Is this a good defense?

12. Parke-Davis was held liable for the wrongful death of Mrs. Stevens because of the failure of their "detail men" to adequately warn Dr. Breland of the possible harmful side effects of their drug, chloromycetin. On appeal Parke-Davis argued that they had complied with the regulations as to warnings issued by the FDA, and also that the negligence of Dr. Breland was an intervening cause that exonerated them from liability. Should this case be reversed?

13. Mr. Pike was 40 feet behind the paydozer with his back to it when it backed up and struck him. The paydozer operator had looked to the rear before backing, but he had not seen Pike because of a blind area created by the cab. An engineer testified that the blind area could have been eliminated by the use of two rearview mirrors. The Hough Company, manufacturer, contended that it had no duty to install safety devices to protect against such an obvious danger. Is this contention sound?

14. Robinette died from pneumonia caused by his exposure to the elements arising in the course of his employment as a gas station attendant. A lower court held that his death was not compensable under Workmen's Compensation Act since it was not a result of an "occupational disease." The court said for his death to be compensable under the Act, his employ-

ment conditions must have exposed him to hazards to a degree beyond that of the public at large. Should this case be reversed on appeal?

15. A nearby gravel pit was in existence and occasionally operated prior to the time the Bies purchased their home. Later, Ingersoll began operating an asphalt plant. At the time the plant commenced operations, the area was zoned as residential, but was rezoned as industrial for the specific purpose of accommodating the plant. In a suit to abate the plant's operation, Bie and other residents testified that the plant's operation caused a noxious odor in the area and created extensive dust. The plant had the conventional pollution abatement equipment for the industry. On appeal from a judgment for Bie, Ingersoll argued that the plant was not offensive, and that since their use was within the zoning ordinance, the court was precluded from holding the operation to be a nuisance. Should the judgment stand?

Part III

Contracts

chapter 5

Introduction

Nature of Contract

Basis of Contract. The basis of a contract is a promise or a group of promises. A promise looks to the future, and the person to whom it is made is justified in expecting that it will be fulfilled. In their everyday relationships with their fellow members of society, people make many promises, some of which, for various reasons, will not be performed. The seriousness of one's failure to carry out his or her promise will depend on the nature of the justified expectation of the person to whom it is made and the social importance of its fulfillment. Many promises made in the regular course of human relations may have material significance to the parties involved but have little or no effect on the welfare of society. The failure to discharge the duty created by a promise will not give rise to a right of action in court unless it has those characteristics which make its nonperformance injurious to the general welfare of society. In general, a promise, the performance of which has economic significance, gives rise to rights which will be protected by court action.

Evolution of the Contract. The courts and law writers have given us many definitions of a contract, all of which recognize the promise, or the agreement which is the result of promises, as an element. A generally accepted definition is: "A contract is a promise or a set of promises for the breach of which the law gives a remedy or the performance of which the law in some way recognizes as a duty."[1] The contract has been accepted as the basis of commercial transactions from the earliest times. It was known to and enforced by the Egyptians and Mesopotamians 3,000 or 4,000 years before Christ.

By 1603 the common-law courts of England recognized the enforceability of the simple contract, that is, a promise not under seal. The courts, however,

---

[1] American Law Institute, *Restatement of the Law of Contracts* (Ten. Draft 1973) Sec. 1.

93

recognized that it would be not only impractical but also undesirable to grant a remedy to the promisee in all instances in which a promise, not under seal, was not performed. After a long period of development the courts finally began to accept the presence of consideration as the test for the enforceability of the simple contract. Today the requirements for a valid contract are (1) an offer, (2) an acceptance of the offer, (3) supported by consideration (with some exceptions), (4) by parties having capacity to contract, and (5) the objective of the contract must be legal. In all cases the promise or promises (offer and acceptance) which are the basis of the contract must be made voluntarily. In addition, in some cases an otherwise valid contract is not enforceable unless it has been reduced to writing. Each of these elements will be discussed in subsequent chapters.

Changing Role of Contracts

Role at Turn of Century.   The laissez-faire economic theories espoused by 18th and 19th century classical and neoclassical economists had an important influence on the evolution of Anglo-American contract law in the 19th and the first half of the 20th centuries. Under these theories the private contract was to be the major mechanism by which economic plans were to be effectuated. Neither the legislative branches of government nor the courts should "tamper" with business contracts because they represented the voluntary choices of the parties in an economy stressing individualism and free choice. Free contracting was viewed as an essential ingredient of the decentralized economic planning that was supposed to take place in a laissez-faire market controlled economy.[2]

The high pedestal this "free contract" concept occupied in law was summarized in 1875 in the frequently quoted words of Sir George Jessel:

> If there is one thing more than any other which public policy requires, it is that men of full age and competent understanding shall have the utmost liberty of contracting, and that contracts when entered into freely and voluntarily, shall be held good and shall be enforced by courts of justice.[3]

These strict hands-off policies of the courts meant businessmen had an ideal legal mechanism for effectuating economic plans which were enforceable in the

---

[2] This was noted by Justice Frankfurter in *AFL v. American Sash & Door Co.,* 335 U.S. 538, 540 (1949): ". . . (In the 19th century) Adam Smith was treated as though his generalizations had been imparted to him on Sinai and not as a thinker who addressed himself to the elimination of restrictions which had become fetters upon initiative and enterprise in his day. Basic human rights expressed by the constitutional conception of liberty were equated with theories of laissez-faire. The result was that economic views of confined validity were treated by lawyers and judges as though the framers had enshrined them in the constitution. . . ."

[3] *Printing and Numerical Registering Co. v. Sampson,* 19 L.R. *Eq.* 462, 465 (1875).

courts. These policies also provided businessmen with a means, within broad limits, for shifting or limiting many of their economic risks. During this period the courts, except in extreme circumstances, would not consider claims or defenses to contract litigation based on alleged "inequality" of bargaining power or "unfairness" in the terms of contracts.

Contracts After 1900. The first basic change has been the widespread adoption of form contracting by business. Llewelyn recognized and summarized the reasons for this development in 1931 when he wrote:

Standardized contracts in and of themselves partake of the general nature of machine-production. They materially ease and cheapen selling and distribution. They are easy to make, file, check and fill. To a regime of fungible goods is added one of fungible transaction—fungible not merely by virtue of simplicity (the over-the-counter sale of a loaf of bread) but despite complexity. Dealings with fungible transactions are cheaper, easier. One interpretation of a doubtful point in court or out gives clear light on a thousand further transactions. Finally, from the angle of the individual enterprise, they make the experience and planning power of the high executive available to cheaper help, and available forth with, without waiting through a painful training period.[4]

Concurrently with the development of form contracting the Industrial Revolution was changing the entire nature and institutional structure of our economy. New theories of "imperfect" and "monopolistic" competition challenged the validity of utilizing laissez-faire economic theories as a basis for public policy in a modern industrial-urban society. The courts began to be persuaded by arguments that inequalities in bargaining power had developed which justified the "intervention" of public agencies into various economic relationships including many types of contracting relationships.[5]

The Uniform Commercial Code (discussed later) contains a provision (2–302) which makes "unconscionability" a defense in all legal and equitable sale of goods actions based on contracts. In a recent law review note discussing the Code, the writer states:

Form contracts generally reflect complete control of negotiations by the party drafting the instrument and almost total lack of bargaining power in the other party. Section 2–302 is designed to avoid exploitation of such situations by limiting the stronger party's ability to enforce the terms he dictates, thus forcing him to exercise restraint in drafting.[6]

---

[4] Karl N. Llewelyn, *"What Price Contract—An Essay in Perspective,"* 40 *Yale L. J.* 704, 731 (1931).

[5] Many important legal relationships formerly left to bargaining between the parties to private contracts are substantially or fully controlled by legislation. As an example, consider all of the federal and state laws that now establish or condition the terms of an ordinary employment relationship entered into by a corporation engaged in interstate commerce. Not only are there laws prohibiting various forms of discrimination and establishing safety standards; there also are laws influencing or controlling the level of compensation. The employee rights established include those related to minimum pay, maximum hours, job injuries, and unemployment and retirement benefits. The trend has been for "legislated" rights and duties to replace, or modify, rights and duties created by private contract in an increasing number of important areas.

[6] Note 63 *Yale L. J.* 560, 562 (1954).

Today a growing number of courts may refuse to enforce; or even may rewrite terms in private contracts if this is deemed necessary to protect the real or presumed victims of one-sided or unfair contracts. For example, disclaimer of liability clauses found in many form sales contracts or so-called warranties given with the sale of goods, now are strictly construed against sellers so as to afford maximum protection to consumers. In an increasing number of circumstances, disclaimers and other "boiler-plate" terms are found to be against public policy and hence invalid. Despite these modern trends the agreement reached by the parties still provides the fundamental basis for the rules and for the enforcement of private contracts. These rules and policies are discussed along with modern trends in the chapters that follow.

Classification of Contracts

To aid in the analysis of contractual problems contracts have been classified according to their various characteristics. These classifications are not all-inclusive or all-exclusive and the same contract may be classified under more than one category.

Formal and Informal or Simple.　Contracts under seal, negotiable instruments, and recognizances are classified as formal contracts. All other contracts, whether oral or written, are classed as informal or simple contracts.

Unilateral and Bilateral.　As the terms indicate, a *unilateral contract* is one in which only one of the parties makes a promise, whereas in a *bilateral contract,* both of the contracting parties make promises. A unilateral contract may be a promise for an act or an act for a promise. For example, a promise to pay a reward for the return of lost property is a promise for an act. The person offering the reward makes a promise and the person returning such property performs the requested act. And a promise to repay money loaned is an act for a promise. The lender performs the act of paying the borrower who in return promises to repay the money. A promise to sell and deliver goods given in exchange for a promise to pay the agreed purchase price at some future date is a bilateral contract or a promise for a promise.

Valid, Unenforceable, Voidable, Void.　A valid contract is one which fulfills all the legal requirements for a contract. A court will lend its aid to the enforcement of a valid contract.

An unenforceable contract is one which satisfies the basic requirements for a valid contract, but which the courts deny enforcement because of some statutory requirement or some rule of law. Such a contract may create, in an indirect way, a duty of performance. An oral contract required by statute to be in writing, is an example of an unenforceable contract. Under some circumstances, such a contract, although not enforceable, may give rise to rights on which a cause of action may be based.

A voidable contract is one which binds one of the parties to the contract, but gives to the other party the right, at his election, to withdraw from the contract. For example, a person who has been induced by fraudulent representation to make a promise is given the right to elect not to be bound by his promise. If he elects to perform his promise, however, he can hold the other party to the performance of his duties under the contract.

The term *void* is applied to a contract which is a nullity due to the lack of some essential element of a contract, that is, it has no legal force or effect. In some respects, it is inaccurate to call such a promise a contract. A promise to murder a person given in exchange for a promise to pay an agreed sum would be termed a void contract.

Executed and Executory.   A contract becomes executed when all the parties to the contract have fulfilled all their legal obligations created by the contract. Until all such legal obligations have been fulfilled, the contract is executory. If one of the parties has partially fulfilled his obligations under the contract, the contract is often referred to as a partially executed contract. The contract might be executed as to one of the parties to the contract and executory as to the other party.

Express and Implied.   An express contract is one in which the promise or promises are stated or declared in direct terms, that is, set forth in words. They may be stated orally or put in writing. An implied contract is one in which the promise or promises are not stated in direct words but are gathered by necessary implication or deduction from the circumstances, the general language, or the conduct of the parties. For example, suppose you go to the dentist and ask him to fill a tooth for you, and say nothing at the time about paying him. You would, under the circumstances, have impliedly promised to pay him the standard fee for such services. You would be bound by a contract implied in fact.

Summary

The basis of a contract is a promise but all promises do not give rise to contractual obligations. The modern concept of a contract was developed in the English law after the 15th century and the simple contract did not attain its present characteristics until the 19th century. The role of contracts changed as our society changed from an agrarian to an industrial-urban society. The courts now are more inclined to review and even modify contract terms—particularly where form contracts are utilized.

Contracts are divided into classes in order to aid in analysis of contractual problems. The recognized classifications are formal and informal or simple;

unilateral and bilateral; valid, unenforceable, voidable and void; executed and executory; and express and implied.

Quasi Contracts

Historical Development.   During the early formative period of the common law, the courts tended to stress stability and continuity in the principles of law being developed. It will be recalled that the inflexibility of common law rules was a principal factor behind the development of courts of equity. Even after courts of equity developed, however, there were special fact situations not adequately covered by existing rules.

For example, if Able through an honest mistake conferred a benefit on Baker under circumstances where Baker knowingly received the benefit, Able had no remedy in either contract or tort law. To preserve the general consistency of the existing rules and yet to avoid the resulting injustice, the common law judges resorted to a fiction: they held that a promise had been made or was implied in law. These obligations based on promises implied in law are known as "quasi contracts." The basis for a recovery in an action in quasi contract is the unjust enrichment of one party at the expense of another. In most cases the remedy is a money judgment for the amount of the unjust enrichment.

Measure of Damages.   The measure of damages for the breach of a contract is, as a general rule, the sum of money which is necessary to place the injured party in substantially the same position he would have occupied had the contract been performed. In quasi contract the court, as a general rule, awards a judgment for an amount equivalent to the unjust enrichment of the party defendant. Some courts allow the plaintiff to recover for the reasonable value of detriment incurred even where no benefit is conferred on the defendant.

Basis for Recovery.   The cases which come under the heading of quasi contracts are of infinite variety, and it is impossible to list the situations that may arise which will justify a recovery in quasi contract. In any situation in which a party is justified in believing that a binding contract exists and the party performs under such belief, thereby benefiting the other party, he or she may recover for the benefits conferred in a suit in quasi contract.

If the parties have entered into a valid contract, the courts will not add to or alter the terms of the contract or allow additional recovery by the application of the principles of quasi contract.

One cannot recover in quasi contract for benefits voluntarily conferred on another without his knowledge or consent, or under circumstances which justify him in accepting the benefits believing them to be a gift. Suppose Parks paints Oren's house when Oren is away on his vacation. Parks cannot recover for the benefits conferred on Oren in a suit in quasi contract. One cannot force benefits on another without the knowledge and consent of the other person and then force him to pay for the benefits.

Summary

The purpose of granting a remedy in quasi contract is to prevent unjust enrichment of one party at the expense of another. The amount of the recovery is based on the amount of the unjust enrichment. Quasi contract cannot be brought where there is an express or implied valid contract covering the subject matter. Some cases now allow recovery for detriment incurred where special facts exist.

Gebhardt Bros., Inc. v. Brimmel

143 N.W.2d 479 (Sup. Ct. Wisc. 1966)

This was an action in quasi contract by Gebhardt Bros., Inc. (plaintiff) against Brimmel (defendant) for the value of fill delivered. Judgment for Gebhardt and Brimmel appealed. Reversed.

Gebhardt entered a subcontract with Semrow, a general contractor, whereby Gebhardt was to supply fill for construction work to be done by Semrow on Brimmel's land. The prime contract included the cost of this fill work. Semrow failed to pay Gebhardt for the fill delivered and Gebhardt sued Brimmel.

HEFFERMAN, JUDGE.   We have previously held that, though there is no express contract, there may be circumstances where, by conduct of the parties, it becomes unjust or inequitable for one party to fail to pay for the goods or services furnished by another. We have previously stated that three elements must be established in order that a plaintiff may establish a claim based on unjust enrichment. These elements are: (1) a benefit conferred upon the defendant by the plaintiff; (2) an appreciation or knowledge by the defendant of the benefit; and (3) the acceptance or retention by the defendant of the benefit under such circumstances as to make it inequitable for the defendant to retain the benefit without payment of its value.

The first of these two elements have been adequately proved, and the finding that 150 loads of earth were delivered to Brimmel's property is not contrary to the great weight and clear preponderance of the evidence. We cannot, however, concur with the learned trial judge's legal conclusion that under the circumstances it was inequitable for the defendant Brimmel to retain the benefit without the payment of its value. That conclusion overlooks the clear and undisputed testimony of Brimmel that the cost of the fill was included in the price agreed upon between him and the general contractor. The evidence could support no other finding. The facts also show that there was an express contract between Gebhardt and Semrow, the general contractor, for the payment of the fill. That Gebhardt recognized this is apparent from the fact that no effort was made to collect from Brimmel until efforts to collect on the express contract with Semrow had proved to be fruitless.

. . . This case is directly governed by our decision in *Superior Plumbing Co. v. Tefs* (1965). We therein held that a subcontractor must resort for payment to the principal contractor and not to the owner of the property and that the owner is not liable on an implied contract simply because he has received goods or services or knows that the services have been rendered.

The Uniform Commercial Code

Purpose of the Code. The aim of the Uniform Commercial Code is to establish a coordinated code covering most of commercial law and to establish a means of continuing revision to improve it and keep it up to date. The Uniform Commercial Code is the product of the combined efforts of the American Law Institute and the National Conference of Commissioners on Uniform State Laws. By 1969 the Code had been adopted in all of the states except Louisiana. In addition, it had been adopted in the District of Columbia and in the Virgin Islands.

Scope of the Code. The scope of the Code is stated in the comment to the title of the Code (p. 3, *1962 Official Text* with comments) as follows: "This Act purports to deal with all the phases which may ordinarily arise in handling a commercial transaction, from start to finish."

The Code is divided into 10 articles: Article 1, General Provisions; Article 2, Sales; Article 3, Commercial Paper; Article 4, Bank Deposits and Collections; Article 5, Letters of Credit; Article 6, Bulk Transfers; Article 7, Warehouse Receipts, Bills of Lading and Other Documents of Title; Article 8, Investment Securities; Article 9, Secured Transactions, Sales of Accounts, Contract Rights and Chattel Paper; and Article 10, Effective Date and Repealer.

Although the Code does not purport to affect any areas of the law other than those specifically stated, its adoption brings about some changes in other areas of law. The Code requires a higher standard of conduct for merchants by imposing a duty to act in "good faith." The duty to act in "good faith" is defined as honesty in fact including the observance of reasonable commercial standards of fair dealing in the trade. The duty to act in "good faith" is imposed on every contract or duty falling within the Code.

The Code recognizes that most contracting today is done by means of forms usually prepared by one of the parties. In some situations the terms may be one-sided or oppressive. The Code stipulates that the courts may find that such terms are "unconscionable" and deny enforcement. The Code further provides that the obligations of good faith and reasonableness may not be disclaimed by contract.

There are other sections of the Code which restrict the right of one or both parties as to the use of specific types of contract terms. In the case of certain types of terms the party signing a form must initial particular terms separately or he will not be bound. In other cases disclaimer of liability terms must be in "conspicuous" print and specific words must be used or the disclaimer terms will not be effective. These latter requirements reduce the possibility that a person will bind himself inadvertently in the signing of these form contracts.

It should be kept in mind that although the general provisions of the Code have application to most business transactions, some major parts of the Code do not apply to some important business transactions. For example, neither contracts to sell real estate nor contracts to provide services are covered under Article 2 (Sales) of the Code because the application of Article 2 is limited to contracts for the sale of goods.

In addition, many provisions of the Code provide one set of rules for merchants selling or buying goods and a different set of rules where one or both parties to the sales agreement are not merchants. Even a merchant may not be subject to the rules provided for merchants unless in the particular transaction, the goods he is selling are those which he customarily sells as a merchant.

Finally, even though the Code may not apply to some types of business transactions, a number of courts have applied various parts of the Code by analogy to transactions not covered by the Code. Because of these complexities it is essential that each part of the Code be studied carefully to determine its possible application to each area of law under study. Selected sections of the Code are printed in full in the Appendixes of this text.

Summary

The Uniform Commercial Code sets out the law for a major part of all business transactions. The Code governs in every state but Louisiana. Topics covered are: sales; commercial paper; bank deposits and collections; letters of credit; bulk transfers; warehouse receipts and other documents of title; investment securities; secured transactions; sale of accounts, contract rights, and chattel paper; and some general provisions. The sales provisions of the Code do not apply to contracts for the sale of real estate or the sale of services. Special rules apply to sales by merchants.

Questions and Problem Cases

1. Into what two general classes may we divide promises?
2. Define a contract.
3. What is the difference between an unilateral and a bilateral contract?
4. What is the difference between an unenforceable contract and a voidable contract?
5. In 1955, La Maita agreed on his retirement to sell his two-family house and garage to

Misisco. At the time the two apartment parts of the house brought in $62.50 per month. Misisco moved into one of these units paying $30 per month. Later he rented both units paying $100 per month. Misisco spent about $5,000 over the next few years improving the property with the knowledge and consent of La Maita. In 1961, La Maita brought eviction proceedings and had Misisco evicted. Misisco brought a suit in quasi contract for the reasonable value of benefits conferred; but the trial court ruled that since there was no written contract no recovery could be had by Misisco. Was this ruling correct?

6. What are some of the advantages businesses can gain from the use of form contracts?

chapter 6

Offer

Introduction

The significant changes in the law of offer as applied to sale of goods contracts subject to the Code will be discussed at the end of this chapter.

Nature of Offer. Before parties enter into a contractual relationship they usually engage in informal negotiations. Whether these informal negotiations result in the creation of a contractual relationship will depend on whether the parties reach a mutual agreement and on the presence of other essential elements.[1] Although these informal negotiations may not be a part of the final agreement, they do indicate the intent of the parties.

To have an agreement, two or more persons must arrive at a mutual understanding with one another. Generally, this is accomplished by the making of a proposition by one party and the acceptance of that proposition by the other. A proposal or offer looks to the future and is an expression of what the party making the offer—the offeror—promises shall be done or happen or shall not be done or happen, provided the party to whom the offer is made—the offeree—complies with stated conditions.

Form of Offer. The expression by the offeror may be made in any form which will serve to communicate his proposition to the offeree. It may be made by acts, by spoken words, by written words, or by any combination of these. All that is necessary is that the one making the offer communicate his proposition, by some means, to the offeree.

Businessmen frequently use a standard form of purchase order in making an offer to buy. Such forms usually include a statement of the terms of the offer to purchase.

Intent. Since a contract is based on an obligation voluntarily assumed, the

---

[1] Consideration, parties having capacity to contract, and a legal objective.

offeror must make his proposition with the intent to contract, thus making "intent" an essential element of an offer. In the law, intent is always tested by an objective standard. In determining the presence of intent, the circumstances surrounding the parties, their acts, their words, and any other facts which may aid the courts in reconstructing the situation are offered in evidence, and from this reconstruction of the entire happening, the court decides whether a reasonable man familiar with the business being transacted would be justified in believing that an offer had been made.

It is not essential that the party be conscious of the legal effect of his words and acts. It is essential, however, that the acts manifesting the making of the offer be done intentionally, and that they be done voluntarily.

Certainty of Terms.   An offer, the terms of which are incomplete or vague, cannot serve as the basis for a contract. Judges frequently make the statement that if the parties have not made a contract, the courts will not make one for them. The offeror need not state the terms of his offer with absolute certainty. However, they must be sufficiently definite to enable the court to determine the intention of the parties and to fix the legal rights and duties arising therefrom. An offer need not state time, price, quantity, or other terms with mathematical exactness, but it must state a formula or basis whereby such matters can be determined with reasonable certainty.

Omission of Terms.   If the contracting parties omit from their agreement material terms or leave material terms for future agreement, the court will hold that because of uncertainty of terms, no contract results. The omission of minor or immaterial terms will not affect the validity of an offer; and under some circumstances, what appears to be an omitted term may be supplied by usage of trade.

These common law requirements that the parties to contracts must have manifested their intent with a reasonable degree of certainty without any omissions of material terms have been relaxed to an as yet undetermined extent for sale of goods contracts subject to the Code.[2]

Usage of Trade.   Usage of trade is defined in the Uniform Commercial Code (1–205 [2]) as follows: "A usage of trade is any practice or method of dealing having such regularity of observance in a place, vocation or trade as to justify an expectation that it will be observed with respect to the transaction in question.[3] The existence and scope of such a usage are to be proved as fact." When a contract is negotiated the presumption is that the parties intend any usage of trade to be a part of the contract. If the parties do not wish to be bound by an established usage of trade they must make it clear by their words or acts that they do not wish to be so bound.

---

[2] This matter is explored subsequently.

[3] The numbers in parentheses refer to the sections of the Uniform Commercial Code.

Preliminary Negotiations. There are times when one may wish to enter into a contract with another person but, instead of making an offer, will try to induce the other party to make the offer. To accomplish this, he will extend an invitation to negotiate.

In the negotiation of a sale, it is a common practice for the seller to make statements of what he thinks he should receive for the property, and for the buyer in turn to make statements as to his idea of the value of the property, without either party making a clear-cut proposition which would be interpreted as an offer. This is what is known as "dickering," and the courts have recognized that in the transaction of business it is often to the advantage of the parties to dicker.

Advertisements. As a general rule the courts have held that an advertisement of goods for sale at a stated price is not an offer to sell the goods at that price, that it is merely an invitation to negotiate for the sale of the goods. Likewise, they have held that the distribution of a price list, either through the mails or by general advertisement, or a mere quotation of a price is not an offer to sell the goods at the listed price. However, if an advertisement contains a positive promise and a positive statement of what the advertiser demands in return, the courts will generally hold that it is an offer.

Rewards. Advertisements of rewards for the return of lost property or for the capture of criminals are common examples of offers made through advertising. Such offers are offers for unilateral contracts. The offer is accepted by the performance of the requested act—the return of the lost property or the capture of the criminal.

Bids. When one advertises for bids on construction work, the advertisement is an invitation to make offers. One may expressly state in the advertisement for bids that the job will be let to the lowest responsible bidder without reservation. In such a situation as this, the advertisement is an offer to let the job to the lowest bidder unless the party advertising for bids can prove lack of responsibility on the part of the low bidder.

As a general rule the advertising for bids and the letting of contracts by governmental units are controlled by statute, and general contract law does not apply. Such statutes usually set out the method of advertising to be used and the form to be followed in making the bid, and provide that the contract is to be let to the lowest responsible bidder.

Auctions. Unless, in the terms governing the auction, language is used which clearly expresses the intention to sell without reservation to the highest bidder or to the lowest bidder, as the case may be, the bidder will be the offeror, and the seller will be free to accept or reject bids, as the case may be. In the ordinary auction, no contract is made until the auctioneer strikes the goods off to the highest bidder. In Section 2–328 of the Uniform Commercial Code the rules of law which apply to an auction of goods are set out.

Summary

The offer must state (1) what the offeror promises, and (2) what he demands in return. It may be made in any manner whereby the offeror can communicate his proposition to the offeree. It must be made with "intent" to contract, and its terms must be reasonably certain. General business practices and common usages play an important role in determining whether an offer has been made. Since dickering is common in the transaction of business, an indication of a willingness to negotiate will not be interpreted as an offer; and as a general rule, advertisement of goods for sale are not offers.

An advertisement offering to pay a reward is usually an offer. An advertisement for bids is, as a general rule, a solicitation of offers, and substantially the same rule applies to sales at auction. Whether or not an offer is made by an advertisement will depend on its wording.

O'Keefe v. Lee Calan Imports, Inc.

262 N.E.2d 758 (Ct. App. Ill. 1970)

O'Keefe (plaintiff) brought this action as administrator of the estate of O'Brien against Lee Calan Imports, Inc. (defendant). Judgment for defendant and O'Keefe appealed. Affirmed.

On July 31, 1966, Calan Imports advertised a 1964 Volvo station wagon for sale in the *Chicago Sun-Times.* Calan had instructed the newspaper to advertise the price of the automobile at $1,795. However, through an error of the newspaper and without fault on part of Calan, the newspaper inserted a price of $1,095 for the automobile in the advertisement. O'Brien visited Calan's place of business, examined the automobile and stated that he wished to purchase it for $1,095. One of Calan's salesmen at first agreed, but then refused to sell the car for the erroneous price listed in the advertisement. O'Brien brought suit against Calan for an alleged breach of contract. O'Brien died subsequent to the filing of the lawsuit, and the administrator of his estate was substituted in his stead.

McNamara, Justice.   It is elementary that in order to form a contract there must be an offer and an acceptance. A contract requires the mutual assent of the parties.

The precise issue of whether a newspaper advertisement constitutes an offer which can be accepted to form a contract or whether such an advertisement is merely an invitation to make an offer, has not been determined by the Illinois courts. Most jurisdictions which have dealt with the issue have considered such an advertisement as a mere invitation to make an offer, unless the circumstances indicate otherwise. As was stated in *Corbin on Contracts* § 25 (1963):

It is quite possible to make a definite and operative offer to buy or to sell goods by advertisement, in a newspaper, by a handbill, or on a placard in a store window. It is not customary to do this, however; and the presumption is the other way. Neither the advertiser nor the reader of his notice understands that the latter is empowered to close the deal without further expression by the former. Such advertisements are understood to be mere requests to consider and examine and negotiate; and no one can reasonably regard them otherwise unless the circumstances are exceptional and the words used are very plain and clear.

In *Craft v. Elder & Johnston Co.,* defendant advertised in a local newspaper that a sewing machine was for sale at a stated price. Plaintiff visited the store, attempted to purchase the sewing machine at that price, but defendant refused. In holding that the newspaper advertisement did not constitute a binding offer, the court held that an ordinary newspaper advertisement was merely an offer to negotiate. In *Ehrlich v. Willis Music Co.,* defendant advertised in a newspaper that a television set was for sale at a mistaken price. The actual price was ten times the advertised price. The court found that no offer had been made, but rather an invitation to patronize defendant's store. The court also held that defendant should have known that the price was a mistake. In *Lovett v. Frederick Loeser & Co.,* a newspaper advertisement offering radios for sale at 25% to 50% reductions was held to be an invitation to make an offer.

We find that in the absence of special circumstances, a newspaper advertisement which contains an erroneous purchase price through no fault of the defendant advertiser and which contains no other terms, is not an offer which can be accepted so as to form a contract. We hold that such an advertisement amounts only to an invitation to make an offer. It seems apparent to us in the instant case, that there was no meeting of the minds nor the required mutual assent by the two parties to a precise proposition. There was no reference to several material matters relating to the purchase of an automobile, such as equipment to be furnished or warranties to be offered by defendant. Indeed the terms were so incomplete and so indefinite that they could not be regarded as a valid offer.

*   *   *   *   *

In *Johnson v. Capital City Ford Company,* defendant advertised that anyone who purchased a 1954 automobile could exchange it for a 1955 model at no additional cost. Plaintiff purchased a 1954 automobile and subsequently attempted to exchange it for a 1955 model, but was refused by defendant. The court held that the advertisement was an offer, the acceptance of which created a contract. However, in that case, the advertisement required the performance of an act by plaintiff, and in purchasing the 1954 automobile, plaintiff performed that act. In the case at bar, the advertisement did not call for any performance by plaintiff, and we conclude that it did not amount to an offer. . . .

Chu v. Ronstadt

498 P.2d 561. (Ct. App. Ariz. 1972)

Sam Chu (plaintiff) brought suit against Ronstadt and others (defendants) for breach of contract concerning an alleged farmland lease by Chu to the defendants. Judgment for the defendants and Chu appealed. Affirmed.

After some preliminary discussions Ronstadt sent Chu the following letter dated July 7, 1969:

Dear Mr. Chu:

As discussed with you on July 4, 1969, with Dick Little and myself, we will enter into a lease on your 150 acres of plowed barley adjacent to your store.

It is our understanding you will lease this land for fall lettuce and that it is immediately available. The price for this land will be $50.00 per acre, and we will reimburse you for the plowing you have done at the rate of $8.00 per acre.

If these conditions are correct, attached hereto is our check of earnest money for $500.00 as you requested, which amount will be applied to the payments that will be due under the lease upon its conclusion.

The other party involved with us on this lease will be here Sunday or Monday next week and we will proceed then to finalize this lease.

Very truly yours,
/s Karl G. Ronstadt

The voucher stub to the $500 check contained the following:

"7/7/69 Earnest money toward rental of 150 acres of farm land near Marana for fall lettuce crop. $500."

HATHAWAY, JUDGE. Chu relies heavily on the contents of the letter of July 7th as forming and representing the alleged contract. We must carefully scrutinize this letter in order to decide the existence or nonexistence of the alleged lease contract. The word used by Ronstadt upon which Chu so strongly relies is "earnest." This word is defined in *Black's Law Dictionary* as follows: "The payment of a part of the price of goods sold, or the delivery of part of such goods, for the purpose of *binding the contract.*" (Emphasis added)

Chu would have us rule that Ronstadt by using the words "earnest money" absolutely bound himself to the technical legal definition of such words and therefore committed himself to the performance of the alleged lease contract. It is elementary in contract law that the manifested objective intention of the parties is the controlling factor in the interpretation of the wording of a writing. The character of contracts must be determined by their provisions rather than by labels. It is therefore incumbent upon us to interpret the meaning of these words in light of the intention of the parties as shown by the whole writing, and not to isolate the words and give them a meaning foreign to such intention.

Chu points to paragraph one of the letter of July 7th, set out above, as clearly establishing a present intention to enter into a contract; the words relied upon specifically read ". . . we will enter into a lease on your 150 acres of plowed . . ." The Arizona Supreme Court, when called upon to rule whether a writing was sufficient to establish a lease contract, decided that words similar to the ones in the letter of July 7th (We *will* pay you . . .) were not, standing alone, sufficient to establish a present intention to enter into a lease contract.

The last paragraph of the July 7th letter clearly shows that Ronstadt had no present intention of entering into a contract but did have an intention of finalizing an agreement some time in the future. Of course, a contract will not be prevented from so operating by the mere fact that the parties also manifest an intention to prepare and adopt a written memorial thereof. If all the conditions of the postponed writing are specified in such agreement, it is an agreement *in praesenti,* and as such becomes immediately enforceable. But where the conditions of the deferred contract are not set out in the provisional one, or where material conditions are omitted, it is not a contract *in praesenti* because the minds of the parties have not met and may never meet. Chu urges this court to interpret this last paragraph as merely showing an intention to formalize a present agreement in the future. In order for us to do so, it is necessary to find that no material conditions have been omitted from the deferred contract. In the case of *Cypert v. Holmes,* our Supreme Court stated:

It may be conceded that an agreement to enter into a lease will neither be enforced in equity nor at law if it appears from the face of the agreement that any of the terms of the lease, no matter how unimportant they may seem to be, are left open to be settled by future conferences between the lessor and lessee. In such cases there is no complete agreement; the minds of the parties have not fully met; and, until they have, no court will undertake to give effect to those stipulations that have been settled, or to make an agreement for the parties respecting those matters that have been left unsettled.

The last paragraph of the July 7th letter, coupled with the limited terms agreed upon in the letter, clearly shows that the parties intended to settle other pertinent and important terms of the lease agreement at sometime in the future.

Terms Included in Offers

Tags, Tickets, Folders, Etc.   An offer has not been communicated until the offeree has knowledge of the proposition. The writing and mailing of a letter stating the offeror's proposition is not effective as an offer until it is received by the offeree. If one writes a letter in which he or she makes an offer but the letter is lost and never delivered, no offer has been made. A more difficult situation arises when the offeror prints his or her proposition on a tag attached to goods shipped, on a ticket delivered to the purchaser of a service, on an invoice sent for goods shipped, or on a folder delivered with monthly bills or distributed as handbills. When has a proposition made in some such manner been communicated to the offeree? No clear-cut rules can be extracted from the decided cases, but the courts have developed standards which aid in solving the problem. If the offeree actually reads the terms, or if he does not read them, but under the circumstances should know as a reasonable person that the tag, ticket, invoice, or handbill contains the terms of the offeror's proposition, the proposition has been communicated to him. However, if the offeree has no reason to know that the printed matter on the tag, ticket, invoice, or handbill contains a proposition and he does not read it, there has been no communication. There is presumption against the inclusion in contracts of terms located in unusual places or printed in microscopic print.

Summary

An offer must be communicated to be effective. Only the offeree has the right to accept an offer. Whether a proposition printed on a tag, ticket, invoice, or handbill has been communicated depends on the facts and circumstances of each individual case, but the test is what reasonable men or women would have intended.

Cutler Corp. v. Latshaw

97 A.2d 234 (Sup. Ct. Pa. 1954)

This was a petition by Jennie Latshaw (plaintiff) against Cutler Corporation (defendant) to set aside a judgment. Judgment for Cutler Corp. and Latshaw appealed. Reversed.

On November 20, 1951, Latshaw contracted in writing to pay Cutler Corp. the sum of $6,456 for certain work to be done and material to be furnished in repairing her premises in Philadelphia. Dissatisfied with the manner in which the work was being performed, Latshaw ordered the employees of the Cutler Corp. to cease operation until defects in the work were corrected.

On July 23, 1952, Cutler Corp. confessed judgment against Latshaw in the sum of $5,238.56 under an alleged warrant of attorney contained in the contract. Latshaw petitioned for a rule to show cause why the judgment should not be stricken from the record; the lower court made the rule absolute; and Cutler appealed.

The contract consisted of five form sheets carrying certain printed matter. The face of each sheet began with a standardized identification of the parties and the designation of Latshaw and Cutler, respectively, as "buyer" and "contractor."

Then followed in small type the wording: "Upon your acceptance below, you are hereby requested by the undersigned owner of the installation premises, hereinafter called 'Buyer,' to furnish and install the materials shown in the following specifications at the installation premises mentioned below (subject to conditions on reverse side)."

In the middle of the sheet, in large type, appeared the single word: "Specifications." Beneath this word, *in handwriting,* followed a list of the various items of work to be done and materials to be supplied by Cutler.

The reverse side of each sheet carried in very small type eight paragraphs, No. 6 of which spelled out a warrant of attorney with confession of judgment. Although each reverse sheet also carried the word, "Specifications," with "continued" in parentheses, no specifications were listed—in spite of the fact that the entire list of the specifications could not be contained on the first sheet and had to go over to other sheets. In fact, with the exception of the printing indicated, the reverse sides of the sheets were blank.

MUSMANNO, JUSTICE. A warrant of attorney authorizing judgment is perhaps the most powerful and drastic document known to civil law. The signer deprives himself of every defense and every delay of execution, he waives exemption of personal property from levy and sale under the exemption laws, he places his cause in the hands of a hostile defender. The signing of a warrant of attorney is equivalent to a warrior of old

entering a combat by discarding his shield and breaking his sword. For that reason
the law jealously insists on proof that this helplessness and impoverishment was voluntarily accepted and consciously assumed.

The case at bar falls short of producing evidence that Miss Latshaw was even aware
that a warrant of attorney was remotely contemplated. The physical characteristics of
the five-page document demonstrate that the reverse sides were entirely ignored. Although the sizeable blank spaces on the reverse pages could have been utilized for the
continuing enumeration of specifications, the parties adopted additional sheets, writing
only on the faces thereof, for that list. In the absence of any explanation as to why
five pages were used when three would have sufficed (employing the reverse sides), the
conclusion is inescapable that the parties purposely intended not to make the reverse
sides of the sheets any part of the contract.

The mere physical inclusion of the warrant of attorney in a mass of fine type verbiage
on each reverse sheet does not of itself make it part of the contract. In the case of
Summers v. Hibbard Co., the question arose as to whether certain printed phrases on
a letterhead became part of the contract entered into between the involved parties. The
Supreme Court of Illinois held:

> The mere fact that appellants wrote their acceptance on a blank form for letters at the top
> of which were printed the words, "All sales subject to strikes and accidents" no more made those
> words a part of the contract than they made the words there printed, "Summers Bros. & Co.,
> Manufacturer of Box-Annealed Common & Refined Sheet Iron," a part of the contract. The
> offer was absolute. The written acceptance which they themselves wrote, was just as absolute.
> The printed words were not in the body of the letter, or referred to therein. The fact that they
> were printed at the head of their letter heads would not have the effect of preventing appellants
> from entering into an unconditional contract for sale.

One of the most hateful acts of the ill-famed Roman tyrant Caligula was that of
having the laws inscribed upon pillars so high that the people could not read them.
Although the warrant of attorney in the numerous sheets of the contract at bar was
within the vision of Latshaw, it was so placed as to be completely beyond her contemplation of its purport. An inconspicuously printed legend on a contract form or letterhead which is obviously fortuitous, irrelevant or supefluous is no more part of the
agreement entered into than the advertisements on the walls of the room in which the
contract is signed.

Diminutive type grossly disproportionate to that used in the face body of a contract
cannot be ignored; it has its place in law, and, where space is at a premium, it allows
for instruction, guidance and protection which might otherwise be lost, but where it
is used as an ambush to conceal legalistic spears to strike down other rights agreed
upon, it will receive rigorous scrutinization by the courts for the ascertainment of the
true meaning, which may go beyond the literal import.

Termination of Offer

Duration of Offer. When an offeror makes an offer, he thereby confers
on the offeree the power to create a contract by the acceptance of the offer;

but for practical as well as legal reasons, such a power cannot exist for an indefinite period. The power to convert an offer into a contract may be terminated in the following ways: (1) by provisions in the offer, (2) by lapse of time, (3) by revocation, (4) by rejection of the offer, (5) by death or insanity of the offeror or offeree, (6) by destruction of the subject matter of the proposed contract, or (7) by the performance of the proposed contract becoming illegal.

Provisions in Offer.   When the offeror states in his offer that the offer must be accepted within a designated time, the offeree does not have the privilege of accepting after the expiration of the designated time. After the stated time has elapsed, it is impossible for the offeree to comply with all the terms of the original offer. Often, in limiting the time for acceptance, the offeror will use such expressions as "by return mail," "for immediate acceptance," and "prompt wire acceptance." "By return mail" does not of necessity require the acceptance to go out by the next mail, especially in large cities where mails are leaving hourly; but it does require an answer the same day the offer is received unless received too late to be answered that day, and in that event the acceptance must be dispatched on the opening for business the succeeding day. "Immediate acceptance" and "prompt wire acceptance" give the offeree a shorter time than "by return mail." The time would depend to some extent on the nature of the transaction; in any event, a few hours at the longest would be the limit of time allowed in which to accept.

An offeror may state that the offer must be accepted within a specified number of days without expressly stating the date from which the time shall start to run. For example, an offer may contain a provision that the offer must be accepted or rejected within ten days. This creates an ambiguity, and the courts have not been in accord in their holdings. One view is that the offer is not communicated until it is received and therefore the time does not start to run until the offer is received. The opposing view is that the offeror is imposing the time limit for his own benefit and that the time should begin to run from the date of the offer.

An attempt to accept an offer after it has terminated due to the lapse of the time stated therein is, in legal effect, an offer to contract on the terms of the original offer. If the original offeror is still willing to contract on the terms of his original offer and indicates his willingness to the original offeree, a contract will result.

Lapse of Time.   If no time for acceptance is stated in the offer, the offer terminates on the lapse of a reasonable time. This rule of law has been developed by the courts and is based on practical grounds. In effect, it writes into an offer which contains no provision for its termination a provision that the offer must be accepted within a reasonable time. The length of time which is reasonable must depend on the circumstances of the case. Each case will have to be decided as a separate proposition, and general rules will be of little help.

If the parties are trading on the floor of the stock or commodity exchanges, any offer made will have to be accepted immediately. Under such circumstances, trading is very rapid, and anyone trading on the exchange knows that offers made are not intended to be held open for more than a very short time. If the offer is made relative to the sale of real estate, a reasonable time for acceptance might well be counted in days. But if the offer is made relative to the sale of a commodity for which there is an established market, the court will hold that the offeree has waited an unreasonable time if he delays his acceptance until he can determine the price trends in the market.

If an offer is made when the parties are negotiating face to face, the time for acceptance will not extend beyond the period of the negotiations unless special words or circumstances clearly indicate that the offeror intends to hold his offer open after they part.

In cases of offers of reward for the capture of criminals, the offer may be open for acceptance for a very long time. In one case in which there was an offer to pay a reward for the capture of the person who had committed a particular crime, the court held that the offer would not lapse until the running of the statute of limitations on the crime. Offers made by trade associations to pay rewards to persons capturing criminals who have committed crimes against members of the association may continue for years.

Revocation. As a general rule the offeror may revoke his offer at any time before acceptance. This rule applies even though the offer states that it will remain open or the offeror promises to hold it open for a stated period of time. However, if the offeror contracts to hold the offer open for a stated period of time, that is, promises for a consideration to hold it open, the offer is irrevocable for the agreed period. This is known as an option. Also, in those states which enforce contracts under seal, a promise under seal to hold an offer open for a stated period is irrevocable for the stated period. An increasing number of courts have held that if an offer is made under such circumstances that the offeror knows or should know that the offeree will change his position in reliance on the offer and he does change his position in justifiable reliance on the offer, the offeror will be estopped from withdrawing his offer for a reasonable time. This exception is usually treated under the doctrine of promissory estoppel.

Communication of Revocation. If the offeror wishes to revoke his offer, he must communicate his revocation to the offeree. The rules which apply to the communication of an offer also apply to the communication of a revocation. In all but a few states, a letter, telegram, or message of revocation is not effective until it is received by the offeree. In a few states a revocation is effective when dispatched.

If the offeror has offered to sell designated property to the offeree and thereafter, but before the offer has terminated, the offeror sells the property to another and this is known to the offeree, the courts have held that the offeree cannot, by giving notice of acceptance, create a contract. The knowledge on the part of the offeree that the offeror has changed his position in such a manner that he can no longer perform the promise in his offer has been held as equivalent to notice of revocation.

Revocation of Offer to Public.   An offer to the general public is communicated by making a general announcement of the offer. This announcement may be made through the newspapers, magazines, posters, handbills, radio, or any other means suitable to the purpose of the offeror. If the offeror, after having made the offer, wishes to withdraw it, he must announce his withdrawal in substantially the same manner as that used in announcing the offer. The fact that one read or heard the offer but did not read or hear the withdrawal is of no moment. If the same publicity has been given to the revocation as was given to the offer, the offer is revoked as to the entire public, and an attempt to accept after the publication of the withdrawal is ineffective.

Revocation of Offer for Unilateral Contracts.   The general rule that an offer may be revoked at any time before acceptance applies to some types of offers for unilateral contracts, but there is some question whether the courts will apply the rule in all cases. If an offer for a reward is made and the offeror revokes the offer before the reward is claimed, the revocation will be effective.

If the act requested is of such a nature that an appreciable period of time is required for its performance, should the offeror be permitted to revoke the offer an instant before the act is performed and the offer accepted? If the nature of the act is such that the offeror receives benefits from the performance, a recovery for the benefits conferred will be allowed in a suit in quasi contract. If the act is such that, although the performance is detrimental to the offeree, it is not beneficial to the offeror, no recovery can be had in quasi contract. Justice would dictate in such a case that the offer should be held to be irrevocable until the offeree, having started performance, would have a reasonable time to complete the performance.

Cases involving the revocation of offers for unilateral contracts are not very common. Business contracts are generally bilateral; and the courts, if the facts permit, will interpret a contract to be bilateral rather than unilateral.

Rejection.   When the offeree rejects an offer, it is terminated, and any subsequent attempt to accept it is inoperative. The offeree may reject the offer by expressly stating that he will not accept it, or he may indicate his rejection by acts or words or by conduct which will justify the offeror in believing that the offeree does not intend to accept the offer.

If the offeree replies to the offeror by making a counteroffer or a conditional acceptance, the offer is terminated. A counteroffer is a statement by the offeree that he will enter into the transaction only on the terms stated by him in his counteroffer. A conditional acceptance is a statement by the offeree that he will accept the offer only if certain changes are made in the terms of the offer. Both, by implication, are rejections of the original offer.

Inquiry regarding Terms. An inquiry by the offeree regarding the terms of the offer is neither a counteroffer nor a conditional acceptance, and it will not terminate the offer. An unequivocal acceptance of an offer accompanied by statements that the terms of the offer are harsh or unreasonable or that better terms should be granted (a grumbling acceptance) is not a counteroffer or a conditional acceptance. Whether the offeree has made an inquiry as to the terms of an offer, a counteroffer, a conditional acceptance, or an unequivocal acceptance accompanied by statements regarding the terms of the offer is a matter of interpretation to be decided according to the facts of each case.

If an offeror makes an offer to be accepted within a certain time and then further states that he will consider counteroffers made within the time limit without such counteroffers terminating the offer, a counteroffer will not be a rejection if it comes within the terms of the offer.

Death or Insanity. There are some situations over which the parties have no control which will terminate an offer. It is a well-established rule that the death or insanity of either party will terminate the offer. This rule was developed in the English courts at the time that a "meeting of the minds" of the parties was the test of the existence of a contract. After death there is no mind; and at that time the courts held that an insane person had no mind. Consequently, if one of the parties died or became insane, it was impossible to have the essential "meeting of minds."

In the case of death the courts have held that the notice of the death is not necessary to terminate the offer. This rule is not in full accord with the general rules governing the termination of offers and sometimes results in injustice, but it is so well established that it will no doubt require legislative action to change it.

Destruction of Subject Matter. If the subject matter of a proposed contract or subject matter essential to the performance of a proposed contract is destroyed without the knowledge or fault of either party, after the making of an offer but before its acceptance, the offer is terminated. For example, suppose Ames has a stack of hay on his farm which he offers to sell to Ball and, without the knowledge or fault of either party, the stack of hay is destroyed by fire before Ball has accepted the offer. The courts will hold that when the stack of hay burned, the offer terminated.

Keep in mind that while destruction of essential subject matter may terminate offers, such destruction does not necessarily terminate liability on contracts. The effect of such events on contracts is discussed in subsequent chapters.

Intervening Illegality. If the performance of a proposed contract becomes illegal after the making of the offer but before the acceptance, the offer is terminated. For example, suppose Ames offers to kill and sell to Ball 60 wild rabbits each week during the month of December, and before Ball accepts the offer the state legislature enacts a statute making the sale of wild rabbits illegal. The courts will hold that when the state made the sale of wild rabbits illegal, the offer was terminated.

Summary

An offer confers on the offeree the power to create a contract by acceptance of the offer. The duration of an offer is limited. It may be terminated by the terms of the offer. If the offer contains no stated time for acceptance, it terminates on the lapse of a reasonable time. Unless the offer is under seal, or unless there is a valid contract to hold the offer open for a stated period, the offeror may revoke the offer at any time before acceptance. With few exceptions a revocation is not effective until communicated to the offeree. An offer is terminated if rejected by the offeree. A counteroffer or conditioned acceptance terminates an offer, but an inquiry does not. Death or insanity of either the offeror or the offeree, destruction of the subject matter of the proposed contract, or intervening illegality terminates an offer; but different rules apply if the same events take place after completion of a contract.

Board of Control of Eastern Mich. Univ. v. Burgess

206 N.W.2d 256 (Ct. App. Mich. 1973)

Action for specific performance of an alleged contract to convey real property brought by Eastern Michigan University (plaintiff) against Burgess (defendant). Burgess appealed from a ruling for the plaintiff. Reversed and remanded.

On February 15, 1966, Burgess signed a document which purported to grant to Eastern Michigan University (E.M.U.) a 60-day option to purchase her home. That document, which was drafted by Burgess' agent, acknowledged receipt . . . of "One and no/100 ($1.00) Dollar and other valuable consideration." E.M.U. concedes that neither the one dollar nor any other consideration was ever paid or even tendered to Burgess. On April 14, 1966, E.M.U. delivered to Burgess written notice of its intention to exercise the option. On the closing date Burgess rejected E.M.U.'s tender of the purchase price. Thereupon, E.M.U. commenced this action for specific performance.

BURNS, JUDGE. Options for the purchase of land, if based on valid consideration, are contracts which may be specifically enforced. Conversely, that which purports to be an option, but which is not based on valid consideration, is not a contract and will not be enforced. In the instant case defendant received no consideration for the purported option of February 15, 1966.

A written acknowledgment of receipt of consideration merely creates a rebuttable presumption that consideration has, in fact, passed. Neither the parol evidence rule nor the doctrine of estoppel bars the presentation of evidence to contradict any such acknowledgment.

It is our opinion that the document signed by Burgess on February 15, 1966, is not an enforceable option, and that Burgess is not barred from so asserting.

The trial court premised its holding to the contrary on *Lawrence v. McCalmont* (1844). That case is significantly distinguishable from the instant case. Mr. Justice Story held that "[t]he guarantor acknowledged the receipt of one dollar, and is now estopped to deny it." However, in reliance upon the guaranty substantial credit had been extended to the guarantor's sons. The guarantor had received everything she bargained for, save one dollar. In the instant case Burgess claims that she never received any of the consideration promised her.

That which purports to be an option for the purchase of land, but which is not based on valid consideration, is a simple offer to sell the same land. An option is a contract collateral to an offer to sell whereby the offer is made irrevocable for a specified period. Ordinarily, an offer is revocable at the will of the offeror. Accordingly, a failure of consideration affects only the collateral contract to keep the offer open, not the underlying offer.

A simple offer may be revoked for any reason or for no reason by the offeror at any time prior to its acceptance by the offeree. Thus, the question in this case becomes, "Did defendant effectively revoke her offer to sell before plaintiff accepted that offer?"

Defendant testified that within hours of signing the purported option she telephoned plaintiff's agent and informed him that she would not abide by the option unless the purchase price was increased. Defendant also testified that when plaintiff's agent delivered to her on April 14, 1966, plaintiff's notice of its intention to exercise the purported option, she told him that "the option was off."

Plaintiff's agent testified that defendant did not communicate to him any dissatisfaction until sometime in July 1966.

If defendant is telling the truth, she effectively revoked her offer several weeks before plaintiff accepted that offer, and no contract of sale was created. If plaintiff's agent is telling the truth, defendant's offer was still open when plaintiff accepted that offer, and an enforceable contract was created. The trial judge thought it unnecessary to resolve this particular dispute. In light of our holding the dispute must be resolved.

An appellate court cannot assess the credibility of witnesses. We have neither seen nor heard them testify. Accordingly, we remand this case to the trial court for additional findings of fact based on the record already before the court.

Sunshine v. Manos

496 S.W.2d 195 (Ct. App. Tex. 1973)

Howard Sunshine (plaintiff), a loan broker, sued Manos (defendant) for compensation due. Judgment for Manos and Sunshine appealed. Reversed and remanded.

On April 12 Manos and Sunshine signed the following agreement:

This is your authorization to proceed to secure for our benefit a mortgage loan secured by the above project and property. The terms and conditions of said loan can be: Loan Amount: $560,000.00 to $575,000.00—Rate: 9.67% (constant, or better).

From the above date you are authorized to work in our behalf exclusively for a period of not less than thirty (30) calendar days. If at the end of the thirty day period, you have in progress the processing of said loan, there will be an automatic extension of fifteen calendar days.

In consideration of your efforts in our behalf, and upon delivery of a commitment in accordance with the terms above stated, or terms as modified and agreed to by us, we agree to accept the commitment and to pay Sunshine Exploration Company, or assigns, a fee equivalent to one (1%) percent of the loan amount for services rendered.

If you are successful in placing this loan, we shall consider that lender your exclusive lender for a period of two (2) years from the date the loan commitment was issued, and we shall not seek to obtain a loan from him without going through you, or your assigns, as broker for us.

. . . On the day the agreement was executed Sunshine commenced performance by contacting the Oak Cliff Savings and Loan Association and requesting a loan on behalf of Manos.

On April 18, 1972, Sunshine called Manos and told Manos that he could procure a loan in the amount of $560,000.00 at 9% interest amortized over a period of twenty-eight years. . . . In the course of the conversation, Manos then requested that Sunshine cease efforts to procure the loan and on April 19, 1972, Manos wrote a letter to Sunshine advising him to cease work on the loan. Sunshine sued for compensation due.

MOORE, JUSTICE.   Where a contract is unilateral on its face, it does not come into existence as a binding contract until the broker has performed, or at least partly performed, his duties under the agreement. Prior to that time, it is nudum pactum and may be revoked by the offeror at any time.

The principal may of course revoke a unilateral offer but there is a distinction between his power to revoke and his right to revoke. He may at any time before full performance revoke the authority of an agent so the agent will lose his authority to bring the principal into legal relations with a third party. However, if he has no right to revoke it, he will be liable for damages suffered by the agent by reason of the wrongful revocation.

The specific question to be resolved in this case is whether the acts and conduct of Sunshine constituted part performance amounting to an acceptance of the offer and a sufficient consideration to make the offer irrevocable, or turn it into a bilateral contract. It has been held that in order to prove partial performance, it must be shown that there was an expenditure of time and money. On the other hand it has been held that a mere making of a local telephone call does not amount to a sufficient part performance so as to cause a unilateral offer to ripen into a binding contract. Practically all of the cases in other jurisdictions hold that the expenditure of time and effort is sufficient. While most of the authorities on the subject deal with real estate brokerage contracts, we think the same legal principles are applicable here. We hold that the expenditure of time and effort is sufficient consideration to make a unilateral contract binding and irrevocable. It is undisputed that Sunshine expended at least some time and effort in attempting to obtain the loan prior to the time Manos rescinded the offer. For this reason we believe that under the foregoing authorities the unilateral offer in this instance ripened into a binding contract.

* * * * *

Changes under the Uniform Commercial Code

The Offer. Under the provisions of the Code an offer or a contract for the sale of goods does not fail for indefiniteness of terms even though one or more terms are left open if the parties have intended to make a contract and there is a reasonably certain basis for giving an appropriate remedy. (2–204 [3].) As under the general rules of contract law, the contract may be made in any manner sufficient to show agreement, including conduct of both parties which recognizes the existence of such contract. (2–305 [1].)

The Comment of the American Law Institute and the National Conference of Commissioners on Uniform Law states:

Subsection (3) states the principle as to "open terms" underlying later sections of the Article. If the parties intend to enter into a binding agreement, this subsection recognizes that agreement as valid in law, despite missing terms, if there is any reasonably certain basis for granting a remedy. The test is not certainty as to what the parties were to do nor as to the exact amount of damages due the plaintiff. Nor is the fact that one or more terms are left to be agreed upon enough of itself to defeat an otherwise adequate agreement. Rather, commercial standards on the point of "indefiniteness" are intended to be applied, this Act making provision elsewhere for missing terms needed for performance, open price, remedies and the like.

The more terms the parties leave open, the less likely it is that they have intended to conclude a binding agreement, but their actions may be frequently conclusive on the matter despite the omissions.

As was previously stated, a promise to hold an offer open which is not supported by consideration is unenforceable under the common law. Merchants in their dealings commonly rely on such a promise. In recognition of this, it is provided in the Code that an offer by a merchant to buy or sell goods in a signed writing which by its terms gives assurance that it will be held open is not revocable for lack of consideration during the time stated, or if no time is stated, for a reasonable time, but in no event may such period of irrevocability exceed three months. (2–205.) To assure that a promise to hold an offer open is consciously and intentionally made, the Code further provides that if the promise is included in a form supplied by the offeree it must be separately signed by the offeror.

E. A. Coronis Assocs. v. M. Gordon Constr. Co.

216 A.2d 246 (Sup. Ct. N.J. 1966)

This was an action for breach of contract brought by E. A. Coronis Associates (plaintiff) against M. Gordon Construction Company (defendant). A summary judgment was entered in favor of E. A. Coronis Associates (Coronis) and M. Gordon Construction Company (Gordon) appealed. Reversed.

. . . Coronis brought suit on three contracts not here pertinent. Gordon admitted liability thereon, but counterclaimed for breach of a contract to supply and erect structural steel on one of its projects. Gordon is a general contractor. In anticipation of making a bid to construct two buildings for Port Authority . . ., Gordon sought bids from subcontractors. Coronis . . . sent the following letter to Gordon:

April 22, 1963

Dear Mr. Ben Zvi:

We regret very much that this estimate was so delayed. Be assured that the time consumed was due to routing of the plans through our regular sources of fabrication.

We are pleased to offer:

All structural steel including steel girts and purlins
Both Buildings delivered and erected $155,413.50
All structural steel equipped with slips for wood girts & purlins
Both Buildings delivered and erected 98,937.50
NOTE:

This price is predicated on an erected price of .1175 per Lb. of steel and we would expect to adjust the price on this basis to conform to actual tonnage of steel used in the project.

Thank you very much for this opportunity to quote.

Very truly yours,

E. A. CORONIS ASSOCIATES

/s/ Arthur C. Pease

Gordon contends that at some date prior to April 22 the parties reached an oral agreement and that the above letter was sent in confirmation.

Bids were opened by the Port Authority on April 19, 1963, and Gordon's bid was the lowest. He alleges that Coronis was informed the same day. The Port Authority contract was officially awarded to Gordon on May 27, 1963, and executed about two weeks later. During this period Gordon never accepted the alleged offer of Coronis. Meanwhile, on June 1, 1963, Coronis sent a telegram, in pertinent part reading:

Due to conditions beyond our control, we must withdraw our proposal of April 22nd 1963 for structural steel Dor Buildings 131 and 132 at the Elizabeth-Port Piers at the earliest possible we will resubmit our proposal.

Two days later, on June 3, 1963, Gordon replied by telegram as follows:

Ref your tel. 6–3 and for the record be advised that we are holding you to your bid of April 22, 1963 for the structural steel of cargo bldgs 131 and 132.

Coronis never performed. Gordon employed the Elizabeth Iron Works to perform the work and claims as damages the difference between Coronis' proposal of $155,413.50 and Elizabeth Iron Works' charge of $208,000.

Collester, J. A. D.   Gordon contends that the April 22 letter was an offer and that Coronis had no right to withdraw it. Two grounds are advanced in support. First, Gordon contends that the Uniform Commercial Code firm offer section precludes withdrawal and, second, it contends that withdrawal is prevented by the doctrine of promissory estoppel.

Prior to the enactment of the Uniform Commercial Code an offer not supported by consideration could be revoked at any time prior to acceptance. The drafters of the Code recognized that the common law rule was contrary to modern business practice and possessed the capability to produce unjust results. The response was section 2–205 which reverses the common law rule and states:

> An offer by a merchant to buy or sell goods in a *signed writing which by its terms gives assurance that it will be held open* is not revocable, for lack of consideration, during the time stated or if no time is stated for a reasonable time. . . . (Emphasis added.)

Coronis' letter contains no terms giving assurance it will be held open. We recognize that just as an offeree runs a risk in acting on an offer before accepting it, the offeror runs a risk if his offer is considered irrevocable. In their comments to section 2–205 of the Code the drafters anticipated these risks and stated:

> However, despite settled courses of dealing or usages of the trade whereby firm offers are made by oral communication and relied upon without more evidence, such offers remain revocable under this Article since authentication by a writing is the essence of this section. Uniform Commercial Code, comment, par. 2.

We think it clear that Coronis' writing does not come within the provision of section 2–205 of a "signed writing which by its terms gives assurance that it will be held open."

Having so concluded, we need not consider the question of whether the Coronis letter was an offer or whether the letter dealt with "goods." We note in this connection that Coronis quoted the price for structural steel delivered and erected.

Gordon also argues that even if Coronis' writing of April 22 is not a firm offer within the meaning of section 2–205, justice requires that we apply the doctrine of promissory estoppel to preclude its revocation. *Restatement, Contracts,* § 90 provides:

> A promise which the promisor should reasonably expect to induce action of forbearance of a definite and substantial character on the part of the promisee and which does induce such action or forbearance is binding if injustice can be avoided only by enforcement of the promise.

Gordon argues that it relied on Coronis' bid in making its own bid and that injustice would result if Coronis could now revoke. Thus, Gordon contends that Coronis' bid is made irrevocable by application of the doctrine of promissory estoppel.

The authorities are not uniform in applying the doctrine of promissory estoppel to situations comparable to that before us. We believe the better line of authority applies the doctrine.

The *Drennan* case involved an oral bid by a subcontractor for paving work at a school project on which plaintiff general contractor was about to bid. Defendant's paving bid was the lowest, and the general contractor computed his own bid accordingly. Plaintiff was the successful bidder but the following day was informed by defendant it would not do the work at its bid price. The California Supreme Court, per Justice

Traynor, applied the doctrine of promissory estoppel to prevent defendant's revocation of its bid, stating:

> When plaintiff used defendant's offer in computing his own bid, he bound himself to perform in reliance on defendant's terms. Though defendant did not bargain for this use of its bid neither did the defendant make it idly, indifferent to whether it would be used or not. On the contrary, it is reasonable to suppose that defendant submitted its bid to obtain the subcontract. It was bound to realize the substantial possibility that its bid would be the lowest, and that it would be included by plaintiff in his bid. It was to its own interest that the contractor be awarded the general contract; the lower the subcontract bid, the lower the general contractor's bid was likely to be and the greater its chance of acceptance and hence the greater defendant's chance of getting the paving subcontract. Defendant had reason not only to expect plaintiff to rely on his bid but to want him to. Clearly defendant had a stake in plaintiff's reliance on its bid. Given this interest and the fact that plaintiff is bound by his own bid, it is only fair that plaintiff should have at least an opportunity to accept defendant's bid after the general contract has been awarded to him.

To successfully establish a cause of action based on promissory estoppel Gordon must prove that (1) it received a clear and definite offer from Coronis; (2) Coronis could expect reliance of a substantial nature; (3) actual reasonable reliance on Gordon's part, and (4) detriment. *Restatement, Contracts,* § 90.

The Law Division did not think promissory estoppel would apply in the situation *sub judice.* Therefore we reverse.

Problem Cases

1. On Thursday, Surplus Store published the following advertisement in the newspaper: "Saturday 9 A.M. Sharp—3 Brand New Fur Coats—Worth to $100—First Come First Served—$1 Each." The following Thursday, Surplus Store again published an advertisement in the same paper as follows: "Saturday 9 A.M.—2 Brand New Pastel Mink 3-Skin Scarfs—Selling for $89.50—Out they go—Saturday Each . . . $1—1 Black Lapin Stole—Beautiful, worth $139.50 . . . $1—First Come First Served." On each Saturday following publication Lefkowitz was the first one to present himself at Surplus Store and each time demanded the coat and stole so advertised, offering the $1. On both occasions, Surplus refused to sell, stating on the first occasion that by a "house rule" the offer was intended for women only, and on the second that Lefkowitz knew Surplus's house rules. Lefkowitz sued Surplus for breach of contract and won a judgment. Can Surplus win a reversal on appeal?

2. Giarraputo gave the Willmotts a six-month option to buy property. The option agreement described the property, the price, and the amount of the purchase-money mortgage, but provided with respect to that mortgage that "the payment of interest and amortization of principal shall be mutually agreed upon at the time of entering into a more formal contract." When the Willmotts elected to exercise the option, Giarraputo's lawyer submitted a contract to them, which they declined to sign because it did not contain a prepayment term. Their lawyer then modified the contract by inserting a prepayment term, and they signed and returned it to Giarraputo, who refused to sign the modified contract. The Willmotts then instituted an action for specific performance. They appeal from a dismissal of their complaint. Should the case be reversed?

3. Deere advertised a repossessed tractor for sale at auction, stating that the tractor would be sold to the highest bidder at the sale. At the sale Drew bid $1500 but the auctioneer did not accept the bid; instead he announced that Deere had itself bid $1600 and accordingly struck down the tractor to Deere. Drew sued Deere for breach of contract claiming that Deere was disqualified to bid because it had not announced intention to bid in advance and, in effect, resting his case on the theory that the auction was "without reserve," where the owner may not withdraw the property after commencement of the bidding. Should Drew succeed?

4. Molitch sued to recover $125,000 in damages that she claims she sustained when she fell, or was dropped, down the exit ramp of one of Irish International Airlines' planes at John F. Kennedy International Airport in New York. The plane was owned and operated by Irish International Airlines, and Molitch paid for, and was issued, an individual passenger ticket. The accident on which Molitch's claim is based occurred on May 8, 1966. Suit was not commenced until January 30, 1969, more than two years after the accident. The lower court, while holding that the Warsaw Convention was applicable to this action, held that the two-year statute of limitations in Article 29 of that convention was not a bar because Molitch's passenger ticket did not contain adequate notice of the applicability of the provision. Is it necessary that the ticket inform the passenger of the statute of limitations for it to be operative?

5. Westside and Humble entered into a written 60-day option agreement concerning some real estate. Shortly thereafter Humble wrote Westside that they were exercising the option but proposed an amendment concerning the extension of utilities to the property. Twelve days later, and still within the 60-day period, Humble wrote another letter to Westside saying again that they intended to exercise their option but that the exercise was unqualified and Westside could disregard the proposed amendment. Westside refused to convey, alleging that Humble terminated the offer. Humble sued for specific performance. Who should prevail?

6. Meyers was employed by Josselyn, a public accountant, at a salary of $150 per week plus a bonus. The bonus was to be 25 percent of a "bonus pool" to be set up by Josselyn. The bonus pool was to be created from the profits of the office after an allowance to Josselyn for his services and capital contribution. There was no minimum figure set for the bonus pool and no maximum figure placed on the amount Josselyn could allow himself for services and capital investment. This left these two figures in the sole discretion of Josselyn.

   Josselyn paid Meyers $1,170 as bonus. Meyers brought suit to recover additional bonus on the ground that $12,974.20 in fees owed to Josselyn by a client, La Veck, was not included when Josselyn computed the profits of the office. Is Meyers entitled to a judgment for additional bonus payment?

7. Ramsey offered to sell certain real estate to Herndon and gave him until January 15, 1965, to accept the offer. Herndon was attempting to arrange a loan so that he could purchase the property, and this was known to Ramsey. Herndon had not completed the arrangements for his loan by January 15, 1965, and Ramsey sold the property to Armstrong. Herndon completed the arrangements for his loan on January 17, 1965, and tendered performance to Ramsey who informed Herndon of the sale to Armstrong. Herndon brought suit against Ramsey for damages for breach of contract. Is Herndon entitled to a judgment?

8. Erickson offered to sell a building to Podnay. The offer was "a continuing option to purchase the building for the consideration of $20,000 in cash." Podnay, intending to accept the offer, wrote Erickson: "Notice is hereby given that I accept your offer to purchase your property for $20,000 cash. Will you please furnish me with abstract brought down to date

so that I may have the title examined before completing the transaction and paying the money?" Was this an unconditional acceptance of the offer?

9. Beach offered to contribute $2,000 to a church building fund on condition that the church would first raise $8,000. Before the church had raised $8,000, Beach was adjudged insane and committed to an asylum for the insane. Later the church raised $8,000, but the conservator of Beach's estate refused to pay the promised $2,000. The church sued to recover a judgment for $2,000. Is the church entitled to a judgment?

10. On September 21, 1942, Gentry executed to New Headley Tobacco Warehouse Company (Warehouse Co.) a lease of property in Lexington for a term of 21 years 6 months. The lease contained no provision for renewal or extension. On March 24, 1952, Gentry addressed the following letter to Warehouse Co.:

> In the event you build within the next five years (from March 1st, 1952) an addition to your warehouse at cost of not less than $25,000.00 on the property you have under lease from me, I agree,
>
> First, to extend your present lease so you will have a total term of twenty-two years (22 years) from March 1st of the year the addition is built.
>
> Second, the extended term of lease shall carry a net rental to me of Sixteen Hundred ($1,600.00) per annum instead of the present net rental of Twelve Hundred Dollars per annum.
>
> Third, in all other respects the terms and conditions of the extended lease shall be the same as the present lease.

Warehouse Co. had not made any response or started construction of the building before Gentry died on September 29, 1955. On April 16, 1956, Warehouse Co. communicated their acceptance of Gentry's offer to the executor of Gentry's estate. The executor refused to extend the lease, and Warehouse Co. brought an action to force the executor to extend the lease. Does Warehouse have a lease?

11. Apex Parts Company sent its salesman Nelson to solicit parts orders from Green Distributing Company. Green placed an order for $5000 and signed the order form provided by Nelson. The order form contained many terms but one term stated, "All orders are subject to approval home office and buyer agrees this order will remain firm for 30 days from date placed." Green signed the form at the bottom. Ten days later Green wrote Apex asking that the order be cancelled. Apex immediately notified Green that the parts were being shipped. Green refused to accept delivery and Apex sued for breach of contract contending Green had made a firm offer. Is Apex right?

chapter 7

Acceptance

The Acceptance

The significant changes in the law of acceptance as applied to sale of good contracts subject to the Code will be discussed at the end of this chapter.

Requirements for Acceptance. The basis of a contract is the mutual consent of the parties to the contract. This consent is manifested by one party—the offeror—making an offer to another party—the offeree—and by the offeree indicating, either expressly or by implication, his or her willingness to be bound on the terms stated in the offer. The offeree has no legal right to insist that the proposition made to him or her be reasonable, practical, or sensible. The proposition is that of the offeror, and if the offeree wishes to accept it, he must agree to all of its terms. Any attempt on the part of the offeree, in his acceptance, to alter the terms of the offeror's proposition will terminate the offer.

The common law rule is that the offeree's acceptance must correspond in all respects with the offer. This does not mean that the offeree must, in accepting an offer, repeat the words of the offer; but it does mean that he must, by his words or acts, clearly manifest his intent to comply in all respects with that which the offeror has stipulated as the return he demands for his promise or act.

Offer in Unilateral Contract. An offer in a unilateral contract is, as a general rule, a promise for an act. To accept such an offer, the offeree must perform the act as requested. Any material variance between the requested act and the tendered performance will result in no acceptance. If the nature of the requested act is such that it will take a substantial period of time for its completion, there will have been no acceptance of the offer until the act has been completed. Under some circumstances, if the offeree has started performance of the requested act, the offer may be irrevocable until he or she has had

125

a reasonable opportunity to complete the performance. If the offeree has started performance and the offeror revokes his offer before performance is completed, the offeree can recover in a suit in quasi contract for benefits conferred.

Offer in Bilateral Contract.   An offer for a bilateral contract states or implies the promise which the offeror requests the offeree to make if he wishes to accept the offer. Except for the provisions of the Code stated below relative to offers for contracts for the sale of goods, if the offeree wishes to accept the offer he must make the promise requested, as requested. No other or different promise than that stated in the offer will suffice as an acceptance. If the offeree, in attempting to accept the offer, makes a promise which adds to, subtracts from, or alters the terms of the promise requested, it is a counteroffer or conditional acceptance, and no contract results.

When a Writing Is Anticipated.   Frequently, the parties negotiating a contract will have a written draft of the agreement drawn and signed. Whether a binding contract is entered into by the parties before they sign the written draft or at the time they sign, depends entirely on the intentions of the parties. Their intention will be determined by the application of the objective standard of what a reasonable person familiar with the facts and circumstances would be justified in believing the parties intended.

Usually, where the parties have completed their negotiations and have reached an agreement on all the material provisions of their transaction, the courts have held that a binding contract results. A decision to have a written draft of the agreement drawn and signed by the parties will not affect the time at which the binding contract came into existence. If the parties do not agree on the terms of the written draft, their disagreement will not discharge them from their liability on the contract into which they have already entered. If they agree on the terms of the written draft and sign it, the writing will be accepted in court as the best evidence of the terms of their contract.

Where the parties are negotiating a complicated agreement and make rough drafts of the agreement for the purpose of correcting mistakes and making alterations, the courts usually will hold that a binding contract does not result until the final written draft is approved by the parties. Such final approval is usually indicated by the signing of the written draft.

If the circumstances are such that it is clear that the parties do not intend to be bound until a written contract is signed, yet they begin to perform after the writing is drafted but before it is signed by one or both of the parties, the courts will hold that they are bound by the terms of the writing.

Silence as Acceptance.   The legal principle that one cannot impose a contractual obligation on another without the consent of that person, either expressed or implied, is well established. The application of this legal principle prevents the offeror from so wording his offer that the offeree will be forced to act or be bound by a contract. Mere silence on the part of the offeree, as a general rule, is not acceptance.

The relation of the parties, the course of dealing, usage of trade, a prior agreement, or other special circumstances may impose on the offeree a duty to reject an offer or be bound by it. If this is true, the offeree's silence will amount to an acceptance, and a contract will result.

Intention to Accept. In order to have a valid acceptance of an offer, the offeree must have performed the act or made the promise requested in the offer with the intention of accepting the offer. The same standards are applied in determining the intentions of the offeree as are applied in determining the intentions of the offeror. The objective test of what a reasonably prudent person would be justified in believing under the circumstances is the test applied.

In the case of a unilateral contract, where an act is required for an acceptance, the offeree must have performed the act with the intention of accepting the offer, or the offeror will not be bound.

Some courts have held that the offer of a reward for the apprehension of a criminal is an offer to pay a bounty, not an offer to contract. These courts allow a recovery if the requested act is performed, and knowledge of the offer of a reward is immaterial. And a few courts have refused to apply the intent test in all reward cases, holding that if the person offering the reward received the benefits he desired, public policy would demand that he pay the promised reward.

In the case of a bilateral contract an offer is accepted when the offeree makes the promise requested in the offer. If the offeree's reply is not a definite statement that he or she accepts the offer, the court must determine whether or not his or her reply indicates an intention to accept.

Summary

An offeree, in order to accept an offer, must perform the requested act as requested or make the requested promise with the intent to accept the offer. In the case of a unilateral contract the offeree must perform the requested act, and in the case of a bilateral contract the offeree must make the requested promise. If a written draft of the agreement is anticipated, whether the parties are bound before the signing of the written draft or at the time of the signing will depend on the intention of the parties. As a general rule, silence on the part of the offeree is not an acceptance. However, by the agreement of the parties, by usage of trade, or by course of dealing, the offeree may owe a duty to reject an offer, in which case his failure to give notice of rejection will amount to an acceptance. In order to have an acceptance of an offer, the offeree must have performed the requested act or made the requested promise with the intention of accepting the offer. In determining intention, one must apply the objective test of what a reasonably prudent person would be justified in believing the offeree intended.

Swingle v. Myerson

509 P.2d 738 (Ct. App. Ariz. 1973)

Appeal by Swingle (defendant) from a judgment of $6,000 for a "finder's fee" in favor of Myerson (plaintiff). Affirmed.

In May, 1969, Swingle was a vice-president of Tucson Federal Savings & Loan Association. Myerson was a Tucson businessman related by marriage to the Capin family of Nogales, Arizona, who then controlled the Security Savings and Loan Association. While Swingle and Myerson were at lunch with several other persons, Myerson remarked to Swingle that it was too bad that Swingle's company was not interested in a savings and loan company that he knew was available for acquisition. Swingle then told Myerson that although his company was not interested, he was. After lunch Swingle accompanied Myerson to the latter's office at which time Swingle inquired about the savings and loan company and gave Myerson two conditions which had to be met before he would consider purchasing its stock. The conditions were that a Tucson branch of the savings company be established and that he acquire at least 51% of the stock. He also told Myerson that he must remain anonymous because he was still employed by Tucson Federal Savings & Loan Association.

Myerson then called Capin and told him that Myerson had a good savings and loan man who was interested in buying the stock of Security Savings and Loan. At this time Myerson also advised Swingle that he expected to be compensated for bringing these people together if a transaction was effected. The stock of Security Savings and Loan was acquired by Swingle with the aid of Myerson but Swingle refused to pay Myerson.

HOWARD, JUDGE.   Swingle contends that since the court found no "express contract" Myerson cannot recover. We do not agree. It is clear that the judgment was based on an *implied contract.* There is no difference in the legal effect between an express contract and an implied contract. . . . But there are different modes of expressing assent.

If the agreement is shown by the direct words of the parties, spoken or written, the contract is said to be an express one. But if such agreement can only be shown by the acts and conduct of the parties, *interpreted* in the light of the subject matter and the circumstances, then the contract is an implied one. These terms, however, do not denote different kinds of contracts, but merely have reference to the evidence by which the agreement between the parties is shown.

There is a well-defined rule of law, applicable to contracts in general, that where the relations between the parties have been such as to justify the offeror in expecting a reply, or where the offeree has come under some duty to communicate either a rejection or acceptance, his failure to communicate his rejection may result in a legal assent to the terms of the offer.

Restatement, Contracts § 72, states:

(1) Where an offeree fails to reply to an offer, his silence and inaction operate as an acceptance in the following cases and in no others:

(a) Where the offeree with reasonable opportunity to reject offered services takes the benefit of them under circumstances which would indicate to a reasonable man that they were offered with the expectation of compensation.

* * * * *

When Myerson made the initial call to Capin and communicated to Swingle his terms and expectation of compensation, Swingle was under a duty at that time to reject Myerson's services. He did not do so. Although Myerson only agreed to find a business opportunity for Swingle, he did more. He accompanied Swingle to the office of the Secretary-Treasurer of the company, discussed the financial aspects of the proposed transaction, and arranged a meeting in his office between Capin and Swingle which resulted in Swingle's offer to buy the controlling shares. A later progress report meeting was held in Myerson's office with the Secretary-Treasurer and Swingle. Swingle sat back idly, accepting Myerson's efforts, and never indicated to Myerson rejection of his proposal. The evidence supports the trial court's conclusion that *quantum meruit** is a proper measure of the value of the services agreed upon.

Corbin-Dykes Electric Co. v. Burr

500 P.2d 632 (Ct. App. Ariz. 1972)

This is an action by Corbin-Dykes Electric Company (plaintiff) against Burr (defendant) for failure to give them a subcontract. Judgment for Burr and Corbin-Dykes appealed. Affirmed.

General Motors Corporation requested bids from general contractors to construct the central air-conditioning plant at its Mesa plant. Burr, a general contractor, was interested in obtaining the contract and as a result received bids for the electrical subcontract. One of the bids received by Burr was from Corbin-Dykes.

Burr incorporated Corbin-Dykes' subcontract bid, which was the low bid, into his general contract bid and submitted it to General Motors Corporation. All bids were rejected by General Motors because they exceeded the cost estimate; and the project was rebid. The second bid submitted by Burr also included the Corbin-Dykes subcontract bid; however, prior to submitting the second bid, Burr had received another bid from Sands. This bid matched the Corbin-Dykes bid but also provided that, in the event Sands could work the proposed project in conjunction with its current project at the [plant], they would reduce their subcontract bid by $4,000. When the second round of bids was opened, Burr was awarded the general contract, and since Sands' other project at the plant was not yet completed, Burr accepted Sands' bid for the electric subcontract as the low bid.

Corbin-Dykes objected to this selection of Sands as the subcontractor and sued Burr for breach of their alleged subcontract.

---

* Based on the value of services rendered.

EUBANK, JUDGE.   In Arizona the law is clear that Corbin-Dykes' bid to Burr was nothing more than an offer to perform the subcontract under specified terms, and that it did not ripen into a contract until it was voluntarily accepted by Burr. The law and its related problems are well stated in the 53 *Virginia L. Rev.* 1720 (1967).

From the time a general contractor (general) receives bids from subcontractors (subs) until he formally accepts one of those bids, the parties are not adequately protected by the common law. Although they are forced by the commercial context to rely upon each other during this period, at common law their relationship cannot be contractual until the general responds with the requisite promise of acceptance. To some extent the promissory estoppel doctrine has alleviated the general's problems by binding the sub to perform according to the terms of his bid. But this protection is one-sided, and despite the view of some courts that promissory estoppel is a panacea, it appears that in confining the scope of protection to the general, the doctrine in fact raises serious problems.

Corbin-Dykes relies on no evidence of the acceptance of their offer by Burr except . . . custom and usage. As we have seen, a "voluntary acceptance" is required to bind Burr. It is also clear from the cited case law that such custom and usage evidence cannot be used to initially establish acceptance or the manifestation of mutual assent.

In our opinion the record shows no evidence of a voluntary acceptance of the offer involved, since the inclusion of Corbin-Dykes' subcontract bid as a part of the general contract bid did not constitute such an acceptance, and the offer never was accepted by Burr in any other manner.

Crouch v. Marrs

430 P.2d 204 (Sup. Ct. Kan. 1967)

This was a suit by Phillip Crouch (plaintiff) against Roy Marrs, Purex Corporation and others (defendants) to establish Crouch's rights in regard to a certain building. From a judgment for the defendants; Crouch appealed. Reversed.

On February 26, 1964, Crouch wrote to the Purex Corporation asking for their lowest price if they were interested in selling an old plant building and its contents located in Meade, Kansas. The letter read in part:

I would be interested in buying the old building that housed the plant and what other items that are still left. The items that are still left are: two crushers, furnace and the elevator is about all that is left.

On March 4, 1964, Crouch received a letter of reply from Purex Corporation signed by Frank Knox which stated:

We will sell this building and the equipment in and about that building for a total of $500.

On March 19, 1964, Crouch wrote to Frank Knox, Purex Corporation, stating that the building was in "pretty bad condition" and asking, "Would you consider taking $300 for what is left?" This letter was not answered.

Later, on April 16, 1964, Crouch addressed another letter to Frank Knox, Purex Corporation, which read:

I guess we will buy the building for the amount you quoted, $500.

I am sending you a personal check for this amount.

It will be 2 or 3 weeks before we can get started; and I presume that we will be allowed all the time that we need to remove the material.

On April 17, 1964, the Purex Corporation, through Frank Knox, wrote a letter to Martin Asche which stated:

In anwer to your inquiry about our property approximately six miles north of Meade, Kansas.

We will sell for $500.00 the mine building and whatever machinery and equipment which remains in or about that building. A condition of sale will require that the property purchased be removed from the premises within forty-five days.

If this price is acceptable we will be pleased to receive a cashier's check to cover.

On April 23, Knox, on behalf of Purex Corporation, endorsed and cashed the check which Crouch had mailed on April 16.

On April 24, 1964, Asche wrote a letter accepting the offer of April 17, which read:

We are enclosing a cashier's check for $500 and the bill of sale of mine buildings with the agreement of option to purchase property.

If the corporation has any other property and machinery in this area for sale, we would be pleased to deal with the corporation. It was our pleasure to deal with the Purex Corporation.

On April 27, 1964, Frank Knox sent Crouch the following telegram:

Your counter offer received April 23 is unacceptable. Your check mistakenly deposited by Purex will be recovered and returned to you or Purex check will be issued to you if your check cannot be located.

There followed a letter dated May 16, 1964, which read:

This is a follow-up to our telegram to you of April 27, advising you that your check which we received on April 23 was not acceptable, but that it had been deposited by mistake. Since we were unable to recover your check, we herewith enclose our check for $500 to reimburse you.

We wish to explain, that the reason we could not accept your counter-offer of $500 for the mine building and machinery at Meade, Kansas was because we had received and accepted an offer from another party prior to receipt of yours on April 23.

In the meantime Martin Asche had entered into a contract to sell the building to Roy Marrs who owned the land surrounding the building site for $500 and had entered into a contract to sell the equipment to the C. & D. Used Truck Parts for $800.

Crouch started to salvage the building but Roy Marrs put a lock on the gate and would not allow Crouch to enter.

Crouch then brought an action to enjoin Marrs from interfering with his salvage operations.

HATCHER, COMMISSIONER.   Marrs contends that Crouch's check was cashed through inadvertence or an error in office procedure and under such circumstances the cashing of the check did not constitute an acceptance of Crouch's offer. The difficulty with this contention is that there was no evidence of any character as to why the check was cashed. Neither would the error void the contract unless mutual mistake was pleaded.

Crouch suggests that the statement in the letter of May 6, 1964, to the effect "we have received and accepted an offer from another party prior to receipt of yours" was a "falsehood" as Asche's acceptance was dated one day after Crouch's check was in the Los Angeles Clearing House. We need not speculate as to the binding effect of Purex Corporation's offer to Asche. The question is whether the endorsing and depositing of Crouch's check constituted an acceptance of his offer to buy. We think it did.

The endorsing and depositing of a check constitutes an acceptance of the offer to buy which accompanies it because the act itself indicates acceptance. An offer may be accepted by performing a specified act as well as by an affirmative answer. Also, where the offeree exercised dominion over the thing offered him—in this instance the check —such exercise constitutes an acceptance of the offer.

Johnson v. Star Iron and Steel Co.

511 P.2d 1370 (Ct. App. Wash. 1973)

Johnson (plaintiff) sued Star Iron and Steel Company (defendant) for compensation under an alleged contract whereby Johnson was to help Star Iron procure some loan funds. Judgment for Star Iron and Johnson appealed. Affirmed.

In a letter dated September 29, 1969, Johnson offered to arrange loan funds for Star Iron in the amount of $500,000. Paragraph 3 stipulated that the funds were to be in the form of "bank book deposits in a local bank of our choice." In a letter dated October 3, Star Iron accepted on condition that "in a local bank of our choice" be changed to read "Bank of Tacoma." On October 8, Star Iron notified Johnson that Star Iron was withdrawing its conditional acceptance. By a letter dated October 8 and mailed October 9, Johnson notified Star Iron that he agreed to the paragraph 3 change included in Star Iron's letter of October 3. Johnson sued when Star Iron refused to proceed with the transaction.

PEARSON, CHIEF JUDGE.   It is axiomatic that an expression of assent that changes the terms of an offer in any material respect may operate as a counter-offer, but is not an acceptance. The issue then raised is whether the exceptions noted above were *material* modifications of the offer.

In *Northwest Properties Agency, Inc. v. McGhee,* this court held that if a "condition *added* by the intended acceptance can be implied in the original offer then it does not constitute a material variance so as to make the acceptance ineffective." (Italics ours.) Otherwise, the condition is a material variance. In our view, this principle applies equally to variances in the acceptance that would change terms of the offer. Using this test, the change in paragraph 3 was clearly material.

The modification of paragraph 3 meant that Johnson's performance would be entirely dependent on the willingness of the Bank of Tacoma to extend credit on the basis of a plan which had been worked out in the Bank's absence. The original offer gave Johnson the option of completing his performance through any local bank. The limitation on the scope of performance effected by the alteration of paragraph 3 in the purported acceptance does not even remotely resemble the scope of performance afforded by the terms of the original offer. Consequently, the paragraph 3 revision must be characterized as a material variance.

Communication of Acceptance

Requirements for Communication. The acceptance of a unilateral contract, as a general rule, requires the doing of an act, although under some circumstances it may require the making of a promise. The acceptance of a bilateral contract requires the making of the requested promise. The law does not recognize as valid an uncommunicated promise; consequently, if the acceptance of an offer requires the making of a promise, the acceptance is not effective until the promise is communicated to the offeror. If the offeror, in his offer, stipulates the time, place, or method of communicating the acceptance, the offeree must comply fully with these terms if he wishes to accept. An attempt to accept at a time or place, or in a manner other than that stipulated, would be, in legal effect, a counteroffer.

If a method or place of communication is merely suggested and not stipulated, acceptance may be communicated by a different method or at a different place, provided it is delivered to the offeror before the offer terminates.

If the offer is silent as to the time, place, or method of communicating the acceptance, the offeree may accept within a reasonable time, at any place, and by any recognized method of communication, provided the acceptance is received by the offeror before the offer terminates.

When Acceptance Is Communicated. Under some circumstances, it becomes important to determine the place and exact time at which a contract comes into existence. A contract comes into existence at the time the offer is accepted and at the place in which the last act is performed which creates the contract. This raises the question of when an acceptance is communicated.

If the parties are dealing face to face, the contract comes into existence at the time the words or acts of acceptance are spoken or performed and at the location of the two parties at this time. If the parties are negotiating over the telephone, the contract comes into existence at the time the offeree speaks the words of acceptance into the telephone and at the location of the offeree at this time.[1]

If the parties are using some agency of communication such as the mails or telegraph, there will be a time lag between the dispatching and the receipt of the acceptance. There will also be a risk that the message of acceptance will never reach its destination—the offeror. Since the offeror is in a position to

---

[1] *Wilson v. Scannavino,* 159 Cal. App.2d 369, 324 P.2d 350 (1958).

include any provisions in his offer he wishes, he may so word the offer that the acceptance is not operative until it is actually received.

Authorized Means of Communication.   An acceptance is effective and a contract arises when the acceptance is dispatched, provided the offeree uses the means of communication authorized by the offeror. If the offer states no agency of communication, the means of communication used by the offeror to communicate the offer is the authorized means of communication. That is, if the offer is sent by mail, the offeree is authorized to use the mail to communicate his or her acceptance, and an acceptance sent by mail is effective, and a contract arises at the time the letter of acceptance is dropped into an official depository for mail. Likewise, if the offeror in his offer expressly authorizes the offeree to send his acceptance by a designated means of communication, an acceptance sent by the designated means of communication is effective, and a contract arises at the time the acceptance is dispatched.

The courts have distinguished between a stipulated means of communication and an authorized means of communication. Whether a means of communication mentioned in an offer is stipulated or authorized will depend on the language of the offer interpreted in relation to trade usage and the surrounding circumstances. If the offeror has, in effect, stated in his offer *"you must"* use this means of communication, the means of communication is stipulated; but if the offeror has, in effect, stated in his offer *"you may"* use this means of communication, the means of communication is authorized. In all events the acceptance must be communicated before the offer terminates.

When Acceptance Is by a Means Not Authorized.   If an acceptance is sent by a means of communication other than that authorized by the offeror, the acceptance is not effective until it is received by him and then only if it is received by him within the time the acceptance would have been received had the authorized agency of communication been used. By using a means of communication not authorized by the offeror, the offeree assumes all the risks of the means he has selected.

Summary

An acceptance is not effective until it has been communicated to the offeror. If, as a part of an offer, the time, place, and method of communication of the acceptance are stipulated, such stipulation must be complied with by the offeree in accepting the offer. If the offer is silent in respect to time, place, and method of communication of the acceptance, the offeree may communicate his or her acceptance to the offeror at any reasonable time, to any reasonable place, by a method of communication of his or her own choosing.

If a means of communication is used by the offeror to communicate his offer, he, by implication, authorizes the offeree to use the same means of communication to communicate the acceptance; and if the offeree uses such means of communication, the acceptance is effective, and a contract results when the acceptance is delivered to the means of communication. The offeror, in his offer, may expressly authorize the offeree to use a particular means of communication to communicate his acceptance, or a means of communication may be authorized by usage of trade. If the offeree uses the authorized means of communication to communicate his acceptance, the acceptance is effective, and a contract results when the acceptance is delivered to such means of communication. The offeror accepts all the risks of the means of communication.

If the offeree uses an unauthorized means of communication he assumes all the risk of the communication of the acceptance. The acceptance is not effective until it is received, and then only provided it is received within the time an acceptance by the authorized means would have been received had it been delivered in the ordinary course.

Morello v. Growers Grape Products Assoc.

186 P.2d 463 (Ct. App. Cal. 1947)

This was an action by Euginio Morello (plaintiff) against Growers Grape Products Association and others (defendants) to recover damages for the breach of an alleged contract to sell brandy. Judgment on a directed verdict for Growers Grape Products Association, and Morello appealed. Judgment reversed.

Morello and Growers Grape Products Association (Association) entered into a contract under which Morello processed brandy for Association. This contract provided that Association would give Morello an opportunity to purchase the brandy which he processed. By the terms of this contract Association was to notify Morello when they had decided to sell the brandy and the price at which they were selling, and Morello was to have five days in which to accept the offer. On November 9, 1942, Association wrote Morello as follows: "The unsold brandy of your distillation remaining in the pool, according to our records, amounts to approximately 23,902—46 original proof gallons. This amount, which is subject to our final verification, or any quantity thereof, is offered to you at $1.25 cash, per original proof gallon, f.o.b. the storage racks within the Internal Revenue Bonded Warehouse where it is now held, provided: "1. That you accept this offer in writing or by telegraphic notification delivered within five days from the date of this letter."

On November 13, 1942, Morello called Association by telephone and attempted to accept the offer but Association told Morello that his acceptance must be in writing or by telegraphic notification. On November 13, 1942, Morello mailed his acceptance at Fresno, California. Association claims that it did not receive the letter of acceptance until Monday, November 16, 1942. The offices of Association are in San Francisco and they were closed on Sunday, November 15. Association claims that no contract resulted because Morello did not accept its offer in writing within five days.

GOODELL, JUSTICE.   Morello testified that he telephoned his acceptance to Association on the 13th and was told that he must put it in writing. The offer called for either written or telegraphic notification, so the telephonic "acceptance" has to be disregarded. However, if Morello's letter dated the 13th was mailed even as late as the 14th—the fifth day—it was within time, although not *received* in San Francisco until Monday, the 16th. Neither paragraph 13 nor the offer itself specifies that the acceptance must be *received* within five days; they call for an acceptance *delivered* within five days.

It is elementary that a contract is complete when the letter of acceptance is posted. The word "delivered" in the offer creates only an apparent, not a real difficulty, because under the law dealing with the formation of contract *delivery of an acceptance to the post office operates as delivery to the person addressed,* except in unusual cases.

There are many cases holding substantially that the deposit by one party in the mails of an instrument properly addressed to the other party, with postage thereon prepaid, constitutes a *delivery* to the other party, *at the place where* and the *time when it is so deposited.*

The post office was clearly the agent of the offeror, for the offer was itself sent by mail and it called for an acceptance in writing and thereby invited the use of the same medium as that chosen for the offer.

Changes under the U.C.C.

The Code attempts to make the enforceability of business contracts depend more on the intent of the parties and less upon technical rules and legal formalities. A contract for the sale of goods may be made in any manner sufficient to show agreement even though the moment of its making cannot be determined. A contract may exist even though many terms are left open. (2–308—2–311.)[2] The only requirement is that there must be a "reasonably certain basis" for giving an "appropriate" remedy. (2–204.)

The fact that the price is left unsettled, is later to be agreed upon, or is to be set by one of the parties does not defeat the contract. (2–305.) Output, requirements, and exclusive dealing contracts are rendered more enforceable. (2–305.) In all of these "loose" or informal contractual situations the basic duty to act in good faith and in accordance with standards of commercial reasonableness helps to define the obligations of the parties.

The mercantile practice of using forms in the buying and selling of goods has created some problems. For example, A may use a form in offering to buy goods from B, and B may use a form in accepting the offer, and the terms of acceptance may differ in some respects from those of the offer. Under the common law no contract resulted. However, with some exceptions, merchants were inclined to ignore these differences and proceed to perform.

The Code has been drafted on the assumption that agreements should be enforced if they have been consummated by commercial understanding. To implement this view the Code provides: A definite and seasonable expression

---

[2] The numbers in parentheses refer to the sections of the Uniform Commercial Code, 1962.

of acceptance or a written confirmation which is sent within a reasonable time operates as an acceptance even though it states terms additional to or different from those offered or agreed upon, unless acceptance is expressly made conditional on assent to the additional or different terms. (2–207 [1].) Under this provision, if the offeree expressly states that his different or additional terms must be agreed to by the offeror, such an attempt to accept would be a counteroffer and would terminate the original offer.

If the negotiating parties are merchants and the acceptance includes additional or different terms, such terms will be treated as proposals for additions to the contract, and the offeror will be bound by such terms unless one of three circumstances occur. The offer must either expressly limit acceptance to the terms of the offer, or the proposed additional or different terms must materially alter the terms of the offer, or the offeror must give reasonable notification of his objection to the changed terms. (2–207 [2].) If the parties, by their conduct, recognize the existence of a contract when their writings do not otherwise establish one, the terms of the particular contract consist of those terms on which the writing of the parties agree, together with any supplementary terms incorporated under any other provision of the Code. (2–207 [3].)

The rules relative to the means used to communicate an acceptance have been relaxed under the provisions of the Code. Unless the offeror expressly stipulates that a designated agency of communication must be used, the offeree may accept in any manner or by any medium reasonable under the circumstances. (2–206.) If an offer is made by mail and the acceptance is made by telegram, the acceptance would be effective and the contract would be consummated when the telegram was dispatched, provided a telegraphic acceptance was reasonable under the circumstances.

If a buyer orders goods for prompt shipment, his or her offer can be accepted either by a prompt promise to ship or by the shipment of conforming goods. The failure of the seller to either promptly notify or to promptly ship causes the offer to lapse. A shipment of nonconforming goods is not an acceptance if the seller notifies the buyer that he or she is shipping nonconforming goods as an accommodation. (2–206–1 [b].) If a seller receives an order or offer to purchase goods for prompt shipment and the seller ships nonconforming goods without giving the buyer the required notice, the shipment of the goods is an acceptance and since the seller has shipped nonconforming goods, the seller will be liable for breach of the contract.

Summary

The Code gives greater weight to the intentions of the parties and less weight to technical form requirements. The "matching terms" concept is replaced by (2–207) which permits a contract to exist even though no full agreement exists. Acceptance may be by any reasonable means and orders for immediate shipment must be handled promptly either by notice or by shipment. If a seller ships nonconforming goods in response to an order for immediate shipment, the seller will be deemed to have accepted the buyer's original order unless he or she notifies the buyer that the nonconforming goods are being shipped for the buyer's accommodation.

Southwest Engineering Co. v. Martin Tractor Co.

473 P.2d 18 (Sup. Ct. Kan. 1970)

This is an action by Southwest Engineering Company (plaintiff) against Martin Tractor Company (defendant) to recover damages for breach of contract. Judgment for Southwest and Martin appealed. Affirmed.

In April, 1966, Southwest was interested in submitting a bid to the Corps of Engineers for the construction of certain runway lighting facilities at an Air Force Base at Wichita. However, before submitting a bid, and on April 11, 1966, Southwest's construction superintendent, Cloepfil, called the manager of Martin's engine department, Hurt, asking for a price on a standby generator and accessory equipment. Hurt replied that he would phone him back which he did quoting a price of $18,500. This quotation was reconfirmed by Hurt over the phone on April 13.

Southwest submitted its bid on April 14, 1966, using Hurt's figure of $18,500 for the generating equipment, and its bid was accepted. On April 20, Southwest notified Martin that the bid had been accepted. Hurt and Cloepfil thereafter agreed over the phone to meet in Springfield on April 28.

At the Springfield meeting it developed that Martin had upped its price for the generator and accessory equipment from $18,500 to $21,500. Despite this change of position by Martin, the two men continued their conversation and, according to Cloepfil, they arrived at an agreement for the sale of a D353 generator and accessories for the sum of $21,500. In addition it was agreed that if the Corps of Engineers would accept a less expensive generator, a D343, the aggregate price to Southwest would be $15,000.

A memorandum with these terms was drawn at that time but there was no definite agreement concerning the exact time and method for payment. Hurt later refused to deliver a D353 generator as requested by Southwest, and Southwest had to procure one from another source. Southwest secured the generator equipment from Foley Tractor Co. at a price of $27,541 and then filed suit seeking damages of $6,041 for breach of the contract.

FONTRON, JUSTICE. It is quite true, as the trial court found, that terms of payment were not agreed upon at the Springfield meeting. Hurt testified that as the memorandum was being made out, he said they wanted 10 percent with the order, 50 percent on delivery and the balance on acceptance, but he did not recall Cloepfil's response. Cloepfil's version was somewhat different. He stated that after the two had shaken hands in the lobby preparing to leave, Hurt said their terms usually were 20 percent down and the balance on delivery; while he (Cloepfil) said the way they generally paid was 90 percent on the tenth of the month following delivery and the balance on final acceptance. It is obvious the parties reached no agreement on this point.

However, a failure on the part of . . . Hurt and Cloepfil to agree on terms of payment would not, of itself, defeat an otherwise valid agreement reached by them. K.S.A. 84–2–204(3) reads:

> Even though one or more terms are left open a contract for sale does not fail for indefiniteness if the parties have intended to make a contract and there is a reasonably certain basis for giving an appropriate remedy.

The official U.C.C. Comment is enlightening:

> Subsection (3) states the principle as to "open terms" underlying later sections of the Article. If the parties intend to enter into a binding agreement, this subsection recognizes that agreement as valid in law, despite missing terms, if there is any reasonably certain basis for granting a remedy. The test is not certainty as to what the parties were to do nor as to the exact amount of damages due the plaintiff. Nor is the fact that one or more terms are left to be agreed upon enough of itself to defeat an otherwise adequate agreement. Rather, commercial standards on the point of "indefiniteness" are intended to be applied, this Act making provision elsewhere for missing terms needed for performance, open price, remedies and the like.
>
> The more terms the parties leave open, the less likely it is that they have intended to conclude a binding agreement, but their actions may be frequently conclusive on the matter despite the omissions.

The above Code provision and accompanying Comment were quoted in *Pennsylvania Co. v. Wilmington Trust Co.,* where the court made this observation:

> There appears to be no pertinent court authority interpreting this rather recent but controlling statute. In an article . . . Mr. Williston wanted to limit omissions to "minor" terms. He wanted "business honor" to be the only compulsion where "important terms" are left open. Nevertheless, his recommendation was rejected. . . . This shows that those drafting the statute intended that the omission of even an important term does not prevent the finding under the statute that the parties intended to make a contract.

So far as the present case is concerned, K.S.A. 84–2–310 supplies the omitted term. This statute provides in pertinent part:

> Unless otherwise agreed.
> (*a*) payment is due at the time and place at which the buyer is to receive the goods even though the place of shipment is the place of delivery . . .

In our view, the language of the two Code provisions is clear and positive. Considered together, we take the two sections to mean that where parties have reached an enforceable agreement for the sale of goods, but omit therefrom the terms of payment, the law will imply, as part of the agreement, that payment is to be made at time of delivery. In this respect the law does not greatly differ from the rule this court laid down years ago.

*   *   *   *

We do not mean to imply that terms of payment are not of importance under many circumstances, or that parties may not condition an agreement on their being included.

However, the facts before us hardly indicate that Hurt and Cloepfil considered the terms of payment to be significant, or of more than passing interest.

In re Doughboy Industries, Inc.

233 N.Y.S.2d 488 (Sup. Ct. N.Y. App. Div. 1962)

Pantasote Company (plaintiff) brought suit to require Doughboy Industries, Inc. (defendant) to arbitrate a dispute. Doughboy appealed from the trial court's denial of its motion to stay arbitration. Reversed for Doughboy.

On two occasions prior to May 6, and on May 6, Doughboy ordered and received shipments of film from Pantasote. On each of these occasions Doughboy had used a purchase order form which stated: "ALTERATION OF TERMS—None of the terms and conditions contained in this Purchase Order may be added to, modified, superseded or otherwise altered except by a written instrument signed by an authorized representative of Buyer and delivered by Buyer to Seller, and each shipment received by Buyer from Seller shall be deemed to be only upon the terms and conditions contained in this Purchase Order except as they may be added to, modified, superseded or otherwise altered, notwithstanding Buyer's act of accepting or paying for any shipment or similar act of Buyer."

Pantasote accepted each order by sending an acknowledgment form which stated: "IMPORTANT—Buyer agrees he has full knowledge of conditions printed on the reverse side hereof, and that the same are part of the agreement between buyer and seller and shall be binding if either the goods referred to herein are delivered to and accepted by buyer, or if buyer does not within ten days from date hereof deliver to seller written objections to said conditions or any part thereof."

The reverse side of Pantasote's acknowledgment form contained a general arbitration clause binding both parties to submit any dispute arising under the contract to arbitration. A dispute arose over the May 6 contract and Pantasote brought suit to require that Doughboy submit the dispute to arbitration.

BREITEL, JUDGE.   This case involves a conflict between a buyer's order form and a seller's acknowledgment form, each memorializing a purchase and sale of goods. The issue arises on whether the parties agreed to arbitrate future disputes. The seller's form had a general arbitration provision. The buyer's form did not. The buyer's form contained a provision that only a signed consent would bind the buyer to any terms thereafter transmitted in any commercial form of the seller. The seller's form, however, provided that silence or a failure to object in writing would be an acceptance of the terms and conditions of its acknowledgment form. The buyer never objected to the seller's acknowledgment, orally or in writing. In short, the buyer and seller accomplished a legal equivalent to the irresistible force colliding with the immovable object.

* * * * *

The dispute, which has arisen and which the parties wish determined, the seller by arbitration, and the buyer by court litigation, is whether the buyer is bound to accept all the goods ordered on a "hold basis." The arbitration would take place in New

York City. The litigation might have to be brought in Wisconsin, the buyer's home state.

Recognizing, as one should, that the businessmen in this case acted with complete disdain for the "lawyer's content" of the very commercial forms they were sending and receiving, the question is what obligation ought the law to attach to the arbitration clause. And in determining that question the traditional theory is applicable, namely, that of constructive knowledge and acceptance of contractual terms, based on prior transactions and the duty to read contractual instruments to which one is a party. . . .

But, and this is critical, it is not only the seller's form which should be given effect, but also the buyer's form, for it too was used in the prior transactions, and as to it too, there was a duty to read. Of course, if the two commercial forms are given effect, they cancel one another. (Certainly, the test is not which is the later form, because here the prior form said the buyer would not be bound by the later form unless it consented in writing. It needs little discussion that silence, a weak enough form of acceptance, effective only when misleading and there is a duty to speak, can be negatived as a misleading factor by announcing in advance that it shall have no effect as acceptance. . . .)

Consequently, as a matter of law there was no agreement to arbitrate in this case, if one applied existing principles. But the problem of conflicting commercial forms is one with which there has been much concern before this, and a new effort at rational solution has been made.

. . . The draftsmen's comments to section 2–207 are in precise point. Thus, it is said:

3. Whether or not additional or different terms will become part of the agreement depends upon the provisions of subsection (2). If they are such as materially to alter the original bargain, they will not be included unless expressly agreed to by the other party. If, however, they are terms which would not so change the bargain they will be incorporated unless notice of objection to them has already been given or if given within a reasonable time. . . .
6. If no answer is received within a reasonable time after additional terms are proposed, it is both fair and commercially sound to assume that their inclusion has been assented to. Where clauses on confirming forms sent by both parties conflict each party must be assumed to object to a clause of the other conflicting with one on the confirmation sent by himself. As a result the requirement that there be notice of objection which is found in subsection (2) is satisfied and the conflicting terms do not become a part of the contract. The contract then consists of the terms originally expressly agreed to, terms on which the confirmations agree, and terms supplied by this Act, including subsection (2).

On this exposition, the arbitration clause, whether viewed as a material alteration under subsection (2), or as a term nullified by a conflicting provision in the buyer's form, would fail to survive as a contract term. In the light of the New York cases, at least, there can be little question that an agreement to arbitrate is a material term, one not to be injected by implication, subtlety or inveiglement. And the conclusion is also the same if the limitation contained in the offer (the buyer's purchase order) is given effect, as required by paragraph (a) of subsection 2 of the new section.

Accordingly, the order denying Doughboy's motion to stay arbitration should be reversed, on the law, with costs to Doughboy and the motion should be granted.

Problem Cases

1. Jaybe and other contractors were invited to bid on a state project. Beco, without solicitation, sent a letter to Jaybe quoting a price for a specified portion of the job. Jaybe received the contract and telephoned Beco to tell them that Jaybe had received the contract which included the Beco quote. Jaybe said that they would send a formal contract for Beco's signature. A request was made for Beco to "shave" their original quote, if possible. Beco, upon later learning that they would be unable to substitute certain equipment, sent Jaybe a new price and refused to sign Jaybe's contract or to do the job at the original price. Another subcontractor completed the job for $1,000 over Beco's original price. Jaybe sued Beco for damages and won a judgment for $1,000. Should the judgment be upheld on appeal?

2. Jones advertised five parcels of real estate for sale on closed bids. The terms of the sale were that a bidder could bid on all or any combination of the parcels. Friel filed a bid in which he listed a bid on parcel 1, 3, and 4 as single parcels, on a combination of parcels 2 and 5, on 1, 2, 3, and 4, and on 1, 2, 3, 4, and 5. Friel, in submitting his bid stated: "The bidder reserves the right to limit his purchase to not more than two of the above parcels or combination of parcels." Friel was high bidder on his combined bid on parcels 2 and 5 and on his bid on parcel 4. He was awarded parcels 2 and 5 but was refused parcel 4. Friel brought suit for specific performance of the contract to sell parcel 4. Jones contends that Friel's bid was a counteroffer and that no contract resulted. Was Friel's bid a counteroffer?

3. Dohman offered his residence for sale. Sullivan was interested and offered to buy the property for $10,250 cash. Dohman was in Florida and negotiations were carried on by letter and telegrams. When negotiations were completed, Dohman sent to the broker who was representing him a contract embodying the terms agreed upon. Sullivan signed the contract and it was returned to Dohman for his signature. Dohman refused to sign and refused to convey the residence to Sullivan. Sullivan brought suit asking specific performance of the contract. Dohman set up a defense that he had not signed the formal contract. Is the defense good?

4. James obtained a contract to lay sewer lines. He then subcontracted to Price the related paving work. Price wrote James stating the terms of the subcontract. James after some delay said he would not accept these terms and wrote new ones which he gave to Price. Price said that he could not accept James' terms, but that he would attach a supplement and sign James' terms with the supplement. The supplement provided that James would pay Price for any repair due to trench settlement. James received the signed terms and supplement but never indicated his acceptance of the supplement. Price proceeded with the work and incurred additional costs for repaving the subsequent settlement from tamped trenches. Price sued James for this cost and won a judgment. Should the judgment be upheld on appeal?

5. Brooks hired Conkey to construct an apartment building according to the specifications set forth by Ratner, his architect. Brooks had given Ratner the authority to change plans of construction and to grant extensions in completion deadlines, limited only by Brooks' "express disapproval." When the apartment building was not completed according to schedule, Brooks sued Conkey for damages. In his defense, Conkey stated that on several occasions he had requested that Ratner give him an extension of time and that Ratner had not replied, but had encouraged him to continue to work. Conkey said he had relied on

Ratner's acquiescence since Brooks had made no express disapproval. Is this a good defense?

6. Duckett had an automobile insurance policy with Reserve Insurance Company, whose agent was Davis. In accordance with the usual practice, Davis sent Duckett a letter 30 days prior to the expiration of the Reserve policy with a request for payment of a renewal premium, enclosing self-addressed envelopes for Duckett's use in making payment. Duckett was uncertain in regard to the exact time he mailed the money order for the premium, prior to the expiration date of the Reserve policy, stating "I would say four or five days." September 6 was the policy expiration date and on September 7 Duckett had an accident. On September 8 a policy identical to the original one was issued to Duckett, marked "renewal." Reserve Insurance Company refused to pay Duckett's accident claim, alleging that his coverage was nonexistent at the time of the accident. Duckett sued, asserting that the renewal notice from Davis was an offer from Reserve which he had accepted by making the renewal premium, which gave rise to a binding contract between Reserve and Duckett to issue an insurance policy. Was the offer properly accepted?

7. Fuller had stored hay in a barn on a farm leased by Bowley. Bowley contemplated purchasing the hay but decided not to do so. On March 11, Bowley gave Fuller written notice to remove the hay by March 15, and that a charge of $4 per day storage would be made after that date. Fuller did not remove the hay until April 1. Bowley claims that he is entitled to $4 per day storage from March 15 to April 1. Is Bowley entitled to storage charges as claimed?

8. Harvey wrote Marclay on March 21 offering her a position stating, "You will confer a favor on me by giving me your answer by return mail." Marclay claimed that she wrote Harvey the next day, accepting the offer, and gave the card to an errand boy to mail. The card was postmarked March 25. Harvey refused to employ Marclay, and she brought suit to recover damages for breach of contract. Is Marclay entitled to a judgment?

9. A salesman of Harvester Company solicited from Hendrickson an order for a machine. The order was subject to the approval of Harvester Company at its home office. The order was received by Harvester Company, but it took no action thereon, and it did not ship the machine. After waiting a reasonable time, Hendrickson brought suit to recover damages for breach of the contract. Harvester set up as a defense that it never accepted Hendrickson's offer. Did a contract result?

10. Carpet Mart placed orders for carpet by telephone with C&A. In each instance C&A promptly sent Carpet Mart one of its acknowledgment forms which stated that all acceptances of orders were "subject to the terms and conditions on the face and reverse side hereof, including arbitration, all of which are accepted by buyer." Carpet Mart accepted the shipments and never objected to the terms on the acknowledgment forms. A dispute arose and Carpet Mart sued claiming damages for fraud. C&A made a motion that the suit be stayed pending arbitration as required on the acknowledgment form. The trial court ruled that there was no contract to arbitrate because C&A failed to give unconditional acceptance when C&A used the words "subject to" on its acknowledgment forms. Was this trial court ruling correct?

chapter 8

Reality of Consent

Introduction

Nature of Real Consent. One of the fundamental requirements for holding a person liable for the nonperformance of a contractual promise is that the promise must have been made voluntarily. Honesty and fair dealing are essential to the success of a free, competitive economy. Under our contract law a person receives protection against sharp dealing in contracts by the law dealing with misrepresentation, fraud, duress, or undue influence. In negotiating contracts the promisor will be required to exercise reasonable caution and judgment, and he will seldom be permitted to escape from promises carelessly made. Standards have been developed by the courts which are used as the basis for determining whether or not the promisor should be held to his promise.

Closely related to a promise induced by misrepresentation, fraud, duress, or undue influence is the promise based on a mistake of fact. If both parties to an agreement have acted in the erroneous assumption as to the existence or nonexistence of a material fact relating to their agreement, the courts have, as a general rule, granted whatever relief the circumstances of the case warranted.

Misrepresentation and Fraud

Misrepresentation. If one person, by words or acts or by any other conduct, has created in the mind of another an impression which is not in accordance with the facts, such person is guilty of misrepresentation. Misrepresentation of a material fact justifiably relied on is ground for holding a contractual promise voidable. Knowledge of the falsity on the part of the person making the misrepresentation is not essential, and the method by which the misrepresentation is made is not material.

The misrepresentation must be of a material fact. To be material, the fact need not be the sole fact which induced the injured party to make the contractual promise, nor need it be the major inducement. It must be a contributing factor, however, and the circumstances must be such that it is reasonable to presume that the party would not have made the contractual promise had he known the true facts.

The misrepresentation must be of an existing or past fact. An expression of future happenings is prospective and is not a statement of fact. Likewise, arguments intended to convince a party that the transaction is a "good deal" are not statements of fact. In general, a "factual" representation is one concerning a matter that is reasonably subject to exact knowledge. A representation concerning a used car asserting, "This is the finest used car in town," is obviously not reasonably subject to exact knowledge, and hence is a statement of mere opinion. A representation, "The motor of this car has been rebuilt" is a statement of fact.

A party, in order to be entitled to a remedy, must have justifiably relied on the misrepresentations. If the party knows that the statements are erroneous, or if the facts and circumstances are such that, in the exercise of reasonable prudence, he or she should have investigated and discovered the falsity of the statements, he or she is not justified in relying on the statements.

As a general rule, if both parties have equal knowledge and equal opportunity to learn the true facts, neither party is justified in relying on statements made by the other party. But if the party making the misrepresentations has superior knowledge and is in a position to know the facts, the other party will, as a general rule, be justified in relying on the statements.

The remedy available to a party who is induced by misrepresentation to make a contractual promise is rescission—that is, the injured party may return what he has received and recover what he has given in performance of the contract, or its value. If no performance has been rendered, the injured party may give notice that he disaffirms the contract; and if suit is brought against him for breach of contract, he may set up the misrepresentation as a defense.

In all cases of misrepresentation the injured party must act seasonably. Failure to rescind or disaffirm within a reasonable time after the injured party learns of the misrepresentation amounts to waiver of the right to rescind or disaffirm.

Fraud.   Fraud is an intentional misrepresentation of a material fact made for the purpose of inducing another, in reliance upon it, to part with some valuable thing belonging to him, or to surrender a legal right. If one party, through misrepresentations knowingly made, creates a mistaken belief as to the existence or nonexistence of a fact material to a transaction and thereby influences the action of the party to whom the representation is made, the party making the misrepresentation is guilty of fraudulent conduct.

The method used to create the mistaken belief is immaterial. It may be by words, acts, concealment, or any other method. The result is important, not the method whereby the result is attained. The terms *misrepresentation* and *fraud* are frequently used synonymously; however, misrepresentation, as used in law, signifies innocent misrepresentation, whereas fraud signifies intentional misrepresentation.

If a person is induced to make a contractual promise by fraudulent representations, he or she may rescind the contract, since the right to rescind is based on misrepresentation. However, if the elements of an actionable deceit are present—(1) misrepresentation of a material fact, (2) knowingly made, (3) with intent to defraud, (4) justifiably relied on, (5) with resulting injury—the injured party has an election of remedies. He may rescind the contract, or he may affirm the contract and bring an action in tort to recover damages for the deceit.[1] Damages for deceit include compensation for all injury resulting directly from the deceit and may include punitive damages. As in misrepresentation, the injured person must act seasonably, and his failure to give notice within a reasonable time after he learns of the deceit will amount to a waiver of his rights.

Summary

A contract induced by innocent misrepresentations or by fraud does not bind the party induced to enter the contract by such means.

The remedy for misrepresentation is rescission. At common law persons guilty of deceit were subject to an election of remedies on the part of the party defrauded.

Sharp v. Idaho Investment Corp.

504 P.2d. 386 (Sup. Ct. Idaho 1972)

Dr. Sharp (plaintiff) brought this action for damages for alleged fraudulent misrepresentations by Idaho Investment Corporation (defendant) in selling certain stock to Dr. Sharp. The trial court found for Dr. Sharp and Idaho Investment appealed. Reversed.

McFADDEN, JUSTICE.   Although the district court found that misrepresentations had been made in the "pitch kit," prospectus, sales material, bulletins and "other

---

[1] The modern trend is to allow the defrauded party to pursue these remedies in sequence. Thus, if an action in deceit results in an unsatisfied judgment, the defrauded may then seek rescission unless, of course, the rights of innocent third parties have intervened.

written material," there is no indication which statements in particular were false. In reviewing the numerous exhibits we conclude that there are no misrepresentations. True enough, optimism and enthusiasm pervade the sales material. However, Dr. Sharp has not carried his burden of producing clear and convincing evidence of the falsity of any statement in the written material he supposedly relied on.

As a final basis for imposing liability on Idaho Investment . . . we must consider the omission of facts material to the transaction which deprived Dr. Sharp of exercising his business investment judgment. The district court found that Idaho Investment . . . "omitted certain facts" which deprived Dr. Sharp of a "fair and honest" opportunity to evaluate the stock. First, we are unable to determine whether such omissions were intentional or negligent. Second, we are unable to discover the extent or exact nature of the omissions. Third, there is no evidence showing that such omissions, if there were any, were material. . . . Furthermore, Dr. Sharp did not read the prospectus or offering circular until after he had purchased the stock. Thus, any omission in the prospectus was not material to his decision to purchase.

Reliance is a fundamental element of fraud which must be proven by clear and convincing evidence. On direct examination Dr. Sharp was asked: "Doctor, would you tell me why you purchased stock in the Idaho Investment?" Dr. Sharp replied, "Because I believed Mr. Neilson. I was acquainted with Mr. Frazier and other officers of Sierra Life. I knew the officers and expected it to be a profitable venture." From Dr. Sharp's own testimony it is evident that rather than relying on representations or misstatements by Idaho Investment and its agents he relied on expectations based on his experience with another corporation.

Perry v. Woodall

438 P.2d 813 (Sup. Ct. Utah 1968)

This was an action brought by Lowell Perry (plaintiff) against Earl Woodall (defendant) to collect payments due on a contract to purchase a drugstore. Woodall counterclaimed for damages for fraud. Perry appealed from a judgment against his payment claim and in favor of Woodall's counterclaim. Held reversed as to both claim and counterclaim.

Prior to April 1, 1964, Perry was the owner of all the corporate stock of Buy Wise Drugs, Inc., which operated a drugstore in the Rose Park area of Salt Lake City. Perry managed the business on behalf of the corporation and Woodall had been for a number of years a pharmacist employed at the drugstore. From time to time prior to April 1964, Perry and Woodall discussed the possibility of Woodall purchasing the business. These discussions resulted in a written offer by Woodall dated March 13, 1964, to purchase Perry's stock upon certain terms set out in the offer. The offer was accepted on March 14, 1964, and Woodall took over the management and assumed control of the business on April 1, 1964.

* * * * *

Prior to the making of the contract of sale, Woodall had been furnished a report by an inventory service which reported the merchandise and physical assets of the store as being in excess of $47,000. Woodall had also been furnished a balance sheet as of February 10, 1964, prepared by the corporate bookkeeper, which showed liabilities of about $47,000, including current liabilities on trade accounts payable of over $20,000.

On July 18, 1964, Perry furnished to Woodall an affidavit which listed the liabilities of the business as being in the sum of approximately $61,000. After receipt of the affidavit, Woodall communicated to Perry through his attorney by letter, which communication pointed out that a number of items listed on the affidavit were personal debts rather than corporate liabilities. The communication also contained a new proposal by Woodall to purchase the business. In the new offer Woodall proposed to pay to Perry the sum of $10,000 for the latter's interest in the assets and inventory. Woodall had failed to pay to Perry all of the sums due under the first offer.

The negotiations between the parties did not result in a second agreement. Woodall continued to operate the business until September 7, 1964, at which time he was appointed receiver in an action commenced by one of the creditors of the business. Woodall continued to act as receiver until January 1966, at which time he resigned and a successor was appointed. Woodall continued to manage the business for the successor receiver until March 1966, at which time he purchased the assets of the business at a receiver's sale for the sum of about $45,000.

TUCKETT, JUDGE.   The court found that Woodall elected to rescind the purchase agreement in July after he had received the affidavit of Perry setting out all of the obligations of the business. We are of the opinion that the record does not support the finding of the court in this regard. One who claims he has been deceived and elects to rescind his contract by reason of the fraud or misrepresentation of the other contracting party must act promptly and unequivocally in announcing his intention. The facts in this case would indicate that Woodall, after learning of the extent of the indebtedness of the corporation he had purchased in July 1964, did not elect to rescind the contract at that time, but rather expressed dissatisfaction with his purchase of the business and offered to renegotiate the terms of that purchase agreement. Woodall, after learning all of the facts, if he then considered that he had been defrauded, had a duty to notify Perry promptly of his election to rescind the contract and to also tender back to Perry the assets of the corporation, as well as the corporate stock involved in the transaction. The law is well settled that one electing to rescind a contract must tender back to the other contracting party whatever property of value he has received. Woodall elected to retain possession of the corporate assets and to carry on the business until it was taken over in the receivership proceedings. We are of the opinion that Woodall waited too long, and that he cannot now rescind the contract. . . .

The judgment of the trial court is reversed and the case is remanded to that court for a new trial. Perry is entitled to costs.

Griffith v. Byers Construction Co. of Kansas, Inc.

510 P.2d 198 (Sup. Ct. Kan. 1973)

Mr. and Mrs. Griffith (plaintiffs) sued Byers Construction Company (defendant) for damages for fraud. Plaintiffs appealed from adverse judgment. Reversed.

Byers Construction Company developed land and then sold lots to home building contractors. These home building contractors built houses on the lots and then sold the houses and lots to home buyers. Mr. and Mrs. Griffith purchased a house and lot from one of the building contractors and then sued Byers (the developer) when they discovered that the soil was defective.

FROMME, JUSTICE.   This court has held that the purchaser may recover on the theory of fraud from a vendor-builder for nondisclosure of defects. In *Jenkins v. McCormick,* it is stated:

Where a vendor has knowledge of a defect in property which is not within the fair and reasonable reach of the vendee and which he could not discover by the exercise of reasonable diligence, the silence and failure of the vendor to disclose the defect in the property constitutes actionable fraudulent concealment.

This *Jenkins* rule approximates that stated in *Restatement, Second, Torts,* § 551:

(1) One who fails to disclose to another a thing which he knows may justifiably induce the other to act or refrain from acting in a business transaction is subject to the same liability to the other as though he had represented the nonexistence of the matter which he has failed to disclose, if, but only if, he is under a duty to the other to exercise reasonable care to disclose the matter in question.

(2) One party to a business transaction is under a duty to disclose to the other before the transaction is consummated.

(3) Facts basic to the transaction; if he knows that the other is about to enter into the transaction under a mistake as to such facts, and that the other, because of the relationship between them, the customs in the trade, or other objective circumstances, would reasonably expect a disclosure of such facts.

A similar rule has been recognized in other states. See *Bethlahmy v. Bechtel,* where a drainage ditch underlay a garage and was not disclosed to the purchaser. . . . We see no reason why the rule in *Jenkins* should not be extended in the present case to a developer of residential lots.

Defendant Byers next contends, without agency, there can be no privity and without privity there can be no duty to disclose. Here, of course, the plaintiffs never dealt with . . . Byers. The duty to disclose the saline nature of the soil must extend to the plaintiffs if their fraud claims are to be upheld. However, the doctrine of privity provides no defense to . . . Byers if the plaintiffs were within a class of persons Byers intended to reach. Liability for misrepresentation is not necessarily limited to the person with whom the misrepresenter deals. The rule is embodied in *Restatement, Second, Torts,* § 531:

One who makes a fraudulent misrepresentation is subject to liability for pecuniary loss

(a) To the persons or class of persons whom he intends or has reason to expect to act or to refrain from action in reliance upon the misrepresentation; and

(b) For pecuniary loss suffered by them through their reliance in the type of transaction in which he intends or has reason to expect their conduct to be influenced.

Under the alleged facts of our present case, . . . we must assume . . . Byers had knowledge of the saline content of the soil of the lots it placed on the market. After the grading and development of the area this material defect in the lots was not within the fair and reasonable reach of the vendees, as they could not discover this latent defect by the exercise of reasonable care. The silence of . . . Byers, and its failure to disclose this defect in the soil condition to the purchasers could constitute actionable fraudulent concealment.

Duress and Undue Influence

General Nature. Duress is unlawful constraint exercised upon a person whereby he or she is coerced to do some act that he or she otherwise would not have done. Undue influence is closely related to duress. It exists where one party is under the domination of another and is induced, by the unfair persuasion of the dominant party, to follow a course of action which he would not have followed of his own free will.

A contractual promise made under duress or undue influence is voidable. The reason for this is that since the party making the promise has been deprived of his ability to exercise a free choice, he should not be bound by his promise. In both duress and undue influence the parties are not bargaining on an equal basis. As a general rule the equality of the bargaining power of the parties to a contract is immaterial. The parties are presumed to be capable of protecting their own interests, and the courts will not assume the role of arbiters of the equality of bargaining powers in the everyday give-and-take of the marketplace. However, when the situation is such that the inequality cannot, in fairness and good conscience, be ignored, the courts will grant relief by declaring voidable the contractual promise made under the pressure of duress or induced by undue influence.

Duress. Duress had its origin in the law of crimes and torts. In the early stages of its development the test of duress was the threat of physical injury sufficient to overcome the will of a constant man of ordinary courage made by one having the power to execute the threat. The modern cases have not developed a clear rule or test for the existence of duress.

As a general rule the courts have stated that the means used must be wrongful. An analysis of the cases reveals that the word *wrongful* is not confined to criminal or tortious acts but may also include unconscionable conduct. In applying this test, the court must determine, in the exercise of its judicial discretion, where the line shall be drawn. Each case is treated as presenting a separate problem. If the act is wrongful, and if it deprives the coerced person of his ability to make a free choice, the courts will, as a general rule, grant relief.

Threats of criminal prosecution made to coerce a person into making payment of a claimed defalcation or to compensate for claimed unlawful gains have been held to be duress if the person making the threat gains thereby advantages to which he is not lawfully entitled.

The courts have generally held that the threat of a civil suit does not constitute duress. However, if the bringing of a civil suit is clearly an abuse of civil process, it may amount to duress. The threat to bring suit on an unfounded claim, when the person threatening suit knows that the financial situation of the person threatened is such that a suit would, in all probability, bring financial ruin to him, would be held by some courts to amount to duress.

The unjustified withholding of a person's goods for the purpose of forcing him to pay an unreasonable charge has been held to be duress. In the earlier cases the courts held that the refusal of a common carrier to deliver goods unless an unreasonable carriage charge was paid amounted to duress. This concept has been extended to other similar situations; and today, "duress of goods," the unjustified withholding of goods unless exorbitant charges are paid, is generally held to be duress. The person paying the excessive charges to obtain possession of the goods is permitted to recover the amount of the overcharge.

Undue Influence. The objective of the defense of undue influence is to protect the aged, the timid, and the physically or mentally weak from the unscrupulous who succeed in gaining their confidence and take advantage of them. There is no precise definition of undue influence. It is a form of coercion. Before the courts will grant relief on the ground of undue influence, there must be a difference in the bargaining ability of the parties. The victim of undue influence must have the mental capacity to contract but at the same time not have the ability to protect himself or herself against unscrupulous persons who gain his or her confidence.

In most of the cases involving undue influence, we generally have a situation in which a close relative or long-time friend takes advantage of the relationship and induces his weakened victim to make a gift or transfer property to him for a wholly inadequate consideration. The principal test is whether the confidential relationship was used to divert property from its normal course, in view of all the circumstances, to the person exercising the undue influence.

Summary

Duress is the obtaining of an advantage over a person by means of coercion brought to bear which deprives that person of his or her ability to make a free choice. A contractual promise obtained by duress is voidable. In contract law, if the means of executing the pressure is wrongful and the contractual promise is unjust or unconscionable, the courts will grant relief. The relief granted may be rescission of the contract or the granting of a judgment for any sum obtained over and above that to which the coercing party was, in fairness and honesty, entitled. Tort damages are not recoverable for duress.

Undue influence is based on a confidential relationship wherein one party dominates the other and wherein the dominant party owes a duty to look for the interests of the servient party. If such a relationship exists and the dominant party, in breach of his duty, uses his position to benefit himself at the expense of the servient party, the courts will hold the transaction voidable on the ground of undue influence.

In both duress and undue influence, the party with superior bargaining power takes advantage of the situation and gains an economic advantage which is so unequal and unfair that it is, as the courts frequently state, shocking to the conscience of man. The modern trend is for the courts to expand duress to include many of the more subtle forms of coercion not recognized at common law.

Laemmar v. J. Walter Thompson Co.

435 F.2d 680 (7th Cir. 1970)

Suit by Laemmar and others (plaintiffs) against J. Walter Thompson (defendant) seeking rescission of an agreement to sell stock. Judgment for Thompson and Laemmar appealed. Reversed.

Laemmar and others were employees-at-will of (defendant) J. Walter Thompson Company for many years. For several years the plaintiffs purchased shares of Class B common stock of the defendant corporation. It is undisputed that all of such stock purchases were subject to an option retained by Thompson to repurchase the stock if the plaintiffs' employment were terminated for any reason.

In 1965 various officers of Thompson solicited plaintiffs to resell their stock either to Thompson or to certain officers of Thompson. Plaintiffs rejected this solicitation and were told, "expressly and by innuendo," that they would be discharged from their employment unless they executed the sale in accordance with an offer then outstanding. Plaintiffs unwillingly sold the stock to Thompson in March of 1965 because of the threat of losing their employment, receiving therefor corporate notes payable over three years at six and one-half per cent interest for the purchase price offered by Thompson.

Plaintiffs remained in Thompson's employ until, after having notified defendant on May 8, 1969, of their desire to rescind the resale together with a tender of the purchase price (including interest) and having been refused the return of the stock, they filed a lawsuit in state court seeking rescission and were then discharged by defendant upon its receipt of a summons.

SWYGERT, CHIEF JUDGE.   In sum, it is the theory of the plaintiffs that the agreement to sell their stock may be rescinded because they were under duress at the time of the making of the agreement. They postulate that the threatened termination of their employment so deprived them of the exercise of free will that the contract to sell the stock is rendered voidable. We agree that, as a matter of law, the threat of discharge from one's employment may constitute duress which would make voidable a contract executed while a party was under such a threat. Whether the threat did constitute duress in this instance, however, is a question of fact which must be resolved by the trier of fact upon remand.

There is no dispute that if duress exists at the creation of a contract the requisite voluntariness of the party subject to duress is absent, rendering the agreement voidable. The Illinois rule was recently restated by the Illinois Supreme Court in *Kaplan v. Kaplan* (1962):

Duress has been defined as a condition where one is induced by a wrongful act or threat of another to make a contract under circumstances which deprive him of the exercise of his free will, and it may be conceded that a contract executed under duress is voidable.

The question thus becomes whether a threat to pursue an action to which one is legally entitled may constitute duress under Illinois law if made as an inducement to execute an agreement. We conclude that it may. The Illinois case law amply illustrates the proposition that pressure generated by noncriminal acts and threatened acts of a party may constitute duress where their undoubted effect was to undermine the ability of another to refuse to execute an agreement.

As the Illinois Supreme Court has observed, adopting the general theory of duress argued by plaintiffs herein:

Under modern views and developments . . . duress is no longer confined to situations involving threats of personal injury or imprisonment, and the standard of whether a man of ordinary courage would yield to the threat has been supplanted by a test which inquires *whether the threat has left the individual bereft of the quality of mind essential to the making of a contract.* (*Kaplan v. Kaplan.*)

Applying the *Kaplan* test to the facts pleaded in the verified complaint, we hold that plaintiffs' allegations of duress by means of threatened discharge from employment are legally sufficient to withstand defendant's motion for judgment on the pleadings. Whether duress actually existed in this instance must be determined by the trier of fact, however, for "the issue of duress generally is one of fact, to be judged in light of all the circumstances surrounding a given transaction."

Link v. Link

179 S.E.2d 697 (Sup. Ct. N.C. 1971)

Action by Mrs. Link (plaintiff) to set aside her transfer of her interest in certain stock and debentures to her husband (defendant). Mrs. Link won in the trial court but the Court of Appeals ordered a new trial. Mrs. Link appealed to the Supreme Court of North Carolina. Held. Reversed in favor of Mrs. Link.

LAKE, JUSTICE.   The complaint in the present action alleges, and the answer denies, that the defendant induced the plaintiff to transfer to him the securities in question by fraudulent concealment and that he "coerced" and "extracted" her signature to the transfers by threats and abuse. The allegations of the complaint are sufficient to justify the submission to the jury of the questions of fraud, duress, and undue influence.

These are related wrongs and, to some degree, overlap. They are, however, not synonymous. Proof of facts sufficient to show one does not necessarily constitute proof of either of the other two.

Mrs. Link and Mr. Link were married in 1948. They lived together until December 2, 1967, when he left home following a discussion, in the course of which, according to his allegation and testimony, she informed him she had been guilty of adultery. Their three children were then 15, 13, and 10 years of age, respectively. She instituted this action to have declared void assignments by her to him of 147½ shares of common stock of Royal Crown Bottling Company of Charlotte and of three 5% debentures of the Royal Crown Bottling Company of Houston, Texas, in the amount of $1,000 each. She alleges that the assignments were obtained by fraud, duress and undue influence. It is alleged and admitted that Mr. Link was, and is, an experienced businessman and that she, while well educated, had no business experience.

Where a transferee of property stands in a confidential or fiduciary relationship to the transferor, it is the duty of the transferee to exercise the utmost good faith in the transaction and to disclose to the transferor all material facts relating thereto and his failure to do so constitutes fraud. Such a relationship "exists in all cases where there has been a special confidence reposed in one who in equity and good conscience is bound to act in good faith and with due regard to the interests of the one reposing confidence." Intent to deceive is not an essential element of such constructive fraud. Any transaction between persons so situated is "watched with extreme jealousy and solicitude; and if there is found the slightest trace of undue influence or unfair advantage, redress will be given to the injured party."

As Justice Sharp said in *Eubanks v. Eubanks,* "The relationship between husband and wife is the most confidential of all relationships, and transactions between them, to be valid, must be fair and reasonable."

In addition to the husband-wife relationship, Mr. Link was the president . . . of the corporation whose stock was being transferred and so had full information of its value. He knew that Mrs. Link had neither such information nor general understanding of corporate securities.

It has been said, "Duress exists where one, by the unlawful act of another, is induced to make a contract or perform or forego some act under circumstances which deprive him of the exercise of free will." Unquestionably, an essential element of duress is a wrongful act or threat.

Ordinarily, it is not wrongful and, therefore, not duress for one to procure a transfer of property by stating in the negotiations therefor that, unless the transfer is made, he intends to institute or press legal proceedings to enforce a right which he believes, in good faith, that he has.

The law with reference to duress has, however, undergone an evolution favorable to the victim of oppressive action or threats. The weight of modern authority supports the rule, which we here adopt, that the act done or threatened may be wrongful even though not unlawful, per se; and that the threat to institute legal proceedings, criminal or civil, which might be justifiable, per se, becomes wrongful, within the meaning of this rule, if made with the corrupt intent to coerce a transaction grossly unfair to the victim and not related to the subject of such proceedings.

The above cited section of the *Restatement* says: "[A]cts that involve abuse of legal remedies or that are wrongful in a moral sense, if made use of as a means of causing fear, vitiate a transaction induced by that fear, though they may not in themselves be legal wrongs." Professor Williston says, in section 1607 of his treatise,

> [M]eans in themselves lawful, may be used so oppressively as to constitute an abuse of legal remedies. . . . [I]t is not duress to threaten or make *good faith* use of legal processes available or the remedies prescribed under a contract. But where a threat of civil action or use of an available remedy is made *only* for the purposes of extortion duress may be found.

An announcement by a husband, to whom the wife has confessed her adultery, that he intends to separate from her and to institute legal proceedings to obtain the sole custody of their children would not, per se, constitute duress when the transaction induced by such statement of intent was the execution of a separation and custody agreement. The situation is completely different, however, when the threat to take the children from the wife is for the purpose of coercing her into transferring, without consideration, her individual property to the husband, the proposal being to leave the children in her custody if she make such transfer. Thus, in the present case, there was evidence to support a finding of duress, even if the jury had found that there was no concealment of facts justifying a finding of fraud.

In *Edwards v. Bowden* this Court quoted with approval the following statements from Pomeroy on *Equity Jurisprudence:*

> Where there is no coercion amounting to duress, but a transaction is the result of a *moral, social* or *domestic* force exerted upon a party, controlling the free action of his will and preventing any true consent, equity may relieve against the transaction on the ground of undue influence, even though there may be no invalidity at law. In the vast majority of instances, undue influence naturally has a field to work upon in the conditions or circumstances of the person influenced, which renders him peculiarly susceptible and yielding—his dependent or fiduciary relation towards the one exerting the influence, his mental or physical weakness, his pecuniary necessities, his ignorance, lack of advice, and the like.

Mistake

Nature of Mistake. Mistake applies only to those situations where the contracting party or parties believe that a present or past fact which is material to their transaction exists when it does not, or believe that it does not exist when it does. Mistake must not be confused with ignorance, inability, or poor judgment.

Likewise, if a person makes a contractual promise to perform a service or bring about a designated result but finds that he is mistaken as to his capacity and that he is unable to perform the service or accomplish the promised result, the court will not relieve him from his obligation on the ground of mistake. This is not mistake but only inability.

When a person has entered into a transaction which is less beneficial than expected or which proves detrimental, the courts will not relieve the party from his or her obligations on the ground of mistake. This may be a mistake of judgment, but the courts do not relieve from mistakes of judgment.

The courts will not grant relief merely on the ground that one or both of the parties deem the contract a bad deal or, in other words, made a mistake when they entered into the agreement; nor is the court very apt to grant relief when the mistake is due to the negligence of the party.

Two closely related yet distinguishable situations have been recognized as justifying relief on the ground of mistake. One is a mistake resulting from ambiguity in the negotiation of the transaction. The other is a mistake as to a material fact which induced the making of the contractual promise.

Mistake Resulting from Ambiguity.   In negotiating a contract, it may happen that the parties will use language which is susceptible equally to two interpretations. In such a situation, if one party honestly places one interpretation on the language and the other party, with equal honesty, places the other interpretation on it, the courts will generally hold that the parties did not, in fact, reach a mutual agreement, and as a result there was no contract.

Mistake as to Material Fact.   A mistake as to a material fact is fundamentally a matter of the mind. A person may believe that a fact exists which does not, or he or she may believe that a fact does not exist when it does. To justify the courts in granting relief, the fact must be material, and, as in fraud cases, it must be as to a present or past fact. A mistake as to the happening of future events is never ground for relief from the obligations of a contractual promise.

In deciding cases involving mistake of fact, the courts give great weight to the fact situation in each case. Although some general rules have been formulated and some attempt has been made to classify the cases, it is apparent that the justice of the individual case has played a more important role in deciding each case than has a formal rule.

Mutual Mistake.   Mutual mistake of material fact is ground for granting relief both in law and in equity. To come within this rule, both of the parties must have contracted in the mistaken belief that certain material facts existed. A court might grant relief if the mistake was as to future happenings; but as a general rule, it is presumed that the contracting parties assume the risks of future events.

Unilateral Mistake.   Whether or not the court will grant relief when only one of the contracting parties is in error as to the existence or nonexistence of a material fact depends on the surrounding circumstances. If one of the parties knows or should know that the other party is mistaken in his belief that certain facts exist and enters into the contract for the apparent purpose of taking advantage of the situation, the courts will grant relief. As a general rule, if the mistake is the result of the negligence of the party in error, the courts will not grant relief. However, even though the mistake is the result of slight negligence, if relief can be granted to the party in error without imposing material loss on the other party, the courts will grant relief, especially if the enforcement of the contract would impose unwarranted hardship on the party in error. As in fraud cases, if a party wishes to be relieved of the burden of a mistake, he or she must act as soon as he or she discovers the mistake. An unreasonable delay in asking relief will amount to a waiver of the right to rescind the contract.

Mistakes in Drafting Writing. Courts will grant relief in those cases in which a mistake has been made in drafting a written contract, deed, or other document. Suppose Arnold bargains to sell Barber a vacant lot which adjoins Arnold's home. The vacant lot is "Lot 3, block 1"; Arnold's house is on "Lot 2, block 1." In drawing the contract the stenographer strikes the wrong key, and the contract reads "Lot 2, block 1." Neither Arnold nor Barber notices this error when they read and sign the contract. A court will reform the contract. Usually, no relief will be granted if one of the parties is mistaken as to the meaning of the language used in a contract; however, if the language is ambiguous, or both parties are mistaken as to the meaning and it does not express the intentions of the parties, no contract is formed.

Mistakes of Law. Mistake as to one's legal rights under a contract is not generally accepted as sufficient justification for granting relief. If the mistake of law is coupled with mistake of fact, relief may be granted. Some courts have attempted to distinguish between mistake of law—error of judgment as to legal rights—and ignorance of law—lack of knowledge of the existence of the law. Such a distinction is difficult to apply and has no secure foundation, because one's error in judgment as to his or her legal rights usually is the result of some degree of ignorance of the law.

Summary

Under some circumstances the courts will relieve a party of a contractual obligation on the ground of mistake. Mistake as to the subject matter of a contract is generally accepted as ground for holding that no contract came into existence, since the parties, as the result of the mistake, never reached an agreement. Mistake of fact is fundamentally a matter of mind. Relief will be granted only if the facts and circumstances make the enforcement of the contract unjust and if the parties can be restored to their original positions without injury to innocent third persons.

As a general rule the courts will grant either the remedy of rescission or the remedy of reformation of a contract entered into under a mutual mistake of a material fact. If the mistake is unilateral, that is, only one of the parties is negotiating under a mistaken conception of fact, the courts will grant no relief. However, the courts grant relief if the circumstances are such that justice and fair dealing demand it.

If one party is mistaken as to the existence or nonexistence of a material fact and the other party knows or should know of the mistake, he or she will not be permitted to take advantage of it. If the mistaken party has proceeded with reasonable care and the mistake is the result of a clerical error and not an error in judgment, relief will be granted if necessary to avoid grave injustice.

Mistakes made in drafting a writing will be corrected through the remedy of reformation. Before a writing will be reformed to correct a claimed mistake, there must be clear and convincing evidence that it was a mistake in drafting the instrument and not merely a lack of understanding of the language used. The statement frequently made that the courts will not relieve from mistakes of law is the generally accepted rule. However, the rule is subject to some exceptions, and relief may be granted if necessary to avoid serious injustice.

Davey v. Brownson

478 P.2d 258 (Ct. App. Wash. 1970)

Action for rescission of a contract to purchase a motel brought by Davey (plaintiff) against Brownson (defendant). Brownson appealed from a trial court judgment granting the rescission. Affirmed.

In January 1968, Davey, looking for some type of family business, answered an ad in the *Spokesman-Review*. It turned out to be the Bluebird Motel in which Davey and her family had stayed on a number of occasions. Davey dealt with Robisch of Johns Realty. On July 15, 1968, Davey and Brownson executed a real estate contract and security agreement covering the motel and its contents for a purchase price of $125,000, of which $12,898.90 was paid. The balance was payable in installments commencing September 1, 1968. The contract gave Davey possession on July 15, 1968.

The contract contained the following provision:

The buyer realizes the condition of said Bluebird Motel and further agrees to upgrade the condition of the buildings within a reasonable time to the best of their ability. The buyer has examined the books and records of said motel and has made this purchase on the basis of her own investigation and not on the basis of any representations of the seller or any agent of the seller.

In September 1968, Davey and her husband were about to repair a loosened tile in a shower stall at the request of a motel guest. They discovered other tiles were also loose due to moisture, and when they tried to replace them found it impossible because of rotten wood. They notified Robisch and later sought legal advice. In October 1968, at Davey's request, William A. Senske, a pest control expert, examined the premises and discovered extensive termite infestation which would require substantial structural repair.

Davey made installment payments on the contract of $1,000 about August 1; $1,250 on September 1; and $1,250 on October 1. No payments were made after Senske's initial examination. On December 10, 1968, Davey brought suit for rescission.

GREEN, JUDGE.   It seems evident, as the trial court concluded, the parties both bargained for a motel in fair-to-good condition and structurally sound. The contemplated upgrading was in terms of cleaning, painting and minor repairs. It is clear the parties were mistaken when it was discovered the motel was extensively infested with termites. Senske, the expert, testified termite infestation would not be discovered by a layman on reasonable inspection because of its concealment. Since this condition went to the very heart of the subject matter of the transaction, we believe the trial court properly granted rescission.

In *Lindeberg v. Murray,* the court said:

We think it is elementary that, where there is a clear *bona fide* mistake regarding material facts, without culpable negligence on the part of the person complaining, the contract may be avoided, and equity will decree a rescission. We take it that the true test in cases involving mutual mistake of fact is whether the contract would have been entered into had there been no mistake.

Because neither Davey nor Brownson had knowledge of the termite condition when the sale agreements were executed, it is Brownson's position the doctrine of caveat emptor applies to bar rescission. Brownson relies upon *Hughes v. Stusser,* wherein the court said:

[C]aveat emptor, means nothing more than saying that the risks of latent defects in residences ought to fall on the purchaser rather than the vendor *where those defects are unknown to the vendor.*

In *Hughes,* a residence was sold for cash. Shortly thereafter, the purchaser discovered termites and brought an action for damages. The theory was fraudulent mispresentation and concealment. The trial court ruled on a challenge to the sufficiency of the evidence that fraud and concealment had not been proved by clear, cogent and convincing evidence and dismissed the complaint. This was affirmed on appeal. The language cited by Brownson from *Hughes* is dictum since the purchaser in *Hughes* failed in its burden to prove fraud and concealment.

The instant case is distinguishable from *Hughes* because here Davey seeks rescission based on mutual mistake. The elements of mutual mistake are different than the elements of fraud. As in *Hughes,* Davey in this case was unable to prove the elements of fraud; rescission for this reason was denied. However, the trial court properly concluded both Davey and Brownson dealt under a mutual mistake as to the actual condition of the property since both considered it to be in fair-to-good condition, free of a need for structural repair.

Brownson contends if the instant agreement can be rescinded, then any contract can be set aside under a set of circumstances rendering a building no longer attractive to a purchaser. To the contrary, we hold a purchaser is bound by facts a reasonable investigation would normally disclose. However, in the instant case it is clear a reasonable investigation by a layman would not have disclosed termite infestation, nor does the record show that a purchaser making a reasonable investigation should employ an expert to investigate the premises for termites. Consequently, the contention of Brownson is without merit.

Reed's Photo Mart v. Monarch Marking System Co.

475 S.W.2d 356 (Civ. App. Tex. 1971)

This was an action for the price of 4,000,000 small, gummed, price labels ordered by Reed's Photo Mart (defendant) from Monarch Marking System Company (plaintiff). Judgment for Monarch and Reed's appealed. Reversed.

Reed's Photo Mart is a small photography store, dealing in photographic supplies and camera equipment in El Paso, Texas. Monarch is a nationwide manufacturer and supplier of pricing and product identification labels.

Monarch received a purchase order from Reed on February 26, 1968. The order listed a request for five different types of labels, four of the five ordered categories specifying "2M" while the fifth specified "4MM," and it is this fifth item which is the subject of this suit. The record reflects a capital "M" is the Roman numeral designation for 1,000, and is so used and understood in the industry. Thus, the purchase order was for four (4) types of labels, 2,000 of each type, while the fifth (5) category was for 4,000 by Reed's intentions or 4,000,000 as understood by Monarch. There is no question but that Reed intended to order 4,000 labels, and that his use of "MM" was a mistake.

Monarch's salesman transferred the information from the purchase order to a company order form and forwarded it to his company's California factory. In doing that, he changed the "4MM" designation to "4,000M," and he changed the requested method of shipment from "Parcel Post" to "best way," and the instructions to ship "at once" to "as soon as possible."

On April 10, 1968, a truck arrived at Reed's store with seven large packages from Monarch. Reed refused to accept delivery, and immediately notified Monarch by telephone that "a terrible mistake had been made." The purchase price of 4,000 labels was some $13, while the price of 4,000,000 was $2,680.

PRESLAR, JUSTICE.   Most of the Texas cases allowing relief for a unilateral mistake involve bids. *Taylor, etc. v. Arlington Ind. School District* is such a case, and there the conditions under which equitable relief will be granted against a unilateral mistake were listed as:

(1) The mistake is of so great a consequence that to enforce the contract as made would be unconscionable;

(2) The mistake relates to a material feature of the contract;

(3) The mistake must have been made regardless of the exercise of ordinary care; and,

(4) The parties can be placed in status quo in the equity sense, i.e., rescission must not result in prejudice to the other party except for the loss of his bargain.

The Court also said: "There may be other circumstances which will govern or influence the extension of relief, such as the acts and extent of knowledge of the parties."

It is well settled that a party need not be actually aware of a certain fact, but that knowledge may be imputed or constructive. *Williston on Contracts,* 3rd Ed., Sec. 94, p. 343, states that: "And the same principle is applicable in any case where the offeree should know that the terms of the offer are unintended or misunderstood by the offeror. The offeree will not be permitted to snap up an offer that is too good to be true."

While the bid cases are distinguishable in that the parties are able to be placed in the status quo, we feel the principle of such applies in the present case. . . .

Numerous circumstances are woven throughout the case at bar that point to the conclusion that at the very least, Reed's order was amiss, and at the most, that a grievous error had been made. . . .

Reed's order specified on its face "—we reserve the right to refuse merchandise not in strict accordance with this order." Monarch's salesman testified that he knew that it would be uneconomical for a customer if his company were to break down a 622 pound shipment into 20 pound cartons and ship it by parcel post, and that as a practical matter, his company did not do it. He was well aware of the discrepancy in the quantity and the parcel post shipping instructions for he testified: "I felt I was acting in their best interests."

He testified that he had never received an order as large as four million labels of one catalogue number, and that the largest order he had ever received before February 22, 1968, was one for a million labels, these not to be shipped at one time but in intervals of several months. . . . Monarch has a policy of checking orders received from their salesmen by going into the records of what a customer has ordered in the past if "there is some discrepancy," and the original of Reed's order went to the factory with the order. Mr. Reed testified that he had been doing business with Monarch as an individual since "in the 50s" and as a Corporation since 1961, and that he had never ordered over 4,000 labels at any one time of any one item. Neither he, nor his employees, had any knowledge of "MM" meaning one million, but used it in the business as meaning millimeter to designate the size of photo lens. The explanation of the error was that the order was partially made up, there were interruptions to wait on customers in the photo shop, and later in the day, the "4MM" item was added to the order.

As the Court stated in *Cox v. Hall:* "Courts of equity are not bound by cast-iron rules, but are governed by rules which are flexible and adapt themselves to particular exigencies, so that relief will be granted when, in view of all the circumstances, to deny it would permit one party to suffer a gross wrong at the hands of the other."

Problem Cases

1. Kennedy contracted to sell his business for 4,000 shares of Flo-Tronics stock having a market value of $8.50 per share. Under the contract, Kennedy was obliged to retire the $17,500 in debts he then owed. Kennedy claimed that he was induced to enter the contract by the assurance of Flo-Tronics that their stock would rise to $25 a share within a year. The stock increased to $17 within 3 months, but under SEC regulation Kennedy was required to hold the stock for 6 months. The stock subsequently dropped to $3 a share causing severe financial problems for Kennedy. Is he entitled to rescission on the grounds of misrepresentation?

2. Welsh was engaged in the business of selling automobile tires and accessories at retail. In 1970, he entered into a written contract with Kelly-Springfield Tire Company whereby Welsh agreed to purchase all his tires, tubes, and other automobile accessories from Tire Company. This contract contained a provision permitting Welsh, in the event of the

termination of the contract, to return for credit at invoice price all goods purchased from Tire Company. Similar contracts were executed by the parties in subsequent years.

On January 2, 1973, Welsh executed a contract with Tire Company, but the contract did not include the clause providing for the return of goods in the event of termination. The contract was terminated, and Tire Company refused to accept returned goods. Tire Company brought suit to recover an unpaid balance for goods sold to Welsh. Welsh claimed credit for goods on hand, but Tire Company refused to accept them. No specific representations were made. Welsh did not read the contract, and Tire Company did not point out to him the change in the contract. Is Welsh entitled to credit for goods on hand?

3. Stone contracted to build a home for Batey. During the construction Batey closely supervised the work, although there were periods of up to two or three weeks at a time when he was not present. After completion of the home and payment under the contract, Batey discovered several defects and sued Stone for fraud. Evidence at the trial revealed that Stone, the contractor, was aware of defective waterproofing, which he had concealed with dirt and paneling; that the driveway had less than the stipulated thickness and base in some areas; that some beams had sagged because of inadequate size; that the paint and other finishes were improperly and inadequately applied; that portions of the house had sunk as much as 3 inches, and had cracked and malfunctioned due to fill dirt underneath; and that these defects were not apparent until after Batey had occupied the house. In his defense Stone alleged that his duties were defined solely by the contract, that he had fulfilled them as such, and that no fraud had been perpetrated. Is this a valid defense as Batey's allegation of fraud?

4. Franklin, an oil supply company, entered into an agreement with Servicios, a Venezuela corporation, to purchase all of the capital stock of Peticon, another Venezuela corporation. It was agreed that Franklin would assume control on May 1, 1971, and that the purchase price of the stock would be the book value of the stock as of April 30, 1971. The parties agreed to employ Peat, Marwick, Mitchell and Co. (P.M.M.), Servicio's auditors, to perform the audit. On May 1, Franklin paid $50,000 in cash and gave Peticon guaranteed notes for $1,000,000—a total book value of $1,050,000, as reported by P.M.M. In January 1972, Franklin dishonored the first note and in July filed suit to rescind the Peticon transaction, asserting overvaluation of inventory. Franklin also alleged that P.M.M. did not perform an independent audit because the audit was in charge of one Southerland, who was both an employee of P.M.M. and an alternate director of Servicios and who had formerly been a director of Peticon. Because of this and the failure of P.M.M. to formally disclose these facts, P.M.M. was charged with having acted in violation of a fiduciary relationship and in violation of an implied duty of independence. Should the transaction be set aside on the ground of constructive fraud?

5. Hannes had his property surveyed and learned that the driveway encroached on a neighbor's property. When he decided to sell the house he did not disclose the encroachment to the realtor. Franchey became interested in the property and visited several times, but Hannes disclaimed knowledge of the boundary markers and, in fact, at one meeting away from the site misrepresented the boundaries. Franchey bought the property and sued for damages upon learning about the encroachment. Did Hannes have a duty to inform Franchey of the encroachment?

6. Sirkle was engaged in the wholesale tobacco business. He was placing the tobacco tax stamps on the packages of tobacco by hand when Pitney, who sold tobacco stamping machines, told Sirkle that one of his tax-stamping machines would be a great timesaver. He said that it could be operated by one man and would stamp 30,000 packages of tobacco

an hour. In reliance on these statements, Sirkle purchased a machine, but when he set it up and started operations, he found that it took two men to operate it and that, during a period of thirty days, he was able to stamp only 27,000 packages of cigarettes. Pitney admitted that the machine showed best results when operated by two men and that it would not stamp 30,000 packages of tobacco per hour. Sirkle rescinded the contract. Pitney contends that his statements were sales talk and that Sirkle is bound by the contract. Does Sirkle have a right to rescind the contract?

7. Ware owned three adjoining tracts of land lying within or near the limits of the city of Tulsa. The larger tract, consisting of about eight acres, was formerly occupied and utilized by a brick and tile manufacturing company. On the north part of this tract was a pit from which clay and shale had been removed for use in making brick. The two smaller adjoining tracts, totaling approximately one-half acre, lay in the southeast corner of the tract.

    The description of the eight-acre tract was by metes and bounds and was quite intricate and lengthy, requiring more than a page and a half of typing. The description of the two smaller tracts was by section subdivision and was relatively short.

    The city of Tulsa negotiated for purchase of the entire property. The negotiations culminated in a lease of the eight-acre tract with an option to purchase it for $17,500. Appraisers had found the market value of the three tracts to be $19,000. City of Tulsa exercised its option to buy the eight-acre tract, and it was deeded to the city on September 30, 1954.

    On February 4, 1955, the city of Tulsa brought suit, alleging that in its negotiations it was negotiating for all three tracts and that through mutual mistake of the parties and through omission of the scrivener only the eight-acre tract was deeded to the city. The city asked that the deed be reformed to include all three tracts. Should the deed be reformed as requested by the city of Tulsa?

8. Anderson advertised a dredge specially designed and built for cutting narrow trenches underwater through submerged stumps, rocks, and so forth in a magazine. O'Meara wanted a dredge capable of digging wide channels for access to offshore well sites. He saw the advertisement and sent a representative, who was an expert on engines but knew nothing of dredges, to examine it. After checking the dredge engines and talking by telephone with O'Meara, the representative signed an agreement on behalf of O'Meara to buy the dredge. Upon delivery it soon became obvious that it would require serious modification for O'Meara's need. After Anderson refused to contribute toward the modifications, O'Meara sued for rescission alleging mutual mistake. Is rescission appropriate?

9. Anna Voboril's husband owed International Harvester Company for machinery purchased. The account was past due, and an agent of the company told Anna that if she did not give her notes, payable to the company for the amount of her husband's debt, the company would have her husband arrested and put in jail. Anna was uneducated, a foreigner, and knew nothing about court procedure. She did not know that her husband could not be imprisoned for debt. Anna executed the notes and, on the due date, refused to pay them. When sued on the notes, she set up duress as a defense. Is the defense good?

10. Coal Co. leased land from Johnson for the purpose of mining coal. They agreed to pay Johnson rent plus royalties on the mined coal. Coal became hopelessly in debt, owing Johnson $75,000 and the SBA $250,000 among others. Vickers, a stockholder in Coal, persuaded Johnson to agree to lease the same properties to a new company he planned to form—Vickers agreeing to make Johnson "whole" as to Coal's debts. Johnson had informed Vickers that as landlords they held a lien on Coal's $500,000 mining equipment, and that under local law this took precedence over the SBA claim. It later developed that Johnson's

claim on the equipment was subordinate to the SBA lien, making it valueless. Vickers did not carry out his agreement to pay Johnson for Coal's debts. However, the trial judge dismissed Johnson's subsequent breach of contract suit on the grounds that there was a mutual mistake of law and fact as to Johnson's lien which excused Vickers from performing. Should the dismissal be upheld on appeal?

11. Grant purchased a newly constructed apartment house from Morris, the builder, for $525,000. After owning the apartment house for two years, Grant asked the court to rescind the contract on the grounds of mutual mistake. The defects which were the basis for the claim of mutual mistake could be remedied for $5,000. Should the court rescind the contract?

12. Curran submitted a bid of $102,171.98 on a project to add an addition to a campus building at Plymouth State Teachers College. The bid had been computed on a hand operated, ten-key adding machine by an experienced employee. When the bids were opened on July 23, 1964, Curran's bid was over $55,000 under the next lowest bid. Realizing the possibility that a mistake had been made, Curran totaled the bids again that evening and discovered that the adding machine used would not add over $99,999.99 and thus omitted $100,000.00 in the cost estimates. On July 24, Curran notified the state of error and asked that his bid be canceled. Curran was then informed that he would be held to his bid. Curran sued to have the contract set aside. Can Curran win?

chapter 9

Consideration

History and Function of Consideration

Historical Development. During the early period of the development of the law of contracts in England, only those promises which were in writing and sealed were enforced. As trade expanded and the law merchant began to be absorbed into the common law of England, the courts were frequently called upon to determine the rights of the parties to a simple contract, and the law of covenants (promises under seal) was inadequate.

At the beginning of the 18th century several tests for the determination of the enforceability of simple promises were tried. Out of this trial and error approach came one basic test which has proven to be satisfactory in most situations. It was borrowed from the law merchant and was termed the bargain theory of consideration. Today the general rule is that a promise is not enforceable by court action unless it is supported by consideration; and the general test for consideration applied by the courts is whether or not detriment to the promisee or benefit to the promisor has been bargained for and given in exchange for the promise.

Under some special circumstances, however, promises are enforced which are not supported by consideration as it is defined above. Two exceptions which are generally recognized are: (1) a situation in which the promisee has justifiably relied on the promise to his injury, termed injurious reliance or promissory estoppel, and (2) a situation in which the right to enforce the promise by court action is barred by operation of law and the obligor makes a promise which removes the bar to the enforcement of the obligation. Under the Code (2–209) no consideration is required for an agreement to modify a contract involving the sale of goods.

Detriment or Benefit

Analysis of Test.   The test mentioned heretofore, "detriment to the promisee or benefit to the promisor," is an important guide in determining the presence or absence of consideration. But this test in no way aids us in determining what the nature of the detriment or of the benefit must be in order to satisfy the requirements for consideration. Obviously, not all those things and experiences which might be classed as detriment or benefit are included.

Legal Detriment.   Legal detriment is the surrendering of a legal right or the assuming of a legal burden. In our society each individual has the right to do or not to do many things. When a person surrenders one of these rights or obligates himself or herself to do something which he or she has a legal right not to do, he has suffered a legal detriment. In the transaction of business the parties to a deal are exchanging legal rights. In the ordinary business contract each party suffers a legal detriment, and each party enjoys a legal benefit. For example, suppose a customer buys a radio from a merchant for $50. The customer suffers a legal detriment—surrenders his right to keep the $50. The merchant also suffers a legal detriment—he surrenders his right to keep the radio. Each gains a benefit—the customer gains the right to the radio, and the merchant gains the right to the $50.

Legal Benefit.   In the majority of situations, if the promisee has suffered a legal detriment, the promisor has enjoyed a corresponding legal benefit. Detriment to the promisee, without a corresponding benefit to the promisor, has been held by the courts to be sufficient as consideration.

For example, Able owes Baker $500 and Baker threatens a suit to collect the debt. Carl, a friend of Able, offers to pay Able's debt within 30 days if Baker will refrain from bringing suit. If Baker accepts Carl's offer, Baker is suffering a legal detriment which is consideration for Carl's promise to pay the debt. Observe that Carl, the promisee of Baker's promise to refrain from suit, receives no benefit from the performance of Baker's promise. Thus consideration need not involve an exchange of things having economic value, and need not confer a benefit on the promisee. A simple and reasonable test of consideration sufficient to support a promise is "detriment to the promisee, bargained for and given in exchange for a promise."

Summary

Consideration under the bargain theory may be defined as "detriment to the promisee or benefit to the promisor, bargained for and given in exchange for a promise." Detriment, as used in this definition, is the surrendering of a legal right or the assumption of a legal obligation. As a general rule, when the promisee has suffered a detriment, the promisor has enjoyed a corresponding benefit. Detriment to the promisee, standing alone, has been held to be sufficient consideration.

Investment Properties of Asheville, Inc. v. Norburn

188 S.E.2d 342 (Sup. Ct. N.C. 1972)

Action by Investment Properties of Asheville, Inc. (plaintiff) against Norburn (defendant) to recover on a written promise of guaranty made by the latter. Investment appealed from a judgment for Norburn. Reversed and remanded.

On May 10, 1965, Allen, sister of Norburn, leased a tract of land to Investment. The lease provided that the lessee should have complete control in grading, reshaping, and developing the land, as well as full responsibility for listing and paying taxes. Investment attempted to obtain financing for the construction of a motel on this property, but found that the lease was not in the proper form to permit such financing. On June 17, 1965, Investment met with Norburn, who was acting as agent for his sister, and informed Norburn that the grading of the property had reached such a point that the machinery might have to be removed if a revised and satisfactory lease could not be obtained. To avert this circumstance Norburn signed the following paper:

This is to certify that I will stand personally liable for the Conduit grading and necessary expenses (at actual cost) for the land preparation of the Action property now owned by my sister, in case the lease is not continued after June 1, 1966.

Charles S. Norburn

Investment continued work on the tract spending a total of $19,456.88 on the grading work. Investment was unable to obtain a new lease and in October 1967 the Allen tract was leased to another development company. Investment sued Norburn on his guaranty, and the trial court jury found that Norburn had received no consideration for his promise to pay.

MOORE, JUSTICE. A guaranty of payment is an absolute promise by the guarantor to pay a debt at maturity if it is not paid by the principal debtor. This obligation is separate and independent of the obligation of the principal debtor, and the creditor's cause of action against the guarantor ripens immediately upon the failure of the principal debtor to pay the debt at maturity. The language in the guaranty signed by defendant Norburn created an unconditional promise to pay in cash for the actual cost of the land preparation of Allen's property in case the lease (of 10 May 1965) was not continued after 1 June 1966. The determinative issue then is: Did defendant Norburn receive valuable consideration from Investment for the execution and delivery of this guaranty agreement?

It is well-settled law in this State that in order for a contract to be enforceable it must be supported by consideration. A mere promise, without more, is unenforceable. . . . As a general rule, consideration consists of some benefit or advantage to the promisor or some loss or detriment to the promisee. However, as stated by Chief Justice Stacy in *Stonestreet v. Southern Oil Co.:* "It has been held that "there is a consideration if the promisee, in return for the promise, does anything legal which he is not bound to do, or refrains from doing anything which he has a right to do, whether there is any actual loss or detriment to him or actual benefit to the promisor or not."

It is not necessary that the promisor receive consideration or something of value himself in order to provide the legal consideration sufficient to support a contract.

Forbearance to exercise legal rights is sufficient consideration for a promise given to secure such forbearance even though the forbearance is for a third person rather than that of the promisor. In a guaranty contract, a consideration moving directly to the guarantor is not essential. The promise is enforceable if a benefit to the principal debtor is shown or if detriment or inconvenience to the promisee is disclosed.

The court in the charge to the jury in this case correctly stated: "There must be a sufficient consideration in order to support a contract or legal agreement. Any benefit, right or interest accruing to the one who makes the promise or guaranty, or any forbearance, detriment or loss suffered or undertaken by one to whom the promise for guaranty is made is a sufficient consideration to support such guaranty or contract." Thereafter, the court charged the jury: "I charge you that if the plaintiffs have satisfied you by the greater weight of the evidence that the defendant Norburn received a valuable consideration for the execution and delivery of the guaranty it will be your duty to answer the issue 'Yes.' If the plaintiffs have failed to so satisfy you it would be your duty to answer the issue 'No.' " Under this charge the jury might well have understood that they were required to find that defendant Norburn himself received a valuable consideration to support his guaranty. In view of the facts in this case, this was too restrictive.

The jury should also have been instructed that if, by reason of the guaranty signed by defendant Norburn, Allen received benefits from Investment by their furnishing additional work on her property, including fertilizing, seeding, and additional leveling, or if Investment, at the request of plaintiffs, did additional work upon the Allen property and thereby incurred added expense by reason of this guaranty, either would be sufficient legal consideration to support such guaranty.

Preexisting Obligation

Nature of Preexisting Obligation. A preexisting obligation, as used in the law of consideration, is an obligation which the promisor already owes at the time he makes a promise to assume such obligation. When a party promises to do or does that which he is already legally obligated to do, or promises to refrain or does refrain from doing that which he has no right to do, he is suffering no detriment, and his promise or act is not sufficient consideration to support a promise.

Although the question of a preexisting obligation may arise in an infinite variety of situations, such obligations fall roughly into four general groups: (1) acts which are criminal or tortious, (2) acts which the holder of an office is under a duty to perform, (3) acts which the promisee is under a contractual duty to the promisor to perform, and (4) acts which the promisee has already obligated himself by contract to perform, but the performance of which, owing to unforeseen and unforeseeable factors, is more burdensome than either of the contracting parties contemplated.

Criminal and Tortious Acts. Since each individual in our society is under a duty to refrain from the commission of a crime or tort, a promise to refrain or a refraining from the commission of such an act cannot be sufficient consideration to support a promise. The commission of a criminal or tortious act or the promise to commit such an act cannot, for obvious social reasons, be considered sufficient consideration to support a promise. A contract to commit a crime or tort is void.

Holder of an Office.   The cases in which the question of whether or not the performance of an official duty is sufficient consideration to support a promise have involved mostly holders of public office, although there have been cases which involved corporate officers, trustees, and others who were acting in an official capacity.

Public Officers.   A person, by accepting a public office, obligates himself to perform those official acts which are incidental to the office. The performance of an act which the holder of a public office is obligated to perform is universally held not to be legal detriment and not sufficient consideration to support a promise. This position is supported by both logic and public policy. If the officeholder does only that which he is duty bound to do, he has given nothing in payment for a promise to compensate him—he has suffered no legal detriment in exchange for the promise. If holders of public office were permitted to accept pay from individuals for performing their official duties, there would be an incentive on the part of the officeholders to delay performance until they had received additional compensation or to render services to those who paid the most for the services.

If the holder of a public office does acts which are similar to, but not a part of, his or her official duties, the performance of the act will be legal detriment and will be sufficient consideration to support a promise. For example, suppose First Bank offers a reward for the arrest of a bank robber, and the sheriff of the county apprehends and arrests the robber in the regular course of the performance of his duties as sheriff. The sheriff has suffered no legal detriment in making the arrest and has not given sufficient consideration to support the bank's promise to pay the reward. But suppose the sheriff, while on vacation in a state other than that in which he holds office, should apprehend and cause the arrest of a criminal for whose apprehension a reward had been offered, the sheriff, in such a case, would be entitled to the reward.

Contractual Obligations.   If a person is under a legal duty, created by contract, to perform an act, and the person to whom the duty is owed promises to pay additional compensation for the performance of that act, such performance is not a legal detriment to the person obligated to perform, since he or she already owes a duty to do so. The doing of that which a person is already legally bound to do is not sufficient consideration to support a promise. If such were recognized as sufficient consideration, fraudulent practices would be encouraged, in that if one of the parties to a contract were in a position where he or she would suffer serious injury in case performance was not completed, the other party could take advantage of the situation and force payment of additional compensation by refusing to perform.

Exceptions.   There are exceptional circumstances, however, under which the courts have enforced such promises. Suppose, for example, the parties enter into a contract on the assumption that certain conditions exist but, after performance is started, encounter unforeseen and unforeseeable difficulties. If a new promise is made to pay additional compensation for the performance of the contract, the courts will, as a general rule, enforce the new promise.

New Contract.   The parties to a contract may, by mutual agreement, terminate a contract and enter into a new one whereby the obligations of one party are the same as under the terminated contract but the obligations of the other are greater. In such a situation the courts require clear and convincing evidence that the old contract was terminated by mutual agreement of the parties and that the entire transaction was free from fraud, duress, or undue influence.

Summary

The doing of an act which a person is already under a legal obligation to do is not sufficient consideration to support a promise. On the grounds of logic and public policy the courts have held that the performance of an act which is a part of the official duties of the holder of a public office is not sufficient consideration to support a promise. Likewise, the performance of contractual obligations by one of the parties to a contract is not sufficient consideration to support a promise on the part of the other party to pay additional compensation. The courts have recognized exceptions to this latter statement. If unforeseen and unforeseeable conditions are encountered in the performance of a contract and the promisor promises to pay additional compensation to offset the additional burden of performance resulting from such conditions, the courts will enforce the promise if justice and fair dealing demand that it be enforced. The parties may terminate a contract by mutual agreement and thereafter enter into a new contract covering the same subject matter as that covered by the terminated contract.

Robert Chuckrow Construction Co. v. Gough

159 S.E.2d 469 (Ct. App. Ga. 1968)

This was an action by Ralph Gough (plaintiff) against Robert Chuckrow Construction Company (defendant) to collect for work done on trusses. Judgment for Gough and Construction Company appealed. Reversed.

Gough was a subcontractor of Construction Co. on a construction job known as the Kinney Shoe Store, having agreed with Construction Co. in a written contract dated April 30, 1965, to perform carpentry work required by the drawings and specification for that building. By the express provisions of the written contract, Gough undertook to "provide all labor and materials, scaffolding, tools, equipment and all other things necessary for the prosecution and completion of the work in strict accordance with the drawings and specification and job control chart." Gough's employees had erected approximately 38 trusses on May 15, 1965, when 32 of them fell off the building. On the following Monday, Gough was told by Construction Co. representative to remove the fallen trusses from the building, disassemble, inspect, rebuild, and re-erect them and to submit an additional bill for this work. Gough proceeded to do so. He also erected the balance of the trusses required to complete the roof truss structure and completed the carpentry work on the project. He was paid by Construction Co. all sums owed under the written contract but given nothing for the costs incurred by him in connection with the fallen trusses.

QUILLIAN, JUDGE.   The pivotal question on which the decision of the present case turns is whether the evidence adduced upon the trial showed the parol contract sued upon to be an enforceable agreement. Assent of the parties to the terms of the contract and a consideration for the performance of the same are essential requisites to its validity. Where either of these elements is lacking the contract is not binding or enforceable.

Gough, under the terms of the parol agreement, assumed no obligation or duty that he was not bound to perform under the written contract he had previously entered into with the defendant. Under both the written contract and the oral agreement Gough assumed the obligation to erect and properly place the same number of trusses to support the decking for the roof of the building.

The Supreme Court held in *Johnson v. Hinson*, "An agreement on the part of one to do what he is already legally bound to do is not a sufficient consideration for the promise of another."

It should be noted that the cause of the trusses' falling was unexplained and there was no evidence that their collapse was due to Construction Co.'s fault or any deficiency in the specifications as to how the trusses were to be erected.

Debt, Compromise, and Composition

Liquidated Debt.   The courts have consistently held that a promise to discharge a liquidated debt on payment of part of the debt at the place where the debt is payable and at or after the time the debt is due is not enforceable because of lack of consideration. This rule is the result of following to its logical conclusion the rule that the performance of an act which one is already bound to perform is not sufficient consideration to support a promise. The courts have expressed dissatisfaction with the rule on the ground that it is contrary to general business practices; yet the rule is so firmly established that the courts hesitate to overrule it.

This rule applies only if all the following requirements are satisfied:

1. The debt must be liquidated; that is, the parties must be in complete agreement as to the amount. For example, suppose you receive a bill for $50 from your doctor for services she has rendered you while you were ill. You feel that the doctor has charged too much and tell her so. After some time, you and the doctor agree on $40 as the amount of the bill. The debt, which up to the time of the agreement was unliquidated, now becomes liquidated—the amount is certain and undisputed.

2. Payment must be made at or after the due date. If the debtor pays any part of the debt before the due date in exchange for the creditor's promise to accept a lesser sum in full payment, the debtor has done something he or she is not legally obligated to do—pay before due date—and this is sufficient consideration to support the promise of the creditor to accept a lesser sum.[1]

3. Payment must be made at the place where the debt is payable. Payment at any other place, if made in exchange for a promise by the creditor to accept a lesser sum, is sufficient to support such promise.

4. Payment must be made in the same medium of exchange as that provided for in the contract. Payment in any other medium, if done in exchange for a promise to accept such payment in discharge of the debt, is sufficient consideration to support such promise.

In those cases in which a creditor has promised (without new consideration) to extend the due date of an obligation, the courts have held that since the debtor (promisee) has suffered no detriment, the promise is unenforceable for lack of consideration. The rule has been applied only to contracts requiring the payment of money or the delivery of fungible goods—goods of which any unit is from its nature or by mercantile usage treated as the equivalent of any other unit.

A creditor may accept a lesser sum and make a gift of the unpaid balance. If the creditor does make a bona fide gift of the balance, he or she cannot at a later date repudiate the gift and recover the balance. To have a bona fide gift of property, there must be a delivery. Since a debt is intangible property, no physical delivery can be made, and some of the earlier decisions held that it was impossible to make a gift of a debt. However, the courts of today hold that a certificate of gift delivered to the debtor, or to someone representing the

---

[1] In some states payment must have been requested by the creditor.

debtor, is sufficient delivery. The giving of a receipt marked "payment in full" is not a certificate of gift.

Compromise (Accord and Satisfaction).   A compromise is the settlement of a disputed claim by the mutual agreement of the parties. In legal terminology an agreement to settle a disputed claim is an "accord," and the fulfillment of the agreement is a "satisfaction." A compromise is referred to as an "accord and satisfaction."

If there is an honest dispute as to the amount of a debt or as to the existence of a debt, the debt is unliquidated. In such a case the parties have a the right to submit the dispute to the courts for adjudication. But if the parties arrive at a mutual agreement of settlement without court action, each has suffered a legal detriment, since each has surrendered his or her right to have the claim submitted to the courts for adjudication, and the surrender of this right is legal detriment and is sufficient consideration to support the mutual promises to pay and accept the agreed sum in full satisfaction of the disputed claim. Therefore a promise to pay an agreed sum in discharge of an unliquidated debt is supported by consideration and is enforceable by court action.

If a person has two claims against another, one admitted and the other disputed, payment of the admitted claim is not sufficient consideration to support a promise to discharge the disputed claim. In such a situation the debtor, in paying the admitted claim, has done nothing which he or she is not already obligated to do.

Composition.   A composition is an agreement between a debtor and two or more of his or her creditors whereby the debtor agrees to pay each creditor who is a party to the agreement a pro rata portion of his claim, and the creditors agree to accept the amount in full satisfaction of their claims. Under such an agreement the debtor has discharged liquidated claims by the payment of a lesser sum at or after the due date. Some courts have held that the consideration to support the agreement is found in the mutual promises of the several creditors to accept the lesser sum. Under this reasoning the legal detriment is found in the surrendering of a portion of a creditor's claim, and this is accepted as consideration to support the promises of the other creditors who are parties to the agreement to surrender a like portion of their claims. Other courts have enforced composition agreements as exceptions to the general rule based on a public policy of encouraging such out of court settlements. A composition agreement which is free from misrepresentation and fraud will be enforced by court action.

Summary

A promise to discharge a liquidated debt on the payment of a lesser sum on the due date and at the place where the debt is payable is not supported by sufficient consideration and, consequently, is not enforceable by court action. An agreement to settle a disputed claim—an unliquidated debt—is supported by consideration and therefore is enforceable by court action. A composition agreement between a debtor and two or more of his or her creditors, if free of misrepresentation, fraud, duress, or undue influence, is enforceable by court action.

Studstill v. American Oil Co.

191 S.E.2d 538 (Ct. App. Ga. 1972)

Action by Studstill (plaintiff) against American Oil (defendant) for damages Studstill suffered when his automobile collided with a truck driven by an agent of American. American set up accord and satisfaction as a defense and Studstill appealed from an adverse judgment. Reversed.

Studstill was injured in an automobile collision due to the negligence of the operator of an American Oil Company truck. American promptly paid for Studstill's automobile and has never claimed that this was more than a payment or partial settlement relating to property damage only. Thereafter, on April 27, 1970, it mailed a $10,000 check to Studstill with a letter stating that this was "in settlement of the above claim for injury and damage" and that "we are willing to do this without obligation on your part to sign releases or agreements." The instrument itself had five possible check boxes for purpose of payment; "Ind. Dam." was checked; "Med." and "Final" were not. It was never cashed. According to Studstill, he attempted during the next six weeks to contact American's agent with whom he had been dealing to ascertain whether the check was intended to be a part payment or a full settlement, but was unable to make contact and eventually employed counsel.

Studstill's attorney wrote the company on June 18, 1970, asking for clarification, stating that $10,000 would not constitute an equitable settlement and that Studstill was holding the draft pending clarification of the company's position. On August 4 he wrote again, stating that he had been promised written confirmation of a telephone statement by the agent that the check might be cashed as part payment of the claim. On August 25, the agent replied, apologized for the delay, and stated that the $10,000 must be considered a final settlement. This was followed on October 12, 1970 by a demand that Studstill either accept the offer and negotiate the check or else return it. On November 9 Studstill's attorney replied advising that Studstill definitely would not settle for $10,000 but offered to continue discussions. He did not return the draft. Studstill filed suit April 22, 1971. On May 5 and 13 American requested that the check be returned and Studstill's counsel, to whom Studstill had turned over the instrument, refused to surrender it. He did, however, return it by mail on July 29 after American had filed a motion for summary judgment based on accord and satisfaction. American promptly returned it to Studstill's attorney on August 3; Studstill's attorney returned it to American on August 11; and American then stated he was holding it pursuant to Studstill's order.

DEEN, JUDGE.   While it is clear that an executed accord and satisfaction, by accepting money or cashing a check given in full settlement for less than the amount of the demand, is in bar of an action to collect any excess and while retaining a check for an unreasonable length of time may lead to the legal conclusion that it has in fact been accepted as payment, nevertheless, "an agreement by a creditor to receive less than the amount of his debt cannot be pleaded as an accord and satisfaction, unless it be actually executed by the payment of the money, . . . or some other new consideration."

It follows that if it is intended to accept a check as payment of a demand, that check should be promptly presented for payment, usually within a 30-day period. Where, in the absence of circumstances suggesting a contrary state of facts, the check, although not cashed, is kept for a period greatly in excess of this time, such retention may of itself cause the debtor to rely on the theory that his offer (accord) has been accepted (satisfaction), in which case the creditor no longer has a right of action for the excess. That, however, is not the situation here. It was perfectly clear to both parties as long as six months after the initial action of the company in forwarding the check that the plaintiff had not and would not accept it if it was to be construed as an accord and satisfaction. This is shown by the letter of October 12 which commences: "I must assume that your client, Mr. Jack Studstill, Jr., has chosen not to accept our offer, as Mr. Studstill had not negotiated our draft." By that time the check was already stale, since a bank is under no obligation to a customer to pay a check, other than a certified check, which is presented more than six months after its date.

. . . The rule is stated in *Pan-American Life Ins. Co. v. Carter* that it matters not whether the tender be of cash or a check; *if the check is accepted in full settlement* an accord and satisfaction will result. Here the evidence is clear that the plaintiff never at any time considered accepting $10,000 in full settlement of his individual damage.

Baggett v. Chavous holds that retention of a check for an unreasonable time without cashing *and without indicating a refusal to accept it as an accord and satisfaction* will constitute an acceptance.

Mere retention of a stale check, where the evidence demands a finding that there was knowledge on the part of the debtor at the time that the creditor refused to accept it in full satisfaction of the unliquidated liability, and where the check was never cashed and was, at the time of the summary judgment order, in the hands of the maker, will not support a judgment of accord and satisfaction.

Baillie Lumber Co. v. Kincaid Carolina Corp.

167 S.E.2d 85 (Ct. App. N.C. 1969)

Baillie Lumber Company sued Kincaid Carolina Corporation for the unpaid balance on an account. Kincaid appealed from an adverse judgment. Affirmed.

In April 1967, Kincaid ordered cherry lumber from Baillie and was billed by Baillie in the amount of $2,447.61. Five months later Kincaid's attorneys wrote to Baillie and other creditors of Kincaid, informing them that Kincaid was insolvent and was offering a 35% compromise settlement to its creditors.

On February 27, 1968, Kincaid forwarded its check number 4985 in the amount of $428.33 to Baillie with the words "first installment of agreed settlement" on the face of the check, which was endorsed by Baillie "with reservation of all our rights."

On April 2, 1968, Kincaid forwarded its check number 5118 in the amount of $428.33 to Baillie with the words "final installment of agreed settlement" on the face of the check, which was endorsed by Baillie "with reservation of all our rights."

On May 2, 1968, Baillie entered suit against Kincaid for $1,590.95, which is the difference between the amount of plaintiff's statement of April 6, 1967, and the two checks forwarded to Baillie by Kincaid.

MALLARD, CHIEF JUSTICE.   G.S. § 1–540 reads as follows:

By agreement receipt of less sum is discharge.—In all claims, or money demands, of whatever kind, and howsoever due, where an agreement is made and accepted for a less amount than that demanded or claimed to be due, in satisfaction thereof, the payment of the less amount according to such agreement in compromise of the whole is a full and complete discharge of the same.

By the words of this statute, G.S. § 1–540, a compromise and settlement is indicated; and a compromise, as distinguished from accord and satisfaction, must be based on a disputed claim while accord and satisfaction may be based on an undisputed or liquidated claim.

*   *   *   *   *

An accord and satisfaction is compounded of two elements: An accord, which is an agreement whereby one of the parties undertakes to give or perform and the other to accept in satisfaction of a claim, liquidated or in dispute, something other than or different from what he is or considers himself entitled to; and a satisfaction, which is the execution or performance of such agreement.

It should be noted that G.S. § 1–540 applies as a compromise and settlement when an agreement is made and accepted. In the case before us Kincaid in the letter of its attorney made a conditional offer to Baillie. The condition was to pay thirty-five per cent if a sufficient number of creditors accepted the proposal within sixty days from 16 August 1967. In reply thereto on 25 August 1967, Baillie made a conditional acceptance of the offer. The conditions were to accept if Kincaid's letter contained all of the relevant information and if payment was made to Baillie on or before 20 September 1967. Thus, it is seen that Baillie did not accept the offer of Kincaid as made. The counterproposal as made by Baillie was not accepted by Kincaid.

The checks involved herein were in payment of part of a liquidated and undisputed debt which was already due. Kincaid has paid but a part of its indebtedness and suffers no detriment. By these partial payments, Baillie has received no more than it was entitled to receive for its lumber sold and delivered to Kincaid. No consideration exists for the discharge of the balance due Baillie for its lumber. Consideration must in some form or other be present in an accord.

Baillie contends that the provisions of G.S. § 25–1–207 are applicable. This section of the statute is a part of the Uniform Commercial Code and reads:

Performance or acceptance under reservation of rights.—A party who with explicit reservation of rights performs or promises performance or assents to performance in a manner demanded or offered by the other party does not thereby prejudice the rights reserved. Such words as "without prejudice," "under protest" or the like are sufficient.

Applying the provisions of G.S. § 25–1–207 to the facts of this case, it is clear that Baillie by indorsing the checks, "With reservation of all our rights," complied with that portion of the statute requiring an explicit reservation of rights. Apparently, Kincaid was claiming a right to settle under its rejected offer of payment of thirty-five percent of Baillie's claim. Baillie contended that such was unwarranted and that it was entitled to payment of its account. We hold that Baillie, by its indorsement with explicit reservations, did not accept the second check in full payment but in the manner provided in G.S. § 25–1–207 reserved its right to collect the remainder of its unpaid bill.

We also hold that the checks sent by Kincaid and accepted by Baillie, under the circumstances presented by this record, do not as a matter of law result in an accord and satisfaction of the undisputed and liquidated account owed Baillie by Kincaid, and the trial court found and concluded that they did not. It follows, therefore, that Baillie had the right to enforce collection of the unpaid balance of its original claim.

Forbearance To Sue

Right to Bring Suit. Every member of our society has the legal right to bring to the courts for enforcement any claim which he or she may have against other members of society. If a person has a claim which he or she reasonably and honestly believes is valid, he or she has a right to bring suit to enforce the claim, and the postponing of or refraining from bringing suit is sufficient consideration to support a promise.

Valid Claims and Reasonable Claims. Forbearance to bring suit on a wholly spurious claim is not sufficient consideration to support a promise. The promisee must honestly believe that his or her claim is valid, and the circumstances must be such that a reasonable person in his or her position would be justified in believing the claim to be valid. The fact that the claim may be doubtful does not prevent forbearance to sue from being sufficient consideration to support a promise.

Summary

Forbearance to bring suit on a claim which the promisee is justified in believing is a valid claim is legal detriment and is sufficient consideration to support a promise. A promise made by a third party may be supported by the promisee's forbearance to sue.

Frasier v. Carter
437 P.2d 32 (Sup. Ct. Idaho 1968)

This was an action by Lena Frasier (plaintiff) against D. L. Carter (defendant) for damages for breach of contract. Judgment for the plaintiff and the defendant appealed. Affirmed.

Lena Frasier brought this action against Carter, a practicing attorney, upon the following letter agreement:

D. L. Carter
Lawyer
May 12, 1962

Dear Lena

This is to advise and confirm our agreement—that in the event the J. W. Frasier estate case now on appeal is not terminated so that you will receive settlement equal to your share of the estate as you would have done if your waiver had been filed in the estate in proper time, that I will make up any balance to you in payments as suits my convenience and will pay interest on your loss at 6%.

Sincerely
/s/D. L. Carter

By his will, her husband has devised and bequeathed all of the separate and community property to Lena and the three children. The specific devises and bequests to Lena were more valuable than her interest in the community property. However, the specific devises and bequests were conditioned upon a waiver by Lena of her interest in the community property, and the will provided that if she failed to waive her community property rights then she would receive her interest in the community property and nothing more.

No such waiver was executed by Lena and under the decree, distribution was made to Lena of her half share of the community property in lieu of the specific devises and bequests provided for by the will.

TAYLOR, JUSTICE. The principal ground urged for reversal is that the promise of Mr. Carter to pay to Mrs. Frasier any loss she sustained by reason of failure to waive her community interest in the Frasier estate, was without consideration. We think consideration was sufficiently established. The promise was in writing, which is presumptive evidence of consideration, and the burden of showing want of consideration sufficient to support the written promise was upon Carter.

Mrs. Frasier contends that Carter's promise to pay was supported by her forbearance from prosecuting an action against him for his negligence in failing to advise her properly respecting her interest in the Frasier estate. Waiver of, or forbearance to exercise, a right which is not utterly groundless is sufficient consideration to support a contract made in reliance thereon.

Mere forbearance without any request to forbear, or circumstances from which an agreement to forbear may be implied, is not a consideration which will support a promise.

However, an agreement to forbear may be implied, and actual forbearance is some evidence of an agreement to forbear.

Bargain and Exchange

The Bargain.   Whether or not a detriment or benefit has been bargained for will depend on the intent of the parties. Nothing will be held to be consideration unless the parties intend it to be such. In determining intent, that is, in determining whether the promise or act has been bargained for and given in exchange for the promise, the same standards are applied as would be applied in determining the intent to make or accept an offer.

Adequacy of Consideration.   The statement that the courts will not inquire into the adequacy of the consideration is frequently made. However, this statement cannot be accepted as a rule of law which will be followed under all circumstances. It is true that if the parties are dealing on an equal basis and the transaction is free from misrepresentation, fraud, duress, undue influence, or mistake, the courts will not refuse to enforce the contract solely on the ground that a burdensome duty was assumed in exchange for a relatively small consideration. This is especially true if the exchange does not involve items of a readily determinable economic value. In general, each party to a contract has the right to judge the value of the exchange according to his own standards, and the court will not substitute its judgment of values for that of the parties to the contract.

The courts will take into consideration the relative value of the things exchanged in those cases in which a promise is made to exchange a larger amount of money or fungible goods for a lesser amount of the same medium of money or the same kind and quality of fungible goods at the same time and place.

If the purported consideration is of such a nature that it can have no value, the courts will hold that no consideration has been given. Also, if the difference in the value of the exchanges is great, this fact may be taken into consideration in determining the existence of fraud, duress, or undue influence; however, inadequacy of consideration standing alone is not sufficient to justify the setting aside of a transaction on the ground of fraud, duress, or undue influence. Since the granting of an equitable remedy rests in the sound discretion of the court, if the bargain imposes an unconscionable burden on one of the parties, or if it appears that one of the parties has a definite bargaining advantage over the other party and has taken advantage of his position to "drive a hard bargain," the court, in the exercise of its discretionary powers, will refuse to grant an equitable remedy to the party who has taken the unconscionable advantage of the other party.

Nominal Consideration.   Nominal consideration refers to the recitation of consideration in a writtten agreement when, as a matter of fact, the consideration recited is not actually bargained for and given in exchange for the promise but is written into the contract to give the appearance of consideration when there is not sufficient consideration given to support the promise.

Writings which recite one dollar or other small sums as the consideration have given rise to many conflicting decisions by the courts. For example, in a written agreement the consideration for a promise made may be recited as "one dollar in hand paid, receipt of which is hereby acknowledged." If it is reasonably certain from the relation of the parties and the surrounding circumstances that the "one dollar" was actually bargained for and given in exchange for the promise, the courts are uniform in holding that the consideration is adequate. On the other hand, if it is reasonably clear that the recitation of consideration was included in the writing to give it the appearance of validity, and the consideration was not bargained for and given in exchange for the promise, a majority of the courts hold that the promise is not supported by sufficient consideration and that it is not enforceable by court action.

Summary

If the parties do not intend as consideration the legal detriment given in exchange for a promise but intend it as a gratuity, it will not be sufficient consideration to support the promise. The courts will not inquire into the adequacy of the consideration so long as a sufficient consideration is given; but if in addition to the gross inequality of the exchange there is evidence of unfair dealing, the court will refuse to enforce the promise on the ground of misrepresentation, fraud, duress, or undue influence.

The recitation of a consideration in a writing is not sufficient to support a promise if no consideration has, in fact, been bargained for and given in exchange for the promise.

Trengen v. Mongeon

206 N.W.2d 284 (Sup. Ct. N.D. 1973)

Suit to recover six quarters of land brought by Alice Trengen (plaintiff), brought as guardian on behalf of Louis and Margaret Mongeon (the parents of Alice) against Pearl Mongeon (defendant), the widow of Ernest Mongeon, Alice's dead brother. Alice appealed from an adverse judgment. Affirmed.

On May 9, 1967, . . . Louis and Margaret executed a warranty deed for approximately 960 acres of land to Ernest and Pearl. The deed contains a recital and an acknowledgment of the receipt of $38,400 as consideration for the conveyance. At the same time an agreement was entered into between the two parties whereby Ernest and Pearl agreed to pay to Louis and Margaret the sum of $1,800 annually for as long as both or the survivor of them shall live. The agreement stated that: . . .

the consideration for this agreement is the conveyance of approximately nine hundred and sixty (960) acres of land to the said Ernest Mongeon and Pearl Mongeon, his wife, this date, said land having been devised to the said Ernest Mongeon by the Wills of said Louis J. Mongeon and Margaret E. Mongeon. . . .

Louis and Margaret were 87 and 83 years old respectively at the date of the agreement.

TEIGEN, JUDGE. The final issue is the plaintiffs' contention . . .

that the Court erred in finding the consideration adequate for the six quarters of land in that

$1800 per year for the lives of Louis Mongeon and Margaret Mongeon who were of the age of 87 and 83 years old respectively at the time, is so shocking and inequitable that it taxes the credibility.

It is a general principle of contract law that courts will not ordinarily look into the adequacy of the consideration in an agreed exchange. Equity will, however, grant relief where the inadequacy of consideration is particularly glaring.

The court in *Rose* cancelled the defendants' quitclaim deed and land contract assignment where the entire consideration for the transfer of equity in the property worth approximately $12,000 amounted to $1.05.

In the present case the consideration is of an indeterminable value. Monetarily, payment of the sum of $1,800 was made in the fall of 1967, and that sum will continue to be payable on or before November 1 of every year for as long as both or the survivor of the plaintiffs shall live. Payments received by the plaintiffs to the present time total $10,800.

Whether the consideration for a deed is adequate ordinarily rests with the parties. Since adequacy of consideration is not necessary to sustain a deed, and any valuable consideration, however small, is sufficient, the consideration need not equal the value of the property conveyed, especially where no creditor's rights are affected. Indeed, the merely nominal consideration of one dollar, which is frequently recited in deeds, evidences a sufficient consideration. . . . The ordinary standard for testing the adequacy of consideration to support a transfer of property is not applicable to a deed conveying realty on condition that the grantee care for the grantor during the remainder of the grantor's life because of the uncertainty of life involved in such agreements.

The trial court also found that the plaintiffs' love and affection for their son Ernest was both a motivating factor and part of the consideration for the transaction.

Natural love and affection has always been held to be sufficient consideration for a deed where the relationship of the parties is such as to justify the presumption that love and affection exist.

Past Consideration

Nature of Past Consideration.   The term *past consideration* is applied to a situation in which the parties attempt to support a present promise on a benefit conferred at some time in the past. This involves a consideration of terms, because, as a matter of fact, past consideration is not sufficient consideration. At the time the promise is made, the promisee is under no obligation to the promisor and suffers no legal detriment in exchange for the promise. The parties attempt to support a present promise on a legal detriment which was suffered at some time past.

Implied Promises to Compensate.   Past consideration cases must be distinguished from those cases in which a promise is made to pay a sum certain in discharge of an existing but unliquidated obligation. Such a promise is supported by sufficient consideration. It differs from an "accord and satisfaction" only in one respect: the claim is not a disputed claim. The promise merely makes definite the unliquidated obligation.

Summary

Past consideration is an attempt to support a present promise on a benefit conferred in the past. Past consideration will not support a present promise. Past consideration cases should not be confused with those cases in which a promise is made to pay a sum certain in discharge of an existing but unliquidated obligation. Such promises are supported by sufficient consideration and are enforceable.

Consideration in Bilateral Contracts

Mutual Obligation.   The parties to a bilateral contract exchange promises, each is promisor and each is promisee. The test of consideration is not merely one of determining whether there has been an exchange of promises but whether the promises exchanged have created a binding obligation the performance of which will be a detriment to the promisee or a benefit to the promisor. If the obligation created by the promise is one which the promisor is already legally bound to perform, the promise cannot be sufficient consideration to support an exchange promise.

Illusory Promise.   An illusory promise is one which is so worded that the fulfillment of the promise is left to the election of the promisor. It is not sufficient consideration to support a bilateral contract. Since the promisor may or may not fulfill the promise, depending on his own desires and wishes, he or she has not made a binding promise.

Right to Cancel Contract.   If one or both parties to a contract reserve the right to cancel it at will, the contract is not a binding contract, since, by canceling the contract, one or both of the parties may avoid the binding effect of any promises made. If the contract provides that it will remain in force for a stipulated period of time after notice of cancellation is given, the promises are mutual, since both parties are bound for at least the time that elapses from the time of the making of the contract until the notice of cancellation becomes effective. If one of the parties is given the right to cancel the contract on the happening of a stated event, such a provision does not give the promisor the right to cancel at will, and his or her promise is sufficient consideration to support the promise given in exchange.

The courts have also held that infants' contracts and contracts induced by misrepresentation, fraud, duress, or undue influence are not void for lack of consideration. Even though one of the parties has the right to disaffirm the contract and thereby escape liability, he is bound until he exercises his right to disaffirm, and he will be bound if he does not exercise his right to disaffirm within a reasonable time.

Summary

If a bilateral contract is to be valid, both contracting parties must make legally binding promises. If one of the parties is not bound, the other is not bound. If the promise of one of the parties to a bilateral contract is so worded that the performance of the promise depends on that party's will, wish, or desire, the promise is not a legally binding promise and cannot be sufficient consideration to support a bilateral contract. If the right to cancel a contract at will is reserved by either or both of the parties, the contract is void for lack of consideration.

Streich v. General Motors Corp.

126 N.E.2d 389 (App. Ct. Ill. 1955)

Streich (plaintiff) brought this action for damages for breach of contract against General Motors (defendant). Judgment for General Motors and Streich appealed. Affirmed.

G.M. placed purchase order No. 11925, an order for air magnet valves, with Streich. The order provided as follows:

This Purchase Order is issued to cover shipments of this part, to be received by us from September 1, 1948 to August 31, 1949 as released and scheduled on our series 48 'Purchase Order release and Shipping Schedule' No. 478412 attached and all subsequent Purchase Order releases.

This order provided that the order, including the terms and conditions on the face and reverse side, constitute "the complete and final agreement between Buyer and Seller and no other agreement in any way modifying any of said terms and conditions will be binding upon Buyer unless made in writing and signed by Buyer's representative."

On the reverse side are twenty-three provisions, among which are the following:

Deliveries are to be made both in quantities and at times specified in schedules furnished by Buyer. Buyer will have no liability for payment for material or items delivered to Buyer which are in excess of quantities specified in the delivery schedules. Buyer may from time to time change delivery schedules or direct temporary suspension of scheduled shipments.

Buyer reserves the right to cancel all or any of the undelivered portion of this order if Seller does not make deliveries as specified in the schedules, or if Seller breaches any of the terms hereof including the warranties of Seller.

On April 19, 1949, order No. 11925 was cancelled by General Motors.

McCORMICK, PRESIDING JUDGE.   There is no question but that under the law a contract properly entered into whereby the buyer agrees to buy all its requirements of a commodity for a certain period, and the seller agrees to sell the same as ordered, is a valid and enforceable contract and is not void for uncertainty and want of mutuality.

The contract in the instant case is not such a contract. Purchase Order No. 11925 states that it is issued to cover "shipments of this part, to be received by us from September 1, 1948 to August 31, 1949 as released and scheduled on our series 48 'Purchase Order release and Shipping Schedule' No. 478412 attached and all subsequent Purchase Order releases." Construing the letter of April 1, 1948 as an integral part of the contract, the provisions therein contained are merely that it "now becomes necessary to issue our 48 series 'Open End' purchase order for our requirements from September 1, 1948, through August 31, 1949." Reading and construing the two documents together, notwithstanding the detailed provisions contained on the reverse side of the purchase order, the result is an agreement on the part of the seller to sell a certain identified valve at a certain fixed price in such quantities as the buyer may designate, when and if it issues a purchase order for the same. The word "release" as used throughout these documents is treated by both parties as equivalent to "order."

In *Corbin on Contracts*, Vol. 1, Sec. 157, the author says:

> In what purports to be a bilateral contract, one party sometimes promises to supply another, on specified terms with all the goods or services that the other may order from time to time within a stated period. A mere statement by the other party that he assents to this, or "accepts" it, is not a promise to order any goods or to pay anything. There is no consideration of any sort for the seller's promise; and he is not bound by it. This remains true, even though the parties think that a contract has been made and expressly label their agreement a "contract." In cases like this, there may be no good reason for implying any kind of promise by the offeree.

Here, the buyer proffers purchase order 11925, with its twenty-five or more clauses, to the seller for acceptance. In the instrument it makes no promise to do anything. On the surface it appears to be an attempt to initiate a valid bilateral contract. The seller accepts, and as by a flash of legerdemain the positions of the buyer and the seller shift. The buyer now becomes the promisee and the seller the promisor. The promise of the seller to furnish identified items at a stated price is merely an offer and cannot become a contract until the buyer issues a release or order for a designated number of items. Until this action is taken the buyer has made no promise to do anything, and either party may withdraw. The promise is illusory, and the chimerical contract vanishes. "An agreement to sell to another such of the seller's goods, wares, and merchandise as the other might from time to time desire to purchase is lacking in mutuality because it does not bind the buyer to purchase any of the goods of the seller, as such matter is left wholly at the option or pleasure of the buyer."

In the instant case, when the seller accepted purchase order No. 11925, no contract came into being.

In this case the use of the contract is extended to cover commodities which must be manufactured before they are available for sale. According to the admitted statements in the complaint, special tools had to be manufactured in order to produce the item herein involved. The seller here, misled by the law ordinarily applicable to an enforceable bilateral contract, undoubtedly, as he alleged in his complaint, did go to considerable expense in providing tools and machines, only to find that by the accepted agreement the buyer had promised to do absolutely nothing. A statement of expectation creates no duty. Courts are not clothed with the power to make contracts for parties, nor can they, under the guise of interpretation, supply provisions actually lacking or impose obligations not actually assumed.

Professor Fuller, in a note to *Alexander Hamilton Institute v. Jones,* . . . discussing insurance and correspondence school contracts, says:

> One often has the impression of a kind of running battle between draftsmen and the courts, with much shifting of ground on the part of both.
> Back of this development lies a problem that touches the basic philosophy of contract law. The law of contracts is founded generally on the principle that it is the business of the courts to interpret and enforce the agreements that the parties have negotiated. This theory confronts the social reality that in many cases no real negotiations take place, and the terms of the contract are in fact set by the will of one party alone. This situation may arise where one party is indifferent or ignorant, or it may result from a superiority of bargaining power on one side. In such situations, there seems to be emerging a principle of law not yet frankly acknowledged which might be phrased something as follows: where one party to a contract has the power to dictate its terms, the terms of the contract are subject to judicial review, and may be modified by the court if they are unduly harsh. Fuller, *Basic Contract Law,* p. 260.

The agreement contained in purchase order No. 11925 was artfully prepared. It contains, in print so fine as to be scarcely legible, more than twenty-three clauses, most of which are applicable to bilateral contracts. It has all the indicia of a binding and enforceable contract, but it was not a binding and enforceable contract because the promise was defective. Behind the glittering facade is a void. This agreement was made in the higher echelons of business, overshadowed by the aura of business ethics. To say the least, the agreement was deceptive.

Nevertheless, as the law is today, on the pleadings in the instant case, the trial court could do nothing but sustain the motion to dismiss the complaint.

When Consideration Unnecessary

Promise Inducing Substantial Action. Where a promisor makes a promise which he or she, as a reasonable person, should expect would induce the promisee, in justifiable reliance thereon, to take some action or forbearance of a definite and substantial character, which would be detrimental to him or her, the courts will enforce the promise although it is not supported by consideration. The enforcement of such promises is based on broad concepts of equity and fair dealing and they are enforced to avoid injustice.

Charitable Subscriptions. A charitable subscription is a promise to make a gift for a charitable, educational, or eleemosynary purpose. In England, such promises are held to be unenforceable; but in the United States, such promises are enforced provided the institution to which the promise is made has incurred obligations in reliance on the promise. Until obligations are incurred in reliance on the promise, the promisor may withdraw his promise without liability. The holdings of the courts are justified on the basis of public policy.

Business Promises.   The courts now enforce promises made in business transactions on the ground that the promisee justifiably relied on the promise in a growing number of cases where the dictates of justice and fair dealing demand that the promise be enforced. Business contracts and business subscription agreements are, as a general rule, bilateral in nature and are supported by sufficient consideration. The traditional attitude of the courts toward promises made in business transactions has been that they are not enforceable unless they are supported by sufficient consideration as tested by the bargain theory of consideration.[2]

Debts Barred by Statute of Limitations.   The states are not in accord in their holdings relative to the enforceability of an unconditional promise to pay a debt barred by the statute of limitations. In general, such a promise is enforceable although the promise is not supported by consideration. In some, but not all, states a voluntary payment on the debt or a securing of the debt will be held to be an unconditional promise to pay the debt, and such new promise will be enforceable by court action until the statute of limitations has run against it for a second time.

Debts Discharged in Bankruptcy.   If a debtor makes an unconditional promise to pay a debt or some portion thereof after he or she has been adjudged a bankrupt or after the debt has been discharged in bankruptcy, such a promise will be binding only as to that debt. A few states require that such a promise, if it is to be enforceable, need be in writing. A promise to pay a debt discharged in a composition agreement is not enforceable unless it is supported by a new consideration.

Promise to Perform a Conditional Duty.   If the happening of a condition or event is made a condition precedent to the promisor's duty to conform and the condition is not fulfilled and thereafter a promise is made by the promisor to perform, such promise will be enforced, and no new consideration will be required.

Summary

To avoid injustice certain promises not supported by consideration are enforced. Promises justifiably relied on by the promisee, which induce substantial action on his or her part, will be enforced if a refusal to enforce would result in substantial injustice. In the United States charitable subscriptions are enforced provided the beneficiary of the promise has changed his or her position in reliance thereon. Promises made in business transactions are not usually enforced unless supported by sufficient bargain theory consideration.

Promises to pay debts barred by the statute of limitations or discharged in

[2] Code provisions and other case trends suggest that the courts may be somewhat less rigorous in regard to their requirement for bargain theory consideration in future cases.

bankruptcy are enforced. A promise to pay a debt discharged in a composition agreement will not be enforced unless supported by a new consideration.

Hoffman v. Red Owl Stores, Inc.

133 N.W.2d 267 (Sup. Ct. Wis. 1965)

Hoffman (plaintiff) sued Red Owl Stores, Inc. for breach of contract. Red Owl appealed from a judgment for Hoffman. Affirmed.

Lukowitz, an agent for Red Owl, represented to Hoffman that Red Owl would build a store building in Chilton and stock it with merchandise for Hoffman to operate in return for which Hoffman was to invest a total sum of $18,000. In reliance upon these representations Hoffman sold his grocery store and purchased the building site in Chilton and rented a residence for himself and his family in Chilton.

After Hoffman had sold his grocery store and paid the $1,000 on the Chilton lot, the $18,000 figure was changed to $24,100. Then in November, 1961, Hoffman was assured that if the $24,100 figure were increased by $2,000 the deal would go through. Hoffman was induced to sell his grocery store fixtures and inventory in June 1961, on the promise that he would be in his new store by fall. In November, Hoffman sold his bakery building on the urging of defendants and on the assurance that this was the last step necessary to have the deal go through.

CURRIE, CHIEF JUSTICE.   Originally the doctrine of promissory estoppel was invoked as a substitute for consideration rendering a gratuitous promise enforceable as a contract. In other words, the acts of reliance by the promisee to his detriment provided a substitute for consideration. If promissory estoppel were to be limited to only those situations where the promise giving rise to the cause of action must be so definite with respect to all details that a contract would result were the promise supported by consideration, then the defendants' instant promises to Hoffman would not meet this test. However, sec. 90 of *Restatement, 1 Contracts,* does not impose the requirement that the promise giving rise to the cause of action must be so comprehensive in scope as to meet the requirements of an offer that would ripen into a contract if accepted by the promisee. Rather the conditions imposed are:

(1) Was the promise one which the promisor should reasonably expect to induce action or forbearance of a definite and substantial character on the part of the promisee?

(2) Did the promise induce such action or forbearance?

(3) Can injustice be avoided only by enforcement of the promise?

We deem it would be a mistake to regard an action grounded on promissory estoppel as the equivalent of a breach of contract action. As Dean Boyer points out, it is desirable that fluidity in the application of the concept be maintained. While the first two of the above listed three requirements of promissory estoppel present issues of fact which ordinarily will be resolved by a jury, the third requirement, that the remedy can only be invoked where necessary to avoid injustice, is one that involves a policy decision by the court. Such a policy decision necessarily embraces an element of discretion.

We conclude that injustice would result here if plaintiffs were not granted some relief because of the failure of defendants to keep their promises which induced plaintiffs to act to their detriment.

Consideration under the Uniform Commercial Code

In General. It will be recalled that a promise in writing to hold open an offer made between merchants is enforceable even though it is not supported by consideration. (2–205.) And likewise an agreement modifying a contract to sell goods needs no consideration to be binding. (2–209.)

Lunsford v. Wilson

149 S.E.2d 515 (Ct. App. Ga. 1966)

This was an action by W. C. Lunsford, Jr. (plaintiff) against E. C. Wilson (defendant) for the purchase price of certain "furniture and fixtures" which Lunsford sold to Wilson under a written contract. Judgment for Lunsford and Wilson appealed. Reversed and remanded.

EBERHARDT, JUDGE.   Wilson alleged that the contract sued upon had been modified orally and there was testimony as to monthly payments inconsistent with the terms of the original agreement. He denied that demand had been made for strict performance of the original agreement. Lunsford challenged this defense on the ground that there was no allegation of consideration for the modification. Assuming that the items contracted for were "goods" as defined by the Sales Article of the Uniform Commercial Code [see 2–105(1) and 2–107(2)], no consideration was necessary for the agreement of modification [Code 2–209(1)], and Wilson raised a valid defense. If upon the trial of the case it is shown that some of the items were not "goods," 2–209(1) would not be applicable as the agreement sued upon was an entire contract.

Problem Cases

1. Finley contracted with Insurance Company to solicit life insurance. He was to receive 50 percent of the initial net premium and, in addition, contingent commissions during the life of the policy on all insurance written by him. After five years he stopped writing for Insurance Company. Insurance Company then wrote him that, although they believed under the contract that his contingent commissions should cease as of the date he terminated writing policies for them, they were sending him the contingent commissions for the balance of that year "in full and final settlement for contingent commissions due under

our contract." They enclosed a check which on its face read: "Received as full payment of all money due as contingent commission under the contract between Finley and Insurance Co." Finley cashed the check. Can Insurance Company successfully raise accord and satisfaction as a defense to a suit by Finley to recover the balance of the contingent commissions accruing on his policies?

2. Hanson, a skilled pressman, had been employed by Central Printing for many years. Central's business was often slack in the winter, occasionally resulting in temporary layoffs for Hanson. When he was offered steady employment with Stoyles Printing, Hanson asked Central if they would have steady work for him. After some negotiations, Central gave Hanson a letter stating that they would "guarantee (Hanson) 40 hours work per week throughout the entire year each year until you retire of your own choosing." Hanson then elected to remain with Central and did so for two years when he was discharged without cause. Can Hanson successfully recover damages for breach of contract?

3. Lipsey managed Co-op for 31 years. In 1958 the directors of Co-op decided to relieve Lipsey of his duties and to pay him retirement benefits for 30 months, provided he cooperated with the directors and the new management. Lipsey somewhat reluctantly accepted the offer and did not encourage opposition from his friends who were Co-op members. He spent some time each day for two months aiding the new manager. Co-op terminated the retirement payments after five months alleging the promises were without consideration. Is Co-op correct?

4. Signs was employed by Insurance Company as a selling agent. The contract of employment set out in detail the commissions to be paid to Signs on business produced by him, and it provided that the stipulated commissions were "full and complete compensation" for all business produced. In December, Insurance Company put out a bulletin stating that the company would distribute $1,000,000 to deserving agents, and that agents selling $20,000 worth of life insurance during the month of December would receive $10,000. Signs sold in excess of $20,000 during the month of December but the company refused to pay him a bonus. Signs brought suit against Insurance Company to recover a judgment for $10,000. Insurance Company set up lack of consideration as a defense. Is the defense good?

5. A. W. Jenkins, an attorney, during his lifetime performed legal services for L. C. Jones Trucking Company, Inc. After the death of A. W. Jenkins, Ruth Jenkins, administratrix of the estate of A. W. Jenkins, deceased, found two bills in the files of A. W. Jenkins for services rendered to L. C. Jones Trucking Company, Inc. One statement was for $500, and a pencil notation on the statement indicated that $300 had been paid thereon. The other statement was for $1,750, and a notation indicated a payment of $700 thereon.

   L. C. Jones Trucking Company, Inc., contended that prior to the death of A. W. Jenkins the officers of Trucking Company had a conference with A. W. Jenkins and at this conference an agreement as to the amount A. W. Jenkins would accept in full settlement as payment for his services was reached and that Trucking Company had paid this amount in full.

   Ruth Jenkins, as administratrix, brought suit to recover an unpaid balance of $1,250 shown to be due on the two statements. She contended that the payment of a lesser sum does not discharge the entire claim. Is the entire claim discharged?

6. Petty made numerous purchases from Field Lumber Company during the period June 6, 1968, through January 23, 1970. Field's ledger statement showed a balance of $1,752.21 in October 1970. Petty acknowledged a balance of $1,091.96 but disputed the difference of $660.25 which represented an allegedly unauthorized $292.60 purchase by an employee

and a 1 percent per month finance charge. In early October 1970, a check in the amount of $500 was mailed to Field with the following letter:

> Field Lumber Co.   Oct 3
> 1970
>
> Gentlemen:
>
> Our client, above named, has asked us to transmit to you the enclosed check in the sum of $500.00 in full settlement of your claim against him.
>
> We realize this check represents a little less than 50% of your claim, but in the present market, Mr. Petty has been unable to sell his real estate, or unable to obtain an offer in excess of his cost, or to obtain a figure representative of his equity.
>
> He has been able to borrow the amount enclosed herewith, which is tendered to you, solely upon the condition that it is accepted in full settlement of your claim and your endorsement and collection of the enclosed check will evidence your agreement to that effect.
>
> If the above is not acceptable, will you please return the check without delay.
>
> Yours truly,
> COOK, FLANAGAN & BERST

Field cashed the check and sued for $1,252.21. Petty set up accord and satisfaction as a defense. Is this a good defense?

7. Mrs. O'Neill contracted with a contractor for the erection of a prefabricated home costing about $30,000. Mrs. O'Neill's stove, refrigerator, washing machine and dryer would not fit into the kitchen as designed, and this necessitated the replacement of some seven kitchen cabinets. The contractor ordered these from Frederick Trading Company (Frederick). Before the contractor completed the house he became insolvent. Frederick prepared to file a mechanic's lien against the house, and Mrs. O'Neill promised Frederick if it would not file a mechanic's lien she would pay them for the cabinets. Frederick, in reliance on Mrs. O'Neill's promise, did not file a mechanic's lien on the house. Mrs. O'Neill then refused to pay for the cabinets and Frederick brought suit. Mrs. O'Neill set up lack of consideration as a defense. Is this a good defense?

8. In 1951, Western Star Mill Company (Mill Co.) entered into an oral contract with Burns to the effect that he should have the exclusive sales agency for Mill Co.'s products in Pontotoc County, Texas. Burns claims that he was to have an exclusive agency so long as he promoted or pushed Mill Co.'s feed and paid his bills. There was no mention of how long the contract would remain in effect. Burns was not required to handle Mill Co.'s feed only, and he continued to handle Purina Feeds. Burns was free to buy whatever amount he wanted and sell at any price he chose. Mill Co. terminated relations with Burns and when sued set up as a defense that the sales agency was void for lack of consideration. Is this a good defense?

9. Portland Gasoline Company entered into a contract with Superior Marketing Company, Inc., whereby Superior contracted to market all the butane-propane gas mixture produced by Portland at a natural-gas processing plant owned by it. Superior failed and refused to market all the butane-propane gas mix produced by Portland, and Portland brought suit to recover damages for breach of contract. Superior set up lack of consideration as a defense. Is this a good defense?

10. Jordan signed a pledge to Mount Sinai Hospital and failed to pay. Mount Sinai sued Jordan for the amount of the pledge. The pledge stated that it was made "in consideration of and to induce the subscriptions of others" and made no reference as to the purpose of the gift. Is this pledge enforceable?

chapter 10

Capacity of Parties

Introduction

Capacity. The term "capacity" as used in the law denotes the ability to perform legally valid acts, that is, the ability to incur legal liability or to acquire legal rights. In ancient times, relatively few persons had full legal capacity, but modern law aims to confer such capacity as widely as possible.

Since some persons, due to natural incapacities, are considered incapable of protecting their interests in our economy, laws have been developed the objective of which is to protect such persons and prevent the dissipation of their estates.

Parties to Contract. Parties having capacity to contract are essential to the validity of a contract, and there must be at least two persons—the promisor and the promisee—as parties to a contract. An individual cannot contract with himself. Nor can he as an individual contract with himself as an official. For instance, Bell cannot contract in his individual capacity with himself in his official capacity as administrator or executor of an estate. A stockholder or officer of a corporation may contract in his or her individual capacity with the corporation since a corporation has an existence separate and apart from its officers and stockholders.

Although there are only two parties to a contract, there is no legal limit to the number of persons (individuals, corporations, and so forth) who may join as promisors or promisees. There is a practical limit, however, since it must be possible to identify each party to the contract with reasonable certainty.

Presumption as to Capacity. Where suit is brought to enforce a contractual promise, the plaintiff need not allege and prove that the parties to the contract have capacity to contract, since lack of capacity to contract is the exception rather than the rule. Any party seeking to base a claim or a defense on incapacity has the burden of alleging and proving the incapacity. The principal classes of persons afforded some degree of special protection on their contracts include (1) infants, (2) insane persons, (3) drunken persons, and (4) married women.

Summary

Capacity is the ability to perform legally valid acts. In modern society, persons with natural incapacities to perform legally valid acts are under legal incapacities.

To have a binding contract, there must be two parties to the contract—a promisor and a promisee. The same person cannot act in both capacities. There may be more than two promisors and more than two promisees. There is no legal limit to the number of persons who may be parties to a contract.

Everyone is presumed to have capacity to contract; consequently, in bringing suit on a contract, it is not necessary to allege and prove contractual capacity. Lack of capacity is a matter of defense and must be affirmatively set out as a defense in the pleadings.

Infants' Contracts

Theory of Infants' Incapacity.   Since the courts have recognized from an early date that a person of immature years does not have the capacity to compete on an equal basis with mature persons, they have granted to an infant the privilege of dissaffirming his or her contracts. The infant's contract is voidable only at the option of the infant. Any adult contracting with an infant finds himself or herself in the precarious legal position of being bound on the contract unless it is to the advantage of the infant to disaffirm the contract.

Period of Infancy.   At common law the age of infancy was fixed at 21 years for both men and women. In counting time, the law generally disregards parts of days. Under this rule an infant becomes of age at the first moment of the day before the 21st anniversary of his or her birth. In a few states an infant becomes of age on his or her birthday.

Twelve states now make 18 the age for reaching majority. Another dozen states allow most adult rights (except the right to drink alcoholic beverages) to vest at age 18. Ten other states have modified the common law in more limited respects, such as allowing married women most of the adult rights at age 18. The impetus for many of these changes came from the passage in 1971 of federal legislation giving 18-year-olds the right to vote.

As a general rule the statutes defining the period of infancy fix a definite age at which a person reaches his or her majority. From a practical standpoint, it is desirable to have a simple rule whereby the period of infancy may be determined with certainty.

Emancipation.   As a general rule the father of an infant has the right to the infant's services and can collect the infant's wages. If the father is dead, the widowed mother succeeds to the father's rights in this respect. A person who employs an infant is not discharged of liability to the parent by payment of wages to the infant unless the infant is emancipated. When a parent emancipates a child, he or she surrenders his or her right to the child's wages. There are no formal requirements for emancipation. All that is necessary is that the parent expressly or impliedly consent to the infant's entering into a contract of employment. If an infant has been emancipated, he or she can recover, either on the contract or on the basis of quasi contract, for services rendered. Emancipation does not enlarge the infant's capacity to contract.

General Rule.   An infant's contract binds both the infant and the adult unless the infant exercises his or her right to elect to disaffirm the contract; consequently, infants' contracts are voidable, not void. If the infant elects to be bound by the contract, the relation existing between the infant and the other contracting party is the same as that existing between contracting parties who have full capacity to contract. If an infant, on reaching his or her majority, elects to ratify a contract entered into while an infant, no new promises are involved, and no new consideration need be given. The infant, by ratifying the contract, has exercised his or her privilege of election, and thereafter both parties are bound by the contract.

Business Contracts.   As a general rule an infant is not liable on his business contracts, even though he may be dependent on the income from the business for his living. In a few cases the courts have held infants liable for equipment which has been purchased for the purpose of aiding in earning a living, such as machinery necessary to operate a farm or a truck to be used in trucking operations, but these cases are clearly exceptions to the general rule. The courts have usually held infants liable for the reasonable value of tools of a trade which have been purchased for the purpose of following a trade. Contracts for such equipment have been classed as contracts for necessaries and not as business contracts.

Infant Partner.   An infant may become a member of a partnership, or a partnership may be composed of members all of whom are infants, and it will in no way affect the validity of partnership contracts. An infant partner may withdraw from the partnership without liability to his or her copartner or copartners for damages for breach of the contract of partnership. However, the infant partner cannot withdraw his or her original investment in the partnership capital if such withdrawal will injure partnership creditors. If an infant purchases the capital stock of a corporation, he or she has the right to disaffirm the purchase, return the stock, and recover the amount paid for it even though the capital of the corporation has been impaired in the interim.

Summary

An infant has the privilege of disaffirming his or her contracts. The period of infancy is, with few exceptions, 21 years.

A parent is entitled to the services of an infant child unless he emancipates the child—that is, unless he gives his consent to permit the infant child to enter into employment contracts and to collect his own wages. Emancipation does not enlarge an infant's capacity to contract.

An infant's contracts are voidable, not void, and they are held to be valid until the infant has exercised his or her privilege and disaffirmed the contract. The adult party to a contract is bound by the contract until the infant disaffirms it. As a general rule an infant may disaffirm her business contracts, even though she has engaged in the business as a means of supporting herself. Many states by statute have altered, in some respects, an infant's capacity to contract. These statutes are not uniform in their terms or coverage.

An infant may become a member of a partnership. An infant partner may disaffirm the partnership agreement without liability to his partners for breach of such agreement, and he may disaffirm his personal liability to partnership creditors, but he may not withdraw his capital investment to the injury of such creditors.

Necessaries

Liability for Necessaries.   An infant is liable for the reasonable value of necessaries furnished him, but his or her liability is quasi contractual in nature. If an infant contracts for necessaries and the contract price is greater than the reasonable value of necessaries furnished, the infant is liable only for their reasonable value. His or her liability is not based on his or her contractual promise.

Nature of Necessaries.   Necessaries are confined to those things which are personal to the infant, that is, things which are essential to the infant's continued existence and general welfare. Generally, necessaries are food, clothing, shelter, and medical care, suitable to the infant's station in life, and a basic education or vocational training and the tools of his or her trade.

An infant's liability for necessaries is limited to the reasonable value of necessaries actually furnished to the infant. For example, if an infant contracts to rent a room for one year and occupies it for only three months, the infant's liability would be the reasonable rent for the room for the three months he or she occupied it. Also, if an infant is furnished with adequate necessaries by his or her parent or guardian, the infant will not be liable for necessaries furnished him or her by other persons. Since his needs are already supplied by his parent or guardian, any items for which he contracts, even though they might fall into the classification of necessaries, will be held not to be necessaries.

Summary

An infant is liable for the reasonable value of necessaries actually furnished to him or her. Only those things that are necessary to the existence of the infant and to his or her future development are classed as necessaries. Generally, necessaries are limited to food, clothing, shelter, and medical care, suitable to his or her station in life, and basic education and training for a trade and tools of the trade. If an infant is adequately supplied with necessaries by his parents or guardian, he will not be liable for necessaries furnished him by other persons.

Gastonia Personnel Corp. v. Rogers

172 S.E.2d 19 (Sup. Ct. N.C. 1970)

Rogers, age 19, was emancipated and married. For assistance in obtaining suitable employment, Rogers went to the office of Gastonia, an employment agency, on May 29, 1968, where he signed a contract containing the following:

If I ACCEPT employment offered me by an employer as a result of a lead (verbal or otherwise) from you within twelve (12) months of such lead even though it may not be the position originally discussed with you, I will be obligated to pay you as per the terms of the contract.

Under the contract, Rogers was free to continue his own quest for employment. He was to become obligated to Gastonia only if he accepted employment from an employer to whom he was referred by Gastonia.

Gastonia referred Rogers to an employer and Rogers accepted the job offered. Rogers then refused to pay Gastonia the agreed fee of $295.

BOBBITT, CHIEF JUSTICE.   An early commentary on the common law, after the general statement that contracts made by persons (infants) before attaining the age of twenty-one "may be avoided," sets forth "some exceptions out of this generality," to wit: *"An infant may bind himselfe to pay for his necessary meat, drinke, apparell, necessary physicke, and such other necessaries,* and likewise for his good teaching or instruction, whereby he may profit himselfe afterwards." (Our italics.) [Coke on Little-ton, 13th ed. (1788), p. 172.] If the infant married, "necessaries" included necessary food and clothing for his wife and child.

* * * * *

In general, our prior decisions are to the effect that the "necessaries" of an infant, his wife and child, include only such necessities of life as food, clothing, shelter, medical attention, etc. In our view, the concept of "necessaries" should be enlarged to include such articles of property and such services as are reasonably necessary to enable the infant to earn the money required to provide the necessities of life for himself and those who are legally dependent upon him.

To establish liability, planitiff must satisfy the jury by the greater weight of the evidence that defendant's contract with plaintiff was an appropriate and reasonable means for defendant to obtain suitable employment. If this issue is answered in plaintiff's favor, plaintiff must then establish by the greater weight of the evidence the reasonable value of the services received by defendant pursuant to the c ntract. Thus, plaintiff's recovery, if any, cannot exceed the reasonable value of its services to defendant.

* * * * *

Disaffirmance of Contract

Right to Disaffirm. An infant's right to dis ffirm his or her contracts is absolute and is personal to the infant. As a general rule, the infant's right to disaffirm his contracts is not conditioned on the infant's ability to return the consideration he has received or on his ability to fulfill other conditions, and the infant or his personal representative (administrator of a deceased infant or a guardian) are the only ones who can exercise the right to disaffirm.

Time of Disaffirmance. The infant may (rcise his right to disaffirm his executed contracts, except contracts affectin to real estate, at any time from the time he enters into the contract until sonable time after he reaches his majority. The infant cannot disaffirm a co ract affecting title to his real estate until he reaches his majority. In some states an infant may repossess real estate which she has sold and conveyed to another, but she cannot disaffirm the conveyance during infancy. If the infant, after she reaches her majority, disaffirms a sale of real estate, the adult must account to the infant for the rents and profits during the period she (the adult) was in possession.

If the infant does not disaffirm within a reasonable time after he or she reaches majority, he or she will be bound. The contracts of an infant are valid until he or she exercises his or her right to disaffirm, and if the infant does not exercise this right reasonably, he or she thereby waives the right. What is a reasonable time for disaffirmance is a question of fact, and the time allowed the infant to disaffirm will depend on the facts and circumstances of each case. No general rule can be stated.

Return of Consideration. The objective of the law in giving an infant the right to disaffirm his or her contracts is the protection of the infant's estate from dissipation during his or her infancy, but the courts will not permit the infant to use this right to defraud adults. There is considerable diversity in the decisions as to the relative rights of the parties if the infant disaffirms his or her contract.

If the disaffirmed contract is wholly executory, the disaffirmance cancels all the legal obligations brought into existence by the contract. If the infant has received consideration, he will be required, on disaffirmance of the contract, to return any of the consideration or the benefits from such consideration which he still has in his possession at the time he disaffirms the contract. However, his right to disaffirm his contract does not depend, as a general rule, on his ability to return the consideration he has received.

Infants' Rights on Disaffirmance.   At common law, when an infant disaffirmed his contract, he had the right to recover from the adult any consideration which he had given or its value. This right was not conditioned on his returning the consideration he had received or on his placing the adult *in statu quo.* However, if the infant had in his possession at the time he disaffirmed his contract any of the consideration he had received, or if his estate had been enhanced by the transaction, the infant would not be permitted to retain the benefits and at the same time recover the consideration given. The courts in some states and the statutes of other states require the infant, on disaffirmance of his or her contract, to pay for the benefits received or to place the adult *in statu quo.* This duty is limited under some circumstances.

If an infant disaffirms his contract, he can recover what he has parted with, even though it has been transferred to an innocent third-party purchaser. This rule, however, does not apply to goods sold by an infant where the sale is subject to the Uniform Commercial Code. Under the Code, a good-faith purchaser for value from a seller having a voidable title acquires good title.[1]

In determining the rights and liabilities of an infant on his or her contract, the courts in equity cases have not followed the strict rule of the common law. Generally, the courts have, in such cases, applied the equitable principle (anyone who asks equity must do equity) and have required the infant to do whatever is equitable and just under the circumstances of the case. The interests of the infant are protected by the court and are paramount to those of the adult.

Misrepresentation of Age.   The misrepresentation of his or her age by the infant does not, as a general rule, estop the infant from exercising his or her right to disaffirm the contract induced by the fraud. In some cases in equity the courts have held that an infant, who by misrepresentation of his or her age has induced the adult to enter into the contract, will not be granted an equitable remedy on disaffirmance of the contract.

Some courts will permit an infant, who by misrepresenting his or her age has induced the adult to enter into a contract, to disaffirm the contract and recover what he or she has given without requiring the infant to account for benefits received. But the majority of the courts now require the infant to restore the consideration received and to account for its use and its depreciation in value.

---

[1] Sec. 2–403.

Summary

An infant has the right to disaffirm his or her contracts, except those affecting title to his or her real estate. He may exercise this right at any time from the time he enters into the contract until a reasonable time after he reaches his majority. An infant will not be permitted to use his infancy as a means of enhancing his estate; consequently, on disaffirmance, the infant must return to the adult any consideration received which he still has or any amount by which his estate has been enhanced. However, the infant's right to disaffirm is not conditioned on his putting the adult *in statu quo.* If the infant has dissipated the consideration received, he or she can, under the majority rule, recover the consideration parted with without reimbursing the adult. In equity cases, as a general rule, the strict common law rule is not followed, but the court, on disaffirmance by the infant, will work out a solution to the case which is fair and equitable to all parties involved. The courts have held, with few exceptions, that misrepresentation of his age does not estop an infant from disaffirming the contract induced by the misrepresentation. However, a majority of the courts will require the infant, on disaffirmance, to return the consideration received and to account for its depreciation and for the value of its use.

Ratification

Nature of Ratification. An infant cannot ratify a contract until he or she reaches his or her majority. During infancy the infant is incapable of making a binding contractual promise. If he were permitted to ratify his contracts during the period of infancy, he would be able to remove his disability by his own act. This the courts will not permit him to do.

Requirements for Ratification. There are no formal requirements for the ratification of an infant's contract. The infant's ratification, on reaching his or her majority, may be either expressed or implied. Any words or acts on the part of the infant, after reaching his or her majority, which indicate with reasonable clarity the infant's intent to be bound by the contract, are sufficient.

If the contract is executed, the retaining of the consideration by the infant for an unreasonable time after the infant attains his or her majority amounts to a ratification. If an infant accepts benefits of tendered performance, or if he performs his part of the contract after reaching majority, it will be evidence of intention to ratify, although either one standing alone would not necessarily be conclusive. The courts have generally held that if an infant, after he becomes of age, indicates an intent to ratify his contract, he cannot escape the effects of his ratification by showing that he did not know that he had a right to disaffirm his contract. In this situation the courts have usually applied the rule that ignorance of the law is no excuse.

If the contract is executory, some courts have held that mere inaction on the part of the infant after he or she reaches majority does not amount to a ratification. Other courts have held that since an infant's contract is valid until it is disaffirmed, failure to disaffirm within a reasonable time amounts to a waiver of the rights to disaffirm and is a ratification.

The circumstances of the case are of major importance in determining whether or not a contract has been ratified. For example, an infant signed a note as surety. The note was not paid when due, but the infant was not given notice of default. Approximately ten years after the infant reached his majority, suit was brought against him on the note. The defense of infancy was set. The court held that the infant had not ratified the contract. In one real estate transaction the court held that failure to avoid the sale within a year amounted to a ratification, whereas in another case the court held that failure to avoid the sale for five years was not a ratification.

Effect of Ratification.   A ratification makes the contract valid from its inception. When an infant ratifies a contract after reaching his majority, he thereby exercises his right to elect whether or not he wishes to be bound by the contract. Having exercised the right to elect and having elected to be bound, the infant cannot thereafter disaffirm the contract. He is bound by his election.

Summary

An infant cannot ratify a contract until the infant reaches majority. All that is necessary for ratification is an indication of an intention to be bound. If the contract is executed, inaction for an unreasonable time will, as a general rule, amount to a ratification. If the contract is executory, some courts have held that mere inaction will not amount to a ratification. Ratification makes the contract valid from its inception.

Robertson v. Robertson

229 So.2d 642 (Ct. App. Fla. 1969)

A suit by father (plaintiff) against son (defendant) on son's agreement to repay father for college expense. Judgment for father and son appealed. Affirmed.

During the son's last year of high school, at age 18, the subject of the son's future education was seriously discussed between the parties. At the conclusion of this discussion, the father agreed to lend his son enough money to finance the son through college.

To adequately meet the expenses of his son's premedical and postgraduate education, the father whose employment was that of a salesman, mortgaged his home and took out loans against existing life insurance policies.

The son graduated from dental school in 1962. The father did not attempt to demand repayment of the monies he had expended for the son's education until June 1964, at which time he wrote to his son a letter which recited his appraisal of the circumstances surrounding their mutual obligations, and concluded by requesting that the son begin repaying to him the sum of $30,000.00. Repayment was requested by installments in the amount of $400.00 per month.

After the son received the letter, he and his father had telephone conversations. On June 28, 1964, the son wrote to his father a letter in which he agreed to repay a total debt of $24,000.00 at the rate of $100.00 per month. The letter read in pertinent part:

Four hundred dollars is a lot of money to write a check for each month. According to my memory I offered to pay $100 per month to help re-pay some of the expenses of my college education. We will be happy to pay $100 each month to you, as I had originally promised. However we cannot afford to pay any more than this.

Accordingly, the son paid the sum of $100.00 per month for the next three years until September 1967, at which time he stopped after he had paid a total sum of $3,846.00.

HENDRY, JUDGE.   As to the issue of whether an infant's contract is void or voidable, see the case of *Lee v. Thompson,* Therein the court stated:

Since the contracts of an infant are voidable, . . . subject to the possibility of disaffirmance, it follows that when the infant attains his majority and ratifies a contract made in infancy its infirmity is removed and it will be treated as valid from inception and the optional right to disaffirm abandoned. Ratification does not now require a new consideration to make it binding.

Thus, our attention is next focused on the issue of whether or not the father proved that the son, having attained majority, thereafter ratified the contractual agreement to repay his father for the amounts expended for education. The jury had before it evidence that the son had received and accepted the benefits of his father's contractual agreement, i.e., to pay for educational and related expenses, for a period of four years after obtaining his majority; evidence of oral affirmances by the son that the agreement he made during his infancy was valid and binding, such affirmances having been made after he attained majority; the hand-written letter . . . which affirmed the agreement and the obligation therein; and evidence showing monthly payments over a period of three years, specifically noted as "college payment," and "education refund." It appears that the trial court was eminently correct in submitting the case to the jury on the issue of whether or not the son had ratified the act committed during infancy, after he had attained majority. The jury determined that he had so ratified, and its finding should stand.

Infants' Tort Liability

Nature of Liability.   An infant is liable for his or her torts and crimes. The general rule applied in determining an infant's liability for tort, including negligence, is whether or not he or she used that degree of care ordinarily exercised by children of like age, mental capacity, and experience. This is usually a question of fact for the jury. In determining an infant's criminal liability, the statutes of the state in which the crime is committed must be consulted.

Insane and Drunken Persons

Nature of Liability. The basic theory of the liability of insane persons is the same as that of infants; that is, it is presumed that the insane person, like the infant, does not have the capacity to protect his or her interests in the give-and-take of a market economy. As a general rule, the drunken person is dealt with in the same manner as though he were insane, but before he will be considered drunk, he must be intoxicated to such an extent that he does not have the mental capacity to comprehend the business at hand.

Some states do not follow the general rule, and in such states the fact that one of the parties to the contract was drunk at the time he or she entered into the contract is not ground for the disaffirmance of the contract. In the states which recognize the right of a drunken person to disaffirm his contract, such person must prove that at the time he entered into the contract, he was so intoxicated that he could not comprehend the business at hand, that he was taken advantage of because of his condition, and that the contract was not a fair and just contract, and the drunken person must, on disaffirmance, put the other party *in statu quo.*

Test of Insanity. The courts recognize that persons have varying degrees of mental capacity and that no simple rule whereby mental capacity may be tested can be formulated. The test usually applied is whether or not the contracting party had, at the time the contract was entered into, sufficient mental capacity to comprehend the business involved. The same test is applied in determining the contractual capacity of drunken persons.

The nature of the mental weakness of the contracting party is immaterial. The incapacity may result from lunacy, idiocy, senility, or other defects or diseases of the mind. A person may have periods of insanity and be lucid at all other times. A contract made during a lucid interval is binding. A person may be laboring under insane delusions, but his or her contracts will be binding unless the insane delusions are so connected with the subject matter of the contract as to render him or her incapable of comprehending its nature.

Effect of Adjudication of Insanity. In most states the contracts of a person who has been adjudged insane are void. The statutes of some states expressly provide that the contracts of a person who has been adjudged insane are void, and in others the same result has been reached by judicial decision.

This rule applies only where there has been a regular hearing before a court having jurisdiction over such cases, and where, after due investigation, the court has adjudged the person to be of unsound mind and incapable of managing his or her estate and has appointed a guardian or conservator of the estate. If a person is sued on a contract and he or she sets up as a defense insanity at the time he or she entered into the contract, a finding that the person was insane at the time he or she entered into the contract would not be an adjudication of insanity. Such a finding is binding only as to the case being tried.

Necessaries. An insane person is liable for the reasonable value of necessaries furnished him. The rules relative to what are necessaries and the liability for necessaries generally are the same as those applying to infants.

Disaffirmance of Contract. If a person contracts with an insane person and does not know or does not have reasonable cause to know of the person's insanity, and if the contract is fair and entered into in good faith, the insane party cannot disaffirm the contract unless he or she can put the sane party *in statu quo.*

If the sane party knows or, in the exercise of reasonable care, should know, of the insanity of the other party, the insane party can disaffirm the contract without putting the sane party *in statu quo.* However, he or she must return to the sane person any portion of the consideration which he or she still has. The rule in such cases is the same as the rule governing infants' contracts.

Ratification of Contract. A contract entered into by a person while he or she is insane may be ratified by that person if and when he or she regains his sanity, or it may be ratified by one's personal representative in the event the insane person is adjudged insane or dies. The ratification of an insane person's contract has the same effect on the rights of the parties to the contract as has the ratification of an infant's contract. The contract will be considered as valid from its inception.

Summary

The contracts of an insane person entered into while insane are voidable unless the party has been adjudged insane by a court having jurisdiction of the case, in which event the majority of jurisdictions hold that the contract is void.

If a contracting party does not have sufficient mentality to comprehend the nature of the business being transacted, he or she is insane, irrespective of the cause of his or her mental weakness. An insane person cannot disaffirm a fair contract entered into with a person ignorant of the insanity unless he or she puts the party *in statu quo.* Knowledge of the insanity on the part of the sane person gives the insane party the same rights to disaffirm a contract as an infant has.

A person who, at the time he or she enters into a contract, is intoxicated to such a degree that he or she cannot comprehend the business at hand, is, in most states, treated the same as an insane person.

Cundick v. Broadbent

383 F.2d 157 (10th Cir. 1967)

This was an action brought by Irma Cundick (plaintiff), guardian *ad litem* for her husband, Darwin Cundick, to set aside an agreement for the sale of (1) livestock and equipment; (2) shares of stock in a development company; and (3) base range land in Wyoming to J. R. Broadbent (defendant). The alleged grounds for nullification were that at the time of the transaction Cundick was mentally incompetent to execute the agreement. Judgment for Broadbent and Cundick appealed. Affirmed.

MURRAH, CHIEF JUDGE.   At one time, in this country and in England, it was the law that since a lunatic or *non compos mentis* had no mind with which to make an agreement, his contract was wholly void and incapable of ratification. But, if his mind was merely confused or weak so that he knew what he was doing yet was incapable of fully understanding the terms and effect of his agreement, he could indeed contract, but such contract would be voidable at his option. But in recent times courts have tended away from the concept of absolutely void contracts toward the notion that even though a contract is said to be void for lack of capacity to make it, it is nevertheless ratifiable at the instance of the incompetent party. The modern rule, and the weight of authority, seems to be as stated in 2 Jaeger's *Williston on Contracts,* 3d ed., § 251, ". . . the contractal act by one claiming to be mentally deficient, but not under guardianship, absent fraud, or knowledge of such asserted incapacity by the other contracting party, is not a void act but at most only voidable at the instance of the deficient party; and then only in accordance with certain equitable principles."

In recognition of different degrees of mental competency the weight of authority seems to hold that mental capacity to contract depends upon whether the allegedly disabled person possessed sufficient reason to enable him to understand the nature and effect of the act in issue. Even average intelligence is not essential to a valid bargain. In amplification of this principle, it has been said that if a maker of a contract ". . . has sufficient mental capacity to retain in his memory without prompting the extent and condition of his property and to comprehend how he is disposing of it and to whom and upon what consideration, then he possesses sufficient mental capacity to execute such instrument." The Wyoming court adheres to the general principle that "mere weakness of body or mind, or of both, do not constitute what the law regards as mental incompetency sufficient to render a contract voidable. . . . A condition which may be described by a physician as *senile dementia* may not be insanity in a legal sense."

Against the background of medical and lay evidence tending to show Cundick's incompetency on the crucial date, there is positive evidence to the effect that at the time in question he was 59 years old, married and operating a sheep ranch in Wyoming; that in previous years he had sold his lamb crop to Broadbent and on a date prior to this transaction the parties met at a midway point for the purpose of selling the current lamb crop. Although there is innuendo concerning what transpired at the meeting, neither party testified and no one else was present. We do know that the meeting resulted in a one page contract signed by both parties in which Cundick agreed to sell all of his ranching properties to Broadbent. It is undisputed that Cundick and his wife thereafter took this one page contract to their lawyer in Salt Lake City who refined and amplified it into an eleven-page contract providing in detail the terms by which the sale was to be consummated. The contract was signed in the lawyer's office by Cundick and Broadbent in the presence of Cundick's wife and the lawyer. The lawyer testified that the contract had been explained in detail and that all parties apparently understood it.

The narrated facts of this case amply support the trial court's finding to the effect that Broadbent did not deceive or overreach Cundick. In the absence of any evidence that Broadbent knew of Cundick's mental deficiency, the only evidence from which it can be said that Broadbent took advantage or overreached him is the proof concerning the value of the property sold under the contract. As to that, there is positive evidence that the property was worth very much more than what Broadbent paid for it. But as we have noted, there was evidence to the effect that after the original contract was signed and some complaint made about the purchase price, the parties agreed to raise the price and the contract was so modified.

Married Women's Contracts

Contractual Capacity at Common Law. At common law a married woman could not contract. When a woman married, her legal existence ceased, the husband being the sole representative of the family. It is often said that under the common law the husband and wife were one, and the husband was that one. At an early date the courts of equity recognized the right of the wife to a separate estate, and through equitable proceedings a separate estate could be created for the wife.

Married Women's Statutes. This disability has been partially or totally removed by statutes adopted by the various states. Some statutes give a married woman full power to contract, whereas others are so drafted that she cannot enter into contracts of suretyship or contracts with her husband. To determine the limits of married women's power to contract, one must consult the statutes of the various states.

Problem Cases

1. Spaulding, a minor living with his wife and child, purchased $1,500 worth of household goods and furniture from Furniture Company on a conditional sales contract. After paying

$400, Spaulding defaulted, and Furniture Company repossessed the items. Spaulding sued to recover the $400. Furniture Company contended that the items were necessities and that Spaulding was liable on the contract. Who should prevail?

2. Kabler, an infant, was killed while driving a Simco, Inc.'s, truck under a lease agreement whereby Kabler used the truck to sell ice cream products supplied to him by Simco, Inc. Suit was brought by Byrne, administratrix of Kabler's estate. Byrne charged Simco, Inc., with failure to maintain the truck in safe operating condition.

   Simco, Inc., set up as a defense the written contract between it and Kabler, in which Kabler agreed to hold Simco, Inc., harmless for any injury suffered by him arising from the use of the truck.

   Byrne contends that since Kabler was an infant the contract was not binding and that Simco, Inc.'s, defense is not valid. Is the provision in the contract binding on Kabler or his estate?

3. Adams, age 20, traded in an Opel and paid $975 in cash on a 1960 Chevrolet which she bought from Barcomb. After two weeks, she was dissatisfied with the car and asked Barcomb for her money back. Barcomb refused and Adams brought suit. The car sat idle at Adam's home for six weeks, whereupon Adams operated it again for two months—having turned 21 in the meantime. She then let the car sit idle again. Barcomb argued that by operating the car after she became 21 she lost the benefits of her disaffirmance. Should Barcomb prevail?

4. Fletcher, while an infant, purchased on land contract an unimproved city lot. The contract required him to make payments of $12.50 per month until a total of $300 was paid. He made the monthly payments before he attained his majority. About two months after attaining his majority, he wrote Koch, the seller, asking him for information concerning the amount of the county and state taxes. And eight months after he attained his majority he gave Koch notice that he disaffirmed the contract. Koch contends that Fletcher had ratified the contract. Did Fletcher's conduct amount to a ratification of the contract?

5. Charles and Margret were married in 1946. They separated in 1965, and Charles filed a divorce petition. About a month later, the two encountered each other at a tavern and agreed to discuss divorce matters that afternoon at the office of Charles' lawyer. At the meeting the couple agreed to a fair property settlement and Margret and Charles signed all the necessary papers, including a warranty deed that conveyed their interests in some jointly owned real estate to Mabel, a straw party who would after finalization of the divorce convey the property to Charles as part of his share. Charles died before the divorce was consummated, and Margret now claims that she had drunk nine beers and was so intoxicated that she has trouble remembering the specific events that took place in Charles' lawyer's office. Can Margret have the deed she signed set aside on the ground that she was intoxicated at the time she signed?

6. Hurley and his grandmother, Elizabeth Price, inherited as co-owners 575 shares of the common stock of Edison Company. At the time of inheritance, Hurley was a minor of the age of 20 years and lived with his grandmother. On December 11, 1955, the grandmother requested Hurley to sign a dividend order authorizing Edison Co. to pay all dividends due on the shares of stock to Elizabeth Price and Hurley signed the dividend orders without receiving any consideration therefor and without knowing the nature of the document being signed. Elizabeth Price died December 27, 1970, and it was not until March 18, 1971, that Hurley first learned that he was co-owner of the stock. On March 20, 1971, Hurley gave notice to Edison Co. that he disaffirmed the dividend order which he had signed earlier and demanded that the Edison Co. pay his one half of all dividends paid on the stock since he

became co-owner thereof. The Edison Co. refused to pay and Hurley brought suit. Edison Co. contends that Hurley did not disaffirm within a reasonable time after he became of age. Does Hurley have the right to disaffirm the contract?

7. Rotondo, on August 8, 1953, purchased a diamond ring from Kay Jewelry Company (Kay) informing the latter that he was a minor 19 years of age and that he was buying it as an engagement ring. Rotondo made a part payment of $94.49 on the ring. On that same day he presented the ring to his fiancée.

   On April 10, 1954, the engagement was terminated but the ring was not returned. Rotondo testified that he asked Kay to repossess the ring shortly after the engagement was broken, but there was no evidence that the ring was repossessed.

   On July 6, 1954, Rotondo, while still an infant, brought this suit to recover the payment made on the ring. Can Rotondo recover his payments?

8. Earlier in a criminal proceeding Davis had been found not guilty on the grounds of insanity. He was committed to a hospital for the criminally insane but in a mental health proceeding was not declared to be insane. He escaped from the hospital about five years before the bringing of this suit. During that time he had married and had established a trucking business. In connection with the trucking business he had bought equipment from the Colorado Kenworth Corporation (Kenworth) as follows: Kenworth tractor $15,000—paid on purchase price $9,058.90; trailer—paid $8,693.74; refrigeration unit, purchase price $17,450; tires $1,125, paid $242.50. Davis sold his business, including this equipment for $1,600, the value of his equity in the equipment. Notice of disaffirmance was given but no offer was made to place the parties *in statu quo*. Davis contends that since he was found to be insane in the criminal proceedings all his contracts are void. Is Davis right?

chapter 11

Illegality

Introduction

Nature of Illegality. A bargain is illegal if either its formation or its performance is detrimental to the general public interest. We recognize and protect the individual's right to bargain, but public welfare is paramount to individual rights, and whenever the bargain of individuals, either in its formation or in its performance, is criminal, tortious, or contrary to accepted standards of morality, it will be declared to be illegal and will not be enforced by court action. In general, illegal bargains are void; however, there are exceptions to the rule. (Note: In legal treatises and judges' opinions, the term "illegal contract" is commonly used. We have used "bargain" in preference to "contract" because "bargain" is a neutral word. "Illegal contract" is a contradiction of terms, and its use tends to be confusing.)

Classification. There are an infinite number of situations which give rise to illegal bargains. However, for the purpose of discussion, illegal bargains may be roughly classified into the following categories: (1) bargains in violation of positive law,[1] (2) bargains made void by statute, and (3) bargains contrary to public policy.

Presumption. In determining the legality of a bargain, the courts will presume that the parties intended a legal result and will interpret the bargain so as to hold it legal, unless it is clear that the parties intended an illegal bargain. All doubts are resolved in favor of the legality of the bargain.

Summary

A bargain is illegal if either its formation or its performance is detrimental to public policy. Bargains to commit a crime or tort, or bargains which are

---

[1] Law actually and specifically enacted or adopted by proper authority for the government of an organized jural society. *Black's Law Dictionary,* 4th ed. (St. Paul, Minn.: West Publishing Co., 1951), p. 1324.

contrary to accepted standards of morality, are illegal. Such bargains are generally declared to be void; however, there are exceptions to this rule. The courts, in interpreting a bargain, will presume that the parties intended to negotiate a legal contract.

Lachman v. Sperry-Sun Well Surveying Company
457 F.2d 850 (10th Cir. 1972)

Lachman (plaintiff) appealed from an order of the District Court, dismissing his suit for damages for breach of contract against Sperry-Sun Well Surveying Co. (defendant). Affirmed.

Lachman had an oil and gas lease on a tract in Oklahoma on which an oil and gas well had been drilled. In April 1967 he contracted with the Sperry Co. for a directional survey of the well. This contract forbade the Sperry Co. to communicate information concerning the survey or well to any third party. Sperry Co. completed the survey and submitted its report which indicated that the well deviated from the vertical to such an extent that it was bottomed on a neighboring tract of land the oil and gas rights to which belonged to third parties.

At the time of the survey the well was producing oil and gas from the adjoining tract. Some time after learning that Lachman's well deviated into the subsurface of the adjoining tract, employees of Sperry Co. notified the owners of the oil and gas rights on the adjoining tract of such deviation. These parties then brought suit against Lachman in the state court, and won a judgment establishing their rights to the proceeds of all oil and gas produced by the well and causing Lachman to plug the well back to his own boundary line.

Lachman later brought this suit against Sperry-Sun alleging a breach of contract by the disclosure of the results of the directional survey to the adjoining owners, the direct result of which was the adverse judgment referrred to above.

SETH, CIRCUIT JUDGE.   It is apparent that the basic issue in this appeal does not fall neatly within any well recognized legal category. While it is axiomatic that an agreement in violation of law is illegal and void, we are not presented here with a contract which, on its face, contravenes Oklahoma law. The Sperry Co. however contends that the effect of its contract with Lachman, if Lachman prevails, would make possible the undetected and wrongful depletion of the oil and gas under another's property. It suggests that the state has such an interest in preventing such an act that the contractual silence was properly broken.

An agreement, the object of which is the commission of a civil wrong against a third person, is also illegal and void although such wrong may not be an indictable offense or crime. In the present case the parties did not of course execute the contract for the purpose of harming the adjoining property owners, but it is clear that non-disclosure of the deviation would have had this result. Should the consequences be the same as if the fact were known when the contract was executed? At 6A Corbin, Contracts, § 1455, the author states: ". . . A bargain is illegal if it is made for the purpose of defrauding one or more third persons, or if its terms are such that it will have such an effect." The *Restatement of Contracts,* § 577 states: "A bargain, performance of which would tend to harm third persons by deceiving them as to material facts, or by defrauding them, or without justification by other means is illegal." The lack of fraud or deception in the present case, strictly speaking, removes it from these rules of contract law. They are cited, however, to indicate the law's reluctance to enforce contracts which have the effect of injuring third persons, whether such a possibility is anticipated or not. It is apparent that it is the silence contracted for in view of the facts found by the survey that creates a condition not contemplated by the parties and, had it been, the agreement for silence would be unenforceable.

*   *   *   *   *

In the instant case there is no assertion of dishonesty on the part of Lachman, and he characterizes his own trespasses as being unintentional and therefore "innocent." The trespasses, however characterized, worked substantial economic injury to the adjoining property owners, and were in violation of Oklahoma law.

In *Singer Sewing Machine Co.* v. *Escoe,* (1937) the defendant was accused by Singer of embezzlement. Defendant's uncle agreed to make up the loss and gave a promissory note in return for Singer's promise to conceal the crime. The Oklahoma Supreme Court held that the note given to one who knows of the commisssion of a crime for the purpose of compounding or concealing the crime or of preventing prosecution therefor is void.

These cases indicate that Oklahoma has expressed a stronger interest in the punishment of wrongful behavior than in the strict enforcement of contracts when the two interests collide.

*   *   *   *   *

It is public policy in Oklahoma and everywhere to encourage the disclosure of criminal activity, and a ruling here in accordance with the argument advanced by Lachman would serve to frustrate this policy. The distinction between a crime and a mere tort can often, as here, be a difference brought about by time, and knowledge. In the present case, the Sperry Co. may reasonably have felt that in adhering to the terms of its contract with Lachman it was silently watching a crime being committed or facts developing into such an act. The fact that Lachman did not release Sperry Co. from its promise once it was on notice that the well was pumping gas from adjoining tracts or to have taken some action themselves may have led Sperry Co. to believe that they planned to take advantage of the adjoining owners.

*   *   *   *   *

Bargains in Violation of Positive Law

Bargain to Commit a Crime.   It is axiomatic that a bargain which requires the commission of a crime is illegal. Also, a bargain which does not require the commission of a crime, but which is of such a nature that it tends to induce the commission of a crime, is illegal. The fact that a party to a bargain might benefit from the bargain if he or she commits a crime will not, as a general rule, make the bargain illegal, but if the inducement is strong enough to endanger the welfare of society, the bargain is illegal.

The nature of the bargain may be such that its formation is a crime. Connivance is a crime; and a bargain whereby one party, for a consideration, agrees to "look the other way" while the other party commits a crime is an illegal bargain. Also, if parties enter into a series of bargains, each innocent in itself but each a part of a plan to accomplish a criminal result, all of the bargains are illegal. For example, suppose the creation of a monopoly is made a crime under the statutes of the state. Arthur, Burton, Clayton, and Dyer own all the theaters in the area. They enter into a bargain to form a partnership to operate their theaters. The purpose of the partnership is to obtain a monopoly of the theater business in the area so that they can charge higher prices. The bargain is illegal, although a bargain to form a partnership to operate a theater is, standing by itself, legal, and the bargains to convey the theaters owned by the parties are, standing by themselves, legal. All of the bargains taken together are illegal, since the objective of the series of bargains is to create a monopoly in violation of positive law.

Bargain to Commit a Tort. The commission of a tort is clearly detrimental to the general public welfare; consequently, a bargain which cannot be performed without the commission of a tort is illegal. The fact that a tort may be committed during the performance of the bargain does not make it illegal. For example, suppose Adams contracts to build a large office building. During the course of the construction of the building an employee of Adams may negligently injure a pedestrian who is passing the building. The fact that such a tort may be committed in the performance of the construction contract does not make the contract illegal.

Summary

If the formation or the performance of a bargain requires a violation of positive law, it is illegal. The commission of a crime or a tort is a violation of positive law. If the formation or the performance of a bargain requires the commission of a crime or will induce the commission of a crime, the bargain is illegal. If a bargain cannot be performed without the commission of a tort, it is illegal. The fact that a tort may be committed in the performance of a contract does not render the contract illegal.

Bargains Made Illegal by Statutes

Types of Statutes.   The statutes affecting the legality of bargains may be divided into three classes: (1) criminal statutes, (2) statutes expressly declaring contracts void, and (3) regulatory statutes. All of these statutes are, as a general rule, so drafted that a penalty is imposed for the violation of the statute; consequently, they are basically criminal in nature. This classification considers as criminal statutes only those statutes the violation of which involves moral turpitude.

Wagering Statutes.   All states have enacted statutes prohibiting or regulating wagering. Such statutes are of special significance in the law of contracts. There is a thin line of distinction between wagering, risk shifting, and speculative bargaining. Risk shifting and speculative bargaining are legal; wagering is illegal. When the parties create a risk, which has no prior existence, for the purpose of bearing it, such a bargain is a wager or bet and is usually prohibited by wagering statutes.

A bargain for insurance is a typical example of a risk-shifting bargain and is, of course, legal. If the insured does not have an insurable interest in the insured property, then the bargain to insure is a wagering bargain and is illegal. In the case of property insurance the insured's relation to the property insured must be such that he or she will suffer pecuniary loss on the happening of the event against which the property is insured. The recovery of the insured is based on the principle of indemnity; and, as a general rule, his or her recovery cannot be greater than the pecuniary loss suffered. The pecuniary interest is not important in life insurance. In life insurance the relationship between the insured and the person obtaining the insurance must be such as to negate the existence of an intent to speculate in human life.

Stock and Commodity Market Transactions.   A good-faith transaction on the stock or commodity market is not illegal. It may be a speculative bargain, but it is not a wager. A wager based on the fluctuation in the price of a stock or commodity is illegal. The primary difference between the two is that in the valid stock or commodity market transaction, the stock or commodity is purchased, and the seller is bound to deliver the shares of stock or quantity of commodity bargained for, and the buyer is obligated to accept delivery and pay the agreed price; whereas in the wager transaction, no stock or commodity is purchased. It is merely a bargain to pay an amount based on the fluctuation in the price of a stock or commodity.

Marginal transactions are not illegal. In such a transaction the purchaser pays a portion of the purchase price to the broker who acts as his or her agent in buying the stock or commodity. When the broker buys the stock or commodity, he or she pays the purchase price in full. He or she then borrows the money to pay the difference between the margin paid by the purchaser and the full purchase price, and pledges the stock or commodity as security for the loan. The pledge agreement provides that if the market price of the stock or commodity declines below a certain point, the purchaser will pay additional margin to the broker, and on his or her failure to do so, the broker will sell the stock or commodity and from the proceeds pay the loan and pay over to the purchaser any surplus remaining. The purchaser may at any time order the broker to resell the stock or commodity, in which event the broker will do so, and from the proceeds discharge the loan and pay the balance over to the purchaser.

The fact that the purchaser may intend never to accept delivery of the stock or commodity does not affect the validity of the transaction. However, if there is an understanding between the broker and the purchaser to the effect that the purchaser will not be obligated to accept delivery of the stock or commodity, the transaction will be interpreted as a wager and will be illegal.

Statutes Declaring Bargains Void. State legislatures have enacted statutes which declare certain defined classes of bargains, or bargains made under certain circumstances, to be void. In some instances, it is clear from the wording of the statute and the surrounding circumstances that the legislative intent is to declare the bargain to be voidable, not void. There is little uniformity in the provisions of such statutes or in the subject matter included. In general, there is no moral turpitude involved in the violation of such statutes, and, with some exceptions, no penalty is imposed for their violation.

Usury laws and Sunday laws are examples of such statutes. Both have been generally adopted. The usury laws provide that if a charge for the use of money is made which is in excess of a stated amount, the lender will be subject to a penalty. The penalty imposed ranges from forfeiture of principal and interest to forfeiture of any amount of interest charged in excess of the legal rate of interest. In several states the usury laws do not apply to loans to corporations.

The Sunday laws prohibit the performance of certain labors and the transaction of business on Sunday. These statutes are not uniform in their provisions. The commoner forms of Sunday statute prohibit all contracts and sales not of necessity or charity. The Sunday statutes of several states follow the pattern of the early English statute and prohibit bargains which are of the "ordinary calling" of the parties. Ordinarily, only bargains which are completed on Sunday come within the prohibitive provisions of these statutes. A bargain negotiated on Sunday but closed on a secular or business day is not illegal. The courts have generally held that a bargain closed on Sunday but renegotiated or adopted on a secular or business day is not illegal.

Regulatory Statutes. A variety of statutes have been passed by Congress and the state legislatures regulating the dealings in a particular article of commerce. These statutes are not uniform either in their wording or in their scope, but certain types of statutes predominate. The commonest type of regulatory statute requires the obtaining of a license before a person, partnership, or corporation engages in the regulated activity. The purpose of such statutes is to protect the public against dishonest and unskilled persons. Lawyers, doctors, dentists, and other professional men and women are required to pass examinations before they are granted a license to practice their profession. In most states, real estate brokers, stock brokers, insurance agents, and others who are engaged in performing special services for the public are required to prove that they are of good character, and they may also be required to pass some type of examination or test of skill before they are granted a license.

Barbers, beauty parlor operators, building contractors, electricians, plumbers, and others performing skilled services may be required to obtain a license before they engage in their trade. In addition, some businessmen, such as pawnbrokers, retailers and wholesalers of liquor and tobacco, and sellers of other special commodities, are required to obtain a license before they engage in the regulated business. If a person bargains to perform services or engages in a regulated business without first having obtained a license, his or her bargain is illegal.

Revenue-Raising Statutes.   Some licensing statutes have as their objective the raising of revenue. Whether a statute requiring the obtaining of a license is a regulatory statute or a revenue-raising statute depends on the intention of the legislature. Some statutes are so worded that the intent of the legislature is not clearly expressed. However, if the statute requires proof of character and skill and imposes a penalty on a person who engages in the regulated activity before he or she first obtains a license, the statute, as a general rule, will be interpreted as a regulatory statute. But if the statute imposes a substantial license fee and provides that a license shall be issued to anyone paying the fee, and if the penalty imposed is a percentage of the fee or an interest charge based on the fee, the statute, as a general rule, will be interpreted as a revenue-raising statute. The failure to obtain a license required by the provisions of a revenue-raising statute in no way affects the validity of the bargains of the unlicensed person.

Summary

There are three classes of statutes which affect the legality of bargains: (1) criminal statutes, (2) statutes expressly declaring the bargain to be void, and (3) regulatory statutes.

Wagering bargains are illegal. A wager is the creation of a risk for the purpose of bearing it. Risk-shifting bargains are not illegal. Stock market and commodity market transactions entered into in good faith are not illegal; and likewise, margin transactions entered into in good faith are not illegal. However, if the principal purpose of a bargain is to wager on the fluctuation in the market price of a stock or commodity, it is illegal.

A wide variety of bargains and especially those involving certain subject matter are made void by state statute. If a person bargains to perform any of the skilled services which require a license without first obtaining a license, his or her bargains are illegal. However, if the licensing statute is a revenue-raising statute instead of a regulatory statute, the bargains of the unlicensed person are not illegal.

Schara v. Thiede

206 N.W.2d 129 (Sup. Ct. Wis. 1973)

Schara (plaintiff) brought an action seeking damages for breach of contract to lease a tavern against Thiede (defendant). An appeal was taken from a judgment for Schara. Reversed.

Thiede operated a tavern in Fond du Lac, Wisconsin and was interested in retiring and disposing of his tavern business. Glanz, in December of 1969, approached Thiede and proposed the acquisition of the business. It was agreed that Glanz would rent the tavern premises from Thiede for $300 per month, and Thiede would continue to live in the upstairs apartment. At the time of these negotiations, Thiede had a liquor license which was due to expire on June 30, 1970. For their mutual financial benefit, it was agreed that Glanz would operate the business for the remainder of the license term under Thiede's license. By so doing Glanz did not have to incur the expense of obtaining a license. Thiede asked his attorney to reduce the entire agreement to writing. The attorney never produced a formal contract, but Thiede obtained the attorney's rough draft, which he and Glanz signed as a memorandum agreement. The agreement purported to be an employment contract under which Glanz was to serve as "manager" of the tavern for Thiede. It provided that Glanz would retain the receipts from the operation in excess of $300 a month and would be responsible for paying the tavern bills. The memorandum also provided that, if Glanz performed faithfully as manager until June 30, 1970, he would be given a one-year lease on the tavern at a rental of $300 and could thereafter operate the business as his own. In fact, however, it was clearly understood from the very beginning that Glanz was to lease the tavern and operate it as his own without any control or supervision on the part of Thiede.

Under this arrangement, and operating under Thiede's license, Glanz operated the tavern until the spring of 1970. At that time, he entered into negotiations with Schara, who wished to buy out Glanz. Schara agreed to pay Glanz $7,500 for the business, which price was to cover the liquor and supplies on hand, as well as furniture and equipment belonging to Glanz. Thiede agreed to the substitution of Schara for Glanz as the operator of the tavern.

Since Schara also wanted to operate until June 30, 1970, without incurring the expense of securing a license, Glanz's rights under the agreement with Thiede were assigned to Schara. The original agreement was altered by striking out the name of Glanz and substituting therefor the name of Schara. Schara operated the tavern under the color of Thiede's license for the balance of the license year.

Within a short period of time, Schara ran into financial difficulties. When he attempted to secure a license in his own name for operating the premises subsequent to July 1, 1970, the common council of the city of Fond du Lac deferred the granting of the license to Schara and postponed the decision on the application until after the expiration of the license year.

Schara persisted in his attempt to get the license and to extend the lease. Thiede refused the tender of the rent check and leased the tavern to Singleton. By this time, the common council had rejected Schara's license application and accepted Singleton's. Schara sued Thiede for damag   r breach of contract.

HEFFERNAN, JUSTICE. De.   .he facial legality of an agreement, parol evidence is admissible to show that a w.   .ng valid on its face is a mere cover for an illegal transaction.

The evidence adduced at trial established that the written contract had little similarity to the parties' actual agreement as they understood it. Both Schara and Thiede, as well as Glanz, testified that there was never any intention that the operator of the tavern act as "manager" for Thiede. On the contrary, the parties contemplated that Glanz, and subsequently Schara, would operate the tavern as his own business and that the agreement was a lease and not a contract of employment.

While they denied that they knew that the arrangement was illegal, all parties to the contract recognized that the agreement was a subterfuge to cover the fact that both Glanz and Schara were operating the tavern without a proper license.

The resolution of this case is governed by *Sponholz v. Meyer* and *Brill v. Salzwedel* (1940). In both of these cases, the parties had entered into a partnership for the operation of a bar. In both cases, the agreement provided that only one of the partners was to obtain the license required by law, despite the statutory requirement that the names of all partners be submitted to the licensing authorities. The court found that such an arrangement to circumvent the licensing law was illegal, and in both cases denied recovery to a partner who sued for breach of the partnership agreement. Both *Sponholz* and *Brill* point out the public policy factors which compel a court to hold illegal any contract which has as its purpose the concealment from the public and the licensing authority of the identity of the true operator of an establishment for the sale of liquor.

We conclude, therefore, that the contract herein was so permeated with illegality that, in accordance with the principles set forth in *Swartzer v. Gillett,* the parties to the contract should be left by the court "just as it found them." *Swartzer* also points out that parties to an illegal contract:

[M]ust not expect that a judicial tribunal will degrade itself by an exertion of its powers to shift the loss from one to the other, or to equalize the benefits or burdens which may have resulted from the violation of law.

Standard Oil Co. v. Williams

288 N.E.2d 170 (Ct. App. Ind. 1972)

Williams (plaintiff), a holder of a credit card issued by Standard Oil Co. (defendant), filed a class action to recover monies paid to the company, based on usury. The trial court found in favor of Williams and Standard appealed. Reversed.

American Oil Company (a wholly owned subsidiary of Standard Oil Company of Indiana) adopted a "Revolving Charge Account Agreement," which read in part:

* * * * *

Buyer agrees to pay American either (1) the full amount of his outstanding balance within 25 days from his statement closing date (always 30 days from purchase date) in which event no FINANCE CHARGE will accrue or (2) an installment payment based on the following minimum payment schedule in which event a FINANCE CHARGE will be incurred; If outstanding balance is $10 to $100, the minimum payment is $10, or if balance is over $100, the minimum payment is 10% of balance. Balances under $10 are payable in full. Buyer may at any time pay his balance in full.

Buyer agrees to pay a FINANCE CHARGE computed by periodic rates of 1½% per month applied to the first $500 of his previous balance after deducting current payments, credits, and past due insurance premiums, and 1% per month of his previous balance in excess of $500, such FINANCE CHARGE to become part of buyer's outstanding balance.

1½% per month is an ANNUAL PERCENTAGE RATE OF 18%. 1% per month is an ANNUAL PERCENTAGE RATE OF 12%.

* * * * *

In addition, the credit card and sales slips reiterated the substance of the above quoted agreement.

Williams elected to defer payment and had been paying the 1½% Finance Charge prior to the filing of this cause.

ROBERTSON, PRESIDING JUDGE.   The legal basis for this case rests upon the following Indiana statutes:

Legal rates of interest on loans or forbearances.—The interest on loans or forbearance of money, goods, or things in action, shall be as follows:

(a) When the parties do not agree on the rate, interest shall be at the rate of six dollars ($6.00) per year per one hundred dollars ($100);

(b) By agreement in writing signed by the party to be charged thereby, and not otherwise, any obligor other than a corporation may lawfully agree to pay any rate of interest not in excess of eight dollars ($8.00) per year per one hundred dollars ($100); . . . .

Usurious rate of interest in contract—Debtor's recoupment.—When a greater rate of interest than is hereby allowed shall be contracted for, the contract shall be void as to the usurious interest contracted for; and, if it appears that interest at a higher rate than eight per cent (8%) has been, directly or indirectly, contracted for by an obligor other than a corporation, the excess of interest over six per cent (6%) shall be deemed usurious and illegal, and, in an action on a contract affected by such usury, the excess over the legal interest may be recouped by the debtor, whenever it has been reserved or paid before the bringing of the suit.

Williams further relies upon *Wisconsin v. J. C. Penney Co.* (1970), and *Rollinger v. J. C. Penney Co.* Both cases hold that under an agreement similar to the Revolving Charge Account Agreement in this case, the 1½% amounts to forebearance and is, therefore, usurious.

Standard maintains the position that the 1½% is a time-price differential which, under Indiana law, does not constitute usury.

A fair summary of the law upon which Standard relies, is contained in the *Stevens* case, which reads:

> The law is well settled that usury can only attach to a loan of money, or to the forbearance of a debt, and that on a contract to secure the price or value of work and labor done, or to be done, or of property sold, the contracting parties may agree upon one price if cash be paid, and upon as large an addition to the cash price as may suit themselves if credit be given; and it is wholly immaterial whether the enhanced price be ascertained by the simple addition of a lumping sum to the cash price, or by a percentage thereon. In neither case is the transaction usurious. It is neither a loan nor the forbearance of a debt, but simply the contract price of work and labor done and property sold; and the difference between cash and credit in such cases, whether 6,10 or 20 percent, must be left exclusively to the contract of the parties, and no amount of difference fairly agreed upon can be considered illegal."

It is our opinion that Standard's position is legally correct and the trial court erred as a matter of law in ruling as it did.

We are not unmindful of our duty to examine the transaction here involved as to its substance and not, necessarily, as to its form. In so examining we find this transaction, reduced to its most basic form, to be a sale of goods on credit.

Those cases which support Standard indicate the time-price differential has several identifiable attributes. A bona fide sale of property, a difference between cash and credit prices, no second or subsequent agreements as to price, payments in future installments and the absence of a prior existing debt, are but several of the more prominent distinctions. We are of the opinion that each of the aforementioned exist in the present case, thereby creating a time-price differential.

Public Policy

General Concept.   Public policy is one of those broad concepts which gives flexibility to the law where flexibility is needed. In many respects, it is comparable to the concept of the general public welfare. Public policy changes from time to time along with social and economic development. Conduct which may be acceptable in one era may not be acceptable in a later era, and vice versa. Also, the public policy of one state may differ in some degree from that of another.

Our concept of public policy goes beyond that of tortious or criminal conduct. A bargain, the performance of which would require the doing of an immoral or unethical act, would be illegal. There is no simple standard or rule which the court can use as the basis for determining whether or not a bargain is against public policy and illegal. Each case is treated as a separate problem, and the presiding judge has broad discretionary powers in determining the legality of the bargain. The public policy of a nation or state is reflected in its laws and judicial decisions.

Bargains Injurious to Public Service.   Any bargain is illegal if it tends to induce a public servant to deviate in any degree from the duty he or she owes the public. A bargain is illegal if it is a bargain to pay additional compensation to a public servant or if it is a bargain to pay an amount less than the salary provided by law for the performance of the duties of a public office. Any bargain is illegal if it is a bargain by a public officer whereby his or her personal interests in the matter may conflict with his or her duty to the public. A person may make his or her desires regarding legislation known to a member of Congress or a state legislature, but it is illegal to offer a congressman or legislator presents or personal favors to influence his or her decision on legislative matters. Obviously, a bargain to pay a public servant a bribe is illegal.

Bargains to Influence Fiduciaries.   Any bargain is illegal if it tends to induce a fiduciary—trustee, administrator, agent, or partner—to breach his or her fiduciary duties to his or her beneficiary or principal. Such a bargain is basically a fraud on the beneficiary or principal. In general, a fiduciary is not permitted to enter into any transactions whereby his personal interests will conflict with his fiduciary duties, unless he makes full disclosure of his interests to his beneficiary or principal and he effectively consents.

Bargains Relieving from Liability for Negligence.   The legality of a bargain relieving a person from the consequences of his or her own negligence depends on the relation of the parties and the nature of the duties owed. As a general rule a bargain whereby one of the parties attempts to provide against liability for his or her willful negligence or for fraud is illegal. Also, as a general rule a bargain relieving a person from the consequences of his or her negligence in the performance of a duty owed to the public is illegal. For example, if a common carrier bargains to relieve himself from liability for damage to property while in transit, where such damage results from the negligence of his agents or servants, the bargain is illegal. However, the common carrier may bargain to limit, to a reasonable degree, the amount of damages recoverable for injury to property in transit, where the injury is not due to the willful negligence of the carrier's agents or servants, and such a bargain will not be illegal.

If no duty is owed to the public and the parties are bargaining on a fair and equal basis, free from duress and undue influence, a bargain relieving one of the parties from his or her nonwillful negligence is legal. Property damage and public liability insurance contracts are legal. The objective of such contracts is to protect the insured against his or her liability for negligent acts.

Bargains in Restraint of Trade.   Bargains in direct restraint of trade are illegal. Any bargain whereby a person, for a consideration, agrees not to compete in trade with another is illegal. If people could enforce bargains not to compete, free competition could be destroyed.

Bargains are permitted which restrain trade if the restraint is reasonable and if valid interests are protected by the restraint. For example, if a contract for the sale of a business or for employment contains a provision which provides that the seller or employee will not compete with the buyer or employer, such provision is legal, provided the restraint is reasonable. A bargain in restraint of trade, if it is to be legal, must be a part of a contract—that is, ancillary to the contract—, must be for the purpose of protecting interests created by the contract, and must be no greater than is reasonable to protect those interests. If the contract is an employment contract, the restraint must be limited as to both space and time. As a general rule the restraint in a contract for the sale of a business or other property must be limited as to space but need not be limited as to time. However, under some circumstances the limitation must be as to both space and time.

The courts are not in complete accord as to the rights of the parties to a contract which includes a restraint provision which imposes a greater restraint on a party than is reasonably necessary to protect the interests created by the contract. If the restraint provision is divisible, the courts have, as a general rule, enforced that part of the restraint which is reasonable and refused to enforce that part which is unreasonable. In such cases the controversy is usually whether or not the restraint provision is divisible.

If the restraint provision is indivisible and is greater than is reasonably necessary to protect the interests created by the contract, a majority of the courts hold that the provision is illegal and void in its entirety and that it affords the party no protection. A minority of the courts hold that, even though indivisible in terms, the restraint provision is enforceable for as much of the restraint as would be reasonable.

Bargains to create monopolies and bargains which prevent the free alienation of property are in restraint of trade and are illegal. For example, suppose Arnold sells his farm, Willow Brook, to Bates, and Bates, as a part of the contract of sale, promises never to sell or mortgage Willow Brook. This promise is illegal and void.

Miscellaneous Illegal Bargains.   It is impossible to list and discuss all types of bargains which are against public policy and are illegal. Such bargains are limited only by the limitations of the ingenuity of man. Bargains to commit immoral acts, bargains which tend to interfere with marital relations or parental relations, collusive bargains to obtain a divorce, bargains to defraud, bargains which induce the breach of other contracts, and a variety of other bargains, the formation or performance of which would be detrimental to the general welfare, are illegal.

Summary

Bargains opposed to public policy vary so greatly that it is impossible to list them. The public policy of a state or nation is reflected in its constitution, laws, and judicial decisions. In general, any bargain is illegal if its formation or performance will be detrimental to the general welfare. Each case must be decided according to the facts of the case. Bargains are illegal if they tend to induce persons who owe a duty to serve the public to breach their duty. Bargains are illegal if they tend to induce a fiduciary to breach his or her fiduciary duty to his or her beneficiary or principal. Bargains relieving a person from liability for his or her nonwillfull negligence are legal, unless the duty of due care is owed to the public and unless the negligence will result in injury to the public.

From an early period, bargains in restraint of trade have been held to be illegal. However, a bargain in restraint of trade is legal if the restraint is ancillary and is no greater than is reasonably necessary to protect the interests created by the principal contract.

Troutman v. Southern Railway Co.

441 F.2d 586 (5th Cir. 1971)

Troutman, an attorney, (plaintiff) brought this action against the Southern Railway Company (defendant) to recover $200,000 as the reasonable value of legal services rendered. Judgment in the amount of $175,000 for Troutman and Southern appealed. Affirmed.

In 1963 the Interstate Commerce Commission issued an order directing Southern to increase certain rates on grain shipments from the Midwest to the Southeast by approximately 16 percent. The order created a difficult situation for Southern: if allowed to stand, the order, according to Southern, would result in its losing a $13,-000,000 investment in "Big John" railroad cars plus a "tremendous" loss of revenue in the future. Wilbanks, a vice president and assistant to the president of Southern, turned for help to Troutman, who had only recently come to Southern's aid in the Central of Georgia case. Troutman, an Atlanta attorney, had no experience in I.C.C. matters, but he was known to Wilbanks as a personal friend and political ally of President John F. Kennedy. Wilbanks told Troutman that Southern was filing suit in a federal district court in Ohio to enjoin the order of the I.C.C. He asked Troutman to persuade the President and the Department of Justice, then headed by the President's brother, Robert F. Kennedy, to "ditch" the I.C.C. and enter the case on the side of Southern. Troutman's efforts were successful: the Department of Justice filed an answer in the Ohio lawsuit opposing the I.C.C. and supporting Southern's position. As a result of the Ohio litigation (in which Troutman played no further part), the I.C.C. order was struck down. Troutman demanded compensation for his services in the grain rate case and when Southern refused to pay, Troutman filed suit.

WISDOM, CIRCUIT JUDGE.   Southern's first contention is that the district court erred in refusing to grant Southern's motion for judgment notwithstanding the verdict because the evidence conclusively establishes that the contract upon which Troutman sued was "to exert his personal and political influence upon the President of the United States." Southern argues that such a contract is in violation of public policy and unenforceable; therefore, the court erred as a matter of law in failing to render judgment for Southern. We cannot agree.

It is of course true that a contract to influence a public official in the exercise of his duties is illegal and unenforceable when that contract contemplates the use of personal or political influence rather than an appeal to the judgment of the official on the merits of the case. Nevertheless, all citizens possess the right to petition the government for redress of their grievances. (United States Constitution, Amendment I.) To that end, one may employ an agent or attorney to use his influence to gain access to a public official. Moreover, once having obtained an audience, the attorney may fairly present to the official the merits of his client's case and urge the official's support for that position. As the district court well stated in its opinion overruling Southern's motion for summary judgment, it is "only the elements of 'personal influence' and 'sinister means' that will void the contract and deny its enforcement."

Moreover, the illegal or sinister nature of a contract for professional services will not be presumed; the burden of proving the illegality of the contract is clearly upon the party asserting it.

It necessarily follows then that the decision whether to enforce a claim for compensation for these kinds of legal services will depend largely upon the facts of each case. Whether the parties in fact entered into a contract calling for the improper exercise of personal influence upon a public official is therefore a question for the jury, guided of course by proper instructions. In this case the jury concluded that Troutman had agreed with Southern to use his influence merely to gain access to the President and present to him the merits of Southern's case; therefore, the contract was valid and enforceable.

Weaver v. American Oil Co.

276 N.E.2d 144 (Sup. Ct. Ind. 1971)

Weaver (plaintiff) sued American Oil (defendant) for damages for personal injuries suffered as a result of the acts of Hoffer, an employee of American Oil. Weaver appealed from an adverse decision. Reversed.

Weaver first signed a station lease with American in 1956, and subsequently each year signed a new lease brought to him by an American Oil salesman. American Oil owned certain equipment located upon the leased premises; and on occasion when the equipment needed repair, Weaver would call American Oil and they would send a repairman to repair the equipment. Hoffer was a repairman working for American Oil.

On April 27, 1962, Hoffer came onto the leased premises for the purpose of repairing certain gasoline pumps. Following the repair of the gas pumps and during the demonstration thereof by Hoffer, gas was sprayed about and over the person of Weaver and his employee, Miller. The gasoline ignited, burning Weaver and his employee. Weaver filed suit seeking recovery of damages from American Oil for personal injuries. American set up as its defense the following provisions in Weaver's lease:

3. Lessor, its agents and employees shall not be liable for any loss, damage, injuries, or other casualty of whatsoever kind or by whomsoever caused, to the person or property of anyone

(including Lessee) on or off the premises, arising out of or resulting from Lessee's use, possession or operation thereof, or from defects in the premises whether apparent or hidden, or from the installation, existence, use, maintenance, condition, repair, alteration, removal or replacement of any equipment thereon, whether due in whole or in part to negligent acts or omissions of Lessor, its agents or employees; and Lessee for himself, his heirs, executors, administrators, successors and assigns, hereby agrees to indemnify and hold Lessor, its agents and employees, harmless from and against all claims, demands, liabilities, suits or actions (including all reasonable expenses and attorneys' fees incurred by or imposed on the Lessor in connection therewith) for such loss, damage, injury or other casualty. . . .

ATTERBURN, CHIEF JUSTICE. It will be noted that this lease clause not only exculpated the leasor oil company from its liability for its negligence, but also compelled Weaver to indemnify them for any damages or loss incurred as a result of its negligence. The appellate court held the exculpatory clause invalid, 261 N.E.2d 99, but the indemnifying clause valid, 262 N.E.2d 663. In our opinion, both these provisions must be read together since one may be used to effectuate the result obtained through the other. We find no ground for any distinction and we therefore grant the petition to transfer the appeal to this court.

This is a contract, which was submitted (already in printed form) to a party with lesser bargaining power. As in this case, it may contain unconscionable or unknown provisions which are in fine print. Such is the case now before this court.

The facts reveal that Weaver had left high school after one and a half years and spent his time, prior to leasing the service station, working at various skilled and unskilled labor-oriented jobs. He was not one who should be expected to know the law or understand the meaning of technical terms. The ceremonious activity of signing the lease consisted of nothing more than the agent of American Oil placing the lease in front of Mr. Weaver and saying "sign," which Mr. Weaver did. There is nothing in the record to indicate that Weaver read the lease; that the agent asked Weaver to read it; or that the agent, in any manner, attempted to call Weaver's attention to the "hold harmless" clause in the lease. Each year following, the procedure was the same. A salesman, from American Oil, would bring the lease to Weaver, at the station, and Weaver would sign it. The superior bargaining power of American Oil is patently obvious and the significance of Weaver's signature upon the legal document amounted to nothing more than a mere formality to Weaver for the substantial protection of American Oil.

Had this case involved the sale of goods it would have been termed an "unconscionable contract" under sec. 2–302 of the Uniform Commercial Code. . . .

According to the Comment to Official Text, the basic test of unconscionability is whether, in light of the general commercial background and the commercial needs of the particular trade or case, the clauses involved are so one-sided as to be unconscionable under the circumstances existing at the time of the making of the contract. Subsection two makes it clear that it is proper for the court to hear evidence upon these questions.

An "unconscionable contract" has been defined to be such as no sensible man not under delusion, duress or in distress would make, and such as no honest and fair man would accept. There exists here an "inequality so strong, gross and manifest that it is impossible to state it to a man of common sense without producing an exclamation at the inequality of it.""Where the inadequacy of the price is so great that the mind revolts at it the court will lay hold on the slightest circumstances of oppression or advantage to rescind the contract."

It is not the policy of the law to restrict business dealings or to relieve a party of his own mistakes of judgment, but where one party has taken advantage of another's necessities and distress to obtain an unfair advantage over him, and the latter, owing to his condition, has encumbered himself with a heavy liability or an onerous obligation for the sake of a small or inadequate present gain, there will be relief granted. *Stiefler v. McCullough* (1933). . . .

The facts of this case reveal that in exchange for a contract which, if the clause in question is enforceable, may cost Mr. Weaver potentially thousands of dollars in damages for negligence of which he was not the cause, Weaver must operate the service station seven days a week for long hours, at a total yearly income of $5,000–$6,000. The evidence also reveals that *the clause was in fine print* and *contained no title heading* which would have identified it as an indemnity clause. It seems a deplorable abuse of justice to hold a man of poor education, to a contract prepared by the attorneys of American Oil, for the benefit of American Oil which was presented to Weaver on a "take it or leave it basis."

*   *   *   *   *

The traditional contract is the result of free bargaining of parties who are brought together by the play of the market, and who meet each other on a footing of approximate economic equality. In such a society there is no danger that freedom of contract will be a threat to the social order as a whole. But in present-day commercial life the standardized mass contract has appeared. It is used primarily by enterprises with strong bargaining power and position. The weaker party, in need of the good or services, is frequently not in a position to shop around for better terms, either because the author of the standard contract has a monopoly (natural or artificial) or because all competitors use the same clauses.

The law should seek the truth or the subjective understanding of the parties in this more enlightened age. The burden should be on the party submitting such "a package" in printed form to show that the other party had knowledge of any unusual or unconscionable terms contained therein. The principle should be the same as that applicable to implied warranties, namely that a package of goods sold to a purchaser is fit for the purposes intended and contains no harmful materials other than that represented. Caveat lessee is no more the current law than caveat emptor. Only in this way can justice be served and the true meaning of freedom of contract preserved. The analogy is rational. We have previously pointed out a similar situation in the Uniform Commercial Code, which prohibits unconscionable contract clauses in sales agreements.

When a party can show that the contract, which is sought to be enforced, was in fact an unconscionable one, due to a prodigious amount of bargaining power on behalf of the stronger party, which is used to the stronger party's advantage and is unknown to the lesser party, causing a great hardship and risk on the lesser party, the contract provision, or the contract as a whole, if the provision is not separable, should not be enforceable on the grounds that the provision is contrary to public policy. The party seeking to enforce such a contract has the burden of showing that the provisions were explained to the other party and *came to his knowledge* and there was in fact *a real and voluntary meeting of the minds and not merely an objective meeting.*

Central Credit Collection Control Corp. v. Grayson

499 P.2d 57 (Wash. Ct. App. 1972)

Central Credit (plaintiff) brought an action against a former employee, Grayson (defendant), to enforce a restrictive covenant contained in an employment contract. Judgment for Central and Grayson appealed. Affirmed.

Central was engaged in the debt collection business in Pierce County and its surrounding counties. In May, 1964, Central entered into a 6-year employment contract with Grayson which contained this restrictive covenant:

The employee will not, in Pierce County, Washington, or in any county bordering on Pierce County within the State of Washington, directly or indirectly engage in the same or similar line of business as that now carried on by the employer or in which the employer becomes engaged during the term of this contract for a period of two years from and after termination of employment under this contract. [Section 6.]

Another clause of the contract stated the reason that a restrictive covenant was incorporated into the agreement:

The employee agrees that it would be impossible, after having received training afforded by the employer, to work for any other collection agency or credit company without using some or all of the trade secrets and information imparted to the employee by the employer or without disclosing some of the employer's trade practices, secrets, methods of operation and information. It is for this reason that the employee has agreed to not become directly or indirectly engaged in such business for a period of two years after the termination of his employment with the employer named in this contract. [Section 10.]

Employment under the contract terminated in May, 1970, but Grayson continued in Central's employment until October 30, 1970. In July or August of that year, Grayson commenced discussions with others concerning the opening of a competing collection business in Pierce County.

In November, 1970, Grayson organized a collection agency corporation and located its principal office some 73 yards from Central's business location. Subsequently, he commenced handling a number of accounts formerly serviced by Central. In December the total accounts in Grayson's new Corporation amounted to $26,000, and by February, 1971 had risen to approximately $44,000. Collections on accounts were averaging $5,000 to $7,000 per month.

PEARSON, JUDGE. It is well settled that covenants not to compete upon termination of employment are valid, but should not be greater than reasonably necessary to protect the business or good will of the employer.

The contract recited that the employer had expended considerable sums of money in developing business in Pierce, King, Kitsap, Thurston, Mason, Grays Harbor, and Lewis counties. This recitation was not challenged by any testimony to the contrary which might raise a factual issue that the area was broader than necessary to protect Central's business interests.

We think the trial court was warranted in concluding that as a matter of law the act of Grayson in locating his competing business within 73 yards of Central's business was violative of a reasonable area restriction. See *Wood v. May,* where it was held that a court of equity may enforce a covenant not to compete to a reasonable area, even though it was factually demonstrated that the area restriction was unreasonable.

The same rationale applies to the time restriction, which becomes crucial only if an injunction is granted for the full time limit. Where the undisputed evidence presented to the trial court showed that Grayson opened the competing business within one month of the termination of his employment, the trial court was warranted in determining as a matter of law, that for the purposes of granting damages a reasonable time restriction covenant was breached.

Grayson's final contention, that the $5,000 in liquidated damages presented an issue of material fact as to whether that amount was a penalty, is also without merit. The parties agreed that any damages would be severe and extremely difficult to determine and fix. (Section 12.) The unrefuted evidence showed that the damage amount prescribed was less than the equivalent of the first month of collections from Grayson's business. In cases involving a breach of a restrictive covenant between competing businesses, damages are not susceptible of accurate determination and a liquidated damages provision is entirely proper.

Wilson v. Clarke

470 F.2d 1218 (1st Cir. 1972)

The plaintiff, Nordli, Wilson Associates (Nordli) appeals from a decision of the district court refusing to enforce a provision of an employment contract against its former employee Clarke (defendant). Affirmed.

In September, 1964, Clarke signed a letter agreement prepared by Nordli which confirmed his existing employment as a "consulting psychologist" which contained the following provisions:

. . . that if, at any time during a five (5) year period commencing on the day following the termination of your employment, any clients or prospective clients of the firm shall, directly or indirectly, receive professional psychological services of any sort from you, or from any other partnership or association with which you shall become associated in any manner whatsoever, or from any corporation of which you shall become an officer, director, stockholder or employee; then, you shall pay to the firm, for said five (5) year period or such shorter period as you, said other partnership or association or any said corporation shall be, directly or indirectly, performing professional psychological services of any sort for said client or clients, the greater of either (A) an amount equal to fifteen percent (15%) of the gross billings received from said client or clients, by you, by said other partnership or association, or by any said corporation; or (B) an amount equal to fifteen per cent (15%) of the total remuneration received by you by way of income, salary, wages, commissions or otherwise from said client or clients, said other partnership or association or any said corporation."

Clarke's principal duties with Nordli were to make psychological assessments of candidates for positions within its business clientele. Two of these were life insurance companies, for which he mainly assessed persons seeking positions as salesmen (he also assessed some prospects for advancement or termination). For a Buffalo, New York, firm, he assessed candidates for middle or lower-middle management positions, and a few candidates for executive positions.

At the time Clarke began working for Nordli, ITT was not its client. In April 1964, Dr. Beare of ITT called Mr. Wilson, a Nordli partner, to arrange an appointment to discuss Nordli's becoming one of ITT's consulting firms. Wilson could not keep the appointment, and Clarke met with Beare instead. Thereafter, Nordli worked for ITT "in a small way." In September 1965, Dr. Beare called Clarke and asked if he was interested in working for ITT. Beare said that he was planning to leave and was looking for someone to replace him. In October 1965, Clarke, still in Nordli's employ, made two assessments of candidates for ITT employment in New York. In early November 1965, he indicated that he would leave Nordli, and did so early in 1966.

Nordli sued claiming that Clarke's duties with ITT (until August 1969, when it concedes they became "very much different") were such that the latter received "professional psychological service" from Clarke within the terms of the employment contract. As ITT had been a client, Nordli claims that it is entitled to 15% of Clarke's ITT compensation from salary and bonuses from February 1966 until August 1969.

CAMPBELL, CIRCUIT JUDGE. Bargains between employers and employees which place restrictions upon an employee's exercise of a gainful occupation after leaving the employer are, and were at common law considered to be, void as in restraint of trade.

Exceptions are made, however, if the restriction is reasonable, "and not wider than is necessary for the protection to which the employer is entitled."

In cases of agreements forbidding an employee to engage in the same business or line of activity as the employer, attention is often given to whether the agreement is reasonably limited as to area and duration. But such considerations are merely aspects of the rule, quoted above, that the agreement must be no wider than is necessary to afford reasonable protection to the employer. A further, and here more relevant, aspect of the rule is that an employer may not enforce limitations on an ex-employee's engaging in activities which do no damage to the employer.

In two recent decisions, the Massachusetts Court has refused to enforce non-competition covenants in employment agreements where the plaintiff-employer could not prove that it was damaged by the employee's work for another firm.

Clarke's duties at ITT, whether or not designated "professional psychological services," did not injure Nordli by diminishing or dispensing with the need for Nordli's services. Assuming, as we do, that Nordli had every right to protect itself reasonably against Clarke's utilizing his position at Nordli to steal a Nordli client, the facts here do not indicate that that is what happened. It is true that Clarke's Nordli position was a springboard from which his ITT association was launched; and had he left Nordli to become an independent (or ITT hired) consulting psychologist doing assessments for ITT in competition with Nordli, the situation would be different. However, Clarke took over a management function at ITT. The work he managed included the making of assessments. But his role was not that of a consulting psychologist. He was the liaison between higher ITT management and the assessment of ITT executives. He directed and hired people to do what he had once done.

*   *   *   *   *

An employer's right, . . . to place future burdens on an employee merely to forestall or offset the loss of his services is clearly limited:

[A]n employer cannot by contract prevent his employee from using the skill and intelligence acquired or increased and improved through experience or through instruction received in the course of the employment. The employee may achieve superiority in his particular department by every lawful means at hand, and then, upon the rightful termination of his contract for service, use that superiority for the benefit of rivals in trade of his former employer. As was said in *Herbert Morris, Limited, v. Saxelby*: "A man's aptitudes, his skill, his dexterity, his manual or mental ability . . . ought not to be relinquished by the servant; they are not his master's property; they are his own property; they are himself."

Doubtless an employer who has provided specialized training to an employee—as by a course of studies or the like—might reasonably contract with the employee for reimbursement if the employee should quit before the employer achieves any benefit. However, the employer may not require its ex-employee to make payments to it unrelated to the employer's damage, simply as a penalty to discourage or punish a job change. At most, the employer, in appropriate circumstances, might require the employee to reimburse it for a sum or under a formula, reasonably related to what it cost the employer to train him, or to retrain a replacement, or the like.

Effect of Illegality

General Rule. As a general rule a court will not enforce an illegal bargain but will leave the parties where it finds them. They cannot recover damages for breach of the illegal promises, cannot recover consideration from which they have parted, and cannot recover in quasi contract for benefits conferred. The courts do not follow this rule as a means of punishing one of the parties, but for the reason that the results obtained thereby best serve the interests of the public. If the facts and circumstances are such that the interests of the public are best served by allowing a recovery, such recovery will be granted.

Ignorance of Fact or Special Regulation. Even though ignorance is, as a general rule, no excuse, the courts have, in exceptional cases, granted recovery to a party to an illegal bargain if the party has been ignorant of the facts which made the bargain illegal, provided the other party had knowledge of the illegality and provided the illegality does not involve moral turpitude. If both parties are ignorant of the facts which make the bargain illegal, the courts have, in some cases, permitted the parties to recover for performance rendered before they learned of the illegal nature of the bargain. In no case will the courts allow recovery for performance rendered after knowledge of the illegality.

In cases in which one of the parties is ignorant of a special statutory regulation of the other's business and of the violation thereof, the courts will allow recovery for performance rendered by the innocent party before he or she learns of the illegality. For example, suppose Alberts, an actor, contracts to perform for Bates, the operator of a theater. Bates has not obtained a license to operate the theater as required by a penal regulatory statute. Alberts, in ignorance of the violation of the statute by Bates, performs his part of the bargain. Alberts can recover the compensation promised by Bates.

Rights of Protected Parties.   Most regulatory statutes have as their objective the protection of the public. As a general rule, if a bargain is entered into by a person who is guilty of the violation of a regulatory statute with another for whose protection the statute was adopted, such bargain will be declared void as to the party violating the statute but enforceable by the protected party. For example, suppose a foreign corporation does intrastate business in a state without obtaining a license, and the laws of the state expressly provide that the contracts of an unlicensed foreign corporation doing intrastate business in the state shall be void. The corporation, in such a case, cannot enforce a contract made by it while unlicensed, but the other party to the contract can enforce it against the corporation.

If the parties to an illegal bargain are not equally guilty but one of the parties has been induced to enter into the bargain by the other party, the courts will grant recovery to the less guilty person. For example, suppose a confidence man induces his victim to enter into a bargain which is illegal as a means of defrauding him. The victim can recover what he has parted with, unless the illegal act involved moral turpitude.

Knowledge of Illegal Use.   Knowledge that an article sold will be used for an illegal purpose will not make the sale illegal, unless the use to be made of the article is a serious crime. If an article is sold or money is loaned for the purpose of aiding in the commission of a crime, the sale or the loan is illegal, and the party making the sale or the loan cannot recover the sale price of the article or the money loaned. For example, if Alberts loans Bates $50 knowing that Bates intends to play cards for money that evening, Alberts can recover a judgment for the $50 loaned. However, if Bates is at the card table gambling and Alberts loans Bates $50 to enable Bates to continue his gambling, the loan is illegal, and Alberts cannot recover a judgment for the $50 loaned.

Divisible Contracts.   If part of a bargain is legal and part is illegal, the courts will enforce the legal part if the legal can be separated from the illegal. But if the bargain is an indivisible bargain and part of it is illegal, the illegal part will taint the entire bargain, and the whole will be void.

A contract is divisible when it consists of several promises or acts on the part of one party and each promise or act is matched by a corresponding promise or act on the part of the other party so that there is a separate consideration for each promise or act.

If a provision in a contract is illegal but the illegal provision does not affect the principal purpose of the contract, the principal portion will be enforced but the illegal provision will not. For example, suppose Alberts sells his barber shop to Bates. The contract of sale provides that Alberts will not engage in barbering during the remainder of his life. The restraint provision is illegal, but the sales contract, except the restraint provision, will be enforced.

Rescission before Performance of Illegal Act. If one of the parties to an illegal contract rescinds the contract before the performance of the illegal act, he or she may recover any consideration he or she has given. If a party to a bet gives notice of withdrawal and demands the return of his money before the stakeholder has paid it over, he can recover his money. However, if a stakeholder refuses to pay to the winner the money which has been bet, the winner can recover the money. The statutes of some states provide that one who has lost money gambling can recover it.

Summary

As a general rule, if parties have entered into an illegal bargain, neither can recover a judgment if the other party fails to fulfill his or her promises. No recovery is granted in quasi contract for the benefits conferred in the fulfillment of an illegal bargain. If the parties are not equally at fault, the courts may, if the circumstances demand it, grant one party relief.

If one party is justifiably ignorant of the facts which make the bargain illegal or is ignorant of a special regulation, he or she may recover for consideration given. Also, the party protected by a regulatory statute may recover for breach of a contract entered into with a person who has not complied with the provisions of the statute.

As a general rule, knowledge that an article sold will be used illegally does not make the sale illegal, but if the use intended is the commission of a serious crime, the sale is illegal. Also, if the sale is for the purpose of aiding in the commission of a crime, it is illegal.

If a bargain is divisible and part is legal and part is illegal, the courts will enforce the legal parts and not the illegal parts, unless the illegal parts go to the principal objective of the contract. If the bargain is indivisible and part is illegal, the entire bargain is void. A party may rescind an executory illegal bargain before the performance of the illegal act and recover any consideration given.

Lawn v. Camino Heights, Inc.

93 Cal. Rptr. 631 (Cal. Ct. App. 1971)

Action by Lawn (plaintiff) against Camino Heights, Inc. (defendant) for compensation due under a contract. Lawn appealed from an adverse judgment. Reversed in part. Harold Brock and Eleanor Brock were husband and wife and the owners of about 325 acres of agricultural land ("Camino Heights Orchards").They were in serious financial straits and Mr. Brock decided to subdivide the ranch. He consulted the plaintiff who suggested that a subdivision development corporation would be formed to which the Brocks would convey their ranch in exchange for shares of stock. Lawn prepared the articles of incorporation which were filed on November 27, 1961.

On December 18, 1961, Lawn and Camino Heights, Inc., (through Mr. Brock, as its president) entered into the following written agreement:

Camino Heights, Inc. proposes to employ you in the capacity of consultant . . . for a period of two years at $8,400 per year effective immediately and payable in stock of the corporation at the end of each year of employment.

We further agree that when residential lots are developed we will convey to you or your nominee five (5) such lots free and clear provided that you or your nominee agree to start construction within six months of such conveyance. After dwellings have been completed on the above five lots, we will make available to you or your nominee additional residential lots at the regular sales price but on a subordinated basis.

The purpose of the contract was to compensate Lawn for his services in developing the subdivision as neither the Brocks nor the corporation had any money. Lawn never received any of the consideration promised by the corporation in the contract of December 18, 1961.

JANES, ASSOCIATE JUSTICE. Since no permit had been obtained from the Commissioner of Corporations at the time the agreement for such payment was made, defendant corporation's promise to compensate Lawn in stock was illegal and unenforceable even though the parties may have intended to obtain a permit before the stock was issued.

Lawn contends that Camino's further promise to convey five residential lots was severable from its agreement to pay him in stock.

[T]he rule relating to severability of partially illegal contracts is that a contract is severable if the court can, consistent with the intent of the parties, reasonably relate the illegal consideration on one side to some specified or determinable portion of the consideration on the other side. . . .

If any part . . . of several considerations for a single object, is unlawful, the entire contract is void.

Nothing in the written agreement of December 18, 1961, nor in the other evidence before the court, suggested that any *part* of Lawn's services had been promised in exchange for the illegal promise to pay stock, or that the parties had allocated the rest of Lawn's services as consideration for the legal promise to convey lots. Camino's two promises were consideration for a single object—namely, Lawn's promise to serve as a consultant. Therefore, the promise to convey lots was not severable from the illegal promise, and cannot provide the basis for a recovery of damages under the written contract.

Lawn further contends that he was entitled to recover the reasonable value of his services under the common count even though the aforesaid illegality and inseverability of consideration preclude relief under his cause of action for breach of the express contract. His contention must be sustained.

The proper rule, amply supported by authority, is thus stated in 27 *Cal.Jur.* p. 210, § 17:

The law does not imply a promise to pay for services illegally rendered under a contract expressly prohibited by statute. But if the services rendered under a void contract by one party thereto were not intrinsically illegal and the other party fails voluntarily to perform on his part, the former may recover as upon a quantum meruit for what the latter actually received in value, though no recovery can be had upon the contract.

Camino's will be unjustly enriched at Lawn's expense if he cannot recover from it the reasonable value of his services.

Unenforceable Contracts and the Uniform Commercial Code

Unconscionability.   The court may refuse to enforce an unconscionable contract or an unconscionable clause in a contract for the sale of goods. The Code (2–302) provides:

(1) If the court as a matter of law finds the contract or any clause of the contract to have been unconscionable at the time it was made the court may refuse to enforce the contract, or it may enforce the remainder of the contract without the unconscionable clause, or it may so limit the application of the unconscionable clause as to avoid any unconscionable result.

(2) When it is claimed or appears to the court that the contract or any clause thereof may be unconscionable the parties shall be afforded a reasonable opportunity to present evidence as to its commercial setting, purpose and effect to aid the court in making the determination.

An unconscionable contract is one in which one of the parties being in a strategic position takes advantage of the situation and drives a bargain which is unfair and commercially unreasonable. In the past this concept has been applied in equity in that a court will not grant specific performance of an unconscionable contract. The expanded concept does not require that the situation involve fraud, duress, or undue influence although elements of fraud and duress frequently are present. The following illustrate some of the situations where various courts have applied Section 2–302 as a basis for denying enforcement of certain contract provisions.

1.   Small print on the back of signature cards prepared by banks which waived the depositor's right to a jury trial in the event of litigation.[2]
2.   A clause in a home improvement contract between a Maine corporation and a Massachusetts citizen which stipulated the New York law would apply.[3]
3.   A clause disclaiming all liability on warranties where the goods were found to be worthless.[4]
4.   Excessively high prices or excessive credit charges.[5]

[2] *David v. Manufacturers Hanover Trust Co.,* 4 U.C.C. Rep. 1145 (N.Y. Civ. Ct. 1968).
[3] *Paragon Homes, Inc. v. Carter,* 4 U.C.C. Rep. 1144 (N.Y. Sup. Ct. 1968).
[4] *Vlases v. Montgomery Ward & Co., Inc.,* 377 F.2d 846 (3rd Cir. 1967).
[5] *Central Budget Corp. v. Sanchez,* 279 N.Y.2d 391 (N.Y. Civ. Ct. 1967).

Additional examples of the application of the "unconscionable" concept are discussed in the case which follows.

Summary

The court may find that a contract or any part of it to be unconscionable and unenforceable as a matter of law. To be unconscionable a clause must be unfair and commercially unreasonable at the time of making of the contract. The principle is prevention of oppression and unfair surprise. The court may enforce the contract in part or limit the application of any unconscionable clause so as to avoid an unconscionable result.

Williams v. Walker-Thomas Furniture Co.

350 F.2d 145 (D.C. Cir. 1965)

Walker-Thomas Furniture Co. (plaintiff) brought these two separate actions (consolidated for purposes of appellate review) against Williams (defendant) to repossess certain furniture sold on credit. Judgment for Furniture Co. and Williams appealed. Reversed.

Furniture Co. operated a retail furniture store in the District of Columbia. During the period from 1957 to 1962, Williams purchased a number of household items from Furniture Co., for which payment was to be made in installments. The terms of each purchase were contained in a printed form contract which set forth the value of the purchased item and purported to lease the item to the customer for a stipulated monthly rent payment. The contract then provided that title would remain in Furniture Co. until the total of all the monthly payments made equaled the stated value of the item, at which time the customers could take title. In the event of a default in the payment of any monthly installment, Furniture Co. could repossess the item.

The contract further provided that:

the amount of each periodical installment payment to be made by purchaser to the Company under this present lease shall be inclusive of and not in addition to the amount of each installment payment to be made by purchaser under such prior leases, bills or accounts; *and all payments now and hereafter made by purchaser shall be credited pro rata on all outstanding leases, bills and accounts* due the Company by purchaser at the time each such payment is made. (Emphasis added.)

The effect of this rather obscure provision was to keep a balance due on every item until the balance due on all items, whenever purchased, was liquidated. As a result, the debt incurred at the time of purchase of each item was secured by the right to repossess all the items previously purchased by the same purchaser, and each new item purchased automatically became subject to a security interest arising out of the previous dealings.

On April 17, 1962, Williams bought a stereo set of stated value of $514.95.[6] She

---

[6] At the time of this purchase her account showed a balance of $164 still owing from her prior purchases. The total of all the purchases made over the years in question came to $1,800. The total payments amounted to $1,400.

defaulted shortly thereafter, and Walker-Thomas sought to replevy all the items purchased since December, 1957.

WRIGHT, CIRCUIT JUDGE.   Williams' principal contention, rejected by both the trial and the appellate courts below, is that these contracts, or at least some of them are unconscionable and, hence, not enforceable. In its opinion the District of Columbia Court of Appeals explained its rejection of this contention as follows:

Williams' second argument presents a more serious question. The record reveals that prior to the last purchase Williams had reduced the balance in her account to $164. The last purchase, a stereo set, raised the balance due to $678. Significantly, at the time of this and the preceding purchases, Furniture Co. was aware of Williams' financial position. The reverse side of the stereo contract listed the name of Williams' social worker and her $218 monthly stipend from the government. Nevertheless, with full knowledge that Williams had to feed, clothe and support both herself and seven children on this amount, Furniture Co. sold her a $514 stereo set.

We cannot condemn too strongly Furniture Co.'s conduct. It raises serious questions of sharp practice and irresponsible business dealings. A review of the legislation in the District of Columbia affecting retail sales and the pertinent decisions of the highest court in this jurisdiction disclose, however, no ground upon which this court can declare the contracts in question contrary to public policy. We note that were the Maryland Retail Installment Sales Act, Art. 83 §§ 128–153, or its equivalent, in force in the District of Columbia, we could grant Williams appropriate relief. We think Congress should consider corrective legislation to protect the public from such exploitive contracts as were utilized in the case at bar.

We do not agree that the court lacked the power to refuse enforcement to contracts found to be unconscionable. In other jurisdictions, it has been held as a matter of common law that unconscionable contracts are not enforceable. While no decision of this court so holding has been found, the notion that an unconscionable bargain should not be given full enforcement is by no means novel.

Congress has recently enacted the Uniform Commercial Code, which specifically provides that the court may refuse to enforce a contract which it finds to be unconscionable at the time it was made. The enactment of this section, which occurred subsequent to the contracts here in suit, does not mean that the common law of the District of Columbia was otherwise at the time of enactment, nor does it preclude the court from adopting a similar rule in the exercise of its powers to develop the common law for the District of Columbia. In fact, in view of the absence of prior authority on the point, we consider the congressional adoption of § 2–302 persuasive authority for following the rationale of the cases from which the section is explicitly derived. Accordingly, we hold that where the element of unconscionability is present at the time a contract is made, the contract should not be enforced.

Unconscionability has generally been recognized to include an absence of meaningful choice on the part of one of the parties together with contract terms which are unreasonably favorable to the other party. Whether a meaningful choice is present in a particular case can only be determined by consideration of all the circumstances surrounding the transaction. In many cases the meaningfulness of the choice is negated by a gross inequality of bargaining power. The manner in which the contract was entered is also relevant to this consideration. Did each party to the contract, considering his obvious education or lack of it, have a reasonable opportunity to understand the terms of the contract, or were the important terms hidden in a maze of fine print and minimized by deceptive sales practices? Ordinarily, one who signs an agreement without full knowledge of its terms might be held to assume the risk that he has entered a one-sided bargain. But when a party of little bargaining power, and hence little real choice, signs a commercially unreasonable contract with little or no knowledge of its terms, it is hardly likely that his consent, or even an objective manifestation of his consent, was ever given to all the terms. In such a case the usual rule that the terms of the agreement are not to be questioned should be abandoned and the court should consider whether the terms of the contract are so unfair that enforcement should be withheld.

In determining reasonableness or fairness, the primary concern must be with the terms of the contract considered in light of the circumstances existing when the contract was made. The test is not simple, nor can it be mechanically applied. The terms are to be considered "in the light of the general commercial background and the commercial needs of the particular trade or case." Corbin suggests the test as being whether the terms are "so extreme as to appear unconscionable according to the mores and business practices of the time and place." We think this formulation correctly states the test to be applied in those cases where no meaningful choice was exercised upon entering the contract.

Problem Cases

1. Mascari, a beer wholesaler, sold Raines, a beer retailer, some beer on credit. Raines gave a promissory note for $1,900 to Mascari as security. A state statute provided that all sales of beer by wholesalers to retailers were to be for cash only. Violations were subject to fine and imprisonment. The intent of the statute was to effectively collect the tax on such sales and to prohibit any form of credit on wholesale beer sales. Raines did not pay the note. Should he be able to set up illegality as a defense to Mascari's suit?

2. Kusche agreed to negotiate a large mortgage loan in behalf of Vulcanized Co. for a 3 percent fee. He successfully secured a commitment for such a loan which he submitted to Vulcanized. However, Vulcanized used this commitment to obtain a similar loan from another bank and refused to pay Kusche the commission. Kusche sued for the commission and Vulcanized set up as defense the Real Estate Brokers License Act which specifically barred instituting a suit to recover for any act prohibited to other than licensed real estate brokers unless the actor was duly licensed, and which included negotiating a loan secured by mortgage on real estate among the prohibited acts. Kusche argued that the loan was a working capital corporate loan and that the mortgage was merely incidental and not the basis for the transaction. Should the defense by Vulcanized be upheld?

3. Smith purchased a used tractor from Dart Company on a conditional sales contract which was on a form provided by Finance Co. and which had their name in bold print at the top. The agreement stated a "Total Cash Price" of $2,350 less $350 down payment plus $50 insurance for a "Balance to be Financed" of $2050. To this was added a "Finance Charge" of $330 for a "Total Time Purchase Price" of $2380, "which Purchaser agreed to pay Seller" in 21 monthly installments of $108. Dart assigned the contract to Finance

Co. the same day. Shortly after Smith took possession of the tractor it broke down and was repossessed by Finance Co. after a series of arguments. Under state law, 12 percent is the maximum legal rate of interest. The above rate is 14.7 percent. However *bona fide* conditional sales contracts are not subject to usury laws. Is the above a *bona fide* conditional sales contract?

4. Moreira leased pumps from Moretrench. The pumps proved defective and delayed Moreira's construction activities. Moreira sued for damages for the delay, basing its claim on certain representations and warranties that the pumps were in good working order. Moretrench counterclaimed for the rent due and contended that the representations and warranties alleged by Moreira were expressly excluded by the contract and, in any event, Moretrench was not liable for delay of Moreira's construction because the contract expressly limited their liability to the free replacement of any defective equipment or parts. The trial court ruled the latter clause was invalid as contrary to public policy. Should this ruling be upheld on appeal?

5. The Chicago, Rock Island, and Pacific Railroad Company, being unable to use its own line to Chicago because of a defective bridge, began to tour its trains over the tracks of the Chicago, Burlington, and Quincy Railroad in accordance with a detour agreement that had previously been signed by the two companies. The import of the all-inclusive language of the agreement was to shift to Rock Island all losses attributable to its occasional exercise of detour privileges, regardless of its culpability. The agreement provided for the broadest possible indemnification coverage. As a result of a defective switching signal under the control of Burlington, a Burlington train ran head-on into a Rock Island train. Should the argument, as set forth by Rock Island, that the indemnity contract should be stricken on the basis of public policy prevail?

6. Conwell brought an action to enjoin its employee, Gutberlet, from accepting a job with its Arundel Corporation. Conwell based its action on a restrictive covenant in Gutberlet's contract of employment, which provided that "Should your employment with us be terminated for any reason you will not accept employment with a competitor or client of ours nor engage in a competing business venture." The District Judge denied Conwell's claim for injunctive relief and dismissed the complaint. On appeal, should the employment contract be enforced?

7. Adelson gave a written guarantee to Wilson Company which guaranteed prompt and punctual payment for any merchandise Wilson delivered to Adelson. The guarantee also contained the following provision: "The records of Wilson Co. shall be conclusive with respect to the amounts, times and places of delivery of any and all merchandise, and the balance due and owing to Wilson Co. by said purchaser." Adelson defaulted on its accounts owed to Wilson and Wilson sued on the guarantee. One of the issues at trial was whether certain merchandise was actually sold and delivered to Adelson. Should Wilson be able to rely on the above provision as conclusive of this issue?

8. Lowe, a married man, gave Quinn a diamond "engagement" ring upon the promise to wed her when and if he became free; Lowe had been living apart from his wife for several years and they contemplated a divorce. About a month after receiving the ring, Quinn told Lowe that she had second thoughts about the matter and had decided against getting married. When Lowe requested the return of the ring, Quinn suggested that he "talk to her lawyer." Convinced of the futility of further discussion, Lowe brought suit to recover the ring or, in the alternative, the sum of $60,000, its assessed value. Can Lowe recover under the common law rule that an engagement ring is a conditional gift that must be returned by a recipient who later breaks the engagement?

9. Carbone instituted a negligence action against his landlord Cortlandt Realty Corporation for damage to his personalty caused by leakage from a steam pipe. Carbone's lease contained in pertinent part the following language: "It is expressly agreed and understood by and between the parties to this agreement, that the Landlord shall not be liable for any injury or damage to person or property caused by or resulting from steam, . . . water, . . . or from any damage or injury resulting or arising from any other cause or happening whatsoever." On appeal should granting of the landlord's motion for summary judgment be upheld?

10. Kaye signed a 20-year consulting agreement with Orkin in 1964, the terms of which contained the following restrictions against competition: ". . . consultant covenants and agrees with the Company, its successors and assigns, until August 31, 1984, whether such consultative services shall cease by reason of the expiration of the term of this contract or by the discharge of consultant by the Company, with or without cause, that he shall not, . . . engage . . . in any business which is at the time competitive with the business or activities conducted by Company or Predecessor on the date of this contract of consultation hereunder in any area in which the Company or Predecessor shall operate on such date." In 1965 Orkin wrote Kaye that the "agreement was terminated." Is Kaye bound by the no-competition clause?

11. Grossman Furniture Company sold defendant Pierre and her husband household furniture, including a bedroom set, a refrigerator, and other items for a cash price of $2,065 and a time-sale price of $2,385. After paying approximately three quarters of the time-sales price, Pierre defaulted in her payments, and under the recapture clause of the signed contract, which was located on the reverse side of the sheet, Grossman instituted action to repossess the furniture. On the motion to show cause, Pierre stated in affidavit that her only source of income was from aid to dependent children benefits, that her husband had deserted her, that most of her furniture had been removed from her home, including the refrigerator in which she kept her food, and that she had no place to keep her own and her children's clothing. Under these circumstances, should the recapture clause be enforced to the benefit of Grossman?

12. Gaster, a contractor, placed orders with Architectural Cabinets, Inc., a plastic fabricator who manufactured kitchen cabinets and counter tops. On each occasion Gaster signed a standardized order form which contained a provision authorizing the entry of a self-confessed judgment against him on default. After delivery of the items ordered, Architectural Cabinets requested payment of the purchase price from Gaster. Upon default in payment, Architectural Cabinets entered judgments by confession as to the amount due. Gaster contends that the confessed judgment clause was unconscionable in this case because of the manner in which the confession clause was set out, which induced him to assume that the paragraph containing the confessed judgment was merely related to the ordering of goods. Is this a valid defense?

13. Acme, through itself and subcontractors, contracted to manufacture recoilless rifles for the government. The government cancelled the contract after three Acme employees were found to have accepted compensation for awarding subcontracts in violation of the Anti-Kickback Act. This act provided for fine or imprisonment for one who makes or receives a kickback and for recovery of the kickback by the United States. However, it did not provide for contract annulment. Should the government be able to use the act as a successful defense against Acme's breach of contract suit?

14. Wilson contracted to sell houses for Stearns in return for a percentage of the sales price. The contract had no specific termination date. Wilson sold 85 houses for Stearns which

generated $17,000 in commissions under the contract. Stearns refused to pay Wilson indicating that the contract violated the Business Code which provided for disciplinary action against a real estate licensee engaged in "the practice of receiving a commission under any exclusive agreement authorizing a licensee to sell real estate *where the agreement does not contain a specific termination date.*" Stearns argued that the contract was against public policy and, therefore, should not be enforced. Should this defense be sustained?

chapter 12

Writing

Statute of Frauds

Introduction. At common law a writing was not essential to the validity of an informal contract, and the same is true today. In England during the 17th century, and for a long period thereafter, any person having an interest in the outcome of a court action was disqualified as a witness and could not testify in the case. Most transactions between persons during this period were oral, since relatively few people could write; as a consequence, if a controversy arose wherein the rights of the parties were litigated, the parties in interest had to prove their case by the testimony of disinterested third-party witnesses. In many cases the only parties having knowledge of the facts of the case were the parties in interest, and since they were disqualified as witnesses, it was impossible for them to prove their cases. As a result of such a condition the practice of offering perjured evidence grew up. This practice, together with other fraudulent practices, became so common that Parliament found it necessary to pass laws aimed at correcting the existing abuses. These laws were comprehensive in their scope and included provisions regulating the making of wills, the creation of trusts involving real estate, and the enforceability of informal contracts.

These laws were enacted in 1677, and the statute embodying them was entitled "A Statute for the Prevention of Frauds and Perjuries" (29 Car. II, c. 3), popularly known as the Statute of Frauds. The principal means of accomplishing the desired reforms was by requiring written proof of an agreement and by denying the courts, in the absence of such written proof, the right to enforce the agreement. The statute defined five classes of contracts and provided that no action should be brought to enforce such contracts unless it was evidenced by some note or memorandum in writing. In the United States the several states have enacted statutes of frauds which have the same objective as the original English statute. These statutes are not uniform in their provisions, but they do follow the general pattern of the English statute.

Provisions of Statute of Frauds. Considered here are only those provisions of the statute of frauds which define certain classes of contracts and declare such to be unenforceable unless evidenced by a writing. The following are the classes of contracts generally included in the statute of frauds: (1) contracts by an executor or administrator to be answerable from his or her own estate for a duty of the decedent's estate; (2) contracts with an obligee to answer to him or her for the debt, default, or miscarriage of his or her obligor; (3) contracts in which the consideration is marriage or a promise to marry, except contracts consisting only of mutual promises by two persons to marry each other; (4) contracts for sale of an interest in land; (5) bilateral contracts, so long as they are not fully performed by either party, which are not capable of performance within a year from the time of their formation; and (6) contracts for the sale of goods or choses in action of a value above an amount fixed by state statutes.

In addition to these classes of contracts, the statutes of a substantial number of states require (1) a promise to pay a debt barred by the statute of limitations or by a discharge in bankruptcy and (2) a contract to pay a commission for the sale of real estate to be evidenced by a note or memorandum in writing and signed by the party to be bound thereby or his or her duly authorized agent.

Interpretation of Statute of Frauds. The common law courts took an antagonistic attitude toward legislation which changed the existing common law. The rule of interpretation adopted was that any statute in derogation of the common law would be strictly construed, that is, it would be given no greater scope than a technical interpretation of the language of the statute demanded. This rule was applied in interpreting the statute of frauds; and as a result, many cases have been brought which have required the courts to determine whether the particular contract came within one of the defined classes and was unenforceable for the lack of the required note or memorandum. The Uniform Commercial Code provides "This Act shall be liberally construed and applied to promote its underlying purposes and policies." (1–102.) This section of the Code controls the construction of the statute of frauds provisions of the Code.

Scope of the Statute of Frauds. The statute of frauds applies only to informal contracts. Consequently, before any question of its application can apply, there must be a valid contract. The statute of frauds does not make illegal a contract falling within the scope of its provisions; it merely makes it unenforceable. If one of the parties to the oral contract has performed, thereby conferring benefits on the other contracting party, and his or her right of action is barred by the statute, the person can recover in quasi contract for the benefits conferred. Under special circumstances a court of equity will hold that part performance will justify the court in decreeing performance of the contract.

The statute of frauds of some states provides that the contract, unless evidenced by the required writing, is void. In most cases, however, the courts have interpreted the statute to mean that the contract will be unenforceable, not void.

Summary

The English Parliament, in 1677, enacted a "Statute for the Prevention of Frauds and Perjuries," which provided that no action could be brought to enforce defined classes of informal contracts unless they were evidenced by a note or memorandum in writing signed by the party to be bound. The several states have enacted statutes which follow the general pattern of the English statute, but they are not uniform in their provisions. The statute of frauds provisions of the Code will tend to bring about more uniformity in those areas to which the Code applies.

The courts have given a strict interpretation to these statutes. The parties must have entered into a valid contract before the statute of frauds applies. The statute makes an oral contract which falls within one of the defined classes unenforceable, not illegal.

Collateral Contracts

Nature of Collateral Contracts. A collateral or secondary contract is one made with an obligee (promisee) in which a third person promises to pay the debt, default, or miscarriage of the obligor (promisor) in the event the obligor fails to perform that duty. Since a contract by an executor or administrator to be answerable from his or her own estate for a duty of the decedent's estate is, under most circumstances, a collateral contract, such contracts will not be discussed as a separate class.

Whether a contract is an original or a collateral contract is primarily a question of the intention of the parties. One must analyze the transaction and from the language used, the relation of the parties, and all the surrounding circumstances determine whether the obligor has contracted to perform in all events or only in the event that some other person fails to perform the duty owed to the obligee. If an oral contract is in fact collateral (or secondary) in character, it is unenforceable if the statute of frauds is used as a defense. If, however, the oral contract is classed as "original," the oral contract is enforceable despite the defense of the statute of fraud.

Original Contracts. Often a three-party transaction may appear to include a collateral contract—that is, a contract to answer for the debt, default, or miscarriage of another—when, in fact, it will include only an original contract. The following are examples of some such transactions:

1. Clark orders from Able flowers to be sent to Brown, Clark promising to pay Able for the flowers. The contract between Clark and Able is an original contract. The fact that Brown receives the consideration given in no way affects the character of the contract.

2. Clark has funds in his possession which he is administering for the benefit of Brown. Able sells a suit to Brown in reliance on Clark's contract to pay for the suit out of the funds which Clark is administering for the benefit of Brown if Brown does not pay for it. The contract between Able and Clark is an original contract. Clark is not obligating his own estate but is promising to use funds available for that purpose to discharge a debt owed by Brown.

3. Brown owns an automobile. Clark enters into a contract with Brown whereby Clark contracts to pay to Brown a sum sufficient to pay Able (or anyone else) the damages Brown may owe to Able in the event Brown, in the operation of the automobile, injures Able and becomes liable to him as a result of the injury. The contract is an original contract (an indemnity contract) between Clark and Brown, and the fact that Able may benefit indirectly does not affect the character of the contract.

4. Brown purchases an automobile from Able on a title-retaining contract by the terms of which Brown agrees to pay Able $100 per month until a $1,000 balance is paid in full. After paying $200 of the indebtedness, Brown sells the automobile to Clark, who contracts with Brown to pay to Able the unpaid balance of $800. The contract between Brown and Clark, whereby Clark promises to pay Able $800, is an original contract. Clark is obligated to pay Able in all events. Able is a third-party creditor beneficiary of the contract.

5. Able owes Brown $100, and Brown owes Clark $100. Able, Brown, and Clark enter into an agreement whereby Able agrees to pay Clark $100; Able thereby discharges his $100 debt to Brown, and Brown discharges his $100 debt to Clark. The resulting Able-Clark contract is an original contract. Able is obligated to pay Clark $100 in all events. This type of transaction is termed a "novation."

6. Clark owns shares of the capital stock in the Brown Corporation. He sells the stock to Able and contracts to guarantee the payment, by Brown Corporation, of an annual dividend of not less than 5 percent. Clark's guarantee contract is an original contract. A corporation owes no obligation to its stockholders to pay a dividend; consequently, Clark's guarantee is not a contract to answer for the debt, default, or miscarriage of another. Instead, it is more in the nature of a warranty of the quality of goods sold.

Suppose, however, that Clark owns 5 percent corporate bonds issued by the Brown Corporation and he sells the bonds to Able and contracts to pay the

5 percent annual interest payment if Brown Corporation defaults. The Clark-Able contract is a collateral contract and is unenforceable unless evidenced by a note or memorandum in writing signed by Clark or his duly authorized agent. Brown Corporation is obligated to pay the interest on the bonds, and Clark's contract to pay in the event Brown Corporation defaults is a contract to answer for the debt, default, or miscarriage of another—in this case, Brown Corporation.

There are other transactions of this same general type which occur less frequently than those described. For example, if Clark contracts to pay Able a debt owed to Able by Brown in consideration of Able discharging Brown, such a contract is an original contract, or if Clark purchases from Able a debt owed to Able by Brown, the contract is an original contract.

Summary

A collateral contract is one made with an obligee to pay the debt, default, or miscarriage of the obligor in the event he or she fails to perform that duty. Whether a contract is original or collateral will depend primarily on the intention of the parties to the contract.

An original contract is one in which a promisor obligates himself or herself to perform in all events. Often a contract in which three persons are involved may appear to include a collateral contract, but an analysis of such a transaction will reveal that only an original contract is involved.

Pravel, Wilson & Matthews v. Voss

471 F.2d 1186 (5th Cir. 1973)

Action by Pravel, Wilson & Matthews (plaintiffs), a law firm, against Voss (defendant) for legal fees. Judgment for plaintiff firm and Voss appealed. Affirmed.

The plaintiff's law firm sued to recover the reasonable value of services rendered in connection with an unsuccessful patent infringement suit filed by V & S Ice Machine Company, a shell corporation organized solely to hold the patent on an "ice blade" and to conduct patent infringement litigation.

Matthews, a member of the plaintiff firm, was hired to represent V & S but upon learning that V & S was a mere shell, Matthews sought assurances from Voss that the firm would be paid for their services.

Matthews told Voss that the case was in "bad shape" and that the firm's fee for handling the case through trial would be between ten thousand and twenty thousand dollars. Voss told Matthews to "go for broke," and agreed to have a second partner work on the case. Voss attended several sessions of the trial, and indicated to Matthews that he was pleased with its progress. During the trial, Voss told Wilson, the other partner, that he viewed the litigation like any other investment, and that he was willing to spend as much as twenty-five thousand dollars in attorneys' fees because he expected that the litigation would yield a "return" of several hundred thousand dollars to him. He told Wilson that he would "take care" of the fee, and that if the lawyers were successful, they would be rewarded by a trip to Las Vegas which Voss said he had used as an incentive in some of his other business dealings.

V & S lost the patent infringement suit. The law firm withdrew from the case, and sent several bills for approximately fourteen thousand dollars in attorneys' fees to Voss at both his home and business addresses. After the bill had gone unpaid for several months, Wilson telephoned Voss and told him that the firm was looking to him personally for payment. Voss did not dispute his personal liability, but said that the bill was larger than he had expected it to be. He later refused to pay anything.

THORNBERRY, CIRCUIT JUDGE.   Voss' statute of frauds argument is untenable, for several reasons. First, there is nothing in the record or in the trial court's findings to support Voss' claim that he promised to answer for a debt owed by the corporation. Voss clearly and repeatedly promised the lawyers that he personally would pay their fee. Thus, the statute of frauds is simply inapplicable to this case on its facts.

But even if the record did disclose evidence that Voss promised to answer for a corporate debt, the law firm would nevertheless be entitled to a recovery. In the first place, the courts afford recovery in quantum meruit as an alternative remedy for breach of promises rendered unenforceable by the statute of frauds.

Secondly, even if Voss did promise to answer for a debt of the corporation, his "leading object" in making the promise was to secure a direct, personal benefit (i.e., to protect his share of the contemplated recovery), and the promise was enforceable notwithstanding the statute of frauds.

Some cases have refused to apply the "leading object" exception when the promisor was a shareholder in the corporation whose debt he guaranteed and the only benefit accruing to him by reason of his promise was the prospect of continued corporate prosperity, which benefitted all stockholders alike.

The promisor's purpose, however, is a question of fact and the courts have not hesitated to apply the leading object exception in cases involving stockholders where, as here, the record compels the conclusion that the promisor could have been acting only to protect his personal interests.

Guinn Co. v. Mazza

296 F.2d 441 (D.C. Cir. 1961)

This was an action by Guinn Company (plaintiff) against Mazza (defendant) to recover damages for breach of an oral agreement to advance money to Togor Publications. Judgment for Mazza and Guinn appealed. Affirmed.

Togor Publications was heavily indebted to Guinn for printing prior issues of *Bounty* magazine and Guinn refused to extend further credit unless payment or "acceptable assurances" were forthcoming. Mazza was a board member of Togor. On July 2 and 3, 1956, Mazza agreed to lend Togor $150,000 and expressed this promise to Guinn assuring Guinn that it could rely on this loan. Mazza told Guinn "to go ahead with printing the August 1956 issue of *Bounty.* "Mazza was to get stock in Togor for making the advance of $150,000.

Guinn printed the magazine in reliance on the oral "promise, statements and assurances" of Mazza; but Mazza has never advanced any money to Togor and Togor has not paid Guinn.

Guinn sued Mazza on his oral promises to advance the money and Mazza set up the statute of frauds as his defense.

BURGER, CIRCUIT JUDGE.   To the extent Guinn relies on the oral communication from Mazza, whether we view this as an "assurance" or a "promise" or an "agreement" it is an undertaking which falls squarely within the controlling New York Statute of Frauds. There is no claim here that Mazza was to pay Guinn for printing costs; Mazza simply gave "assurances" or "guarantees" to Guinn that Mazza would advance money to Togor and that payment would ultimately be made by Togor. Togor remained originally liable on the debt. Since the authorities agree that if as between all the parties the original debtor remains primarily liable, the oral undertaking by the new promisor (here Mazza) is a promise to answer for the debt of another and thus is barred by the statute of frauds unless put in writing. . . .

The settled law of the matter is stated at 3 *Williston, Contracts:*

> Ordinarily, there is no individual liability on the part of a stockholder for the debts of a corporation. His promise to pay such a debt is in a strict sense the promise to answer for the debt of another; and such a promise, if oral, is unenforceable under the Statute of Frauds.
>
> In other words, where the oral promise of a stockholder to pay the debt of a corporation is collateral in form and effect, and the consideration, therefore, is not to secure or promote some personal object or advantage of the promisor, as distinguished from the indirect benefit to him from the mere fact of his being a stockholder of the corporation, the promise is within the statute.

Interest in Land

Scope of Provision.   One of the provisions of the statute of frauds requires contracts for the sale of an interest in land to be evidenced by a memorandum in writing and signed by the party to be bound thereby or his or her duly authorized agent. Although the statute of frauds is worded "interest in land," the courts have interpreted land to mean real estate, and any contract, the performance of which will affect the ownership rights in real estate, comes within the statute of frauds. Contracts to sell, to mortgage, to permit the mining and removal of minerals on the land, and to give easements fall within this class. Leases fall within this class, but in most states, leases are provided for by a special provision of the statute. Contracts to insure buildings, to erect buildings, to organize a partnership to deal in real property, and similar contracts are not within this class because they do not affect an interest in the real property.

Summary

If the performance of the contract will require the transfer of any interest in real property, it comes within the provisions of the statute and is not enforceable unless it is evidenced by a writing. The distinction between real property and personal property is a part of the law of property and is discussed in chapter 29.

Gene Hancock Construction Co. v. Kempton & Snedigar Dairy

510 P.2d 752 (Ct. App. Ariz. 1973)

Suit by Hancock Construction Co. (plaintiff) against Kempton & Snedigar Dairy (defendants) on an oral contract for the sale of realty and on an oral authorization to sell realty. The plaintiffs appealed from an adverse judgment. Affirmed.

Hancock Construction Company alleged that Dairy acting through its authorized agent Snedigar, entered into an oral contract for the sale of certain real property, and Hancock specifically asked Snedigar whether the contract was considered to be binding and one upon which Hancock could rely. Snedigar answered in the affirmative and shook hands on it. In reliance on this oral contract Hancock immediately had engineering studies of the property made and made arrangements to obtain a loan of $292,-830.00. Dairy refused to go through with the deal and when sued set up the defense of the statute of frauds. Hancock argued that part performance had removed the statute of frauds defense.

HATHAWAY, CHIEF JUDGE.   The pertinent provisions of A.R.S. § 44–101 are:

No action shall be brought in any court in the following cases unless the promise or agreement upon which the action is brought, or some memorandum thereof, is in writing and signed by the party to be charged, or by some person by him thereunto lawfully authorized:

* * * * *

6. Upon an agreement for leasing for a longer period than one year, or for the sale of real property or an interest therein. Such agreement, if made by an agent of the party sought to be charged, is invalid unless the authority of the agent is in writing, subscribed by the party sought to be charged.

7. Upon an agreement authorizing or employing an agent or broker to purchase or sell real property, or mines, for compensation or a commission.

Part performance necessary to take an oral contract out of the statute of frauds must be unequivocably referable to the contract. Unless the acts of part performance are exclusively referable to the contract, there is nothing to show that the party seeking to enforce it relied on the contract or changed his position to his prejudice so as to give rise to an estoppel. In this jurisdiction, *Restatement of Contracts* § 197, has been cited with approval. This section states:

Where, acting under an oral contract for the transfer of an interest in land, the purchaser with the assent of the vendor (a) makes valuable improvements on the land, or (b) takes possession thereof or retains a possession thereof existing at the time of the bargain, and also pays a portion or all of the purchase price, the purchaser or the vendor may specifically enforce the contract.

Adverting to the allegations of the complaint, the "part performance" relied upon by Hancock, was obtaining financing and having engineering studies made of the subject property. The sufficiency of the particular acts to constitute part performance can be decided as a matter of law. An act which admits of explanation without reference to the alleged oral contract does not constitute part performance. We believe Hancock's acts are not unequivocally referable to the oral contract and therefore the trial court did not err in ruling, as a matter of law, that the doctrine of part performance did not preclude the defense of the statute of frauds. Since the contract was unenforceable, not only did Hancock's claim for specific performance fail, but likewise its claim for damages.

Hancock refers to the allegation in its complaint that Snedigar offered to have his attorney prepare the necessary documents to memorialize the contract. Even if this allegation can be construed as a promise to make a memorandum that would satisfy the statute of frauds, an agreement to reduce to writing a contract within the statute of frauds must itself be in writing to be enforceable.

*　*　*　*　*

Not To Be Performed within One Year

Scope of Provision. This provision applies only to executory bilateral contracts. If Allen loans Bates $100 and Bates orally promises to repay the loan in two years, the contract is a unilateral contract and need not be evidenced by a writing. Likewise, if a bilateral contract has been fully performed, the fact that the contract was oral and could not be performed within a year of the making thereof would in no way affect the rights acquired by the parties to the performed contract. Since the statute is worded in the negative, "*not* to be performed within one year," the courts have held that if, under the terms of the contract, it is possible to perform the contract within a year of the making thereof, it need not be evidenced by a writing to be enforceable. The fact that it is highly improbable that performance will be completed or that performance was not completed within one year is not controlling.

The one-year period is computed from the time the contract comes into existence, not from the time performance is to begin. For example, a contract entered into on July 1, 1972, whereby the promisor agrees to work for the promisee for one year, work to begin on July 3, 1973, cannot be performed within one year from the making thereof and, if it is to be enforceable, would have to be evidenced by a memorandum in writing signed by the party to be bound or his duly authorized agent.

Computing Time. In computing time, as a general rule, parts of days are not counted. A contract entered into today to work for one year, work to begin tomorrow, can be performed within one year under the rule generally followed. However, if such a contract were entered into on Saturday, work to begin the following Monday, it could not be performed within one year from the making thereof. In a few states the day the contract is entered into is counted. In these states if a contract to work for one year is entered into today, work to begin tomorrow, it cannot be performed within one year from the making thereof.

Contracts to Extend Time of Performance. In determining whether or not a contract to extend the time for the performance of an existing contract can be performed within one year, time is computed from the day the contract to extend the time of performance is entered into until the time the performance under the extended time contract will be completed. For example, on July 1, 1970, Able contracts to work for Brown for six months beginning on July 2, 1970. On September 1, 1970, Able and Brown enter into a contract whereby Able agrees to work for Brown for an additional 11 months after the performance of the existing contract. The contract for the extension of time cannot be performed within one year from the making thereof.

An Indefinite Time Stated. When the time of performance of the contract is stated in indefinite terms, such as "for life" or "as long as needed," and under existing conditions it is possible to perform the contract within one year, it need not be evidenced by a writing to be enforceable, even though the actual time of performance is more than one year.

The courts are not in accord in their interpretation of contracts to support someone and contracts to refrain from action. All courts hold that a contract whereby Ames contracts to support Barnes for life need not be in writing. They reason that the contract will be fully performed on the death of Barnes and this may occur within a year.

A majority of the courts hold that a contract whereby Ames contracts not to compete with Barnes for a period of five years must be evidenced by a writing to be enforceable whereas a few courts hold that the contract will be completely performed on the death of Ames and that this may occur within a year and that no writing is required.

Summary

The provision of the statute of frauds which requires that a contract must be in writing if it cannot be performed within one year from the making thereof applies only to bilateral contracts. Since it is worded in the negative, "not fully performed," no writing is required if it is possible, under the terms of the contract, to complete performance within one year. Time is computed from the time of the formation of the contract, not from the time the promisor is to begin performance. A contract to extend the time of performance of an existing contract must be evidenced by a writing if the time from the formation of the contract to extend time of performance until the time of complete performance of the contract, under the terms of the contract, exceeds one year. If the time for performance is stated in indefinite terms, such as "for life" or "for long as needed," the courts hold, in the absence of a special statute, that no writing is required, since the contract, under its terms, may be performed within one year.

Frontier Ins. Agency, Inc. v. Hartford Fire Ins. Co.

499 P.2d 1302 (Sup. Ct. Ore. 1972)

A declaratory judgment proceeding was brought to determine the relative rights and liabilities between Hartford Fire Insurance Company, its agent, Frontier Insurance Agency, Inc., and the insured Gillespie Decals, Inc. The trial court found that Hartford was liable to Gillespie and Hartford appealed. Affirmed.

Gillespie was in the printing business in Portland prior to August 1968. Frontier is an independent insurance agency which represents a number of insurance companies, including Hartford. On May 16, 1968, Hartford issued to Gillespie, through Frontier, its fire policy #52 FS 155139 for a term of three years, insuring for the sum of $50,000 a stock of merchandise located at 1910 S.W. Stevenson Road.

In August 1968 Gillespie expanded its business into a second location. At that time Locke, Gillespie's General Manager, and Cheatham, Frontier's President, discussed the insurance changes necessary because of Gillespie's expansion into the additional location. It was agreed that the insurance coverage at the new location would include $50,000 fire insurance on the stock of merchandise and fire insurance on some new machinery, a Friden computer, and the accounts receivable records. All the new insurance was to be effective at the time of the move in August 1968. Cheatham advised Gillespie that the stock of merchandise at the new location would be insured by adding the coverage to Hartford's policy #52 FS 155139.

For some unexplained reason, Frontier apparently made no effort to obtain the additional insurance for Gillespie until about March 1, 1969. At about that time Cheatham ordered from Hartford's Portland office a fire insurance policy covering the equipment at the new location, including the computer, and a new policy covering those items for $37,000 was issued by Hartford.

Although Frontier could order new policies from Hartford's Portland office, it was necessary that amendments to existing policies be ordered from Hartford's Seattle office. Cheatham testified that he sent a memorandum dated March 3, 1969, to Hartford's Seattle office requesting Hartford to amend policy #52 FS 155139 to provide $50,000 fire coverage on the stock of merchandise at Gillespie's new location. Hartford contends that it never received the memorandum and therefore took no action to provide the insurance requested therein. Frontier did not follow up its request and no insurance was written on the Gillespie stock at the new location.

MCALLISTER, JUSTICE.   Hartford concedes that Frontier had at least apparent authority to commit the company to additional coverage, but it contends that nevertheless it was entitled to a judgment in its favor as a matter of law. First, Hartford argues that because policy # 52 FS 155139 had more than a year to run after March 3, 1969, the contract for $50,000 additional coverage was a contract not to be performed within a year and was, therefore, unenforceable under the statute of frauds. . . . In *Osburn v. De Force,* it was held that an oral modification of a written contract which was within the statute, because it was not to be performed within a year, was unenforceable. We do not believe the *Osburn* rule is applicable in this case because the original policy was not within the statute. That policy includes the provisions of the statutory fire insurance policy, including the following: "This policy shall be canceled at any time at the request of the insured. . . . This policy may be canceled at any time by this company by giving to the insured a five days' written notice of cancellation. . . ." This cancellation provision means that neither party to the contract need be bound for more than a year. in *Bickel v. Wessinger,* the opinion states: ". . . It is only where the agreement shows by its terms or within the contemplation of the parties that it cannot be performed within a year that the statute intervenes."

In *Duniway v. Wiley,* the court said that a contract which is capable of performance within a year, even though performance within that time was not probable and was not expected, is not within the statute.

There is a division of authority as to whether a contract provision for termination at will, or upon the happening of a contingency which may occur within a year, takes a contract out of the statute of frauds. According to Williston, the majority of courts holds that it does not, but there is a strong minority position to the contrary.

The cases following the majority position reason that termination of a contract, even though provided for by its terms, is not performance but merely excusable non-performance.

Courts following the minority rule consider termination according to the terms of the contract to be a form of, or equivalent to, performance. . . . We believe the minority view is in harmony with the spirit of the decisions in this and other jurisdictions which hold that if, according to the terms of the contract, performance within a year is possible, the contract is not within the statute.

Lucas v. Whittaker Corporation

470 F.2d 326 (10th Cir. 1972)

Lucas (plaintiff) sued Whittaker (defendant) to recover the balance due him on an alleged two-year oral employment contract. Whittaker denied the existence of the contract and also relied on the statute of frauds as a defense, claiming it was an agreement not to be performed within a year. The trial court held that under the circumstances the doctrine of equitable estoppel prevented Whittaker from asserting the statute as a defense. Whittaker appealed. Affirmed.

PICKETT, CIRCUIT JUDGE.   The contract having been consummated in California, Colorado law requires the application of California law in determining its validity. In California the doctrine of estoppel to assert the statute of frauds is applied to prevent fraud that would result from a refusal to enforce an oral contract. It is said that such fraud may inhere in the unconscionable injury that would result from denying enforcement of the contract after one party has been induced by the other seriously to change his position in reliance on the contract.

The nub of Whittaker's argument is that Lucas gave up no more than any person who leaves his present employment for what he thinks is a better job. The trial court held that Lucas' detrimental reliance on the two-year contract in moving to Colorado was more than that suffered in the ordinary change of jobs.

Lucas, in accepting the offered employment by Whittaker, resigned from what appeared to be a secure job with a company for whom he had worked for nine years, including incidents of that employment—medical and life insurance benefits, stock options, accrued vacation time and a college tuition supplement for eligible dependents. He sold a custom-built house in which he and his family lived for only eight months. He gave up business and social contacts. All of this obviously was lost because of Lucas' reliance on the oral agreement. The trial court's fact finding of unconscionable injury is not clearly erroneous. That Lucas earned more during his thirteen months with Whittaker than he would have earned in two years at his old job is irrelevant in determining unconscionable injury.

Whittaker also contends that Lucas failed to meet his burden of proof in showing that Whittaker breached the employment contract and that the trial judge erred in not instructing the jury on whether Lucas was discharged for cause. Although it is generally held that an employee claiming breach of an employment contract has the burden of proving the employer's breach . . . when the employee establishes the breach, the burden is on the employer to show justification.

The evidence establishes that Whittaker discharged Lucas before the expiration of the period of employment. Whittaker offered no evidence to show that Lucas' discharge was for cause and no issue was present for the jury. . . .

The Writing

Nature of Writing Required.   The statutes of fraud of the several states are not uniform in their provisions for writing. In most of the states the statutes require "a memorandum," or "a note of memorandum," but in some of the states the statutes require "a contract in writing."

If a memorandum, or note of memorandum, is required, it may be made at any time up to the time suit is filed. If it has been signed but has been lost, its loss and its content may be proven by parol evidence. It may be in any form, such as, for instance, a formal contract, letters, telegrams, receipts, or any other writing accurately stating the material provisions of the contract.

The memorandum, or note of memorandum, may consist of several documents, in which case the documents must show, either by attachment physically or by the content or references in the documents themselves, that they all refer to the same transaction. If a contract in writing is required, it must include all the material provisions of the agreement, and must be made with the intent to bind the party signing it. The memorandum, or note of memorandum, need not be made with the intent that it be binding.

Content of the Memorandum. The note or memorandum, in order to be sufficient, must state the names of the parties, or designate them so that they can be identified from the content of the writing, must describe the subject matter of the contract with reasonable certainty (a more detailed description of real property than of personal property is required), must state the price to be paid (with some exceptions), and must state credit terms, if credit is extended, and all other terms that are material. The statutes of frauds of some states expressly provide that the consideration need not be stated in the memorandum; however, if price is a material term, it must be stated.

It is immaterial in what order the terms are stated or how the parties are indicated. The parties may be indicated by their signatures on the memorandum, by the appearance of their names in the heading of the memorandum, by an address on an envelope in which the memorandum is mailed, or by a statement in the memorandum expressly setting out the names of the parties.

Under the provisions of the Uniform Commercial Code (discussed later), the requirements for the note or memorandum of a contract to sell goods[1] are not as strict as are those required in general.

The Signing. The statute of frauds in force in most of the states provides that the memorandum must be signed by the *party* to be bound or his or her duly authorized agent. Since the statute is worded in the singular, the memorandum need not be signed by both parties but must be signed by the party who is being sued or by his or her agent. Unless the statute expressly provides that the memorandum or contract must be signed at the end thereof, the signature may appear any place on the memorandum.

In a sale at auction the auctioneer and his or her clerk are impliedly authorized to sign the note or memorandum as agent for both the buyer and the seller. However, this implied authority continues only during the auction sale.

Oral Variation of Contract. By the great weight of authority, an oral variation of a contract, for which contract a sufficient note or memorandum exists, is not enforceable. The contract may be enforced as originally negotiated, but the variation is not enforceable. However, a mutual oral agreement to cancel a contract, for which a sufficient memorandum exists, is effective.

Summary

A note or memorandum in writing is generally a sufficient writing to satisfy the statute of frauds. It may be made at any time prior to the bringing of suit to enforce the contract and need not be in any particular form. If several

[1] Uniform Commercial Code, § 2–201 (1) and (2).

documents are relied on, they must be physically attached together, or it must be clearly indicated from their contents that they refer to the same transaction. The note or memorandum must include the names of the parties and describe the subject matter of the contract with reasonable certainty and in addition must contain all the material provisions of the contract.

The note or memorandum must be signed by the party to be charged or his or her duly authorized agent; that is, it must be signed by the party who sets up the statute of frauds as a defense. No particular place or mode of signing is stipulated by the statute. An agent may sign in his or her principal's name or in his or her own name. An auctioneer or his clerk has implied authority to sign for both the buyer and the seller. An oral variation of a contract, where such contract is evidenced by a sufficient note or memorandum, is not enforceable.

Babdo Sales v. Miller-Wohl Co.

440 F.2d 962 (2nd Cir. 1971)

In an action brought to determine whether Babdo Sales (plaintiff) was entitled to continued use and occupancy of certain departments of Miller-Wohl Company's (defendant) stores under contracts entered into by the two parties, the court granted judgment in favor of Babdo Sales and Miller-Wohl appealed. Affirmed.

Babdo Sales is a corporation engaged in retail sale of records, novelties, and other merchandise which obtains licenses or leases from department stores to conduct business on their premises in return for a percentage of its gross sales. For some years Babdo had concededly valid written agreements with Miller-Wohl and occupied space in a number of Miller-Wohl stores throughout the country. In 1968 the parties entered into negotiations as to a lease in Miller-Wohl's new store soon to be opened in Springfield, Ohio. Agreement was reached as to the terms of this new lease, and at the same time the parties agreed to a renewal of the previously existing leases in eleven other stores until February 28, 1975 in consideration of an increase in rentals based on the terms of the Springfield negotiations.

On February 12, 1969, Fortgang, a vice-president of Miller-Wohl sent an unsigned internal memorandum to the company's assistant comptroller informing him as to the terms of the new agreements which would become effective on March 1, 1969. Sometime thereafter in March or April Miller-Wohl sent to Babdo ten separate formal agreements and requested that they be signed and returned. These were dated February 28, 1969. On April 7, 1969, Miller-Wohl's assistant comptroller sent Babdo a letter entitled "Final Accounting under Existing Leases" setting forth the balance due to Babdo under the terms of the previously existing leases which had been terminated as of March 1, 1969.

In the meantime new management had taken over control of Miller-Wohl and decided that in the future Miller-Wohl would operate its own departments rather than license others, and the executives of Miller-Wohl were instructed as to this policy in a memorandum dated May 5, 1969. Miller-Wohl never executed the ten letter agreements which had been signed by Babdo and returned. Instead Miller-Wohl informed Babdo that it regarded the renewals as ineffective and that the existing licensing agreements would not be renewed upon their expiration. Babdo contends that binding agreements had been entered into and seeks a declaratory judgment to this effect.

SMITH, CIRCUIT JUDGE.   Once two parties have reached agreement on the material terms of a contract, it may or may not become binding at that point depending solely on the intention of the parties. Professor Corbin has noted:

One of the most common illustrations of preliminary negotiation that is totally inoperative is one where the parties consider the details of a proposed agreement, perhaps settling them one by one, with the understanding during this process that the agreement is to be embodied in a formal written document and that neither party is to be bound until he executes this document. Often it is a difficult question of fact whether the parties have this understanding; and there are very many decisions holding both ways.

*   *   *   *   *

In the present case the evidence strongly suggests that both parties considered the new leases binding and in force as of March 1, 1969. Thus the Fortgang memorandum of February 12, 1969 states: "We have today negotiated a new license agreement . . . the above agreement will be effective as of March 1, 1969." Likewise the April 7, 1969 letter of Miller-Wohl's assistant comptroller to Babdo begins: "In accordance with our agreement, we are terminating your existing leases in the Welles Stores as of February 28, 1969 in order to initiate the new leases as of March 1, 1969.

Assuming that a binding oral agreement is found to exist, the next question . . . is whether the agreement is nevertheless void under the statute of frauds. Section 5–701(1) of the New York General Obligations Law provides:

Every agreement, promise or undertaking is void, unless it or some note or memorandum thereof be in writing, and subscribed by the party to be charged therewith, or by his lawful agent, if such agreement, promise or undertaking:
(1) By its terms is not to be performed within one year from the making thereof or the performance of which is not to be completed before the end of a lifetime.

In applying the statute of frauds it is well to remember that the purpose of the statute is not to permit fraud to take place. As Professor Corbin has noted:

Such gain in the prevention of fraud as is attained by the statute is attained at the expense of permitting persons who have in fact made oral promises to break those promises with impunity and to cause disappointment and loss to honest men. It is this fact that has caused the courts to interpret the statute so narrowly as to exclude many promises from its operation on what may seem to be flimsy grounds. The courts cannot bear to permit the dishonest breaking of a promise when they are convinced that the promise was in fact made.

Babdo and the court below relied on the . . . decision in *Crabtree v. Elizabeth Arden Sales Corp.,* which stated:

The statute of frauds does not require the "memorandum . . . to be in one document. It may be pieced together out of separate writings, connected with one another either expressly or by the internal evidence of subject-matter and occasion."

*   *   *   *   *

None of the terms of the contract are supplied by parol. All of them must be set out in the various writings presented to the court, and at least one writing, the one establishing a contractual relationship between the parties, must bear the signature of the party to be charged, while the unsigned document must on its face refer to the same transaction as that set forth in the one that was signed. Parol evidence—to portray the circumstances surrounding the making of the memorandum—serves only to connect the separate documents and to show that there was assent, by the party to be charged, to the contents of the one unsigned.

The lower court correctly found that the signed letter of Miller-Wohl's assistant comptroller dated April 7, 1969 which included the reference to "our agreement . . . to initiate the new leases" was sufficient to come within the *Crabtree* requirement that the signed document "establish a contractual relationship between the parties" and that the unsigned documents of February 12th and the agreements dated February 28, 1969 set forth all the material terms of the contract. . . .

Effect of Failure to Comply

General Effect. The statute of frauds does not, as a general rule, declare an oral contract which comes within the scope of the statute's provisions void or voidable if it does not comply with the requirements of the statute; it declares such a contract unenforceable. If suit is brought to enforce an oral contract which comes within the provisions of the statute of frauds and the party defendant does not plead noncompliance with the statute as a defense, he or she thereby waives his or her defense, and the court will proceed in the same manner as though the statute of frauds had been complied with.

Rights of Parties to Oral Contract. If the parties have entered into an oral contract which comes within the provisions of the statute of frauds and one party has performed, thereby conferring benefits on the other party, he or she can recover for the benefits conferred in an action in quasi contract.

The courts of equity recognize and enforce the statute of frauds; yet a court of equity may refuse to permit a party to raise the defense of the statute of frauds if such refusal is necessary to prevent the perpetration of a fraud. The refusal to permit the defense of the statute of frauds is based on general concepts of fairness and justice. The idea is expressed in the equitable maxim that he who asks equity must do equity.

Part performance will take the contract out of the statute of frauds in cases involving the purchase of real property where the purchaser has been given possession of the property and has made extensive improvements to it. Part performance may limit the statute of frauds defense in some cases involving sale of goods (discussed next) to the extent that there is either part payment or part delivery. Absent special facts, part performance does not remove the statute of frauds defense where either the "one year" or "promises to answer" statutes are involved.

If an oral contract which comes within the statute of frauds has been fully performed, neither party will be permitted to rescind the contract and recover the consideration given. Once the contract has been performed, the transaction is a closed deal and cannot be reopened on the ground of noncompliance with the provisions of the statute of frauds.

Summary

An oral contract which comes within the provisions of the statute of frauds is unenforceable, not void or voidable. If one of the parties to an oral contract which is within the statute of frauds performs, thereby conferring benefits on the other party, the party who has performed can recover in quasi contract for the benefits conferred. In transactions concerning real estate, if there has been part performance of an oral contract, a court of equity may grant specific performance if the circumstances are such that specific performance is necessary to avoid an unjust result. If the parties have performed an oral contract which comes within the provisions of the statute of frauds, neither party can rescind the contract on the ground of noncompliance with the statute of frauds.

Sale of Goods and the Code ✗ *important*

The Memorandum.   The statute of frauds in the Code which applies to the sale of goods in the amount of $500 or more is Sec. 2–201. Such an oral contract is not enforceable by way of action or defense unless the requirements of the statute of frauds are complied with. These requirements can be met by the execution of a memorandum signed by the party against whom enforcement is sought or by his or her authorized agent or broker. The memorandum satisfies the requirements of the statute of frauds if it is "some writing sufficient to indicate that a contract of sale has been entered into between the parties." It is not insufficient because it omits or incorrectly states a term agreed upon. A sales contract is not enforceable beyond the quantity of goods stated in the memorandum. (2–201[1].)[2]

As between merchants, if an oral contract has been negotiated and one of the parties, within a reasonable time thereafter, sends a written confirmation, sufficient to bind him or her, to the other party, such writing is sufficient to bind the receiver. Even if the receiver does not sign it, if he or she has reason to know its contents, the receiver loses the defense of the statute unless written notice of objection to its contents is given within ten days after it is received. (2–201 [2].)

---

[2] The numbers in the parentheses refer to the sections of the Uniform Commercial Code, 1962.

Part Payment or Part Delivery. Under the Code, part payment or delivery of part of the goods satisfies the statute of frauds but only "with respect to goods for which payment has been made and accepted or which have been received and accepted." (2–201 [3] [c].) This provision of the statute makes the oral contract of the parties enforceable only to the extent that payment has been made and accepted or that the goods have been received and accepted; it does not make the oral contract enforceable in its entirety.

Admissions in Pleadings or Court. Although a sufficient writing has not been executed and no part payment or part delivery has been made, if the party being sued admits in his or her pleadings or in court that an oral sales contract was entered into, he or she can be held liable. The oral contract is not enforceable, however, beyond the quantity of goods admitted. (2–201 [3] [b].)

Specially Manufactured Goods. Oral contracts for goods to be specially manufactured are enforceable (1) if the goods are not suitable for sale in the ordinary course of the seller's business, and (2) if the seller, before notice of repudiation is received and under circumstances which reasonably indicate that the goods are for the buyer, has made a substantial beginning of their manufacture or commitment for their procurement. (2–201 [3] [a].) Under this section of the statute of frauds a wholly executory oral contract for goods to be specially manufactured is unenforceable.

Effect of Noncompliance. The statute of frauds does not declare oral contracts which come within its scope void or voidable if they do not comply with the requirements of the statute, but it does declare such contracts unenforceable. If suit is brought to enforce an oral contract for the sale of goods for the price of $500 or more, the party sued, if he wishes to avail himself of the protection of the statute, must plead it specially in the trial court. If the contract has been completely performed, neither party will be permitted to rescind the contract and recover the consideration given.

Summary

An oral contract for the sale of goods for the price of $500 or more is unenforceable unless evidenced by a writing signed by the party against whom enforcement is sought or his or her authorized agent or broker. The writing need not set out all the terms of the agreement but must be sufficient to indicate that a contract was entered into. It is not enforceable beyond the quantity stated. It may be satisfied by part payment or part delivery or by admission in the pleadings or in court but not for a quantity beyond payment made, goods received and accepted, or admitted. A written confirmation sufficient to bind the sender will bind the receiver unless he or she objects to its terms within ten days of its receipt. The statute of frauds declares the contract coming within its provisions unenforceable and the party defendant must plead the statute as a matter of defense in the trial court if he or she wishes to avail himself of its protection.

Reich v. Helen Harper, Inc.

3 U.C.C. Rep. 1048 (Civ. Ct. N.Y. 1966)

This was an action brought by Reich (plaintiff) against Kaplan (defendant) for the breach of an oral contract to purchase 11,500 yards of India madras for 75 cents per yard. Held: Kaplan's motion to dismiss on grounds of the statute of frauds denied.

A document entitled "Rate Confirmation" was sent by Amtec to both Kaplan and Reich. It described the goods, stated the quantity, the price per yard, and that Amtec, upon whose printed stationery this appeared, was acting as sales agent for Ricky Fabrics (a designee of Reich), and that the goods were being sold to Kaplan. On January 9, 1966, Reich sent Kaplan a bill for 11,528 yards of madras at 75 cents a yard on the printed bill form of Brian Mills, a name under which Reich does business. On February 18, 1966, Kaplan sent a letter to Brian Mills, attention of Mr. Reich, reading as follows:

Brian Mills, 152 W. 27th St., New York, N.Y.
Att: Mr. Elliott Reich
Gentlemen:
Replying to your letter of the 18th, please be advised that we examined a few pieces of merchandise that were billed to us against your invoice No. 10203, and found that it was not up to our standard.
We are, therefore, unable to accept this shipment, and we also wish to advise that the few pieces that we examined are also being held for return to you.
     Very truly yours,
     /s/ Isidor Kaplan

GOLD, JUDGE. The Code makes it necessary for a merchant buyer or merchant seller to watch his mail and to act promptly if he is not to be bound by a contract for sale with respect to which he has signed no writing. It deprives the party who fails to answer the confirmation, by rejecting it, of the defense of the statute of frauds. The burden of persuading the trier of the facts that a contract was in truth made orally prior to the written confirmation is unaffected.

In *Harry Rubin & Sons, Inc. v. Consolidated Pipe Company,* the Supreme Court of Pennsylvania stated:

As between merchants, the present statute of frauds provision (i.e., under § 2–201[2]) significantly changes the former law by obviating the necessity of having a memorandum signed by the party sought to be charged. The present statutory requirements are: (1) that, within a reasonable time, there be a writing in confirmation of the oral contract; (2) that the writing be sufficient to bind the sender; (3) that such writing be received; (4) that no reply thereto has been made although the recipient had reason to know of its contents. Section 2–201 (2) penalizes a party who fails to 'answer a written confirmation of a contract within ten days' of the receipt of the writing by depriving such party of the defense of the statute of frauds.

It becomes necessary now to determine whether the document sent by Amtec is "sufficient against the sender." In short, would it bind Reich so that he, Reich, would be deprived of the statute of frauds as a defense were Kaplan the party suing herein? The court finds that the document would in and of itself so bind Reich to the transaction. Moreover, this commitment would be reinforced by Reich's invoice to Kaplan.

Whether examined together with Reich's invoice or standing alone, the sales confirmation would also bind Kaplan so as to deprive him of the defense of the statute of frauds in light of Kaplan's failure to give written notice of objection to its contents within ten days from the receipt thereof. The invoice rendered by Reich to Kaplan promptly after the sending of the sales confirmation would leave not the slightest doubt that the written confirmation was complete and that Kaplan would in effect forfeit the right to utilize the statute of frauds if he failed to make timely written objection to its contents.

The contention of Kaplan that the sales confirmation is not "signed" and is therefore not binding upon the sender and therefore cannot be binding upon the recipient is without basis in law. The authorities clearly hold to the contrary.

The term "signed," used in UCC, § 2–201, is defined in UCC, § 1–201 (39) in part as follows:

" 'Signed' includes any symbol executed or adopted by a party with present intention to authenticate a writing. . . ."

The question remaining then is whether the sale confirmation sent to Kaplan was "signed." In the context of the facts here present, the question may also be posed in the following manner: Was there an intent to authenticate the writing? This court believes so.

In the instant transaction not only was there the printed name of the agent, "Amtec," but in addition the name of the seller's principal was hand-lettered thereon.

The court is likewise of the opinion that the statute of frauds is not available to Kaplan for the further reason that Kaplan's letter, written some forty-five days after the receipt of the sale confirmation and some forty days after receipt of Reich's bill, may in and of itself constitute a sufficient memorandum to satisfy § 2–201 of the Uniform Commercial Code.

It has long been held that a memorandum sufficient to satisfy the statute of frauds need not be contained in one document but "It may be pieced together out of separate writings, connected with one another either expressly or by the internal evidence of subject matter and occasion." If the writings so conjoined meet the three requirements of the code, that a contract is evidenced, it is signed and the quantity of goods is specified, then the agreement is enforceable.

In re Augustin Bros. Co.

460 F.2d 376 (8th Cir. 1972)

This is an action by Wright (plaintiff) against Augustin Bros. Co. (defendant) to recover damages for an alleged breach of oral contract. Judgment for Augustin and Wright appealed. Affirmed.

Wright operates a grain elevator, its principal business being the storage, processing, and sale of corn for use as cattle feed. Wright filed suit against Augustin, alleging in substance that Augustin had incurred liability to it in the amount of $64,187.95 due to its breach of an oral contract to purchase corn for cattle feed.

In April 1967, Wright and Augustin entered into an oral arrangement by which it was agreed that Wright would acquire any corn available on the market and thereafter Augustin would buy it at Wright's cost plus four cents per bushel for handling.

During the next four months, Wright increased its stored corn inventory substantially. In August the market price fell sharply. Shortly before October, however, due to financial difficulties, Augustin declined to honor the oral commitment to purchase the corn held in inventory although at that time Augustin had made a prepayment in the amount of $27,882.24. Wright was forced to liquidate its corn inventory at a lower market price. It sustained a substantial loss both as compared to the oral contract price it would have received and as compared to its acquisition cost.

BRIGHT, CIRCUIT JUDGE.   The Statute of Frauds bars enforcement of the overall oral contract between the parties which called for Augustin to purchase all of Wright's inventory of corn. The Statute of Frauds does, however, permit partial enforcement of this contract under the doctrine of part performance.

The statute U.C.C. § 2–201, as is here pertinent, provides:

(1) Except as otherwise provided in this section a contract for the sale of goods for the price of five hundred dollars ($500) or more is not enforceable by way of action or defense unless there is some writing sufficient to indicate that a contract for sale has been made between the parties and signed by the party against whom enforcement is sought or by his authorized agent or broker. A writing is not insufficient because it omits or incorrectly states a term agreed upon but the contract is not enforceable under this paragraph beyond the quantity of goods shown in such writing.

*   *   *   *   *

A contract which does not satisfy the requirements of subsection (1) but which is valid in other respects is enforceable . . . (c) *with respect to goods for which payment has been made and accepted or which have been received and accepted.* . . . (Emphasis supplied.)

"Partial performance" as a substitute for the required memorandum can validate the contract only for the goods which have been accepted or for which payment has been made and accepted.

Receipt and acceptance either of goods or of the price constitutes an unambiguous overt admission by both parties that a contract actually exists.

The language of the statute, and of the official comment, makes it clear that part performance of an oral contract for the sale of goods that is capable of apportionment is enforceable only as to that portion that has been either fully or partially performed.

We agree with the conclusion of the district court that enforcement of an oral contract for goods in which an advance payment has been made by the buyer is limited to that quantity of goods which the advance payment would buy at the market price.

We therefore conclude that Augustin by making a part payment, and Wright by accepting that part payment, made an enforceable contract only as to that quantity of goods that could have been purchased by that part payment.

Under this principle, Wright could have called upon Augustin to take delivery of an additional 21,783 bushels at $1.28 per bushel. When Augustin repudiated the contract Wright's right to damages was limited to that part of the contract recognized as enforceable by the express provisions of the Statute of Frauds contained in the Uniform Commercial Code.[3]

Interpretation

Necessity for Interpretation. Interpretation of a contract is the process of discovering and explaining the meaning of words and other manifestations used by the parties to the contract. If suit is brought to enforce a right claimed under a written contract, the court must interpret the meaning of the writing in order to determine the existence of a contract and the rights and duties of the parties to the contract.

Basic Standards of Interpretation. The courts have adopted broad, basic standards of interpretation which they follow in determining the meaning of contracts and agreements which are expressed in writing. They will, as a general rule, give the writing the meaning that the contracting parties would be expected to give it under the circumstances surrounding the making of the contract. And they will give to the words and phrases used the meaning usually given to them by the business, trade, or profession in which the parties are engaged.

Rules of Interpretation. If the language used in a contract is clear and definite, the interpretation of the writing is a matter for the judge; but if the writing is uncertain and ambiguous, and parol evidence is introduced in aid of its interpretation, the question of its meaning should be left to a jury.

When the court is asked to interpret a writing which is being litigated it will attempt first to determine, by reading the writing in its entirety, the principal objective of the parties. Ordinary words will be given their usual meaning and technical words will be given their technical meaning unless it clearly appears that a different meaning was intended. Each clause and provision will be interpreted with regard to its relation to the principal objective of the contract.

If the parties have used general terms followed by special terms, the court will assume that the special terms qualify the general terms. If the parties have used a form contract, or a contract which is partly printed and partly written, and there is a conflict between the printed and the written terms, the written terms will control. If there is an ambiguity in a contract and one of the parties has drawn the contract, the contract will be construed more strongly against the party who has drawn it.

Usage. Usage is a uniform practice or course of conduct which is followed in a line of business or profession or in a locality and which is either known

---

[3] The court ordered Wright to refund to Augustin that part of the prepayment which exceeded the actual damages suffered on the enforceable part of the contract. Assuming Wright sold the corn elsewhere at $1.18 per bushel, Wright would be entitled to $2,178.30 damages on the enforceable part of the contract. The balance of the prepayment would be due to Augustin.

to the parties or so well established that the parties must be presumed to have acted with reference thereto.

Usage may give to certain words a meaning different from the general meaning of the words. It may add to a written contract provisions not actually written into the writing. The courts have generally held in such cases that there is a presumption that the parties did not intend to reduce the entire agreement to writing but intended to contract with reference to those known usages. If both contracting parties live in the same community or are members of the same trade or association, the presumption is that they contract with reference to the usage of the community or trade and that they are both familiar with such usages. If the parties do not wish so to contract, they should express an intention not to be bound by such usages. Where the parties are not residents of the same community or members of the same trade group, the presumption is that they contract in regard to general usages and not in respect to local or special usages. It may be shown, however, that the local or special usages were known to both parties and that they contracted in reference to them. Where different usages prevail in different sections, the presumption is that the parties contracted in reference to the usage prevailing at the place where the contract was made and was to be performed.

Summary

Interpretation of a contract is the process of determining the meaning of words and other manifestations used by the parties to the contract. If an action is based on a writing, the writing must be interpreted in order to determine the rights and duties of the parties thereto. As guides to the court in the interpretation of written instruments, general standards and rules of interpretation have been adopted. Usage plays an important role in the interpretation of contracts. Usage is a uniform practice or course of conduct followed in a business or profession or in a locality, and may give to the language used a special meaning, or it may add terms to the contract.

Stender v. Twin City Foods, Inc.

510 P.2d 221 (Sup. Ct. Wash. 1973)

Action by Stender (plaintiff), a grower, against Twin City Foods (defendant), a food processor, for damages for breach of contract. Twin City appealed from an adverse decision made by the Court of Appeals. Reversed and the trial court judgment for Twin Foods affirmed.

The contract required Twin Foods to harvest and vine the peas at proper maturity and pay a stipulated price but gave the processor option to divert at a substantially lower price, such portion of the grower's acreage for seed or feed purposes as quality

". . . of salvage might dictate in the event of *adverse weather conditions that might delay harvest of pea crop beyond optimum maturity for processing."* The weather resulted in an unexpected maturation of the entire crop. Twin Foods claimed the right to divert Stender's crop under the "adverse weather" clause.

WRIGHT, JUSTICE. Determination of the intent of the contracting parties is to be accomplished by viewing the contract as a whole, the subject matter and objective of the contract, all the circumstances surrounding the making of the contract, the subsequent acts and conduct of the parties to the contract, and the reasonableness of respective interpretations advocated by the parties.

Both Stender and Twin City were heavily involved in the Washington pea industry, Stender as a grower with 8 years of experience and Twin City as a large processor. This fact would indicate that the contract should be construed in light of the usages of the pea industry existing at the time the contract was executed.

As the trial court indicated, it was the well-established plan of all the pea processors in the Skagit County area to plant the peas in a staggered manner in order to avoid the entire crop maturing at once. This system was in wide use and known by all the individual growers. In fact, Stender testified as to his knowledge of the custom of staggered planting and the planning and calculation of harvest scheduling. Thus, Stender must be held to have had knowledge of the existence of other pea contracts with Twin City Foods, the staggered planting schedule and the reasons therefor.

The record supports the trial court's conclusion that the reason that Twin City bypassed Stender's crop is that the weather conditions increased the size of the crops ready for processing beyond any reasonable expectations.

The definition of adverse weather conditions must be determined in light of reasonable industry custom and usage. Once a contract is established, usage and custom are admissible into evidence to explain the terms of the contract. And, parol evidence is admissible to establish a trade usage even though words in their ordinary or legal meaning are unambiguous. In view of custom and usage of the pea industry, it can be most reasonably stated that the term "adverse weather conditions" includes unusual temperature fluctuations resulting in an unexpected maturation of an entire pea crop which has been systematically planted with the objective of partial maturation over a period of time to allow for orderly harvesting. This construction of the term in question is especially valid when both parties to the contract were well aware that the purpose of scheduling crops was to avoid maturity of all the contract crops at once and to provide for systematic harvesting.[4]

Parol Evidence

Scope and Purpose of Parol Evidence Rule. Under the parol evidence rule, oral or extrinsic evidence is not admissible to add to, alter, or vary the

---

[4] Three judges dissented. The case demonstrates the importance of having unambiguous language in contracts.

terms of a written contract. The purpose of the parol evidence rule is to lend stability to written agreements by excluding from consideration any evidence of facts tending to show that the parties intended something different from that set out in the written contract. When the parties have expressed their contract or agreement in a writing free from ambiguity, such writing is the best evidence of their intent; all preliminary negotiations are merged in the writing.

The parol evidence rule has been made a part of the law of sales in those states which have enacted the Uniform Commercial Code. (2–202.)

Admissible Parol Evidence. Parol evidence is admissible if it is offered to prove that the writing is not a valid contract because it was induced by misrepresentation, fraud, duress, or undue influence, or to prove that the contract is illegal. In all such instances, oral evidence is offered to prove that the contract is voidable or is based on an illegal bargain, and not to add to, alter, or vary the terms of the contract. Parol evidence is also admissible to prove that a writing was executed on the condition that it was not to be operative unless or until an agreed, uncertain future event happened.

Subsequent Contracts. An oral contract, entered into subsequent to the making of the written contract, may be proved by oral evidence even though the terms of the oral contract are such that they cancel, subtract from, or add to the obligations of the prior written contract. Such parol evidence is not offered to alter, vary, or add to the written contract but is offered to prove the existence of a valid oral contract entered into subsequent to the making of the written contract.

Partial Writings. If a writing is incomplete and such fact is apparent from a reading of the writing in the light of the relation of the parties, the subject matter of the contract, and the surrounding circumstances, parol evidence is admissible to fill in the gaps. However, the parol evidence admitted must not tend to alter, vary, or contradict the written terms of the contract.

As to sales contracts the U.C.C. rejects the assumption that because a writing has been set out which is final as to some, or even as to most terms, it is to be taken as including *all* matters agreed upon. Under the U.C.C. 2–202 (b) the court must find that the *parties intended* the writing to be the *complete and exclusive* statement of the terms of the agreement before the writing can operate to exclude parol evidence of additional terms consistent with those written.

Ambiguous Contracts. Parol evidence is admissible to clear up ambiguities in a written contract or agreement. Such evidence is limited to testimony of facts and circumstances surrounding the making of a contract which will aid the court in interpreting the contract. Likewise, if there is nothing in the writing which indicates that the parties did not intend to contract in accordance with an existing usage, oral evidence of a business usage is admissible.

Summary

The parol evidence rule is a rule of substantive law. Under the parol evidence rule, oral evidence is not admissible to add to, alter, or vary the terms of a written contract. Oral evidence is admissible to prove the writing is voidable or illegal; to prove that at the time it was executed it was agreed that it would not be operative unless a specified future, uncertain event happened; to prove a subsequent contract; or to clear up an ambiguity in the contract.

From a practical standpoint a person should read a proposed writing carefully before he or she signs it and be certain that all the terms of the agreement are expressed in clear, concise language. If there are any provisions or words in the writing which a person does not understand, an explanation should be demanded concerning their meaning before signing.

Under the U.C.C. the court must find that the parties intended no additions to the written sales contract before the parol evidence rule will be used to exclude additional terms not inconsistent with those written.

Flamm v. Scherer

198 N.W.2d 702 (Ct. App. Mich. 1972)

Suit for breach of contract brought by Flamm (plaintiff) against Scherer (defendant). Flamm appealed from an adverse judgment. Affirmed.

The parties entered into an agreement on April 28, 1966, and a supplementary agreement on the same day. Under the terms of an April 28 agreement Scherer agreed to sell to Flamm all pickling cucumbers grown on 80 acres during the 1966 season from seed furnished by Flamm. The price of the pickle seed furnished by Flamm was to be deducted from the first payment. The final paragraph of the agreement read as follows:

It is expressly understood that BUYER WILL NOT BE RESPONSIBLE for any promises or conditions, statements or representations OTHER THAN THOSE CONTAINED HEREINABOVE.

A dispute arose between the parties in May at the time Flamm's field man, Ott, delivered the seed pursuant to the terms of the contract. The seed delivered was SMR 18 while Scherer was desirous of planting SMR 58. Scherer testified that he told Ott that he would not use the seed because Flamm had orally agreed to furnish SMR 58. Scherer bought his own seed and later sold his pickles to one of Flamm's competitors at a much higher price than was called for in the contract.

TARGONSKI, JUDGE. It is Flamm's contention that the contract could not be modified except by a written instrument under the provisions of Section 2209 of the Uniform Commercial Code—Sales which reads in pertinent part as follows:

(2) A signed agreement which excludes modification or rescission except by a signed writing cannot be otherwise modified or rescinded, but except as between merchants such a requirement on a form supplied by the merchant must be separately signed by the other party.

Flamm further contends that if the above section is not applicable then parol evidence relative to type of seed was still not admissible because it tended to contradict the written terms of the agreement rather than explaining or supplementing them as permitted by Section 2202 of the Uniform Code . . . which reads:

Sec. 2202. Terms with respect to which the confirmatory memoranda of the parties agree or which are otherwise set forth in a writing intended by the parties as a final expression of their agreement with respect to such terms as are included therein may not be contradicted by evidence of any prior agreement or of a contemporaneous oral agreement but may be explained or supplemented. . . .

(a) by course of dealing or usage of trade (section 1205) or by course of performance (section 2208); and

(b) by evidence of consistent additional terms unless the court finds the writing to have been intended also as a complete and exclusive statement of the terms of the agreement.

It is Scherer's contention that the trial court properly admitted testimony concerning the type of seed under the terms of Section 2202, to explain and supplement the agreement and that Section 2209, does not apply because the parol testimony offered regarding the variety of seed did not constitute a modification nor a rescission of the agreement.

Scherer's contentions are supported not only by a reading of the cited statutes and the trial court's opinion, but also by comments of the National Conference of Commissioners and the American Law Institute, which are recorded in M.S.A. following Section 2202. The portions of such comments as are pertinent to the issues in this matter appear as follows:

Purposes:

1. This section definitely rejects:

(a) Any assumpton that because a writing has been worked out which is final on some matters, it is to be taken as including all the matters agreed upon;

(b) The premise that the language used has the meaning attributable to such language by rules of construction existing in the law rather than the meaning which arises out of the commercial context in which it was used; and

(c) The requirement that a condition precedent to the admissibility of the type of evidence specified in paragraph (a) is an original determination by the court that the language used is ambiguous.

* * * * *

3. Under paragraph (b) consistent additional terms, not reduced to writing, may be proved unless the court finds that the writing was intended by both parties as a complete and exclusive statement of all the terms. If the additional terms are such that, if agreed upon, they would certainly have been included in the document in the view of the court, then evidence of their alleged making must be kept from the trier of fact.

The contract prepared by the plaintiff is silent on the question of the type of seed that was to be furnished by him although it does specify that he was to furnish the seed. Consequently, there is no contradiction, modification, or rescission arising out of the oral testimony pertaining to an agreement on the variety of seed to be furnished. Such testimony was supplementary or explanatory. . . .

Problem Cases

1. Executive Action, an employment agency, contacted Hudgens Realty regarding an employment opportunity. According to testimony of Executive Action, Hudgens advised that the "employer would pay the placement fee." On the same day the agency interviewed a potential employee who signed a contract agreeing to pay Executive Action the fee. This third party was eventually hired by Hudgens to fill the above-discussed vacancy. Executive Action billed Hudgens for the claimed amount of the placement fee and the realty company refused to pay. Hudgens admitted talking with Executive Action but denied that he had ever made any oral promise to pay the fee, although conflicting evidence would authorize a finding that an oral promise was made to pay the fee. Is this parol promise one that is within the statute of frauds, and thus unenforceable?

2. Colonial Distributors, a sundries business, attempted to establish a credit account with Star Sales, a wholesaler in 1958. Star was unwilling to grant credit to Colonial but was satisfied with the financial responsibility of Arnoult, one of the partners, and agreed to bill Arnoult personally for goods purchased by Colonial. All invoices were thereafter billed in Arnoult's name. Colonial was soon after incorporated with Arnoult and the other partners becoming stockholders. Payments on the account were made by Colonial before and after incorporation and the checks were co-signed by Arnoult until 1960 when Arnoult withdrew from the company. Thereafter, although Arnoult did not sign any checks, no change in the billing of the account was made. Late in 1960 Star discontinued the account because of delinquency accruing after Arnoult's departure. Shortly thereafter Colonial notified Star that they were going into bankruptcy, whereupon Star reclaimed merchandise equivalent to 40 percent of the debt. Star sued Arnoult for the deficiency and Arnoult set up the statute of frauds as a defense. Should Arnoult be held liable for the balance?

3. Ryle entered a written contract with Cunningham Associates, a prime contractor, whereby Cunningham was to build Ryle a home. Cunningham subcontracted the cement work to Carvitto. After Carvitto started work he found that Cunningham had written some bad checks, and he told Ryle that he and his crew were going to stop work. Ryle said, "You boys don't do that. I'll see that you get your money." Carvitto completed the work and sued Ryle when Cunningham was unable to pay the bills. Ryle set up the statute of frauds. Is this a good defense?

4. White promised Wolfson that, if he would continue with him as vice president and sales manager, he would receive a salary of $300 per week, expenses, and 1 percent of the annual gross receipts in excess of $1,000,000. Although Wolfson then remained, White refused to comply with the 1 percent provision and refused to give Wolfson any information which would tell him if any amount was due. Wolfson's employment was to be on a "permanent" basis but was not to continue for any specified period. Wolfson resigned upon request and sued White for breach of an oral employment agreement. White argued that the agreement violated the statute of frauds. Should White's argument succeed?

5. In 1954 Ortega entered an oral employment contract with Kimbrell Foods. One of the terms of the employment agreement concerned benefits which Ortega would receive upon retirement when he reached the age of 65. After retirement, Kimbrell refused to pay Ortega the retirement pension and Ortega sued for breach of contract. At the trial, Kimbrell argued

that the suit was barred by the statute of frauds, which prohibits the enforcement of an oral agreement not to be performed within one year of the making. Will this defense prohibit the enforcement of the alleged contract in regard to retirement benefits?

6. Rhodes brought suit against Wilkins for specific performance of a purported option agreement to purchase approximately 1.862 acres of land and damages for a claimed breach of the agreement. The purported agreement was prepared on a printed "Purchase Agreement" form that the parties had converted into an option agreement by deletions and addendums. The property was described as "approximately 1.862 acres being in the SE ¼ of the SW ¼ of SE ¼ of Sec. 10, R 6 E, T W 8 N, City of _____, County of Bernalillo, State of New Mexico, including vacant land." Is this agreement alone sufficient to satisfy the requirements of the statute of frauds, and thus, to be enforceable?

7. Olympic made suits for Crystal and received the following letter from Crystal:

> January 7, 1965
>
> Mr. Paul D Allesandro
> Olympic Juniors
> Newark, New Jersey
>
> Dear Paul:
>
> As a result of the discussion we had in my office Thursday, January 7th, I am writing this letter to you to confirm the agreement that we reached at this time.
>
> The agreement constitutes a contract between us; if and when David Crystal is sold that Olympic Juniors will be part and parcel of that sale and that it will be at a price that will be satisfactory to both you and your partner. A working employment contract will be required from you and your partner at a salary suitable to both you and your partner for a period of five years after the sale takes place.
>
> You have been an important factor in the growth of our suit business over many years, and it is my earnest desire to see that you remain with us.
>
> Sincerely yours,
> David Crystal, Inc.
>
> /s/ Philip Crystal
> Philip Crystal, Vice President

Crystal sold out but made no arrangement concerning Olympic. Olympic sued for breach of contract and Crystal set up the statute of frauds. Olympic contends that the letter is a sufficient memo of the transaction. Is Olympic correct?

8. After considerable negotiations American orally agreed to meet with Transport to work out terms for Transport's purchase of American's foundry. This conference terminated with American agreeing to prepare the necessary papers and to submit them to Transport. Transport, at American's suggestion, arranged a lease for part of the plant to Hartz who was presently a tenant in another American property. The lease was to be assigned to American as further security for the purchase-money mortgage. At American's request Transport also supplied a letter of credit from Irving Trust for $100,000. However, after a newly hired real estate manager informed American that $575,000 was grossly inadequate for the plant, American informed Transport that they would have to substantially increase their offer. Transport refused and American terminated the negotiations. Transport sued

for specific performance and American set up the statute of frauds. American argued that its part performance removed the defense. Is American correct?

9. Erving Paper manufactured and sold paper napkins in reusable polyethylene bags. Erving decided to purchase a special packaging machine from Sharp Machine Co. in order to meet the increase demand for these napkins. Through oral negotiations with Sharp a price of $11,000 per machine was accepted by Erving. Erving placed a written order, specifying the exact package sizes the machine had to be able to wrap, the exact production rate (per minute) desired, and that the machine be equipped with change parts required to fit a second size of wrapping. A few days before the promised delivery date, Sharp informed Erving by letter that their Engineering Dept. was unable to design a machine that would meet the special requirements of the packaging job. Erving Paper sued for damages for breach of contract and Sharp set up the statute of frauds. Is this a good defense?

10. Nofaras purchased a used car from Leveridge Motors. He signed a sales agreement which provided in part that "I have examined said auto and accept it in its present condition and agree that there are no warranties, express or implied, not specified herein, respecting said auto." On a blank portion of the form, Edison, a Leveridge salesman, had written, "30-day warranty-repair clutch as needed not to exceed $100-date no later than Feb. 24, 1963." A few days later Nofaras had Leveridge do other work totaling $70 for which he gave a personal check but later stopped payment on it. A few days after that (within 30 days of purchase) the car broke down whereupon Nofaras sued Leveridge to recover the purchase price contending Leveridge had breached the oral warranty. Leveridge argued that Nofaras was violating the parol evidence rule by trying to introduce evidence of the oral warranty. Is Leveridge correct?

11. The Secretary of the Interior issued four oil and gas leases to Essley. Each lease was for five years and contained a provision which required that the lessee should pay "a rental of 50 cents per acre for each acre for the first year; and a rental of 25 cents for each subsequent lease year." Essley paid 50 cents per acre the first year and maintained that the government was entitled to only 25 cents total (for each tract) for subsequent years. Section 17 of the Mineral Leasing Act provided inter alia that all leases were conditioned upon a payment of not less than 25 cents per acre. The bases stated that they were entered into pursuant to the Mineral Leasing Act which was made a part of the lease provided that "such regulations are not inconsistent with any express and specific lease provision." In an action by the government to recover the balance of the rent, should the government recover the 25 cents per acre or per tract?

chapter 13

Rights of Third Parties

Assignment of Contracts

Introduction.   In many early systems of the law the obligation of a debtor was personal in a literal sense, in that the body of the debtor could be taken by his creditors. In England, if a debtor did not fulfill his obligations, he could be imprisoned for debt. The accepted attitude toward one who did not pay his honest debts was that he was in effect a thief. This general attitude, together with the right of a creditor to have his debtor imprisoned if he failed to pay his debt, emphasized the personal nature of debt. At this time the courts held that a contract was personal to the parties and that neither party could assign his rights under the contract to a third person.

With the development of trade and the attainment of higher standards of commercial morality, the practice of extending credit, especially in the area of commercial transactions, became common. The needs of merchants demanded procedural reforms in the courts in relation to commercial cases. The courts began to recognize the right to assign contract rights, yet any suit on the contract had to be brought in the name of the party to the contract and not in the name of the assignee. By gradual development the rules of law regarding the assignment of contracts became more liberal, and now the assignability of contracts which are not personal to the parties are recognized. Under the procedural statutes now in force in most states, the assignee of a contract may bring suit in his or her own name to enforce the contract.

Contracts Not Assignable.   An assignment is a transfer, to the assignee, of the rights which the assignor has under a contract. The assignee has the right to have the performance of the contract rendered to him or her. From the beginning of the law of contracts, we have recognized that the promisee cannot demand of the promisor a performance which differs in any material respects from that promised; consequently, if the duties of the promisor will be altered in any material respect by the assignment of the contract, the contract is not assignable. Only those contracts can be assigned, the performance of which can be rendered by the promisor to the assignee without materially altering or increasing the burdens of performance.

Any contract which is personal in nature cannot be assigned, since the nature of the contract is limited by the personality of the original promisee, and the substitution of the assignee changes the nature of the performance required by the promisor.

Any contract the performance of which involves personal skill, judgment, or character is not assignable. A contract to support for life cannot be assigned. A property insurance policy cannot be assigned before the loss of the material insured because such policies are based in part on the character of the insured. A sharecrop lease is not assignable, since the rent received depends directly on the skill, ability, and honesty of the tenant.

If a contract contains a provision expressly prohibiting the assignment of the contract, the courts will hold that the contract is not assignable. The modification of this rule under the U.C.C. is discussed subsequently.

Contracts Which Are Assignable.   The typical example of an assignable contract is one in which a promisor has obligated himself or herself to pay money to a promisee. In such a contract the promisor's duty to pay is fixed, the burden of performance is not increased by requiring payment to the assignee instead of to the promisee, and a minimum of personal relationship is involved. As a general rule a contract to sell and deliver goods or to sell land is assignable. However, if the contract to sell goods is what is known as a "needs" or "output" contract, such a contract is, as a general rule, held not to be assignable, since the assignee's "needs" or ability to produce may vary materially from that of the promisee.

Contracts not to compete with the buyer of a business or with an employer have been held by the majority of the courts to be assignable. The purpose of such a restraint clause is to protect the goodwill of a business. The goodwill is an asset which may be sold with the business; consequently, the courts have held that a contract not to compete can be assigned as an incident of the sale of the business to be protected.

The Delegation of Duties.   The courts have held that the duties under a contract cannot be assigned but under some circumstances may be delegated. For instance, the courts have recognized the validity of the delegation of the duty to do building or engineering work, if the work is of such a nature that it may be performed by many persons, and if its performance does not depend on the skill, training, or character of an individual or group of individuals. The promisor cannot, however, relieve himself or herself from his or her obligation under a contract by delegating his or her duties to some third party. He or she can still be held liable for breach of the contract if the party to whom the duties are delegated fails to perform.

The right to delegate the duties created by a contract to sell goods is expanded by Section 2–210 of the Code.

Summary

In the early period of the development of our law, if a debt was not paid, the debtor could be imprisoned. Under the law the contractual relation was held to be highly personal, and no contract was assignable. As the country developed and trade expanded, the extension of credit became a common practice, especially in connection with commercial transactions. By gradual development the right to assign contracts was recognized, and today a contract is assignable if it does not involve the performance of personal services or the skill or character of the promisor, and if the duties of the promisor will not be materially altered by the assignment. A contract to receive money is a typical example of an assignable contract. Duties under a contract cannot be assigned, but they can be delegated if they are wholly impersonal in character. The promisor cannot relieve himself from his obligations under a contract by the delegation of his duties.

Although the basic principles of law relative to the assignment of contracts are not changed under the provisions of the Code, some aspects of the law are simplified and made more flexible and more practical.

Munchak Corporation v. Cunningham

457 F.2d 721 (4th Cir. 1972)

In a suit of Munchak Corporation (plaintiff), owner of a professional basketball club, to enjoin Cunningham (defendant) from performing services as a player for any other basketball club, the lower court denied relief and plaintiffs appealed. Reversed.

For the first year of the contract Cunningham was to receive a salary of $100,000, for the second year $110,000, and for the third year $120,000. Additionally, Cunningham was to receive $125,000 as a bonus for signing the contract. Cunningham refused to play for the Cougars contending that his contract was assigned illegally to Munchak Corporation, the new owner of the Cougars.

WINTER, CIRCUIT JUDGE.   Cunningham's contention that his contract was not assignable and that by reason of a purported assignment he is excused from performance arises from these facts. Cunningham's contracts with the Cougars were made at a time when Southern Sports Corporation, owned and operated primarily by James C. Gardner, was the owner of the Cougars' franchise. His contract with Southern Sports Corporation prohibited its assignment to another *"club"* without his consent, but it contained no prohibition against its assignment to another owner of the same club. In 1971, Southern Sports Corporation assigned its franchise and Cunningham's contracts to Munchak. Cunningham was not asked to consent, nor has he consented, to this assignment. While Cunningham's contracts require him to perform personal services, the services were to the club.

We recognize that under North Carolina law the right to performance of a personal service contract requiring special skills and based upon the personal relationship between the parties cannot be assigned without the consent of the party rendering those services.

But, some of such contracts may be assigned when the character of the performance and the obligation will not be changed. To us it is inconceivable that the rendition of services by a professional basketball player to a professional basketball club could be affected by the personalities of successive corporate owners. Indeed, Cunningham had met only Gardner of Southern Sports Club, and had not met, nor did he know, the other stockholders. If Gardner had sold all or part of his stock to another person, Cunningham could not seriously contend that his consent would be required.

The policy against assignability of certain personal service contracts is to prohibit an assignment of a contract in which the obligor undertakes to serve only the original obligee. This contract is not of that type, since Cunningham was not obligated to perform differently for plaintiffs than he was obligated to perform for Southern Sports Club. We, therefore, see no reason to hold that the contract was not assignable under the facts here. . . .

Rose v. Vulcan Materials Company

194 S.E.2d 521 (Sup. Ct. N.C. 1973)

In an action for breach of contract to supply stone at a specified price, the court entered judgment in favor of Vulcan Materials Company (defendant) and Rose (plaintiff) appealed. Reversed.

Rose owned and operated a stone quarry and ready-mix cement business in Yadkin County, North Carolina. He used stone from his quarry in his cement business. Dooley was also in the rockcrushing business in Yadkin County in competition with Rose. Late in 1956 Dooley contracted to buy Rose's rockcrushing business and to lease his quarry for ten years. The purchase contract obligated Dooley to provide Rose with enough stone to meet his business requirements for ten years at favorable listed prices. Sometime prior to 12 April 1960, Dooley advised Rose that he had an offer from Vulcan Materials Company to purchase his quarry operations and requested Rose to release him from the contract so he could consummate the sale. Rose declined to do so and advised Dooley he would not release him unless Vulcan Materials Company would agree in writing to comply with all of Dooley's obligations.

In April 1960 Vulcan purchased the quarry operations and all of the assets and obligations of Dooley. Vulcan then sent Rose a letter which stated that they intended to carry out Dooley's obligations. In 1961, however, Vulcan notified Rose that all prices for stone sold to Rose would have to be increased above the prices listed in the Rose-Dooley contract. Rose paid the higher prices under protest and then sued Vulcan for breach of contract.

HUSKINS, JUSTICE.   In most states, the assignee of an executory bilateral contract is not liable to anyone for the nonperformance of the assignor's duties thereunder unless he expressly promises his assignor or the other contracting party to perform, or "assume," such duties. . . . These states refuse to *imply* a promise to perform the duties, but if the assignee expressly promises his assignor to perform, he is liable to the other contracting party on a third-party beneficiary theory.

And, if the assignee makes such a promise directly to the other contracting party upon a consideration, of course he is liable to him thereon.

A minority of states holds that the assignee of an executory bilateral contract under a general assignment becomes not only assignee of the rights of the assignor but also delegatee of his duties; and that, absent a showing of contrary intent, the assignee *impliedly* promises the assignor that he will perform the duties so delegated. This rule is expressed in *Restatement, Contracts,* § 164 (1932) as follows:

(1) Where a party under a bilateral contract which is at the time wholly or partially executory on both sides purports to assign the whole contract, his action is interpreted, in the absence of circumstances showing a contrary intention, as an assignment of the assignor's rights under the contract and a delegation of the performance of the assignor's duties.

(2) Acceptance by the assignee of such an assignment is interpreted, in the absence of circumstances showing a contrary intention, as both an assent to become an assignee of the assignor's rights and as a *promise to the assignor to assume the performance of the assignor's duties.* (Emphasis added.)

This Court has never expressly adopted the Restatement Rule (§ 164) in North Carolina. However, . . . [we] apparently recognized the rule of implied assumption that later became the Restatement Rule.

This rule is regarded as the more reasonable view by legal scholars and textwriters. Professor Grismore says:

It is submitted that the acceptance of an assignment in this form does presumptively import a tacit promise on the part of the assignee to assume the burdens of the contract, and that this presumption should prevail in the absence of the clear showing of a contrary intention. The presumption seems reasonable in view of the evident expectation of the parties. The assignment on its face indicates an intent to do more than simply to transfer the benefits assured by the contract. It purports to transfer the contract as a whole, and since the contract is made up of both benefits and burdens both must be intended to be included. It is true the assignor has power only to delegate and not to transfer the performance of duties as against the other party to the contract assigned, but this does not prevent the assignor and the assignee from shifting the burden of performance as between themselves. Moreover common sense tells us that the assignor, after making such an assignment, usually regards himself as no longer a party to the contract. He does not and, from the nature of things, cannot easily keep in touch with what is being done in order properly to protect his interests if he alone is to be liable for nonperformance. Not infrequently the assignor makes an assignment because he is unable to perform further or because he intends to disable himself for further performance. The assignee on the other hand understands that he is to carry out the terms of the contract as is shown by the fact that he usually does, most of the decided cases being those in which the other party objected to performance by the assignee. In view of these considerations is it not reasonable to infer that the assignee tacitly promises to perform?

In addition, with respect to transactions governed by the Uniform Commercial Code, an assignment of a contract in general terms is a delegation of performance of the duties of the assignor, and its acceptance by the assignee constitutes a promise by him to perform those duties. *See* G.S. § 25–2–210(4). Our holding in this case maintains a desirable uniformity in the field of contract liability.

We further hold that the other party to the original contract may sue the assignee as a third-party beneficiary of his promise of performance which he impliedly makes to his assignor, under the rule above laid down, by accepting the general assignment. . . . When Vulcan accepted such assignment it thereby became delegatee of its assignor's duties under the contract and impliedly promised to perform such duties.

Rights Acquired by Assignee

General Rule.   An assignment of a contract is in legal effect a sale to an assignee of an assignor's rights under a contract. The assignee takes the place of the assignor and is entitled to all the rights of the assignor. He or she can, however, acquire no greater rights than the assignor has at the time of the assignment, that is, he or she takes the contract subject to all the defenses that the promisor has to the contract.

Notice of Assignment.   If the assignee wishes to protect the rights acquired by the assignment, the assignee, or someone acting in his behalf, must give the promisor notice of the assignment. If the promisor is not given notice of the assignment and he renders performance to the original promisee, the promisor will have discharged his duty and will not be liable to the assignee under the contract. In such a situation the original promisee, having accepted performance of the assigned contract, is liable to the assignee for the value of the performance received by him. When notice is given to the promisor, he or she becomes liable at this time to render to the assignee any performance due the promisee.

Successive Assignments.   If a promisee assigns rights to one assignee and at a later date wrongfully assigns the same rights to a second assignee, who takes for value and without notice or knowledge of the prior assignment, the question then arises as to which of the respective assignees has the better right. There are two views on this point.

Under the rule known as the "American rule," the courts have held that the first assignee has the better right. This view is based on the rule of property law that a person cannot transfer greater rights in property than he has. Under the rule known as the "English rule," the assignee who first gives notice of the assignment of the contract has the greater right. Under this rule, the giving of notice is considered equivalent to the taking of possession of tangible property. Under the Code, if the same item of property is sold to two different innocent purchasers for value, the first to take possession has the better right.

Assignment of Wages.   Under the common law an assignment of future wages was void unless the assignor had a contract of employment. This rule has been relaxed, and now, as a general rule, if the assignor is regularly employed, the courts will enforce an assignment of the future wages of such employee.

However, substantially all the states have enacted statutes regulating the assignment of future wages. These statutes range from those which make all assignments of future wages void to those which place various limitations on such assignments.

Summary

The assignee of a contract can acquire by the assignment no greater rights than those had by the assignor at the time of the assignment. If the assignee wishes to protect the rights acquired by the assignment, notice of the assignment must be given to the promisor. The rights acquired by the assignment will be such rights as the assignor had against the promisor at the time notice of the assignment was given to the promisor. In most states the assignment of future wages is regulated by statute.

General Factors, Inc. v. Beck[1]

409 P.2d 40 (Sup. Ct. Ariz. 1965)

This action was brought by General Factors (plaintiffs) as assignees of a claim for construction materials sold by Tempe Gravel Company to A. Deal Beck (defendant). Judgment for Beck and General Factors appealed. Reversed.

In early October, Beck purchased from Tempe Company certain materials for use by Beck in his construction business. Invoices representing these purchases were then sent to General Factors, Inc., under an alleged assignment and factoring account. General Factors paid for these invoices, between the 10th and 31st of October, and mailed these invoices to Beck at his place of business.

The invoices bearing the name of Tempe had at the bottom the following statement: "Accounts due and payable 15th of month following purchase."

General Factors affixed a sticker to each invoice which read as follows: "Pay only to General Factors, Inc., 3500 North Central Avenue, Phoenix, Arizona. This account and the merchandise covered hereby is assigned and payable only to said corporation, to which notice must be given of any merchandise returns or claims of any kind."

And also stamped to the invoice was the following: "To facilitate our accounts receivable bookkeeping, this invoice has been factored with General Factors, Inc., 3500

---

[1] Note: This case reversed the Court of Appeals decision used in the last edition of this text.

North Central Building, Suite 332 in Phoenix, Arizona. Make payment directly to factor."

Invoices were received by Beck's bookkeepeer and the bookkeepeer merely opened the letters and checked the amounts on the invoices to determine any set-offs or "charge-backs." The bookkeeper did not have the authority to draw checks for payment of the invoices or any other accounts. These invoices were not handed to Beck until sometime between the 7th and 15th of November, 1960.

In the meantime, Tempe was experiencing financial difficulties and Beck paid off this account with Tempe.

VOALL, JUSTICE.   Thus, the primary issue in this case concerns the question of notice of an assignment under the statutes and laws of the State of Arizona. The pertinent Arizona statute is A.R.S. § 44–805, subsec. A, which provides as follows:

If a debtor, *without actual notice* that an assignment of his account has been made, makes full or partial payment of his debt to the assignor, his debt shall thereby be extinguished or reduced. [Emphasis supplied]

The requirement of actual notice in the above statute would seem to import that the notice actually reach the debtor. Otherwise, where the debtor has paid his creditor prior to actual notice, his debt is extinguished or reduced according to the amount paid.

General Factors gave written notice addressed to Beck personally that the account was being factored with them. The invoices were received at Beck's usual place of business by an employee who opened the letters, checked the amount due, and presented at a later date the invoices to Beck for payment.

There is support for the proposition that an agent or clerk ostensibly in charge of the place where the principal's business is carried on has apparent authority to accept notification in relation to the business.

It has been held that an employee in charge of the receipt of mail may accept written notification. The cases split as to the effect of notification served upon bookkeepers.

If the law is to be practical, it must recognize other channels through which notice may be served. The phrase "actual notice" is properly distinguishable from "actual knowledge" and includes notice to an authorized agent as well as generally the communication of any information enabling the recipient to acquire therefrom, by the exercise of reasonable diligence, actual knowledge.

We therefore hold there was actual notice to the debtor under the facts of this case by the notification received by the employee within the meaning of A.R.S. § 44–805, subsec. A (1956). . . .

Nassau Discount Corp. v. Allen

255 N.Y.S.2d 608 (Sup. Ct. N.Y. 1965)

This was an action brought by Nassau Discount Corp. (plaintiff), as an assignee of a book purchase contract, against Allen (defendant). Judgment for Allen.

In April 1963, a salesman representing Educational Guild went to Allen's house and convinced her that she was required to buy certain books for use by her school-age child. He did this by falsely representing that he was connected with the Board of Education.

Allen signed an installment purchase contract which stated on its reverse side:

> Buyer will settle all mechanical, service, and other claims of whatsoever character with respect to the sale evidenced hereby, directly with Seller (and not with any such Assignee) and will not set up any such claim(s) as a defense or counterclaim to any action for payment or possession which may be brought by an Assignee who acquires this Contract in good faith and for value. . . .

On April 30, 1963, Discount Corp., took an assignment of the contract for value. On May 5, 1963, Discount mailed to Allen a Notice of Assignment requesting Allen to notify Discount in writing within ten days from the date of the mailing of the notice of any defense that she might have arising out of the sale or otherwise be barred from asserting such defense in an action by Discount. Discount received no written response to its Notice of Assignment. However, Allen upon receipt of the notice immediately returned Discount's coupon payment book by mail. Allen refused to pay any installments of the contract.

HELLER, JUDGE.　The broad issue presented for determination by this court is whether Allen is barred by the waiver of defenses clause contained within the contract from asserting her defenses of fraud and non-delivery against plaintiff assignee. Subsidiary to the determination of this broad issue is whether the fraud alleged is fraud in factum, the real defense of fraud, or fraud in the inducement, and furthermore, whether Discount Corp. takes subject to the real defense of fraud.

Fraud in factum exists where one is induced to sign an instrument of a different nature or character than that he was led to believe was before him. In the present case Allen does not assert that she was deceived as to the nature of the paper she was signing but rather that she was *induced* to sign the contract through the fraudulent misrepresentations of the salesman. Therefore, the fraud involved in this case is fraud in the inducement of the contract and we need not decide whether plaintiff takes subject to the real defense of fraud.

More accurately phrased, the issue is whether Allen has waived her defenses of fraud in the inducement of the contracts and non-delivery. The controlling statute in the resolution of this issue is Section 403, subdivision 3(a) of the Personal Property Law which provides in substance that no contract shall contain any provision whereby the buyer agrees not to assert against an assignee a claim or defense arising out of the sale, but it *may* contain such a provision as to an assignee who acquires the contract in good faith and for value and to whom the buyer has not mailed written notice of the facts giving rise to a claim or defense within ten days after the assignee has mailed notice of the assignment to the buyer. Subdivision 3(a) further provides stringent requirements for the contents of the notice of assignment, all of which have been complied with by plaintiff.

Good faith necessarily requires that the assignee be "not so identified with the seller, to an extent that it could fairly be said that the dealings of one are inextricably interwoven with that of the other." *Public National Bank and Trust Co. of New York v. Fernandez.* The court further stated: "Certain unmistakable indicia point inevitably that this plaintiff, far from being a bona fide assignee of a chose in action, was in fact a principal in the transaction. . . ." It was pointed out that the contract provided that all installments be paid to the plaintiff assignee; that the title to the merchandise was to be retained by the holder, who was defined as either the seller or the assignee; that the assignment was made even before the goods were delivered to the buyer and that the sale and assignment were physically encompassed within the same document. The court concluded: "From all the above it would appear that the bank, rather than being a bona fide purchaser of the contract in question, was to all intents and purposes a party to the original agreement."

When contracts are supplied by an assignee, complete with the assignee's name printed thereon, it is obvious that the assignee is a specific assignee, vitally interested in the sale, so closely related that it is almost as if the assignee were "looking over the parties' shoulders when the sale was consummated." Form contracts supplied by a specific assignee containing waiver of defenses clauses inescapably point to the conclusion of a pre-formed intention upon the part of the assignee to defeat the rights of the buyer so as to negate the requirement of good faith.

It can fairly be said that Allen and Discount in the circumstances of this case were so inextricably intertwined as to impugn Discount's good faith status. This court, therefore, finds as an ultimate fact that an implied agency existed under the terms of the contract and that Discount is subject to the defenses of fraud in the inducement and nondelivery.

Assignor's Liability to Assignee

Implied Warranties. When an assignor assigns a contractual claim for value to an assignee, the assignor impliedly warrants to his immediate transferee that the claim is a valid claim, that is, that the parties have capacity to contract, that the claim is not void for illegality, and that it has not been discharged prior to the assignment or rendered unenforceable for any reasons known to the assignor. The assignor also impliedly warrants that he has good title to the claim and that he has passed good title to the assignee.

If the claim is represented by a written instrument, the assignor impliedly warrants that the instrument is genuine and is in all respects what it purports to be. The assignor also impliedly agrees to do nothing which will defeat or impair the value of the assignment. The assignment does not warrant the solvency of the promisor. These implied warranties may be limited or enlarged by the express agreement of the parties.

General Liability. If, after the assignment of a contract, payment is made to and received by the assignor, he or she holds the money as trustee for the assignee and is liable to the assignee for the money collected. If the assignor makes successive assignments of the same claim to two or more assignees, the assignor is liable to the assignee or assignees who acquire no right against the promisor for the damages such assignee or assignees may have suffered as a result of the fraud.

Summary

An assignor impliedly warrants that the claim he assigns is a valid, subsisting claim and that he will do nothing to defeat or impair the value of the assignment. The assignor does not warrant the solvency of the promisor.

If the assignor collects the assigned claim, he is liable to the assignee for all moneys collected. If the assignor makes successive assignments of the same claim, he is liable to the defrauded assignees for the damages they have suffered.

Third-Party Beneficiary

Classes of Third-Party Beneficiary Contracts.   Where the performance of the promise in a contract will benefit some person other than the promisee, the party benefited is a third-party beneficiary. As a general rule a person who is not a party to a contract has no rights in the contract, even though he or she may derive some advantage from its performance. However, if the parties to the contract enter into the contract with the intent of benefiting a third party, the beneficiary under the contract may enforce it by court action. Third-party beneficiaries have been divided into three classes: (1) donee beneficiaries, (2) creditor beneficiaries, and (3) incidental beneficiaries.

Donee Beneficiaries.   If the primary purpose of the promisee, in contracting for performance to be rendered to the third person, is to make a gift of the performance to the third person, the third person is a donee beneficiary. In a donee beneficiary contract the promisee furnishes the consideration, and the promise of the promisor is made to the promisee, but the promise of the promisor is to confer a stipulated benefit on the beneficiary, who must be named or indicated with reasonable certainty. If the promisor does not perform his promise, both the promisee and the beneficiary have a cause of action against him. The beneficiary can recover a judgment for the value of the promised performance. The promisee can recover a judgment for any damage he or she can prove he suffered as a result of the promisor's failure to render performance to the beneficiary. As a general rule the promisee can recover only nominal damages.

A life insurance contract whereby the insurance company, in consideration of premiums paid, contracts to pay to the named beneficiary the amount of the policy on the happening of a stipulated event, usually the death of the insured, is a common form of the donee beneficiary contract. If the insurance company does not pay on the happening of the contingency, the beneficiary can bring suit in his or her own name and recover a judgment.

Creditor Beneficiaries. A person is a creditor beneficiary if the performance of the promise will satisfy an actual or supposed legal duty of the promisee to the beneficiary. The primary distinction between a donee beneficiary and a creditor beneficiary is that the benefits conferred on one, the donee beneficiary, are a gift, whereas the performance of the promise in the case of the creditor beneficiary is intended to discharge a duty or supposed duty by the promisee. The duty need not be the payment of money but may be any type of obligation.

For example, Anson buys a car on an installment contract from Sharp Motor Company. Anson then sells the car to Baker and Baker agrees to assume Anson's indebtedness to Sharp as a part of the purchase price. Sharp is a creditor beneficiary of the Baker-Anson agreement and may hold either one or both of them liable on the installment contract. Sharp, of course, can collect no more than the full amount owing on the debt.

Incidental Beneficiaries. An incidental beneficiary is one who will benefit in some way from the performance of a contract which has been entered into by the promisee for his or her own benefit and without any intent of benefiting a third person. The purpose of the contract is to obtain the benefits for the promisee, not for a third person. An incidental beneficiary has no rights in the contract and cannot recover damages in a suit for breach of contract.

For example, suppose Adams contracts with Ball to dig a ditch which will drain a low place on Adams' farm. The low place extends over onto Clark's farm, and the drainage ditch will be of benefit to Clark also.

If Ball then breaches his contract with Adams and does not dig the ditch, Clark will not be allowed to recover damages in an action against Ball for breach of the contract. Although Clark would have benefited from the performance of the contract, he was not a party to the contract, nor was the contract entered into with the intent of benefiting Clark. Clark is an incidental beneficiary and has no rights under the contract.

Municipal or Governmental Contracts. As a general rule the members of the public are incidental beneficiaries of contracts entered into in the regular course of the carrying-on of the functions of the municipality or governmental unit. A member of the public cannot recover a judgment in a suit against the promisor, even though as a taxpayer he or she will suffer some injury from nonperformance. However, a municipality or governmental unit may enter into contracts which have as their objective the protection of the individual members of the public. If a member of the public is injured by breach of such a contract, he can recover damages in a suit brought in his own name.

Summary

A contract may expressly provide that performance shall be rendered to a named third person who is not a party to the contract, or a third person who is not a party to the contract may be benefited by the performance of the contract without being named. Such persons fall into three groups: (1) donee beneficiary, (2) creditor beneficiary, and (3) incidental beneficiary.

If the purpose of the promisee is to make a gift to a named third person of part or all of the performance of the promisor, such third person is a donee beneficiary. If the purpose of the promisee is to impose on the promisor an obligation to pay a debt owed to a third person by the promisee, such third person is a creditor beneficiary. Both donee beneficiary and creditor beneficiary have the right to bring suit on the contract. If a third person will benefit from the performance of the contract without any intent on the part of the promisee to confer such benefits, such person is an incidental beneficiary and has no rights in the contract.

United States v. State Farm Mutual Automobile Ins. Co.

455 F.2d 789 (10th Cir. 1972)

Action by U.S. (plaintiff) against State Farm (defendant). U.S. appealed from trial court judgment for State Farm. Reversed.

On November 24, 1969, Mack was injured in a car accident near Fort Sill, Oklahoma. Mack then owned a State Farm automobile liability insurance policy. He was treated free of any personal cost or expense at Government medical facilities. Such free hospital and medical services for servicemen are prescribed in 10 U.S.C.A. § 1074. The medical expenses incurred by the United States for Sergeant Mack were $1,855.00.

The United States sued State Farm claiming that it is entitled to collect as a third party beneficiary under Mack's State Farm Policy.

The pertinent provisions of the policy are as follows:

COVERAGE C—MEDICAL PAYMENTS

To pay reasonable medical expenses incurred for services furnished within one year from the date of the accident:

Division 1. to *or for* the first *person* named in the declarations . . . who sustains *bodily injury,* caused by accident, while *occupying* the owned motor vehicle. . . .

POLICY CONDITIONS
7. Payment of Claim; Autopsy-Coverages C, M, S, T, and U. Under coverages C and M *the company may pay the injured person or any person or organization rendering the services* and such payment shall reduce the amount payable hereunder. Any payment shall not constitute admission of liability of the insured or, except hereunder, of the company. (Emphasis ours.)

BARRETT, CIRCUIT JUDGE.   It is a general rule that where the third-party beneficiaries are so described as to be ascertainable, it is not necessary that they be specifically named in the contract in order to recover thereon and it is not necessary that they are identifiable at the time the contract is made.

In *United States v. United Services Automobile Association,* the minor son of an Air Force officer was injured by a car and was treated free of cost at Government facilities as provided by 10 U.S.C.A. § 1076. The United States and the officer sued the officer's insurance company under the medical payments provision of the policy. The policy required the insurance company to pay all reasonable medical expenses incurred within a year of any accident to or for the named insured. It also provided, as in the State Farm policy, that the Company may pay any person or organization rendering the services for the insured. The Court found that the United States was entitled to sue and recover as a third-party beneficiary.

We hold that the United States qualifies as a third-party beneficiary under the policy in that it is an "organization rendering the services."

"Organization" is defined as a corporation, government or governmental subdivision or agency. Where a contract creates a right or imposes a duty in favor of a third party, the law presumes that the parties intended to confer a benefit on the party and allows the party a remedy.

The United States is entitled to recover from State Farm for the reasonable value of those medical services it rendered to Sergeant Mack. To hold otherwise we must ignore the clear language of the policy, thus granting State Farm a windfall represented by that portion of Sergeant Mack's premium payments for coverage which, under the facts of this case, State Farm, in effect, contends he really did not need. . . .

Assignment under the Uniform Commercial Code

Scope of Application. Article 9 of the Code applies to any sale of accounts, contract rights or chattel paper. (Section 9–102.) It does not apply, however, to a sale of accounts, contract rights, or chattel paper as a part of a sale of the business out of which they arose, or an assignment of accounts, contract rights, or chattel paper which is for collection only, or a transfer of a contract right to an assignee who is also to do the performance under the contract. (9–104[f].) The assignment of accounts, contract rights, and chattel paper are treated primarily from the standpoint of secured transactions. Under the provisions of the Code, the basic principles of the assignment of contracts are retained. The primary purpose of the Code is to clarify, simplify, and make more practical the law relative to the sale or assignment of accounts, contract rights, and chattel paper. The provisions of the Code affecting assignment and sale of accounts, contract rights, and chattel paper will be discussed in greater detail in Chapter 42, "Secured Transactions."

Assignment. The main provisions relative to the assignment of contracts for the sale of goods are to be found in Section 2–210 of the Code. This section provides that duties may be delegated unless the other party has a "substantial interest" in having the original party perform or control the acts required in the sales contract. All rights are assignable except where the assignment would "materially" change the duties of the obligor or "materially" increase his risks. A right to damages for breach of a sales contract may be assigned despite an agreement prohibiting any assignment. Unless the circumstances indicate a contrary intent, a clause prohibiting assignment of a contract will be construed as barring only the delegation of duties. An assignment of "all of my rights" normally will operate as a delegation of duties. The other party may treat any assignment which also delegates duties as grounds for demanding assurances from the assignor. Section 9–206 applies to sale of goods contracts where the seller has retained a security interest.

Summary

In general, contract rights are assignable under the U.C.C. A right to damages for breach of a sales contract may be assigned despite terms in the contract prohibiting any assignment. Rights cannot be assigned where such assignment materially changes the duties of the obligor or materially increases his or her risks. Duties may be delegated in some contracts but the person delegating the duties remains liable on the contract.

First National Bank of Elgin v. Husted

205 N.E.2d 780 (Ct. App. Ill. 1965)

This was an action brought by First National Bank (plaintiff) against Husted (defendant) to recover payments due on a car purchase installment contract which Husted had entered with Reed Motors. Reed Motors assigned the contract to First National Bank.

The contract provided: "Buyer agrees to settle all claims against Seller directly with Seller and will not set up any such claims against Seller as defense, counterclaim, set off, cross-complaint or otherwise in any action for the purchase price or possession brought by any assignee of this contract."

DAVIS, JUSTICE.   The Uniform Commercial Code provides:

(1) Subject to any statute or decision which establishes a different rule for buyers of consumer goods, an agreement by a buyer that he will not assert against an assignee any claim or defense which he may have against the seller is enforceable by an assignee who takes his assignment for value, in good faith and without notice of a claim or defense, except as to defenses of a type which may be asserted against a holder in due course of a negotiable instrument under the Article on Commercial Paper. (Article 3.) A buyer who as part of one transaction signs both a negotiable instrument and a security agreement makes such an agreement.

(2) When a seller retains a purchase money security interest in goods the Article on Sales (Article 2) governs the sale and any disclaimer, limitation, or modification of the seller's warranties." (9–206)

The first sentence of this subsection permits a contractual waiver of certain defenses by the buyer, and it is in accord with prior Illinois case law. While this section provides that either the legislature or the courts may establish a different rule, we view this as a legislative function, the exercise of will rather than judgment, and we are reluctant to change the prior decisional law.

The defenses which may be asserted against a holder in due course are:

(a) infancy, to the extent that it is a defense to a simple contract; and
(b) such other incapacity, or duress, or illegality of the transaction, as renders the obligation of the party a nullity; and
(c) such misrepresentation as has induced the party to sign the instrument with neither knowledge nor reasonable knowledge nor reasonable opportunity to obtain knowledge of its character or its essential terms; and
(d) discharge in insolvency proceedings; and
(e) any other discharge of which the holder has notice when he takes the instrument (3–305[2])

Thus, a buyer may contractually waive, as against an assignee, any defenses except those enumerated in articles [Sections] 3–305(2) and 9–206(2). In absence of allegation in Husted's affidavit that First National Bank did not take the assignment for value, in good faith, and without notice of claim or defense, and in view of the date of the contract and assignment, we believe that First National Bank is an assignee for value, in good faith, and without notice of claim or defense.

The buyers' defenses of failure of consideration, and subsequent promise and failure to repair the car were waived, as against First National Bank, under article [Section] 9–206 of the Uniform Commercial Code.

Problem Cases

1. Paalzow owned a large office building in Chattanooga which the Bergers wished to lease. After extensive negotiations and after investigation revealed that the Bergers were experienced managers of office buildings and millionaries, Paalzow contracted to lease the building to them. The Bergers assigned the contract to their niece. A lease drafted in accordance with the contract and naming the niece as lessee was refused execution by Paalzow. The Bergers sued for specific performance and Paalzow set up the defense that the contract to lease was not assignable. Who should prevail?

2. The architect firm of Rossetti, DiCorcia, and Mileto signed a contract with the City of New Britain to prepare the plans and specifications for a new police station and courthouse. Although the contract was signed in the name of the firm, Rossetti negotiated the entire agreement and was in charge of the project. After approximately 30 percent of the project had been completed and the blueprints turned over to the city authorities, the architect firm dissolved, and Rossetti and Mileto formed a partnership under the terms of the dissolution, the new partnership assumed responsibility for fulfilling the contract with New Britain. At this point New Britain instructed Rossetti and Mileto that the contract would no longer be honored. New Britain alleged that the agreement with Rossetti, DiCorcia, and Mileto was a personal service contract and that the duties thereunder were not assignable to the Rossetti and Mileto partnership. Is this a valid defense to a breach of contract action?

3. Rosier purchased a car of gasoline from Chanute on open account for $1,516.58. Chanute assigned the account to Sinclair. At the time of the assignment, Rosier had paid Chanute $289.70 on account and he had also paid $1,477.30 in inspection fees under a statute which had been declared unconstitutional. The inspection fees should have been returned to Rosier. Rosier refused to pay Sinclair. Sinclair sued Rosier on the assigned account. Is Sinclair entitled to a judgment?

4. Certain individuals entered home building contracts with Burns, a contractor. They desired to obtain loans whereupon Burns directed them to Washington Savings. The prospective homeowners filed loan applications and Burns provided assistance by furnishing surveys, credit reports, title insurance, and plans and specifications to Washington Savings. Savings gave written commitments to each applicant and informed Burns by letter that they had done so. Savings then refused to make the loans. The new homeowners defaulted on their payments to Burns and he was forced to take over the residences he had built and to sell them at a loss. Burns sued Washington Savings contending that he was a third party beneficiary of the loan-commitment contracts. Should he recover?

5. Maryland Corporation encountered financing problems and sought additional loan-insurance commitments from FHA. FHA agreed to these commitments provided Maryland agreed in writing to guarantee the refund of all deposits received from purchasers where Maryland failed to complete their homes. Maryland then failed to complete the home of Hobstetter and also failed to refund his deposit. Hobstetter sued Maryland claiming that he was a third party beneficiary of the Maryland-FHA agreement. Should he succeed?

6. Bilich was a contractor, and he entered into a contract with Reliable Trucking Company, whereby Bilich agreed to install designated sewer lines for Reliable Trucking Company and Reliable Trucking Company agreed that they would have Barnett prepare survey lines and grade sheets covering the work that was to be done by Bilich for Reliable Trucking Company. Barnett prepared survey lines and grade sheets and submitted them to Bilich. The grade sheets were negligently prepared and were an inaccurate representation of the grade lines on the property. Bilich relied on the grade sheets and discovered, on the completion of the grading, that the excavation was not as it should have been according to plans and specifications. As a result of the errors, Bilich was required to fill in part of the excavation and incur additional expenditures of $382. Bilich sued Barnett to recover a judgment of $382 on the theory that Bilich was a third-party beneficiary of the contract between Reliable Trucking Company and Barnett. Is Bilich a third-party beneficiary of the contract?

7. Auto-Lite Co. entered into a collective bargaining agreement with Metal Polishers Union. According to this agreement: (1) 8 consecutive hours except for lunch constituted a "normal" work day and 40 hours of 5 consecutive days (Monday-Friday) constituted a "normal" work week; (2) when a reduction in the work force becomes necessary, probationary employees were to be laid off first followed by others according to seniority to maintain "normal" work days and weeks.

   Auto-Lite's chief customer cut its orders severely; and, as a result, the company decided to cut production to a four-day week without a reduction in work force. Wesley, third man in seniority in the Union was laid off for seven consecutive Fridays as was the rest of the work force. Wesley sued for wages lost in violation of the bargaining agreements. Can Wesley collect?

chapter 14

Performance and Remedies

Conditions

Introduction. The requirements essential to the making of a valid and enforceable contract have been discussed and the rules followed by the courts in determining the rights and duties of the parties to the contract. The next step is to determine what action is required by the promisor if the promisor is to perform the duties imposed in the contract.

In determining whether or not a contract has been performed, the court is faced with an exceedingly complex problem. The relation between the parties, standard practices in the trade, usage in the community, business, or trade, prior dealings between the parties, and a multitude of other possible relations and circumstances must be analyzed and weighed.

Nature of Conditions. As a general rule the duty of performance arises at the time the contract is entered into although the time of the performance of the duty does not arise until some future date. The parties may provide in their contract that no duty to perform shall arise until the happening of some future, uncertain event. Such a provision is a condition precedent. Likewise, the parties may provide in their contract that on the happening of some future, uncertain event the party on whom is imposed the duty of performance will be relieved of that duty. Such a provision is a condition subsequent.

In some contracts the terms of the contract and the accompanying circumstances are such that the courts will imply a provision that the parties will perform simultaneously. Such an implied provision is a concurrent condition.

Creation of Conditions. A condition in a contract is, as a general rule, created by an express provision in the contract. Although no particular language need be used to create a condition, a conditional clause will, as a general rule, be introduced by words such as "provided that," "on condition that," "if," "when," "while," "after," or "as soon as."

Conditions may also be implied from the nature of the performance promised. If a person contracts to unload the cargo of a ship which is at sea, there is an implied condition that the ship will arrive in port.

Concurrent conditions are usually implied by law. In a contract to sell for cash, the law implies concurrent conditions, that is, the seller's duty to deliver the goods is conditioned on the buyer's tender of the purchase price, and the buyer's duty to pay the purchase price is conditioned on the seller's tendering delivery of the goods. If neither party makes a tender within a reasonable time, both are discharged from their duty under the contract.

Independent Promises.   In many contracts the promises are independent; that is, the duty of one of the parties to perform is not conditioned on the happening of any event or on the other party's tender of performance. In all contract situations, if one of the parties is guilty of a material breach of the contract, the injured party will be discharged from his or her duty to perform. The effect of a breach of contract will be discussed under "Performance and Breach."

Summary

The determination of the nature and scope of a promisor's duty under a contract requires the analysis of many complex situations.

A condition in a contract is a stipulation that on the happening of some future, uncertain event the promisor will owe a duty of performance—a condition precedent—or will be relieved from an existing duty—a condition subsequent. A concurrent condition requires simultaneous performance by the parties. Conditions may be created by express promises or by implication, or may be implied by law.

Clarkson v. Wirth

481 P.2d 920 (Ct. App. Wash. 1971)

Action by Clarkson (plaintiff), a real estate broker, against Wirth (defendant) to recover a commission. Clarkson appealed from an adverse judgment. Affirmed.

Wirth signed an exclusive listing contract with Clarkson which gave Clarkson the right to sell certain real estate owned by Wirth for a period of thirty days. Clarkson asked for and received a verbal extension of this listing and finally on July 20, 1965, arranged to have Grimnes and Wirth sign an earnest money agreement which contained the following provision:

This offer to purchase is made subject to purchasers disposing of certain properties upon which deals are now pending and said deals to be closed prior to the closing of this deal. Legal description of these properties will be furnished sellers upon request. Sale to be closed not later than October 1st, 1965.

All parties to the contract understood the down payment of $30,000 would have to come from the proceeds of those properties owned by the purchasers, upon which deals were then pending. Clarkson agreed to aid the Grimnes brothers in selling their property. He attempted to do so by advertising their property to other brokers but was unable to generate a sale by October 1, 1965.

In April 1966 the Grimnes brothers, learning that the Wirth property had not yet been sold, and still being interested, joined with two other men in an offer to purchase the Wirth property. The parties negotiated the sale without the benefit of Clarkson's services, and the sale was closed on August 26, 1966.

Upon learning of this sale Clarkson brought suit for a commission.

*   *   *   *   *

EVANS, JUDGE.   Clarkson is not entitled to any commission from Wirth in that the earnest money agreement entered into between Clarkson and Grimnes is unenforceable for the following two reasons, to wit:

(a) The offer to purchase was made subject to the purchasers disposing of certain properties on which deals were then pending with said deals to be closed prior to the closing of the transaction contained in the earnest money agreement, said transactions never being closed.

(b) The offer to sell and the offer to purchase were clearly made subject to the condition that the sale was to have been closed not later than October 1, 1965.

In *Ross* v. *Harding,* the court established the following test to determine whether a particular promise to perform is conditional:

Whether a provision in a contract is a condition, the nonfulfillment of which excuses performance, depends upon the intent of the parties, to be ascertained from a fair and reasonable construction of the language used in the light of all the surrounding circumstances. 5 Williston, *Contracts* (3d ed.) § 663, p. 127.

Any words which express, when properly interpreted, the idea that the performance of a promise is dependent on some other event will create a condition. Phrases and words such as "on condition," "provided that," "so that," "when," "while," "after," or "as soon as" are often used.

It is clear from the evidence that it was the understanding of Grimnes as purchaser, and Wirth as seller, that performance by the purchasers was conditioned upon the sale of the Grimnes property by October 1, 1965.

Clarkson contends, however, that he obtained the Grimnes . . . as purchaser, and his offer was accepted by Wirth, and even though the Grimnes . . . was unable to obtain adequate financing to purchase before October 1, 1965, Clarkson was still entitled to his commission upon execution of the earnest money agreement. Clarkson bases this contention upon the holding in *Dryden v. Vincent D. Miller, Inc.,* where the court stated:

We have held that, when a real-estate broker has procured a prospective purchaser who is accepted by the seller, and the seller promises to pay the broker a certain commission for services rendered, the broker has earned the commission, and the promise to pay it may be enforced.

In *White & Bollard, Inc. v. Goodenow,* the court made the following observation concerning the above stated rule in *Dryden:*

Implicit in this rule is the requirement that the purchaser be willing to purchase, and that in contracting with the seller, he has agreed to purchase the property. Here we do not have such an unqualified promise, but rather a conditional promise, and the respondent's right to collect his fee was also made conditional upon the purchaser's obtaining satisfactory financing. *The securing of such financing was a condition precedent. Until it had occurred, the respondent was not obliged to sell, and the purchaser was not obliged to buy the property, and the appellant was not entitled to its fee.*

Architects' and Engineers' Certificates

Requirement of Certificate. The building or construction contracts in common use usually contain a clause making the payments provided for in the contract conditional on the production of the certificate of a named architect or engineer. The courts enforce such a provision and will deny the contractor the right to recover in a suit on the contract unless he produces the certificate or can excuse his failure to produce it.

When Failure to Produce Certificate Is Excused. Failure to produce the certificate is excused by showing that the named architect or engineer is dead, insane, or otherwise incapacitated and cannot issue the certificate, or that the certificate is fraudulently, collusively, or arbitrarily withheld; and in some instances the courts have excused the production of the certificate if it can be shown that the withholding is unreasonable. As a general rule, if the architect or engineer is acting honestly and has some reason for withholding the certificate, the courts will not allow a recovery unless it is produced. The parties have contracted for the expert judgment of the named architect or engineer, and if he has exercised that judgment honestly, the courts will not substitute their judgment for that of the architect or engineer and hold that the architect or engineer is mistaken or that his decision is incorrect. If a mistake has been made in computation, the courts will correct it.

Summary

When a contract makes the production of an architect's or engineer's certificate a condition precedent to payment, the certificate must be produced before a duty of immediate payment arises. However, the death or incapacitating illness of a named architect or the fraudulent or unjustified withholding of the certificate will excuse the failure to produce the certificate.

Performance and Breach

Duty of Performance. A promisor is obligated to perform as promised; however, his or her performance may range from perfection to no performance at all. In attempting to solve the problems relative to the performance of contractual obligations, the courts have attempted to set up practical, workable standards. As a general rule, they recognize three degrees of performance: (1) complete or satisfactory performance, (2) substantial performance, and (3) material breach.

Complete or Satisfactory Performance.   Some types of contractual obligations can be completely performed; others cannot. Such obligations as the payment of money, delivery of a deed, and, in some instances, the delivery of goods can be performed either exactly or to a high degree of perfection, whereas such obligations as the erection of a building, the construction of a road, the cultivation of a crop, and many similar obligations cannot be performed without some slight deviation from perfection, due to the limitations of human ability.

The standard set up by the courts as a measure of the degree of perfection of performance to which the promisee is entitled is the test of "reasonable expectation." The promisee is entitled to that degree of perfection which is standard for the type of obligation owed by the promisor. If the promisor owes the promisee $10, the promisee is justified in expecting the obligation to be discharged by the payment of $10. The payment of $9.99 will not satisfy the requirement of "reasonable expectation." However, if the promisor's obligation is to erect a building of several stories according to plans and specifications, the promisee is not justified in expecting a building which deviates in no degree from the plans and specifications. All the promisee is justified in expecting is a building which is built in a "good and workmanlike manner"—that is, one which comes up to the accepted standards of the degree of perfection attained in the erection of that type of building.

Substantial Performance.   Substantial performance is a degree of perfection of performance which is slightly below that of complete or satisfactory performance. If the promisor has made an honest effort to perform but, due to lack of ability or other reasons beyond his or her control, has deviated in some slight degree from accepted standards, and if, in addition, the consideration given to the promisee is such that it cannot be returned to the promisor, the courts will hold that the promisor has substantially performed the contract. The promisor will, as a general rule, be entitled to the contract price less any damage the promisee has suffered as a result of the defective performance. Each case involving substantial performance must be decided on the basis of the facts of that individual case.

Material Breach.   The promisor will be guilty of a material breach of contract if his or her performance or tendered performance fails to reach that degree of perfection which the promisee is justified in expecting under the circumstances. If the promisor has materially breached the contract, the promisor has no right of action on the contract, unless the promisee has accepted the defective performance without objection. If defective performance is tendered, and the circumstances are such that the promisee can reject the tender, he has a right to do so. If performance is defective to such a degree that it amounts to a material breach but the circumstances are such that it is impractical for the promisee to reject the defective performance, the promisor may be able to recover for benefits conferred on the promisee in an action in quasi contract.

Prevention of Performance.   The promisor assumes all the risks incident to the performance of the contract. However, if the circumstances are such that a condition precedent will be implied, the promisor will owe no duty of performance until the condition is fulfilled, and in some situations the promisor may be discharged completely from his duty of performance on the ground of impossibility.[1]

The promisee owes a duty to cooperate with the promisor in the performance of the contract. The extent of the promisee's duty to cooperate will depend on the subject matter of the contract and the surrounding circumstances. If the promisee fails to fulfill his or her duty of cooperation, or if the promisee is guilty of affirmative acts which materially hinder or delay performance on the part of the promisor, the promisee will be guilty of a material breach of the contract, and the promisor will be relieved of a duty of further performance.

Time Is of the Essence.   The time within which the promisor is to complete his or her performance may or may not be expressly stated in the contract. If no time for performance is expressly stated or implied in the contract, the courts will hold that performance must be completed within a reasonable time. What is a reasonable time is a question of fact and must be determined from all the surrounding circumstances. If the time for performance is stated or implied in the contract, the promisor's failure to perform within the allotted time is a breach of the contract.

Under some circumstances a failure to perform on time will be held to be a material breach on the part of the promisor, and such breach will relieve the promisee of his or her duty of reciprocal performance. If failure to perform on time is a material breach of the contract, then "time is of the essence" of the contract. The contract may expressly stipulate that time is of the essence of the contract, in which case the courts will enforce the provision, unless its enforcement would impose on the promisor an unjust and burdensome penalty. If the circumstances are such that the promisee will derive little or no benefit from late performance, the courts will hold that time is of the essence of the contract even though the contract does not expressly so provide.

If time is not of the essence of the contract, the promisee will be required

---

[1] Impossibility is discussed later in this chapter.

to accept late performance, provided performance is completed within a reasonable time after that stipulated in the contract. If the promisee has suffered an injury as the result of a delay in performance, he or she is entitled to set off against the contract price the loss he or she has suffered.

Performance to Personal Satisfaction. The promisor may obligate himself or herself to perform to the personal satisfaction of the promisee. Such contracts fall into two categories: (1) those situations in which personal taste and comfort are involved, and (2) those situations in which mechanical fitness or suitability for a particular purpose is involved.

If personal taste and comfort are involved, the promisee has the right to reject the performance without liability to the promisor, if the promisee is honestly dissatisfied with the performance rendered or tendered.

If mechanical fitness or suitability is involved, the court will apply the "reasonable man" test; and if the court holds that a reasonable person would be satisfied with the performance rendered or tendered, the promisee must accept the performance and pay the contract price.

Good Faith Performance under the U.C.C. The Code (1–204) provides that every contract or duty within its provisions imposes an obligation of *good faith* in its performance or enforcement. Farnsworth defines this obligation of good faith as:

> . . . an implied term of the contract requiring cooperation on the part of one party to the contract so that another party will not be deprived of his reasonable expectations.[2]

At common law buyers and sellers dealt at "arms' length." Just how great a departure from the common law this adoption of "good faith" duties represents, remains to be determined by the courts.

Summary

A promisor is obligated to perform as promised. Since performance may range from perfection to no performance at all, the courts recognize three stages of perfection of performance: (1) complete or satisfactory performance, (2) substantial performance, and (3) material breach. Complete or satisfactory performance is performance up to accepted standards; substantial performance falls short of complete performance only in minor respects, and the promisee is not deprived of a material part of the consideration bargained for. The promisor is guilty of material breach if his or her performance is defective in some major respect.

If the performance is complete or satisfactory, the promisor is entitled to the contract price; if substantial, the promisor is entitled to the contract price

---

[2] Farnsworth, "Good Faith Performance and Commercial Reasonableness under the Uniform Commercial Code," 30 *Chicago L. Rev.* 666, 669 (1963).

less damage resulting from defects. If he or she is guilty of a material breach, he or she cannot recover on the contract but may be entitled to some recovery in a suit in quasi contract.

The promisor may be relieved from duty of performance by an implied condition precedent, by impossibility, or by interference on the part of the promisee.

If time is of the essence of a contract, failure to perform within the permitted time is a material breach of the contract, and such breach will relieve the promisee from his or her obligations under the contract. If time is not of the essence, the promisee must accept late performance, if completed within a reasonable time, in which event he or she will be compensated in damages for injury suffered.

If personal taste and comfort of the promisee are involved, the promisee need not accept performance if he or she is honestly dissatisfied. If fitness or utility is involved, the "reasonable man" test is applied. The Code imposes a broad obligation to perform in "good faith" on all contracts and duties within the Code.

Lowy v. United Pacific Insurance Co.

429 P.2d 577 (Sup. Ct. Calif. 1967)

This was an action for damages for breach of an excavation and grading contract brought by Lowy and others (plaintiffs) against Wolpin and others (defendants). Wolpin filed a cross complaint for payments due. Judgment for Wolpin and Lowy appealed. Affirmed.

Lowy entered into a contract with Wolpin, a licensed contractor, for certain excavation and grading work on lots and streets, together with street improvement work. After Wolpin had performed 98 percent of the contracted excavation and grading work, a dispute arose between the parties regarding payment of $7,200 for additional work, consisting of importing dirt for fills, necessitated by changes made by Lowy in the plans.

Wolpin ceased performance and Lowy immediately employed others to do street improvement work called for by the contract and thereafter sued Wolpin and his bonding company for breach of contract.

McCOMB, ASSOCIATE JUSTICE.   Lowy agreed to pay Wolpin for the excavation and grading work (including street grading work) the sum of $73,500, as set forth in Exhibit "A" of the contract and they agreed to pay Wolpin for the paving of the streets and the installation of curbs and gutters (all commonly called "street improvement work") pursuant to the unit prices set forth in Exhibit "B" of the contract.

Accordingly, since the consideration was apportioned, the contract was a severable or divisible one.

Under the circumstances, the fact that Wolpin did not perform the second phase of the contract does not prevent his recovering for work done under the first phase.

Wolpin did not entirely perform under the first phase of the contract. However, the doctrine of substantial performance, ordinarily applied to building contracts, is here applicable, since the evidence shows that Wolpin completed 98 percent of the work under the first phase and was prevented from completing the balance through the fault of Lowy.

Where a person agrees to do a thing for another for a specified sum of money, to be paid on full performance, he is not entitled to any part of the sum until he has himself done the thing he agreed to do, unless full performance has been excused, prevented, or delayed by the act of the other party.

In *Thomas Haverty Co. v. Jones,* we held that in the case of a building contract where the owner has taken possession of the building and is enjoying the fruits of the contractor's work in the performance of the contract, if there has been a substantial performance thereof by the contractor in good faith, if the failure to make full performance can be compensated in damages to be deducted from the price or allowed as a counterclaim, and if the omissions and deviations were not wilful or fraudulent and do not substantially affect the usefulness of the building or the purpose for which it was intended, the contractor may, in an action upon the contract, recover the amount of the contract price remaining unpaid, less the amount allowed as damages for the failure of strict performance.

Clayton McLendon, Inc. v. McCarthy

186 S.E.2d 452 (Ct. App. Ga. 1971)

McLendon (plaintiff), a real estate broker, brought an action against Bonny Corp. and McCarthy (defendants), the vendor and purchaser on a certain real estate contract for a commission. McCarthy, the purchaser, counterclaimed for his earnest money deposit. McLendon and Bonny Corp., the seller of the land, appealed from a judgment in favor of McCarthy on his counterclaim. Affirmed.

The real estate sales contract contained provisions for the payment of a $26,250 commission to McLendon upon a consummation of the sale, which commission is equivalent to the earnest money deposited by McCarthy, the purchaser, at the time of the signing of the contract. The contract provided:

It is further understood and agreed that this contract is subject to and contingent upon subject property being served by the necessary storm and sanitary sewers to service the type development referred to in No. 7 above at a cost to purchaser which purchaser considers to be reasonable and economically feasible. If it cannot be then this contract shall be null and void and earnest money shall be refunded to purchaser and purchaser shall have no liability to seller whatsoever.

BELL, CHIEF JUDGE. We need not reach the question as to whether there was any anticipatory breach of the contract for the contract is unenforceable. By the express terms of the above quoted special condition, the purchaser was only bound to perform if in his uncontrolled judgment the cost of the sewers was "reasonable and economically feasible." This shows that the contract is lacking in mutuality. The condition made the contract contingent upon the event which may or may not happen at the pleasure of the buyer. Until that contingency has occurred there is no obligation on the part of the purchaser to purchase or the seller to sell.

DEEN, JUDGE (concurring specially). *Commercial Mortgage & Finance Corp. v. Greenwich Savings Bank* . . . , states: "Contracts requiring that one party's performance be 'satisfactory' or 'acceptable' to the other party in certain specified respects, are not illusory in character or void for lack of mutuality, but impose upon the party to be satisfied positive obligations conditioned upon his satisfaction in the exercise of an honest judgment." 5 Williston on *Contracts* (3d Ed.) § 675A is quoted in part: "Since, however, such a promise is generally considered as requiring a performance which shall be satisfactory to him in the exercise of an honest judgment, *such contracts have been almost universally upheld.*" Cases are grouped which held contracts had mutuality although conditioning a lease renewal as being satisfactory to the owner, a land sale on the buyer's satisfaction with the condition of the property, a construction contract on the work being done to the owner's satisfaction and a sale of goods subject to the satisfaction of the buyer. The *Commercial Mortgage* case involved a sale to persons "whose credit rating shall be satisfactory to" and title insurance "written by companies acceptable to" the plaintiff. The fact that such a contract is not void and does not lack mutuality, although it may be unenforceable where it takes the form of a condition precedent, is shown by *Stribling v. Ailion:* "Where in a contract one party agrees to perform to the satisfaction of the other party in a matter involving judgment, the latter shall be the sole judge of his satisfaction." The case then cites *Atlanta Realty Co. v. Campion,* where it was said:

Where one contracting party agrees to perform services "to the satisfaction of" or "satisfactory to" the other party, compliance with the contract is not shown unless it appears that the thing done or the article furnished does in fact satisfy the other party. An exception to this rule, of course, is where dissatisfaction is feigned merely for the purpose of avoiding the contract. That has been held not to be dissatisfaction, but fraud.

Thus it appears that a contract is not void or lacking in mutuality because it specifies that in connection therewith something must be done which one of the parties may accept or reject in his discretion. The contract is valid; the exercise of an honest judgment is the question at issue. Further, the discretionary acceptance may be phrased in either of two ways—as a condition precedent, in which case no rights arise on either side until the judgment is exercised one way or the other, or as a condition subsequent, in which case the contract is valid until the contracting party exercises his discretion to annul it, the burden then being on the opposite party to show that the discretion was not fairly exercised if he wishes to insist on enforcement.

The present case is a good example of a discretionary stipulation contained in a condition subsequent: the sale is contingent upon subject property being served by the necessary storm and sanitary sewers "at a cost to purchaser which purchaser considers reasonable and economically feasible. If it cannot be then this contract shall be null and void." Obviously, all parties considered the contract viable, subject to its cancellation if, in the opinion of the purchaser honestly exercised, sewer connections were found not to be economically feasible.

* * * * *

I therefore disagree with the second division of the opinion, holding the contract void for lack of mutuality. The cited cases are not in point. There the contracts did not become effective until the purchaser did some unrelated act—in one instance, sell another house which he owned; and in the other obtain a certain described mortgage loan, there being no duty cast on him to initiate either act. In those cases the contracts simply never came into existence because a stated condition precedent failed to occur.

However, on this motion for summary judgment I think McCarthy prima facie established (a) that he elected to rescind the contract because in his opinion the cost of sewer installation was not satisfactory to him because not economically feasible, and (b) a logical, objective reason for his having arrived at this opinion. McLendon offered no evidence either that McCarthy, the purchaser, did not exercise his discretion in the matter or that it was arbitrarily and unfairly exercised so as to be fraudulent. For this reason alone I concur in the judgment.

Impossibility of Performance

Nature of Impossibility.   The common law legal concept of impossibility is narrower than the popular concept. Impossibility means: "It cannot be done," not "I cannot do it." If a person contracts to perform an obligation, inability to perform or intervening hardship will not discharge the obligation. If the person fails to perform, he or she will be liable to the promisee for any injury resulting from such failure.

The courts recognize three situations in which the promisor will be discharged from failure to perform on the ground of impossibility: (1) incapacitating illness or death of the promisor, (2) intervening illegality, and (3) destruction of the subject matter essential to performance. Some courts have recognized a fourth ground for discharging the promisor from the obligation, that of commercial frustration.

The Uniform Commercial Code (2–615) adopts less rigorous standards for excusing nonperformance of sales of goods contracts. Nonperformance is excused if the performance as agreed has been made "impracticable by the occurrence of a contingency the nonoccurrence of which was a basic assumption on which the contract was made or by compliance in good faith with any applicable foreign or domestic governmental regulation or order." The Code further provides, however, that if the contingency affects only a part of the seller's capacity to perform, the seller must allocate production and deliveries among his customers in a "fair and reasonable" manner. The seller is also required to give buyers reasonable notice of any delay and of any limited allocation of the goods.

Illness or Death of Promisor.   The promisor is discharged from the obligation to perform on the ground of impossibility only if the contract is personal in nature. If the obligations under the contract are such that they can, under the law of assignment of contracts, be delegated, the incapacitating illness or death of the promisor does not discharge the contract. It can be performed by the agents or personal representatives of the promisor.

An incapacitating illness is one that renders the party incapable of performing his or her ordinary duties. Whether the illness of the promisor is of such nature as will justify him or her in terminating the contract will depend on all the facts and circumstances of the case, such as the nature of the work to be done, the urgency of the work, the probable duration of the illness, and other special factors.

A promisor may be relieved from liability on the grounds of impossibility if the promisor has contracted to have a named person perform special services and that person is prevented from performing due to his or her death or illness. For example, in one case in which a booking agency had contracted to furnish the services of a certain entertainer who was well known and the entertainer became ill and was unable to perform, the court held that the booking agency was discharged of its obligation.

Performance Declared Illegal.   In some instances, parties may enter into a contract the performance of which is legal when entered into but later becomes illegal because of an intervening statute or official order before performance is due. In such a case, performance is not impossible, but since it is illegal, the promisor is excused from his or her duty to perform. The increased powers of regulating business granted to the federal government during World War I and World War II gave rise to many cases involving the application of this rule. As a general rule, if a regulatory statute or rules and regulations promulgated under a regulatory statute prevent the performance of the contract, the promisor is excused from his or her duty to perform; but if the performance of the contract is merely rendered more difficult or less profitable, the promisor is not so excused.

Destruction of Subject Matter.   If the performance of the act required by the contract to be performed is necessarily dependent on the continued existence of a specified thing, the destruction of such thing before performance of the required act without the fault of the promisor will excuse the nonperformance of the contract. For example, the destruction of a warehouse after a contract to reroof it is entered into but before the contract is performed would excuse the nonperformance of the contract. If a contract is partially performed at the time the subject matter essential to the performance of the contract is destroyed, the recipient of the benefits of the partial performance must pay, as a general rule, on a pro rata basis for the part performance. Neither party is liable in damages for the nonperformance of the contract.

Commercial Frustration.   Some courts have extended the scope of impossibility to include those cases in which performance by the promisor would be impractical due to unforeseen developments having made performance of no value to the promisee. And some courts have included in the scope of impossibility cases in which the cost of performance to the promisor would be great, due to some extreme or unreasonable difficulty, expense, injury, or loss, and the benefits to the promisee would be of little or no value.

Summary

Impossibility of performance should be distinguished from inability to perform. The impossibility must arise after the contract is entered into, and it must be due to the nature of the thing to be done. Impossibility of performance arises in three situations: (1) incapacitating illness or death of promisor if contract requires performance of personal service, (2) intervening statutes or governmental regulation making performance illegal, and (3) destruction of subject matter essential to the performance of the contract without fault of either party. The U.C.C. adopts less rigorous standards for excusing nonperformance of sales of goods contracts.

Death always terminates a contract for personal service. Whether illness will justify termination of the contract will depend on the nature of the work, the term of the employment, the seriousness of the illness, and the duration or probable duration of the illness.

Before a statute or governmental regulation can be used to excuse nonperformance, it must be such that the performance of the contract will be illegal. A statute or governmental regulation which makes performance more difficult or less profitable will not excuse the promisor from performance on the ground of impossibility.

Destruction of the subject matter which is essential to the performance of the contract will excuse the promisor from performance. Destruction of subject matter which the promisor expects to make use of in the performance of the contract but which is not essential to the performance of the contract will not be an excuse for nonperformance.

In some recent cases the promisor has been discharged from his or her obligation to perform on the ground of commercial frustration.

Parker v. Arthur Murray, Inc.

295 N.E.2d 487 (Ct. App. Ill. 1973)

Parker (plaintiff) sued to have dancing lesson contracts he had signed with Arthur Murray, Inc. (defendant) rescinded. Judgment for Parker and Arthur Murray appealed. Affirmed.

In November, 1959 Parker went to the Arthur Murray Studio in Oak Park to redeem a certificate entitling him to three free dancing lessons. At that time he was a 37-year-old college-educated bachelor who lived alone in a one-room attic apartment in

Berwyn, Illinois. During the free lessons the instructor told Parker he had "exceptional potential to be a fine and accomplished dancer" and generally encouraged further participation. Parker thereupon signed a contract for 75 hours of lessons at a cost of $1000. At the bottom of the contract were the bold-type words, **"Non-cancellable Negotiable Contract."** This initial encounter set the pattern for the future relationship between the parties. Parker attended lessons regularly. He was praised and encouraged regularly by the instructors, despite his lack of progress. Contract extensions and new contracts for additional instructional hours were executed. Each contained the bold-type words, **"Non-cancellable Contract."** Some of the agreements also contained the bold-type statement, **"I Understand that no Refunds Will be Made under the Terms of this Contract."**

On September 24, 1961, Parker was severely injured in an automobile collision, rendering him incapable of continuing his dancing lessons. At that time he had con-tracted for a total of 2734 hours of lessons, for which he had paid $24,812.80.

STAMOS, PRESIDING JUDGE.   Parker was granted rescission on the ground of impossibility of performance. The applicable legal doctrine is expressed in the *Restate-ment Contracts,* 459, as follows:

A duty that requires for its performance action that can be rendered only by the promisor or some other particular person is discharged by his death or by such illness as makes the necessary action by him impossible or seriously injurious to his health, unless the contract indicates a contrary intention or there is contributing fault on the part of the person subject to the duty.

Similarly, 460 of the *Restatement* states:

(1) Where the existence of a specific thing or person is, either by the terms of a bargain or in the contemplation of both parties, necessary for the performance of a promise in the bargain, a duty to perform the promise . . . (b) is discharged if the thing or person subsequently is not in existence in time for seasonable performance, unless a contrary intention is manifested, or the contributing fault of the promisor causes the nonexistence.

In Illinois impossibility of performance was recognized as a ground for rescission in *Davies v. Arthur Murray,* wherein the court nonetheless found for the defendant because of the plaintiff's failure adequately to prove the existence of an incapacitating disability.

Arthur Murray does not deny that the doctrine of impossibility of performance is generally applicable to the case at bar. Rather they assert that certain contract provi-sions bring this case within the *Restatement's* limitation that the doctrine is inapplicable if "the contract indicates a contrary intention." It is contended that such bold type phrases as **"Non-cancellable Contract," "Non-cancellable Negotiable Contract"** and **"I Understand that No Refunds Will Be Made under the Terms of this Contract"** manifested the parties mutual intent to waive their respective rights to invoke the doctrine of impossibility. This is a construction which we find unacceptable. Courts engage in the construction and interpretation of contracts with the sole aim of deter-mining the intention of the parties. We need rely on no construction aids to conclude that plaintiff never contemplated that by signing a contract with such terms as **"Non-cancellable"** and **"No Refunds"** he was waiving a remedy expressly recognized by Illinois courts. Were we also to refer to established tenets of contractual construction, this conclusion would be equally compelled. An ambiguous contract will be construed most strongly against the party who drafted it. Exceptions or reservations in a contract will, in case of doubt or ambiguity, be construed least favorably to the party claiming the benefit of the exceptions or reservations. Although neither party to a contract should be relieved from performance on the ground that good business judgment was lacking, a court will not place upon language a ridiculous construction. We conclude that Parker did not waive his right to assert the doctrine of impossibility.

American Trading and Production Corporation v. Shell International Marine, Ltd.

453 F.2d 939 (2nd Cir. 1972)

In a proceeding on a claim against Shell International (defendant) American Trading & Production Corp. (plaintiff) appealed from a dismissal of its claim. Affirmed.

On March 23, 1967, American entered into a voyage charter with Shell whereby Shell hired American's tank vessel, *Washington Trader,* to deliver a cargo of lube oil from Texas to Bombay, India. On June 5th, American cabled the ship's master advising him of various reports of trouble in the Suez Canal and suggested delay in entering it pending clarification. On that very day, the Suez Canal was closed due to the state of war which had developed in the Middle East. American then communicated with Shell on June 5th through the broker who had negotiated the charter party, requesting approval for the diversion of the *Washington Trader* which then had proceeded to a point about 84 miles northwest of Port Said, the entrance to the Canal. On June 6th the charterer responded that under the circumstances it was "for owner to decide whether to continue to wait or make the alternative passage via the Cape since Charter Party obliges them to deliver cargo without qualification." In response the owner replied on the same day that in view of the closing of the Suez, the *Washington Trader* would proceed to Bombay via the Cape of Good Hope and "we are reserving all rights for extra compensation." The vessel proceeded westward, back through the Straits of Gibraltar and around the Cape and eventually arrived in Bombay on July 15th (some 30 days later than initially expected), traveling a total of 18,055 miles instead of the 9,709 miles which it would have sailed had the Canal been open. The owner billed $131,978.44 as extra compensation which Shell has refused to pay.

MULLIGAN, CIRCUIT JUDGE.   On appeal and below American argues that transit of the Suez Canal was the agreed specified means of performance the voyage charter and that the supervening destruction of this means rendered the contract legally impossible to perform and therefore discharged the owner's unperformed obligation (*Restatement Contracts* § 460 (1932)). Consequently, when the *Washington Trader* eventually delivered the oil after journeying around the Cape of Good Hope, a benefit was conferred upon the charterer for which it should respond in *quantum meruit.* The validity of this proposition depends upon a finding that the parties contemplated or agreed that the Suez passage was to be the exclusive method of performance, and indeed it was so argued on appeal. We cannot construe the agreement in such a fashion. The parties contracted for the shipment of the cargo from Texas to India at an agreed rate and the charter party makes absolutely no reference to any fixed route. It is urged that the Suez passage was a condition of performance because the ATRS rate was based on a Suez Canal passage, the invoice contained a specific Suez Canal toll charge and the vessel actually did proceed to a point 84 miles northwest of Port Said. In our view all that this establishes is that both parties contemplated that the Canal would be the probable route. It was the cheapest and shortest, and therefore it was in the interest of both that it be utilized. However, this is not at all equivalent to an agreement that it be the exclusive method of performance. The charter party does not so provide and it seems to have been well understood in the shipping industry that the Cape route is an acceptable alternative in voyages of this character.

This leaves us with the question as to whether American was excused from performance on the theory of commercial impracticability. Even though American is not excused because of strict impossibility, it is urged that American law recognizes that performance is rendered impossible if it can only be accomplished with extreme and unreasonable difficulty, expense, injury or loss. There is no extreme or unreasonable difficulty apparent here. The alternate route taken was well recognized, and there is no claim that the vessel or the crew or the nature of the cargo made the route actually taken unreasonably difficult, dangerous or onerous. American's case here essentially rests upon the element of the additional expense involved—$131,978.44. This represents an increase of less than one third over the agreed upon $417,327.36. We find that this increase in expense is not sufficient to constitute commercial impracticability under either American or English authority.

Discharge

Nature of Discharge.   A contract is discharged where the parties to the contract are released from all obligations of the contract, and in the majority of contractual transactions this is brought about by complete performance by the parties to the contract.

Earlier in this chapter, the discharge of a contract by the occurrence or nonoccurrence of a condition precedent or subsequent, by material breach, and by impossibility of performance was discussed. A contract may also be discharged by agreement. The agreement may be in the form of a mutual agreement to cancel, a rescission, an agreement to forgo rights, a substitute contract, a novation, or a waiver. Under some circumstances a contract may be discharged or the right of action to enforce the contract may be barred by operation of law.

Discharge by Agreement.   A contract is created by the mutual agreement of the parties, and it may be discharged in like manner, unless rights of third parties will be involved. Any agreement to discharge a party to a contract from obligations under the contract must be supported by consideration if such agreement is to effect a discharge. Mutual promises to rescind an executory contract will make the rescission valid since such an agreement is supported by consideration, in that both parties surrender their rights under the contract.

Waiver.   A party to a contract may voluntarily relinquish a right which he or she has under the contract. Such a relinquishment is known as a "waiver." If one party tenders an incomplete performance and the other party accepts such defective performance without objection, knowing that the defects will not be remedied, he or she will have waived the right to strict performance. If the party wishes to insist on strict performance, he should object to the incomplete or defective performance. In any instance in which performance is defective, notice should be given within a reasonable time that the defects must be remedied or damages will be claimed. If failure to give notice will justify a belief that strict performance will not be claimed, failure to give notice will amount to a waiver.

Discharge by Alteration.   If a party to a written instrument intentionally alters it in any material respect, the other party to the instrument is discharged from all his or her duties. If the instrument is altered by one not a party to it and without the knowledge and consent of either of the contracting parties, the alteration does not affect the rights of the parties. If an alteration is made by one of the contracting parties with the consent of the other contracting party, or if the other contracting party consents to the alteration after she learns of it, the party consenting to the alteration is not discharged from her duties.

Discharge by Statute of Limitations.   From the earliest times the courts have refused to grant a remedy to one who has delayed an unreasonable time in bringing suit. In modern times the various states have by statute declared that an action must be brought within a stated time after the action accrues. Such statutes are known as "statutes of limitations." ← *certain time limit*

The time limit for bringing suit for breach of contracts differs in the various states, and in many states the statutes distinguish between oral contracts and written contracts; for example, in Indiana the time limit for bringing suit on an oral contract is six years, whereas on a contract in writing it is ten years. In Illinois the time limit is five years on oral contracts and ten on written contracts. The time is computed from the time the cause of action accrues.

If one is incapacitated or beyond the jurisdiction of the court, the time during which the incapacity continues or the time during which one is beyond the jurisdiction of the court is not, by the terms of many statutes, counted in computing the statutory time for bringing suit.

Uniform Commercial Code.   The Code provides "any claim or right arising out of an alleged breach can be discharged in whole or in part without consideration by a written waiver or renunciation signed and delivered by the aggrieved party." (Section 1–107.)

Sec. 2–309 (2) (3) are the only parts of the Code which specifically treat termination rights and liabilities. Subsec. (2) states that where a contract "provides for successive performances but is indefinite in duration it is valid for a reasonable time but unless otherwise agreed may be terminated at any time by either party." Subsec. (3) "provides termination of a contract by one party except on the happening of an agreed event requires that reasonable notification be received by the other party and any agreement dispensing with notification is invalid if its operation would be unconscionable."

Comment 7 to Subsec. (2) by the editorial board which drafted the Code states that when an arrangement has been carried on over many years the reasonable time "can continue indefinitely and the contract will not terminate until notice." Comment 8 to Subsec. (3) states that this subsection:

. . . recognizes that the application of principles of good faith and sound commercial practice normally call for such notification of the termination of a going contract relationship as will give the other party reasonable time to seek a substitute arrangement. An agreement dispensing with notification or limiting the time for the seeking of a substitute arrangement is, of course, valid under this subsection unless the results of putting it into operation would be the creation of an unconscionable state of affairs.

Comment 10 states: ". . . The requirement of notification is dispensed with where the contract provides for termination on the happening of an 'agreed event.' 'Event' is a term chosen here to contrast with 'option' or the like."

The Code (2–725) stipulates a four-year statute of limitations for contracts involving the sale of goods.

Summary

A contract is discharged when the parties to a contract are released from their obligations under the contract. A contract is generally discharged by performance. The promisor is generally discharged from his or her duty to perform by a material breach of the contract, by the failure of the event to occur, which event has been stipulated in a condition precedent, by the occurrence of the event stipulated in a condition subsequent, or by impossibility. A contract may be discharged by mutual agreement, rescission, substitute contract, novation, or waiver. Under some circumstances a contract may be discharged by operation of law.

The Code requires that reasonable notification be given where sales of goods contracts provide for successive performances but are of indefinite duration. Any agreement dispensing with notification is invalid if its operation would be unconscionable.

Franchises

Termination of Franchises. A franchise system has been defined in marketing-management terms as an organization composed of distributive units established and administered by a supplier as a medium for expanding and controlling the marketing of his products. It is an integrated business system. Franchised dealers are legally independent but economically dependent units of the system.

The franchise approach offers a supplier a highly effective means of gaining rapid market expansion with minimum capital outlay. The growth rate and profitability of many franchise systems has been fantastic. Since most franchised dealers have the major investment in their outlets strong profit and loss incentives are present.

The franchise method of distribution first gained national recognition and success in the automobile industry. The standard form of franchise contract formerly used by automobile manufacturers did not require the dealer to whom the franchise was given to represent the manufacturer for any specified period of time nor did it provide that the dealer would purchase any automobiles. These franchises provided that either party could cancel on relatively short notice "with or without cause" or on causes left to the sole judgment of the franchisor. Many franchises currently used in other industries were modeled after automobile dealer franchises.

Until recent times the courts, with few exceptions, ruled that such franchises were not enforceable as contracts.[3] This strict-enforcement-of-contracts approach allows franchisors to exercise a maximum of control over their franchisees with a minimum of legal risks. Franchisees failing to follow policies can be canceled or threatened with cancellation, and those with highly specialized investments in particular franchises can ill-afford to have their franchise canceled.

After extensive hearings concerning the one-sided nature of automobile dealer franchises, Congress in 1956 enacted legislation imposing liability on manufacturers of automobiles if they exercise coercion against a dealer to the damage of the dealer.[4] The U.C.C. (1–203) requires the exercise of "good faith" in franchise relationships involving the sale of goods. In addition, Section 2–309 of the Code requires the giving of reasonable notice of termination of a sales contract which provides for successive performances but is indefinite as to duration. An agreement dispensing with notice will not be enforced if it is unconscionable.

The trend in contract law, particularly in franchise relationships, appears to be away from the strict and technical application of the rules of contract law relative to consideration and requirements of definiteness. Rights may be granted even though, from a technical standpoint, the contract or franchise may be indefinite or lacking in consideration, or may have been canceled or not renewed.

---

[3] See the classic case, *Ford Motor Company v. Kirkmyer Motor Co., Inc.,* 65 F.2d 1001 (1933).

[4] United States Code, Annotated, Title 15, §§ 1221–25.

Summary

Many franchises have been held to be unenforceable as contracts because of indefiniteness and lack of consideration. The Code tends to make more of these loose informal arrangements enforceable as contracts. Franchisors with one-sided contracts may encounter cancellation or termination difficulties under the Code provisions dealing with good faith, unconscionability, and reasonable notice requirements.

Sinkoff Beverage Co., Inc. v. Jos. Schlitz Brewing Co.

273 N.Y.S.2d 364 (Sup. Ct. N.Y. 1966)

This was an action brought by Sinkoff Beverage Co. (plaintiff) against Joseph Schlitz Brewing Co. (defendant) to enjoin Schlitz from selling to others in Suffolk County. Held preliminary injunction denied.

In 1960 the parties contracted in writing regarding Sinkoff's wholesale purchase of beer from Schlitz. The agreement specifically provided that it might be terminated at any time without cause or notice by either party. No exclusive rights were granted, but Sinkoff is nevertheless claiming the existence of an "understanding" making it Schlitz's exclusive Suffolk County distributor from the time of the 1960 agreement to date. As a practical matter, for six years Sinkoff was actually Schlitz's exclusive distributor in Suffolk County. However, on June 8, 1966, Schlitz notified Sinkoff that it was discontinuing its sales and deliveries to Sinkoff, in ten days.

STANISLAW, JUDGE.   Sinkoff devotes considerable of its facilities just to the handling of the business the result of six years of exclusive distribution of Schlitz's products. It claims the privilege, nowhere to be found in the agreement with Schlitz, of a year's notice of termination of the relationship. First, the diminution of its gross sales and net profit is alleged to be serious enough to raise a question of its ability to continue in business altogether. Then too, Sinkoff believes itself entitled to more than the ten days' notice of termination it received based upon the continuing, exclusive-in-fact relationship. Sinkoff argues that reasonable notice is required in these circumstances, and that a reasonable period would be one year.

Schlitz responds not only by pointing to the terms of the 1960 agreement but also by showing that it had expressed dissatisfaction with Sinkoff's wholesaling of its product in November, 1965, and several more times until it finally terminated the relationship. Furthermore, Schlitz denies the existence of any parol understanding or arrangement between the parties. In addition, Schlitz notes that the contract refutes any such possibility as either emanating from it or available at all other than in writing.

As to the extra-contractual, verbal franchise Sinkoff relies upon we find ourselves, and even more particularly Sinkoff, bound by the writing which expresses no such exclusivity and in fact acknowledges the complete absence of such status. In the face of these terms Sinkoff has not shown enough to extricate itself by properly establishing other than a simple distributorship.

The auxiliary issue presented is apparently one of first impression. Relying on section

2–309(3) of the Uniform Commercial Code, Sinkoff argues that it is entitled to "reasonable notification" of the termination of the contract. The cited section so provides, "except on the happening of an agreed event . . . an agreement dispensing with notification is invalid if its operation would be unconscionable." The court has the power to determine the issue of unconscionability and may limit the application of a clause found to be so in order to avoid an unconscionable result (Uniform Commercial Code, section 2–302). A hearing may be directed to aid the making of such determination (Uniform Commercial Code, section 2–302). The official comment for this section of the Code advises that "The basic test is whether, in the light of the general commercial background and the commercial needs of the particular trade or case, the clauses involved are so one-sided as to be unconscionable under the circumstances existing at the time of the making of the contract." Further on, the comment visualizes the power extended the courts as directed against one-sided, oppressive and unfairly surprising contracts, but not against the consequences of uneven bargaining positions or even simple old-fashioned bad bargains.

It seems, too, that the hearing called for is mandatory rather than discretionary once the court has initially accepted a possibility of unconscionability (see 1 *Anderson's Uniform Commercial Code,* section 2–302:5). Therefore, the precise question must at first be whether we can see a specter of oppression in the termination clause of the instant contract *as of the time the contract was made.*

Applying the required limitation of time to the question we may not take into consideration the volume increase in Sinkoff's business and Sinkoff's subsequent expansion and development of facilities and expense due to and in reliance upon its continued relationship with Schlitz. For all that appears the mere creation of any relationship between Sinkoff and Schlitz was, at that first point in time, of great benefit to both and perhaps even particularly favorable (and thus especially inoppressive) to Sinkoff.

We find no basis for a reasonable belief that the termination clause of the contract might have been unconscionable. The motion for a preliminary injunction is denied, without prejudice (noting the absence of any data relevant to conditions existing when the contract was executed in 1960).

Shell Oil Co. v. Marinello

307 A.2d 598 (Sup. Ct. N.J. 1973)

This was an action by Marinello (plaintiff) to enjoin Shell Oil Co. (defendant) from terminating his service station lease and product franchise. Judgment for Marinello and Shell appealed. Affirmed.

In 1959 Shell leased a station to Marinello, and at the same time entered into a written dealer-franchise agreement with the lessee. The original lease was for a one-year term and was regularly renewed in writing for fixed terms. The last lease between Shell and Marinello was dated April 28, 1969, and ran for a three-year term ending May 31, 1972, and from year-to-year thereafter, but was subject to termination by Marinello at any time by giving at least 90 days' notice and by Shell at the end of the primary period or of any subsequent year by giving at least 30 days' notice. The last dealer agreement was also dated April 28, 1969, and was for a three-year term ending May

31, 1972, and from year-to-year thereafter, but was subject to termination at any time by giving at least ten days notice.

By letter dated April 14, 1972, Shell notified Marinello that it was terminating the lease and the dealer agreement pursuant to the provisions in each agreement effective May 31, 1972. Marinello immediately filed suit seeking to have Shell enjoined from taking this proposed action. Shell then filed a summary dispossess complaint for possession of the service station premises.

SULLIVAN, JUDGE.   We are in full agreement with the basic determination of the trial court that Shell had no legal right to terminate its relationship with Marinello except for good cause, *i.e.,* the failure of Marinello to substantially comply with his obligations under the lease and dealer agreement. However, we conclude that it was unnecessary to have granted specific reformation of the lease and dealer agreement. The same end result is reached from consideration of the instruments themselves, the relationship between Shell and Marinello created thereby, and the public policy of this State affecting such relationship.

Marinello testified that when the station was offered to him in 1959 he was told by the Shell representative that the station was run down, but that a good operator could make money and that if he built up the business his future would be in the station. Shell's own witnesses admitted that it was Shell's policy not to terminate its relationship with a lessee-dealer except for good cause, which was described as not running the station in a good and businesslike manner.

Viewing the combined lease and franchise against the foregoing background, it becomes apparent that Shell is the dominant party and that the relationship lacks equality in the respective bargaining positions of the parties. For all practical purposes Shell can dictate its own terms. The dealer, particularly if he has been operating the station for a period of years and built up its business and clientele, when the time for renewal of the lease and dealer agreement comes around, cannot afford to risk confrontation with the oil company. He just signs on the dotted line.

Where there is grossly disproportionate bargaining power, the principle of freedom to contract is nonexistent and unilateral terms result. In such a situation courts will not hesitate to declare void as against public policy grossly unfair contractual provisions which clearly tend to the injury of the public in some way.

In *Ellsworth Dobbs, Inc. v. Johnson,* (1967) we said:

Courts and legislatures have grown increasingly sensitive to imposition, conscious or otherwise, on members of the public by persons with whom they deal, who through experience, specialization, licensure, economic strength or position, or membership in associations created for their mutual benefit and education, have acquired such expertise or monopolistic or practical control in the business transaction involved as to give them an undue advantage. Grossly unfair contractual obligations resulting from the use of such expertise or control by the one possessing it, which result in assumption by the other contracting party of a burden which is at odds with the common understanding of the ordinary and untrained member of the public, are considered unconscionable and therefore unenforceable. . . . The perimeter of public policy is an ever increasing one. Although courts continue to recognize that persons should not be unnecessarily restricted in their freedom to contract, there is an increasing willingness to invalidate unconscionable contractual provisions which clearly tend to injure the public in some way. (Citing cases)

. . . It is clear that the provisions of the lease and dealer agreement giving Shell the right to terminate its business relationship with Marinello, almost at will, are the result of Shell's disproportionate bargaining position and are grossly unfair.

It is a fallacy to state that the right of termination is bilateral. The oil company can always get another person to operate the station. It is the incumbent dealer who has everything to lose since, even if he had another location to go to, the going business and trade he built up would remain with the old station.

We hold (1) that the lease and dealer agreement herein are integral parts of a single business relationship, basically that of a franchise, (2) that the provision giving Shell the absolute right to terminate on 10 days' notice is void as against the public policy of this State, (3) that said public policy requires that there be read into the existing lease and dealer agreement, and all future lease and dealer agreements which may be negotiated in good faith between the parties, the restriction that Shell not have the unilateral right to terminate, cancel or fail to renew the franchise, including the lease, in absence of a showing that Marinello has failed to substantially perform his obligations under the lease and dealer agreement, *i.e.,* for good cause, and (4) that good cause for termination has not been shown in this case.[5]

Nature of Remedies

Objective in Granting Remedy. When a party has failed to perform his or her obligations under a contract and the other party to the contract has suffered a resulting injury, the injured party is entitled to be put, as nearly as is practical, in the same position as that he or she would have occupied had the contract been performed. If the injured party is granted a money judgment for the value of the thing he contracted to acquire or for the profit which he would have realized had the contract been performed, the injured party will be in substantially the same position he or she would have held had the contract been performed. Consequently, the remedy usually granted is the legal remedy of damages.

If the circumstances are such that the legal remedy of damages is inadequate, the court may grant the injured party an appropriate equitable remedy. The equitable remedy of specific performance of the contract is the one most frequently granted for breach of a contract.

Enforcement of Remedy. When a money judgment has been granted, the creditor is entitled to the aid of the court in the enforcement of the judgment if the debtor does not pay it. In the enforcement of the judgment the clerk of the court will issue either a writ of execution or a writ of garnishment.

---

[5] Author's Note: It is doubtful that this case would be followed by a majority of the courts. On January 11,1974 the U.S. District Court in New Jersey ruled that the State's "public policy" preventing dealer leases and franchises from being terminated without "good cause" conflicted with the rights of trademark owners under the *Lanham Act.* In a separate case, however, the U.S. Supreme Court refused to review Shell's appeal from the New Jersey Supreme Court's decision.

A writ of execution directs the sheriff to take into his possession and sell so much of the judgment debtor's property which is not exempt from execution as is necessary to satisfy the judgment. All states have exemption laws, although they vary widely, which provide that certain property or property of a stated value shall be exempt from levy of execution.

Garnishment is also statutory and is supplemental to the execution. In general, it is used to reach property or credits of the judgment debtor which are in the hands of a third person, and the procedure varies with the different states. As a general rule, garnishments are used to reach bank accounts, wages due, or accounts receivable; however, under some statutes, one can reach goods in storage, the redemption value of pawned goods, and other similar assets.

Under some circumstances the plaintiff may have the sheriff seize property of the defendant at the time suit is started. This procedure is called an "attachment." The grounds for attachment are generally set out by statute and are not uniform throughout the United States.

Uniform Commercial Code.   The remedies available to the parties to a contract which comes within the scope of the provisions of the Code are set out as follows:

(1) The remedies provided by this Act shall be liberally administered to the end that the aggrieved party may be put in as good a position as if the other party had fully performed but neither consequential or special nor penal damages may be had except as specifically provided in this Act or by other rule of law.

(2) Any right or obligation declared by this Act is enforceable by action unless the provision declaring it specifies a different or limited effect. (Section 1–106.)

The remedies of both the buyer and the seller in the event of a breach of the sales contract are set out in detail in Part 7 of Article 2, "Sales." Special remedies available to the parties are set out in the other articles of the Code.

These remedies are discussed in detail in subsequent chapters.

Summary

The remedy usually granted for breach of contract is a judgment for damages, but if the remedy at law is inadequate, an equitable remedy may be granted.

A judgment is enforced by levy of execution, garnishment, or attachment.

Remedies available for breach of those contracts which come within the scope of the Code are, for the most part, defined in the Code.

Classification of Damages

Introduction.   The different classes of damages awarded by the court as a remedy for injury resulting from breach of contract are known as (1) compensatory, (2) consequential or special, (3) liquidated, and (4) nominal.

Compensatory damages are damages which can be compensated for by the payment of a sum of money which will make good or replace the loss caused by the wrong or injury. They are the damages which would normally and usually result from the breach of a contract such as that into which the parties have entered.

Consequential or special damages are those damages which do not flow directly or immediately from the breach of the contract but only from some of the special or unusual circumstances of the particular contractual relation of the parties.

Liquidated damages is the term applicable when a specific sum of money has been expressly stipulated by the parties as the amount of damages to be recovered by the injured party in the event the contract is breached.

Nominal damages are those damages awarded to the injured party where there is a technical breach of the contract but still no actual loss suffered as a result of the breach.

Mitigation of Damages. If the defendant has breached the contract, the plaintiff owes a duty to the defendant to make a reasonable effort to avoid damages. If the plaintiff can avoid or minimize the damages he will suffer as a result of the defendant's breach without undue risk, expense, or humiliation, the plaintiff owes a duty to the defendant to avoid the damage.

In employment contracts, if the employer wrongfully discharges an employee before the end of the term of the employment, the employee is entitled to recover his or her wages for the remainder of the term. However, the employee owes a duty to make a reasonable effort to obtain similar employment elsewhere and minimize the damages. If the employee is employed as a skilled plumber, the employee would not be expected or required to accept employment such as digging sewers to minimize the damages; but he would be required to make a reasonable effort to obtain other employment as a skilled plumber in the same locality.

Liquidated Damages. The courts will not enforce a provision in a contract for liquidated damages unless (1) the damages to be anticipated are uncertain in amount or difficult to prove, (2) the parties intended to liquidate the damages in advance, and (3) the amount stipulated is a reasonable one, that is, not greatly disproportionate to the presumable loss or injury. If the amount stipulated to be paid in the event of the breach of a contract is disproportionate to the loss or injury suffered, the courts will declare it to be a penalty and refuse to enforce it.

If a liquidated damage provision in a contract is declared to be a provision for a penalty or a forfeiture and therefore unenforceable, the injured party will be granted compensatory damages, provided the person can prove that he or she suffered a loss as the direct result of the breach of the contract and can prove with reasonable certainty the amount of the resulting loss.

Nominal Damages.   The courts have held that failure to perform a contractual duty is, in itself, a legal wrong. As a result a wronged party who is unable to prove actual damages will not be denied a judgment on the ground that the law will not be concerned with trifles. He or she will be granted a judgment for nominal damages, which may be an amount ranging from one cent to one dollar, depending on the policy of the courts trying the case.

Summary

Damages awarded for the breach of a contract may be (1) compensatory, (2) consequential (special), (3) liquidated, or (4) nominal. Damages are awarded on the basis of the reasonable contemplation of the parties at the time the contract is entered into. The measure of compensatory damages is the value of the unfulfilled promise less the cost to the injured party of fulfilling the promise. The measure of consequential (special) damages is the loss suffered by the injured party as the direct result of the default. Loss of profit may be allowable as an element of damages if such loss can be established with reasonable certainty. In all instances the injured party owes a duty to make a reasonable effort to minimize the damages he or she suffers by reason of a default. The measure of liquidated damages is the amount stipulated by the parties, and they are allowed by the court unless the amount stipulated is unreasonable, that is, it amounts to a penalty. Nominal damages is a token amount awarded for the breach of a contract in those cases when the injured party establishes the breach of the contract but cannot prove with reasonable certainty that he or she suffered a loss as the direct result of the breach.

Parker v. Twentieth Century-Fox Film Corporation

474 P.2d 689 (Sup. Ct. Cal. 1970)

Shirley MacLaine Parker (plaintiff) brought this action against Twentieth Century-Fox (defendant) to recover her agreed compensation under a contract for her services in a motion picture. Fox Film appealed from an adverse judgment. Affirmed.

BURKE, JUSTICE.   Under the contract, dated August 6, 1965, Parker was to play the female lead in Fox Film's contemplated production of a motion picture entitled "Bloomer Girl." The contract provided that Fox Film would pay Parker a minimum "guaranteed compensation" of $53,571.42 per week for 14 weeks commencing May 23, 1966, for a total of $750,000. Prior to May 1966 Fox Film decided not to produce the picture and by a letter dated April 4, 1966, it notified Parker of that decision and that it would not "comply with our obligations to you under" the written contract.

By the same letter and with the professed purpose "to avoid any damage to you" Fox Film instead offered to employ Parker as the leading actress in another film tentatively entitled "Big Country, Big Man" (hereinafter, "Big Country"). The compensation offered was identical, as were 31 of the 34 numbered provisions or articles of the original contract. Unlike "Bloomer Girl," however, which was to have been a musical production, "Big Country" was a dramatic "western type" movie. "Bloomer Girl" was to have been filmed in California; "Big Country" was to be produced in Australia. Also, certain terms in the proffered contract varied from those of the original. Parker was given one week within which to accept; she did not and the offer lapsed. Parker then commenced this action seeking recovery of the agreed guaranteed compensation.

As stated, Fox Film's sole defense to this action which resulted from its deliberate breach of contract is that in rejecting its substitute offer of employment Parker unreasonably refused to mitigate damages.

The general rule is that the measure of recovery by a wrongfully discharged employee is the amount of salary agreed upon for the period of service, less the amount which the employer affirmatively proves the employee has earned or with reasonable effort might have earned from other employment.

However, before projected earnings from other employment opportunities not sought or accepted by the discharged employee can be applied in mitigation, the employer must show that the other employment was comparable, or substantially similar, to that of which the employee has been deprived; the employee's rejection of or failure to seek other available employment of a different or inferior kind may not be resorted to in order to mitigate damages.

In the present case Fox Film has raised no issue of *reasonableness of efforts* by Parker to obtain other employment; the sole issue is whether Parker's refusal of defendant's substitute offer of "Big Country" may be used in mitigation. Nor, if the "Big Country" offer was of employment different or inferior when compared with the original "Bloomer Girl" employment, is there an issue as to whether or not Parker acted reasonably in refusing the substitute offer. Despite Fox Film's arguments to the contrary, no case cited or which our research has discovered holds or suggests that reasonableness is an element of a wrongfully discharged employee's option to reject, or fail to seek, different or inferior employment lest the possible earnings therefrom be charged against him in mitigation of damages.

. . . It is clear that the trial court correctly ruled that Parker's failure to accept Fox Film's tendered substitute employment could not be applied in mitigation of damages because the offer of the "Big Country" lead was of employment both different and inferior, and that no factual dispute was presented on that issue. The mere circumstance that "Bloomer Girl" was to be a musical review calling upon Parker's talents as a dancer as well as an actress, and was to be produced in the City of Los Angeles, whereas "Big Country" was a straight dramatic role in a "Western Type" story taking place in an opal mine in Australia, demonstrates the difference in kind between the two employments; the female lead as a dramatic actress in a western style motion picture can by no stretch of imagination be considered the equivalent of or substantially similar to the lead in a song-and-dance production.

Additionally, the substitute "Big Country" offer proposed to eliminate or impair the director and screenplay approvals accorded to Parker under the original "Bloomer Girl" contract . . . and thus constituted an offer of inferior employment. Judgment for plaintiff in the amount of $750,000 plus interest and costs affirmed.

Equitable Remedies

Specific Performance. The granting of the equitable remedy of specific performance rests in the sound discretion of the court. The court will not grant specific performance of a contract if a money judgment, the remedy at law, is adequate. Since the remedy is equitable, the court has the power to withhold it when the ends of the law will thus be best served.

Injunction. The injunction is an equitable remedy designed to protect property or other rights from irreparable injury by commanding acts to be done or prohibiting their commission. It is used in a multitude of situations and affords the court of equity a flexible remedy which may be resorted to in a variety of situations. For example, if one having exceptional skills contracts to employ those skills exclusively for a party and then threatens, in violation of the contract, to employ those skills for others, the court may enjoin the use of such skills for anyone except the one with whom he or she contracted.

Summary

If the remedy at law, a judgment for damages, is inadequate, the injured party may be entitled to one of the remedies in equity. The remedy of specific performance may be granted if it is very difficult to determine the effect of the breach of the contract or if it is difficult to estimate the damages. Courts will, as a general rule, grant a decree of specific performance of a contract to sell land. They will not grant a decree of specific performance of a contract to sell personal property unless the property contracted for has a sentimental value or unless it is very difficult or impossible to obtain a duplicate elsewhere.

The injunction is issued to prevent hardship. As a general rule, it is in the form of a court order ordering a party threatening to breach a contract to refrain from his threatened course of action.

DeBauge Bros. Inc. v. Whitsitt

512 P.2d 487 (Sup. Ct. Kan. 1973)

DeBauge (plaintiff) brought an action for specific performance against Whitsitt (defendant) on a contract for the sale of a beverage bottling business. Whitsitt appealed from an adverse judgment. Affirmed.

In 1970 DeBauge offered to buy Whitsitt's Coca-Cola plant and franchise, located in Emporia, Kansas, for $172,000. Whitsitt accepted this offer subject to the approval of the Coca-Cola Co. As part of the contract DeBauge agreed to employ Whitsitt and/or his sons as consultants for six years at $1000 per month. Coca-Cola Co. approved the franchise transfer, but Whitsitt then notified DeBauge that the deal was off and demanded the return of the keys to the plant. DeBauge sued for $200,000 damages in lost rents and profits and asked for specific performance of the contract.

On appeal, Whitsitt argued that the trial court erred in ordering specific performance because the contract contained provisions for personal services and was unenforceable since it provided for making a separate contract for these services, and because specific performance was not necessary because DeBauge had an adequate remedy at law for damages.

OWSLEY, JUSTICE. We find no merit to these contentions. DeBauge had no adequate remedy in money damages since the real and personal properties to be conveyed were unique and were not available to DeBauge from any other source. Land conveyances are frequently the subject of specific performance due to the unique properties of each parcel which cannot be duplicated. Franchises are by their very nature unique and exclusive, which is the source of their value to the possessor. A contract for sale or transfer of such a retail franchise, along with the real property necessary to operate the business, is a proper subject for specific performance.

Whitsitt further contends the court erred in ordering specific performance because the contract included provisions for personal services and, to be complete, required execution of an additional contract for those services. It is our conclusion that the provisions for personal services of Whitsitt were only incidental to the intent of the parties. It is clear that services of this kind by Whitsitt have some monetary value, but the payment provided for them in the contract is clearly out of proportion to such value. In an equitable proceeding for specific performance of a contract, the court looks to the real intent of the parties and enforces the contract accordingly. Consulting services might be temporarily valuable following change of ownership, but it is obvious that after an initial period of operation, much less than six years, these consulting services will grow valueless as vendee's experience in the manufacture, sale and distribution of beverages increases. We conclude the real purpose of the payment of $12,000 per year was not for consulting services, but was a method of enforcing the agreement not to compete for that period.

The purchaser indicated in its brief that payment of the total consideration, including the deferred payments, was not dependent upon consulting services of the seller; and in argument before this court stated its willingness to pay the whole purchase price regardless of the availability of such services. It is a recognized principle of equity that a vendee, in an action brought by him for specific performance of a contract, may waive the performance on the part of the vendor of portions of his contract, and may elect to take a partial performance if he himself is willing to perform fully.

Problem Cases

1. Leach signed an agreement with Cahill to purchase a house for $18,000 and paid a deposit of $1,000. The contract contained the following provisions: "This agreement is contingent upon buyer being able to obtain a mortgage of $12,000 on the premises and have immediate occupancy of the property." Leach made an honest effort to borrow $12,000 on the security of the house, but he was unable to do so. Cahill refused to repay the $1,000 deposit and Leach brought suit to recover a judgment for the $1,000. Is Leach entitled to a judgment?

2. Herbert contracted to build a house for Dewey according to designated plans and specifications. Three payments were to be made during the course of the work and all payments

were to be made on the production of the architect's certificate. The architect gave his certificate for the first three payments but refused to give a certificate for the final payment. Herbert sued Dewey to recover a judgment for the final payment, claiming that the work was done in a workmanlike manner and in accordance with the plans and specifications. Dewey set up as a defense Herbert's failure to get the architect's certificate. Is the defense good?

3. Cramer contracted to remodel a house for Essivein. In performing the contract, Cramer installed only seven radiators instead of eight as specified in the contract, leaving the bathroom without a radiator. He failed again to carry out the terms of the contract when he installed in the bathroom a used bathtub and a used washbasin, whereas the contract provided that both be new. Essivein refused to pay Cramer, and Cramer brought suit on the contract to recover the contract price for work and material. Is Cramer entitled to a judgment under the doctrine of substantial performance?

4. Plaintiff, Armour and Company, brought an action against defendant contractor, Nord, for delay damages caused by Nord's alleged breach in the performance of a written cost-plus building construction contract. Nord alleged that Armour was not entitled to damages for delay when it terminated Nord under article 314 of the contract which provided for termination without cause. In essence, Nord claimed that since Armour chose to terminate under the "without cause" provisions, Armour elected to pursue that exclusive remedy and thereby waived any other remedy it may have had. In its defense Armour relied on a nonwaiver clause in the contract. Under the contract should the termination "without cause" provision be adjudged as Armour's exclusive remedy for breach?

5. Jones hired Hillin to serve as a sales representative for five years. The employment contract authorized Jones to terminate Hillin's employment should he at any time fail in Jones' discretion to perform his duties in accordance with standards of reasonable care and prudence. Two years prior to the termination date in the contract Jones fired Hillin claiming that he was dissatisfied with the caliber of his performance. Hillin sued Jones for damages claiming that he had performed prudently and that the reason he was fired was because Jones had decided to drop the entire territory. If Hillin is correct can he collect damages?

6. Hood contracted with Ferro for the designing and construction of a tunnel kiln. The design and construction was completed in January 1958. Ferro supervised the operation of the kiln-making adjustment for its operation. However, the operation was not satisfactory and the last of the Ferro people did not depart until December 1958. Hood was forced to make large expenditures in attempting to modify the kiln to achieve operation within the specifications in the contract both during and after Ferro's departure. Hood sued Ferro for (1) the expenditures for modification, and (2) Hood's business losses and profits caused by the failure of the kiln to perform to specifications. Should they recover for either loss? The contract expressly provided that Ferro would not assume liability for consequential damages.

7. Lee contracted to buy a Kirby vacuum cleaner for $269. As an inducement for the purchase, Kirby had included a "New Home" Sewing Machine for $200 and allowed Lee $200 in trade for her used vacuum cleaner. At the time of the sale the Kirby salesman left the new vacuum cleaner and a "Modernaire" Sewing Machine and took their trade-in cleaner. The next day Lee discovered that the sewing machine was a Modernaire rather than a New Home although it was of comparable value. When this was brought to Kirby's attention, Kirby offered to immediately exchange the Modernaire for a New Home. Lee refused and insisted the contract be cancelled. Kirby sued to recover the contract price and Lee set up material breach as a defense. Should Lee be forced to pay?

8. Perry leased a gasoline filling station to Champlain Oil Co. for a term of fifteen years. The stipulated rent was one cent per gallon of gasoline sold. At the time the lease was executed, Champlain Oil Co. had a franchise to sell "Sunoco" products, but seven months later, it terminated the "Sunoco" franchise and substituted for it a franchise with City Service products. This change resulted in a decrease in sales. The lease did not designate the brand of gasoline and other products which should be sold at the station. Perry brought suit to cancel the lease on the ground of commercial frustrations. Should the lease be canceled?

9. Otinger contracted with City Water Board to construct a pump and water station on Catona Creek. Due in part to flood conditions on the Catona, Otinger went over the time specified for completion. The contract contained a provision stating that time was of the essence and authorizing the City to withhold $50 per day for every day, including Sundays and holidays, which the work remained uncompleted beyond the date specified. The $50 was stated to represent not liquidated but actual stipulated damage which the City would have sustained. The total amount of the contract was $120,000. Otinger maintained that the City waived the time limit when, in reply to his letter requesting an extension, they instructed him to "proceed with the unfinished work with reasonable and continual progress until completion" and stated that upon completion they "would gladly have you appear for a review of the delay and assure you of full consideration of the circumstances." Otinger sued for a balance due on the contract and the City counterclaimed for overpayment because the amount of the stipulated damages had exceeded this balance. Who should prevail?

10. Tisdale entered into a contract with Elliott for the construction of a house on a lot owned by Tisdale. The house was to be in accordance with the plans and specifications provided by Tisdale. During the construction it was agreed that drain tiles would be installed around the foundation of the house. At the time Tisdale occupied the house, water leakage into the basement was observed. Upon Elliott's promise to remedy the situation, Tisdale made the final payment. When Elliott's repair efforts proved futile, Tisdale hired another contractor who dug out to the bottom of the foundation and discovered that the drainage tile had been improperly laid. The tiles were repaired and, thereafter, the leakage problem stopped. Tisdale brought suit against Elliott to recover the cost of repair and damages he had suffered from the leakage. In his defense Elliott argued that the defects in Tisdale's house were known to him at the time of acceptance, and that the acceptance of the house by final payment under the construction contract constituted a waiver of the known defects. Is this a valid defense?

11. Columbus Milk Co-op. purchased some milk from milk producers under a contract that did not stipulate the price to be paid. The price Columbus paid was under the going competitive price for the area and pursuant to a special statute the State Department of Agriculture ruled that Columbus would have to pay the milk producers the going competitive price. Columbus took this ruling into court contending that the purchase agreement was an open price contract under the U. C. C., and that since the Department of Agriculture had made no finding of "bad faith," the price set by Columbus was set in "good faith" in accordance with the U. C. C. Sec. 2-305 (2). Is Columbus correct?

12. Goodman and McKinley entered into a contract whereby Goodman agreed to manage a lunch counter for McKinley for a term of one year, beginning September 1, 1964. After Goodman had worked one month, she was discharged without cause. Goodman made no effort to obtain similar employment in the city; had she done so she could have easily obtained a comparable position. On the expiration of the year, Goodman sued McKinley to recover a judgment for the unpaid portion of the full year's salary which McKinley had contracted to pay her. Is Goodman entitled to the amount of damages claimed?

13. In 1966, Tele-Controls and Ford Industries entered into a dealer agreement making Tele-Controls the exclusive sales agent in the Chicago area for Code-a-phones, a telephone-answering device manufactured by Ford Industries. Paragraph 13 (*b*) of the contract provided:

> Either party hereto may terminate this Agreement at any time, with or without cause, by giving to the other party a written notice of intention to terminate at least thirty (30) days prior to the effective date of termination specified in such notice. In the event of termination by Code-a-phone, Dealer shall continue to maintain the sales and service facilities previously maintained until the effective date of the termination.

On February 1, 1967, Ford Industries sent a notice of termination to Tele-Controls effective at the close of business on March 10. Tele-Controls sued for damages and for an injunction claiming that Sec. 1–203 of the U.C.C. imposes an obligation of good faith on franchisors exercising termination rights. Tele-Controls offered no evidence of "bad faith" on the part of Ford although Ford offered evidence that Tele-Controls was an inferior franchisee. Can Tele-Controls prevail?

Part IV

Agency

chapter 15

Creation of Relation and Authority

Introduction

Background. Agency law grew out of the desire of people to extend their activities beyond the physical limits of their own bodies. In simple societies this desire was primarily for additional labor—through slaves or servants. Kings and high churchmen in early England also deputized others to transact business for them. For example, the king customarily issued letters of credit enabling others to borrow money and promise repayment in his name. As commerce grew in importance merchants and traders also began to transact business through others. Brokers and factors began to play a prominent role in business in England by the latter part of the 17th century. Such persons are now typical examples of agents but were originally treated by the English courts as servants. By the 19th century the law began to distinguish between servants and agents.

Nature of the Relation. An agency relationship arises when two people consent that one shall act for the benefit of the other and under the latter's direction. Although there need be no contract nor explicit agreement, the relationship is one of mutual consent as evidenced by the acts of the parties rather than whatever may be their subjective intent. Although termination of the relationship may involve a breach of contract, generally either party may terminate it at will. Either or both parties—the principal, who is the person in control, or the agent, who is the party serving the principal—may be corporations. Indeed, a corporation can act only through agents since it is merely a creation of law. Once the relationship is found to exist, a developed body of law which defines the rights and liabilities of the parties in their relations to each other and to third persons then becomes applicable.

Scope. The legal problems to which agency law is addressed include questions such as the following: When is the dominant person (principal or master or employer) liable on contracts made by the subordinate person (agent or servant or employee)? When is the dominant person liable for the torts of the subordinate person? What duties does each person in the relationship owe to the other? Differences in the nature of the services rendered and the degree of control which the dominant person in the relationship is entitled to exercise has led to terms of classification which are sometimes confusing.

Master and Servant.   The term "principal and agent" is often used in the law to include both the relationship of principal and agent and that of master and servant. It has been common to distinguish agents from servants (employees) according to the nature of the services rendered: agents conduct business transactions such as selling and buying, while servants perform physical acts such as operating a machine or using a tool. However, this distinction tends to lead to confusion in considering when the dominant person is liable for the torts committed by the subordinate person. For this purpose, the important determination is whether the dominant person has the right to control the subordinate's physical activities. If so, the latter is a *servant* in legal terminology, even though he or she may be president of a corporation, and his or her employer (the corporation) will be liable for the person's torts. Because the legal term *servant* connotes servility in common speech, the terms *employee* and *employer* are tending to replace *master* and *servant* even in the law. Therefore, this text will generally use the terms *employee* and *employer.*

It is not uncommon for an employee to be directed to do work for another employer, with the original employer being paid for the services of his or her employee. The question arises as to which employer (master) is liable for a tort committed by an employee (servant) in this situation. The inference is that the *"loaned servant"* remains the employee of the original employer, who will be liable to the employee for his or her pay and will remain the employer under most statutes, such as social security, unemployment, and workmen's compensation. However, if the primary right of control is shifted to the special employer, under the "loaned servant doctrine," the special employer becomes liable for the employee's torts. Which employer has the right of control is frequently a difficult question of fact.

Principal and Agent.   As indicated above, the term *agent* may, in its broadest legal sense include an employee who does nothing but manual labor. However, it is usually applied to one who conducts business transactions for his or her *principal.* Such an agent may be one who is an employee of a corporation or a person who is an independent business person, perhaps employing other people. Agents of the latter type are sometimes called *professional agents.* Manufacturers' representatives, realtors, stockbrokers, auctioneers, and attorneys fall into this category. With respect to such agents the principal's control is limited to determining the objectives and limitations of the agent's authority in the business the agent is transacting for the principal, and he or she has no right to control the agent's physical acts. Whether the agent travels by automobile or airplane or takes three hours for lunch is not within the realm of control by the principal.

General and Special Agents.   Agents are often further classified as general or special agents. A *general agent* is a person who acts for the principal in a number of transactions over a period of time. He or she may be given authority to act for the principal in a rather wide range of matters, such as the manager of a business unit, or may be authorized to handle all transactions of a certain class for the principal, such as a general purchasing agent. A *special agent,* on the other hand, is one who is authorized to act either in a single transaction or a limited series of transactions.

Franchising and Other Relationships.   The terms *agent* and *agency* are sometimes used to refer to relationships which do not come within the law of agency. For example, a merchant who has a franchise to sell the products of the Ford Motor Company is often referred to as a Ford agent, and the business is referred to as a Ford agency; but the merchant is not an agent of the Ford Motor Company, and the relationship between the Ford Motor Company and the merchant is not that of agency. Such a person is an independent contractor dealing in Ford Motor Company products.

Independent Contractor.   The term *independent contractor* is used in contrast to that of employee (or servant). Although the relationship is common in the building trades, it includes an individual, or a partnership or corporation, who contracts to do something for another but who is not an employee. The distinction between employee and independent contractor is based upon the degree of control over the physical conduct of the one performing the service, and the principal is generally not liable for the torts of an independent contractor.

Whether a person is acting as an independent contractor is often a difficult question of fact.[1] If Archer needs a new machine, he may build it in his own shop, in which case those persons who build the machine will be Archer's employees. Archer may submit the specifications for the machine to Burch, who will contract to build the machine according to the specifications and for an agreed price. In this case, Burch will not be an employee of Archer, since Burch has contracted to produce a result and is free to proceed by whatever method he may wish in producing that result. Burch's physical conduct is not under the control of Archer. Burch is an independent contractor. The employee is subject to the direction of his or her employer, the independent contractor is obligated to produce a result and is free to pursue self-chosen methods in the performance of the work.

Summary

Agency law grew out of the desire of people to extend their activities, both in performing labor and in transacting business, beyond the physical limits of

---

[1] See the criteria applied by the court in *Flick v. Crouch, infra.*

their own bodies. Agency is a relationship which exists when two parties agree that one shall act for the benefit and under the control of the other. When created the relationship brings into play a body of developed law governing the relationship of the parties to each other and to third persons.

The term *agency* includes both the relation of master and servant and that of principal and agent. The employer has the right to control the physical activities of an employee (servant). The term *agent* is most commonly applied to one who conducts business transactions such as buying or selling for his or her principal. The agent may be an employee or may be independent and not controlled by the principal as to his or her physical activities. If the latter, the agent may be called a *professional agent.* A general agent acts for the principal in a number of transactions over a period of time and has greater apparent authority than does a special agent.

An independent contractor is one who produces a stipulated result for his or her employer, the employer having little control over the employee's physical conduct. The independent contractor determines the methods used in the work.

Flick v. Crouch

434 P.2d 256 (Sup. Ct. Okla. 1967)

This was an action by Mrs. Flick (plaintiff) against Elmer Crouch (defendant) for the wrongful death of her husband while employed by Crouch. Crouch's motion to dismiss was sustained and Flick appealed. Reversed.

Mrs. Flick's husband was killed at a well site when a derrick suddenly collapsed. She claimed the collapse was due to faulty welds at the base of the derrick. The welders who did the work had been procured by Crouch.

Crouch would not be subject to suit if he were an employee of the Parker Drilling Company, as he claimed, since he would be immune under the Workmen's Compensation Act. Mrs. Flick argued that Crouch was an independent contractor.

Crouch owned a truck and welding equipment and supplied his own welding rods and arc. He operated under the trade name of Crouch Welding Company, and had been in the welding business for 15 years. All of the work he did was for Parker Drilling Co., and he had stopped doing work for others because Parker kept him "busy." Crouch maintained his own insurance coverage. He billed Parker monthly at the rate of $7.00 per hour, keeping his own time records. He was not required to work regular hours. Crouch had signed the invoices submitted by the other welders who were employed for the job on the derrick. Crouch was not told by Parker how to use his equipment or what kind of equipment to use but was given a sketch from which the size of the steel to be used to reinforce the derrick could be determined.

MCINERNEY, JUSTICE.   According to the widow's contention, these welders were independent contractors. The widow complains that under the evidence . . . the status of the welders in relation to Parker presented a jury question. She asserts error in treating that issue as one of law.

As a general rule the line of demarcation between an independent contractor and a servant is not clearly drawn. The question of such a relationship must be determined from the facts peculiar to each case. The various elements to be considered, as set forth in *Page v. Hardy,* are:

(a) the nature of the contract between the parties, whether written or oral; (b) the degree of control which, by the agreement, the employer may exercise on the details of the work or the independence enjoyed by the contractor or agent; (c) whether or not the one employed is engaged in a distinct occupation or business and whether he carries on such occupation or business for others; (d) the kind of occupation with reference to whether, in the locality, the work is usually done under the direction of the employer or by a specialist without supervision; (e) the skill required in the particular occupation; (f) whether the employer or the workman supplies the instrumentalities, tools and the place of work for the person doing the work; (g) the length of time for which the person is employed; (h) the method of payment, whether by the time or by the job; (i) whether or not the work is a part of the regular business of the employer; (j) whether or not the parties believe they are creating the relationship of master and servant; and (k) the right of either to terminate the relationship without liability.

An independent contractor is one who engages to perform a certain service for another, according to his own method and manner, free from control and direction of his employer in all matters connected with the performance of the service, except as to the result thereof. Those who render service but retain control over the manner of doing it are not servants. Where the defendant's status forms a material issue in the case and the facts bearing on that issue are disputed, or *where there is room for reasonable difference of opinion as to the proper inference to be drawn from the known facts,* the issue is for the jury under proper instructions by the court. [Emphasis added by court.]

Kuchta v. Allied Builders Corp.

98 Cal. Rptr. 588 (App. 1971)

This was a suit by Joseph G. Kuchta and his wife (plaintiffs) against Allied Builders Corporation and its franchisee, Raphael Weiner, (defendants) for fraud and breach of a building contract. Allied's primary defense was that Weiner was an independent contractor. Judgment was granted the Kuchtas on jury verdicts for $5,585 in general damages against Allied and Weiner jointly and $3,750 punitive damages against each of them individually. Judgment affirmed.

Mr. and Mrs. Kuchta saw a sign on the lawn of a neighbor's home indicating that Allied had just constructed an outdoor living area attached to the neighbor's house. Desiring a similar facility and not finding an Allied listing in Orange County, they phoned Allied in Los Angeles. They were told by the vice president of Allied that they should contact Allied's branch in Anaheim, and he gave them Weiner's phone number. Weiner appeared two days after they phoned the Anaheim office. He represented that he was from Allied Builders, and a few days later the Kuchtas entered into a written contract with Allied Builders System. It provided that the franchisee, as contractor, would furnish all labor and materials for $5,671, that construction would conform to local and state codes and that Allied would obtain necessary building permits.

The plans were submitted by Weiner to the building department of Orange County but were not approved because the planned structure would extend to the property line while the applicable zoning restrictions prohibited building within five feet of the lot line except for a fence. Without the knowledge of the Kuchtas, a second set of plans was submitted by Weiner to the building department. They omitted the roof and side supports provided for in the contract and called for only a slab. Nevertheless, the construction followed the original plan. About five months later the Kuchtas received notice of violation of the building code and were required to demolish the addition and to restore the property to its original condition.

KERRIGAN, ACTING PRESIDING JUSTICE.   The law is clear that a franchisee may be deemed to be the agent of the franchisor (citations). In the field of franchise agreements, the question of whether the franchisee is an independent contractor or an agent is ordinarily one of fact, depending on whether the franchisor exercises complete or substantial control over the franchisee (citations).

In the case under review, there was evidence that Allied Builders exercised strong control over Weiner. The franchise agreement itself gave Allied Builders the right to control the location of the franchisee's place of business, to prescribe minimum display equipment, to regulate the quality of the goods used or sold, to control the standards of construction, to approve the design and utility of all construction, and to assign persons to see that the franchisee performed according to the franchisor's standards. Additionally, Allied enjoyed the right of inspection over the franchisee's plans and specifications, the franchisee's work in progress, and finished jobs, as well as the right to train Weiner's salesmen. Moreover, Allied Builders was entitled to share in the profits of the franchisee and to audit Weiner's books. These elements of control were sufficient to support an implied finding of agency.

The trial court also properly instructed the jury on the doctrine of ostensible agency. An agency is ostensible when the principal intentionally, or by want of ordinary care, causes a third person to believe another to be his agent who is really not employed by him. Ostensible authority is such as a principal, intentionally or by want of ordinary care, causes or allows a third person to believe the agent to possess.

There was formidable evidence establishing Weiner's ostensible authority. When the plaintiffs first contacted Allied Builder's vice president in Los Angeles, they were referred to Allied's "branch office" in Anaheim. The vice president characterized the Los Angeles office as the "main office." Both the main office and the branch office answered their phone in the same manner, to wit, "Allied Builders." Both the franchisor and the franchisee did business under the same name at that time, to wit, Allied Builders System. The contract listed "Allied Builders System" as the contractor. Both offices employed common advertising in newspapers and in the yellow pages of the telephone book. Calls to the main office brought swift and certain reaction from the franchisee. Weiner represented to plaintiffs that the firm had been in business for over 50 years, which covered the entire span of Allied's experience in the building business.

The plaintiffs' check for payment on the contract price was endorsed and deposited to the account of "Allied Builders System." Consequently, there was ample evidence that Allied Builders either intentionally, or by want of ordinary care, led third persons, including plaintiffs, to believe that the franchisee and Allied Builders were part of the same business operation.

While Allied Builders argues that no agency relationship existed by virtue of the franchise agreement, in that the agreement itself stated that no such agency relationship was created, the declarations of the parties in the agreement respecting the nature of the relationship are not controlling.

Allied also takes the position that the plaintiffs elected to hold Weiner alone responsible in that they contracted solely with him and, therefore, are estopped from holding the principal liable. There is authority that if, at the time the contract is made in the name of the agent, the third party has knowledge of the identity of the principal and nevertheless proceeds to contract with the agent, there is no "undisclosed" principal, and this has sometimes been considered as an election to hold the agent alone. However, it is equally well settled that knowledge of the identity of the principal is not conclusive, and the election to hold the agent must be established by other evidence of actual intent. The evidence herein reflects that both the franchisor and the franchisee held themselves out to the public as one construction firm and that the plaintiffs contracted with Allied on that basis. Consequently, the trial court was correct in not requiring the plaintiffs to make an election.

Creation of Relation

Requirement to Create Agency. As a general rule, no formality is required to create the relationship of master and servant or principal and agent. Whether or not such a relationship exists is a question of fact, and if, from the circumstances, it appears that one person is acting for the benefit and under the control of another, the courts will hold that an agency exists. The relation may be created without either party being aware of its existence and even though the parties have expressly stated that they do not intend to create it.

In by far the majority of instances the relationship of master and servant, and that of principal and agent, is created by contract. However, the fact that an agent is acting gratuitously and that no enforceable contract of agency has been entered into between the principal and agent will in no way affect the validity of the contracts negotiated in the name of the principal by the agent. The gratuitous agent owes to his or her principal a fiduciary duty and is responsible to the principal for any failure to exercise due care in the transaction of the business entrusted to him. The gratuitous agent may terminate the relationship at any time without incurring liability.

Statutory Requirement. In many states the authority of an agent to sell and convey, to mortgage, or to create a trust in real property is required by statute to be in writing. In a few states an agent must be authorized in writing to execute, in the principal's behalf, any contract which, to be enforceable, is required to be evidenced by a writing.

Summary

As a general rule, no formality is required to create the relation of employer and employee or principal and agent; it may be created by the mutual consent of the parties, or it may be implied from their conduct. However, the fact that an agent is acting gratuitously does not affect his or her power to bind the principal, nor does it relieve the agent from the fiduciary duty owed to the principal. Under the statutes of some states, written evidence of the agent's authority is required.

Capacity of Parties

Infants and Insane Persons as Principals.   Since the relation of principal and agent is not necessarily contractual, it is not necessary that the principal have, when appointing an agent, the capacity to contract. However, agency is a consensual relation; consequently, the principal must have sufficient legal capacity to give the consent essential to the creation of the relation.

A person of limited capacity cannot enlarge his or her legal capacity by appointing an agent and acting through the agent. The infant or insane person is bound by the acts of a person who has been appointed and authorized to act as agent only to the extent that the infant or insane person would be bound had either acted in person.

Unincorporated Associations as Principals.   Under the common-law rule an unincorporated association is not recognized as an entity having legal capacity. It cannot, as a general rule, sue, be sued, own property, or enter into a contract. Under special statutes, however, such associations have been made subject to suit and their assets are subject to execution. This is especially true of labor unions. If an unincorporated association is not liable to suit under the provisions of a statute, its members who have legal capacity may be held liable. If a person is appointed an agent for an unincorporated association, such person may be the agent of all of its members or of only certain ones of them. If the person appointing or authorizing the agent to act has been authorized to do this by all of the members of the association, then such an agent binds all of the members while acting within the scope of his or her authority. A class action, or action against a representative group of the members on behalf of all members, is the means to enforce the liability of all the members for the acts of an agent acting within his authority. A judgment in such an action is good against the assets of the association. Whether one is acting for the entire membership of the unincorporated association or for only a group of the members will depend on the circumstances of the particular case.

Capacity to Act as Agent.   A person may have capacity to act as an agent even though he or she does not have the capacity to contract. In the transaction of business through an agent the principal is the party to the transaction, not the agent. The agent's capacity is immaterial so long as he or she has sufficient ability to carry out the principal's instructions. A partnership, as a general rule, can act as an agent. Corporations frequently act as agents although whether they have the right to do so depends upon the powers granted in their articles of incorporation. A husband or wife may act as the agent of the spouse but there is no agency merely by virtue of the marital relationship. The liability of a husband for the necessities purchased by his wife is an aspect of the marital relationship itself and does not constitute the wife an agent for her husband.

Business Organizations as Principals.   Business organizations, such as corporations, partnerships, and business trusts, which have the power to contract have the capacity to appoint agents. All the business of a corporation is, in fact, transacted through its agents. And although the partnership is not recognized as an entity, each partner acts as the agent of the copartners in the transaction of partnership business. One who has been appointed the agent of a partnership by a member of the partnership who is authorized so to act is the agent of all the partners.

Summary

An infant, insane person, or other persons may appoint agents and act through such agents to the same extent as they might act in person, but they cannot enlarge their legal capacity by acting through agents. The courts have held infants liable for the torts of their agents provided the agent's acts have been directed by the infant.

At common law an unincorporated association had no capacity to contract and could not appoint an agent. This has been changed by statute in many states, at least as to some types of associations. Members of unincorporated associations may act through an agent and be bound by his or her acts. Business organizations such as corporations and partnerships may appoint agents.

Authority to Bind Principal

Authorization.   An agent is authorized to act for a principal when the principal has by his or her acts or conduct made it manifest to the agent that the principal intends the agent to act on the principal's account. The authority of the agent to bind the principal is based on the conduct of the principal. In general, the authority to act on the account of the principal may be conferred on the agent by written or spoken words or by other conduct of the principal which, reasonably interpreted, causes the agent to believe that the principal intends the agent so to act on the principal's account.

In analyzing the power of an agent to bind the principal, the courts and writers have not been consistent in the terms used. This analysis shall follow a three-part classification: (1) express authority, (2) implied authority (also referred to as incidental authority), and (3) apparent authority (also referred to as ostensible authority and similar to "authority by estoppel").

Express Authority.   Express authority is that authority which is explicitly conferred on the agent by the principal. It may be conferred either orally or in writing, but in either event the principal must express to the agent the acts he or she wishes the agent to perform. For example, if the principal instructs the agent, either orally or in writing, to draw a check payable to Tucker for a stated sum and to sign the check in the principal's name and deliver it to Tucker, the agent will have express authority to draw, sign, and deliver the check.

Implied Authority.   In almost all situations the agent will have authority to perform some acts not included in his or her express authority. Expressly to include every act which an agent is to perform in the carrying out of the mission would be almost impossible. An agent is appointed by the principal to accomplish an objective. If the agent is a special agent—that is, if the agent is appointed to conduct a single transaction or to conduct a number of transactions which do not involve continuity of services—the express authority may include the majority of acts the agent is authorized to perform. If an agent is authorized to sell a piece of real property or several pieces of real property and this authority is in writing, the express authority may be sufficiently detailed to include most of the acts to be performed by the agent. However, it will not include every detail of the transaction authorized. If the agent is a general agent—that is, if the agent is appointed to conduct a series of transactions involving a continuity of services—the express authority, even though carefully worded to cover the agent's duties in detail, cannot include more than the major acts the agent is to perform. In carrying out the objective of the agency, the agent will be authorized to do many acts not detailed in the express authority.

Unless the principal limits the authority of the agent by express instructions or by clear implication, the authority to negotiate a transaction includes the authority to do those acts which are usually or customarily done in conducting transactions such as the agent is authorized to transact or to do those acts which are reasonably necessary to accomplish the objective of the agency. Such authority is generally termed "implied authority" or "incidental authority."

In determining the scope of the agent's express and implied authority, the measure used is the justified belief of the agent. The same principles apply to the interpretation of an agent's authority as apply in interpreting an offer to contract. The nature of the agency, whether special or general, usages of trade, prior relations between the principal and agent, and such other facts and circumstances as are material in the particular case are weighed in determining what authority the agent is justified in believing the principal intended to confer on him or her.

Apparent Authority.   Whereas the scope of an agent's express or implied authority is determined by analyzing the relation between the principal and the agent, an agent's apparent authority is determined by analyzing the relation between the principal and a third person. An agent's apparent authority may be less than, coextensive with, or greater than his or her express or implied authority. An agent's apparent authority, sometimes termed ostensible authority, is the authority which the principal by his or her conduct has led the third person, acting as a reasonable and prudent person, justifiably to believe is conferred on the agent by the principal.

Apparent authority is created by the same method as that by which express or implied authority is created except that the manifestations of the principal must be made to the third person or to the community rather than to the agent. In holding the principal liable on the ground of the apparent authority of the agent, the third person must prove that the principal was responsible for the information which justified the third person in believing that the agent was authorized to act and that the third person relied upon it. The information on which the third person justifies his or her belief may come directly from the words or conduct of the principal; it may be based on standard practices of trade; or it may result from the principal entrusting certain documents to the agent or from the appointment of the agent to a position which carries with it the implication of authority. Also, apparent authority may be established by showing that the agent has been conducting similar transactions or doing similar acts to the knowledge of and without objection by the principal.

Summary

The authority of an agent to act for a principal is based on the manifestation of the principal. Authority may be conferred by written or spoken words, or by other conduct of the principal. The authority of the agent may be express, implied, or apparent. The agent has the express authority explicitly conferred upon him or her by the principal. The agent has, in addition, the implied authority which he or she, as a reasonable person familiar with the business to be transacted, is justified in believing the principal intended to confer. This would include authority to do those acts which are reasonably necessary to accomplish the objective of the agency. The agent has such apparent authority as the principal, by conduct, has led the third person, acting as a reasonable person familiar with the business to be transacted, justifiably to believe has been conferred on the agent.

Jennings v. Pittsburgh Mercantile Co.

202 A.2d 51 (Sup. Ct. Pa. 1964)

This was an action by Dan R. Jennings, a real estate broker, and his associate, Daniel B. Cantor (plaintiffs), against Pittsburgh Mercantile Company (defendant) to recover a real estate brokerage commission for the alleged consummation of a sale and lease-back of all of Mercantile's real property. Judgment for Jennings and Cantor, and Mercantile appealed. Judgment reversed.

In April 1958, Egmore, Mercantile's Vice President and Treasurer-Comptroller, and Stern, its financial consultant, met with Jennings, explained Mercantile's desire to raise cash for store modernization, and provided Jennings with financial information. At the meeting Egmore represented that the Executive Committee, of which he was a member, controlled Mercantile, that this committee would determine whether the company would accept any offers produced by Jennings, and that subsequent Board of Directors approval would be automatic. Egmore outlined preliminary terms of an acceptable offer, and promised payment of a commission if Jennings produced an offer acceptable to the Executive Committee.

In July and August 1958, Jennings brought Egmore three offers, none of which met the originally specified terms. The first two were quickly rejected, but the third came close to the original terms. On November 4, 1958, Jennings was informed by Stern that the Executive Committee had "agreed to the deal." However, within a week Egmore informed Jennings that the third offer had been rejected. Mercantile refused to pay Jenning's bill for commission of $32,000 and suit was instituted. Mercantile claimed that Egmore and Stern had no authority to accept the offer for sale and leaseback, thereby binding it to payment of the brokerage commission.

COHEN, JUSTICE. At the outset, we note that for Mercantile this proposed sale and leaseback was not a transaction in the ordinary course of business. Rather, it was unusual and unprecedented. The transaction envisaged Mercantile's relinquishment of ownership of all its real property, worth approximately $1.5 million, for a period of 30 years. Hence, the apparent authority which Jennings seeks to establish is the apparent authority to accept an offer for an extraordinary transaction.

Apparent authority is defined as that authority which, although not actually granted, the principal (1) knowingly permits the agent to exercise or (2) holds him out as possessing.

Jennings strongly contends that Egmore's representations gave rise to the apparent authority asserted. We do not agree. Without regard to the extraordinary nature of a transaction, a disclosed or partially disclosed principal cannot be bound on the doctrine of apparent authority by virtue of the extrajudicial representations of an agent as to the existence or extent of his authority or the facts upon which it depends. An agent cannot, simply by his own words, invest himself with apparent authority. Such authority emanates from the actions of the principal and not the agent. Therefore, the representations upon which Jennings relies so heavily do not support his contention.

Jennings further argues that apparent authority arose by virtue of (1) certain prior dealings of Egmore and (2) the corporate offices held by Egmore. However, the evidence advanced in support of this argument is insufficient to permit a reasonable inference of the existence of apparent authority in Egmore to accept Jennings' offer.

Focusing on the first of these factors, in order for a reasonable inference of the existence of apparent authority to be drawn from prior dealings, these dealings must have (1) a measure of similarity to the act for which the principal is sought to be bound, and, granting this similarity, (2) a degree of repetitiveness. Although the required degree of repetitiveness might have been present here, the prior acts relied upon consisted solely of Egmore's provision of financial information to Jennings and other brokers with regard to the sale and leaseback, and Egmore's solicitation of offers through them. The dissimilarities between these acts and the act of accepting the offer in issue are self-evident, and apparent authority to do the latter act cannot be inferred from the doing of the former.

As to the second of the above factors, the corporate offices of Vice President and Treasurer-Comptroller, which Egmore held, do not provide the basis for a reasonable inference that Mercantile held out Egmore as having the apparent authority to accept the offers produced by Jennings. [Cases cited.] Each of these cases involved a suit against a corporation for a brokerage commission for securing a purchaser for all of the corporation's realty. The principal issue in each was the apparent authority possessed *virtute officii* to consummate an extraordinary transaction. On facts stronger than those present here, the claims of apparent authority were rejected. We hold likewise on the present facts, for any other conclusion would improperly extend the usual scope of authority which attaches to the holding of various corporate offices, and would greatly undercut the proper role of the Board of Directors in corporate decision-making by thrusting upon them determinations on critical matters which they have never had the opportunity to consider.

Finally, the extraordinary nature of this transaction placed Jennings on notice to inquire as to Egmore's actual authority, particularly since Jennings and Cantor were an experienced real estate broker and investment counselor-attorney team. Had inquiry been made Jennings would have discovered that the Board never considered any of the proposals and obviously did not delegate actual authority to accept offers.

Southwestern Portland Cement v. Beavers

478 P.2d 546 (Sup. Ct. N.M. 1970)

This suit was brought by Southwestern Portland Cement (plaintiff) against A. E. Beavers, B. C. Glasgow, and P. G. Adams, d/b/a Plains Sand and Gravel, (defendants) to collect payment on account. Judgment for Southwestern, and Beavers and Glasgow appealed. Affirmed.

In February 1968, Beavers and Glasgow formed Plains Sand and Gravel as a partnership to provide concrete for a construction project at Cannon Air Force Base. In March the partnership entered into an oral agreement with Adams to use his ready-mix concrete batching plant and delivery trucks to mix and deliver concrete to the project. Arrangements were made with Southwestern to furnish bulk cement to Adams at his plant. The method of payment for the delivered concrete was for the general contractor, Wilkerson-Webb, to issue its check payable jointly to Plains Sand and Gravel and to Southwestern.

On March 20, 1968, and on April 30, 1968, Southwestern delivered cement to Adams' plant for the partnership account. Adams received these deliveries at his plant and signed truck tickets for the cement on behalf of Plains Sand and Gravel for the Cannon Air Force job. These two deliveries of cement were paid for by Wilkerson-Webb's joint check in the amount of $1,052.70.

On July 10, 13, and 16, Adams again ordered cement from Southwestern telling it that the order was for Plains Sand and Gravel. Adams received the three deliveries at his plant, signed truck tickets for receipt of the cement on behalf of Plains Sand and Gravel for the Cannon Air Force job.

It was established during trial that prior to the last three deliveries by Southwestern, Adams' equipment broke down, and he was unable to deliver the concrete to the job site and Plains Sand and Gravel made other arrangements with another firm to deliver the concrete. However, Southwestern was not informed of this prior to the last three deliveries. After the last of the three deliveries, Southwestern contacted Wilkerson-Webb to "confirm" the amount of concrete usage on the job and to "reconfirm" the guarantee of payment. It was then informed that only a negligible amount of concrete was supplied by Plains Sand and Gravel for the job, and Wilkerson-Webb refused to issue a joint check for the delivered cement. Thereupon, Southwestern called one of the partners, who denied that Adams had authority to order the cement.

Southwestern then sued Beavers, Glasgow, and Adams in the amount of $1,647.00 for the last three loads delivered.

McKENNA, JUSTICE.   For reversal, Beaver and Glasgow argue that there was no substantial evidence to support the finding that Adams had apparent authority from the course of dealing to order the last three loads of cement and Southwestern was negligent by not inquiring into the scope of Adams' authority and this negligence precluded Southwestern from any recovery.

* * * * *

Obviously, the course of dealing was not lengthy, and was limited, in terms of time span and deliveries, but this must be viewed in light of the limited business relationship which was involved—it was for only one project at Cannon Air Force Base. It is equally obvious that the component acts in the course of dealing were identical and reflected a common pattern. Each of the deliveries made to Adams by Wilkerson-Webb was for the account of Plains Sand and Gravel for use on the particular project in accordance with the prearranged procedure. Each delivery was made to the same location; each was receipted for by Adams for the partnership. If Southwestern had not been paid for the first two loads, it would have been warned or alerted—at least the law would so view it—but having been paid for the first two loads by the very procedure agreed upon, Southwestern could reasonably construe this as ratification of the previous course of business. We cannot say that under these circumstances Southwestern acted in bad faith or without reasonable prudence in delivering the last three shipments. As between Southwestern and the partners, it is the latter's conduct which fails to meet the test of reasonable prudence, for not only did they have the responsibility for the relationship, they neglected to notify Southwestern that they had made different arrangements for delivery of the concrete when Adams' equipment broke down. If they had done this, Southwestern's delivery of the last three shipments would have been at its peril.

An agent's scope of authority embraces not only his actual authority but also that apparently delegated. A settled course of conduct does serve to create apparent authority in the agent binding upon the principal where the acts are not timely disavowed and a third party is thereby induced to rely on the ostensible authority of the agent and does so in good faith and with reasonable prudence. The doctrine is based upon an estoppel: the principal will not be permitted to establish that the agent's authority was less than what was apparent from the course of dealing for when one of two innocent parties must suffer, the loss must fall upon the party who created the enabling circumstances.

Ratification

Nature of Ratification.   Ratification in the law of agency is the subsequent adoption and affirmance by one person of an act which another, without authority, has previously assumed to do for the first while purporting to act as his or her agent. Ratification is equivalent to a previous authorization and relates back to the time when the act ratified was done, except where intervening rights of third parties are concerned. Any act which the principal could have authorized at the time the act was done may be ratified.

Requirements for Ratification.   To have a valid ratification, the following conditions must be satisfied: (1) The person ratifying must have had the present ability to do the act himself or herself or authorize it to be done, (2) the person for whom the act was done must have been identified or the circumstances must have been such that he or she was capable of identification, (3) the person acting must have acted as agent of the principal or the person represented to be the principal, (4) the principal or person represented to be the principal must have been in existence at the time the act was done and must have been competent to do or authorize the act done, (5) the principal or person represented to be the principal must have had knowledge of all the material facts at the time he or she ratified, (6) the third party must not have canceled the transaction, and (7) the circumstances must have been such that the intervening rights of third persons were not cut off by the ratification.

There are no formal requirements for ratification. It may be expressed or implied from the acts of the principal. Usually, acceptance of benefits or failure to repudiate within a reasonable time will be convincing evidence of intent to ratify, provided the principal, at the time, has knowledge of all the material facts.

What Acts May Be Ratified. As a general rule, any act which the principal could have done or authorized at the time the act was done or authorized may be ratified. The principal may ratify an illegal act of his or her agent. If the act ratified is both a tort and a crime, ratification by the principal will make the principal liable for the tort, but it will not alone make the principal liable for the crime. Ratification by the principal of an agent's illegal act will not relieve the agent from individual tort or criminal liability.

Since ratification relates back to the time the act was done, and since the principal must have been in existence at that time, it naturally follows that a proposed but nonexistent corporation, when it comes into existence (receives its charter), cannot ratify the acts done by the promoters in the name of the proposed but nonexistent corporation. It may, however, as discussed in Chapter 24, adopt such acts when it comes into existence.

Effect of Ratification. When a principal ratifies the unauthorized acts of his or her agent, the principal then accepts and receives all responsibility for such acts from the time they were done. When the principal has effectively ratified the acts of the agent, the principal cannot at a later time repudiate the ratification.

Ratification releases the agent from liability to both the principal and third persons for having exceeded his or her authority. It also gives the agent the same rights against the principal as to compensation that the agent would have been given had the acts been previously authorized. In return the principal is entitled to receive from the agent everything to which the principal would have been entitled had the act been originally authorized.

Under the rule generally followed in the United States, the third person has the right to cancel or withdraw from the unauthorized transaction at any time before the principal ratifies it, but not afterward.

Ratification Must Be Entire. If the principal wishes to ratify, the entire transaction must be ratified. The principal cannot ratify those portions of the contract which are beneficial and repudiate those parts which are detrimental.[1] On ratification the principal will be bound in the same manner and to the same extent as he or she would have been if the agent had had full authority in the first instance.

Summary

Ratification is the subsequent adoption of an act which was unauthorized originally. In order to make the ratification valid, the existing and identifiable

---

[1] See *Navrides v. Zurich Insurance Co.,* p. 349.

principal, with knowledge of the material facts, must indicate his or her intention to be bound by the agent's unauthorized acts done in the name of the principal. All that is necessary for ratification is that the principal, either expressly or impliedly, indicate an intention to be bound by the originally unauthorized act of the agent. Any act which could have been done or authorized by the principal may be ratified. The principal must have been in existence at the time the act was done.

A ratification is retroactive and supplies the authority lacking at the time of the commission of the act. Unless third parties have acquired rights which would be cut off by ratification, the effect of ratification is to place all involved parties in the position they would have held had the act been authorized at the time it was done. If the principal wishes to ratify, the transaction must be ratified in its entirety.

Problem Cases

1. Crudup was a distributor of gasoline for Texaco, from whom he leased storage facilities. His contract with Texaco provided that he would purchase at least a certain number of gallons per year, but not more than a specified greater quantity, that the gasoline would be sold to Crudup on consignment, that he would deliver it to Texaco dealers in the area and bill them on forms furnished by Texaco, banking their payments in a Texaco account. It declared that Crudup was an independent contractor. The distributorship telephone was listed in Texaco's name. Texaco required Crudup to follow a printed manual which laid down procedures for the operation of the distributorship, including every step in the handling, storage, and unloading of gasoline, the manner of extending credit and making collections and prescribed the forms to be used. Texaco retained the power to terminate the contract with Crudup on five days' notice and to make inspections three times per month.

   Approximately 100 gallons of gasoline were spilled during unloading from a Texaco railroad car at the distributing plant. It entered a ditch which extended under a feed mill owned by Burriss. The gasoline caught fire and damaged the mill. A state law required a separation box to prevent the entrance of flammable liquids into public drainage ditches and made failure to comply negligence per se.

   Can the owner of the feed mill recover from Texaco on the grounds that Crudup is Texaco's agent?

2. Delta Savings and Loan Association furnished the uniforms and equipment for a baseball club which was a member club of a local league which played baseball in the local parks. The uniforms had "Delta Savings and Loan Association" written across the front of the shirts. While playing a game, Philip Hudson, a member of the team who was wearing a shirt having "Delta Savings and Loan Association" written across the front, negligently batted a ball which struck Howard Toms in the left eye, causing him to lose the sight of the eye. Toms sued Delta Savings and Loan Association to recover damages. Toms contends that Hudson was, at the time he batted the ball, an agent or employee of Delta Savings and Loan Association and that the principal or employer is liable for the torts of its agent or employee. Was Hudson an agent or employee of Delta Savings and Loan Association?

3. Weisbein appointed Lichtenstein as his agent to continue Weisbein's business during his absence. The appointment was in the form of a general power of attorney, granting Lichtenstein authority to do those things necessary in the operation of the business. Claflin claimed that Weisbein had obtained goods from him through fraud and demanded that Lichtenstein return the goods and settle the account. Lichtenstein returned the goods still in stock and settled the balance of the claim by delivering to Claflin goods at a discount of 24 percent off cost. Before making the settlement, Lichtenstein showed Claflin his power of attorney. On his return Weisbein brought an action in conversion to recover a judgment for the value of the goods given to Claflin. Weisbein claims that Lichtenstein, under the power of attorney, had no authority to settle the claim of Claflin. Is Weisbein entitled to a judgment?

4. Barton was sales manager for Bonanni, who manufactured hosiery and sold it through door-to-door salesmen. Barton was authorized to hire and supervise salesmen employed by Bonanni. Barton contracted with Hinkson to employ him as a salesman for Bonanni. Barton, as agent for Bonanni, agreed to pay Hinkson a 5 percent commission on the amount of all orders taken and submitted to Bonanni. Barton took Hinkson on a sales demonstration trip for four days during which time Hinkson was paid $10 per day. Hinkson took orders and submitted them to Bonanni but due to a shortage of materials Bonanni was unable to fill a substantial percentage of the orders submitted by his salesmen. Bonanni paid Hinkson the agreed commission on orders filled but refused to pay commissions on orders submitted but not filled. Hinkson sued Bonanni to recover a judgment for such commissions. Bonanni set up as a defense that Barton had no authority to contract to pay a commission on orders submitted but not filled. Did Barton have authority to contract to pay a commission on such orders?

5. Elmo Bonneval and Paul Kiefer owned and operated a used-car lot under the firm name of Bonneval Motors. There was a large sign on the lot reading "Bonneval Motors." Rubins, who was working the lot, sold a used car to Vicknair at a price above the legal maximum permitted by price-ceiling regulations. In making the sale Rubins used Bonneval Motors billheads and stationery. Also, in the chattel mortgage signed before Viosca, a notary public, Paul Kiefer appeared as the duly authorized agent of the vendor, Bonneval Motors, and the documents were signed by Paul Kiefer. Vicknair brought suit against Bonneval Motors to recover for the overpayment and penalties, and Bonneval Motors set up as a defense that Rubins was an independent dealer selling his own cars and that they merely permitted him to carry on his business on their lot. Is Vicknair entitled to a judgment against Bonneval Motors?

6. Sprague Electric Company had, for about three years, been purchasing carbon rings from Continental-Wirt used in the manufacture of some of Sprague's products. Continental-Wirt decided to discontinue production of the rings, and its executive vice president, Lifson, so notified Kerouac, materials manager for Sprague, who had been purchasing the rings for Sprague and was Continental-Wirt's only contact at Sprague. Kerouac then wrote Lifson asking if Continental-Wirt would sell its manufacturing equipment for this product to Sprague. Lifson offered the machinery, instruction in its use, and the services of an experienced foreman for a reasonable time for $20,000. Kerouac then phoned Lifson and told him that Sprague had decided to buy the equipment, that a purchase order was being forwarded, and the call was being made in advance because Kerouac knew that Lifson was anxious to dispose of the equipment. Lifson then sent a letter confirming the sale. The following day Kerouac wrote Lifson that the sale was off because upper management had reversed its original thinking.

    Sprague refused to complete the purchase and when Continental-Wirt sued on the alleged contract, Sprague claimed Kerouac had authority only to buy raw materials. Did he have apparent authority to buy the equipment?

7. Mrs. Fendler parked her Chrysler Imperial in front of a "No Parking" sign and next to a shop in the Chris-Town shopping center. Her car and two others parked next to it were towed away at the request of Chris-Town by Charles Swinford, who operated a towing service in connection with his Texaco station. Mrs. Fendler sued Texaco for conversion, alleging Swinford was its ostensible or apparent agent because of the signs and other indicia that Texaco was operating the station and the tow truck. If Swinford did wrongfully remove the auto, could Texaco be liable under the doctrine of apparent authority?

8. Gaines listed a house and lot for sale with Michael, a real estate broker. The listing contract authorized Michael to find a purchaser for the property; but it did not authorize him to execute, in behalf of Gaines, a contract of sale or to close any deal. Michael contracted, in Gaines' name, to sell the property to Murphy and gave Murphy possession of the property. Murphy moved into the house. When Gaines learned of this, he refused to confirm the sale and brought suit against Murphy to recover possession of the house and damages for withholding possession of the house from Gaines. Murphy set up as a defense the contract of sale and the permission granted to him by Michael, Gaines' agent. Is Gaines entitled to possession of the house?

9. Weingart drove his Cadillac to the door of the Directoire Restaurant at 160 East 48th Street in Manhattan and gave the key to his car to Douglas who was standing in front of the door in a uniform consisting of doorman's cap and matching jacket. He asked Douglas to park the car for him while he was in the restaurant and gave him a $1 tip. Douglas gave him a claim check. When Weingart left the restaurant about 45 minutes later and presented Douglas with the claim check, Douglas was unable to find the automobile. The restaurant had been open only nine days but Weingart had patronized it previously and had his car parked in a similar manner. When sued for the loss of the automobile, the restaurant's defense was based upon the fact that Douglas was not its employee. He furnished his own uniform and parked autos for several restaurants in the block. The manager of the restaurant was aware of Douglas' activities and had not objected to them. Is the Directoire Restaurant liable for the loss of the automobile?

10. Larry Wilks traded a Plymouth automobile to Stone in part payment for a Chevrolet convertible and gave a check for $1,695 for the balance. According to Stone, Larry represented that he was acting for his mother, Hazel Wilks. The check was returned marked "no account," and Stone discussed the check with Hazel. Stone alleges that she told him she knew of the exchange and that "the matter would be straightened out and consummated." Hazel denies that Larry was her agent or that she indicated she would make good on the check. Stone sues Hazel for the amount of the check. If Stone's allegations can be proved, would Hazel be held liable?

chapter 16

Relation of Principal and Third Person

Disclosed or Partially Disclosed Principal

Liability of Agent of Disclosed Principal. A principal is disclosed when both the existence of the agency and the identity of the principal are known to the third person. If the agent is acting for a disclosed principal, the third person will, as a general rule, intend to contract with the principal, not the agent. For that reason the principal is bound by all contracts which are negotiated by the agent in the name of the principal, provided the agent has acted within the scope of his or her authority, express, implied, or apparent, or if the principal has ratified the acts of the agent. The third person does not intend to contract with the agent, and the agent is not bound by such a contract.

An agent may make a contract in his or her own name, in which event the agent is one of the contracting parties and is liable on the contract; the agent may join the principal as joint obligor in the making of the contract, in which case the agent is jointly liable with the principal; or the agent may guarantee the performance of the contract by the principal, in which event the agent is liable as surety. The mere fact that an agent, in negotiating a contract, uses such expressions as "I will sell" or "I will build," when it is clearly understood that he or she is acting for and in the name of the principal, will not make the agent a party to the contract or a surety for the principal.

Liability of Agent of Partially Disclosed Principal. A principal is partially disclosed when the existence of the agency is known to the third person but the identity of the principal is not known. The agent for the partially disclosed principal will, in the usual situation, be a party to the transaction he or she is negotiating. Since the identity of the principal is unknown to the third person, such third person will not, as a general rule, be willing to rely wholly on the credit and integrity of an unknown party. The third party will desire the promise of the agent either as a guarantor or as a copromisor. In such a situation, both the principal and the agent will be liable to the third person. The agreement may, however, expressly state that the agent is not liable and that the third person will look solely to the principal for performance.

Execution of Writings. An agent for a disclosed or partially disclosed principal need not sign an informal writing in any particular manner in order to make the writing binding on the principal. In the event the writing is drafted and signed in such a manner that it is not clear who the parties to the contract are, the courts will admit parol evidence to clear up the ambiguity. Good business practices, however, dictate that the principal should be named in the body of the writing as the party to be bound by the writing, and the agent should sign it in such a way as clearly to indicate that he or she is executing the writing for the principal in a representative capacity. For example, the following would clearly indicate the relations of the parties:

> I, Peters, hereby * * *.
> (Signed) Peters
> By Archer, his agent

Only persons whose names appear on negotiable instruments can be held as parties to them. Therefore, if the principal is not disclosed on the instrument he or she will not be liable on it.

Summary

A principal is disclosed when the existence of the agency and the identity of the principal are known to the third person; a principal is partially disclosed when the existence of the agency is known to the third person, but not the identity of the principal. In the usual situation the agent of a disclosed principal will not be a party to the transaction, provided the agent is acting within the scope of his or her authority, expressed, implied, or apparent. The agent may, by express agreement, make himself or herself a party to a transaction being negotiated for the principal. The agent of the partially disclosed principal is, together with the principal, a party to the transaction being negotiated unless it is understood that the agent is not to be liable.

To avoid doubt, the agent should sign in the customary manner indicated. A principal is not bound on a negotiable instrument unless his or her identity is disclosed on it.

Undisclosed Principal

Nature of Relation. A principal is undisclosed if both the existence of the agency and the identity of the principal are unknown to the third person. In such a situation, if the common-law rules of contract law were followed, the principal, not being a party to the contract, could not be held liable on it.

However, under the law of agency, the undisclosed principal is held liable as if a party to the contract, provided the agent intends, in negotiating the transaction, to act for the undisclosed principal and has acted within the scope of his or her powers. The liability of the undisclosed principal is imposed by operation of law.

Rights of the Third Person.   Since, in the case of an undisclosed principal, the agent is the contracting party, he or she is liable on the contract. If the third person discovers that an agency exists and learns the identity of the principal, the third person has the right to recognize the agency and hold the principal liable or to pursue his or her rights on the contract against the agent. The third person must make an election to hold either the principal or the agent liable; they are not both liable.

Just when the third person has made an election as to whether to pursue his or her rights under the contract and hold the agent liable or recognize the agency and hold the undisclosed principal liable will depend, primarily, on the circumstances of each case. Obviously, the third person cannot make an election until he or she learns of the existence of the agency and knows the identity of the principal. If the agent or the principal has fully performed the contract, the third person will have no occasion to make an election. If the contract is not fully performed, the third person may, under the majority rule, proceed against the principal.

Some courts have held that if the third person has brought suit against the agent and obtained a judgment against the agent before the third person learns of the agency, he or she may elect to abandon a judgment against the agent and bring suit against the principal. If the third person knows of the agency and the identity of the principal at the time suit is brought and it is brought against the agent, this is strong evidence that an election has been made.

There is a conflict in the decisions as to the third person's rights against an undisclosed principal who has settled accounts with his or her agent. The better rule is that the undisclosed principal remains liable to the third person regardless of the fact that the principal has settled accounts with the agent. However, this would not be true if the third person, after learning of the existence of the agency and the identity of the principal, follows a course of action which justifies the principal in believing that the third person intends to hold only the agent, and the principal then, in reliance on such course of action, settles with the agent. This rule is supported by the argument that the principal stands to benefit from the transaction, and further that the principal selected the agent and has an opportunity to gain protection through bonding or other devices not open to the third person.

The third person can set off against the principal claims the third person has against the agent if the agent was authorized not to reveal the existence of the principal. This is in addition, of course, to the third person's right to set off claims he or she has against the principal.

Scope of Liability of Undisclosed Principal. The liability of an undisclosed principal for the transactions of the agent is the same as that of a disclosed principal where the acts of the agent are authorized. However, an undisclosed principal runs a greater risk that the agent will bind him or her on transactions exceeding the principal's authority because the principal is unable to put a third person on notice of limitations on the authority of the agent. If the agent is a general agent, the undisclosed principal is liable for acts done on his account if usual or necessary in conducting the business entrusted to the agent even if the acts are forbidden by the principal. For example, if Prindle does not wish to be disclosed and appoints Agnew to manage a retail food business, Agnew will bind Prindle on groceries purchased on credit from Terman even though Prindle instructed Agnew to buy only for cash and specifically not to buy from Terman.

Rights of Undisclosed Principal. The undisclosed principal is given substantially the same rights in a transaction negotiated by an agent as is given an assignee or beneficiary of a contract. The undisclosed principal takes the rights subject to all the outstanding equities as they exist at the time the third person learns of the existence of the agency and the identity of the principal. That is, he takes the transaction subject to all defenses, such as setoff, counterclaims, and payment, which the third person would have against the agent had the agent brought suit on the contract at the time the third person learned of the agency and the identity of the principal.

Summary

A principal is undisclosed if both the existence of the agency and the identity of the principal are unknown to the third person. When the third person who has entered a transaction with the agent of an undisclosed principal discovers the existence of the agency and identifies the principal he or she may elect to hold either the agent or the principal. Under the majority rule the principal remains liable even after settling accounts with the agent unless the third person by conduct, justifiably relied upon, has led the principal to believe that the third person intends to hold the agent instead of the principal.

An undisclosed principal may be liable for unauthorized, as well as authorized, acts of the agent provided such unauthorized acts are done for the account of the principal and are usual or necessary for carrying out the transaction entrusted to the agent.

Howell v. Smith

134 S.E.2d 381 (Sup. Ct. N.C. 1964)

This was an action by Hubert M. Howell (plaintiff) against Herbert Smith (defendant) to recover a judgment for petroleum products sold. Smith set up as a defense that the petroleum products were sold to the Atlantic Building Block Company, Inc. Judgment for Howell and Smith appealed. Judgment affirmed.

Howell sold petroleum to A. J. Marlow, trading as Atlantic Building Block Company. Marlow sold the business to Smith, who was introduced to Howell as the purchaser of the business, and Howell continued to sell petroleum products to Smith. Smith incorporated the business but Howell was not notified that it had been incorporated, and he continued to carry the account in the name of Atlantic Building Block Company and to make out invoices in that name. Several checks given in payment of invoices were signed "Atlantic Building Block Company, Inc.," and were signed by Smith, but he did not indicate that he was signing the checks in a representative capacity. When sued, Smith set up as his defense that he was acting as agent for Atlantic Building Block Company, Inc., and that this was known to Howell.

SHARP, JUSTICE.   An agent who makes a contract for an undisclosed principal is personally liable as a party to it unless the other party had actual knowledge of the agency and of the principal's identity. The disclosure of the agency is not complete so as to relieve the agent of personal liability unless it embraces the name of the principal. The duty is on the agent to make this disclosure and not upon the third person with whom he is dealing to discover it. It will not relieve the agent from personal liability that the person with whom he dealt had means of discovering that the agent was acting as such. . . . . The cases are in substantial accord that the use of a trade name is not as a matter of law a sufficient disclosure of the identity of the principal and the fact of agency.

The liability of the agent is not exclusive. When the principal becomes known, the other party to the contract may elect whether he will resort to him or to the agent with whom he dealt unless the contract is under seal, a negotiable instrument, or expressly excludes him. Ordinarily, however, it is an alternative liability. The principal and agent are not jointly liable unless the agent has, by contract or by his conduct, added his own liability to that of the principal. It is competent for an agent, although fully authorized to bind his principal, to pledge his own personal responsibility instead. The aggrieved party seeking damages must elect whether he will hold the principal or the agent liable; he cannot hold both.

The right of the third party to sue the agent is not impaired by a discovery of the identity of the principal after the contract was made. The disclosure of the principal comes too late to discharge the agent after the third party has extended credit, performed services, or entered upon the performance of an indivisible contract.

Liability on Special Transactions

Basis of Liability.   In transactions negotiated by an agent, the basis of the principal's liability is the authority of the agent. It is sometimes difficult to determine the scope of this authority, even though it is set out in writing. The nature of the business entrusted to the agent, standard practices of business, and the circumstances surrounding the transaction will be considered in determining the scope of an agent's authority, both implied and apparent. The third person is bound by notice or knowledge of limitations on the agent's authority and has the burden of proving that the agent had authority to bind the principal.

Presumptions as to an agent's authority or lack of authority in relation to certain common types of transactions have been developed by the courts. Such presumptions apply only in the absence of credible evidence as to the agent's actual authority or lack of authority.

Liability for Agent's Representations.   In the ordinary course of transacting business, statements and representations relative to the business at hand will be made by the negotiators. An agent has implied authority to make such statements and representations as are reasonably necessary to accomplish the objective of the agency, and has apparent authority to make such statements and representations as are usual and customary in the transaction of the business entrusted to the agent. If the principal has instructed the agent not to make certain statements and representations, or has informed him or her of defects in goods entrusted to him or her for sale, but the agent, in violation of instructions or in violation of his or her duty not to misrepresent, makes the statements and representations he or she has been instructed not to make, or represents the goods as free from defects, the principal will be bound if the statements and representations are within the scope of the agent's apparent authority, and if the third person has no notice or knowledge of the limitations on the agent's authority or of the violation by the agent of his or her instructions.

A third person has the right to rescind a contract into which he or she has entered in reliance on false representations made by the agent. According to the better view, this is true despite the use of what is sometimes referred to as an "exculpatory clause" in the contract. Many businessmen, in seeking to avoid liability for misrepresentations of salesmen (as well as to control the contract price), adopt the practice of limiting their salesmen to soliciting written offers from their customers on preprinted forms which must be accepted by them as principal in order to complete the sales contract. The offer form includes a clause which specifically states that the salesman has no authority to make oral representations and that only such representations as appear on the offer form in writing will be binding.

Courts have tended to take the view that even though the seller has done all he or she reasonably can in such a case to give notice to the customer of the limitation on the agent's authority, it would be unjust to permit the principal to enjoy the benefit of a misrepresentation and yet disclaim responsibility for it. A few recent cases have even permitted the buyer to recover damages for fraudulent misrepresentations of the agent despite such an exculpatory clause.[1]

---

[1] See, for example, *Brunswick Corp. v. Sittason,* 167 So.2d 126 (Ala. 1964).

Liability for Agent's Warranties. A principal is liable for warranties made by his or her agent in a sale of goods if such a warranty is customarily made on such goods in the market in which the goods are sold. The principal is also liable on warranties made by the agent which are no more extensive than those implied by law. The principal is not liable on an unauthorized warranty which is unusual or extraordinary in nature. The third person is bound by any limitations or instructions given the agent of which the third person has knowledge or notice.

Liability for Payment to Agent. The fact that an agent has negotiated a transaction does not, as a matter of law, confer on the agent the authority to collect. Such authority arises when it is the usual and reasonable incident of the business to be transacted. As in other cases, it may be shown that the agent has express, implied, or apparent authority to collect; but as a general rule, authority to sell does not confer on the agent authority to collect or receive payment. A sales agent who has authority to solicit orders for future delivery does not thereby have the authority to collect the purchase price of the goods. However, it is generally held that if the selling agent has possession of the goods, he has implied authority to collect the purchase price of goods sold. Also, it is generally held that an agent making over-the-counter sales has authority to collect. Usage of trade, course of dealing, or the acts of the principal may confer on the agent authority to collect.

Possession of an instrument evidencing the debt is strong, yet not conclusive, evidence of authority to collect. If the agent has negotiated a loan, sold property, or transacted other similar business for the principal and has received from the third person a negotiable instrument payable to the principal, the agent has apparent authority to receive payment and discharge the instrument if the principal permits the agent to retain possession of the instrument. However, in several cases the courts have held that payment to the agent before the due date does not discharge the debt. If the agent has not been permitted to retain the instrument evidencing an indebtedness, the third person is put on notice that the agent does not have authority to collect.

Liability for Credit Contracted by Agent. The agent, in the absence of express authority, will not have authority to purchase on the principal's credit. This rule is not absolute. If the agency is general, and if, in order to carry out the purpose of the agency, it becomes necessary for the agent to borrow money or purchase goods on the principal's credit, the principal will be bound. If the principal has held the agent out as having authority to borrow money or purchase goods on his or her credit or has knowingly permitted the agent to borrow money or purchase goods on his or her credit, the principal will be bound.

If the agent is given money by the principal to purchase goods and the third person accepts the agent's personal check without knowledge that the principal has furnished funds to pay for the goods, the third person cannot recover from the principal if the check is not honored. If the agent is authorized to purchase the goods but is not furnished the money with which to pay for the goods, the agent will have implied authority to purchase on the credit of the principal.

Liability on Negotiable Instruments.   The negotiable instrument is given a separate and distinct place in the business world. The nature of the negotiable instrument and the liability of the parties to it are such that the authority to sign, or to endorse and negotiate, or to cash such instruments is sparingly conferred on an agent, unless the agent represents a corporation.

Express authority to sign or endorse negotiable instruments is strictly construed and will not be enlarged by interpretation. The authority to sign or endorse negotiable instruments will not be implied unless the nature of the business entrusted to the agent is such that it cannot be effectively carried on without the signing or endorsing of negotiable instruments. An authorization "to transact any and all business" does not expressly or impliedly authorize the agent to sign or endorse negotiable instruments unless such acts are essential to the carrying-on of the business entrusted to him or her.

Only in exceptional cases will the courts hold that an agent has apparent authority to sign or endorse negotiable instruments. The fact that an agent is given a special title, such as president, secretary, treasurer, general manager, or cashier of a corporation, does not as a general rule give him or her apparent authority to sign or endorse negotiable instruments in the name of the corporation. A member of a partnership has the authority, under partnership law, to sign or endorse negotiable instruments in the partnership name, unless such authority is withheld by the terms of the partnership agreement.

Summary

Where the scope of the agent's authority is not specified or is ambiguous, the law makes certain presumptions as follows: generally the principal is liable for representations of his or her agent which are reasonably necessary to accomplish the objective of the agency or are customary in the transaction of such business, provided they are relied upon by the third person. The third person has the right to rescind a transaction where misrepresentations are made even if they were unauthorized or expressly forbidden by the principal.

The principal is bound by the warranties made by a selling agent, provided they are of the nature usually made in the trade, but the principal is not liable for unusual warranties made by the agent.

Authority to sell does not confer on the agent authority to collect the purchase price. Authority to make a loan does not imply authority to accept payment and discharge the debt when the loan falls due. If negotiable paper is left in the hands of the agent, it is evidence of authority to accept payment on the due date, but it is not evidence of authority to accept payment before the due date.

As a general rule an agent does not have authority to pledge his principal's credit. Such authority is not implied unless there is a clear necessity for such action. Nor does the agent have authority to sign or endorse negotiable instruments in the principal's name unless the authority is express or unless the nature of the business entrusted to the agent is such that it is necessary to sign or endorse negotiable instruments in order to transact the business. A strong case is necessary to establish apparent authority to sign or endorse negotiable instruments.

Harnischfeger Sales Corp. v. Coats

48 P.2d 662 (Sup. Ct. Calif. 1935)

This was an action by Harnischfeger Sales Corporation (plaintiff) against E. C. Coats (defendant) to recover the balance due on a conditional sales contract. Judgment for Harnischfeger Sales Corporation and Coats appealed. Judgment reversed.

Coats entered into a conditional sale contract for the purchase of a power shovel from Harnischfeger Sales Corporation (Harnischfeger). The contract was negotiated by an agent of Harnischfeger and contained the following provision: "This agreement shall not be considered as executed, and shall not become effective until accepted by the vendee, and executed and approved by the president, or vice president or secretary of the vendor, and it is hereby further declared, agreed and understood that there are no prior writings, verbal negotiations, understandings, representations or agreements between the parties, not herein expressed." Coats, when sued, set up that the agent induced him to execute the contract by making fraudulent representations, and he counterclaimed for tort damages for the fraud. The jury brought in a verdict in favor of Coats on his counterclaim for $2,500. The court set the verdict aside and gave judgment for Harnischfeger for the full amount of its claim.

LANGDON, JUSTICE. It seems clear that this stipulation limits the authority of the agent to make representations, and purports to absolve the principal from all responsibility therefor. The question is whether such a stipulation may be given effect.

This problem was the subject of conflicting decisions in California until recently, when this court, in *Speck v. Wylie* announced the governing rule. It was there held that an innocent principal might by such a stipulation protect himself from liability in a tort action for damages for fraud and deceit, but that the third party would nevertheless be entitled to rescind the contract. This is the rule declared in the *Restatement of the Law of Agency,* §§ 259 and 260. The distinction between the two situations is a sound one. The principal would normally be liable in tort for misrepresentations by an agent acting within the scope of his actual or ostensible authority, and by stipulating in the contract that the agent has no such authority, the principal has done all that is reasonably possible to give notice thereof to the third party. Under such circumstance the innocent principal may justly be relieved of liability for the agent's wrong. But where the principal sues to recover on the contract, he is seeking to benefit through the agent's fraud. This he cannot be permitted to do. His personal liability may be avoided, but the fraudulently procured contract is subject to rescission.

In the instant case, the counterclaim, which seeks the affirmative relief of damages, is objectionable for the same reason that an independent tort action would be. However, the principle followed in *Speck v. Wylie,* supra, warrants relief for fraud whether the injured party sets it up in an affirmative action for rescission, or as defensive relief in an action by the other party to enforce the contract; that is to say, the right of the aggrieved buyer to rescission exists regardless of which party initiates the proceeding on the contract. That the buyer may set up a claim for rescission in the seller's action has recently been held by the District Court of Appeal. The defensive relief must not be such as to subject the plaintiff to affirmative liability for damages; nor would it be proper, under the rule just discussed, to permit an award of damages to offset liability for the balance of the purchase price. Coats's relief is limited to rescission of the contract. Hence the affirmative verdict in favor of Coats on his counterclaim for damages is improper; but Coats may be entitled, because of the fraud, to be placed in *statu quo,* by restoration of the consideration or its equivalent by both parties.

Navrides v. Zurich Insurance Co.

488 P.2d 637 (Sup. Ct. Cal. 1971)

This was an action by Audrey Navrides (plaintiff) against Zurich Insurance Company (defendant) to recover the proceeds of a check in settlement of her tort claim which had been paid to her attorney. Judgment for Navrides and the insurer appealed. Judgment reversed.

Audrey Navrides had been injured on the premises of one Crancer who was insured by the Zurich Insurance Company. She employed an attorney, Robert S. Forsyth, who filed an action for damages on her behalf. Forsyth negotiated with Zurich a compromise settlement of the claim. Miss Navrides rejected the settlement of $9,000 but Forsyth represented to Zurich that she had approved it. Zurich then submitted to Forsyth for signature a release of all claims, a request for the dismissal of the pending action and a draft for $9,000 payable to Navrides and Forsyth. Forsyth retained the draft and returned the release, purportedly signed by Navrides, together with the request for dismissal. The latter document was then filed and the action dismissed. Three days later the settlement draft, bearing the purported endorsements of Navrides and Forsyth, was cashed and in due course charged to Zurich's bank account in Chicago.

Miss Navrides' signature on the draft and on the release were forgeries by Forsyth, and she received none of the settlement money. About a year later she discovered that her personal injury action had been dismissed and the draft had been delivered to her attorney. She was unable to recover from him and then filed an action against Zurich.

SULLIVAN, JUSTICE. The trial court's conclusion that plaintiff's signature on the draft was a forgery is amply supported by the findings and the evidence. Unfortunately, however, the court nowhere indicates any legal theory explaining its leap from its findings and first conclusion of law to its second conclusion that Zurich owed plaintiff $9,000 plus interest. It is a fair assumption that the trial judge, relying on former Civil Code section 3104, concluded that the forged endorsement was wholly inoperative and that as a consequence Zurich still owed plaintiff $9,000.

Although Forsyth clearly had no authority, express or implied, to compromise plaintiff's claim, the record before us establishes as a matter of law that plaintiff, by bringing the instant action against Zurich for the $9,000, ratified the settlement. . . .

It is well settled that a client may ratify the unauthorized actions of his attorney (citations); that a principal may ratify the forgery of his signature by his agent (citations); and that a principal may ratify the unauthorized act of an agent by bringing suit based thereon (citation).

By virtue of such ratification, there then existed between plaintiff and Zurich a *valid* compromise agreement which was fully performed on the part of plaintiff by Forsyth's delivery of the release and dismissal to Zurich. The true and indeed only tenable theory of plaintiff's action thus emerges: that Zurich owes her $9,000 under the settlement agreement and that she has not been paid. . . . However, inherent in the ratification of the settlement is ratification of Forsyth's authority to settle the claim, which, as we explain, *infra,* necessarily includes authority to receive and collect the payment of the settlement on behalf of plaintiff.

Unfortunately for plaintiff, she cannot stop at this point. She must reckon with the elementary rule of agency law that a principal is not allowed to ratify the unauthorized acts of an agent to the extent that they are beneficial, and disavow them to the extent that they are damaging. If a principal ratifies part of a transaction, he is deemed to ratify the whole of it (citations). The reason for the rule is obvious. Ratification is approval of a transaction that has already taken place. Accordingly the principal has the power to approve the transaction only as it in fact occurred, not to reconstruct it to suit his present needs.

* * * * *

The foregoing authorities support the now-settled rule that where an agent authorized to collect a debt owing his principal accepts in lieu of cash a valid check *payable to the agent,* the debtor is discharged upon payment of the check, although the agent absconds with the proceeds, since payment to the agent is equivalent to payment to the principal. . . .

The crucial question presented to us in the instant case is whether the above rule applies where the attorney receives a check payable to the *client* or to the *client* and the *attorney together.*

* * * * *

Zurich argues, a proper correlation of these competing principles is found in section 178 of the *Restatement Second of Agency* the effect of which is to relieve the maker where the payee's endorsement has been forged by his agent authorized to receive the check.

* * * * *

The twofold justification for this rule, which amply demonstrates its wisdom, is best articulated in two similar cases. In *Burstein v. Sullivan* (1909), one Melle, the general manager of a garage, had authority to render bills and receive payments, but not to sign checks. He presented a bill to defendant, who delivered to the manager a check payable to the garage for the amount of the bill. Melle endorsed the check by using a rubber stamp of the firm's name in connection with which he signed his name as manager. The court said: "A payment to Melle in cash would have been a payment to the plaintiff's though he had stolen the money; and the defendant should not be compelled to pay twice, or subjected to the hazard of a lawsuit with the bank, for having taken the precaution to protect the plaintiffs by making a check payable to their order. . . ."

In *McFadden v. Follrath* (1911) the court explained the justification for this rule in terms of business practice and its need for negotiable paper. "It would be a novel burden if the drawer of a check given in the usual course of business, to the authorized agent of the payee, upon such check being indorsed by such agent, were charged with the duty of determining that the indorsement on the check was authorized."

* * * * *

The rule articulated by the line of authority of which the foregoing decisions are a part has been expressly adopted in the *Restatement Second of Agency.* Section 178(2) thereof provides: "If an agent who is authorized to receive a check payable to the principal as conditional payment forges the principal's endorsement to such a check, the maker is relieved of liability to the principal if the drawee bank pays the check and charges the amount to the maker."

Notice to or Knowledge of Agent

Effect of Notice to Agent. Generally, notice to the agent is notice to the principal if the information acquired by the agent relates to the business that he or she is transacting for the principal. The duty to communicate to the principal with respect to matters coming to the agent's notice which are within the scope of the agency and material to the principal for protection or guidance is imposed on the agent by law for reasons of public policy. If the agent fails to perform his duties, the principal rather than the innocent third person should bear any resulting loss. The agent is not required to communicate to the principal every rumor or detailed fact which comes to the agent's notice, regardless of the reliability of the source. Notice to the agent of matters not within the scope of the agency is not binding on the principal unless the agent does in fact communicate it to the principal.

Knowledge of Agent. Knowledge of the agent includes knowledge gained in transactions for the principal and knowledge which, by the exercise of reasonable prudence, the agent should have obtained. Knowledge of facts material to the agency gained during the transaction of business unrelated to the agency may be imputed to the principal if it was present in the mind of the agent and used to the advantage of the principal during the agency. Of course, the agent has no duty to disclose confidential information obtained while serving another principal. Knowledge gained by the agent after the termination of the agency is not binding on the principal unless the agency is a continuing one. In such a case the principal will be bound by notice given to the agent by a third person who has dealt with the agent during the agency and at the time he or she gave the notice was unaware of the termination of the agency.

Limitations on the Rule. The rule does not apply in those situations in which it is clear that the agent would not communicate the knowledge to the principal. The courts have held that if the agent's interests conflict with the interests of the principal and the agent's interests will be furthered by not communicating a fact to the principal, the principal will not be bound by the knowledge of the agent. If, however, an innocent third person will be injured if the principal is not bound by the uncommunicated knowledge of the agent, the courts will hold that the principal is bound. If the agent and the third person collusively or fraudulently withhold knowledge from the principal, the principal will not be bound.

Under this rule the knowledge of the agent is imputed to the principal; hence the principal's knowledge is constructive, not actual. The principal cannot be held criminally liable where knowledge is an essential element of the crime if the agent has not communicated such knowledge to the principal and the principal does not have actual knowledge.

Summary

Notice of facts given to the agent regarding business being transacted by the agent for the principal is binding on the principal. Notice of facts given to the agent regarding matters unconnected with the business entrusted to the agent is not binding on the principal unless communicated to him or her. Knowledge of the agent, at the time the agent is transacting business for the principal, will be imputed to the principal.

If the agent's personal interests conflict with the duties owed to the principal, or if the agent and third person are in collusion to defraud the principal, the knowledge of the agent will not be imputed to the principal.

A principal cannot be held criminally liable for an act of an agent if knowledge is an essential element of the crime, even though the agent has knowledge but has not actually communicated that knowledge to the principal.

Southern Farm Bureau Casualty Insurance Co. v. Allen

388 F.2d 126 (5th Cir. 1967)

This was an action by Southern Farm Bureau Casualty Insurance Company (plaintiff) against Betty Allen (defendant) for a declaratory judgment that an automobile liability policy issued by it was void and that it had no liability under it. Judgment for Allen and Southern appealed. Reversed and remanded.

Southern had rejected the application for a policy by Joe Jezisek, a minor who had a record of a previous accident and two "moving violations." Jezisek then arranged to transfer the title of the automobile to his brother who was carrying insurance with Southern. The registration slip which was shown to a secretary in the office of the insurance agent showed that title had been transferred for insurance purposes. The insurance application showed that the auto would be kept in the town where Joe lived rather than where his brother lived several hundred miles away. There was testimony that the insurance agent, Wattenbarger, had suggested or at least approved the suggestion of the change of title.

The policy was issued to Joe's brother and then forwarded to Joe, who paid the premiums. Three months later Joe was involved in an accident with the auto which resulted in the death of Cecil Allen. The trial court found that the insurance agent was aware of the transaction between the Jeziseks and that this knowledge was imputed to Southern.

WISDOM, CIRCUIT JUDGE. The general rule in insurance cases and other cases, of course, is that "notice to the agent is notice to the principal." Two conditions are necessary for the application of this rule, however: (1) The agent must be acting within the scope of his authority and in reference to a matter over which his authority extends; and (2) the insured (or applicant) must not be involved with the agent, even informally, in perpetrating a fraud against the insurer.

The authorities are uniform to the effect that a principal is not affected by notice to an agent who is acting adversely to the interests of his principal, and either for his own benefit or for the benefit of a third party.

If a person colludes with an agent to cheat the principal, the latter is not responsible for the acts or knowledge of the agent. The rule which charges the principal with what the agent knows is for the protection of innocent third persons, and not those who use the agent to further their own frauds upon the principal.

The defendants (Allen) in the trial below argued, and the trial court found, that Wattenbarger actively participated in the scheme whereby paper title to the Chevrolet was transferred to George Jezisek for insurance purposes, with the insurance policy to be listed in his name, knowing that Joe Jezisek was to be the actual owner and sole operator of the vehicle. In the least, Wattenbarger is "placed in the light of having assisted in bringing about the consummation of the fraudulent transaction. . . . Such action is sufficient to constitute collusion." We therefore find Southern Farm not estopped to avoid the policy on account of its agent's knowledge.

Liability for Acts of Subagents

Appointments of Subagents. The liability of a principal for the acts of a subagent or employee (servant) will depend on the relation between the appointing agent and his or her principal. The agent may be authorized to appoint agents or employees for the principal, or the agent may have apparent authority to make such appointments. The circumstances may be such that the agent will be authorized to delegate to subagents or employees certain acts which the agent is authorized to perform for the principal. For example, the personnel officer of a corporation is authorized to appoint employees for his or her principal, the corporation. Such persons are the employees of the corporation, not of the personnel officer. Likewise, when the sales manager appoints sales agents they are the agents of the corporation. The agent of an insurance company who operates his own insurance business may appoint agents and employees to whom the agent may delegate certain functions. Such agents and employees are answerable to the agent and are not the agents or employees of the insurance company.

Liability of Principal for Acts of Subagents.   If an agent is authorized to appoint agents or employees for the principal, the persons appointed, provided the agent has acted within the scope of his or her authority, are the agents and employees of the principal and are under the principal's direct control; consequently, the principal is liable for the acts of such persons to the same extent as if the principal had made the appointments himself. In this situation the appointing agent is not liable for the acts of the appointed agents or employees unless the appointing agent has failed to exercise reasonable care and skill in selecting the appointees, in which case liability is based on failure by the agent to exercise care and skill, and is not a direct liability for the acts of the appointees. Suppose, for instance, Parker is engaged in the business of selling merchandise door to door, and she appoints Alexander as her agent and authorizes him to hire and supervise crews of door-to-door salesmen in the name of Parker. Such salesmen hired by Alexander will be the agents of Parker and will be subject to her control.

The circumstances may be such that the agent will be authorized to delegate to agents and employees of his selection certain acts required in the performance of his duties to the principal. Such appointees are the agents and employees of the original agent and as such are under his control, and he is liable for their acts. However, the original principal is liable indirectly for their acts which are done at the direction of or are delegated to them by the original agent, provided such acts are within the scope of the authority of the original agent. For example, suppose Albert is the agent of Perfect Insurance Company and he appoints Bates as his agent, authorizing him to prepare and execute insurance policies of Perfect Insurance Company in fulfillment of applications for insurance which Albert has approved. If Bates prepares and delivers a policy of insurance in the name of Perfect Insurance Company which is issued within the scope of Albert's authority, Perfect Insurance Company will be liable on the policy. But suppose Bates, when on his way to deliver the policy, operates his automobile in a negligent manner and injures a pedestrian. Perfect Insurance Company will not be liable to the injured pedestrian.

If the principal, in appointing an agent, makes the appointment in reliance on the discretion, judgment, skill, or character of the appointee, such agent cannot delegate his or her authority to a subagent or to a third person and any attempt to delegate such authority is a nullity. Acts which involve no discretion but which are ministerial in nature may, as a general rule, be delegated.

Summary

The variation in the authority to appoint subagents and employees is so great that no specific rules can be formulated. The authority to make such appointments will depend on the circumstances of the particular case. The agent may be authorized to make appointments in behalf of the principal, in which event such appointees will be under the control of the principal and will be his or her agents or employees. The agent may be authorized to perform portions of his or her duties to the principal by delegating certain functions to others. In such a situation the appointees will be the agents and employees of the original agent, and the original principal will be liable indirectly for the acts of such appointees only to the extent that they are performing delegated acts which the original agent is authorized to delegate.

An agent cannot delegate his authority if the principal has selected the agent on the basis of judgment, discretion, skill, or character. As a general rule, ministerial acts may be delegated.

Liability for Torts and Crimes

Agents Who Are Employees.   Today, most agents are employees, and thus the principal (employer) is liable for their torts committed within the scope of the employment under the doctrine of *respondeat superior.* The meaning of this very old legal doctrine is "let the master answer," and it imposes liability on the employer without fault on his part. The employer cannot escape liability by proving that he exercised the greatest of care in the selection of the employee, that the employer trained the employee in safety measures or that the employer gave the employee specific instructions not to do the act or to make the representation that was tortious.

Scope of Employment.   Whether or not a tort committed by an employee was committed within the scope of the employment is frequently a difficult question of fact. Several factors are examined in making the determination. One factor is whether the tort was committed within the time and space limits of the employment. A second factor is whether the employee was actuated, in part at least, by the purpose of serving the employer. A third is whether the act is of the same general nature as or incidental to the authorized conduct.

As a general rule, an employer is not liable for the torts committed by an employee who has abandoned his or her employment temporarily. The courts have distinguished between degrees of digression from the employment. The employer remains liable for torts committed during a mere deviation from the employment. For example, if a truck driver while making deliveries takes a one- or two-block detour and stops only briefly at the home of a friend, the employer would be liable for damages due to injuries suffered by a pedestrian resulting from negligent driving of the truck just before the trucker reaches the friend's house. However, if after the trucker arrives at the friend's house they decide to go fishing and they have started off in a new direction toward a lake at the time the pedestrian is struck, the employer would not be liable.

There is considerable diversity in the decisions as to when the employee has returned to his employment after a temporary abandonment. In the fishing trip example, some courts would hold that the driver had returned to his employment as soon as he started toward his next delivery. Others would hold that he had not returned until he was at or near a point on his original route.

Liability for Torts of Professional Agent.   A professional agent, such as a manufacturer's representative or stockbroker, is not an employee of the person for whom he or she conducts transactions. A professional agent is an agent with respect to those transactions for which he is employed by his principal. The principal is not liable for the torts of the professional agent which result from misconduct in respect to physical acts, such as negligence in driving his or her automobile, but the principal may be liable for other torts committed in the course of the negotiation of the principal's business.

Liability for Deceit of Agent.   The trend of court decisions has been toward holding the principal liable for fraudulent representations when it is usual in that trade for agents to make representations or when the agent commits the deceit while apparently acting within his or her authority unless the reliance upon the representation by the third party was unreasonable. A number of cases have held banks liable for fraudulent schemes of their officers, such as the sale of stolen negotiable bonds, perpetrated on customers of the bank even though the bank had no material connection with the scheme except for the position of the officer and the wrongful use of its name. There is, of course, no doubt that the principal is liable for any deceit which he or she directs, causes, or participates in. Likewise, if the principal ratifies an unauthorized transaction in which a tortious act occurred, the principal is liable for the tort.

Intentional Torts.   In the past, the employer was generally held not liable for an intentional physical act of an employee which was tortious, such as striking or shooting a third person, unless the employer authorized the act. However, courts today are much more likely than earlier to find an employer liable for an intentional tort. If use of force is foreseeable by the employer, this is generally sufficient for liability, and some courts let the question of scope of employment go to the jury without regard to foreseeability.

Tort Liability Is Joint and Several.   The principal or employer and the agent or employee are jointly and severally liable for the torts of the agent or employee. That is, the principal and agent or employee may be joined in the same action, or they may each be sued in a separate action. However, the injured party is entitled to only one satisfaction. When the injured party has been compensated for injuries, whether he or she recovers from the principal or from the agent or employee, there is no further right of action.

Crimes.   The older view was that an employer could not be liable for crimes committed by an employee unless the employer directed or participated in the crime at least to the extent of being an accessory. A number of recent cases have held the employer liable for crimes requiring intent where the person who did have the requisite intent was a high level managerial employee. Where no intent or knowledge of the law is required for an illegal act of an employee, liability may be imposed on the principal for statutory penalties.

Summary

The employer is liable without fault on his or her part for the torts of employees if the tort is committed within the scope of the employment. If the tortious act is committed by the employee while the employee is engaged in the performance of his or her duties and the act is viewed as aiding in some way or is incidental to the task assigned him by the employer, the employer is likely to be held liable.

The principal is not liable for tortious physical acts of a professional agent but is liable for fraudulent representations if it is customary in the trade for agents to make representations or if the agent is acting within his apparent authority. Although generally employers have not been held liable for intentional physical acts of their agents, the trend is toward finding liability more frequently.

The liability of the principal or employer for the torts of an agent or employee is joint and several.

Although generally employers have not been held liable for crimes of employees where intent is required, the trend is toward liability if the crime is committed by a high managerial employee.

Kugler v. Romain

266 A.2d 144 (Super. Ct. Ch., N.J. 1970)

This was a suit brought by Kugler, Attorney General of New Jersey (plaintiff), against Romain (defendant), doing business as Education Services Co., under the New Jersey Consumer Protection Act. Romain is enjoined from further fraud or deceptions and directed to cancel default judgments granted him on certain contracts. Recision of the contracts of those testifying in the action and penalties against Romain in the amount of $2400 are also granted. [Note: Upon appeal by Kugler, the New Jersey Supreme Court held that all consumers signing sales contracts were entitled to recover.[2]]

Romain, a member of the New York bar, conducted a book sales operation door to door in New Jersey. The sales solicitors operated in teams under the direction of a crew leader who would drive them from New York City to a New Jersey neighborhood and back each day. Their function was to take orders for a group of 15 books, including *Questions Children Ask* and four volumes of *High School Subjects Self-taught,* plus French and Spanish records and a flash-card set. The contract price was $279.95 plus $2.94 each for ten annual supplements. This was payable by a down payment of $9.00 and 24 monthly installments of $11.50. Few were sold at the cash price of $249.50. The court estimated the cost of the "package" to Romain to be $35 to $40.

Sales people were paid strictly on a commission basis, the commission on each sale varying from $16.50 to $33.00, depending upon the extent to which the following four points were satisfied: (1) securing a down payment of $9.00, (2) securing a home phone number for the customer, (3) securing a customer who is not self-employed, and (4) securing a customer who has been employed for 1½ years. The crew leader received a commission plus a $5.00 over-ride on each approved order.

Several customers testified to various fraudulent practices on the part of sales personnel. Romain and several witnesses denied that such practices were either authorized or used and alleged that the sales people were independent contractors.

MINTZ, JUDGE. I am mindful of the . . . testimony offered by the defendant and his witnesses. I simply did not believe them. I was particularly unimpressed by the testimony of Miss Florence Yeoman, a lady who has taught school for many years and who categorically denied making any misrepresentations. She still is in the defendant's employ. She impressed me as a polished, suave, over-talkative lady who would not hesitate to misrepresent in order to induce the execution of a contract.

. . . Defendant contends that he did not participate in any prohibited sales practices and that if any in fact occurred, they were committed by independent contractors. He argues that he cannot be responsible for their acts. Alternatively, defendant asserts that if the sales personnel were his agents, they were not authorized to misrepresent and therefore he cannot be held accountable.

I am satisfied that the sales representatives were defendant's agents. The contention that they were independent contractors is without merit. The sales people were employed by defendant for the sole purpose of representing him in transactions arising out of his business. They made no investment of capital incident to a separate business and assumed no financial business risks. An agency relationship must be determined in the light of the totality of the facts. The form contract used by defendant shows a recognition of defendant's responsibility in that the name of defendant Educational Service Company, with its address and phone number, appears on its heading. The sales personnel sign the contracts as "representatives" of defendant. The absence of direct

---

[2] 279 A.2d 640 (1971).

control over the sales representatives regarding the manner in which they solicit business is insignificant in the overall view of the circumstances.

Defendant denies authorizing the sales personnel to engage in any fraudulent practices. A principal is accountable for the authorized acts of his agent and for any acts which he may have ratified. The testimony indicates that defendant was apprised of the misrepresentations committed by two of his key sales representatives, Miss Florence Yeoman and a Martin Gross. He took no affirmative action against them. Also, in some instances defendant personally applied pressure tactics in attempting to make collections after being informed of the consumers' complaints. While I am mindful of the testimony that at no time did defendant instruct his representatives to misrepresent, I am satisfied that the vast number of complaints received from consumers and the resistance to his demands for payment (defendant initiated suit in approximately 70 percent of the contracts with New Jersey consumers) made him fully aware of the repeated fraudulent practices.

. . . Alternatively, as to the vast majority of purchasers who have paid moneys to Romain, I find that he has ratified those transactions and is responsible for them. Defendant cannot escape responsibility if he accepts and retains the "fruits" of the fraud.

Lange v. National Biscuit Co.

211 N.W.2d 783 (Sup. Ct. Minn. 1973)

This was an action by Lange (plaintiff) against National Biscuit Company (defendant) for damages resulting from an assault upon him by an employee of Nabisco. Appeal from a decision granting judgment for Nabisco notwithstanding a jury verdict for Lange. Reversed.

Lange was the manager of a small grocery store. Lynch was hired by Nabisco as a cookie salesman-trainee in October 1968, and in March 1969 was assigned his own territory which included Lange's store. Between March 1 and May 1 Nabisco received numerous complaints from grocers served by Lynch that Lynch was overly aggressive and that he was taking shelf space reserved for competing cookie companies.

On May 1 while Lynch was stocking Lange's shelves with Nabisco products an argument developed between them over Lynch's activities in the store. Lynch became very angry and started swearing. Lange told Lynch either to stop swearing or leave the store, as children were present. Lynch then became uncontrollably angry, saying, "I ought to break you neck." He went behind the counter and dared Lange to fight. Lange refused, whereupon Lynch proceeded to assault him viciously. Upon completion of the assault, Lynch proceeded to throw merchandise around the store and then left.

Todd, Justice.   There is no dispute with the general principle that in order to impose liability on the employer under the doctrine of respondeat superior it is necessary to show that the employee was acting within the scope of his employment. Unfortunately, there is a wide disparity in the case law in the application of the "scope of employment" test to those factual situations involving intentional torts. The majority rule as set out in *Annotation,* 34 A.L.R. 2d 372, 402, includes a twofold test: (a) Whether the assault was motivated by business or personal considerations; or (b) whether the assault was contemplated by the employer or incident to the employment.

Under the present Minnesota Rule, liability is imposed where it is shown that the employee's acts were motivated by a desire to further the employer's business. Therefore, a master could only be held liable for an employee's assault in those rare instances where the master actually requested the servant to so perform, or the servant's duties were such that that motivation was implied in law.

*   *   *   *   *

Respondeat superior or vicarious liability is a principle whereby responsibility is imposed on the master who is not directly at fault. Its derivation lies in the public policy to satisfy an instinctive sense of justice. It has been explained most frequently under the "entrepreneur theory." This justification holds that an employer, knowing that he is liable for the torts of his servants, can and should consider this liability as a cost of his business. He may then avoid the cost by insuring against such contingencies, or by adjusting his prices so that his patrons must bear part, if not all, of the burden of insurance. In this way, losses are spread and the shock of the accident is dispersed. A secondary consideration lies in the fact that an employer, knowing that he is responsible, will be alert to prevent the occurrence of such injuries.

In developing a test for the application of respondeat superior when an employee assaults a third person, we believe that the focus should be on the basis of the assault rather than the motivation of the employee. We reject as the basis for imposing liability the arbitrary determination of when, and at what point, the argument and assault leave the sphere of the employer's business and become motivated by personal animosity. Rather, we believe the better approach is to view both the argument and assault as an indistinguishable event for purposes of vicarious liability. . . .

Attempts, in cases where altercations arise, to distinguish the doctrine of respondeat superior on the theory that at some point the argument becomes personal and not related to the scope of employment are unduly restrictive and attribute to the employee, enraged by reason of his employment, a rational decision, that he is crossing some imaginary line to pursue personal business. Whether the nature and character of the dispute change from a work-related incident to a personal assault, and, if so, when they do, is not dispositive of the issue.

We hold that an employer is liable for an assault by his employee when the source of the attack is related to the duties of the employee and the assault occurs within work-related limits of time and place. The assault in this case obviously occurred within work-related limits of time and place, since it took place on authorized premises during working hours. The precipitating cause of the initial argument concerned the employee's conduct of his work. In addition, the employee originally was motivated to become argumentative in furtherance of his employer's business. Consequently, under the facts of this case we hold as a matter of law that the employee was acting within the scope of employment at the time of the aggression and that Lange's post-trial motion for judgment notwithstanding the verdict on that ground should have been granted under the rule we herein adopt. To the extent that our former decisions are inconsistent with the rule now adopted, they are overruled.

Among other states which have abandoned the "motivation test" and allow recovery for assaults arising out of or ancillary to the work being done by the employee are Mississippi, California, Kentucky, Illinois, Alabama, Connecticut, and Montana.

Problem Cases

1. Leahy, who was a shareholder and director of Multi-Krome Corporation, loaned $1,000 to the corporation. The note bore the stamped name of the corporation, and immediately below were the signatures of C. E. McManus, Jr., and C. E. Delauney without any indication that they signed in a representative capacity. By resolution of the board of directors, checks and notes of the corporation were to be signed by McManus, who was chairman of the board, and Delauney, the treasurer. The corporation became insolvent and Leahy sued McManus individually. McManus defended on the ground that he signed in a representative capacity and that this was known by Leahy. Is McManus liable?

2. Oswald wished to purchase a block of lots from Holding Company, but it would not sell the lots to him. Oswald later induced Chapin to purchase the lots for him. The lots were to be purchased by Chapin in his own name and were to be conveyed to Oswald at some later date. Oswald authorized Chapin to pay $51,000 for the lots. Chapin contracted to pay $51,000 for the lots and, in addition, contracted to pay for the street improvements to be made by Holding Company. The street improvements were made but not paid for. Holding Company learned that Oswald was the undisclosed principal of Chapin and sued Oswald to recover a judgment for the street improvements. Oswald set up as a defense that he did not authorize Chapin to contract to pay the street improvements. Is Oswald liable for the cost of the street improvements?

3. Letbetter purchased merchandise from a salesman representing United Laboratories, Inc. The contract of sale expressly provided that no representations of the salesman should be binding upon the seller unless written into the order. It contained a recital that the seller expressly denied liability and assumed no responsibility for the application or resale of the material purchased on the order. The salesman made representations regarding the suitability of the materials for certain uses but the materials were not suitable for the purposes as represented. The representations were not included in the sales orders. Letbetter refused to pay for the materials and when sued set up the representations of the salesman as a defense. United Laboratories contends that the representations were not authorized, that Letbetter had notice of the lack of authority and that it is not bound by the representations. Is United Laboratories bound by the salesman's representations?

4. Kjome, a sales agent for Arntson, sold 200 gallons of Shell Oil Company's Weed Killer No. 20 to Start, a commercial grower of lily bulbs. At the time of the transaction Start had told Kjome that he wanted a weed killer for use on a field in which he had planted lily bulblets. Kjome expressly warranted that the weed killer could be used safely on the field. However, when applied the weed killer killed most of the bulblets. When sued for damages on breach of warranty, Arntson's defense was that Kjome had no authority to warrant the product. Is Arntson liable on the warranty?

5. Gray Lumber Company engaged Wetherbee to manage its planing mill and commissary and to haul logs from the woods to the sawmill and lumber from the sawmill to the planing mill. He was paid $100 per month and a stipulated price per 1,000 feet for logs and lumber hauled. Wetherbee purchased from Motor Company on the credit of Gray Lumber Co., a truck and

also parts and supplies for the truck which was to be used in hauling logs and lumber. Wetherbee had no express authority to purchase on the credit of Gray Lumber Co. Is Gray Lumber Co. liable to Motor Co. for the purchase price of the truck, parts, and supplies?

6. Wagner, who was president of Wagner Trading Company, a corporation, endorsed 15 checks payable to the order of Wagner Trading Co. by writing thereon "Wagner Trading Co., C. J. Wagner, Pres.," and deposited them in his personal account in Park Bank. Wagner Trading Co. sued Park Bank for the value of the checks. Wagner Trading Co. claims that Wagner had no authority to endorse the checks and deposit them in his personal account. Is Park Bank liable?

7. Beane Plumbing Company had been employed to make a hookup to the city water system. Sandman, an employee of the city water works came to the job to inspect the refilling of the excavation of the water main. He jumped down into the excavation to show Brunssen, one of Beane's employees, that the filling had been done improperly. An argument developed and Sandman hit Brunssen. Another of Beane's employees, who had been shoveling dirt into the hole, then injured Sandman by striking him on the head with a shovel. Is Beane liable for the harm done to Sandman?

8. Mr. and Mrs. Rubin purchased a five-acre tract, zoned commercial in Scottsdale, Arizona, from Mr. and Mrs. Jerger for $125,000. During the negotiations Stamper, the realtor acting for the Jergers, told the Rubins that the purchase would be particularly attractive because Shell Oil Company had agreed to purchase a corner of the property for $75,000 but that for tax reasons the Jergers needed to sell the entire five acres as a unit. He told the Rubins that the Shell purchase would be closed "back-to-back" with their purchase of the tract. The purchase by the Rubins was completed in June and the down payment of $36,250 was paid. The Rubins inquired several times of Stamper concerning the status of the Shell Oil purchase. He advised them that he believed he could obtain $85,000 and so had not closed the deal. In January the Rubins told him to accept the original offer of $75,000. He then advised them that Shell decided not to buy the property because of a Scottsdale sign ordinance but that he had another purchaser at $65,000. When this sale fell through the Rubins contacted another realtor who requested Stamper to show him his files concerning the property. They did not show evidence of any negotiations with Shell, and Shell denied ever having any interest in or negotiating with respect to the property.

   The Rubins brought an action for rescission on grounds of Stamper's misrepresentation as the Jerger's agent. The Jergers had not authorized and were unaware of the misrepresentation. Are the Rubins entitled to rescission?

9. Saxton was employed by Better Maid Dairy Products to deliver its products to various retail food stores including Brazelton Brothers, Inc. Better Maid had installed a large cooler in Brazelton's and assumed responsibility for keeping it stocked. It furnished Saxton books of invoice blanks on which to record the quantities of items delivered to its customers and authorized him to collect on those invoices. For a period of two years Saxton presented invoices which were paid by Brazelton for daily deliveries in excess of the capacity of the cooler. Other invoices were presented by Saxton and paid by Brazelton when no products had been delivered. Upon discovery of the shortages it was determined from the records of Brazelton and Better Maid that the loss to Brazelton was at least $28,000. When Better Maid failed to pay this sum, Brazelton sued. Can it recover?

chapter 17

Relation of Agent to Third Person

Liability on Authorized Contracts

Disclosed Principal. An agent who is acting for a disclosed principal and who acts within the scope of his or her authority and in the name of the principal is ordinarily not liable on the contract he or she makes. If the agent expressly or impliedly makes himself a party thereto or contracts to act as surety for the principal, the agent becomes liable on the contract. The fact that the agent, in the negotiation of the contract, uses such expressions as "I will sell" or "We will buy" in negotiating a contract for the principal will not make the agent a party to the contract.

Partially Disclosed or Undisclosed Principal. If the principal is partially disclosed—that is, the existence of the agency is known to the third person but the identity of the principal is unknown—the agent is a party to the contract and liable on it. However, the third person and the agent may overcome this rule by agreement—for example that the agent is to remain liable only until he reveals the principal. Otherwise, if the agent wishes to escape liability, the agent must give such complete information concerning the principal's identity at the time of the making of the contract that the principal can be easily identified, and the agreement with the third person must clearly indicate that the agent is not to be bound.

If the principal is undisclosed, the contract is between the agent and the third person. Since the third person does not know of the existence of the agency, it is clear that the third person intended to contract with the agent, and the agent is liable on the contract. On the discovery of the existence of the agency and the identity of the principal, the third person may elect to hold the principal, as discussed in the previous chapter. The defenses available to an agent held liable on a contract are discussed later in this chapter.

363

Summary

The agent of a disclosed principal is not liable to the third person unless otherwise agreed. An agent is a party to a contract negotiated for an undisclosed principal, and, generally, the agent is a party to the contract if he or she is acting for a partially disclosed principal.

Agent's Liability on Unauthorized Contracts

General Rule. When a third person is negotiating with an agent of a disclosed principal, a third person expects and is entitled to an obligation binding on the principal. If the agent exceeds his or her authority, or if no agency exists, the principal will not be bound, in which event the third person will be injured to the extent that he does not get the benefit of an obligation binding on the principal. If the third person has acted in good faith, without notice or knowledge of the lack of authority and in justifiable reliance on the misrepresentation of authority, and if the principal has not ratified the transaction, the agent will be liable for any resulting loss.

Remedies against the Agent. If the person purporting to be acting as an agent knowingly and intentionally misrepresents his or her authority, a third person justifiably relying on the misrepresentation may recover for any resulting injury under the tort law of deceit. If the person purporting to be acting as an agent acts honestly in the mistaken belief that he has been authorized or justifiably believes the principal will ratify his acts, then a third person relying upon the misrepresentation may recover from the agent on an implied warranty of authority should the principal refuse to ratify. There is no implied warranty of authority if the parties have so agreed or if the third party knows that the agent's acts are not authorized.

If an agent who is uncertain as to the scope of his authority makes a full disclosure to the third person, the agent escapes liability. For example, if the agent shows his contract of employment or power of attorney to the third person, and the third person decides that the agent has authority to bind the principal, the agent is not liable to the third person even if, in fact, the agent does not have such authority. There is neither a misrepresentation nor a warranty as to the scope of the agent's authority.

Ratification or Knowledge of Third Person. Since ratification by the principal relates back to the time the transaction was negotiated, the relation of the parties after ratification is the same as it would have been had the agent had full authority to bind the principal at the time the transaction was negotiated. Since the principal is bound, the agent is not liable to the third person either in tort or on the theory of implied warranty.

The agent's liability to the third person is based on misrepresentation of authority by the agent, justifiably relied on by the third person. If the third person knows or, in the exercise of ordinary prudence, should know that the agent is not authorized to negotiate the transaction in behalf of the principal, the agent will not be liable to the third person, since such third person is not justified in relying on the agent's misrepresentation.

Transactions Not Binding on Principal. The courts have also held that if the principal will not be bound, even if the agent is authorized to negotiate the contract, the agent cannot be held liable. Suppose Allen, acting without authority, enters into an oral contract in the name of Plum as principal to purchase a tract of land from Turner. Turner cannot hold Allen liable if Plum refuses to carry out the contract. The contract is unenforceable under the statute of frauds because there is no note or memorandum of the agreement; and even if Allen had had authority to purchase for Plum, Plum would not have been bound.

Summary

If a person purports to act as agent for a party when he or she has no power to bind such party, the agent will become liable on the contract to the third person upon an implied warranty of authority. If the agent intentionally misrepresents the existence of the agency or the scope of his authority, he will be liable in tort for his or her deceit.

If the third person knows that the agent does not have authority, or if the agent informs the third person that he is uncertain as to the scope of his authority or reveals the facts and circumstances of the agent's authorization, the agent will not be liable to the third person for misrepresentation of the authority nor for breach of implied warranty of authority.

If the principal will not be bound by a contract which the agent has authority to negotiate, the agent will not be liable to the third person.

Killinger v. Iest

428 P.2d 490 (Sup. Ct. Idaho 1967)

Action by Gale Killinger (plaintiff) against Case Iest and A. W. Tadlock (defendants) to recover for furnishing and installing an irrigation pump. Motion for dismissal granted and Killinger appealed. Affirmed as to Iest, reversed and remanded as to Tadlock.

Iest owned a farm near Twin Falls, Idaho, and Tadlock was his tenant under an oral lease. Tadlock telephoned Killinger, who operated an electric appliance repair shop, to repair a malfunctioning irrigation pump used on the farm. The pump was taken to his shop by Killinger. The next day Tadlock went to inspect the pump which needed extensive repairs. Believing that it would take a long time to repair the pump, he decided that a new, more efficient pump should be installed immediately. At this time he informed Killinger that he was Iest's tenant but asserted that he had authority to repair the pump or to purchase a pump and that Iest would pay the agreed price.

A few days later Killinger installed a new pump and sent the bill for $2,048 to Iest. This was Iest's first knowledge of the new pump. He refused to pay and denied that Tadlock had authority to bind him on the purchase. A major expenditure for a concrete pipeline earlier installed had been ordered personally by Iest. Tadlock once had a broken shaft repaired on Iest's tractor, but Tadlock himself paid the bill without consulting Iest.

SMITH, JUSTICE.   Killinger first contends that the trial court erroneously ruled that Tadlock's declarations as to the existence and scope of his authority would not be binding on Iest, the alleged principal. That ruling was proper. The declarations of an alleged agent, standing alone, are insufficient to prove the grant of power exercised by him and to bind his principal to third parties.

The statements by the alleged agent, as to the scope of his authority, are admissible if, at the time the statements are offered in evidence, the existence of the agency has been proven by independent evidence.

Killinger adopted the position at trial that, even if Tadlock originally lacked authority to act as Iest's agent in purchasing the pump, Iest subsequently ratified the transaction by accepting and retaining benefits resulting from Tadlock's use of the pump. Killinger established that Tadlock irrigated the 1963 crops with the new pump, but Killinger nevertheless failed to prove that Iest in any way benefited from Tadlock's use of the pump. The benefits must accrue directly to the principal as the proximate result of the unauthorized transaction in order to constitute ratification by the principal.

Although the dismissal of Killinger's action against Iest was proper, the dismissal of the action against Tadlock stands upon different grounds. Killinger's evidence, particularly his own testimony, established that Tadlock had represented he had authority as Iest's agent "to make this extensive repair and improvement," "to repair the pump or purchase a pump," and to bind Iest for the agreed purchase price. The testimony of Ralph Taylor, Killinger's assistant, corroborated appellant's testimony, and this evidence remained uncontradicted through the examination of Iest and Tadlock.

A party entering into a contract in his self-assumed capacity as agent, with no actual authority from the purported principal, or in excess of an existing authority, is personally liable to the other contracting party who acted in good faith and in reliance on the false representations. The liability terminates only if the purported principal is estopped to deny the authority or subsequently ratifies the transaction.

Lack or Limitation of Capacity of Principal

Nonexistent Principal.   If an agent purports to act for a legally nonexistent principal, the agent will be personally liable as a party to the contract unless the parties expressly agree that the agent will not be liable. In that event, there is no binding contract due to lack of mutuality. A common example of an agent acting for a nonexistent principal is afforded in the case of a promoter of a corporation contracting in the name of the corporation prior to the time it receives its charter. As a general rule the promoter is personally liable on such contracts. The liability of a promoter is discussed in detail in Chapter 24.

Principal Lacking in Capacity. An agent who purports to act for a person who is wholly incompetent, such as a person who has been officially adjudged insane, is liable as a party to the contract. However, an agent acting for a person who does not have full capacity to contract, as in the case of a minor, is not liable to the third person on the contract unless the agent misrepresents or conceals the status of his or her principal's capacity. If the agent knows that the third person is unaware of the principal's lack of capacity, the agent's failure to inform the third person may amount to concealment.

Defenses Available to Agent. The defenses available to an agent who is a party to a contract will depend on the terms of the contract and the relation of the parties. In general, the agent will have all the defenses which arise out of the transaction itself, such as fraud, misrepresentation, nonperformance, payment, accord and satisfaction, infancy, and setoff, together with illegality if the third person is a party to a collusive agreement or other plan which requires or permits the agent to violate his or her fiduciary duty to his or her principal. In addition, the agent will have the defenses which are personal in nature and which exist between the agent and the third person.

If the agent is a party to a contract as surety for his or her principal, the rules of law relative to a surety's rights and duties apply in determining the agent's defenses against the third person.

Summary

A person who purports to act for a nonexistent or wholly incompetent principal is personally liable to the third person in a transaction involving such principal unless it is the understanding of the parties that the agent is not to be held liable.

If the principal lacks full capacity to contract, the agent is not liable on the contract he or she negotiates for the principal and is not liable to the third person on the contract unless the agent misrepresents the capacity of the principal or conceals the fact that the principal does not have full capacity.

As a general rule, all defenses which arise out of a transaction and all defenses, personal in nature, which exist between the agent and third person are available to the agent when sued on the contract. If the agent is a party to a contract as surety, the laws of suretyship apply in determining his or her liability to the third person.

Dixie Drive It Yourself System v. Lewis

50 S.E.2d 843 (Ct. App. Ga. 1948)

This was an action by Dixie Drive It Yourself System (plaintiff) against John G. Lewis (defendant) to recover a judgment for the damage to a rented station wagon. Judgment for Lewis and Dixie Drive It Yourself System appealed. Judgment reversed.

John G. Lewis, principal of Hapeville High School, rented two station wagons from Dixie Drive It Yourself System to be used in transporting students engaged in athletic activities. The rental contract was signed, "Hapeville High School, John G. Lewis, Principal." One of the terms of the contract was that the customer would pay for any damage which might occur to the vehicle while in his possession. During the rental of these two station wagons, a wreck occurred and damaged one of them to the extent of $400. Dixie Drive It Yourself System sued Lewis and he set up as a defense that he signed the contract as agent for Hapeville High School. The trial court held that Lewis was not liable and Dixie Drive It Yourself System appealed.

GARDNER, JUDGE.   The only question presented here for decision is whether the contract in question is the individual undertaking of Lewis. It is clear that both parties to the contract knew that the Hapeville High School had no legal entity. It could not sue or be sued. So neither Dixie Drive It Yourself System nor Lewis were misled. They were both bound by this knowledge. This is true, even though the Hapeville High School is a unit of the Fulton County school system. Therefore, as a legal entity the Hapeville High School was nonexistent. The question before us was discussed at length in *Hagan v. Asa G. Candler, Inc.* The court in that case said: "One who professes to contract as agent for another, when his purported principal is actually nonexistent, may be held personally liable on the contract, unless the other contracting party agrees to look to some other person for performance." In a similar case, *Wells v. Fay & Egan Co.*, the Supreme Court said: "If one contracts as agent, when in fact he has no principal, he will be personally liable." This court, in *Harris v. Stribling*, said: "The note sued on is signed 'Harris-Stribling Sales Company, L.S., by J. D. Stribling, L.S.' It is alleged that at the time of the execution of the note there was no such person, corporation, or other legal entity as 'Harris-Stribling Sales Company,' and that J. D. Stribling is personally liable on the note. The note, on its face, purports to have been signed by J. D. Stribling. He signed it 'Harris-Stribling Sales Company,' by himself, 'J. D. Stribling.' If 'Harris-Stribling Sales Company' is not a person or corporation or other legal entity, it is a purely fictitious name, and the note being signed by J. D. Stribling as such constitutes his individual obligation." We do not think that the decision sustains the contentions of Lewis. Upon reading the other cases relied on by Lewis, it will be found that in each of those cases there was an existing principal and legal entity. Not so in the instant case. That is the distinction. A nonexistent legal entity can have no agent. This principle was ruled very clearly in *Hagan v. Asa G. Candler, Inc.*, where the Supreme Court said: "At the time the contract was executed and at the time the suit was filed, no such corporation as Food Shops, Inc. was in existence, but this fact was unknown to the plaintiff. By reason of these facts, the contract was one between Asa G. Candler, Inc. and H. G. Hagan, individually." In that case

H. G. Hagan represented that the Food Shops, Inc. was a corporation and that he had a right to sign the contract "Food Shops, Inc., by H. G. Hagan." Under those circumstances, this court held that this was an individual undertaking of H. G. Hagan, and on *certiorari* the Supreme Court affirmed the judgment of the Court of Appeals. In view of the authorities cited and the record in the instant case, the contract was the individual undertaking of Lewis.

Agent's Liability for Torts and Crimes

General Rule.   As a general rule the fact that an agent is acting within the scope of his or her authority or at the direction of the principal does not relieve the agent from personal liability for tortious or criminal acts. An agent may escape tort liability when exercising a privilege of the principal or a privilege held by the agent for the protection of the principal. For example, if the principal has an easement of right-of-way over the land of another, the agent would not be liable to the owner of the land if the agent uses the right-of-way in carrying on the business of the principal, provided the agent does not exceed, in using the right-of-way, the principal's rights under it. The tort liability of a principal and an agent is joint and several. The injured party can recover from either but, of course, is not entitled to more than one satisfaction.

Liability for Deceit and Duress.   An agent is liable to an injured third person if the agent knowingly makes misrepresentations in the transaction of the principal's business or knowingly assists the principal or other agents of the principal in defrauding the third person. However, if the agent is innocent and does not know, and in the exercise of reasonable prudence would not know, that the representations he or she makes are false, the agent is not personally liable. For example, suppose Parker authorizes Arnold to sell his house. He tells Arnold that the house is fully insulated with rock wool when it is not. Arnold does not know that the house is not insulated, and he would not discover such fact on an ordinary inspection. If Arnold, in making a sale of the house to Thomas, tells Thomas that the house is fully insulated with rock wool, Arnold will not be liable to Thomas in an action of deceit.

In making a sale, an agent may use use sales talk and puff his principal's goods in the same manner and to the same extent as may the principal, in which case the agent is not liable to the third person for deceit.

The same general rules which apply regarding an agent's liability for deceit apply in determining the agent's liability for duress.

Liability for Conversion.   An agent is personally liable for the conversion of another's goods, and this is true even though at the time the agent takes possession of the goods he or she has reason to believe that the principal is entitled to the possession of the goods. For example, suppose Parker has loaned his plow to Thomas, and Parker tells Arnold, his employee, to get the plow. Arnold goes to Thomas' tool shed and gets a plow which he believes is Parker's plow but which really belongs to Thomas. Arnold is liable to Thomas for the conversion of the plow.

If a principal delivers to his agent for safekeeping goods which the principal has wrongfully taken from a third person, and later, the agent, without knowledge of his principal's wrongdoing, redelivers the goods to the principal, the agent is not liable to the third person for the conversion of the goods. However, if the third person gives the agent notice of the third person's right to the goods and demands the return of the goods and thereafter the agent returns the goods to the principal, the agent is liable to the third person for the conversion of the goods.

Liability for Negligence. An agent is liable to a third person for any injury the third person may suffer as a result of the negligence of the agent. If the principal furnishes the agent a defective instrument and the agent does not know and by the exercise of reasonable care would not know of the defects in the instrument, and owes no duty to third persons to discover such defects, the agent will not be liable to third persons for injuries resulting from the defects in the instrument.

Liability to Third Persons for Breach of Duty to Principal. Although courts have not been in full agreement, the trend of decisions has been to hold that agents who fail to perform their duties to their principal and thereby cause physical harm to third persons or their property are liable to them if they have relied upon the performance owed the principal. For example, a consulting engineer, employed by the owner to inspect a building, who negligently fails to find structural defects is liable to a tenant who is injured due to its collapse. Generally, courts have not held an agent liable for economic harm to others caused by a failure to perform duties owed to the principal.

A number of cases have involved accountants engaged to audit the books of a business. If the accountant is negligent in making the audit, those relying upon the audited financial statements may suffer a loss. The question is whether third parties can hold the accountant liable for their losses resulting from the accountant's errors and omissions. Earlier cases had found no liability. Later, liability was imposed if the accountant had been grossly negligent on the theory of constructive fraud. More recently a few courts have gone further and have held the professional agent liable for his or her negligence to anyone relying on his or her work who is in the class of persons or is the person for whose benefit or guidance the work was prepared. Accountants may also be held liable to third parties for failure to disclose information under the federal securities laws.[1]

---
[1] See Chapter 27.

Liability for Crimes. The fact that one is acting under instructions from his or her principal or employer does not relieve one of liability for any crime which he or she may commit. This is true whether the crime is one deriving from the common law, such as murder, assault and battery, or larceny, or a crime defined under a regulatory statute, such as price fixing under the Sherman Act. The agent or employee's duty to society overrides his duty to follow the instruction of the principal or employer. As discussed in Chapter 16, the principal directing the commission of a crime would also be liable.

Summary

An agent is liable to third persons for his or her torts, and the fact that the principal may also be liable does not relieve the agent.

The agent is liable for deceit for false representations knowingly made even though the agent does not profit personally therefrom. The agent is not personally liable for making statements which he has no reason to know are false and which are based on statements made to the agent by his principal.

An agent is liable for conversion even if he or she is following the instructions of the principal in the wrongful taking of the goods and is not aware that the act is wrongful.

An agent is liable for injury resulting from his own negligent conduct but not for injury resulting from the negligence of his principal if the agent has not been negligent.

An agent, as a general rule, is not liable to a third person for injury resulting from the agent's failure to perform a duty owed to the principal. However, professional agents such as accountants have in some instances been held liable to third persons who might be expected to and do rely on their work.

An agent is liable for his or her crimes even when they are committed under direction of the principal.

Rusch Factors, Inc. v. Levin

284 F.Supp. 85 (D.R.I. 1968)

This was an action by Rusch Factors, Inc. (plaintiff) against Leonard Levin (defendant), an accountant, to recover damages sustained as a result of alleged negligence in the preparation of financial statements. Motion to dismiss for failure to state a cause of action (and other grounds not here considered) denied.

In late 1963 and early 1964, a Rhode Island corporation sought financing from Rusch. Rusch requested certified financial statements to determine the financial condition of the company. The corporation employed Levin to prepare the statements. They represented the corporation to be solvent by a substantial amount. In fact, the corporation was insolvent. Relying on the certified statements, Rusch loaned the corporation

$337,000. Subsequently, the corporation went into receivership, resulting in a loss to Rusch of $121,000.

PETTINE, DISTRICT JUDGE.   No appellate court, English or American, has ever held an accountant liable in negligence to reliant parties not in privity. The reluctance of the courts to hold the accounting profession to an obligation of care which extends to all reasonably foreseeable reliant parties is predicated upon the social utility rationale first articulated by Judge Cardozo in the *Ultramares* case. In that case the defendant accountants were employed by a company to perform the company's yearly audit. The defendants negligently overvalued the company's assets in the balance sheet upon which the plaintiffs, creditors of the company, subsequently relied. In holding the defendant accountants free from liability for their negligence, Judge Cardozo stated:

> If liability for negligence exists, a thoughtless slip or blunder, the failure to detect a theft or forgery beneath the cover of deceptive entries, may expose accountants to a liability in an indeterminate amount for an indeterminate time to an indeterminate class. The hazards of a business conducted on these terms are so extreme as to enkindle doubt whether a flaw may not exist in the implication of a duty that exposes one to these consequences.

The wisdom of the decision in *Ultramares* has been doubted. Why should an innocent reliant party be forced to carry the weighty burden of an accountant's professional malpractice? Isn't the risk of loss more easily distributed and fairly spread by imposing it on the accounting profession, which can pass the cost of insuring against the risk on to its customers, who can in turn pass the cost onto the entire consuming public? Finally, wouldn't a rule of foreseeability elevate the cautionary techniques of the accounting profession?

This Court need not, however, hold that the Rhode Island Supreme Court would overrule the *Ultramares* decision, if presented the opportunity, for the case at bar is qualitatively distinguishable from *Ultramares*. There, the plaintiff was a member of an undefined, unlimited class of remote lenders and potential equity holders not actually foreseen but only foreseeable. Here the plaintiff is a single party whose reliance was actually foreseen by the defendant. The case at bar is, in fact, far more akin to the case of *Glanzer v. Shephard,* another Cardozo opinion and the first case to extend to persons not in privity, liability for negligent misrepresentation causing pecuniary loss. In *Glanzer* a professional weigher contracted with a bean seller to weigh a shipment of beans and certify the weight to the bean buyer. The plaintiff bean buyer paid his seller for the beans in accordance with their weight as represented by the defendant's certificate. When it turned out that the weigher had overweighed, and hence that the buyer had overpaid, the Court allowed the buyer to recover the difference from the misrepresenting weigher. In fact, the *Glanzer* principle has been applied to accountants. The tentative drafts of the *Restatement (Second) of Torts* § 552 state the rule of law as follows:

1.   One who, in the course of his business, profession or employment, or in a transaction in which he has a pecuniary interest, supplies false information for the guidance of others in their business transactions, is subject to liability for pecuniary loss caused to them by their justifiable reliance upon the information, if he fails to exercise reasonable care or competence in obtaining or communicating the information.

2. Except as stated in subsection (3), the liability stated in subsection (1) is limited to loss suffered

    a. by the person or one of the persons for whose benefit and guidance he intends to supply the information, or knows that the recipient intends to supply it; and

    b. through reliance upon it in a transaction which he intends the information to influence, or knows that the recipient so intends, or in a substantially similar transaction.

3. The liability of one who is under a public duty to give the information extends to loss suffered by any of the class of persons for whose benefit the duty is created, in any of the transactions in which it is intended to protect them.

With respect then to the plaintiff's negligence theory, this Court holds that an accountant should be liable in negligence for careless financial misrepresentations relied upon by actually foreseen and limited classes of persons. According to the plaintiff's complaint in the instant case, the defendant knew that his certification was to be used for, and had as its very aim and purpose, the reliance of potential financiers of the Rhode Island corporation. The defendant's motion is, therefore, denied. The Court does not rule upon, but leaves open for reconsideration in the light of trial development, the question of whether an accountant's liability for negligent misrepresentation ought to extend to the full limits of foreseeability.

Third Person's Liability to Agent

Agent's Right of Action on Contract. An agent who is acting for a disclosed principal and who has negotiated a contract within the scope of his or her authority and in the name of the principal has no right to bring an action in his own name against the third party to the contract to recover a judgment for breach of such contract. The principal may assign a contract or negotiate a negotiable instrument to the agent and thereby make the agent the owner of the right, in which case the agent may, under the laws of most states, bring the action in his own name.

An agent acting for an undisclosed or partially disclosed principal will be a party to the contract and may bring an action on the contract in the agent's own name. However, if the undisclosed or partially disclosed principal wishes to bring the action in his or her name instead of the agent's, the principal has the right to do so.

Exceptional Situations. If the agent is a party to the contract, other than as a surety for the principal, the agent will be a party in interest and as such may bring an action in his or her own name to recover for a breach of the contract.

An auctioneer or commission merchant (factor) who has sold goods for the principal may, by custom, bring suit in his or her own name to collect the purchase price of the goods.

An agent who is entrusted with goods by his or her principal and whose possession is tortiously interferred with by a third person may bring an action in his or her own name for the unlawful interference with his possession. Likewise, if a third person has the possession of goods owned by the principal when the agent is entitled to their possession, the agent has the right to bring an action in his own name to recover possession of the goods. In both of these situations the agent is basing the action on his personal right to possession.

Summary

An agent acting within the scope of his or her authority and contracting in the name of the principal cannot bring an action in his own name to recover for the breach of the contract. An agent who is acting for an undisclosed or partially disclosed principal, or who is acting for a disclosed principal but at the same time is a party to the contract other than as surety for the principal, may bring an action in his own name for breach of the contract. An auctioneer or factor, as a general rule, may bring an action in his own name. An agent may bring an action in his own name against a person who has interfered with his possession of the principal's goods or who has wrongfully injured the agent.

Problem Cases

1. Williams, as agent for Planters Company, contracted to sell Oil Company 25 carloads of cottonseed at $11 per ton to be delivered during the season. The memorandum of sale was in writing and signed "Planters Company by Eugene Williams, agent." Williams had no authority to sell cottonseed, and Planters refused to fill the order. Oil Company sued Williams to recover a judgment for the loss resulting from its failure to get the cottonseed. Is Williams liable?

2. Letha Johnson, who was employed as a saleswoman by Village Realty, told Evelyn Zanner, a broker with Glendale Realty, that Village Realty had a listing for sale of an acreage on Bainbridge Island. Mrs. Zanner proposed that if Glendale procured a buyer any resulting commission be divided equally. Letha Johnson said she would consult Village Realty. She then called back the same day and advised Zanner that Village Realty would not accept an equal division but would agree to 60 percent for the office that did the work on the transaction and 40 percent for the other office. Mrs. Zanner accepted the proposal and ten days later they met to inspect the property together. When Mrs. Zanner returned from the inspection, she told a Glendale saleswoman about the opportunity. This saleswoman brought a prospective customer to Letha Johnson who, when asked, told him that either office could handle the transaction. He bought the property through Letha Johnson and Village Realty was paid a commission of $8,500. When Glendale Realty claimed 40 percent of the commission from Village Realty it discovered that Letha Johnson had never discussed the proposed split of commission with Village Realty. Can Glendale Realty recover 40% of the commission from Letha Johnson?

3. Anderson, assuming to act for the owner of real estate, listed it for sale with Brawley, who found a buyer ready, willing and able to buy the property at the price fixed by Anderson. Anderson was not authorized to act for the owner of the property, and instead of submitting

the purchaser's written offer to the owner of the property, he returned it to Brawley. Brawley brought suit against Anderson to recover a judgment for the commission he would have earned had Anderson been authorized to list the property. Can Brawley recover from Anderson the commission he would have earned had Anderson been authorized to list the property?

4. The telephone users of Benton County held a mass meeting and organized themselves into the Telephone Federation for the purpose of combating a raise in telephone rates. Officers were elected and those present at the meeting voted to employ an attorney. The officers employed Cousin, an attorney, and promised him $2,000 to represent the Telephone Federation in the rate case. Cousin was not paid, and he sued the officers and 15 members of the Telephone Federation to recover a judgment for the promised fee. They set up as a defense that they had acted as agents of the Telephone Federation and were not personally liable. Is the defense good?

5. Weisbein appointed Lichtenstein as his agent to continue Weisbein's business during his absence. The appointment was in the form of a general power of attorney, granting Lichtenstein authority to do those things necessary in the operation of the business. Claflin claimed that Weisbein had obtained goods from him through fraud and demanded that Lichtenstein return the goods and settle the account. Lichtenstein returned the goods still in stock and settled the balance of the claim by delivering to Claflin goods at a discount of 24 percent off cost. Before making the settlement, Lichtenstein showed Claflin his power of attorney. On his return Weisbein brought an action in conversion to recover a judgment for the value of the goods given to Claflin. Weisbein claims that Lichtenstein, under the power of attorney had no authority to settle the claim of Claflin. Is Weisbein entitled to a judgment?

6. Chandler, Inc., leased a business building to Food Shops Inc. The lease was signed in the name of Food Shops Inc., by Hagan as its president. At the time the lease was signed Hagan represented that Food Shops Inc. was a corporation, that he was its president, and that he had been authorized to sign the lease by the board of directors. It is admitted that no corporation existed and that Hagan acted for a nonexistent principal. Is Hagan personally liable on the lease?

7. Odom, acting as agent for Sulton, took possession of property belonging to Friedman and delivered the property to Sulton. The taking of the property was a conversion of it. Friedman sued Odom in the tort action of conversion to recover a judgment for the value of the property, and Odom set up as a defense that when he took the property he was acting under the direction of Sulton and as his agent. Is the defense good?

8. The owner of real property known as 7005 Shore Road listed it for sale with Southern, a licensed real estate broker. Southern interested Sperling in the property but he refused to pay the listed price for it. He, however, made a counteroffer to Southern upon terms more favorable to him (Sperling) and delivered to Southern a check for $1,000 as earnest money on the proposed contract. The owner of the property thereafter agreed to accept Sperling's offer. Subsequently Sperling refused to complete the contract. Under the terms of the listing contract, Southern was not entitled to a commission unless a sale of the property was completed; consequently Southern was not entitled to a commission from the owner. Southern sued Sperling to recover the commission he would have earned had the deal been completed—$14,250. Is Southern entitled to a judgment?

chapter 18

Relation of Principal and Agent

Duties of Agent in General

Sources of Duties. Most agency relationships are created by contract. In addition to the duties imposed by the contract, the agent, as a fiduciary, has a duty of loyalty to the principal. The agent also has the duty of obedience, which is derived from the nature of the relationship, and the duties of care and diligence in carrying out the principal's instructions. The terms of the contract may relieve the agent of some of the duties he or she might otherwise, by the law of agency, owe the principal. However, courts are reluctant to interpret contractual provisions as eliminating or even substantially diminishing the agent's fiduciary duties.

Gratuitous Agent. The fiduciary duties of a gratuitous agent are basically the same as a paid agent, and a gratuitous agent has the same power to bind the principal and may exercise the same rights as a paid agent. The difference is that the gratuitous agent has no obligation to act for the principal unless the agent causes the principal reasonably to rely upon him or her to perform certain acts. For example, suppose Astor agrees as an accommodation to his friend Pogue to submit a written bid for a certain parcel of real estate in Pogue's behalf at an auction. Astor fails to do so and the bid would have been successful. If Pogue does not learn of the failure to act until too late to submit another bid, Astor is liable for Pogue's damages on account of his failure to act. The standard of care imposed upon a gratuitous agent may be somewhat less than that imposed upon an agent who is paid.

Summary

In addition to contractual duties, an agent owes the principal the fiduciary duty of loyalty and also the duty to follow directions and the duties of exercising care and diligence. These duties may be modified by contract, except that courts are likely to hold that a duty of loyalty still remains. A gratuitous agent does not escape the duties of loyalty and obedience, but ordinarily such an agent has no obligation to act for the principal.

Agent's Duty of Loyalty

Conflicts of Interest.   The agent's duty of loyalty requires him or her to exercise scrupulous honesty in dealings with the principal, to use his best efforts to further the principal's interests, and to avoid getting into a position where the agent's own interests are in conflict with those of the principal.

An agent who is authorized to buy or sell property for the principal will not be permitted to buy from or sell to himself or herself unless the agent makes a full disclosure of all the material facts to the principal and the principal consents to the transaction. Contracts which put the agent, directly or indirectly, in the position of buying from or selling to the principal without the assent of the principal are voidable at the election of the principal, unless a custom in the trade of which the principal is aware permits such action. For example, if an agent has sold to a corporation of which he is a substantial shareholder or to a relative or someone who has agreed to sell the property to the agent at a later date, the principal may get the transaction set aside when he learns of it. This right is not affected by the fact that the price was the best obtainable.

Even if the principal acquiesces in the agent's acting on his own account in dealing with the principal, the agent has the duty to deal fairly with the principal and to disclose to him or her all facts which might have a bearing on the desirability to the principal of the transactions.

Unless there is agreement by the principal, the agent may not compete with the principal with respect to the subject matter of the agency. If employed to purchase certain property, the agent may not buy it himself nor may the agent, while still employed, solicit the principal's customers while making plans to enter a competing business for himself.

Duty to Act for Only One Party to Transaction.   As a general rule an agent will not be permitted to act as an agent for both parties to a transaction without first disclosing the agent's double role and obtaining the consent of both parties. An exception is where the agent is merely acting as a middleman to bring the parties together so that they may negotiate their own contract.

Confidential Information.   The agent has a duty not to disclose to others or use for his or her own benefit confidential information acquired by him as an agent. Although in the absence of a restrictive agreement, the agent is free to compete with the principal after termination of the agency, the agent may not use or disclose confidential information. Such information includes trade secrets such as mechanisms, formulae, and processes and may include customer lists or special knowledge about customers. However, an agent may use, in competition with his former principal, the skills and general knowledge of a line of business the agent has learned while working for the principal.

Agent's Right to Compensation and Profits.   If the agent is acting for both parties without the knowledge and consent of both, the agent is not entitled to compensation. If only one of the parties knows of and consents to the agent's acting for both parties to the transaction, the party having knowledge and giving his or her consent is bound, but the other party may elect to have the transaction set aside. In such a situation the agent is not entitled to compensation from either party. The agent has breached his duty to the party not consenting, and the agreement between the agent and the party consenting is a fraud on the other party, is against public policy, and is illegal.

A similar situation arises if a third person agrees to pay an agent a secret commission, make him or her a gift, or compensate an agent in any way. A promise on the part of a third person to benefit an agent in any respect is a fraud on the principal and is illegal. Any benefits given the agent by the third person may be claimed by the principal, whether the benefits are in the form of a secret commission or a gift.

Summary

The agent's duty of loyalty to the principal requires the agent to be honest, to use his best efforts to further the principal's interests, and to avoid conflicts between the agent's own interests and the principal's. The agent may not buy from or sell to the principal directly or indirectly without the assent of the principal after full disclosure. Without such disclosure such contracts are voidable by the principal.

Generally the agent may not act as agent for both parties to a transaction unless both parties agree after full disclosure, although the agent may serve as a middleman. If the agent acts for both parties without the consent of both he or she is not entitled to compensation from either. The principal is entitled to any gift or compensation paid the agent by a third person who is dealing with or wishes to deal with the principal.

The agent may not use for his or her own benefit or disclose to others confidential information acquired in the agency relationship even after termination of the agency. Nor may the agent compete with the principal during the existence of the relationship.

Rushing v. Stephanus

393 P.2d 281 (Sup. Ct. Wash. 1964)

This was an action by Eugene Rushing and wife (plaintiffs) against Paul Stephanus (defendant) alleging negligence, fraud, and breach of Stephanus' fiduciary duty as an agent, and seeking recovery of commissions and excessive loan expenses. Judgment for Rushing and Stephanus appealed. Judgment affirmed.

Rushing was a sewer contractor with a fifth-grade education. He wanted to borrow $1,800 for use in his business, and he and his wife went to Stephanus, doing a mortgage loan brokerage business as the Prudential Mortgage Co. Stephanus indicated that he could secure a first mortgage loan for them at 8 percent interest which would refinance the preexisting $3,200 mortgage on Rushing's home and provide $1,800 in cash. He asked Rushing and his wife to sign a stack of papers, representing that the loan application, which was on top, was in several copies. In this manner the Rushings signed blank forms not only for a loan application but a note, a mortgage and a hold harmless agreement. Stephanus filled in the application to show the loan amount as $6,600.

Although the proposed loan was marketable, Stephanus did not place it promptly. After a month, the Rushings expressed concern and were told that there was a problem with the title to the home, and Stephanus suggested an interim loan of $1,000. The Rushings again signed another stack of papers in blank. On this loan Stephanus received a commission of $160. Finally, a month later a savings and loan association accepted the original loan. Stephanus advised the association prior to the closing that he held a recorded mortgage on the premises (one of the papers Rushings signed) which had an unpaid balance of $660. This was actually his $660 commission, and it was paid in the closing transactions. By the use of this device, Stephanus' commissions were not noticed by the Rushings.

As a result of all of these transactions the Rushings received $1,560 and increased their debt on their house from $3,200 to $6,600, and Stephanus received $820 in commissions plus $85 in closing fees, appraisal and other fees. The Rushings recovered in the trial court the $905 which had gone to Stephanus plus $480 in expenses on the interim loan.

FINLEY, JUDGE.   The entire $905 received by Stephanus as agent is forfeit, including the commissions and the $85 in "fees," only a few dollars of which were ever shown to have been passed on to third parties. The record is ample to support the findings of fraud and breach of an agent's fiduciary duty. The obtaining of signatures by trickery, misrepresentation and concealment of mortgages and fees, which appear staggering from the standpoint of amount alone, are all elements found by the trial court on substantial evidence. The broker must fully reveal the nature and extent of his fees to the client for whom he acts, and the failure to do so will render him liable. Where there has been a breach of the fiduciary relationship in addition to the partial concealment of fees, the rule is stated as follows in the *Restatement, Agency* (2d), § 469:

"An agent is entitled to no compensation for conduct which is disobedient or which is a breach of his duty of loyalty; if such conduct constitutes a wilful and deliberate breach of his contract of service, he is not entitled to compensation even for properly performed services for which no compensation is apportioned."

Stephanus is likewise liable, as a loan broker, for the expenses imposed upon his clients as a result of his failure to exercise due diligence or care. The item of $840 represents the loss caused when Stephanus failed to exercise reasonable diligence in obtaining the first mortgage as agreed, but also affirmatively acted to secure an expensive interim loan which the trial court found was totally unnecessary. This interim loan was arranged at a 20 percent discount, a 10 percent interest rate, and a penalty for a pay-off prior to maturity, despite the fact that Stephanus knew it was to be paid off with the proceeds of the $6,600 loan as soon as possible. Reviewing the above evidence, we cannot say that there was insufficient evidence of negligence to support the finding of the trial court.

Barber's Super Markets, Inc. v. Stryker

500 P.2d 1304 (Ct. App. N.M. 1972)

Action by Barber's Super Markets, Inc. (plaintiff) against Robert Stryker and Stryker Realty, Inc. (defendants) for breach of fiduciary duties and on other grounds. Trial court directed a verdict for Stryker and Barber's appealed. Reversed.

J. C. Horn was president and general manager of Barber's and was authorized to purchase real estate for a supermarket in Las Cruces, New Mexico. In early 1967 Wanda Hyatt, a licensed broker and an employee of Stryker Realty told the owner, Robert Stryker, that Horn was looking for a site for a supermarket, and they agreed to try to interest him in a tract of 18 acres owned by Mrs. Chisholm. After looking at several tracts Horn told Hyatt that his first choice was 4½ acres of the Chisholm tract. However, Horn testified that he was unable to get a firm offer on the 4½ acres. In July or August, Stryker involved himself with Horn and said he would try to help Hyatt get a deal on the property. Thereafter, several price quotations for the tract were relayed to Horn by Hyatt but each was higher than the last.

On August 25, Chisholm agreed to sell the 18-acre tract for $150,000 to I. E. Shahan, who had been a salesman for Stryker until the end of April. Hyatt earned a commission on this sale but it had not been paid at the time of trial. However, Stryker did not have a listing on it, and Chisholm had never been told of Barber's interest in the tract.

On September 22, Horn for the first time asked Stryker to get a price on the entire 18-acre tract. Stryker then contacted Shahan who set the price at $275,000. This was relayed to Horn. Horn was satisfied with it, and on September 25 he came to Las Cruces to try to complete the deal. Stryker introduced Horn to Shahan and they agreed upon a lease with option to purchase because Shahan was unwilling to sell for six months because of tax consequences.

The contract was signed on October 27 after Stryker had had numerous phone conversations and much correspondence with Barber's attorney. . . . Stryker had no oral or written agreement with Barber's for a commission but Shahan agreed to pay Stryker a 5 percent commission.

The trial court directed a verdict for Stryker on Barber's claim for damages for violation of his fiduciary duties as agent for Barber's by failing to inform Barber's that Stryker was acting as a broker for Shahan and that Shahan had contracted to buy the property from Chisholm in August. Stryker's position was that he was only a middleman rather than Barber's agent in the transaction, merely bringing Shahan and Horn together, and thus owed no fiduciary duties to Barber's.

SUTIN, JUDGE. Stryker's main contention is that he was a "middleman." Therefore, no fiduciary relation existed between Barber's and Stryker.

The only case in New Mexico on the issue of a "middleman" is *Ross v. Carr,* (1909). Ross sought to recover a commission on the sale of timberlands by Carr to third parties. Ross had solicited the aid of another real estate broker named Wirtz in Milwaukee, Wisconsin, to try and find purchasers for the timberlands, and Carr gave Ross a letter agreeing to pay him a commission of 5 percent of any sale made with Wirtz and his associates. The land was sold to associates of Wirtz, but Wirtz acquired no interest in the property. Ross recovered his commission. In affirming, the court said:

> A full examination of the record shows that in effecting the sale Ross did not act as a broker, but only as a middleman. He was instrumental in bringing the buyers and sellers together, but was not expected to and did not take any part in the negotiations between them, and the final bargain was made without his aid or intervention. Indeed, it is in evidence that Ross did not know the price at which the land was sold until the written contract was offered in evidence. Ross, being only a middleman, could therefore legally have taken a commission from both buyers and sellers. *McLure v. Luke* (1907); *Knauss v. Godfried Krueger Brewing Co.*

McLure and *Knauss,* supra, support the contention that the real estate agent, to be a "middleman," must be employed for the mere purpose of bringing the possible buyer and seller together so that they may negotiate their own contract. The agent has only limited authority. He has no power to and does not negotiate the terms on which the principals will deal. However, he is no longer a "middleman" if he is invested with the least discretion in the matter of advising or negotiating the sale or purchase of property, or where the principal has the right to rely on the broker for the benefit of his skill or judgment, or in any such case where the agent is employed by the other side in a similar capacity, or in one where, by possibility, his duty and his interest might clash. "The whole matter depends upon the character of his employment," because the duty of an agent for the vendor is to sell property at the highest price, and the duty of an agent for the purchaser is to buy it at the lowest. If the agent is a "middleman," no fiduciary relation to either principal exists.

The facts heretofore set out would sustain a determination that Stryker was employed by Barber's to try to procure the Chisholm tract from Shahan. He was also employed by Shahan to sell the tract. He brought Shahan and Horn together. Horn concentrated on closing the deal himself, and they orally closed the deal. Before the deal was closed, Stryker obtained a price for Barber's. After the deal was closed, Stryker aided and assisted Barber's and acted as its trustee. From all of the evidence in the record we believe an issue of fact exists whether Stryker was a "middleman," whether he "was not expected to and did not take any part in the negotiations between them, and the final bargain was made without his aid or intervention."

Stryker was not a "middleman" as a matter of law. The trial court erred in so holding.

* * * * *

We have previously pointed out that where there is a duty of disclosure, both Stryker and Shahan could be liable for constructive fraud, based on nondisclosure of material facts. The duty of disclosure depends upon Stryker's relationship to Barber's. If Stryker was an agent, and not a middleman, he may be held liable for his nondisclosure. If

Shahan had knowledge of Stryker's relationship with Barber's as an agent, and nevertheless hired him, he may also be liable to Barber's regardless of whether he was Stryker's employee.

Agent's Duty to Obey Instructions and to Use Care and Skill

Duty to Obey Instructions. The agent owes a duty to follow faithfully all lawful and reasonable instructions given to the agent by the principal. The agent is engaged to transact business or perform services for his or her principal, and the principal has the right, within the limits of legality, to have the business transacted or the services performed as he or she wishes. If the agent, even though it be a gratuitous agency, fails or refuses to follow the legitimate instructions of the principal, the agent will be liable to the principal for any damages suffered by the principal as the result of the agent's failure to act as instructed. In addition, the agent's failure or refusal to follow instructions will, as a general rule, justify the principal's termination of the agency.

There are some situations in which the agent may be justified in not following instructions. If an emergency arises and the agent cannot consult with the principal, the agent may be justified in using his or her own judgment, especially if following instructions would clearly result in injury to the principal; but if no emergency has arisen, the agent must follow instructions, even though the agent deems the course of action designated by the principal to be clearly injurious to the principal. If the principal instructs the agent to do an illegal or criminal act, the agent is not bound to follow instructions. If the agency is general in its nature and the principal has not given the agent detailed instructions, the agent must use his or her own judgment in following that course of action which will best further the principal's interests.

Standard of Care and Skill. In the absence of an agreement imposing on the agent a duty of a greater or lesser degree, the agent owes a duty to act with standard care and skill. That is, the agent must possess and exercise the care and skill which is standard in the locality for the kind of work he or she is employed to perform. If the agent is acting gratuitously, this fact may be taken into consideration in determining whether the agent has acted with reasonable care and skill. In all instances the paid agent owes a duty to exercise at least the skill that the agent represents himself as having. The agent may warrant that his undertakings will be successful or that his performance will be satisfactory to the principal, but in the absence of such a warranty, the agent does not assume the risk of the success or satisfaction of his or her performance.

Duty to Communicate Notice or Knowledge. The principal is bound by notice given to the agent or knowledge acquired by the agent during the transaction of the principal's business. Therefore, the agent owes a duty to communicate to the principal all notice which is given to him or her in the course of the transaction of the principal's business and to disclose all facts within his knowledge which are material to the matters entrusted to the agent by the principal and which do not violate a confidence. Failure to communicate notice or to disclose knowledge is a breach of duty and will render the agent liable to the principal for any resulting injury.

Duties of Agents in Certain Transactions.   Agents employed to buy or sell have a duty to obtain terms which are most advantageous to the principal even when the principal has fixed a price, unless the agent is directed to adhere to the price fixed. An agent making collections has a duty to exercise reasonable diligence and to accept payment only in the medium customary. This will usually be money or the debtor's check, but the situation may require a certified check. An agent making collections or receiving goods for the principal has the duty to use care to keep them safely and to remit or deliver them in accordance with the principal's instructions. An agent making loans is not an insurer of the loans made but must use care in investigating the credit standing of the borrower and, if customary to require security, to investigate its adequacy.

Summary

An agent owes a duty to follow and obey the instructions of his or her principal, provided the principal does not instruct the agent to do a criminal or illegal act. In an emergency, when the agent cannot communicate with the principal, an agent may be justified in not following instructions if doing so would result in injury to the principal.

The standard of care and skill required of the agent is that which is standard in the locality for the work to be performed or at least the skill the agent represents himself or herself as having. In the absence of a warranty, the agent does not assume the risk of the success of his performance.

An agent owes a duty to communicate to the principal all notices received in the course of the transaction of the principal's business. The agent also owes a duty to disclose all facts material to the purpose of the agency which come to the agent's knowledge during the performance of his duties.

Nash v. Sears, Roebuck and Co.

174 N.W.2d 818 (Sup. Ct. Mich. 1970)

Mary Nash (plaintiff) brought an action against Sears, Roebuck and Company, Heidt's Protective Service, Inc., and Art Keolian (defendants) for false arrest and assault and battery on a customer. Judgment for Mrs. Nash against all three defendants and against Sears on its cross claim against Heidt's. Sears appealed. Reversed and remanded with respect to the judgment on the cross claim.

Keolian was an employee of Heidt's Protective Service serving as a uniformed security guard in a Sears' store. Both Heidt's and Sears gave Keolian detailed instructions and both retained the right to supervise and direct him and to discharge him from further work for Sears. Keolian had been instructed not to arrest unless he himself witnessed a shoplifting incident but was expected to respond to information received from Sears' employees.

Based upon information from a Sears' saleslady who allegedly witnessed a woman identified by her as Mary Nash shoplifting, Keolian confronted Mrs. Nash and requested her to accompany him back to the store. She refused and started to walk away. Keolian shoved her to the ground, straddled her body, and pinned her arms above her head. Police arrived and took both Keolian and Mrs. Nash to the police station. A subsequent investigation proved the shoplifting charge to be without foundation. Sears filed a cross claim against Heidt's for reimbursement for any liability it was found to have. Sears alleged that the contract with Heidt's required Heidt's to furnish a qualified guard and that Keolian was not qualified and had not performed his work properly. The trial judge submitted to the jury the question whether there had been an agreement between Sears and Heidt's that a qualified guard was to be sent over. Sears appealed urging this as error.

T. M. KAVANAGH, JUSTICE.   Every contract of employment includes an obligation, whether express or implied, to perform in a diligent and reasonably skillful workmanlike manner. The general rule is fully stated in Am. Jur.2d as follows:

As a general rule, there is implied in every contract for work or services a duty to perform it skillfully, carefully, diligently, and in a workmanlike manner. Moreover, a contracting party may be bound by the terms of the contract to perform it in a good and workmanlike manner.

With respect to the skill required of a person who is to render services, it is a well-settled rule that the standard of comparison or test of efficiency is that degree of skill, efficiency, and knowledge which is possessed by those of ordinary skill, competency, and standing in the particular trade or business for which he is employed. Where the contract does not provide for a degree of skill higher than this, none can be required. Where skill as well as care is required in performing the undertaking, and where the party purports to have skill in the business and he undertakes for hire, he is bound to exercise due and ordinary skill or, in other words, to perform in a workmanlike manner. In cases of this sort he must be understood to have engaged to use a degree of diligence and attention and skill adequate to the performance of his undertaking. It seems, however, that he is not liable for an error due to an honest mistake of judgment, and not to gross ignorance. Nor, in the absence of an express provision to that effect, does he become a guarantor of the results.

Failure to comply with the implied duty to perform in a skillful and workmanlike manner may not only defeat recovery but may entitle the other party to damages resulting from the unskillful and unworkmanlike performance.

An independent contractor, undertaking to discharge a contractual duty to his or her employer, is bound to proceed with skill, diligence, and in a workmanlike manner, as is any employee under the common-law rule above quoted. This necessary implication of any contract of employment, if not expressly provided for by the parties, will be supplied in law by construction.

We hold that the trial judge committed reversible error when he instructed the jury that they were to determine whether Heidt's obligated itself to send over a qualified guard.

Agent's Duty to Account

Duty to Account for Money and Property. Both the agent's duty of loyalty and the agent's duty of exercising care require him or her to account to the principal for any money or property coming into his or her possession in the course of the agent's transaction of the principal's business. The principal may demand an accounting at any time he or she wishes, and the agent owes a duty to make such an accounting. If the nature of the business entrusted to the agent involves collections, receipts, expenditures, and similar transactions, the agent owes a duty to keep accurate accounts and to render such accounts to his or her principal.

Duty to Keep Principal's Property Separate. An agent owes a duty not to commingle the property of the principal with the agent's own property, and if the agent does, he or she will be liable to the principal for any resulting loss. If the commingled property—grain or money, for example—cannot be separated, the agent must satisfy the legitimate claim of the principal even if this results in the principal taking the entire mass of commingled property.

An agent owes a duty not to deposit the principal's money in the agent's own name or in his or her own personal bank account. The agent should either use the principal's name or the form, "Ames, in trust for Peters."

Liability for Use of Principal's Property. If an agent uses his or her principal's property with the intent of depriving the principal of it, the agent will be guilty of the crime of embezzlement. If the agent has used the principal's property or failed to keep it separate, the principal may claim his or her property if the principal can identify it, or the principal may hold the agent liable for the value of the property in the tort action of conversion.

If the agent has used the principal's money for his or her own purposes, the principal is entitled to a judgment against the agent for the amount of the money used, or if the agent has purchased property with the principal's money, the principal may, at his or her election, claim such property, even though it has increased in value since the agent acquired it. For example, suppose Alden, acting as agent for Pape, collects $5,000 for Pape and, instead of remitting the money to him, purchases corporate stock with it. Pape, if he can prove that Alden purchased the stock with his money, may claim the stock even though it has increased in value since Alden purchased it, or he may hold Alden accountable for the money collected.

Summary

An agent owes a duty to keep a true and accurate account of all property and money of the principal coming into his or her possession. The agent owes a duty not to commingle the principal's property or money with the agent's own. If the agent commingles the principal's property with his own, deposits the principal's money in the agent's own name, or uses the principal's money or property for the agent's own use and benefit, the agent is liable for any and all resulting loss.

Bain v. Pulley

111 S.E.2d 287 (Sup. Ct. Va. 1959)

This was an action by Marion T. Bain and Harry L. Bain (plaintiffs) against Douglas H. Pulley (defendant) asking for an accounting. Judgment for Pulley and the Bains appealed. Judgment reversed and remanded.

The Bains were trustees of the Thomas L. Bain, deceased, estate, which was composed of a business and farms. The Bains as trustees employed Pulley as agent to operate and manage the business and farms. Pulley continued in the employ of the Bains from June 1936 to January 1, 1956. During this time Pulley kept and maintained books and records pertaining to the estate business and properties. The books and records were kept entirely in Pulley's handwriting. Over the years, substantial profits from the operation were paid to the beneficiaries of the estate.

From January 1952, and continuing through January 1956, Pulley rendered an annual income report. These reports were not verified or checked with the records by the accountants or the trustees or the beneficiaries. No audit of Pulley's accounts was made between 1943 and 1956, when Pulley resigned as agent and manager of the estate. This action was brought asking for an accounting. Pulley contended that since he had rendered an annual report the Bains were not entitled to an accounting.

EGGLESTON, CHIEF JUSTICE.   The general duty of an agent who is required to handle money is thus laid down in *Restatement of the Law of Agency*, 2d, Vol. 2, § 382, p. 185:

Unless otherwise agreed, an agent is subject to a duty to keep, and render to his principal, an account of money or other things which he has received or paid out on behalf of the principal.

Where such fiduciary relation exists the principal may invoke the aid of a court of equity in requiring an accounting by his agent.

In an action for an accounting, the agent has the burden of proving that he paid to the principal or otherwise properly disposed of the money or other thing which he is proved to have received from the principal.

We do not agree that the acceptance by the beneficiaries of the income reports for the years 1951 to 1955, both inclusive, was a valid and sufficient reason for denying the prayer for an accounting. Clearly, these reports did not constitute an annual accounting between the parties and a settlement of their transactions. As has been said, the reports merely showed a list of items of income and disbursements and the amount of cash in bank for the respective years. There was no showing that the stated amount of cash had been reconciled with the records of the estate or those of the bank. Nor was there any evidence that the trustees, beneficiaries, and Pulley agreed or considered that they were final accountings for the respective years.

But even if the furnishing and acceptance of these reports be considered an account stated for the respective years, it does not constitute an estoppel but is subject to impeachment for mistake or error clearly proved.

Neither do we agree with the trial court's holding that since the beneficiaries knew of and acquiesced in Pulley's "method of bookkeeping and the method in which the business was conducted," they are estopped to demand an accounting of him. There is no showing that his method of keeping his books and conducting the business were improper. Indeed, he insists in his brief that these were proper and that his records correctly show his transactions. Nor is there any evidence that the beneficiaries had actual or implied knowledge of, or acquiesced in, the discrepancies disclosed by the evidence, or the lack of records and vouchers which might have explained and accounted for such discrepancies. Not until they received the auditors' preliminary report in August 1956, did the beneficiaries know of these alleged discrepancies and lack of adequate records. Within a few months thereafter the present suit was brought. Hence, there is no showing that the beneficiaries were guilty of laches which would preclude their right to require an accounting of Pulley for the recent period in controversy, from 1951 to 1955, both inclusive.

Principal's Duties to Agent

Duty to Compensate Agent. Most agency relations are created by contract, and the contract ordinarily stipulates the compensation the agent is to receive for his or her services. Controversies as to the amount of compensation due are then settled by applying rules of law for contract interpretation. Where the agency agreement is implied or the contract omits reference to compensation, whether the agent is to be compensated is determined from the relation of the parties and the surrounding circumstances. In such cases the rate of compensation would be the reasonable value of the services.

The courts have held that the agent is not entitled to compensation (1) if the agent is also representing interests adverse to those of the principal without the knowledge or consent of the principal, (2) if the agent is guilty of fraud or misrepresentation, (3) if the agent is negligent in the performance of his or her duties and the agent's negligence results in material injury to the principal, or (4) if the agent is transacting business which is illegal.[1]

Contingent Compensation. Frequently, the agent's compensation is contingent on his or her accomplishment of a stipulated result. In such cases, the

---

[1] See the earlier discussion in this chapter under Agent's Duty of Loyalty.

agent is not entitled to compensation until he or she has accomplished the result, regardless of how much effort the agent expends in attempting to do so. If the agent is to be paid on a contingent basis, the principal must cooperate with the agent in the accomplishment of the result and must not do anything which will prevent the agent from earning the agreed upon compensation. If the principal by his or her acts prevents the agent from accomplishing the stipulated result, the agent will be entitled to the designated compensation.

When the agent has accomplished the stipulated result, the agent is entitled to his or her compensation even though the principal is not benefited by the agent's performance. For example, suppose a salesman is to be paid a commission on all orders accepted and approved by the principal. The principal has accepted and approved orders taken by the salesman but, as the result of a shortage of materials, is unable to produce and ship the goods. The principal must pay the agent the agreed commission on the orders taken and approved. On the other hand, no matter how hard the salesman works, if no orders are obtained, he or she is entitled to no compensation.

Compensating Professional Agents.   The basis of compensation for professional agents varies according to custom for different types of agents in different geographical areas. Statutes in some states require that contracts of employment of certain types of professional agents, for example real estate brokers, must be in writing or the agent is not entitled to compensation.

The courts have decided many controversies over the compensation, if any, due real estate brokers and other agents who are employed on a contingent basis. Certain general rules have evolved which are subject to variation according to jurisdiction and, of course, subject to express contract agreement. Only a few of these rules are stated here.

Where the principal gives the broker what purports to be his or her complete terms and the broker finds a buyer (or seller) "ready, willing and able" to buy (or sell) on those terms, the broker is entitled to the commission, even if the principal refuses to contract with the third party, provided that the broker is the "effective cause" of accomplishing the result. If the principal provides the broker with only incomplete terms, the principal may terminate negotiations without liability for the commission if no agreement is reached with the third party on additional terms, unless the principal acts in bad faith. Unless the contract with the agent provides otherwise, the agent is entitled to his or her commission even if the third party defaults in carrying out a promise to buy or sell. A provision stating that the principal is to receive a certain net price is usually interpreted as imposing not only the condition that the offer from the broker's customer provide that sum to the principal but also that the sum be paid before the agent is entitled to the commission.

Reimbursement for Expenditures.   If the agent has made advancements in behalf of the principal in the transaction of the principal's business and within the scope of the agent's authority, the agent is entitled to reimbursement for all such advancements. Also, if the agent has suffered losses in the conduct of the principal's business, the principal is legally bound to indemnify the agent for such losses, provided the agent has acted within the scope of his or her authority.

Summary

The principal owes a duty to pay the agent any compensation due him or her by the terms of the contract of employment. If there is no agreement as to the compensation to be paid to the agent and it is clear that the agency is not gratuitous, the principal must pay the reasonable value of the agent's services.

If the agent's compensation is made contingent on accomplishing a stipulated result, the principal must cooperate with the agent in its accomplishment.

There are certain rules adopted by the courts to interpret contracts with real estate brokers and other agents employed on a contingent basis that do not clearly specify under what circumstances the agent has earned his or her commission.

The principal must reimburse the agent for all money advanced and expenditures made in the course of the performance of the agent's duties, if the advances or expenditures are expressly or impliedly authorized.

Axilbund v. McAllister

180 A.2d 244 (Sup. Ct. Pa. 1962)

Action by Jacob Axilbund and partners (plaintiffs) against McAllister and 917 Filbert Street Corp. (defendants) to recover a commission on the sale of the Filbert building. The trial court gave judgment to Filbert (McAllister had died) notwithstanding a verdict for Axilbund. Reversed and new trial directed.

Axilbund learned that Filbert wished to sell its building, and McAllister, president of Filbert, promised Axilbund that "if they produced a purchaser for the premises for $300,000 net, the usual brokerage commission would be paid." Axilbund told McAllister that he had a client named Gross who could use the building. He showed Gross the building, informed him it was available at $315,000, and provided him with additional information. He talked to Gross on the telephone several times over several months, even after Gross told him he was not interested in the building. Unknown to Axilbund, Gross purchased the building directly from McAllister for $295,000.

Filbert's defense to Axilbund's claim to the commission was (1) that the sale was induced by direct contact between Gross and McAllister and (2) that if there was any contract between Axilbund and Filbert it was a "special contract," that is, that Axilbund was retained on a nonexclusive basis to sell the building for not less than $300,000 net and that Axilbund had not performed that condition of the contract.

JONES, JUSTICE.   In this area of the law certain principles are well established: (1) a broker cannot recover a commission, even though he brought the seller and buyer together, unless he can prove a contract of employment, express or implied, oral or written, between himself and the buyer (or seller) or an acceptance and ratification of his acts by the buyer (or seller); in the absence of an exclusive agency, if the actions of a broker constitute the efficient cause of the production of a buyer (or seller), he is generally entitled to his commission even though the sale was finally concluded and completed by the seller (or buyer) himself, or another broker; (3) the mere fact that the broker has carried on negotiations with a prospective buyer (or seller) does not entitle the broker to a commission unless his efforts constituted "the efficient procuring cause of the sale"; (4) where the prospective buyer (or seller) and the seller (or buyer) or the broker-agent fail to reach an agreement and there is a *break in their negotiations,* and, at a later date, the property is sold to (or bought by) the same prospective buyer, the original broker is not entitled to a commission.

. . . Filbert contends that this oral contract was a "special contract," which constitutes an exception to the principles usually applied in this area of the law.

Section 447 of the *Restatement of the Law, Agency,* recognizes this exception: "An agent whose compensation is conditional upon procuring a transaction on specified terms is not entitled to such compensation if, as a result of his efforts, a transaction is effected on different or modified terms, although the principal thereby benefits." Comment a, Section 447 states: ". . . a clearly expressed condition that the principal will pay a commission only if the agent's services result in a transaction with another on specified terms is binding, and the agent is not entitled to a commission if the principal, acting in good faith, . . . enters into a transaction with another procured by the agent, but with terms less favorable to the principal." *Restatement of Law 2d, Agency,* § 447, p. 354.

There is adequate evidence on this record that Axilbund brought Gross and Filbert together but there is no evidence that Gross was ready and willing to pay such price for the building as would *net* Filbert $300,000 *and* yield a commission to Axilbund. Therefore, Axilbund did not perform in accordance with the terms of the contract. Under such circumstances, the sale by Filbert to Gross of this building for $295,000 *net* would not entitle Axilbund to a commission *unless Filbert had acted fraudulently or in bad faith.* Whether Filbert acted fraudulently or in bad faith was never submitted to nor passed on by the jury in the court below.

Termination of Agent's Powers

Termination by Will of Parties.   Since an agent's authority is derived from the will of the principal, such authority terminates when the agent knows, or the circumstances are such that the agent should know, that the principal does not wish the agent to continue to exercise the authority vested in him or her. No formalities are necessary for such termination. All that is needed is that the principal indicate that he or she does not wish the agent to represent the principal or that the agent indicate that he does not intend to represent the principal. This may be brought about by the mutual consent of the parties or in violation of an existing contract of employment. If the termination constitutes a breach of the contract of employment, the terminating party is liable in damages to the injured party.

Termination of Contract Provisions. A contract of agency will terminate at the time or upon the happening of an event stated in the contract, and if no time or event is stipulated, it terminates after a reasonable time. An agency created to accomplish a specified result terminates when that result is accomplished.

Termination by Change of Circumstances. Certain changes or happenings may cause the termination of the agency. The courts have held that, as a general rule, the agency is terminated by (1) the death of either the principal or the agent, (2) the insanity of the principal (to continue for the period of insanity), (3) the bankruptcy of the principal (as to matters affected by the bankruptcy), (4) the bankruptcy of the agent (under limited circumstances), (5) the objective of the agency becoming illegal, (6) impossibility of performance, (7) the disqualification of principal or agent (e.g. loss of license when license is required), (8) loss or destruction of subject matter of agency, or (9) changes in values or in business conditions.

In general, the basis for holding that the agency is terminated on the happening of the events listed above is that it is reasonable to believe that the principal, if he or she knew the circumstances, would not wish the agent to act further, or that the event is such that the accomplishment of the objective is rendered impossible or illegal. In most of the situations mentioned, there may be circumstances which justify the courts in holding that the general rule does not apply.

Termination of Powers Given as Security. An agency power given as a security, sometimes called an agency coupled with an interest, cannot be terminated without the consent of the agent. The commonest example of such an agency is a secured transaction in which the secured party or some person acting for his or her protection is authorized to sell the property pledged as security in the event of default. For instance, suppose Allen loans Peters $1,000, and Peters pledges his diamond ring as security for the repayment of the loan. Such a pledge agreement usually authorizes Allen to act as Peters' agent to sell the ring at public or private sale in the event that Peters fails to repay the loan. In such a case Allen is said to have "a power given as security," and the power to sell is irrevocable by Peters and is not terminated by the death or loss of capacity of either Peters or Allen. Of course, the power to sell is terminated when the loan is repaid. It may also be terminated by the agent, Allen, (or if three parties are involved, by either the agent or the beneficiary) if he voluntarily surrenders his power.

A situation where a power is given as security must be distinguished from one where the agent has only an expectation of profits to be realized. An agent promised a commission cannot prevent the termination of the agency merely because this will bar the agent from earning the commission.

Notice to Third Persons. An agent may have apparent authority to bind the principal after the termination of the agency. If the agency is general, third persons who have transacted business with the principal through the agent are justified in believing that the agent still has authority to represent the principal unless they have notice or knowledge of the termination of the agency. If the principal wishes to be protected against the results of the acts of a former agent, he or she should give third persons who have dealt with him through the agent personal notice of the termination of the agency. As to all other persons, notice by publication is usually sufficient.

If the agency is terminated by the death of the principal, the agent will not have the power to bind the estate of the deceased principal; and as a general rule, any act of the agent after the death of the principal will not bind the deceased principal's estate even though at the time of the transaction neither the agent nor the third person had notice of the principal's death.

This rule places a heavy burden on innocent agents and third persons who act without notice or knowledge of the principal's death. In some states the rule has been relaxed by statute. In general, the rule is not applied to banks that pay checks which have been issued prior to the drawer's death but presented for payment after his or her death and before the bank has notice of the death, or to checks which are in the process of being collected at the time of the drawer's death. (Uniform Commercial Code, Section 4–405.)

Summary

The relationship of principal and agent may be terminated at the will of either the principal or the agent. If the termination of the agency is a breach of the contract of employment, the injured party is entitled to a judgment for the resulting damage. The agency may be terminated by the terms of the appointment, the accomplishment of its objective, the death of the principal or agent, the illegality of the objective, the loss or destruction of the subject matter of the agency, or the happening of events which would make it reasonably clear that the principal would not wish the authority of the agent to continue.

A power given as security is created when the power is granted for the protection of the power holder or third person. It is not revocable by the grantor of the power nor is it usually affected by his or her death or incapacity.

If notice of the termination of the agency is not given to third persons who have been dealing with the agent, and they have no knowledge of the termination, the principal will be bound by the acts of the agent. At common law, this rule did not apply if the agency was terminated by the death of the principal, and the common-law rule applies today with some exceptions, especially as to the payment of checks.

Problem Cases

1. Mrs. Jones, a check-out counter cashier at Acme Markets, was $11.18 short in her cash register receipts at the end of the day. Acme sought to recover this amount from her, but did not allege conversion on her part. Is she liable to Acme for negligence in handling her transactions?

2. Queen Fisheries, Inc., was in financial difficulty. To satisfy creditors its majority shareholder transferred his voting rights to Williams, giving Williams control. At Williams' instigation additional directors were elected to the board, and the new board passed a resolution in December 1965 stating that Williams was employed by Queen for three years as president and general manager at a minimum salary of $20,000 per year. In the spring of 1966, Williams and an associate entered into the lighterage business under his own name but using Queen's equipment and employees. He intended to keep this business as his own upon leaving Queen but intended to turn over the net profits of the 1966 season to Queen.

   In November 1966, having made new financial arrangements, the majority shareholder notified Williams that he had been relieved of all management responsibilities and that he was no longer an officer nor a director. His employment was terminated at the end of the year. Williams sued for breach of the employment contract. Queen's defense was that Williams had violated his fiduciary duty to Queen in operating the lighterage business and sought recovery of salary already paid. Was the trial court in error in holding that Queen had no liability under the employment contract but permitting Williams to keep the salary already paid for 1966?

3. Arnold's Ice Cream Company employed three salesmen and four drivers to sell and deliver its products to about 190 retailers of ice cream. The drivers' duties included delivering orders previously phoned in and making route sales to individual customers. They were supplied with pricing and product information and customer names. At the end of March two of the drivers resigned, effective immediately. In the previous two months their wives had incorporated an ice cream business and delivery trucks were acquired. During March they solicited Arnold's customers on behalf of the new corporation, and during the last ten days of March their sales for Arnold's had dropped more than 25 percent. By the end of April, 45 former customers had ceased to buy from Arnold, and 85 others had been solicited and some had bought from the new corporation, threatening Arnold's with a loss of one third of its sales. Is Arnold's entitled to a preliminary injunction on the grounds that the customer lists were trade secrets being used by the former employees and the new corporation?

4. A. M. Franco carried the titles of chief engineer, director of fabrication and vice president of Stein Steel Company, which was engaged in the design, fabrication, and sale of structural steel. Instead of apportioning his salary and expenses in establishing the prices for structural steel he sold for Stein, Franco had billed and collected direct from Stein's customers for his services. Stein sought to enjoin Franco from continuing to collect directly from Stein's customers. Franco's defense was that he was a consulting engineer and not an employee of the company and was entitled to the compensation. Is Franco correct?

5. Gilbert, acting as broker for Mason, took an order for a carload of beans from Lexington Company. It later canceled the order by giving notice of the cancellation to Gilbert. At the time of the giving of the notice the beans had not been shipped. Gilbert failed to give notice of the cancellation to Mason, and he shipped the beans from Colorado to the Lexington Company in Kentucky. The beans could not be disposed of on their arrival in Kentucky and had to be reshipped to Colorado. The resulting loss was $500. Mason sued Gilbert to recover a judgment for the $500 loss. Is Mason entitled to a judgment for the $500 loss?

6. Vasilios Diamantopoulos, known in his community as Barber Bill, lived by himself in the back of his barber shop. After both legs were amputated as a result of complications of diabetes, he went to live in the home of William Dakouras, who was his godson through rites in the Greek Orthodox Church. He executed a power of attorney which gave Dakouras ". . . full power and authority to do and perform all and every act and thing whatsoever required and necessary to be done as fully as I might do if personally present . . ." At the time the power of attorney was given, Barber Bill had a bank account of $10,415. He delivered the bank book to Dakouras who, in less than eight months, made four withdrawals which completely exhausted the account. Barber Bill died 17 months later. An executor was appointed for the estate who, learning of the facts, commenced an action for conversion against Dakouras, who moved for a nonsuit contending the power of attorney had the effect of a gift. Is Dakouras correct?

7. Rotella listed his restaurant for sale with Lange, a real estate broker. It was an exclusive listing for 45 days and the offering price was established at $9,000 cash. The listing agreement indicated that Rotella held a three-year lease on the property where the restaurant was operated. Lange obtained an offer in writing to buy the business for $9,000, part in cash and the balance in monthly payments secured by a chattel mortgage. Rotella rejected the offer. Armstrong's later offer of $7,000, all cash, was also rejected as was a subsequent offer for $9,000 cash subject to the following provisions: "The offer to be binding only if Armstrong can obtain an A.B.C. license, a health permit and a five-year lease," a provision which was in the two prior offers and to which Rotella made no objection in refusing the earlier offers. Lange claimed he had found a buyer ready, willing, and able to buy on the terms stated in the listing. Can Lange recover his commission?

8. Ayrshire Corporation purchased a 215-acre tract of unimproved land which it planned to subdivide and plot into city lots. On February 1, 1946, Wall entered into a contract with Ayrshire Corporation under the terms of which he was given the exclusive sales agency to sell the lots into which the property should thereafter be subdivided. Wall was to receive a 5 percent commission on the sale price of all lots plotted and sold. In 1957, Ayrshire gave Wall notice of the termination of the contract. Wall sued to recover commissions on lots and acreage sold after the termination of the contract. Is Wall entitled to the commissions?

9. McBride and Pogue, the principal stockholders, and Delta Lumber Company, a corporation engaged in the building business which was having financial difficulty, entered into a credit agreement with Village Bank to make unsecured loans to the corporation up to $50,000 in the aggregate. Borrowing was necessary to permit Delta to perform its contracts and wind up its business. In the contract McBride and Pogue appointed each other as attorney in fact to execute notes under the terms of the credit agreement. By its terms any party could terminate the agreement upon ten days written notice to the others, at which time all indebtedness would become due and payable. Over a period of 19 months a number of loans were made by the bank to Delta and, as required by the credit agreement, Delta obtained bank approval before entering new building contracts.

   Delta became insolvent and Village Bank sought to hold McBride on the last note. McBride had refused to sign this note but it had been signed for him by Pogue as attorney in fact under the authority granted in the credit agreement. The credit agreement had not been terminated. Is McBride liable?

Part V

Partnerships

chapter 19

Creation of Partnership

Introduction

Historical Background. The basic concept of partnership, two or more people joining forces to carry on a business, was in use in ancient times. The Code of Hammurabi—2300 B.C.—included provisions regulating partnerships. The concept was highly developed in Roman law, and the Justinian Code defines a partnership in a manner similar to our Uniform Partnership Act. During the Middle Ages in Europe much of the trade between nations was conducted by partnerships, and partnership law became a well-developed part of the law merchant.

Nature of Partnership. Businessmen and their accountants have tended to view the partnership as an entity—a body distinct from its members. This is the view of the law in France and other civil-law countries. However, the English common-law courts tended to treat the partnership as an aggregate of the individuals composing it. Under this view partners hold property in joint or common tenancy and are joint obligors on their contracts. However, through the equity courts, principles of the entity theory were introduced into the law of partnership. The result was a great deal of confusion in the decisions and demand for statutory clarification. This led to the passage of the Partnership Act in England in 1890, and in this country the Commissioners on Uniform State Laws, as one of their earliest efforts, completed the Uniform Partnership Act in 1914. Its companion law, the Uniform Limited Partnership Act was adopted by the Commissioners in 1916.

The original draft clearly adopted the entity theory even in its definition of a partnership, but the final form of the Uniform Partnership Act does not do so, nor does it provide for suits in the firm name. However, it contains a number of provisions consistent with the entity theory: it permits ownership of property in the firm name, accounting is between the firm and the partners rather than merely between partners, and the firm is permitted to continue to operate in situations where the aggregate theory would suggest immediate dissolution and discontinuance. In addition, responsibility for the acts of the partners is initially placed upon the partnership rather than the partners, and creditors of the partnership are given priority in partnership assets.

The Uniform Partnership Act has been adopted by 44 states, although some have made modifications in enacting it. Four have adopted it since 1970. The Uniform Limited Partnership Act has been substantially adopted by 47 states. Only Alabama and Louisiana have adopted neither act.

Louisiana, following the civil-law tradition, accepts the entity theory. Nebraska has modified the Uniform Partnership Act by defining a partnership as an entity, and several states by separate statute permit suits by and against the partnership in the firm name. A few provide for continuity after the death of a partner.

Summary

The partnership was known from early recorded history. There has been inconsistency in both the English and American law because of conflicting concepts of a partnership—between the entity theory that the firm is separate from its members and the view that it is merely an aggregation of its members. The Uniform Partnership Act, which has been adopted in 44 states, does not fully adopt the entity theory but several of its provisions appear to treat the partnership as something different from its members.

Creation of Partnership

Tests of Existence of Partnership.   The Uniform Partnership Act (UPA) (6[1])[1] defines the relationship as follows: "A partnership is an association of two or more persons to carry on as co-owners a business for profit." No formalities, such as registration with the state or even a written agreement between the partners, are required. However, receipt by a person of a share of the profits of a business is prima facie evidence he or she is a partner in the business. This presumption may be rebutted, according to the UPA (7[4]), by showing that a share of the profits was received (1) as payment on a debt, (2) as wages or as rent, (3) as an annuity to a widow or representative of a deceased partner, (4) as interest on a loan, or (5) as consideration for the sale of the goodwill of a business.

Following is a discussion of the characteristics of a partnership. However,

---

[1] The numbers in the parentheses refer to the sections of the Uniform Partnership Act (UPA), which is reprinted in the Appendix.

the most critical factor is whether the parties are sharing in profits and the management of a business. If they are, they are almost certain to be held to be partners.

Intent. Partnership is a voluntary relationship. It cannot be imposed, as for instance by the inheritance of property. Frequently it is said by courts that there must be intent to form a partnership. However, the subjective intent of the parties is immaterial. Intent is determined by the words and acts of the parties interpreted in the light of surrounding circumstances. Therefore, even an explicit, written statement that the parties do not intend to form a partnership is not conclusive.

Carrying on a Business. The carrying on of a business is usually considered to require a series of transactions directed toward a definite end and conducted over a period of time. This requirement is referred to by the draftsmen of the UPA in their commentary. At least one court has held that engaging in a single venture, such as constructing buildings on several lots of land, is not carrying on a business even though the venture involves several transactions.[2] However, frequently if short-term ventures are before the courts, they will be treated as joint ventures and partnership law will be applied, as discussed later in this chapter.

Any trade, occupation, or profession is treated as a business for the purpose of partnership determination. For example, ownership of unimproved land as an investment would not ordinarily be carrying on a business but the operation of an apartment house would probably be so treated. If a group of farmers joined together to buy supplies in order to get lower prices this would probably not be viewed as carrying on a business. However, if they bought harvesting equipment with which they performed custom harvesting for others for a fee, this would probably be considered a business.

Even if the endeavor might otherwise be treated as a business, if it is carried on by a charitable or nonprofit association, those participating in it will not be considered to be partners since their objective is not profit.

Co-ownership. The ownership must be of the business as such. There is no requirement that there be co-ownership of the capital or other property, real or personal, used in the business. It may be entirely owned by one of the partners so long as there is co-ownership of the business itself. "Community of interest" may be a more descriptive term for the requirement than "co-ownership." In a partnership there is a community of interest in both the profits of the business and in the control of the business. However, a partnership may be found even if one (or a group) of the partners is by agreement given the management of the business.

A voice in management standing alone is not conclusive proof of the exis-

---

[2] *Walker, Mosby & Calvert, Inc. v. Burgess,* 151 S.E. 165 (Va. 1930).

tence of a partnership. For example, a creditor may be granted considerable control in a business, such as a veto power and the right of consultation, without becoming a partner.

A clearly expressed intent not to share losses is evidence inconsistent with the partnership relation but is not conclusive. A failure to make provision for sharing losses is of no effect since the possibility of loss is seldom in the contemplation of the parties as they undertake to form a business.

Persons may be simply co-owners of property and not be partners. For example, assume that Allen and Beech inherit a commercial building and own it as tenants in common. If they merely rent the building to a tenant and share income and expenses, it is not likely they would be held to be partners since the partnership relation is consensual and cannot be imposed by another. However, if they then go on to buy other buildings and one or both of them become active in seeking out tenants, they would probably be held to be partners since it appears they are in the business of providing commercial space rather than just holding a building as an investment.

As a general rule, an owner of a farm and his or her tenant who own livestock and equipment together and who divide income and expenses are not deemed to be partners, since this is a very common method of farm tenancy. However, if the farm owner participates regularly in determining crops to be planted or when the livestock is to be sold, the farm owner may be held to be a partner and bound by acts of the tenant such as purchases made.

Where there is a clear agreement to be partners, partnership liability is found even though the business itself never gets underway. A partnership may also be found if associates operate a business without carrying out an intention to incorporate it.

Summary

There is no simple test for the existence of a partnership. The major requirements of a partnership are: intent, co-ownership of the business, and carrying on the business for a profit. No formalities are required to create a partnership.

The intent required is not the intent to form a partnership but the intent to perform acts which are viewed as constituting the establishment of a partnership. Sharing in profits is prima facie evidence of the existence of a partnership although this presumption may be rebutted. The co-ownership requirement applies to the business. It is not necessary that there be co-ownership of the property used in the business. Co-ownership implies a voice in management but partners may agree to appoint a managing partner or partners. Conducting a trade, occupation, or profession is considered to be carrying on a business. There is no partnership if the activities are conducted by a nonprofit group.

As a general rule, the sharing of profits together with having a voice in the management of a business are sufficient evidence of the existence of a partnership.

Rosenberger v. Herbst

232 A.2d 634 (Sup. Ct. Pa. 1967)

This was an action by Rosenberger d/b/a Clover Leaf Mill (plaintiff) against Herbst (defendant) on account for grain, feed and fertilizer. Judgment for Clover Leaf Mill and Herbst appealed. Reversed.

Clover Leaf Mill had sold farm supplies to Parzych who operated a farm owned by Herbst. Parzych operated the farm under an agreement which gave him use and occupancy of the farm and acknowledged his indebtedness to Herbst in the amount of $6,000, repayable with 5 percent interest per annum. Herbst and Parzych were to equally share net profits and losses and the actual farming operation was to be "under the full control of Parzych." The agreement further recited that "the parties do not intend by this agreement to establish a partnership of any kind or type, but rather (a relation) of Debtor and Creditor and Landlord and Tenant." Parzych failed to pay for farm supplies purchased from Clover Leaf and Clover Leaf demanded payment for these debts from Herbst.

HOFFMAN, JUDGE. The Uniform Partnership Act, § 12(4), specifically provides:

The receipt by a person of a share of the profits of a business is prima facie evidence that he is a partner in the business, *but no such inference shall be drawn if such profits were received in payment:* (a) As a debt by installments or otherwise, (b) As . . . rent to a landlord . . . (d) As interest on a loan, though the amount of payment vary with the profits of the business. . . . [Emphasis supplied.]

As previously noted, Parzych's indebtedness to Herbst was to be repaid from the proceeds of the farming operation. Furthermore, the agreement specifically provided that Herbst's remuneration was to be considered rental payments. Accordingly, no inference of partnership may be drawn from Herbst's receipt of a fractional share of the proceeds of the farming operation.

The construction of this contract must, ultimately, be determined by reference to the intent of the parties. Our Supreme Court has held: "[W]here [the parties] expressly declare that they are not partners this settles the question, for, whatever their obligations may be as to third persons, the law permits them to agree upon their legal status and relations [as between themselves]." In light of the parties' express statement of intention, coupled with the inconclusive nature of the remainder of the agreement, we hold that defendant Herbst and Eugene Parzych were not partners *inter se.*

There is testimony in the record that Parzych represented himself as Herbst's partner to Clover Leaf, at some unspecified date, and that Clover Leaf allegedly relied on Herbst's credit, for some unspecified period of time. There is nothing in the record, however, to suggest that Herbst, himself, by words spoken or written or by conduct, ever made or consented to such a representation. Parzych's unauthorized statement, without more, cannot give rise to an estoppel against Herbst.

Borum v. Deese

26 S.E.2d 538 (Sup. Ct. Ga. 1943)

This was an action by H. B. Deese and others (plaintiffs) against V. B. Borum and others (defendants) asking a decree partitioning certain real estate. Judgment for Deese and Borum appealed. Judgment affirmed.

Charlie Borum owned in his lifetime a lot with a residence thereon. Under the terms of his will this property was devised to his wife for life, the remainder to his four children. Charlie Borum died in 1929. The wife and four children occupied the premises as their home until the death of the wife after which the children continued to live together in the house. They agreed among themselves to occupy the residence as a home and to share equally the paying of taxes, insurance, repairs, improvements, and other expenses. In addition, they agreed to share jointly in their living expenses, including food and necessaries of life with the exception of clothing. The arrangement continued for several years.

H. B. Deese, claiming to have contributed $1,200 more than the others toward these purposes, brought this action asking that the property be sold and that out of the proceeds he be reimbursed for the $1,200 and that the balance be divided among the parties. Borum defended on the ground that the parties were partners and that the proper action was dissolution and winding-up of the partnership.

REID, CHIEF JUSTICE.   To constitute a partnership as between members there must ordinarily be more than mere common ownership or interest. So it is found that the term is used with reference to some business enterprise, or the joint pursuit of some objective, profit at least having some connection with it. This is not to be understood as an exact or embracing definition of a partnership, or even as a definition at all; but it is intended merely to point out what we generally have in mind when a partnership is referred to. Definitions may be found in 31 *Words and Phrases* as indexed on page 166, where it is pointed out at page 217 that "Partnership is the relation which subsists between persons carrying on a business in common with a view of profit. It is necessary to note the significance of the words 'carrying on a business,' which implies a relation entirely different from the enforced relation of tenants in common, as the owners of a ship or of a house, who must either let the property lie idle or keep it in some way occupied or used, deriving a return from such occupation or use. . . ." Likewise the distinction between the relation of cotenancy and that of partnership has been pointed out in 40 Am. Jur. 129, ¶ 5, in the following language:

While partnership property has many characteristics of an estate in common and of joint tenancy or cotenancy, the interest of the partners therein is neither that of joint tenants, tenants in common, nor cotenants. Their interest in the firm property is *sui generis*. Each is possessed of a joint interest in the whole, but does not own any separate part, and each has an undivided interest in the property of the partnership only after the debts are paid. A mere tenancy in common does not create a partnership, and a partnership will not be implied from the joint ownership or joint purchase of land, even when accompanied by an agreement to share the profits and losses of selling it; yet tenants in common may become partners, like other persons, where they agree to assume that relation towards each other.

It will be noted that the language of our Code on the subject speaks of a partnership which may arise "from a joint ownership, use, and enjoyment of the profits of undivided property." In the present case, that these joint owners agreed to be equally responsible for taxes and upkeep of the property added nothing to the relation which already obtained between them, they being joint owners in equal parts. The only additional undertaking on their part as between themselves, appearing from Borum's petition, was that they would share living expenses. This, it seems to us, to be purely incidental to the other relation, and had no connection with the ownership of the land itself, and as such constituted no burden upon the land. Certainly no profit was contemplated by any agreement or facts which appear. . . .

Capacity To Be a Partner

Minors and Insane Persons. A minor may become a member of a partnership, but since a minor's contracts are voidable, a minor has a right to disaffirm the contract and withdraw at any time. The courts are divided as to whether the minor, upon disaffirmance, can recover from his or her adult partners the full amount of his investment or must bear his proportionate share of losses up to, but not exceeding the amount of the minor's investment. There is agreement that the minor is not permitted to recover his capital contributions unless creditors' claims can be satisfied. The fact that a member of a partnership is a minor does not permit disaffirmance of the contracts of the partnership.

The UPA (32) provides that upon the application of or for any partner, dissolution of a partnership shall be decreed if a partner has been adjudged insane. However, until there is dissolution by court action or by withdrawal of a partner, an insane person probably is in the same position in a partnership as is a minor.

Corporations. The UPA (2 and 6 [1]) includes corporations as persons who may form partnerships. The Delaware statute, the Model Business Corporation Act, and other modern corporation statutes explicitly permit corporations to join partnerships. However, in past years some courts held that corporations had no implied power to enter a partnership, and a number of secretaries of state refused to accept proposed articles of incorporation which expressly conferred such power on the corporation. It was argued that to join a partnership was to delegate to other partners some of the responsibility of the directors to manage.

Summary

A minor may become a member of a partnership, but he or she may disaffirm the contract of partnership and withdraw. Courts differ as to whether a minor must bear losses beyond his investment. If a partner is adjudged insane, this is a basis for dissolution by court action. Under modern corporation statutes a corporation can become a member of a partnership.

Persons Represented To Be Partners

Effect of Holding Out as Partner.   Some of the earlier cases held that a person could become a member of a partnership by being held out as a partner, even though he or she never consented to becoming a partner and never actually participated in the affairs of the partnership. This theory of ostensible partnership has been abandoned. The UPA (7 [1]) provides: "(1) . . . persons who are not partners as to each other are not partners as to third persons." However, a person not a partner may, by holding himself or herself out or permitting himself or herself to be held out as a partner, incur liability to a third person who has dealt with the partnership in reliance on such holding out. The liability is based on the theory of estoppel, not on the theory that the party is a member of the partnership. In order to recover against a party as if he or she were a partner, a person must prove (1) that the party held himself out or permitted himself to be held out as a partner, (2) that the person dealt with the partnership in justifiable reliance on the holding out, and (3) to the person's injury. The only person who can hold a party liable as a partner is one who knows of the holding out and in justifiable reliance thereon has dealt with the partnership to his injury.

Holding Out or Consenting to Holding Out.   The cases are not in accord as to what acts on the part of a person who has been held out to be a partner will amount to permission. Some of the earlier cases have held that if one is held out to be a partner and is aware of that fact, and yet does not take affirmative action to stop it, and also takes no action to notify the public that he or she is not a partner, this amounts to permitting oneself to be held out as a partner. The later cases and the UPA take the view that to be held liable as a partner, one must consent to the holding out. Under this view, knowledge that one is being held out as a partner, without other facts, will not amount to consent.

Summary

Persons who are not partners as to each other are not partners as to third persons. However, if a person holds himself or herself out as a partner or permits himself to be held out as a partner, that person will be liable to a party who in justifiable reliance on the holding out has dealt with the partnership to his or her injury.

Unless the party being held out as a partner acquiesces in the holding out, thereby contributing to the creation of the appearance that he or she is a partner, that party cannot be held liable as a partner.

Wisconsin Telephone Co. v. Lehmann

80 N.W.2d 267 (Sup. Ct. Wisc. 1957)

This was an action by Wisconsin Telephone Company (plaintiff) against Walter R. Lehmann (defendant) to recover a judgment for the unpaid balance of a telephone bill. Judgment for Wisconsin Telephone Company, and Walter R. Lehmann appealed. Reversed and judgment entered for Walter R. Lehmann.

Walter R. Lehmann had been in business with his son, Wayne R. Lehmann. They were doing business under the name of W. R. Lehmann and Son but by February 1952, Wayne had withdrawn and gone into business for himself as a dealer in calves. Wayne lived across the road from his father, Walter R. Lehmann, and had his business headquarters in a building on his father's farm over which was a sign, "W. R. Lehmann & Son—Dairy Cattle." Telephone No. 196W was located in that building.

Commencing in February 1952, Wisconsin Telephone Company (Telephone Co.) carried telephone No. 196W in the name of Wayne R. Lehmann. The bills were sent to and paid by Wayne. In May 1953, Wayne requested Telephone Co. to list telephone 196W under the name of W. R. Lehmann & Son. The change was made, and thereafter bills were sent to W. R. Lehmann & Son, R. R. 4, Watertown (which was also Wayne's address), and were paid by check signed by Wayne. The bill for December 1954, in the amount of $1,261.16, was not paid, and Telephone Co. sued Walter R. Lehmann to recover a judgment for this bill. There was no showing that Walter R. Lehmann knew that Wayne was going to list telephone No. 196W in the name of W. R. Lehmann & Son or that he consented thereto. Telephone Co. never billed Walter R. Lehmann for the service of telephone No. 196W until Wayne failed to pay the December bill.

WINGERT, JUSTICE. The general principle applicable to cases of this kind is stated by a leading authority as follows:

A person who is not actually a partner may render himself liable as though he were one, by so conducting himself as to reasonably induce third persons to believe that he is a partner and to act upon that belief. This rule is based upon the same principle as that which has been discovered in the law of Agency,—that a person may become liable for the acts of another who was not really his agent, if he has so conducted himself as to lead others reasonably to believe that such person was his agent. It is a case in which the principle of estoppel applies.

The principle has been codified in the Uniform Partnership Act, under the heading "Partnership by estoppel."

(1) When a person, by words spoken or written or by conduct, represents himself, or consents to another representing him to any one, as a partner in an existing partnership or with one or more persons not actual partners, he is liable to any such person to whom such representation has been made, who has, *on the faith of such representation, given credit to the actual or apparent partnership,* and if he has made such representation or consented to its being made in a public

manner he is liable to such person, whether the representation has or has not been made or communicated to such person so giving credit. . . .

(2) When a person has been thus represented to be a partner in an existing partnership . . . he is an agent of the persons consenting to such representation to bind them . . . with respect to persons who *rely upon the representation.* . . .

The liability of the nonpartner being based on estoppel, it is essential to the cause of action that the party asserting liability must have been induced by the misleading appearance to change his position to his detriment.

It (partnership by estoppel) involves some express or implied representation by the person in question that he is a partner, in reasonable and bona fide reliance upon which the person now seeking to hold him liable as such has extended a credit, or otherwise changed his position, in such a manner that he will now be prejudiced if the representation be denied. . . . The party seeking to hold him liable as a partner must, in the exercise of reasonable prudence and good faith, have relied upon such condition or thing and been misled by it. Metchem, *Elements of Partnership.*

Estoppel *in pais* is an equitable doctrine, and in general does not operate against one unless his conduct has induced another to change his position to his prejudice.

Application of this principle to the evidence in the present case leads to the conclusion that there was no basis on which the jury could find for Telephone Co. There is no evidence in the record that Telephone Co. did anything it would not have done or refrained from doing anything that it otherwise would have done, had it known the true facts relative to the relationship between Walter R. Lehmann and Wayne. There is no evidence that Telephone Co. would not have furnished the service to telephone No. 196W or would have cut it off sooner if it had known that Wayne Lehmann was not a partner or authorized agent of Walter R. Lehmann. The service had theretofore been rendered when the telephone was listed in Wayne's name, and there is no showing that Telephone Co. would not have continued to render the service as long as the bills were paid, had it known that only Wayne would be responsible for payment. There is nothing to show that in changing the listing from Wayne's name to that of W. R. Lehmann & Son, Telephone Co. relied in any way on Walter R. Lehmann's credit.

Since Telephone Co. was seeking to hold Walter R. Lehmann liable by estoppel it had the burden of proving the elements of estoppel. Having failed to offer any proof of change of position to its prejudice in reliance on the misleading appearance Telephone Co. failed to make a *prima facie* case for the jury. Therefore, Walter R. Lehmann's motion for nonsuit should have been granted.

Limited Partnership and Related Forms

Nature of Limited Partnership. A limited partnership can be created only by compliance with statutory requirements. Such a partnership is composed of one or more general partners and one or more limited partners. The management of the firm is in the hands of the general partners and they have the unlimited personal liability for partnership debts which is characteristic of a general partnership. The liability of a limited partner, on the other hand, is restricted to his or her contribution of capital to the limited partnership.

The Uniform Limited Partnership Act. The Uniform Limited Partnership Act has been adopted by 47 states. The other states also have statutes permitting this form of business organization, and their requirements are similar. To attain the status of limited partners under the ULPA, a certificate must be filed with the county recorder or some other designated official in the state in which the partnership will operate. Included in the information required in the certificate is the name of the partnership, the character of its business, the location of its principal place of business, the term for which it exists, its capitalization, and the capital contribution of each limited partner. General partnership law applies to limited partnerships except as changed by the applicable statute.

The exemption from personal liability of a limited partner is conditional upon his or her avoiding participation in the management of the business of the firm. However, the limited partner is permitted to be an employee of the firm. Unfortunately, the decisions do not make it very clear as to how far the limited partner can go in giving advise or reviewing management decision-making without losing the exemption. There is no requirement that a limited partnership so designate itself in its name or otherwise in its dealings. The surnames of limited partners may not be used in the firm name.

Nature of Joint Venture. Courts frequently distinguish joint ventures (sometimes called joint adventures, joint enterprises, or syndicates) from partnerships. A joint venture may be found where a court is reluctant to call an arrangement a partnership because the purpose is not to establish an ongoing business involving many transactions but is limited to a single project. For example, an agreement to buy and resell for profit a particular piece of real estate, perhaps after development, is likely to be viewed as a joint venture rather than a partnership. Corporate promoters transacting business prior to incorporation may be treated as joint venturers, although some courts call them partners. Like a partnership, there must be a business (profit-seeking) purpose. However, a "joint enterprise" is sometimes found in vehicle tort cases where profit is not an objective.

The legal implications of the distinction between a partnership and a joint venture are not entirely clear either. Generally, partnership law applies. For example, all participants in the venture are personally liable for debts, and the same fiduciary duties as are imposed on partners are owed by joint venturers to each other. Distinctions have been made in the power of the individual members to bind other joint venturers, there appearing to be greater reluctance by courts to find apparent authority. This is related to the tendency of courts to put less emphasis upon common control of the enterprise than in the case of partnerships. Although less likely to be treated as entities, joint ventures are treated as partnerships for income tax purposes. A joint venturer, like a partner, is entitled to an accounting in equity.

Two or more corporations frequently join together to form a corporation to conduct some business in which both are interested. These are frequently referred to as joint ventures, but since incorporated they fall under the rules of corporation rather than partnership law.

Mining Partnership.   A mining partnership, as recognized in some states, is a distinct relationship somewhat similar to a joint venture. In these states when co-owners share expenses and the proceeds of operation of mining property, a mining partnership is formed. A partner in a mining partnership can charge the other partners with necessary expenses but his or her agency powers are less than in an ordinary partnership. Unlike an ordinary partnership, bankruptcy or death of a partner does not work a dissolution, and membership is freely transferable by assignment.

Summary

A limited partnership is a statutory form of business organization composed of one or more general partners and one or more limited partners. Limited partners are not liable for partnership debts in excess of their capital contribution unless statutory formalities are not followed in formation or they participate in the management of the business.

A joint venture is similar to a partnership but tends to be limited to a single project rather than an ongoing business. In some states the development and operation of a mine by co-owners of the property constitutes a mining partnership. Participants in joint ventures and mining partnerships have rights and duties similar to partners but they differ principally in the power of one party to bind his or her associates.

Davis v. Davis

429 P.2d 808 (Sup. Ct. Ore. 1967)

This was an action by Robert Davis (plaintiff) against James Davis (defendant, who is no relation to Robert) seeking dissolution of a partnership and equal distribution of its assets. Judgment for Robert Davis; James Davis appealed. Judgment affirmed.

Robert and James were engaged in a trucking business. They had signed a certificate of limited partnership but did not file this certificate with the county clerk as required by statute. Throughout the years, Robert and James had assumed equal liability on debts of the partnership and had shared equally in the profits of the growing firm. During the last two years, Robert devoted more time to the actual running of the business than did James; however, during the middle period of the business relationship both partners had devoted equal time to its affairs. James elected to terminate the partnership and insisted that Robert was only a limited partner and entitled only to return of his original investment and his undistributed share of partnership profits. Robert claimed to be a general partner and sued for an equal distribution of the partnership assets.

GOODWIN, JUSTICE. James relies primarily upon two facts in seeking to reverse the trial court's decision. First, it is conceded that in all the banking and other business transactions of the enterprise, the name "Davis Company, Oreg. Ltd." was used. Although this name is some evidence of the type of association intended, it is not conclusive. A name, if it does not reflect the true facts, cannot be used to the prejudice of the rights of third parties. In a case of an intramural dispute between the partners themselves, we believe that an inconsistency between the name of the enterprise and the method of doing business is even less significant than it would be if strangers were involved.

In addition to using a business name suggesting a limited partnership, the parties had, as noted, executed a certificate of limited partnership. The certificate was not filed with the county clerk as required by statute, however, and this failure to file tends to cast doubt on the effect the parties intended the certificate to have. Further, the certificate is merely a document required by statute for the effective formation of a limited partnership. Its purpose is to give notice to third parties dealing with the business. It does not purport to embody the entire business arrangement between the parties. Therefore, it is not as persuasive as evidence of intent as a comprehensive agreement would be.

When the evidence shows that the parties for many years conducted the business in every respect as a general partnership, and at no time as a limited partnership, any inference created by the certificate is quickly overcome. Whatever may have been the intention of the parties when they started the enterprise, their conduct proved beyond doubt that the parties were general partners from and after 1957.

Misco-United Supply, Inc. v. Petroleum Corp.
462 F.2d 75 (5th Cir. 1972)

Action by Misco-United Supply, Inc. (plaintiff), a seller of oil-well construction supplies, against Petroleum Corporation (Petco), C. J. Pinner, and others alleged to be joint venturers (defendants) for the purchase price of supplies furnished. Appeal from judgment against Pinner but in favor of the other defendants. Affirmed.

Pinner and Petco agreed to drill a test well—the Persons well—and a development well—the Youngblood well—on two parcels of ground under lease to Pinner. In connection with the drilling, which was to be conducted by him, Pinner ordered supplies in the amount of $141,716.61 on his account. The account was not paid and learning later of Petco's participation, Misco sued Petco and others who had agreed to participate in the well drilling.

The agreement between Pinner and Petco involved two written contracts that appeared to be inconsistent in part. The agreement required Pinner to give 60 days' notice and evidence of marketable title before drilling the Youngblood well. This was not done. The agreement also provided that Petco could elect not to participate further in drilling at the Persons site after expending $82,200, its share of the cost of drilling to an agreed upon depth. This depth was reached on February 24, 1969, and the following day Petco elected not to participate further. No supplies were delivered by Misco to the Persons well until after that date.

BELL, CIRCUIT JUDGE. If a joint venture exists under Texas law, one joint venturer has the authority to bind other joint venturers by contracts made in furtherance of the joint enterprise. Misco's case is dependent on the establishment of a joint venture among Pinner and the defendants or some of them. If the joint venture is established, the venturers would then be jointly liable for the cost of the goods sold to Pinner. If the defendants were merely owners of an interest in realty, or owners who have contracted for the operation of a lease by another, they would not be liable for the contracts of the operator or drilling contractor. A joint venture or mining partnership would not be created. The nonoperators would have only a contractual liability to the operator predicated upon the terms of the operating agreement, and not to third persons. Furthermore, and as Misco concedes, whether a particular agreement constitutes a joint venture depends upon the intentions of the parties thereto.

The matter of disagreement, however, is whether in the present case the question of intent should have been presented to the jury.

Opposing inferences from contractual provisions as to the intentions of the parties regarding the creation of a joint venture will ordinarily give rise to a question of fact. Whether such opposing inferences exist in the first place is a question of law. Here the contracts were of great length and were complex. Conflicting descriptions and definitions were used to describe the relationship of the parties. The language defining the liabilities of the parties and the conditions precedent to liability were open to more than one interpretation. Which parts of the agreement were to be in effect at a given time is not by any means clear. The conflicting inferences are apparent with respect to the joint venture liability asserted against the defendants. The district court did not err in allowing evidence as to the intention of the parties.

With respect to Petco, there was ample evidence of record to support the submission to the jury of the question of intent to enter into a joint venture with Pinner in the Youngblood well and to support the jury's finding. For example, we have previously noted the evidence which supports the position that Petco's obligations as to the Youngblood well were contingent upon Pinner's performance with respect to notice and title. Contrary to Misco's argument, it is a matter of substantive law in Texas that conditions precedent had to be met before a joint venture was created. "(Where) an agreement is made for a future partnership, but the partnership is to go into effect only after stipulated things are done, no partnership exists until the conditions are fulfilled." *Shell Petroleum Corp. v. Caudle* (1933).

As to Petco's participation in the Persons well, the matter is posed in a different context. The jury found that Petco did intend to participate in this well as a joint venturer. However, the jury also found that Misco delivered no equipment prior to noon, February 25, 1969. Upon consideration of Petco's letter to Pinner, delivered prior to noon, on February 25, 1969, by which Petco declined to participate further in the Persons well, the court entered judgment for Petco.

Misco challenges the effectiveness of Petco's withdrawal, contending that its liability could not be limited without first giving notice to third parties. While we agree with the proposition that a private agreement between partners will not limit their liability to third parties, we deem this rule to be inapposite on the present facts. Petco's right to withdraw from further participation in the Persons well was specifically provided for in the written agreement of the parties. Reliance by a third party, the *sine quo non* of the rule, is totally absent here. Misco never, in any way prior to delivering the supplies, had knowledge of the participation in the well of any person other than Pinner. Under these circumstances, the district court was correct in giving effect to Petco's withdrawal.

Problem Cases

1. Bulasky was one of three owners of a partnership which had two accounts in a bank which failed. After the Federal Deposit Insurance Corporation had paid off the insured portion of the accounts, the partnership still had a claim against the bank for $21,724.68 as a general creditor. Prior to its closing the bank had loaned Bulasky $30,000, for which he had given his personal promissory note. Bulasky seeks to offset the $21,724.68 against the $30,000 he owes the receiver. May he do so?

2. Anthony and Thomose Felice operated, as partners, Felice Office Equipment Co. Dorothy Felice, wife of Anthony Felice, was an employee of the partnership. On September 27, 1951, she suffered an accident which arose out of and in the course of her employment, and she subsequently sought workmen's compensation. Her petition was dismissed on the ground that an employee who is the wife of a partner is not entitled to the benefits of workmen's compensation since a contract of employment between spouses would be void. On appeal Dorothy contended that under the workmen's compensation act a partnership is considered to be a person and that she was an employee of the partnership, not of her husband, and is entitled to compensation. Is Dorothy Felice entitled to workmen's compensation?

3. Jaworsky, a veterinarian, entered into an agreement with LeBlanc, an operator of a lumber-yard and race-horse owner who was not a veterinarian, to sell at Breaux Bridge, Louisiana, veterinary medicines and supplies which could be purchased only by a veterinarian. The agreement provided that (1) LeBlanc would provide office space for Jaworsky in one of his lumberyard buildings in Breaux Bridge, (2) Jaworsky would purchase $1,000 worth of medicines and supplies, (3) LeBlanc would advance the money for their purchase and for additional inventory as needed, (4) LeBlanc would sell them at prices set by Jaworsky, (5) LeBlanc could retain all of the profits derived from sales until his $1,000 had been returned plus $350 "interest," (6) thereafter profits would be divided equally, and (7) LeBlanc would pay only cost for medicines and supplies used on his own horses and they would receive Jaworsky's veterinary services at reduced rates. Was this arrangement a partnership?

4. From 1941 until the death of Rafael Cavazos in June 1956, he and his son Martin together operated a farm owned by May. They signed the lease jointly as tenants. The operation of the farm was the only job that either Rafael or Martin had. Both of them had control over the operations. They jointly purchased farming equipment for the farm as well as fuel and feed, and jointly incurred living expenses and other expenses for the farm. All of these expenses were financed by loans from the Victoria bank. Notes and chattel mortgages on the crops and farming equipment were executed by both Rafael and Martin to secure repayment of the advances, and the loans were paid out of the farming operations. The administrator of Rafael's estate claims one half of the farming equipment and crops as assets of Rafael's estate. Martin claims that a partnership existed and that the farming equipment and crops are partnership property. Did a partnership exist?

5. James Romer procured a loan at the Gruver State Bank after providing the bank with an instrument which recited that he was an agent of RMC, a partnership consisting of certain named persons, with power to negotiate the loan. The instrument was signed by each of

the named partners. After default, the bank sued the alleged partners on the note which had been signed by James Romer on behalf of RMC. The alleged partners assert that there was insufficient evidence to support a finding that they are partners. Are they correct?

6. John Taber and Delmar Coombs were partners doing business as Hamilton Lumber Sales Company. They needed capital for the operation of the firm. John Taber and C. J. Taber obtained a loan from Ravalli Bank, and the money was used to finance the firm. The money obtained by the loan was deposited in the Ravalli Bank to the credit of Hamilton Lumber Sales, and checks on the account were to be countersigned by C. J. Taber.

    Hamilton Lumber Sales made arrangements to purchase lumber from Grizzly Bear Lumber Co. At the time the arrangements were made, John Taber represented that C. J. Taber was a member of the partnership and gave Grizzly Bear Lumber the telephone number of Hamilton Lumber Sales and of C. J. Taber's office and represented that he (John Taber) was C. J. Taber. C. J. Taber told John not to use his name again but made no effort to inform Grizzly Bear Lumber that he was not a partner of John Taber and Delmar Coombs.

    Before shipping lumber to Hamilton Lumber, Grizzly Bear Lumber obtained a credit report from Ravalli Bank which showed that C. J. Taber was a partner in the firm of Hamilton Lumber Sales. Grizzly Bear Lumber shipped five cars of lumber to Hamilton Lumber Sales which were paid for with checks countersigned by C. J. Taber. A sixth car of lumber was not paid for, and Grizzly Bear Lumber sued John Taber, Delmar Coombs, and C. J. Taber as partners doing business as Hamilton Lumber Sales. C. J. Taber set up as a defense that he was not a member of the partnership. Is C. J. Taber liable as a partner?

7. Hacienda Farms, Limited, was organized as a limited partnership with de Escamilla as general partner and Russell and Andrews as limited partners. It was arranged with the bank that any two of the partners could sign checks on the partnership account. Russell and Andrews visited the truck farm about twice a week and discussed, among other things, crops to be raised. There was evidence that they insisted that peppers, eggplant, and watermelons be planted, although de Escamilla thought the soil unsuitable. The partnership went into bankruptcy, and the trustee in bankruptcy sought a court ruling that Russell and Andrews were liable to creditors of the partnership as general partners. Are they liable?

8. The Pennsylvania Railroad Company had abandoned a branch line, and Johnson, Hicks, and Fenwick negotiated with the railroad to purchase the ballast and ties. The railroad would deal only with a corporation, so Johnson, Hicks, and Fenwick asked a corporation to sign the contract with the railroad, indemnifying it from loss if they should fail to carry out the contract. Although discussions had included the whole line, the contract covered only one section of it. The ballast and ties were removed on that section and sold at a profit which was shared by the three men with the corporation under an agreed formula. Subsequently, the corporation signed another contract with the railroad covering another section of the line. Fenwick, but not Johnson, participated in this transaction, and Johnson sued for an accounting and his share of the profits on the second section. Is he entitled to a share?

9. Fitzhugh, Thode, and Harnagel entered into a written agreement by which they were to purchase certain real estate, subdivide it, and sell the building lots. Fitzhugh was to furnish the down payment, title was to be held in his name. Thode was to survey the property, plant it, lay out roads and sidewalks, advertise, and sell the lots. The lots did not sell well and ten years later, stating he would sell the property at the best price obtainable, Fitzhugh gave notice of termination of the contract and demanded that Thode and Harnagel share the loss. Is this a joint venture which would make Thode and Harnagel liable for their share of the loss?

chapter 20

Relation of Partners between Themselves

Relation between Partners

Nature of Duty. Most partnerships arise from an oral or written agreement to form a partnership, although courts occasionally find the relationship between associates to be a partnership despite their lack of such a purpose or even the contrary subjective intent. The duties the partners owe to each other are subject to the contract between them. They may, for example, provide by agreement for unequal sharing of profits and losses, for the payment of salary or interest or some minimum compensation to some of the partners, and for unequal shares in management decision-making. Different classes of partners (such as junior and senior partners) may be established.

However, agency law provides a body of rules which will determine the relations between the partners if their agreement does not. Furthermore, partnership law—like agency law—imposes fiduciary duties which arise from the relationship itself and need not be specified in the agreement. They can be modified to some extent by the agreement but they cannot be eliminated.

Articles of Partnership. Although not required for the existence of a partnership, written articles of partnership are highly desirable for the same reasons written contracts are generally to be preferred. The process of preparing the agreement, if done properly, requires the parties to consider and provide for contingencies, such as the possibility of losses and the death of one or more partners, for which they might not otherwise plan. A written partnership agreement also tends to eliminate disagreements arising from misunderstanding and failure of memory. Many lawsuits involving partnerships could have been avoided if the partners had followed this practice. However, even in the most carefully drawn articles of partnership it is impossible to anticipate all of the contingencies which may arise in conducting the business. As to these, general partnership law will apply.

Articles of partnership usually include provisions covering at least the following matters: name of the firm, business to be carried on, place at which the business is to be conducted, term of the partnership, capital investment of each partner, how the profits and losses will be shared, how the business will be managed, how the books will be kept, salary and drawing accounts, definition of authority of the partners to bind the firm, provisions for withdrawal of partners and for dissolution and winding up of the business and, frequently, for continuing the business after the death or withdrawal of one of the partners.

Unless another rule is provided by the agreement, a partnership agreement can be modified only by the unanimous consent of the partners.

Summary

Partners may, by agreement, define their relationship to each other within certain limits, and it is desirable to have written articles of partnership. They cannot, however, relieve themselves of the fiduciary duties they owe each other. Partnership law determines their relations in situations not covered by a provision in the partnership agreement.

Partnership Property

What Is Partnership Property?   Most partnerships need to use property in the conduct of the business, whether they are engaged in manufacturing, in trade, or in providing a service. Usually, a partnership commences with capital, either in cash or other property, contributed by the partners. However, the partnership, as such, may own no property other than the business, and all the other tangible and intangible property used by the partnership may be individually or jointly owned by one or more of the members of the partnership or rented from third parties by the partnership. To determine what is partnership property becomes essential not only when the partnership is dissolved and the assets are being distributed but also when both the partnership and one or more of the partners are insolvent, since partnership creditors have first claim on partnership property and individual creditors have first claim on individual property.

The Uniform Partnership Act (UPA) (8)[1] provides that "(1) all property originally brought into the partnership stock or subsequently acquired by purchase or otherwise, on account of the partnership, is partnership property, and (2) unless the contrary intention appears, property acquired with partnership funds is partnership property."

Application of this rule is not always easy. Fundamentally, intent of the

---

[1] The numbers in the parentheses refer to the sections of the Uniform Partnership Act (UPA), which is reprinted in the Appendix.

partners controls. To provide a record of that intent with respect to the original property used by the partnership is one of the major advantages of having a written partnership agreement. A well-kept set of books for the partnership will show the partnership assets, and those assets appearing there will be presumed to belong to the partnership. It is also presumed that money used by a partnership as working capital is partnership property in the absence of clear evidence that it was intended to be merely a loan. The presumption is very strong that property purchased with partnership funds and used in the partnership is partnership property. In contrary decisions it usually appears that the court was strongly influenced by the rights of nonpartners. The presumption applies even when the property is not necessary to the partnership business or where partnership property rather than cash is exchanged for the asset.

Title to Partnership Property.   The task of determining ownership is made especially difficult because under common law the firm had no existence separate from its members. Therefore, title to real estate could not be carried in the firm name. Despite the contrary provision of the UPA (8[3]) and statutory provisions in most states which have not adopted the UPA, it is not uncommon for individual partners to take or retain title in partnership property because they believe this to be more convenient.

If title is taken in the partnership name it will be presumed that the property is partnership property. However, because of the common law rule, the presumption is not as strong that property held in the name of a partner is individual property.

Other Indicia.   The mere fact that property is used by the partnership creates no presumption that it is partnership property. This applies equally to personal as well as real property. The payment of taxes, or insurance, or the making of repairs by the partnership, and deduction of these expenses on the partnership income tax return will be used as indications of the intent of the parties with respect to property not held in the name of the partnership. Of similar effect is the making of improvements on such property or mortgaging of crops or rentals by the partnership. Listing the property on a partnership financial statement given to a prospective lender may be treated as an admission of the partners. Frequently such indicia are in conflict, complicating a determination of ownership.

Ownership and Possession of Partnership Property.   The partnership owns the partnership property as a unit; the partners as individuals do not own proportionate interests in separate items of partnership property. The UPA (25) states that this form of ownership makes the partners "tenants in partnership."

Each partner has the right of possession of partnership property for partnership purposes. If a partner takes possession of partnership property for his or her own purposes without the consent of the other partners and to their exclusion, the partner will have violated his duties as a partner, and the wrongful acts may be ground for the dissolution of the partnership. Although a partner has wrongfully deprived the partnership and his or her partners of the possession of partnership property, the other partners cannot maintain a possessory action, such as replevin, against the wrongdoing partner, since the only remedy available to partners for breach of partnership duties is the remedy of dissolution and accounting.

Creditors of Individual Partner. A partner cannot assign any interest in separate items of partnership property, nor are they subject to levy of execution or attachment by the creditors of an individual partner. Prior to the general adoption of the UPA the courts of different jurisdictions disagreed on how a creditor of an individual partner might reach his or her interest. Section 27 provides that a partner may assign his interest but that this does not dissolve the partnership nor terminate the assignor's participation in it. It entitles the assignee to receive the assigning partner's share of the profits and does not even give him a right to inspect the books or to information about its affairs.

Section 28 authorizes a court granting a creditor a judgment against a partner to enter an order charging that partner's interest in the partnership with payment of the unsatisfied amount of the judgment. The court may also and frequently does appoint a receiver to receive the profits for the creditor and to look after the creditor's interest. If the profits are insufficient, the court may order foreclosure and sell the partner's interest to satisfy the charging order. Again such a sale does not automatically dissolve the partnership but would entitle the purchaser to dissolve a partnership which is at will. Provision is also made for the payment of the judgment by other members of the partnership so that it can be relieved of the charging order.

Summary

Whether property used by the partnership or purchased with partnership funds is partnership property is fundamentally a question of the intent of the parties. A partnership may operate with all its tangible and intangible property except the business itself owned individually by its partners or others. There is a very strong presumption that property purchased with partnership funds and used in the partnership is partnership property. If title is taken in the partnership name, it is presumed that it is partnership property.

Each partner has the right to possess partnership property for partnership purposes, but a partner has no right to use it for his or her own purposes without the consent of the other partners. Partnership property is owned by the partners as tenants in partnership.

Neither the assignment of the interest of a partner in the partnership nor the imposition of a charging order on that interest by a court dissolves the partnership. An assignee during the existence of the partnership is entitled only to the profits which would otherwise be due the assigning partner. A court may decree foreclosure, and if it is a partnership at will the purchaser will then have the right to dissolve the partnership.

Tupper v. Kroc

494 P.2d 1275 (Sup. Ct. Nev. 1972)

Proceedings on a motion by Tupper (defendant in action for dissolution of a partnership) to set aside a judicial sale of his interest in three limited partnerships which had been made pursuant to a charging order obtained by Kroc (plaintiff). Motion denied. Affirmed.

Tupper was the general partner and Kroc the limited partner in three limited partnerships formed for the purpose of owning and leasing certain parcels of real estate. Each held a fifty percent interest. On several occasions Tupper had been unable to pay his share of partnership obligations, and on those occasions Kroc paid the full amount and in return accepted interest bearing notes from Tupper for one half the amount. Kroc filed an action alleging that Tupper had mismanaged the partnerships and had misappropriated funds from them. He asked that the partnerships be dissolved and that a receiver be appointed. The court appointed a receiver pending the outcome of that action.

Later Kroc filed an action against Tupper to recover on the notes and was awarded a judgment for $54,609. He then sought and was granted a charging order under section 28 of the Uniform Partnership Act. The sheriff was directed to sell Tupper's interest in the three partnerships. Tupper was served with notice of the sale to be held June 27, 1969, and Kroc purchased Tupper's interest at the sale for $2,500.

In March 1970, Kroc filed a motion to terminate the receivership, contending that the need for it had ceased since he was sole owner of the partnerships. Tupper then objected to Kroc's motion and moved to set aside the sale.

BATJER, JUSTICE. Pursuant to the provisions of the statute the district court was authorized to appoint a receiver to act as a repository for Tupper's share of the profits and surplus for the benefit of Kroc, or as the court did here, order the sale of Tupper's interest. In Kroc's application for the order charging Tupper's interest in the partnerships he requested an order directing a sale of that interest. Likewise in the notice to Tupper and his attorneys they were advised that Kroc was seeking a sale of Tupper's interest. The application and notice afforded Tupper an opportunity to take whatever steps he deemed necessary to either limit the charging order or prevent the sale. Tupper was allowed 30 days to file an appeal from the order charging his interest in the partnerships and ordering the sale. He did not appeal from that order, but instead waited nearly a year after the sale was made before filing a motion to set it aside. He is now estopped to question the propriety of the charging order.

Although Tupper concedes that the charging order is not under attack he continues a collateral attack by insisting that the sale of his interest in the partnerships authorized by the charging order was void. One of those contentions of irregularity is based upon the fact that an accounting "to determine the nature and extent of the interest to be sold" was not required by the district court before it entered its order authorizing the sale. An accounting prior to the sale of Tupper's interest was not compelled in this case.

Tupper also contends that his interest in the partnership was inadequately described. Anyone reading or relying on the notice of sale was, as a matter of law, deemed to understand that by statute the sale of Tupper's interest in the partnerships consisted of a sale of his share of the profits and surplus and no more.

* * * * *

Tupper's contention that the price paid by Kroc for Tupper's interest in the three partnerships is inadequate, is without merit. The mode for determining the value of Tupper's interest in the partnerships was by a public sale. The fair market value of $2,500 was established by Kroc's bid at the sheriff's sale. Kroc was under no duty or obligation to support or justify that price and the entire burden was upon Tupper to prove its inadequacy. Thus it became a question of fact to be determined by the trial judge who heard the testimony and observed the witnesses. We will not substitute our judgment for that of the trial judge as to the weight given to evidence.

Tupper contends that the sale amounted to an involuntary assignment of his interest in the partnerships and is in violation of the partnership agreements which preclude a partner from assigning his interest. We do not agree. A sale made pursuant to a charging order of a partner's interest in a partnership is not an assignment of an interest in a partnership. Furthermore, the partnership agreements could not divest the district court of its powers provided by statute to charge and sell an interest of a partner in a partnership.

Finally Tupper contends that because he retained an equity in the partnerships' business and assets, the district court erred when it discharged the receiver. Unfortunately for Tupper this is not true. After Kroc bought all of Tupper's interest in the partnerships, i.e. all of his right and title to the profits and surplus, Kroc was entitled to all of the profits and all of the surplus. After the sale Tupper had no immediate or future rights to any profits or surplus or any equity whatever in the partnership property, and therefore he had no valid reason to insist on a continuation of the receivership.

Although as a matter of law Tupper was entitled to have the receivership terminated and the receiver discharged, the wisdom of that request, short of the dissolution of the partnerships, is questionable, for as soon as the receiver was discharged Tupper had the authority under the statute, as well as the partnerships' agreements, to assert his right to participate in the management. By purchasing Tupper's interest in the partnerships Kroc did not divest Tupper of his other property rights.

The receiver was appointed at the request of Kroc. Now Tupper wants the receiver to be reappointed to protect Tupper as a general partner from liability that might be incurred through excessive partnership debts. At a glance it might seem that Tupper's fears have some merit. However, as a matter of law, at the moment the receiver was discharged Tupper's right to participate in the management of the partnerships was restored, and as the general partner he would, at least theoretically, be able to prevent the partnerships from incurring liabilities in excess of assets.

Management of Business and Compensation

Voice in Management. In the absence of an agreement to the contrary, each partner has an equal voice in the management of the business. The vote of the majority of the partners controls in making decisions related to the normal business of the partnership. However, by agreement the partners may grant authority to manage the business to one or more partners, or they may set up an organization in which the authority to manage certain defined activities of the business is given to one or more of the partners.

Even if the management is in the hands of less than all the partners, any major change in the nature of the business of the partnership or its location which would materially alter the risks of the business must be approved by all the partners.

Right to Compensation. In the absence of a contrary agreement, each partner owes a duty to devote his or her entire time and energy to the partnership business. This does not mean that a partner cannot have outside interests, but it does mean that the partner must not engage in outside activities which will interfere with the performance of the duties he or she owes to the other partner or partners. A partner must not engage in activities which are in competition with the partnership business or which will be injurious to it.

A partner is not ordinarily entitled to salary or wages, even if quite disproportionate amounts of time are spent by certain partners in conducting the business of the partnership. Unless there is a contrary agreement, actual or implied, a partner's compensation is presumed to be his or her share in the profits of the business. The same principle applies to rent for the use by the partnership of property belonging to one of the partners. A surviving partner, however, is entitled to reasonable compensation for winding up partnership affairs UPA (18 f).

If a partner does not perform his or her duty to serve, he may be charged with the cost of hiring an employee to perform his expected services or the other partners may be allowed compensation. A partner's breach of duty may also be ground for dissolution.

Profits and Losses. In the absence of an agreement defining the partner's rights in the profits of the partnership business, profits are distributed equally, irrespective of the capital contributions of the partners. Likewise, each partner is liable for an equal share of any losses suffered by the partnership.

If the partnership agreement sets out the proportions by which the profits of the business will be divided among the partners but is silent as to the way the liability for losses will be divided, each partner will be liable for losses according to the proportion in which he or she shares in the profits.

Summary

In the absence of a contrary agreement, each partner has an equal voice in the management of the business. A majority of the partners have the right to make decisions regarding the everyday operation of the business. However, all partners must consent to the making of fundamental changes.

A partner is not entitled to wages for services rendered to the partnership or rent for property used by the partnership except by agreement. A partner's share of the profits is presumed to be his or her only compensation. In the absence of agreement profits and losses are distributed equally. If there is an agreement only with respect to profits, losses will be shared in the same proportion.

Hauke v. Frey

93 N.W.2d 183 (Sup. Ct. Neb. 1958)

This was an action by Albert P. Hauke (plaintiff) against John H. Frey (defendant) asking that Frey be enjoined from taking possession of assets claimed by Hauke to be his individual property. Judgment for Frey and Hauke appealed. Judgment affirmed.

Hauke owned a certain lot on which he constructed a building in which bowling alleys were installed. A business known as Bowl Arena was operated in the building by Frey and Hauke. Frey managed the business and received a salary of $425 a month and Hauke received $500 as rent for the building and equipment. The parties planned to organize a corporation to operate the business but this plan was never carried out. Hauke claimed that he was sole owner of the business and that Frey was his employee.- Hauke gave Frey notice that he was discharged and brought this action asking that Frey be enjoined from taking possession of the assets of the business or in any manner interfering with the management or operation of the business. The court held that Hauke and Frey were partners in the operation of the business and denied the injunction.

YEAGER, JUSTICE.   The conclusion reached is that here was a partnership although there is not in evidence an agreement containing either complete details of organization or of functions after organization. This court said in *Bard v. Hanson,* "The scope of a partnership may be evidenced by written or oral agreement, or implied from the conduct of the parties and what was done by them." The acts of the parties and what was done, as disclosed by the testimony of Hauke, indicated a partnership which was to continue until plans could be worked out and a corporation organized to take its place.

This being a partnership Hauke could not by injunction deprive Frey of his possession of the partnership property and his rights in the management of the partnership business.

Section 67–318(*e*), R.R.S. 1943, (UPA Sec. 18[e]) provides: "All partners have equal rights in the management and conduct of the partnership business."

The general rule is that one partner may not maintain an action against his copartner on account of a partnership transaction where there has been no settlement of the partnership accounts and business.

Fiduciary Duties

Loyalty and Good Faith.   The partnership relation is one of trust and confidence, and partners owe to each other the highest degree of loyalty and good faith in all partnership matters. This is a duty imposed by law and need not be provided for in the partnership agreement. Nor can a partner be relieved of this duty by contract.

A partner may deal with the firm or the individual members of the firm provided he or she deals in good faith and makes a full disclosure of all matters which affect the transaction and which a partner should know are not known to the other party. A partner must return to the partnership any profit made in a transaction with the partnership where he or she has used misrepresentation or concealment. If a partner, in contemplation of the organization of the partnership, acquires property which will be needed by the partnership when organized, he will not be permitted to sell the property to the partnership at a profit.

A partner is liable to his or her copartners if he uses partnership property for his individual purposes, misappropriates partnership funds, makes a secret profit out of the transaction of partnership business, engages in a competing business without the knowledge and consent of the copartners, accepts a secret commission on partnership business, or uses information gained as a partner to the detriment of the partnership.

Duty in Transacting Partnership Business.   In transacting partnership business, each partner owes a duty to use reasonable care and skill and not to exceed the authority granted him or her by the partnership agreement. A partner is not liable to his partner or partners for losses resulting from honest errors in judgment, but a partner is liable for losses resulting from his negligence or lack of care and skill in the transaction of partnership business, and for losses resulting from unauthorized transactions negotiated in the name of the partnership. For example, suppose Arnold, Bond, and Cline are partners and the partnership agreement provides that no partner shall accept in the partnership name any draft for the accommodation of a third person. Suppose Arnold then accepts a draft in the name of the partnership for the accommodation of Thomas and the partnership has to pay the draft, thereby suffering a loss. Arnold will have to bear the loss.

Books of Partnership.   The UPA (19) provides for the keeping of partnership books, and further provides that such books shall be kept at the principal place of business and that "every partner shall at all times have access to and may inspect and copy them." The books to be kept are determined by the agreement of the partners. Each partner owes a duty to keep a reasonable record of all business transacted by him or her for the partnership and to make such records available to the person keeping the partnership books. Under some circumstances a partner may be entitled to a formal accounting.

Disclosure of Information. Each partner owes a duty to disclose to the other partner or partners all information material to the partnership business. He or she owes a duty to inform the partner or partners of notices he has received which affect the rights of the partnership. Partners are presumed to have knowledge of matters appearing on the books of the partnership, and failure to inform a partner of such matters is not a breach of duty.

If one partner is selling his or her interest in the partnership to a copartner, he owes a duty to disclose to the buying partner all the facts having a bearing on the value of the interest in the partnership which are not open to the buying partner. Likewise, the buying partner owes the same duty of full disclosure to the selling partner. Neither the buying nor the selling partner owes a duty to disclose facts appearing on the books or in the records of the partnership.

Duty to Account. Partners have a right to be reimbursed for expenditures they properly make on behalf of the partnership from personal funds. They also have a duty to account for their expenditures of partnership funds and their use or disposal of partnership property, as well as for any benefit or profit derived by them without the consent of the other partners UPA (21).

In addition to a right to inspect the books of the partnership, a partner has a right to a formal account ("or an accounting") as to partnership affairs. Under the UPA (22) this right arises when a partner is excluded from the partnership business or possession of its property, when the right arises under the terms of an agreement, when there have been benefits or profits received by a partner without the consent of the other partners, and whenever other circumstances make it just and reasonable. If a partner asks his or her copartners for an accounting and they refuse or he is dissatisfied with it, a partner may bring an action for an accounting.

Actions by the partnership against a partner for breaches of duty to the partnership are not permitted except through an accounting. The same applies to actions by a partner against the partnership.

Summary

Each partner owes to the partnership loyalty and good faith, a duty to use due care and a duty to account. These fundamental duties cannot be eliminated by contract. A partner cannot make a secret profit in engaging in the business of the partnership or in dealing with it. A partner is liable for losses to the partnership resulting from his or her negligence or from making unauthorized transactions.

Each partner is entitled to free access to all the books and records of the partnership. A partner owes a duty to disclose to the other partner or partners all matters affecting the partnership business which are not disclosed by the books and records of the partnership. A partner also has a right to a formal accounting under certain circumstances and may ask the court to order and supervise the accounting.

Elle v. Babbitt

488 P.2d 440 (Sup. Ct. Ore. 1971)

This was a suit brought by Ralph Elle and others (plaintiffs) against E. J. Babbitt, Beall Pipe and Tank Corporation, and others (defendants) seeking an accounting between the corporation and certain of the partners and the partnership. Appeal from judgment for plaintiffs. Affirmed as modified (reversed as to issue reported here).

Beall Pipe and Tank Corporation was a family concern which had been in the pipe-making business for many years. John Beall was president and owned 55 percent of the stock. His cousin Franklin Beall was executive vice president and owned 40 percent of the stock. The corporation determined that it needed new pipe-making equipment but did not have enough capital to buy it. John Beall proposed the formation of a partnership to buy the mill and lease it to the corporation. John and Franklin and 13 other employees of the corporation plus a customer formed a partnership, purchased the mill, and leased it to the corporation in 1954 for a rental of one cent per inch of diameter for each lineal foot produced.

In May 1963, the corporation was preparing a bid on a large pipeline job for Cascade Natural Gas. It was known that competition would be keen and Ralph Elle, chief engineer and estimator for the corporation, concluded that it would not be possible to get the job unless the rentals paid to the partnership were cut in half. At a meeting in the corporation's offices attended by four partners—the two Bealls, Elle, and Ben Wilkins, sales manager of the corporation—it was agreed that only half the usual rental rate would be paid for pipe produced for the pipeline job.

All of the partnership business was conducted in the corporation's office and the partners, except for the two Bealls and a few of the corporation's key employees, did not take an active part in the affairs of the partnership. These were left largely to the management of John Beall.

The corporation decided to terminate the lease of the mill in 1965 and offered to buy it from the partnership. After prolonged negotiations the final purchase offer of the corporation was refused, and it installed a new mill. Thereafter the suit for an accounting was brought. The complaining partners sought $8,289.62 for the partnership—the half of the normal rental which was not paid on the pipeline job—on the ground that the agreement with the corporation was made without authority and was not binding on the partnership.

MCALLISTER, JUSTICE.   Elle does not contend that there was any fraud or bad faith involved, but vigorously contends that the partners who decided to reduce the partnership royalties on the Cascade job were, in fact, acting for the corporation and that they had no authority to agree to the reduced royalty payments on behalf of the partnership.[2]

The management of partnership affairs in its dealings with third parties is governed in part by statute. ORS 68.310 provides:

The rights and duties of the partners in relation to the partnership shall be determined, subject to any agreement between them, by the following rules:

* * * * *

(5) All partners have equal rights in the management and conduct of the partnership business.

* * * * *

(8) Any difference arising as to ordinary matters connected with the partnership business may be decided by a majority of the partners; but no act in contravention of any agreement between the partners may be done rightfully without the consent of all the partners.

The power of a single partner to bind the partnership in dealings with third parties is covered by ORS 68.210:

(1) Every partner is an agent of the partnership for the purpose of its business, and the act of every partner, including the execution in the partnership name of any instrument, for apparently carrying on in the usual way the business of the partnership of which he is a member binds the partnership, unless the partner so acting has in fact no authority to act for the partnership in the particular matter, and the person with whom he is dealing has knowledge of the fact that he has no such authority.

* * * * *

(4) No act of a partner in contravention of a restriction on authority shall bind the partnership to persons having knowledge of the restriction.

Elle claims that the partners who were not consulted about the royalty reduction were deprived of their right to participate equally in the management of the partnership business. The rule stating this right is, however, subject to any agreement among the partners. The members of a partnership may, if they wish, agree to leave the management of the business in the hands of a single managing partner. Such an agreement may be implied from the parties' course of conduct.

During the years the partnership leased the pipe mills to the corporation the partnership's affairs were handled by those partners who were management-level employees and officers of the corporation under the direction of John Beall. None of the partners ever objected to this manner of conducting the partnership business; John Beall became, by tacit agreement among all the partners, the managing partner with authority to conduct the ordinary business of the partnership. In the present case the decision to agree on behalf of the partnership to a temporary reduction in royalty in order to enable the corporation to make a successful bid on a large job was clearly part of the ongoing management of the partnership's business affairs. John Beall, by virtue of the other partners' long acquiescence in his exercise of management, had the authority to make that decision and to bind his copartners by agreement with the corporation. It

---

[2] Authors' Note: There is no indication in the opinion that the complaining partners explicitly alleged breach of fiduciary duty by John Beall or the other partners who were key employees of the corporation. Would such an allegation have changed the result?

is also significant that the plaintiff Elle agreed to the reduction in royalty and so testified. It appears that the other partner Wilkins either agreed or did not object.

The award of $8,289.62 for unpaid royalties was in error.

Problem Cases

1. George and J. B. Wilson were brothers and had been in business together most of their lives. During the 1930s they got into farming, operating as a partnership in the name of "Wilson Brothers." At various times in the 1940s and early 1950s several tracts of land were purchased which were farmed by the brothers and some of the land resold. At the time of George's death there were 670 acres, all of which was held in George's name. George's heirs sought an accounting of the partnership assets, mostly livestock, and J. B. filed a cross complaint alleging that the land was also part of the partnership assets and was held in trust for the partnership by George.

   The testimony at the trial was voluminous (1,189 pages in the record) and frequently conflicting, but there was no testimony as to why title was taken by George. Neighbors testified that they thought the land was owned by the partnership and that both George and J. B. referred to the land as "ours" or "Jay's and mine." There had been several checking accounts used in connection with the farming operation. One had been in the name of a daughter of George. Most of the checks were signed merely "George Wilson" but many were signed "George Wilson by J. B." and "Wilson Brothers by George" or "Wilson Brothers by J. B." A common practice was for George to give J. B. a book of blank checks already signed by George. However, there was no documentary evidence as to whether the accounts were personal or partnership accounts. Some witnesses testified that they dealt only with J. B. with respect to land clearing and other transactions related to the land. J. B. identified checks which he testified were payments on land contracts or for improvements and were drawn on partnership funds. The land was assessed in the name of Wilson Brothers, and George had prepared the assessment for at least several of the years involved. An abstractor testified that about a year before George's death J. B. had requested her to prepare a deed for George conveying to J. B. one-half interest in the land and that when she contacted George he told her not to prepare the deed because it was his land and he was leaving it to his wife and daughters.

   Was the land partnership property?

2. Terry and Simmons were Portland, Oregon, businessmen who, in 1965, agreed to become partners in buying parcels of real estate as investments. Within two years two business buildings and a medical services building had been purchased with the down payments made jointly by the two partners. Shortly thereafter Simmons learned that a piece of property owned by the city was to be put up for sale. On it was a service station which Simmons was leasing for his business as a gasoline distributor. He told Terry of its availability, and after Terry had looked at it, they agreed to try to buy it as partners. Simmons then made the required $500 deposit. When it was offered at public auction a month later, he was the only bidder at the established minimum price of $75,000. Two months later a land contract providing for payments over five years was signed by Simmons in his name alone, and he paid the balance of the $7,500 down payment.

   Terry brought a suit in equity against Simmons, claiming an equal partnership interest in the property. Simmons' defense was that Terry had not paid his half of the $500 deposit although Simmons had asked for it several times. Simmons testified that Terry said each time that he didn't have the cash or a blank check and that he, Simmons, then dropped the matter. Simmons also defended on the ground that an oral agreement to create an interest in land is unenforceable under the statute of frauds. Does Terry have a partnership interest in the land?

3. Sanborn and Packard were operating a grocery business as partners. The constable levied on certain fixtures of the partnership business an execution which had been issued on a judgment obtained against Packard individually. Did the constable have the right to levy such execution on specific items of partnership property?

4. Boyd, Walker, and others entered into an oral partnership agreement to engage in the practice of law. There was a continuing disagreement between Boyd and his fellow partners as to the profits of the partnership and the consequent compensation due Boyd. The relationship was finally terminated and Boyd sued for an accounting, asserting that his compensation was to be based upon a percentage of profits of the partnership business and consequently an accounting is necessary to determine the amount due him. Does Boyd have a cause of action?

5. Lehman, a machinist, and Alford, a physician, formed a partnership to manufacture a small tractor using certain parts on which Lehman was to obtain a patent. Alford was to pay $20,000 into the venture. Lehman was to contribute the patents when obtained and the use of his machine shop, equipment, and tools. Lehman was to have complete management of the business and was to devote full time to it. The written partnership agreement provided that Lehman "shall be allowed an annual salary in an amount or amounts to be agreed upon by the parties hereto."

   The venture was a complete failure and the $20,000 was gone. Lehman never devoted full time but continued with other work. Upon dissolution Lehman claimed he was entitled to a credit of $17,500 as salary. The parties had never agreed upon a salary for Lehman. Alford claimed Lehman was to have no salary unless the business made a profit. Is Lehman entitled to compensation for his services?

6. Mrs. Babray, who had operated a tavern and had other business experience, put some of her business affairs in the hands of Charles Carlino, a small-town banker, after the death of her husband. She bought stock in the bank on Carlino's recommendation and bought U.S. Treasury bonds through him. Carlino suggested that she might be interested in investing in a motel and becoming a one-third partner with him and Mrs. Alongi, who was introduced to her by Carlino and who would live in and manage the motel. Mrs. Babray invested $30,000. Some time later there were disagreements between the partners with respect to the management of the motel. Mrs. Babray wanted to operate the motel tavern, but Mrs. Alongi would not agree. Carlino asked Mrs. Babray if she would be willing to sell out to Mrs. Alongi, who would borrow enough to return Mrs. Babray's investment plus $10,500, and that Carlino would sell to Mrs. Alongi on the same basis. Mrs. Babray asked for time to consider and then agreed. She was represented by an experienced attorney in the sale, and the documents involved in the settlement, including a release by each to the others from all claims growing out of the partnership and the motel purchase, were signed in his office.

   Shortly thereafter Mrs. Babray brought suit against Carlino, seeking to rescind the sale of the motel and the release and for an accounting. She alleged that Carlino had taken advantage of her in arranging the purchase and sale of the motel. Is she entitled to an accounting and a constructive trust?

7. Gardner was a member of a partnership dealing in notes and other securities. Gardner purchased, in the name of the partnership, certain notes issued to Winner of Kansas City. The notes were not paid when due and Gardner, acting for the partnership, accepted renewal

notes. Winner was adjudged bankrupt. The partnership suffered a $15,000 loss on the notes purchased by Gardner. A suit in equity was brought by the partners asking that Gardner be ordered to reimburse the partnership for the $15,000 loss suffered on account of the poor investment. There is no showing of dishonesty or bad faith on the part of Gardner. Is Gardner liable?

8. Lester was a distributor of petroleum products, which entitled him to buy such products at a discount. He and Liggett formed a partnership to conduct a service station. In order to take advantage of the discount, it was arranged that Lester would order and pay for the petroleum products required by the service station. Shortly after the formation of the partnership, Lester acquired a bulk plant which entitled him to receive an additional jobber's discount of up to one and one-half cents per gallon of gasoline. Liggett was not told of this additional discount, and it was not passed on to the partnership. When Liggett learned of the extra discount a dispute arose which resulted in dissolution. Liggett then sued for an accounting and then recovery for the partnership of the additional discount. Lester argues that the partnership agreement only included the distributor's discount and that the jobber's discount represented only a reasonable return on his investment in the bulk plant, which could not have been financed by the partnership. Is Liggett entitled to a share in the extra discount?

chapter 21

Relation of Partners
to Third Persons

Partner as Agent of Partnership

General Powers of Partner. The relations of the partnership to third persons, and the power of a partner to bind the partnership and his or her copartners, are set out in Sections 9–14 of the Uniform Partnership Act (UPA). In the absence of agreement between the partners, every partner is an agent of the partnership for the purpose of conducting the partnership business. However, even where there is such an agreement limiting the power of one or all of the partners to bind the partnership (for example an agreement that partners may not make purchases on behalf of the partnership above some specific sum of money without the concurrence of a majority of the partners) the limitation is not binding on third parties conducting normal transactions with the partnership unless they are aware of the limitation.

There are three kinds of evidence of authority which will give a partner power to bind the partnership: (1) specific agreement between the partners, whether or not contained in the articles of partnership; (2) the course of business of the partnership (that is the way the business has, in fact, been conducted); and, (3) the course of business of similar partnerships in the locality. Therefore, if the partnership is not to be bound by acts of partners which have been customary in the past or which are usual in partnerships of that type in the locality, those doing business with the partnership must be informed of the limitations. In the words of the UPA (9)[1] this general authority includes "the execution in the partnership name of any instrument, for apparently carrying on in the usual way the business of the partnership."

The partnership is bound by admissions or representations made by a partner

---

[1] The numbers in the parentheses refer to sections of the Uniform Partnership Act (UPA), which appears in the Appendix.

concerning partnership affairs which are within the scope of his or her authority. Likewise, notice to or the knowledge of a partner relating to partnership affairs is binding on the partnership.

Partner's Power to Convey Partnership Real Property.   Since each state, by statute, requires certain formalities for the conveyance of real property located within its borders, the power of a partner to convey partnership real property and the manner in which the instrument of conveyance must be signed will be affected by such statutory requirements. To bind the partnership, the conveyance must be made in the regular course of the partnership business. Under the UPA (10) if the real property has been conveyed to the partnership in the partnership name, it may be conveyed by a conveyance executed in the name of the partnership by a partner. If title to the real property is in the name of the partnership, a conveyance signed by a partner in his or her name will pass the equitable interest of the partnership in the property. If title to the real property is in the name of one or more but not all of the partners and the record does not disclose the partnership's rights in the property, a conveyance signed by the partners in whose name the property stands will pass good title to an innocent purchaser for value. If the purchaser, however, has notice or knowledge of the partnership's interest in the property, the purchaser will take subject to such interest. In the same situation, a conveyance executed by one of the partners in the partnership name or in his or her own name passes the equitable interest of the partnership. The same rule applies if the real property is held in the name of a third person in trust for the partnership. If the title to the real property is held in the name of all the partners and the conveyance is executed by all the partners, the conveyance passes all their rights in such property.

Limitations on a Partner's Power.   Certain actions are specifically stated by the UPA (9[3]) not to be binding on the partnership unless all of the partners have authorized them. They include an assignment for the benefit of creditors, disposal of the goodwill of the business, an act which would make it impossible to carry on the partnership business in the usual way (such as the sale of the entire stock of goods of a retailing partnership), confession of a judgment, and (although it now appears quaint)[2] submission of a claim to arbitration. Other acts which would not ordinarily bind a partnership unless authorized by all of the partners because they would not be "apparently for the carrying on of the business of the partnership in the usual way," UPA (9[2]), would be an agreement of suretyship or a guarantee of the debt of another, paying or assuming an individual debt of a partner or, at least under old precedents, making charitable gifts or subscriptions or providing gratuitious services.

---

[2] Courts no longer have the antipathy for arbitration they did when the act was drafted in the early part of this century.

Summary

In the absence of an agreement limiting the authority of a partner, each partner has the power to bind the partnership by acts which are ordinarily done in the carrying on of a business such as that in which the partnership is engaged, but this may be limited by agreement of the partners. In general, agency rules apply to admissions, to representations of a partner, and to notice to or knowledge of a partner. Title to real property which is in the partnership name may be conveyed by a conveyance executed by a partner in the name of the partnership. If title to the real property is in the name of one or more but not all partners, or is held in trust in the name of a third person, a conveyance executed by a partner in the name of the partnership or in his or her own name will convey the equitable interest of the partnership, provided the partner has acted within the scope of his or her power. If the title to the real property is in the name of all partners and the conveyance is executed by all the partners, such conveyance passes all of their rights in the property.

As a general rule, a partner does not have the authority to do acts which will defeat the purposes of the partnership or impose unreasonable burdens on the partnership, such as selling all the partnership assets, obligating the partnership as surety or guarantor for third persons, or paying or assuming an individual debt of a partner.

Borrowing on Partnership's Credit

Trading and Nontrading Partnerships.   The extent of the implied and apparent authority of a partner to bind the partnership depends upon the nature of the business being carried on by the partnership. Although the UPA does not recognize the distinction, a number of courts distinguish between trading and nontrading partnerships. A partnership engaged in buying and selling for profit, such as retailing, wholesaling, importing or exporting, is classed as a trading partnership. A partnership engaged in providing a service, such as the practice of law, medicine, the carrying on of a real estate brokerage or insurance business, would be a nontrading partnership. Businesses such as general contracting, manufacturing, or operating a commercial farm, where working capital is necessary, are treated as trading partnerships.

Partner's Power to Borrow Money.   The distinction between trading and nontrading partnerships is most frequently made in connection with cases involving the borrowing of money or the execution of a negotiable instrument where a partner's act is, in fact, unauthorized by the other partners. Courts making the distinction hold trading partnerships liable for money borrowed in the name of the partnership. Of course, a nontrading partnership may also be held liable if borrowing has been customary by that firm or by similar firms in the locality or appears necessary in the light of the nature of the business. The power to borrow money on the firm's credit will ordinarily carry with it the power to pledge firm assets to secure the repayment of the borrowed money.

If a partner having the power to borrow money does so and then converts it to his or her own use, the partnership will be liable. If, however, money is borrowed in a partner's own name, the fact that it is used for partnership purposes does not create partnership liability.

Partner's Power to Bind Firm on Negotiable Instruments.   Negotiable instruments play such an important role in the carrying on of a business that a partnership will, regardless of the nature of its business, use negotiable instruments to some extent. If the partnership has a commercial account with a bank, a partner will have the power to endorse for deposit in the partnership bank account checks drawn payable to the partnership. As a general rule, a partner will have the power to endorse and cash checks drawn payable to the order of the partnership, and will likewise have the power to endorse drafts and notes payable to the order of the partnership and to discount them.

If the partnership has a checking account, a partner whose name is not on the signature card filed with the bank may bind the partnership on a check signed in the partnership name if such check is issued to a third person who has no knowledge of the limitation of the partner's authority. If a partner has the power to borrow money on the firm's credit, a partner has the incidental power to give a promissory note for that purpose, and if for such a loan it is customary to give security, he or she has the power to pledge the firm's assets.

Under the law of negotiable instruments, Uniform Commercial Code Section 3–305, if a partner signs without authority a negotiable instrument in the firm's name for the accommodation of a third person, the partnership is liable if the holder has paid value and has no notice that it was signed as an accommodation.

Summary

A partner's power to borrow money on the firm's credit will depend primarily on the nature of the partnership's business and whether or not it is standard practice in such business to use borrowed money to aid in financing its operation. The nature of the business is sometimes categorized as a trading or nontrading partnership, and an unauthorized partner will be held to have the power to bind a trading partnership.

Ordinarily a partner has the power to endorse for deposit or for discount negotiable instruments drawn payable to the order of the partnership. A partner's power to issue negotiable instruments in the name of the partnership is closely related to a partner's power to borrow money on the firm's credit.

Reid v. Linder

251 P. 157 (Sup. Ct. Mont. 1926)

This was an action by Edgar P. Reid as receiver of the Bank of Twin Bridges (plaintiff) against A. A. Linder, James P. Darnutzer, Carl Darnutzer and A. J. Wilcomb, partners, doing business as Trout Creek Land Company (defendants), to recover a judgment on partnership notes. Judgment for Reid, and A. A. Linder, James P. Darnutzer and Carl Darnutzer appealed. [Wilcomb did not join in the appeal.] Judgment affirmed.

The Trout Creek Land Company, a partnership, was organized by A. J. Wilcomb, A. A. Linder, James P. Darnutzer, and Carl Darnutzer and at various times during its existence had rented land and raised wheat, purchased land and raised cattle, and speculated on the wheat market. The firm had no capital but borrowed money from the bank to finance its operations. It seems that substantially all of its undertakings resulted in losses which were absorbed by the bank. A. J. Wilcomb was cashier of the bank and handled the finances of the firm. In June 1921, Wilcomb borrowed a total of $16,828.26 from the bank upon four promissory notes signed "Trout Creek Land Company by A. J. Wilcomb." The money was used by Wilcomb to speculate in the grain market and was lost. The bank was declared insolvent and ceased business on May 28, 1923, and this suit was brought by the receiver on the four notes. The partners, except Wilcomb, appeared and set up as a defense (1) that the firm was a nontrading partnership and that the making of the notes was not within the scope of the firm's business and not necessary to the transaction of such business, (2) that the power to borrow money and execute notes was vested only in the members acting together and that no one member had authority to execute a note in the firm name, (3) that no one of the defendants nor the firm received anything of value paid for the notes, and (4) that the bank had knowledge of the limitations on the authority of a partner to act for the firm because Wilcomb was cashier of the bank and a member of its board of directors.

MATTHEWS, JUSTICE. The evidence does not establish a custom of the firm known to the bank, requiring that all notes of the firm be signed by all of the members, for the record discloses notes, acknowledged as firm notes and paid or renewed as such, signed only by one or more members of the firm or signed as were the notes in question and endorsed on the back by the individuals constituting the firm.

It is contended that the firm was a nontrading copartnership. The question is important, as in such a partnership a partner has no implied power to borrow money and give firm mercantile paper therefor.

"The test of the character of the partnership is buying and selling. If it buys and sells, it is commercial or trading; if it does not buy or sell, it is one of employment or occupation." *Lee v. Bank.*

"The partnership must be in a trade or concern to which the issuing or transfer of bills is necessary or usual." *Chitty on Bills.*

And although a firm may ordinarily come within the definition of a nontrading partnership, where the partnership engages in trading requiring capital and the use of credit, the rule as to nontrading partnerships does not apply.

Here no question of fact arises; the facts are undisputed. They show that the firm engaged in buying and selling cattle, as well as in farming and selling grain, and that it required capital and the use of credit; in fact, it operated from the beginning on credit alone and established a custom within itself long prior to the issuance of the notes in question. Whether the firm was a trading or nontrading partnership was but a question of law for the court. It appears that the issuance of negotiable paper was justified by custom and necessity of the firm as well as by the fact that the firm engaged in trading.

As the notes were traced back on the books of the bank as renewals of notes, the proceeds of which were credited to the checking account of the firm, it is apparent that the bald statement made by Linder *et al.,* that neither as individuals nor as members of the firm did they receive any consideration for the notes, presents no issue requiring determination by the jury.

As the firm was a trading partnership, each member of the firm was the agent for the partnership in the transaction of its business and had authority to do whatever was necessary to carry on such business in the ordinary manner and for that purpose could bind the partnership by an agreement in writing; and notes executed by one of the partners for the benefit of the firm became partnership obligations, binding upon all of the members of the firm, in the absence of bad faith on the part of the contracting partner and knowledge thereof on the part of the payee.

But it is contended that Wilcomb used the firm credit for the purpose of playing the wheat market, without authority from the other members of the firm and, in this, acted with bad faith toward his copartners. Even though this be admitted to be true, the borrowing was ostensibly authorized; and, if the bank was a bona fide lender, it was entitled to recover on the notes, even though the partner borrowing was actually obtaining the money for his own use.

It is contended, however, that the bank was not a bona fide lender, as Wilcomb had full knowledge of all the facts regarding the notes and their purpose and that, as Wilcomb acted as agent for the bank in the transaction, his knowledge was imputed to the bank. In passing, it may be said that the record clearly discloses that Wilcomb was superseded as managing agent of the bank three days before the notes were given; but, as the notes were renewals of other notes issued as far back as 1919, this fact may be disregarded.

It is the general rule that knowledge obtained by an officer of a bank while acting for the bank is imputed to the bank but that knowledge obtained by such officer while acting not on behalf of the corporation but for himself, or in a manner antagonistic to the corporation, is not imputable to it.

Enforcement of Partnership Rights and Liabilities

Suits by and against Partnerships. Since partnerships were not considered a legal entity at common law, a partnership could neither sue nor be sued in its own name, but rather all partners had to be joined. Furthermore, since partners are jointly liable on partnership contracts, it was necessary to get personal service on each of the joint obligors. The difficulty this creates when partnerships conduct business in and are formed by people from different jurisdictions has resulted in remedial statutes in most states, but these statutes are not uniform. Some statutes make all joint obligations joint and several, that is, suit may be brought against the partners jointly or against each individual partner. Common-name statutes permit the complainant to proceed to judgment if he or she serves one or more of the partners even though service is not gained over all. The judgment, when obtained, is enforceable against the joint assets of the partnership and against the individual assets of the parties served with process.

In the case of tort liability all partners are individually as well as jointly liable. Therefore, the problem discussed above does not exist and recovery can be had from any one or more of the partners who can be served with process.

Partnership Liability for Torts and Crimes. The standards and principles of agency law are applied in determining the liability of the partnership and of the other partners for the wrongful acts of a partner. If the wrongful act is committed within the scope and in the course of the transaction of partnership business or is a breach of trust, the UPA (14 & 15) provides that the partnership and the partners will be jointly and severally liable. Whether or not the tort was within the scope and was committed in the course of the transaction of partnership business is a question of fact. A partnership is not liable in tort to any of the partners.

If a partner commits a crime in the course of the transaction of partnership business, his or her partners are not criminally liable unless they have participated in the criminal act. The partnership itself, since it is not a legal entity, cannot be held to be criminally liable for the crimes of its partners.

Summary

Partners are jointly liable on contracts of the partnership and jointly and severally liable for torts chargeable to the partnership. At common law all partners had to be served in a suit against the partnership on joint obligations. Most states have changed this by statute to make it possible to reach partnership property if any individual partner can be served and to reach the individual property of all partners personally served with process.

The rules of agency law are applied in determining when the tort of a partner becomes the act of the partnership. A partnership is not liable for the crimes of the partners.

Vrabel v. Acri

103 N.E.2d 564 (Sup. Ct. Ohio 1952)

This was an action by Stephen J. Vrabel (plaintiff) against Florence Acri (defendant) to recover damages for personal injuries. Judgment for Vrabel, and Acri appealed. Judgment reversed and judgment entered for Acri.

Florence Acri and Michael Acri owned and operated a cafe as partners. They had

had domestic difficulties and Florence had sued Michael for divorce. At times Florence had helped in the cafe, but following their domestic troubles, Michael was in complete control of the management of the cafe.

On February 17, 1947, Vrabel and a companion went into the cafe to buy drinks of alcoholic beverages. While Vrabel and his companion were sitting at the bar drinking, Michael, without provocation, shot and killed Vrabel's companion and assaulted and seriously injured Vrabel. Michael was convicted of murder and sentenced to life in the state prison.

Vrabel brought this suit against Florence Acri to recover damages for his injuries on the ground that Florence, as a partner of Michael, was liable for the tort of Michael.

ZIMMERMAN, JUDGE. The authorities are in agreement that whether a tort is committed by a partner or a joint adventurer, the principles of law governing the situation are the same. So, where a partnership or a joint enterprise is shown to exist, each member of such project acts both as principal and agent of the others as to those things done within the apparent scope of the business of the project and for its benefit.

The Uniform Partnership Act provides: "Where, by any wrongful act or omission of any partner acting in the ordinary course of the business of the partnership or with the authority of his copartners, loss or injury is caused to any person, not being a partner in the partnership, or any penalty is incurred, the partnership is liable therefor to the same extent as the partner so acting or omitting to act."

Such section, although enacted after the cause of action in the instant case arose, corresponds with the general law on the subject.

However, it is equally true that where one member of a partnership or joint enterprise commits a wrongful and malicious tort not within the actual or apparent scope of the agency or the common business of the particular venture, to which the other members have not assented, and which has not been concurred in or ratified by them, they are not liable for the harm thereby caused.

We cannot escape the conclusion, therefore, that the above rules, relating to the nonliability of a partner or joint adventurer for wrongful and malicious torts committed by an associate outside the purpose and scope of the business, must be applied in the instant case. The willful and malicious attack by Michael Acri upon Vrabel in the Acri Cafe cannot reasonably be said to have come within the scope of the business of operating the cafe, so as to have rendered the absent defendant accountable.

Since the liability of one partner or of one engaged in a joint enterprise for the acts of his associates is founded upon the principles of agency, the statement is in point that an intentional and willful attack committed by an agent or employee, to vent his own spleen or malevolence against the injured person, is a clear departure from his employment and his principal or employer is not responsible therefor.

Horn's Crane Service v. Prior

152 N.W.2d 421 (Sup. Ct. Neb. 1967)

This was an action by Horn's Crane Service (plaintiff) against Wendell Prior and Orie Cook (defendants) to recover sums due under a written contract and for supplies and services furnished a partnership comprised of Prior, Cook, and C. E. Piper. Piper was not joined in the action. Dismissed for failure to state a cause of action and Horn's Crane Service appealed. Affirmed.

The substance of Horn's theory of recovery was that Prior and Cook were members of a partnership and on that basis individually and jointly liable for the partnership debts. Horn's did not bring suit against the partnership itself and did not allege that the partnership property was insufficient to satisfy the debt.

WHITE, CHIEF JUSTICE.   In an action seeking a personal judgment against the individual members of a partnership or a joint adventure the petition does not state a cause of action if it fails to state that there is no partnership property or that it is insufficient to satisfy the debts of the partnership or joint adventure. There are several reasons for the rule. One of the most obvious is that credit having been extended to the partnership or firm, the members ought to have a right to insist that the partnership property be exhausted first. And to permit a firm creditor to by-pass the partnership property and exhaust the assets of an individual member leaving the partnership property extant, would be an obvious injustice, permit the other partners to profit at his expense, and place him in an adverse position with relation to his copartners.

Problem Cases

1. Mrs. Picone and Mr. Cox formed a partnership to conduct a floor covering business under the name "Gulfport Linoleum Mart." The partnership agreement provided: "Neither partner shall have the right to buy or contract for or on account of the partnership without the consent of his copartner." Cox signed an order in the firm name for floor covering to be shipped by Commercial Paste Company to the partnership's place of business in Gulfport. When it was delivered, Mrs. Picone received the shipment, and when she asked Cox about it, he said the goods were intended for the store he operated in Mobile, to which they were then sent.

    The goods were not paid for, and Commercial Paste Company sued Mrs. Picone and Cox d/b/a Gulfport Linoleum Mart. Mrs. Picone defended on the grounds that (1) under the partnership agreement she was not to be bound unless she consented to the purchase and she had not consented and (2) the goods were actually intended for Cox and Cox had taken the goods. Is either defense good?

2. Lule, Peters, and Barton were partners doing business under the name of Box and Handle Company. The partnership owned and operated a manufacturing business in Tennessee, where it made crates, insulating pins, and "dimensional stock." All these products were made of wood and, to supply its need for lumber, the partnership had purchased a tract of timber which they were in the process of cutting and manufacturing into lumber. The partnership had used in its business all lumber manufactured and had never sold any.

    While in Michigan Barton contracted in the name of Box and Handle to sell a quantity of lumber to Bole. Bole paid Barton $1,500 as a down payment and Barton appropriated the money to his own use. Box and Handle refused to deliver the lumber, and Bole sued the partnership to recover a judgment for breach of contract. Is Bole entitled to a judgment?

3. Wheeler & Company was a partnership engaged in the plumbing contracting business. It did not operate a retail store but purchased from jobbers and manufacturers the plumbing

supplies used in the fulfillment of its contracts and also hired laborers to perform the work necessary in performing the contracts. Wheeler, a partner, executed in the partnership name and issued certain promissory notes. The notes were not paid when due, and suit was brought against the partnership to recover a judgment for the amount of the notes. The partnership set up as a defense that Wheeler had no authority to issue the notes. Is the defense good?

4. Maerklein and Schroeter were partners in farming operations. Maerklein borrowed $1,000 from his brother Edward and gave his brother a promissory note secured by a chattel mortgage on 130 head of sheep which the partnership owned. Both the note and mortgage were signed in the partnership name by Maerklein, but Schroeter did not sign either. The money borrowed was used for partnership purposes. The note was not paid when due and suit was brought. Schroeter contended that since he did not sign the note and mortgage, he was not bound thereby. Is Schroeter liable on the note and mortgage?

5. Maclay brought suit for alienation of the affections of Mrs. Maclay against Kelsey-Seybold Clinic and Dr. Brewer, one of its junior partners. He alleged that between late 1966 and April or May 1967, while their children were being treated by the clinic, an improper relationship developed between Dr. Brewer and Mrs. Maclay and that acts of undue familiarity occured on as well as off of the premises of the clinic. He also alleged that in April he had notified a senior partner of the clinic of Dr. Brewer's actions. Mr. Maclay argues that the partnership is liable both because Dr. Brewer was acting for the partnership at the time the tort was committed and because it breached its duty to act when notified by Mr. Maclay. Is the partnership entitled to a summary judgment?

6. Rankin and Norswing were partners doing business under the name of Rankin Aviation Industries. Rankin, while operating an airplane owned by the partnership, in the furtherance of the partnership business, crashed while taking off, fatally injuring Rankin and injuring one of his passengers, Thompson. The crash was the result of negligence on the part of Rankin. Thompson sued the partnership and Norswing as surviving partner. Is Thompson entitled to a judgment against Norswing?

7. Marjory Pearson and Dr. Robert Pearson were dealing in real estate as partners under the name of Casa Blanca. They exchanged properties with the Nortons. The Pearsons brought suit for damages for deceit in the transaction and the Nortons filed a cross complaint, also for deceit. Judgment was given the Nortons against the partnership and against both Pearsons individually. Marjory Pearson appealed claiming error in the granting of a judgment against her individually since she did not participate in the deceit. Is she entitled to reversal?

8. Willson and Kitchner were partners engaged in the operation of a cattle farm in McCormick County, South Carolina. The partnership delivered to Palmetto Production Credit Association a promissory note secured by a security agreement pledging cattle and equipment of the partnership and by a mortgage on property owned by Willson. The copartnership failed to pay the promissory note, and an action was instituted by Palmetto to foreclose on the real estate and to effect a sale of the other pledged property to satisfy the indebtedness. Willson failed to assert any defenses to this action. Kitchner, on the other hand, filed a separate answer and asserted an individual counterclaim. Will Kitchner's separate answer and counterclaim be allowed in his defense to the action against the partnership?

9. Thomas Felderhoff, Jr., an employee of a partnership in which his father was a general partner, was injured while in the scope and course of his employment as a result of the negligence of his father. He first went into court and had his disabilities of being a minor removed. He then brought suit against the partnership, Felderhoff Brothers, and his father's two partners. Are the defendants entitled to a motion for summary judgment?

chapter 22

Dissolution and Winding Up

Dissolution

Effect of Dissolution. Dissolution is defined in the Uniform Partnership Act (UPA) (29)[1] as "the change in the relation of the partners caused by any partner ceasing to be associated in the carrying on as distinguished from the winding up of the business. Dissolution does not terminate the business; indeed, the business may be carried on without any interruption by the remaining partners, by one of the partners as a sole proprietorship, by a purchaser, or by a corporation formed by all or some of the partners. However, dissolution may have a very significant effect on the business and the value of the partnership interests because, in the absence of an agreement to the contrary, a partner may insist upon liquidation of the partnership assets after dissolution, except when dissolution is caused by a violation of the partnership agreement (38[1]). The value of partnership assets for purposes of liquidation seldom equals the value of the partnership as a going business. The process of liquidation is called "winding up," and usually this involves continuing to operate the business for some period of time. "Termination" does not occur until liquidation is complete.

A partnership may be dissolved without any violation of the partnership agreement; it may be dissolved in violation of the partnership agreement; or it may be dissolved by operation of law.

Dissolution without Violation of Agreement. A partnership dissolves at the end of the term—if one was agreed upon—for which the partnership was created or when its objectives have been accomplished. If no period of time or specific undertaking was agreed upon by the partners, any partner may

---

[1] The numbers in the parentheses refer to sections of the Uniform Partnership Act (UPA), which appears in the Appendix.

dissolve the partnership at any time by so notifying his or her copartners. Of course, the partners may, despite earlier agreement on the term of the partnership or on a specific undertaking, dissolve the partnership at any time by unanimous agreement. Such an agreement may be made at the time the partnership is formed, as in a buy-out agreement, permitting a partner to retire or withdraw and establishing a method of determining the amount to be paid a partner for his or her share by the other partners continuing the business.

Dissolution in Violation of Agreement. Under the UPA (31[2]) a partner has the "power," in contrast to a "right," to dissolve the partnership at any time. If such dissolution is contrary to the partnership agreement, he or she will be liable in damages for its breach to the copartners who are injured thereby. In this event the UPA (38[2]) gives the innocent partners the right to continue the business themselves or with new partners. The partner wrongfully causing dissolution must, nevertheless, be paid the value of his or her interest less damages, or the payment must be secured by a bond and he or she must be indemnified against partnership liabilities. However, the goodwill of the business is not to be taken into account in determining the value of the wrongdoing partner's interest. Courts have tended to treat any dissolution which is "wrongful," as where a partner refuses to carry out his or her financial or service obligations to the partnership, as a dissolution "in contravention" of the agreement so as to give the innocent partners the rights just described.

Dissolution by Operation of Law or Court Decree. Under the UPA (31 [4] and [5]) the death or bankruptcy of any partner automatically dissolves the partnership. The UPA (32) also sets out several grounds for dissolution by judicial decree: insanity of a partner, other incapacity to perform according to the partnership contract, persistence in conduct which is prejudicial to the carrying on of the business, willful or persistent breach of the partnership agreement, and when the business can be conducted only at a loss.

Dissolution after Assignment. An assignment of a partner's interest does not itself dissolve the partnership nor permit the assignee to participate in management or to look at the books. It only entitles the assignee to the assignor's share of the profits (27). However, the assignment of the assignee's interest by a partner or the imposition of a charging order by a creditor permits the partners whose interests have not been assigned or charged to dissolve the partnership by agreement among themselves (31[1] c).

Summary

Any change in the membership of a partnership causes its dissolution. Dissolution, which usually does not involve an interruption in the firm's business, should be distinguished from the winding up and termination of the partnership.

Dissolution without violation of the partnership agreement may be caused by the expiration of the term or by the accomplishment of the objective of the partnership, or if no term or objective is stated, at the will of any partner, or by the mutual agreement of the partners. A partner can withdraw and dissolve the partnership even if it amounts to a breach of the partnership agreement, but he or she is then subject to liability to the other partners for damages.

A partnership is automatically dissolved by the death or bankruptcy of a partner, or it may be dissolved by court decree on a number of grounds stated in the UPA. An assignment of a partner's interest does not automatically dissolve the partnership, but it or the imposition of a charging order permits the other partners in the business to dissolve the partnership by agreement among themselves.

Cox v. Jones

412 S.W.2d 143 (Sup. Ct. Mo. 1966)

This was an action by Dr. William L. Cox (plaintiff) against his former partner, Dr. Charles E. Jones (defendant), seeking an accounting and a share of remaining accounts receivable. Judgment for Dr. Cox and Dr. Jones appealed. Judgment reversed in part (affirmed on issues not here discussed).

Dr. Cox and Dr. Jones were partners in a medical practice. The written partnership agreement provided that a withdrawing partner's capital investment would be purchased by the remaining partner at book value and that for six months following withdrawal all accounts receivable collections would be divided per the existing percentage formula. At the end of this period, all accounts receivable were to become the property of the remaining partner. Following a series of disagreements, Dr. Jones orally informed Dr. Cox that he was leaving as of October 1, 1963. Dr. Cox thereafter sought another doctor to join the practice, but prior to October 1, Dr. Jones gave notice that he had changed his mind and was not leaving. Dr. Jones refused to set a definite termination date and on November 9, 1963, Dr. Cox wrote to Dr. Jones requesting his withdrawal as of December 31, 1963. The letter stated that if Dr. Jones refused to withdraw, Dr. Cox would withdraw as of February 15, 1964. Dr. Jones took no further action, and on February 15, Dr. Cox left the practice. Dr. Cox claimed that he was entitled to the accounts receivable as the remaining partner by reason of Dr. Jones's oral notice of withdrawal as of October 1, 1963.

PER CURIAM.   The letter of November 9, 1963, from Dr. Cox to Dr. Jones, has no legal significance except as a *written* notice of partnership termination by Dr. Cox effective February 15, 1964. It is clear that as of the date of the letter the partnership had not been dissolved by Dr. Jones's acts or conduct as of October 1, 1963. The record shows only that he withdrew his oral notice of dissolution before it was acted upon (accepted) by Dr. Cox. That Dr. Jones could do this is elementary in contract law. Dr. Cox testified that Dr. Jones told him he had changed his mind *before* the oral termination date of October 1, 1963. It thus appears from all the evidence that Dr.

Jones was not the withdrawing partner as of October 1, 1963. Dr. Cox's letter of November 9 could not have the effect of forcing Dr. Jones to give a notice and become a withdrawing partner and thus work a forfeiture of his interest in the accounts receivable, in accordance with paragraph 11 of the April 1, 1962 partnership agreement. On this record we can conclude only that by the November 9, 1963 letter, Dr. Cox became the withdrawing partner as of his own termination date, February 15, 1964. The result which we reach is that Dr. Jones does not forfeit his interest in the accounts receivable, but under the terms of these parties' agreement, each partner must share equally in all the accounts receivable for six months after February 15, 1964, after which the remaining accounts and collections thereon are the property of Dr. Jones.

Cooper v. Isaacs

448 F.2d 1202 (D. C. Cir. 1971)

This was a suit by Cooper (plaintiff) against Isaacs (defendant) seeking dissolution of their partnership. The District Court appointed a receiver to supervise partnership business pending determination on the merits. Affirmed.

Cooper and Isaacs were partners in the sale of janitorial supplies, doing business as Lesco Associates. In 1965, after three years of operations, they entered into a written partnership agreement. The agreement provided that the partnership would continue "until terminated as herein provided." Then followed specific provisions regarding termination by sale of interests, mutual consent, retirement of a partner, death of a partner, or incompetency of a partner.

In 1970 Cooper brought suit under section 32 of the Uniform Partnership Act seeking dissolution of the partnership because of irreconcilable differences between the partners on matters of policy and requesting the appointment of a receiver *pendente lite* and permanently until the business was wound up. Isaacs filed a counterclaim charging that Cooper's filing of his complaint constituted a wrongful dissolution in contravention of the partnership agreement under section 31. Isaacs claimed that under section 38 he was entitled to continue the business in the name of the partnership and sought damages and both a *pendente lite* and a permanent injunction prohibiting Cooper from interfering with the business or engaging in a competing business within a 25-mile radius of the District of Columbia. Then both the partners moved for the *pendente lite* relief they had requested. The District Court granted Cooper's motion and denied Isaacs.

TAMM, CIRCUIT JUDGE.   In determining whether the District Judge's appointment of a receiver *pendente lite* was a permissible exercise of his authority, we must first decide whether appellee Cooper's filing of his complaint requesting dissolution of the partnership on the ground of irreconcilable differences regarding business policy was itself a wrongful dissolution of the partnership in contravention of the partnership agreement. If it was, then appellant Isaacs was entitled to relief under section 38, and the appointment of the receiver was improper as a matter of law.

Section 31 of the Uniform Partnership Act provides:

Dissolution is caused:

*   *   *   *   *

by *decree of court* under section 32. (emphasis added)

Turning to section 32, we find the following provisions:

(1) On application by or for a partner the court shall decree a dissolution whenever—

*   *   *   *   *

(c) a partner has been guilty of such conduct as tends to affect prejudicially the carrying on of the business;

(d) a partner willfully or persistently commits a breach of the partnership agreement, or otherwise so conducts himself in matters relating to the partnership business that it is not reasonably practicable to carry on the business in partnership with him.

*   *   *   *   *

(f) other circumstances render a dissolution equitable.

Courts interpreting these provisions have consistently held that serious and irreconcilable differences between the parties are proper grounds for dissolution by decree of court. Since the Act provides for dissolution for cause by decree of court and Cooper has alleged facts which would entitle him to a dissolution on this ground if proven, his filing of his complaint cannot be said to effect a dissolution, wrongful or otherwise, under the Act; dissolution would occur only when decreed by the court or brought about by other actions.

A partnership agreement can presumably change this result, but the terms of the agreement must be quite specific to effect such a change. . . .

We do not believe it can be said at this time, with the case in its present posture, that the partnership agreement involved here was clearly meant to exclude the possibility of dissolution of the partnership by decree of court under section 32. True, the partnership agreement does discuss certain ways by which the partnership can be terminated and states that the partnership "shall continue until terminated as herein provided." However, it may well be that the parties did not consider the possibility that serious disagreements would arise at the time they made the agreement; the language limiting the methods of terminating the partnership may have been intended only to prevent a partner from dissolving the partnership voluntarily and without good cause. We thus conclude that without further inquiry into the partnership agreement and the claims made by the parties, it is impossible to say that the mere filing of the complaint by Cooper constituted a wrongful dissolution.

Having concluded that the appointment of the receiver *pendente lite* was not invalid as a matter of law, we must now decide whether the District Judge abused his discretion in making the appointment. Although there is some conflict in the opinions as to when it is permissible to appoint a receiver in a case involving the proposed dissolution of a partnership, we believe the action taken here was clearly a proper exercise of judicial discretion. There appears to be no question that very serious disagreements have frequently occurred between the parties to this case. The parties are in conflict as to whether these disagreements threaten the continued success of the business, but considering their apparent seriousness and frequency, the District Judge's conclusion that they do is certainly a reasonable one.

Winding Up Partnership Business

The Process.   If a partnership business is to be terminated, the next step after the dissolution is the winding up of the partnership business. This involves the orderly liquidation of the assets of the business. The partnership continues to exist until the liquidation is completed and the proceeds are distributed. During this period the partners continue to owe a fiduciary duty to each other, especially in negotiating sales or making distribution of partnership assets to members of the partnership. However, the powers of a partner to bind the partnership are limited to those acts which are reasonably necessary to the winding up of the partnership affairs.

Who Winds Up Business?   Under the provisions of the UPA (37), if the dissolution of a partnership is brought about amicably and during the lifetime of the partners, they have the right to wind up the business. If the dissolution is due to the death or bankruptcy of a partner, the surviving partners, or partners not bankrupt, have the right to wind up the business. If the dissolution is by court decree, a receiver is usually appointed to wind up the business. A partner winding up the business is generally entitled to compensation beyond his or her share in the profits only by agreement, unless a partner is the survivor after dissolution by death.

Partner's Power in Winding Up.   The partner or partners who have charge of winding up the partnership business have the power to bind the partnership in any transaction necessary to the liquidation of the assets. They may collect on negotiable paper held by the partnership, collect moneys due, sell partnership property, sue to enforce partnership rights, and do such other acts as the nature of the business and the circumstances dictate. As a general rule, a partner who is winding up a partnership business cannot borrow money in the name of the partnership. However, if by borrowing money and using it to pay partnership obligations a partner can preserve the assets of the partnership or enhance them for sale, he or she will make, renew, or endorse negotiable instruments.

A partner's power to bind the partnership on contracts will depend on the nature of the contract. If the contract is in furtherance of the orderly liquidation of the assets, he or she can bind the partnership; but if it is "new business," the partnership will not be bound.

In addition, a partner who has the right to wind up the business has apparent authority to bind the partnership by any act which would have bound the partnership prior to dissolution unless the other party had knowledge of the dissolution or specified steps to notify him or her had been taken (35). If the other party had been a creditor of the partnership prior to dissolution, that other party must be directly informed of the dissolution or a written notice of the dissolution must be delivered to him or her or to a proper person at his or her residence or place of business. If the other party were merely aware of the earlier partnership, newspaper notice to him or her is sufficient to protect the partnership from liability.

At the death of a partner, right to all partnership property vests in the surviving partner or partners. He or she or they may pass title to real estate held in the partnership name without joinder of the decedent's representatives. In the absence of agreement, the survivors have only the right to wind up the business.

Summary

If the partnership business is to be terminated after dissolution, the partnership relation will continue to exist until the assets of the partnership are liquidated, the partnership creditors are paid, and the remaining assets are distributed to the partners.

In the event the dissolution is caused by the death or bankruptcy of a partner, the surviving partners or those not bankrupt have the right to wind up the business. If the partners cannot agree, a receiver may be appointed for this purpose. After dissolution the partner or partners who are winding up the partnership business have the authority to do those acts which are reasonably necessary to wind up the business, but they do not have authority to engage in new business.

In addition, one winding up the business has broad apparent authority which will bind the partnership to those who may do business with the firm unless they are notified in accordance with the provisions of the UPA.

State v. Ed Cox and Son

132 N.W.2d 282 (Sup. Ct. S.D. 1965)

This was an action by the State of South Dakota for the use of Farmers State Bank (plaintiff) against Ed Cox and Son and William B. Cox (defendants) to recover a judgment for money loaned. Judgment for Farmers State Bank; and Tennefos Construction Company and United Pacific Insurance Company, surety, and Ed Cox and Son appealed. Judgment affirmed.

Ed Cox and Son, a partnership consisting of Ed Cox and William B. Cox, entered into a contract with the State of South Dakota for the construction of a section of highway. Ed Cox and Son executed a performance bond with United Pacific Insurance Company (Pacific) as surety. Tennefos Construction Company was co-contractor with Ed Cox and Son. Ed Cox and Son, prior to June 1, 1956, borrowed money from Farmers State Bank (Bank). Between June 1, 1956, and August 16, 1956, Ed Cox borrowed from Bank further sums and after August 16, 1956, William B. Cox, as surviving partner (Ed Cox died on August 16, 1956), borrowed further sums. Ed Cox and Son owed Bank $108,492.42 at the time of suit. On June 1, 1956, Ed Cox and William B. Cox dissolved the partnership of Ed Cox and Son but Bank was not given notice of dissolution and had no knowledge of it. The money borrowed from Bank by William B. Cox as surviving partner was used to pay for labor and materials necessary to complete the construction contract. Pacific contends that it is not liable for moneys loaned to Ed Cox and Son by Bank after June 1, 1956.

RENTTO, JUDGE.   The death of Ed Cox dissolved the partnership, but it did not terminate it. As declared in SDC 49.0602 the partnership continued until the winding up of its affairs was completed. The dissolution resulting from the death of Ed Cox terminated the authority of William Cox to act for the partnership "Except so far as may be necessary to wind up partnership affairs or to complete transactions begun but not then finished." This is reiterated in SDC 49.0607 wherein it is provided that "After dissolution a partner can bind the partnership . . . (a) By any act appropriate for winding up partnership affairs or completing transactions unfinished at dissolution; . . .". Transactions unfinished at dissolution have been held to include road and other construction contracts. Funds advanced or furnished to the surviving partner for such purpose are legitimate expenses for which the partnership is liable.

Under SDC 49.0609 William Cox as a surviving partner had the right to wind up the affairs of the partnership. In fact it was his duty. He was so engaged when the notes in question were executed. In our view they are proper obligations of the partnership. Ed Cox and Pacific argue that because of the dissolution agreement of June 1st he was not a surviving partner when his father died. This dissolution was secret as far as the bank was concerned and the subsequent conduct of William Cox in his dealings with it was consistent with the partnership's continuation. As to the bank the partnership continued until the death of Ed Cox.

When the Business Is Continued

Advantage of Continuing.   When a partner dies or if he or she desires to or is forced to withdraw from the partnership, all parties involved usually find it advantageous to continue the business because its going concern value is normally greater than its liquidated value. Certainly, for large partnerships (some have more than 100 partners) the necessity of going through a winding up process whenever a partner dies or retires would make this form of organization completely impracticable. The advantage of avoiding liquidation at the demand of any partner or his or her legal representative is so great that a prior agreement for continuing the business is advisable. Frequently, the plan specified in the agreement involves the use of life insurance on the lives of the partners to facilitate a transfer of a deceased partner's interest to the surviving partner or partners.

It is this "going concern" value which accounts for the UPA giving the other partners the right, discussed above, to continue after a partner has dissolved the partnership wrongfully.

Although it is arguable that there is technically a dissolution, many partnerships provide in the original partnership agreement that death or withdrawal of individual partners and the admission of new partners will not dissolve the partnership. The agreement then outlines a plan whereby the financial interests of partners leaving and entering the partnership are protected. Tax consequences to the various parties differ under different arrangements and the needs of the various parties and the business itself also vary so that drafting either a general plan in advance or a continuation agreement for a specific situation is often difficult and must be done with great care.

Liability for Obligations Incurred Prior to Dissolution. Dissolution itself has no effect upon existing liabilities of the partnership or of the partners. Contracts, unless calling for services in which a personal factor is crucial, are ordinarily not affected, and obligations under them must be completed or settled by negotiation during the winding up process.

If the business is to be continued rather than terminated, the original partners or their legal representatives remain liable for obligations incurred prior to dissolution unless there is agreement with the creditor to the contrary. When the business is continued after one or more partners withdraw and assign their rights to others, or when a partner dies or is expelled, creditors of the old partnership are creditors of the person or partnership continuing the business. This gives them equal status with creditors of the new sole proprietorship, corporation, or partnership (41). Creditors of the original partnership are further protected by the UPA (41[8]) by being given priority over separate creditors of a retiring or deceased partner with respect to the consideration due or paid to the former partner or his or her representative.

Usually when the business is being continued the continuing or new partners specifically agree to relieve the withdrawing partner from the obligations of the preceding partnership, the settlement between the original partners taking this into account. Courts have occasionally found an implied agreement to this effect where the assets are retained in the continuing business. Nevertheless, even an express agreement to hold the withdrawing partner harmless is not binding on creditors unless they join in it so as to constitute a novation. However, the withdrawing partner or deceased partner's estate is only secondarily liable as a surety. Mere receipt by a creditor of partial payment or a negotiable instrument from a continuing partner does not release the withdrawing partner, but an agreement by a creditor to hold only the person or partnership continuing the business may be inferred from his or her dealings with the continuing business if he or she has knowledge of the change of membership in the partnership. Acceptance of a negotiable instrument in full settlement of a claim has been held to be an implied novation.

A person joining an existing partnership becomes liable for all previous obligations of the partnership as if he or she had been a partner except that this liability is limited to the partnership assets (17).

Liability for Obligations Incurred after Dissolution.   Former partners or their estates may be liable for obligations incurred by the partnership continuing the business unless the prescribed notice discussed above is given (35) or the new creditor has knowledge of the change. The UPA does not exclude dissolution by death or bankruptcy of a partner from these notice provisions.

Rights of Noncontinuing Partner.   If after dissolution the partnership affairs are wound up and its assets liquidated, the normal sharing of profits and losses continues among the partners. However, when the business is continued, whether by right, agreement, or acquiescence, the noncontinuing partner becomes a creditor of the new partnership (subordinate to other creditors), and his or her interest in the partnership assets is determined at the time of the dissolution. If dissolution results from death or retirement, the noncontinuing partner then has an election, which doesn't need to be made until there is an accounting, so that the noncontinuing partner can determine which of two positions is more favorable: taking the value of his partnership interest at dissolution plus interest or that dissolution value plus a share of subsequent profits based upon the proportion of that value to the total value of the partnership at the time of dissolution (42). This option, of course, provides some incentive for the continuing partners to settle with the noncontinuing partner promptly.

Goodwill.   The determination of the existence and value of the goodwill of a partnership which is transferred when the partnership business is continued after dissolution is frequently difficult. In service partnerships the goodwill may be so closely tied to the individual partners that none carries over with the business. Because of these difficulties and uncertainties, it is usually advisable to include an agreement on this matter in the original articles of partnership. Too frequently courts conclude that goodwill should be ignored unless there is such an agreement or (in the unusual case) goodwill appears in the partnership accounts. The UPA specifically excludes goodwill in providing for valuation of a partner's interest who has wrongfully caused dissolution (38[2]c II).

Summary

The business of financially successful partnerships is usually continued after the death or withdrawal of a partner because it is worth more as a going concern. This makes it wise to have in advance a well-drafted agreement for continuing the business and buying the interest of the partner or partners not continuing.

Dissolution normally does not affect obligations incurred by the partnership, and they must be satisfied. If the business is continued, the original partners or their legal representatives remain liable unless they are released by a nova-tion, which requires the assent of the creditors. Also, unless there is a contrary agreement, the creditors of the previous partnership remain creditors of the continuing business. A person joining an existing partnership assumes liability for its previous obligations but only to the extent of the partnership assets.

If the business is continued after dissolution, the noncontinuing partner becomes a creditor of the new partnership. If the noncontinuing partner retires or dies, he or she or his or her representative has an election whether to be paid interest on the value of the partnership interest or to share in the profits from operations after dissolution.

Credit Bureaus of Merced County, Inc. v. Shipman

334 P.2d 1036 (Sup. Ct. Cal. 1959)

This was an action by Credit Bureaus of Merced County, Inc., (plaintiff) against Russell C. Shipman and Donald E. Davis (defendants) to recover a judgment for partnership debts. Judgment for Credit Bureaus of Merced County, Inc., and Davis appealed. Judgment affirmed.

Donald Davis and Russell Shipman formed a partnership in 1954 under the name of Shipman & Davis Lumber Company. On September 20, 1955, the partnership was dissolved by written agreement. A notice of dissolution was published in a newspaper of general circulation in the county where the business was conducted but no actual notice of dissolution was given to the firms which had extended credit to the partnership at the time of dissolution.

Under the terms of the dissolution agreement Shipman was to continue the business and was to assume and pay all partnership debts. After the dissolution several firms which had previously extended credit to the partnership continued to extend credit to the continued business. Their claims were not paid. Several claimants assigned their claims to Credit Bureaus of Merced County, Inc., and it brought suit against Shipman and Davis. Davis claimed that he was not liable for goods sold or services rendered after the date of dissolution.

SCHOTTKY, JUSTICE. Davis argues first that at the time of the suit he was not liable for the debts sued upon. He contends that no liability exists as to Laird Welding & Manufacturing Works because the amount which was due at the time of dissolution was subsequently paid, and, therefore, no liability existed at the time of suit. As to the repair item incurred on November 3, 1955, which was after the date of the dissolution, Davis would not be liable thereof if Laird Welding & Manufacturing Works had notice of the dissolution. While the evidence is conflicting as to whether the Welding Works had notice of the dissolution at the time the repairs were made, it is sufficient to support the finding of the court that the company did not have notice. The burden is on a defendant relying on dissolution to prove notice of dissolution. Davis cannot rely on the provisions of section 15035.5 of the Corporation Code (U.P.A. Sec. 35) to show actual knowledge. This section provides for publication of notice of dissolution of a partnership. However, as to firms having prior credit dealings with the partnership, actual notice of dissolution is necessary. While publication may be evidence from which actual knowledge could be inferred, publication alone would not compel a finding of actual knowledge. A retiring partner is not justified in placing sole reliance upon the publication of notice of dissolution, but should assure himself that existing creditors who have extended credit to the partnership receive actual notice of such dissolution.

As to the Merced Hardware account it is clear that the debts for the items sued upon were all incurred after February 1956. Davis contends that he is not liable for these items of debt because they were incurred after the dissolution of the partnership. Credit Bureaus in reply points out that section 15035 of the Corporation Code provides that after a dissolution a partner can bind the partnership "By any transaction which would bind the partnership if dissolution had not taken place, provided, the other party to the transaction: I. Had extended credit to the partnership prior to dissolution and had no knowledge or notice of the dissolution." Here again the evidence is conflicting as to whether Merced Hardware & Implement Company had notice of dissolution of the partnership, and we are bound by the court's finding that it did not. There is also evidence that Merced Hardware & Implement Company had previously extended credit to the partnership.

Distribution of Assets

Order of Distribution. The order of distribution of the assets of a partnership is set out in the UPA (40) as follows:

I. Those owing to creditors other than partners,
II. Those owing to partners other than for capital and profits,
III. Those owing to partners in respect of capital,
IV. Those owing to partners in respect of profits.

If the partnership has been operated without losses which impair the capital, few problems are presented in the distribution of the assets. Everyone having an interest in the partnership will be paid in full. If there is a disagreement as to the amount due any party in interest, the dispute will usually be resolved by an audit which will be ordered by the court and which will, as a general rule, settle the fact question of the amount due.

Distribution of Assets of Insolvent Partnership. If the partnership is insolvent, the order of distribution set out above will be followed, but additional problems will be encountered. For example, the relative rights of partnership creditors and individual creditors, and the distribution of losses will be involved. In adjusting the rights of partnership creditors and individual creditors, the rule that partnership creditors have first claim on partnership assets and individual creditors have first claim on individual assets is usually followed.

If a partner has, in addition to contributing capital, loaned money to the partnership, no distinction will be made, on dissolution, between the capital contributed and the money loaned as far as the rights of the partnership creditors are concerned. The only difference which might arise would be in adjusting the rights of the partners. After payment of creditors, a partner, under some circumstances, will be allowed interest on a loan, whereas no interest is allowed on capital contributed.

As an example of distribution of the assets of an insolvent partnership, suppose Alden, Bass, and Casey organize a partnership. Alden contributes $25,000, Bass contributes $15,000, and Casey contributes $10,000. After operating for several years, the firm suffers losses and is insolvent. The assets of the partnership, when liquidated, total $30,000. The partnership owes to partnership creditors $40,000. The accounts of the individual partners are as follows:

	Contributed to Capital of Partnership	Individual Assets	Individual Liabilities
Alden	$25,000	$75,000	$5,000
Bass.	15,000	10,000	2,000
Casey	10,000	2,000	6,000

The $30,000 will be distributed to partnership creditors pro rata, leaving $10,000 of partnership debts unpaid. Alden's individual creditors will be paid in full, leaving a $70,000 balance in Alden's individual estate. Bass's individual creditors will be paid in full, leaving an $8,000 balance in Bass's individual estate. Casey is insolvent; his creditors will receive $33\frac{1}{3}$ percent of their claims.

The losses of the partnership total $60,000 (capital investment, $50,000, plus unpaid debts after distribution of assets, $10,000). In the absence of a provision in the partnership agreement as to distribution of profits and losses, they are distributed equally. Each partner would be liable for $20,000, one third of the loss.

	Capital	Loss	
Alden	$25,000	$20,000	+$ 5,000
Bass.	15,000	20,000	− 5,000
Casey	10,000	20,000	− 10,000

In this case, Bass is legally liable to contribute $5,000 and Casey, $10,000. This sum would be distributed $10,000 to partnership creditors and $5,000 to Alden. In our illustration, Casey is insolvent and can contribute nothing; consequently, his share of losses over and above his capital investment will be redistributed between the solvent partners. However, Bass had only $3,000 in his estate, and the final result will be that Bass will pay $3,000 of his loss and Alden will pay $7,000. Bass will have a claim against Casey for the $3,000 he pays, and Alden will have a claim against Casey for $7,000. If one of the partners is a minor, that fact will alter the distribution of the assets accordingly.

Summary

If a partnership has been operated without a loss, the order of distribution of assets is unimportant, since everyone will be paid in full.

If the partnership is insolvent, the order of distribution is important. Partnership creditors have first claim on partnership assets, and individual creditors have first claim on the individual assets of their debtor. The order of distribution is set out in UPA (40).

Mahan v. Mahan

489 P.2d. 1197 (Sup. Ct. Ariz. 1971)

Helen Mahan (plaintiff) brought this action against T. Gordon Mahan (defendant) for an accounting and division of partnership property. Helen Mahan appealed from a judgment for T. Gordon Mahan. Reversed and remanded.

Helen Mahan's deceased husband, Terrell Mahan, and his brother, T. Gordon Mahan, were partners in an agricultural and construction partnership. In 1964 the partnership traded one of the partnership properties for a home into which Terrell and Helen moved, and Terrell's capital account was reduced by $23,000, leaving a balance of $4,005.45 which was one eighth of the total capital account of $31,308.06. Soon thereafter the partnership became inactive and remained so until Terrell's death in 1966 and the bringing of this suit in 1969.

There was disagreement at the trial as to the market value of the partnership assets, which were carried on the books as follows:

Red Lake Ranch	$15,622.61*
Investments	9,150.00†
Oil Lease	4,000.00‡
Miscellaneous	4,502.00§
	$33,274.61

* Sold in 1961 for $284,200 but sale not completed; appraised for $43,868.44 in 1963; the $15,622.61 was a figure allowed by the I.R.S. for tax purposes after the aborted sale.

† Represents 7,500 shares of Unita Finance Company, which the plaintiff's (and partnership's) accountant testified was worthless, and 180 shares of Arizona Livestock Production Credit Association, which the accountant testified was worth $5.00 per share or $900.

‡ Valueless, according to the accountant.

§ Subject to extreme disagreement on several items.

Gordon claimed Helen was entitled to one eighth of the partnership assets of $33,274.61, or $4,159.29.

CAMERON, JUSTICE.   Helen contends that after payment of the partnership debts, she should share with Gordon on a 50-50 basis. We agree with Helen as long as it is understood that the capital account, as used by the bookkeeper in this case, represents a debt of the partnership.

Upon liquidation, the rules of payment are governed by § 29–240 A.R.S., which decrees that the liabilities of the partnership shall rank in the following order of payment:

(*a*)   Those owing to creditors other than partners.
(*b*)   Those owing to partners other than for capital and profits.
(*c*)   Those owing to partners in respect of capital.
(*d*)   Those owing to partners in respect of profits.

"The capital of the partnership is the amount specified in the agreement of the partners, which is to be contributed by the partners for the purpose of initiating and operating the partnership business." Thus, ordinarily we would look to the initial contributions for a determination of the amounts "owing to partners in respect of capital." While the general rule is that the amount of capital may not be changed absent consent of all the partners, the partners in this case have apparently conceded to adjustments in their capital accounts. Thus, we accept, for purposes of this case, adjustments in plaintiff's and defendant's capital accounts to $4,005.45 and $27,302.61 respectively.

Therefore, whether the money left after satisfaction of creditor's claims and recoupment of partnership capital is termed profits or surplus, the clear mandate of the authorities is that, absent agreement to the contrary, it is divided equally as profits.

Gordon has placed reliance on § 29–242 A.R.S., relating to continuation of the business when a partner dies. In the instant case, the business was not continued by the surviving partner. Quite the contrary. The partnership remained dormant and nothing was done until suit was brought by the plaintiff to compel an accounting. Where the efforts of one partner in the production of profits in an active partnership cease, it is apparent that he no longer bears full entitlement to his respective share of the profits. In this case, however, where the partnership has been and continues to be inactive, any appreciation of worth is due to the nature of the partnership property rather than the effort of the surviving partner. Thus, we hold that any profit or surplus resulting shall be shared equally.

This conclusion is buttressed by the situation confronting Helen and her husband Terrell when they gave up $23,000 of their capital account for a $23,000 home. They knew that the partnership had few or no debts and owned a piece of property that had sold for $284,200 a few years previous. If the value of the land had stayed reasonably constant in the interim, the partnership would have been worth over $300,000. It is highly unlikely that the plaintiff and her husband intended, when they gave up $23,000 of their capital account for a $23,000 house, that they were actually giving up not $23,000 but well over $100,000.

The answer to the question of whether the court erred in accepting the book value of the assets can be answered by looking at the figures we have reconstructed. Every single component of the $33,274.61 book value has been strongly contested. The Red

Lake Ranch, for example, was sold in 1961 for over $280,000, but has an arbitrary book value of $15,622.61. An "investment" valued at $9,150 is made of two investments, one worthless and the other worth only $900. In short, the book values are completely arbitrary and should not have been used.

Our determination that the trial court erred in accepting book value is in accord not only with the Arizona case of *Hurst v. Hurst,* supra, but with general principles of partnership accounting. The normal rule is that book value is only used in ascertaining the respective shares when there is an explicit contractual provision to that effect, and even then is not used where the facts of the case make it inequitable to do so. Here there was no contractual provision mandating the use of book value, and even if there were, the facts show book value in this case to be so disproportionate to possible real values that it would be inequitable for it to be used anyway.

Having decided that book value should not be used in valuing the partnership assets, we are forced to conclude that the trial court should have granted plaintiff's wish to have the assets liquidated.

We hold that the partnership assets must be liquidated, and that the general creditors be paid first. If the assets are insufficient for this purpose, the estate and Gordon should be charged equally for the losses. If the assets are more than sufficient, then the surviving partner should be paid first up to the amount of $23,297.16 to set off the withdrawal from the capital account by Terrell. Any amount left over should be equally divided between Terrell's estate and the surviving partner, Gordon Mahan.

Problem Cases

1. Reynolds, White, and McKellar, among others, were partners in a Houston law firm. In early February, Reynolds and White tendered their resignations. By their terms these resignations were to take effect on June 1, and they were unanimously accepted on February 4. On that day and the days immediately following, the remaining partners, less McKellar, decided to continue the practice of law together without McKellar. There were negotiations between the other remaining partners as to the possibility of McKellar's voluntary withdrawal from the firm. Whether McKellar agreed to withdraw or not was in dispute. McKellar argued that there was no voluntary withdrawal and sued on an alleged breach of the partnership agreement. He included Reynolds and White as defendants. The trial court gave a directed verdict for Reynolds and White. Was the trial court right in excluding Reynolds and White?

2. White and Beal were partners trading as White & Company. The partnership had leased from Long the premises in which it operated its business. The lease provided that the lease could not be assigned and that any attempt to assign it would invalidate it and that the lessor could take possession of the premises. White assigned his interest in the partnership to his son, William. Long brought an action to recover the premises claiming that the assignment by White to his son was a breach of the provision in the lease not to assign. Is Long's claim correct?

3. Jackson and Caldwell were partners in a public accounting firm in which discontent arose among the partners and employees. After a series of meetings which did not resolve the problems, Caldwell advised Jackson that he could have any account and any of the em-

ployees as well as the office space then under lease. Jackson rejected the offer and gradually withdrew from active participation in the partnership. Caldwell then gave formal notice of termination of the partnership. The two partners then immediately agreed upon a division of the assets and that the clients were to follow the accountant of their choice without solicitation, and they each established a new firm. Jackson then brought an action for an accounting to obtain his share of the goodwill of the partnership, which was not mentioned in either the partnership or termination agreement and was not carried as an asset on the partnership books of account. Is Jackson entitled to a settlement for the value of goodwill?

4. B. F. Ibos & Sons, a partnership, was engaged in the business of plumbing contracting. In October 1961, Emile Ibos withdrew from the partnership. Emile testified that at the time he withdrew he went to the office of T. W. Shaw and personally notified Max Pastel, Shaw's manager, of his withdrawal. Both Max Pastel and T. W. Shaw claim that no notice of the withdrawal was given to them. T. W. Shaw extended credit to B. F. Ibos & Sons after Emile's withdrawal. The account was not paid and T. W. Shaw sued B. F. Ibos & Sons and included Emile as a defendant. Is Emile liable?

5. Vitelli and Borelli were partners in a jewelry business. Borelli died July 18, 1961. At the time of Borelli's death, the value of his interest in the partnership was $1,299.22. This sum was set up as a liability in favor of Borelli on the books of the business which Vitelli continued to operate until his death on January 21, 1964. What are the rights of the estate of Borelli in the assets of the partnership which came into the hands of the administratrix of Vitelli's estate?

6. White was a member of an architectural partnership, and he withdrew under an agreement with the two continuing partners under which they assumed the partnership debts and agreed to indemnify White. Among the partnership debts was $20,695 owed Brown for services as a consulting engineer to the partnership. Brown was given notice of the withdrawal and the agreement. Later he accepted a series of 12 promissory notes, each for $2,000 and drawing interest and payable serially, one per month. None of the notes was paid. When Brown sued White, the latter's defense was that Brown had accepted the liability of the continuing partners in lieu of the original partnership. Is Brown entitled to a directed verdict?

7. Fielder and Lohman entered into a partnership to construct and operate a trailer park. They borrowed $6,600 from First Bank. Although the note was signed by both and the proceeds used by the partnership, the partnership name was not included. Fielder died and it developed that neither his personal estate nor the partnership assets were sufficient to pay their respective creditors. First Bank filed a claim against Fielder's personal estate for the amount of the loan and the claim was disallowed. Is First Bank entitled to participate as a creditor of Fielder?

8. Carl Sundstrom and Roy Sundstrom operated, as partners, the *Custer County Chronicle,* a newspaper. Carl alone purchased the physical assets used by the partners, and Roy contributed no capital to the partnership venture. The profits of the business were divided, 55 percent to Carl and 45 percent to Roy. The partnership was dissolved by the death of Roy. In winding up the partnership affairs, Carl contended that he was entitled to depreciation on the physical assets. The partnership agreement was silent as to depreciation on the physical plant, and there was no evidence that the matter of depreciation was ever considered by the partners. Is Carl entitled to credit for depreciation on the physical assets?

Part VI

Corporations

chapter 23

Nature of Corporation and Incorporation

Historical Background and Principal Characteristics

Early History. The general idea is very old that a corporation is a fictitious legal person distinct from the actual persons who compose it. The Romans recognized the corporation, and in England the corporate form was used extensively even before A.D. 1600, although most early corporate charters were granted to municipalities or to ecclesiastical, educational, or charitable bodies. For example, the church used the "corporation sole" as a device for holding the title to land. If the title were in "the Bishop of Exeter," a corporation, rather than in Bishop John Fitzwilliam, then the complications which would arise in regard to the descent of the land upon the death of an individual person as title holder could be avoided, since the corporation's existence would be perpetual.

The famous British trading companies, such as the Hudson's Bay Company, which was chartered as a corporation by the king in 1670 and still operates in Canada, were the forerunners of the modern corporation. They were given monopolistic privileges in trade and even granted governmental powers in the areas they colonized.

Beginning about 1780 the corporate form of organization began to be used in the United States. The early corporations were chartered by the state legislatures, most of them to operate businesses of a public nature such as toll roads, toll bridges, and water systems. In 1811 New York State enacted the first general corporation-for-profit statute. Under this statute any group of persons who complied with the procedures established in the statute would be granted a corporate charter. However, incorporation tended still to be viewed as a privilege and many restrictions were placed upon corporations. Incorporation was permitted for only relatively short periods of time, maximum limits on capitalization were relatively low, the purpose of the business had to be specifically and narrowly defined, and limits on land and personal property holding were often restrictive. Today these restrictive provisions have disappeared in most states and the incorporation statutes are mostly enabling, permitting the controlling persons very great flexibility in establishing, financing, and operating the corporation.

Principal Characteristics. The essential nature of the corporate form of organization has not, however, changed very much from the description in Blackstone's *Commentaries,* which were written before 1765. They are: (1) existence independent of its members and unaffected by their death; (2) right to sue and be sued in the corporate name; (3) right to acquire, hold, and convey property for corporate purposes in the corporate name; (4) right to have a seal; and (5) right to make bylaws.

Classifications. Historically corporations have been of three classes: (1) corporations for profit, (2) corporations not for profit, and (3) governmental corporations. Ordinarily, separate statutes establish procedures for incorporating each class of corporation and for their operation. There is a large body of common law which applies equally to the first two classes and to a lesser extent to governmental corporations.

A corporation for profit is a corporation operated for the purpose of making a profit which may be distributed in dividends to the stockholders. Generally, corporations for profit which operate a business affecting the public interest, such as railroads, banks, insurance companies, building and loan associations, and farm marketing cooperatives, are incorporated under special statutes which impose on such corporations more stringent regulations than are imposed on the ordinary business corporation which is incorporated under the general corporation-for-profit statutes.

Hospitals, schools, churches, lodges, and fraternities are frequently incorporated as not-for-profit. A not-for-profit corporation cannot distribute any surplus it may have to its members or shareholders. Most of these are chartered by states but a few such as the American Red Cross have federal charters.

Governmental corporations include not only municipalities but some, such as the Tennessee Valley Authority and the Federal Home Loan Bank, which are similar to business corporations except that at least some of their directors are appointed by governmental officials and frequently they are financed in part or totally by government. The two examples given are chartered by Congress, but states sometimes establish this hybrid kind of corporation also.

Corporations for profit are frequently divided into publicly held and close (privately held) corporations. The distinction is not clear cut but a close corporation is one where most of the stock is held by and the corporation is managed by a family or a small group of people who are personally known to each other. In contrast, a publicly held corporation (for example, General Motors) is owned by a large number of people who are not personally known to each other. The close corporation in practice is often operated more like the popular stereotype of the partnership than that of the corporation.

Distinction between Corporation and Shareholder. As an artificial legal person a corporation has an existence separate from its shareholders. The shareholders normally have no individual liability for the debts of the corporation. Their liability for loss is limited to their investment in their shares. However, the separateness between corporation and shareholder may be disregarded if the corporate form is adopted to promote fraud, to evade the law, or to accomplish purposes detrimental to society. This problem arises most frequently in the close corporation. If the shareholders' personal transactions are intermingled with those of the corporation and corporate formalities are not observed, if the corporation is established with so little capital as to be unable to meet normal business obligations, or if the corporation is otherwise formed to defraud or to evade existing obligations, courts will disregard the corporate entity or, as it is often phrased, will "pierce the corporate veil." They will hold the shareholders liable on the same basis as if no effort had been made to incorporate. Generally, this means the active shareholders will be held liable as if they were general partners.

Similar principles are followed by the courts in dealing with suits brought against corporations which operate a segment of their business through a subsidiary corporation whose stock is controlled or fully owned by the parent corporation. If, in fact, the two corporations have no separateness except their individual charters or the subsidiary is formed as a shield for a "shady" purpose, the parent corporation will be held responsible for the acts and debts of its subsidiary.

Other Aspects of the Distinction. The corporation has its own domicile separate from its shareholders, which is in the state in which it is incorporated and the place in that state where it has its registered office. Where it is a different place, the site of its principal office is sometimes said to be its "commercial domicile."

Generally, there is no fiduciary duty between the shareholders and the artificial person which is the corporation.[1] The shareholders may deal with the corporation in the same manner and to the same extent as would any other person. The shareholder is not an agent or representative of the corporation by virtue of his or her stock ownership. The courts recognize the separateness of the corporation and its shareholders even though all the shares of the corporation are owned by one person.

---

[1] However, controlling shareholders may owe fiduciary duties, at least when selling control of the corporation, *Perlman v. Feldman* 219 F.2d 173 (2d Cir. 1955); *cf. Essex Universal Corp. v. Yates,* 305 F.2d 572 (2d Cir. 1962). See also the discussion at the end of Chapter 27.

Summary

Early corporations were chartered by the Crown in England and by special enactment of state legislatures in the United States. Today incorporators need only to conform to the procedures established in a general statute, and these impose few limitations in organizing, financing, and operating the corporation.

A corporation is a legal person separate and distinct from its members. A corporation can hold property and sue and be sued in its own name. The members of a corporation are not personally liable for its debts and its existence is not affected by the death of its members.

Shareholders normally have no individual liability for the debts of the corporation so their risk of loss is limited to their investment. However, courts may "pierce the corporate veil" where incorporation is for the purpose of promoting fraud, or to evade the law, or where the business affairs of a close corporation or corporate subsidiary and its shareowners are intermingled.

The corporation has its own domicile and shareholders ordinarily have no fiduciary duties to the corporation.

Fagan v. La Gloria Oil and Gas Co.

494 S.W.2d 624 (Ct. Civ. App. Tex. 1973)

Suit by La Gloria Oil and Gas Company (plaintiff) against Albert E. Fagan and the other stockholders in Cooper Petroleum Corporation (defendants) seeking to hold them personally liable for the debt of the corporation to La Gloria. Judgment for La Gloria appealed. Affirmed.

Cooper Petroleum Corporation was engaged in the marketing of petroleum products. A majority of its shares was owned by Albert E. Fagan. The balance was owned equally by a son and two sons-in-law of Fagan. The four men were also the officers and directors of Cooper. Fagan also owned half of the shares of International Marketing, Inc. (IMI), another corporation engaged in petroleum marketing. The other half of IMI's shares were pledged by him to secure a loan for their purchase price. IMI was heavily indebted to La Gloria for the purchase of petroleum products and went into bankruptcy. The trustee in bankruptcy got a judgment against Cooper Petroleum Corporation and Fagan individually because the court held that as creditors of the bankrupt IMI they had received voidable preferences.

In December 1967, the amount of the judgment against Cooper and Fagan was $220,000. Fagan paid the trustee $100,000 for which he was given a release of the judgment against him and an assignment of the judgment against Cooper. On the basis of the assignment he then filed judgment liens against Cooper in the counties in which it owned realty—mostly service station sites.

La Gloria also filed an action against Cooper as a guarantor of the account owed La Gloria by IMI. It obtained a judgment but was unable to recover because Fagan had already attached Cooper's property under the judgment he had bought from the IMI trustee in bankruptcy.

The present suit against the shareholders, who were also the officers and directors of Cooper Petroleum Corporation, was brought by La Gloria claiming that the shareholders wrongfully diverted Cooper's corporate assets to themselves for the purpose of preventing La Gloria from attaching them and therefore should be personally liable. They alleged and the court found as fact that Cooper was actually insolvent at the end of its fiscal year ending June 30, 1966, because its balance sheet understated its liabilities (not showing La Gloria's judgment against it or La Gloria's pending suit against it which resulted in a judgment for $160,000). It also overstated its assets by listing an account receivable in the amount of $192,000 which was repayable only out of the profits of the debtor, and it was then doubtful there would be profits. However, Cooper continued operating, its gross receipts dropping each fiscal year from seven and one half million dollars in 1966 to one half million in 1971 after which no business was done. Large profit-sharing bonuses were paid to the officers even in years in which no profits were earned and most of the physical assets—mostly service stations—were acquired by another Fagan family corporation engaged in the same business. All accounts receivable were assigned to two of the directors and one of them bought the office furniture and fixtures. The debts owed to the Fagans and to outsiders which had been guaranteed by the Fagans were paid.

TUNKS, CHIEF JUSTICE. It is a basic rule of law that officers and directors of a corporation owe to it duties of care and loyalty. They stand in a fiduciary relationship to the corporation. Such duties, however, are owed to the corporation and not to creditors of the corporation. In ordinary circumstances where an officer or director negligently mismanages corporate business to its injury or takes to himself that which belongs to, or in fairness and equity should be acquired by, the corporation, a cause of action in behalf of the corporation arises. Such cause of action can be prosecuted only by the corporation, itself, or by someone authorized to act in its behalf. Such cause of action under some circumstances may be prosecuted by one standing in the position of the corporation for the benefit of a creditor, but not directly by the creditor himself. Such breaches of duty neither create a cause of action in a creditor of the corporation nor, without more, entitle the creditor to collect his claim from the officers and directors.

There is a well-recognized exception to that basic rule. That exception is frequently called the trust-fund doctrine. Such exception, stated in general terms, is to the effect that when a corporation (1) becomes insolvent and (2) ceases doing business, then the assets of the corporation become a trust fund for the benefit, primarily, of its creditors. The officers and directors hold the corporate assets in trust for the corporate creditors. They are placed in a fiduciary relation to and owe a fiduciary duty to the creditors. That duty obliges them to administer the corporate assets for the benefit of the creditors and to ratably distribute them. The breach of that duty gives rise to a cause of action against the officers and directors which can be prosecuted directly by the creditors.

* * * * *

Under the evidence in this record the trial judge was justified in believing that in July 1966 those in control of Cooper conceived and instituted a scheme whereby they would so manipulate Cooper's affairs that it would continue business solely for the purpose of permitting it to pay the claims which they had against it and to pay the claims of creditors to whom they were secondarily liable. It was part of their scheme so conceived and instituted that they would strip the corporation of any surplus funds that it would otherwise have had with which to pay its creditor, La Gloria, by paying to themselves spurious bonuses. Their scheme also included an intention to acquire for themselves, for other members of their family, and for O.C.M., which they controlled, all of the physical assets which Cooper owned and to transfer to O.C.M. Cooper's business operations. The evidence shows that their scheme so conceived and instituted was fully carried out so that on December 31, 1970, Cooper was an empty shell and La Gloria was unpaid.

Aside from the trust-fund doctrine there is another theory of law that sustains the trial court's judgment. The evidence sustains an implied finding that the defendants appropriated to themselves the assets of Cooper and thereby "denuded" it so that it had nothing left with which to pay La Gloria. To the extent that they, as shareholders of Cooper, took to themselves the corporate assets, they are personally liable on La Gloria's claim. . . .

Kilpatrick Bros., Inc. v. Poynter

473 P.2d 33 (Sup. Ct. Kan. 1970)

This was an action by Kilpatrick Brothers, Inc., and Memphis Motel Furnishings, Inc. (plaintiffs), against W. R. Poynter (defendant). Judgment against W. R. Poynter and he appealed. Affirmed.

W. R. Poynter operated a Ford dealership, Poynter Motors, Inc., all shares in which were registered in the name of his wife, Rosalee. He became interested in mobile motels and in early 1965 he leased as an individual a portion of a building of the Parsons Ordnance Plant for the purpose of manufacturing portable motel units. On March 30, 1965, articles of incorporation for Economotels were filed with the Secretary of State of Kansas. They showed a paid up capital of $1,000 and W. R. Poynter as its only shareholder. The only directors' meeting after organization was held in May 1966, and the only business was the reelection of Poynter as president and treasurer and William Ong as vice president and secretary. Economotels used the space leased by Poynter and manufactured the motel units from June 1965 to January 1966. It continued paying salaries to the officers until May 1966, at which time it ceased all activity while owing $93,726 to unsecured creditors.

On May 27, 1966, articles of incorporation were filed for Standard Buildings, Inc. Rosalee Poynter was the only shareholder. As in Economotels, W. R. Poynter was president and he, Rosalee, and Ong were the directors. Standard Buildings commenced operations in the middle of May in the same leased premises. Its primary product was mobile classrooms, and it continued operations until February 1967, at which time it was indebted to unsecured creditors in the sum of $66,218. On December 12, 1966,

Modern Structures, Inc., was incorporated. Rosalee Poynter was the sole shareholder and W. R. Poynter, she, and Ong were the directors. Modern Structures began building mobile classrooms in the leased premises in February of 1967 and continued until November 1967.

Although each corporation used the leased space at the ordnance plant and took over the equipment, fixtures, and supplies of the preceding corporation, there was no formal sale, written agreement, nor price established between the corporations, nor was any provision made for creditors. When the equipment, supplies, and materials remaining were sold in early 1968 the proceeds went to Poynter Motors to pay loans personally guaranteed by W. R. and Rosalee Poynter. W. R. Poynter completely dominated all three corporations and his wife signed such papers as he instructed her to do. There was no board action with respect to the operations of any of the corporations. On various occasions funds were transferred between the three corporations and Poynter Motors and Tower Bowl, also owned by the Poynters.

The suppliers bringing this action sought to hold the Poynters individually liable on the ground that the corporations were merely their alter ego. The court adopted this view but held only W. R. Poynter liable since Rosalee had participated very little in the business and the shares had been put in her name principally to avoid probate in case of her husband's death.

HARMON, COMMISSIONER.   Thus we see the doctrine of *alter ego* fastens liability on the individual who uses a corporation merely as an instrumentality to conduct his own personal business, such liability arising from fraud or injustice perpetrated not on the corporation but on third persons dealing with the corporation. Under it the court merely disregards corporate entity and holds the individual responsible for his acts knowingly and intentionally done in the name of the corporation.

From the evidence we glean the following in support of the trial court's findings. The building in which all three corporations conducted their business was initially leased by W. R. Poynter as an individual from the federal government. This lease was never transferred or changed by him throughout the corporations' tenure in the building. Corporate undercapitalization has already been mentioned. Poynter contributed what little capital there was. Apparently, as to one of the corporations, the capitalization consisted only of his promissory note. When each corporation ceased functioning, whatever assets it had on hand, including material and equipment, were transferred to the next successive corporation. All of them were engaged in building structures of the same general type. No consideration was paid for these transfers and no arrangement was made toward payment of unsecured creditors of the prior corporation. An airplane initially belonging to Economotels was thereafter used by Standard Buildings and Modern Structures and finally sold and the proceeds applied upon an S.B.A. loan which Poynter had personally guaranteed. When Modern Structures ceased activities its remaining assets were sold and the proceeds turned over to Poynter Motors and used by it to pay on a bank loan personally guaranteed by Poynter. He transferred funds back and forth at will between the various corporations, including Tower Bowl and Poynter Motors. This juggling of assets could scarcely have served the corporation whose funds were being diverted but would be strong indication Poynter regarded all funds as his own. The rent for the building used by the three corporations was paid through Poynter Motors under some kind of vague arrangement made by him as president of Poynter Motors, Standard Buildings, and Modern Structures. Poynter was an officer in all of the corporations involved, set the policies, and made all final decisions. He received varying amounts not in excess of $14,000 as salary each year. No board of directors' meetings of the corporations were held. Corporate reporting was largely disregarded. In his testimony, although he had difficulty in remembering which corporate office he filled in each, he stated he was the policy-making person; he described Economotels as a "vehicle" corporation.

The foregoing amply supports the challenged findings and conclusions of the trial court concerning *alter ego.* Certainly W. R. Poynter conducted business with such unity of interest and ownership that the separate personalities of the corporations and of himself as an individual no longer existed. And if the acts were treated as those of the corporations alone an inequitable result would follow. Poynter himself disregarded corporate entity and we think the trial court was justified in doing the same.

Regulation and Termination of Corporations

State Regulation of Corporations.   The framers of the Constitution decided not to provide for the chartering of business corporations by Congress. Therefore, they have been chartered by the individual states. However, under the Constitution one state cannot grant to its citizens privileges which are to be exercised in another state. Therefore, if a "foreign corporation" (a corporation chartered either by another state or a foreign country) wishes to transact intrastate business, it must first obtain a license permitting it to do business within the state as a foreign corporation. Since interstate commerce is regulated by the federal government, corporations have the right to transact interstate commerce in any state. This distinction and the rights and liabilities of foreign corporations are discussed in Chapter 28.

The right to charter corporations carries with it the right to regulate them. This is done today in every state through a general incorporation law for profit-making corporations. These set up requirements for incorporation, provide for the payment of certain fees and taxes and the filing of annual reports, grant certain powers to the directors in managing the corporation, and establish certain rights and liabilities of shareholders. In part because there is competition among states to become the legal domicile of the larger corporations doing an interstate and perhaps international business, the general corporation statutes of most states have tended to be liberal enabling acts rather than regulatory devices. Delaware has been the leader in this movement over the past 60 years. Effective state regulation tends to be limited to regulation of the activities of corporations, both domestic and foreign, within the state rather than through limitations placed in charters.

Federal Regulation of Corporations. Critics of business, most recently Ralph Nader, have from time to time proposed federal chartering or licensing of the largest corporations so that it might be easier to require them to operate in the public interest. However, the proposal has dropped from public view each time when a federal regulatory statute was passed dealing with the primary concern of that period. These include the Interstate Commerce Act, the Sherman Act, the Clayton Act, the Federal Trade Commission Act, the Securities Act of 1933, and the Securities Exchange Act of 1934.[2] Whether dealing with problems posed by large business through a federal chartering or licensing statute, coupled with a super agency to administer it, would be more successful than a patchwork of statutes and a number of administrative agencies appears problematical at this time. However, the huge size of some corporations and their importance to the livelihood and well-being of the citizenry gives the proposal at least a surface appearance of appropriateness.

Termination. Being a creature of the state, a corporation cannot be unilaterally dissolved; it must have the consent of the state. Today the corporation statutes establish procedures for dissolution, and consent is given in advance if those procedures are followed. For example, the Model Business Corporation Act, which is discussed in some detail later in this chapter, provides five methods of dissolution. They are: by a majority of the incorporators if the corporation has not commenced business (82)[3]; by written consent of all of its shareholders (83); by act of the corporation, which requires a vote of a majority of the shareholders after proper notice of a meeting to be held for that purpose (84); by act of the attorney general for failure by the corporation to file an annual report or pay its franchise tax, for abuse of its corporate authority, or failure to appoint or maintain a registered agent in the state (94); or by a court upon petition of a shareholder or creditor (97).

Bases for dissolution upon petition of a shareholder include deadlock of directors which cannot be broken by the shareholders and irreparable injury is threatened, illegal or oppressive acts by the directors, failure to elect directors for a period including two consecutive annual-meeting dates because of shareholder deadlock and, finally, misapplication or waste of corporate assets. In a few states, courts have dissolved corporations upon petition of a shareholder where it appeared that the main purpose of the corporation was no longer attainable. However, courts tend to be reluctant to order an involuntary dissolution. The end of the term of a corporation chartered for a specific period of time will, of course, also dissolve the corporation. A new charter may be obtained, however, and the business may be continued without interruption.

---

[2] See Chapter 46 for a discussion of the Sherman Act, Chapter 47 for the Clayton Act, Chapter 49 for the Federal Trade Commission Act and Chapter 27 for the securities acts.

[3] The numbers in the parentheses refer to the sections of the Model Business Corporation Act, which appears in the Appendix.

If a corporation merges into another under statutory authority, the former corporation is dissolved. If two corporations consolidate into a new corporation, both of the original corporations are dissolved.

Under the Model Act a creditor may get a court to dissolve the corporation if the corporation is insolvent and execution on a judgment is unsatisfied or the corporation admits in writing that the creditor's claim is due and owing.[4] In addition, a court is given jurisdiction to liquidate the corporation when the attorney general files an action to dissolve.

Summary

The right to charter a corporation for profit is vested in the states. This carries with it the right to regulate the corporation.

Despite numerous proposals there is no law requiring large corporations doing an interstate business to be chartered by or licensed by the federal government. Instead, statutes establishing a regulatory framework and an administering agency for each of several major types of problems between corporations and society have been enacted.

The existence of a corporation may be terminated by: (1) voluntary dissolution, (2) forfeiture of its charter, (3) expiration of its charter, (4) merger or consolidation, and sometimes by suit of (5) minority shareholders or (6) creditors.

Incorporation

Where to Incorporate?   If the business of such corporation is to be primarily intrastate, it will ordinarily be most advantageous to incorporate in the state in which the business is to be carried on. If the business is to be primarily interstate, the promoters of the corporation will usually wish to incorporate in the state which has corporate statutes that best serve the purpose of the proposed corporation.

Comparative taxes are, of course, an important factor. There is a considerable range among states with respect to the imposition of or amount of organization taxes, annual taxes such as franchise and income taxes, and taxes on the issuance and transfer of shares in the corporation. A few states impose a "cessation" or dissolution tax. Of equal or greater concern may be the limitations placed upon the operation of the corporation. The statutes and court decisions in some states, especially Delaware, give promoters and management much greater freedom than do some other states. Such liberality, however, may not always be in the interest of minority shareholders.

---

[4] See Chapter 44 for discussion of the Federal Bankruptcy Act.

Model Business Corporation Act.   In 1946 the Committee on Corporate Laws, a part of the American Bar Association's Corporation, Banking and Business Law Section drafted the Model Business Corporation Act. The Committee was composed of leading corporate lawyers and scholars. The Model Act served both as a stimulus and as a guide to the many states which had not substantially revised their general corporation statutes in the light of current business practices and the changes in incorporation statutes made by the more progressive states. It has been adopted substantially whole by 20 states and in large part by 10 additional states.[5] Several others have used the Model Act as a guide in amending parts of their statute. However, the most popular domicile for large corporation, Delaware (39 percent of the corporations listed on the New York Stock Exchange are incorporated there)[6] does not follow the act; nor do several other major commercial and industrial states, such as New York, Massachusetts, and California.

Since the Model Business Corporation Act comes closest to being a common denominator between the corporation statutes of the various jurisdictions, it will be used as the primary basis for this discussion. However, the discussion will call attention to the Delaware Act where it is substantially different. The Delaware Act differs in some respects merely because it covers nonprofit corporations as well as corporations for profit.

The Model Business Corporation Act follows the policy of granting broad discretion to the incorporators. It is drafted so as to permit them, by adoption of appropriate articles and bylaws, to adapt the corporation to their interests whether the corporation be a close corporation or a large publicly held corporation. For example, although Section 32 provides that normally a quorum for taking action at a meeting of shareholders shall be a majority of the shares, it permits the corporation in its articles to set the quorum as low as one third of the shares or as high as 100 percent. Section 143 permits the corporation to establish a requirement of a higher proportion of shares voting in favor of any corporate action than provided for in the act by so declaring in its articles, thus presumably giving notice to its shareholders.

Who May Incorporate?   Many states require that three natural adult persons serve as incorporators, as did the Model Act prior to amendment in 1962. It now specifies that the incorporators may be "one or more persons, or a domestic or foreign corporation." (53). Delaware specifically permits a partnership or an association to be an incorporator.

Steps in Incorporation.   The steps prescribed by the incorporation statutes of the different states vary but they generally include the following, which appear in the Model Act: (1) preparation of articles of incorporation and

---

[5] The Model Act was extensively revised in 1969 and many of the adopting states have not amended their statutes to conform.

[6] As of January 1973. In January 1965, 35 percent were Delaware corporations.

signing and authenticating the articles by one or more persons or a domestic or foreign corporation; (2) filing of the articles, accompanied by the specified fees, with the Secretary of State; (3) issuance of a certificate of incorporation by the Secretary; and (4) holding an organization meeting of the board of directors named in the articles for the purpose of adopting bylaws, electing officers, and transacting other business.

In addition, in many states, including Delaware, copies of the articles must be filed with a county official in the county where the registered office of the corporation is located and in some states the articles must be published in a newspaper. Furthermore, qualification or registration of the corporation's stock may be required under either the federal or state securities laws or both.[7]

Articles of Incorporation. The statutes of various states also vary somewhat with respect to what must be included in the articles of incorporation, but in general, the requirements are similar to the following which appear in the Model Act (54): (1) name of the corporation; (2) its duration; (3) its purposes; (4) number and classes of shares; (5) if appropriate, designation of classes and relative rights; (6) if appropriate, designation of relative rights between series; (7) if desired, a provision limiting or denying preemptive rights; (8) any additional provisions desired, not inconsistent with law, for the regulation of the internal affairs of the corporation, including any restrictions on the transferability of shares; (9) registered office and registered agent; (10) number of and names and addresses of initial directors; and (11) the name and address of each incorporator.

Name and Seal. The incorporators must give the corporation a name, and it is customary, but not required, that it adopt a seal. Under the Model Act (8) the name must contain the word "corporation," "incorporated," or "limited," or an abbreviation of one of these words. It may not be the same as or deceptively similar to the name of any other corporation incorporated in or authorized to transact business in the state. The Model Act also prohibits the use of a word in the name which indicates that the corporation is organized for any purpose other than those stated in its articles. A number of corporation statutes specifically prohibit the use of a word denoting an activity, such as "bank," "trust," or "insurance," which would indicate that it has been incorporated under a special, more restrictive statute rather than the general corporation statute.

To facilitate the selection of a name unlike those of preexisting corporations, the Model Act (9) provides for advance application to the secretary of state for a desired name. If the name is available, it may be reserved for a period of 120 days while the corporation is being formed.

Many states require the signing on behalf of the corporation of documents

---

[7] See Chapter 27.

pertaining to real estate, such as deeds and mortgages, to be authenticated by a "seal." If the corporation does not adopt a seal, it may be asked to furnish a certificate to that effect when executing such documents. Therefore, it is advisable to adopt a simple seal, which is customarily held in the custody of the corporate secretary and affixed to documents by him or her.

Duration and Purposes.   The Model Act and the Delaware statute permit corporations to have perpetual existence. A few states still impose limitations.[8] If desired, the articles of incorporation may provide for a shorter period even when the applicable statute permits perpetual life.

All jurisdictions require that the corporate purpose or purposes be set forth in the articles. Under the Model Act and the Delaware statute, it is sufficient to state, alone or together with specific purposes, that the corporation may engage in "any lawful activity." Other statutes require corporations to list specific purposes or limit a corporation to a single purpose. Most general corporation statutes, including the Model Act (3), exclude types of activity which require incorporation under special statutes. Otherwise, the limitations as to scope of business placed upon the corporation are self-imposed, and they are stated in the articles for the protection of stockholders.

Financial Structure.   Modern statutes, including that of Delaware and the Model Act, give wide latitude to the incorporators in establishing the capital structure of the corporation. Various classes of shares may be established with or without par value and with or without voting rights (except in the case of certain extraordinary transactions). Certain classes may be subject to redemption by the corporation or may be given convertibility at the option of the holder into a different class of share. Under the Model Act the board of directors may be given authority by the articles to divide the classes of shares into series and establish the different rights and preferences for the various series. Some state statutes are more restrictive and a few do not permit a corporation to limit voting rights of common shares or do not allow no par or convertible shares or liquidation preferences for shares designated as common stock. Some states require that shares designated as preferred stock have some preferential features.

Management.   The Model Act states (35), "The business and affairs of a corporation shall be managed by a board of directors." Many states require a minimum of three directors but Delaware and the 1969 revision of the Model Act (36) permit a corporation to have a single director. They do not require that the directors be shareholders of the corporation, adults, residents of the state of incorporation, or even United States citizens. The articles need only state the number of initial directors and their names and addresses. These directors hold office until the first annual meeting of shareholders. Subse-

---

[8] Arizona: 25 years subject to renewal; Mississippi: 99 years; Oklahoma: 50 years.

quently, the number is to be specified in the bylaws and may be increased or decreased by amendment of the bylaws. Some statutes reserve the power to change the number of directors to the shareholders. Directors must be elected at each annual shareholders' meeting, but the Model Act permits dividing the directors into two or three classes when they number nine or more. When classes are established, one class is to be elected at each annual meeting.

The bylaws are, in effect, private legislation for the structuring and operation of the corporation. Under the Model Act (27) the initial bylaws are to be adopted by the board of directors, and the power to alter them or to adopt new bylaws is vested in the board unless reserved to the shareholders by the articles of incorporation. Delaware vests bylaw-making authority in the shareholders unless given to the directors in the articles. Bylaws, of course, must be consistent with law and the articles of incorporation.

Regulation of the calling of, conduct of, and voting at shareholders' and directors' meetings is also generally specified in the bylaws. Most state corporation laws and the Model Act (29, 43) contain provisions in this respect designed to ensure minimum standards of fairness. The Model Act (50) specifies that there "shall be a president, one or more vice presidents as may be prescribed in the bylaws, a secretary, and a treasurer." It provides that the board of directors may elect or appoint such other officers and assistant officers and agents as may be prescribed in the bylaws and that their duties shall be provided in the bylaws or by resolution of the board of directors. The Model Act (50) permits the same person to hold any two or more offices except those of the president and secretary. Delaware does not specify titles for officers and declares that any number of offices may be held by the same person.

Summary

The incorporators of a business must first decide in which state they wish to incorporate. Since the corporation laws of the states are not uniform, there may be advantages to be gained by incorporating under the laws of a particular state. A majority of the states, but excluding some of those in which the largest number of businesses have incorporated, have adopted all or substantially all of the Model Business Corporation Act, which follows the policy of granting broad discretion to the incorporator or incorporators. A number of states require three natural persons as incorporators.

The corporation statutes will set out the framework within which the business may be incorporated and the steps to be followed. The articles of incorporation and the bylaws define the basic structure of the corporation and, in very general terms, the procedures for its management.

A name which is not confusingly similar to that used by another corporation doing business in the state must be selected, and usually the word "corporation" or some variant of it must be included in the name.

The purpose or purposes of the corporation must be stated in the articles of incorporation but most states permit this to be very general. It is necessary in most states to incorporate under special statutes to conduct special types of businesses, such as banking, railroading, insurance, and building and loan associations.

Corporations *de Jure* and *de Facto*

The *de Facto* Doctrine.   Since the process of incorporation involves a series of steps, courts have frequently been faced with the question of how to classify a business association which holds itself out to be a corporation but which has not completed all of the steps required by statute. The question usually is whether the persons involved are to be given the limited liability of owners of corporate shares or to be treated as partners.

Over the years the courts developed a tripartite classification system: (1) *de jure* corporation, (2) *de facto* corporation, and (3) no corporation.

If the incorporators essentially comply with all of the mandatory provisions of the corporation statute and fulfill in a substantial manner all the required prerequisites for the organization of the corporation, they will create a *de jure* corporation. The validity of a *de jure* corporation is not subject to attack even in a direct action brought by the state despite the fact its organization may not be perfect. Failure to comply with statutory provisions which are considered only directive, not mandatory, will not prevent the organization of a *de jure* corporation.

De Facto Corporation.   If the incorporators fail in some material respect to comply with the mandatory provisions of the corporate statutes, they will not have organized a *de jure* corporation. The courts have held, on the basis of public policy, that a *de facto* corporation is formed when: (1) there is a valid statute under which the corporation could be organized, (2) the parties have made an honest effort to organize under the statute, and (3) they have done business as a corporation. The corporate existence of a *de facto* corporation cannot be collaterally attacked. That is, in a suit by or against the corporation, neither the corporation nor the other party to the suit will be permitted to defend on the ground of the defects in the corporation's organization. However, the state may attack its claim of corporate status in a direct action brought for that purpose (*quo warranto*). A corporation whose charter has expired is usually treated as a *de facto* corporation during the interval before it is renewed. Courts have not been consistent in their treatment of cases when no attempt is made to reinstate the charter.

Estoppel to Deny Corporate Existence.   If persons hold themselves out as doing business as a corporation and induce third persons to deal with them as such, they will not be permitted to set up their lack of incorporation as a defense against the third persons. Likewise, if a third person has dealt with an association of persons as a corporation, such third person will not be permitted to escape liability by setting up the lack of corporate existence as a defense. Having dealt with the persons as a corporation, the third person has impliedly agreed that his or her rights and liabilities will be determined on the basis that such persons are transacting business as a corporation.

This theory of estoppel to deny corporate existence is an extension of the theory of *de facto* corporate existence. However, the theory of estoppel to deny corporate existence applies only in determining the rights and liabilities of the parties in particular transactions, whereas the *de facto* corporation is recognized as having a corporate existence for all corporate purposes.

Statutory Effect on *de Facto* Doctrine. The Model Act (56) states that issuance of a certificate of incorporation by the secretary of state is conclusive evidence of incorporation except against the state, which is permitted to bring an action challenging corporate status. Since it is unlikely that failure to complete steps in the procedure short of the issuance of the certificate would be held to constitute the enterprise a *de facto* corporation, this would appear to eliminate the distinction between a *de facto* and a *de jure* corporation. The Delaware statute does not specifically give the issuance of the certificate this effect.

Liability on Failure to Organize Corporation. If persons attempt to organize a corporation but their efforts are so defective that not even a *de facto* corporation comes into existence, or if they carry on a business for profit representing that they have incorporated the business when they have made no effort to do so, the courts have generally held such persons to be partners and liable as such.

The courts are not in accord as to the liability of a person who purchases stock in a corporation which is so defectively organized that it does not have even the status of a *de facto* corporation. Some courts have held that such a person is a co-owner of the business and as such is liable as a partner. Other courts have held that one who justifiably believes that he or she is purchasing stock in a validly organized corporation will not be held liable as a partner. These courts impose the unlimited liability of a partner on only those stockholders who are actively engaged in the management of the business or who are at fault for the defects in the organization of the corporation.

A third person may be estopped from denying the existence of the corporation and may be denied the right to recover from the stockholders as partners.

Summary

If the organizers of a corporation have substantially complied with the mandatory provisions of the corporation statutes and have fulfilled all the required prerequisites for incorporation, they will have organized a *de jure* corporation. The organization of a *de jure* corporation is not subject even to direct attack by the state.

If a statute exists under which a corporation may be incorporated and persons make an honest effort to incorporate under the statute and do business as a corporation but do not comply with all the mandatory provisions, a *de facto* corporation will have been created. Any attack on a *de facto* corporation must be made by the state in a direct proceeding brought for that purpose.

If persons have held themselves out as doing business as a corporation but either have made no attempt to comply with the corporation statutes or have complied so defectively that they have not formed even a *de facto* corporation, they will be estopped, under some circumstances, from denying their existence as a corporation. Likewise, a third person dealing with such an association of persons will be denied the right to escape liability by setting up the lack of corporate existence of the association.

As a general rule, if persons purport to carry on a business for profit as a corporation but have made no attempt to incorporate or have made an attempt which was so defective that even a *de facto* corporation was not brought into existence, such persons will be liable as partners.

By statute in many states the distinction between *de jure* and *de facto* corporations has been eliminated.

Terrel v. Industrial Commission

508 P.2d 355 (Ct. App. Ariz. 1973)

Petition by Terrel (plaintiff) for a writ of certiorari seeking review of an award by the Industrial Commission of Arizona (defendant) which denied the liability of the major shareholder of an uninsured corporation. Affirmed.

Terrel was injured on February 25, 1969, while employed by AC&C Wreckers, Inc., which was engaged in the business of building demolition. Because it employed three or more persons AC&C was subject to the Arizona workmen's compensation laws, but it had not complied with them. AC&C had filed its articles of incorporation on August 30, 1968, but had neglected to file a certified copy with the county recorder and to publish them in a newspaper as required by statute. AC&C conducted its business as a corporation, kept corporate minutes, and had assets of its own.

Collins, a lawyer who was not in charge of the corporation's business, was the major shareholder. Terrel sought to hold him personally liable because of failure to complete required steps in incorporation.

HAIRE, JUDGE. There is a substantial agreement among the authorities that a *de facto* corporation can result even in the absence of compliance with all of the technical statutory incorporation provisions. The reason generally given for holding such a corporation to have achieved a *de facto* existence is that if rights and franchises have been usurped, they are the rights and franchises of the state, which alone can object.

The authorities are also in agreement that once it has been determined that *de facto* existence has been achieved, then the stockholders cannot be held liable to third persons who deal with the corporation merely on account of the technical defect in the formation of the corporation. The three prerequisites to the creation of a *de facto* corporation are:

1. The existence of a charter or law under which a corporation with the powers which it undertakes to exercise may lawfully exist.
2. An effort in good faith to incorporate thereunder.
3. An actual use or exercise of corporate powers.

The disagreement and the apparent conflict in the decisions arise from the application of the second element to different fact situations to determine just how far the statute must be followed to demonstrate a "good faith effort to incorporate" under the applicable statutory law. Many decisions differentiate between statutory conditions precedent to the actual existence of the corporation as opposed to conditions precedent to its right to commence or do business. Failure to comply with the latter type of condition precedent does not preclude a finding of *de facto* existence.

It is petitioner's contention that AC&C's failure to file a certified copy of its articles of incorporation with the county recorder precludes *de facto* corporate existence. A review of the pertinent Arizona constitutional and statutory provisions discloses the following:

No domestic . . . corporation shall do any business in this State without having filed its articles of incorporation or a certified copy thereof with the Corporation Commission, and without having one or more known places of business and an authorized agent, or agents, in the State upon whom process may be served. (Arizona Constitution, Art. 14, § 8, A.R.S.)

AC&C fully complied with these constitutional filing requirements. A.R.S. § 10–123, set forth in footnote 2, *supra*, adds another filing requirement—the filing of a certified copy of the articles with the county recorder "before doing business." As previously stated, AC&C did not comply with this filing requirement. While it is generally held that there can be no *de facto* corporation where there has been a complete failure to file in any office, it is also generally held that the failure to file in one of two required offices does not preclude *de facto* existence.

Here, petitioner places great reliance upon the language of A.R.S. § 10–123 requiring the omitted filing "before doing business." Similar language has been considered by many courts and held not to preclude *de facto* existence.

Robertson v. Levy

197 A.2d 443 (Ct. App. D.C. 1964)

This was an action by Martin G. Robertson (plaintiff) against Eugene M. Levy (defendant) to recover the balance due on a note signed by Levy as president of Penn Ave. Record Shack, Inc., which had not been incorporated at the time the note was executed. Judgment for Levy and Robertson appealed. Judgment reversed.

Levy agreed with Robertson to form a corporation to purchase Robertson's record store business. An agreement assigning Robertson's lease was made to Penn Ave. Record Shack, Inc., and signed by Levy as president on December 22, 1961. Levy submitted articles of incorporation to the Superintendent of Corporations on December 27. On January 2, 1962, Levy began to operate the business as Penn Ave. Record Shack, Inc. On this same day he received notification that his articles of incorporation were rejected. On January 8, Robertson executed a bill of sale of his assets to the "corporation" and received a note signed in the name of the corporation by Levy as president. A certificate of incorporation of Penn Ave. Record Shack, Inc., was issued on January 17. One payment was made on the note. In June 1962, the corporation ceased doing business and no assets remained.

HOOD, CHIEF JUDGE.   The Business Corporation Act of the District of Columbia is patterned after the Model Business Corporation Act which is largely based on the Illinois Business Corporation Act of 1933. On this appeal, we are concerned with an interpretation of sections 29–291 c and 29–950 of our act. Several states have substantially enacted the Model Act, but only a few have enacted both sections similar to those under consideration. A search of the case law in each of these jurisdictions, as well as in our own jurisdiction, convinces us that these particular sections of the corporation acts have never been the subject of a reported decision.

For a full understanding of the problems raised, some historical grounding is not only illuminative but necessary. In early common law times private corporations were looked upon with distrust and disfavor. This distrust of the corporate form for private enterprise was eventually overcome by the enactment of statutes which set forth certain prerequisites before the status was achieved, and by court decisions which eliminated other stumbling blocks. Problems soon arose, however, where there was substantial compliance with the prerequisites of the statute, but not complete formal compliance. Thus the concepts of *de jure* corporations, *de facto* corporations, and of "corporations by estoppel" came into being.

* * * * *

One of the reasons for enacting modern corporation statutes was to eliminate problems inherent in the *de jure, de facto,* and estoppel concepts. Thus sections 29–921c and 950 were enacted as follows:

§29–921c. (§56 of Model Act) Effect of issuance on incorporation.

Upon the issuance of the certificate of incorporation, the corporate existence shall begin, and such certificate of incorporation shall be conclusive evidence that all conditions precedent required to be performed by the incorporators have been complied with and that the corporation has been incorporated under this chapter, except as against the District of Columbia in a proceeding to cancel or revoke the certificate of incorporation.

§29–950. (§146 of Model Act) Unauthorized assumption of corporate powers.

All persons who assume to act as a corporation without authority so to do shall be jointly and severally liable for all debts and liabilities incurred or arising as a result thereof.

* * * * *

The authorities which have considered the problem are unanimous in their belief that section 29–921c and section 29–950 have put to rest *de facto* corporations and corporations by estoppel. Thus the Comment to section 50 (56 of 1969 revision) of the

Model Act, after noting that *de jure* incorporation is complete when the certificate is issued, states that: "Since it is unlikely that any steps short of securing a certificate of incorporation would be held to constitute apparent compliance, the possibility that a *de facto* corporation could exist under such a provision is remote."

*   *   *   *   *

The portion of §29–921c which states that the certificate of incorporation will be "conclusive evidence" that all conditions precedent have been performed eliminates the problems of estoppel and *de facto* corporations once the certificate has been issued. The existence of the corporation is conclusive evidence against all who deal with it. Under §29–950, if an individual or group of individuals assumes to act as a corporation before the certificate of incorporation has been issued, joint and several liability attaches. We hold, therefore, that the impact of these sections, when considered together, is to eliminate the concepts of estoppel and *de facto* corporateness under the Business Corporation Act of the District of Columbia. It is immaterial whether the third person believed he was dealing with a corporation or whether he intended to deal with a corporation. The certificate of incorporation provides the cutoff point; before it is issued, the individuals, and not the corporation, are liable.

Turning to the facts of this case, Penn Ave. Record Shack, Inc., was not a corporation when the original agreement was entered into, when the lease was assigned, when Levy took over Robertson's business, when operations began under the Penn Ave. Record Shack, Inc., name, or when the bill of sale was executed. Only on January 17 did Penn Ave. Record Shack, Inc., become a corporation. Levy is subject to personal liability because, before this date, he assumed to act as a corporation without any authority so to do. Nor is Robertson estopped from denying the existence of the corporation because after the certificate was issued he accepted one payment on the note. An individual who incurs statutory liability on an obligation under section 29–950 because he has acted without authority, is not relieved of that liability where, at a later time, the corporation does come into existence by complying with section 29–921c. Subsequent partial payment by the corporation does not remove this liability.

Problem Cases

1. Berkson was a wholly owned subsidiary of Consolidated and had been leasing from Oppenstein the premises on which it operated a retail store. The lease was for a term of 26 years. Several years before the expiration of the lease Consolidated changed its relationship to Berkson in a number of respects. It closed the bank account in Berkson's name and all deposits of Berkson were made to an account in Consolidated's name; it pledged all of Berkson's accounts receivable as security for loans to Consolidated; it took over from Berkson all decision-making on buying and merchandising; and all correspondence with respect to the leased premises was on Consolidated's letterhead and it frequently referred to "its lease" and "its rent." Later it closed the retail store on the leased premises and sold its inventory in bulk to Macy's, the proceeds going to Consolidated. However, it continued to maintain Berkson as a separate corporation, holding and keeping minutes of directors meetings (all officers and directors were the officers and directors of Consolidated), filing reports, tax returns, and so forth.

    When neither Berkson nor Consolidated continued to pay rent under the lease, Oppenstein sued both corporations. Is Consolidated liable?

2.   Cornell Company developed a new product and organized FTG Corporation to protect the corporate name which was related to the name of the new product. Later, Urnest was employed by Cornell without a written contract to solve some problems encountered with the new product, and he expressed a desire to acquire an interest in the new business. He was issued 10,000 shares, and he was elected president and a director. Cornell retained 20,000 shares. FTG had no assets except a bank account and the product was manufactured and sold by Cornell, with FTG being paid an arbitrary portion of the receipts from the new product. Urnest's salary was paid from the bank account.

      After a year's employment, Urnest was told he was being discharged and FTG dissolved, and he was outvoted on these decisions in the FTG directors' meeting. Should Cornell be permitted to dissolve FTG?

3.   Area residents sued West Company, Stroud, the president, and Fuller, a director, for damages allegedly sustained from West's blasting activities. Fuller argued that he was merely a director and took no part in the activities complained of and, therefore, should not be held personally liable. Fuller was owner of 50 percent of the stock of the company and Fuller, along with Stroud and Stroud's wife, comprised West's Board of Directors. Stroud, Stroud's wife, and Fuller's wife were West's officers. All physical assets owned by West were leased from Fuller. He was familiar with West's operation, and he maintained daily contact with Stroud. Fuller knew that West was in financial difficulties, that complaints concerning damage had been received, and that insurance coverage for the blasting activities was doubtful. However, Fuller did not tell Stroud to cease blasting. Should Fuller be held personally liable?

4.   Clarks, Inc., operated a chain of stores in Texas. The stores were open seven days a week until the Texas legislature passed a statute prohibiting the sale of certain items (including nearly all of Clarks' merchandise) by any person on consecutive Saturdays and Sundays. Just prior to the effective date of the statute, Clarks entered into an arrangement with Sundaco, a newly formed corporation, whereby Sundaco leased Clarks' premises on every Sunday and "bought" all Clarks' merchandise at 11:59 P.M. each Saturday with an option to return all unsold merchandise on Monday. The contract did not fix a value on Clarks' inventory nor was a physical inventory taken; rather it provided that Sundaco would pay Clarks 75 percent of its gross sales. Signs continued to identify the premises as Clarks. All advertising and telephone response was done as "Sundaco, Exclusive Lessee of Clarks." Prices remained the same as did almost all of the employees. Is Clarks in violation of the Saturday and Sunday statute?

5.   Farrar and Pesterfield each owned 50 percent of the capital stock of Tri-State Inc., of which each was a director. Farrar was president of the corporation, and Pesterfield was secretary-treasurer. The corporation operated a broadcasting station and published a weekly newspaper. The state corporation statutes, the articles of incorporation, and bylaws of the corporation all provided that "the affairs of the corporation shall be managed by a board of three directors, to be elected by the stockholders, and that a majority of the directors shall constitute a quorum for the transaction of business."

      One of the directors of the corporation resigned, and Farrar and Pesterfield, the remaining directors, could not agree on a successor. Farrar and Pesterfield were in complete disagreement as to the operation of the business. Farrar, who had been acting as general manager of the corporate business, was threatening to cease operation of the newspaper and to dispose of the publishing equipment.

      Farrar refused to let Pesterfield examine the books of the corporation or have an audit made. Farrar had employed his wife as an office employee, was paying himself a salary, and had moved the bank account from the usual depository. He had refused to attend stockholders' meetings called by Pesterfield and by so doing had prevented the accomplishment of any business at the meetings because of the absence of a quorum. The corporation owned valuable property but primarily as a result of the existing deadlock it was operating at a loss. Pesterfield brought action asking the court to appoint a receiver and to dissolve the corporation. Should a receiver be appointed and the corporation be dissolved?

6. The corporate charter of PHA, Inc., was amended to increase the maximum authorized number of common shares from 10,000 to 20,000. Paragraph 5 of the charter, which primarily dealt with the minimum authorized capital, had been previously amended to authorize the board of directors to issue any number of shares in such quantities as they judge best, "except that the total number of such shares issued and outstanding shall not exceed 10,000 shares." The board subsequently issued 3,800 shares in addition to the 10,000 already outstanding. Certain shareholders seek to have the 3,800 shares declared void, and the directors enjoined from further issue. The directors contend that the later amendment by implication also increased the limitation in paragraph 5 to 20,000 shares. Should this argument succeed?

7. Chevreau Ltd. sells artificial fur fabrics to garment manufacturers. The stock of the corporation is held, 50 percent each, by the Littmans, who conceived the business and who market the fabrics, and by the Nierenbergs, who procure the fabrics and sell them to the corporation. The directors are equally divided between the two families. The two factions have fundamental disagreements about managing the company. The Littmans brought an action charging the Nierenbergs with trying to lure customers away to their own separate company, as well as with other actions adversely affecting Chevreau. The Nierenbergs countered by suing to dissolve Chevreau, pointing to the Littmans action as evidence of a hopeless division making effective management of Chevreau impossible. The Littmans opposed this action arguing that dissolution would accomplish the Nierenbergs' goal and would require the disposal of Chevreau's inventory with the Nierenbergs' the only potential purchaser and in a position to take advantage of their own alleged misconduct. Should the corporation be dissolved?

8. Montgomery Ward agreed to purchase certain goods from Sutain Corporation in 1960. Sutain claimed that it had performed all the contract terms, but Montgomery Ward refused to comply with the agreement. Sutain sued for damages. During trial it was discovered that Sutain had been dissolved in 1956 by proclamation of the secretary of state for nonpayment of taxes, and Montgomery Ward then claimed that it had no right to sue. However, the dissolution had occurred because of an error made by the secretary of state. Sutain had been reinstated by the secretary in 1963 following institution of the suit but before the trial. Can Montgomery Ward rely on the dissolution as a valid defense?

chapter 24

Organizing and Financing the Corporation's Business

Promoters

Function of Promoters. The function of a promoter is to bring about the incorporation and organization of a corporation. It is a most vital activity in a free enterprise system, and it is unfortunate that a few unscrupulous individuals have given the term a stigma. The promoter initiates the business; finds persons who are willing to finance the project; negotiates all contracts, leases, purchases, and so forth, necessary for the initial operation of the proposed venture; incorporates the business; and gets it started as a going concern.

In its broadest sense the term "promoter" applies to anyone who assumes the task of organizing and starting a corporation. If a member of a going partnership is instrumental in forming a corporation to which the assets of the partnership are transferred in exchange for stock in the corporation, such a person would be a promoter. However, the term is generally applied to one who causes the formation of a corporation for the purpose of carrying on a new business.

Relation of Promoter and Corporation. The relation of a promoter to the corporation and the persons whom he or she interests in the venture is unique. The promoter is not an agent, since he or she is self-appointed. Technically, the promoter cannot be the agent of the proposed corporation, since it is not in existence. The promoter is not the agent of the persons interested in the venture, since they did not appoint him or her and the promoter is not subject to their direction and control in regard to the promotion of the proposed corporation. A few courts have attempted to draw an analogy between the relation of a promoter and the corporation and that of a trustee and the beneficiary, but important elements of a common law trust are missing.

The promoter owes the duty of a fiduciary to the corporation he or she is

479

promoting and to the persons interested in it. In a promoter's dealings he or she owes a duty of perfect candor, full disclosure, the utmost of good faith, and absolute honesty. It would be a breach of this duty to divert money received on stock subscriptions to the payment of promotional expenses, unless agreed to in the subscription contract, or to take a secret profit at the expense of the subscribers or the corporation. Those injured by the breach of duty, including the corporation, if formed, may recover from the promoter.

For example, if the promoter takes an option on property or purchases property in contemplation of selling it to the corporation after its incorporation and he or she misrepresents to the corporation the option or purchase price of the property, thereby making a secret profit, the corporation may recover a judgment against the promoter for the secret profit. However, if the promoter makes a full disclosure to an independent board of directors who purchase at the increased price, the corporation would have no right of action against the promoter. If the board of directors is under the control of and is manipulated by the promoter, the corporation may rescind the transaction or recover damages.

If the misrepresentations are made to the persons interested in the corporation and they, in behalf of the corporation, take up the option or purchase the property, paying the promoter a secret profit, a majority of the courts have permitted the corporation, when it is incorporated, to bring an action to rescind or recover damages. A few courts have held that only the persons who purchased from the promoter have a right of action.

A more confused situation is one in which property is conveyed to the corporation at a greatly inflated value in payment for shares of stock of the corporation, with the knowledge and consent of all persons interested in the corporation, and then the issued stock is sold to the public at a price substantially in excess of its true value. The federal courts have held that in such a situation the corporation has no right of action against the promoters of the corporation who have engineered the deal.[1] However, in such a case brought in the Massachusetts courts, the judge held that the corporation could recover.[2] The Massachusetts court reasoned that when the stock was issued with the intent to sell it to the public, thus bringing in new shareholders, the bringing-in of these new shareholders was the equivalent of creating a new corporation with the same rights as though the promoters had sold to the corporation making a secret profit on the transaction. In a later U.S. Supreme Court case, in which bonds were issued in payment for property purchased at a greatly inflated value, thereby rendering the corporation insolvent from its inception, the court permitted the receiver of the corporation to recover, for the benefit of creditors,

---

[1] *Old Dominion Copper Mining & Smelting Co. v. Lewisohn,* 210 U.S. 206 (1908).

[2] *Old Dominion Copper Mining & Smelting Co. v. Biglow,* 203 Mass. 159, 89 N.E. 193 (1909); *aff'd,* 225 U.S. 111 (1912).

a judgment against the promoters for the secret profit.[3] The preponderance of states have followed the Massachusetts rule permitting recovery by the corporation. The opportunities for illegal manipulation by promoters have been greatly lessened by the adoption of the Securities Act of 1933 and by the Securities Exchange Act of 1934.

Corporation's Liability on Promoter's Contracts.   The corporation, when it comes into existence, does not automatically become liable on contracts made in its behalf by the promoter. It cannot be held liable as principal since it was not in existence when the contracts were made. Except for Massachusetts, American courts have held that a contract made by a promoter in behalf of a corporation to be formed can become binding between the corporation and the second party. They have used various theories to reach this result. All require some action by the corporation after it is formed, if only acceptance of the benefits of the contract. The most common ones are: (1) adoption, (2) ratification, (3) novation, and (4) continuing offer. The adoption and novation theories both appear to depend upon the fourth, that is, that the third party with whom the promoter dealt impliedly made a continuing offer to the corporation to adopt the contract, or in the case of novation, for the corporation to be substituted for the promoter. The ratification theory is based upon the agency concept permitting a principal to ratify the unauthorized acts of the agent, although it is a dubious extension because no principal was in existence when the act was done. Massachusetts, like England, does not accept any of these theories, including implied novation, and requires an express agreement between the three parties after the corporation is formed.[4]

Regardless of which one of these theories the state follows as the basis for finding the corporation liable on promoter's contracts, the corporation will not be held liable if the promoter's contract is illegal, fraudulent, not supported by consideration or is beyond the powers of the corporation. For the corporation to adopt or ratify a promoter's contract, the contract must be a valid, subsisting contract which is within the powers of the corporation. The corporation must accept the contract in its entirety, and the officers or agents who purport to adopt or ratify the promoter's contract must have authority to bind the corporation to such a contract.

Liability of Promoter.   Contracts made by promoters on behalf of proposed corporations have generally been held to bind the promoters. If the corporation is not formed or fails to adopt or ratify the agreement, the promoter remains liable on it. Obviously, the promoter alone is liable if the contract is made by him or her without reference to a proposed corporation but with the intent to assign it to the corporation later.

The effect on the liability of the promoter differs under the adoption and

---

[3] *McCandless v. Furlaud*, 296 U.S. 140 (1935).

[4] *Abbott v. Hapgood*, 22 N.E. 907 (1889); *Henshaw v. McBride*, 2 N.E.2d 445 (1936).

ratification theories. Under the adoption theory the promoter remains liable. The promoter would not, of course, under the novation theory. No agreement between the corporation and the promoter will relieve the promoter of his or her liability unless the third party consents to it, thus establishing a novation. Courts have held in a few cases that neither the third party nor the promoter intended to bind the promoter. Such an arrangement would be only a "gentleman's agreement" rather than a contract and would not bind the third party either.

Summary

The function of a promoter is to bring about the incorporation and organization of the corporation and to do those things necessary to get it operating as a going business.

The relation of the promoter to the corporation is unique. The promoter is neither agent nor trustee, yet he or she owes a fiduciary duty to the corporation and the persons interested in the venture. The promoter will not be permitted to make a secret profit at the expense of the corporation or of the persons interested in the venture. The courts are not in accord as to a corporation's rights against the promoter who conveys property to the corporation at an inflated value in payment of stock issued, with all the parties interested in the corporation having full knowledge of the transaction, the deal being entered into with the intent of selling the issued stock to the public at a price greatly in excess of its true value. Most states permit the corporation to recover.

The corporation is not liable on the promoter's contracts, but it may, by its actions, make itself liable. Ratification, adoption, continuing offer, and novation are theories used to support liability.

The promoter continues liable on preincorporation contracts unless there is a novation. He or she is not relieved from the liability by the adoption of the contract by the corporation.

Park City Corp. v. Watchie

439 P.2d 587 (Sup. Ct. Ore. 1968)

Action by Park City Corporation (plaintiff) against H. R. Watchie and others (defendants) for recovery of alleged secret profits made by Watchie as promoter in the sale of property to the corporation. Judgment for Watchie and the corporation appealed. Modified and remanded.

H. R. Watchie was a real estate broker in Seattle, Washington, who devoted most of his efforts as a finder and developer of property suitable for development as homesites as well as adjacent shopping centers and recreational areas. He transacted much of his business through a corporation wholly owned by him, H. R. Watchie & Associates, Inc., which was also named as a defendant.

In 1960 Watchie became interested in several tracts of property west of Portland, Oregon. It was near the Sunset highway, known as the Skyline property. As was his usual procedure, he made an extensive study of population trends, the availability of utilities, and other data likely to affect the success of a proposed development. He then acquired contracts and options to buy 965 acres at a total price of $729,000. His next step was to interest investors. A group of Seattle investors, hereafter called the syndicate, agreed to put up the money for Watchie to buy the land. It was agreed that Watchie would take title to the land as trustee and that it would be held until he could resell it for the syndicate at double the purchase price. The syndicate did not wish to involve itself in development.

Two years later Watchie acquired options to buy 1600 acres of flat land adjacent to the earlier purchase. He decided to form a publicly owned corporation to acquire and develop both this property and that owned by the syndicate. He organized the Park City Corporation for that purpose after having notified the members of the syndicate of this plan and his participation in it. He also told them that the corporation would buy their property at the earlier agreed upon price of twice the purchase cost, or $1,458,000. This was accepted by the syndicate. He also prepared a stock subscription agreement form setting forth the plans for development of the property in detail, and he sold stock in the corporation at units of $100,000 each. The subscription agreement information included the fact that the property would be acquired by the corporation at cost plus a commission to H. R. Watchie & Associates, Inc.

The venture was not financially successful and in 1965 Watchie resigned as president and a director of the corporation, and a group of Portland shareholders were elected directors and officers. Watchie was not forced to resign but it was thought that having local people in the corporation management might stimulate home and lot sales. Subsequently, the corporation filed this suit alleging that Watchie had sold the Skyline property to the corporation for twice its cost without disclosing the profit to subsequent subscribers.

SLOAN, JUSTICE. Plaintiff's cause of suit is based upon a doctrine originally formulated in this country in the Massachusetts case of *Old Dominion Copper Mining & Smelting Co. v. Bigelow.* We read that case to hold that the promoter of a corporation owes to the corporation, and its subsequent subscribers of stock, a fiduciary duty. This duty is violated if he schemes to and does secretly acquire property or the right to buy property which he knows the corporation will require and sells it to the corporation, while he still retains control of the corporation, at a secret profit which is not disclosed to the later subscribers or to an independent board of directors of the corporation. In that event the corporation may bring an action to recover the secret profits. Oregon has adopted this theory in *Wills v. Nehalem Coal Co.* The doctrine is generally recognized.

*   *   *   *   *

The allegations of the complaint are limited to charges that Watchie was the promoter of plaintiff corporation; that he personally contracted to buy the Skyline property; that he formed plaintiff corporation and while he was in the complete control of it, sold the property to the corporation for double his own purchase price; and that

Watchie "did not disclose to either the Board of Directors or the stockholders of plaintiff corporation that (Watchie) would make a profit of $729,000 by reason of said contract." These are the pertinent allegations of the complaint.

The evidence does not sustain the allegations. In the complete transaction, as described in the evidence, the property was bought by the Seattle syndicate. It was not bought with the scheme or design of selling it to this or any other persons or corporation but it was held for sale at the price specified. Contrary to the allegations, Watchie did not participate in any part of the profit made by the Seattle syndicate in the contract for the sale of the property, except for the commission paid to H. R. Watchie & Associates, Inc. In the contract with plaintiff corporation, Watchie was named as the vendor. But he was acting, admittedly, only as the trustee for the Seattle syndicate. He was not the true vendor or the recipient of any of the profits, as alleged. Nor is there any evidence that at any time, Watchie as an individual or as trustee schemed to overload the profit on unsuspecting subscribers.

However, the evidence did establish that Watchie made a personal profit in the form of the commission he received for the transaction. The commission was actually received by H. R. Watchie & Associates, Inc., but it is Watchie's alter ego. Because of his failure to disclose his dual relationship, he should be required to return this personal profit to plaintiff. This means that he should not be charged with the whole commission received. He should be charged with that part which could be said to result from his nondisclosure.

The subscription agreement informed all subscribers that there would be a commission in the present transaction payable to Watchie or H. R. Watchie & Associates, Inc., by the corporation. This commission was described in the subscription agreement as one ninth of the cost of the property to Watchie or Watchie & Associates, Inc. It also provided that he was to receive his actual costs. Thus everyone that was involved in the venture was aware that there would be a profit to Watchie.

As a result of his nondisclosure, however, there is an ambiguity concerning what was the cost to Watchie for determining the amount of his authorized profit on the transaction; the price at which he purchased the property for the Seattle syndicate or the price he arranged between the syndicate and the plaintiff corporation. Since this ambiguity is solely the result of Watchie's nondisclosure of his relationship with the syndicate it would seem that the proper course would be to resolve the ambiguity against Watchie and in favor of the corporation that the cost referred to in the subscription agreement was the original cost.

Completing Corporate Organization

Organization Meeting. After the charter has been granted, the Model Act (57)[5] requires an organization meeting of the board of directors, which is to be named in the articles. Many statutes specify that the organization meeting shall be held by the incorporators. Delaware provides that the organization

---

[5] The numbers in the parentheses refer to the sections of the Model Business Corporation Act, which appears in the Appendix.

meeting will be held by the incorporators unless the articles specify the initial board of directors instead. Even where the statute does not specifically require one, it is customary to hold an organization meeting although the incorporators, or even, in some cases, the directors, are "dummies" who are associates and employees of the lawyer handling the incorporation. The use of dummies may facilitate completion of the routine business of incorporation, the substitutes then resigning in favor of the operating directors. The organization meeting requires a proper notice. The Model Act requires a call by the majority of the directors named in the articles and the giving of three days' notice by mail to the directors.

Business of Organization Meeting. The business to be transacted at an organization meeting will depend on the nature of the business to be carried on by the corporation, on the laws of the state of incorporation, and on the provisions of the articles of incorporation. The Model Act specifies only that bylaws shall be adopted and officers elected. Where the meeting is held by the incorporators, election of directors would be necessary unless they are named in the articles. Other matters usually included would be adoption of a corporate seal, approval of the form of stock certificates, acceptance of stock subscriptions, authorization of issue of stock, adoption of promoters' contracts, authorization of payment of or reimbursement for incorporation expenses, and fixing the salaries of officers. Action on other matters which are appropriate to get the corporation into operation may also be taken at this time.

Bylaws of Corporation. The power to adopt the initial bylaws is given to various groups in different jurisdictions. While the Model Act (27) gives it to the initial directors named in the articles, some states give it to the incorporators and others to the shareholders or subscribers. In Delaware the initial bylaws may be adopted by the incorporators or by the initial directors if they are named in the articles. The Model Act also gives the power of amendment, repeal, and adoption of new bylaws to the directors unless this power is reserved to the shareholders by the articles of incorporation. Again, there is wide variation among the states. If the statute, as is true in some states, is silent, the power to make and amend bylaws rests with the shareholders. They may delegate this power to the directors, however. To determine who has the authority in any given corporation the statute and the articles of incorporation must be examined.

Although normally the procedures outlined in the bylaws for their amendment must be adhered to, if a different practice is customarily followed with the implied consent of those who could amend it, the courts will treat the bylaw as amended or repealed "by custom and usage."

To be valid, bylaws must be consistent with state law and with the articles of incorporation. They must also be "reasonable" and related to a corporate purpose. Since usually a bare majority may make and amend bylaws, the latter requirement provides the minority with some protection against oppression by the majority.

Persons Bound by Bylaws. Officers, directors, and shareholders of the corporation are bound by bylaws properly adopted. Corporate employees, however, have been held not to be bound unless they have notice or knowledge of them, and the same is true of third persons.

Provisions of Bylaws. The purpose of the bylaws is to regulate the conduct and define the duties of the members toward the corporation and among themselves. They usually include provisions setting out the authority of the officers and directors, the time and place at which the annual shareholders' meeting shall be held, how special meetings of shareholders may be called, defining a quorum, stating how shareholders' meetings shall be organized, and regulating how the voting shall be carried on and how elections shall be conducted. They will also provide for the organization of the board of directors, state the place and time for the regular meetings of the board of directors, set forth how special meetings shall be called, state the officers to be elected or appointed and the duties of the officers, and also state who shall be authorized to sign various kinds of contracts in behalf of the corporation. The bylaws may make provision for special committees, defining the scope of their activities and the membership of such committees. They will set up the machinery for the transfer of shares of stock, for the keeping of stock records, and so forth, and will also make provision for the declaring and the paying of dividends.

Summary

An organization meeting is held after the corporation has been granted its charter. Under the Model Act the initial board of directors are the participants in this meeting. Some statutes specify that the incorporators conduct the meeting. The business to be transacted at the meeting depends upon the laws of the state of incorporation and also the nature of the business and the provisions of its articles of incorporation.

Under the Model Act the initial bylaws and amendments are adopted by the board of directors unless the articles of incorporation give the power of amendment and repeal to the shareholders. Some statutes specify that the incorporators will adopt initial bylaws.

The bylaws usually include provisions regarding annual meetings of shareholders, meetings of the directors, the duties of the officers of the corporation, where the bank account will be kept, and who shall sign checks. They will set up the machinery for the transfer of stock and such other details as the nature of the corporate business warrants.

To be valid bylaws must be consistent with the state law and the articles of incorporation. They are binding on officers, directors and shareholders of the corporation. Third persons, as a general rule, are not bound by any provision of the bylaws of the corporation unless they have notice or knowledge of it.

Financing the Corporation

Sources of Funds.   The initial funds and property for a corporation usually come from the promoters and from other investors. They furnish money and property or settle claims for services rendered in exchange for securities of the corporation, which may be one or more types of stock and possibly bonds as well. However, sometimes a potentially large supplier or customer or a bank may provide money on notes of the corporation, perhaps cosigned by the promoters.

Once the corporation is operating profitably, it may rely heavily on retained earnings for increasing the funds available to the business. In addition, it may use accounts receivable financing, inventory financing, and other means for increasing its available funds. Dollars charged off to depreciation which are not actually spent for replacement, renewal, or additions to plant and equipment also become additional available funds.

There are two main types of securities: equity securities and debt securities. Each type has many variants, and there have been some securities which are hybrids.

Equity Securities.   Every business corporation must issue some stock or equity securities. Traditionally, shareholders were viewed as having a threefold proportionate interest in the corporation: in its earnings, in its control, and in its net assets upon liquidation. However, modern statutes permit corporations to issue more than one class of stock and to vary the preferences, limitations, and rights of the various classes. Most statutes even permit voting rights to be restricted or denied. The Model Act (60, 73, 79, and 84) provides, however, that the articles cannot eliminate the right to vote of any class of stock on certain extraordinary transactions including merger, dissolution, sale of assets not in the normal course of business, and certain amendments to the articles. The shareholder's contract is determined by the articles of incorporation and the bylaws as well as by what may be printed on the certificate.

The equity securities constitute the "capital stock" of the corporation and the value received for these shares appears in the capital accounts in the shareholders' investment section of the corporation's balance sheet. Because of much confusion in terminology and definition with respect to "capital" and "stock," the Model Act uses the term "stated capital." Whatever the term, the value of the capital stock, which may be divided into two or more classes of differing amounts and stated values, is fixed at the time the stock is issued. That value will be the par value or, in case of stock without par value, the value determined by the directors to be the stated value (18 and 21). If the stock is sold for more than the par or stated value, the excess will become capital surplus. The value of the capital stock on the books of the corporation will not be affected by changes in the value of the corporation's assets or the market price of its stock. It can be changed only by amending the articles of incorporation.

Stock may be issued for money, for property—tangible or intangible—or for labor actually performed or services rendered to the corporation under the Model Act (19), but not for promissory notes nor future services. Delaware does not foreclose the use of promissory notes but does by court decision prohibit issuing stock for services to be performed in the future. Subscriptions for shares may be paid by installments so long as the calls are uniform as to all shares of a particular class. Certificates, however, under the Model Act (23) may not be issued until the shares are fully paid.

In order to cope with the problem of "watered" stock (shares issued for an inadequate consideration), it was common in the past to require some public record of the valuation placed upon property exchanged for shares. These requirements have tended to disappear, and the state and federal securities laws are relied upon to deal with the problem.

Certificates are issued to represent the shares of stock, but they are not the stock. There have been recent proposals to eliminate stock certificates due to the burden on brokerage houses in handling a very large quantity of such documents. However, presently under the Uniform Commercial Code (8–105 [1]) all types of corporate securities, including stocks, stock warrants, and bonds are declared to be negotiable instruments, but Article 8 rather than Article 3 of the Code applies.

Debt Securities.   A corporation has the power to borrow money for the purpose of carrying on its operations. The general term for debt securities of corporations is "bonds." However, short-term debt securities may be designated "notes," and evidences of debt which is unsecured may be called "debentures." Debenture holders participate on a pro rata basis with general creditors in the event of insolvency while the holder of a mortgage bond will have priority over general creditors as to the assets covered by the mortgage. The possible variations in the terms of bonds are endless. The rights of the bondholder depends upon the provisions of the contract which constitutes the bond.

Neither the Model Act nor most statutes require authority of the shareholders to issue corporate bonds. Several statutes appear to require shareholder approval if a mortgage of all or substantially all of the assets of the corporation is to be given as security. However, this is not required by the Model Act (78) nor by the Delaware statute.

By the terms of the contract for the bond issue, called an indenture, the corporation may be obligated to pay a fixed rate of interest on the bonds, or it may be obligated to pay interest only in case the corporate income is sufficient to cover the interest on the bonds. Instead of being entitled to a fixed rate of interest, the bondholders may be paid a proportional percentage of the net profits of the corporation. The bondholders, as a general rule, do not have voting rights but may be given voting rights if the interest on the bonds is not paid when due or is not paid for a stated period of time. Also, a bond may be convertible, that is, the holder of the bond may be given the right to take common or preferred stock in payment of the bond on terms stated in the bond. A sinking fund may be provided. The bonds may be issued for a special purpose such as the purchase of certain equipment. In such a case the bond may provide that interest is to be paid only out of the proceeds from the use of the equipment.

Summary

The initial funds and property for the corporation usually come from the promoters and from investors in exchange for securities. There are two major types of securities: equity securities (stock) and debt securities (generally called bonds).

Every business corporation must issue some equity securities or stock and may issue two or more classes and vary their preferences, limitations, and rights so that shareholders do not have their traditional threefold proportionate interest in the corporation: in its earnings, in its net assets, and in its control. Stock certificates are issued to represent the shares but they are not the stock itself.

Bonds represent obligations of the corporations, and the bondholders are creditors of the corporation. If the bonds are secured, in the event of the insolvency of the corporation, the bondholders have priority over general creditors as to the assets pledged as security. Interest may be a fixed obligation, or it may be payable out of profits. In general, bondholders have priority over all classes of stockholders.

Eastern Oklahoma Television Co. v. Ameco, Inc.

437 F.2d 138 (10th Cir. 1971)

In an action for damages brought by Eastern Oklahoma Television Company (plaintiff) against Ameco, Inc. (defendant), in which certain promoters and original subscribers of Eastern Oklahoma Television Co. (KTEN) became third party defendants, the basic issue was whether corporate stock allotted to the promoters in consideration of services rendered and property furnished had been validly issued. There was an appeal from the ruling that the stock was valid. Affirmed.

C. C. Morris, Brown Morris, and Bill Hoover were owners and operators of two radio stations in Ada, Oklahoma. In 1953, they organized KTEN to operate a TV station in Ada. They obtained a channel from the Federal Communications Commission, pledging all of the assets of the radio stations to "undergird" the venture, personally guaranteed payment to Radio Corporation of Amerca in the amount of $240,000 for equipment, designed the facilities, planned the operations and hired and trained personnel. The articles of incorporation authorized 650 shares of Class A voting stock and 650 shares of Class B nonvoting stock, both classes having a par value of $500 per share.

The Class B Stock was sold to the public at par by the promoters, who were also the directors. Each subscriber was told of the necessary organizational services which had been or were to be performed by the directors and that the Class A stock would be allotted to them. The subscriptions and payments on the Class B stock were to be held in escrow in a local bank until the construction permit from the FCC was received. The Class A stock was issued by a resolution of the directors which recited that the consideration was their experience in broadcasting, their standing with the FCC and their personal guarantee of the debt to RCA for equipment.

The early years of operation of KTEN were plagued with financial difficulties. The promoters not only returned 250 shares of Class A stock to the treasury to be sold for working capital but also made personal loans to the corporation. $170,000 worth of preferred stock was also issued. One of the original shareholders contests the validity of the stock issued to Bill Hoover, one of the two major Class A shareholders.

PICKETT, CIRCUIT JUDGE.   It is first argued that the directors in the meeting of January 22, 1954, did not have a quorum and could not vote the issuance of shares to themselves as such action was in contravention of their fiduciary responsibility to the corporation, since at that moment they had a personal interest in the resolution and were hence disqualified as interested directors. A contract between a corporation and an interested director, which in essence is what the stock issuance in the instant case presents, does not render the contract void per se but at most merely voidable at the option of the corporation. . . . It is obvious that the directors and Class A shareholders were completely informed of and had consented to the resolution since they were one and the same as the interested directors who had passed the resolution. Likewise, it was found by the trial court . . . that the Class B shareholders were informed prior to their subscription for shares that the Class A shares were to be issued to the directors for their organizational services and property received by the corporation, all of which was of considerable value to the corporation. Under such circumstances we conclude that the shares were issued with the full knowledge and consent of all parties at the time and the resolution had at least been ratified by the acquiescence of the Class B shareholders.

It is further urged that the issuance of the stock to the directors was in violation of Article 9, Section 3 of the Oklahoma Constitution, and Okl. Stat. Ann. tit. 18, § 1.76 (1953), as having been made without adequate consideration. The record clearly discloses that the stock transfer was for property, goodwill, extensive valuable services rendered, and the personal guaranty given by the directors for the RCA note. That the corporation received valuable services and property from the organizers cannot be doubted. Apparently from the beginning they contributed their time and abilities, together with the risk of all all their personal assets for the corporate success. The goodwill, which included Hoover's experience, expertise, and favorable broadcasting record with the FCC was extremely valuable in the acquisition of FCC permits by KTEN and in the actual construction of the station, including the design and construction of a signal relay system from Oklahoma City. Where goodwill constitutes property as in Oklahoma, Okl. Stat. Ann. tit. 60, § 316 (1963), and if actually existent and of value at the time, it may be included in determining a valid consideration for the issuance of stock. . . .

In objecting to the personal guaranty upon the RCA note as part of the consideration for the issuance of shares, appellants rely on the rule in Oklahoma that a promissory note or other obligation of the subscriber is not valid consideration for such purposes. But here, the guaranty was for an obligation of the corporation. Absent the guaranty, the essential equipment for the operation of a television station could not have been obtained. The organizers personally furnished the security for the purchase of this property. Without it the cost to the corporation would have been substantial if it had been possible to obtain the security by other means. The record clearly indicates that the result of this security was the completion of the station, which eventually led to a successful corporate operation. The guaranty was valuable property or services within the meaning of the Oklahoma Constitution. The purpose of the constitutional and statutory provisions was to require corporations to receive at least actual par value either in money, property, or services for stock issued. There was no intent to limit the kind of property or services which might be received. An expert in the field of television and the promotion of local stations, after consideration of all the facts, testified that in his opinion the value of the services and property rendered by the corporate organizers was considerably more than the par value of the Class A stock received by them. This evidence was admissible and is the customary method of proving the value of services and property to a corporation.

Jones Valley Finance Co. v. Tennille

115 So.2d 495 (Ct. App. Ala. 1959)

This was an action by Tennille (plaintiff) against Jones Valley Finance Co. (defendant) to recover accrued interest on Finance Co.'s securities. Judgment for Tennille and Finance Co. appealed. Reversed and remanded.

Tennille bought securities issued by Finance Co. The certificate stated that he was the owner of 40 shares of preferred stock and it stated that Finance Co. "hereby guarantees the payment of interest, accumulated, on said shares at the rate of 4 percent, payable semi-annually." The articles of incorporation authorized Finance Co. to issue both common and preferred shares. The securities in question were issued pursuant to a resolution of the board of directors, ratified by the shareholders, which read:

That the holders of the Preferred Stock would be entitled to receive, when and as declared by the Board of Directors, Dividends from the surplus or net profits of the corporation at the rate of 4 percent per annum, payable semi-annually on the 1st day of July and the 1st day of January of each year. Dividends on Preferred Stock would be cumulated from the date of issue and would be paid or set apart for payment before any dividend on any other stock of the corporation would be paid or set apart.

Alabama corporations were authorized by statute to create varied classes of stock "including debenture stock and preferred stock of one or more classes." (Debenture stock is a security more common in England than the United States which is similar to a bond secured by a mortgage on corporate property except that it has no maturity date and hence resembles an annuity. Interest in arrears may be recovered by an action against the company.)

CATES, JUDGE.   Our Legislature, in having provided the power in corporations to issue debenture stock, has thereby indicated that the law (on this matter) should put no impediment to corporate ingenuity which may be employed in the bargaining leading up to business financing, nor in the expression of the parties' bargain.

We are satisfied the power to make such a guaranty as was used here exists. The remaining question is solvable by the familiar—and often invisible—rule of ascertaining the intent of the parties to the agreement.

We consider that the instant certificates evidence the ownership of preferred stock as distinguished from a certificate of indebtedness and also do not include a promise to pay interest. Our reasons for this include (1) the legend employed on the certificate itself, using "preferred stock" (words of statutory connotation), coupled with the similar indication found on one of the panels on the reverse of the certificate; (2) the resolution of January 18, 1946, which, by law, is always available for the plaintiff's inspection at convenient hours at the company office; (3) the filing of the statutory certificate (of charter amendment) in the office of the judge of probate making the statement of the recapitalization a matter of public record; and (4) the absence of any compulsory redemption date of the preferred shares.

The expression "guarantees the payment of interest" fitted into the remainder of the text is but a provision calling for a cumulative dividend, which, of course, would mean that the payment would not be available, except upon declaration by the board of directors unless otherwise required under the rule of *Holcomb v. Forsyth:* this because a dividend as distinguished from an absolute promise to pay interest is the normal thing to expect as an incident of the ownership of preferred stock.

Kinds of Equity Securities

Par and No Par.   Most statutes permit corporations to issue either par or no-par stock.[6] If a par value is established, it is done so in the articles. However, par is not always the price at which the corporation will sell par value shares. The Model Act (18) provides that the price of par value stock is to be established from time to time by the directors, but it cannot be less than the value stated in the articles of incorporation except for treasury stock. If sold for more

---

[6] Nebraska prohibits no-par stock.

than par, the overage becomes "capital surplus." A few states permit corporations to issue stock for less than par value in certain circumstances.

The Model Act (18) and the Delaware Act both give to the directors the right to establish the issue price of no-par stock, but this right can be given to the shareholders by an appropriate provision in the articles. Under the Model Act (21) the directors may within 60 days of issue allocate some proportion of the price of no-par stock to capital surplus; otherwise it is all allocated to stated capital.

Common Stock. If a corporation has only one class of stock, it is common stock. When there is more than one class of stock, the common shareholders generally bear the major risks of the venture and stand to profit most if it is successful. Therefore, ordinarily no special contract rights or preferences are granted to common shareholders. They receive what is left over after the preferences of other classes have been satisfied, both with respect to net earnings payable in dividends and net assets upon liquidation. To balance this, they generally have control or the predominant voice in management.

However, there is under the Model Act and most statutes no limit on the ingenuity of promoters and their financial advisors in apportioning preferences, rights, and limitations to suit their interests and those of prospective buyers of the securities. As a result, the distinction between common and preferred stock is frequently blurred. It is not unusual to have one class of common shares with voting rights, perhaps designated "Class A," and another without voting rights except in case of certain extraordinary transactions which might be referred to as "Class B" shares.

Preferred Stock. Classes of stock which have rights or preferences over other classes of stock are called preferred stock. Preferred shareholders are customarily given preference as to dividends and in the distribution of assets on the dissolution of the corporation. In regard to dividends the preferences granted may vary greatly. The stock may be cumulative or noncumulative, and participating or nonparticipating. Dividends on cumulative preferred, if not paid in any year, will be payable later if funds are available for payment of dividends, whereas dividends on noncumulative preferred not earned and paid in any one year are not payable at a later date. Participating preferred has priority as to a stated amount or percentage of the dividends, and after a prescribed dividend is paid to common shareholders, the preferred shareholders participate with the common shareholders in additional dividends paid. Various combinations, such as cumulative participating or noncumulative participating, may be issued. If funds are not available for the payment of dividends, no dividends will be paid on preferred stock regardless of the type of stock. Under the Model Act (45) and the laws of substantially all states, it is unlawful to pay dividends out of capital.

Preferred stock may be made redeemable, and provision may be made for the setting up of a sinking fund for the redemption of such stock. It may be convertible, in which case provision will be made whereby it may be converted into common stock or into other securities of the corporation. Preferred stock may be given voting rights, especially in the event of default in the payment of dividends.

The preferences granted will usually be set out in the articles of incorporation. The Model Act (15 and 16) provides that the preferences of the various classes, if more than one, must be stated in the articles of incorporation but permits the articles to authorize the directors to issue any preferred class of stock in series and to establish variations between the different series with respect to: (1) the rate of dividend; (2) whether the stock may be redeemed, and if so, the price and terms of redemption; (3) the amount payable upon the stock in liquidation; (4) sinking-fund provisions, if any, for redemption of the stock; and (5) the terms and conditions, if any, on which the stock may be converted.

Warrants, Rights, and Options. The Delaware Act and the Model Act (20), as well as other statutes, specifically permit the directors to issue options or rights to purchase shares of the corporation, whether or not in connection with the sale of its other securities. If they are to be issued to directors, officers, or employees, shareholder approval must be secured under the Model Act. In the absence of fraud the judgment of the directors as to the adequacy of the consideration received is conclusive.

Options to purchase stock of a corporation which are evidenced by a certificate are known as warrants. They give the holder the right to buy a specified number of shares of the stock (usually common) at a specified price and they generally have a termination date. Although customarily issued in combination with another security, warrants may be bought and sold alone and may be listed on the American Stock Exchange. Although out of favor for a period after the 1920s, warrants have been used rather extensively in recent years both as a "sweetener" in public- and private-debt placement and as a separate security usually issued as part of a "package" in connection with a merger or acquisition offer.

The term "rights" is usually applied to short-term and often nonnegotiable options. They usually are a device used to give a present security holder the right to subscribe to some proportional quantity of the same or a different security in his corporation, often pursuant to preemptive right requirements.

Summary

Under most statutes corporations may issue common or preferred stock as par or no par shares. If there is more than one class of stock, the common shareholders generally bear the major risks of the venture, stand to gain the most, and have control of the corporation. If there is only one class, it will be common. Usually the common shareholders' claim to both income and assets comes after other investors, but they are generally given the predominant or full right to select the management.

Preferred shareholders are usually given preferences over one or more other classes of stock as to dividends and distribution of assets in case of liquidation. Preferences are stated in the articles of incorporation. The shares may be cumulative or noncumulative as to dividends. Preferred stock may be redeemable either with or without a sinking fund.

Warrants and rights are options to purchase shares.

Stock Subscriptions, Issuance, Transfer, and Redemption

Nature of Stock Subscription. In the absence of statutes most courts have held that preincorporation subscriptions to stock are merely offers which continue open until the corporation is chartered and that subscribers may revoke their offers at any time before the occurrence of that event. Other courts have held that the subscription is a mutual agreement between the subscribers and enforceable unless all subscribers agree to release each other. The Model Act (17) and the statutes of Delaware and many other states make such subscriptions irrevocable for a period of six months in the absence of a contrary provision in the subscription. Several states provide either that the filing of articles of incorporation or the issuance of the certificate constitute acceptance of the subscriptions. Delaware and several other states require all stock subscriptions to be in writing, but the Model Act does not.[7]

If a subscription is made for the unissued shares of stock of an existing corporation, the generally accepted view is that the subscription is an offer to purchase which ripens into a contract on acceptance by the corporation. On acceptance the subscriber immediately becomes a stockholder, even though the delivery of the stock certificates is postponed until the purchase price of the stock is paid. An existing corporation may, in soliciting subscriptions for its unissued stock, so word its subscription agreement that it amounts to an offer to sell which is accepted when the subscriber agrees to purchase.

The subscription may provide for payment of the price of the stock on a specified day or in installments or it may be payable upon call of the board of directors. The Model Act (17) requires that calls for payment must be uniform as to all shares of the same class or series.

Issuing Shares of Stock. When a person has subscribed for stock in a proposed or existing corporation and his or her subscription has been accepted,

---

[7] A preincorporation subscription is not considered a sale of goods covered by the statute of frauds so need not be in writing.

the making of the contract between the subscriber and the corporation is generally termed "issuing stock," and thereafter he or she is a shareholder. If the subscription agreement is a preincorporation agreement and more stock is subscribed than the corporation is authorized to issue, the corporation will, as a general rule, issue stock to the subscribers on a pro rata basis. Under the general rule, stock subscribed for by preincorporation agreement is issued when the corporation is chartered.

Although one can be a shareholder without having been issued a stock certificate and before fully paying for the shares, the Model Act (23) provides that no certificate shall be issued until the shares are fully paid. It also provides (25) that an assignee or transferee of shares or a subscriber in good faith and without notice will not be personally liable to the corporation or its creditors for any unpaid portion of the consideration for the shares. This is consistent with Article 8 of the Uniform Commercial Code, which makes stock certificates negotiable.

Liability of Issuer under U.C.C. A corporation has a duty not to issue more than its authorized shares and often employs a bank or trust company as a registrar to prevent overissue through error in the issuance or transfer of its stock. Overissued shares are void. However, the Uniform Commercial Code (8–104) requires the issuer to obtain identical stock, if reasonably available, and to deliver it to the holder or, if unavailable, to reimburse him for the value paid plus interest. Under the U.C.C. (8–202 and 8–205), the issuer is not liable for a security which is not genuine, but it is liable to a purchaser for value and without notice if an unauthorized signature or a forgery is placed on the security by someone, such as an employee or transfer agent, to whom the security has been entrusted by the issuer.

Transfer of Corporate Stock. Stock certificates have the effect of making the stock registered investment securities under Article 8, since they specifically name the owner or owners. Most stock certificates have an assignment form printed on the back, and this is endorsed by the registered owner to effect a transfer. However, a separate document, often referred to as a "stock power," may be used for assignment. If an assignment of a stock certificate is made without naming a transferee, it becomes transferable by delivery and is called a "street certificate."

Bonds are also covered by Article 8 as investment securities. They may be either registered or bearer bonds. A registered bond is transferred in the same manner as a stock certificate while a bearer bond is transferred by delivery. Interest is paid on the latter upon the presentation to the issuer or its agent of an interest coupon attached to the bond which is due and payable.

Restrictions on Transfer. In the absence of a valid restriction, investment securities are freely transferable. In close corporations, however, the shareholders often wish not only to select carefully their original business associates but to control the future disposition of the stock so that they can choose competent and compatible associates or keep control in the remaining members. Any restriction which would in effect make the stock nontransferable would be against public policy and void. Therefore, the validity of a restriction will turn on whether it is reasonable in objective and degree. Keeping outsiders from becoming shareholders and maintaining the proportionate interests between shareholders are usually held proper. The most common restriction requires the shareholder to offer his or her stock to the corporation and/or proportionately to other shareholders before transferring it to an outsider. The restriction may be imposed in the bylaws or by agreement between the shareholder and the corporation, but it appears from the cases that where there is doubt the restriction is more likely to be enforced if it is stated in the articles of incorporation. To be effective the restriction must be noted conspicuously on the certificate (U.C.C. 8–204).

Corporation's Duty to Transfer.   A corporation owes a duty to register the transfer of any registered security presented to it for registration, provided the security has been properly endorsed and other legal formalities have been complied with. (8–401.) If the corporation refuses to make the transfer, it is liable to the transferee. The nature of the corporation's liability will depend on the laws of the state having jurisdiction of the case and the surrounding circumstances. In some cases the transferee has been able to recover the value of the stock in a suit in conversion, and in other cases the transferee has been granted the remedy of specific performance by a court of equity.

The corporation has the right to make reasonable inquiry and investigation before it transfers stock or registered bonds. It will not be liable for any delay which is reasonably necessary to make whatever investigation the circumstances of the case warrant. If the corporation has a lien on the stock for an obligation owed to the corporation by the shareholder, it has the right to refuse to register a transfer until the obligation is satisfied. However, any lien in favor of the corporation, if it is to be valid against a purchaser of the security, must be noted conspicuously on the security. (8–103.)

If the owner of corporate stock or bonds dies, the ownership of such security passes to his or her estate, and the administrator or executor has the right to transfer the security. The procedure followed will depend on the probate laws of the state of domicile. If the corporate security is held by one acting as trustee, the trustee is the legal owner of the stock, but such trustee may not have the authority to sell. The rights and obligations of the corporation regarding the transfer of registered corporate securities by a trustee are set out in Section 8–403 and 8–404 of the Uniform Commercial Code. The procedure to be followed in obtaining a new registered security or the transfer of a lost, destroyed, or stolen security is set out in Section 8–405.

Redemption and Purchase of Stock by Corporation.   It is quite common for corporations to issue preferred stock subject to call or redemption. Redemption is an involuntary sale by the shareholder at a fixed price. Under the Model Act (15) the right of the corporation to redeem a preferred stock issue and the redemption price must be stated in the articles of incorporation. Redemption is not permitted when the corporation is or would become insolvent or when the prior claim of other shareholders upon its assets would be impaired (66). In a few jurisdictions the statutes are silent on redemption. It has been held that preferred shares may be redeemed in the absence of statute if the articles so provide. The New York statute permits redeemable common shares provided that the corporation has outstanding another class of common shares not subject to redemption. Redemption is usually at the discretion of the corporation but even if mandatory it is still subject to the solvency requirement. Some articles permit a partial redemption of a class of preferred shares.

A corporation may purchase its own common as well as preferred shares from a shareholder willing to sell without specific authorization in its articles. In the Model Act (6) and most other statutes the restrictions safeguarding creditors and other shareholders are more confining than in the case of redemption. The Model Act permits such purchases only out of unrestricted earned surplus or, upon two-thirds vote of shareholders, unrestricted capital surplus may be used. When redeemable shares are reacquired by the corporation, the Model Act (67) requires their cancellation but purchased shares may be held as treasury shares and resold, or they may be canceled (5).

Summary

A stock subscription is an agreement to purchase a stated number of shares of stock when issued. Generally a preincorporation subscription agreement is treated as an offer which is accepted when the corporation is chartered. A subscription to purchase the unissued stock of an existing corporation is an offer to buy stock, and a contract is completed when the corporation accepts the offer. Immediately on acceptance the subscriber becomes a stockholder, irrespective of when the stock certificate evidencing the shares of stock is executed and delivered.

Stock is issued when the contract to purchase it is completed.

The Uniform Commercial Code in Article 8 sets forth the duties and liabilities of the corporation as issuer of stocks and bonds, which are referred to as investment securities and are given characteristics of negotiable instruments. Among these provisions are the following: the issuer who issues more than its authorized shares must obtain identical stock or pay its value; it is liable on a certificate which has been forged by someone entrusted with it; restrictions on transfer of investment securities must be noted conspicuously on the certificate and are valid only if reasonable; the corporation must register the transfer of any security presented to it properly endorsed.

A corporation may usually redeem preferred stock if such a power is reserved in its articles. Generally it may purchase outstanding securities without a provision in the articles.

Van Noy v. Gibbs

318 P.2d 351 (Sup. Ct. Utah 1957)

This was an action by Spencer Van Noy (plaintiff) against Richard Gibbs (defendant) for the balance due on a stock subscription. Judgment for Van Noy and Gibbs appealed. Affirmed with modification not here pertinent.

Van Noy and Gibbs formed a corporation known as Valley Amusement Enterprises. Each owned 1,950 shares of stock. A short time after the corporation was formed a dispute over the management of the business arose between them and each offered to buy the other's interest. Van Noys assigned his shares to Gibbs for $2,000, of which Gibbs paid $750 down. When Gibbs refused to pay the balance, Van Noy filed this action and Gibbs filed a counterclaim seeking to recover the down payment.

At the time the contract between them was made, both parties believed the corporation owned a leasehold interest in the premises it occupied as an amusement center, but it was subsequently discovered that it did not have a valid lease. The corporation had other assets and the articles of incorporation set a value of $6,900 on the property taken into the corporation. The value placed on the leasehold was $3,100.

Gibbs claimed that he was not liable on the contract and was entitled to a return of his down payment because of a mutual mistake of fact as to the existence of the leasehold interest as an asset of the corporation.

TUCKETT, DISTRICT JUDGE.   One who buys stock in a corporation of necessity enters into a contract of a speculative nature and he will not ordinarily be permitted to rescind because the stock turns out to be of less value than the buyer and seller supposed it to be worth. Gibbs received all of Van Noy's interest in the corporation and that is what he bargained for.

Ling and Co. v. Trinity Savings and Loan Ass'n

482 S.W.2d 841 (Sup. Ct. Tex. 1972)

Action by Trinity Savings and Loan Association (plaintiff) against Bruce Bowman and Ling and Company, Inc. (defendants), to recover balance due on a note and to foreclose on Bowman's collateral, which consisted of 1500 shares of Ling and Co. class A common stock. Summary judgment for Trinity affirmed by Court of Appeals. Reversed and remanded.

Ling contended that its articles restricted transferability of the shares. It argued that Bowman's assignment to Trinity violated this restriction and therefore Trinity was not entitled to the shares.

On the front side of the stock certificates in small print, it was stated that the shares were subject to the provisions of the articles of incorporation, that a copy could be obtained from the secretary of the corporation or the secretary of state and that specific references to provisions setting forth preferences, limitations, and restrictions were on the back of the certificate. On the back, also in small type, the reference to the articles was repeated and specific reference was made to article four. It referred to a number of rights and limitations contained in article four, including those which:

Restrict the transfer, sale, assignment, pledge, hypothecation, or encumbrance of any of the shares represented hereby under certain conditions, and which under certain conditions require the holder thereof to grant options to purchase the shares represented hereby first to the Corporation and then pro rata to the other holders of the Class A common stock.

REAVLEY, JUSTICE.   The court of civil appeals struck down the restrictions for three reasons: the lack of conspicuous notice thereof on the stock certificate, the unreasonableness of the restrictions, and statutory prohibition against an option in favor of other stockholders whenever they number more than twenty. These objections will be examined in that order.

CONSPICUOUSNESS

The Texas Business Corporation Act as amended in 1957, V.A.T.S. Bus. Corp. Act, art. 2.22, subd. A, provides that a corporation may impose restrictions on the transfer of its stock if they are "expressly set forth in the articles of incorporation . . . and . . . copied at length or in summary form on the face or so copied on the back and referred to on the face of each certificate . . ." Article 2.19, subd. F, enacted by the Legislature at the same time, permits the incorporation by reference on the face or back of the certificate of the provision of the articles of incorporation which restricts the transfer of the stock. The court of civil appeals objected to the general reference to the articles of incorporation and the failure to print the full conditions imposed upon the transfer of the shares. However, reference is made on the face of the certificate to the restrictions described on the reverse side; the notice on the reverse side refers to the particular article of the articles of incorporation as restricting the transfer or encumbrance and requiring "the holder hereof to grant options to purchase the shares represented hereby first to the Corporation and then pro rata to the other holders of the class A Common Stock . . . " We hold that the content of the certificate complies with the requirements of the Texas Business Corporation Act.

There remains the requirement of the Texas Business and Commerce Code that the restriction or reference thereto on the certificate must be conspicuous. Sec. 8.204, V.T.C.A. Bus. & C., [UCC 8–204] requires that a restriction on transferability be "noted conspicuously on the security." Sec. 1.201(10) [UCC 1–201(10)] of the Business and Commerce Code defines "conspicuous" and makes the determination a question of law for the court to decide. It is provided that a conspicuous term is so written as to be noticed by a reasonable person. Examples of conspicuous matter are given there as a printed heading in capitals . . . [or] larger or other contrasting type or color." This means that something must appear on the face of the certificate to attract the attention of a reasonable person when he looks at it.

Our holding that the restriction is not noted conspicuously on the certificate does not entitle Trinity Savings and Loan to a summary judgment under this record. Sec. 8.204 of the Business and Commerce Code provides that the restriction is effective against a person with actual knowledge of it. The record does not establish conclusively that Trinity Savings and Loan lacked knowledge of the restriction on January 28, 1969, the date the record indicates when Bowman executed an assignment of this stock to Trinity Savings and Loan.

REASONABLENESS

Art. 2.22, subd. A of the Texas Business Corporation Act provides that a corporation may impose restrictions on disposition of its stock if the restrictions "do not unreasonably restrain or prohibit transferability." The court of civil appeals has held that the restrictions on the transferability of this stock are unreasonable for two reasons: because of the required approval of the New York Stock Exchange and because of successive options to purchase given the corporation and the other holders of the same class of stock.

Ling & Company in its brief states that it was a brokerage house member of the New York Stock Exchange at an earlier time and that Rule 315 of the Exchange required approval of any sale or pledge of the stock. Under these circumstances we must disagree with the court of civil appeals holding that this provision of article 4D of the articles of incorporation is "arbitrary, capricious, and unreasonable." Nothing appears in the summary judgment proof on this matter, and the mere provision in the article is no cause for vitiating the restrictions as a matter of law.

It was also held by the intermediate court that it is unreasonable to require a shareholder to notify all other record holders of Class A Common Stock of his intent to sell and to give the other holders a ten day option to buy. The record does not reveal the number of holders of this class of stock; we only know that there are more than twenty. We find nothing unusual or oppressive in these first option provisions. Conceivably the number of stockholders might be so great as to make the burden too heavy upon the stockholder who wishes to sell and, at the same time, dispel any justification for contending that there exists a reasonable corporate purpose in restricting the ownership. But there is no showing of that nature in this summary judgment record.

STATUTORY LIMIT ON OPTIONEES

Art. 2.22, subd. B of the Texas Business Corporation Act provides that, in addition to other reasonable restrictions, any of the following restrictions may be imposed upon the transfer of corporate shares:

1. Restrictions reasonably defining pre-emptive or prior rights of the corporation or its shareholders of record, to purchase any of its shares offered for transfer.
2. Restrictions reasonably defining rights and obligations of the holders of shares of any class, in connection with buy-and-sell agreements binding on all holders of shares of that class, so long as there are no more than twenty (20) holders of record of such class.
3. Restrictions reasonably defining rights of the corporation or of any other person or persons, granted as an option or options or refusal or refusals on any shares.

The court of civil appeals regarded subsection (2) as being applicable to the stock restriction in this case. Since it was stipulated that there were more than twenty holders of record of Class A stock it has been held that the restriction fails for the reason. We disagree. Subsection (2) is not applicable to the Ling & Company restriction. It seems that a "buy and sell agreement" usually refers to a contract between shareholders rather than a restriction imposed by the corporation. In any event, there is no obligation to purchase this stock placed upon anyone, and these restrictions can only be considered as options and not "buy and sell agreements."

The summary judgment proof does not justify the holding that restrictions on the transfer of this stock were ineffective as to Trinity Savings and Loan Association. The judgment below is reversed and the cause is remanded to the trial court.

Problem Cases

1. Parent, Flanders, and Priebusch contracted to purchase all of the assets of a lumberyard for $45,000. They organized a corporation to make the purchase and to operate the business and each agreed to buy 100 shares of $100 per value stock. However, each paid only $2,000 in cash. They borrowed $4,000 from a bank as individual joint debtors to make the $10,000 down payment on the lumberyard. To finance the balance of the purchase price they borrowed an additional $17,000, giving a mortgage on all corporate assets, and gave a second mortgage to the sellers of the lumberyard to secure the remaining $18,000. In December 1958, Killeen was induced to buy 100 shares of stock (one-fourth ownership) for $10,000 upon representations by Parent and Flanders that the value of the business was $65,000 and that they had each paid $10,000 for their stock. The business was adjudged bankrupt in January 1962, and Killeen then learned the purchase price of the business and the actual investment of Parent and Flanders. Can Killeen recover his damages from Parent and Flanders as promoters of the corporation?

2. Cheek learned that Humble would be willing to sell some prime undeveloped land for $275,000. Three other businessmen learned, through a friend of Cheek, of the general availability of the land and approached Cheek about participating in a development venture. Cheek informed them that he had obtained an option on the property for $400,000. After several meetings, visits to the property and examination of aerial maps, the four decided that a corporation should be formed to purchase and develop the property, with each individual having a 25 percent interest. A price of $400,000 for the property was agreed upon after a review of sales of comparable properties. The corporation was formed by Tomlinson. Cheek had not been listed as an incorporator or even as a shareholder in the articles of incorporation but was elected a director two months later. Prior to this time, Cheek had assigned to the corporation his rights in what purported to be an option to purchase the property for $400,000, and the transaction was completed by Humble selling the property to Cheek for $275,000 and Cheek on the same day selling it to the new corporation for $400,000.

   The other three later learned of Cheek's $125,000 secret profit and sued to recover it for the corporation. They alleged that Cheek was a promoter of the new corporation and, as such, owed a fiduciary duty not to make a secret profit at the corporation's expense. Can the corporation recover?

3. Thornton, Jamieson, and Ash formed a joint venture for the purpose of acquiring the business of Litton. After the business was acquired it was reorganized as a corporation, Litton Industries, Inc., with Thornton as president and Jamieson, Ash, and Steele holding the other key-executive posts. Under the reorganization, 100,000 shares of founders' stock were issued to Thornton who distributed 20,000 shares each to Jamieson and Ash and kept 60,000 shares for himself. Prior to the reorganization Thornton had promised Steele the opportunity to purchase the same number of founders' shares as Jamieson and Ash. Thornton never carried out the promise and Steele did not receive any of the founders' stock. Steele brought an action for breach of contract against Litton Industries, Inc., as well as

against Thornton individually. He argued that Thornton's action as a promoter for the reorganization was binding upon the resulting corporation. Should Litton be held liable on Thornton's contract?

4. In August 1969, K&E Company entered an agreement to sell certain property in Hoboken, New Jersey, to K&J Holding Corporation for $750,000 and accepted a check for $10,000. Cohen signed as president of Holding, the buyer—a corporation not yet in existence. The agreement provided for closing the transaction on November 3, 1969. On October 31, incorporation of Holding was completed. On November 3, however, the president of the selling corporation, K&E, wrote to the attorney for Holding, enclosing a check for the amount of the earnest money. He stated that it had been discovered that incorporation papers for Holding had not been filed and that the real estate contract was therefore a nullity.

    Holding sued for specific performance. K&E defended on grounds that since Holding was not in existence at the time of the contract, K&E could not enforce the contract against it and, therefore, it was not bound due to lack of mutuality. Is this a good defense?

5. Dixie Power Association's charter provided that members could vote at the appropriate membership meetings in person or by proxy. A bylaw also provided for voting by proxy. Dixie's board of directors repealed the bylaw and prohibited proxy voting, relying on their power to adopt and amend bylaws for the management and regulation of corporate affairs. The members brought suit against the directors, alleging that the board was without power to impair the proxy right. Did the board exceed its powers?

6. Dorado Corporation constructed and operated golf courses. It agreed to construct and operate Skywest, Inc.'s, public golf course in exchange for 70 percent of Skywest's common stock. Dorado, in serious financial difficulty, negotiated to sell the Skywest shares. One of Skywest's bylaws required a shareholder who desired to sell or transfer to give other Skywest shareholders an opportunity to purchase such shares within 25 days. The bylaw also voided any transfer which did not comply with this right of first refusal. Dorado attempted to obtain waivers from the other shareholders. A number conditioned their waiver on a provision that Dorado would irrevocably dedicate a specified portion of the proceeds from the sale to correcting some serious deficiencies in Dorado's performance of the original Skywest agreement. Dorado did not comply with the waiver conditions, and the shareholders sued to void the transfer. Dorado argued that the bylaw was an unreasonable restraint on the transfer of common stock. Should the bylaw be held invalid?

7. Molina signed a subscription form to buy 40 shares of nonvoting stock in a proposed corporation at $50 per share. He paid the $2,000 to Largosa, the promoter. The corporation later failed. Molina sued Largosa to recover his investment on the grounds that he had not become a shareholder as agreed since shareholders' meetings were never held, that his certificate of 40 shares was never delivered, and that he had subscribed to buy nonvoting shares when the articles of incorporation provided only for one class of stock with "full and equal voting rights." Largosa argued that, as to the first two grounds, Molina's remedy was to compel the meetings and delivery, and as to the last, Molina should not be heard to complain that he received more than he bargained for. Should Molina recover his investment?

8. Eubanks decided to incorporate his trucking business. The new corporation was organized with a stated capital of $75,000, and 100 shares of capital stock with a par value of $750 each were issued—98 to Eubanks and 2 to other members of his family. As consideration for the $75,000, Eubanks transferred title to his trucks and trailers to the corporation and also put in approximately $5,000 in cash. However, it appears that the total capital never

exceeded $50,000. The corporation later failed and filed bankruptcy. Debts against the corporation totalled $7,100 after the liquidation of all corporate assets. The creditors claimed that Eubanks should be held personally liable for this amount on the grounds that he failed to pay into the corporation the capital specified in the corporate charter as required by state law. Should their claim be upheld?

9. Dempsey, a brokerage firm, sold 320,000 shares of Otis Corporation common stock for Tilton. The certificates to these shares had been wrongfully removed from Otis' stock book by the secretary of Otis, who applied facsimile signatures, and negotiated them without authority. They came into Tilton's possession, who transferred them to Dempsey. Otis refused to transfer the shares relying on a Colorado statute which provided that facsimile signatures were acceptable if countersigned by a transfer agent. The certificates had not been countersigned. Dempsey argued that the certificates were negotiable instruments under the U.C.C. and that they were genuine in that they were free from forgery or counterfeiting. Should Otis be required to register the transfer of the shares?

10. First Methodist employed Institutional Finance Company to sell $90,000 in bonds for the construction of a new church, and the church treasurer put her signature on a blank sheet of paper in the presence of the pastor and a trustee of the church and gave it to an officer of Institutional Finance to use as a facsimile signature upon the bonds. The printed bonds contained the facsimile signatures of the church treasurer and an officer of Institutional Finance but had no provision for an authenticating manual signature. Members of the church purchased $45,000 of the bonds but Institutional Finance had difficulty finding buyers for the remainder.

    Hayes, the president of Institutional Finance, pledged $28,800 of the bonds to First Bank as collateral for a personal loan. He had been a previous borrower and the bank had no knowledge of his relationship to Institutional Finance or basis for suspicion that he did not own the bonds. Duplicates of these bonds and others were later ordered printed by Hayes, and they were sold to Christian Foundation Life. Hayes's dishonesty became known when duplicate interest coupons were presented to the bank for payment, and the bank refused to honor them until their validity had been established. Are the bonds held by First Bank binding obligations of the church?

11. Martin Company was a closely held general contracting corporation. Martin owned 416 shares while Van Kampen and Manglos each held 2 shares. The three parties entered into a stockholders agreement which provided in part that in the event of the death of any of the three, the company would buy and the estate of the deceased party would be compelled to sell all of his company stock at book value. Martin died; however, the board of directors repudiated the sales agreement and refused to buy the stock. Van Kampen sued. The board defended its action on the grounds that repurchase of all of Martin's stock would have seriously reduced the company's working capital and jeopardized its operations and this would have been contrary to a state law which provided that no corporation shall use its funds or property for the purchase of its own shares when such use would cause impairment of the corporate capital. Should the defense be sustained?

chapter 25

Operating the Corporate Business

Corporate Powers

Sources of Powers. A corporation obtains its powers from the state, and it cannot have powers that exceed those conferred by the constitution and statutes of the state of its incorporation. Assuming that the statute under which the corporation is chartered is constitutional, then its powers may be determined by consulting that statute and the articles of incorporation. Just as the statute is limited by constitutional provisions, the articles cannot be inconsistent with the statute.

It is usually the function of the secretary of state's office (or that of some other official in a few states) to make at least a perfunctory check of the articles to determine if they are consistent with the statute under which incorporation is sought. In most states, certain businesses such as railroads, insurance companies, and banks must be incorporated under special statutes which include restrictions not applicable to other corporations and frequently provide special governmental supervision because of special public interest in their operation. The articles of incorporation may also limit the powers of the corporation, most frequently by the manner in which its purposes or scope of business are described.

A few states limit or prohibit the acquisition of agricultural land by corporations. Corporations have, in the recent past, been denied altogether the privilege of engaging in some of the professions such as, for instance, that of law, medicine, or dentistry. However, a number of states have recently enacted statutes which permit physicians and other professionals to incorporate in order to take advantage of federal tax laws encouraging establishment of retirement plans by corporations. Some of these statutes expressly provide that individual liability is not limited.

The powers outlined by Blackstone which were referred to in Chapter 23 have long been considered inherent in the corporate form of organization. The trend in this century has been to increase the powers of business corporation by court decision as well as statute. Section 4 of the Model Act sets out the general powers of corporations to be chartered under it. A number of these and the powers added in Sections 5 and 6 are inserted specifically because earlier decisions had denied or raised a doubt about such a power. Examples of provisions to remove doubt include: to make gifts for charitable and educational purposes (4m),[1] to enter a partnership (4p), to indemnify the corporation's officers and directors who are defendants in suits growing out of their performance of corporate duties (5), and to purchase and dispose of its own shares (6). Also the 1969 revision (4n) states that the corporation may "transact any lawful business which the board of directors shall find will be in aid of governmental policy." This was inserted to clarify an earlier provision authorizing the corporation to aid the United States government in time of war. In an era of undeclared wars this provision was too narrow. The revised clause is intended to cover other governmental programs such as the elimination of poverty. Although several states had adopted the "war power" provision, none has yet adopted the broader grant of power.

Limitations in Articles of Incorporation. Under both the Model Act (54) and the Delaware statute it is unnecessary to enumerate in the articles the powers set out in the incorporation statute. It is, however, required to state the corporate purposes. The purposes can be phrased in the broadest and most general terms or "for any lawful purpose." However, the incorporators may desire to use the statement of purpose as a self-imposed limitation. The statement becomes then a promise on the part of the corporation to its shareholders that it will confine the business risks taken by the corporation to those normally incident to the operation of a business such as that defined in the purpose section of the articles of incorporation.

The *Ultra Vires* Doctrine. The original conception of the corporation was that it was an artificial person created by and given limited powers by the state. It was deduced from this view that any act of the corporation which is beyond the authority given it by the state was void as being *ultra vires.* Therefore, any act not permitted by the statute under which it is incorporated or by its articles of incorporation which are consistent with that statute is void for want of capacity. The lack of capacity or power in the corporation could be urged either by the corporation or the other party as a defense to a suit on a contract alleged to be *ultra vires.* Oftentimes it was merely a convenient justification for reneging on an agreement no longer considered desirable.

The Model Business Corporation Act (7) and the Delaware statute have

---

[1] The numbers in the parentheses refer to the sections of the Model Business Corporation Act, which appears in the Appendix.

eliminated such collateral attacks on the capacity of the corporation. The trend in business corporation statutes toward granting corporations very broad powers and for draftsmen of articles of incorporation to use very broad statements of purpose have also diminished the vitality of the *ultra vires* doctrine in the states which have not abolished it.

Under Section 7 direct attacks upon *ultra vires* actions are still permitted. A shareholder may seek an injunction to restrain the corporation from carrying out a proposed action which is beyond its powers, thus seeking to prevent a breach of his or her membership contract with the corporation. The corporation itself, or through a legal representative such as a receiver or shareholder in a representative suit, may bring an action against its officers or directors for damages resulting from *ultra vires* actions taken by them. Also under Section 7, the state's attorney general may enjoin the corporation from transacting unauthorized business, or bring an action to dissolve the corporation as set out in greater detail in Section 94.

Liability under the Doctrine.   One reason for the strong trend toward abolishing the doctrine is that there had been much confusion and uncertainty in the holdings of the courts in regard to *ultra vires* contracts. Courts have generally refused to enforce contracts which are wholly executory but have been unwilling to strike down contracts which are fully executed by both parties even when viewed as being beyond the corporate capacity. The partially executed contracts have been the source of confusion and disagreement. The older rule was that a partially executed contract would not be enforced although a quasi-contractual remedy might be appropriate. A majority of courts have held that such a contract is enforceable if one of the parties has received a benefit.

Summary

The powers of a corporation are limited to those conferred by the constitution and statutes of the state of its incorporation, although certain traditional powers are considered inherent in the corporate form of organization. The trend of modern corporation statutes, including the Model Act, is to broaden the powers of general business corporations.

The articles of incorporation are required to set forth the purpose(s) of the corporation, which may be as broad as permitted by the statute. However, a more restricted statement of purpose acts as a self-imposed limitation for the benefit of the shareholders. Some statutes, including the Model Act, do not require a specific statement of corporate powers in the articles, and the corporation will then have all those powers granted by the statute under which it is formed.

Under the *ultra vires* doctrine any act of a corporation which is beyond the powers given to it by the state or its articles of incorporation is void, and either the corporation or the other party to a contract may allege as a defense that the making of the contract is beyond the powers of the corporation. The Model Act and some other modern statutes have eliminated this defense, but they permit shareholders or the state attorney general to enjoin an *ultra vires* act and the corporation may bring an action against its officers or directors for damages resulting from actions taken beyond the corporation's power.

A major reason for the trend toward abolishing the *ultra vires* doctrine is the confusion in the law regarding the enforceability of *ultra vires* contracts. Courts have generally refused to enforce wholly executory contracts and have not interfered with fully executed contracts. However, partially executed contracts have been a source of confusion and disagreement.

Rio Refrigeration Co. v. Thermal Supply of Harlingen, Inc.

368 S.W.2d 128 (Tex. Civ. App. 1963)

This was an action by Thermal Supply of Harlingen, Inc. (plaintiff), against Rio Refrigeration Company (defendant) to recover a judgment for an account receivable. Judgment for Thermal Supply of Harlingen, Inc., and Rio Refrigeration Company appealed. Judgment affirmed.

Rio Refrigeration Company (Rio) and Coastal Refrigeration Service, a partnership, were competitors in the refrigeration and air-conditioning business. Rio purchased the business, parts, and assets of Coastal Refrigeration Service and as part of the transaction contracted to pay the account owed by Coastal Refrigeration Service to Thermal Supply of Harlingen, Inc. (Thermal Supply), in the amount of $2,161.35. Rio then refused to pay Thermal Supply and it brought suit. Rio set up as a defense that the contract was a guaranty of the debt of a third person and was *ultra vires* and did not bind it.

BARROW, JUSTICE.   Rio Refrigeration was incorporated in 1948, for the purpose of buying and selling goods, wares and merchandise of any description by wholesale and retail. It has never adopted the Texas Business Corporation Act enacted in 1955, which by Art. 2.04, *Vernon's Ann. Civ. St.* abolished the defense of *ultra vires*. It is our opinion however, that this defense is here without merit. It is not ordinarily necessary for the conduct of a corporation's business that it lend its credit to another business, and in the absence of an express charter power, a corporation has no right to stand as surety or guarantor for the debt of another. Here the contract was of direct and material benefit to Rio, in that it eliminated a competitor and purchased parts, supplies, and equipment used in Rio's business. The law is well settled that in all grants of corporate powers there exist not only the powers expressly granted, but also such implied powers as are necessary or reasonably appropriate to the exercise of those powers expressly granted. It is our view that the powers granted Rio would include the power to assume payment of Coastal's account with Thermal Supply as partial consideration for the assets purchased from Coastal.

In any event, Rio is estopped to assert the defense of *ultra vires* in that it had operated under and attained the benefits of the contract.

Management of the Corporation

Authority. The shareholders are the owners of the corporation and have the ultimate power to determine the course of the business through their power to elect directors and to amend the articles. However, they do no have, by virtue of ownership, the right and duty of management. The law g ves these to the directors, who are elected by the shareholders. Shareholders' approval is required for certain extraordinary corporate matters as discussed in Chapter 26 such as changes in the articles of incorporation, sale of assets not in the regular course of business, merger, and dissolution. Other major questions and policies are determined by the directors, who also elect the officers and delegate to them the authority to manage the everyday operations of the business.

This right and duty of the directors to manage the corporation exists under the corporation statutes of all states even when one man owns all of the stock of the corporation and holds the office of president and chief executive or general manager (the latter is an older term which today is used more frequently by small than large corporations). As has been frequently pointed out by students and critics of corporations, even in large, publicly held corporations the chief executive may choose the board members and/or make all policy decisions for the corporation with the board of directors acting merely as a rubber stamp. Even what may be the directors' most important duty, to choose the chief executive's successor, may effectively have been usurped by the training opportunities given to possible candidates within the organization. However, in the long run, acceptance of a rubber stamp role by the board is likely to lead to corporate stagnation and decay, and it may lead to the personal liability of board members for default in carrying out their duties.

Directors

Duties and Powers of Directors. Since directors are given by statute the broad, general duty of "management of the corporation," they have the power to make all decisions for the corporation except those reserved by statute to the shareholders. Under the Model Act as well as other statutes, certain corporate actions can be taken only by authorization of the board. These include: authorizing a change in the registered office or registered agent of the corporation (13); establishing the time of payment of stock subscriptions (17); establishing the price for sale by the corporation of shares of stock, except when the power to establish the price of no-par stock is reserved in the articles to the shareholders (18); establishing the value of noncash consideration received for shares (19); increasing stated capital by transfer of surplus (21); adopting initial bylaws and, unless this power is reserved to the shareholders in the articles, amendment or repeal of bylaws (27); establishing record dates for dividend nd shareholder meeting purposes (30); filling a vacancy on the board of directors (38); declaring dividends (45); electing officers and assigning duties to them not inconsistent with the bylaws (50); removing officers (51); and selling, leasing, or mortgaging assets of the corporation in the normal course of its business (78).

Directors are required under the Model Act to initiate and propose to the shareholders certain major changes affecting the corporation which can be accomplished only with approval of the shareholders. These include: amendments to or restatements of the articles of incorporation (59 and 62); reduction in stated capital (69); merger or consolidation (71 and 72); a sale, lease, or mortgage of substantially all assets of the corporation other than in the normal course of business (79); and a voluntary dissolution of the corporation (84).

Practices of Boards of Directors. Unless the directors are full-time officers of the corporation, they cannot possibly make all management decisions nor if they were full time would it be feasible to make them all in group meeting. Therefore, actions other than the ones which must be taken by the directors, as listed above, are often delegated to the officers and many of those are redelegated to employees of the corporation.

A number of studies have been made as to what boards of the larger corporations do. The Conference Board has made periodic surveys. Although they have found wide variations in the functions of directors, in their 1967 study they found seven to have general acceptance. They were: (1) to establish the basic objectives and broad policies of the corporation; (2) to elect the corporate officers, advise them, approve their actions, and audit their performance; (3) to safeguard, and approve changes in, the corporate assets; (4) to approve important financial decisions and actions and to see that proper reports are made to shareholders; (5) to delegate special powers to officers and employees to sign contracts, open bank accounts, sign checks, borrow money, and perform other such activities; (6) to maintain, revise, and enforce the corporate charter and bylaws; and (7) to assure maintenance of a sound board through selection of the management slate at regular elections and filling interim vacancies.[2] A 1972 survey[3] was not quite comparable but suggests more clearly that directors' meetings tend to deal mostly with important financial transactions of the firm, including the approval of budgets, large capital expenditures, and pension and profit-sharing plans as well as the salaries of corporate officers.

Some boards undertake to approve broad corporate policies in certain areas such as defining the business of the corporation in terms of products and markets and establishing guidelines for product pricing, labor relations, and

---

[2] Conference Board, *Corporate Directorship Practices,* Studies in Business Policy #125 (New York, 1967), pp. 93–94.

[3] James K. Brown, "The Board of Directors and Its Work Routine," *Conference Board Record* 9 (March 1972):36.

so forth. However, one recent study declared that the generally accepted idea that the board selects top executives, determines policy, measures results, and asks discerning questions which uncover weaknesses or stimulate desirable executive action is a myth. The author concluded that what boards do is to advise management (rather than making business decisions), to provide some sort of discipline for management through the necessity of making reports to the board, and to act in emergencies to replace the chief executive when he or she dies or is incapacitated unexpectedly or when the chief executive's performance or the corporation's fortunes are perceived as unusually bad.[4]

Powers and Rights of Director as Individual. An individual director has no management function or power except as he or she may be appointed an agent of the corporation. A director does, however, have the right to inspect corporate books and records, since information concerning the corporation and its affairs is essential for carrying out his or her duties. Although often said to be an absolute right, in contrast to the qualified right of a shareholder, the director's right of inspection may be denied in cases where the director clearly has an interest adverse to the corporation.

Number and Qualifications of Directors. Some states require a minimum of three directors. This requirement in the Model Act was dropped in the 1969 revision and now, along with Delaware and a number of other states, it only requires one director (36). This recognizes the reality that in close corporations it is not unusual for one person to own all or substantially all of the stock and that additional board members are superfluous. Most statutes, including the Model Act, provide that the number of directors may be fixed by either the articles or the bylaws. A few states require directors to be shareholders, and some require that a certain percentage be citizens of the state of incorporation and/or the United States. The Model Act makes no such requirement but permits qualifications to be specified in the articles of incorporation (35).

Most publicly held corporations and not a few close corporations have both "inside" and "outside" directors. The term "inside" director is applied to one who is an officer of the corporation or an affiliated corporation and devotes substantially his or her full time to it. The term is also often applied to controlling shareholders who are not officers. There has been a trend toward having more "outside" members on corporate boards.[5] Even the preeminent example

---

[4] Miles L. Mace, "The President and the Board of Directors," *Harv. Bus. Rev.* 50 (March–April 1972), p. 37.

[5] Conference Board surveys since 1938 have shown a slow but steady increase in firms with a majority of outside directors. In the 1967 report, outside directors predominated on the boards of 63 percent of the manufacturing companies in the survey. The Conference Board, *Corporate Directorship Practices,* pp. 6–7. The 1972 report is not comparable but states, "For all but the smallest companies and in all but 5 of 17 industry groups, outside directors outnumber insiders on the boards we have surveyed." Brown, "The Board of Directors," p. 36.

of the "inside" board, Standard Oil Company of New Jersey (now Exxon), added outside directors in 1966. However, many leading corporations have few or no "outside" directors.

Election of Directors.   Directors are elected by the shareholders at their annual meeting and normally hold office until the succeeding annual meeting or until a successor has been elected and qualified. However, most statutes, including the Model Act, permit a corporation to provide in its articles for staggered terms for directors. Under the Model Act a corporation having a board of nine or more members may establish either two or three approximately equal classes of directors with only one class of directors coming up for election at each annual meeting.

Vacancies occurring on the board of directors can be filled only by the shareholders, absent a provision in the statute, articles or bylaws. Most statutes permit the directors to fill vacancies at least until the next shareholders' meeting. The Model Act (38) provides that a majority vote of the remaining directors, even though less than a quorum, is sufficient to elect persons to serve out unexpired terms. It also explicitly deals with the troublesome question whether if directors have the power to increase the size of board, they may, without a vote by the shareholders, also fill the "vacancy" created. It provides that such "vacancy" may be filled by the directors only until the next election of directors by the shareholders.

Removal of Directors.   Unless there is authorization for such shareholder action in the statute or in articles or bylaws adopted prior to his election, a director may not be removed without cause, that is without misconduct or action contrary to the interests of the corporation. Shareholders, but not directors, have inherent power to remove directors for cause and may do so even if the articles or bylaws give this power to the directors and despite a shareholder agreement. Bylaw provisions establishing the proportion of vote required are upheld, however. A shareholder agreement to elect and maintain in office certain persons as directors would prevent removal without cause by such shareholders. Before removal for cause, the director must be given adequate notice and an opportunity for a hearing.

The Model Act (39) permits shareholders at a meeting expressly called for the purpose to remove directors with or without cause by a majority of the shares entitled to vote.

The rationale of this section is that as owners the shareholders should have the power to judge the fitness of directors at any time. If less than the entire board is to be removed and cumulative voting[6] is in effect, then a removal action fails if the votes cast against the removal of a director would have been sufficient

---

[6] For discussion of cumulative voting, see Chapter 26.

to have elected him or her initially. The Delaware statute has no provision on removal of directors.

Directors' Meetings.   Traditionally, directors can act only when properly convened as a board and cannot vote by proxy or informally, as by a telephone poll. This rule is based upon belief in the value of consultation and collective judgment. Obviously, agreement with a proposal by the chairman is more likely if he talks to each director individually and there is no opportunity to consider the doubts or opposition expressed by a potential dissenter. However, where the statute is silent some courts have upheld action in casual meetings not properly called but attended by all directors and also action taken which has been consented to by all directors without a meeting.

Today the corporation laws of a majority of states, including Delaware, and the Model Act (44) specifically permit action by the directors without a meeting if all directors consent in writing. Although subject to possible abuse, such authorization is useful for routine matters or when formal action is required by a third party and the underlying policy decision has been previously made after full discussion. Close corporations are likely to take advantage of such a method of action more often than large public corporations holding monthly meetings of the board.

Board meetings need not be held within the state of incorporation even under older statutes.

Reasonable notice, including the purpose, is required of special but not of regular meetings. Actual attendance at a meeting by all directors, unless for the limited purpose of raising an objection to the lack of notice, is generally held to cure defects in the notice. Also, directors may waive notice, and it is normal practice for corporate secretaries to obtain signed waivers when notice is defective. To be effective under common law, a waiver of notice must be signed by all directors either before or during the meeting. However, the Model Act (144) makes waivers of notice signed after the meeting equally effective.

Directors each have one vote regardless of their stock holdings. In order for the directors to act, a quorum must be present. The Model Act (40) provides that a quorum shall be a majority of the number of directors fixed by the bylaws. If none is so fixed, then a majority of the number stated in the articles constitutes a quorum. If there is a quorum, the act of the majority of directors present is the act of the board. However, the Model Act permits the corporation to require a greater number for a quorum by a provision in the articles or bylaws.

Committees of the Board.   The bylaws of most large corporations establish an executive committee of the board which is given full authority to act for the board when the entire board is not in session, although this is frequently limited to matters not already acted upon by the board. The executive committee is usually composed of inside directors or board members who can easily be summoned to a meeting on short notice. Thus, the executive committee is available to give a timely formal authorization such as approval of a routine sale of property or a bank transaction. It may also serve as a screening committee for preliminary consideration of complicated or weighty matters prior to presentation to the full board. Other common board committees are salary and bonus, stock option, audit and finance committees.

The Model Act (42) provides that the directors may by resolution establish an executive committee and other committees which may exercise all the authority of the board within the limits established in the resolution or in the articles or bylaws, except that committees shall not have authority to act in connection with extraordinary corporate matters such as amendment of articles, merger, disposition of substantially all of the assets not in the normal course of business or a voluntary dissolution.

Compensation of Directors.   The traditional view was that directors are presumed to perform their ordinary duties as director without compensation and that they have no power to fix their own salaries. The Model Act (35) and other modern statutes permit the directors to fix their compensation unless the articles forbid this. In the Conference Board study only 2 to 3 percent of the companies reported that outside directors served without compensation in 1967.[7]

Summary

Since corporation statutes generally provide that directors have the duty of "management of the corporation" they have the power to make all decisions for the corporation not reserved to the shareholders. The statutes specifically require directors to authorize certain actions. However, generally most other management decisions are delegated to the officers or employees. An individual director as such has no management function or power, although he or she may be appointed an agent of the corporation.

Although a director is said to have an absolute right of inspection of corporate books and records, inspection may be denied where the director clearly has an interest adverse to the corporation.

Some states require a minimum of three directors but the Model Act and Delaware require only one. A few states have other requirements, for example, that they be shareholders in the corporation or citizens of the state or the United States.

Directors are normally elected by the shareholders at their annual meeting and hold office until the next annual meeting. Most statutes and the Model Act

---

[7] Conference Board, *Corporate Directorship Practices* (1967), p. 29.

permit staggered terms. Vacancies are filled by shareholders unless, as is usually the case, the statute, articles, or bylaws give this power to the directors to fill the vacancy until the next shareholders' meeting.

Shareholders have inherent power to remove a director for cause but not without cause unless this power is specifically given in the statute, articles, or bylaws prior to his election.

Generally, directors take action only in a properly convened meeting, but many statutes today specifically permit action without a meeting if all directors consent in writing. Reasonable notice is required for a special meeting but not for a regular meeting of the directors. A majority of the board is usually required to constitute a quorum but many statutes permit the articles or bylaws to establish a higher number for a quorum.

Although traditionally directors serve without compensation, modern statutes permit directors to fix their own compensation unless the articles forbid this, and most outside directors are today paid for their service as a director.

Grossman v. Liberty Leasing Co., Inc.

295 A.2d 749 (Del. Ch. 1972)

Howard Grossman and Maurice Gross and other shareholders (plaintiffs) sought a declaration that the election of certain persons to the board of directors of Liberty Leasing Co., Inc., (defendant) was void and for an injunction to prohibit the management from soliciting proxies. Election held valid and injunction denied.

Liberty is a diversified corporation incorporated in Delaware but based in Chicago. Grossman and Gross and members of their families owned approximately 20 percent of the common stock of Liberty, a publicly held company. They had been directors for about ten years and Grossman had been president and treasurer and Gross executive vice president and secretary. Liberty's bylaws called for five directors, but between April 14, 1970, and December 29, 1971, there were only four. At the annual shareholder meetings in 1970 and 1971 management had recommended that only four directors be elected and that was done. In the fall of 1971 there was discussion of adding a fifth director but the four directors could not agree on a nominee. They finally agreed on December 29, 1971, to amend the bylaws to increase the number of directors to seven and Haas, Malkin, and Roland were elected by the board to fill the vacancy and the new positions. The next day Grossman and Gross wanted to rescind the action but Sachnoff, one of the continuing directors and an attorney, told them this could not be done.

At a board meeting attended by both the old and the newly elected directors on February 21, 1972, all the directors except Grossman and Gross voted to liquidate immediately the equipment leasing division of the company. There was also consideration given to removing Grossman and Gross as executives, but this was deferred. On March 3 the three new directors and Sachnoff voted to oust Grossman and Gross. Haas was then elected chairman of the board, Malkin was made president, and Roland was chosen as executive vice president. Both factions then began soliciting proxies for the annual meeting of shareholders scheduled for May 23.

DUFFY, CHANCELLOR: At the December 29 meeting two new directorships were created. Grossman and Gross concede that such action was within the power of the board under Liberty's bylaws and 8 Del. C. § 223 which provides in part:

Unless otherwise provided in the certificate of incorporation or bylaws, vacancies and newly created directorships resulting from any increase in the authorized number of directors may be filled by a majority of the directors then in office, although less than a quorum, or by a sole remaining director. . . .

But, they argue, a "vacancy" within the contemplation of § 223 requires a previous incumbency. They say at the time of the December 29 meeting there was not such a vacancy and, therefore, the board, as a matter of law, did not have the power to fill the office.

Grossman and Gross rely upon the Supreme Court decision in *Automatic Steel Products, Inc. v. Johnston.* . . .

* * * * *

In Johnston the directors created new directorships and then filled them. The Court viewed the statute as a limitation on the power of directors and held that they could not do what they did. At that time, when "vacancies" were defined in terms of prior incumbency, directors did not have the power to elect or appoint directors; all such power was reserved to stockholders with only one exception: directors in office could choose a director when a vacancy occurred in their number.

. . . However, what was once regarded as the prerogative solely of stockholders is now permissible action under § 223.

* * * * *

Under § 223 directors in office now may fill vacancies in their membership if stockholders do not do so and if other requirements of the statute are met; a prior incumbency is not a condition precedent to such action. In so stating I do not consider any question of fraud upon the stockholders, or an estoppel upon directors to fill a vacancy in their membership, or circumstances amounting to a change by stockholders in the authorized number of directors.

I conclude that Liberty's directors had the power to fill the fifth directorship, and it therefore follows that Malkin, Haas, and Roland were validly elected to the Board.

Grossman and Gross argue also that Liberty's bylaws provide for the filling of vacancies and newly created directorships "at a special meeting called for that purpose" and, they say, the December 29 meeting was not called for either of those purposes. They argue that the actions taken were therefore invalid.

Such bylaw provisions do, of course, serve a useful purpose and they are enforceable. But both the Delaware Corporation Law and the bylaws of Liberty permit waiver of these requirements. . . . And the bylaws provide that any director may waive notice of any meeting, and that attendance of a director at any meeting constitutes a "waiver of notice of such meeting" except when he attends for the express purpose of objecting to the transaction of business because the meeting is not lawfully convened. Since the statute is applicable to "any meeting," it follows that it is applicable to a special meeting.

It is undisputed that Grossman and Gross, together with the other directors, attended the December 29 meeting, voted for the action taken and signed the minutes. Under these circumstances I conclude that they waived any defect with respect to notice of the meeting.

Officers and Employees

Officers of the Corporation. The Model Act (50) provides that the officers of a corporation shall be the president, one or more vice presidents, a secretary, and a treasurer. Some statutes require fewer officers and most allow more if desired. It is increasingly common for a corporation to establish the office of chairman of the board. Under the Model Act any two or more offices may be held by the same person except the offices of president and secretary.

The officers are agents of the corporation, and as such, they will have the express authority which is conferred upon them in the bylaws or by the board of directors. In addition, they will have implied authority to do those things reasonably necessary to accomplish the functions delegated to them. Like any agent they may be held accountable by the corporation for exceeding such actual authority. However, like any agent they also may bind the corporation on the basis of apparent authority, when acting beyond their actual authority.

In addition, courts have held that certain officers may have authority by virtue of their office. The cases are difficult to reconcile, but such *ex officio* powers are much more restricted than laymen are likely to expect. Even the president traditionally had no power to bind the corporation by virtue of his or her office, but merely served as presiding officer in shareholder and director meetings. However, if an executive acts as general manager or chief executive— that is, he or she is given general supervision and control of the business—the executive is vested with broad implied authority to make such contracts and do such other acts as are appropriate in the ordinary business of the corporation.

A vice president has no authority by virtue of that office. However, an executive who is vice president of sales or some other department of the business will have the authority of a manager of the specified department to transact the normal business of the corporation which falls within the functions of that department.

The secretary, or clerk as he or she is called in some states, usually keeps the minutes of director and shareholder meetings and other corporate records and has custody of the corporate seal. The secretary has no authority to bind the corporation by virtue of that office but there is a presumption that a document to which he or she affixes the seal has been duly authorized.

The treasurer has custody of the funds of the corporation and is the proper officer to receive payments to the corporation and to disburse corporate funds for authorized purposes. A treasurer binds the corporation by his or her receipts, checks, and endorsements but does not by virtue of the office alone have authority to borrow money or issue negotiable instruments.

Like any principal, the corporation may ratify the unauthorized acts of its officers. This may be accomplished through a resolution of the board of directors or of the shareholders.

Statutory Liabilities of Officers. The Model Act (136) imposes criminal liability on corporate officers (and directors as well) who sign a report or application filed with the secretary of state which is known by the officer to be false or who refuses to answer truthfully and fully questions asked by the secretary in accordance with his or her duties under the act. Provisions are found in several state statutes which impose either civil or criminal liability upon officers for failure to perform other statutory duties, such as filing proper annual reports for the corporation or denying access to shareholders to the corporate books and records.

Employees of the Corporation. Employees of the corporation who are not officers may also be delegated authority to act as agents for the corporation and the usual rules of agency will apply both to their relationship to the corporation and to third parties. Both officers and other agents can best protect themselves from personal liability by having their authority for conducting out-of-the-ordinary transactions for the corporation stated in writing, either in a bylaw or a specific resolution of the board of directors, and then making it clear in signing as agent for the corporation that they do not intend to join individually. The proper form is, of course:

THE WIDGET CORPORATION
By JOHN DOE, Director of Purchases.

Summary

The Model Act specifies that the officers of a corporation shall be the president, one or more vice presidents, a secretary, and a treasurer and that two or more offices may be held by one person, except the offices of president and secretary. Officers are agents of the corporation and have express, implied, and apparent authority like any agent.

Ex officio powers are limited even for the president. Only if the president acts as general manager does he or she have broad implied authority to make contracts and conduct the ordinary business of the corporation. A vice president has only such authority as he or she may be given as manager of some division of the corporation's business. The secretary's function is to keep minutes and other records, and the secretary has no implied authority except to affix the corporate seal. The treasurer can bind the corporation by his receipts, checks and endorsements but does not, by virtue of his office, have authority to borrow money.

Employees of the corporation other than officers may be delegated to act as agents for the corporation. Statutory criminal or civil liability may be imposed upon officers for failure to perform certain statutory duties such as filing the corporation's annual report with the secretary of state or for making reports known to be false.

Belcher v. Birmingham Trust National Bank

348 F. Supp. 61 (N.D. Ala. 1968)

Action by Charles Belcher, beneficiary of a trust, (plaintiff) against Birmingham Trust National Bank (Trust Bank), trustee (defendant). Trust Bank then cross claimed against Brady Belcher and others to require them to account for using corporate funds for their own benefit and failing to disclose information to other stockholders. Judgment against Brady Belcher and other officers and directors. (Note: the following facts and excerpt from the court's opinion deal only with one of numerous grounds for liability—the taking of evidence during the trial required 60 days, and the court's opinion runs 88 pages, two columns to a page.)

W. E. Belcher founded a lumber business headquartered in Centreville, Alabama, in the early part of the century. It was incorporated in 1941 as the W. E. Belcher Lumber Company, with the founder owning 996 shares and his three sons and one son-in-law each holding one share. After Belcher's death in 1945, his shares were divided among his five children, and in 1949 one of them, Brady Belcher, became president and thereafter acquired a slightly larger shareholding interest than his siblings. The family also organized a number of other corporations and partnerships which were engaged in various enterprises, most of which were related to the lumber business. These included the operation of large tracts of timberland in several states and Costa Rica, sawmills, manufacturing wooden structural members for buildings and furniture, house building, an oil company, and Belcher Motor Company. Charles Belcher, the plaintiff, is the grandson of W. E. Belcher. His father conveyed most of his shares in W. E. Belcher Lumber Company (the Corporation) to a trust and appointed Trust Bank as trustee. It was also trustee for the estate of W. E. Belcher.

During the course of the litigation the facts came to light concerning the Costa Rica Company, organized by Brady Belcher to exploit a timber contract with the government of Costa Rica. The aim was to acquire Central American logs for the production of plywood and veneer. It was to be financed by the Corporation. Extensive road building in public lands would be required.

The board of directors of the Corporation never discussed the formation of the Costa Rican Company and the shareholders, other than the two brothers then active in the business, were unaware of the venture. Brady Belcher when asked at the trial why he had not informed his sister, Mrs. Davis, or the Trustee replied, "I think I would have gotten a 'no' answer on it." The initial investment contemplated by the Corporation was estimated at from $365,000 to $473,000 with an additional average annual capital investment after allowance for depreciation of $198,000 for the ten years of the contract.

GROOMS, DISTRICT JUDGE.   The evidence developed as to this issue portrays an indifference, if not callousness, of those in control of the Corporation towards those who have a common interest but who are not so situated. The least that Brady and W. E. Jr. could have done was to first fully inform their fellow directors and stockholders that the venture *was to be* undertaken, and what was involved in the undertaking, rather than to present them with a *fait accompli,* the chief facts of which would be disclosed only in the course of the trial and which disclosure would serve to further inflame an already overheated controversy.

The facts here found present the primary question of Brady's authority to act for and on behalf of the Corporation.

Assuming that the Corporation under its broad charter powers could have engaged in the Costa Rica venture upon proper authorization of its board of directors, it does not follow that the president and general manager has the power to engage in the venture on behalf of the Corporation.

The bylaws of the Corporation, provides that "The affairs and business of the Company shall be under the control of a Board of five (5) Directors . . . and the President or the Vice President shall sign and execute *all contracts and other commitments* in the name of the Company *when authorized to do so by the Board of Directors.* The President shall have general supervision of the affairs and business of the Company. . . ." (Emphasis supplied) This section also provides that ". . . [The President] shall keep the Board of Directors fully informed and shall freely consult with them concerning the affairs and business of the Company. . . ."

Whatever authority the president of a corporation has must be expressly conferred on him by statute, charter, or bylaws or by the board of directors or be implied from express powers granted, usage or custom, or the nature of the company's business. Unless the authority of a general manager is restricted, his authority and powers "are coextensive with the powers of the corporation itself, and he has authority to do any act on its behalf . . . *in the ordinary course of the company's business.* . . ." (Emphasis supplied.)

* * * * *

While the harvesting of timber and the manufacture of lumber are two of the things the Corporation was organized to do, the Court is, however, of the opinion, and so holds, that the Costa Rica venture, involving actual outlays and contractual commitments, apart from operation charges of almost one million dollars, and further involving prolonged dealings with a foreign government located in an area where tempers are volatile, revolutions frequent, and expropriation not unknown, required the action of the board of directors of the Corporation. The undertaking by Brady purportedly on its behalf was not in the ordinary course of the Corporation's business, was beyond the scope of the authority and power of the president and general manager, and was not authorized by the directors of the Corporation. Accordingly, Brady and W. E. Jr., who was acting with him, must assume this undertaking as their own, and account to and indemnify the Corporation against sums expended and obligations incurred on the Costa Rica project.

Fiduciary Duties of Directors, Officers, and Others

General. Directors as such are not agents of the corporation but hold a position which is *sui generis.* Nevertheless, they and corporate officers are treated as having fiduciary, or at least quasi-fiduciary, duties to the corporation which are essentially similar to the duties to his or her principal of any agent. They may generally be stated as (1) to act within one's authority and within the powers given to the corporation, (2) to act diligently and with due care in conducting the affairs of the corporation, and (3) to act in loyalty and good faith for the benefit of the corporation.

The trend of statutory and case law, and especially of the regulatory activity of the Securities and Exchange Commission, has been to raise the standard of conduct required of directors and officers and to extend some of the prohibitions to employees who are not officers and to controlling shareholders. There also appears to be a trend toward more suits against directors, usually derivative actions by shareholders, for breach of their duties to the corporation.

Acting within Authority. Like any agent, officers have a duty to act within the authority conferred upon them by the articles and bylaws of the corporation and by the directors. Directors must act within authority given to the corporation and to them by statute and by the articles and bylaws, as discussed above in the section on *ultra vires.* Either an officer or director may be liable to the corporation if it is damaged by an act exceeding his or her or the corporation's authority.

If directors honestly believe that a transaction approved by them is within the scope of the corporate business, and they are justified in that belief, they will not be held personally liable for injury to the corporation resulting from the transaction, even if the transaction is held to be *ultra vires.* Also, if the transaction is not illegal and is later ratified by the shareholders, the directors will be relieved of personal liability to the corporation.

Due Care and Diligence. Directors and officers are liable for losses to the corporation resulting from their negligence or lack of attention to their responsibilities. The Model Act does not define the standard of care but the New York statute defines it in a manner similar to that declared by some courts. It states: "Directors and officers shall discharge the duties of their respective positions in good faith and with that degree of diligence, care, and skill which ordinarily prudent men would exercise under similar circumstances in like positions."[8] They may reasonably rely upon others—directors upon officers, both directors and officers upon accountants and lawyers, but lack of knowledge of the actual state of affairs of the corporation is not an adequate defense if the knowledge was obtainable through reasonable diligence.

The cases are in conflict as to whether a person's lack of capacity as a director will save him or her from liability. Certainly the failure to attend directors' meetings or the fact that a director receives no compensation does not permit him or her to escape liability, although if a director receives no compensation, is engaged full time in another business, and lives at a distance from the corporation, these are circumstances that would affect the degree of care and diligence expected. Directors and officers are not liable for mere errors of judgment if they act with care, diligence, and in good faith. This rule is known as the "business judgment rule." However, they are liable for negligence both in taking action and in failing to take appropriate action. This would include liability for negligence in the selection and supervision of officers and employees of the corporation.

Loyalty and Good Faith.[9]   Cardozo in a much quoted opinion well stated the duty to act in loyalty and good faith. He declared that a director:

owes loyalty and allegiance to the corporation—a loyalty that is undivided and an allegiance that is influenced by no consideration other than the welfare of the corporation. Any adverse interest of a director will be subjected to a scrutiny rigid and uncompromising. He may not profit at the expense of his corporation and in conflict with its rights; he may not for personal gain divert unto himself the opportunities which in equity and fairness belong to his corporation. He is required to use his independent judgment. . . . He must, of course, act honestly and in good faith. . . .[10]

The requirement of loyalty and good faith is general and is as broad as the inventiveness of avaricious humans to which it is addressed. Only four kinds of situations where questions of the good faith of directors or officers have been adjudicated will be discussed. They are: (1) transactions with the corporation, (2) usurpation of a corporate opportunity, (3) transactions in the corporation's stock, and (4) oppression of minority shareholders.

Transactions with the Corporation.   Fiduciaries are generally not permitted any type of self-dealing, and earlier decisions held that any transaction with the corporation in which a director was involved directly or indirectly was voidable at the discretion of the corporation. However, transactions in which a director or officer (or another business organization in which he or she has an interest) supplies facilities, products, or services to or is served by the corporation may clearly benefit the corporation. So more recently the majority

---

[8] McKinney, *N.Y. Bus. Corp. Law* 717.

[9] See also "Defense of Good Faith," later in this chapter.

[10] *Meinhard v. Salmon,* 164 N.E. 545, 546 (1928).

of courts have held that such a transaction is voidable only if unfair to the corporation. If the director or officer represents the corporation as well as himself or herself in the transaction or if the director's presence is necessary for a quorum or his or her vote for the approval of the transaction, then a court is less likely to enforce the contract. Failure to disclose fully his or her interest in the transaction is more important and may be fatal to the director's attempt to enforce the contract even if its terms are fair to the corporation.

The Model Act provides (41), and Delaware is similar, that transactions between the corporation and a director (or between it and a corporation in which a director is interested) are not automatically void or voidable under any one of three conditions. These are: (1) with knowledge or after disclosure of the conflicting interest, the board, without counting the vote of interested directors, approves or ratifies; (2) with knowledge or after disclosure the shareholders approve or ratify; or (3) the transaction is fair to the corporation.

Section 35 authorizes the directors to fix their own compensation—a situation where there is an inherent conflict of interest. Neither are such contracts necessarily enforceable if they pass one of these tests. For example, fraud would be a basis for invalidating a transaction even if it had been approved by directors and was fair to the corporation. Section 20 requires any stock option plan which is to issue options to directors, officers, or employees of the corporation to be approved by a majority of the stock but the directors' judgment as to the adequacy of the consideration for the options is declared to be conclusive in the absence of fraud.

Usurpation of a Corporate Opportunity. Directors and officers may not take for themselves business opportunities which come to them in their corporate capacity and which fall within the normal scope of the corporation's business and which it is able to undertake. They may not, for example, buy up land that the corporation could use and then resell it to the corporation at a profit nor may they personally buy the rights to manufacture a product which would fit into the corporation's line. If the corporation is unable to finance the opportunity or accepting it would be *ultra vires* or a noninterested majority of directors vote against accepting it, then a director or officer is free to exploit it personally unless it would result in harmful competition to the corporation.

Transactions in the Corporation's Stock. Directors and officers have access to information affecting the value of the corporation's securities unavailable to other securities holders. Are they entitled to make a profit from that knowledge by buying and selling the corporation's stock or other securities without disclosing this information to the other party in the transaction? In the early cases courts concluded that directors and officers had no fiduciary duty to existing or potential shareholders but only to the corporation. Therefore, they are accountable for their trading profits neither to the corporation, which suffered no loss, nor to the individuals from whom they bought or to whom they sold stock. However, in this century there has been a trend in the court decisions toward finding a duty on the part of the director or officer, and even an employee or controlling shareholder, to disclose inside knowledge as a condition to his or her right to buy or sell. Under this view the other party to the transaction may recover the difference between the stock's value had the information been known and the actual trading price. As will be discussed, this is already the law under the Securities and Exchange Act, but it remains only a minority rule in suits not brought under that act.

Some relatively recent decisions have held that controlling shareholders are liable to their fellow shareholders for breach of a duty to exercise due care to guard their interests against potential looters of the corporate assets and also have permitted shareholders to recover the premium over and above the inherent value of the stock paid the controlling shareholders for sale of control of the corporation.

Oppression of Minority Shareholders.   Directors and officers owe a duty to the corporation to exercise their management functions in the best interests of the corporation as a whole. Although this duty is generally recognized, so also is the right of the majority to manage the corporation with considerable discretion through the "business judgment" rule. Courts are frequently faced with suits, usually involving close corporations, which allege oppression of minority shareholders or attempts to "freeze" them out of the corporation which require balancing these two principles. The means of oppression complained of are many. They include dividend withholding, siphoning off profits in high salaries to controlling shareholders in management, mergers or reorganizations or merely charter amendments which alter the rights and preferences of a certain class or classes of stock and sale or lease of major corporate assets to or from controlling shareholders for an unfair consideration. Generally minority shareholders have been successful in obtaining an injunction or recovering damages only where the acts of directors have been clearly in bad faith, arbitrary, or clearly abuse the discretion allowed them under the "business judgment" rule.

Federal Securities Laws.   The federal securities laws have imposed new duties on directors and officers and Rule 10b-5 of the Securities and Exchange Commission has been said to be the basis of a new federal corporation law. These laws and their effect on the duties of directors, officers, and others who are considered "insiders" are discussed in Chapter 27.

Other Statutory Liabilities of Directors.   The Model Corporation Act (48) imposes personal civil liability to the corporation upon directors for certain acts taken in conducting the internal affairs of the corporation. These acts include: (1) assent to the payment of a dividend or a distribution of assets in violation of the statute or the articles; (2) assent to an improper purchase of its own shares by the corporation, and (3) assent to the distribution of assets during liquidation without providing for the payment of all known debts. For protection, a director who attends a board meeting at which any of these illegal actions is taken must have his or her dissent recorded in the minutes. If the director voted in opposition to the motion, immunity from liability may be gained by filing a written dissent with the secretary of the corporation immediately after adjournment of the meeting.

Defense of Good Faith. The Model Act (48) protects the director if he or she acts in good faith upon financial statements represented to be correct by the president or the officer of the corporation having charge of its books of account or on a written report by an independent public accountant. This appears merely to codify the "business judgment" rule. In a number of cases the courts have held that good faith reliance by an officer or director upon the opinion of counsel is a defense to personal liability, but this defense has perhaps more frequently been rejected and the cases probably cannot be reconciled.

Summary

Although directors are not agents of the corporation, they and corporate officers are treated as having fiduciary duties to the corporation. The trend of the law is toward raising the standard of conduct required of directors and officers and there appears to be an increase in suits brought against them, usually by stockholders, for breach of their duties to the corporation.

Directors and officers must act within their authority and within the powers given to the corporation. They are liable to the corporation for losses due to their negligence or lack of attention to their responsibilities but not for mere errors in judgment. They also owe a duty of loyalty and good faith to the corporation and must put its welfare above their own.

A director or officer may transact business with the corporation but he or she should disclose to the corporation any conflict of interest. The corporation may usually avoid a contract which is unfair to the corporation. A director or officer may not usurp a corporate opportunity by taking for personal advantage some opportunity coming to him or her in his corporate capacity or which may have the effect of putting the director or officer in competition with the corporation.

There is a trend in the case law towards holding that directors and officers may not use information not generally available to the investing public to personally buy and sell the corporation's shares. This is now clearly the law under the Securities Exchange Act.

The duty of good faith is to act for the best interests of the corporation as a whole and if the actions of the directors or officers are taken primarily for the purpose of oppressing minority shareholders or "freezing" them out of the corporation, the minority may be able to obtain injunctive relief or damages.

Nanfito v. Tekseed Hybrid Co.[11]

341 F. Supp. 240 (D.Neb. 1972)

Suit by Nanfito, administrator of the estate of Alice C. Major (plaintiff), against Tekseed Hybrid Company and the five other shareholders who were the directors of Tekseed (defendants) to recover damages under Section 10(b) of the Securities Exchange Act of 1934 for negligent misrepresentation as well as fraud in connection with a corporate merger. Judgment for defendants.

Through inheritance from her husband, who had been a founder of both companies, Mrs. Major owned one fifth of the shares of Tek Annex Co. and of Tekseed, both subchapter S corporations which were located at Tekemah, Nebraska. Tekseed was producing and selling hybrid seed corn and also some alfalfa and sorgum seed. Tex Annex was an inactive corporation which had been partially liquidated, and Mrs. Major sold her shares back to that corporation in 1967. On July 1, 1968, Tek Annex was merged into Tekseed. After consulting with their accountant who had been performing accounting work for Tekseed for 20 years, the directors established the basis for the exchange of shares in the merger solely upon the book values: $106.02 for Tek Annex shares and $73.22 for Tekseed shares. They gave no weight to potential earnings or goodwill of Tekseed because they thought its plant and equipment were obsolete, the plant's location was poor, and it was anticipated that the business manager would leave shortly and no qualified replacement appeared to be available.

The court found no evidence of fraud and disposed of the suit on the allegation of negligence by the directors.

DIER, DISTRICT JUDGE.   It appears to be Nanfito's position that the individual defendants were as fiduciaries for the corporation and all its shareholders under a definite duty to fully consider all factors tending to have a bearing upon the exchange ratio for the stock for merger purposes, and then to advise all the shareholders, particularly Alice C. Major, of what factors were actually used, and the reasons for the use of those factors and the rejection of other factors. Without such information, Nanfito contends, Alice C. Major could not make the truly informed type of investment decision which the federal securities laws, specifically Section 10(b) and Rule 10(b)–5, are intended to encourage.

However, Nanfito goes further, and would require the officers and directors of a corporation, such as Tekseed to not only supply investors and shareholders with full information regarding a major corporation decision affecting the value of its assets and stock, but to also interpret their information and provide an expert opinion as to all the possible ramifications such a decision might have on the investor's interests.

This Court, however, does not read Section 10(b) or Rule 10(b)–5 as requiring any more than full disclosure of all information which the ordinary investor of common business experience would require in making an informed investment decision.

In any event, the primary aspects necessary to make Nanfito's claim cognizable under Section 10(b) are present.

---

[11] *Aff'd,* 473 F.2d 537 (8th Cir. 1973). Although this case was brought under the federal securities laws treated in Chapter 27, the court's discussion of a director's duty of due care is not based upon these statutes.

The Court, therefore, has only to determine whether the individual defendants exercised due care in establishing the exchange ratios for the stock and in advising Alice C. Major of the basis of their decision.

The so-called "business judgment" rule validates corporate management from liability for any transaction within the powers of the corporation, *intra vires,* and the authority of management, and involves the exercise of due care and compliance with applicable fiduciary duties. Under this rule a Court will not interfere with the internal management and substitute its judgment for that of the directors to enjoin or set aside the transaction or to hold the directors responsible for any resulting loss.

Directors and officers of a corporation may become liable to it or the shareholders for negligence in the performance of their corporate duties. However, they are not insurers and are not generally held liable for errors of judgment or mistakes while acting with reasonable skill and prudence.

The standard of care has been variously described as that of a "reasonably prudent man," or of an ordinarily prudent director in a similar business, or "the same degree of fidelity and care as an ordinarily prudent man would exercise in the management of his own affairs of like magnitude and importance."

Directors and officers must act carefully in light of the circumstances which confront them, in light of actual knowledge, and such knowledge as they should have gained by reasonable care and skill.

This Court is of the opinion that the individual defendants used all due care in establishing the exchange ratios of the stock for merger purposes. They, in testifying, explained to this Court's satisfaction why future earnings potential were not significant factors in setting the ratios. There is also evidence that they relied upon the advice and judgment of their accountant, a member of the accounting firm of Peat, Marwick, Mitchell & Co., in setting the ratios. Reasonable reliance on others has been found by some courts to be consistent with the duty of due care imposed upon corporate management.

However, even though the individual defendants exercised all due care in carrying out the merger pursuant to, and in compliance with, statutory and other legal requisites, they must also have provided Alice Major with information which would have enabled her to determine how her interests in the corporation might be altered.

In this latter regard, it must be noted that Alford Major, the husband of Alice C. Major, who predeceased her, was one of the founders of Tekseed Hybrid Company and had been active in its management until the time of his death in 1960. He was undoubtedly quite familiar with the corporation's problems and expectations.

It is at least inferable from this that Alice C. Major acquired from her husband information about the condition and outlook of the company.

In addition, the evidence established that Alice C. Major kept herself relatively well informed about the management of the corporation. She attended shareholders' meetings and was about as active as a minority shareholder in a close corporation can be, for eight years prior to the merger. Since a Subchapter S corporation was involved, she was, of course, quite familiar with the earnings Tekseed Hybrid Company had experienced.

Alice C. Major had also been a stockholder of Tek Annex, having sold her interest in Tek Annex approximately one year before the merger. She was thus aware of the fact that it was a dormant corporation.

By letter of May 21, 1968, Alice C. Major was advised by Raymond Cram, then secretary of Tekseed Hybrid Company, that the management had discussed the financing of worn out facilities and additional facilities for Tekseed Hybrid Company, and had concluded that the most practical solution would be the merger of Tek Annex Company with Tekseed Hybrid Company. Along with the letter was a proposed plan of merger, a notice of a stockholders' meeting, and a proxy for Mrs. Major to sign.

. . . The Court now concludes that Alice C. Major already knew that Tekseed was a going concern with goodwill while Tek Annex was not such a firm. Since Mrs. Major was already aware of the factors which plaintiff deems so important, it would have been a useless gesture for the defendants to advise her thereof.

Thus, all that remained for the defendants to inform Alice C. Major about were the reasons for the merger. This the defendants did. They could not, in this Court's view, be required to go further and analyze the facts for Mrs. Major. Had they done so, they would have been walking on dangerous grounds, because once they assumed the duty to do so, they might possibly have become liable if their analysis had proven incorrect. In short, Alice C. Major, was free to draw her own conclusions about the propriety of the merger and its ramifications on her interests, once she had been fully apprised of the reasons for the merger and the condition of each corporation.

It is, therefore, the opinion of this Court that the defendants herein neither committed an act nor omitted to do an act in regard to the merger, such as would justify a recovery by Nanfito under Section 10(b) of the Securities Exchange Act of 1934 or any other law, state or federal.

Guth v. Loft, Inc.

5 A.2d 503 (Sup. Ct. Del. 1939)

This was a bill in Chancery by Loft, Inc. (plaintiff), against Charles G. Guth, Grace Company and Pepsi-Cola Company (defendants) seeking to impress a trust in favor of Loft upon all of the capital stock of Pepsi-Cola. The Chancellor found for Loft. Affirmed.

Loft manufactured and sold candies, syrups, beverages, and foodstuffs in 115 retail stores on the Middle Atlantic seaboard and its wholesale activities amounted to sales of $800,000. It dispensed Coca-Cola at all of its stores. Guth, a man of long experience in the candy and soft drink business, joined Loft in 1929 and became president and general manager in 1930. In 1931 he tried to persuade Coca-Cola to give Loft a jobber's discount in view of its very large purchases. Coca-Cola refused and Guth learned that Pepsi-Cola syrup could be purchased for about two thirds the price of Coca-Cola. While this was under consideration, the corporation owning the secret formula and trademark for Pepsi-Cola was adjudicated a bankrupt and the man controlling it sought Guth's help in forming a new corporation. This was done with approximately half of the stock going to Grace, a corporation owned by Guth's family which made syrups for soft drinks and which sold one of its syrups to Loft. Most of the rest of the stock came to be owned by Guth through subsequent transactions with the man previously control-ling Pepsi-Cola. During this period Guth was very heavily indebted to Loft, Guth was in serious financial straits, and Grace was insolvent.

Guth used Loft's working capital, its credit, its plant and equipment, and its execu-tives and employees in producing Pepsi-Cola, although Loft was subsequently reim-bursed for wages paid to workers. Loft was Pepsi-Cola's chief customer. It suffered diminution of profits in its retail stores estimated at $300,000 due to discarding Coca-Cola, despite advertising expenditures of $20,000 to promote Pepsi-Cola, which was relatively unknown.

Guth claimed he offered the Loft directors the opportunity to take over Pepsi-Cola but they declined because they did not wish to compete with Coca-Cola, that it was not in line with Loft's business, and that it involved too great a financial risk. However, he also claimed that later the directors authorized the use of Loft facilities and resources upon Guth's guarantee of all advances. No record of either action appeared in the corporate minutes of Loft, and the Chancellor found that the directors were without knowledge of the use of Loft's money, credit, facilities, and personnel in furthering the Pepsi-Cola venture.

LAYTON, CHIEF JUSTICE.   Corporate officers and directors are not permitted to use their position of trust and confidence to further their private interests. While technically not trustees, they stand in fiduciary relation to the corporation and its stockholders. A public policy, existing through the years, and derived from a profound knowledge of human characteristics and motives, has established a rule that demands of a corpo-rate officer or director, peremptorily and inexorably, the most scrupulous observance of his duty, not only affirmatively to protect the interests of the corporation committed to his charge, but also to refrain from doing anything that would work injury to the corporation, or to deprive it of profit or advantage which his skill and ability might properly bring to it, or to enable it to make in the reasonable and lawful exercise of its powers. The rule that requires an undivided and unselfish loyalty to the corporation demands that there shall be no conflict between duty and self-interest. The occasions for the determination of honesty, good faith, and loyal conduct are many and varied, and no hard and fast rule can be formulated. The standard of loyalty is measured by no fixed scale.

If an officer or director of a corporation, in violation of his duty as such, acquires gain or advantage for himself, the law charges the interest so acquired with a trust for the benefit of the corporation, at its election, while it denies to the betrayer all benefit and profit. The rule, inveterate and uncompromising in its rigidity, does not rest upon the narrow ground of injury or damage to the corporation resulting from a betrayal of confidence, but upon a broader foundation of a wise public policy that, for the purpose of removing all temptation, extinguishes all possibility of profit flowing from a breach of the confidence imposed by the fiduciary relation. Given the relation between the parties, a certain result follows; and a constructive trust is the remedial device through which precedence of self is compelled to give way to the stern demands of loyalty.

The rule, referred to briefly as the rule of corporate opportunity, is merely one of the manifestations of the general rule that demands of an officer or director the utmost good faith in his relation to the corporation which he represents.

It is true that when a business opportunity comes to a corporate officer or director in his individual capacity rather than in his official capacity, and the opportunity is one which, because of the nature of the enterprise, is not essential to his corporation, and is one in which it has no interest or expectancy, the officer or director is entitled to treat the opportunity as his own, and the corporation has no interest in it, if, of course, the officer or director has not wrongfully embarked the corporation's resources therein.

Although the facts and circumstances disclosed by the voluminous record clearly show gross violations of legal and moral duties by Guth in his dealings with Loft, Guth makes bold to say that no duty was cast upon him, hence he was guilty of no disloyalty. The fiduciary relation demands something more than the morals of the marketplace. Guth's abstractions of Loft's money and materials are complacently referred to as borrowings. Whether his acts are to be deemed properly cognizable in a civil court at all, we need not inquire, but certain it is that borrowing is not descriptive of them. A borrower presumes a lender acting freely. Guth took without limit or stint from a helpless corporation, in violation of a statute enacted for the protection of corporations against such abuses, and without the knowledge or authority of the corporation's Board of Directors. Cunning and craft supplanted sincerity. Frankness gave way to concealment. He did not offer the Pepsi-Cola opportunity to Loft, but captured it for himself. He invested little or no money of his own in the venture, but commandeered for his own benefit and advantage the money, resources and facilities of his corporation and the services of his officials. He thrust upon Loft the hazard, while he reaped the benefit. His time was paid for by Loft. The use of the Grace plant was not essential to the enterprise. In such manner he acquired for himself and Grace ninety-one percent of the capital stock of Pepsi-Cola, now worth many millions. A genius in his line he may be, but the law makes no distinction between the wrongdoing genius and the one less endowed.

Diamond v. Oreamuno

248 N.E.2d 910 (Ct. App. N.Y. 1969)

This was a derivative action by Diamond (plaintiff) against Oreamuno and Gonzalez (defendants) to compel an accounting to MAI for profits resulting from an alleged breach of fiduciary duty. Motion to dismiss the complaint was denied and Diamond appealed. Affirmed.

MAI was in the business of financing computer installations through sale and leaseback arrangements with commercial and industrial users. Under the leases, MAI was required to maintain and repair the computers. Since it lacked the capacity to do this itself, it contracted with International Business Machines, the manufacturer of its machines, to service them. As a result of a sharp increase by IBM in its charges for such services, MAI's expenses for August 1966 rose considerably and its net earnings declined approximately 75 percent from $262,253 in July to $66,233 in August. This information was not released to the public until October, but before this time Oreamuno, chairman of the board of directors, and Gonzalez, president of MAI, sold 56,500 shares of their MAI stock at the then current market price of $28 per share. When the information concerning the reduction in earnings became known to the public, the price of the stock immediately dropped to $11. Diamond's complaint charged that Oreamuno and Gonzalez were forbidden to use the inside information for their personal advantage and asked that they account to the corporation for the $800,000 difference between the selling price and $11 per share.

FULD, CHIEF JUDGE. It is well established, as a general proposition, that a person who acquires special knowledge or information by virtue of a confidential or fiduciary relationship with another is not free to exploit that knowledge or information for his own personal benefit but must account to his principal for any profits derived therefrom. This, in turn is merely a corollary of the broader principle, inherent in the nature of the fiduciary relationship, that prohibits a trustee or agent from extracting secret profits from his position of trust.

In support of their claim that the complaint fails to state a cause of action, Oreamuno and Gonzalez take the position that, although it is admittedly wrong for an officer or director to use his position to obtain trading profits for himself in the stock of his corporation, the action ascribed to them did not injure or damage MAI in any way. Accordingly, they continue, the corporation should not be permitted to recover the proceeds. They acknowledge that, by virtue of the exclusive access which officers and directors have to inside information, they possess an unfair advantage over other shareholders and, particularly, the persons who had purchased the stock from them but, they contend, the corporation itself was unaffected and, for that reason, a derivative action is an inappropriate remedy.

It is true that the complaint before us does not contain any allegation of damages to the corporation but this has never been considered to be an essential requirement for a cause of action founded on a breach of fiduciary duty. This is because the function of such an action, unlike an ordinary tort or contract case, is not merely to compensate the plaintiff for wrongs committed by the defendant but, as this court declared many years ago, "to *prevent* them, by removing from agents and trustees all inducement to attempt dealing for their own benefit in matters which they have undertaken for others, or to which their agency or trust relates." (Emphasis supplied.)

Just as a trustee has no right to retain for himself the profits yielded by property placed in his possession but must account to his beneficiaries, a corporate fiduciary, who is entrusted with potentially valuable information, may not appropriate that asset for his own use even though, in so doing, he causes no injury to the corporation. The primary concern, in a case such as this, is not to determine whether the corporation has been damaged but to decide, as between the corporation and the defendants, who has a higher claim to the proceeds derived from the exploitation of the information. In our opinion, there can be no justification for permitting officers and directors, such as the defendants, to retain for themselves profits which, it is alleged, they derived solely from exploiting information gained by virtue of their inside position as corporate officials.

In addition, it is pertinent to observe that, despite the lack of any specific allegation of damage, it may well be inferred that the actions of Oreamuno and Gonzalez might have caused some harm to the enterprise. Although the corporation may have little concern with the day-to-day transactions in its shares, it has a great interest in maintaining a reputation of integrity, an image of probity for its management, and in insuring the continued public acceptance and marketability of its stock. When officers and directors abuse their position in order to gain personal profits, the effect may be to cast a cloud on the corporation's name, injure stockholder relations and undermine public regard for the corporation's securities. . . .

Oreamuno and Gonzalez maintain that extending the prohibition against personal exploitation of a fiduciary relationship to officers and directors of a corporation will discourage such officials from maintaining a stake in the success of the corporate venture through share ownership, which, they urge, is an important incentive to proper performance of their duties. There is, however, a considerable difference between corporate officers who assume the same risks and obtain the same benefits as other shareholders and those who use their privileged position to gain special advantages not available to others. . . .

* * * * *

Oreamuno and Gonzalez recognize that the conduct charged against them directly contravened the policy embodied in the Securities Exchange Act but, they maintain, the Federal legislation constitutes a comprehensive and carefully wrought plan for dealing with the abuse of inside information and that allowing a derivative action to be maintained under State law would interfere with the Federal scheme. Moreover, they urge, the existence of dual Federal and State remedies for the same act would create the possibility of double liability.

* * * * *

There is nothing in the Federal law which indicates that it was intended to limit the power of the States to fashion additional remedies to effectuate similar purposes. Although the impact of Federal securities regulation has on occasion been said to have created a "Federal corporation law," in fact, its effect on the duties and obligations of directors and officers and their relation to the corporation and its shareholders is only occasional and peripheral. The primary source of the law in this area ever remains that of the State which created the corporation. Indeed, Congress expressly provided against any implication that it intended to preempt the field by declaring, in section 28(a) of the Securities Exchange Act of 1934 (48 U.S. Stat. 903), that "(t)he rights and remedies provided by this title shall be in addition to any and all other rights and remedies that may exist at law or in equity."

Nor should we be deterred, in formulating a State remedy, by the claim of possible double liability. Certainly, as already indicated, if the sales in question were publicly made, the likelihood that a suit will be brought by purchasers of the shares is quite remote. But, even if it were not, the mere possibility of such a suit is not a defense nor does it render the complaint insufficient. It is not unusual for an action to be brought to recover a fund which may be subject to a superior claim by a third party. If that be the situation, a defendant should not be permitted to retain the fund for his own use on the chance that such a party may eventually appear.

Liability for Torts and Crimes

Torts. The view in the early cases was that torts committed by a corporation's employees were *ultra vires* and, therefore, the corporation was not responsible. Today, as is clear from the cases in Chapter 3, the rule of *respondeat superior* applies to corporations, and the only issue is whether the employee was acting within the scope of his or her authority. The corporation may be liable even though it had expressly instructed its employees to avoid the act. Where the employee's acts are willful, wanton, or malicious and punitive damages would be appropriate, however, there is a split of authority as to whether the corporation will be held liable for punitive damages in the absence of authorization or ratification.

Since neither the directors nor the officers are the principal, they are not personally liable unless they have authorized or participated in the tort.

Crimes. The traditional view of the law was that a corporation could not be guilty of a crime involving intent. Today a number of courts find little difficulty in holding them guilty, particularly where the offense is requested by, authorized by, or performed by the board of directors or an officer or other person having responsibility for formulating company policy or by a high-level administrator having supervisory responsibility over the subject matter of the offense and acting within the scope of his or her employment. The Model Penal Code, for example, distinguishes between an agent and a "high managerial agent" of a corporation and attributes the felonies of only the latter to the corporation.

A number of statutes specifically define crimes which are most likely to be committed by corporations. Examples include the Sherman Act, the Securities Act of 1934, and the Sunday closing laws of a number of states. Others impose penalties for failing to file or filing false reports with taxing or regulatory authorities.

Directors and officers may be held individually guilty if they request, authorize, or aid and abet the commission of a crime by an employee, even if the corporation is acquitted, because they have acted outside the scope of their authority. Likewise, of course, an employee committing an unauthorized crime is individually guilty even though his or her only motive was to benefit the corporation. However, the trend is away from finding lack of authority.

Summary

The general agency rules concerning torts and crimes apply to corporations. A corporation is liable for the torts of its employees done within the scope and in the course of the employment, even when it expressly instructs the employee to avoid the act. Corporations may also be found guilty of crimes, including those requiring intent, if the offense is authorized or performed by policy-making managers or high-level administrators acting within the scope and in the course of employment. Directors and officers may be held criminally liable although the corporation is acquitted because they have acted beyond their authority.

State v. Adjustment Department Credit Bureau

483 P.2d 687 (Sup. Ct. Ida. 1971)

The State of Idaho (plaintiff) prosecuted Adjustment Department Credit Bureau (defendant) for the crime of extortion. The corporation was convicted and it appealed. Reversed and remanded.

Adjustment Department Credit Bureau (Credit Bureau) conducted a bill collection service as part of its operation. A pharmacy assigned to Credit Bureau an open account owed to it by Rodney Price. Credit Bureau designated Howard Short as its employee to handle the claim. He persuaded Price to execute a promissory note, and when it was not paid he obtained a judgment against Price. He then persuaded Price to draw a check, even though Price stated that he had no account in the bank upon which the check was drawn. While Price was employed in another city, Short contacted Mrs. Price about the obligation, and when Price returned for a visit, Short threatened to prosecute him for issuing a bad check if he failed to make a payment on the debt. Price at that time paid $20.

Shortly thereafter Price went to see Short's supervisor, Mr. Slayton, about the threat to prosecute. Slayton told him to deal with Short. Price then filed a complaint and this prosecution resulted.

McFADDEN, JUSTICE.   On this appeal Credit Bureau has made numerous assignments of error. The crucial issue presented by these assignments of error concerns the instruction given by the trial court to the effect that a corporation (which acts only through its agents) can be held criminally liable "for the acts of its agents who are authorized to act for it in the particular matter out of which the unlawful conduct with which it is charged grows or in the business to which it related." It is Credit Bureau's contention that this instruction by the trial court was in error, arguing that the trial court should have instructed that Credit Bureau could have been found guilty only if the agent committed the prohibited acts, and that the agent's acts were authorized, requested, or commanded by another corporate agent having responsibility for formation of corporate policy, or by a managerial agent having supervisory responsibility over the subject matter.

It is our conclusion that there is merit in Credit Bureau's position in regard to these instructions. . . .

By reason of the fact that corporations can only act through their agents, the courts have struggled with the problem of holding a corporation criminally liable in those cases involving crimes where a specific intent is required. The question is, how can a corporation, an artificial being, have the necessary *mens rea* to commit those crimes where specific intent is required. The answer is found in the relationship between the corporation and the agent that performed the acts for which the corporation is being criminally charged, and in the nature of the crime with which the corporation is being charged.

There are certain crimes defined by statute for which a corporation is guilty without regard to any unlawful intent . . .

Some students of the problem of corporate criminal responsibility have drawn a distinction between those types of criminal cases where the crime is one created by statute, and where the crime is a codification of a common law offense. The conclusion of the authors in this discussion is that when a statutory offense is involved, the commission of a crime by a corporate agent within the scope of his authority is a crime of the corporation, regardless of knowledge, acquiescence, or ratification by a higher corporate officer. However, when the crime is a statutory codification of a common-law crime requiring *mens rea* this reasoning as to corporate criminal liability is insufficient to bind the corporation, and more must be established to justify a conviction under this type of crime than a mere proof of an agency relationship.

* * * * *

The corporation in this case could not be bound by the actions of its agent unless that agent's acts were authorized, requested, commanded, performed, or recklessly tolerated by the board of directors or by a high managerial agent acting in behalf of the corporation within the scope of his office or employment.

Thus the instructions given by the trial court to the effect that the corporation could be found guilty if the jury found that the agent was acting within the scope of his authority was not a correct statement of the law under the circumstances of this case; it was not established that Short was in a managerial capacity, and no issue was submitted to the jury as to whether Short's actions were authorized, requested, or commanded by either an agent of the corporation responsible for formation of corporate policy or by a high managerial agent. This error is of a prejudicial nature and the case must be remanded.

Problem Cases

1. Capitol Service, Inc., was in the business of preparing persons to take the civil service examination. It was incorporated under the general incorporation statute of the state. Capitol's purpose was stated in the articles of incorporation as follows: "To aid, assist, advise, and counsel persons seeking employment with governmental agencies, to provide information, pamphlets, and data relating to employment with governmental agencies, to print, publish, sell, and distribute periodicals, pamphlets, papers, brochures, cards, and letters relating to employment with governmental agencies, to manufacture, sell, and deal in books, maps, charts, examination papers, stationery, models, casts, drawings, engravings, instruments, and school supplies of every class and description." Capitol prepared a two-year course of study which included furnishing course outlines and materials, having the trainee prepare and submit lessons, and giving and grading examinations.

    The attorney general brought an action in the nature of *quo warranto* to void Capital's charter, alleging that it was acting as an educational institution and should have been incorporated as an educational institution. Is Capitol Services exercising power in excess of its charter?

2. Thunder Corporation had two shareholders; Cohen owned 80 percent of the stock and Berman owned 20 percent. Thunder was incorporated in May 1966 and in August gave a first mortgage on its apartment property to Equitable Life Insurance Company in the amount of $765,000. In March 1967 it gave a second mortgage to Real Estate Capital Corporation (RECC) and Weissman in the amount of $105,000, but the proceeds were paid to Winthrop Homes, Inc., rather than to Thunder. Cohen, who carried out all of the transactions, was the sole shareholder of Winthrop. Thunder failed to make timely payments on its note and mortgage to Equitable, and RECC made three of them and paid the taxes. RECC then filed action to foreclose its mortgage and to appoint a receiver for Thunder. Berman, the 20 percent shareholder in Thunder, objected that the mortgage was invalid because there was no consideration for it which passed to Thunder and that Thunder had no authority to make a gift. The pertinent corporation law specifically permitted corporations "to guarantee or secure the obligations of any person." Is the mortgage valid?

3. Three of the six directors of Automatic Steel Products, Inc., were removed without cause by a majority vote of Automatic's stockholders. Automatic's certificate of incorporation provided for staggered terms with three classes of two directors each, each director to hold office for three years or until his death or resignation. A bylaw provided that a director might be removed, with or without cause, at anytime by the affirmative vote of the majority in interest of shareholders.

    Essential Enterprises, a substantial shareholder in Automatic, brought an action to determine the validity of the removal. Essential contends that the certificate of incorporation forbids dismissal of the three directors despite the contrary bylaws. Will Essential be successful?

4. Elton Risley, while president, director, and majority shareholder of Dredging Corporation, purchased from the corporation 365 shares, which constituted effective control of Margate Bridge Company at a price of $100 per share, well under its actual value. Without a prior notice, Risley called a meeting of the directors of Dredging to approve the sale. One of the three directors, Harry Kaupp, was in Florida on corporate business and did not attend. Carl Risley and Elton Risley attended, both signing a waiver of notice and statement approving the transaction. Carl Risley claimed he did not favor the sale but merely replied, "What can I do?" when asked in the meeting how he voted. The minutes, signed by Carl Risley as corporate secretary, however, showed a unanimous vote in favor of the sale.

    Dredging brought an action to rescind the stock sale, claiming that the directors' meeting was not valid and therefore the sale had not been ratified. What result?

5. Goldman, a physician, was the sole owner of Ghent Arms Corporation, which owned and operated a nursing home. It had lost money in each but one of its six years. Goldman also owned stock in Coastal Pharmaceutical Company. Coastal had been relatively inactive: it had held no stockholders' or directors' meetings for seven years, had had only one employee, and made sales of only $5,000 in 1969.

    In 1969 Coastal adopted a plan to convert to a minority enterprise eligible for Federal assistance. Gay was employed as manager, and he was also employed as acting administrator of the Ghent Arms nursing home. As a result of increased income through Medicare and better management, Ghent Arms began to show a profit. Gay and Goldman then began negotiating an acquisition of Ghent Arms by Coastal. The proposed merger was discussed at three Coastal stockholders meetings, which were attended by all Coastal directors, and at numerous meetings between Gay and Goldman between January 1970 and January 1971. At a Coastal stockholders meeting attended by all of its directors on January 17, 1971, Goldman and six others were elected as directors of Ghent Arms. On January 22 Gay, acting as president of Coastal, and Goldman for Ghent signed a formal contract, which was dated January 17, stating the terms of the acquisition of Ghent Arms by Coastal. On March 2, Goldman's accountant, who in anticipation of a public stock offering by Coastal had audited the books of both Coastal and Ghent Arms, advised Goldman that the sale of the nursing home was a mistake and that Coastal was on the verge of bankruptcy and would be unable to "go public." Goldman advised Coastal on March 9 that he was rescinding the contract. Goldman based the suit to rescind on the allegation that Coastal's board of directors had never formally authorized its president to execute the acquisition contract.

Will Goldman's suit be successful?

6. Venture Capital Corporation (a loan company) was organized and promoted by Shear, who became majority shareholder, president and chief executive officer, treasurer, and one of the three directors. Juergens, induced by a planned public stock offering, invested $26,000 in Venture stock as an original subscriber. Venture's failure to make a public offering caused Juergens to demand that the corporation buy back his stock. In April, Shear promised Juergens that he would be paid, and Juergens returned all his stock certificates. However, he was paid only $10,000, and Shear promised to pay the remaining $16,000 in June. Venture's balance sheet carried a $16,000 liability entry, "Common Stock Refunds Payable." Venture's bylaws provide that the president "subject to the direction of the board of directors, shall have general charge of the business, affairs, and property of the Corporation and general supervision of its officers and agents." Shear actively managed all the corporation's business, and the other directors permitted him to exercise complete control over management of all corporate affairs. He was also given exclusive authority by the board of directors to sell and issue the corporate stock. Juergens sued Venture for the remaining $16,000. Venture's defense is that Shear had no express or implied authority to enter any refund agreement and that the board of directors never ratified the agreement. Is Juergens entitled to the refund?

7. Some but not all of the owners of lots in a subdivision formed a nonprofit corporation, Aspen Acres Association, to maintain the roads and water system in the subdivision. The developer of the area assigned his interests to Seven Associates, Inc. This included 18 lots, some undeveloped land, a water system, and easements over all of the roads in the subdivision for purposes of water and electric lines. A conflict developed between Aspen Acres and Seven Associates, successor to the developer, as to responsibilities for financing and maintaining the water system and roads. Fundamental to the resolution of the dispute was whether a document alleged to be a contract between the parties was binding. In the document Seven Associates promised to transfer title to the water system to Aspen Acres. It had been signed on behalf of Seven Associates by Walter R. Farmer, who was treasurer and a director of the corporation. Seven Associates claimed it was signed without authorization of its board of directors, and the corporate minute books did not record such an authorization. Was the trial court correct in finding that the document was a binding contract because it was signed by an officer and director?

8. The manager of the television department in a W. T. Grant store in Santa Barbara, California, over a three-year period sold used television sets as new. W. T. Grant was charged with grand theft. It then sought to prohibit further prosecution on ground that probable cause was lacking, contending that there was no criminal intent. Could the corporation be guilty even though evidence is lacking that a higher-level executive was aware of the practice?

9. Allegheny County, Pennsylvania, had for many years levied a tax on machinery and tools used in industrial establishments whether or not attached to the realty. The tax was believed to be detrimental to the expansion of industry, and it had been discontinued in 1953 in

all counties except Allegheny, which heavily relied upon the revenue from this tax. However, in 1957 the county was suffering so severely from reduced industrial activity that it was proposed to eliminate the tax there. The issue was given considerable publicity and was thoroughly discussed, especially the need to provide continued revenue until the county's economy inproved. Several large corporations, of which U.S. Steel was the largest, then volunteered to continue paying the tax on existing but not new machinery if the tax were rescinded by the legislature. Largely because of these commitments the tax was repealed. Thereafter, two shareholders brought a derivative action seeking to hold the directors of U.S. Steel personally liable for the money paid to the county in lieu of the tax.

Are the directors entitled to summary judgment?

10. Case, shareholder of the Gulf, Mobile and Ohio Railroad Company, in 1966 offered to give GM&O information showing that it owned land in an oil field from which oil was being extracted without payment of royalty. The offer, accepted by GM&O, was conditioned upon GM&O being fully satisfied that it was the true owner of the land to be described. Further it was agreed that if GM&O determined to exercise its ownership, Case was to pay $1,000 for a three-eighths interest in the minerals in the land. GM&O examined the statutes under which it had been granted its right-of-way by the United States, which were somewhat ambiguous as to whether the right-of-way was 150 or 200 feet wide, as asserted by Case, or only 100 feet, the width historically claimed by the railroad and on which it was being paid royalties. GM&O decided to "let sleeping dogs lie" and not claim title to the extra width through the oil field because it was feared that an earlier case involving the Illinois Central Railroad might be held applicable as a precedent and that it could lose even its claim to its 100 foot right-of-way.

Case in 1969 again requested GM&O to exercise its claim, which it refused to do. Case then introduced a resolution, which failed to gain a second, in the 1970 shareholders' meeting to require the directors to acknowledge ownership of the additional land. Case then brought a derivative action seeking to assert the claim to the additional land for the railroad.

Is GM&O entitled to a motion to dismiss on the grounds that failure to assert title to the additional land was within the directors' discretion?

11. Redmont was an officer in Abbott Corporation. His primary duty was to persuade architects to use Abbott Corporation ceiling lighting in designing buildings. Abbott's ceiling lights, often called "sky lights," were unique to the area so that once this type of light was adopted by the architect, Abbott would get the job.

Due to a change in business outlook, Redmont left the employ of Abbott and subsequently formed Circle Corporation. Circle entered the skylight-ceiling light business under Redmont's direction. Prior to leaving the employ of Abbott, Redmont solicited several building jobs in which "skylights" were adopted by the architects. Redmont, who had previously submitted Abbott's bids for these jobs, later acquired the job contracts for Circle. Can Abbott recover from Circle the expected profits on these jobs?

12. Blake, Wabell, and Starobin were the only directors and officers of National Research Associates, Inc. (NRA). NRA's charter had been forfeited for failure to pay taxes. At the time of forfeiture, the corporation was inactive and its assets were limited to some patent rights. During this time, Blake and the others voted themselves salaries of $10,000 a year each, but they were not paid. Several years later, NRA was revived and merged into a successor corporation of the same name, National Research Associates, Inc. Blake, Wabell, and Starobin sued the new NRA corporation for the unpaid salaries. Will they recover?

chapter 26

Shareholders' Rights and Liabilities

Shareholders' Meetings

Exercise of Shareholder Functions.   Shareholders of a corporation ordinarily have few functions. Functions which generally are required to be performed by shareholders include: the annual election (36)[1] and the removal of directors (39); the adoption, amendment, and repeal of bylaws under a few statutes but not the Model Act (27); approval of extraordinary corporate matters such as merger or consolidation (73), sale of assets not in the normal course of business (79), reduction of stated capital (69), voluntary dissolution (84), and amendment of corporate articles (59); and under the Model Act (47) approval of loans to officers and approval of stock option plans (20). As will be discussed later in this chapter, certain classes of shares may be denied all voting rights except in specific extraordinary corporate transactions.

The shareholders' functions can generally be exercised only by voting in shareholders' meetings. However, the Model Act (145) and the statutes of many states permit shareholders to act without a meeting if consent to the action in writing is signed by all shareholders. Delaware requires written consent only by the holders of the number of shares required for approval.

Unless a higher proportion is required by the statute, articles, or bylaws, a majority of the shares represented at the meeting will decide issues put to a vote. The Model Act (33) permits including a provision in the articles to give the shareholders of any class more or less than one vote per share.

Annual Meetings.   The general corporation statutes of most states and the Model Act (28) provide that an annual meeting of shareholders shall be held at the time specified in the bylaws. Delaware, however, no longer requires an

---

[1] The numbers in parentheses refer to the sections of the Model Business Corporation Act, which appears in the Appendix.

annual meeting. A failure to hold an annual meeting does not work a forfeiture or dissolution of the corporation. Some statutes provide that if the directors do not call an annual shareholders' meeting within a stipulated period of time, such as 18 months, any stockholder or some stipulated percentage of shareholders may call a meeting. The Model Act specifies that any shareholder may petition a court to order a meeting if none is held for 13 months.

Usually, the most important business at the annual shareholders' meeting is the election of directors. Other matters which may be voted on include amendments to the articles of incorporation, approval of the firm's auditors, approval of a stock-option plan for executives and such resolutions as management or shareholders may propose. It is also customary for one or more members of the top management to give reports with regard to the operation and prospects of the corporation.

Only a few states require that shareholders' meetings be held within the state of incorporation. Some publicly held corporations hold their meetings in their state of incorporation even though few shareholders live nearby, and they are not required to do so. Others seek to encourage shareholder attendance by hiring large halls in convenient locations. A few rotate their meetings between the major cities of the country for the convenience of their shareholders.

Special Meetings.   Special shareholders' meetings may be held whenever corporate matters arise which require shareholders' action. Under the Model Act (28) a special shareholders' meeting may be called by the president, the board of directors or the holders of not less than one tenth of the shares entitled to vote at the meeting. It permits the corporation, in its articles of incorporation or bylaws, to specify that other officers or persons may call a special meeting.

Notice of Meetings.   The Model Act (29) and the statutes of most states set forth the requirements for notice of annual and special meetings of shareholders. The Model Act states that written notice giving the place, day, and hour of the meeting and, for special meetings, the purpose(s) of the meeting must be delivered not less than 10 nor more than 50 days before the date of the meeting to all shareholders entitled to vote at the meeting. For extraordinary changes such as merger, dissolution, or sale or mortgage of assets out of the regular course of business, specific notice of the proposal must be given all shareholders (73, 79, 84). Specific notice must be also given shareholders entitled to vote thereon when a reduction in stated capital (69) is proposed. Those entitled to notice are the shareholders of the class or classes of shares entitled to vote who are "of record," that is, those whose names appear on the stock-transfer book of the corporation. In jurisdictions where the statutes are silent as to notice, notice of a regular meeting is not required if the articles or bylaws specify the place, date, and hour.

If the prescribed notice is not given, any action taken at the meeting is a nullity, unless notice is waived in writing either before or after the meeting (144) or the action taken is later ratified in a properly called meeting. Actual attendance at a meeting, unless merely to object to the transaction of business, constitutes a waiver. Waiver is effective only if all shareholders either attend or waive in writing. Some statutes require written waiver by all shareholders.

Quorum.   In order to be able to conduct business at a meeting, a certain number of shares (a quorum) must be represented in person or by proxy. In the absence of a statute those shares represented, even though a minority, constitute a quorum. However, most statutes define a quorum as the majority of shares outstanding but permit a different requirement to be established in the articles or bylaws. A number of these, including the Model Act (32), establish a minimum of one third of the shares. Delaware establishes no minimum but leaves it to the corporation. Once a quorum is present, a later withdrawal of shareholders will not affect the validity of action taken by those remaining.

Conduct of the Meeting.   The articles or bylaws generally state who shall preside at shareholders' meetings, and this is usually the chairman of the board, if there is such an office, or the president. If there is no such provision, then any shareholder may call the meeting to order and preside while a meeting chairman is elected. In publicly held corporations it is customary to provide inspectors of election whose responsibility it is to determine whether or not a person claiming to be a shareholder is entitled to vote. A few states have statutory provisions dealing with inspectors of election. It is customary and desirable, though not required by statute in most states, to keep minutes of shareholders' meetings, and they are usually recorded and kept by the secretary of the corporation.

Shareholder Proposals and Right to Speak.   Among the rights of shareholders is full participation in shareholders' meetings. This includes the right to offer resolutions,[2] to speak for or against such resolutions as are proposed, and to ask questions of the officers of the corporation. In recent years these rights have been rather systematically pursued by certain shareholders who might be said to fall into two classes. One might be typified by Lewis D. Gilbert, who has made an occupation of attending the shareholder meetings of large corporations and proposing resolutions which are aimed at protecting or enhancing the interests of small shareholders. These proposals include amending the corporate articles to permit cumulative voting for directors, setting ceilings on top-executive pay and limiting charitable contributions by the corporation. More recently, groups seeking social or political changes, such as elimination of the use of napalm in Vietnam, provision of greater opportunities for minority groups, environmental protection, and the elimination of apartheid in South Africa, have introduced or sought to introduce resolutions at shareholders'

---

[2] See Chapter 27 for a discussion of SEC rules on such proposals.

meetings which would limit corporate activity or require publication of certain information. They have also questioned and criticized management in regard to these issues. None of the proposals has drawn more than a few percent of shareholders' votes, and in most cases it appears that calling attention to the issue was the primary motivation of those making them.

Summary

Shareholders generally have few functions. They elect and remove directors and vote on extraordinary corporate transactions such as merger and sale of assets. Under most statutes authority to amend the articles of incorporation is reserved to them.

Annual meetings of shareholders are held at a time specified in the bylaws. All shareholders "of record" of classes entitled to vote are entitled to notice of special meetings and also of regular meetings if the specific time and place is not established in the bylaws.

Most statutes establish a majority of the shares as the quorum for a meeting but permit the number to be established by the corporation as low as one third. Who is to preside at the meeting is usually established by the bylaws.

Shareholders have the right to offer resolutions and to comment and ask questions at shareholders' meetings. Resolutions offered by small shareholders in large corporations generally get few votes.

Darvin v. Belmont Industries, Inc.

199 N.W.2nd 542 (Ct. App. Mich. 1972)

Action by Frank Darvin (plaintiff) for writ of mandamus to set aside actions taken at shareholders' meetings of both Belmont Industries, Inc., and V and F Investment Company (V & F) (defendants). Judgment for Belmont and V & F and Darvin appealed. Reversed and remanded.

Frank Darvin owned 170 out of 700 shares of the stock in Belmont. There were four other shareholders. Underwood, Sychta, and Punturiere each also owned 170 shares and the fifth shareholder owned 20 shares. Underwood, Sychta, Punturiere, and Darvin each owned 3,200 shares out of a total of 12,800 shares outstanding in V and F Investment Company (V & F). The four men comprised the boards of directors of both corporations, and they were officers and employees of both corporations.

A dispute over corporate management arose between Darvin and Underwood, the president. The other three directors concluded they no longer wanted Darvin in the two companies. Accordingly, special shareholders' meetings and boards of directors' meeting of both corporations were scheduled for September 12, 1969. Darvin received notice of the meetings on September 11.

Darvin and his attorney attended the shareholders' meetings of both corporations, and at the beginning of each meeting they objected to the lack of notice. At the meetings the board of directors of each company was reduced to three, and Underwood, Sychta, and Punturiere were elected. The directors then held a meeting and Darvin was eliminated as an officer of each company. He was later terminated as an employee.

The bylaws of each corporation provide that shareholders shall receive notice "at least ten days prior to any meeting." Darvin claims that the actions taken at the shareholders' and directors' meetings are ineffective not only because of the fact he was given notice only one day in advance but also because the Michigan corporation statute requires that the notice give the purpose for a special shareholders' meeting.

LESINSKI, CHIEF JUDGE.   At the outset, we emphasize that this case involves what have traditionally been called "close corporations". . . .

The shareholder in the close corporation faces special problems. If dissatisfied with corporate management, he has no ready market for his shares, as opposed to the shareholder of a corporation the stock of which is publicly traded. He often discovers that the only prospective purchasers of his shares are the very individuals with whom he has disagreed over corporate policy.

*   *   *   *   *

It is in this close-corporation framework, then, that we examine plaintiff Darvin's claims on appeal.

*   *   *   *   *

In relation to notice defects, the bylaws state that "whenever all the shareholders shall meet, in person or by proxy, such meeting shall be valid for all purposes, without call or notice, and at such meeting any corporate action shall not be invalid for want of notice."

*   *   *   *   *

The question that we address, then, is whether plaintiff Darvin's attendance at the meetings, his objections to the lack of notice, and his responses that he did not wish to vote his shares when so asked at the meetings, as testified to by Directors Underwood, Punturiere, and Sychta, constituted a waiver of the notice defects.

A purpose of the time-notice requirement is, of course, to allow a shareholder sufficient time to arrange to attend the meeting. If the shareholder did, in fact, attend the meeting, despite a failure by the corporation to comply with the time-notice requirement, courts have reasoned that he has suffered no harm because he was still able to be present. The purpose-notice requirement serves another function, however. It provides a shareholder with sufficient opportunity to study contemplated action at the meeting and the legality thereof. When the shareholder possesses knowledge of the purpose of a special meeting, he can study the proposal, arrive at a position, and either oppose it or support it. One commentator has even suggested that notice be given of any extraordinary matter that is to be considered at a regular meeting:

> With such notice, the shareholder has the opportunity to think upon, and discuss with other shareholders, the matter and be prepared to vote intelligently upon it. Lattin on *Corporations.*

We find the language of two Michigan Supreme Court cases, although they concern the problem of notice at directors' meetings and not shareholders' meetings, to be relevant to the issue which confronts us here. In *Zachary v. Millin* . . . the Court held that the members of the board not only had to be present, but also had to participate, before a defect in notice would be deemed waived.

The case of *Bourne v. Muskegon Circuit Judge* concerned a purpose-notice requirement at a directors' meeting. Notice of the special directors' meeting was sent out with several purposes enumerated, but no mention was made of the fact that dissolution or receivership proceedings were contemplated by the corporation. The Court held that such omission was fatal to the validity of the notice and pointed out that the situation "was not a dire emergency requiring individual action." That notice of a special shareholders' meeting must include the purpose of the proceeding has long been the law in Michigan. . . .

Courts in other jurisdictions have ruled specifically on the issue at hand, holding that attendance at a meeting, without participation, does not constitute waiver of defective notice.

* * * * *

Although the notice given to plaintiff Darvin in the instant case was sufficient to obtain his physical presence at the meeting, it is plain that it was not sufficient to allow him to ascertain what action was to be taken at the special meeting of defendant corporations, and to determine what steps could be taken to protect his position. The weight of the evidence at trial, although it was contradicted, revealed that Darvin had not voted his shares at the meeting. He specifically refused the opportunity to do so. If he had voted his shares he could have made use of the protection afforded him by M.C.L.A. § 450.–13(3); M.S.A. § 21.13(3) [relative to cumulative voting], which governs reduction of members of the board of directors in this State. With sufficient notice, plaintiff Darvin and his attorney could have had the opportunity to apprise themselves of the existence of this provision which has been recognized as supplying special protection to the minority shareholder in the close corporation.

Accordingly, we hold that plaintiff Darvin's mere attendance at the meeting coupled with the nonvoting of his shares was not sufficient participation to waive the notice requirement under the facts of this case.

Voting Rights

Shareholders Entitled to Vote.   Whether a shareholder is entitled to vote at a shareholders' meeting depends upon statutory provisions and the articles and bylaws of the corporation. The Model Act (15, 33) permits the issuance of a class or classes of nonvoting stock if so provided in the articles. However, such nonvoting classes are entitled to vote on extraordinary corporate transactions (60, 73, 74, 84). The person who has legal title to the stock is the one generally entitled to vote, but it is common in publicly held corporations for the directors to establish a "record date." Those entitled to vote will be those appearing on a voting list prepared as of that date or the directors may close the transfer books for a period of from 10 to 50 days prior to a meeting. A title owner who is not the owner of record may obtain a proxy from the record holder. The Model Act (30) also provides that if none is established, the record date shall be the date of mailing of notice of the meeting.

A corporation may not vote its treasury shares (those once issued and then reacquired) if any, and, of course, unissued stock has no vote. Shares held by a subsidiary in a parent corporation may not be voted since the effect would be the same as the vote of the treasury shares, and this device could be used to perpetuate management. The Model Act (33), following a rule adopted by the courts, so provides.

The fact that a shareholder has a personal interest in the matter being voted will not disqualify him or her from voting or affect the validity of the action taken, since ordinarily shareholders have no fiduciary duty to the corporation. However, controlling shareholders will not be permitted to manipulate the corporate affairs in fraud of the rights of the other shareholders.

Cumulative Voting.   Although most corporations conduct the election of directors on the basis that each share is entitled to one vote for each vacancy, many corporations give shareholders the option to cumulate their votes by giving one candidate as many votes as the number of directors to be elected multiplied by his number of shares. The option to cumulate votes is given to all shareholders by constitutional provisions or statute in almost half of the states. Most of the rest of them permit corporations to provide for cumulative voting in their articles. A few statutes are silent, in which case some courts have permitted cumulative voting if so provided in articles or bylaws. The Model Act (33) offers mandatory and permissive cumulative voting as alternative provisions.

The purpose of cumulative voting is to give minority shareholders an opportunity to be represented on the board of directors. Whether this is desirable is a highly controversial issue. Its opponents argue that unity and stability of management will increase the likelihood of success of the corporation. Few large publicly held corporations are domiciled in states with mandatory cumulative voting, and promoters tend to avoid incorporation in these states.

The formula for determining the minimum number of shares required to elect one director under cumulative voting is:

$$X = \frac{S}{D+1} + 1$$

where S is the number of shares voting and D is the total number of directors to be elected. Obviously, the fewer the number of directors to be elected the larger the minority interest must be to enable a shareholder to elect a director. One device for reducing the effect of cumulative voting is to provide for electing directors by classes, each class to remain in office for three years, the maximum permitted by the Model Act (37).

Proxy Voting.   All state statutes permit shareholders to appoint an agent, known as a proxy, to vote for them. The Model Act (33) requires that the authority to vote as a proxy must be given in writing, but some states permit oral proxies. Both the writing and the person designated to vote for the shareholder are called a proxy. Usually proxies are general, permitting the agent to vote on all matters properly coming before a shareholders' meeting, but they may be limited to a particular matter. Most states put a limit on the duration of a proxy. The Model Act limits it to 11 months from the date of execution unless the writing itself provides otherwise. Generally, proxies are revocable at any time by the shareholder. Exceptions are those "coupled with an interest," such as where the proxy is given to a pledgee of the shares or to a purchaser of the shares under an executory contract. Otherwise, irrevocability is considered against public policy. A proxy is automatically revoked when another proxy is given subsequently. The Securities and Exchange Commission is given rule-making power over solicitation of proxies by the Securities Exchange Act of 1934.

Voting Trust.   The Model Act (34) and most state statutes permit shareholders to establish voting trusts. The purpose of a voting trust is to concentrate shareholder power in one or a few persons who can control the corporation through the election of directors. One frequent use of the device is to give control of the corporation to creditors during corporate reorganization after bankruptcy.[3] Although courts earlier tended to hold voting trusts illegal as against public policy, the modern cases tend to uphold them even in the absence of statute unless the purpose for which the voting trust is formed is illegal, such as to gain a monopoly as in the case of the Standard Oil trust and others near the end of the 19th century, or to defraud minority shareholders.

The Model Act (34) and a number of state statutes require that a voting trust be established by an agreement in writing among the participating shareholders and that it be filed with the corporation. They also establish a maximum life, usually ten years, for the agreement. It is common for voting trust certificates to be given the shareholder in exchange for his or her shares in the corporation and they entitle the holder to a ratable share of dividends and distributions paid by the corporation.

Summary

The voting rights of the shareholder are based on the statutes of the state of incorporation and on the articles and bylaws of the corporation. Nonvoting classes of stock are entitled to vote on certain extraordinary corporate transac-

---

[3] The most notable recent voting trust was established in 1960 at the insistence of Trans World Airlines' creditors to vote the 78 percent of TWA shares owned by Hughes Tool Co.

tions. Shareholders listed on the books of the company on the record date are those who are entitled to vote.

A corporation cannot vote unissued or treasury stock. The personal interest of a shareholder in a matter being voted on does not disqualify him.

Many states require corporations formed under their statutes to grant cumulative voting and most of the rest permit this system of voting, which is designed to give representation to minority shareholders, if provided for in the articles. Proxy voting is generally permitted and the SEC has rule-making power over the solicitation of proxies. Voting trusts are permitted if they have a legitimate purpose and a reasonable length of life.

Levin v. Metro-Goldwyn-Mayer, Inc.

264 F.Supp. 797 (S.D. N.Y. 1967)

This was an action by Levin and other shareholders (plaintiffs) against Metro-Goldwyn-Mayer, Inc., and certain of its directors (defendants) seeking to enjoin methods used by management is soliciting proxies. Injunction denied.

Levin, a director of MGM, and his associates in this action owned 11 percent of the outstanding shares of MGM and were seeking to gain control of the corporation through a proxy contest. They charged the MGM management with wrongfully committing the corporation to pay for the services of attorneys, a public relations firm, and a proxy soliciting organization to secure support from shareholders for the current management. They further claimed that the use of MGM employees and business contacts was improper. No charge was made that any false or fraudulent statements had been made by the management group in connection with proxy solicitation.

RYAN, DISTRICT JUDGE.   It is quite plain that the differences between "the O'Brien [management] group" and "the Levin group" are much more than mere personality conflicts. These might readily be resolved by reasoning and hard-headed, profit-minded businessmen. There are definite business policies advocated by each group, so divergent that reconciliation does not seem possible. They appear so evident from the papers before us that detailed analysis would be a waste of time. However, in such a situation the right of an independent stockholder to be fully informed is of supreme importance. The controlling question presented on this application is whether illegal or unfair means of communication, such as demand judicial intervention, are being employed by the present management. We find that they are not and conclude that the injunctive relief now sought should be denied.

. . . Contrary to the shareholders' unsupported statement that 9,000 MGM employees are at work soliciting proxies, MGM has stated that the total number of employees who on their own time have consented to telephone shareholders to vote is less than 150. We do not find this an unreasonable situation under the circumstances. . . .

The employment of two proxy solicitation firms and the fees agreed to be paid to them were fully disclosed in the MGM proxy statement. Georgeson & Co. is in charge of solicitation of proxies from stockholders directly; the Kissel-Blake Organization is directing its efforts to brokerage solicitation. Here again, MGM states without contradiction that "in every year since 1956, MGM has employed the firms of Georgeson & Co. and the Kissel-Blake Organization, Inc., to solicit proxies for its stockholders' meetings." We do not find basis for injunctive relief in their employment, nor in the employment of Dudley King & Co., as a consultant in connection with corporate matters and stockholder relations. . . .

There have been set forth in paid advertisements statements by actors, directors, writers, and exhibitors supporting and expressing confidence in the present management. MGM states these expressions have been unsolicited and spontaneous and have been published by these persons [and] . . . paid for completely out of their own pockets without any direct or indirect promise of repayment by MGM. There is no proof to challenge this. Certainly, MGM should not be expected to deny or contradict what they regard as well-deserved compliments graciously paid to them. Nor do we find the publication of such unsolicited individual advertisements a violation of the Act of 1934.

. . . MGM engaged the services of Thomas J. Deegan Co., Inc. Deegan is a recognized and reputable public relations firm. The engagement was long before the present proxy contest. The employment is neither unusual nor unreasonable. It does not afford ground for injunctive relief.

Dividends

Introduction. The law assumes that the purpose of a business corporation is to make a profit. Shareholders usually invest in a corporation primarily to share in the expected profit through dividends, although it is not unusual for corporations to retain all earnings over long periods of time and to reinvest them in the business. Such a policy may be attractive to shareholders in the higher income tax brackets if the result is rapid appreciation of the market value of their shares. Retention of earnings in close corporations may permit capital gains treatment if liquidation or sale is anticipated, but this is vulnerable to a heavy penalty under the tax laws. Dividends must be paid ratably on the shares of any class.

Types of Dividends. Dividends are usually paid in cash but assets of the corporation, such as shares in another corporation, may be distributed as a dividend. Such dividends are referred to as "property dividends" or "dividends-in-kind." Distribution of assets, including cash, which amount to a partial liquidation are not included within the meaning of the term dividend as used in the Model Act. "Stock dividends" are distributions of shares in the corporation itself and are of a different nature than the other two types of dividends and will be discussed separately. An "extra dividend" is not a special kind of dividend but is usually so designated by the directors to indicate that it is given in addition to what they consider to be the normal or regular dividend that they expect to be able to maintain.

Funds Available for Dividends.   The corporation statutes of all states specify the sources from which dividends may be paid. The common law rule was that payment of a dividend was illegal if it resulted in the impairment of the capital of the corporation. The ingenuity of corporate promoters and managers in designing various types of shares and methods of establishing their value has made it difficult for the courts and legislatures to accomplish their objective of maintaining the original capital of the corporation as a "trust fund" for the protection of creditors and to help assure stockholders that the corporation may be able to carry out its purposes.

Tests of Validity of Dividend Payments.   There are three principal tests of the validity of dividend payments. They are: (1) the noninsolvency test, (2) the surplus test, based upon the balance sheet, and (3) the current earnings test, based upon the income statement. Some statutes include more than one. For example, the Model Act (45) forbids a dividend which would render a corporation insolvent, that is unable to pay its debts as they fall due as well as limiting dividends to "earned surplus" (although it has an alternative provision which would permit dividends out of unreserved and unrestricted net earnings of the current and next preceding fiscal years). A dividend which would make the corporation insolvent is probably illegal as an invasion of creditors' rights without a statutory provision.

Earned surplus is available for dividends in all states. A number of states permit the use of surplus arising from other sources, a few limiting such dividend payments to preferred shareholders.

The surplus test would permit dividends so long as there is a surplus, even if there are no earnings during the current year. A corporation has a surplus when its assets exceed its liabilities plus its stated capital. A surplus may arise from several kinds of corporate transactions. "Earned surplus" arises from net profits made in the operation of the business. "Paid-in surplus" arises out of the difference between the par value (or stated value in case of no-par shares) and the price the corporation receives when it sells the shares to investors. "Revaluation surplus" is created by an upward revaluation of assets of the corporation. "Reduction surplus" is created by reducing stated capital.

The Model Act (45a) limits dividends to "earned surplus," and it is available for dividends in all states. However, some states allow dividends to be paid from either earned or paid-in surplus and a few permit payment from any kind of surplus.

Some states permit the payment of a dividend out of current net profits regardless of a negative surplus. This is referred to as the "nimble dividend" rule because the dividend must be declared before such net profits are closed to the surplus account, that is charged against the accumulated deficit. A few statutes specifically forbid payment out of unrealized appreciation or require assets to be reduced by unrealized depreciation in computing the source of dividends.

Directors' Discretion in Payment of Dividends. Declaration of dividends is the responsibility of the directors under the Model Act and most statutes, although under some statutes the shareholders may retain this power by an appropriate provision in the articles. Declaration of dividends is discretionary and within the business judgment of the directors. This discretion applies even to shares with a dividend preference, although a clearly worded provision in the articles may make the payment of a dividend mandatory if one can legally be paid. However, dividends are not gratuities handed out to shareholders by a benevolent board of directors; they are the expected returns on capital investment. Although the burden of proof is on the complaining shareholder and courts are hesitant to substitute their judgment for that of the directors, shareholders have occasionally been able to get a court to decree the payment of a dividend when the directors have refused to do so through a flagrant abuse of their discretion.

The federal government imposes heavy punitive taxes upon improper accumulation of corporate earnings, which also limits the discretion of directors. On the other hand, it is very common for lenders to prohibit the payment of dividends or to limit them to funds defined more narrowly than the legal prohibitions.

Dividend Payment on Preferred Stock. The preferred shareholder's right to dividends is based upon his or her shareholder contract, subject to the availability of funds from which dividends can be paid. Considerable confusion exists as to the dividend rights of preferred shareholders under varying conditions, and great care in drafting the contract is essential. Unless the contract is interpreted as making the declaration of a dividend upon a preferred class of shares mandatory, the directors may refuse to declare and pay a dividend even though funds are available from which a dividend could legally be paid if, in their honest judgment, the payment of the dividend would be detrimental to the corporation.

Four types of contractual provisions are found in preferred stock: (1) a mandatory dividend preference entitles the holder to the contractual dividend if payment is legally permissible, leaving no discretion to the directors (such contracts are very rare; in case of ambiguity courts avoid interpreting preferences as mandatory, and at least one court has held such a contract unenforceable[4]); (2) a cumulative dividend preference entitles the shareholder to unpaid dividends for all prior periods before any dividend or distribution may be paid

---

[4] *Lindgrove v. Schulter & Co.*, 176 N.E. 832 (Ct. App. N.Y. 1931).

upon shares which are subordinate with respect to dividend rights; (3) a cumulative-to-the-extent-earned preference entitles the shareholder to unpaid dividends for all prior periods in which there were funds legally available for such dividends before subordinate shareholders may receive dividends or distributions; (4) a noncumulative preference only gives the shareholder the right to dividends in a fiscal period before dividends or distributions are paid to other shareholders.

There is a divergence of authority as to whether the preference on noncumulative shares extends beyond the current fiscal year. Most jurisdictions hold that even though earnings are legally sufficient for a dividend on the preferred shares, directors may retain them for reinvestment in the business. New Jersey, on the other hand, applies the "dividend credit theory" which holds that preferred shareholders have an equity in such reinvested funds. The effect is to treat noncumulative shares as if they were cumulative-to-the-extent-earned. Under the majority rule, directors retaining earnings for a number of years without paying dividends to preferred shareholders may, nevertheless, be subject to a court finding that they have abused their discretion and be ordered to declare dividends.

Whether holders of cumulative preferred shares are entitled to the arrearages in case of liquidation of the corporation depends upon the interpretation of the shareholders' contract. Most courts hold that arrearages must be paid upon liquidation, if assets are sufficient, even though there were insufficient earnings to pay them when due.

Stock Dividends and Stock Splits.   A stock dividend is a distribution to shareholders of additional shares in the corporation and is, in effect, a capitalization of surplus. The shares distributed may be either of the same class as those held or of a different class or series. Under the Model Act (45e) no dividend payable in shares shall be paid to holders of shares of any other class unless the articles of incorporation so provide or such payment is authorized by a majority of the outstanding shares of the class in which payment is to be made. This limitation, of course, is for the protection of the holders of the class of shares being distributed, since such a distribution would dilute their shares. A dividend payable in the same class of shares has no effect on the equity of the shareholders since their interest in the corporation remains proportionately the same. Nevertheless, the total market value of the shareholder's interest frequently increases and shareholders seem to value the additional piece of paper. If the dividend rate remains the same on a per share basis, of course, the effect will be to increase the dividend received by the shareholder.

The difference between a stock dividend and a stock split is that in the former case the par or stated value of the shares distributed must be transferred from the surplus to the capital account (unless treasury shares are distributed) while in the case of a stock split there is no change in the total capital account but only in the par value or stated value of the shares. Payment of a stock dividend in the same class of shares requires only director approval while approval of shareholders is required for the amendment of the articles of incorporation necessary to make a stock split (58i, 60f). A reverse stock split is a decrease in the number of shares of a class such that, for example, two shares become one share. The most common purpose of a stock split is to adjust the market price to fall within the popular $20 to $40 range. It may also mask rapid changes in earnings per share.

Distributions. The Model Act (46) distinguishes a dividend from what it designates as a distribution from capital surplus. Such distribution may be made from capital surplus as distinguished from earned surplus. However, distribution may not be made when the corporation is insolvent, and unless the articles provide for such a distribution, a majority of the shares of each class of shares, whether regularly entitled to voting rights or not, must vote in favor of the distribution. If it is a distribution from capital surplus, that fact must be disclosed to the shareholders when it is received. Other limitations include a provision that no distribution may be made when cumulative dividends have accrued or when the remaining net assets of the corporation would be insufficient to pay off preferential shares in a voluntary liquidation.

In addition, this section of the Model Act permits, without a shareholder vote or authorization in the articles, distributions from capital surplus to discharge cumulative dividend rights of preferred shareholders so long as insolvency is avoided.

Dividend Declaration. A dividend is declared by formal action of the board of directors. Once declared, a lawful cash dividend becomes a debt owing to the shareholders, although a Massachusetts case has held that the directors may rescind their action prior to the time the declaration has become known to shareholders.[5] Thereafter, should the corporation become insolvent, the shareholders may share in the assets with other creditors to the extent of the dividend. However, stock dividend declarations, since they do not actually change the shareholders' interest in the corporation, are held to be revocable. Dividends other than stock dividends may be paid in cash or property of the corporation, such as stock in another corporation.

Effect of Transfer on Right to Dividend. As between the corporation and the shareholder, the corporation may treat the shareholder of record as the person entitled to receive the dividend. As between the transferor and transferee, the right to the dividend will depend on the agreement between the parties. In the absence of agreement the transferor is entitled to the dividend if the sale was made after the record date. If the sale is made on a stock exchange, the transferee is entitled to the dividends unless he or she buys the

---

[5] *Ford v. Easthampton Rubber Thread Co.,* 32 N.E. 1036 (Mass. 1893); cf. *Brown v. Luce Mfg. Co.,* 96 S.W.2d 1098 (K.C. Ct. App. Mo. 1936).

stock after it is declared "ex dividend," which is five business days before the record date for the dividend.

Summary

Shareholders usually expect to share in the profits of a corporation through dividends. These are normally paid in cash but may be paid in property, such as shares in another corporation. A distinction is drawn between a distribution in partial liquidation and a dividend.

Corporation statutes usually specify the sources from which dividends may be paid. Earned surplus is available for dividends in all states but a dividend may not be paid if the result would be to make the corporation insolvent. Three principal tests of the validity of dividends are used: (1) the noninsolvency test, (2) the surplus test, and (3) the current earning test.

Declaration of dividends is the responsibility of the directors and is subject to their business judgment even with respect to shares with a dividend preference, except in the rare case of a mandatory dividend. Three other types of dividend preferences are: cumulative, cumulative-to-the-extent-earned, and noncumulative. Most courts hold that arrearages on cumulative shares must be paid upon liquidation of the corporation, if assets are sufficient, even though earnings were insufficient at the time the dividends were due.

A stock dividend is a distribution of additional shares in the corporation and is, in effect, a capitalization of surplus. A stock split does not change the total capital account but only the par or stated value of the shares.

Under the Model Act a distribution is distinguished from a dividend and may be made from capital surplus while a dividend must be charged against earned surplus. Distributions may be used to discharge cumulative dividend rights.

Once declared a cash dividend becomes a debt but a stock dividend declaration may be rescinded.

The corporation may treat the stockholder of record as entitled to the dividend. In the absence of an agreement the transferee of shares bought on a stock exchange is entitled to the dividend unless he buys after it is declared "ex dividend."

Dodge v. Ford Motor Co.

170 N.W. 668 (Sup. Ct. Mich. 1919)

This was an action by John F. Dodge and Horace E. Dodge (plaintiffs) against Ford Motor Company and others (defendants) to force the directors of Ford Motor Company to pay a special dividend. Judgment for Dodge, and Ford Motor Company appealed. Judgment affirmed in part and reversed in part.

Dodge *et al.* were stockholders in the Ford Motor Company. From the beginning in 1903 to July 31, 1916, the corporate business had been profitable. The capital stock had been increased from $150,000 in 1903 to $2,000,000 in 1908. A regular dividend of 5 percent per month on its capital stock of $2,000,000 had been paid since 1911, and in addition thereto special dividends had been paid which ranged from $1,000,000 to $10,000,000 per year and which totaled $41,000,000 for the years 1911 to 1915 inclusive. In 1916 the directors decided to continue to pay the regular dividend of 5 percent per month on the corporation's capital stock of $2,000,000 but to discontinue all special dividends. At this time the corporation had a surplus of $112,000,000; its yearly profits were $60,000,000; its total liabilities including capital stock were less than $20,000,000; it had cash on hand of $54,000,000; and all planned improvements would cost approximately $24,000,000. This action was brought to force the directors to pay a special dividend.

OSTRANDER, CHIEF JUSTICE.   The rule which will govern courts in deciding these questions is not in dispute. It is, of course, differently phrased by judges and by authors; and, as the phrasing in a particular instance may seem to lean for or against the exercise of the right of judicial interference with the actions of corporate directors, the context, or the facts before the court, must be considered. This court, in *Hunter v. Roberts, Throp & Co.,* recognized the rule in the following language:

It is a well-recognized principle of law that the directors of a corporation, and they alone, have the power to declare a dividend of the earnings of the corporation, and to determine its amount. Courts of equity will not interfere in the management of the directors unless it is clearly made to appear that they are guilty of fraud or misappropriation of the corporate funds, or refuse to declare a dividend when the corporation has a surplus of net profits which it can, without detriment to the business, divide among its stockholders, and when a refusal to do so would amount to such an abuse of discretion as would constitute a fraud, or breach of that good faith which they are bound to exercise towards the stockholders.

The record, and especially the testimony of Mr. Ford, convinces that he has to some extent the attitude towards shareholders of one who has dispensed and distributed to them large gains and that they should be content to take what he chooses to give. His testimony creates the impression, also, that he thinks the Ford Motor Company has made too much money, has had too large profits, and that, although large profits might be still earned, a sharing of them with the public, by reducing the price of the output of the company, ought to be undertaken. We have no doubt that certain sentiments, philanthropic and altruistic, creditable to Mr. Ford, had large influence in determining the policy to be pursued by the Ford Motor Company—the policy which has been herein referred to.

In discussing this proposition, counsel have referred to decisions such as *Hawes v. Oakland, Taunton v. Royal Ins. Co., Henderson v. Bank of Australia, Steinway v. Steinway & Sons, People v. Hotchkiss.* These cases, after all, like all others in which the subject is treated, turn finally upon the point, the question whether it appears that the directors were not acting for the best interests of the corporation. We do not draw in question, nor do counsel for the Dodges do so, the validity of the general proposition stated by counsel nor the soundness of the opinions delivered in the cases cited. The case presented here is not like any of them. The difference between an incidental humanitarian expenditure of corporate funds for the benefit of the employees, like the building of a hospital for their use and the employment of agencies for the betterment of their condition, and a general purpose and plan to benefit mankind at the expense of others, is obvious. There should be no confusion (of which there is evidence) of the duties which Mr. Ford conceives that he and the stockholders owe to the general public and the duties which in law he and his co-directors owe to protesting, minority stockholders. A business corporation is organized and carried on primarily for the profit of the stockholders. The powers of the directors are to be employed for that end. The discretion of directors is to be exercised, in the choice of means to attain that end and does not extend to a change in the end itself, to the reduction of profits or to the nondistribution of profits among stockholders in order to devote them to other purposes.

There is committed to the discretion of directors, a discretion to be exercised in good faith, the infinite details of business, including the wages which shall be paid to employees, the numbers of hours they shall work, the conditions under which labor shall be carried on, and the price for which products shall be offered to the public.

It is said by Ford Motor Company that the motives of the board members are not material and will not be inquired into by the court so long as their acts are within their lawful powers. As we have pointed out, and the proposition does not require argument to sustain it, it is not within the lawful powers of a board of directors to shape and conduct the affairs of a corporation for the merely incidental benefit of shareholders and for the primary purpose of benefiting others, and no one will contend that, if the avowed purpose of the directors was to sacrifice the interests of shareholders, it would not be the duty of the courts to interfere.

The directors of Ford Motor Company say, and it is true, that a considerable cash balance must be at all times carried by such a concern. But, as has been stated, there was a large daily, weekly, monthly receipt of cash. The output was practically continuous and was continuously, and within a few days, turned into cash. Moreover, the contemplated expenditures were not to be immediately made. The large sum appropriated for the smelter plant was payable over a considerable period of time. So that, without going further, it would appear that, accepting and approving the plan of the directors, it was their duty to distribute on or near the 1st of August, 1916, a very large sum of money to stockholders.

Inspection of Books and Records

Common Law Right to Inspect.   Disputes are frequent between corporations and shareholders who seek to examine records of the corporation. These may arise when a challenge to management through a proxy campaign is suspected, when management fears a use of the information which may be harmful to the corporation or sometimes just because of a general desire for secrecy.

At common law, shareholders have the right to inspect corporate books and records, including shareholders' lists, books of account, minute books, and the properties of the corporation, so long as it is exercised for a proper purpose. However, even if his or her purpose were proper, the shareholder might suffer much delay and find it very expensive to obtain a remedy, which is usually a writ of mandamus.

The line between proper and improper purposes is not always clear, and in the earlier cases the courts put the heavy burden of proving a proper purpose upon the shareholder. Requests to inspect the books of account to determine the value of shares or the propriety of dividends and to inspect the stock ledger to identify fellow shareholders in order to communicate with them concerning corporate affairs—including an effort to replace management—are clearly proper purposes. On the other hand, to learn business secrets, to aid a competitor, to get the names of shareholders for a "sucker list," or to obtain prospects for a personal business would clearly be improper purposes. Bare ownership of stock in a competing corporation would not, in itself, however, be sufficient grounds for denying access to the records. Mere curiosity or even a desire to be informed about corporate affairs has been held an insufficient purpose, especially where other means of gaining information, such as attendance at shareholders' meetings, have not been fully utilized.

Statutory Inspection Rights.   Statutes giving inspection rights usually aim to make it more difficult for a corporation to resist or delay proper requests by shareholders. Some give shareholders an absolute right of inspection, particularly with respect to the stock ledger or shareholder list.

The Model Act (31) gives an absolute right of inspection of a complete record of shareholders entitled to vote at a meeting and their shareholdings. This must be made available at the meeting. The act (52) also provides that the corporation's books of account, minutes of shareholders' and directors' meetings, and a shareholder list must be kept available at its registered office. Upon a written demand stating his or her purpose, any shareholder of record for the preceding six months or who holds five percent of the outstanding shares may examine these records which are relevant for any proper purpose. Any official who denies a proper demand may be liable for a penalty of ten percent of the value of the stockholder's shares plus damages unless the requesting shareholder has made an improper use of information gained from a similar request within the past two years.

In addition, the act specifically recognizes the power of a court, upon proof of a proper purpose, to grant inspection rights without regard to the length of time the petitioner has been a shareholder. It also provides that upon written request the corporation must mail to a shareholder its most recent financial statements showing in reasonable detail its assets and liabilities and the results of its operations.

Delaware requires that the shareholder list be available for ten days before the shareholders' meeting. It gives shareholders the right of inspection of corporate records without regard to the size of their holdings or the holding time. In the case of a demand to inspect the list of shareholders, it puts the burden of proof that the purpose is not proper on the company.

Summary

At common law shareholders have the right to inspect corporate books and records and the properties of the corporation so long as it is for a proper purpose. Statutes usually seek to make it more difficult for a corporation to resist or delay proper requests by shareholders and often give an absolute right to inspect the voting list of shareholders. The Model Act imposes penalties in addition to provable damages on corporate officers or agents who refuse proper requests.

State ex rel. Pillsbury v. Honeywell, Inc.

191 N.W.2d 406 (Sup. Ct. Minn. 1971)

Mandamus action on behalf of Charles Pillsbury (petitioner) to compel Honeywell, Inc., (respondent) to produce its original shareholder ledger, current shareholder ledger and all corporate records dealing with weapons and munitions manufacture. Relief denied and Pillsbury appealed. Affirmed.

Pillsbury attended a meeting on July 3, 1969, of a group opposed to American involvement in Vietnam who believed that a substantial part of Honeywell production consisted of munitions used in that war. Pillsbury had long opposed the Vietnam involvement, but it was at this meeting that he first learned of Honeywell's production of antipersonnel fragmentation bombs. He was upset to learn that such bombs were produced in his own community by a company he had known and respected. On July 14 he purchased 100 shares of Honeywell stock for the sole purpose of gaining a voice to persuade Honeywell to cease producing munitions. Later he learned that he was beneficiary of a trust with an interest in 242 shares of Honeywell.

He then made two formal demands on the corporation for shareholder records and all corporate records dealing with weapon and munitions manufacture. Honeywell refused and this petition resulted.

KELLY, JUSTICE. The trial court ordered judgment for Honeywell, ruling that Pillsbury had not demonstrated a proper purpose germane to his interest as a stockholder. Pillsbury contends that a stockholder who disagrees with management has an absolute right to inspect corporate records for purposes of soliciting proxies. He would have this court rule that such solicitation is per se a "proper purpose." Honeywell argues that a "proper purpose" contemplates concern with investment return. We agree with Honeywell.

* * * * *

. . . But for his opposition to Honeywell's policy, Pillsbury probably would not have bought Honeywell stock, would not be interested in Honeywell's profits, and would not desire to communicate with Honeywell's shareholders. His avowed purpose in buying Honeywell stock was to place himself in a position to try to impress his opinions favoring a reordering of priorities upon Honeywell management and its other shareholders. Such a motivation can hardly be deemed a proper purpose germane to his economic interest as a shareholder.

The fact that Pillsbury alleged a proper purpose in his petition will not necessarily compel a right to inspection. . . . Neither is inspection mandated by the recitation of proper purpose in his testimony. Conversely, a company cannot defeat inspection by merely alleging an improper purpose. From the deposition, the trial court concluded that Pillsbury had already formed strong opinions on the immorality and the social and economic wastefulness of war long before he bought stock in Honeywell. His sole motivation was to change Honeywell's course of business because that course was incompatible with his political views. If unsuccessful, Pillsbury indicated that he would sell the Honeywell stock.

We do not mean to imply that a shareholder with a bona fide investment interest could not bring this suit if motivated by concern with the long- or short-term economic effects on Honeywell resulting from the production of war munitions. Similarly, this suit might be appropriate when a shareholder has a bona fide concern about the adverse effects of abstention from profitable war contracts on his investment in Honeywell.

In the instant case, however, the trial court, in effect, has found from all the facts that Pillsbury was not interested in even the long-term well-being of Honeywell or the enhancement of the value of his shares. His sole purpose was to persuade the company to adopt his social and political concerns, irrespective of any economic benefit to himself or Honeywell. This purpose on the part of one buying into the corporation does not entitle Pillsbury to inspect Honeywell's books and records.

Pillsbury argues that he wishes to inspect the stockholder ledger in order that he may correspond with other shareholders with the hope of electing to the board one or more directors who represent his particular viewpoint. . . .

While a plan to elect one or more directors is specific and the election of directors normally would be a proper purpose, here the purpose was not germane to Pillsbury's or Honeywell's economic interest. Instead, the plan was designed to further his political and social beliefs. Since the requisite propriety of purpose germane to his or Honeywell's economic interest is not present, the allegation that Pillsbury seeks to elect a new board of directors is insufficient to compel inspection.

Preemptive Rights

General. The shareholders' proportionate interests with respect to dividends, control, and assets are adversely affected by the nonproportionate issue of additional shares. A sale of additional shares at a price lower than book value would reduce the book value of existing shares and even a sale above book value may not necessarily result in earnings per share equal to the rate previously enjoyed. If there is but one class of shares these problems can be minimized if existing shareholders are given an opportunity to add proportionately to their holdings whenever new shares are to be sold by the corporation. The preemptive rights doctrine was evolved by the courts to accomplish this purpose, and many of the corporation statutes have codified the principal. Briefly stated, the doctrine gives the shareholder an option of subscribing to a new allotment of shares, in proportion to his or her holding of outstanding shares, before the newly alloted shares are offered to the public.

Application of Preemptive Rights. Generally, courts have held that preemptive rights do not apply to treasury shares, shares issued in connection with a merger or consolidation or issued for a noncash consideration. There is a conflict of authority with respect to shares which are unissued but which were authorized when the corporation was chartered. The rationale of courts holding that preemptive rights do not apply is that there was an implied agreement with original subscribers that these shares would be sold to raise capital for the business. If the sale of these shares is long postponed, the rationale breaks down and they are probably subject to preemptive rights. A common device used to give effect to preemptive rights is the issuance of short-term warrants or stock rights which entitle the holder to purchase a specified number of shares at a price fixed somewhat below the anticipated market price. The warrants are transferable and permit the shareholder to sell them if he or she does not wish to purchase the additional shares.

Preemptive Rights under the Model Act. The Model Act (26) contains alternative provisions permitting a legislature to choose the provisions which are consistent with its policy. One alternative recognizes no preemptive rights except to the extent provided in the articles of incorporation. The other gives preemptive rights but permits a corporation to limit or deny them in its articles. The latter alternative exempts from preemptive rights shares sold to officers and employees under terms which have been approved by shareholders (for example, a stock-option plan) and shares sold otherwise than for cash. Certain other shares are also excluded. Even when shareholders are not entitled to preemptive rights courts will grant relief necessary to hold directors and majority shareholders to a high standard of reasonableness and fairness in issuing new shares. They will not be permitted to issue additional shares to themselves or to some favored group in order to gain an advantage over other shareholders.

Summary

A shareholder's preemptive right is the option of subscribing to a new allotment of shares, in proportion to his or her holding of outstanding shares. Preemptive rights have generally been held not to apply to treasury shares,

shares issued in connection with a merger or issued for a noncash consideration. There is a conflict of authority with respect to shares which are unissued but which were authorized when the corporation was chartered.

Many statutes permit a corporation to avoid preemptive rights.

Extraordinary Corporate Transactions

Introduction. At common law the corporate charter was considered as a contract between the state and the corporation, between the corporation and the shareholders and among the shareholders, and it could not be changed without the consent of all the parties, including unanimous consent of the shareholders. Modern corporation statutes [Model Act (149)] reserve the right to the legislature to change the statutes and regulations, thus changing the corporate charter, and to permit the corporation itself to change its articles and to make substantial changes in the nature of its business and the rights of its shareholders with approval of less than all of the shareholders. Thus the "vested rights" doctrine no longer is a bar to extraordinary corporate transactions, including amendment of articles, merger and consolidation, sale or mortgage of assets, and dissolution.

Procedure for Amending Articles. To amend the articles of incorporation, the procedure set out by the statutes of the state of incorporation must be complied with. The Model Act (59, 60) requires that a written notice setting forth the proposed amendment or a summary of the changes to be affected by it must be given to all shareholders entitled to vote and that the amendment be approved by a majority of the shares. The act (60) further provides that the holders are entitled to vote as a class on certain amendments which would affect the value or rights of any class of shares. Such changes include changing the number of authorized shares of the class, changing the par value of those shares, changing the preferences or rights of the shares of the class, changing the shares into the different number of shares or a different class, creating a new class with preferences superior to an existing class, limiting or denying existing preemptive rights or canceled accrued dividends of that class of shares. Such amendments, however, require only a majority vote under the act unless greater voting requirements are established in the articles (143).

Other Extraordinary Transactions. The statute of the state of incorporation must also be complied with in other extraordinary corporate transactions. The Model Act establishes similar procedures to effect a merger or consolidation (71–73), a sale of substantially all of the assets other than in the regular course of business (79), or a voluntary dissolution of the corporation (84). The procedure includes approval of the board of directors, notice to all shareholders whether or not entitled to vote, and a majority vote of shareholders entitled under the articles or bylaws to vote on the proposal. A higher percentage of favorable votes may be required by the articles or bylaws.

In case of merger or consolidation, shareholders are entitled to vote as a class, whether or not otherwise entitled to vote, if their shares would be affected in a manner similar to one of the amendments to the articles of incorporation specified in Section 60. However, under Section 75 a merger between a parent and subsidiary at least 90 percent of whose shares are owned by the parent may be accomplished by the directors without a vote of the shareholders of either corporation.

Appraisal Rights. Most state corporation statutes, including Delaware, as well as the Model Act, give shareholders who disapprove of certain extraordinary transactions the right to demand payment of the value of their shares. The Model Act (80, 81) gives this right in connection with a merger or consolidation or a sale of substantially all of the corporate assets other than in the normal course of business. However, this right does not apply in the case of a merger of a parent and subsidiary corporation where the parent owns 90 percent of the shares of the subsidiary, nor does it apply when the corporation's shares are registered on a national securities exchange. A few states give appraisal rights in case of certain amendments to the articles of incorporation, such as change in corporate purposes, change in the rights of shares, and extension of corporate life.

There has been litigation in a few states on the question whether an acquisition by one corporation of all the assets of another, together with assumption of the second corporation's liabilities, in exchange for the stock of the first corporation, is a de facto merger such that appraisal rights apply. The Delaware court has held that there is no merger and no right of appraisal,[6] but other courts have taken the opposite view.

The Model Act requires a dissenting shareholder to file a written objection with the corporation prior to the shareholder vote. If the proposal is approved, the corporation must so advise the dissenting shareholders and give them an offer for their shares at what it considers to be their fair value. If any dissenting shareholder is unwilling to accept the offer, he or she may petition a court in the county where the corporation's registered office is located to determine the fair value of the shares. All dissenting shareholders, wherever they live, must be made parties to the suit and will be bound by the judgment. Costs of the action may be assessed against any or all dissenting shareholders if the corporation made an offer and the refusal was arbitrary or vexatious. However, if the corporation made no offer or one which was materially less than the judgment, the court is authorized to require it to pay the reasonable compensation of any expert employed by the dissenters in the proceedings. The act (5) exempts the

---

[6] *Harton v. Arco Electronics, Inc.*, 182 A.2d 22(1962), *aff'd* 188 A.2d 123 (1963).

purchase of shares from dissenters from the requirement that purchase of its own shares may be made only from unrestricted earned surplus.

Summary

The fundamental structure and purpose of the corporation may not be changed without the shareholders' consent. Corporation statutes today provide for amendment of the articles of incorporation with the approval of the owners of some proportion of the voting shares, usually two thirds, but a majority under the Model Act. If the proposed amendment substantially affects the rights of a nonvoting class of shares, most states give that class a vote. Approval of voting shares is also usually required for extraordinary transactions such as merger, consolidation, sale of assets not in the normal course of business and for voluntary liquidation.

Dissenting shareholders are entitled to payment for the value of their shares in some of these situations. The Model Act gives the right of appraisal in case of merger or consolidation and in case of a sale of assets.

In re Watt & Shand

304 A.2d 694 (Sup. Ct. Pa. 1973)

Petition by Watt & Shand, a corporation (plaintiff), to determine the fair value of the shares of Laura Watt O'Connor, who dissented from a plan to amend the articles of incorporation. The trial court adopted the findings of the appraiser it had appointed, and Mrs. O'Connor appealed. Reversed and remanded. Upon remand the court itself established a fair value of $102.15 per share. Mrs. O'Connor again appealed. Remanded.

Mrs. O'Connor was a shareholder in Watt & Shand, a closely held family corporation which operated department stores in Lancaster, Pennsylvania. At the annual shareholders' meeting on April 24, 1969, the majority of the shares amended the articles of incorporation to eliminate cumulative voting. Pennsylvania law gave dissenting shareholders the right to be paid the "fair value" of their shares when the articles of Pennsylvania corporations are amended to eliminate this voting right. It also provided:

The costs and expenses of any such proceeding shall be determined by the court and shall be assessed against the corporation, but all or any part of such costs and expenses may be apportioned and assessed as the court may deem equitable against any or all of the dissenting shareholders who are parties to the proceeding to whom the corporation shall have made an offer to pay for the shares if the court shall find that the action of such shareholders in failing to accept such offer was arbitrary or vexatious or not in good faith. Such expenses shall include reasonable compensation for and reasonable expenses of the appraisers but shall exclude the fees and expenses of counsel for and experts employed by any party, but if the fair value of the shares as determined materially exceeds the amount which the corporation offered to pay therefor, or if no offer was made, the court in its discretion may award to any shareholder who is a party to the proceeding such sum as the court may determine to be reasonable compensation to any expert or experts employed by the shareholder in the proceedings.

Mrs. O'Connor made her demand on the corporation pursuant to the statute and Watt & Shand offered to pay her $93.46 per share, which she refused.

The corporation petitioned the court to appraise the stock. The court appointed an appraiser to take evidence of the fair value of the shares. Mrs. O'Connor's expert witness testified that the fair value was $145.00 per share. He arrived at this figure by multiplying $11.35 (agreed by both parties as the earnings per share for the year 1969) by 15, and then, because the stock was not freely traded, he discounted this figure of $170.35 by 14.7 percent to arrive at the value of $145.00. Watt & Shand's expert used ten as the multiplier and then applied a 25 percent discount and reached a valuation of $85.13. Earnings per share for the previous four years had been $17.13 in 1968 (more than half from gain on sale of its parking lot to the city of Lancaster), $8.32 in 1967, $10.75 in 1966 and $4.81 in 1965. The court adopted the appraiser's figure of $84.56 per share. Upon remand, the parties agreed to go on the record made originally, and the trial court entered judgment for $83,047.95 or $102.15 per share without interest and with costs other than cost of counsel and expert witness fees to be paid equally by the parties. Still dissatisfied, Mrs. O'Connor appealed again.

EAGEN, JUSTICE.   Preliminarily it should be observed that while the term "fair value" is hardly self-executing in its clarity, the object of an appraisal proceeding is to determine the value of the dissenter's shares on a going concern basis. In determining what figure represents this true or intrinsic value, consideration must be given to all factors and elements which reasonably might enter into the fixing of value.

* * * * *

In an attempt to render the unwieldy, wieldable, courts have distilled all of these factors into three principal methods of valuation which have been variably used, commonly in combination, in the actual judicial determination of intrinsic value: (1) net asset value; (2) actual market value, and (3) investment value.*

Upon remand the trial judge undertook to conduct the appraisal as was his right. His opinion indicates that while he studied closely the valuations of the respective experts who testified, he did not choose to adopt either conclusion, opting instead to work out his own valuation. By taking the annual earnings of $11.35, multiplied by

---

* *Net Asset Value* is the share which the stock represents in the value of the net assets of the corporation. Such assets include every kind of property and value, whether realty or personalty, tangible or intangible, including goodwill and the corporation's value as a going concern.

Investment Value is an estimate of present worth in light of past, present, and prospective financial records of the company and is obtained by capitalizing earnings. There are two basic steps in the capitalization process: calculation of a representative annual earnings figure, and choice of capitalization ratio which reflects the stability and predictability of earnings of the particular corporation.

Market Value refers to the price at which the stock was selling on the market prior to the action which is objected to, disregarding any change in price due to the action.

This case presents an instance where a certain method of valuation has no applicability whatever. Watt & Shand is a closely held family corporation having unlisted stock and therefore, no public market. Shares are sold too infrequently for market value to play any part in these proceedings, a fact correctly realized by the lower court.

10, or $113.50 less a 10 percent discount, the trial judge reached a fair value figure of $102.15.

The lower court used but a single year (the year ended January 1969) to obtain the average earnings of Watt & Shand. In our judgment this was an error, but since neither party complains of the action, we will not review it.

However, we do point out that in this kind of proceeding "[i]t is best to average earnings over several years to avoid undue emphasis on one exceptionally good or bad recent year." The purpose of any average is to balance off extraordinary profits against extraordinary losses, in order that a hypothetical figure of what might be considered the ordinary profit or inherent earning capacity of the business may become discernible.

* * * * *

The capitalization ratio used instantly was ten which we feel is within the range of reason.

Mrs. O'Connor also contends that the determination of fair value was incorrect because the lower court placed little or no significance on the net asset or book value of this stock. As the lower court's opinion noted, the book value on January 25, 1969, was $126 per share and when adjusted for an up-to-date appraisal of the real estate became $141.91 per share.

While net-asset value must be given significance, especially in situations where there is no reliable market value for the stock, courts must be extremely judicious with respect to the amount of weight assigned this factor. As one authority has pointed out "[t]here is nearly complete agreement that book value does not accurately represent the fair value of the corporate assets." This is so for the reason that the balance sheet usually lists assets at original cost, which may differ greatly from present useable value or the present cost of equivalent assets. Normally, the total assets are worth more than the sum of their parts, because they include qualities useful in the context of a particular business that they would lose if put to different uses.

In its opinion the lower court expressed reservation about factoring in discount in this particular case, a reservation which we share because of the opinion's conclusion that "book value is not inflated but very conservatively stated." We feel a more appropriate weight can be given to net assets by not employing a discount in this situation. Hence, the fair market value of the stock is $113.50.

We also conclude the lower court erred in declining to award Mrs. O'Connor interest and costs. At one time Pennsylvania law made no provision for the award of interest and our court uniformly refused to allow it. In 1959 certain amendments were added to the Corporation Code which rectified this situation.

We believe the better view, as well as the intent of the statute, is to allow interest as a matter of course in all cases absent the existence of some inequitable situation. "Since the corporation has had the use of the dissenter's money without his consent from the time he demanded appraisal, it seems that interest is justified."

Despite the fact that the lower court declined to make these awards, there was no explicit finding that Mrs. O'Connor's refusal to accept Watt & Shand's offer was arbitrary, vexatious, or not in good faith, nor is there a shred of evidence in the record to support such a finding. The difference between the corporation's offer and the trial judge's undiscounted appraisal is $16,292.52. This figure materially exceeds the amount the corporation offered to pay and, therefore, Mrs. O'Connor should also receive reasonable expenses for the employment of experts. Mrs. O'Connor further requests reimbursement for attorney's fees but the statute does not permit it.

Bove v. Community Hotel Corp.

249 A.2d 89 (Sup. Ct. R.I. 1969)

Action by Bove and other dissident preferred shareholders (plaintiffs) against Community Hotel Corporation of Newport, Rhode Island (defendant), to enjoin a merger between Community Hotel and a subsidiary corporation. Appeal from dismissal of the action. Affirmed.

Community Hotel was incorporated in 1924 to erect and operate hotels. It had 4,335 shares of $100 par-cumulative preferred stock outstanding of which Bove and the other plaintiffs had held 900 shares since 1930 or earlier. There were also 2,106 no-par common shares outstanding. No dividends had been paid on the preferred stock for 24 years and the arrearage totalled $645,000 or approximately $149 per share.

In order to be in a position to obtain additional capital, Community Hotel incorporated a wholly owned subsidiary, Newport Hotel Corp., for the purpose of merging with it. The merger plan called for eliminating the arrearage on the preferred shares by converting them into five shares of common stock of Newport. Under the Rhode Island statute such a merger could be effected if two thirds of the shares of each class of stock in Community Hotel were voted in favor of it.

JOSLIN, JUSTICE. It is true, of course, that to accomplish the proposed recapitalization by amending Community Hotel's articles of association under relevant provisions of the general corporation law would require the unanimous vote of the preferred shareholders, whereas under the merger statute, only a two-thirds vote of those stockholders will be needed. Concededly, unanimity of the preferred stockholders is unobtainable in this case, and the plaintiffs argue, therefore, that to permit the less restrictive provisions of the merger statute to be used to accomplish indirectly what otherwise would be incapable of being accomplished directly by the more stringent amendment procedures of the general corporation law is tantamount to sanctioning a circumvention or perversion of that law.

The question, however, is not whether recapitalization by the merger route is a subterfuge, but whether a merger which is designed for the sole purpose of cancelling the rights of preferred stockholders with the consent of less than all has been authorized by the legislature. The controlling statute is section 7–5–2. Its language is clear, all-embracing and unqualified. It authorizes any two or more business corporations *which were or might have been organized* under the general corporation law to merge into a single corporation; and it provides that the merger agreement shall prescribe

. . . the terms and conditions of consolidation or merger, the mode of carrying the same into effect . . . *as well as the manner of converting the shares of each of the constituent corporations into shares or other securities of the corporation resulting from or surviving such consolidation or merger,* with such other details and provisions as are deemed necessary. [Italics ours.]

Nothing in that language even suggests that the legislature intended to make *underlying purpose* a standard for determining permissibility. Indeed, the contrary is apparent since the very breadth of the language selected presupposes a complete lack of concern with whether the merger is designed to further the mutual interests of two existing and nonaffiliated corporations or whether alternatively it is purposed solely upon effecting a substantial change in an existing corporation's capital structure.

Moreover, that a possible effect of corporate action under the merger statute is not possible, or is even forbidden, under another section of the general corporation law is of no import, it being settled that the several sections of that law may have independent legal significance, and that the validity of corporate action taken pursuant to one section is not necessarily dependent upon its being valid under another.

We hold, therefore, that nothing within the purview of our statute forbids a merger between a parent and a subsidiary corporation, even under circumstances where the merger device has been resorted to solely for the purpose of obviating the necessity for the unanimous vote which would otherwise be required in order to cancel the priorities of preferred shareholders.

A more basic problem, narrowed so as to bring it within the factual context of this case, is whether the right of a holder of cumulative preferred stock to dividend arrearages and other preferences may be cancelled by a statutory merger.

[The Court then reviews Delaware decisions on the question whether a shareholder may prevent a recapitalization that eliminates dividend arrearages and certain Rhode Island decisions.]

On the basis of our own precedents we conclude that the merger legislation, notwithstanding its effect on the rights of its stockholders, did not necessarily constitute an improper exercise of the right of amendment reserved merely because it was subsequent.

Shareholders' Actions

Shareholders' Individual Actions.   As a general rule a shareholder has no right to bring an action in his or her own name to recover a judgment for the impairment of his or her investment as a shareholder where such impairment resulted from a wrong to the corporation. In such a case the person wronged is the corporation and it has the cause of action. If individual shareholders were permitted to sue for their proportional share of a wrong to the corporation, there could be a multiplicity of suits and shareholders might benefit to the detriment of creditors.

The courts have, however, recognized the shareholder's right to sue in his or her own name under some circumstances in which, although the wrong is based on corporate rights, the injury is primarily to the shareholder and rights of the creditors are not affected. For instance, where all but a small number of shareholders have participated in a misappropriation of funds, the nonparticipating shareholders have been allowed to recover a judgment sufficient to place them on a par with the participating shareholders.

The shareholder has the right to bring an action in his or her own name to prevent or redress a breach of his or her shareholder contract. For example, a shareholder may sue to enforce his right to inspect the books, to recover dividends paid but not declared, to enjoin the corporation from committing an *ultra vires* act, and to enforce his preemptive rights.

Shareholder Class Action Suits.   When a number of people have a right or claim against the same defendants growing out of the same or substantially the same event or transaction, courts have long permitted some of them to maintain an action for the benefit of all. An example might be a preferred shareholder bringing an action in behalf of all holders of that security seeking the payment of a dividend. The number of class actions by shareholders (as well as consumers, environmentalists, and others) has greatly increased since Rule 23 of the Federal Rules of Civil Procedure was amended in 1966 and many states relaxed their requirements for class actions. Most of the shareholder actions have been brought under the federal securities laws, which are discussed in the next chapter.

Rule 23 requires: (1) that there be questions of law and fact which are common to all members of the class, (2) that the class be so large that it be impracticable to force them to join as parties, (3) that the claims of the representatives of the class be typical of the class, and (4) that the plaintiff(s) must fairly and adequately represent the class (for example, must have suffered the wrong complained of, have no interests adverse to the class, and have competent counsel).

Any recovery in a class action is distributed to members of the entire class, according to such rules and procedures as may be established by the court.

Shareholders' Derivative Actions.   One or more shareholders are also permitted under certain circumstances to bring an action for the benefit of the corporation when the directors have failed to pursue a claim not of the shareholders directly but of the corporation. For example, if the corporation has a claim against its chief executive for wrongfully diverting corporate assets to his or her own use but because the chief executive controls the directors the corporation is unlikely to bring an action, a shareholder may bring a derivative action. A derivative action may also be used against an outsider. If a judgment is obtained, it ordinarily goes to the corporate treasury for the benefit of the corporation and the creditors as well as all shareholders.

Although the possibility of a derivative action may be a major deterrent to wrongdoing on the part of officers and directors, it is also susceptible to abuse. "Strike suits" brought to gain an out-of-court settlement for the complaining shareholder personally or to earn large attorney's fees rather than a recovery for the corporation have not been uncommon. The U.S. Supreme Court long ago established several requirements for actions brought in federal courts to discourage abuse.[7] Under these rules the shareholder bringing the action must have held his or her shares or acquired them by operation of law (such as inheritance) from someone who held them at the time the alleged wrong was committed. He or she must also show that intracorporate remedies have been exhausted by a prior demand upon the directors and, if appropriate, a demand on the shareholders. By statute or court rules many of the states have adopted these and additional safeguards. The Model Act (49) contains the contemporaneous ownership requirement, and it also provides that the corporation may require the plaintiff(s) to post security for reasonable expenses and attorneys' fees which may be incurred by it and other defendants unless the plaintiff(s) own 5 percent of the outstanding shares or their shares have a market value in excess of $25,000. It also authorizes the court to assess the defendants' expenses and attorneys' fees whether or not security has previously been given, and whether or not it finds that the action was brought without reasonable cause. To prevent benefit only to the shareholder bringing the action, statutes in a number of states and the federal rules require approval of the court of any settlement as well as notice to all shareholders.

Occasionally, the officers or managers will refuse to defend a suit brought against a corporation. If a shareholder shows that the corporation has a good defense to the suit and that the refusal or failure of the directors or managers to defend is a breach of their fiduciary duty to the corporation, the courts will permit a shareholder to defend for the benefit of the corporation, its shareholders, and its creditors.

Reimbursement in Class and Derivative Actions. A plaintiff in a class action or derivative action who gets a judgment or who gains a benefit for the class or the corporation is entitled to be reimbursed by the corporation for his or her reasonable expenses, including attorneys' fees. Otherwise, a shareholder could hardly afford to sue, since ordinarily the cost of the suit will far exceed the benefit to the shares alone. The result often is that the attorneys' fees and expenses of both plaintiffs and defendants are paid out of corporate funds should the suit be successful, and if the court thinks the suit is unreasonably brought, it may under Section 43a and similar statutes assess the costs of both parties to the unsuccessful shareholder complainant.

Minority Shareholder Suits. The right to control the affairs of a corporation is vested in the holders of a majority of the shares, subject to the requirements of some statutes or the articles of incorporation for approval of a higher proportion of shares or even unanimous approval for certain corporate actions.

---

[7] *Hawes v. Oakland,* 104 U.S. 450 (1882).

However, if the majority of shareholders pursue a course which will operate to deprive minority shareholders of their rights in the corporation, a court of equity will, on suit by minority shareholders, grant whatever relief the circumstances of the case demand. The courts are reluctant to interfere in the internal affairs of a corporation, and they will grant relief to minority shareholders only when the conduct of the majority shareholders amounts to a fraud on the minority shareholders.

Dissolution at Suit of a Minority Shareholder.   In a number of cases, although there is authority to the contrary, courts have appointed a receiver for the corporation upon the petition of a minority shareholder. In a few cases courts have decreed dissolution of the corporation without specific statutory authority. These cases have included situations where: (1) those in control of the corporation are benefiting themselves at the expense of the other shareholders in a cavalier manner or actually defrauding them; (2) corporate functions have been abandoned or the corporation has been inactive since organization; (3) the main purpose of the corporation can no longer be carried on without utter ruin or because the business has become illegal; and (4) there has been such a deadlock among directors and shareholders that corporate functions cannot be carried on. The Model Act (94, 102) gives statutory authorization for liquidation and dissolution in all of these situations but the third. However, the power given is discretionary and would be exercised only if the court were convinced that liquidation and dissolution would benefit the shareholders as a whole.

Summary

As a general rule a shareholder has no right to bring a suit in his or her own name to recover damages for the impairment of his investment resulting from a wrong to the corporation. A shareholder may bring an action in his or her own name to redress or prevent a breach of his membership contract, or under certain conditions a shareholder may bring a class action representing himself or herself and a large group similarly harmed.

A shareholder may bring a derivative suit for the benefit of the corporation, its stockholders, and creditors if the directors and managers of the corporation have, in breach of their fiduciary duty, refused or failed to bring suit, and if their failure to bring suit will result in injury to the corporation.

Although courts are reluctant to interfere in the internal affairs of a corporation, they will grant relief to minority shareholders if the conduct of the majority amounts to a fraud upon them. In a number of cases, courts have appointed a receiver and have sometimes decreed the dissolution of a corporation upon the suit of a minority shareholder. Some statutes specifically authorize dissolution in certain circumstances.

Shareholder Liability

Shareholder Liability on Shares. A shareholder is liable to the corporation on his or her share subscription contract, and a receiver or trustee of an insolvent corporation may recover the unpaid balance for the benefit of creditors. However, a shareholder who has paid a lawful agreed price for nonassessable shares is not liable for creditors' claims. The Model Act (25) makes all paid up shares nonassessable, that is not subject to further call for contribution, but at one time it was common for bank shares to be assessable. If the stock is "watered," that is, less than lawful consideration was given for it, then the shareholder is likely to be held liable either to the corporation or to creditors for the difference between what he or she paid and what would constitute lawful payment. In the absence of statute, courts apply several different theories which result in different conclusions in some situations.

Statutes also vary. The Model Act (19) recognizes neither promissory notes nor future services as payment for shares, but property and services actually performed are valid consideration. It makes the judgment of directors or shareholders as to the value of property or services received for shares conclusive in the absence of fraud.

The record holder of the shares is usually the one subject to shareholder liabilities. A transferee who in good faith believes that full consideration has been paid is not liable to the corporation or its creditors for any unpaid portion of the consideration (25).

Shareholder Liability on Illegal Dividends and Distributions. Dividends received by a shareholder with knowledge of their illegality may be recovered on behalf of the corporation even though he or she had no part in their declaration. However, despite lack of knowledge of the illegality, a shareholder is liable for a dividend received if the corporation were insolvent at the time the dividend was declared. Under the Model Act (48) primary liability is placed upon the directors who declared the dividend. However, any director against whom a claim is asserted for the wrongful payment of a dividend or distribution of assets of the corporation is entitled to contribution from shareholders who received a dividend or distribution knowing it was illegally declared.

Shareholder Liability for Corporate Debts. A number of states at one time imposed personal liability on shareholders for wages due to corporate employees, even though their shares were fully paid for and nonassessable. New York still imposes this liability but not in case of publicly owned corporations and only upon the ten largest shareholders. In several states shareholders may be held liable for corporate debts if business is commenced before the required capital is paid in or the certificate of incorporation filed.

Duties of Controlling Shareholders.   A question which has been extensively discussed by legal scholars is whether controlling shareholders have any obligation to other shareholders when selling control of the corporation. They have been held liable where control was sold to persons they should have known would not act in the best interests of the corporation,[8] and in another case the controlling shareholders were held liable to other shareholders for the premium paid for control.[9] Also controlling shareholders have been held liable for not giving other shareholders an opportunity to participate in recapitalization which resulted in large profits to the controlling shareholders.[10]

Summary

The shareholder remains liable to the corporation on any unpaid portion of his or her subscription and may become liable on "watered" stock. Creditors may enforce the right of the corporation.

Dividends received by a shareholder knowing of their illegality may be recovered on behalf of the corporation. Shareholders may be held liable for corporate debts if business is commenced before certain requirements for incorporation are met. A few states still impose personal liability on shareholders for wages due to corporate employees. The extent of liability of controlling shareholders to other shareholders in selling control is the subject of dispute.

Jones v. H. F. Ahmanson & Co.

460 P.2d 464 (Sup. Ct. Cal. 1969)

Class action by June Jones (plaintiff), a minority shareholder in the United Savings and Loan Association of California, against H. F. Ahmanson & Company, United Financial Corporation of California, and others (defendants) seeking to recover for economic injuries suffered by minority shareholders. Judgment for defendants on demurrer. Reversed.

United Savings and Loan Association of California (the Association) converted from a mutual to a stockholder owned savings institution in 1956. Of the 6,568 shares issued, 987 (14.8 percent) were purchased by depositors, including June Jones, through warrants issued in proportion to the amount of their deposits at that time. The shares allocated to unexercised warrants were sold to the then chairman of the board who resold them to H. F. Ahmanson & Co., which became the controlling shareholder, and to others. The Association retained most of its earnings in reserves so that book value of the shares increased to several times their 1956 value. Because of high book value and the fact the shares were closely held there was little buying and selling of shares, and these sales were mostly among existing shareholders.

---

[8] *Gerdes v. Reynolds,* 28 N.Y.S.2d 622 (NY Co. Sup. Ct. 1941).

[9] *Perlman v. Feldman,* 219 F.2d 50 (2d Civ. 1955).

[10] *Jones v. H. F. Ahmanson Co.,* 460 P.2d 464 (Cal. 1969).

Savings and loan stocks which were publicly traded were enjoying a steady increase in market price in 1958, but not those of the Association. To take advantage of this opportunity for profit H. F. Ahmanson & Co. and a few other shareholders of the Association incorporated United Financial Corporation of California (United) in 1959 and exchanged their Association shares for shares in United. United then owned more than 85 percent of the shares of the Association. The minority shareholders, including June Jones, were not given an opportunity to exchange their shares.

United then made a public offering of its stock in 1960, and the following year the original shareholders in United made a secondary public offering of a block of their shares. However, Ahmanson remained in control. By mid-1961 trading in United shares was very active while sales of Association shares decreased to half of its formerly low level. In 1960 United offered to purchase Association stock for $1,100 per share while those who had exchanged their shares for United stock had shares worth $3,700 for each share originally held in the Association. In 1959 and in 1960 the Association had paid extra dividends of $75 and $57 per share but after 350 shares were purchased by United pursuant to its offer, United caused the Association president to announce to the minority shareholders that in the near future only the $4.00 regular dividend would be paid. In 1961 United proposed to exchange United stock showing a book value of $210 and earnings at the rate of $134 per year for the Association stock of the minority shareholders which then had a book value of $1,700 per share and annual earnings at the rate of $615 per share. At this time the United shares of the former majority shareholders in the Association had a market value of $8,800.

TRAYNOR, CHIEF JUSTICE.   Defendants take the position that as shareholders they owe no fiduciary obligation to other shareholders, absent reliance on inside information, use of corporate assets, or fraud. This view has long been repudiated in California. The Courts of Appeal have often recognized that majority shareholders, either singly or acting in concert to accomplish a joint purpose, have a fiduciary responsibility to the minority and to the corporation to use their ability to control the corporation in a fair, just, and equitable manner. Majority shareholders may not use their power to control corporate activities to benefit themselves alone or in a manner detrimental to the minority. Any use to which they put the corporation or their power to control the corporation must benefit all shareholders proportionately and must not conflict with the proper conduct of the corporation's business.

* * * * *

The rule that has developed in California is a comprehensive rule of "inherent fairness from the viewpoint of the corporation and those interested therein." The rule applies alike to officers, directors, and controlling shareholders in the exercise of powers that are theirs by virtue of their position and to transactions wherein controlling shareholders seek to gain an advantage in the sale or transfer or use of their controlling block of shares. Thus we held in *In re Security Finance,* that majority shareholders do not have an absolute right to dissolve a corporation, although ostensibly permitted to do so by Corporations Code, section 4600, because their statutory power is subject to equitable limitations in favor of the minority. We recognized that the majority had the right to dissolve the corporation to protect their investment *if* no alternative means were available *and* no advantage was secured over other shareholders, and noted that "there is nothing sacred in the life of a corporation that transcends the interests of its shareholders, but because dissolution falls with such finality on those interests, above all corporate powers it is subject to equitable limitations."

* * * * *

. . . Had defendants afforded the minority an opportunity to exchange their stock on the same basis or offered to purchase them (sic) at a price arrived at by independent appraisal, their burden of establishing good faith and inherent fairness would have been much less. At the trial they may present evidence tending to show such good faith or compelling business purpose that would render their action fair under the circumstance. On appeal from the judgment of dismissal after the defendants' demurrer was sustained we decide only that the complaint states a cause of action entitling plaintiff to relief.

In so holding we do not suggest that the duties of corporate fiduciaries include in all cases an obligation to make a market for and to facilitate public trading in the stock of the corporation. But when, as here, no market exists, the controlling shareholders may not use their power to control the corporation for the purpose of promoting a marketing scheme that benefits themselves alone to the detriment of the minority. Nor do we suggest that a control block of shares may not be sold or transferred to a holding company. We decide only that the circumstances of any transfer of controlling shares will be subject to judicial scrutiny when it appears that the controlling shareholders may have breached their fiduciary obligation to the corporation or the remaining shareholders.

Newmark v. RKO General, Inc.

332 F. Supp. 161 (S.D.N.Y. 1971)

Proceeding on petition of attorneys for Margot Newmark (plaintiff) to recover from RKO General, Inc., (defendant) attorneys' fees and costs after recovering judgment for Newmark in behalf of Frontier Airlines. Attorneys' fees and disbursements of $750,000 awarded to the law firm of Kaufman, Taylor, Kimmel and Miller.

Margot Newmark, a securities holder in Frontier Airlines, Inc., brought a derivative action under Section 16(b) of the Securities Exchange Act of 1934 to recover short-swing profits made by RKO General, Inc., at the time of the merger of Central Airlines, Inc., into Frontier. She recovered a judgment of over $7,920,000 plus interest of more than $553,000 on behalf of Frontier.

BONSAL, DISTRICT JUDGE.   Frontier and RKO also suggest that since RKO owns 56% of Frontier, the benefit of the judgment to Frontier's public stockholders is limited to 44% thereof, and that the Kaufman attorneys' fee should be based on the recovery attributable to Frontier's public stockholders. However, the court holds that Kaufman's fee should be based on Frontier's recovery, exclusive of postjudgment interest.

Kaufman contends that the amount sought of $2,500,000 in legal fees and $16,000 in disbursements is fair and reasonable in view of the successful outcome of this litigation. Frontier contends that a generous fee should not exceed $575,000, and RKO contends that the fee should not exceed $300,000. Some of the letters from Frontier stockholders which were filed in this proceeding suggest a fee of 10% of the amount recovered.

The court invited the Securities and Exchange Commission to file a brief *amicus curiae* on the amount of the fee. On April 6, 1971, the Commission filed a memorandum in which it stated, ". . . the Commission believes that an allowance of $2,500,000 in counsel fees, as requested by plaintiff's attorneys, would be excessive."

* * * * *

It is true that there have been a number of Section 16(b) cases in this court in which the plaintiff's attorneys have been awarded fees ranging from 20% to 50% of the amount recovered, where the amounts recovered ranged from $70,000 to $190,000. However, as pointed out by the Securities and Exchange Commission in its memorandum *amicus,*

. . . there comes a point where, as in the present case, the judgment is so large that a fee based primarily on a percentage of recovery exceeds the limits of reasonable compensation for the attorneys' efforts.

In determining a reasonable fee for Kaufman, the court has considered the following factors: (1) the amount of the recovery; (2) the novelty and complexity of the legal issues; (3) the skill with which the services were performed, and the standing of Kaufman; (4) the benefits to Frontier; (5) the contingent nature of Kaufman's employment; (6) the hours reasonably expended by Kaufman.

Problem Cases

1. The bylaws of Tank Cleaners, Inc., provided that a meeting of stockholders for the election of directors be held on the 27th of October each year and that notice be mailed to the shareholders "ten day prior thereto." Shannon, president and general manager of Tank Cleaners, ordered a meeting for the election of directors be held on October 8, and notice was mailed on September 30. At the meeting, which was attended by all shareholders and chaired by Shannon, he was replaced as a director and at a meeting of directors held immediately thereafter, he was replaced as president and general manager. Shannon brought an action to have the meeting declared illegal because it was held at a date other than that set by the bylaws and because "ten days' notice" of the meeting was not given. Was the meeting illegal?

2. At a shareholder meeting of Climax Molybdenum Company, called for the purpose of voting on a proposed merger with American Metal Company, 1,781,564 shares were counted by the inspectors of election as favoring the merger. Climax had 2,580,000 shares outstanding and two thirds (1,720,000) were required to effect a merger under the applicable statute. Alice Schott, a dissenting shareholder, brought suit to have the merger declared void. Schott contended that 62,834 proxies voted in favor of the merger should not have been counted because they were rubber stamped with the registered owner's (usually a brokerage house) name rather than signed. She also contended that in a number of cases a series of proxies was given by a single broker and that the entire series was counted when only the last proxy should have been counted. If either group of contested proxies was invalid, then there were insufficient favorable votes to permit the merger. Are these proxies valid?

3. Schnell, a stockholder in Chris-Craft Industries, Inc., a Delaware corporation, wrote Chris-Craft's management desiring to obtain a copy of the company's stock ledger or to be furnished with a list of its stockholders. Schnell's purpose was to solicit proxies for the next shareholders' meeting in order to change the company's management. Delaware law expressly requires corporations to supply such lists for valid purposes, such as proxy solicitation. Chris-Craft refused to supply the lists. The company claimed that Schnell's membership on an independent stockholders committee which included David Cohen made it contrary to the company's best interests to supply the lists. Cohen was previously employed as counsel for Chris-Craft, and an employee of his was currently bringing a suit against Chris-Craft for another client. The company suspected that Cohen was aligning himself behind Schnell in a battle for management control. It alleged that such action by Cohen would violate certain canons of professional ethics relating to lawyer-client confidences. Schnell asked a Delaware court to order Chris-Craft to produce the lists. He argued that his purpose in obtaining the lists was lawful. He also argued that Cohen had not represented him as attorney in this case, and therefore, suspicion of any joint overthrow attempts by Schnell and Cohen were unfounded. Should the court order delivery of the lists?

4. Malone owned 15 percent of the shares of each of six corporations; five of them owned apartments and Dimco Corporation was a land developer. Dimino owned 70 percent and Santandrea the other 15 percent of the shares in each. Malone had been active in all six corporations and received a salary from Dimco. Without the knowledge of the other shareholders, Malone formed a real estate corporation of his own and shortly thereafter purchased land adjacent to acreage owned by Dimco and for which it once had a contract to purchase that was never consumated. His employment with Dimco was terminated, and thereafter Malone sought a court order permitting inspection of the books and records of the corporations. In the meantime, through his new corporation and other interest, Malone became a competitor of the six corporations. There had been intermingling of funds between the six corporations and Frank Dimino, Inc., a construction company solely owned by Dimino.

   The corporations resisted Malone's demand for inspection rights on the ground that he was a competitor. Is this a sufficient ground for denial?

5. Mutual Telephone Company's authorized capital stock was 1,000 common shares, of which 356 were outstanding. An investment group headed by Carlson purchased 203 of the outstanding shares at $200 per share. Shortly thereafter, the directors of Mutual voted to dispose of the 644 unsold shares "to such parties as the board of directors may approve at $40 per share, and upon the condition that before any such parties sell said stock they will first offer it to the corporation." Relatives, friends, and employees purchased 225 additional shares, thereby divesting the Carlson group of their majority interest.

   The articles of incorporation provided, "When the outstanding capital is increased, additional stock shall be offered to existing stockholders in proportion to their then holdings. . . ."

   Carlson brought suit to enforce his preemptive rights and Mutual argues that the words "outstanding capital" and "capital stock" are used as the equivalent of each other and that preemptive rights guaranteed to stockholders are limited to situations where the authorized capital is increased, and that preemptive rights do not apply to the original authorization of 1,000 shares. Is Carlson entitled to buy his proportion of the shares being offered for sale?

6. Rath Packing Company sought to combine with Needham Packing Company to form Rath-Needham Corporation. The plan designed to accomplish this combination was called "Plan and Agreement of Reorganization." A group of minority shareholders of Rath sought to enjoin the combination, contending that the plan was a merger and that the shareholder vote was insufficient for a merger. If the reorganization plan were effected, former Needham shareholders would hold a 54 percent interest in Rath-Needham.

The Iowa statutes required an affirmative vote of two thirds of the shares to accomplish a merger but only a majority for an amendment to the articles, which could include change of corporate name, establishment of new classes of securities, and so forth. The plan involved several amendments to Rath's articles but was not designated nor did it follow the statutory procedure for a merger. The affirmative vote on the proposed amendments to the articles by the Rath shareholders was 60.1 percent of the outstanding shares (77 percent of those voting).

Is the plan a merger?

7. Mr. and Mrs. Fred Saigh, stockholders of Anheuser-Busch Inc., brought a derivative suit against the corporation and its president, A. A. Busch, Jr., seeking to require Busch to return to the corporation the value of salary and perquisites provided him in excess of the reasonable value of his services as president of the corporation.

The Saighs alleged that Busch had been given benefits in the form of salary, bonuses, stock-purchase options, expense allowances not to be accounted for, personal club dues, life insurance, retirement annuity, yachts, private railroad cars, automobiles, residences, servants, and so forth, which far exceeded the reasonable value of his services.

Busch asked the court to dismiss the suit because the Saighs had failed to try to get the directors to take the desired action. The Saighs argued that the directors were controlled by Busch and an attempt to change the board would be useless because Busch and the board controlled communication with shareholders.

Are Busch and the corporation entitled to a summary judgment?

8. Royal Enterprises of Pensacola, Inc., was a close corporation in which Miller owned 51 percent of the stock and Hebert and Levine owned the remainder. Hebert, Levine, Miller, and a nominee of Miller were the directors. Hebert and Levine got into an irreconcilable conflict with Miller over management policies for the corporation, and the directors were deadlocked.

The Florida Corporation statute provided that if the voting power of a corporation is evenly divided into two independent interests and the number of directors is even and equally divided respecting management of the corporation, with one half of the ownership favoring a course advocated by one half of the directors and the other directors favoring the course of the other half of ownership, a court may entertain a petition from any shareholder for involuntary dissolution of the corporation.

Are Hebert and Levine entitled to have the corporation dissolved?

9. Seyler and Beary were the principal shareholders in Seekay, Inc. In 1945 Seekay paid cash dividends of more than $55,000 which rendered the corporation insolvent. Seekay's income-tax assessment for 1945 of $22,000 went unpaid due to the insolvency. The United States brought an action against Seyler and Beary, as shareholders, to recover the unpaid tax liability of Seekay. Are the shareholders liable?

chapter 27

Securities Regulation

Introduction

Background and Objectives. The major federal laws dealing with securities were passed in response to studies of the stock market crash of 1929, which ended a period of extravagant speculation in corporate securities by a rather broad segment of the American population. The purposes of this legislation were to provide investors with more information to help them make buy-sell decisions and to prohibit some of the unfair, deceptive, and manipulative practices which had resulted in substantial losses to the less-informed and less-powerful investors during the stock market debacle at the end of the 1920s.

The two principal statutes are the Securities Act of 1933 and the Securities Exchange Act of 1934.[1] They impose duties and liabilities upon certain corporations and their directors, officers, and controlling shareholders as well as upon certain persons involved in issuing and distributing securities to the public, such as underwriters, stockbrokers, accountants, and lawyers. The Securities and Exchange Commission (SEC) was established by the 1934 Act to administer the 1933 and 1934 Acts, and it has subsequently been given the administration of other related statutes. The SEC was granted and has exercised rather broad rule-making power under these statutes. The discussion of these acts will emphasize their impact upon corporations and upon their officers and directors rather than upon those engaged in the marketing and trading of securities.

The securities legislation and the body of rules and practices developed by the SEC constitute a very complex body of law. Indeed, it is so complex that most of the law practiced in this area, both in advising clients and in registering

---

[1] Other federal statutes applying to securities and security issuers, such as the Public Utility Holding Company Act of 1935 and the Investment Company Act of 1940, will not be discussed here because they apply only to certain kinds of businesses. Nor will the Securities Investor Protection Act of 1970, which was passed to protect investors from financial failure of brokerage firms, be discussed.

securities, is handled by a relatively small number of specialists, most of whom are located in large financial centers. All the businessman or business student who is not directly involved in the securities industry can expect is to obtain sufficient information to understand some of the terminology and to become generally familiar with the requirements the statutes impose upon corporations and their officers and directors.

What Is a Security? Although corporate stocks and bonds are the most common types of securities, they are not the only kinds of contract covered by the securities regulation statutes. The 1933 Securities Act (2[1]) defines a security in broad language in part as follows:

. . . any . . . note, stock . . . evidence of indebtedness, certificate of interest or participation in any profit-sharing agreement, . . . investment contract, . . . voting trust certificate, . . . fractional undivided interest in . . . mineral rights, or in general, any interest or instrument commonly known as a "security," . . .

The 1934 Act definition is similar. Many of the state statutes are equally broad. Under such definitions contracts not generally thought of as securities have been held subject to regulation. Sales of limited partnerships, of live animals with contracts to care for them, of restaurant properties and citrus groves with management contracts and contracts involving the bottling and selling of whiskey have all been held to constitute investment contracts subject to the Federal securities law. If an investment involves participation with others in an enterprise in which the investor is led to expect profits solely from the efforts of the promoter or some third person rather than his or her own efforts, the arrangement falls within the United States Supreme Court's definition of an investment contract.[2] The fact that there is no certificate or that what is being offered for sale purports to be tangible property is immaterial. Of course, all offers or sales of such contracts do not come under the securities laws because certain exemptions may apply.

Exemptions. There are a number of exemptions from the requirements of the Securities Act of 1933 for the filing with the SEC of a registration statement and furnishing investors with a prospectus. The exemptions are of two types: one exempts certain kinds of securities; the other exempts certain transactions in securities. Examples of the first include exemptions of securities which are part of an exclusively intrastate issue and small offerings where the aggregate offering price does not exceed $300,000, although in the latter case the SEC prescribes certain conditions. Among numerous other exemptions are securities issued by religious, educational, charitable, and other eleemosynary institutions and those which are exchanged by the issuer exclusively with its existing shareholders where no commissions are paid for soliciting the exchange.

---

[2] *SEC v. W. J. Howey Co.*, 328 U.S. 293, 298–99 (1946).

The intrastate exemption applies only if the issuer and all of the offerees reside in the same state. If the issuer is a corporation it must be incorporated and doing business in the same state as the residence of the offerees. If only one of the offerees is a resident of another state or intends to resell the security to a nonresident, the exemption is lost. Issuers intending to rely on this exemption usually require an "investment letter" from each purchaser. In such a letter the investor declares that he or she is purchasing the securities for investment and not for resale.

The *transactions* exempted include transactions by persons other than an issuer, underwriter, or dealer. This exemption covers individual investors, although officers, directors, or those in control of the issuer may not be able to sell their securities without registration. Also exempt are "transactions by an issuer not involving any public offering"—the so-called private offering.

Private Offerings. An issuer may avoid the rather considerable difficulty and expense as well as the need to make the public disclosures required in a registration statement if the offering of a security is limited to a "private offering." The interpretations by the SEC and the courts do not provide highly specific criteria for determining when this exemption applies. Perhaps most important is whether the offerees of the securities already have available to them the kind of information provided by a registration statement and whether the securities are likely to be resold to the public. Although the SEC has stated that the number of offerees is relevant to the exemption only in determining whether they have the requisite knowledge of the issuer, a 1935 opinion of the SEC general counsel mentioned the number 25. Since then legal advisors have tended to take the position that when the number exceeds 25, the risk of relying on the exemption increases considerably. However, if the offerees are highly sophisticated investors, such as large banks and insurance companies, the number of offerees could be substantially higher without endangering the exemption. Also, the number of units and the amount of securities offered are relevant factors in determining whether the exemption applies. The smaller the denominations of the securities and the larger the size of the offering, especially if the securities are of a class already held by the public, the less likely the exemption will be held to apply.

It is customary in private offerings, as well as when the intrastate exemption is being utilized, for the issuer to require an "investment letter" from each purchaser. With respect to stock, such securities are known as "letter stock" or "investment stock." Usually, the certificates representing such securities will carry a notice of restriction against transfer. However, the intent of the purchaser, as determined later by the SEC or a court, rather than the existence of a letter or the length of time the securities are held before resale determines the applicability of the exemption. Resale by purchasers, except possibly to others who also agree to hold for investment or where the original investor has suffered a substantial change of circumstances making resale desirable, may result in a loss of the exemption unless considerable time has elapsed. No definite time has been established by the SEC but knowledgeable advisors often suggest that no resale be attempted in less than two years.

Summary

The purposes of the Securities Act of 1933 and the Securities Exchange Act of 1934 are to provide investors with adequate information and to prohibit unfair, deceptive, and manipulative practices which had caused losses to ordinary investors. The securities laws and the rules of the SEC constitute a complex body of law which tends to be the province of legal specialists.

The law applies a broad definition of "security." It includes any sort of investment which involves participation with others in an enterprise holding out the expectation of profit from the efforts of the promoter or others rather than the investor's own efforts.

There are two types of exemptions from the registration and other requirements of the 1933 Act. One exempts certain types of securities such as those sold only intrastate, those of nonprofit institutions, and those which are offered in exchange for those held by existing shareholders. The other exempts certain transactions, including "private offerings" and sales by individual investors rather than distributions by underwriters and dealers. The criteria for meeting the "private offering" exemption are not very explicit.

SEC v. Glenn W. Turner Enterprises, Inc.

474 F.2d 476 (9th Cir. 1973)

This was a suit by the Security and Exchange Commission (plaintiff) against Glenn W. Turner Enterprises, Inc., (defendant) to enjoin violation of the federal securities laws by selling unregistered securities. Appeal from a preliminary injunction. Affirmed.

Dare To Be Great, Inc., (Dare) was a wholly owned subsidiary of Glenn W. Turner Enterprises. Dare offered courses designed to improve an individual's self-motivation and sales ability. The basic course, called Adventure I, provided the purchaser with a portable tape recorder, 12 tape-recorded lessons and certain printed material presented in notebook form. The purchaser was also entitled to attend a 12- to 16-hour series of group meetings. The cost was $300. For an additional $700 the purchaser also received Adventure II, which included 12 more tape recordings and permitted him to attend 80 hours of group sessions. For $2,000 the buyer also received Adventure III which gave him six more tape recordings, a notebook of written material called "The Fun of Selling," as well as other written instructions and 30 more hours of group sessions. In addition, after fulfilling a few nominal requirements, the Adventure III purchaser became an "independent sales trainee" empowered to sell the Adventures. He received $100 for each Adventure I, $300 for each Adventure II, and $900 for each Adventure III that he sold.

For $5000 a purchaser received Adventure IV as well as the lesser ones. Besides receiving additional tapes he had the opportunity to attend two week-long courses in Florida and might sell Adventure IV for which he received $2500. An alternative Plan selling for $1000 was rather similar to Adventure II but permitted the purchaser to sell it to others if he first brought two purchasers to the person who sold him the Plan. After that he would receive $400 for each additional sale that he made. If he brought three purchasers into the Plan he might sell the $1000 Plan without buying it himself.

DUNIWAY, CIRCUIT JUDGE.   The trial court's findings, which are fully supported by the record, demonstrate that defendant's scheme is a gigantic and successful fraud. The question presented is whether the "Adventures" or "Plan" enjoined are "securities" within the meaning of the federal securities laws.

*   *   *   *   *

It is apparent from the record that what is sold is not of the usual "business motivation" type of courses. Rather, the purchaser is really buying the possibility of deriving money from the sale of the plans by Dare to individuals whom the purchaser has brought to Dare. The promotional aspects of the Plan, such as seminars, films, and records, are aimed at interesting others in the Plans. Their value for any other purpose is, to put it mildly, minimal.

Once an individual has purchased a Plan, he turns his efforts toward bringing others into the organization, for which he will receive a part of what they pay. His task is to bring prospective purchasers to "Adventure Meetings."

These meetings are like an old-time revival meeting, but directed toward the joys of making easy money rather than salvation. Their purpose is to convince prospective purchasers, or "prospects," that Dare is a sure route to great riches. . . . Films are shown, usually involving the "rags-to-riches" story of Dare founder, Glenn W. Turner. The goal of all this is to persuade the prospect to purchase a plan, especially Adventure IV, so that he may become a "salesman," and thus grow wealthy as part of the Dare organization. It is intimated that as Glenn W. Turner Enterprises, Inc., expands, high positions in the organization, as well as lucrative opportunities to purchase stock, will be available. After the meeting, pressure is applied to the prospect by Dare people, in an effort to induce him to purchase one of the Adventures or the Plan.

*   *   *   *   *

In *SEC v. W. J. Howey Co.,* the Supreme Court set out its by now familiar definition of an investment contract:

The test is whether the scheme involves an investment of money in a common enterprise with profits to come solely from the efforts of others.

In *Howey* the Court held that a land sales contract for units of a citrus grove, together with a service contract for cultivating and marketing the crops, was an investment contract and hence a security. The Court held that what was in essence being offered was "an opportunity to contribute money and to share in the profits of a large citrus-fruit enterprise managed and partly owned by respondents." The purchasers had no intention themselves of either occupying the land or developing it; they were attracted only "by the prospects of a return on their investment." It was clear that the profits were to come "solely" from the efforts of others.

For purposes of the present case, the sticking point in the *Howey* definition is the word "solely," a qualification which of course exactly fitted the circumstances in *Howey*. All the other elements of the *Howey* test have been met here. There is an investment of money, a common enterprise, and the expectation of profits to come from the efforts of others. Here, however, the investor, or purchaser, must himself exert some efforts if he is to realize a return on his initial cash outlay. He must find prospects and persuade them to attend Dare Adventure Meetings, and at least some of them must then purchase a plan if he is to realize that return. Thus it can be said that the returns or profits are not coming "solely" from the efforts of others.

We hold, however, that in light of the remedial nature of the legislation, the statutory policy of affording broad protection to the public, and the Supreme Court's admonitions that the definition of securities should be a flexible one, the word "solely" should not be read as a strict or literal limitation on the definition of an investment contract, but rather must be construed realistically, so as to include within the definition those schemes which involve in substance, if not form, securities. Within this context, we hold that Adventures III and IV, and the $1,000 Plan are investment contracts within the meaning of the 1933 and 1934 Acts.

Shimer v. Webster

225 A.2d 880 (Ct. App. D.C. 1967)

Action by H. A. Shimer and others (plaintiffs) against Sherwood F. Webster (defendant) to rescind a contract for the sale of stock and to recover the price paid. Shimer appealed from a decision for Webster. Reversed.

Webster, who had formerly worked in the stock brokerage business, was the "assistant to the president" of LaForce, Inc., a corporation located in Burlington, Vermont, involved in the invention and marketing of an improved engine and carburetor. Webster, whose office was in Washington, D.C., during the spring and summer of 1961 sold some 25,000 shares in LaForce to approximately 80 persons at $5 per share. Shimer invested $11,500, others invested as little as $500. They were told that because of some difficulty with the SEC they would receive the certificates in January 1962, when the stock was registered. However, no effort was made to have the stock registered. After numerous phone calls and a formal demand for shares, the shares were delivered to Shimer and others in December 1964, but they were informed that the stock was not registered. By this time it was worthless.

Webster's defense to the alleged violation of the Securities and Exchange Act of 1934 was that the transaction was exempt as a private offering. This view was accepted by the trial court.

CAYTON, JUDGE.   In *Garfield v. Strain* a private sale was found invoking the following useful criteria:

(a) smallness of the offering ($10,500) and the small number of offerees;
(b) fewness of the units offered;

(c)   close relationship and past dealings of the parties;
(d)   former business and social contacts of the parties;
(e)   the fact that the investor initiated the transaction;
(f)   the investor's varied business experience including the stock market and prior ownership of stocks similar to the one upon which the suit was founded;
(g)   an investor such as this did not need the protection of the Act.

We adopt the following as a correct statement of law here applicable: "Whether a transaction involves a public offering of stock is a question of fact involving many aspects. An important factor . . . is whether the securities have come to rest in the hands of an initially informed group or whether the purchasers are merely conduits for wider distribution." 14 Fletcher, Corporations § 6754. In determining the nature of the offering "all the circumstances are to be considered."

The number of offerees not the number of purchasers is the significant factor. "The offering of many units in small denominations . . . indicates the issuer recognizes the possibility, if not probability, of a public distribution." 1 Loss, Securities Regulation at 665. Since the *Ralston* case ". . . the Commission will normally not agree that an offering to, say, more than 30 persons is a private sale unless it is shown that all the offerees are well informed regarding the issuer. An offering to 80 or 90 institutional investors or millionaires might be regarded as an exempt private offering, because investors of this character do not buy securities without demanding and obtaining full information." Mulford, 13 Bus. Law 297, 300. Similarly, it would probably be permissible to offer privately to fifty to seventy vice-presidents and other senior executives. . . . "An offering to 100 commercial banks is probably not public but an offering to 10 individuals including one old lady unversed in financial matters probably is. . . ."

"To mention a closer case, the Commission was recently persuaded that an offering to some 40 members of a family which, or the ancestors of which, had owned or controlled the issuer for many years, and most of whom were residents of the area where the issuer operated, was exempt as a private offering. . . . In another recent case, the Commission held that an offering to 40 persons whose only affinity was that all were friends or acquaintances of the promoters of the issuer was a public offering." Mulford.

*   *   *   *   *

. . . It appeared that there were no past dealings among the parties; that their relationship was impersonal and not based on friendship; that only Shimer could have received adequate information; and that the investment experience of the investors was either limited or nonexistent (thus making them particularly needful of complete information in order to fend for themselves). The transactions were initiated by Jordan and Webster and the inspection of the corporation's inventions was delayed and incomplete. Finally, while the offering of LaForce stock was not technically systematic, the close dealings of Webster and Jordan, Webster's former work in the brokerage field and the substantial number of shares involved cast an unfavorable light on the manner of Webster's offering. We think it must be held as a matter of law, therefore, that this is precisely the type of stock offer requiring registration under the Securities and Exchange Act and that Shimer and the other investors clearly fall within the ambit of its protection. It follows that the decision in favor of defendants was erroneous.

Requirements of Issuers

Registration under the 1933 Act.   The 1933 Act requires the registration of any issue of securities (subject to exemptions discussed above) with the SEC prior to offering that issue for sale. A very large amount of historical and current data about the issuing company and its business (including certified financial statements) must be filed along with full details about the securities being offered, how the proceeds of the issue are to be used (if a new issue), agreements between the parties involved in the distribution of the securities and copies of important contracts to which the issuer is a party which were not made in the usual course of business. In addition, a copy of the prospectus which is required to be given to those to whom the securities are offered for sale must be filed with the SEC. The registration statement must be signed by the issuing company, its principal executive officer, its principal financial officer, its principal accounting officer, and by at least a majority of its board of directors. In addition, any expert named in the registration statement as having prepared or certified information must sign a consent. Such experts would include the accountant certifying the financial statements and the lawyer certifying to the legality of the security, plus others such as mining experts who estimate mineral reserves or the value of other assets.

The statute provides that the registration becomes effective on the 20th day after filing, but the SEC may advance the date or require an amendment which will start the 20-day period running again. The effective date normally is later than 20 days after filing. Since the offering price and the "spread" or commission for the underwriters and dealers usually aren't finally determined until just before the securities are to go on sale, the issuer almost always files at least one amendment. However, it is ordinarily possible to schedule the date of issue so that SEC approval is secured promptly upon the filing of this final amendment.

The approval of the SEC only attests to the completeness of the registration statement and prospectus. It does not indicate any opinion about the worth of the securities or even whether the statements in the filed documents are accurate, although if the staff doubts their accuracy the SEC will usually delay approval and ask for more information.

Registration under the 1934 Act.   Under an amendment to the 1934 Act (12g), corporations having total assets exceeding \$1,000,000 and a class of equity securities held by 500 or more shareholders must register that security under the act even if it is not traded on a public stock exchange. Registration under the 1933 Act is essentially a registration of a transaction. It covers a particular issue at a particular time, and later sale by the corporation of another issue of the same class of securities would require a new registration. In contrast, registration under the 1934 Act provides registered status for the entire class of securities until action is taken to deregister it.

The information required in the registration statement is similar to that required under the 1933 Act. Companies registered under the 1934 Act become subject to certain further requirements which will be discussed later in this chapter, such as the rules pertaining to the solicitation of proxies and the filing of certain periodic reports. The 1934 Act also subjects directors and officers to the recapture of "short-swing profits" (as defined later in this chapter) and requires them to report monthly any transactions in the stock of the company.

The Prospectus. The instrument by which investors are to be given the information required by the 1933 Act is the prospectus. It must be filed with the SEC along with the registration statement. The required contents include much of the information required in the registration statement, and it must be furnished to every purchaser of the security being registered for distribution through underwriters and brokers prior to or concurrently with the transmission of the security to him. During the waiting period before the registration statement becomes effective, a preliminary or "red herring" prospectus may be used. The term is applied because a legend on the cover of the preliminary prospectus (which ordinarily will contain blanks instead of the offering price and the "spread" or commission going to those in the channels of distribution) is required to be printed in red ink. It warns that the document is incomplete and that securities may not be sold until the registration becomes effective. If 90 days have elapsed and the distribution of the issue is complete, a prospectus is no longer required in dealer sales of the security.

"Prospectus" is defined in the 1933 Act as being any notice, circular advertisement, letter, or radio or TV statement which offers a security for sale. The use of a "prospectus" thus defined is prohibited except when such information is given to one to whom a proper written document, confusingly also known as a prospectus, has been given. The purpose is to prevent a company planning to issue stock from "conditioning the market" by publicizing favorable news. Therefore, a prospective issuer and its directors and officers acting as individuals must be careful to avoid publicity about the company before the distribution of a new issue is completed. While the registration and distribution processes are under way, press releases, brochures, advertisements, speeches, and press conferences which have any relation to the issue or the prospects for the company may be dangerous and, if used, should be carefully prepared under expert legal guidance. An announcement called a "tombstone advertisement" is permitted during distribution. These are commonly seen in financial periodicals and merely give the name of the issuer, the type of security and its price, and tell from whom a proper prospectus can be obtained.

Periodic Reports. The Securities Exchange Act of 1934 (15d) requires registrants under the 1933 Act to file periodic reports with the SEC. Firms meeting certain criteria specified in Section 12 of the 1934 Act (presently total assets exceeding $1,000,000 and a class of equity securities held by 500 shareholders or a listing of securities on a national stock exchange) must file such reports even if they have no securities registered under the 1933 Act. These reports include: an annual report (form 10–K), a quarterly report (form 10–Q) and, when applicable, a current report (form 8–K).

Under SEC rules the 10–K report must include audited financial statements for the fiscal year plus current information about the conduct of the business and the management and the status of its securities. In effect, the 10–K report is intended to bring up to date the information required in the registration statement. The quarterly report, 10–Q, requires only a summarized and unaudited operating statement and unaudited figures on capitalization and shareholders' equity. The 8–K report is required within 10 days of the end of any month in which any of certain specified events occur, such as changes in the amount of securities, a default under the terms of an issue of securities, acquisition or disposition of assets, changes in control of the company, revaluations of assets, or "any materially important event."

Proxy Statements and Annual Reports. SEC rules require that a corporation registered under the 1934 Act furnish a proxy statement containing certain information with the proxy if it solicits proxies for a shareholders' meeting. If directors are to be elected, any employment contract with the nominee, pension benefits, and any options to purchase the corporation's shares held by him or her must be disclosed in the proxy statement as well as any material transaction between the corporation and any officer, director, nominee or holder of 10 percent or more of any class of shares of the company. The proxy form itself must give the shareholder a "two-way" choice on matters to be acted upon and a place to insert the date.

If the corporation does not solicit proxies, it must send all shareholders entitled to vote at the meeting an "Information Statement," which contains substantially the same information. A preliminary form of the proxy statement or information statement must be filed with the SEC at least 10 days before mailing to shareholders. If the proxy or information statement is issued in connection with an annual meeting of shareholders at which directors are to be elected, it must be preceded by a mailing of an annual report containing audited figures including a balance sheet and comparative operating statement of the current and immediately preceding fiscal years.

If misleading statements are made in the proxy solicitation, a court may enjoin the holding of the meeting or void the action taken. This statutory remedy is in addition to the common law remedy for breach of fiduciary duty to shareholders.

The corporation must furnish a shareholder who wishes to solicit proxies in competition with the management either a shareholder list or send his proxy material to the shareholders for him or her. It must also include in its own proxy a proposed resolution submitted by a shareholder. If the management opposes the proposal, it must include in its proxy statement a comment by the shareholder of not more than 200 words supporting the proposal. Management may omit proposals which are beyond the power of the corporation to effectuate, proposals which are not proper subjects for action by shareholders under the laws of the corporation's domicile, and proposals for action with respect to matters relating to the conduct of the ordinary business of the firm. A proposal which has been included in the proxy within the last three calendar years may also be omitted unless it has received 3 percent or more of the vote. If it has been voted upon twice, it must be included in the proxy only if it received 6 percent of the vote the last time it was submitted. After the third year, if the proposal has been voted on twice, it must be included on the proxy only if 10 percent of the shares favored it when last presented.

Summary

The Securities Act of 1933 requires corporations preparing to issue securities to provide the SEC and prospective investors with a great deal of information through a registration statement, as well as a prospectus, which must be furnished to every purchaser prior to or concurrently with the transmission of the security to him or her. Securities cannot be sold until the registration statement is in effect after being filed with the SEC. The SEC approves the registration statement and prospectus only in the sense of determining that they are complete.

Registration under the 1934 Act is a registration of a transaction only; it applies only to the sales of a particular issue of securities made at a certain point in time. Companies of a certain size must register even though their securities are not traded on an exchange. Registration requirements are similar to the 1933 Act. In addition, requirements as to proxy solicitation and periodic reporting to the SEC are imposed.

Rather elaborate rules have been issued by the SEC with respect to the solicitation of proxies for voting at shareholders' meetings, and the proxy statement must be filed in advance with the SEC.

Escott v. BarChris Construction Corp.

283 F. Supp. 643 (S.D.N.Y. 1968)

An action by Escott and other investors (plaintiffs) against BarChris Construction Corporation, the corporate directors—including its legal counsel, certain officers, the underwriters and its public auditors (defendants). Recovery was sought for losses suffered due to allegedly false statements and omissions in a prospectus which would constitute a violation of Section 11 of the Securities Act of 1933. Held for investors, with additional issues not here pertinent being reserved for later decision. (Note: The excerpts from the opinion deal only with those defendants indicated in the subheads.)

BarChris was in the business of constructing bowling centers. With the introduction of automatic pin-setting machines in 1952 there was a rapid growth in the popularity of bowling, and BarChris's sales had increased from $800,000 in 1956 to over $9,000,000 in 1960. By 1960 it was building about 3 percent of the lanes constructed while Brunswick Corporation and AMC were building 97 percent. Unlike its larger competitors, BarChris did not manufacture bowling equipment. Its method of operation was to contract with a customer for the construction and equipping of a bowling alley, requiring a relatively small down payment in cash and taking the balance, after the work was completed, in notes which it discounted with a factor. The factor held back part of the face value of the notes as a reserve and could call on BarChris to repurchase the notes if the debtors were in default. In 1960 it began to offer an alternative method of financing which involved selling the equipment to a factor, James Talcott, Inc., which would then lease it back either to BarChris's customer or to a subsidiary of BarChris which would then sublease to the customer. Under either financing method BarChris made substantial expenditures before receiving reimbursement and was, therefore, in constant need of cash, which grew as operations expanded.

In December 1959, BarChris sold additional common stock, but by early 1961 it needed more working capital. It determined to offer debentures, and part of the proceeds of the debentures was to be devoted to this purpose. The preliminary registration statement was filed with the SEC in March, it became effective on May 16, and the closing was held on May 24, 1961. By that time BarChris was experiencing difficulties in collecting amounts due it from some of its customers, and others were in arrears on their payments to the factors. Due to overexpansion in the number of bowling alleys, many operators failed. The result was that on October 29, 1962, BarChris itself filed a petition under the Bankruptcy Act and defaulted on the payment of interest on the debentures.

The court found that BarChris had in the prospectus overstated sales and earnings and also its current assets in its 1960 financial statements. It also understated, the court found, its contingent liabilities by $375,795 as of December 31, 1960, and by $618,853 as of March 31, 1961. First quarter 1961 earnings were overstated by $230,755 (92%) and the March 31, 1969 backlog was overstated by $4,490,000 (185%) the court held. It also found that the prospectus was in error in stating that loans from officers had been paid off, finding loans outstanding of $386,615. Further, the court held that: $1,160,000 of the proceeds of the debentures were used to pay off old debts and this was not disclosed in the prospectus; BarChris had a potential liability to factors due to customer delinquencies of $1,350,000 which it did not disclose; and it misrepresented the nature of its business by failing to disclose that it was already engaged and was about to become more heavily engaged in the operation of bowling alleys to try to minimize its losses from customer defaults.

Each of the defendants had either signed the registration statement or had consented to being named in it as an "expert." Each except BarChris asserted in his defense that he had acted with due diligence as defined in Section 11b (3).

McLEAN, DISTRICT JUDGE.   I turn now to the question of whether defendants have proved their due diligence defenses. The position of each defendant will be separately considered:

Trilling

[Trilling] was BarChris's controller. He signed the registration statement in that capacity, although he was not a director. Trilling entered BarChris's employ in October 1960. He was Kircher's (BarChris's treasurer) subordinate. When Kircher asked him for information, he furnished it.

Trilling was not a member of the executive committee. He was a comparatively minor figure in BarChris. The description of BarChris's "management" on page 9 of the prospectus does not mention him. He was not considered to be an executive officer.

Trilling may well have been unaware of several of the inaccuracies in the prospectus. But he must have known of some of them. As a financial officer, he was familiar with BarChris's finances and with its books of account. He knew that part of the cash on deposit on December 31, 1960, had been procured temporarily by Russo for window-dressing purposes. He knew that BarChris was operating Capitol Lanes in 1960. He should have known, although perhaps through carelessness he did not know at the time, that BarChris's contingent liability on Type B lease transactions was greater than the prospectus stated. In the light of these facts, I cannot find that Trilling believed the entire prospectus to be true.

But even if he did, he still did not establish his due diligence defenses. He did not prove that as to the parts of the prospectus expertised by Peat, Marwick he had no reasonable ground to believe that it was untrue. He also failed to prove, as to the parts of the prospectus not expertised by Peat, Marwick, that he made a reasonable investigation which afforded him a reasonable ground to believe that it was true. As far as appears, he made no investigation. He did what was asked of him and assumed that others would properly take care of supplying accurate data as to the other aspects of the company's business. This would have been well enough but for the fact that he signed the registration statement. As a signer, he could not avoid responsibility by leaving it up to others to make it accurate. Trilling did not sustain the burden of proving his due diligence defenses.

Auslander

Auslander was an "outside" director, i.e., one who was not an officer of BarChris. He was chairman of the board of Valley Stream National Bank in Valley Stream, Long Island. In February 1961, Vitolo asked him to become a director of BarChris. Vitolo gave him an enthusiastic account of BarChris's progress and prospects.

In February and early March 1961, before accepting Vitolo's invitation, Auslander made some investigation of BarChris. He obtained Dun & Bradstreet reports which contained sales and earnings figures for periods earlier than December 31, 1960. He caused inquiry to be made of certain of BarChris's banks and was advised that they regarded BarChris favorably. He was informed that inquiry of Talcott had also produced a favorable response.

On March 3, 1961, Auslander indicated his willingness to accept a place on the board. Shortly thereafter, on March 14, Kircher sent him a copy of BarChris's annual report for 1960. Auslander observed that BarChris's auditors were Peat, Marwick. They were also the auditors for the Valley Stream National Bank. He thought well of them.

Auslander was elected a director on April 17, 1961. The registration statement in its original form had already been filed, of course without his signature. On May 10, 1961, he signed a signature page for the first amendment to the registration statement which was filed on May 11, 1961. This was a separate sheet without any document attached. Auslander did not know that it was a signature page for a registration statement. He vaguely understood that it was something "for the SEC."

At the May 15 directors' meeting, however, Auslander did realize that what he was signing was a signature sheet to a registration statement. This was the first time that he had appreciated the fact. A copy of the registration statement in its earlier form as amended on May 11, 1961, was passed around at the meeting. Auslander glanced at it briefly. He did not read it thoroughly.

At the May 15 meeting, Russo and Vitolo stated that everything was in order and that the prospectus was correct. Auslander believed this statement. . . . Auslander knew that Peat, Marwick had audited the 1960 figures. He believed them to be correct because he had confidence in Peat, Marwick. He had no reasonable ground to believe otherwise.

As to the [remainder of the prospectus], however, Auslander is in a different position. He seems to have been under the impression that Peat, Marwick was responsible for all the figures. This impression was not correct, as he would have realized if he had read the prospectus carefully. Auslander made no investigation of the accuracy of the prospectus. He relied on the assurance of Vitolo and Russo, and upon the information he had received in answer to his inquiries back in February and early March. These inquiries were general ones, in the nature of a credit check. The information which he received in answer to them was also general, without specific reference to the statements in the prospectus, which was not prepared until some time thereafter.

It is true that Auslander became a director on the eve of the financing. He had little opportunity to familiarize himself with the company's affairs. The question is whether, under such circumstances, Auslander did enough to establish his due diligence.

Section 11 imposes liability in the first instance upon a director, no matter how new he is. He is presumed to know his responsibility when he becomes a director. He can escape liability only by using that reasonable care to investigate the facts which a prudent man would employ in the management of his own property. In my opinion, a prudent man would not act in an important matter without any knowledge of the relevant facts, in sole reliance upon general information which does not purport to cover the particular case. To say that such minimal conduct measures up to the statutory standard would, to all intents and purposes, absolve new directors from responsibility merely because they are new. This is not a sensible construction of Section 11, when one bears in mind its fundamental purpose of requiring full and truthful disclosure for the protection of investors.

Peat, Marwick

The part of the registration statement purporting to be made upon the authority of Peat, Marwick as an expert was, as we have seen, the 1960 figures. But because the statute requires the court to determine Peat, Marwick's belief, and the grounds thereof, "at the time such part of the registration statement became effective," for the purposes of this affirmative defense, the matter must be viewed as of May 16, 1961, and the question is whether at that time Peat, Marwick, after reasonable investigation, had reasonable ground to believe and did believe that the 1960 figures were true and that no material fact had been omitted from the registration statement which should have been included in order to make the 1960 figures not misleading. In deciding this issue, the court must consider not only what Peat, Marwick did in its 1960 audit, but also what it did in its subsequent "S–1 review." The proper scope of that review must also be determined.

Peat, Marwick's work was in general charge of a member of the firm, Cummings, and more immediately in charge of Peat, Marwick's manager, Logan. Most of the actual work was performed by a senior accountant, Berardi, who had junior assistants, one of whom was Kennedy.

Berardi was then about 30 years old. He was not yet a CPA. He had had no previous experience with the bowling industry. This was his first job as a senior accountant. He could hardly have been given a more difficult assignment.

It is unnecessary to recount everything that Berardi did in the course of the audit. We are concerned only with the evidence relating to what Berardi did or did not do with respect to those items which I have found to have been incorrectly reported in the 1960 figures in the prospectus. More narrowly, we are directly concerned only with such of those items as I have found to be material.

First and foremost is Berardi's failure to discover that Capitol Lanes had not been sold. This error affected both the sales figure and the liability side of the balance sheet. Fundamentally, the error stemmed from the fact that Berardi never realized that Heavenly Lanes and Capitol were two different names for the same alley. . . . Berardi assumed that Heavenly was to be treated like any other completed job.

*   *   *   *   *

Berardi testified that he inquired of Russo about Capitol Lanes and that Russo told him that Capitol Lanes, Inc., was going to operate an alley some day but as yet it had no alley. Berardi testified that he understood that the alley had not been built and that he believed that the rental payments were on vacant land.

I am not satisfied with this testimony. If Berardi did hold this belief he should not have held it. The entries as to insurance and as to "operation of alley" should have alerted him to the fact that an alley existed. He should have made further inquiry on the subject. It is apparent that Berardi did not understand this transaction.

The burden of proof on this issue is on Peat, Marwick. Although the question is a rather close one, I find that Peat, Marwick has not sustained that burden. Peat, Marwick has not proved that Berardi made a reasonable investigation as far as Capitol Lanes was concerned and that his ignorance of the true facts was justified.

The purpose of reviewing events subsequent to the date of a certified balance sheet (referred to as an S–1 review when made with reference to a registration statement) is to ascertain whether any material change has occurred in the company's financial position which should be disclosed in order to prevent the balance sheet figures from being misleading. The scope of such a review, under generally accepted auditing standards is limited. It does not amount to a complete audit.

*   *   *   *   *

Berardi made the S–1 review in May 1961. He devoted a little over two days to it, a total of 20½ hours. He did not discover any of the errors or omissions pertaining to the state of affairs in 1961 which I have previously discussed at length, all of which were material. The question is whether, despite his failure to find out anything, his investigation was reasonable within the meaning of the statute.

What Berardi did was to look at a consolidating trial balance as of March 31, 1961, which had been prepared by BarChris, compare it with the audited December 31, 1960, figures, discuss with Trilling certain unfavorable developments which the comparison disclosed, and read certain minutes. He did not examine any "important financial records" other than the trial balance.

In substance, what Berardi did is similar to what . . . Ballard did. He asked questions, he got answers which he considered satisfactory, and he did nothing to verify them. . . .

Berardi had no conception of how tight the cash position was. He did not discover that BarChris was holding up checks in substantial amounts because there was no money in the bank to cover them. He did not know of the loan from Manufacturers Trust Company or of the officers' loans. Since he never read the prospectus, he was not even aware that there had ever been any problem about loans from officers.

During the 1960 audit, Berardi had obtained some information from factors, not sufficiently detailed even then, as to delinquent notes. He made no inquiry of factors about this in his S–1 review. Since he knew nothing about Kircher's notes of the executive committee meetings, he did not learn that the delinquency situation had grown worse. He was content with Trilling's assurance that no liability theretofore contingent had become direct.

There had been a material change for the worse in BarChris's financial position. That change was sufficiently serious so that the failure to disclose it made the 1960 figures misleading. Berardi did not discover it. As far as results were concerned, his S–1 review was useless.

Accountants should not be held to a standard higher than that recognized in their profession. I do not do so here. Berardi's review did not come up to that standard. He did not take some of the steps which Peat, Marwick's written program prescribed. He did not spend an adequate amount of time on a task of this magnitude. Most important of all, he was too easily satisfied with glib answers to his inquiries.

This is not to say that he should have made a complete audit. But there were enough danger signals in the materials which he did examine to require some further investigation on his part. Generally accepted accounting standards required such further investigation under these circumstances. It is not always sufficient merely to ask questions.

Here again, the burden of proof is on Peat, Marwick. I find that that burden has not been satisfied. I conclude that Peat, Marwick has not established its due diligence defense.

Requirements of Directors, Officers, and Others

Reports of Stock Transactions.   Section 16a of the 1934 Act requires that the directors and officers of a corporation registered under the act and shareholders holding 10 percent or more of any class of its equity securities file individually a statement disclosing the amount of such holdings. Thereafter, they must report any transactions in such securities within ten days following the end of the month in which the transaction occurs. Purchases and sales made before or after one becomes obligated to report transactions must also be reported if they are made within six months of transactions made while an officer, director or 10 percent shareholder. Those required to report are also prohibited from making short sales of the securities (sales of shares not owned at the time of sale).

"**Short-Swing Profits.**"   Section 16b of the 1934 Act provides that any profit made by anyone required to report their transactions in the stock belongs to the company if it resulted from the purchase and sale or sale and purchase of its securities within less than a six-month period. Either the corporation itself or a holder of its securities may file a suit to recapture the profit for the corporation. This provision was designed to remove temptation from insiders to make short-term profits in the corporation's securities by buying and then selling, or the reverse, in order to take advantage of short-term price swings resulting from events concerning which they have advance information. However, the application of the provision is without regard to intent. In a number of cases courts have held inadvertent or otherwise innocent sales and sales made without the benefit of inside knowledge, to be subject to the provision, although recently the United States Supreme Court exempted a transaction involving a corporation which had been the object of an unsuccessful acquisition bid.[3]

Tender Offers.   After a wave of corporate acquisitions through tender offers, the Williams Act amendments to the 1934 Act were passed in 1968 to provide investors with more information in these situations. Under these amendments anyone—which, of course, includes corporations—seeking to gain ownership of more than 10 percent of a class of equity securities registered under the 1934 Act must file with the SEC and provide shareholders of the "target company" certain information. This includes information about the offeror and his or her background, shares held by the offeror and his associates, agreements made to gain support for the tender offer, sources of funds, the purpose in making the offer, and, if the purpose is control, specific plans for liquidation or merger of the "target company." The amendments also give the shareholder an opportunity to withdraw the tender of his or her shares within certain time limits. They also require the offeror to accept shares tendered during the first ten days of the offer on a pro rata basis and to extend any increased offering price to tenders made earlier. If the target company management wishes to make a recommendation on the offer to its shareholders, it must make a filing with the SEC. An antifraud provision specifically applying to tender offers was added in Section 14e.

---

[3] *Kern County Land Co. v. Occidental Petroleum Corp.* 411 U.S. 582 (1973).

Summary

Directors, officers, and holders of 10 percent or more of any class of equity securities of a corporation must file reports of their shareholdings and transactions in the stock with the SEC, and they are prohibited from making "short sales." "Short-swing profits," or those made from buying and selling within a six months' period by such "insiders," may be recovered by the corporation. The Williams Act amendments impose numerous requirements upon those making tender offers for shares of a corporation and upon management of the "target company."

Kern County Land Co. v. Occidental Petroleum Corp.

411 U.S. 582 (U.S. Sup. Ct. 1973)

Suit by Kern County Land Company (plaintiff) to recover "short-swing" profits from Occidental Petroleum Corporation (defendant) under Section 16(b) of the Securities Exchange Act of 1934. Judgment for Kern County Land Company (New Kern) on its motion for summary judgment. Reversed by Court of Appeals. Affirmed.

Occidental sought to negotiate a merger with Kern County Land Company (Old Kern), which had extensive real estate and farming operations and interests in manufacturing. After being rebuffed, Occidental on May 8, 1967, made a tender offer for 500,000 (over 10 percent) of the 4,328,000 shares outstanding in Old Kern at a price of $83.50 per share. The market price at that time was about $64 and the range in prices in the period since January 1, 1964, had been from a low of 51¾ to a high of 76¼. It extended its tender offer, and at the close on June 8, 1967, Occidental owned 887,549 shares.

Management of Old Kern sought to frustrate the takeover attempts by wiring shareholders advising them against tendering their shares to Occidental. It then undertook merger discussions with Tenneco, Inc., another large, diversified company with extensive interests in the oil and gas industry. The proposal provided for the incorporation of New Kern to take over the assets and continue the business of Old Kern, with the shareholders of Old Kern receiving a share of cumulative convertible preference stock in Tenneco in exchange for each share of Old Kern common. Occidental, in a report to its shareholders, estimated the value of the Tenneco preference shares at $105.

Occidental, fearing that it would be locked into a minority position in Tenneco, negotiated an arrangement with Tenneco whereby it granted Tenneco an option to purchase at $105 per share all of the Tenneco preference stock to which it would become entitled when and if the merger were consummated. To secure the option a $10 per share premium was paid immediately to Occidental, but if the option were exercised the premium would be credited to the purchase price. The option was not exercisable until a date more than six months after the expiration of Occidental's tender offer for Old Kern shares. However, the option agreement was entered into within six months of the time Occidental had acquired more than 10 percent ownership of Old Kern through its tender offer.

The option was exercised by Tenneco, which resulted in a total profit to Occidental of $19,506,419 on the Old Kern shares obtained through its tender offer. New Kern filed suit to recover these profits under Section 16(b) of the Securities Exchange Act of 1934.

MR. JUSTICE WHITE.   Section 16(b) provides, *inter alia,* that a statutory insider must surrender to the issuing corporation "any profit realized by him from any purchase and sale, or any sale and purchase, of any equity security of such issuer . . . within any period of less than six months." As specified in its introductory clause, § 16(b) was enacted "[f]or the purpose of preventing the unfair use of information which may have been obtained by a [statutory insider] . . . by reason of his relationship to the issuer." Congress recognized that short-swing speculation by stockholders with advance, inside information would threaten the goal of the Securities Exchange Act to "insure the maintenance of fair and honest markets." Insiders could exploit information not generally available to others to secure quick profits. As we have noted, "the only method Congress deemed effective to curb the evils of insider trading was a flat rule taking the profits out of a class of transactions in which the possibility of abuse was believed to be intolerably great." *Reliance Electric Co. v. Emerson Electric Co.* As stated in the report of the Senate Committee, the bill aimed at protecting the public "by preventing directors, officers and principal stockholders of a corporation . . . from speculating in the stock on the basis of information not available to others."

Although traditional cash-for-stock transactions that result in a purchase and sale or a sale and purchase within the six-month, statutory period are clearly encompassed within the purview of § 16(b) the courts have wrestled with the question of inclusion or exclusion of certain "unorthodox" transactions. The statutory definitions of "purchase" and "sale" are broad and, at least arguably, reach many transactions not ordinarily deemed a sale or purchase. . . .

* * * * *

Occidental was, after all, a tender offeror, threatening to seize control of Old Kern, displace its management, and use the company for its own ends. The Old Kern management vigorously and immediately opposed Occidental's efforts. Twice it communicated with its stockholders, advising against acceptance of Occidental's offer and indicating prior to May 11 and prior to Occidental's extension of its offer, that there was a possibility of an imminent merger and a more profitable exchange. Old Kern's management refused to discuss with Occidental officials the subject of an Old Kern-Occidental merger. Instead, it undertook negotiations with Tenneco and forthwith concluded an agreement, announcing the merger terms on May 19. Requests by Occidental for inspection of Old Kern records were sufficiently frustrated by Old Kern's management to force Occidental to litigation to secure the information it desired.

There is, therefore, nothing in connection with Occidental's acquisition of Old Kern stock pursuant to its tender offer to indicate either the possibility of inside information being available to Occidental by virtue of its stock ownership or the potential for speculative abuse of such inside information by Occidental. Much the same can be said of the events leading to the exchange of Occidental's Old Kern stock for Tenneco preferred, which is one of the transactions that is sought to be classified a "sale" under

§ 16(b). The critical fact is that the exchange took place and was required pursuant to a merger between Old Kern and Tenneco. That merger was not engineered by Occidental but was sought by Old Kern to frustrate the attempts of Occidental to gain control of Old Kern. Occidental obviously did not participate in or control the negotiations or the agreement between Old Kern and Tenneco. Once agreement between those two companies crystalized, the course of subsequent events was out of Occidental's hands. Old Kern needed the consent of its stockholder, but as it turned out, Old Kern's management had the necessary votes without the affirmative vote of Occidental. The merger agreement was approved by a majority of the stockholders of Old Kern, excluding the votes to which Occidental was entitled by virtue of its ownership of Old Kern shares.

Antifraud Provisions

Introduction.   To accomplish its objective of preventing fraud, unfair, deceptive, and manipulative practices and providing remedies to the victims of such practices, Congress included a number of provisions in the securities acts. These provisions are not all mutually exclusive in their application. Rule 10b–5 has come to be used by plaintiffs more than any other provision.

Antifraud Provisions of 1933 Act.   Section 11a of the 1933 Act provides civil liabilities for damages resulting to an investor who finds, after acquiring a security, that the registration statement for the security contained an untrue statement or an omission of a material fact. Those potentially liable for such misleading or false information in the registration statement are all who signed it, all directors (whether or not they signed), every "expert" who gave consent to be named in the registration statement as having prepared or certified part of it and the underwriters of the distribution of the security. Among the defenses permitted is what has come to be known as the "due diligence defense." If a defendant can show that after making a reasonable investigation he had reasonable grounds to believe that the statements in it were true and there was no omission of a material fact, he will not be held liable.

Section 12(2) prohibits making untrue or misleading statements in a prospectus or in oral communication in connection with the offering or sale of a security. This is not limited to securities which are required to be registered and it applies to anything which is held under the Act to be a prospectus, not just the formal document usually so named. Section 17a broadly prohibits the use, in connection with an offer or sale of any security (again whether or not required to be registered), of any device or scheme to defraud or the use of any untrue or misleading statement. Section 17b is designed to deal with the evils of the "tipster" sheet. It requires anyone who publicizes a security in a newspaper, magazine, and so forth, for a consideration to disclose that fact and give the amount of pay he is receiving.

All of these provisions apply to the use of the mails or any means of transportation or communication in interstate commerce. This has been interpreted to include the use of the telephone even when both buyer and seller are in the same city.[4]

Antifraud Provisions of 1934 Act. Section 9 specifically prohibits a number of deceptive practices which had previously been used to cause security prices to rise or fall by stimulating market activity. Prohibited practices include sales involving no change in beneficial ownership and certain other actions seeking to affect the price of a security.

Section 10b is an extremely broad provision prohibiting the use of any manipulative or deceptive device in contravention of any rules the SEC may prescribe as necessary or appropriate in the public interest.

Rule 10b–5. This rule was adopted under Section 10b of the 1934 Act. It couples the broad language of Section 10b with the somewhat more detailed language of Section 17a of the 1933 Act so as to make the prohibitions of 17a apply to purchasers as well as sellers. The rule speaks in very general terms as follows:

It shall be unlawful for any person, directly or indirectly, by use of any means or instrumentality of interstate commerce or of the mails, or of any facility of any national securities exchange, (*a*) to employ any device, scheme, or artifice to defraud, (*b*) to make any untrue statement of a material fact or to omit to state a material fact necessary in order to make the statements made, in the light of the circumstances under which they were made, not misleading, or (*c*) to engage in any act, practice, or course of business which operates or would operate as a fraud or deceit upon any person, in connection with the purchase or sale of any security.

Its sweeping language and the recognition in 1946[5] of an implied right of an injured party to recover under it have encouraged imaginative counsel for private plaintiffs as well as the SEC and sympathetic courts to expand the scope of its applicability so wide that the case law interpreting the rule is frequently described as a federal law of corporations. It is applicable to nonregistered securities, to those not listed on an exchange and to face-to-face transactions as well as those transactions completed on an exchange.

The boundaries of its applicability remain rather uncertain, and the decisions under it are not easy to reconcile—a not unusual situation in new and rapidly growing areas of the law. Also, lack of precision is, of course, a continuing and necessary characteristic of the related tort law of fraud, due to the unlimited ingenuity of those who would deceive.

Section 10b–5 has been used to deal with both of the evils to which the securities laws are principally addressed—deceptive practices and lack of sufficient information by the ordinary investor. In applying the rule to deceptive

---

[4] *Myzel v. Fields,* 386 F.2d 718 (8th Cir. 1967).

[5] *Kardon v. National Gypsum Co.,* 73 F.Supp. 798 (E.D. Pa. 1946), *modified* 83 F.Supp. 613 (E.D. Pa. 1947).

practices, courts have interpreted the prohibitions to be much broader than common law fraud.

A number of the cases brought under 10b–5 allege conduct that would amount to fraud. For example, a manager of a business which had been unprofitable induced shareholders to sell their stock to him by representing that the business would continue to decline although he knew that it had become potentially profitable, and in fact he sold the business at a very large profit to himself.[6] Other false statements or misleading statements, such as those published by a company to promote its product just prior to going public, may be violations of 10b–5 even though not common law fraud.[7]

Efforts to manipulate stock prices which do not involve false statements, such as reducing dividends for the purpose of depressing stock prices,[8] are also violations. Action by company executives to manipulate the price of the company's stock by transactions on behalf of an employee stock-bonus trust for which they were trustees has also been declared a violation.[9]

Although an early case held that there was no right of action under Rule 10b–5 against directors for mismanagement, some breaches of fiduciary duty by company insiders have been successfully attacked under 10b–5. One such case involved issuance of shares by directors to themselves at a price below the fair value.[10]

Failure to meet requirements of other sections of the securities laws have been held to violate Rule 10b–5. In one case, for example, failure to file required information on form 10–K, the annual report, was so treated although company officials did not trade in the stock at that time.[11]

Many cases involve concealment or failure to disclose information known to an insider. Some of these involve face-to-face transactions between an insider and another shareholder, as where two directors acquired all of the outstanding stock of the corporation without disclosing the existence of a written agreement with a third party to sell the company's assets at a much higher value.[12] Others, such as the famous *SEC v. Texas Gulf Sulphur Co.* case, below, involve trading on a stock exchange by persons in possession of information which has not been disclosed generally.

The *Texas Gulf Sulphur* case clearly holds that it is a violation to buy or sell either on an exchange or in a direct transaction when one is privy to "material" information which is not generally available to the investing public.

---

[6] *Janigan v. Taylor,* 344 F.2d 781 (1st Cir., 1965).

[7] *SEC v. Electrogen Industries, Inc.,* CCH ¶92,156 (1967–69 Transfer Binder).

[8] *Cochran v. Channing Corp.,* 211 F.Supp. 239 (S.D.N.Y. 1962).

[9] *SEC v. Georgia–Pacific Corp.,* CCH ¶91,692 (1964–66 Transfer Binder).

[10] *Weitzen & Epstein v. Kearns,* 271 F. Supp. 616 (S.D.N.Y. 1967).

[11] *Heit v. Weitzen,* 402 F.2d 909 (2d Cir. 1968).

[12] *Kardon v. National Gypsum Co.,* 73 F.Supp. 798 (E.D. Pa. 1947).

This applies to almost anyone, not just those usually viewed as insiders, such as directors, officers, and those who own a major interest in the company. It would include secretaries, employees such as researchers or geologists and their supervisors. Included also are outside consultants, lawyers, engineers, financial and public relations advisors, and others given "inside" information for special purposes, such as news reporters and personnel of government agencies. Furthermore, "tippees" (those who are given or acquire the information without a need to know) such as stockbrokers or financial analysts and even relatives or friends of those acquiring the information for a corporate purpose are forbidden to trade and are subject to recovery of their profits if they do. Although stock exchanges have rules as to when issuers must release "material" information, the cases so far merely hold that the securities laws forbid trading while in possession of unreleased information which is material.

The test for materiality of corporate information has been variously stated but in essence it is any information which is likely to have an impact upon the price of a security in the market. The SEC has said that a fact is material if its disclosure would reasonably be expected to affect the market price of the stock or would materially affect the decision of a prospective buyer or seller whether to buy, sell, or delay. Certainly such matters as proposed mergers, tender offers for the corporation's stock, plans to introduce an important new product or indications of an abrupt change in the profit expectations of the company are examples of what would be considered material facts. A more difficult question, which troubled the courts in the *Texas Gulf Sulphur* case, is when information with some element of uncertainty about it becomes material or how early in the development of a plan or trend a disclosure or abstention from buying or selling is required.

Summary

Both the 1933 and 1934 acts include antifraud provisions. The most used is Section 10b of the 1934 Act, under which Rule 10b–5 of the SEC has been issued. It has been used extensively both to impose liabilities for failure to provide an investor with adequate information and for the use of deceptive practices. Practices which would not amount to common law fraud are covered by this section.

SEC v. Texas Gulf Sulphur Co.

401 F.2d 833 (2d Cir. 1968)

This was an action by the Securities and Exchange Commission (plaintiff) against the Texas Gulf Sulphur Company (TGS) and thirteen of its officers, directors, and employees (defendants) alleging violations of Section 10b of the Securities Exchange Act of 1934. The District Court found that two of the individuals, Clayton and Crawford, had violated the act but otherwise dismissed the complaint. On appeal the judgment was affirmed as to Clayton and Crawford and reversed as to all other parties but one, Murray, who was held not to have committed a violation. The case was remanded to determine whether TGS had violated the act and to determine remedies.

TGS had for several years made serial geophysical surveys in eastern Canada followed by drilling exploratory cores into geological formations that looked promising. On November 12, 1963, the core from the first drilling on a parcel of land near Timmins, Ontario, was fabulously high in copper content as well as in zinc and silver. Diversionary holes were then drilled elsewhere until the balance of the land covered by the formation could be acquired by TGS. The land-acquisition program had progressed far enough for TGS to resume drilling in the area on March 31, 1964. The next two cores also showed substantial quantities of the same minerals and additional rigs were put to work drilling more holes beginning on April 8. Meanwhile, rumors of a major ore strike were circulating in Canada and on Saturday, April 11, two major New York papers printed reports of TGS activity and appeared to infer a rich strike from the fact that the drill cores were being flown to the United States.

Following this publication on Saturday, Stephens, the president of TGS, and Fogarty, the executive vice president, were concerned by the publicized rumors and talked with Mollison, the TGS vice president who was in charge of the operations near Timmins. He had left the drilling on Friday and was at his home near New York City for the weekend. As a result on Sunday a news release was distributed for use on Monday, April 13. The release stated that most of the drilling in eastern Canada had shown nothing of value with a few holes indicating small or marginal ore bodies. It said that shipment of the cores to the United States was routine. It then added:

> Recent drilling on one property near Timmins has led to preliminary indications that more drilling would be required for proper evaluation of this prospect. The drilling done to date has not been conclusive, but the statements made by many outside quarters are unreliable and include information and figures that are not available to TGS.
>
> The work done to date has not been sufficient to reach definite conclusions and any statement as to size and grade of ore would be premature and possibly misleading. When we have progressed to the point where reasonable and logical conclusions can be made, TGS will issue a definitive statement to its stockholders and to the public in order to clarify the Timmins project.

On April 16 at 10:00 A.M. TGS held a conference for the financial press and disclosed that the ore body would run to at least 25,000,000 tons of ore. This information was published on the Dow-Jones tape at 10:54 A.M.

Some of the individual defendants had purchased stock or calls upon stock in TGS between the time the results were known to them of the first core drilled on the site and the appearance of the second release on the Dow-Jones tape. Others, including Stephens and Fogarty, had accepted options to buy TGS stock from the corporation's stock-option committee of the board of directors which was unaware of the find. The market price of TGS stock rose from approximately $18 per share on November 12, 1963, to $58 on May 15, 1964. In addition to alleging a violation of the Securities Exchange Act by the individuals, the SEC claimed that the first press release of TGS, issued April 12, was deceptive and misleading in violation of the Act.

WATERMAN, CIRCUIT JUDGE. . . . The essence of the Rule is that anyone who, trading for his own account in the securities of a corporation has "access, directly or indirectly, to information intended to be available only for a corporate purpose and not for the personal benefit of anyone" may not take "advantage of such information knowing it is unavailable to those with whom he is dealing," that is, the investing public.

Insiders, as directors or management officers are, of course, by this Rule, precluded from so unfairly dealing, but the Rule is also applicable to one possessing that information who may not be strictly termed an "insider" within the meaning of Sec. 16(b) of the Act.

Thus, anyone in possession of material inside information must either disclose it to the investing public, or if he is disabled from disclosing it in order to protect a corporate confidence, or he chooses not to do so, must abstain from trading in or recommending the securities concerned while such inside information remains undisclosed. So, it is here no justification for insider activity that disclosure was forbidden by the legitimate corporate objective of acquiring options to purchase the land surrounding the exploration site: if the information was, as the SEC contends, material, its possessors should have kept out of the market until disclosure was accomplished. . . . Material facts include not only information disclosing the earnings and distributions of a company, but also those facts which affect the desire of investors to buy, sell, or hold the company's securities.

* * * * *

In each case, then, whether facts are material within Rule 10b–5 when the facts relate to a particular event and are undisclosed by those persons who are knowledgeable thereof will depend at any given time upon a balancing of both the indicated probability that the event will occur and the anticipated magnitude of the event in light of the totality of the company activity.

Here, notwithstanding the trial court's conclusion that the results of the first drill core, K–55–1, were "too 'remote' . . . to have had any significant impact on the market, that is, to be deemed material," knowledge of the possibility, which surely was more than marginal, of the existence of a mine of the vast magnitude indicated by the remarkably rich drill core located rather close to the surface (suggesting mineability by the less expensive open-pit method) within the confines of a large anomaly (suggesting an extensive region of mineralization) might well have affected the price of TGS stock and would certainly have been an important fact to a reasonable, if speculative, investor in deciding whether he should buy, sell or hold.

We hold, therefore, that all transactions in TGS stock or calls by individuals apprised of the drilling results of K–55–1 were made in violation of Rule 10b–5.

* * * * *

Appellant Crawford, who ordered the purchase of TGS stock shortly before the TGS April 16 official announcement, and defendant Coates, who placed orders with and communicated the news to his broker immediately after the official announcement was read at the TGS-called press conference, concede that they were in possession of material information. They contend, however, that their purchases were not proscribed purchases for the news had already been effectively disclosed. We disagree. . . . Before insiders may act upon material information, such information must have been effectively disclosed in a manner sufficient to insure its availability to the investing public. Particularly here, where a formal announcement to the entire financial news media has been promised in a prior official release known to the media, all insider activity must await dissemination of the promised official announcement.

Assuming that the contents of the official release could instantaneously be acted upon, at the minimum Coates should have waited until the news could reasonably have been expected to appear over the media of widest circulation, the Dow-Jones broadtape, rather than hastening to insure an advantage to himself and his broker son-in-law.

* * * * *

Contrary to the belief of the trial court that Kline had no duty to disclose his knowledge of the Kidd project before accepting the stock option offered him, we believe that he, a vice president, who had become the general counsel of TGS in January 1964, but who had been secretary of the corporation since January 1961, and was present in that capacity when the options were granted, and who was in charge of the mechanics of issuance and acceptance of the options, was a member of top management and under a duty before accepting his option to disclose any material information he may have possessed, and, as he did not disclose such information to the Option Committee we direct rescission of the option he received.

* * * * *

II. The Corporate Defendant

[I]t seems clear from the broad legislative purpose Congress expressed in the Act, and the legislative history of Section 10b that Congress when it used the phrase "in connection with the purchase or sale of any security" intended only that the device employed, whatever it might be, be of a sort that would cause reasonable investors to rely thereon, and, in connection therewith, so relying, cause them to purchase or sell a corporation's securities. There is no indication that Congress intended that the corporations or persons responsible for the issuance of a misleading statement would not violate the section unless they engaged in related securities transactions or otherwise acted with wrongful motives; indeed, the obvious purposes of the Act to protect the investing public and to secure fair dealing in the securities markets would be seriously undermined by applying such a gloss onto the legislative language.

Absent a securities transaction by an insider it is almost impossible to prove that a wrongful purpose motivated the issuance of the misleading statement. The mere fact that an insider did not engage in securities transactions does not negate the possibility of wrongful purpose; perhaps the market did not react to the misleading statement as much as was anticipated or perhaps the wrongful purpose was something other than the desire to buy at a low price or sell at a high price. Of even greater relevance to the Congressional purpose of investor protection is the fact that the investing public may be injured as much by one's misleading statement containing inaccuracies caused by negligence as by a misleading statement published intentionally to further a wrongful purpose.

* * * * *

To render the Congressional purpose ineffective by inserting into the statutory words the need of proving, not only that the public may have been misled by the release, but also that those responsible were actuated by a wrongful purpose when they issued the release, is to handicap unreasonably the Commission in its work.

*   *   *   *   *

. . . [T]he investing public is hurt by exposure to false or deceptive statements irrespective of the purpose underlying their issuance. It does not appear to be unfair to impose upon corporate management a duty to ascertain the truth of any statements the corporation releases to its shareholders or to the investing public at large.

Accordingly, we hold that Rule 10b–5 is violated whenever assertions are made, as here, in a manner reasonably calculated to influence the investing public, for example, by means of the financial media, if such assertions are false or misleading or are so incomplete as to mislead irrespective of whether the issuance of the release was motivated by corporate officials for ulterior purposes. It seems clear, however, that if corporate management demonstrates that it was diligent in ascertaining that the information it published was the whole truth and that such diligently obtained information was disseminated in good faith, Rule 10b–5 would not have been violated.

*   *   *   *   *

In the event that it is found that the statement was misleading to the reasonable investor it will then become necessary to determine whether its issuance resulted from a lack of due diligence. The only remedy the Commission seeks against the corporation is an injunction, and therefore we do not find it necessary to decide whether a lack of due diligence on the part of TGS alone, absent a showing of bad faith, would subject the corporation to any liability for damages. . . .

We hold only that, in an action for injunctive relief, the district court has the discretionary power under Rule 10b–5 and Section 10(b) to issue an injunction, if the misleading statement resulted from a lack of due diligence on the part of TGS. The trial court did not find it necessary to decide whether TGS exercised such diligence and has not yet attempted to resolve this issue. . . .

It is not altogether certain from the present record that the draftsmen could, as the SEC suggests, have readily obtained current reports of the drilling progress over the weekend of April 10–12, but they certainly should have obtained them if at all possible for them to do so.

However, even if it were not possible to evaluate and transmit current data in time to prepare the release on April 12, it would seem that TGS could have delayed the preparation a bit until an accurate report of a rapidly changing situation was possible.

At the very least, if TGS felt compelled to respond to the spreading rumors of a spectacular discovery, it would have been more accurate to have stated that the situation was in flux and that the release was prepared as of April 10 information rather than purporting to report the progress "to date." Moreover, it would have obviously been better to have specifically described the known drilling progress as of April 10 by stating the basic facts. Such an explicit disclosure would have permitted the investing public to evaluate the "prospect" of a mine at Timmins without having to read between the lines to understand that preliminary indications were favorable—in itself an understatement.

The choice of an ambiguous general statement rather than a summary of the specific facts cannot reasonably be justified by any claimed urgency. The avoidance of liability for misrepresentation in the event that the Timmins project failed, a highly unlikely event as of April 12 or April 13, did not forbid the accurate and truthful divulgence of detailed results which need not, of course, have been accompanied by conclusory assertions of success.

* * * * *

We conclude, then, that having established that the release was issued in a manner reasonably calculated to affect the market price of TGS stock and to influence the investing public, we must remand to the district court to decide whether the release was misleading to the reasonable investor and if found to be misleading, whether the court in its discretion should issue the injunction the SEC seeks.

SEC v. Scott Taylor & Company, Inc.

183 F. Supp. 904 (S.D.N.Y. 1959)

Action by the Securities and Exchange Commission (plaintiff) against Scott Taylor & Company, Inc., Stephen N. Stevens, and Theodore Landau (defendants) seeking to enjoin them from violating Section 17 of the Securities Act of 1933 and Section 10b of the Securities Exchange Act of 1934 and Rule 10b–6. Injunction issued.

Scott Taylor & Co., through Stevens, its owner, had been using the mails from April until the SEC filed its complaint in August 1959, to offer for sale and sell shares of stock in Anaconda Lead & Silver Company to residents of various states. These shares had been obtained from Landau. The company had been organized as a Nevada corporation in 1948 and had offices in Denver, Colorado. It had not been in operation nor had it any income since 1952. There were slightly more than 7,000,000 shares outstanding. Some stock had transferred at 40 cents per share at about this time and the president and the attorney for the company, both having sizable holdings in the stock, advised Stevens prior to his sales efforts that the stock had a value of from 25 to 40 cents for trading purposes. Scott Taylor (Stevens) sold 33,000 shares at prices ranging from $4.25 to $4.75.

Stevens, in his efforts to sell the stock, told customers that the company was a subsidiary of or controlled or backed by the Anaconda Company, a well-known copper company. Landau placed bids on Anaconda Lead & Silver Company stock in the National Daily Quotation sheets on every business day but one during the period of April 30 to August 7, 1959, at prices ranging from $4.00 to $4.25 until the end of July when some lower bids were entered. The bids were pursuant to an order from Scott Taylor to purchase shares for its account.

BICKS, DISTRICT JUDGE.   In the course of sales to numerous customers, Stevens, on behalf of himself and as an officer of Scott Taylor, made and caused to be made certain statements (with respect to an association with Anaconda Copper) which are the basis for the action under Section 17(a) of the Securities Act of 1933 . . . Said statements were false and untrue to the knowledge of Stevens. Each of these untrue statements constitutes a violation of Section 17(a).

The Commission alleges further that the defendants violated Rule 10b–6, promulgated under Section 10(b) of the Securities Exchange Act of 1934, which statutory section proscribes "manipulative or deceptive" devices or contrivances. Manipulative and deceptive are defined in Rule 10b–6 as including those transactions in which a person who participates in the distribution of securities, directly or indirectly, bids for the securities of the same class or purchases them for an account in which he has a beneficial interest.

Manipulation was one of the basic evils with which Congress was concerned in enacting statutes to regulate the securities market. Manipulation was often accomplished by those about to sell securities or already engaged in selling securities bidding on the market for the same securities, thereby creating an unjustifiable impression of market activity which would facilitate the sale at artificially high prices. This was one of the practices which the Securities Exchange Act was designed to eradicate, and it is the practice which is covered by Rule 10b–6.

Stevens' and Scott Taylor's activities come within the prohibitions of Rule 10b–6 as involving a "broker, dealer, or other person who has agreed to participate or is participating in" a particular distribution of securities. The stock sold to the public by Scott Taylor was an aggregate of approximately 33,000 shares. These sales constituted a "distribution" within Rule 10b–6.

At the same time that Stevens and Scott Taylor were engaged in distributing Anaconda Lead & Silver securities they caused Landau to insert bids in the National Daily Quotation sheets. Stevens and Scott Taylor thereby violated Rule 10b–6, even though the bids were made indirectly.

. . . As might be expected in cases of this type, there is no direct evidence of an agreement between Scott Taylor and Stevens on the one hand and Landau on the other to engage in this joint venture. But circumstantial evidence is competent to prove the necessary agreement. The circumstantial evidence here clearly establishes such a common concert, plan, or agreement.

Myzel v. Fields

386 F.2d 718 (8th Cir. 1967)

Separate actions by Harry Fields, Samuel King, Rita Vertelney, and Gordon Cohen (plaintiffs) seeking damages for violation of Section 10b of the Securities Exchange Act of 1934 against Benjamin Myzel, the Levines, and others (defendants) were consolidated for trial before a jury. Verdicts totalling $411,000 were returned in favor of Fields, King, Vertelney and Cohen. Affirmed.

Fields and King each purchased 30 shares at $50 per share in Lakeside Plastics and Engraving Co. (LPE), a close corporation, of Duluth, Minnesota, when it was founded in 1946. Vertelney purchased 100 shares and Cohen 40 shares. They had made the investment upon the advice of their close friend, Benn Myzel, who was also a relative of Zelman Levine, one of the founders of the company. Myzel was an early director of the company, going off the board in 1949 but returning to it in 1954. At all times relevant to the case he served the corporation as a financial advisor. The company made advertising signs, and from 1946 to 1951 it struggled for sales, made little profit and paid the shareholders nothing on their investment. The shareholders were discouraged and in the 1949 shareholders' meeting Fields made a motion for dissolution. In 1952 sales increased substantially but not to a record level and a profit of $7,500 was made, after which the company still showed a $43,000 deficit. The company secured a large contract with Blatz Brewing Company and in the first four months of 1953 the company earned a profit of $30,000 but this interim financial statement was not disclosed at the June shareholders' meeting.

Myzel and his brother, who acted as his undisclosed agent, using the telephone and personal solicitation, bought the shares of Fields, King, Vertelney and Cohen toward the end of 1953 and in early 1954 at prices from $6.67 to $45.00 per share. In each instance the Myzels made representations that the stock was not worth anything, that the company was not making money and that Benn Myzel was "going to get out of the company" or suggested that the company was on the verge of bankruptcy.

Myzel later sold the shares at a substantial profit to the Levines who came to own all of the shares of the company. In addition, he received other substantial amounts from the Levines for his service in buying the stock. After 1953 the sales of LPE increased very greatly and large profits came shortly thereafter.

LAY, CIRCUIT JUDGE.   Both Section 10 of the Act and Rule 10b–5 require as a jurisdictional basis "the use of *any means or instrumentality of interstate commerce or of the mails,* or any facility of any national securities exchange." The evidence is undisputed that the telephone was used only on an intrastate basis in the solicitation or purchase of (the) stock. . . . We hold . . . that intrastate use of the telephone comes within prohibition of the Act.

Proof of affirmative misrepresentation, generally an essential element of common-law fraud, is not required in actions brought under Rule 10b–5, since the rule expressly prohibits material omissions as well. Several undisclosed facts in the present case assume relevance when coupled with the factual statements and reckless opinions offered by the Myzels. Among facts the jury could find not disclosed in the purchases were (1) the increased sales in 1953, (2) the April 1953 interim financial statements showing the successful Blatz contract and $30,000 profit, (3) the potential of 1954 sales or at least Zelman Levine's (President of LPE) optimism over prospects for the future, and (4) the identity of the controlling purchasers.

These nondisclosures assume materiality when considered in the context of the affirmative representations made severally to Fields, King, Vertelney, and Cohen. Phil Myzel's statement to Vertelney that Benn was "going to get out" of the company could be considered actionable as a misstatement of another's intent or state of mind. Benn's statements to King that he himself had sold his stock, that it was worthless and that the company wasn't making any money were misleading. Phil's statements to Fields that the company was on the "verge of bankruptcy" or "in bad shape" were material in view of the nondisclosures. And Benn's statements to Cohen that "he was not getting any money from the company" become significant with the discovery of Benn's commissions commencing in August 1953.

Proof of "scienter," that is, knowledge of the falseness of the impression produced by the statements or omissions made, is not required under Section 10(b) of the Act.

Under the circumstances we conclude, although not without great difficulty, that all of the appellees presented sufficient proof of an "assortment" of nondisclosures and positive misrepresentations to carry their respective cases to the jury.

Liabilities and Penalties

Civil Liabilities.   Section 12 of the 1933 Act imposes civil liability upon persons selling securities which are required to be but have not been registered or who use untrue or misleading statement in any filing under the 1933 Act. In addition, an implied right of action for damages has been found as stated above, for violation of rules such as 10b–5 or sections of the statute which do not include explicit penalties such as 14a.[13]

Criminal Sanctions.   Criminal penalties are also provided. Section 24 of the 1933 Act provides for a fine up to $5,000 for willful violations of the provisions of that 1933 Act or rules issued under it. Section 32 of the 1934 Act provides for a fine of not more than $10,000 and not more than two years imprisonment for willful violations of that 1934 Act or the related SEC rules.

United States v. Simon

425 F.2d 796 (2d Cir. 1969)

Prosecution by the United States of Carl Simon, Robert Kaiser and Melvin Fishman (defendants) under Section 32 of the Securities Exchange Act of 1934 for conspiring to draw up and certify a false and misleading financial statement. Appeal from conviction. Affirmed.

Continental Vending Machine Corporation (Continental) and Valley Commercial Corporation (Valley) were dominated by Harold Roth, who was president of Continental, supervised the day-to-day operations of Valley and owned about 25 percent of the stock in both corporations. Valley was engaged in lending money to Continental and others in the vending machine business. Continental's stock was listed on the American Stock Exchange. Since 1956 its auditors had been Lybrand, Ross Bros. & Montgomery, an internationally known accounting firm. Simon was a senior partner of the firm and had become the partner in charge of the Continental audit in 1960, having been "second partner" on the account previously. Kaiser was a junior partner and first dealt with Continental as "audit manager" for the 1961 audit. Fishman had been assigned to the Continental audit in 1957 as a junior accountant and was promoted to be manager of the audit in 1962.

Valley had $1 million lines of credit with each of two banks. Continental would issue notes to Valley, and Valley would use them as collateral to borrow from the banks. Valley would then transfer the discounted amounts of the notes to Continental. These transactions, dating from 1956, gave rise to what was referred to by the accountants

---

[13] *J. I. Case Co. v. Borak,* 377 U.S. 426 (1964).

as "the Valley payable." Continental also made loans to Valley beginning in mid-1967, and this account was known as "the Valley receivable." Roth used these latter loans to finance his personal transactions in the stock market. At the close of fiscal 1962 the amount of the Valley payable was $1,029,475, of which $543,345 was due within a year. The amount of the Valley receivables at that time was $3.5 million and on February 15, 1963, the date when Lybrand certified the 1962 statement of Continental, it had risen to $3.9 million. At the certification date the auditors were aware that Valley could not repay its debt to Continental and so arranged that collateral would be posted by Roth and members of his family.

The 1962 Continental earnings statement showed an operating loss of $867,000 plus write-offs of approximately $3 million. The balance sheet, certified by Lybrand, showed the Valley receivable and the Valley payable. Note 2, relating to the Valley payable and the Valley receivable, stated,

> The amount receivable from Valley Commercial Corp. (an affiliated company of which Mr. Harold Roth is an officer, director and stockholder) bears interest at 12% a year. Such amount, less the balance of the notes payable to that company, is secured by the assignment to the Company of Valley's equity in certain marketable securities. As of February 15, 1963, the amount of such equity at current market quotations exceeded the net amount receivable.

The financial statements were mailed on February 20, 1963. By then the market prices of Continental's securities (and therefore the value of Roth's collateral) were dropping rapidly. On the day after Washington's Birthday holiday it had dropped to $395,000 (against a debt of $3.9 million) and a Continental check to the internal revenue service bounced. Two days later the Government padlocked Continental's plant and the American Stock Exchange suspended trading in Continental stock. Bankruptcy came shortly thereafter.

The Government in its case against the accountants contended that the note to the 1962 balance sheet should have stated that the Valley receivable was uncollectible since Valley had loaned approximately the same amount ($3.5 million) to Harold Roth who was unable to pay and that by the date of certification the obligation had increased to $3.9 million. It should also have cautioned that Continental's liability to Valley (the Valley payable) could not be offset against Valley's debt to Continental because Continental's notes had been endorsed in blank to the two banks as collateral for the cash Valley had loaned to Continental. Further, the Government contended that the note should have included the information that 80 percent of the securities pledged by Roth as collateral for his debt to Valley were issued by Continental and that as of the date of certification they had a market value of $2,978,000.

There was evidence that all three accountants knew that Roth had, in effect, been using the Continental loans to Valley for his stock market operations as well as knowing or being alerted so that they should have known the facts that the Government contended should have been contained in Note 2.

FRIENDLY, CIRCUIT JUDGE.   We join defendants' counsel in assuming that the mere fact that a company has made advances to an affiliate does not ordinarily impose a duty on an accountant to investigate what the affiliate has done with them or even to disclose that the affiliate had made a loan to a common officer if this has come to his attention. But it simply cannot be true that an accountant is under no duty to disclose what he knows when he has reason to believe that, to a material extent, a corporation is being operated not to carry out its business in the interest of all the stockholders but for the private benefit of its president. For a court to say that all this is immaterial as a matter of law if only such loans are thought to be collectible would be to say that independent accountants have no responsibility to reveal known dishonesty by a high corporate officer. If certification does not at least imply that the corporation has not been looted by insiders so far as the accountants know, or, if it has been, that the diversion has been made good beyond peradventure (or adequately reserved against) and effective steps taken to prevent a recurrence, it would mean nothing, and the reliance placed on it by the public would be a snare and a delusion. Generally accepted accounting principles instruct an accountant what to do in the usual case where he has no reason to doubt that the affairs of the corporation are being honestly conducted. Once he has reason to believe that this basic assumption is false, an entirely different situation confronts him.

* * * * *

Turning to the failure to describe the collateral, defendants concede that they could not properly have certified statements showing the Valley receivable as an asset when they knew it was uncollectible. That was why Roth proposed collateralization and they accepted it. As men experienced in financial matters, they must have known that the one kind of property ideally unsuitable to collateralize a receivable whose collectibility was essential to avoiding an excess of current liabilities over current assets and a two-thirds reduction in capital already reduced would be securities of the very corporation whose solvency was at issue—particularly when the 1962 report revealed a serious operating loss. Failure to disclose that 80% of the "marketable securities" by which the Valley receivable was said to be "secured" were securities of Continental was thus altogether unlike a failure to state how much collateral were bonds or stock of General Motors and how much of U.S. Steel.

* * * * *

Even if there were no satisfactory showing of motive, we think the Government produced sufficient evidence of criminal intent. Its burden was not to show that the defendants were wicked men with designs on anyone's purse, which they obviously were not, but rather that they had certified a statement knowing it to be false.

State Securities Legislation

Purpose and History. State securities laws are frequently referred to as "blue-sky" laws, since the early statutes were designed to protect investors from promoters and security salesmen who offered stock in companies organized to pursue visionary schemes or to exploit uncertain resources. However, even legitimate ventures typically provided the investor with little hard information and most investors are not educated in the intricacies of corporate organization and finance. The first state to enact such a law was Kansas in 1919. Thirty-two states presently have such legislation.

Types of Statutes. There are three basic types of state statutes. Some combine two or more of these approaches. Those which might be called the "fraud type" provide penalties for fraudulent sales and injunctive proceedings to protect investors from further or anticipated fraudulent acts. Some state official, usually the attorney general, is given broad investigative powers and criminal penalties are provided for selling fraudulent securities and conducting fraudulent transactions. The second type of law regulates the seller. It provides licensing of security salesmen and requires proof of financial responsibility of dealers. It puts a duty upon dealers to disclose pertinent facts about the securities they are selling and to avoid sales of fraudulent securities. The third type controls the issuer. It requires the filing by the issuer of certain information with the state regulatory agency and prohibits sales without such filings. The Uniform Securities Act, which has been adopted in whole or in part by 25 states, combines all three types. It contains antifraud provisions, requires broker-dealer registration, and also requires the registration of securities.

The Securities Act of 1933 specifically permits concurrent jurisdiction by state agencies. However, a number of states with registration of securities (issuer control) provisions exempt securities which have been registered with the SEC under the 1933 Act.

Summary

Securities regulation statutes, commonly called blue-sky laws, were passed by a number of states before the federal legislation. Such laws are now in effect in 32 states. Three basic types of regulation are used: (1) prohibition of fraud and misrepresentation, (2) licensing of securities sellers, and (3) requiring of issuers the disclosure of information relevant to the security. The Uniform Securities Act, adopted in whole or in part by 25 states, includes all three types of regulation.

Problem Cases

1. Charles Timm was a real estate broker in Minneapolis who also participated in oil ventures on a limited scale. Thompson, an acquaintance of Timm who made his living from investments, advised Timm he was interested in buying an oil lease and asked Timm to let him know if he learned of one that might seem attractive. While in Oklahoma, Timm learned that Pierce owned a one-sixteenth interest in an oil and gas lease on land known as Tract No. 1, which he offered to sell for $19,000. Timm obtained more information by letter which he passed on to Thompson and to Collier, a friend of Thompson. Timm insisted that Thompson and Collier make their own independent investigation and decision. Timm drove with them to Oklahoma to see the property and to check the drilling and production records, at which time they bought the one-sixteenth interest and Timm received a 5 percent commission.

   Shortly thereafter, Anderson, a friend of Timm, inquired of him concerning oil leases and Timm told him he had learned while in Oklahoma with Thompson and Collier of another one-sixteenth interest in Tract 1 being available from a different owner. In a similar fashion Timm served as intermediary in the sale of three more fractional interests in the lease on Tract 1, in two cases the acquaintances of Timm not visiting the leased property but relying upon the judgment of a friend who was an earlier purchaser. Several months later, Timms arranged similar sales to Thompson, Collier, and Anderson in two other tracts. In all there were five different buyers and four different sellers through Timm.

Operating and development expenses on the leases exceeded income and Thompson, Collier, and Anderson brought suit against Timm to recover their investments and the amounts by which expenses exceeded income, alleging that the leases were unregistered securities sold in violation of the Securities Act of 1933. Is Timm's defense that the sales were exempt as private offerings good?

2. The domesticated-beaver fur industry had been started in 1950 by Mark Weaver, who claimed to have learned the secrets of raising beavers in captivity. He developed an aggressive advertising campaign which described the beaver-fur industry as "the royal road to riches." Buyers could establish their own beaver ranches, but they were encouraged to leave them at whichever one of Weaver's ranches they were located at the time of sale since the suggested ranching techniques required for each pair of beavers a private swimming pool, patio, den, and nesting box. Services of a veterinarian, dental technician, and breeding specialist were also required for success. Weaver and his associates had formed separate corporations to operate the beaver ranches and formed Continental Marketing Corporation to sell the live beavers.

The SEC sought to enjoin Continental from offering securities for sale in violation of Section 17(a) of the Securities Act of 1933. Continental argued that since it was only in the business of selling beavers and did not conduct ranching operations, its business could not possibly involve the sale of an investment contract or securities. Is Continental involved in selling securities?

3. Several Montana dentists purchased stock in a corporation being organized in that state to market a background music device. Dr. Belhumeur, one of these investors, demonstrated the device at a dentist's convention at Sun Valley and interested Dr. Winn, a dentist who resided in Idaho, in the corporation. Winn purchased $5,000 worth of stock in the corporation by means of a sale to Belhumeur who endorsed the certificate over to Winn. The securities were not registered with the SEC. Dr. Winn seeks to rescind the sale under the Securities Act of 1933. The corporation argues that since it only sold stock to residents of Montana, its securities are exempted from the act. Is this argument good?

4. Between April 1961 and March 1962, Gamble-Skogmo, Inc., acquired 50.1 percent of the common stock of General Outdoor Advertising (GOA). GOA at this time was the largest outdoor advertising company in the United States. Shortly thereafter, Skogmo decided that GOA's advertising plants could not be operated profitably and should be sold. By the end of 1962 Skogmo had sold 23 of the original 36 GOA plants at prices well in excess of their book values, resulting in considerable profits for GOA. In May 1963, Skogmo decided to carry out a statutory merger with GOA. A proxy statement was sent to the shareholders of both companies in advance of special meetings to be held on October 11 at which approval of the merger by the shareholders of both companies would be sought. The proxy statement said that once the merger became effective, Skogmo intended to continue the business of GOA including the policy of considering offers for the sale of plants, with the proceeds of any such sales being used to further expand and diversify operations now being conducted. It went on to state that there had been expressions of interest in buying many of the remaining GOA plants but no agreement had been made and no negotiations were

presently being conducted with respect to the sale of any plant. Thus the minority share-holders of GOA were required to make an investment choice between (1) retaining their shares in GOA, a firm with poor earnings prospects if it remained in the outdoor advertising field but also with the possibility of substantial extraordinary profits from the liquidation of that business, or (2) exchanging them for a small premium for the Skogmo convertible preferred, a security involving much less risk but with a correspondingly reduced interest in the profit potentially available through sales of the plants.

On October 9, two days before the GOA shareholders' meeting which approved the merger, arrangements were made to sell the Chicago and New York plants. On December 2, Skogmo sold the Philadelphia and Washington plants, and by July 13, 1964, Skogmo had contracted to sell the remaining U.S. plants of GOA. Minority shareholders of GOA brought a class-action suit against Skogmo claiming that the merger was procured by a false and misleading proxy statement in violation of SEC Rule 14a–9. It was alleged to be misleading because it failed to disclose the true value of the GOA plants and the intention of Skogmo to sell those plants immediately after the merger at an anticipated large profit, thus depriving the GOA shareholders of an undiluted interest in the capital gains. Did the proxy statement violate the securities laws?

5. A noted industrialist, Arthur Vining Davis, transferred all of his real estate holdings on Florida's Gold Coast to the Arvida Corporation. This was announced in press releases by Arvida in New York, Florida, and several other areas of the country. The press releases and related news coverage stated that the Arvida Corp. was controlled by the very success-ful Mr. Davis and his associates, that a registration statement for the SEC was being prepared, that the new corporation would be provided with $25 million to $30 million capital, and stated the names of the underwriters. The SEC brought suit seeking an injunc-tion to prevent Arvida from offering to sell securities and other actions in violation of the 1933 Securities Act. Should the injunction be issued?

6. RKO General owned 56 percent of the outstanding common stock of Frontier Airlines. In April 1967, the managements of Frontier and Central Airlines reached a tentative agreement to merge the two companies through an exchange of stock. On May 3, RKO contracted with several major shareholders of Central to purchase 49 percent of its out-standing shares at $8.50 per share and to buy $500,000 of Central's debentures convertible into enough additional shares to give RKO roughly the same proportion of ownership in Central that it had in Frontier. Shareholder approval of the proposed merger was, therefore, a foregone conclusion, and the Civil Aeronautics Board also gave approval. On September 18, RKO performed its contract with the Central shareholders and paid them the contract price of $7,550,082, and the merger of Central into Frontier was completed. On October 1, 1967, the Central certificates, including those acquired by RKO, were exchanged for Frontier certificates under the merger agreement.

Newmark, an owner of Frontier debentures and warrants, sued RKO under Section 16(b) of the 1934 Act for the difference between RKO's purchase price of the Central shares and debentures and the market price of their equivalent in Frontier shares on the date of the merger plus a control premium of 15 percent. Does the purchase of Central securities and their exchange for Frontier securities constitute a purchase and sale subjecting RKO to liability under Section 16(b)?

7. Bailey, officer and stockholder of Black Company, had a contract for the right of first refusal upon a majority of Black Co. stock from James Black, company founder and majority stockholder. Upon Black's death, Continental Bank, executor of Black's estate, participated in a transaction which transfered all assets of Black Co. and all the stock except Bailey's to Meister Brau, Inc. Black was then consolidated with Meister Brau, Inc. and ceased to

have a separate identity. Black Co. received in exchange for the assets $440,000 worth of Meister Brau stock. However, Bailey argued that Black Co. was worth $1,870,000 as a going concern and that the transaction operated as a fraud upon him in violation of Section 17(a) of the Securities Act of 1933 and of Rule 10b–5. Meister Brau contended that the particular violations alleged require deception, which was not present since full disclosure of the transaction was made to the Black Co. directors. Further, it was contended that the statute and regulations were intended to apply only to security transactions in the open market and not to the transfer of securities as a vehicle for the sale of a going business. Bailey countered that the individual board members were all involved in a conflict of interest and that their knowledge of the transaction could not, therefore, be imputed to the corporation, and that the security laws should apply to any security transaction. Do the security laws apply to this dispute?

8. Murchison was able to gain control of Alleghany Corporation from Kirby in 1961 after a vigorous proxy fight. Murchison and associates owned directly 34.5 percent of the stock while Kirby remained the largest single owner with 33 percent. In deference to his holdings, Murchison offered Kirby two seats on the new board. However, Kirby refused and launched an active program to regain control, which included public and private criticism of Murchison's management policies. Murchison became discouraged over the conflict with Kirby and in October 1962, agreed to an offer from Gamble to sell a majority of his personal holdings at $10 per share. An option to buy his remaining shares plus those of his associates at the same price prior to the end of 1963 was also granted. Although the market price for Alleghany stock was only $8 per share at this time, an investment banker advised Gamble that it was worth $10 to $12 based upon net asset value. After the initial sale, Gamble and his attorney were elected to the board and in December 1962, Murchison resigned and Gamble was elected president; however, the Murchison group continued to control the remaining eight seats through 1963, at times rejecting Gamble's proposals.

During 1963 Gamble was not successful in establishing a workable relationship with Kirby either for himself or the Murchisons. Therefore, while he did exercise his option for the remaining Murchison holdings, he sold nearly one half of them to Kirby on the same day at $10.50 per share. This enabled Kirby to gain firm control of the corporation. Shortly thereafter, a stockholder's derivative action was brought against Murchison to recover the "control premium" over the market price realized by Murchison. The minority shareholders alleged that Murchison realized the $2 per share premium in exchange for the sale of the corporate offices and control of the corporation and that he withheld material information from other stockholders (the agreement with Gamble) in violation of Rule 10b–5 and other security regulations. The Alleghany stock had meantime climbed from $8 in July 1962, when the Murchison-Gamble agreement was negotiated to $13 in January 1963. Did Murchison violate the security regulations in his dealings with Gamble?

9. Volk purchased stock in Belock Corporation in reliance upon the financial data contained in Belock's Annual Report, press releases, and other documents filed with the SEC. Belock, as it later turned out, did not disclose that a substantial amount of its income reported in these documents was derived from overcharges on government contracts. Volk brought suit against Belock's directors seeking to represent all shareholders who purchased Belock stock and sold it or were holding it at a loss. He alleged that these directors violated Rule 10b–5 by not disclosing the overcharges. The action was dismissed by the trial court on the grounds that these overcharges were part of a fraudulent scheme directed at the government and not intended to perpetrate a fraudulent practice associated with the sale of securities, and that none of the corporate or individual defendants was engaged in the sale or purchase of Belock securities and that, therefore, the "in connection with the purchase or sale of

any security" requirement of Rule 10b–5 was not satisfied. Should this dismissal be upheld on appeal?

10. BarChris acquired all of the stock of Victor Billiard Company in December 1961, through an exchange of stock. The only shareholders of Victor were Frank Lanza, Jr., and his two sisters. The financial data concerning BarChris which had been furnished the Lanzas included the 1960 annual report, the May 16, 1961, debenture prospectus, and BarChris's earnings statement for the six months ending June 30, 1961, which had been revised downward because of the bankruptcy of a bowling alley built by BarChris and not yet paid for. On October 1962, BarChris filed a petition in bankruptcy. The Lanzas sought to recover their shares in Victor in a recission action and, failing that, brought an action for damages against former officers and directors of BarChris, including Coleman, under SEC Rule 10b–5.

Coleman, a partner in Drexel & Company, an investment and brokerage firm which had been the lead underwriter of the debenture offering by BarChris in the spring of 1961, had joined the BarChris board of directors in connection with that transaction in April of 1961. He served until he resigned in March 1962. He had not participated in any of the negotiations concerning the Victor acquisition. He had not attended the board meeting which authorized BarChris representatives to enter into a contract with the Lanzas nor the closing when the stock was exchanged. He had, however, attended the board meeting on November 27 when the exchange agreement had been approved, but there was no discussion then of the negotiations with the Lanzas, which had extended over a period of several months.

The Lanzas argue that Coleman is liable because he was aware, through a board of directors' meeting on December 6 (8 days before the closing with the Lanzas), that Bar-Chris's financial condition had deteriorated since the issuance of the prospectus and financial statements and that there was dissension in management. Coleman argues that as an outside director who did not participate in the negotiations he had no duty to warn the Lanzas.

Is Coleman liable under Rule 10b–5?

11. American Foods, a franchisor, sued Goldsmith, to whom it had granted a franchise, to recover on a note for certain operating expenses. Goldsmith raised as a defense that the franchise agreement was an investment contract subject to the provisions of the state security act, and that, since American had not registered the agreement under the act, he was entitled to avoid the agreement. Under the agreement Goldsmith was licensed to operate a restaurant under American's trademark in return for a stipulated monthly royalty. American granted Goldsmith a lease in a building with equipment and furnished services such as the training of his employees and provided him with certain supplies. Goldsmith testified that he spent approximately eight hours a day at the restaurant trying to make it a success.

Under the state securities act an investment contract is construed as a security if the scheme involves an investment of money in a common enterprise with profits to come solely from the efforts of others. Is the franchise agreement a security so as to absolve Goldsmith of liability?

chapter 28

Foreign Corporations

Rights of Foreign Corporations

Introduction. A corporation is a "domestic corporation" in the state or country which has granted it its charter and is a "foreign corporation" in all other states, territories, countries, or subdivisions of countries. It may not be a domestic corporation in more than one state.

A corporation has no right to transact business except in interstate commerce in a state other than the one granting its charter. However, all states permit foreign corporations to become "domesticated" (licensed or qualified) to do intrastate business within the state upon compliance with general statutes. They may impose in such statutes any reasonable condition upon foreign corporations seeking the privilege to do intrastate business. Some require certain kinds of corporations providing important public services, such as railroads, to incorporate a subsidiary within the state. The term "domesticate" is sometimes used in this limited sense.

Under the Commerce Clause of the Constitution the power to regulate interstate commerce is given to the federal government, and states have no power to exclude or to discriminate against foreign corporations which are engaged solely in interstate commerce. Nor can a state deny a foreign corporation due process of law or equal protection of the laws if it is admitted to do intrastate business. However, even if it is engaged only in interstate commerce, a foreign corporation is subject to nondiscriminatory regulations of business activities such as sanitary standards for food products, regulations on truck size and usury laws, and under recent Supreme Court decisions, it is subject to a suit in the state growing out of its activities and to taxation.

The Model Act. The provisions which apply to foreign corporations in the Model Business Corporation Act are set out in sections 106 to 124. Similar to most such statutes, section 110 requires the foreign corporation to apply for a certificate of authority from the secretary of state, giving information similar to that required in an application for a charter from a domestic corporation and to file a copy of its articles.

The foreign corporation must maintain a registered office and a registered agent upon whom service of process upon the corporation may be served. The registered agent may be and frequently is a corporation which makes a business of providing such representation. The foreign corporation must also make an annual report.

A license fee, based upon the number of authorized shares of stock of the corporation apportioned according to the relative value of its property located in the state and outside and its gross income inside and outside of the state, must be paid at the time of filing for certificate of authority to do business in the state. An additional license fee is required when the articles are amended to authorize additional shares. In addition, a franchise tax is payable annually based upon the proportion of its property in and business done within the state.

If the taxes are not paid, if the reports are not submitted, or if other requirements are not met, the secretary of state, under the Model Act and most state statutes, may revoke the certificate of authority of the foreign corporation to do business in the state. The penalties for failing to obtain a certificate of authority when required are discussed later in the chapter.

Summary

A corporation is a domestic corporation in the state which grants it its charter and a foreign corporation elsewhere. A corporation has a right to engage in intrastate business only in the state granting its charter, but generally it has a right under the Commerce Clause to conduct interstate business throughout the country.

To qualify to do intrastate business a foreign corporation must apply for a certificate of authority giving information similar to that required of a domestic corporation seeking a charter and must maintain a registered agent within the state. License and franchise fees must be paid to the state in which it is qualified.

"Doing Business"

Introduction. The courts recognize three general types of "doing business" by foreign corporations. They are: (1) that which subjects the foreign corporation to suit in the state courts, (2) that which subjects the foreign corporation to taxation by the state, and (3) that which requires that the foreign corporation comply with statutes granting it permission to do intrastate business in the state. More business activity within a state is required to subject a corporation to admission (or qualification or license) as a foreign corporation than for either service of process or taxation, but it is difficult to say today that more activities are necessary to subject the foreign corporation to taxation than to subject it to service of process. Although there have been literally thousands of cases, clear standards have not been arrived at by the courts in any one of the three categories. What is "doing business" is a question of fact determined by all the circumstances in a particular case and apparently inconsistent decisions by the same court are not infrequent. The trend has been to require fewer local activities for any of the three types than in earlier times.

Subjecting Foreign Corporations to Suit. The leading case on the issue whether a foreign corporation can be hailed into court in the state is *International Shoe Company v. State of Washington.*[1] There the court rejected the traditional "doing business" test and held that an unlicensed foreign corporation could be subjected to suit if to do so would not offend traditional notions of fair play and substantial justice. Jurisdiction of the state court depends, under this decision, as much upon matters of convenience to the parties, location of witnesses and the expense of producing them within the state, and the place where the events leading up to the suit took place as upon the extent of business activities with the state. Some local activity, or "minimum contacts" with the state, by the corporation are necessary, however, to give the state courts jurisdiction and then only with respect to a suit based upon or resulting from those contacts.

As a result of this decision, most states have passed so-called long-arm statutes to take advantage of the broadened jurisdictional power permitted in the *International Shoe* case. These statutes frequently specify several kinds of corporate activities which make the foreign corporation subject to suit within the state, such as the commission of a tort, the making of a contract or the ownership of property. Most of the statutes grant jurisdiction with respect to causes of action growing out of any doing of business or any transaction within the state, and some grant jurisdiction in product liability cases if the foreign corporation should have expected use of the product in the state. Others, like Rhode Island's statute, are general rather than specific and seek to assert the full extent of jurisdiction granted by the constitution as interpreted by the *International Shoe* case. It subjects any nonresident to jurisdiction who has "the necessary minimum contacts with the state." Such a statute turns each case into an exercise in interpretation of the Due Process Clause of the Fourteenth Amendment, each being decided upon its particular facts.

Taxing Foreign Corporations. A foreign corporation which is not required to apply for a certificate of authority to do business within the state may be subject to taxation by that state. There has never been any doubt that the

---

[1] *International Shoe Co. v. State of Washington,* 326 U.S. 310 (1945).

property of the corporation stored in or otherwise located in the state is subject to taxation even though it is used in carrying on the corporation's interstate business.

More troublesome for the courts have been attempts by states to impose income taxes upon foreign corporations conducting only an interstate business and, therefore, not required to obtain a certificate of authority. The Supreme Court had tended toward permitting taxation with fewer and fewer activities within the state until its decision in *Northwestern States Portland Cement Co. v. Minnesota.*[2] In that case the court upheld the imposition by Minnesota of an apportioned, nondiscriminatory net income tax on a corporation engaged solely in interstate commerce in Minnesota and which had not qualified in Minnesota as a foreign corporation.

As a result of what it appeared to think was a too liberal decision by the court, Congress enacted the Federal Interstate Income Law in 1959.[3] It prohibits taxing bodies, state or local, from imposing net income taxes on income which is derived from interstate commerce in which the only activity in the taxing jurisdiction is the solicitation of orders to be accepted and shipped from another state. Also under the act a foreign corporation may employ an independent contractor who represents more than one principal as sales agent, even if he has an office in the state, without becoming subject to taxation.

Admission of a Foreign Corporation. Subjection of the foreign corporation to the necessity of becoming domesticated (being admitted or qualifying) is dependent upon the wording of the statute, but so long as it limits its activities in the state to interstate commerce, a corporation is protected by the Constitution from the necessity of obtaining a certificate of admission. The Supreme Court, of course, has the final determination of what constitutes interstate commerce.

The Model Act (106)[4] provides that "no foreign corporation shall have the right to transact business in this State until it shall have procured authority to do so. . . ." It then lists a number of activities which the foreign corporation may carry on which will not be considered transacting business for the purposes of the act. These activities include: bringing or defending suit, holding corporate meetings, maintaining bank accounts, soliciting sales through independent contractors, soliciting orders by mail or agents if the orders require acceptance outside of the state, collecting debts, conducting isolated transactions completed within 30 days if they are not in the course of a number of repeated transactions of like nature, as well as transacting business in interstate commerce.

---

[2] *Northwestern States Portland Cement Co. v. State of Minnesota,* 358 U.S. 450 (1959).

[3] U.S.C. §§ 381–384.

[4] The numbers in parentheses refer to the sections of the Model Business Corporation Act, which appears in the Appendix.

It is difficult to state a general rule as to what activities constitute intrastate commerce. The following frequently quoted rule hardly seems to clarify the matter: "A foreign corporation is doing, transacting, carrying on, or engaging in business within a state when it transacts some substantial part of its ordinary business therein."[5] Generally, the maintenance of a stock of goods within a state even though the orders filled from the stock are accepted outside the state is treated as doing business. Even peddling goods from a truck sent in from outside the state or mere ownership of real estate have been held to require qualification. Statutory definitions such as Section 106 of the Model Act may not reach as far in requiring qualification as the Constitution has been interpreted to permit.

Penalty for Failure to Obtain Permission.   Generally, the states impose by statute a penalty on foreign corporations which do intrastate business without first obtaining permission. The statutory penalties usually include one or more of the following: a fine imposed upon the corporation, its agent in the state or its officers; denial to the corporation of the right to bring suit in the state courts; and holding officers, directors, or agents personally liable on contracts made within the state. In addition a few states declare contracts made within the state to be void. Nevada denies even the right to defend a suit brought against the corporation in the state.[6] The Model Act (124) denies the right to bring an action in the state courts plus the penalty for failure to pay fees and franchise taxes. Generally, if a corporation complies with the statute of the state after having transacted intrastate business without obtaining permission, such compliance will be retroactive and will cure the defect in such prior transactions.

Under the majority rule, if the intrastate contracts of a foreign corporation doing business in a state without having qualified are declared to be void by the state statute, such contracts are not enforceable by the corporation but may be enforced against it. These statutes are for the protection of the public; if the corporation were permitted to set up illegality as a defense to such contracts, it would be taking advantage of its own wrong, and the statutes would, in effect, penalize rather than protect the public.

Summary

The courts recognize three general types of "doing business" by foreign corporations: (1) that which subjects the foreign corporation to suit in the state courts, (2) that which subjects the foreign corporation to taxation by the state, and (3) that which requires qualification by the foreign corporation. More business activity is necessary to require the corporation to qualify to do intra-

---

[5] *Royal Insurance Co. v. All States Theatres,* 6 So.2d 494 (Ala. 1942).
[6] Nevada Rev. Stat., 80.210(1).

state business than for either service of process in a lawsuit or for taxation. There are no clear standards in any of the three situations but the trend has been toward requiring fewer local activities.

Under the most recent decisions of the U.S. Supreme Court, whether a foreign corporation can be subjected to suit within a state depends as much on matters of convenience to the parties as on the extent of the defendant corporation's business activities within the state. A single contract entered into within the state or a single tort committed within the course of the corporation's business within the state, even if the business is essentially interstate, will give jurisdiction to local courts.

The right of a state to tax property of a foreign corporation located in the state even though used solely in carrying on its interstate business has long been upheld. Recent decisions, however, have permitted states to impose income taxes on foreign corporations doing only interstate business, although limitations on such taxation have been established by Congress.

States cannot require qualification by a foreign corporation which does only an interstate business in the state as defined by the Supreme Court in interpreting the Commerce Clause. States frequently penalize foreign corporations which fail to qualify when necessary by denying them the right to bring suit in state courts and/or by fines.

International Shoe Co. v. State of Washington

326 U.S. 310 (U.S. Sup. Ct. 1945)

This was an action by the Office of Unemployment Compensation and Placement of the State of Washington (plaintiff) against International Shoe Company (defendant) to recover money alleged due as contributions under the Unemployment Compensation Act. Shoe Company appealed from a decision of the Washington Supreme Court affirming judgment for the State. Affirmed.

Shoe Company maintained neither an office nor a stock of goods in Washington, and it made no deliveries in intrastate commerce there. During the years in question it employed eleven to thirteen salesmen in Washington who were under the direct supervision of sales managers located in its headquarters office in St. Louis. The salesmen occasionally rented rooms in hotels or other buildings in which they displayed samples of Shoe Company's merchandise. They solicited orders on terms fixed in St. Louis for acceptance or rejection there. When accepted the merchandise was shipped f.o.b. to the Washington customers from points outside Washington. The salesmen had no authority to make collections and merchandise was invoiced at the place of shipment.

Shoe Company argued that its activities within the state were not sufficient to manifest its "presence" there and that in its absence the state courts were without jurisdiction, and, therefore, it was a denial of due process for the state to subject it to suit.

MR. CHIEF JUSTICE STONE. Due process requires only that in order to subject a defendant to a judgment *in personam,* if he be not present within the territory of the forum, he have certain minimum contacts with it such that the maintenance of the suit does not offend "traditional notions of fair play and substantial justice."

Since the corporate personality is a fiction, although a fiction intended to be acted upon as though it were a fact, it is clear that unlike an individual, its "presence" without, as well as within, the state of its origin can be manifested only by activities carried on in its behalf by those who are authorized to act for it. To say that the corporation is so far "present" there as to satisfy due process requirements, for purposes of taxation or the maintenance of suits against it in the courts of the state, is to beg the question to be decided. For the terms "present" or "presence" are used merely to symbolize those activities of the corporation's agent within the state which courts will deem to be sufficient to satisfy the demands of due process. Those demands may be met by such contacts of the corporation with the state of the forum as to make it reasonable, in the context of our federal system of government, to require the corporation to defend the particular suit which is brought there. An "estimate of the inconveniences" which would result to the corporation from a trial away from its "home" or principal place of business is relevant in this connection.

Finally, although the commission of some single or occasional acts of the corporate agent in a state sufficient to impose an obligation or liability on the corporation has not been thought to confer upon the state authority to enforce it, other such acts, because of their nature and quality and the circumstances of their commission, may be deemed sufficient to render the corporation liable to suit.

Applying these standards, the activities carried on in behalf of International Shoe in the State of Washington were neither irregular nor casual. They were systematic and continuous throughout the years in question. They resulted in a large volume of interstate business, in the course of which International Shoe received the benefits and protection of the laws of the state, including the right to resort to the courts for the enforcement of its rights. The obligation which is here sued upon arose out of those very activities. It is evident that these operations establish sufficient contacts or ties with the state of the forum to make it reasonable and just according to our traditional conception of fair play and substantial justice to permit the state to enforce the obligations which International Shoe has incurred there. Hence we cannot say that the maintenance of the present suit in the State of Washington involves an unreasonable or undue procedure.

Youngblood v. Citrus Assoc. of N.Y. Cotton Exch., Inc.

276 So.2d 505 (Ct. App. Fla. 1973)

Class action by Youngblood and others (plaintiffs) against Citrus Associates of the New York Cotton Exchange, Inc. (defendant), seeking damages for actions of Citrus Associates which limited trading in frozen concentrated orange juice. Appeal from order quashing service of process. Affirmed.

Citrus Associates is a commodity exchange. Its only business is to furnish facilities for the trading in frozen orange juice futures, which is conducted in New York City.

It does not own or lease property or maintain an office, telephone listing, bank account, or any records in Florida. All meetings of its board of directors and its executive committee take place in New York. Investigations of prospective members of Citrus Associates have taken place in Florida and meetings of the frozen concentrated orange juice committee and warehouse committees have occasionally taken place in Florida. The function of the committees is to make recommendations to the board of directors. Citrus Associates has also held one cocktail party in Florida for one of its members.

The complaint in this action was personally served in the state of Florida on the first vice president of Citrus Associates. Citrus Associates filed a motion to void the service. Youngblood argues that Citrus Associates is subject to suit in Florida under the Florida "long-arm" statutes.

CROSS, JUDGE.   In determining a question of jurisdiction which arises under the Florida "long-arm" statutes, we must consider that the provisions for making foreign corporations subject to service of process and subject to the jurisdiction of the Florida courts is a matter within the legislative discretion of the state lawmaking body. Legislatures have, generally speaking, enacted three types of long-arm statutes: those which require more activities or contracts than are currently required by the United States Supreme Court, those which are coextensive with the limits of the due process concept, and those which go beyond the due process limits and are hence unconstitutional.

The Florida "long-arm" statutes are, generally speaking, of the first type; that is, they require more activities or contacts to sustain service of process than are currently required by the decisions of the United States Supreme Court. Therefore, any analysis of the question of whether jurisdiction in personam has been acquired over a foreign corporation must necessarily start with an analysis of the statutes.

We deal first with Youngblood's contention that service is sustainable under Florida Statute § 48.081, F.S.A. In [this case] service was made upon a vice president of the foreign corporation pursuant to Florida Statute § 48.081 (1) (1971), [which states] that process against any private corporation, domestic or foreign, may be served on the vice president of the corporation. No requirement that the corporation be doing business in this state or that the cause of action arise from the corporation's activities in this state is found in this section.

Upon the absence of language to the above effect, Youngblood bases his argument that process served according to the terms of Florida Statute § 48.081(1) confers in personam jurisdiction over a foreign corporation upon Florida courts provided that the corporation so served possesses minimum contacts with the State of Florida as defined by *International Shoe Co. v. Washington,* and subsequent cases, notwithstanding the fact that the corporation does not do business in the State of Florida, or that the cause of action did not arise out of any transaction or operation connected with or incidental to the corporation's business in the State of Florida.

To adopt Youngblood's interpretation or construction of Florida Statute § 48.081(1), F.S.A., would render the statute quite similar in effect to a California statute, thus creating the same problems. For example, every case would automatically be turned into a constitutional problem of defining, according to the facts of each particular case, "minimum contacts." In addition, such a statute would probably be subject to constitutional infirmities as men of common intelligence would necessarily have to guess as to its meaning and differ as to its application. This statute, under the circumstances of the instant case, cannot be applied alone, as to do so would be to violate a fundamental maxim of statutory construction, that statutes are to be construed to avoid a declaration of unconstitutionality or grave doubts on that score. Therefore, we determine that the requirements of doing business and connexity as delineated in Florida Statute § 48.181 (1971), F.S.A., must be read in *pari materia* with Florida Statute § 48.081 (1971), F.S.A. . . .

Under this construction, Florida Statute § 48.081, F.S.A. (with the exception of subsection 5) then merely provides an alternative method of service. Therefore, to serve a foreign corporation not qualified to do business in Florida but which is doing business in Florida, where the cause of action arose out of the corporation's activities in Florida, service may be made either constructively upon the secretary of state, or personally upon those persons listed in § 48.081 (1)–(3).

In summary, the burden of proof to sustain the validity of service of process is upon the person who seeks to invoke the jurisdiction of the court. This party must show, when attempting to serve a foreign corporation not qualified to do business in the State of Florida, that the requirements of Florida Statute § 48.181, F.S.A. (namely, doing business and connexity) have been met and that process has been served upon a person qualified to accept such process. We would note at this point that the question of due process or "minimum contacts" is not properly discussed if a showing of doing business requirement necessarily includes the concept of minimum contacts. Wherefore, as Youngblood argues that connexity is not required, while in fact it is required, and as no showing of connexity has been made, service cannot be sustained under Florida Statute § 48.081, F.S.A., when read with § 48.181 (1971).

Northwestern States Portland Cement Co. v. State of Minnesota

358 U.S. 450 (U.S. Sup. Ct. 1959)

This action was brought by the state of Minnesota (plaintiff) against Northwestern States Portland Cement Company (defendant), a foreign corporation, to collect income taxes. Judgment for Minnesota affirmed.

Cement Company was an Iowa corporation which regularly solicited orders in Minnesota for its products, each order being subject to acceptance, filling, and delivery by it from its plant at Mason City, Iowa. It sold only to building material supply houses, contractors, and ready-mix companies. Forty-eight percent of its total sales were made in Minnesota in this manner. It leased an office in Minneapolis and furnished it with its own furniture and fixtures. The office was occupied by an employee-salesman designated a "district manager" and two other salesmen and a secretary. Two additional salesmen were supervised from the office. It had not qualified to do business in Minnesota. Cement Company had no bank account, owned no real estate and warehoused no merchandise in Minnesota but it did furnish two automobiles to its salesmen. It filed no tax returns.

Minnesota imposed a tax upon the taxable net income of four classes of persons, including domestic and foreign corporations whose business consisted "exclusively of foreign commerce, interstate commerce, or both." Ratios were used in determining the portion of net income taxable under the law: proportion of its total sales assignable to Minnesota, proportion of its total tangible property in the state, and proportion of its total payroll in the state.

Cement Company argued that imposition of the income tax on purely interstate commerce violated the Commerce Clause of the Constitution and also the Due Process Clause of the Fourteenth Amendment.

MR. JUSTICE CLARK.   The taxes are not regulations in any sense of that term. Admittedly they do not discriminate against nor subject either corporation to an undue burden. While it is true that a State may not erect a wall around its borders preventing commerce an entry, it is axiomatic that the founders did not intend to immunize such commerce from carrying its fair share of the costs of the state government in return for the benefits it derives from within the State. The levies are not privilege taxes based on the right to carry on business in the taxing state. . . .

While the economic wisdom of state net income taxes is one of state policy not for our decision, one of the "realities" raised by the parties is the possibility of a multiple burden resulting from the exactions in question. The answer is that none is shown to exist here. This is not an unapportioned tax which by its very nature makes interstate commerce bear more than its fair share. . . . We cannot deal in abstractions. In this type of case the taxpayers must show that the formula places a burden upon interstate commerce in a constitutional sense. This they have failed to do.

Nor will the argument that the exactions contravene the Due Process Clause bear scrutiny. The taxes imposed are levied only on that portion of the taxpayer's net income which arises from its activities within the taxing State. These activities form a sufficient "nexus between such a tax and transactions within a state for which the tax is an exaction."

Eli Lilly and Co. v. Sav-On-Drugs, Inc.

366 U.S. 276 (U.S. Sup. Ct. 1961)

This was an action brought in New Jersey by Eli Lilly and Company (plaintiff) against Sav-On-Drugs, Inc., (defendant), to enjoin Sav-On, a retailer, from selling Lilly's products at prices lower than fixed under the New Jersey Fair Trade Act. Judgment for Sav-On because Lilly was doing business in New Jersey without being qualified and, therefore, had no standing to sue was affirmed by the New Jersey Supreme Court. Affirmed.

Lilly, an Indiana corporation, sold its products in interstate commerce to certain selected wholesalers in New Jersey. The wholesalers in turn sold them in intrastate commerce to hospitals, retail drug stores and physicians. Lilly maintained an office in its name in Newark. Its district manager there supervised 18 "detail men" who were paid on a salary basis and whose function it was to visit retail pharmacists, physicians, and hospitals to acquaint them with Lilly's products and to encourage them to purchase them from the wholesalers. They also made available to retail druggists, free of charge, advertising and promotional material.

Lilly sought to enjoin Sav-On from selling its products below the Fair Trade prices.

Lilly opposed Sav-On's motion to dismiss and urged that its business in New Jersey was entirely in interstate commerce and that to require it to obtain a certificate for its New Jersey business was forbidden by the Commerce Clause of the Federal Constitution.

MR. JUSTICE BLACK. It is well established that New Jersey cannot require Lilly to get a certificate of authority to do business in the State if its participation in this trade is limited to its wholly interstate sales to New Jersey wholesalers. . . . On the other hand, it is equally well settled that if Lilly is engaged in intrastate as well as in interstate aspects of the New Jersey drug business, the State can require it to get a certificate of authority to do business. In such a situation, Lilly could not escape state regulation merely because it is also engaged in interstate commerce.

We agree with the trial court that "[t]o hold under the facts above recited that plaintiff [Lilly] is not doing business in New Jersey is to completely ignore reality." Eighteen "detailmen," working out of a big office in Newark, New Jersey, with Lilly's name on the door and in the lobby of the building, and with Lilly's district manager and secretary in charge, have been regularly engaged in work for Lilly which relates directly to the intrastate aspects of the sale of Lilly's products. These eighteen "detailmen" have been traveling throughout the State of New Jersey promoting the sales of Lilly's products, not to the wholesalers, Lilly's interstate customers, but to the physicians, hospitals and retailers who buy those products in intrastate commerce from the wholesalers. . . . And they sometimes even directly participate in the intrastate sales themselves by transmitting orders from the hospitals, physicians, and drugstores they service to the New Jersey wholesalers.

Problem Cases

1. Julia Cosmetics, Inc., a Louisiana corporation, designed and intended to market a line of cosmetics associated with the character of "Julia" portrayed by Diahann Carroll, a National Broadcasting Company owned television show. NBC, a Delaware corporation, held trademark rights to "Julia"; therefore, Julia entered into a licensing contract with NBC to use the name and to associate its product with the show. NBC was to receive 5 percent of Julia's gross sales and reserved the right to approve Julia's products and marketing procedures. Julia found it extremely difficult and frustrating to get approval from NBC. Miss Carroll later notified Julia that she, too, must approve the cosmetics. Julia failed to receive approval from NBC, for a period of almost one year.

   Julia then filed an action in federal court in Louisiana against NBC for breach of the licensing contract. NBC moved to quash service of process for lack of jurisdiction. NBC claimed that it did not have "sufficient contacts" with Louisiana to fall under its long-arm statute. NBC had entered into contracts with six independent television and seven independent radio stations located in Louisiana to broadcast NBC network programs, but it owned no property, had no office or agent, nor did it advertise or solicit advertising in Louisiana.

Since the licensing contract was negotiated and completed in New York, NBC claimed that the contract had no connection with Louisiana. Louisiana law provided for jurisdiction over a cause of action arising from a nonresident "causing injury or damage in this state by an offense or quasi offense committed through an act or omission outside of this state, if he regularly does or solicits business, or engages in any other persistent course of conduct, or derives substantial revenue from . . . this state." Does the court have jurisdiction over NBC?

2. Babbitt Brothers, Inc., a Wisconsin corporation, was engaged in the interstate trucking business. In compliance with the Federal Motor Carrier Act, Babbitt had a designated agent to receive service of process in each state in which it operated. On November 17, 1968, a truck owned and operated by Babbitt collided with a vehicle driven by Ervin Clark, A South Carolina resident. The accident occurred in Kentucky. Clark filed suit against Babbitt in a South Carolina court to recover for his damages. Service was accomplished by delivering the notice to the South Carolina agent of Babbitt required by the FMCA. South Carolina's long-arm statute grants jurisdiction over foreign corporations which are "doing business" in South Carolina. Babbitt moved to quash the service, contending that South Carolina has no jurisdiction. It is undisputed that Babbitt had ceased its trucking operations in South Carolina on September 7, 1968. Babbitt contends that since it no longer operates in South Carolina, neither the state long-arm statute nor service on an alleged agent whose purpose has expired, can operate to confer jurisdiction. Will Babbitt's motion to quash be sustained?

3. J. C. Penney Company was sued by several customers who suffered injuries in June of 1966 from Penney merchandise. Penney purchased the merchandise from Malouf Company in March 1966. In the purchase contract, Malouf warranted the goods as fit and safe for consumer use and to "indemnify and hold the company (Penney) harmless from all claims, liability, loss, damage, and expense incurred or sustained by company (Penney) by reason of any breach of such warranty." In a cross-claim, Penney sought to join Malouf, pursuant to its warranty contract, as a third-party defendant, Malouf claims that the Georgia court does not have jurisdiction over it since Malouf is a foreign corporation. Georgia's long arm statute became effective in April of 1968. This litigation began in May 1968. Malouf's only contact with Georgia was the March 1966 shipment to Penney and the warranty contract. Does Georgia have jurisdiction over Malouf?

4. Ace Novelty Company brought suit in the State of Washington against M. W. Kasch Company to recover $24,530.92 for merchandise allegedly sold and delivered to Kasch. Ace is a Washington corporation and Kasch is a Wisconsin corporation. At no time had Kasch ever done business within the State of Washington. It had neither salesmen nor officers within the state, and all aspects of the transaction between Ace and Kasch occurred outside the state through Kasch's agent in Chicago. Ace had writs of garnishment and attachment issued and served upon several corporations which conduct business in Washington and with Kasch. These corporations allegedly were debtors of Kasch. The debts were unrelated to Ace's claim.

   Kasch moved to dismiss the complaint for lack of jurisdiction, claiming that the only possible link between it and the State of Washington is the relationship between Kasch and its debtors. What result?

5. George R. Williams brought suit in the State of Washington against Canadian Fishing Company, a Canadian corporation, to recover for the sinking of his vessel *Starling* due to a collision in the waters of British Columbia with a ship owned by Canadian. Canadian challenges the complaint on jurisdictional grounds. Canadian neither has offices nor conducts business in Washington. Williams seeks to show the requisite "minimum contacts" for jurisdiction through Canadian's relationship with its parent corporation, New England Fish Company of Seattle, a Washington corporation. Canadian is a wholly owned subsidiary

of New England, and New England's president is a member of Canadian's board of directors. Is Canadian subject to the court's jurisdiction?

6. Du-Wald Steel Company, a Colorado corporation, contracted with Dorsid Trading Company, a Texas corporation, to buy steel angles through the Port of Houston. Dorsid obtained the steel in Houston and shipped it to Du-Wald in Colorado. Du-Wald refused to accept delivery in Denver. Dorsid filed suit in Texas on the alleged breach of contract by Du-Wald. Service of process was obtained under the Texas long-arm statute, which states: ". . . shall be deemed doing business in this State by entering into contract by mail or otherwise with a resident of Texas to be performed in whole or in part by either party in this State . . .". Du-Wald does not have an office or any employee in Texas. Du-Wald had on occasion sold scrap metal to Texas buyers and also had previously transacted business similar to the contract involved with Dorsid. The contract was prepared and signed by Dorsid in Houston. After mailing, it was signed in Denver by Du-Wald and returned to Houston. The contract provided for arbitration, if desired, in Houston, Texas. It also stated that Texas law was to govern the contract. Did service of process under the Texas statute meet the due process requirements?

7. Golden Dawn Foods is a wholesale grocery firm incorporated in Pennsylvania. All of its warehouses are in Pennsylvania and it neither owns nor leases any real property in Ohio. Salesmen dispatched from its Pennsylvania office sell to approximately 50 stores in Ohio and 100 independent retail stores in Pennsylvania. It did not provide merchandising or other services to its customers in Ohio. One of its Ohio customers defaulted upon a promissory note and Golden Dawn sued. The defense was that Golden Dawn had no right to maintain an action in Ohio since it was an unregistered foreign corporation doing business in Ohio. Was Golden Dawn doing business in Ohio so as to be required to register?

8. N. L. Blaum Construction Company was the general contractor for the construction of a school in Houston County, Alabama. Blaum contracted with Computaflor Company, a subcontractor, to install four wooden gymnasium floors. A Florida corporation, Computaflor agreed to furnish all the necessary labor and materials to substantially complete the floors for $25,500. Computaflor filed an action against Blaum in Alabama for breach of contract, claiming $10,404 of the contract price was unpaid. Blaum's defense was that Computaflor, as a foreign corporation, had failed to qualify to do business in Alabama and, therefore, was not entitled to recover. Computaflor asserted that the contract was one of interstate commerce (the building materials came from Michigan) and, therefore, Alabama law did not restrict its right to recover. Section 232 of the Alabama Constitution provided:

> No foreign corporation shall do any business in this state without having at least one known place of business and an authorized agent or agents therein, and without filing with the secretary of state a certified copy of its articles of incorporation or association.

An Alabama statute stated that all contracts or agreements made and entered into in the state by foreign corporations which have not qualified to do business in the state "shall be held to be void at the suit of such foreign corporation." The statute excepted corporations engaged in or transacting business of interstate commerce only within the state. Computaflor had never registered with the secretary of state nor appointed an agent. Can Computaflor recover in Alabama?

Part VII

Property

chapter 29

Personal Property

Nature and Classification

Nature of Property.   Property or ownership may be defined as the right to possess, enjoy, and dispose of objects or rights having economic value. Property, in its legal sense, has a variety of meanings. It may refer to an object having a physical existence; it may refer to legal rights connected with and growing out of an object having physical existence; or it may refer to legal rights which are of economic value but not connected with a physical object.

A tract of land is property. If the owner leases the land, the lease is also property. The lease grants to the lessee the right to use the land, a right connected with and growing out of the physical object of land. A patent right is property; yet the patent right does not refer to or grow out of a physical object.

In the United States the legal concept of property is synonymous with ownership. To have property in the legal sense, it is necessary to have an organized society which has developed some concepts and some laws relative to property and ownership. A careful analysis of our concepts of property and ownership reveals that property or ownership is based on a bundle of legal rights recognized and enforced by society. People commonly refer to the physical object or to the specific right as the property, but from a legal sense, property is the right to the physical object or the right to enjoy the benefits flowing from the exercise of the specific right.

For example, people say that the house is John's property. From a legal standpoint the physical object is not property. The property is really the legal right which John has to use, enjoy, sell, mortgage, or rent the physical object, the house. Likewise, people say the patent is John's property. A patent has no physical existence. It is a bundle of rights which protects one in the enjoyment of the benefits flowing from the exclusive right to reproduce the patented object.

The owner of the patent may sell the patent, he or she may license others to produce the patented article, or he or she may produce it himself. The total of these rights is the patent.

Under our free competitive society, private ownership of property is of primary importance. This concept is written into the Constitution of the United States. The Fourteenth Amendment provides that no state shall "deprive any person of life, liberty, or property without due process of law." This concept recognizes and protects the individual in his or her right to acquire, enjoy, and dispose of property; yet the concept does not grant anyone unlimited property rights. Under the philosophy of a free competitive society the individual is encouraged to use his or her best efforts to produce; and our laws are framed to secure the fruits of his or her labors to one who has produced something beneficial to society. It is also recognized that if each individual is to reap the greatest reward for his or her efforts, restrictions are necessary; consequently, one must pursue a course which does not deprive other individuals in society of their right of freedom of action. Our property laws have developed out of this philosophy of a free competitive society.

Possession.   The importance of possession in the law of property is indicated in the old saying, "Possession is nine points of the law." In any primitive society, possession is the equivalent of ownership. In the development of our law the courts have held that in a case of violation of property rights, the right violated is the right of peaceful possession, not the right of ownership.

In our modern society, possession is used with such a variety of meanings that it is futile to attempt to define it in precise terms. In its simplest sense, possession signifies that a person has manual control over a physical object; however, in law this simple concept is inadequate. In connection with possession of personal property, two elements are of general importance: (1) manual control, and (2) intent to claim property rights. The courts recognize legal possession, which is the legal right to control the physical object; manual control is not an essential element of legal possession. If a person is wearing his watch, he has both legal and manual control of the watch. He has possession of the watch in the popular sense of the word, and he also has legal possession. If he leaves his watch in his house while he is on vacation, he does not have manual control of the watch but does have legal control. He has legal possession, and anyone taking the watch from his house without his consent has invaded his right of possession.

A servant or an agent may have manual control of his or her employer's or principal's property yet not have legal possession of the property. The servant or agent has only custody of the property; the employer or principal has legal possession. For example, if a storekeeper gives a clerk the day's receipts to count in the storekeeper's presence, the clerk has custody of the receipts, but the storekeeper has legal possession.

The term "possession," when used in the abstract, includes such a multiplicity of situations that it loses its significance. Possession may indicate one factual and legal situation when one says that "to have a valid levy of execution, the sheriff must take possession of the property," another when one says that "to create a bailment of property, possession must be delivered to the bailee," and still another when one says that "the crime of larceny involves the felonious taking possession and carrying away of another's property."

Real and Personal Property.   Because of the breadth of the subject of property and the varied incidents of ownership, property has been divided into various classes. These classes are not mutually exclusive; the same piece of property may, owing to its various characteristics, fall into more than one classification.

The most important classification is that of "real" and "personal" property. The earth's crust and all things firmly attached thereto are real property, while all other objects and rights capable of ownership are personal property.

Although the distinction as stated is simple, the problems arising are frequently complex because that which is real property can be converted into personal property by severance and that which is personal property can be converted into real property by attachment. Stone in the ground is real property, but when quarried, it becomes personal property; and if it is used in the construction of a building, it will again become real property. Perennial products, such as trees, grass, and fruit trees which need not be seeded each year, are, as a general rule, treated as part of the land. Crops resulting from annual labor, such as potatoes, corn, oats, and annual vegetables are in many cases treated as personal property, although generally they pass with the land. If perennial products are severed from the land, they become personal property.

Tangible and Intangible Property.   Property may be classed as "tangible" or "intangible"—sometimes termed "corporeal" or "incorporeal." The basis for classifying property as tangible or intangible is the physical nature of the property. Property which has a physical existence, such as land, buildings, and furniture is tangible; and property which has no physical existence, such as patent rights, easements, and bonds, is intangible. This distinction is important in determining the right to tax, in the probating of estates, and in similar situations. As a general rule, tangible property is subject to taxation by the state in which it is located, whereas intangible property is taxable at the domicile (home) of the owner.

Public and Private Property.   Property is also classed as "public" or "private." The classification of property into public and private is based on the ownership of the property. If the property is owned by the government or a political division thereof, it is classed as public property; but if the property is owned by an individual, a group of individuals, a corporation, or some other business organization, it is classed as private property.

Summary

Property, or more specifically ownership, is the exclusive right to possess, enjoy, and dispose of objects or rights having economic value. In law, property is a bundle of legal rights to things having economic value, which rights are recognized and protected by society.

The concept of possession is of outstanding importance in our society; however, possession is used with such a variety of meanings that it is futile to attempt to define it in precise terms. Basically, it is the right to control things having physical existence.

Property is classified according to its various characteristics. The earth's crust and all things firmly attached thereto are classed as real property; all other objects and rights subject to ownership are classed as personal property.

Those things which have a physical existence are classed as tangible or corporeal property. Rights which have economic value but which are not related to things having a physical existence and rest solely in contemplation of law are classed as intangible or incorporeal property.

Property owned by the government or a government unit is classed as public property, whereas property owned by any person or association, even though used exclusively for public purposes, is classed as private property.

Acquisition of Personal Property

Production or Purchase.   A person owns the product of his or her own labors unless he or she has agreed to perform labor for another, in which event the employer is the owner of the product of the labors. This rule of law is so well-established and so generally accepted in the United States that it is almost never the subject of litigation.

The most common means of acquiring ownership of personal property, other than by production, is by purchase. A special body of law regarding the purchase and sale of personal property has been developed which is treated under the heading of "Sales."

Taking Possession.   Ownership of personal property was acquired, in the very early times, by taking possession of property which was unowned. This right to acquire ownership of unowned property by taking possession thereof is recognized today; however, it is of relatively little importance in modern society. Wildlife and abandoned property are classed as unowned property, and the first person to take possession of such property becomes the owner thereof.

To acquire ownership of a wild animal by taking possession thereof, a person must attain such a degree of control over it as will deprive it of its freedom. Manual control is not necessary. A mortally wounded animal becomes the property of the person wounding it, even though he has not as yet obtained manual control of it. Animals in a trap or fish in a net have been held to be the property of the person who set the trap or net. However, if a captured animal escapes and is again caught by another person, that person becomes the owner unless he or she knows that the animal is an escaped animal and that the prior owner is pursuing it with the intent of recapturing it.

If property is abandoned by the owner, it then becomes unowned property, and the first person who takes possession of it with the intention of claiming ownership thereof becomes the owner of it.

Gift. A gift is a voluntary transfer of property by one person to another without any consideration being given for the transfer. To make a valid gift, the donor must presently deliver the property to the donee or to some third person, who holds the property for the donee, and this delivery must be unconditional and must be made with the intent of vesting ownership in the donee. Delivery is the transfer of possession from one person to another, and, as a general rule, there can be no gift without delivery. If the delivery is to a third person, who holds for the donee, the delivery must be made with the intent of divesting the donor of all rights in the property. After the delivery the third person must hold the property as trustee for the donee. If the donor reserves rights in the property, the third person will be held to hold as agent for the donor, and a valid gift will not result.

If the donee is already in possession of the property, a clear declaration by the donor that he or she gives the property to the donee is sufficient to make the gift valid. In some instances the courts have recognized symbolic delivery. For example, the delivery of the keys to a strongbox is symbolic delivery of the contents of the strongbox.

A gift of intangible property requires the execution and delivery of a certificate of gift. If the intangible property is evidenced by a stock certificate or a negotiable instrument, the delivery of the stock certificate or the negotiable instrument properly endorsed, if endorsement is required, is sufficient delivery.

In determining whether a gift has actually been made, the law places great importance on "delivery." Surrender of possession through delivery to the donee or a third person should make clear to the donor the significance of his or her act, that he or she is giving up ownership of his or her property without obtaining anything in return. Basic contract law requires consideration in order to make a promise enforceable. Gift law compliments contract law by refusing to acknowledge a mere promise to make a gift and insisting on completion of the gift through delivery before recognizing the validity of the gift.

Two types of gifts are recognized: gifts *inter vivos,* and gifts *causa mortis.* A gift *inter vivos* is a gift between living persons; a gift *causa mortis* is a gift in contemplation of death. A gift *causa mortis* has some of the elements of a testamentary disposition of property.

If a gift *causa mortis* is to be valid, the donor must make the gift in contemplation of death in the immediate future, and he or she must comply with all the requirements for a valid *inter vivos* gift. However, the gift *causa mortis* is a conditional gift and is subject to three conditions implied by law, the occurrence of any one of which will defeat the gift: (1) recovery of the donor from the peril or sickness under fear of which the gift was made, (2) revocation of the gift by the donee before his or her death, and (3) death of the donee before the donor. When one of these events takes place, title and the right to possession are immediately revested in the donor.

Lost Property.   Lost property becomes the property of the finder as against all persons except the original owner. If Abbott loses his ring and Birge finds it, and later Birge loses the ring and Crum finds it, Birge may claim the ring from Crum; but Abbott, the original owner, has the superior right to the ring and may claim it from either Birge or Crum.

If the finder of lost property knows the identity of the person who lost it yet appropriates it to his own use, he is guilty of larceny. If he does not know the identity of the owner and does not have reasonable means of discovering his identity and appropriates the property to his own use, he will be liable to the owner in conversion for the value of the property if the owner later proves his or her right to it. Some states have enacted statutes which permit the finder of lost property to clear his or her title thereto by complying with the statutory procedure.

The courts have made a distinction between lost property and mislaid property. If Abbott, while in Birge's store, drops his wallet in the aisle, the wallet will generally be classed as lost property; but if he lays it on the counter and, forgetting it, leaves the store, it will be classed as mislaid property. If the wallet is mislaid, Birge will become bailee thereof. If Crum finds the wallet in the aisle, he will have the right to take possession of it; but if Crum discovers the wallet on the counter, Birge will have the right to take possession of it. The distinction between lost and mislaid property was developed to increase the chance the property would be returned to its real owner where he or she knowingly placed it down but had forgotten to pick it up and might well be expected to remember later where he or she had left it and return for it. It is very difficult to distinguish between lost property and misplaced property; consequently, the cases on the subject are not in accord.

Confusion.   Title to personal property may be acquired by confusion or by accession. Confusion of goods is the inseparable intermixture of goods belonging to different owners. For example, suppose crude oil belonging to several persons is mixed in one tank. If the mixing is by common consent or inevitable accident, each party will be deemed the owner of a proportionate part of the mass. If the mixing is by willful, tortious act, the innocent party will be protected, and the entire mass will become the property of the innocent party if such action is necessary to protect his or her interest. In case of accidental confusion, if one of the owners is guilty of negligence, he or she will have to bear any loss resulting from the confusion.

Accession. Literally, "accession" means that something has been added, and as applied to property, it means that new value has been added to existing property by labor or by the addition of other property or by a combination of both. As a general rule, the owner of the original property will become the owner of the improvements. If Birge repairs Abbott's automobile by adding some new parts, Abbott will be the owner of the automobile when repaired and will also be the owner of the new parts which Birge has added.

Difficulty arises where one person improves the property of another by labor or by the addition of materials, or both, when the owner has not contracted for or consented to the improvement. The decisions of the courts in regard to the rights of the parties in such a situation are not in accord, and in many respects they are confusing. As a general rule, if one person has tortiously taken property of another and, by his labor or the addition of his materials, or both, improved the property, the owner of the original property may recover it in its improved state and will not be obligated to compensate the tort-feasor for his labor or materials.

If the person making the improvement honestly but mistakenly believes that he is the owner of the property at the time he makes the improvement, the courts will, as a general rule, permit recovery for the benefits conferred on the true owner of the property as a result of the improvement. If the owner of the property wishes, he may sue the wrongdoer in tort for conversion of his property and recover a judgment for the value of the unimproved property. Whether the property itself can be recovered, after payment of due compensation to the improver for his improvements, will depend on: (1) the relative increase in value, (2) whether the form or identity of the property has been changed, and (3) whether the improvements can be separated from the original property.

Summary

Ownership of personal property may be acquired by (1) production, (2) purchase, (3) taking possession, (4) gift, (5) finding, (6) confusion, and (7) accession.

A person owns property produced by his own labor or by the labor of persons whom he hires to work for him.

The owner of personal property may sell or barter his or her property to another, and the purchaser then becomes the owner of the property.

The person who first reduces unowned property—wildlife or abandoned property—to possession with the intent of claiming ownership of the property acquires ownership thereof.

A gift is the transfer of the ownership of property from the donor to the donee without any consideration being given by the donee. To have a valid gift, the donor must deliver the possession of the property to the donee or to some third person with the intent of vesting ownership in the donee.

The finder of lost property acquires ownership of the property against everyone except the original owner. A distinction, which is not clear cut, is made between lost property and mislaid property.

If a person confuses his or her property with that of another, the other party may acquire ownership of the entire mass.

If property is improved by the labor and addition of materials by another without the owner's consent, the owner of the original property becomes the owner of the property in its improved state.

Lieber v. Mohawk Arms, Inc.

314 N.Y.S.2d 510 (Sup. Ct. N.Y. 1970)

This was an action by Lieber (plaintiff) against Mohawk Arms, Inc., (defendant) to recover possession of several items of personal property. Mohawk Arms moved for summary judgment. The motion was denied and the court granted summary judgment to Lieber.

The facts are given in the opinion.

LYNCH, JUDGE.   In 1945 the plaintiff, then in the United States Army, was among the first soldiers to occupy Munich, Germany. There he and some companions entered Adolph Hitler's apartment and removed various items of his personal belongings. The plaintiff brought his share home to Louisiana. It included Hitler's uniform jacket and cap and some of his decorations and personal jewelry.

The plaintiff's possession of these articles was publicly known. Louisiana newspapers published stories and pictures about the plaintiff's collection, and he was the subject of a feature story in the *Louisiana State University Alumni News* of October, 1945. There is some indication that the articles were occasionally displayed to the public.

In 1968 the collection was stolen by the plaintiff's chauffeur who sold it to a New York dealer in historical Americana. The dealer sold it to the defendant who purchased in good faith. Through collectors' circles the plaintiff soon discovered the whereabouts of his stolen property, made a demand for its return that was refused, and commenced this action seeking the return.

The defendant resists and asks summary judgment on the ground that the plaintiff cannot succeed in the suit since he "never obtained good and legal title to this collection," that "the collection properly belongs to the occupational Military authority and/or the Bavarian Government."

This defense, title in a third party, was at one time effective. . . . But it did not survive the enactment of the Civil Practice Law and Rules, Section 7101 of which provides for the recovery of a chattel by one who has the superior right to possession. In proposing the elimination of this defense the draughtsmen of the CPLR sought to prevent the very thing being attempted by the defendant here.

The present law thus allows a defendant who has a lesser right to possession than the plaintiff to keep the property and withstand a replevy by asserting the superior right of a third person, even though there is no assurance that he will turn over the property to the third person. There is no good reason to perpetuate this situation, for if the holder of a chattel is genuinely concerned about the rights of the true owner, he may employ the modern procedural device of interpleader to protect them, or may merely notify the person who claims to be the true owner and the latter may intervene. (Fourth Preliminary Report of the Advisory Committee on Practice and Procedure, Legislative Document No. 20, p. 254.)

The question presented by an action to recover a chattel is "whether or not a plaintiff has such a title in the cause of action so that a recovery or satisfaction by it will protect the defendant from the claims of third parties. . . ." Applying this test we find that the plaintiff must recover possession of the chattels. The defendant, despite its good faith, has no title since its possession is derived from a thief (Uniform Commercial Code, § 2–403). The plaintiff's possession prior to the theft and since 1945 is unquestioned. He further benefits from Article 3509 of the Louisiana Civil Code which provides that when "the possessor of any movable whatever has possessed it for ten years without interruption, he shall acquire the ownership of it without being obliged to produce a title or to prove that he did not act in bad faith."

Dolitsky v. Dollar Savings Bank

118 N.Y.S.2d 65 (City of N.Y. Mun. Ct. 1952)

This was an action by Betty Dolitsky (plaintiff) against Dollar Savings Bank (defendant) to recover $100 allegedly found by Dolitsky. Judgment for Dollar Savings Bank.

Betty Dolitsky rented a safe-deposit box from Dollar Savings Bank. The safe-deposit vault of the bank is in the basement, and the vault area is walled off from all other parts of the bank. Only box renters and officers and employees of the bank are admitted to this area. To gain access to the area a box renter must obtain an admission slip, fill in his box number and sign the slip, have the box number and signature checked by an employee against the records of the bank, and then present the slip to a guard who admits the renter to the safe-deposit vault area.

On November 7, 1951, Dolitsky requested access to her box and the procedure as outlined was followed. While Dolitsky was in the booth she was looking through an advertising folder which had been placed there by the bank and found a $100 bill which she turned over to the attendant. Dolitsky waited one year and during that time the rightful owner of the $100 bill made no claim for it. Dolitsky then demanded that the bank surrender the bill to her claiming that she was entitled to the bill as finder. The bank claims the bill is mislaid property and that they owe a duty to keep the bill for the rightful owner.

TRIMARCO, JUSTICE.   At common law property was lost when possession had been casually and involuntarily parted with, so that the mind had no impress of and could have no knowledge of the parting. Mislaid property was that which the owner had voluntarily and intentionally placed and then forgotten.

Property in someone's possession cannot *be found in the sense of common-law lost property.* If the article is in the custody of the owner of the place when it is discovered it is not lost in the legal sense; instead it is mislaid. Thus, if a chattel is discovered anywhere in a private place where only a limited class of people have a right to be and they are customers of the owner of the premises, who has the duty of preserving the property of his customers, it is in the possession of the owner of the premises.

In the case of mislaid property discovered on the premises of another, the common-law rule is that the proprietor of the premises is held to have the better right to hold the same for the owner, or the proprietor has custody for the benefit of the owner; or the proprietor is the gratuitous bailee of the owner. The effect of the cases, despite their different description of the relationship, is that the proprietor is the bailee of the owner. Thus, the discoverer of mislaid property has the duty to leave it with the proprietor of the premises, and the latter has the duty to hold it for the owner. New York statutory requirements do not change this rule.

The bank is a gratuitous bailee of mislaid property once it has knowledge of the property. As such the bank has the duty to exercise ordinary care in the custody of the articles with a duty to redeliver to the owner.

The recent case of *Manufacturers Savings Deposit Co. v. Cohen,* which held that property found on the floor of a booth located in an outer room used by a safe-deposit company in conjunction with a bank, access thereto not being limited to box holders or officials of the safe-deposit company, was lost property and as such should have been turned over to the property clerk of the Police Department, can be distinguished from the present case. In the *Cohen* case the court found that the booth on the floor of which the money was found was not located within the safe-deposit vault but rather in an outer room adjoining said vault and in a part of the bank which was accessible to the ordinary customer of the bank for the purchase of bonds and the opening of new accounts; as such the court considers the room in which the booth was located a public place which was not restricted to safe-deposit officials and persons having safe-deposit boxes in the vault. The case is further distinguished from the present case since its facts disclose that the money was found on the floor of the booth which indicated to the court that the money was not mislaid. The court points out that the testimony shows the money to have been found on the floor of the booth and not on any table or other normal resting place.

Nature and Creation of Bailment

Essential Elements.   Normally, in a bailment the title of personal property is in one person, the bailor, and the right of possession is in another person, the bailee. Not all transactions in which there is a division of title and possession are bailments. These essential elements must be present in order to have a bailment: (1) the title to the property or a superior right to possession must be in the bailor, (2) the bailee must have lawful possession without title, and (3) the bailee must owe a duty to return the property to the bailor or dispose of it as directed by him or her. The bailment is a common transaction, and frequently a bailment exists when the parties to the transaction are not aware of its existence. For instance, if you loan your lawn mower to your neighbor, a bailment arises.

Creation of Relation.   As a general rule a bailment is created by a contract. Whether or not a bailment exists must be determined from all the facts and circumstances of the case. The test generally applied is whether possession has been delivered and whether the person into whose possession the article has been delivered intended to assume custody and control over the object and has expressly or impliedly promised to return the article to the owner or to dispose of it as directed by the owner. Usually, if one goes into a restaurant or barber shop or like place and hangs his hat and coat on a rack provided for that purpose, no bailment will arise; but if the circumstances are such that it can be established that the owner of the establishment either expressly or impliedly assumes control over the hat and coat, the existence of a bailment may be established. If a checkroom is provided and the hat and coat are checked with the attendant in charge, a bailment will arise.

The courts have held that if a person parks his automobile in a parking lot, retaining the keys to his automobile and having the privilege of getting it himself whenever he wishes, the transaction is a lease and not a bailment. However, if a person takes his automobile to a parking garage and surrenders it to an attendant who parks it and returns it to the owner when the owner calls for it, a bailment is created.

Custody of Servant or Agent.   The distinction between custody and possession of personal property is technical and is based on the law of master and servant. If a master (employer) entrusts his or her property to a servant, the master technically retains the legal possession of the property and the servant has the custody. For instance, a clerk working in a store has custody of the goods entrusted to him or her for sale, but the master has possession of the goods. In such a situation, no bailment exists since, in contemplation of law, there is no surrender of the possession of the goods.

Summary

A bailment is created when the owner of personal property, the bailor, delivers the possession of the property to another, the bailee, who is obligated to return the property to the bailor or to dispose of it as directed by the bailor.

A bailment is created by contract, expressed or implied. Whether or not a bailment is created will depend on the facts and circumstances of the case.

Delivery of goods by a master to his or her servant does not, as a general rule, create a bailment. The servant has custody of the goods, not possession.

Kuchinsky v. Empire Lounge, Inc.

134 N.W.2d 436 (Sup. Ct. Wis. 1965)

This was an action by Kuchinsky (plaintiff) against Empire Lounge (defendant) to recover for the loss of Kuchinsky's coat. The trial court dismissed the complaint and Kuchinsky appealed. Affirmed.

Kuchinsky entered the Empire Lounge as a customer and hung his coat on a clothes tree near his table. His coat was stolen while he ate.

CURRIE, CIRCUIT JUDGE. A case very much in point is *Montgomery v. Ladjing.* There the plaintiff entered the restaurant kept by the defendant with a party of friends; he removed his overcoat and hung it on a hook affixed to a post near the table at which he seated himself; the attention of neither the defendant nor of any of his employees was called to the coat in any way; and fifteen minutes later the coat was missing. The court held that the plaintiff had wholly failed to show failure on the part of the defendant to exercise ordinary care, and declared:

The rule to be deduced from all these cases therefore is that, before a restaurant keeper will be held liable for the loss of an overcoat of a customer while such customer takes a meal or refreshments, it must appear either that the overcoat was placed in the physical custody of the keeper of the restaurant or his servants, in which cases there is an actual bailment, or that the overcoat was necessarily laid aside under circumstances showing, at least, notice of the fact and of such necessity to the keeper of the restaurant, or his servants, in which case there is an implied bailment or constructive custody, that the loss occurred by reason of the insufficiency of the general supervision exercised by the keeper of the restaurant for the protection of the property of customers temporarily laid aside.

In *National Fire Insurance Co. v. Commodore Hotel,* the plaintiff was a guest at a luncheon held at the defendant's hotel. She hung her mink jacket in an unattended cloakroom on the main floor across from the lobby desk. After the luncheon and ensuing party the plaintiff went to the cloakroom to retrieve her jacket and discovered it was gone. The court held that no negligence had been established against the defendant and stated:

. . . In any event, we do not feel that it is incumbent upon a hotel or restaurant owner to keep an attendant in charge of a free cloakroom for luncheon or dinner guests or otherwise face liability for loss of articles placed therein. The maintenance of such rooms without attendants is a common practice, and where the proprietor had not accepted control and custody of articles placed therein, no duty rests upon him to exercise any special degree of care with respect thereto.

Likewise, failure to post a warning disclaiming responsibility would not seem to constitute negligence when, as here, a guest is aware that a cloakroom is unattended, adjacent to the lobby, and accessible to anyone; and has used it under similar circumstances on many prior occasions. The absence of such warning signs does not appear to have been material in a number of decisions absolving proprietors from liability although when posted they appear to be regarded as an added factor in establishing such nonliability.

Weinberg v. Wayco Petroleum Co.

402 S.W.2d 597 (Ct. App. Mo. 1966)

This was an action by Weinberg (plaintiff) against Wayco Petroleum Company (defendant) for the theft of personal property which occurred while Weinberg's car was parked in Wayco's parking garage. The circuit court awarded Weinberg a $500 judgment. Reversed.

Weinberg was the holder of a "Parkard" issued by Wayco for which he paid $10.50 per month and which entitled him to park his automobile at Wayco's garage located in St. Louis. This garage had five stories and entrance was gained by inserting the "Parkard" into a slot causing the entrance gate to open. This was a so-called self-park garage and there were no attendants on duty at the time Weinberg parked his automobile at about 11:30 P.M. on September 25, 1962. After securing admission to the garage with the Parkard, Weinberg parked his own car, locked it, and took the keys with him. When he returned to his automobile in the evening of September 27th, he found it had been broken into and certain personal property stolen from it. The automobile had not been moved.

The "Parkard" stated: "This card licenses the holder to park one automobile in this area at holder's risk. Lock your car. Licensor hereby declares himself not responsible for fire, theft, or damage to or loss of such automobile or any article left therein. Only a license is granted hereby, and no bailment is created." Weinberg testified that prior to this occurrence he had read this language on the card and knew what it said.

BRADY, COMMISSIONER. With respect to cases involving automobiles and the contents thereof when loss occurs after the automobile is left in a parking lot, the relationship between the parties is usually one of bailment or license, and whether it is one or the other depends upon the circumstances of the particular case and especially upon the manner in which the parking lot in question is being operated and with whom control of the allegedly bailed article or articles is vested.

A "bailment" in its ordinary legal sense imports the delivery of personal property by the bailor to the bailee who keeps the property in trust for a specific purpose, with a contract, express or implied, that the trust shall be faithfully executed, and the property returned or duly accounted for when the special purpose is accomplished or that the property shall be kept until the bailor reclaims it. This court has said that ". . . the term 'bailment' . . . signifies a contract resulting from the delivery of goods by bailor to bailee on condition that they be restored to the bailor, according to his directions, so soon as the purposes for which they were bailed are answered."

It is obvious from the facts in the instant case that there was no delivery to Wayco sufficient to create the relationship of bailee and bailor between the parties here involved. Cases of the nature here involved are to be distinguished from those where the parking operation is such that the attendants collect a fee and assume authority or control of the automobile by parking it and/or retaining the keys so that the car can be moved about to permit the entrance or exit of other automobiles and where the tickets that are given to the owner of the automobile are issued for the purpose of identifying the automobile for redelivery. In such instances a bailment relationship is almost invariably held to exist. In the instant case Wayco never secured control or authority over Weinberg's automobile. No agent or employee of Wayco parked it or kept the keys to it or issued any ticket whereby the automobile could be identified by comparison of a portion of the ticket left with the automobile when it was parked. Weinberg parked his own automobile, locked it, and took the keys with him. Certainly Wayco, the alleged bailee, did not have the right under these circumstances to exclude the purposes of the owner or even of anyone else who might have had the keys. In the instant case Weinberg never made a delivery, actual or constructive, of the automobile to Wayco under circumstances leading to the creation of a bailee-bailor relationship between them.

Rights and Liabilities of Parties

Bailee's Duty of Care.   In determining the liability of the bailee for damage to or loss of the bailed property, bailments have been divided into three classes: (1) mutual benefit bailments, (2) bailments for the sole benefit of the bailor, and (3) bailments for the sole benefit of the bailee.

All commercial bailments are mutual-benefit bailments, that is, both the bailee and the bailor receive benefits from the relation. For example, if goods are stored in a warehouse, the warehouseman (the bailee) is compensated for his services, and the owner of the goods (the bailor) has his or her goods cared for during the period of storage. The mutual benefit bailee owes a duty of ordinary care and is liable for damage to or loss of the goods only if such damage or loss is the result of his negligence. Ordinary care has been defined as that care which a person of ordinary prudence would take of his or her goods of like nature under the same or similar circumstances.

A bailment for the sole benefit of the bailor is one in which the bailee renders some service in respect to the bailed property without receiving a return benefit. For instance, if you permit your neighbor to put his automobile in your garage while he is away on a trip, and he pays you nothing for the privilege, the bailment is for the sole benefit of the bailor. In such a bailment the bailee owes a duty of slight care. The bailee will be liable for damage to or loss of the bailed goods only if he does little or nothing to protect them when it is apparent that they will be damaged or lost and when the bailee could prevent the damage or loss without any substantial cost or sacrifice on his part.

A bailment for the sole benefit of the bailee arises when the owner of goods permits another to use his or her goods free of charge. For instance, if you loan your lawn mower to your neighbor, the bailment is for the sole benefit of the bailee. In such a bailment, the bailee owes a duty of great care. If the bailee is negligent in any respect in his or her use or care of the bailed goods, and as the result of such negligence the goods are damaged or lost, the bailee is liable.

Recently some courts have moved away from the three classes of bailments with their distinctions as to degree of care which sound fine in theory but are often difficult to apply in practice. Instead, these courts require a reasonable amount of care on the part of all bailees. What is reasonable care in any given situation depends on: (1) the nature and value of the bailed property, (2) who the bailee is—for example, whether he or she is a professional bailee, and (3) whether the bailment was paid for or whether it was gratuitous.

Alteration of Liability by Contract. The liability of the bailee may be either increased or decreased by the contract of the parties. The extent to which a bailee may relieve himself from his liability for his own negligence is limited. Under the law of contracts, a contract whereby a person relieves himself of liability for his own negligence may be against public policy and void. The courts have, as a general rule, enforced provisions in contracts of bailment whereby the bailee is relieved from specific perils; but the courts have been reluctant to enforce provisions in such contracts whereby the bailee is relieved from all liability for his negligent acts.

The effect of the posting of notices, the printing of terms on a check or receipt given to the bailor, or the doing of other similar acts by the bailee in an attempt to limit his liability was discussed in Chapter 6, "Offer." The question is primarily one of communication of the terms of the contract. The knowledge of the bailor of the facilities of the bailee or of his method of doing business or the nature of prior dealings may give rise to an implied agreement as to the duties of the bailee. The bailee may, if he wishes, assume all the risks incident to the bailment and contract to return the bailed property undamaged or to pay any damage to or loss of the property.

Bailee's Duty to Return Property. On the termination of the bailment, the bailee owes a duty to return the bailed property in an undamaged condition to the bailor or to dispose of it as directed by the bailor. If the bailee cannot return the property to the bailor in an undamaged condition, he may excuse his failure by showing that the goods were damaged or destroyed without negligence on his part. If the bailed property is taken from the bailee by legal process, the bailee should notify the bailor and must take whatever action is necessary to protect the bailor's interest.

If a third person claims to have, in the bailed property, rights which are superior to the rights of the bailor and demands possession of the bailed property, the bailee is in a dilemma. If the bailee refuses to deliver the bailed property to the third-person claimant and the third-person claimant is entitled to the possession of it, the bailee will be liable to such claimant. If the bailee delivers the bailed property to the third-person claimant and the third-person claimant is not entitled to possession, the bailee is liable to the bailor. The circumstances may be such that the conflicting claims of the bailor and the third-person claimant can be determined only by judicial decision. In some cases the bailee may protect himself by bringing a bill of interpleader, but this remedy is not available in all cases. The bailee cannot set up a claim to the bailed property which is adverse to the rights of the bailor if the claim is based on rights which existed at the time the property was bailed. By accepting the property as bailee, the bailee is estopped from denying the bailor's title to the bailed property.

Bailee's Right to Compensation. The bailee's right to compensation will depend entirely on the agreement or understanding of the parties. If the bailment is a gratuitous bailment, the bailee will be entitled to no compensation even though the bailment is for the sole benefit of the bailor. If the bailment is created by the rental of personal property, the bailee will be obligated to pay the agreed rent. If the bailment is for the storage or repair of property, the bailee will be entitled to the contract price for his or her services. If there is no agreement as to compensation, the bailee will be entitled to recover the reasonable value of the services rendered. In many situations the bailee, if entitled to compensation, will have a lien on the bailed property for the reasonable value of his or her services.

Bailor's Liability for Defects in Bailed Property. If personal property is rented or loaned to a bailee, the bailor impliedly warrants that there are no defects in the property which will make it unsafe for use.

If the bailment is a mutual-benefit bailment, that is, if the property is rented to the bailee, the bailor must use reasonable care in inspecting the property and in seeing that it is in a safe condition for use for the purpose for which it is rented. The bailor is liable to the bailee or an employee of the bailee for damages resulting from the use of the defective property if the bailee should have, in the exercise of due care, discovered the defect.

If the bailment is for the sole benfit of the bailee, as is the case when the bailor loans property to the bailee, the bailor is liable for injuries resulting from defects in the bailed property only if the bailor has knowledge of the defects and fails to give the bailee notice of the defects.

Summary

The bailee owes a duty of due care to prevent loss of or damage to the bailed property. In determining whether or not due care has been exercised by the bailee, the nature of the bailment is of outstanding importance.

The parties within the limits of the legality of their contract, may, by agreement, increase or decrease the scope of the liability of the bailee.

On the termination of the bailment the bailee must return the bailed property to the bailor or dispose of it according to the direction of the bailor. If a third person having a right of possession superior to that of the bailor demands the surrender of the property to him or her, the bailee is obligated to deliver the property to such third person.

The bailee is entitled to reasonable compensation for services rendered in the care of the property. If the contract of bailment stipulates the compensation, the bailee is entitled to the stipulated compensation.

If the bailor rents property to the bailee, the bailor owes a duty to inspect the property to see that it is free from dangerous defects. If the bailor loans the property to the bailee, he or she owes a duty to warn the bailee of any known dangerous defects in the property.

Allen v. Southern Pacific Co.

213 P.2d 667 (Sup. Ct. Utah 1950)

This was an action by Frank J. Allen (plaintiff) against Southern Pacific Company (defendant) to recover a judgment for $2,190, the value of a traveling bag and contents. Judgment for Allen for $25 and Allen appealed. Reversed.

Allen checked his traveling bag with its contents at the parcel-checking room of Southern Pacific Company (Pacific) in the Union Station at Portland, Oregon. When he presented his claim check and asked for its return, it could not be found. At the time the bag was checked Pacific gave Allen a parcel check or receipt which had printed on one side the following:

Notice—Liability for loss of, damage or delay to any parcel limited to not to exceed $25.00 unless at time of deposit value is declared and paid for at the rate of 10 cents for each $25.00 or fraction thereof for thirty days or less. No parcel valued in excess of $250.00 will be accepted.

On the reverse side was printed:

Date and time of delivery.
For Excess Liability See Notice on Opposite Side.

There was also posted a sign at this parcel room to the same effect as the printing on the check.

At the time Allen checked his bag his attention was not called to the provisions printed on the claim check or to the sign, and he did not read either. Pacific claims that its liability is limited to $25. Allen claims that, since his attention was not called to the provisions limiting liability and since he had no knowledge of them at the time he checked his bag, he is not bound by them.

WADE, JUSTICE. The sole question before this court is: Was the court correct in holding that respondent's liability was limited by contract?

Ordinarily, a bailee for hire is responsible for the value of the goods entrusted to him if they are lost or destroyed. However, the parties may enter into a valid agreement to modify the obligations which would otherwise arise from the relationship of bailor and bailee if it ". . . does not violate the law or contravene public policy, and so long as it is actually a part of the contract of bailment and is expressed in clear and unmistakable language. . . ." 6 Am. Jur., Bailments, Sec. 174, page 268.

The great weight of authority is that a bailee cannot entirely exempt himself by contract from liability due to his negligence and contracts limiting his liability for negligence during the course of a general business with the public are usually regarded as being against public policy. But even where such contracts are not against public policy there must be actual assent to the conditions modifying the bailee's liability growing out of the contract of bailment.

In the instant case the court, as the trier of the facts, found that Allen did not see or read the notice posted at the parcel room, nor did he read the check, that he had no actual knowledge of the limitations contained therein, nor were such limitations or conditions called to his attention. Under such a state of facts, it cannot be said that Allen actually assented to the limitations contained in the notice and check.

Pacific contends that the rules that a bailee may not exempt himself from liability for loss due to his negligence because such a contract is against public policy and that he may not limit his liability unless the contract is fairly and freely made and the bailee has actual knowledge of such limitations do not apply to the type of contract made herein where the limitations of liability varies in amount in direct proportion to the value declared and the charge paid by the bailor. In support of this argument it cites a number of United States Supreme Court cases. We have carefully read each of these cases and find that they deal with baggage or other personal property involved in a contract of carriage in interstate commerce and which are subject to the rules and regulations of the Interstate Commerce Commission and applicable laws of Congress. Under these rules the railroads have to file schedules giving the rates, charges and fares for transportation between different points and these cannnot be changed by contract. These cases and the reasoning therein are distinguishable from the cases where the railroad company acts as a warehouseman, where the baggage is left for care and not for transportation. As stated by the court in *Boston & M. R. R. v. Hooker,* in holding that where baggage is in interstate commerce it is subject to published rates and even though the shipper was not aware of the fact that there were different rates for different valuations of the property, the common carrier's liability was limited to the amount actually provided by the different scheduled rates:

It is to be borne in mind that the action as tried and decided in the state court was not for negligence of the railroad company as a warehouseman for the loss of the baggage after its delivery at Sunapee Lake station, but was solely upon the contract of carriage in interstate commerce.

A checkroom business is not part of the business of a common carrier and when it acts in that capacity it is acting as a warehouseman.

In the instant case the court found as facts that Allen did not actually know of the printed conditions and that such conditions were not called to his attention by Pacific's agent. Under such a state of the facts the court erred in concluding that as a matter of law a contract was entered into limiting liability to $25.

Edward Hines Lumber Co. v. Purvine Logging Co., Inc.

399 P.2d 893 (Sup. Ct. Ore. 1965)

This was an action by Edward Hines Lumber Company (plaintiff) against Purvine Logging Company, Inc., (defendant) to recover a judgment for the value of a donkey engine destroyed by fire. Judgment for Purvine Logging Co., Inc., and Edward Hines Lumber Co. appealed. Judgment affirmed.

Edward Hines Lumber Co. (Hines) was the owner of a donkey engine. Purvine Logging Co., Inc., (Purvine) was a logger engaged in the performance of a logging contract for Hines. Hines delivered the donkey engine to Purvine to be used in the performance of the logging contract. The written agreement entered into by the parties provided in part that the "equipment (donkey engine) shall be kept in good operating condition maintained by contractor (Purvine) and . . . redelivered . . . in as good condition as of this date, reasonable wear and tear excepted. . . ." The donkey engine was destroyed by fire of unknown origin.

HOLMAN, JUSTICE.   The trial court in the case at bar correctly applied the common-law rule. A contract to return in good condition, reasonable wear and tear excepted, does not make the bailee an insurer of the goods. The parties may by contract place the risk of loss as they see fit, but in the absence of an agreement to the contrary, the common-law rule applied. An agreement to return in good order, fair wear and tear excepted, is not an agreement to shift the risk of loss.

Hines argues further that, even if the bailee is not to be held liable without fault, a doctrine akin to that of *res ipsa loquitur* applies the necessary inference of negligence and shifts to the bailee the duty of explaining the fire in a manner consistent with the exercise of due care on the part of the bailee. This question was probed in detail in *National Fire Ins. Co. v. Morgan et al.* We held that, after it had been shown that the goods had not been returned, the burden of going forward with the evidence shifted to the bailee. We also observed, in passing, that if the bailee could explain why the goods were not returned, as by showing that a fire occurred without fault on the bailee's part, such a showing would absolve the bailee from liability. We adhere to the view expressed in *National Fire Ins. Co. v. Morgan et al.*

In the case at bar, the trial court correctly concluded that the bailee had gone forward with a sufficient explanation of the fire to show that it had occurred under circumstances which were fully consistent with the exercise of due care by the bailee. The fire started on a weekend when woods operations were shut down. The logging site was near a public highway, and the area was accessible to fishermen, picnickers, and the like. The trial court believed that the fire was of an unknown, and unknowable, cause and that under the circumstances any inference of negligence that might arise initially under *National Fire Ins. Co. v. Morgan et al.* was overcome by the bailee's evidence that due care had been exercised. The ultimate burden of proof of negligence remained on Hines, and the trial court found that negligence had not been proven.

Moore v. Ellis

385 S.W.2d 261 (Ct. Civ. App. Tex. 1964)

This was an action by Harold Ellis (plaintiff) against John J. Moore and H. R. Wardlaw (defendants) to recover a judgment for personal injuries. Judgment for Ellis, and Moore and Wardlaw appealed. Judgment reversed and judgment entered for Moore and Wardlaw.

Moore and Wardlaw furnished a tractor and disk to Harper for use in disking land. The hydraulic cylinder lift used to raise and lower the disk was not operating properly. The disk could be raised by the three-point hitch lift. However, if the disk was overloaded with dirt when lifted with the three-point lift, it would cause the front end of the tractor to raise up. Upon disengaging the clutch or releasing the gas throttle, the front of the tractor would then come down. Moore informed Harper that the hydraulic cylinder lift was inoperative. Harper hired Harold Ellis to operate the tractor and disk. The ground being disked at the time was wet and this wet condition was causing the disk to become overloaded. Twice on the day before the accident the front of the tractor reared up. Ellis was told by McCrary, an employee of Moore and Wardlaw, and he knew that the hydraulic cylinder lift (which was safe to use if in working order) was defective and would not work. The fourth time the tractor reared up when Ellis lifted the disk it flipped over, pinning Ellis underneath and injuring him seriously.

DUNAGAN, CHIEF JUSTICE.   In the case of *Nesmith v. Magnolia Petroleum Co.,* the court said:

> One who supplies directly or through a third person a chattel for another to use, is subject to liability to those whom the supplier should expect to use the chattel with the consent of the other or to be in the vicinity of its probable use, for bodily harm caused by the use of the chattel in the manner for which and by a person for whose use it is supplied, if the supplier (a) knows, or from facts known to him should realize, that the chattel is or is likely to be dangerous for the use for which it is supplied; (b) and has no reason to believe that those for whose use the chattel is supplied will realize its dangerous condition; and (c) fails to exercise reasonable care to *inform* them of its dangerous condition or of the facts which make it likely to be so. These general principles apply alike to donors, lenders, and lessors of chattels. . . .

Therefore, all three of the above elements must exist concurrently before liability can be assessed against Moore and Wardlaw.

In the case at bar it is undisputed that Harold Ellis knew of the inoperable cylinder lift, and it is further undisputed that McCrary told Harold Ellis about the inoperable cylinder lift. Furthermore, the jury found that at the time and on the occasion in question, Harold Ellis knew that the cylinder lift was not in operating condition. Therefore, elements (b) and (c) did not exist, but, rather, the evidence showed that the duty imposed was fulfilled and not breached.

Special Bailment Situations

Bailment of Fungible Goods.   As a general rule the bailee is required to return to the bailor the identical goods he or she deposited. If the parties enter into a contract whereby the party to whom the goods are delivered has the right to surrender other goods, though of the same kind and value, the transaction is a sale, not a bailment. This rule has not been applied to the storage of grain and other fungible goods. The courts hold that if grain of several persons is stored in a common mass in an elevator and the operator of the elevator contracts to return to the depositor an equal quantity of grain of the same kind and quality, the transaction is a bailment.

The courts are not in complete accord as to the nature of the transaction if the storage contract permits the payment of the purchase price of the grain in lieu of delivery. They are in accord in holding that the transaction is a bailment if the depositor has the absolute right to demand the return of grain of the same kind and quality or to demand the payment of the market price at the time he or she makes his or her demand in lieu of accepting delivery of the grain. But most of the courts hold that the transaction is a sale if the depositary (the elevator) has the right, at the time the demand is made, to pay the market price of the grain in lieu of delivery of the grain. Some courts hold that if the depositary is given an option to purchase at the market price at the time the depositor returns his or her receipt and demands delivery, the transaction is a bailment until such time as a demand is made and the option to purchase is exercised, at which time it becomes a sale.

Safe-Deposit Boxes.   In the operation of a safe-deposit box, the box and the property in the box are in the manual possession of the bank. However, neither the bank nor the renter can gain access to the contents of the box without the consent and cooperation of the other. To open the box, two keys are used. One of the keys is kept by the bank and the other by the renter. The bank need have no knowledge of the nature, amount, or value of the property in the safe-deposit box. Although there is some diversity of opinion as to the nature of the relationship, some courts have held that the renter is a bailor and the bank is a bailee.

Involuntary Bailments.   Sometimes a person finds himself in possession of the personal property of another without having consented to accept such possession. For instance, the personal property of one person may be deposited on the premises of another by storm or flood, or the animals of one person may stray onto the premises of another. In such cases a few courts have held that no bailment arises, whereas other courts have held that an involuntary bailment arises.

There are no well-established rules as to the rights and duties of the involuntary bailee. He or she does not have a right to destroy the property willfully, convert it to his or her own use, or refuse to redeliver it to the owner. The affirmative duties of the involuntary bailee are uncertain and, in many instances, do not require him or her to assume control over the goods. Under the circumstances of some cases the duties imposed are those of the bailee in a bailment for the sole benefit of the bailor. Each case must be decided according to the facts of the case.

Common Carrier.   A person is a common carrier if he holds himself out to carry, for hire, the property of any person who chooses to employ him. A person is a private carrier if he carries the property only for those whom he selects. Both common carriers and private carriers are bailees. The common carrier is held to a standard of responsibility higher than of the private carrier. This distinction is historical and is based on the social conditions which existed in England during an early period. To prevent collusion between the carrier and highwaymen, the carrier was held to be the insurer of the property he carried. This imposed an absolute liability on the carrier for the damage or loss of property he carried.

This rule is in force in the United States today; however, there are several exceptions to the general rule. The common carrier is not liable if the damage or loss is the result of an act of God, an act of the public enemy, an act of the state, or an act of the shipper, or if the damage or loss is caused by the nature of the goods.

Innkeepers.   The hotel owner or innkeeper is one who holds himself out to provide food and lodging to transients. He is obligated to serve the public, and like the common carrier, is held to a responsibility greater than that of the ordinary bailee. The hotel owner or innkeeper is not a bailee in the strict sense of the word, since the guest does not surrender the exclusive possession of his or her property to the hotel owner or innkeeper; but the hotel owner or innkeeper is the insurer of the guest's property. Losses resulting from acts of God or acts of public enemies, and losses suffered by guests resulting from the acts of members of their own parties, are exceptions to this strict liability. Many states have enacted statutes which relieve the hotel owner or innkeeper from this strict liability or, in other words, limit his or her liability.

Summary

The courts have held a transaction to be a bailment if fungible goods of several persons are stored in a common mass and the depositary is to return an equal quantity of goods of the same kind and quality. Most courts have held the transaction to be a sale if the depositary has the right, at the time demand for return of the goods is made, to pay the market price in lieu of returning the goods.

The courts are not in accord as to the relation between the bank and the renter of a safe-deposit box. Some courts have held the relation to be that of bailor and bailee.

A person may become an involuntary bailee if the goods of another are deposited on his land by storm or flood or by the acts of third persons, or if the domestic animals of another stray onto his or her land. Such a bailee owes a minimum of duty. He cannot willfully destroy the property or convert it to his own use.

A common carrier is the insurer of the goods he carries against loss or damage unless such loss or damage is caused by an act of God, an act of the public enemy, an act of the state, or an act of the shipper, or by the nature of the goods.

An innkeeper is an insurer of the goods of his or her guests. Many states have statutes permitting innkeepers to limit their liability.

Problem Cases

1. Oil Company held oil leases on land located in the State of Illinois which the state taxed as tangible property. Oil Company contends that the oil leases are intangible property since they convey only the right to drill for oil and gas and to take oil and gas if discovered. Are the oil and gas leases tangible or intangible property?

2. Liesner shot and mortally wounded a previously wounded wolf. Before Liesner could reach the wolf, Warnie, with his gun pointed within 3 feet of the wolf, fired the finishing shot. Liesner had the wolf in such condition that escape was improbable if not impossible. Who owned the wolf, Liesner or Warnie?

3. P. B. Porterfield, aged 87, went to his bank and purchased a certificate of deposit which provided in pertinent part: "P. B. Porterfield has deposited in this bank twelve thousand five hundred and no/100 dollars, $12,500, payable to the order of Jesse or Dildy Porterfield, Payee(s), in current funds on the return of this certificate properly endorsed 12 months after date with interest at 5½% per annum. . . . Nonnegotiable." Mr. Porterfield kept the certificate in a box at his home and did not notify his sons, Jesse and Dildy, of the certificate. On Porterfield's death his sons claimed ownership of the certificate of deposit and his widow and other children claimed the certificate was part of the estate. Did Porterfield make a valid *inter vivos* gift to his sons?

4. Blanchard, who worked in a hotel owned by Hamaker, found three $20 bills on the floor in the public lobby of the hotel. She turned them over to Hamaker on his representation that he knew the guest who had lost them. He did not know who had lost the bills and they were not reclaimed. Hamaker refused to return the bills to Blanchard. Is Blanchard entitled to the return of the bills?

5. Jackson, a chambermaid in a hotel owned by Steinberg, found eight $100 bills under the paper lining of a dresser drawer in a room. She turned the money over to Steinberg who was unable to locate the true owner. Jackson demanded the return of the money to her, and Steinberg refused the demand. Is Jackson entitled to the return of the money?

6. Ochoa's Studebaker automobile was stolen. Eleven months later the automobile through some unaccountable means found its way into the hands of the U.S. government which sold it at a "junk" auction for $85 to Rogers. At the time it was purchased by Rogers no part of the car was intact. It had no top except a part of the frame; its steering rod was without a wheel; it had no tires, nor rims, no cushions, no battery; the motor was out of

the car, but included in the junk, as was also the radiator; one headlight was entirely gone, the other was useless; part of the gears were out, and one wheel was gone, as was one axle; the fenders were partly gone and had to be entirely replaced; the differential was beyond repair, and the frame, or chassis, was there, but broken. It was no longer an automobile but a pile of broken and dismantled parts of what was once Ochoa's car. Having purchased these parts, Rogers used them in the construction of a delivery truck, at an expense of approximately $800. When the truck was completed, he put it in use in his furniture business. Several months later, Ochoa, passing Rogers' place of business recognized the machine from a mark on the hood and another on the radiator and discovered that the serial and engine numbers matched those on the car he had owned. Ochoa demanded the car from Rogers, who refused to surrender it. Ochoa brought suit to recover possession of the property, or, in the alternative, for the value thereof at the time of the suit, which he alleged to be $1,000, and for the value of the use of the car at the rate of $5 per day from the time Rogers purchased it from the government. Can Ochoa recover?

7. Grana worked as a waitress in the Mid-Top Restaurant and was required to wear a Mid-Top waitress uniform. She and the other waitresses were provided with a locker room adjacent to the dining room where they could change into the uniforms and ready themselves for work. In the middle of the locker room was a large rack and on one wall were several small metal lockers. Grana was assigned one of the lockers and was provided with one key to it; Mid-Top also retained a key to the locker. Street clothes and other items were generally hung on the rack or placed under it and smaller items were placed in the lockers, which on some occasions were left open. Employees of Mid-Top, other than waitresses, cleaned the locker room which could be entered only through a single door which was left unlocked. The restaurant was destroyed by fire as were all of the personal belongings of the waitresses in the locker room. If the Mid-Top Restaurant was the bailee of the waitresses, they can recover for their losses under a fire insurance policy carried by Mid-Top. Was Mid-Top the bailee of their clothes and personal belongings left in the locker room?

8. Simkins owns a thoroughbred racehorse named Cider Dave. Because she was unable to train or race Cider Dave, she sent him to the Ritters on the understanding that Cider Dave was to be returned to Simkins when he was finished racing. The Ritters were to pay the entire cost of Cider Dave's upkeep and in return they were to retain all of his earnings. Simkins sent the Ritters the jockey club certificate of registration which she had signed in blank. Kate Ritter placed her name on Cider Dave's registration as the transferee and inserted the date of transfer as June 8, 1970. Simkins contends that the transfer of foal registration is frequently done in the racing business to allow someone else to race a horse. Was this transaction a sale or a bailment?

9. Plaintiff, a permanent resident of defendant's hotel, had her son take two diamond rings from her apartment and deposit them with the hotel clerk for safekeeping. In accordance with customary practice in performing the service, the rings were exhibited to the clerk and placed in a sealed "safety deposit envelope" used by the hotel for depositing valuables belonging to guests. Plaintiff's son received a depositor's check stub which bore a number corresponding to the one on the envelope and signed his name on the envelope. The stub and his signature were both necessary for the return of the envelope. The envelope was kept in a safe located in the hotel's front office, 4 or 5 feet behind the registration desk. The safe was used not only to keep valuables of guests, but also cash for use in the hotel's cafe, bar, and coffee shop. Although the safe was equipped with a combination lock, during the 16 years that defendant operated the hotel, the safe door, while customarily closed, was never locked. A clerk was on duty at the registration desk at all times. Subsequently, the hotel was robbed by two armed men at 3:30 A.M. and the rings taken from the safe.

Plaintiff sues for value of rings. The hotel claims the robbery was a supervening cause, relieving it of any liability. Can plaintiff recover?

10. Hyde parked his automobile in a parking lot operated by Parking, Inc., and while parked there the windshield of the automobile was broken. The parking lot in question is located in an uptown section of Washington, D.C. A large sign fronting on an adjacent street invites passing motorists to "Park and Lock." At the entrance there are printed directions instructing the incoming party to remove a "claim check," stamped with the time of arrival, from an automatic dispensing apparatus. He may then proceed onto the parking area and occupy any available space, locking his car or not as he chooses. The motorist makes his only contact with lot personnel at the time of departure. He drives to the cashier's booth by the exit and presents the check by means of which the attendant computes the amount of the parking charge.

Hyde brought suit against Parking, Inc., to recover a judgment for the damage resulting from the breaking of the windshield on his car while it was parked on the parking lot of Parking, Inc. At the trial Hyde offered evidence to prove that at the time he parked his car the windshield was unbroken and that when he returned to get his car the windshield was broken. Parking, Inc., offered no evidence in its defense but denied liability. Is Parking, Inc., liable to Hyde for the broken windshield?

11. Hightower delivered his Cadillac automobile to Auto Auction for sale and while on Auto Auction's lot it was damaged. At the trial Hightower offered evidence of the delivery of the Cadillac automobile to Auto Auction's lot in good condition and its subsequent damaged condition. Auto Auction contended (1) that no bailment was created, (2) that Hightower did not allege and prove that the damage to his Cadillac automobile was caused by the negligent acts of Auto Auction, and (3) that the damage was caused by the negligence of a third party. There was evidence that a Mrs. Tune drove her automobile on Auto Auction's lot to sell it and parked it as directed by the attendant in charge of the lot; and that when Mrs. Tune alighted from her automobile it started to roll down an incline on the lot and although she attempted to stop it she was knocked down and the automobile continued to roll down the incline and struck Hightower's Cadillac broadside and damaged it. Is Auto Auction liable to Hightower for the damage to his Cadillac automobile?

12. Equipment Company was negotiating the sale of a crane to Lumber Company and during the negotiations it let Lumber Co. have the crane for trial and inspection. Roy, an employee of Lumber Co., experienced in the operation of cranes, was assigned the duty of operating the crane and inspecting it, and while doing so, he slipped, fell, and was injured. The circumstances were as follows:

> There was a catwalk, twelve- or thirteen-inches wide, around the sides and rear of the crane, and a grab handle at the door of the cab. The flow of fuel into the engine, for the purpose of operating the crane, was regulated by a throttle located high inside the cab. There was a place in the cab for the operator to stand, or he could sit, and, in operating the crane, he would reach for the throttle over his head with his right hand. Roy, when he was injured, was endeavoring to reach for the throttle from where he was standing on the catwalk. He was holding the door jamb with his left hand and was reaching into the cab for the throttle with his right. It had been raining up to about an hour before, and the catwalk was wet. Roy's feet slipped, causing him to fall backward and sustain his injuries.

Roy sued Equipment Co. claiming that it had not used reasonable care to see that the crane was reasonably safe for use in the manner and for a purpose reasonably to be anticipated. Is Equipment Co. liable to Roy?

chapter 30

Real Property

Fixtures

Nature of Fixture. A fixture is personal property which is so attached to or used with real estate that it is considered to be a part of that real estate. The term *fixture* is also used to designate personal property, such as, for instance, a store fixture, which may appear to be a part of the real estate but is not attached thereto and is removable. A wide variety of fact situations have been before the courts in controversies which arise when one person claims that an article of personal property has become a fixture and another claims that the article continues as personal property. The courts have developed standards for determining issues regarding fixtures and have consistently applied these standards.

In the modern cases the courts apply the reasonable-man standard, which is: Would a reasonable man familiar with the community and with the facts and circumstances of the case be justified in assuming that the person attaching or using the personal property with the real estate intended it to become a fixture? The intention of the parties, determined by the application of this objective test, is controlling in all the cases. In applying this standard, all the facts of the case, such as the time, place, usage, relation of the parties, mode of attachment, and adaptability for use with the particular premises, must be considered, and the case must be decided by a common-sense application of this accepted standard.

Express Agreement. Since intention of the parties is controlling, if the parties have, by express agreement, indicated their intention as to whether or not an article of personal property shall or shall not become a fixture, the courts will, within limits, enforce the agreement of the parties. Parties cannot, however, by their agreement convert into personal property such property as a city lot or a farm, nor can they convert into a fixture an article which is in no way attached to or used with real property. The courts have held that if articles of personal property, such as brick, stone, beams, and girders, are permanently built into a building so that they become an integral part of the building, they become a part of the real property, irrespective of any express agreement by the parties to the contrary.

Mode of Attachment. In some of the early cases the courts held that attachment was the sole test for determining whether or not an article of personal property had become a fixture. Today, attachment is of outstanding importance, but it is not conclusive in determining the intention of the parties.

As already noted, if an article of personal property is built into a building so that it becomes an integral part of the building, it loses its character as personal property and becomes real property, irrespective of any declared intention of the parties. If an article of personal property is firmly attached to the real property in such a manner that its removal will substantially destroy the article and will also injure the real property to which it is attached, the court will consider such attachment as very strong evidence that the parties intended the article to become a fixture. If attachment is slight and the article can be removed without injury to the article or to the real property, such attachment is of little importance as evidence.

An article which is attached to the land only by gravity may become a fixture. For example, a building set on blocks on top of the ground and a statue weighing several tons set on a cement foundation, but not attached to the foundation, have been held to be fixtures.

Use with Real Property. The appropriateness of the use of the article of personal property with the real property is important as evidence of the intention of the parties. As a general rule, some degree of attachment is considered as necessary to indicate an intention that an article is to become a fixture, but the courts have held certain articles to be fixtures, even though the articles are not attached to the real property, if such articles would be of little or no value except as used with that particular property. Such articles as keys to doors, storm windows, and screens for windows have been held to be fixtures although not attached to the real property.

In one case, in-a-door beds, refrigerators, stoves, cabinets, and similar items, which were installed in an apartment house, were held to be fixtures even though they were so attached to the real property that they could be easily removed. In such a case the appropriateness of the use of the article with the real property is given great weight in determining the intentions of the parties.

Additions by Owner. The relation of the parties is also of outstanding importance. If the owner of real property improves it by the addition of personal property, there is an all but conclusive presumption that he intended the improvement to become a part of the real property; and if he or she sells or mortgages the real property without reservation, the courts have held that the additions are fixtures and pass as real property to the purchaser or mortgagee.

If the owner of real estate purchases personal property, the seller retaining a security interest in such property as security for the payment of the purchase price, and attaches the personal property to his or her real estate, the seller's security interest in the attached property will, under the Uniform Commercial Code, have priority over all persons having an interest in the real estate, provided the seller's security interest has been perfected. On default, the seller may remove the personal property but he or she will be liable to third parties, such as prior real estate mortgagors, for damage to the real estate caused by its removal.[1]

Additions by Tenants.   As between landlord and tenant, the earliest cases held that any improvement made by a tenant became a part of real property; but the courts soon began to make a distinction between attachments made by tenants of business property for trade purposes and those made by tenants of other kinds of real property. This distinction is important today. The courts have generally held that personal property brought onto premises leased for business purposes, for use in the carrying on of the business for which the premises are leased, remains personal property irrespective of the mode of attachment. Such property is known as trade fixtures. However, if the personal property is so built into the real property that its removal will weaken the structure, the courts have held that it becomes a part of the real property.

In cases involving domestic and agricultural tenancies, the general rule of intention has been applied. However, the presumption that the property which is attached to the real property is to remain personal property is usually not so strong in the case of domestic and agricultural tenancies as in the case of business tenancies.

In all cases in which a tenant has added trade, domestic, or agricultural fixtures, if the tenancy is for a definite period, the tenant must remove the article before the expiration of his or her term, and if he or she does not, the article becomes the property of the landlord. This rule had its origin in the early English land law and has been recognized by the courts ever since. Two reasons for the rule have been given: (1) that the failure to remove is conclusive indication of an intention to abandon the article, and (2) that after the expiration of the term the tenant would be a trespasser if he or she entered the land to remove the article.

If the tenancy is for an indefinite period, such as a tenancy for life or a tenancy at will, the tenant will have a reasonable time after the termination of the tenancy to remove such property. The courts have held that if there is an express agreement that articles attached by the tenant shall remain personal

---

[1] Uniform Commercial Code, Article 9, Section 9–313.

property and may be removed by him, he will have a reasonable time after the expiration of his term in which to remove the articles.

Summary

A fixture is personal property which by attachment to or association in use with land is regarded as real property. The reasonable-man standard is applied by the courts in determining whether or not an article of personal property has become a fixture. The objective intent of the parties is the basic test.

Within reasonable limits the courts enforce the agreement of the parties relative to whether an article of personal property shall or shall not become a fixture.

Mode of attachment is important as evidence to be considered in determining the intention of the parties. If there is no attachment, that fact is prima facie evidence that the article of personal property is not a fixture.

The appropriateness of use with the real property is a fact which is always considered in determining the intention of the parties. In exceptional cases, appropriateness of use with the real property, without attachment, may be sufficient to justify holding that the article is a fixture.

The relation of the parties is always of outstanding importance. If an owner attaches his own personal property to his real property for the purpose of improving the real property, the article becomes a fixture.

Under the Uniform Commercial Code if one sells personal property to be attached to real estate, retaining a security interest in such property, his or her lien will have priority over rights of third persons provided it is perfected.

Tenants who have added to the leased premises articles of personal property which are classed as trade, domestic, or agricultural fixtures may remove the articles on the termination of the lease. If the lease is for a definite term, the articles must be removed before the expiration of the term; if the lease is for an indefinite term, the articles must be removed within a reasonable time after the expiration of the lease.

Sherburne Corp. v. Town of Sherburne

207 A.2d 125 (Sup. Ct. Vt. 1965)

This was an action by Sherburne Corporation (plaintiff) against the Town of Sherburne (defendant) to determine whether a ski lift was personal property or real estate. The lower court held it was personal property and Sherburne Corporation appealed. Reversed.

Sherburne Corporation erected a ski lift on land leased from the state. The Town of Sherburne taxed the ski lift as personal property and Sherburne Corporation brought an action asking that the ski lift be declared a fixture and not subject to tax by the Town of Sherburne. Additional facts are stated in the judge's opinion.

BARNEY, JUSTICE.   The resolution of this case depends upon the classification of the lift facilities as either real property or personal property. This decision is necessarily preemptory, because the facilities are perhaps truly neither, or a little of both. The requirements of such classification have presented such an acute problem in the law, that a special subgrouping has accumulated its own identity as a device to determine which side of the arbitrary boundary between chattels and real estate the nature of a given object places it. This is the law of fixtures. Fixtures are usually classed as real estate; trade fixtures, an exception to the rule, are usually classed as personal property.

When a scheme of classification is used to serve more than one purpose, internal conflicts frequently develop. The object of classification is to define categories so that like objects invariably fall into the same class. But "likeness" may vary as the purpose for classification varies. The incentive to class an object as either real estate or chattel for tax purposes may call for a result contrary to that arrived at when done in the context of a bailment.

However, in *First National Bank v. Nativi,* certain tests for resolving the classification of things as real or personal property have been set out as general rules: (1) the annexation, actual or constructive, of the article to the real estate; (2) its adaptation to the use of the realty to which it is annexed; and (3) whether or not the annexation has been made with the intention to make it a permanent accession to the freehold. By applying these tests in the first instance, we can decide what the character of the property at issue is under the law generally, without the pressures brought to that determination by possible tax consequences or the identity of the parties.

The characteristics of the lift installations appear from the findings. The lifts, including towers, cables, chairs, railings, and platforms, are integrated devices for providing uphill transportation. Each one is a substantial structure, the longest lift being 6,300-feet long. The towers are designed according to the topography of the line of the particular lift, and each tower is embedded in a heavy cement base. They cannot be removed without permanent damage to the real estate. Over half of the cost of the lifts was for installation, amounting, in one case, to more than $120,000. These lifts could not be moved without a loss of a substantial portion of the installation investment. The buildings associated with the lifts are uniquely adapted to the land upon which they are located, are set upon heavy cement foundations and also cannot be moved without substantial damage to the real estate.

From the established facts already stated, annexation to the real estate and adaptation to the use of the real estate to which the property is annexed are amply evidenced. This satisfies the first two criteria previously set out. The remaining issue concerns intention to make the property a part of the real estate. This is crucial, since if the intention to make it a permanent accession is doubtful, it remains a chattel.

It is also clear from the findings that these lifts are items used in the trade or business conducted on the premises by the lessee. This is a characteristic typical of trade fixtures, which retain the nature of chattels, and may be removed at the end of a lease. As such, they are an exception to the rule pertaining to fixtures generally.

However, when we use this sort of test to arrive at an article's classification, we are ascertaining the intention of the parties by inference. Declarations in the documents representing the transaction may be useful to shed light on equivocal situations, or to directly contradict inferred intentions.

Here we have a lease. Sherburne Corp. lays great emphasis on the provision which states that the lift facilities shall be deemed to be real estate and the property of the State upon erection. Town, on the other hand, stresses the provisions that require the State to pay for the lifts in the future. From this Town argues that the provision "deeming" the facilities real estate is without real substance and a mere tax evasion device.

A reading of the lease does not bear out Town's view. The statement that the lift facilities be deemed real estate on construction is reinforced by the balance of the lease. The basic ingredient necessary to make such property trade fixtures is a right to remove them at the expiration of the lease. The entire contemplation of this lease is that the lifts cannot be removed by the lessee in any event.

Rights and Interests in Real Property

Fee Simple.   The basic land ownership interest in the United States is the fee simple which entitles the owner to the entire property for an unlimited duration of time with the unconditional power to dispose of it during his life or upon his death and which will descend to his heirs if he dies without making a will. The holder of a fee simple may grant many rights to others without changing the nature of his interest. For example, Archer, who owns land in fee simple, may give Burch a mortgage on the land, grant Clark an easement of right-of-way over the land, and lease the land to Fox for a period of years. Archer has granted rights to Burch, Clark, and Fox; but Archer still owns the land in fee simple. On the termination of the rights of Burch, Clark, and Fox, such rights revert to the owner of the fee and merge into the fee, and may again be granted by the owner.

Life Estate.   A life estate is an interest in land which is limited in time to the life or lives of persons in being. A life estate may be for the life of the holder or for the life or lives of another or others. The life tenant has the right to use the property, but he or she does not have a right to do acts which will result in permanent injury to the property.

Leasehold.   A leasehold gives the lessee the right to occupy and possess a given piece of real property. This right may be for a fixed period of time, such as a month or a year, in which case it is known as a "periodic tenancy," or for what is known as a "tenancy at will" where the time period is not fixed in advance and either the lessor or the lessee can terminate the leasehold after giving notice to the other party of his intention to do so.

Easements.   An easement is the nonpossessory right to use or enjoy the land of another person. It may be an easement appurtenant or an easement in gross. An easement appurtenant is the right which the owner of a particular parcel of land has, by reason of such ownership, to use the land of another for a specific purpose. The land benefited by the easement is known as the "dominant tenement," and the land subject to the easement is known as the "servient tenement." For instance, if the owner or occupier of land, tract A, has an easement of right-of-way over the land, tract B, tract A is the dominant tenement, and tract B is the servient tenement.

An easement may be created which is not accessory to adjoining land. Such an easement is known as an "easement in gross." If the easement in gross is granted to an individual, it will, as a general rule, be held to be personal to him or her and not assignable, transferable, or inheritable, although in a few cases such an easement has been held to be transferable. Easements to utility companies are usually easements in gross.

An easement may be an affirmative or a negative easement. An affirmative easement is the right to make certain uses of the land of another. The right to drive across, to run a sewer across, or to drill for gas and oil on the land of another are affirmative easements. A negative easement is the right to have an adjoining landowner refrain from making certain uses of his or her land. The right to have an adjoining landowner refrain from erecting a structure on his or her premises which would cut off light and air from your buildings is a negative easement.

An easement may be acquired by an express grant, by a reservation in a grant, by implication, by estoppel, by necessity, or by prescription (adverse possession). Since an easement is an interest in land, it is within the purview of the statute of frauds and usually must be evidenced by a writing if it is to be enforceable. Under the statutes of most states, the grant of an easement must be executed with the same formalities as is the grant of a fee simple in real property. However, nonexpressly granted easements such as those by implication, necessity, estoppel, or prescription are enforceable even though they are not in writing.

Licenses. A license is similar in some respects to an easement; however, it is not an interest in land and may be created orally and, unless coupled with an interest, may be revoked at the will of the licensor. Permission to cross the land of another or to hunt or fish on the other's land is a license. A person entering on the land of another for the purpose of transacting business is a licensee. If a person purchases from another trees which are to be cut and hauled away, the purchaser would have an irrevocable license to go onto the land for the purpose of cutting and hauling the logs. There are innumerable situations in which one person has a license to go onto the land of another. A license, as a general rule, creates a temporary right to use another's land in a limited and specific manner.

Summary

Ownership in fee simple is the highest estate a person can hold in land. It is the original source of all rights in land and is not limited in time.

A life estate is a freehold estate for the life or lives of persons in being.

A leasehold is the right to occupy and possess real property and is limited in time.

An easement is a nonpossessory right in the land of another. An easement in gross is an easement which is not accessory to adjoining land and an easement appurtenant is accessory to adjoining land. An affirmative easement gives the owner of the easement the right to make certain uses of another's property, and a negative easement gives the owner of the easement the right to have another refrain from making a certain use of his land.

An easement may be acquired by an express grant, by a reservation in a grant, by implication, by estoppel, by necessity, or by prescription. It is an interest in land, and to be enforceable, it usually must be evidenced by a writing.

A license creates a temporary privilege to make some specific use of another's land, and it is not an interest in land.

Helton v. Jones

402 S.W.2d 694 (Ct. App. Ky. 1966)

This was an action by Jones (plaintiff) to enjoin Helton (defendant) from interfering with a passway easement Jones claimed to have over Helton's land. Judgment for Jones. Affirmed.

Prior to 1929 Tom Noe owned a single tract of ground bounded on two sides by parallel highways. Across Noe's land was a roadway approximately 125 feet in length connecting the two highways and which for more than fifty years had been used for access to the principal parallel highway. In 1929 Noe died and his land was divided into two tracts. Since that time the owners and occupants of the tract now owned by Jones have continued to use the roadway over the other tract now owned by Helton. Prior to the time Jones acquired the property in 1943, a gate was put up across the road. Sometimes this gate was locked by Helton but Jones was given a key to it. Then in 1964 Helton put a new lock on the gate and did not give Jones a key. Jones sued Helton to enjoin him from blocking the road.

CLAY, COMMISSIONER. Helton's contention is that the use of this passway (for a period of fifty years) has always been *permissive* and therefore the use of it never ripened into an easement. Jones contends that when the lands were originally divided an easement was created, but in any event, the long-continued use matured into an absolute right.

The facts in this case are almost identical with those in *Delong v. Cline.* It was therein held that upon a division of a tract of land under the same circumstances we have here, an easement will pass by implication "as if he had a deed thereto" to the party who acquired the parcel whose enjoyment required the use of a preexisting passway over another parcel.

This principle amply supports the Chancellor's finding of the existence of an easement although his finding appears to have been based on his conclusion that appellee had acquired his rights by prescription or adverse possession. Such alternate ground of the decision is also amply supported by the record. The circumstances would justify no other conclusion but that appellee had a permanent easement as a matter of right. The existence of the gate may have restricted the scope of the easement but certainly did not destroy it.

Co-ownership of Real Property

Nature of Co-ownership.   Co-ownership of real property exists when two or more persons own an undivided interest in such property. The co-owners do not have separate rights in any portion of the real property; each has a share in the whole property.

There are seven kinds of co-ownership of real property recognized in the United States today: (1) tenancy in common, (2) joint tenancy, (3) tenancy by the entirety, (4) community property, (5) tenancy in partnership (6) condominiums, and (7) cooperatives.

Tenancy in Common.   A tenancy in common is created when real property is deeded to two or more persons as tenants in common or when two or more persons inherit real property. In most states, if real property is conveyed to two or more persons and the instrument of conveyance does not state how they shall hold the property, they will hold as tenants in common.

The interest which the tenants in common hold in the property is known as an estate of inheritance, that is, each tenant holds his interest as his individual property, and on his death his interest will descend to his heirs or devisees. Each tenant may sell or encumber his interest in the property, and it is subject to levy of execution by a judgment creditor. The shares of tenants in common need not be equal, that is, one tenant may own a two-thirds interest in the property and his or her cotenant may own the remaining one-third.

The only common right of tenants in common is the right of possession. Each tenant has the right to possess and use the common property, but he has no right to exclude his cotenants from equal rights of possession and use. If the property is rented, the cotenants share ratably in the income from the property and must make a ratable contribution to the taxes, the repairs, and the upkeep.

A tenant in common may petition the court to divide the property. In such an action the property will be physically divided if it is practical, and each tenant will receive his or her proportionate share in kind. If this is not practical, however, the court will order the property sold, and the proceeds from the sale will be divided according to the share of each tenant. The tenants may divide the property by mutual agreement.

Joint Tenancy.   A joint tenancy is created when equal interests in real property are conveyed to two or more persons by one instrument which expressly states that the persons take as joint tenants. The outstanding characteristic of the joint tenancy is the right of survivorship; that is, on the death of one of the joint tenants, his or her interest passes to the surviving joint tenant or tenants. The interest of a joint tenant cannot be devised by will.

The interest of a joint tenant is subject to levy by his or her creditors, and the jointure may be destroyed by a conveyance by one of the joint tenants. If a joint tenant conveys his or her interest, the conveyee holds as a tenant in common with the other joint tenant or tenants.

The right of use, possession, contribution, and partition of joint tenants is the same as that of tenants in common.

The joint tenancy with right of survivorship has been abolished in some states and is not generally favored by the law. It is thought that on the death of an owner his or her interest in property should pass to his or her estate and not to a joint tenant. Moreover, in many cases where people acquire property as concurrent owners, they are not fully aware of the right of survivorship.

Tenancy by the Entirety.   Tenants by the entirety must be husband and wife. This is fundamentally a joint tenancy with rights of survivorship. It can be created only by a conveyance to persons who are husband and wife at the time of the conveyance. A tenancy by the entirety cannot be destroyed by the acts of either party. Real property owned by the entirety cannot be sold under execution issued on a judgment rendered against either the husband or the wife individually, but it may be sold on execution issued on a judgment rendered against them on a joint obligation. Neither can convey the real property by deed unless the other joins, and neither can dispose of the property by will. Tenancies by the entirety are not recognized in all states.

Community Property.   In some states, what is known as the "system of community property" prevails. The principal characteristic of the system is that whatever property is acquired by the efforts of either the husband or the wife during marriage becomes a common fund or, as it is called, "community property." Either the husband or the wife may own, in addition to his or her interest in the community property, "separate property." Generally, separate property includes that property owned prior to marriage or acquired after marriage by gift, devise, or descent, or in exchange for property owned as separate property. The details of the system are set out by the statutes of each of the community property states.

Tenancy in Partnership.   Tenancy in partnership was discussed in Chapter 20. The incidents of the tenancy in partnership are set out in Section 25 of the Uniform Partnership Act.

Condominium Ownership. In resort and urban areas the form of ownership known as the condominium has come into extensive use. In a condominium, the purchaser gets title to the apartment or townhouse unit he or she occupies and also becomes a tenant in common of the facilities shared in common with the other owners such as hallways, elevator and utility shafts, swimming pools, and parking areas. The condominium owner pays property taxes on his individual unit, he can take out a mortgage on his unit, and he is generally free to sell the unit without having the prospective buyer approved by the other owners. He also makes a monthly payment to cover the maintenance of the common areas. For federal income tax purposes he is treated like the owner of a single-family home and is allowed to deduct his property taxes and mortgage interest expenses.

Cooperative ownership. In a cooperative, the entire building is owned by a group of people or by a corporation. Usually the buyer of a unit buys stock in the corporation and holds his apartment under a long-term lease which he can renew. Frequently the cooperative owner must obtain the approval of the other owners in order to sell or sublease his or her unit.

Summary

Seven types of co-ownership of real property are recognized: (1) tenancy in common, (2) joint tenancy, (3) tenancy by the entirety, (4) community property, (5) tenancy in partnership, (6) condominiums, and (7) cooperatives.

Tenants in common need not hold equal shares. On the death of a tenant in common, if he dies intestate, his or her interest passes to his heirs. A tenant in common may devise his interest by will. Tenants in common have the right to possess and use the property, and each is entitled to his proportionate share of the income. Each must contribute to taxes, repairs, and upkeep in proportion to his or her share or interest.

Joint tenants hold equal interests which must be created by the same instrument at the same time. They have the right of survivorship. In other respects, their rights are substantially the same as the rights of tenants in common.

Tenants by the entirety must be husband and wife. On the death of either, his or her interest passes by the right of survivorship to the other. Neither party can destroy the tenancy by his or her individual acts, and the property is not subject to the individual debts of either.

Community property is a type of ownership by husband and wife. The rights are created by statute, and the details of the system are set out by the statutes of the state.

Condominiums and cooperatives are forms of joint ownership developed relatively recently to allow apartment dwellers many of the advantages of individual home ownership.

Acquisition of Real Property

Origin of Title to Real Property. Original title to land in the United States was acquired either by grant from the federal government or by grant from a country which held the land prior to its acquisition by the United States. The land which was within the boundaries of the original 13 states was land which had, for the most part, been granted by the king of England to the colonies or to certain individuals. The Northwest Territory was ceded by the states to the federal government. Original title to this land was a patent from the federal government signed by the president. Most of the land in Florida and sections of land in the Southwest were held by Spain, and the ownership of this land is based on Spanish grants.

Acquisition by Purchase. One of the rights of ownership is the right to sell (the right of alienation). Under our law any agreement or restriction which deprives the owner of land of his right to alienate his land is against public policy and is void. Most persons who own real property today have acquired their title by purchasing the property from a prior owner. Each state has the right to regulate the formal requirements for the transfer of the ownership of the lands within the state.

Acquisition by Gift. Ownership in real property may be acquired by gift. The donor of such property must deliver to the donee, or to some third person for the benefit of the donee, a deed which complies with all the statutory requirements of the state in which the property is located. It is not necessary for the donee, or some third person acting for the donee, to take actual physical possession of the property. The essential element of the gift is the delivery of the deed. If the donor makes deeds to real property and leaves them in his or her safe-deposit box to be delivered to the named donee after the death of the donor, the gift will fail for lack of delivery.

Acquisition by Adverse Possession. Title to real property may be acquired by adverse possession. The statutory law of the states provides that no action shall be brought for the recovery of the possession of land after a stated number of years, which varies from 5 to 20 years. If a person holds land by open, continuous, and adverse possession for the statutory period, he or she can acquire title to the land by complying with certain statutory requirements. In order to acquire title by adverse possession, there must be (1) actual occupancy, (2) which is hostile to the owner's title, (3) with open claim to title, (4) continuously for the statutory period. In some states the claimant must, in addition to the four requisites set out above, pay the taxes. The same person need not occupy the land for the entire period, but the adverse possession must be continuous. Suppose, for instance, Bixby takes possession of land owned by Altman and claims title to the land and remains in possession for four years, at which time Bixby sells his interest to Clay, who immediately takes possession and remains in possession for six years. If the statutory period is 10 years, Clay can acquire title to the land at the end of his 6-year occupancy. He acquired Bixby's rights which, added to his rights, satisfy the statutory requirement. It is Altman's responsibility to take legal action to remove the trespasser from his property prior to the expiration of the statutory period; his failure to act as the owner and to remove the trespasser means that the law will recognize as the true owner of the property the person who acts like an owner for the statutory period.

Acquisition by Tax Sale. If the taxes assessed on real property are not paid, they become a lien which is prior to the claims of all persons having an interest in the property. After a stated period of time, if the taxes remain unpaid, the state will sell the property at a tax sale, and the purchaser at such sale will acquire title to the property. The entire procedure is statutory, and there is no uniformity in the tax laws of the several states.

Acquisition by Will or Descent. The owner of real property has the right, subject to some restrictions which will be discussed in a later section, to dispose of his or her real property by will. The will, to be effective, must be drawn and executed in accordance with the statutory requirements of the state in which the real property is located. If the owner of real property dies without having made a will, the land will descend to his or her heirs according to the laws of the state in which the real property is located.

Summary

Original title to all lands in the United States was acquired either by grant from the federal government or by grant from a government which held the land prior to its acquisition by the United States.

Real property is usually acquired by purchase. The formal requirements for the transfer of real property are determined by the statutes of the state in which it is located.

Real property may be acquired by gift. To have a valid gift, the donor must deliver to the donee, or to some third person for the benefit of the donee, a deed which complies with the statutory requirements of the state in which the property is located.

To acquire ownership of real property by adverse possession, the claimant must have had open, adverse, and continuous possession of the property for the statutory period.

If the taxes on real property are not paid, the property, under the laws of most states, will be sold for taxes, and the purchaser at the tax sale will be given a tax deed which, if valid, cuts off all prior claims to the real property.

The owner of real property may dispose of such property on his or her death by will. If the owner leaves no will, the ownership descends according to the statutes of the state in which it is located.

Converse v. Kenyon

132 N.W.2d 334 (Sup. Ct. Neb. 1965)

This was an action by George N. Converse and others (plaintiffs) against Guy E. Kenyon and others (defendants) to establish the boundaries of land. Kenyon claimed that he had acquired title to approximately twenty acres of the land by adverse possession. Judgment for Kenyon and Converse appealed. Affirmed.

Kenyon and Converse owned adjoining tracts of land. Kenyon owned the east half of the section of land and Converse owned the west half. Converse claimed that the line fence dividing their land had been moved to the west of the actual boundary and that the true line should be established, whereas Kenyon claimed that the fence had been in the same location for over 21 years and claimed the land east of the fence by adverse possession. Converse claimed that he had paid the taxes on the entire southwest quarter of the section, which included the land in dispute. In 1962 Kenyon wrote Converse that he would move the fence but that he did not know when he could get it done.

Kenyon had farmed the east half of the section including the disputed tract from 1934 until 1956 when he leased the land to his son who has farmed it since that date.

BROWER, JUSTICE. "What is sufficient to meet the requirements for actual possession depends upon the character of the land and all of the circumstances of the case.

Acts of dominion over land must, to be effective against a true owner, be so open, notorious, and hostile as to put an ordinarily prudent person on notice of the fact that his lands are in the adverse possession of another. . . .

Where one, by mistake as to the boundary line, constructs upon and takes possession of land of another, claiming it as his own to a definite and certain boundary by an actual, open, exclusive, and continuous possession thereof under such claim for ten years or more, he acquires title thereto by adverse possession.

The fact that one claiming title by adverse possession never intended to claim more land than is called for in his deed is not a controlling factor. It is the intent with which possession is held, rather than the intention to hold in accordance with the deed, that is controlling. The claim of adverse possession is founded upon the intent with which the occupant has held possession, and this intent is ordinarily determined by what he has done in respect thereto.

In 3 Am. Jur. 2d, Adverse Possession, § 240, p. 339, it is said:

After the running of the statute, the adverse possessor has an indefeasible title which can only be divested by his conveyance of the land to another, or by a subsequent disseisin for the statutory limitation period. It cannot be lost by a mere abandonment, or by a cessation of occupancy, or by an expression of willingness to vacate the land, or by the acknowledgement or recognition of title in another, or by subsequent legislation, or by survey.

In *Martin v. Martin,* this court held: "One who has acquired absolute title to land by adverse possession for the statutory period does not impair his title by thereafter paying rent to the owner of the paper title." In the opinion of the cited case it was stated: "The law is well settled that recognition of title in the former owner by one claiming adversely after he has acquired a perfect title by adverse possession will not divest him of title."

Transfer by Sale

Steps in a Sale. The major steps normally involved in the sale and purchase of real property are: (1) contracting with a real estate broker to sell the property or to locate suitable property for sale; (2) negotiating and signing a contract to sell the property; (3) arranging for the financing of the purchase and satisfaction of other contingencies such as a survey or acquisition of title insurance; and (4) closing the sale, at which time the purchase price is paid and the deed is signed, delivered, and recorded.

Real Estate Brokers. Although it is not necessary to engage a broker, commonly a prospective seller of real estate will enter into a listing agreement with a real estate broker. The broker's job is to locate a buyer ready, willing, and able to buy the property on the seller's terms and to work out the details of the transfer of the property. The listing agreement should be in writing, specify the length of the listing period, and provide for the amount or percentage of the commission. Generally a seller must pay the commission regardless of who actually sells the house, so long as the broker produces a ready, willing, and able buyer, even if the seller decides not to go through with the sale.

Contract for Sale. The agreement between the seller and the buyer to purchase real property should be in writing to be enforceable under the statute of frauds. The agreement commonly spells out such things as the purchase price, the type of deed the purchaser will get, and what items of personal property such as appliances and carpets are included. It may also make the "closing" of the sale contingent on the buyer's finding financing at a specified rate of interest and the seller's procurement of a survey, title insurance, and termite insurance.

Financing the Purchase. The various arrangements for financing the purchase of real property such as mortgages, land contracts and deeds of trust are discussed in Chapter 43.

Transfer by Deed. Since the states have the power to regulate the conveyance of land within their borders, each state has enacted statutes which set out the formalities with which the parties should comply in such conveyance. As a general rule the conveyance of land is accomplished by the execution and delivery of a deed; and in the law of real property a deed is an instrument in writing whereby the owner of land (the grantor) conveys to another (the grantee) some right, title, or interest in real property.

Quitclaim and Warranty Deeds. Two types of deeds are in general use in the United States: the quitclaim and the warranty deed. When the grantor conveys by a quitclaim deed, he conveys to the grantee whatever title he has at the time he executes the deed, but he does not, by the form of the deed, claim to have good title or, in fact, any title; and if the title proves to be defective, or if the grantor has no title, the grantee has no action against him or her under the deed. Quitclaim deeds are frequently used to cure a technical defect in the chain of title to property. In such a case the grantor may claim no right, title, or interest in the property.

A warranty deed may be a deed of general warranty or of special warranty. A warranty deed contains covenants of warranty; that is, the grantor, in addition to conveying title to the property, binds himself or herself to make good any defects in the title he or she has conveyed. In a general warranty deed the grantor warrants against all defects in the title and all encumbrances, whereas in a special warranty deed the grantor warrants against only those defects in the title or those encumbrances which arose after he or she acquired the property. If the property conveyed is mortgaged or subject to some other encumbrance, such as an easement or long-term lease, it is a common practice to give a general warranty deed which contains a provision excepting from the warranty specific encumbrances.

Form and Execution of Deed. Some states have enacted statutes setting out the form of deed which may be used in that state. These statutes have been held to be directive, not mandatory; that is, a deed may be valid even though it does not follow the statutory form. The statutory requirements of the different states for the execution of deeds are not uniform, but they do follow a similar pattern. As a general rule a deed states the name of the grantee, contains a recitation of consideration and a description of the property conveyed, and is executed by the grantor. In most states the deed, to be eligible for recording, must be acknowledged by the grantor before a notary public or other officer authorized to take acknowledgment.

No technical words of conveyance are necessary; any language is sufficient which indicates with reasonable certainty an intent to transfer the ownership of the property. The phrase "give, grant, bargain, and sell" and the phrase "convey and warrant" are in common use.

A consideration is recited in a deed for historical reasons. At an early time in England, if the deed did not recite a consideration, the presumption was that the grantee held the land in trust for the heirs of the grantor, and for that reason it became standard practice to recite a consideration in the deed. The consideration recited is not necessarily the purchase price of the real property; it may be "one dollar and other valuable consideration."

The property conveyed must be described in such a manner that it can be identified. In urban areas, descriptions are as a general rule by lot, block, and plat. In rural areas the land, if it has been surveyed by the government, is usually described by reference to the government survey; otherwise, it is described by metes and bounds.

Delivery is essential to the validity of a deed. Whether or not a deed has been delivered is, in cases of dispute, a question of fact. If a person executes deeds to his or her real property and puts them in his or her safe-deposit box together with a note directing that the deeds be delivered to named persons after his or her death, the deeds are inoperative and pass no title by delivery after the death of the grantor. A deed, to be valid, must be delivered in the lifetime of the grantor.

Recording Deeds.   The several states have recording statutes which establish a system for the recording of all transactions affecting the ownership of real property. The statutes are not uniform in their provisions; but in general, they provide for the recording of all deeds, mortgages, and other such documents, and further provide an unrecorded transfer is void as against an innocent purchaser or mortgagee for value. Under this system, it is customary in some states for the seller to give the buyer an abstract of title certified to date. The abstract is a history of the title of the real property according to the records and is not a guarantee of title. The buyer, for his or her own protection, should have the abstract examined by a competent attorney who will render an opinion as to the title held by the grantor. The opinion will state whether or not the grantor has a merchantable title to the property; and if the title is defective, the nature of the defects will be stated. In many states the buyer obtains this protection by acquiring title insurance; in many cases where the purchase of the property is being financed by a third party, the lender will require a policy of title insurance for his or her protection.

Several of the states have adopted the "Torrens system." Under this system the person who owns the land in fee will obtain, through the procedure set up by the statute, a certificate of title from the designated official; and when the real property is sold, the grantor will deliver a deed and his or her certificate of title to the grantee, who delivers the deed and certificate of title to the designated official and receives a new certificate of title. All liens and encumbrances against the property will be noted on the certificate of title, and the purchaser is assured that his or her title is good except as to liens and encumbrances noted thereon. In some states, some encumbrances, such as liens for taxes, short-term leases, and highway rights, are good against the purchaser even though they do not appear on the certificate.

Warranties in the Sale of a House.   Traditionally, unless there was an express warranty of the habitility or condition of a house, or unless there was some fraud or misrepresentation involved, the purchaser of a house was subject to the doctrine of *caveat emptor*. This was based on the fact that buyer and seller dealt at arm's length and the buyer had the opportunity to acquaint himself with the condition and quality of the property he or she was acquiring. Thus, the buyer either had to obtain an express warranty as to quality, or he or she took at his or her own risk.

Recently, several courts have abandoned the *caveat emptor* doctrine in the sale of new homes by builder-sellers as far as latent defects are concerned and have adopted the doctrine of *caveat venditor.* This tends to put the buyer of a new home in roughly the same position the buyer of goods is in—that he or she gets an implied warranty of merchantable fitness or habitibility. The court decisions to date have not dealt with the quality of the realty itself, but rather they have separated out the new home and treated it like any other manufactured product.

Summary

Any agreement affecting an interest in land and a conveyance of real property is required to be in writing.

Two forms of deed are in general use in the United States: the quitclaim deed and the warranty deed. In a quitclaim deed the grantor conveys his or her interest, whatever it may be. In a warranty deed the grantor conveys his or her interest and, in addition, warrants his or her title to be free from all defects except those stated in the deed.

A deed, to be valid, must comply with certain formal requirements. These requirements are not uniform, but as a general rule the deed must name the grantee, contain words of conveyance, recite a consideration, describe the property, and be executed by the grantor. It will usually be acknowledged, may be sealed and witnessed, and must be delivered.

Smith v. Old Warson Development Co.

479 S.W.2d 795 (Sup. Ct. Mo., 1972)

This was an action brought by Frank and Catherine Smith (plaintiffs) against the Old Warson Development Company (defendant) to recover damages sustained by the abnormal settling of a new house sold to the Smiths by defendant. The trial court granted defendant's motion for a directed verdict and the Smiths appealed. Reversed and remanded. The Court of Appeals filed an opinion reversing the trial court and then transferred the case up to the Supreme Court which affirmed the action the Court of Appeals had taken.

Old Warson Development Co. owned a tract of land in St. Louis which it subdivided for sale as residential lots. It had a home constructed on one of the lots which it sold to the Smiths in February of 1963. The sales contract contained the following provision:

Property to be accepted in its present condition unless otherwise stated in contract. Seller warrants that he has not received any written notification from any governmental agency requiring any repairs, replacements, or alterations to said premises which have not been satisfactorily made. This is the entire contract and neither party shall be bound by representation as to value or otherwise unless set forth in contract.

Within a few months the Smiths noticed that the doors in a section of the house containing a bedroom and bathroom were sticking. Soon they noticed the caulked space between the bathtub and wall was enlarged. Eventually a space developed between the baseboard and the floor, and cracks developed in the wall. All problems were limited to the two rooms, which were constructed on a 4-inch concrete slab, completely surrounded by but not attached to, foundation walls. The remainder of the house rested on a foundation and experienced no difficulties. The slab had settled or sunk as much as 1¾ inches. Although the builder made some attempts to repair the visual problems, there was no attempt to correct the basic problem—the settling of the slab.

MORGAN, JUDGE.   We accepted transfer of this cause after the filing of an opinion by the Court of Appeals, St. Louis District, because the result reached therein evidenced a departure, although limited, from a strict application of the doctrine of *caveat emptor*. The court's reasoning was expressed in an opinion by Smith, J., which was as follows:

This appeal presents squarely the question of whether implied warranties of merchantable quality and fitness exist in the purchase of a new home by the first purchaser from a vendor-builder. We hold such warranties do exist.

* * * * *

. . . Although considered to be a "real estate" transaction because the ownership to land is transferred, the purchase of a residence is in most cases the purchase of a manufactured product—the house. The land involved is seldom the prime element in such a purchase, certainly not in the urban areas of the state. The structural quality of a house, by its very nature, is nearly impossible to determine by inspection after the house is built, since many of the most important elements of its construction are hidden from view. The ordinary "consumer" can determine little about the soundness of the construction but must rely upon the fact that the vendor-builder holds the structure out to the public as fit for use as a residence, and of being of reasonable quality. Certainly in the case here no determination of the existence of the defect could have been made without ripping out the slab which settled, and maybe not even then. The home here was new and was purchased from the company which built it for sale. The defect here was clearly latent and not capable of discovery by even a careful inspection. Defendant was the developer of the subdivision in which the house was located, and built this home to demonstrate to the public the type of quality residence which could be erected in the subdivision. It was held to the public as "luxurious" and was shown as a model to the public. Common sense tells us that a purchaser under these circumstances should have at least as much protection as the purchaser of a new car, or a gas stove, or a sump pump, or a ladder.

* * * * *

We turn to the "present condition" provision of the contract, and respondent's contention that that provision excluded any implied warranties. On its face it does not indicate that it has reference to implied warranties. Respondent contends that the language "Property to be accepted in its present condition unless otherwise stated in contract" is an exclusion of warranties. We cannot so interpret it. The reasonable interpretation of that provision is that vendor assumes no obligation to do any additional work on the house unless specified. Such a provision would preclude purchasers from insisting that the vendor promised to paint the house a different color, or add a room, or retile a bathroom or correct an obvious defect. We do not believe a reasonable person would interpret that provision as an agreement by the purchaser to accept the house with an unknown latent structural defect.

Disposition on Death of Owner

Statutes of Descent and Distribution.   If a person does not make a will, his property, on his death, will be distributed according to the statutes known as statutes of descent and distribution. His real property will be distributed according to the statutes of the state in which it is located, and his personal property will be distributed according to the statutes of the state in which he is domiciled. A person dies intestate if he dies without leaving a will. In the event a person dies intestate and leaves no heir or next of kin who can take under the statutes of descent and distribution, his property will escheat to the state.

Right of Disposition by Will. The right to dispose of property by will is statutory. Under the feudal system of land tenure in England the king was the title owner of all the land, and the lords and knights held only a life estate in the land. On the death of a landholder, his rights in the land which he held terminated, and no rights in the land descended to his heirs. In 1215 the king granted to the nobility the right to pass their interest in the land which they held to their heirs.

Today, we recognize the theory of basic ownership by the state, and on the basis of this theory the courts have upheld the right of the state and the federal government to tax the estate of a deceased person and to tax an inheritance. Also, the right of the state to prescribe the formalities which must be complied with in the devising of property by will has been firmly established.

Execution of Will. Although the statutes concerning wills are not uniform in the different states, they are similar in their basic requirements. The courts have been strict in interpreting these statutes, and they will declare a will to be void unless all the requirements of the statute have been complied with in the execution of the will, in which case the property of the deceased will be distributed according to the statutes of descent and distribution.

Only persons of sound mind and of full age are permitted to dispose of property by will. In some states the age at which a person may make a valid will is stated in the statute and is as low as 18 years. The required formalities vary with the different states, and the laws of the states which may affect the will should be consulted before the will is executed. Formalities which are required by many states are: (1) The will must be in writing; (2) it must be witnessed by two or three witnesses; (3) it must be signed and sealed by the testator; (4) it must be published by the testator—as a general rule, all that is required for publication is a declaration by the testator, at the time of signing, that the instrument is his or her will; and (5) the testator must sign in the presence and in the sight of the witnesses, and the witnesses must sign in the presence and in the sight of the testator and in the presence and in the sight of each other. If the statutory formalities are not all complied with, the will is not valid. As a general rule an attestation clause, stating the formalities which have been followed in the execution of the will, is written following the testator's signature.

Some states recognize the validity of holographic wills, and some recognize the validity of nuncupative wills. A holographic will is one which is wholly written, signed, and sealed in the testator's or testatrix's own hand. The statutes of a few states recognize these wills as valid without formal execution or attestation. A nuncupative will is an oral will. In many states the oral wills made by sailors at sea or by soldiers in actual service are recognized as valid for the purpose of disposing of the personal estate in the actual possession of the testator at the time of the making of the will.

Limitations on Disposition by Will.   A person who takes property by will takes it subject to all outstanding claims against the property, both legal and equitable. Also, the rights of creditors are superior to the rights of a beneficiary under the will. If the deceased person is insolvent, persons named as beneficiary take nothing by virtue of the will.

Under the laws of most states the widow or widower of the deceased has statutory rights in the property of the deceased spouse which cannot be defeated by will. As a general rule a widow is given the right to claim certain personal property of the deceased husband, is given the right to the use of the home for a stated period, usually a year, and is given a portion of his real estate or a life estate in a portion of his real estate. In many states the widow's share in the husband's real property is a one-third interest or a life estate in one third of his real property. In some states the husband of a deceased wife is given an interest in her property, and this right cannot be defeated by will. In the community property states, each spouse has a one-half interest in the community property, and the rights of the surviving spouse cannot be defeated by will.

Revocation of Will.   One distinguishing feature of a will is that it conveys no interest in the maker's property until his death and the will has been probated. All wills are revocable at the option of the maker; and a will, at the time it is executed, does not confer any present rights in the property devised or bequeathed. A person may revoke his will by destroying or canceling it or by making a later will, duly executed, in which he expressly states that he thereby revokes all former wills executed by him. Under the statutes of the state, certain changes in relationship may operate as a revocation of a will. In some states the marriage of a man or a woman will revoke a will made by such person while single. The birth of a child after the execution of the will may, under the laws of some states, revoke a will or operate as a partial revocation of a will.

Summary

If a person dies intestate, that is, dies without having made a will, his property will be distributed according to the statutes of descent and distribution. His personal property will be distributed according to the statutes of the state of the deceased's domicile, and his real property according to the statute of the state in which it is located.

If a person disposes of real property by will, the statutory requirements of the state in which the real property is located must be complied with if the will is to be valid; and if a person disposes of personal property by will, the statutory requirements of the state of the domicile of the testator must be complied with.

There are statutory limitations on a husband's and a wife's right to dispose of their property by will.

A will transfers no interest in property until the death of the maker, and the maker may revoke his or her will at any time. A will may be revoked by operation of law as the result of the change in the status of the maker.

Public Controls on the Use of Land

While the owner of an interest in real property may generally make such use of his property as he desires, he does not have an unlimited right to do so. Society places a number of restraints on the owner of real property: (1) The owner cannot use his or her property in such a way as to unduly injure others; (2) through the use of the "police power," governmental units have the right to impose reasonable regulations on the use of property; and (3) society retains the right to divest ownership through the power of eminent domain.

Nuisance Control. When different uses are made of separate parcels of land, those uses may come into conflict and one or more of the users may become very unhappy. For example, the owner of a grove of orange trees finds that the dust from a nearby cement mill is forming a crust on his oranges, or the owner of a drive-in movie finds that the spotlights at a nearby auto racetrack are interfering with his patrons' enjoyment of the movies, or a housewife finds the noise from a nearby airport is interfering with her peace of mind. In some cases the courts have granted damages and injunctive relief to such aggrieved persons on the grounds that the use on the other property constitutes a nuisance which interferes substantially with the enjoyment of the property of the aggrieved person.

Zoning and Subdivision Ordinances. State legislatures commonly delegate to political subdivisions the police power to impose reasonable regulations designed to promote the public health, safety, morals, and the general welfare of the community. Zoning ordinances are an exercise of such a power to regulate. Normally, zoning ordinances divide the political subdivision into a number of districts, specify or limit the use to which property in those districts can be put, and restrict improvements and use on the land.

Such restrictions and controls may be of four basic types:

1. Control of Use. Regulation of the activity on the land such as single family dwellings, multi-family dwellings, commercial, light industry or heavy industry.
2. Control of Height and Bulk. Control of the height of buildings, the setback from front, side, and rear lot lines, and the portion of a lot that can be covered by a building.
3. Control of Population Density. Control over the amount of living space that must be provided for each person and specification of the maximum number of persons who can be housed in a given area.
4. Control of Aesthetics. Commonly used to control billboards, but also may be used to enforce similarity or dissimilarity of buildings as well as to preserve historical areas or communities.

When zoning ordinances are passed they have only a prospective effect so that already existing uses and buildings are permitted to continue. However, the ordinance may provide for the gradual phasing out of such uses and buildings that do not conform to the general zoning plan. If a property owner later wants to use his property in a way other than that which is permitted by the zoning ordinance, he must try to have the ordinance amended by showing that his proposed changes are in accordance with the overall plan or by obtaining a variance on the ground the ordinance creates an undue hardship on him by depriving him of the opportunity to make a reasonable use of his land. Such attempts to obtain amendments or variances often conflict with the interests of other nearby property owners who have a vested interest in the zoning status quo and produce heated battles before the zoning authorities.

Many local governments also have ordinances dealing with proposed subdivisions. The ordinances often require that the developer meet certain requirements as to lot size, street and sidewalk layout, and provision for sanitary facilities, and that the city approve the proposed development. In addition, the ordinance may in some cases require the developer to dedicate land to the city for streets, parks, and schools. The purpose of such ordinances is to protect the would-be purchasers in the subdivision as well as the city population as a whole by ensuring that minimum standards are met by the developer.

Some urban planners feel that it is undesirable to totally segregate the living, working, shopping, and entertainment areas as is commonly done with a zoning scheme. They argue that a more livable environment is one that mixes these uses so as to insure the vitality of an area for the vast part of each day. In response to this philosophy, cities and counties are allowing "planned unit developments" and "new towns" which mix such uses so long as the plans are submitted to the authorities and approved pursuant to general guidelines established for such developments.

People are also becoming more aware of the shortcomings of making our land-use decisions on a piecemeal basis at the local level. Airports, major shopping centers, highways, and new towns require a regional, rather than local, planning focus. Moreover, sensitive ecological areas, such as marshes, can readily be destroyed if encroached in a piecemeal manner. Accordingly, a number of states and the federal government have passed, or are considering, legislation to put some land-use planning on a regional or a statewide basis.

Eminent Domain.   The Constitution provides that private property shall not be taken for public use without just compensation. Implicit in this statement is the power of the state to take property for public use by paying "just compensation" to the owner of the property. This power of eminent domain makes possible our highways, water control projects, municipal and civic centers, public housing, and urban renewal.

Currently, there are several major problems inherent in the use of the eminent domain power. The first is what is meant by "just compensation." A property owner now receives the "fair market value" of his property; but some people feel that this falls short of reimbursing the owner for what he has lost since it does not cover the lost "goodwill" of a business or the emotional attachment a person may have to his home.

A second problem is deciding when a "taking" has occurred. The answer is easy where the owner is completely dispossessed by a governmental unit. It is much more difficult where (1) the zoning power has been utilized to restrict the permissible use of a given piece of property only for a narrow and publicly beneficial use, such as a parking lot, or (2) where the government uses nearby land in such a way as to almost completely destroy the usefulness of adjoining, privately owned land as sometimes occurs in the case of municipal airports.

A third problem is determining when the eminent domain power can be properly exercised. Clearly where the governmental unit itself uses the property, as in the case of municipal building or a public highway, the use of the power is proper. However, where as in the case of urban renewal, the condemned property may be resold to a private developer or the condemned property is not substandard, the use of the power is not so clearly justified.

Summary

Society places a number of restraints on the ownership of real property. First, a person may not create a nuisance on his property such that it unreasonably interferes with another person's enjoyment of his own land. Second, legislative bodies may use the constitutionally provided police power to impose reasonable regulations on property designed to promote the public health, safety, morals and general welfare. Third, the government through the eminent domain power may divest ownership entirely of property it desires to use for public purposes by paying just compensation to the private owner.

Spur Industries, Inc. v. Del E. Webb Development Co.

4 Envir. Rep. Cases 1052 (Sup. Ct. Ariz. 1972)

This was an action brought by Del E. Webb Development Company (plaintiff) against Spur Industries, Inc., (defendant) to enjoin the operation of Spur Industries' feedlot on the grounds it constituted a nuisance substantially interfering with the homeowners' enjoyment of their property in a retirement community developed by Del Webb. A judgment granting a permanent injunction was appealed by Spur and cross appealed by Webb. Judgment was affirmed in part and reversed in part.

In 1956 Spur's predecessor began operating a small cattle-feeding operation of some 6,000 to 7,000 head in an area that included about 25 cattle pens within a 7-mile radius. About one-and-a-half miles away was the city of Youngstown, a retirement community appealing primarily to senior citizens. In 1959 Del Webb acquired some 20,000 acres, a portion of which was located between Youngstown and Spur's predecessor's property, and began to build Sun City, a retirement community. In 1960 Spur acquired the feedlot and began expanding the acreage from 35 to 114 acres and by 1967 was feeding between 20,000 and 30,000 head of cattle. Del Webb in the meantime had acquired additional property between his original acreage and the Spur operation which Webb intended to sell as residential lots. There was considerable sales resistance to about 1,300 lots in the area closest to the Spur operation. Del Webb then brought suit against the Spur feeding operation, complaining that it constituted a public nuisance because of the flies and the odors which drifted or were blown over onto the Webb property. Webb contended that even with good feedlot management the citizens of Sun City were unable to enjoy the outdoor living they had been promised, and that the feedlot should be enjoined.

CAMERON, VICE CHIEF JUSTICE.   Although numerous issues are raised, we feel that it is necessary to answer only two questions. They are:

1.   Where the operation of a business, such as a cattle feedlot is lawful in the first instance, but becomes a nuisance by reason of a nearby residential area, may the feedlot operation be enjoined in an action brought by the developer of the residential area?

2.   Assuming that the nuisance may be enjoined, may the developer of a completely new town or urban area in a previously agricultural area be required to indemnify the operator of the feedlot who must move or cease operation because of the presence of the residential area created by the developer?

* * * * *

The difference between a private nuisance and a public nuisance is generally one of degree. A private nuisance is one affecting a single individual or a definite small number of persons in the enjoyment of private rights not common to the public, while a public nuisance is one affecting the rights enjoyed by citizens as a part of the public. To constitute a public nuisance, the nuisance must affect a considerable number of people or an entire community or neighborhood. *City of Phoenix v. Johnson.*

Where the injury is slight, the remedy for minor inconveniences lies in an action for damages rather than in one for an injunction. *Kubby* v. *Hammond*. Moreover, some courts have held, in the "balancing of conveniences" cases, that damages may be the sole remedy. See *Bonner v. Atlantic Cement Co.*

Thus it would appear from the admittedly incomplete record as developed in the trial court, that, at most, residents of Youngstown would be entitled to damages rather than injunctive relief.

We have no difficulty, however, in agreeing with the conclusion of the trial court that Spur's operation was an enjoinable public nuisance as far as the people in the southern portion of Del Webb's Sun City were concerned.

* * * * *

There was no indication in the instant case at the time Spur and its predecessors located in western Maricopa County that a new city would spring up, full blown, alongside the feeding operation and that the developer of that city would ask the court to order Spur to move because of the new city. Spur is required to move not because of any wrongdoing on the part of Spur, but because of a proper and legitimate regard of the courts for the rights and interests of the public.

Del Webb, on the other hand, is entitled to the relief prayed for (a permanent injunction) not because Webb is blameless, but because of the damage to the people who have been encouraged to purchase homes in Sun City. It does not equitably or legally follow, however, that Webb, being entitled to the injunction, is free of any liability to Spur if Webb has in fact been the cause of damage Spur has sustained. It does not seem harsh to require a developer who has taken advantage of the lesser land values in a rural area as well as the availability of large tracts of land on which to build and develop a new town or city in the area, to indemnify those who are forced to leave as a result.

Having brought people to the nuisance to the foreseeable detriment of Spur, Webb must indemnify Spur for a reasonable amount of the cost of moving or shutting down. It should be noted that this relief to Spur is limited to a case wherein a developer has, with foreseeability, brought into a previously agricultural or industrial area the population which makes necessary the granting of an injunction against a lawful business and for which the business has no adequate relief.

Ferguson v. City of Keene

238 A.2d 1 (Sup. Ct. N.H. 1968)

This was an action by Ferguson (plaintiff) to recover for injury to her property from the noise and vibration emanating from the airport owned by the City of Keene (defendant). The trial court refused to hold as a matter of law that Ferguson had no cause of action in "inverse condemnation." The Supreme Court reversed, holding that no claim of inverse condemnation was stated, but that Ferguson had stated a cause of action in nuisance.

The airport had been established in 1942 and Ferguson acquired her property in

1947. In 1956 the airport was enlarged and part of Ferguson's property was taken for this purpose. Ferguson alleged that the use of a "warm-up apron" located opposite her house resulted in such noise and vibration as to cause windows to break, to make conversation or sleep in the house impossible, and life generally unbearable. She further alleged that this use of the airport constituted a taking of her property for which she was required to be compensated.

DUNCAN, JUSTICE.   It is the settled law of this jurisdiction that a municipality, like any property owner, is bound to use its property in a reasonable manner, and is liable if its use results in a private nuisance. The City of Keene contends, however, that no taking of Ferguson's property can properly be alleged, since she admits that the flight path of aircraft does not cross it, and damage alone without an actual taking requires no compensation. The City further argues that its use of the airport is "proper," and that subjection of airports to liability for claims such as this would unduly impede the progress of air transportation in the state. Ferguson asserts that the allegations of its writ include all of the classic elements of nuisance, and also that the defendant's conduct of the airport gives rise to a cause of action for "inverse condemnation," even though no overflights occur.

Inverse condemnation is a term used to describe "a cause of action against a governmental defendant to recover the value of property which has been taken in fact by the governmental defendant, even though no formal exercise of the power of eminent domain has been attempted by the taking agency."

Pertinent cases decided by the United States Supreme Court have not gone beyond the point of holding that there may be recovery in inverse condemnation for damages occasioned by direct flights of aircraft over a claimant's property. *U.S. v. Causby.* As was pointed out in Dunham, *Griggs v. Allegheny County* in *Perspective: Thirty Years of Supreme Court Expropriation Law:* "The question whether those (claimants) adjacent to airports, but not in any flight path, should be compensated thus remains an open one so far as the Supreme Court decisions are concerned. But the logic of *Causby* and its idea of fairness would seem to require compensation even where planes do not fly directly over the objector's land." However, in *Batten v. United States,* the Court of Appeals declined to extend the doctrine to a case where overflights did not occur, relying upon the proposition that the federal Constitution requires compensation for a "taking" only. . . .

Since there is hardly a government act which could not cause someone substantial damage, an arbitrary boundary line must be drawn between compensable and noncompensable injury." Under the federal Constitution, the line has been drawn at compensation for a taking of property. "The Fifth Amendment . . . requires just compensation where private property is taken for public use . . . (but) does not undertake . . . to socialize all losses. . . .

A genuine distinction may reasonably be thought to exist between the nature of the injury suffered by the owner whose land is subjected to direct overflight, and that suffered by his neighbor whose land is not beneath the flight path. Only the former has lost the use of the airspace above his land, and he is subjected to risks of physical damage and injury not shared by the latter.

To what extent the nuisance of which Ferguson complains is essential to the public use of the City's airport is a question which is not determinable at this stage of this litigation. The question whether a defendant in circumstances such as these should be compelled by inverse condemnation to acquire an "easement" and compensate Ferguson therefore presents issues of social policy which might well be the subject of legislative study and appropriate enactment.

GRIMES, JUSTICE (dissenting).   Ferguson's writ alleges that

the noise from the planes "warming up" for take off, make such a great amount of noise that it is impossible for the people in the house to converse or talk on the telephone, the house vibrates and the glass in the windows shake and that more than 20 panes of glass have been broken by said vibration in the winter of 1963–1964, that it is often times impossible to sleep and there is no peace or quiet in their home and that life has become unbearable because of said noise.

The majority of the court says this declaration does not set forth a cause of action based on inverse condemnation. I disagree.

Our court long ago decided that in our state at least, the term "property" refers to "the right of any person to possess, use, enjoy, and dispose of a thing" and is not limited to the thing itself, and that a person's property is "taken" for public use so as to entitle him to "just compensation" under our Constitution when a physical interference substantially subverts one of these rights even though the thing itself is not taken.

I am unimpressed with the rationale of those cases which confine inverse condemnation to overflights. A person's property rights can be damaged as greatly by sound waves traveling horizontally as by those traveling vertically, and to draw a distinction is to ignore reality.

We are dealing here with an important and fundamental individual right, the roots of which reach back to Magna Carta. It is one which deserves to be stoutly defended and liberally construed. It is one which we should not deny to Ferguson because the means by which her property was taken was neither known to nor foreseen by the Barons of England or the Framers of our Constitution.

The court while denying the constitutional right has at least recognized that Ferguson has set forth a cause of action based on nuisance. This I think is a poor substitute from the standpoint of both parties.

Problem Cases

1.   Kelm owned a building which he leased to Timper. The first floor of the building had always been used as a tavern. The upper floor of the building was a rooming house. When Timper originally leased the building, an old-fashioned bar was situated against one of the walls on the building. Timper, without the knowledge or consent of Kelm, removed this old bar and installed a new 60-foot circular bar in the center of the room. This bar was worth about $2,000. Timper borrowed money from Loan Company and as security gave it a chattel mortgage which covered certain items in the tavern and rooming house, including the 60-foot circular bar. Timper later defaulted on the chattel mortgage and abandoned the lease on the building. Loan Co. claimed a lien on the bar and Kelm claimed that the bar

was a fixture and that the mortgage was void as to it. By removing the bar there would be left in the floor twelve holes differing in diameter from one to six inches. These holes were made so that the bar could have the necessary electrical, water and sewage facilities and so that the beer could be piped from the basement. A bottle chute had also been installed. Should the bar be considered a fixture?

2. William D. Robinson left a will in which he devised all his real estate as follows: "Third: I give all of my real estate to my wife, Lela S. Robinson, and at her death it goes to Frank M. Robinson, and at his death to his two boys, David Robinson and Richard Robinson." Caldwell and the other heirs of Lela S. Robinson claim that a fee simple title vested in Lela and that Frank M. Robinson takes nothing. Is this claim correct?

3. Henry Steitz owned, in Placeville, improved real estate of the value of $10,000. On March 13, 1944, Steitz went to the office of his attorney, J. D. Elliot, and told him that Frank B. Irwin and his wife had been very kind to him and that he wished to give them his Placeville property. Steitz directed Elliot to draw a deed conveying the real estate to Frank B. Irwin and his wife as tenants by the entirety. Elliot drafted the deed and Steitz executed it. Steitz was described in the deed as an unmarried man. After Steitz executed the deed he handed it to Elliot and told Elliot to keep the deed until his (Steitz's) death and then to deliver it to the Irwins. Elliot, in compliance with the directions of Steitz, placed the deed in his safe where it remained until the trial of the case. After the execution of the deed, Steitz told several people, including the Irwins, that he had given his Placeville property to the Irwins.

    On June 23, 1947, Steitz married his present wife. On the same date, Steitz and his wife, without the knowledge of the Irwins, joined in a purported deed of conveyance of the Placeville real estate to Janis H. Benson, and the deed was recorded the same day. Janis H. Benson then purported to reconvey the property to Henry Steitz and his wife as tenants by the entirety, and this deed was also immediately recorded. Frank B. Irwin and his wife brought suit against Henry Steitz, his wife, and Janis H. Benson to have the deeds of June 23, 1947, cancelled. Should these deeds be ordered cancelled?

4. Floyd, 84 years of age, was suffering from an incurable cancer and was confined to his bed at the time he executed his will. He conversed for about one-half hour with the two men who witnessed the will, talking about their families and other topics. The will was read to him topic by topic and he approved each item as read and said at the conclusion of the reading that that was the way he wanted his property distributed. He had left a life estate in all of his property to his wife, and the fee to his grandson and his wife. They had cared for Floyd during his last illness. Objections were filed to the probate of the will on the ground of mental incapacity to make a will. Should the will be admitted to probate?

5. Norman owned Lot 6 and in 1910 he built town houses on the lot. The houses faced Twelfth Street. From this street, he built a walk which led to a flight of three steps and then continued to the rear of the houses. From the tops of the flight of steps he built walks to the front entrance of each house and at the rear of the walk he built walks to the rear entrance of each house. The walk between the houses was 35 inches wide; it was 35 inches from the south house and 27 inches from the north house. In 1935, Early purchased the south house, and the south one half of Lot 6 was deeded to him. In 1945, Kovack purchased the north house, and the remaining north one half of Lot 6 was deeded to Kovack. Shortly after purchasing the north house, Kovack erected a picket fence on the lot line extending from the rear lot line to the top of the concrete steps. This act on the part of Kovack resulted in locating substantially all of the concrete walk on Kovack's side of the fence. After the building of the fence, Early had only about 12 inches of the walk over which to pass in entering upon or leaving the flared apron leading to his front entrance and only about 12

inches of the walk leading to his back door. Early brought an action to force Kovack to remove the fence claiming he had an easement of right of way over that portion of the concrete walk that was on Kovack's side of the dividing line. The walk had been used from the time it was built until Kovack built the fence, by the occupants of the two houses and their guests and by tradesmen serving the houses. Does Early have an easement of right of way as he claims?

6. DuBose contracted to sell Bishop timber to be cut by Bishop from a tract of land owned by DuBose. The contract was in writing and, in addition to stating the price per thousand feet to be paid for the logs cut, provided that the seller had the right to direct the portion of the tract from which the trees were to be cut. It did not state the quantity of timber to be cut, nor did it state that all merchantable timber on the tract was to be cut. After Bishop had cut between 30,000 and 40,000 feet of timber, DuBose ordered him to cease cutting timber and denied him the right to come onto the land. Bishop sued DuBose to recover damages for breach of contract. Bishop claimed that he had acquired title to the timber on the tract. DuBose claimed that the contract was unenforceable for uncertainty of terms and that Bishop had only a license to cut timber. Was DuBose's claim correct?

7. In 1935, the state purchased a tract of land for park purposes. It developed the tract to the edge of a cliff along the Columbia River. It fenced the property and built shelter houses and cared for it generally. No improvements were made from 1945 to 1947, but the park was open to the public. In 1947, Stockdale purchased an adjoining tract of land and at this time it was discovered that the portion of the state park along the cliff was included in the deed to the tract purchased by Stockdale. The statute of limitations is ten years. The state claims the land along the cliff by right of adverse possession. Is the state the owner of the disputed tract?

8. Hobbs kept two horses in the backyard of her home in a residential section of Jefferson County, Colorado. The local zoning ordinance permitted the keeping of two horses on property in this area. Hobbs used reasonable skill and care in maintaining the horses, and no health regulations were violated. However, the horses did attract flies to the general area and noxious smells also permeated the area. Smith, who owns the adjoining property, sues Hobbs claiming the horses constitute a nuisance which should be abated. What arguments will Hobbs and Smith each make? How will the court rule?

9. Mid-West Freight owns a piece of property in the City of Chicago bordered partly by a residential area and partly by a manufacturing area. Across some railroad tracks from Mid-West is an area designated for motor freight terminals, the entrance to which is located about one mile from Mid-West's property. There are three other areas in the city designated for motor freight terminals in order to prevent traffic congestion, and to regulate noise, air pollution, and heavy use of streets. Mid-West's property is zoned "light industrial," a category that excludes motor-freight terminals. Mid-West currently uses its property to repair and paint its freight moving equipment, and it has no dock or freight storage equipment on the premises. Mid-West seeks to have its property rezoned in order to permit expansion of its current use to include freight handling, a change that would bring it into the motor-freight terminal category. Mid-West contends that only a small change from its present use is involved, that it will suffer financial injury if not allowed to change, and that the city has no justification for refusing to change its present zoning classification of Mid-West's property. As a judge how would you evaluate this situation?

10. Sanborton, New Hampshire, is located on the shore of Lake Winnisquam and is near several other recreational lakes as well as a number of ski resorts. It has a year-round population of about 1000 people living in some 330 regular homes and has another 400 seasonal homes.

Steel Hill Development acquired 510 acres of land in an area zoned for "agriculture and general residential," where the minimum permissible lot size is 35,000 square feet or about three fourths of an acre. Steel Hill then prepared plans calling for the construction of about 500 recreational housing units on its property, both in conventional and cluster arrangements. The Sanborton Planning Board, over the objection of many town residents, approved the subdivision of 37 conventional lots. Then, responding to community pressure, it rezoned about 70 percent of Steel Hill's acreage into a zoning category requiring a 6-acre minimum lot size. This was done in order to preserve the rural nature of the town and to avoid the environmental and growth problems threatened by the recreational home development. Steel Hill contends that the rezoning so greatly reduces the value of its land as to constitute a "taking" without due compensation and that it is also an abitrary and discriminatory restriction of development. Should Steel Hill's contentions be sustained by the court?

chapter 31

Landlord and Tenant

Leases

Landlord-Tenant Relationship.   The relationship of landlord and tenant, which has been with us for a long time, is an area of the law which is rapidly changing. In England and in early America, farms were the most common subjects of leases; the primary object was to lease land on which crops could be grown or cattle grazed. Any buildings on the leased property were frequently of secondary importance to the land itself, and they generally were rather simple structures built without such modern conveniences as plumbing and wiring. The tenant would have dominion over the entire property and would be responsible for its upkeep. The landlord and the tenant would normally have similar knowledge of the condition of the property at the time the lease was entered into. Accordingly, traditional landlord-tenant law looked at a lease mainly as a conveyance of land and gave relatively little attention to its contractual aspects.

Today, the landlord-tenant relationship is typified by the lease of an apartment in a large building located in an urban area. The tenant occupies only a small portion of the total property; he is likely to have signed a form lease dictated by the landlord; and he is less likely than his grandfather to be adept at making the kind of repairs that might be required in the apartment. In the rundown sections of cities the tenant's situation is commonly exacerbated by the presence of rats and filth and by his or her relatively meager economic status.

The law had been slow to recognize the essentially changed nature of the landlord-tenant relationship. The rule of *caveat emptor* in lease situations was eventually grafted with exceptions, and the emphasis changed from focusing on the lease as a conveyance of land to focusing on its contractual aspects. In recent years, the courts, legislatures, and local governing bodies have provided

687

a plethora of new rules to govern the relationship. Accordingly, this chapter will be concerned not only with the time-developed common law of landlord and tenant but also with recent statutory and case-law developments.

Nature of Lease. A leasehold is an interest in land and is created by a lease which, as a general rule, need not be executed with the same formalities as are followed in the execution of a deed. In some respects a leasehold interest in real property is treated as personal property. In probating an estate after the death of a lessee, any leasehold interest which the lessee held at the time of his or her death is treated as personal property. Also, in some states the courts treat the breach of a lease as a breach of contract and assess damages accordingly.

Execution of Lease. A lease, to be valid, need not conform to any specific formal requirements. Basically, a lease is a contract, and in most states, if the lease is for a term of more than one year from the making thereof, it must, under the statute of frauds, be evidenced by a writing if it is to be enforceable. In some states, however, the statute of frauds expressly provides that leases for a term of three years or less need not be evidenced by a writing to be enforceable.

The statutes of many states provide for the recording of long-term leases— five or ten years, or longer—and further provide that such leases, to be eligible for recording, must be executed with the same formalities as are used in the execution of a deed. The failure to execute a long-term lease with the formalities set out in the statute does not render it a nullity, the only effect of such failure is to render the lease ineligible for recordation.

In the leasing of real estate, good business practice demands that the parties execute a carefully drafted lease which defines their respective rights. Such a lease will contain covenants covering such essential matters as the use permitted by the tenant, who shall make repairs, the landlord's right to enter the premises, and the purposes for which the landlord may enter, the rent to be paid, warranties as to the condition of the premises, and whether or not the lease may be assigned or the premises sublet.

Rights, Duties, and Liabilities of the Landlord. The rights, duties, and liabilities of the landlord, as well as of the tenant, must be considered in three different situations: (1) where there is no applicable and enforceable lease clause, (2) where there is an applicable and enforceable lease clause, and (3) where there is an applicable statute. The discussion in this section of the text relates primarily to the law which applies in the absence of a lease clause or statute, and it should be kept in mind that a lease clause or statute may supercede the common law rule in any given situation.

When a landlord leases his or her premises, the landlord impliedly warrants that he will give the tenant possession of the premises, or at least that the tenant will have the right to possession, and that the tenant's possession shall not be interfered with as the result of any act or omission on the part of the landlord or as a result of any defects in the landlord's title. In the absence of covenants in the lease to the contrary, the landlord has no right to enter onto the premises during the term of the lease, and if the landlord does, he or she is a trespasser.

Under traditional law, the landlord does not warrant the condition of the premises, nor does he or she warrant that the premises are suitable for the purposes of the tenant. The tenant takes the premises as he or she finds them. Since the landlord has no duty as to the condition of the premises, the landlord is not liable to the tenant or his or her family for injuries or property damage due to obvious defects or failure to repair. To this general rule, the courts created some very important exceptions: (1) The landlord remains liable to use due care for those common areas of a building in which he or she retains control; (2) the landlord must disclose concealed defects known to him or her and not discoverable on a reasonable inspection by the tenant and is liable for those defects not disclosed that cause injury; (3) the landlord remains liable for the consequences of any negligently made repairs, even though he or she was not obligated to make them; (4) the landlord who rents a fully furnished dwelling for a short period impliedly warrants that the premises are safe and habitable.

The emergence of substantial housing problems in large cities has led many cities and states to pass statutes imposing the duty to repair residential properties on the landlord. Failure to make the repairs may result in landlord liability for injuries or give the tenant the right to withhold rent until the repairs are made or to move out.

The landlord is entitled to the agreed rent, and at the expiration of the term of the lease, has the right to the surrender of the premises in as good condition as when leased, normal wear and destruction by the elements excepted.

Rights and Duties of the Tenant. The tenant may use the leased premises for any lawful purpose which is reasonable and appropriate, unless the purpose for which they may be used is expressly set out in the lease. Under the common law rule the tenant has the exclusive right to the possession and use of the premises during the term of the lease, and if the landlord comes onto the premises without the consent of the tenant, he or she will be guilty of trespass. The tenant is fully responsible for the care and upkeep of the premises and traditionally owed a duty to make all ordinary repairs so that the premises would be returned in the same condition as rented except for normal wear and tear. Again, this duty for the upkeep of residential property has been changed by statute in many jurisdictions and put on the landlord. The tenant has no duty to make major repairs except where he or she was negligent, but the tenant must take steps to prevent damage from the elements as when a window breaks or a roof leaks.

The tenant is normally liable to persons injured or property damaged because of the tenant's negligence on that part of the property over which he or she has control.

The tenant has in the leased premises a property interest which he or she may transfer to another by the assignment of the lease unless the lease expressly provides that it shall not be assigned. If the tenant assigns the lease, he does not relieve himself from any contractual obligations under the lease, but the tenant does divest himself of his property interest in the leased premises. The tenant may sublease the premises or a part thereof. If the tenant subleases the premises or a part thereof, the tenant does not divest himself of his property interest therein, and the tenant remains liable to the landlord on all the covenants in the lease. The tenant's relation to his or her sublessee is that of landlord. The tenant cannot grant to a sublessee greater rights than he has under the original lease, and if the original lease contains a provision denying the tenant the right to sublease the premises or any part thereof, such provision is enforceable.

Termination of the Lease.   Normally, a lease is ended by "surrender" of the premises by the tenant to the landlord and "acceptance" of the premises by the landlord. However, sometimes the tenant may be forced out by the landlord prior to the end of the lease period or the tenant may vacate the premises before the end of the lease period.

If the premises become uninhabitable because of the acts of the landlord, then under the doctrine of "constructive eviction" the tenant may, after giving the landlord a reasonable opportunity to correct the defect, move out and incur no further liability for rent. The tenant must move out within a reasonable amount of time. For example, if the furnace breaks down in the middle of the winter and the apartment is without heat for February and March, the tenant cannot use this as an excuse for breaking the lease in August.

If the tenant abandons the premises before the end of the lease, the consequences vary from state to state. In some states the landlord is under an obligation to mitigate damages and must attempt to rerent or will lose any claim for further rent against the original tenant. In other states, the landlord may continue to collect rent from the tenant without rerenting, but loses the right if he does rerent. As a result, many leases contain a clause maintaining the landlord's right to the rent whether or not he tries to rerent and continuing the tenant's liability for any difference in rents if the landlord does rerent.

Summary

As a general rule, no formalities are required for the execution of short-term leases—one to three years—but leases for a longer period of time are required by the statute of frauds to be in writing. Long-term leases—five to ten years or longer—are required by the statutes of some states to be recorded, and such leases must be executed with the same formalities as are used in the execution of deeds to real property.

A landlord, in leasing premises, impliedly warrants that the tenant will have possession and quiet enjoyment of the premises. Under the common law rule, the landlord does not warrant the condition of the premises or their suitability for the tenant's purposes but this has been changed by statute or judicial decision in many jurisdictions. Unless the landlord agrees to make ordinary repairs, he or she has no duty to do so under the common law rule; however, many statutes now require landlords to keep residential property in repair.

In the absence of covenants in the lease to the contrary, the tenant has the exclusive right to the possession of the premises and is responsible for the upkeep. The tenant has the right to make any lawful use of the premises he or she wishes, provided the use does not result in permanent injury to them.

Normally a lease is terminated by surrender by the tenant and acceptance by the landlord at the end of the lease term. However, if the premises become uninhabitable through the acts of the landlord, the tenant may move out within a reasonable time after giving the landlord notice to remedy the defects. If the tenant abandons the premises prior to the end of the lease, he or she may remain liable for the rent.

Lemle v. Breeden

462 P.2d 470 (Sup. Ct. Hawaii 1969)

This was an action brought by Henry Lemle (plaintiff) against V. E. Breeden (defendant) to recover a deposit and advance payment of rent. Judgment for Lemle was affirmed on appeal.

Mrs. Breeden owned a home fronting on the water in the Diamond Head area of Honolulu. On September 21, 1964, Lemle was shown the fully furnished house by a realtor. After a half-hour inspection, during which Lemle saw no evidence of rodent infestation, he signed a rental agreement covering September 22, 1964, to March 20, 1965, and April 17, 1965, to June 12, 1965, at a monthly rental of $800. Lemle tendered a check for $1,190 and moved his family in the next day. That evening he became aware that there were rats in the dwelling and on the roof. As a consequence, Lemle and his family vacated their bedrooms and slept in the living room over the next three nights. The landlord was notified of the problem and efforts by both the landlord and Lemle to alleviate the rat problem were unavailing. Consequently, three days after the lease began, Lemle and his family vacated the premises and demanded the return of their money.

LEVISON, JUSTICE. The application of an implied warranty of habitability in leases gives recognition to the changes in leasing transactions today. It affirms the fact that a lease is, in essence, a sale as well as a transfer of an estate in land and is, more importantly, a contractual relationship. From that contractual relationship an implied warranty of habitability and fitness for the purposes intended is a just and necessary implication. It is a doctrine which has its counterparts in the law of sales and torts and one which when candidly countenanced is impelled by the nature of the transaction and contemporary housing realities. Legal fictions and artificial exceptions to wooden rules of property law aside, we hold that in the lease of a dwelling house, such as in this case, there is an implied warranty of habitability and fitness for the use intended.

Here the facts demonstrate the uninhabitability and unfitness of the premises for residential purposes. For three sleepless nights the plaintiff and his family literally camped in the living room. They were unable to sleep in the proper quarters or make use of the other facilities in the house due to natural apprehension of the rats which made noise scurrying about on the roof and invaded the house through the unscreened openings.

*   *   *   *   *

It is a decided advantage of the implied warranty doctrine that there are a number of remedies available. The doctrine of constructive eviction, on the other hand, requires that the tenant abandon the premises within a reasonable time after giving notice that the premises are uninhabitable or unfit for his purposes. . . . This is based on the absurd proposition, contrary to modern urban realities, that "(a) tenant cannot claim uninhabitability, and at the same time continue to inhabit." . . . Abandonment is always at the risk of establishing sufficient facts to constitute constructive eviction or the tenant will be liable for breach of the rental agreement. Also the tenant is forced to gamble on the time factor as he must abandon within a "reasonable" time or be deemed to have "waived" the defects.

Some courts have creatively allowed for alternatives to the abandonment requirement by allowing for a declaration of constructive eviction in equity without forcing abandonment. . . . Other courts have found partial constructive eviction where alternative housing was scarce, thus allowing the tenant to remain in at least part of the premises. . . .

By adopting the view that a lease is essentially a contractual relationship with an implied warranty of habitability and fitness, a more consistent and responsive set of remedies are available for a tenant. They are the basic contract remedies of damages, reformation, and rescission. These remedies would give the tenant a wide range of alternatives in seeking to resolve his alleged grievance.

In considering the materiality of an alleged breach, both the seriousness of the claimed defect and the length of time for which it persists are relevant factors. Each case must turn on its own facts. Here there was sufficient evidence for the trier of fact to conclude that the breach was material and that the plaintiff's action in rescinding the rental agreement was justifiable. The plaintiff gave notice of rescission and vacated the premises after the landlord's early attempts to get rid of the rats failed. When the premises were vacated, they were not fit for use as a residence. Nor was there any assurance that the residence would become habitable within a reasonable time.

Garcia v. Freeland Realty, Inc.

314 N.Y.S.2d 215 (Civ. Ct. N.Y.C. 1970)

This was an action brought by Jose Garcia (plaintiff) against Freeland Realty, Inc., (defendant) to recover for materials furnished and labor performed by tenant Garcia in connection with the replastering and painting of rooms in an apartment owned by landlord Freeland Realty. Judgment for Garcia.

Garcia rented the apartment pursuant to an oral lease. He had two small children that he discovered were eating paint and plaster that was flaking off the walls in two of the rooms in the apartment. Garcia complained about the condition to the landlord, and when the landlord did nothing to remedy the situation, Garcia purchased paint and plaster and replastered and repainted the offending walls. He spent $29.53 for materials and also claimed $1.60 an hour (the minimum wage) for 10 hours labor.

GOODELL, JUDGE.   The issue here, in the light of the uncontested facts, is whether a recovery by the plaintiff is barred as a matter of law in view of the common-law rule that the landlord, in the absence of an express covenant is not obligated to repair or paint. . . . While statutory duties to repair and paint have been imposed upon the owner by sections 78 and 80 respectively of the Multiple Dwelling Law, it has been held that these duties are enforceable by the municipality only and, therefore, that neither is the basis of a claim by the lessee against the lessor for reimbursement of the cost of repairs made by the lessee.

* * * * *

The court takes judicial notice of the facts, now notorious and a matter of common knowledge in New York City, that in New York City slum apartments "as successive layers of paint peel away, the paint underneath becomes a menace to any young child who can pick off the flakes and put them in his mouth" (*New York Post,* May 15, 1970, p.6); such plaster and paint contain lead; that lead poisoning is limited mainly to the children of the poor in New York City; and that the eating of such plaster and paint flakes by children leads to lead poisoning with the consequences of mental retardation and death.

This, therefore, is not a case involving painting for the sake of comfort or enjoyment of the premises. It is different and more than that. It concerns a situation of emergency and menace to the health and life of children.

The practical question that faced the plaintiff, a father of small children, in December 1969 and January 1970, was whether he was bound to sit by and do nothing despite the landlord's inactivity and the delays of a municipality beset by a multiplicity of problems and conflicting demands for its attention or whether he should take prompt steps to prevent irreparable damage to his children and charge the cost to his landlord.

In these circumstances, in my view, the plaintiff had the right to remove the menace to the health and life of his children and to charge the cost, to the extent hereafter noted, to the landlord, for the following reasons.

While it has been held, as noted, that despite sections 78 and 80 of the Multiple Dwelling Law, the making of repairs by a tenant, does not entitle the tenant to reimbursement from the landlord in the absence of an express covenant by the landlord, the landlord is nevertheless liable for injuries suffered by the tenant or members of his family as a result of the landlord's failure to make repairs. . . .

Just as in the case of a falling ceiling or a defective step, so the defendant could foreseeably have been exposed to a tort action for damage had the plaintiff's children suffered the result of continuing ingestions of plaster and paint because of the defendant's failure to act after notice and demand for action.

The plaintiff, therefore, by his act, prevented the commission of an actionable tort that might have resulted from inaction.

If damage based upon the commission of a tort is an appropriate award, then in my view, it is proper and desirable to reimburse a plaintiff for the reasonable cost of preventing or averting the commission of a tort after a defendant has had a reasonable opportunity to act and failed to do so in circumstances calling for action on his part. As Prosser has said in his discussion of "prevention":

> The "prophylactic" factor of preventing future harm has been quite important in the field of torts. . . . While the idea of prevention is seldom controlling, it very often has weight as a reason for holding the defendant responsible. (Prosser, *Law of Torts,* (3d ed.), p.23).

In the circumstances of this case involving the concurrent conditions of an immediate threat to the health and life of children and a critical shortage of housing, it is my view that the prevention of an actionable tort by the plaintiff warrants his reimbursement for the cost of materials and the reasonable value of labor applied to the accomplishment of that result.

Brown v. Southall Realty Co.

237 A.2d 834 (Ct. App. D.C. 1968)

This was an action brought by Southall Realty (plaintiff) to evict Mrs. Brown (defendant) for nonpayment of rent. Mrs. Brown contended that no rent was due under the lease because it was an illegal contract. The trial court held for the landlord, Southall Realty. Judgment reversed on appeal, holding that no rent was owed by the tenant.

QUINN, JUDGE.   The evidence developed, at the trial, revealed that prior to the signing of the lease agreement, Southall was on notice that certain Housing Code violations existed on the premises in question. An inspector for the District of Columbia Housing Division of the Department of Licenses and Inspections testified that the violations, an obstructed commode, a broken railing, and insufficient ceiling height in the basement, existed at least some months prior to the lease agreement and had not been abated at the time of trial. He also stated that the basement violations prohibited the use of the entire basement as a dwelling place. Counsel for Southall Realty at the trial below elicited an admission from Brown that "he told the defendant after the lease had been signed that the back room of the basement was habitable despite the Housing Code Violations."

This evidence having been established and uncontroverted, Mrs. Brown contends that the lease should have been declared unenforceable because it was entered into in contravention to the District of Columbia Housing Regulations, and knowingly so.

Section 2304 of the District of Columbia Housing Regulations reads as follows:

No persons shall rent or offer to rent any habitation, or the furnishings thereof, unless such habitation and its furnishings are in a clean, safe and sanitary condition in repair, and free from rodents or vermin.

Section 2501 of these same Regulations, states:

Every premises accommodating one or more habitations shall be maintained and kept in repair so as to provide decent living accommodations for the occupants. This part of the Code contemplates more than mere basic repairs, and maintenance to keep out the elements; its purpose is to include repairs and maintenance designed to make a premises or neighborhood healthy and safe.

It appears that the violations known by appellee to be existing on the leasehold at the time of the signing of the lease agreement were of a nature to make the "habitation" unsafe and unsanitary. Neither had the premises been maintained or repaired to the degree contemplated by the regulations, that is, "designed to make a premises . . . healthy and safe." The lease contract was, therefore, entered into in violation of the Housing Regulations requiring that they be safe and sanitary and that they be properly maintained.

In the case of *Hartman v. Lubar,* the court stated that,

the general rule is that an illegal contract, made in violation of the statutory prohibition designed for police or regulatory purposes, is void and confers no right upon the wrongdoer.

. . . To this general rule, however, the courts have found exceptions. For the exception, resort must be had to the intent of the legislature, as well as the subject matter of the legislation.

A reading of Sections 2304 and 2501 infers that the Commissioners of the District of Columbia, in promulgating these Housing Regulations, were endeavoring to regulate the rental of housing in the District and to insure for the prospective tenants that these rental units would be "habitable" and maintained as such. . . . To uphold the validity of this lease agreement, in light of the defects known to be existing on the leasehold prior to the agreement (that is, obstructed commode, broken railing, and insufficient ceiling height in the basement), would be to flout the evident purposes for which Sections 2304 and 2501 were enacted. The more reasonable view is, therefore, that where such conditions exist on a leasehold prior to an agreement to lease, the letting of such premises constitutes a violation of Sections 2304 and 2501 of the Housing Regulations, and that these Sections do indeed "imply a prohibition" so as "to render the prohibited act void."

Problem Cases

1. Burnstein owned two buildings at 5045–57 Broadway, Chicago, which he leased to Lapkin for a term of five years commencing November 1, 1956, and expiring October 31, 1961, at a rental of $132,000 payable at the rate of $2,200 per month. Paragraph Two of the lease provided, in part, as follows:

Lessee has examined and knows the condition of said premises, and has received the same in good order and repair, and acknowledges that no representations as to the condition and repair thereof, have been made by the Lessor or his agent prior to or at the execution of this lease, that are not herein expressed or endorsed hereon; Lessee will keep said premises including all appurtenances, in good repair . . . and will without injury to the roof, remove all snow and ice from the same when necessary. . . . Upon receipt of written request from Lessee, the Lessor shall, during the term of this lease, make any and all necessary repairs to the roof and exterior walls of the premises demised herein. . . .

On March 31, 1958, Lapkin filed suit to rescind the lease. He claimed that on taking possession (November 1, 1956) he spent large sums decorating the premises and that the roof leaked and damaged the interior of the building and damaged his property stored therein. (The buildings were used as a salesroom for new automobiles and a garage.) He based his right to rescind the lease on: (1) constructive fraud in the inducement of the lease in that Burnstein did not disclose to him the condition of the roof during the negotiations for the lease, and (2) constructive eviction, since Burnstein had failed to repair the roof. Burnstein had, after Lapkin took possession, paid an independent contractor $8,000 to repair the roof and walls of the buildings.

Should the lease be rescinded?

2. Winslow rented an apartment from Landlord and signed a lease which provided, in part, that "Landlord or Landlord's agents shall not be responsible for the presence of bugs, vermin, or insects, if any, in the premises, nor shall their presence affect this lease." Some mice appeared in Winslow's apartment and despite efforts to get rid of them, they continued their presence in the apartment. Winslow moves out, claiming construction eviction, and cites § 227 of the *Real Property Law* of New York which provides: "Where any building, which is leased or occupied, is destroyed or so injured by the elements or any other cause as to be untenable, and unfit for occupancy, and no express agreement to the contrary has been made in writing, the lessee or occupant may if the destruction or injury occurred without his fault or neglect, quit and surrender possession of the leasehold premises. . . . and he is not liable to pay to the lessor or owner, rent for the time subsequent to the surrender." Landlord sues Winslow for rent for the unexpired portion of the lease. Is Winslow liable for the remaining rent?

3. Ross constructed a steep outdoor stairway on a house prior to leasing it to Sargent. Sargent's four-year-old child fell from the dangerously steep stairway and was killed. Sargent sued Ross for damages, saying that he could not have remedied the defect himself since he did not own the house or have the authority to alter it. Ross contended that he had no "duty" to the deceased child since the stairway was not leased for public use, did not contain a hidden defect, and was not under his control. How should the judge decide this case?

4. Anna had leased a third-floor tenement apartment from Santo for about 15 years. Under Connecticut law, Santo was required to keep all public halls in the tenement lighted, but Anna had found it necessary to complain frequently about the adequacy of the lighting. One night Anna returned from work to the apartment house about 1:30 A.M. All of the hall lights were out. The light in the lower hall was turned on by a wall switch. The lights in the upper halls were operated by pull chains. None of the lights lighted the stairs adequately. She turned on the light in the lower hall and ascended the stairs. While reaching for the pull chain to turn on the light in the upper hall, she lost her balance and fell down the entire flight of stairs. Anna brought suit to recover damages for the personal injuries

suffered. Santo claims that there was no breach of duty on his part and that Anna should also be precluded from recovering because she was contributorily negligent or had assumed the risk. Should Anna recover?

5. On April 2, 1969, Ireland entered into a one-year lease for an apartment in a two-family duplex owned by Marini for a monthly rental of $95. The lease did not include a specific covenant for repairs. On June 25, Ireland discovered the toilet in the apartment was cracked, and water was leaking onto the bathroom floor. Ireland tried unsuccessfully to notify Marini of the problem and then on June 27 hired a plumber to repair the toilet. Ireland paid the plumber $85.72 for this work and deducted it from her next rent payment. Marini now seeks to have Ireland dispossessed for nonpayment of rent since Ireland refuses to pay the $85.72 he offset. What argument will Marini make? What argument will Ireland make? Who should prevail?

6. In 1965, Miss Kline moved into an apartment house in Washington, D.C. At the time she signed the lease a doorman was on duty at the main entrance 24 hours a day, at least one employee manned a desk in the lobby from which all persons entering the elevators could be observed, and attendants were stationed at the entrance of the garage. By mid–1966, the main entrance had no doorman, the lobby desk was unattended much of the time, and the garage entrances were generally unlocked and unattended. This was true despite the fact an increasing number of assaults and robberies were being perpetrated against tenants in the hallways of the apartment. At 10:00 P.M. on November 17, 1966, Kline was assaulted and robbed just outside her apartment of the 535-unit apartment building. Two months before another tenant had been similarly attacked in the same hallway. Kline sues the landlord because of injuries she sustained in the assault. What arguments will Kline and the landlord make? What result should the court reach?

7. Richstone entered into a lease with Landlord that prohibited any alterations without the consent of the Landlord and which provided that even papering the walls or changing the color of wall paint was a prohibited alteration and breach of a substantial obligation of the lease. Richstone subsequently spent more than $5,000 for new metallic wallpaper, removal and replacement of kitchen cabinets, a new "hanging ceiling" in the living room, and candlelight fixtures. Richstone contended that his modifications enhanced the value of the property and would cost only $250 to remove. Landlord sues to have Richstone evicted for substantial breach of the lease. What result should the court reach?

8. Glyco rented a house and 30 acres to Schultz under an oral month-to-month lease that stipulated a rent of $200 per month. When Schultz moved into the house in September 1970 there were serious and substantial violations of the housing code. The electrical system was underserviced and in a state of disrepair, the steps were deteriorating, the floor was weak, and the furnace often failed to work or on occasions emitted smoke that ruined furniture. The steps collapsed when Schultz's mother stepped on them, and they had to be repaired. Several electrical appliances, including a television set, burned up in electrical fires caused by the inadequate wiring. Schultz notified Glyco by letter on at least three occasions as to the need for repairs; but Glyco refused to inspect, repair, or reimburse Schultz for the cost of repairs. In August 1971, a farmer claiming under a lease from Glyco, entered the property and began plowing, including areas Schultz used as a garden, strawberry patch, and pasture for his pony. Then Schultz stopped using that part of the property. In November 1971, Schultz began paying only one half of the rent each month in order to try to secure repairs. This continued until March when Glyco brought suit to have him evicted for nonpayment of rent and to obtain the back rent owed. Schultz counterclaimed for damages. What decision should the court reach?

9. On October 1, Zankman entered into a two-year lease with Landlord for rental of an apartment which he intended to use not only as a residence but also as a place to make and receive business calls and correspondence. The lease was executed not only in Zankman's name but also in the name of New Jersey Steel Products. He paid his October and November rent but on December 1 notified the landlord that he would be late with his December rent payment. On December 29 he received a telegram advising him that unless his rent was paid by 11 A.M. the next day his apartment would be padlocked. On December 30, Zankman left to go to the drugstore to have a prescription filled and when he returned, his apartment had been padlocked. He was not allowed to remove his belongings until January 8. A New Jersey statute provides that "with regard to any property occupied solely as a residence by the party in possession, such entry shall not be made in any manner without the consent of the party in possession unless the entry and detention is made pursuant to legal process." Zankman claims the entry to his apartment to padlock it was unlawful. What conclusion would a court reach?

10. Mr. Gurian rented an apartment from East Haven Associates, Inc., on May 26, 1963, under a lease running until November 30, 1966. Early in 1965 the air-conditioning and incinerating systems began spewing material onto Gurian's terrace, rendering it unusable. In July 1966, Gurian vacated the apartment and refused to pay rent for the remaining four months of the lease. East Haven filed an action for this amount. What are the possible defenses available to Gurian and what are his chances of success?

chapter 32

Environmental Law

Introduction

Historical Perspective. The 1970s have become the decade of the environment as our nation, and indeed the world, has moved to reverse the longstanding degradation of our surroundings and to improve the quality of life. Historically people have assumed that the air, water, and land around them would absorb their waste products. But in recent times it has become clear that nature's capacity to assimilate people's wastes is not infinite. Burgeoning population, economic growth, affluence, and synthetic products that resist natural decomposition have contributed to environmental deterioration.

Concern about the environment existed long before the 1970s. In medieval England, Parliament passed "smoke control" acts making it illegal to burn soft coal at certain times of the year. Where the owner or operator of a piece of property is using it in such a manner as to unreasonably interfere with another owner's (or the public's) health or enjoyment of his or her property, the courts have long entertained suits to abate the nuisance. Nuisance actions, which are discussed in Chapters 4 and 30, are frequently not ideal vehicles for dealing with widespread pollution problems. Rather than a hit-or-miss approach, a comprehensive across-the-board approach is required. Realizing this, the federal government, as well as many state and local governments, had passed air-and-water-pollution abatement laws by the late 1950s and 1960s. As the 1970s began, an explosion of interest and concern over the quality and future of our environment produced new laws and a strong demand that action be taken to reverse the degradation.

The Environmental Protection Agency. In December 1970, the President created the Environmental Protection Agency (EPA) to consolidate the federal government's environmental responsibilities. This was an explicit recognition that the problems of air and water pollution, solid waste disposal, water supply, pesticides and radiation control were interrelated and required a coordinated approach. Hard on the establishment of EPA, Congress passed comprehensive new legislation covering, among other things, air and water pollution, pesticides, ocean dumping, and noise pollution. Among the factors prompting these laws were: protection of human health, esthetics, economic costs of continued pollution, and protection of natural systems. The public, acting through Congress, had expressed a strong desire for action. The next steps lay largely in the hands of federal, state, and local agencies, and in industry. As the laws are implemented, the consequences are felt by the individual citizen through environmental improvement on the one hand and through increased prices and changes in his or her lifestyle on the other hand. The next few years will find adjustments being made in our environmental laws and regulations as society decides how clean it wants its environment, how quickly it wants to proceed, and what costs it is willing to bear. Inherent in these societal decisions are questions of which resources to use, and at what rate, and which resources must be protected.

The National Environmental Policy Act.   The National Environmental Policy Act (NEPA) was signed into law on January 1, 1970. In addition to creating the Council of Environmental Quality in the Executive Office of the President, the act required that an environmental impact statement be prepared for every recommendation or report on legislation and in every major federal action significantly affecting the quality of the environment. The environmental impact statement must: (1) describe the environmental impact of the proposed action; (2) discuss impact that cannot be avoided; (3) discuss the alternatives to the proposed action; (4) indicate differences between short- and long-term impacts; and (5) detail any irreversible commitments of resources. NEPA has proven to be one of the most significant pieces of environmental legislation. For the first time federal agencies were required to consider the environmental impact of their actions before they undertook them. And, other federal, state, and local agencies, as well as interested citizens, have an opportunity to comment on the environmental impact of the project before the agency can proceed. Where the process is not followed, citizens can, and have, gone to court to force compliance with NEPA. Adherence by all governmental units, industry, and citizens to the NEPA concept—that the environmental impact of actions should be understood and minimized before they are undertaken—would do much to reduce environmental degradation. A number of states and local governments have passed their own environmental impact laws requiring NEPA-type statements for major public and private developments.

Summary

This decade has seen the passage of many new laws designed to protect the environment and the creation of new administrative agencies to enforce those laws. Older tools for protecting human health and welfare—such as the action to abate a nuisance—have to some extent been supplanted by comprehensive legislation prescribing across-the-board measures to deal with the major kinds and sources of pollution. The NEPA was passed to require the federal government to take into account the environmental effects of actions it proposes to take.

Daly v. Volpe

350 F.Supp. 252 (D.C. Dist. Col. 1972)

This was an action by Daly and others (plaintiffs) against the Secretary of Transportation, John Volpe, and the Washington State Department of Highways (defendants) to enjoin the construction of a federally funded highway on or near plaintiffs' property. Plaintiffs contended, among other things, that defendants had violated the provisions of the National Environmental Policy Act and in particular had failed to take into account the impact the highway would have on a wildlife preserve, Kimball Creek Marsh. Judgment for plaintiffs that the act had not been complied with.

BEEKS, JUDGE.   Plaintiffs contend that defendants failed to follow the required procedures with respect to drafting and filing an environmental impact statement. NEPA, which became law on January 1, 1970, requires that

all agencies of the Federal Government shall: . . .
  (C) include in every recommendation or report on proposals for legislation and other major Federal actions significantly affecting the quality of the human environment, a detailed statement by the responsible official on—
    (i)   the environmental impact of the proposed action.
    (ii)   any adverse environmental effects which cannot be avoided should the proposal be implemented.
    (iii) alternatives to the proposed action.
    (iv) the relationship between local short-term uses of man's environment and the maintenance and enhancement of long-term productivity, and
    (v)   any irreversible and irretrievable commitments of resources which would be involved in the proposed action should it be implemented.

*   *   *   *   *

The state's first-draft environmental impact statement was drafted in the form required by statute, but was ambiguous and self-contradictory. Paragraph one, concerning the environmental impact of the highway, failed to discuss Kimball Creek Marsh, and was too general and ambiguous.

The second paragraph was inadequate. All adverse environmental effects should be listed, and harmful effects which cannot be avoided must be discussed to indicate what measures can be taken to minimize the harm. The state's draft environmental impact statement was far too general and not sufficiently detailed.

*   *   *   *   *

The fifth paragraph of the draft impact statement is totally unsatisfactory. It should list, among other things, (1) the cost of land, construction materials, labor, and other economically measurable costs which cannot be retrieved once a highway is constructed; and (2) the resources which may be irretrievably lost, and the nature of each such loss, to which a dollar value cannot be readily assigned—for example, the loss of forested recreational land.

It is the judgment of the court that defendants have failed to conform to the procedural requirements of 42 U.S.C. (4332) [2] [C]. The state must prepare a draft environmental impact statement which conforms to those requirements, circulate it among interested agencies, and make it available to the public prior to another public location hearing. The state shall then prepare a final environmental impact statement, append to it a compilation of the comments received, and submit these, together with a new application for approval of the state's suggested location of I–90, to the Regional Federal Highway Administrator. Federal defendants shall then process the application according to existing regulations. Both the state and federal defendants shall carefully consider the ecological effects of the highway upon Kimball Creek Marsh.

Air Pollution

Introduction. The combustion of fuel, industrial processes, and solid waste disposal are the major contributors to air pollution. People's initial concern with air pollution related to that which they could see—visible or smoke pollution. In the 1880s, Chicago and Cincinnati enacted smoke control ordinances. As the technology became available to deal with smoke and particulate emissions, attention turned to other less visible gasses which impact human health and vegetation. The first federal legislation came in 1955 when Congress authorized $5 million each year for air pollution research. In 1963 the Clean Air Act was passed to provide assistance to the states and to deal with interstate air pollution; it was amended in 1965 and 1967 to provide for among other things, controls on pollution from automobiles. The comprehensive legislation enacted into law in December 1970 now provides the basis for our approach to the air pollution problem; its provisions are central to the discussion that follows.

1970 Clean Air Act. The 1970 Clean Air Act separates air pollution controls into essentially two categories: (1) controls on mobile or transportation sources, and (2) controls on stationary sources. The major pollutants from mobile sources such as automobiles and airplanes are carbon monoxide, hydrocarbons, and nitrogen oxides. Carbon monoxide is a colorless, odorless gas which can dull mental performance and even cause death when inhaled in large quantities. Hydrocarbons, which essentially are unburned fuel, combine with nitrogen oxides under the influence of sunlight to become photochemical oxidants—known as smog.

Automobile Pollution. The 1970 Clean Air Act required a reduction by 1975 of 90 percent in the amount of carbon monoxide and hydrocarbons emitted by automobiles and a likewise 90 percent reduction of nitrogen oxides by 1976. The administrator of EPA was empowered to grant a one-year extension of this deadline if technology to achieve the reduction is not available and if the manufacturers make a good-faith effort to meet the deadline. The act also provided for regulation and registration of fuel additives such as lead, as well as for regulation of emissions from aircraft.

Pollution from Other Sources. The 1970 Clean Air Act established a comprehensive approach for dealing with air pollution from stationary sources. The EPA was required to set national ambient air-quality standards for the major pollutants which have an adverse impact on human health—that is, to set the amount of a given pollutant that could be present in air around us. The ambient air-quality standards were to be set at two levels: (1) *primary* standards which are designed to protect public health from harm; and (2) *secondary* standards which are designed to protect vegetation, materials, climate, visibility, and economic values. Pursuant to this statutory mandate, EPA set ambient air-quality standards for carbon monoxide, nitrogen oxide, sulfur oxide, hydrocarbons, photochemical oxidents, and particulates.

The country was divided into air-quality regions, and each region was required to have an implementation plan for meeting the national ambient air-quality standards. This necessitates an inventory of the various sources of air pollution and their contribution to the total air pollution in the air-quality region. The major emitters of pollutants are then required to reduce their emissions to a level that will enable the overall air quality to meet the national standards. The states have the responsibility for deciding which activities must be regulated or curtailed to meet the national standards.

The act also requires that new stationary sources must install the best available technology for reducing air pollution. EPA was required to establish standards to be met by new stationary sources and has done so for the major types of stationary sources of air pollution. The primary responsibility for enforcing the air-quality standards lies with the states, but the federal government also has the right to enforce the standards where the states fail to do so. The Clean Air Act also provides for suits by citizens to force industry or the government to fully comply with the act's provisions.

Summary

The Clean Air Act of 1970 separates air pollution controls into two categories: (1) mobile sources; and (2) stationary sources. The act sets out time schedules by which certain control measures must be instituted in order to protect human health and the general welfare from harm attributable to air pollution.

International Harvester Co. v. Ruckelshaus

478 F.2d 615 (D.C. Cir. 1973)

This was an action brought by International Harvester Company, General Motors Corporation, Ford Motors Corporation, and Chrysler Corporation (plaintiffs) against the Administrator of the U.S. Environmental Protection Agency, William D. Ruckelshaus (defendant) challenging the administrator's May 1972 decision not to grant them a one-year postponement of the 1975 standards set by the Clean Air Act of 1970. Judgment for plaintiffs.

LEVENTHAL, CIRCUIT JUDGE: These consolidated petitions of International Harvester and the three major auto companies—Ford, General Motors, and Chrysler— seek review of a decision by the Administrator of the Environmental Protection Agency denying petitioners' applications, filed pursuant to Section 202 of the Clean Air Act, for one-year suspensions of the 1975 emission standards prescribed under the statute for light duty vehicles in the absence of suspension.

The tension of forces presented by the controversy over automobile emission standards may be focused by two central observations:

(1)   The automobile is an essential pillar of the American economy. Some 28 percent of the nonfarm workforce draws its livelihood from the automobile industry and its products.

(2)   The automobile has had a devastating impact on the American environment. As of 1970, authoritative voices stated that "[a]utomotive pollution constitutes in excess of 60 percent of our national air pollution problem" and more than 80 percent of the air pollutants in concentrated urban areas.

Congressional concern over the problem of automotive emissions dates back to the 1950s, but it was not until the passage of the Clean Air Act in 1965 that Congress established the principle of Federal standards for automobile emissions. Under the 1965 act and its successor, the Air Quality Act of 1967, the Department of Health, Education and Welfare was authorized to promulgate emission limitations commensurate with existing technological feasibility.

The development of emission control technology proceeded haltingly. The Secretary of HEW testified in 1967 that "the state of the art has tended to meander along until some sort of regulation took it by the hand and gave it a good pull. . . . There has been a long period of waiting for it, and it hasn't worked very well."

The legislative background must also take into account the fact that in 1969 the Department of Justice brought suit against the four largest automobile manufacturers on grounds that they had conspired to delay the development of emission control devices.

On December 31, 1970, Congress grasped the nettle and amended the Clean Air Act to set a statutory standard for required reductions in levels of hydrocarbons (HC) and carbon monoxide (CO) which must be achieved for 1975 models of light duty vehicles. Section 202(b) of the Act added by the Clean Air Amendments of 1970, provides that, beginning with the 1975 model year, exhaust emission of hydrocarbons and carbon monoxide from "light duty vehicles" must be reduced at least 90 percent from the permissible emission levels in the 1970 model year. In accordance with the Congressional directives, the administrator on June 23, 1971, promulgated regulations limiting HC and CO emissions from 1975 model light duty vehicles to .41 and 3.4 grams per vehicle mile respectively. 36 Fed. Reg. 12,657 (1971). At the same time, as required by section 202(b) (2) of the Act, he prescribed the test procedures by which compliance with these standards is measured.

Congress was aware that these 1975 standards were "drastic medicine," designed to "force the state of the art." There was, naturally, concern whether the manufacturers would be able to achieve this goal. Therefore, Congress provided, in Senator Baker's phrase, a "realistic escape hatch": the manufacturers could petition the Administrator of the EPA for a one-year suspension of the 1975 requirements.

* * * * *

This case inevitably presents, to the court as to the administrator, the need for a perspective on the suspension that is informed by an analysis which balances the costs of a "wrong decision" on feasibility against the gains of a correct one. These costs include the risks of grave maladjustments for the technological leader from the eleventh-hour grant of a suspension, and the impact on jobs and the economy from a decision which is only partially accurate, allowing companies to produce cars but at a significantly reduced level of output. Against this must be weighed the environmental savings from denial of suspension. The record indicates that these will be relatively modest. There is also the possibility that failure to grant a suspension may be counterproductive to the environment, if there is significant decline in performance characteristics.

Another consideration is present, that the real cost to granting a suspension arises from the symbolic compromise with the goal of a clean environment. We emphasize that our view of a one-year suspension, and the intent of Congress as to a one-year suspension, is in no sense to be taken as any support for further suspensions. This would plainly be contrary to the intent of Congress to set an absolute standard in 1976. On the contrary, we view the imperative of the Congressional requirement as to the significant improvement that must be wrought no later than 1976, as interrelated with the provision for one-year suspension. The flexibility in the statute provided by the availability of a one-year suspension only strengthens the impact of the absolute standard. Considerations of fairness will support comprehensive and firm, even drastic, regulations, provided a "safety valve" is also provided—ordinarily a provision for waiver, exception or adjustment, in this case a provision for suspension. "The limited safety valve permits a more rigorous adherence to an effective regulation." *WAIT Radio v. FCC, supra,* 418 F.2d at 1159. To hold the safety valve too rigidly is to interfere with the relief that was contemplated as an integral part of the firmness of the overall, enduring program.

Water Pollution

Introduction. History is replete with plague and epidemics brought on by poor sanitation and polluted water. Indeed, preventing waterborne disease has through time been the major reason to combat water pollution. Among the more tragic symbols of our time are the oil-soaked seagull, a river that catches on fire, a rapidly euthrophying Lake Erie, and a "No Swimming—Water Polluted" sign near a swimming hole. Water pollution can affect public health, recreation, commercial fishing, agriculture, water supplies, and esthetics. Accordingly, our current efforts to combat water pollution have a broad range of reasons to support them.

Federal Legislation.   Federal water pollution legislation dates back to the 19th century when Congress enacted the River and Harbor Act of 1886. In fact this act, recodified in the River and Harbor Act of 1899, furnished the legal basis for the EPA's initial enforcement actions against polluters. The act provided that anyone discharging or depositing "refuse" into a navigable waterway had to obtain a discharge permit first from the Corps of Engineers. Under contemporary court decisions even hot water discharged from nuclear power plants was considered "refuse." The permit system established pursuant to the "Refuse Act" has subsequently been replaced by a permit system set up by the Federal Water Pollution Control Act Amendments of 1972.

The initial Federal Water Pollution Control Act (FWPCA) was passed in 1948. Amendments to the FWPCA in 1956, 1965, 1966, and 1970 increased the federal role in water pollution abatement and strengthened its enforcement powers. Gradually, the federal government has begun to pay a larger and larger share of the costs of building municipal sewage treatment plants; under the 1972 Amendments the federal share is now 75 percent with the remainder being put up by state and local governments.

Clean Waters Act of 1972.   The 1972 Amendments to the FWPCA were as comprehensive in the water pollution field as the 1970 Clean Air Act was in the air pollution field. They proclaimed two general goals for this country: (1) to achieve wherever possible by July 1, 1983, water that is clean enough for swimming and other recreational uses, and clean enough for the protection and propagation of fish, shellfish, and wildlife; and (2) by 1985 to have no discharges of pollutants into the nation's waters. The goals reflected a national frustration with the progress made to date in dealing with water pollution and a commitment to end such pollution. The new law set out a series of specific actions to be taken by certain dates by federal, state, and local governments, and by industry and also provided strong enforcement provisions to back up the deadlines.

The 1972 Amendments left the primary responsibility for preventing, reducing, and eliminating water pollution with the states but provided that they had to do it within a national framework with the EPA empowered to move in if the states do not fulfill their responsibilities. The law set a number of deadlines to control water pollution from industrial sources: (1) industries discharging wastes into the nation's waterways must install the "best practicable" water pollution control technology by July 1, 1977, and must have the "best available" technology on line by July 1, 1983. New sources of industrial pollution must use the "best available demonstrated control technology." In each instance EPA is responsible for issuing guidelines as to the "best available" and "best practicable" technologies. Industries that discharge their wastes into municipal systems are required to pretreat their wastes so that they will not interfere with the biological operation of the plant or pass through the plant without treatment.

The 1972 law continues and expands the previously established system of setting water quality standards which define the uses of specific bodies of water—such as recreational, public water supply, propagation of fish and wildlife, and agricultural and industrial water supply. Then the maximum daily loads of various kinds of pollutants are set so that the water will be suitable for the designated type of use. The 1972 law requires that all municipal and industrial dischargers must obtain permits which will spell out the amounts and types of pollutants the permit holder will be allowed to discharge and any steps it must take to reduce its present or anticipated discharge. Polluters are also required to keep records, install and maintain monitoring equipment, and sample their discharges. Penalties for violating the law range from a minimum of $2,500 for a first offense up to $50,000 per day and two years in prison for subsequent violations.

Citizen Suits.   Any citizen or group of citizens whose interests are adversely affected has the right to take court action against anyone violating an effluent standard or limitation or an order issued by EPA or a state. Citizens also have the right to take court action against the EPA if it fails to carry out mandatory provisions of the law.

Ocean Dumping.   The Marine Protection, Research, and Sanctuaries Act of 1972 set up a permit system regulating the dumping of all types of materials into ocean waters. Thus the nation's concern over the impact of people's actions on the environment is extended to marine areas contiguous to our shores.

Summary

Water pollution has posed potential health problems for people for many years. Federal water pollution control legislation was first passed in 1948 and has been amended five times since then. The 1972 amendments set two major goals for this country: (1) swimmable water wherever possible by 1983, and (2) no discharge of pollutants into the nation's waters by 1985. To facilitate achievement of these goals, the amendments set out a series of strict interim deadlines which must be met by governments and private industry.

Reserve Mining Co. v. Minnesota Pollution Control Agency

2 E.R.C. 1135 (Minn. Dist. Ct., Lake County 1970)

This was an action brought by the Reserve Mining Company (plaintiff) against the Minnesota Pollution Control Agency (defendant) to obtain a variance from a regulation limiting discharges of effluent to Lake Superior. The variance was granted subject to continued jurisdiction of the Court.

Reserve Mining is a taconite mining and processing company which in the course of its operations discharged about 67,000 tons per day of an industrial waste called taconite tailings into Lake Superior along with 600,000 gallons of water. In 1947, Reserve was given permits by the Minnesota Pollution Control Agency and the Minnesota Department of Conservation allowing it to discharge the tailings and wastewater into a 9-square-mile area of Lake Superior where they would be carried into a deep trough in the lake some 600–900 feet deep. In 1956 and in 1960, the permits were amended to increase the amount of water Reserve Mining could withdraw from the lake and the amount of wastewater and tailings that could be discharged. In reliance on the permits, Reserve Mining increased its investment at the site until at the time of the suit its capital investment totalled $350,000,000, and it employed 3,300 people.

In 1969, under pressure from the federal government and after conducting public hearings, the Minnesota Pollution Control Agency adopted Regulation WPC 15 which limited discharges of solids to Lake Superior to 30 milligrams per liter of water. The Reserve Mining discharge has a concentration of about 28,000 milligrams per liter. Reserve Mining then went to court to appeal the application to it of WPC15, claiming present enforcement would be unreasonable and would constitute an unconstitutional taking of its property.

ECKMAN, DISTRICT JUDGE.   Minnesota Statutes § 115.01, Subd. 5, defines pollutions as follows:

Pollution means the contamination of any waters of the state so as to create a nuisance or render such waters unclean, or noxious, or impure so as to be actually or potentially harmful or detrimental or injurious to public health, safety or welfare, to domestic, commercial, industrial or recreational use, or to livestock, wild animals, birds, fish or other aquatic life.

In applying this statutory definition to the voluminous evidence, both oral and documentary; the court concludes that there was lacking the required substantial evidence by the Control Agency to convince this court that the discharge of tailings by Reserve after 15 years of operation, had "rendered the waters unclean or noxious or impure thereby."

The only exception of convincing quality was the increased display of the "green water phenomenon" and the disappearance of a proportion of the scud, a small shell creature which serves as a food for smelt and small trout. Although measurable, these conditions were of minimal significance or materiality.

The question of potential harm to the lake water then became the greatest concern of the court. This facet also became the main thrust of the Control Agency's attack. Control Agency's experts, while admitting there had been no measurable deterioration of water quality to date, maintained that the chemical and bacterial content of the tailings were of such significance that they would result in eutrophication by nutrient feeding of algae, and paradoxically, the reduction of algae in the zone of discharge as a limiting factor. They opined, therefore, that the tailings had or would have a pollutant effect on the lake. These findings and opinions were denied by Reserve's experts. And so the court, completely lacking in personal expertise, found itself in the impossible position of being required to analyze, weigh, and choose between these controversial points of view. There was scant consolation to the court in the remark of Dr. Donald Mount who, evidently recognizing the court's dilemma, stated while testifying, "The court has my sympathy."

In view of the absence of definitive measurements of pollution in quantity or time, with consideration to the assimilative capacity of Lake Superior, the court would be indulging in speculation to make a determination that the discharge was or was not a potential source of pollution to Lake Superior. Nevertheless, the vital importance of maintaining the lake in its present oligotrophic state demands that definitive steps be taken to remedy any condition that may possibly be a source of even potential irremedial damage. It is in fact a socio-legal problem and is entitled to those remedies. And so, in view of the refusal or inability of the parties to negotiate, compromise, or agree on even temporary solutions, the court has concluded that Reserve Mining Company's present method of discharge must not be allowed to continue as it has over the next 40 years—and neither must the Control Agency be given the instrument that would in effect require prohibitive compliance.

The court's continuing jurisdiction is essential to insure the establishment of a modified method of discharge by good-faith cooperative discussions between the parties. The type and extent of Reserve's modifications are not for the court to dictate at this time. The minimum efforts in that regard are set forth in some limited detail in Reserve's Exhibit 67 entitled "Engineering Task Force Report," and will require Reserve to assume the burden of expending millions of dollars in capital outlay and expense of operation. The public is entitled to this.

In the judgment of this court, any modification must insure the flocculation of the fine tailings and the deposit of all the tailings by conduit to the floor of the great trough, where they will remain, eliminating thereby their dispersion to other parts of Lake Superior, and elimination of complaints of aesthetic loss, net or shore slime, drinking-water contamination, or eutrophication by increased algal growth. In support of this solution, the court has gleaned from the Control Agency's experts that the deposit of the tailings on the lake floor in a relatively quiescent condition would substantially remove their apprehensions as to their effect upon the lake's ecology, aesthetics, or navigation.

Pesticides and Toxic Substances

Introduction. The vast increase in productivity over the past few decades of the American farmer has in large measure been attributable to the farmer's use of chemicals to kill the insects, pests, and weeds that have historically competed with him or her for his or her crops. Some of the chemicals, like pesticides, were a mixed blessing. They enabled people to dramatically increase productivity and to conquer disease. On the other hand, dead fish and birds provided evidence that some of the chemicals were building up in the food chain and were proving fatal to some species. Gradually people awoke to the realization that man was introducing millions of pounds of chemicals into the environment each year with little or no appreciation of the long term consequences or effects.

Federal Pesticide Legislation.   The federal responsibility for dealing with pesticides was given to the EPA in December of 1970. EPA enforces the Federal Insecticide, Fungicide, and Rodenticide Act of 1947 (FIFRA) as amended recently by the Federal Environmental Pesticide Control Act of 1972 (FEPCA). This act gives EPA the authority to register pesticides before they can be sold, to provide for certification of applicators of pesticides designated for "restrictive" use, to set tolerances on the amount of pesticide residue on crops that provide food for people or animals, and to register and inspect pesticide manufacturing establishments.

Suspension and Cancellation.   When the administrator of EPA has reason to believe that continued use of a particular pesticide poses an "imminent hazard" he or she may suspend its registration and remove it from the market. In those situations where the administrator believes there is less than an imminent hazard but where the environmental risks of continuing to use a pesticide outweigh its benefits, the administrator may initiate a cancellation of registration proceeding. This proceeding affords all interested persons—manufacturers, distributors, users, environmentalists, and scientists—an opportunity to present evidence on the proposed cancellation. Cancellation of the registration occurs when the administrator finds that the product will cause "unreasonable adverse effects on the environment."

Toxic Substances.   Other current legislation is focused on other toxic substances—such as mercury—and some of the new chemical compounds developed each year. The thrust of this legislation, like that concerning pesticides, is that people should have some idea of the anticipated impact on the environment release of a new chemical or substance will have before releasing it. This philosophy relates to the philosophy behind the NEPA, that people should carefully consider the environmental consequences of any major step he plans to take.

Summary

Use of agricultural chemicals in the last few years has led to vast increases in productivity and at the same time posed increased risks to the environment. The Federal Environmental Pesticide Control Act of 1972 gives the EPA the responsibility to register pesticides before they can be sold, to restrict their use, to set tolerances on residues on food products, and to provide for the certification of applicators. Pesticides whose risks outweigh their benefits may have their registration cancelled or suspended.

Consolidated DDT Hearings
Opinion and Order of the Administrator

37 Fed. Reg. 13369 (1972)

This was an action taken by the administrator of the Environmental Protection Agency cancelling the registration of most of the uses of DDT.

On January 15, 1971, the Environmental Protection Agency commenced formal administrative review of all registrations for DDT products and uses pursuant to section 4(c) of the Federal Insecticide, Fungicide, and Rodenticide Act. Thirty-one companies holding DDT registrations challenged the EPA's cancellation of DDT use registrations. The U.S. Department of Agriculture intervened on the side of the registrants, and the Environmental Defense Fund intervened along with the EPA to help present the case for cancellation.

After a lengthy public hearing, on April 25, 1972, the hearing examiner issued an opinion recommending to the administrator of EPA that all "essential" uses of DDT be retained and that cancellation be lifted. The administrator took the opinion under advisement and received oral and written briefs both supporting and taking exception to the hearing officer's findings of fact and conclusions of law. The administrator then issued his opinion and order cancelling virtually all uses of DDT as of December 31, 1972, except for use on several minor crops and its use for disease control and health-related uses.

WILLIAM D. RUCKELSHAUS, ADMINISTRATOR.   This hearing represents the culmination of approximately 3 years of intensive administrative inquiry into the uses of DDT.

* * * * *

Background. DDT is the familiar abbreviation for the chemical (1,1,1,trichloro-phenyl ethane), which was for many years the most widely used chemical pesticide in this country. DDT's insecticidal properties were originally discovered, apparently by accident, in 1939, and during World War II it was used extensively for typhus control. Since 1945, DDT has been used for general control of mosquitoes, boll-weevil infestation in cotton-growing areas, and a variety of other uses. Peak use of DDT occurred at the end of the 1950's and present domestic use of DDT in various formulations has been estimated at 6,000 tons per year. According to Admission 7 of the record, approximately 86 percent or 10,277,258 pounds of domestically used DDT is applied to cotton crops. The same admission indicates that 603,053 pounds and 937,901 pounds, or approximately 5 percent and 9 percent of the total formulated by 27 of the petitioners in these hearings, are used respectively on soybean and peanut crops. All other uses of the 11,966,196 pounds amount to 158,833 of the total, or little over 1 percent.

For the above uses it appears that DDT is sold in four different formulations: emulsifiable sprays; dust; wettable powder; and granular form.

Public concern over the widespread use of pesticides was stirred by Rachel Carson's book *Silent Spring* and a natural outgrowth was the investigation of this popular and widely sprayed chemical. DDT, which for many years had been used with apparent safety, was, the critics alleged, a highly dangerous substance which killed beneficial insects, upset the natural ecological balance, and collected in the food chain, thus posing a hazard to man, and other forms of advanced aquatic and avian life.

* * * * *

Application of risk-benefit to crop uses of DDT. The Agency and EDF have established that DDT is toxic to nontarget insects and animals, persistent, mobile, and transferable and that it builds up in the food chain. No label directions for use can completely prevent these hazards. In short, they have established at the very least the risk of the unknown. That risk is compounded where, as is the case with DDT, man and animals tend to accumulate and store the chemical. These facts alone constitute risks that are unjustified where apparently safer alternatives exist to achieve the same benefit. Where, however, there is a demonstrated laboratory relationship between the chemical and toxic effects in man or animals, this risk is, generally speaking, rendered even more unacceptable, if alternatives exist. In the case before us the risk to human health from using DDT cannot be discounted. While these risks might be acceptable were we forced to use DDT, they are not so trivial that we can be indifferent to assuming them unnecessarily.

The evidence of record showing storage in man and magnification in the food chain is a warning to the prudent that man may be exposing himself to a substance that may ultimately have a serious effect on his health.

As Judge Leventhal recently pointed out, cancer is a "sensitive and fright-laden" matter and noted earlier in his opinion that carcinogenic effects are "generally cumulative and irreversible when discovered." *EDF v. EPA.* The possibility that DDT is a carcinogen is at present remote and unquantifiable; but if it is not a siren to panic, it is a semaphore which suggests that an identifiable public benefit is required to justify continued use of DDT. Where one chemical tests tumorigenic in a laboratory and one does not, and both accomplish the same risk, the latter is to be preferred, absent some extenuating circumstances.

The risks to the environment from continued use of DDT are more clearly established. There is no doubt that DDT runoff can cause contamination of waters and given its propensity to volatilize and disperse during application, there is no assurance that curtailed usage on the order of 12 million pounds per year will not continue to affect widespread areas beyond the location of application. The agency staff established as well, the existence of acceptable substitutes for all crop uses of DDT except on onions and sweet potatoes in storage and green peppers.

Registrants attempted but failed to surmount the evidence of established risks and the existence of substitutes by arguing that the buildup of DDT in the environment and its migration to remote areas has resulted from past uses and misuses. There is, however, no persuasive evidence of record to show that the aggregate volume of use of DDT for all uses in question, given the method of application, will not result in continuing dispersal and buildup in the environment and thus add to or maintain the stress on the environment resulting from past use. The Department of Agriculture has, for its part, emphasized DDT's low acute toxicity in comparison to that of alternative chemicals and thus tried to make the risk and benefit equation balance out favorably for the continued use of DDT. While the acute toxicity of methyl parathion must, in the short run, be taken into account, it does not justify continued use of DDT on a long-term basis. Where a chemical can be safely used if label directions are followed, a producer cannot avoid the risk of his own negligence by exposing third parties and the environment to a long-term hazard.

Accordingly, all crop uses of DDT are hereby canceled except for application to onions for control of cutworm, weevils on stored sweet potatoes, and sweet peppers.

Noise Pollution and Radiation Control

Noise Control Act of 1972. Noise pollution—or unwanted sound—has become an undesirable and sometimes dangerous aspect of modern life. Although there is some local and federal legislation now on the books dealing with noise pollution, our efforts to control it are very much in the embryonic stage. In the Noise Control Act of 1972 Congress mandated the Federal Aviation Administration and the Environmental Protection Agency to prescribe standards and regulations for the control and abatement of aircraft noise and sonic boom; the Department of Transportation and the EPA were directed to promulgate standards and regulations relating to noise emissions of interstate railroad and motor carriers. The act further authorizes the administrator of EPA to set regulations for products designated as major noise sources where such standards are feasible.

Local ordinances sometimes specify the hours each day during which construction work on buildings and streets may be performed and commonly require mufflers on motor vehicles. The noise pollution area is of considerable interest to the prospective businessman because it is a factor he is likely to have to take into account in the design of his products and in the operation of his business.

Radiation Control. The rapidly escalating demand for energy combined with the finite availability of fossil fuels has intensified the need for nuclear-fueled power plants. This need has coincided with increased citizen concern with radioactivity. Citizen concerns specifically related to nuclear plants include: possible release of radioactivity into the environment during normal operation of the nuclear reactor, possible accidents through human error or mechanical failure, and the disposal of the radioactive wastes generated by the reactor. There is also concern that the discharge of heated water used to cool the reactor—thermal pollution—may cause irreversible damage to the environment.

Currently, the problems of reactor safety are under the jurisdiction of the Atomic Energy Commission which exercises licensing authority over nuclear power plants. The Environmental Protection Agency has the responsibility for setting standards for radioactivity in the overall environment and for dealing with the radioactive waste disposal problem. The thermal pollution problem is handled by EPA pursuant to its water pollution control authorities.

Summary

As the amount of unwanted noise present in our environment has increased, the federal and local governments have enacted legislation aimed at controlling some of the most offensive sources of noise. As the demand for energy increases, the country is utilizing more and more nuclear energy to satisfy the demand. The regulation of radiation problems occasioned by nuclear reactors is largely done at the federal level by the Environmental Protection Agency and the Atomic Energy Commission.

Northern States Power Co. v. Minnesota

447 F.2d 1143 (8th Cir. 1971)

This was an action brought by the Northern States Power Company (plaintiff) against the State of Minnesota and the Minnesota Pollution Control Agency (defendants) seeking a judgment declaring Minnesota to be without authority to regulate radioactive wastes from a nuclear power plant Northern States was constructing. Judgment for Northern States. Affirmed.

Northern States Power Company, which produces, transmits, and sells electric power in several states, was constructing a nuclear power plant at Monticello. The plant was in compliance with the federal regulations regarding the release of radioactive wastes, but the State of Minnesota sought to impose substantially more stringent requirements regarding such release than those of the U.S. Atomic Energy Commission.

MATTHES, CHIEF JUDGE.   The central question posed by this litigation is whether the United States government has the sole authority under the doctrine of preemption to regulate radioactive waste releases from nuclear power plants to the exclusion of the states. The United States District Court for the District of Minnesota answered affirmatively and its decision is here for review. We affirm.

* * * * *

In urging reversal of the district court's judgment, Minnesota asserts that the regulation of radioactive waste releases to the environment is within the State's traditional power under the Tenth Amendment to protect and promote the health, safety and general welfare of its citizens. Minnesota also vigorously maintains that the Atomic Energy Act of 1954, as amended, neither expressly nor impliedly preempts the State's authority to regulate radioactive waste releases by nuclear power plants. Finally, Minnesota contends that even if Congress did intend to preempt this area of regulation, this would not preclude concomitant regulation by the State. Conversely, in support of the district court's judgment, Northern asserts that the Act, as amended, together with its legislative history, evince a clear Congressional intent that the AEC have exclusive authority and control over the disputed field of regulation. In support of its position of federal preemption, Northern also argues that the development and utilization of nuclear energy is an area demanding uniform policies and controls which can only properly be effectuated on a national scale.

It is appropriate to observe that the question of federal preemption of the subject matter involved is one of first impressions in the federal appellate courts. We realize too that our decision may affect future relationships between other states and other public utility companies who enter the still evolutionary field of nuclear-reactor energy production. The many amici briefs filed in this appeal have not only been helpful in our consideration of this case, but have served as an indicator of the widespread interest generated by this litigation. Finally, we are cognizant that apart from the significant and controlling legal issue, the subject of this appeal is collaterally pervaded by currently compelling controversies concerning the need to supply power to an ever-burgeoning population, coupled with the newly recognized importance of maintaining an ecological balance and also with the whole Pandora's box of problems in the area of federal–state relationships and responsibilities.

The doctrine of federal preemption has its roots in Article VI, Clause 2 of the United States Constitution, the "Supremacy Clause," which elevates federal law above that of the States. It provides:

This Constitution, and the Laws of the United States which shall be made in Pursuance thereof; and all Treaties made, or which shall be made, under the Authority of the United States, shall be the supreme Law of the Land; and the Judges in every State shall be bound thereby, any Thing in the Constitution or Laws of any State to the Contrary notwithstanding.

On the other hand, under the Tenth Amendment to the Constitution "[t]he powers not delegated to the United States by the Constitution, nor prohibited by it to the States, are reserved to the States respectively, or to the people."

* * * * *

The nature of the subject matter regulated and the need for uniform controls in order to effectuate the objectives of Congress are additionally supportive of a finding of preemption. In enacting the Atomic Energy Act of 1954, Congress made specific findings concerning the development, use, and control of atomic energy. Included in these findings are a number of statements to the effect that the processing and utilization of source, by-product, and special nuclear material must be regulated by the United States in the national interest because of their effect upon interstate and foreign commerce and in order to provide for the common defense and security and to protect the health and safety of the public.

However, Minnesota vigorously maintains that the subject matter regulated in the instant case is confined to the narrow area of pollution control over the radioactive effluents discharged from the Monticello plant and that this is peculiarly related to the public health and safety of its state's citizens and therefore within their police powers to control. (See *Huron Portland Cement Co. v. Detroit,* 362 U.S. 440 (1960).) They contend that this is not an area which by its very nature admits only of national supervision nor one demanding exclusive federal regulation in order to achieve uniformity vital to national interests. (*Florida Lime & Avocado Growers, Inc. v. Paul.*)

We cannot acquiesce in this microcosmic approach to the subject matter to be regulated. As discussed earlier, regulation of the radioactive effluents discharged from a nuclear power plant is inextricably intertwined with the planning, construction, and entire operation of the facility. As Northern points out and as the record reveals, major generating plants not only produce electric power for customers in their own and neighboring states but are part of an interstate transmission system which makes possible the purchase and sale of electric power between major systems across the nation. Congressional objectives expressed in the 1954 Act evince a legislative design to foster and encourage the development, use, and control of atomic energy so as to make the maximum contribution to the general welfare and to increase the standard of living. (42 U.S.C. §§ 2011, 2012.) However, these objectives were to be effectuated "to the maximum extent consistent with the common defense and security and with the health and safety of the public." (42 U.S.C. § 2013.) Thus, through direction of the licensing scheme for nuclear reactors, Congress vested the AEC with the authority to resolve the proper balance between desired industrial progress and adequate health and safety standards. Only through the application and enforcement of uniform standards promulgated by a national agency will these dual objectives be assured. Were the states allowed to impose stricter standards on the level of radioactive waste releases discharged from nuclear power plants, they might conceivably be so overprotective in the area of health and safety as to unnecessarily stultify the industrial development and use of atomic energy for the production of electric power.

Problem Cases

1. The Interstate Commerce Commission (ICC) has the power to approve or to set the tariff rates to be charged shippers by railroads. As a result of past ICC approval, the railroad tariffs call for higher shipping charges to carry scrap metals and paper than for carrying virgin materials. This disparity operates as an economic discrimination against recycled goods. A group of law students have formed an organization known as SCRAP (Students Challenging Regulatory Agency Procedures). SCRAP is concerned that the ICC approved rate structure discourages the environmentally desirable use of recycled goods. On April 24, 1972, the ICC approved a 2.5 percent across the board surcharge on railroad shippinig rates and indicated that no environmental impact statement was necessary because there was "no environmental impact." SCRAP is concerned that the increase will further the discrimination against used materials. Should an environmental impact statement be required?

2. Washington D.C.'s National Airport is owned by the Federal government and operated by the Federal Aviation Administration. A group of citizens who lived and worked in the vicinity of National Airport were concerned about the congestion, noise, and air pollution accompanying the heavy use of National while two other area airports, Dulles and Friendship, were substantially underutilized. In 1968, the FAA permitted the airlines servicing National to replace 727–100 model planes with the 727–200 model planes known as "stretch jets." The 727–200 is about 15–20 feet longer and can carry 120 passengers, as opposed to the 98 carried by the 727–100. There is some evidence that the 727–200 is quieter, safer, and rarely, if ever, loaded to a gross maximum weight greater than that of the 727–100.

The group of citizens filed suit against the FAA, contending that the introduction of "stretch jets" required an environmental impact statement pursuant to NEPA. Should an impact statement be required?

3. Bortz Coal Company operates 70 beehive coke ovens which were built in 1898. The ovens emit a considerable amount of air pollutants in the form of particulate matter. Beginning in 1963, the state air-pollution control authorities began discussing Bortz's violation of the state air-pollution control law. Finally, in 1970 the Air Pollution Commission issued an abatement order requiring Bortz to comply with the state law and to conduct their operations in such manner that the air contaminants produced were not detectable beyond the plant's property line. Bortz appeals the order to the court, contending that it cannot practically or feasibly meet the standards and will be forced out of business. This result, Bortz contends, constitutes a confiscation of its property without due process of law. The state agrees that there is no known way for old beehive ovens to be controlled so as to meet the standards set by the state to protect the health of the inhabitants. Should the court decide that Bortz has been illegally deprived of its property?

4. Conkey owns a farm through which run Mill Creek and Goose Ditch. For years the City of Walla Walla has been depositing treated effluent from its sewage treatment plant into Mill Creek and Goose Ditch, and for years Conkey, whose property is located downstream from the plant, has been using the water for farm-irrigation purposes. In 1927, a court decree required the City of Walla Walla to "treat, purify or otherwise sterilize" its sewage waters to the end that they "may be used for irrigation purposes." This decree benefits the property owned by Conkey. Because of increased population and industrial expansion, sewage was created far in excess of amounts the city could treat and purify at their treatment plant. As a result, Conkey's sprinkling system became plugged, the pollution covered the creek and ditch bed with a slimy material, and the area was permeated by noxious odors. What action might Conkey take against the City?

5. In 1958 Congress passed the Federal Aviation Act establishing the Federal Aviation Agency and vesting it with "plenary authority to (a) allocate airspace and control its use by both civil and military aircraft." The House Report on the act stated in pertinent part that "The principal purpose of this legislation is to establish a new federal agency with powers adequate to enable it to provide for the safe and efficient use of the navigable airspace and control its use by both civil and military operations." The City of Burbank enacted an ordinance prohibiting the takeoffs by jet aircraft from the Hollywood-Burbank Airport between 11:00 P.M. and 7:00 A.M. The airlines using the Hollywood-Burbank Airport challenge the ordinance, contending that the federal government had preempted the field of regulation of air traffic so as to invalidate the ordinance. What arguments would you make on behalf of the airlines? How should the court decide the question?

6. In 1931, the Tweed-New Haven Airport opened as a turf airport, without paved runways or navigational aids, other than a few lights. In 1941, two paved runways were constructed, one of which has remained unchanged since then and the other of which has been twice enlarged. During the 1950s various navigational aids were installed and in 1969 a control tower was constructed. The airport has always been used by private aircraft; during the 1950s and 1960s commercial traffic was instituted by several major airlines which currently operate jets in and out of Tweed-New Haven seven times a day. A group of local residents who purchased their houses in the flight path to the airport in 1954, 1956, 1959, and 1962, respectively, now bring suit against the airport complaining that the noise, smoke, soot, and fumes constitute a nuisance substantially interferring with their use of their property. Other nearby residents also join the suit complaining in addition about broken windows and fear of airplane crashes in their neighborhood. The residents seek an injunction against further operation of the airport. Should the injunction be granted?

Part VIII

Sales

chapter 33

Formation and Terms
of Sales Contracts

Introduction

Nature of Sales and the Law of Sales. A sale, as the term is used in the law of sales, consists of the transferring of the ownership of goods, for a consideration, from one person to another. Modern courts do not attempt to distinguish between a sale and a contract to sell since the technical sale is preceded or accompanied by an agreement, which is supported by consideration, to transfer the ownership of the goods.

A majority of the rules and standards of law relating to the sale of goods deal with the formation, terms, obligations, performance and remedies of the sales contract. The law of sales is based on the fundamental principles of contract and personal property law. However, the vast variety of transactions involved in the marketing of goods has necessitated the development of special rules and standards which apply primarily to sales transactions. The developments in the law of sales have kept pace with the practices of merchants. Many of the technical requirements recognized and enforced in contract and property law serve no purpose in the marketplace and have been replaced with rules which assure to the merchant a more just and equitable result.

Uniform Commercial Code—Sales. Article 2 of the Uniform Commercial Code—Sales—does not follow the organization of the Uniform Sales Act nor does it adhere to its philosophy. The objective of the drafters of Article 2 of the Code was to clarify the law of sales and to recognize the developments which had taken place during the 50 years the Uniform Sales Act had been in force. The law of sales was not revolutionized by the adoption of the Code but some important changes were made.

It will be recalled from the chapters treating the principles of contract law that special Code rules are set out for the formation of contracts involving sale of goods, and these rules provide standards for testing the existence of an enforceable contract. Many of the provisions of the Code apply only to merchants or to transactions between merchants. Actions are measured by such concepts as "good faith" and what is "commercially reasonable," and the court is expressly given the right to refuse to enforce an unconscionable contract or an unconscionable clause in a contract.

Some of the important changes the Code makes in contract law include the following with references given to the pages in this text where these changes are discussed.

1. Firm Offers (see p. 119).
2. Statute of Frauds (see p. 256).
3. Unconscionable Contracts (see p. 232).
4. Additional Terms in Acceptances (see p. 136).
5. Modification (see p. 188).

Terms of the Contract

General Terms. Within broad limits the parties to a contract to sell goods may include any terms, not illegal, upon which they agree. In the everyday transactions of business many practices have become common, and the courts have ruled that in the absence of a provision in the contract stating the parties' agreement on the particular matter the presumption is that the parties intended the established practice to control. In the Code the rights of the parties when certain terms are used are set out in some detail, and those terms apply unless the parties agree otherwise. If a contract includes an open-price clause or if nothing is said about price, the price would be what would be considered reasonable at the time of delivery. If the price is to be fixed by either the buyer or seller, such party, in fixing the price, must act in good faith. If a price is to be fixed otherwise than by agreement of the parties and one of the parties, through his acts, prevents the fixing of the price, the other party may, at his option, treat the contract as canceled or fix a reasonable price. If it is clear from their negotiations that the parties do not intend to be bound unless they agree on a price and the price is not agreed or fixed, no contract results. (2–305[4].)[1]

Terms in a sales contract which measure the quantity of goods sold on the basis of output or need are enforceable. In determining the quantity, the rule of good faith applies. Also, if the parties have entered into a lawful contract for exclusive dealing in certain goods, the seller is obligated to use his best efforts to supply the goods to the buyer and the buyer is obligated to use his best efforts to promote their sale. (2–306.)

If no time for performance is stated in the sales contract, the time for

---

[1] The numbers in the parentheses refer to the sections of the Uniform Commercial Code, 1962.

performance shall be a reasonable time. Where the contract provides for successive performances for an indefinite period of time the contract is valid for a reasonable time but unless otherwise agreed it may be terminated at any time by either party. Reasonable notice is required to terminate a contract in which the time is for an indefinite period. A clause in such a contract dispensing with notice is declared by the Code to be unconscionable and invalid. (2–309.)

Delivery and Payment Terms. Standardized shipping terms which through mercantile practice have come to have a specific meaning are customarily used in sales contracts. The Code includes provisions setting out these terms and their legal effect on the rights and duties of the parties when included in a sales contract.

The terms f.o.b. (free on board) and f.a.s. (free alongside) are basic delivery terms. If the delivery term of the contract is f.o.b. or f.a.s., the seller is obligated to deliver to the carrier goods which conform to the contract and which are properly prepared for shipment to the buyer and he must make a reasonable contract of carriage on behalf of the buyer. Under such delivery terms, the goods are at the risk of the buyer during transit. If the term is f.o.b. destination, the seller must deliver the goods to the designated destination and they are at the seller's risk during transit. Risk of loss will be discussed in more detail later in this chapter.

Title

Introduction. At common law and under the Uniform Sales Act most of the problems relative to risks, insurable interests in goods, remedies and other similar rights and liabilities were determined on the basis of who was technical title owner at the particular moment the right or liability arose. After such determination the general rule of property law, that rights and liabilities relative to property followed ownership, was then applied.

Under the Code the rights of the seller and buyer and of third persons do not depend on the technicality of who has title, and such rights are determined irrespective of such technicality unless the provision of the Code expressly refers to title. Under some circumstances who has title to the goods becomes important, for instance, a situation in which the rights of the seller's or the buyer's creditors in the goods must be determined. And, under some state statutes, the rights of the parties may be made to depend on who has title to the goods. (2–401.)

Provisions for Passing of Title. Rules as to the passing of title to goods are set out in the Code. Title to goods cannot pass from the seller to the buyer until the goods are identified to the contract. For example, if S agrees to sell B 50 chairs and S has 500 such chairs in his warehouse, title to 50 chairs will not pass from S to B until the 50 chairs which B has purchased are selected and identified as the chairs sold to B. The reservation by the seller of a security interest in the goods sold does not affect the passing of title. (2–401 [1].)

Unless otherwise specifically agreed, title passes from the seller to the buyer when the seller has completed his performance as to delivery of the goods. If the sales contract requires the seller to ship the goods, title passes when the seller delivers conforming goods to the carrier, but if the sales contract requires the seller to deliver the goods to the buyer, title does not pass until the goods are delivered and tendered to the buyer. (2–401 [2].) If the goods are in the possession of a third person as bailee and a negotiable document of title has been issued for the goods, title passes to the buyer on the endorsement, if endorsement is necessary, and delivery of the document of title to the buyer. If no negotiable document of title has been issued by the bailee and the goods at the time of contracting are already identified to the contract, title passes at the time and place of contracting. (2–401 [3].) If the buyer, whether justified or not, refuses to accept or retain the goods or if he justifiably revokes his acceptance, title reverts, by operation of law, in the seller. (2–401 [4].)

Summary

Rules as to the passing of title are set out in the Code. Title cannot pass until goods are identified to the contract, and retention by the seller of a security interest in the goods does not affect the passing of title. Unless otherwise agreed, title passes when the seller has completed his performance. If he is to ship goods, title passes on delivery to the carrier; if he is to deliver the goods, title passes on delivery and tender. If the goods are in the possession of a bailee and a negotiable document of title has been issued, title passes on delivery of the document of title. If no negotiable document of title has been issued and the goods are identified, title passes at the place and time of the making of the contract. Rejection of the goods by the buyer reverts title in the seller.

Newhall v. Second Church and Society of Boston

209 N.E.2d 296 (Sup. Jud. Ct. Mass. 1965)

This was an action by Newhall (plaintiff) to enjoin the sale of five pieces of silver from Second Church and Society (defendant) to the Henry Francis duPont Winterthur Museum of Winterthur, Delaware, (defendant). The question before the court was whether for purposes of injunctive relief the Second Church and Society by special act effectively sold five silver vessels. The trial judge held that title had not passed. Affirmed on this point on appeal.

The contract was completed by telephone and payment had been made by check. Terms as to delivery then negotiated did not appear in the contract. However, a letter from the curator of the Winterthur Museum tended to show that the contract included the obligation to deliver the silver pieces to the buyer's representative in Boston:

Confirming our telephone conversation of this afternoon, I have made arrangements for Charles F. Hummel, associate curator of the Museum, to act on Mr. duPont's behalf in receiving from you the five pieces of silver. Mr. Hummel is of medium build and dark haired. He will meet you at the Shawmut Branch Bank, Beacon Street and Park Drive. I have asked him to bring a carbon copy of this letter with him and to have you sign a receipt form upon picking up the silver.

WHITTEMORE, JUSTICE.   On this record we think that the Uniform Commercial Code, § 2–401 (2), is applicable. This provides: "(2) Unless otherwise explicitly agreed title passes to the buyer at the time and place at which the seller completes his performance with reference to the physical delivery of the goods, despite any reservation of a security interest and even though a document of title is to be delivered at a different time or place; and in particular despite any reservation of a security interest by the bill of lading. . . ." It follows that § 2–401 (3) is *inapplicable:* "Unless otherwise explicitly agreed where delivery is to be made without moving the goods . . . (b) if the goods are at the time of contracting already identified and no documents are to be delivered, title passes at the time and place of contracting."

Rights of Third Parties

Introduction.   One of the fundamental rules of property law is that one cannot pass better title to goods than he has. There are, however, several exceptions to this rule, as is the case with most general rules, and three of the most generally accepted are: (1) one having a voidable title can pass good title to a bona fide purchaser for value, (2) one purchasing goods in the regular course of a retailer's business takes free from outstanding equities created by his seller, and (3) one purchasing goods in the ordinary course of a dealer's business takes free from the claim of one who has entrusted his goods to such dealer. A corollary to the general rule is that a creditor cannot by legal process acquire greater rights in his debtor's goods than the debtor has.

Creditor's Rights.   If a seller, after he has sold goods or identified them to the contract, retains possession of them and the sale is, under any statute of the state, made for the purpose of delaying or defeating the rights of creditors, the sale or identification is void as to the seller's creditors. However, if possession of the goods is retained in good faith and for only a commercially reasonable time, the seller's creditors can acquire no rights in the goods. This rule applies to the seller's creditors and not to purchasers in the regular course of the seller's business. Also, if the sale or identification of the goods to the contract is bona fide, the buyer has the right to claim the goods.

A creditor having a perfected security interest in goods will have priority over a buyer and also over a buyer who takes goods in payment of a past due claim if the transfer is fraudulent or a voidable preference. (2–402.)

Transfer of Voidable Title.   A seller having a voidable title has the power to pass good title to a good faith purchaser for value. A seller has a voidable title to goods if he has obtained his title through fraudulent representations. If a person has obtained goods by impersonating another, or if he has obtained the goods by giving a check or draft in payment for them and the check or draft is dishonored, or if he has obtained the goods without paying the agreed purchase price when it was agreed that the transaction was to be a "cash sale," such a person has a voidable title but can pass good title to a good faith purchaser for value. A buyer who takes goods in payment of a past obligation is a purchaser for value.

Buyer in Ordinary Course of Business.   A "buyer in ordinary course of business" is defined in Section 1–201 (9) of the Code. The definition is broad in its scope and includes good faith purchases from persons in the business of selling goods of the kind purchased, but it expressly eliminates purchases from pawnbrokers. Any person entrusting his goods to a merchant who deals in such goods confers on such merchant the power to pass good title to such goods to a buyer in the ordinary course of such merchant's business. For example, if O takes his watch to S, a retail jeweler, to have it repaired and S sells the watch to B, B would acquire good title to the watch. Since O entrusted his watch to S, who was a merchant dealing in such goods, O conferred on S the power to pass good title to B, a buyer in the ordinary course of S's business. However, a merchant seller cannot pass good title to stolen goods even though the buyer is a buyer in ordinary course of business. (2–403.)

Summary

A good faith buyer has priority over the creditors of a seller to goods identified to the sales contract even though the goods are left in the possession of the seller for a commercially reasonable time. A sale and identification of goods to a sales contract made for the purpose of delaying or defeating the rights of the seller's creditors is void as to such creditors.

One acquiring a voidable title to goods through false representations, giving a check or draft which is dishonored or on a "cash sale" without paying the agreed price can pass good title to a bona fide purchaser for value. A buyer in the ordinary course of business acquires good title to goods which have been entrusted to a merchant who deals in such goods.

Independent News Co. v. Williams

293 F.2d 510 (3rd Cir. 1961)

This was an action by the distributor, publisher and copyright owner of certain comic books (plaintiffs) to enjoin the sale of the comics by Williams (defendant). Judgment for Williams and the plaintiffs appealed. Affirmed.

The wholesaler of comic books, after receiving unsold comics back from retailers, was supposed to remove the covers from the unsold comics and return them to the distributor, Independent News, for credit. As to the remaining portion of the comics, the wholesaler was obligated by contract to see that they were mutilated so as not to be resold as publications but only as waste paper. The contract between the distributor and the wholesaler provided that:

"Title to all copies from which covers have been detached as above provided shall remain with the Company until the same are so destroyed or mutilated so as to be unusable for any purpose except waste. The use of such copies for any purpose other than waste is unauthorized and contravenes this agreement."

The wholesaler sold cover-removed comics to a waste paper dealer who—rather than selling them as waste paper—sold them to Williams, a distributor of secondhand books and magazines.

McLAUGHLIN, CIRCUIT JUDGE. The first proposition upon which plaintiffs rely is conversion. They argue that after the covers of the comics are removed and returned to Independent for full credit, title to the insides of the magazines as "literary works" reverts to Independent. . . .

The district court rejected this argument and expressly found that the reservation of title in the contract had no effect upon the waste paper dealer who was a buyer in the ordinary course of business; the whole agreement between the parties was "at best, a sale or return transaction"; no agency relationship ever arose; and the waste paper dealer and in turn the defendant acquired the full complement of property rights in the comics.

Under the Uniform Commercial Code, adopted in Pennsylvania, Section 2–403 (2), provides

"(2) Any entrusting of possession of goods to a merchant who deals in goods of that kind gives him power to transfer all rights of the entruster to a buyer in ordinary course of business."

That section of the Code has broadened the protection of buyers in the ordinary course of business and has changed prior Pennsylvania law.

In the case at bar, plaintiffs ". . . conceded that plaintiffs have 'entrusted' the magazines in question to the Wholesaler-Agent." However, they dispute the applicability of Section 2–403 (2) stating:

"(a) Wholesaler-Agent is not a 'merchant who deals in goods of the kind . . .' " and

"(b) neither the waste paper house nor the defendant is a 'buyer in the ordinary course of business' as defined by the Code."

The first assertion seeks to distinguish between the wholesaler ". . . selling new publications prior to or during the publication period," and the wholesaler selling the cover-removed magazines. The argument is specious. The wholesaler deals in comics, and the fact that the covers are present or not is irrelevant. His regular business is dealing with comics and as such he is a "merchant who deals in goods of that kind."

The interrelated second contention, namely, that neither the waste paper dealer nor the defendant are buyers in the ordinary course of business is equally without merit. In defining this concept, Section 1–201 (9) of the Code provides:

"(9) 'Buyer in ordinary course of business' means a person who in good faith and without knowledge that the sale to him is in violation of the ownership rights or security interest of a third party in the goods buys in ordinary course from a person in the business of selling goods of that kind. . . ."

The district court's finding of fact forms a proper basis for the determination that the waste paper dealer is within that definition.

And there is no evidence in the record . . . that shows that the waste paper dealer had any notice of any restriction whatsoever on the cover-removed comics purchased from the wholesaler. It follows, that when the wholesaler sold these coverless comics to the waste paper dealer, the waste paper dealer, under Section 2–403 (2) of the Code, obtained the totality of property rights in the comics which included the right to use or sell them as reading material.

Risks

Introduction.   In the event that goods which are the subject matter of a sales contract are damaged or destroyed, the question frequently arises as to which of the parties, the buyer or seller, must stand the loss. At common law and under the Uniform Sales Act the risk of loss was on the technical title owner of the goods unless the parties had indicated in their agreement a contrary intention. As a general rule, businessmen in negotiating a sale neither express nor indicate an intention as to when title to the goods is to pass. Rules of presumption as to the time of the passing of the title to the goods were developed by the courts and these rules were incorporated into the Uniform Sales Act. The basing of risks on title to the goods was unrealistic and the decisions of the courts were inconsistent in many respects. Under the provisions of the Code the parties may by their agreement shift the allocation of the risk or divide the risk (2–303) unless the provision in the agreement would be void as an unconscionable clause under Section 2–302.

Explicit Agreements.   In some instances the parties to a contract may by the terms of their agreement indicate an intention as to which of the parties shall bear the burden of the risk. In other instances usage of trade or course of dealing may determine on which party the risk is to be placed. Under the Code title is relegated to a secondary position and the circumstances of the case are of primary importance. If the parties include delivery terms in their agreement such terms will indicate which party will bear the risk of loss while the goods are in transit. If delivery terms are f.o.b., f.a.s., c.i.f., or c. & f., the risks shift to the buyer on the delivery of the goods to the carrier and the making of a commercially reasonable contract of carriage. (2–319 and 2–320.) If the delivery terms are f.o.b. destination or delivery ex-ship the seller bears the risk. (2–319 [1] [*b*] and 2–322.)

Identification and Insurable Interest.   The general practice of insuring risks is recognized and provided for under the Code. Provision is made whereby the buyer may protect his interest in goods which are intended as the subject matter of a sales contract before the title to the goods vests in the buyer. The buyer obtains a special property interest and an insurable interest in existing goods when they are identified to the contract even though they are nonconforming. Identification of goods to a sales contract is the indication either by the agreement of the parties or, in the absence of an agreement, under the applicable provisions of the Code, that certain goods will be the subject matter of the contract. The goods may be nonconforming at the time of the identification and the seller may substitute other goods for those identified to the contract.

In the absence of an explicit agreement identifying the goods to the sales contract identification occurs when the contract is made if the goods are in existence and identified. If the goods are future goods, except growing crops or the young of animals, the goods are identified when they are shipped, marked or otherwise designated by the seller as the goods to which the contract refers. Crops are identified to the contract when planted, and the young of animals when conceived if the young are to be born within one year of the making of the contract or if the crops are to be harvested within one year or the next normal harvesting period. (2–501 [1].) The seller retains an insurable interest in goods so long as title or a security interest remains in him. (2–501 [2].)

A buyer who has paid for or has made a payment on identified goods which have not been shipped may, in the event of the insolvency of the seller within 10 days of the time payment was made, by making and keeping good a tender of the payment of any balance due, recover the goods identified to the contract. If the buyer has identified the goods to the contract he can recover the goods only if the goods identified to the contract conform to the sales contract. (2–502.)

Risks of Loss—General Rules. Since goods can readily be lost, stolen, or damaged while in transit, the risk of loss is an important aspect of any sales situation. General rules relative to risks of loss are subject to the contrary agreement of the parties. In the absence of an agreement the risk of loss passes to the buyer on the delivery to the carrier of conforming goods unless the seller has agreed to deliver the goods at a particular destination, in which event the risk of loss passes to the buyer when the carrier so tenders the goods as to enable the buyer to take delivery. If the goods are in the possession of a bailee and are not to be moved, the risk of loss passes to the buyer on delivery to him of a negotiable document of title for the goods and if no negotiable document of title has been issued when the bailee acknowledges the buyer's right to the possession of the goods.

If the transaction is such that it does not fall within the situations discussed above, the risk of loss passes to the buyer on receipt of the goods if the seller is a merchant and if he is not a merchant on the tender of delivery of the goods. (2–509.)

When a seller tenders goods which do not conform to the contract and the buyer would have the right to reject the goods, the risk of loss remains with the seller until any defect is cured or until the buyer accepts the goods. Where the buyer rightfully revokes his acceptance, the risk of loss is with the seller from the beginning to the extent that the loss is not covered by the buyer's insurance. This rule gives the seller the benefit of any insurance carried by the buyer. Where a buyer repudiates a contract for conforming goods identified to the contract, the risk of loss, to the extent the loss is not covered by the seller's insurance, is on the buyer for a commercially reasonable time after the repudiation. (2–510 [3].)

Summary

Goods which are the subject matter of a sale may be damaged or destroyed and the question of which of the parties to the sales contract must bear the loss frequently arises. The parties to the sales contract may by explicit agreement designate who shall bear such loss or how the risk of loss shall be divided. The inclusion in the sales contract of delivery terms will indicate which of the parties shall bear the risk of loss during transit. The buyer acquires a property interest in goods identified to the sales contract and has an insurable interest in them even though they may be nonconforming.

If there is no explicit agreement identification occurs when the contract is made if the goods are in existence and identified, if they are future goods, then when they are shipped, marked or otherwise designated by the seller, if growing crops then when planted, and if young of animals, when conceived, provided the crops will be harvested or the young of animals will be born within one year.

A buyer who has made payment on goods identified to the contract may claim them if the seller becomes insolvent within 10 days of such payment. If transactions are not covered by the above rules and there is no agreement relative to who shall bear the risks of loss, such risk passes to the buyer on delivery of the goods to the carrier unless the seller has agreed to deliver the goods, then on delivery at destination. If goods are in the possession of a bailee and not to be moved, the risk passes to the buyer on delivery of a negotiable document of title and, if none, when the bailee acknowledges the buyer's rights. Nonconforming goods are at the risk of the seller. If the buyer repudiates the contract the goods are at the risk of the buyer for a commercially reasonable time. Insurance on the goods inures to the benefit of the party who must bear the loss.

Ninth Street East, Ltd. v. Harrison

259 A.2d 772 (Cir. Ct. Conn. 1968)

This was an action brought by Ninth Street East, Ltd. (plaintiff) against Harrison (defendant) to recover the purchase price of merchandise sold by Ninth Street East to Harrison. Judgment for Ninth Street East.

Ninth Street East was the manufacturer of men's clothing with a principal place of business in Los Angeles, California. Harrison was the owner and operator of a men's clothing store, located in Westport, Connecticut, known as "The Rage."

Pursuant to orders received by Ninth Street East in Los Angeles on November 28, 1966, Harrison ordered a variety of clothing items. On November 30, 1966, Ninth Street East delivered the merchandise in Los Angeles to a common carrier known as Denver-Chicago Trucking Company, Inc. (Denver) and received a bill of lading from the trucker. Simultaneously, Ninth Street East mailed Harrison four invoices, all dated November 30, 1966, covering the clothing, in the total sum of $2216. All the invoices bore the notations that the shipment was made "F.O.B. Los Angeles" and "Via Denver-Chicago" as well as the printed phrase, "Goods Shipped at Purchaser's Risk." Denver's bill of lading disclosed that the shipment was made "collect,"—namely, that Harrison was obligated to pay the freight charges from Los Angeles to Westport. Denver subsequently transferred the shipment to a connecting carrier known as Old Colony Transportation Company (Old Colony) for ultimate delivery at Harrison's store in Westport. The delivery was attempted by Old Colony at Harrison's store on December 12, 1966. Harrison's wife requested the Old Colony truck driver to deliver the merchandise inside the door of defendant's store. The truck driver refused to do so. The dispute not having been resolved, Old Colony retained possession of the eight cartons comprising the shipment, and the truck thereupon departed from the store premises.

Harrison later reported its refusal to accept delivery. The merchandise was subsequently lost by the carrier. Ninth Street East filed a claim against the carrier but as of the date of the trial, it had not been reimbursed. In this action Harrison claimed that since the merchandise had never been delivered into his place of business, he was not liable for the loss or disappearance of the shipment or its purchase price, and that the risk of loss was on Ninth Street East.

LEVINE, JUSTICE.   The basic problem is to determine the terms and conditions of the agreement of the parties as to transportation, and the risks and hazards incident thereto. The court finds that the parties had originally agreed that the merchandise would be shipped by common carrier F.O.B. Los Angeles, as the place of shipment, and that the defendant would pay the freight charges between the two points. The notations on the invoices, and the bill of lading, previously described, make this clear. The use of the phrase "F.O.B.," meaning free on board, made this portion of the agreement not only a price term covering defendant's obligation to pay freight charges between Los Angeles and Westport but also a controlling factor as to risk of loss of the merchandise upon delivery to Denver and subsequently to Old Colony as the carriers. General Statutes § 2–319, comment 1. Title to the goods, and the right to possession, passed to defendant at Los Angeles, the F.O.B. point. Upon delivery to the common carrier at the F.O.B. point, the goods thereafter were at defendant's sole risk. § 2–509 (1).

It is highly significant that all the invoices sent to defendant contained the explicit notation "Goods Shipped at Purchaser's Risk." This was, initially, a unilateral statement by plaintiff. The validity of this phrase, as expressing the understanding of both parties, was, however, never actually challenged by defendant, at the trial or in his brief. The contents of the invoices therefore confirm the statutory allocation of risk of loss on F.O.B. shipments.

The arrangements as to shipment were at the option of plaintiff as the seller. § 2–311 (2). Plaintiff duly placed the goods in possession of a carrier, to wit, Denver, and made a reasonable contract for their transportation, having in mind the nature of the merchandise and the remaining circumstances. Notice of the shipment, including the F.O.B. provisions, was properly given to defendant, as required by law, pursuant to the four invoices. § 2–504; Uniform Commercial Code § 2–504, comment 5.

The law erects a presumption in favor of construing the agreement as a "shipment" contract, as opposed to a "destination" contract. Uniform Commercial Code § 2–503, comment 5. Under the presumption of a "shipment" contract, plaintiff's liability for loss or damage terminated upon delivery to the carrier at the F.O.B. point, to wit, Los Angeles. The court finds that no persuasive evidence was offered to overcome the force of the statutory presumption in the instant case. Thus, as § 2–509 (1) indicates, "[w]here the contract requires or authorizes the seller to ship the goods by carrier (a) if it does not require him to deliver them at a particular destination, the risk of loss passes to the buyer when the goods are duly delivered to the carrier." Accordingly, at the F.O.B. point, when the risk of loss shifted, Denver and Old Colony, as carriers, became the agents or bailees of defendant. The risk of subsequent loss or delay rested on defendant, and not plaintiff. A disagreement arose between defendant's wife and the truck driver, resulting in nondelivery of the merchandise, retention thereof by the carrier, and, finally, disappearance of the shipment. The ensuing dispute was fundamentally a matter for resolution between defendant and the carriers, as his agents. Nothing in the outcome of that dispute could defeat or impair plaintiff's recovery against defendant.

Defendant has urged that, since plaintiff pressed a damage claim against the carrier, this constitutes an assertion of an ownership interest by plaintiff, and responsibility for loss thereof, inconsistent with plaintiff's present claim against defendant. The court does not agree. Even though the risk of loss, subsequent to delivery to the carrier, had passed to defendant, plaintiff nevertheless had the privilege of pressing the damage claim against the trucker. Any recovery on the claim would, however, be held by plaintiff, subject to its own interest, as a fiduciary for defendant. § 2–722 (b). In this connection, the evidence demonstrated that plaintiff first made an effort to secure defendant's cooperation in asserting the damage claim but was unsuccessful.

The court entertains substantial doubt about the credibility of the defense. Defendant initially professed an urgent need for the merchandise, for holiday sales. When, however, the delivery was tendered, on December 12, 1966, only some two weeks prior to Christmas, defendant, acting by his wife, saw fit to refuse the merchandise for the alleged reason that the truck driver was obligated to carry the cartons inside defendant's door. The defense arising out of the refusal is without merit. Defendant knew, or should have known, that his rejection exposed the shipment to time consuming delays and disputes. Hence, delivery in time for holiday business was actually frustrated, not by plaintiff, but rather by the action of defendant and his agent, based on a disagreement over a relatively minor item. Wholly apart from the conclusion, previously stated, that such refusal was at the sole risk of defendant, the court finds that defendant's conduct was wrongful, arbitrary, and unreasonable, under all the circumstances.

In view of defendant's wrongful rejection, following the shifting of the risk of loss to him, he is liable to plaintiff for the entire purchase price of the merchandise. Thus, § 2–709 provides in part: "(1) When the buyer fails to pay the price as it becomes due the seller may recover . . . the price (a) . . . of conforming goods lost or damaged within a commercially reasonable time after risk of their loss has passed to the buyer." In *Lewis v. Scoville* the court said: "Refusal by the defendant to receive the goods did not revest title in the plaintiff, and he is . . . entitled to recover the contract price."

Sales on Trial

Sale on Approval. If goods are delivered to a buyer under an agreement that he may test or use the goods for the purpose of determining whether or not he wishes to buy them, the sale is a sale on approval. (2–326.) In a sale on approval, unless otherwise agreed, the risk of loss and the title do not pass to the buyer until acceptance. The buyer may use the goods in a manner consistent with the purpose of the trial but an unwarranted exercise of ownership over the goods is an acceptance. Also, failure to notify the seller of election to return the goods is an acceptance; and if the goods conform to the contract, acceptance of any part is acceptance of the whole.

After due notification of election to return the goods, the return is at the seller's risk and expense but a merchant buyer must follow any reasonable instructions given by the seller for the return of the goods. Since the risk of loss and title remain with the seller, goods held on approval are not subject to the claims of the buyer's creditors until approval. (2–326 and 2–327.)

Sale or Return. If delivered goods may be returned by the buyer even though they conform to the contract, the sale is a sale or return where the goods are delivered primarily for sale. Under a sale or return, unless otherwise agreed, the risk of loss and title to the goods are in the buyer and are subject to the claims of the buyer's creditors while in his possession. The buyer's option to return extends to the whole or any commercial unit of the goods while substantially in their original condition, but such option must be exercised seasonably. The return of the goods is at the buyer's risk and expense. (2–326 and 2–327.)

If delivered goods may be returned by the buyer even though they conform to the sales contract, the transaction is "sale on approval" if the goods are delivered primarily for use. If the goods are delivered primarily for resale the transaction will be deemed sale or return.

Sale on Consignment or on Memorandum.   Where goods are delivered to a person "on consignment" or "on memorandum" for resale and such person maintains a place of business at which he deals in goods of the kind involved, under a name other than the name of the person making delivery, then with respect to claims of creditors of the person conducting the business the goods are deemed to be on sale or return. For example: Jones operates a retail music store under the name of City Music Store. Baldwin Piano Company delivers to Jones a piano on consignment and no notices are posted indicating that it is so delivered. A judgment creditor could acquire a lien on the piano by levy of execution on it. However, the creditors of the person conducting the business may not so treat the goods if the person making delivery complies with an applicable law providing for a consignor's interest or the like to be evidenced by a sign, or establishes that the person conducting the business is generally known by his creditors to be substantially engaged in selling goods for others, or complies with the filing provisions of Article 9, Secured Transactions. (2–326.)

Summary

In a sale on approval the goods are delivered to the buyer for use or trial and the risk of loss and title remain in the seller. A sale or return is one where the goods are sold to the buyer for resale. The risk of loss and title is in the buyer and he may at his option return to the seller all or any commercial unit of the goods which is in substantially the same condition as when received. The return of the goods is at the buyer's risk and expense.

Goods delivered "on consignment" or "on memorandum" are subject to the claims of the creditors of the person to whom they are delivered if he operates a business selling like goods in a name other than that of the party delivering the goods. The person delivering the goods can protect his interest by posting notice as required by the state statute or filing under Article 9. Also, if the person to whom the goods are delivered is known to his creditors to be substantially engaged in selling goods for others the creditors cannot obtain an interest in the goods.

Collier v. B & B Parts Sales, Inc.

471 S.W.2d 151 (Civ. App. Tex. 1971)

This was an action brought by B & B Parts Sales, Inc. (plaintiff) against Collier (defendant) to recover the balance allegedly due on a sale to Collier of stereo tapes, cartridges and equipment. Judgment for B & B Parts Sales, Inc. Affirmed on appeal.

At the time B & B's salesman delivered the stereo tapes, cartridges and equipment, he gave Collier an invoice that had printed on it "sold to" followed by Collier's name and address in handwriting. Also written in by hand was the notation "Terms 30–60–90 this equipment will be picked up if not sold in 90 days." Collier's service station was burglarized shortly afterwards and most of the merchandise was stolen.

Collier maintained that he held the merchandise on consignment and thus the risk of loss was on the consignor. B & B maintained that the transaction was a sale and that Collier was bound to pay for it.

MCKAY, JUSTICE.   The transaction here was a "sale or return," and under section (c) of Article 2.326 [UCC § 2–326 (3)] and section (b) (1) and (2) of Article 2.327 [UCC § 2–327 (2) (a) and (b)] of the Uniform Commercial Code, it became a sale, and therefore title passed to the appellant. The notations "Terms 30–60–90" and "this equipment will be picked up if not sold in 90 days" do not constitute a consignment. We construe the language to mean that there was a sale of the items listed on the invoices; but the seller agreed to pick up items which had not been sold in 90 days.

In Anderson's Uniform Commercial Code, Vol 1, Sec 2–326:1, p. 258, it is stated: "The type of 'sale or return' involved herein is a sale to a merchant whose unwillingness to buy is overcome only by the seller's engagement to take back the goods (or any commercial unit of goods) in lieu of payment if they fail to be resold." And in Sec 2–326:4, p. 260, of the same work is found: "Unless otherwise agreed, a transaction under which goods delivered primarily for resale may be returned to the seller even though they conform to the contract is a sale or return." In 50 CJ2d, Sales, § 22, page 277, we find this statement:

Under the Uniform Commercial Code, many transactions that might have been regarded as consignments under former law will be regarded as sales. This is because of a code provision stating that where goods are delivered to a person for sale and he maintains a place of business where he deals in goods of the kind involved, under a name other than that of the person making delivery, the goods are deemed to be on sale or return, as regards claims of creditors of the person conducting the business. In other words, many transactions whereby a consignor sends goods to a dealer in goods of that kind will be regarded as sales transactions, and not consignments, under the code. . . .

The intention of the parties seems to be no longer determinative of the question of whether a transaction was a sale or a consignment under the Uniform Commercial Code. In addition, under Article 2.327 (b) (2), supra, when a transaction is a sale or return agreement the return is at the buyer's risk.

Bulk Transfers

Bulk transfer legislation was enacted in order to prevent fraud on creditors. The principal type of commercial fraud which this legislation is intended to prevent occurs most often where a merchant, owing debts, sells out his stock in trade for cash, pockets the proceeds, and then disappears, leaving his creditors unpaid. Although many states adopted bulk sales laws, there was no uniform bulk sales act ever drafted and adopted by the states. Article 6 of the Uniform Commercial Code—Bulk Transfers—attempts to simplify and make uniform the bulk sales laws of the states that adopt the Code.

This Article of the Code covers any transfer "in bulk" and not in the ordinary course of the transferor's business of a major part of the materials, supplies, merchandise or other inventory of an enterprise. A transfer of a substantial part of equipment is a bulk transfer if such transfer is part of a bulk transfer of inventory. The enterprises subject to this Article are all those whose principal business is the sale of merchandise from stock and those that manufacture and sell from stock their manufactured products such as, for instance, a retail bakery which makes and sells at retail its baked goods. (6–102.)

Transfer for security, assignments for the benefit of creditors, transfers in settlement of liens, transfers by executors, administrators, receivers, trustees in bankruptcy, and like persons acting under judicial process, transfers as part of a corporate reorganization and like transfers are excepted from the operation of this Article. (6–103.)

The general plan of the Article is to give creditors notice in advance of the transfer and provide a plan for their protection. The transferor is required to give the transferee a schedule of the property to be transferred and a sworn list of his creditors. The transferee is required to give the creditors on the list and any additional known creditors notice of the pending transfer at least 10 days before he takes possession of the goods.

A choice of plans is made available to the adopters of the Code. They may adopt the New York plan, under which the giving of notice is all that is required, or the Pennsylvania plan, under which the proceeds of the sale are distributed to the transferor's creditors. (6–106.) If the parties fail to comply with the requirements of this Article the transferee holds the goods in trust for the creditors of the transferor.

Special provision is made for the regulation of sales by auction. (6–108.)

A short statute of limitations provides that no action shall be brought or levy made more than six months after the date on which the transferee took possession of the goods unless the transfer has been concealed. (6–111.)

Adrian Tabin Corp. v. Climax Boutique, Inc.

338 N.Y.S. 2d 59 (Sup. Ct. N.Y. 1972)

This was an action brought by Adrian Tabin Corp. (plaintiff) against Climax Boutique, Inc. (defendant) to recover money owed to Adrian Tabin by L.D.J. Dresses which had made a bulk sale of its business to Climax Boutique. Trial court found for

Adrian Tabin on the ground that Climax Boutique had not satisfied the Bulk Sales provisions of the U.C.C. Reversed on appeal.

Additional facts are stated in the opinion.

SHAPIRO, JUSTICE. The novel issue posed by this appeal is whether a purchaser at a bulk sale, who receives an affidavit of "no creditors" is nevertheless under a duty to make careful inquiry as to the possible existence of creditors, of whom he has no actual knowledge. The plaintiff, a creditor of the seller, was not notified of the sale and hence seeks an adjudication that, as to it, the sale is void.

Defendant L.D.J. Dresses, Inc. (hereinafter referred to as "the seller") operated a dress shop in Jamaica, Queens. The seller was indebted to the plaintiff, a garment supplier, at the time it sold its business in bulk to defendant Paul Warman, who in turn sold the business to defendant Climax Boutique, Inc., in which he was a principal. (Warman and Climax will hereafter be referred to as "the purchasers.")

Prior to the consummation of the bulk sale the purchasers received an affidavit from Joseph Marino, the president of the seller, which stated that the seller was not indebted to anyone and had no creditors. The purchasers caused a lien search to be conducted and determined that there were no outstanding liens.

At the trial, the purchasers' attorney testified as follows:

I knew . . . the attorney for the seller for at least fifteen years, knew him well, had seen him in court maybe once a month for fifteen years so knew his voice well. In fact I had matters with him too from the past. At the closing . . . (the seller's attorney) and I spoke on the telephone and I said, "What about the general creditors? You have told me already there are none but I think I should have some necessary affidavit to cover." Then he said, "Well, to begin with," he said, "I am going to give you a bill of sale sworn to by the seller and notarized by me as an attorney that there are absolutely no creditors. He has shown me checks that he had sent to all his creditors because I checked it with him in order to close out the business for the end of the year and I am satisfied that there are none and as an attorney I would never let my client sign such an affidavit if I thought there were, and there are no creditors."

The parties stipulated that the purchasers had no knowledge of the plaintiff prior to the sale.

In setting aside the sale the Special Term noted that the purchasers had not requested an examination of the seller's books and had not questioned the source of the garments involved in the sale. It held that the purchasers had not made careful inquiry of the seller as to existing creditors and that, failing such careful inquiry, the purchasers had acted at their peril.

A bulk sale is ineffective against creditors of the seller unless the purchaser requires the seller to furnish a list (signed and sworn to or affirmed) of his existing creditors (Uniform Commercial Code, § 6–104) and notifies such creditors of the impending sale (Uniform Commercial Code, §§ 6–105, 6–107). . . .

Subdivision (3) of § 6–104 of the Uniform Commercial Code provides that "responsibility for the completeness and accuracy of the list of creditors rests on the transferor, and the transfer is not rendered ineffective by errors or omissions therein unless the transferee is shown to have had knowledge." Section 1–201 of the Uniform Commercial Code, the general definitions section of that code, provides, in subdivision (25), that "a person 'knows' or has 'knowledge' of a fact when he has actual knowledge of it." It is therefore apparent that a bulk sale may not be set aside as to creditors not listed by the seller in the affidavit requested by the purchaser, of whom the purchaser had no actual knowledge. As the purchasers concededly had no actual knowledge of the plaintiff, the possibility of whose existence as a creditor was denied by the seller in an affidavit (the purchasers having no reason to disbelieve the truthfulness of the affidavit), the bulk sale may not be set aside as to the plaintiff.

We note, in passing, that even were the purchasers under a duty to make careful inquiry, they complied with that responsibility in this case by making a lien search and by making inquiry of the seller's attorney, who represented that all creditors had been paid and that he had seen the checks sent out to them in payment of the seller's obligations.

MUNDER, JUSTICE (dissenting).   The issue here is simply whether an affidavit of "no creditors" relieves the purchaser at a bulk sale of the duty to make careful inquiry as to the possible existence of creditors of whom he had no actual knowledge, under § 6–104 of the Uniform Commercial Code.

I conclude the answer is no.

A purchaser or transferee of the entire stock of a going business knows the seller more than likely has some creditors. He should at least inquire into the sources of the inventory. Otherwise, the opportunity for fraud upon creditors is too great. Here, the purchasers made no such inquiry. They relied upon an oral assurance by the seller's attorney that there were no general creditors and a statement to the same effect by the seller's president. The statement, although in affidavit form, was not notarized.

Problem Cases

1. Buyer sent a purchase order to Seller ordering 150 lawn mowers and instructing Seller to "Ship direct to 30th & Harcum Way, Pitts., Pa."—30th & Harcum Way being Buyer's address. The mowers were delivered to a carrier for shipment by Seller and were received and paid for by Buyer. At what point did title to the mowers pass to Buyer?

2. Mr. Lane, a dealer in new and used boats, sold a new boat and trailer to Mr. Johnson. Mr. Johnson paid for the boat and trailer by check, which was later dishonored. Mr. Johnson then resold the boat to Mr. Honeycutt. Lane attempts to get the boat and trailer from Honeycutt. Can Lane recover the boat?

3. Chamberlin, a dealer in mobile homes in Popular Bluff, Missouri, sold Crowder a new camper unit for $1,757.74. Crowder gave Chamberlin a check in full payment. Crowder loaded the unit on a pickup truck that was too small to properly accommodate it and left Chamberlin's place of business without obtaining a bill of sale or title. Crowder drove to Jonesboro, Arkansas, where he sold the unit to Hollis, who was a dealer in used mobile homes. Hollis paid $500, knew the camper unit was new and worth at least $1,000, asked no questions about why the camper was affixed to the truck as it was, and asked for no title or bill of sale from Crowder except for requesting a bill of sale from Crowder to him. Crowder's check was dishonored and Chamberlin wants to recover the unit from Hollis. Can he do so?

4. Sherman, a used car dealer, sold and delivered two Volkswagens to Miller, also a used car dealer. Miller agreed not to resell the cars until his check given in payment cleared the bank. Miller, however, violated this agreement and sold the cars for cash to Kresge, another dealer. The Miller check was dishonored and Sherman attempted to get the cars from Kresge. Can Sherman recover the cars from Kresge?

5. In February of 1967 Hayward purchased a yacht from Postma for $10,000. They agreed that the yacht was to be delivered to a nearby lake in April of 1967. In early 1967, prior to delivery, a fire at Postma's yacht showroom destroyed the yacht. Who must bear the burden of the loss and why?

6. Bell Aerospace Corp. sold Ellis a helicopter for $102,000. Ellis paid the purchase price, registered the aircraft with the FAA and came to pick it up at the Bell plant and to receive a five flight training program included in the sale. During the first of these flights, the helicopter crashed and was severely damaged. Who bears the burden of this loss?

7. Debs, Inc. a dress manufacturer, sold Rose Stores, Inc. 288 dresses. The order was on a Rose Stores' printed form which stated, "Ship via Stuarts Express Inc." Stuarts Express picked up the dresses at Debs, Inc. and one week later wrote Debs, Inc. a letter informing them that the entire shipment was lost. Since Stuart's liability is extremely limited by the shipping contract who absorbs the loss?

8. Consolidated Company sold Jaco Corporation a piece of used machinery. The Jaco purchase order for the machine, described it at length, and contained the following terms "sold as per our inspection, f.o.b. purchasers truck, $11,500, to be paid in full at time of shipment probably within two or three weeks maximum; shipping instructions to follow." One month later the machine was destroyed by vandals. Consolidated files suit for the $11,500 claiming that the risk of loss transferred to Jaco after the three-week maximum had elapsed and no shipping instructions were forthcoming. Can Consolidated recover?

9. In October 1964, Mincow and Finale entered into a written contract, by the terms of which Finale agreed to deliver to specified chain and department stores throughout the country such merchandise as Finale might see fit, for sale in those stores for the account of Mincow, as Finale's consignee. Title to the merchandise and the proceeds thereof was to be "always vested in Finale" and such merchandise was to be "at all times subject to and under the direction and control of Finale." Finale was to bear all risk of loss and Mincow was to remit sales proceeds, less commission, to Finale. The assignee for benefit of Mincow's creditors claims that he is entitled to the merchandise or proceeds thereof in preference to Finale's rights by reason of U.C.C. Section 2–236. Should the goods be turned over to Mincow's assignee for the benefit of creditors?

10. Halifax Finance Company sold all of its assets to Credithrift Financial Corporation. Included in the sale were several promissory notes held by Halifax valued at $230,000. Jones, who had been an unsecured creditor of Halifax brings an action to set aside the sale of the notes two months later. Under what theory should he proceed and will he be successful?

chapter 34

Warranty and Product Liability

Nature of Warranties

Representations. When a person is making an effort to sell goods, he usually makes some statements relative to the merits of the goods. Such statements are representations and may range in their legal effect from statements which are mere sales talk to statements which are fraudulent misrepresentations. In determining the legal effect of representations made by a seller, all of the facts and circumstances must be taken into consideration.

In the early period of the development of the law of sales, business was carried on in such a manner that the seller and the buyer negotiated face-to-face in the presence of the goods. Frequently, the seller was an itinerant merchant who would leave for parts unknown as soon as he had sold his wares. Also, the sale was quite often looked upon as a test of wits, the seller doing his best to drive a sharp bargain and the buyer exercising all of the cunning at his command to get a good buy. Under such conditions, neither party placed much faith in the statements of the other. All representations made by a seller were accepted as sales talk and not binding on him unless he clearly and unequivocally assumed responsibility for the quality of the goods he was selling.

With the development of commerce, business methods changed, and there was a shift from the face-to-face sale in the presence of the goods to sales made by the seller's representative, who called on the customer and described or displayed samples of the goods the seller was offering for sale. Since the buyer, under this system of selling, could not examine the goods he was buying before he contracted to buy, he had to rely on the representations of the seller or his agent.

By gradual evolution, merchandising has progressed from a system in which the seller was not held responsible for representations made regarding the goods offered for sale to a system in which a high degree of responsibility is placed on a seller for such representations.

Under the law as it has developed, a seller is not responsible if he, in representing his goods, confines his statements to "sales talk" or "puffing," such as "It is a good buy," "These goods are high class," or "You should be happy with this." Also, the seller is not responsible if he merely expresses an opinion relative to the nature or quality of the goods. Whether a statement made by a seller will be interpreted as an opinion or a representation will depend, in many instances, on the relative experience and knowledge of the parties. If the seller is one who deals in goods such as he is selling, and the buyer does not deal in such goods and knows little about them, a statement relating to the quality or character of the goods might be interpreted as a warranty, whereas if the buyer is a dealer in such goods and has had experience and knowledge substantially equal to that of the seller, the same statements might be interpreted as statements of opinion.

Warranties—General. In its broadest sense a warranty is the assumption of responsibility, by the seller, for the quality, character, or suitability of goods sold. The seller may assume such responsibility by express agreement, in which case the warranty is created by contract and the rights and liabilities are contractual in nature. Such a warranty is called an express warranty.

If the seller has knowingly misrepresented the goods with intent to defraud and the buyer has justifiably relied on the representations to his injury, the seller will be liable to the buyer in damages in an action in tort for deceit. If the seller is guilty of deceit, the buyer may elect to pursue either his remedy for breach of warranty or his remedy for damages for deceit.

Under some circumstances a degree of responsibility for goods sold is imposed on the seller by operation of law, in which case the nature and extent of the seller's responsibility will be determined by the nature of the transaction. Such responsibility is quasi-contractual in nature. The warranty is included in the sales agreement by operation of law, and such warranties are known as implied warranties.

Summary

As a result of the change in the method of doing business, we have developed rules of law under which a seller is held responsible for representations made to induce a buyer to purchase goods.

A warranty is the assumption by the seller of goods of the responsibility for the quality, character, and suitability of goods sold. A warranty may result from representations made by the seller, or it may be imposed on the seller by operation of law.

Express Warranties

Nature of Express Warranty.   An express warranty is based on contract and is the result of negotiation of the terms of the sales contract. It may be broad in its scope and include all phases of the quality, character, suitability and ownership of the goods involved or it may go to only one or more character-istics of the goods. When the seller has expressly warranted the goods, the courts have generally held that such warranty represents so clearly the intent of the parties that they will not interpret any language in the sales contract whereby the seller attempts to relieve himself from liability for the warranty as being effective if the language is general in its terms or is included in a form contract.

Creating an Express Warranty.   To create an express warranty it is not necessary that the seller use the words "warrant" or "guarantee," nor is it necessary that he intend to make a warranty. Any affirmation of fact or promise made by the seller to the buyer which relates to the goods and becomes a part of the bargain creates an express warranty that the goods shall conform to the affirmation or promise. An affirmation merely of the value of the goods or a statement purporting to be merely the seller's opinion or commendation of the goods does not create a warranty. Whether or not affirmations or statements made by a seller to a buyer in the negotiation of a sale are warranties or merely statements of opinion or commendation of the goods will depend to a large extent on the relation of the parties, their experience and knowledge, and all the facts and circumstances of the case.

In the negotiation of a sale the seller may use descriptive terms to convey to the buyer an idea of the quality or characteristics of the goods or he may use pictures, drawings, blueprints, or technical specifications. When a seller uses descriptive terms as the basis of the sales contract he will have expressly warranted that the goods delivered will conform to the description. If a sample or model is made a part of the basis of the bargain, the seller will have expressly warranted that the goods delivered will conform to the sample or model. If a sample is used, the court, in determining the scope of the seller's liability on the warranty, will take into consideration whether the sample is drawn from the bulk of the goods or is merely illustrative of the goods. (2–313.)[1]

Summary

To expressly warrant goods such words as "warrant" or "guarantee" need not be used. Any affirmation of fact or promise, any description of the goods or a sample or model of the goods used as a basis of the bargain is an express warranty. An affirmation merely of the value of the goods or a statement

---

[1] The numbers in the parentheses refer to the sections of the Uniform Commercial Code, 1962.

purporting to be merely the seller's opinion or commendation of the goods does not create an express warranty.

Wat Henry Pontiac Co. v. Bradley

210 P.2d 348 (Sup. Ct. Okla. 1949)

This was an action to recover the sum of $324.56 damages for breach of an express oral warranty of a used car purchased by Mrs. Joe Bradley (plaintiff) from the Wat Henry Pontiac Co. (defendant). The trial resulted in a judgment against the Wat Henry Pontiac Co. in the sum of $279.56. Affirmed on appeal.

JOHNSON, JUSTICE.   Mrs. Bradley testified that on October 22, 1944, she went to the Wat Henry Pontiac Company; that she contacted the manager of salesmen in charge of the used cars; that she made a deal for the car; that she was with her brother; and that the brother was present during her negotiations for the purchase of the car; that she asked many questions about the car; that the seller assured her that the car was in good condition; that he had driven the car; that "this is a car we know; this is a car I can recommend"; that "it is in A-1 shape." She informed him that her husband was in Camp Shelby, Mississippi, and that her child was only seven months old; and that she wanted to be sure she was going to get there. Wat Henry further assured her that he knew the car, he knew the man who had brought it in, that it was "mechanically perfect" and that it would get her any place she wanted to go. That she asked to drive the car and try it out, but was told that gas rations were very short and they were not allowed to send cars out for trial, but that she had no cause to fear this car, that it was all right; that she could not see the connecting rods or crankshaft or rings; that she was not a mechanic, but was a trained nurse.

The salesman who sold the car testified in substance that he had been an auto mechanic for about twelve years before becoming a salesman; that he was engaged in demonstrating and selling cars; that he did not warrant the car, but explained to the buyer that the sale was without a warranty, but did state that after the deal was closed that he told Bradley, "I would not be afraid to start, and I wouldn't have been afraid to start any place in the car, because it ran as nice as you would expect a car that age to run. There wasn't anything to indicate to me that there was anything wrong with the car, if there was anything wrong with it."

The rule is that to constitute an express warranty no particular form of words is necessary, and any affirmation of the quality or condition of the vehicle, not uttered as a matter of opinion or belief, made by a seller at the time of sale for the purpose of assuring the buyer of the truth of the fact and inducing the buyer to make the purchase, if so received and relied on by the buyer, is an express warranty.

This court in *International Harvester Co. v. Lawyer,* said:

" 'Warranty' is a matter of intention. A decisive test is whether the vendor assumes to assert a fact of which the buyer is ignorant, or merely states an opinion, or his judgment, upon a matter of which the vendor has no special knowledge, and on which the buyer may also be expected to have an opinion and to exercise his judgment. In the former case there is a warranty; in the latter case there is not."

The facts in this case bring it squarely within the above well-settled principles of law, and the jury was justified in finding that there was an oral warranty.

*   *   *   *   *

The buyer here was ignorant of the facts, and the defects were hidden and not open to discovery by the buyer. The seller was an expert in handling automobiles, having served for a long period of time as an automobile mechanic before becoming a salesman; and his statements as to the condition of the car and where it could be driven constituted a warranty and not mere opinion.

Warranty of Title

Nature of Warranty of Title. A warranty of title differs from other warranties in that it protects the buyer in his ownership of the goods he has bought whereas other warranties go to the quality of the goods sold. Unless the buyer knows from the circumstances that the seller does not have title to the goods but is selling in an official capacity and purports to sell only such title as a third person has, a warranty of title attaches to the sale. A warranty of title may be excluded or modified but only by specific language. The courts have generally held that unless the language of a disclaimer of warranty clearly and unequivocally includes the warranty of title, the buyer is justified in believing that the intent is to disclaim warranties of quality and not warranties of title. (2–312 [2].)

Scope of Warranty of Title. In a contract for sale the seller warrants that the title conveyed shall be good, and its transfer rightful; and that the goods shall be delivered free from any security interest or other lien or encumbrance of which the buyer at the time of contracting has no knowledge. If the goods are encumbered by an outstanding secured interest or lien, the contract of sale may provide that the sale is subject to the encumbrance. If it does not so provide, the seller is obligated to discharge any outstanding encumbrance before time for the delivery of the goods. Although the warranty of title provision of the Code does not expressly warrant against disturbance of quiet possession, the language of the provision is such that a disturbance of quiet possession is a breach of the warranty of title. (2–312 [1].)

A seller who is a merchant regularly dealing in goods of the kind sold warrants that the goods shall be delivered free of the rightful claim of any third person by way of infringement or the like, unless such warranty is disclaimed by the contract. A buyer who contracts with a seller for the purchase of goods which comply with specifications furnished by him must hold the seller harmless against any claim of infringement or the like which arises out of compliance with the specifications. (2–312 [3].)

Summary

A warranty of title differs in some respects from other warranties. Unless the buyer knows that the seller is acting in an official capacity or does not have title or the warranty of title is excluded or modified in clear and unequivocal language, it attaches. In a sale the seller warrants that the title conveyed shall be good, that the goods when delivered shall be free from encumbrances of which the buyer has no knowledge, and, if the seller is a merchant dealing in goods of the kind, that the goods will be free from rightful claim of infringement. A buyer who furnishes specifications to a seller must hold the seller harmless from claims of infringement which arise out of compliance with the specifications.

Implied Warranties

Nature of Implied Warranty. Under present methods of merchandising and because of the complexity of goods sold, the buyer either has little or no opportunity to examine the goods or is not in a position to adequately test the goods to determine their quality. A merchant dealing in such goods is in a much better position than a buyer to make a thorough examination of the goods or to make tests to determine their quality. Therefore, in the interest of trade certain responsibilities are imposed on the seller, especially if he is a merchant dealing in such goods, relative to the quality, character and suitability of the goods sold. This responsibility is not assumed by the seller, either by express promise or by the making of representations relative to the goods, but is imposed on him by operation of law. The responsibility imposed is the same, in its general nature, as that assumed by the seller when he expressly warrants goods. In fact the responsibility is a warranty implied in law.

This responsibility is not absolute. It attaches only under certain circumstances and the seller may contract against it. The courts, however, favor implied warranties, and if the seller wishes to relieve himself from the responsibility imposed on him by the implied warranties attaching to a sale, it must be clearly established that the parties to the sale did not intend it to attach.

There are two implied warranties of quality recognized under the Code: the implied warranty of merchantability and the implied warranty of fitness for a particular purpose. These two warranties overlap and under some circumstances the seller may be held liable for breach of warranty under either or both.

Implied Warranty of Merchantability. An implied warranty of merchantability attaches to a sale made by a merchant dealing in goods of the kind sold. The implied warranty may be excluded or modified by an appropriate agreement. (2–314 [1].) Under this section of the Code the serving for value of food or drink to be consumed either on the premises or elsewhere is a sale.

This provision in the Code resolves the controversy as to whether or not the serving of food in a restaurant or hotel dining room is a sale. Under this provision of the Code it is a sale and the server, if the food or drink is unwholesome, may be held liable either for breach of implied warranty of merchantability or implied warranty of fitness for a particular purpose.

At common law and under the Uniform Sales Act the term "merchantable" was not clearly defined and there was little uniformity in the standards applied in determining whether or not goods were of merchantable quality. In an attempt to give more certainty to an uncertain situation six tests of merchantability are set out in the Code. Goods to be merchantable must be at least such as (1) pass in the trade under the contract description; (2) in the case of fungible goods, are of fair average quality within the description; (3) are fit for the ordinary purpose for which such goods are used; (4) run, within the variations permitted by the agreement, of even kind, quality and quantity within each unit and among all units involved; (5) are adequately contained, packaged, and labeled as the agreement may require; and (6) conform to promises or affirmations of fact made on the container or label if any. (2–314 [2].)

Implied Warranty of Fitness for Particular Purpose.   To give rise to an implied warranty of fitness for a particular purpose the seller must at the time of contracting have reason to know the particular purpose for which the goods are required by the buyer and that the buyer is relying on the seller to select goods suitable for that purpose.

If the buyer gives the seller technical specifications of the goods he wishes to buy or in some other manner clearly indicates the particular goods desired, there would be no evidence of reliance on the seller's judgment and no implied warranty of fitness for a particular purpose. An implied warranty of fitness for a particular purpose may arise whether or not the seller is a merchant. (2–315.)

Summary

There are two implied warranties of quality—that of merchantability and that of fitness for a particular purpose. The implied warranty, unless excluded or modified, becomes a part of the sales contract by operation of law.

Accompanying a sale by a merchant dealing in goods of the kind sold, there is, unless excluded or modified, an implied warranty of merchantability. The warranty imposes on the seller liability if the goods are not of fair average quality. Six tests of merchantability are set out in the Code. The serving for value of food or drink is a sale.

The implied warranty of fitness for a particular purpose is based on the seller's having reason to know the particular purpose for which the buyer wishes the goods and the buyer's reliance on the seller's skill and judgment in selecting the goods suitable for his purpose. The warranty may be excluded or modified. The seller need not be a merchant to have the warranty attach.

Hunt v. Ferguson-Paulus Enterprises

415 P.2d 13 (Sup. Ct. Ore. 1966)

This was an action by Hunt (plaintiff) against Ferguson-Paulus Enterprises (defendant) to recover damages for injury allegedly sustained through a breach of warranty. Judgment for Ferguson-Paulus and Hunt appealed. Judgment affirmed.

Hunt purchased a cherry pie from Ferguson-Paulus through a vending machine owned and maintained by them. On biting into the pie one of Hunt's teeth was broken when it encountered a cherry pit.

LUSK, JUSTICE. If the cherry pie purchased by Hunt from Ferguson-Paulus was not reasonably fit for human consumption because of the presence of the cherry pit there was a breach of warranty and Hunt was entitled to recover his damages thereby caused.

In the consideration of similar cases some of the courts have drawn a distinction between injury caused by spoiled, impure, or contaminated food or food containing a foreign substance, and injury caused by a substance natural to the product sold. In the latter class of cases, these courts hold there is no liability on the part of the dispenser of the goods. Thus in the leading case of *Mix v. Ingersoll Candy Co.,* the court held that a patron of a restaurant who ordered and paid for chicken pie, which contained a sharp sliver or fragment of chicken bone, and was injured as a result of swallowing the bone, had no cause of action against the restauranter either for breach of warranty or negligence. Referring to cases in which recovery had been allowed the court said:

All of the cases are instances in which the food was found not to be reasonably fit for human consumption, either by reason of the presence of a foreign substance, or an impure and noxious condition of the food itself, such as for example, glass, stones, wires or nails in the food served, or tainted, decayed, diseased, or infected meats or vegetables.

The court went on to say that:

. . . despite the fact that a chicken bone may occasionally be encountered in a chicken pie, such chicken pie, in the absence of some further defect, is reasonably fit for human consumption. Bones which are natural to the type of meat served cannot legitimately be called a foreign substance, and a consumer who eats meat dishes ought to anticipate and be on guard against the presence of such bones.

Further the court said:

Certainly no liability would attach to a restaurant keeper for the serving of a T-bone steak, or a beef stew, which contained a bone natural to the type of meat served, or if a fish dish should contain a fish bone, or if a cherry pie should contain a cherry stone—although it be admitted that an ideal cherry pie would be stoneless.

Other courts have rejected the so-called foreign-natural test in favor of what is known as the "reasonable expectation" test, among them the Supreme Court of Wisconsin, which, in *Betehia v. Cape Cod Corp.* held that a person who was injured by a chicken bone in a chicken sandwich served to him in a restaurant, could recover for his injury either for breach of an implied warranty or for negligence. "There is a distinction," the court said, "between what a consumer expects to find in a fish stick and in a baked or fried fish, or in a chicken sandwich made from sliced white meat and in roast chicken. The test should be what is reasonably expected by the consumer in the food as served, not what might be natural to the ingredients of that food prior to preparation. What is to be reasonably expected by the consumer is a jury question in most cases; at least, we cannot say as a matter of law that a patron of a restaurant must expect a bone in a chicken sandwich either because chicken bones are occasionally found there or are natural to chicken."

In view of the judgment for the defendant, we are not required in this case to make a choice between the two rules. Under the foreign-natural test the plaintiff would be barred from recovery as a matter of law. The reasonable expectation test calls for determination of a question of fact. The Court has found the fact in favor of the defendant and this court has no power to disturb the finding.

Corneliuson v. Arthur Drug Stores, Inc.

214 A.2d 676 (Sup. Ct. Conn. 1965)

This was an action by Corneliuson (plaintiff) against Arthur Drug Stores, Inc. (defendant), for breach of an implied warranty of fitness of a home permanent waving lotion purchased by Corneliuson from Arthur. Corneliuson claimed that, as a result of her use of the lotion, she sustained a severe dermatitis with concomitant physical and neurotic injuries. The jury returned a verdict for Corneliuson which the trial court refused to set aside. Reversed on appeal.

HOUSE, JUSTICE. In *Crotty v. Shartenberg's-New Haven, Inc.,* we held that under our statute there may be an implied warranty that the goods sold shall be reasonably fit for a particular purpose, or that the goods shall be of merchantable quality and that the existence, nature and extent of either implied warranty depends on the circumstances of the case. We noted that some jurisdictions hold that if the article sold can be used by a normal person without injury, there is no breach of the implied warranty of reasonable fitness, while others adopt the theory that the seller is not absolved from liability under the implied warranty created by the statute by the mere fact that only a small portion of those who use the product suffer injuries from its use. We concluded that the term "reasonable fitness" must, of necessity, be considered one of degree and that the term must be "related to the subject of the sale."

Rejecting the rule limiting the application of the term "reasonable fitness" to a class or group designated as normal persons, we adopted the test of injurious effect to "an appreciable number of people." We held that not only the causal connection between the product and the injury must be established but also the plaintiff must be a member of a class who would be similarly affected by the product, identifying that class as an appreciable number of people.

In the course of the opinion we used the following language:

To establish a breach of the warranty, the plaintiff must show (1) that the product contains a substance or ingredient which has a tendency to affect injuriously an appreciable number of people, though fewer in number than the number of normal buyers, and (2) that he has, in fact, been injured or harmed by the use of the product. . . . The burden is on the plaintiff to establish these facts. Proof of the harmful propensities of the substance and that it can affect injuriously an appreciable number of persons is essential to his case. . . . If a buyer has knowledge, either actual or constructive, that he is allergic to a particular substance and purchases a product which he knows or reasonably should know contains that substance, he cannot recover damages for breach of an implied warranty. Nor can he recover if he suffers harm by reason of his own improper use of the article warranted. . . . When a manufacturer puts into a product to be sold for human use a substance which has deleterious qualities and a tendency to harm an appreciable number of its users, the manufacturer, and not the user, should shoulder the risk of injurious consequences. The same risk should be borne by the retailer who sells the article to a prospective user who, relying on the retailer, is entitled to believe that the article is reasonably fit for the purpose for which it is sold.

. . . Although there was evidence from which the jury could find that the Ogilvie Sisters lotion did cause injury to Corneliuson there was no evidence from which they could find that this lotion as compounded had a tendency to affect injuriously an appreciable number of people. Proof of both injury to Corneliuson and such injurious tendency are necessary for Corneliuson to prevail. Proof that all permanent waving lotions generally contain certain basic chemicals compounded in varying strengths in the different brands and that in the strength used in some of them the chemicals may injuriously affect some people is not alone a reasonable basis for a conclusion that any specific lotion, even though it contains in some form those same basic chemicals, has the injurious tendency requisite to establish liability and that that lotion is not "reasonably fit" or of "merchantable quality" as those terms are used in the statute on implied warranties. The basic test must be applied to the particular product as compounded, which necessarily includes any incorporated substance or ingredient in the strength and quantity used in the particular product, not in the strength and quantity which such substances or ingredients may be used in some other products.

Exclusions, Modification, or Conflict of Warranties

Common Law Rule. At common law the parties to a sales contract were free, by mutual agreement, to relieve the seller from all liability arising from warranties, either express or implied. The courts gave a narrow construction to exclusion clauses and held that a disclaimer of "all warranties stated herein" or similar language included in a sales contract did not exclude implied warranties. If the circumstances were such that it was clear that both parties were aware of the exclusion clause and agreed to it the court would enforce it. There were no general provisions in the Uniform Sales Act relating to exclusion or modification of warranty clauses in the sales contract. Section 15(3) of the act did provide: "If the buyer has examined the goods there is no implied warranty as regards defects which such examination ought to reveal."

Exclusions or Modifications. The drafters of the Code recognized that the parties should, if they desired to do so, have the right to relieve the seller from all or any phase of his liability. Experience, however, demonstrated the need of protecting the buyer from the inclusion in a sales contract of an exclusion or modification clause unless the buyer was fully aware of the inclusion and freely consented thereto.

In framing the provisions of the Code relative to exclusion or modification of warranties, the drafters recognized the desirability of distinguishing between different types of warranties. An express warranty made in the negotiation of a sales contract or in the formal draft of it, and words or conduct tending to negate or limit the warranty shall be construed whenever reasonable as consistent with each other; but negation or limitation is inoperative to the extent that such construction is unreasonable. (2–316.) If a sales contract includes an express warranty and also includes a clause which seeks to exclude "all warranties, express or implied," such clause would be inoperative since it would be unreasonable. Also, if the sales contract is in writing, oral evidence of an agreement to exclude or modify warranties included in the written contract would not be admissible. (2–202.)

To exclude an implied warranty of merchantability or any part of it the language must mention merchantability and in case of a writing must be conspicuous. To exclude or modify an implied warranty of merchantability, where the sales contract is in writing, the exclusion clause would have to be printed or written into the contract in larger type or letters or in ink of a different color so that one reading the contract would not be likely to overlook it. If the seller wishes added protection he should have the buyer separately sign the exclusion clause. (2–316 [2].)

To exclude or modify an implied warranty of fitness for a particular purpose the exclusion must be in writing and conspicuous. Language to exclude all implied warranties of fitness is sufficient if it states, for example, that "There are no warranties which extend beyond the description on the face hereof." However, such clause in the contract, to be effective, would have to be printed or written in conspicuous type or letters. (2–316 [2].)

Unless circumstances indicate otherwise, all implied warranties are excluded by expressions like "as is," "with all faults," or other language which in common understanding calls the buyer's attention to the exclusion of warranties and makes plain that there are no implied warranties. (2–316 [3] [*a*].)

When the buyer, before entering into the contract, has examined the goods or a sample or model as fully as he desires or has refused to examine the goods, there is no implied warranty with regards to defects which an examination ought in the circumstances to have revealed to him. If the seller merely makes the goods available to the buyer for examination and the buyer neglects to examine them, the seller would not be protected under this provision of the Code. The seller should not only make the goods available for examination but he should demand or follow a course equivalent to a demand that the buyer examine the goods. (2–316 [3] [*b*].)

An implied warranty can also be excluded or modified by course of dealings, or course of performance or usage of trade. (2–316 [3] [*c*].)

Conflict of Warranties. Frequently in a sales contract implied warranties supplement express warranties. The Code provides that warranties whether express or implied shall be construed as consistent with each other and as cumulative, but if such construction is unreasonable the intention of the parties shall determine which warranty is dominant. In case of conflict the court must determine from all the facts and circumstances which warranty was intended by the parties to be dominant. To aid the court in determining intention the Code provides: Exact or technical specifications displace an inconsistent sample or model or general language of description. A sample from an existing bulk displaces inconsistent general language of description. Express warranties displace inconsistent implied warranties other than an implied warranty of fitness for a particular purpose. (2–317.)

Summary

Language of a disclaimer in a sales contract is ineffective where such language is inconsistent with an express warranty included therein. To exclude or modify an implied warranty of merchantability, merchantability must be mentioned and in the case of a writing must be conspicuous. To exclude or modify an implied warranty of fitness for a particular purpose the exclusion must be in writing and conspicuous. Implied warranties are excluded by expressions like "as is" or "with all faults." If the buyer examines the goods or a sample or model or a demand is made that he examine them and he refuses, there is no implied warranty with regards to defects which the examination ought to reveal. An implied warranty can also be excluded or modified by course of dealing or course of performance or by usage of trade.

Express and implied warranties will be construed as consistent and cumulative unless such construction is unreasonable, and if unreasonable, the intention of the parties as to which warranty shall be dominant shall control.

Weisz v. Parke-Bernet Galleries, Inc.

325 N.Y.S. 2d 576 (Civ. Ct. N.Y.C. 1971)

This was an action brought by Dr. Arthur Weisz and David and Irene Schwartz (plaintiffs) against the Parke-Bernet Galleries, Inc. (defendant) to recover the purchase prices of paintings that plaintiffs had purchased at a Parke-Bernet auction. Judgment for plaintiffs.

On May 16, 1962, Dr. Arthur Weisz attended an auction conducted by the Parke-Bernet Galleries, Inc., where he ultimately bought for the sum of $3,347.50 a painting listed in the auction catalogue as the work of Raoul Dufy. Some two years later, on May 13, 1964, David and Irene Schwartz bought for $9,360.00 at a Parke-Bernet auction a painting also listed in the catalogue as the work of Raoul Dufy.

Several years after the second auction, as a result of an investigation conducted by the New York County District Attorney's office, the plaintiffs received information that the paintings were in fact forgeries. When this was called to Parke-Bernet's attention, Parke-Bernet denied any legal responsibility, asserting among other things that the conditions of sale for both auctions included a disclaimer of warranty as to genuineness, authorship and the like.

In each instance the auction catalogue contained several pages of print entitled "Conditions of Sale." The second of 15 numbered paragraphs provided as follows:

The Galleries has endeavored to catalogue and describe the property correctly, but all property is sold "as is" and neither the Galleries nor its consignor warrants or represents, and they shall in no event be responsible for, the correctness of description, genuineness, authorship, provenience or condition of the property, and no statement contained in the catalogue or made orally at the sale or elsewhere shall be deemed to be such a warranty or representation, or an assumption of liability.

SANDLER, JUSTICE. The most substantial of the defenses interposed by Parke-Bernet is that the conditions of sale for the auctions, appearing on a preliminary page of each catalogue, included a disclaimer of any warranty and that the plaintiffs are bound by its terms.

This issue embraces two separate questions, each of which merits careful examination.

First, did the plaintiffs in fact know of the disclaimer, and, if they did not, are they legally chargeable with such knowledge.

Second, if the answer to either part of the first question is yes, was the disclaimer effective, under all the circumstances of the auctions, to immunize Parke-Bernet from the legal consequences that would normally follow where a sale results from a representation of genuineness that is thereafter disclosed to be completely inaccurate.

* * * * *

As to the first auction, I am satisfied that Dr. Weisz did not in fact know of the conditions of sale and may not properly be charged with knowledge of its contents. I accept as entirely accurate his testimony that in his prior appearances at Parke-Bernet auctions he had not made any bids, and that on the occasion of his purchase he did not observe the conditions of sale and was not aware of its existence.

The test proposed for this kind of issue by Williston, quite consistent with the decided cases, is whether "the person . . . should as a reasonable man understand that it contains terms of the contract that he must read at his peril." 1 Williston on Contracts, Sec. 90D (1937).

The most obvious characteristic of the two Parke-Bernet auctions is that they attracted people on the basis of their interest in owning works of art, not on the basis of their legal experience or business sophistication. Surely it is unrealistic to assume that people who bid at such auctions will ordinarily understand that a gallery catalogue overwhelmingly devoted to descriptions of works of art also includes in its preliminary pages conditions of sale. Even less reasonable does it seem to me to expect a bidder at such an auction to appreciate the possibility that the conditions of sale would include a disclaimer of liability for the accuracy of the basic information presented throughout the catalogue in unqualified form with every appearance of certainty and reliability.

For someone in Dr. Weisz's position to be bound by conditions of sale of which he in fact knew nothing, considerably more was required of Parke-Bernet to call those conditions of sale to his attention than occurred here.

As to the Schwartz case, I am satisfied from the evidence that Mrs. Schwartz knew of the conditions of sale, and that both Schwartz plaintiffs are chargeable with that knowledge since they both participated in the purchase.

This factual conclusion leads to consideration of the extremely interesting question whether the language of disclaimer relied upon as a bar to the actions should be deemed effective for that purpose. No case has come to my attention that squarely presents the issue raised by the underlying realities of this case.

What is immediately apparent from any review of the evidence is that notwithstanding the language of disclaimer, Parke-Bernet expected that bidders at its auctions would rely upon the accuracy of its descriptions, and intended that they should. Parke-Bernet, as the evidence confirms, is an exceedingly well-known gallery, linked in the minds of people with the handling, exhibition and sale of valuable artistic works and invested with an aura of expertness and reliability. The very fact that Parke-Bernet was offering a work of art for sale would inspire confidence that it was genuine and that the listed artist in fact was the creator of the work.

The wording of the catalogue was clearly designed to emphasize the genuineness of the works to be offered. The list of artists followed by catalogue numbers, the black-and-white reproductions of the more important works, the simple listing of the name of the artist with the years of his birth and death could not have failed to impress upon the buyer that these facts could be relied on and that one could safely part with large sums of money in the confident knowledge that a genuine artistic work was being acquired.

Where one party in a contractual relationship occupies a position of superior knowledge and experience, and where that superior knowledge is relied upon and intended to be relied upon by the other, surely more is required for an effective disclaimer than appears here.

After reassuring the reader that Parke-Bernet endeavored to catalogue the works of art correctly, there follow highly technical and legalistic words of disclaimer in a situation in which plain and emphatic words are required. And this provision, in light of the critical importance to the buyer of a warning that he may not rely on the fact that a work attributed to an artist was in fact his creation, is in no way given the special prominence that it clearly requires.

The language used, the understated manner of its presentation, the failure to refer to it explicitly in the preliminary oral announcement of the auction all lead to the conclusion that Parke-Bernet did not expect the bidders to take the disclaimer too seriously or to be too concerned about it. I am convinced that the average reader of this provision would view it as some kind of technicality that should in no way derogate from the certainty that he was buying genuine artistic works, and that this was precisely the impression intended to be conveyed.

In denying legal effect to the disclaimer I am acting consistently with a whole body of law that reflects an increasing sensitivity to the requirements of fair dealing where there is a relationship between parties in which there is a basic inequality of knowledge, expertness or economic power.

Who Benefits from Warranty

General Rule. The courts, in determining who is entitled to the benefit of a warranty, have considered the warranty as contractual. In many situations the seller expressly promises to assume responsibility for the failure of the goods to measure up to certain defined standards. Such a warranty is contractual. However, a warranty may arise as the result of representations which are not promissory in nature, and an implied warranty may attach by operation of law. Nevertheless, all suits for damages for breach of warranty are actions in contract, not in tort. Proceeding from the accepted theory that a warranty is contractual, the courts have applied the general rule of contract law, that one not a party to a contract has no right to enforce the contract. Traditionally, this has meant that a person who did not himself purchase the defective goods did not have a cause of action for breach of warranty and even the purchaser of defective goods could sue only his immediate seller and not the manufacturer with whom he was not in privity of contract.

Demise of the Privity Doctrine. Today there is a growing tendency on the part of courts to allow recovery by an injured purchaser directly from the manufacturer or processor. In most cases the manufacturer or processor has control over the state of the product when it reaches the buyer's control and should be held liable for defects in it. The fact that the ultimate consumer may bring suit against the manufacturer or processor in no way relieves the retailer from his responsibility for the fitness or merchantability of the goods. In many states the buyer has been permitted to sue both the retailer and the manufacturer or processor in the same suit.

The manufacturers of many products give a manufacturer's warranty to the ultimate purchaser of their products in which they warrant their products against certain defined defects and in which they expressly limit their liability for breach of the express warranty. A manufacturer who has given such a warranty is liable on the warranty in a direct suit brought by the ultimate purchaser to whom the warranty is addressed.

Uniform Commercial Code. The drafters of the Code took no position on whether an injured purchaser could directly sue the manufacturer; instead, they left the development of the law on this point open to the courts, which as indicated above tend to allow such direct actions.

The Code, in Section 2–318, does extend warranty protection to "any natural person who is in the family or household of his buyer or who is a guest in his house if it is reasonable to expect that such person may use, consume, or be affected by the goods and who is injured in person by breach of warranty." The Code further provides that the seller may not exclude or limit his liability to the members of the buyer's household or his guests for breach of warranty. (2–318.)

Summary

Under the general rule a seller is liable for damages for breach of warranty to his immediate purchaser and to no one else.

The courts are now tending to hold manufacturers and processors liable to the ultimate consumer for damages for breach of warranty.

A manufacturer is liable to an ultimate purchaser for breach of a warranty directed to the ultimate consumer.

The Code extends the scope of a seller's warranty to include any natural person who is in the family or household of his buyer or is a guest, and further provides that the seller may not exclude or limit his liability to such persons.

Henningsen v. Bloomfield Motors, Inc.

161 A.2d 69 (Sup. Ct. N.J. 1960)

This was an action for breach of warranty by Claus and Helen Henningsen (plaintiffs) against Chrysler Corporation and Bloomfield Motors (defendants). The trial court awarded damages to the Henningsens. Affirmed on appeal.

Claus Henningsen purchased a new 1955 Plymouth from Bloomfield Motors as a gift for his wife, Helen. At the time of purchase Claus signed a purchase order that included an express warranty against defects in material and workmanship but which limited Chrysler's obligation to replacing the defective parts. The "warranty clause" went on to say that this warranty was "expressly in lieu of all other warranties expressed or implied, and all other obligations or liabilities on its part." This statement was made in fine print on the reverse side of the purchase order as of the seventh of ten paragraphs. Shortly after the purchase and while Helen Henningsen was driving the car on a smooth dry pavement, she heard a loud noise as if something cracked, the steering wheel spun in her hands, and the car veered sharply to the right, crashing into a brick wall. This action was then initiated against Chrysler and Bloomfield Motors, and the trial court awarded judgment to the Henningsens. The defendants appealed, arguing among other things (1) that no implied warranties ran from Chrysler to the Henningsens, (2) that there was an effective disclaimer of the implied warranties, and (3) that Helen Henningsen's lack of privity with the defendants barred a breach of warranty action against them.

FRANCIS, JUSTICE

I. The Claim of Implied Warranty against the Manufacturer. Preliminarily, it may be said that the express warranty against defective parts and workmanship is not inconsistent with an implied warranty of merchantability. Such warranty cannot be excluded for that reason.

Chrysler points out that an implied warranty of merchantability is an incident of a contract of sale. It concedes, of course, the making of the original sale to Bloomfield Motors, Inc., but maintains that this transaction marked the terminal point of its contractual connection with the car. Then Chrysler urges that since it was not a party to the sale by the dealer to Henningsen, there is no privity of contract between it and the plaintiffs, and the absence of this privity eliminates any such implied warranty.

There is no doubt that under early common-law concepts of contractual liability only those persons who were parties to the bargain could sue for a breach of it. In more recent times a noticeable disposition has appeared in a number of jurisdictions to break through the narrow barrier of privity when dealing with sales of goods in order to give realistic recognition to a universally accepted fact. The fact is that the dealer and the ordinary buyer do not, and are not expected to, buy goods, whether they be foodstuffs or automobiles, exclusively for their own consumption or use. Makers and manufacturers know this and advertise and market their products on that assumption; witness, the "family" car, the baby foods, etc. The limitations of privity in contracts for the sale of goods developed their place in the law when marketing conditions were simple, when maker and buyer frequently met face to face on an equal bargaining plane and when many of the products were relatively uncomplicated and conducive to inspection by a buyer competent to evaluate their quality. With the advent of mass marketing, the manufacturer became remote from the purchaser, sales were accomplished through intermediaries, and the demand for the product was created by advertising media. In such an economy it became obvious that the consumer was the person being cultivated. Manifestly, the connotation of "consumer" was broader than that of "buyer." He signified such a person who, in the reasonable contemplation of the parties to the sale, might be expected to use the product.

As far back as 1932, in the well known case of *Baxter v. Ford Motor Co.,* the Supreme Court of Washington gave recognition to the impact of the existing commercial practices on the straitjacket of privity, saying:

> It would be unjust to recognize a rule that would permit manufacturers of goods to create a demand for their products by representing that they possess qualities which they, in fact, do not possess, and then, because there is no privity of contract existing between the consumer and the manufacturer, deny the consumer the right to recover if damages result from the absence of those qualities, when such absence is not readily noticeable.

Accordingly, we hold that under modern marketing conditions, when a manufacturer puts a new automobile in the stream of trade and promotes its purchase by the public, an implied warranty that it is reasonably suitable for use as such accompanies it into the hands of the ultimate purchaser. Absence of agency between the manufacturer and the dealer who makes the ultimate sale is immaterial.

II. The Effect of the Disclaimer and Limitation of Liability Clauses on the Implied Warranty of Merchantability. What effect should be given to the express warranty in question which seeks to limit the manufacturer's liability to replacement of defective parts, and which disclaims all other warranties, express or implied? . . .

* * * * *

The warranty before us is a standardized form designed for mass use. It is imposed upon the automobile consumer. He takes it or leaves it, and he must take it to buy an automobile. No bargaining is engaged in with respect to it. In fact, the dealer through whom it comes to the buyer is without authority to alter it; his function is ministerial—simply to deliver it. The form warranty is not only standard with Chrysler but, as mentioned above, it is the uniform warranty of the Automobile Manufacturers Association.

The gross inequality of bargaining position occupied by the consumer in the automobile industry is thus apparent. There is no competition among the car makers in the area of the express warranty. Where can the buyer go to negotiate for better protection? Such control and limitation of his remedies are inimical to the public welfare and, at the very least, call for great care by the courts to avoid injustice through application of strict common-law principles of freedom of contract.

* * * * *

V. The Defense of Lack of Privity against Mrs. Henningsen. Both defendants contend that since there was no privity of contract between them and Mrs. Henningsen, she cannot recover for breach of any warranty made by either of them. On the facts, as they were developed, we agree that she was not a party to the purchase agreement. Her right to maintain the action, therefore, depends upon whether she occupies such legal status thereunder as to permit her to take advantage of a breach of defendants' implied warranties.

In the present matter, the basic contractual relationship is between Claus Henningsen, Chrysler, and Bloomfield Motors, Inc. The precise issue presented is whether Mrs. Henningsen, who is not a party to their respective warranties, may claim under them. We are convinced that the cause of justice in this area of the law can be served only by recognizing that she is such a person who, in the reasonable contemplation of the parties to the warranty, might be expected to become a user of the automobile. Accordingly, her lack of privity does not stand in the way of prosecution of the injury suit against the defendant Chrysler.

It is our opinion that an implied warranty of merchantability chargeable to either an automobile manufacturer or a dealer extends to the purchaser of the car, members of his family, and to other persons occupying or using it with his consent. It would be wholly opposed to reality to say that use by such persons is not within the anticipation of parties to such a warranty of reasonable suitability of an automobile for ordinary highway operation. Those persons must be considered within the distributive chain.

Section 2–318 of the Uniform Commercial Code proposes that the warranty be extended to "any natural person who is in the family or household of his buyer or who is a guest in his home if it is reasonable to expect that such person may use, consume or be affected by the goods and who is injured in person by breach of the warranty." And the section provides also that "A seller may not exclude or limit the operation" of the extension. A footnote thereto says that beyond this provision "the section is neutral and is not intended to enlarge or restrict the developing case law on whether the seller's warranties, given to his buyer, who resells, extend to other persons in the distributive chain."

It is not necessary in this case to establish the outside limits of the warranty protection. For present purposes, with respect to automobiles, it suffices to promulgate the principle set forth above.

Product Liability

Liability of a manufacturer based on breach of warranty is only one theory of liability included in the area of product liability—the liability of a manufacturer of goods to the user of goods for personal injury or property damage resulting from the use of the goods. Product liability encompasses negligence and so-called strict liability in tort as well as warranty. The scope and nature of the liability of a manufacturer to the user of his product is in a state of continual change and development.

Negligence.   The early rule was *caveat emptor,* that the buyer had to make his own inspection, rely on his own judgment and assume the risk of any defect in the goods he purchased. Gradually, American courts came to do away with this rule and to hold that a seller of goods is under a duty to exercise the care of a reasonable man to see that the goods do no harm to a buyer.

An important case in this line of cases was *McPherson v. Buick Motor Co.*[2] decided in 1916 by the New York Court of Appeals. In that case the manufacturer, Buick Motor Company, was held liable to a subpurchaser for injuries sustained when a wheel collapsed. The court found that Buick was negligent in its inspection of the wheel and was liable in tort on a negligence theory.

Subsequent courts have found liability based on negligence not only where there was a failure to inspect but also for (1) misrepresentation as to the character of the goods or their fitness for a particular purpose, (2) failure to disclose known defects or to warn about known dangers, and (3) failure to use due care in designing and preparing the goods for sale.

In many cases, it would be extremely difficult for an injured person to show the circumstances in the seller's plant at the time a defective product was manufactured. At this point, the doctrine of *res ipsa loquitor* often comes to the injured person's aid. To invoke this doctrine he must show that the cause of the injury was something that lay within the responsibility of the defendant-manufacturer, thus putting the burden on the manufacturer to show it did exercise due care in the circumstances. The defendant-manufacturer can prevail against a suit based on negligence if it can show the defect was one that could not be discovered or avoided by the exercise of all reasonable care or that under the facts and circumstances all reasonable care was in fact exercised.

In the earliest cases the courts held that the manufacturer was liable only to the person with whom he contracted. Today a substantial number of courts allow an injured consumer to recover from the manufacturer in a direct suit. The requirement of privity is dispensed with and the decisions have been, as a general rule, based on concepts of public policy or a conduit theory, that is, that the retailer is the conduit through which the product is distributed and that the manufacturer owes the duty of reasonable care directly to the consumer.

Strict Liability.   Once negligence became established as a basis for liability of sellers to the ultimate consumers, an effort was begun to carry the seller's

---

[2] 111 N.E. 1050 (Ct. App. N.Y. 1916).

responsibility even further and to hold the seller liable even though he had exercised reasonable care—in effect making him an insurer of the safety of his product. According to Prosser, the rationale for strict liability which has proved convincing to those courts which have accepted it consists of three main arguments:[3]

1. The public interest in human life and safety demands the maximum possible protection that the law can give against dangerous defects in products which consumers must buy, and against which they are helpless to protect themselves; and it justifies the imposition, upon all suppliers of such products, of full responsibility for the harm they cause, even though the supplier has done his best. This argument, which in the last analysis rests upon public sentiment, has had its greatest force in the cases of food, where there was once popular outcry against an evil industry, injuries and actions have multiplied, and public feeling is most obvious. It is now being advanced as to other products, such as automobiles.

2. The maker, by placing the goods upon the market, represents to the public that they are suitable and safe for use; and by packaging, advertising or otherwise, he does everything that he can to induce that belief. He intends and expects that the product will be purchased and used in reliance upon this assurance of safety; and it is in fact so purchased and used. The middleman is no more than a conduit, a mere mechanical device, through whom the thing sold is to reach the ultimate user. The supplier has invited and solicited the use; and when it leads to disaster, he should not be permitted to avoid the responsibility by saying that he has made no contract with the consumer.

3. It is already possible to enforce strict liability by resort to a series of actions, in which the retailer is first held liable on a warranty to his purchaser, and indemnity on a warranty is then sought successively from other suppliers, until the manufacturer finally pays the damages, with the added costs of repeated litigation. This is an expensive, time-consuming, and wasteful process, and it may be interrupted by insolvency, lack of jurisdiction, disclaimers, or the statute of limitations, anywhere along the time.

The essential aspects of strict liability are expressed in Section 402A of the *Restatement of Torts* (Second):

§ 402A. Special Liability of Seller of Product for Physical Harm to User or Consumer.

(1) One who sells any product in a defective condition unreasonably dangerous to the user or consumer or to his property, is subject to liability for physical harm thereby caused to the ultimate user or consumer, or to his property, if
  (a) the seller is engaged in the business of selling such a product, and
  (b) it is expected to and does reach the user or consumer without substantial change in the condition in which it is sold.
(2) The rule stated in Subsection (1) applies although
  (a) the seller has exercised all possible care in the preparation and sale of his product, and
  (b) the user or consumer has not bought the product from or entered into any contractual relation with the seller.

As can be seen from the *Restatement,* the lack of privity of contract is not a defense available to the seller. The crucial elements of strict liability are a "defective condition" at the time the product leaves the seller's hands and

---

[3] William L. Prosser, *Handbook of the Law of Torts* (4th ed.; St. Paul, Minn.: West Publishing Co.), p. 651.

which causes harm to a user and which is "unreasonably dangerous" to him or his property—that is, that it is more dangerous than the ordinary consumer would contemplate.

It is important to note that strict liability is not presently accepted by all states with regard to all types of products and all types of defects. Strict liability finds its most common acceptance with sales of food and drink, but is gradually being extended to a wide variety of products that can prove to be unreasonably dangerous because of defective manufacture. And, as presently applied, strict liability can be used against retailers as well as manufacturers of such defective products.

Summary

Product liability encompasses negligence and strict liability as well as warranties. A seller of goods is under a duty to use due care in the design, manufacture or preparation, inspection, and sale of goods; failure to do so may give rise to a cause of action for negligence by a person injured by a defective product.

Strict liability is imposed by some states on the sellers of some types of products. It arises when a product is sold in a defective condition unreasonably dangerous to a user or consumer or to his property and the defective product results in damage to the person or property. Neither lack of privity nor exercise of all possible due care are defenses to an action for strict liability.

Larsen v. General Motors Corp.

391 F.2d 495 (8th Cir. 1968)

This was an action by Erling David Larsen (plaintiff) against General Motors (defendant) to recover damages resulting from an alleged negligent design of the steering assembly of a Corvair automobile manufactured and sold by defendant. The District Court rendered summary judgment for General Motors and Larsen appealed. Reversed.

Larsen received severe bodily injuries while driving, with the consent of the owner, a 1963 Chevrolet Corvair. A head-on collision, with the impact occurring on the left front corner of the Corvair, caused a severe rearward thrust of the steering mechanism into Larsen's head.

Larsen did not contend that the design caused the accident but that because of the design he received injuries he would not have otherwise received or, in the alternative, his injuries would not have been as severe. The rearward displacement of the steering shaft on the left frontal impact was much greater on the Corvair than it would be in other cars that were designed to protect against such a rearward displacement. Larsen's complaint alleged (1) negligence in design of the steering assembly; (2) negligent failure to warn of the alleged latent or inherently dangerous condition to the user of the steering assembly placement; and (3) breach of express and implied warranties of merchantability of the vehicle's intended use. General Motors contended that it had no duty to design and manufacture a vehicle safe to occupy during collision impacts.

GIBSON, CIRCUIT JUDGE.   General Motors contends that it has no duty to produce a vehicle in which it is safe to collide or which is accident-proof or incapable of injurious misuse. It views its duty as extending only to producing a vehicle that is reasonably fit for its intended use or for the purpose for which it was made and that is free from hidden defects; and that the intended use of a vehicle and the purpose for which it is manufactured do not include its participation in head-on collisions or any other type of impact, regardless of the manufacturer's ability to foresee that such collisions may occur.

Larsen maintains that General Motors' view of its duty is too narrow and restrictive and that an automobile manufacturer is under a duty to use reasonable care in the design of the automobile to make it safe to the user for its foreseeable use and that its intended use or purpose is for travel on the streets and highways, including the possibility of impact or collision with other vehicles or stationary objects.

There is a line of cases directly supporting General Motors' contention that negligent design of an automobile is not actionable, where the alleged defective design is not a causative factor in the accident. The latest leading case on this point is *Evans v. General Motors Corp.* A divided court there held that General Motors in designing a "X" body frame without perimeter support, instead of an allegedly more safe perimeter body frame, was not liable for the death of a user allegedly caused by the designed defect because the defendant's design could not have functioned to avoid the collision.

In *Shumard v. General Motors Corp.,* the United States District Court for the Southern District of Ohio held there was no liability where the alleged design defects in a 1962 Corvair automobile caused it to erupt into flames on impact, killing the plaintiff's decedent. That Court said: ". . . No duty exists to make an automobile fireproof, nor does a manufacturer have to make a product which is 'accident-proof' or 'fool-proof.' "

Generally, as noted in 76 A.L.R. 2d 93, Anno.: Products Liability—Duty As to Design, the manufacturer has a duty to use reasonable care under the circumstances in the design of a product but is not an insurer that his product is incapable of producing injury, and this duty of design is met when the article is safe for its intended use and when it will fairly meet any "emergency of use" which is foreseeable.

Accepting, therefore, the principle that a manufacturer's duty of design and construction extends to producing a product that is reasonably fit for its intended use and free of hidden defects that could render it unsafe for such use, the issue narrows on the proper interpretation of "intended use." Automobiles are made for use on the roads and highways in transporting persons and cargo to and from various points. This intended use cannot be carried out without encountering in varying degrees the statistically proved hazard of injury-producing impacts of various types. The manufacturer should not be heard to say that it does not intend its product to be involved in any accident when it can easily foresee and when it knows that the probability over the life of its product is high, that it will be involved in some type of injury-producing accident. O'Connell in his article "Taming the Automobile," 58 *Nw. U. L. Rev.* 299, 348 (1963) cites that between one-fourth to two-thirds of all automobiles during their use at some time are involved in an accident producing injury or death. Other statistics are available showing the frequency and certainty of fatal and injury-producing accidents. It should be recognized that the environment in which a product is used must be taken into consideration by the manufacturer.

We think the "intended use" construction urged by General Motors is much too narrow and unrealistic. Where the manufacturer's negligence in design causes an unreasonable risk to be imposed upon the user of its products, the manufacturer should be liable for the injury caused by its failure to exercise reasonable care in the design. These injuries are readily foreseeable as an incident to the normal and expected use of an automobile. While automobiles are not made for the purpose of colliding with each other, a frequent and inevitable contingency of normal automobile use will result in collisions and injury-producing impacts. No rational basis exists for limiting recovery to situations where the defect in design or manufacture was the causative factor of the accident, as the accident and the resulting injury, usually caused by the so-called "second collison" of the passenger with the interior part of the automobile, all are foreseeable. Where the injuries or enhanced injuries are due to the manufacturer's failure to use reasonable care to avoid subjecting the user of its products to an unreasonable risk of injury, general negligence principles should be applicable. The sole function of an automobile is not just to provide a means of transportation, it is to provide a means of safe transportation or as safe as is reasonably possible under the present state of the art.

Filler v. Rayex Corp.

435 F.2d 336 (7th Cir. 1970)

This was an action brought by Michael Filler and his mother, Barbara Mitchell (plaintiffs) against Rayex Corp. (defendant) to recover damages for loss of Michael's right eye and medical expenses. The U.S. District Court granted judgment for the plaintiffs. Rayex appealed. Judgment affirmed.

The facts are given in the opinion:

CUMMINGS, CIRCUIT JUDGE.   When his injury occurred, Michael Filler was a 16-year-old student at Oak Hill High School, near Marion, Indiana. While he was practicing for a varsity baseball game in the late afternoon of June 10, 1966, fungoes were being lofted to him by a fellow player. Filler lost a fly ball in the sun, although he was wearing flipped-down "baseball sunglasses" manufactured by defendant. After tipping the top of his baseball glove, the ball struck the right side of the sunglasses, shattering the right lens into sharp splinters which pierced his right eye, necessitating its removal nine days later.

Filler's coach was Richard Beck, an experienced ballplayer, whose first baseball season at Oak Hill was in 1965. During that season, Beck would not allow his players to use sunglasses, considering them too dangerous. However, before the 1966 season, he read the following advertisement of defendant in *Sporting News:*

"PLAY BALL!
and Flip for Instant Eye Protection with
RAYEX
Baseball
SUNGLASSES
Professional
FLIP-SPECS"

The advertisement also stated:

Scientific lenses protect your eyes with a flip from sun and glare anywhere . . . baseball, beach, boat, driving, golfing, fishing, just perfect for Active and Spectator Sports—World's finest sunglasses.

After seeing this material, Beck decided to buy six pairs of defendant's flip-type baseball sunglasses for use by his outfielders and second basemen. Each pair of sunglasses was in a cardboard box labeled "Baseball Sunglasses—Professional Flip-Specs," stating "simply flip . . . for instant eye protection." The guarantee inside each box provided:

Rayex lenses are guaranteed for life against breakage. If lens breakage occurs mail glasses and 50¢ (Postage Handling Charge) for complete repair service.
Rayex Sunglasses are guaranteed to:
1.   Eliminate 96% of harmful ultra-violet and infra-red rays.
2.   Protect your eyes against reflected glare from smooth surfaces, roads, water, snow, etc.
3.   Retain clear, undistorted vision.

Except for the flip feature and elastic tape at the rear of the frame, the glasses resembled ordinary sunglasses. The thinness of the lenses was shielded by the frames and therefore not obvious to users.

These glasses were stored in the glove compartment of coach Beck's car, and in accordance with the custom of his teammates, Filler removed a pair of the sunglasses from the coach's car and was using them at the time of his injury. Neither Filler, nor Beck, nor indeed even defendant's president knew the lenses would shatter into sharp splinters when hit by a baseball.

After a bench trial, the district judge awarded Filler $101,000 damages and his mother $1,187.75 for her consequential damages. In an unreported memorandum opinion, the district judge supported this result on three independent grounds: implied warranty, strict liability, and negligence.[4] Under any of those theories, privity between the manufacturer and plaintiff is not required by controlling Indiana law.

We agree that defendant is liable for breach of an implied warranty of fitness for a particular purpose. Indiana has adopted the implied warranty provision of the Uniform Commerical Code dealing with fitness for a particular purpose:

Implied Warranty—Fitness for particular purpose.—Where the seller at the time of contracting has reason to know any particular purpose for which the goods are required and that the buyer is relying on the seller's skill or judgment to select or furnish suitable goods, there is unless

---

[4] The court reserved judgment on an express warranty count, and we also do not consider that theory.

excluded or modified under the next section an implied warranty that the goods shall be fit for such purpose. Burns Indiana Stat Ann § 19–2–315.

These sunglasses were advertised as baseball sunglasses that would give "instant eye protection." Although they were intended for use by baseball fielders, the thickness of the lenses ranged only from 1.2 mm to 1.5 mm, so that shattering into exceedingly sharp splinters would occur on their breaking. Since they lacked the safety features of plastic or shatterproof glass, the sunglasses were in truth not fit for baseball playing, the particular purpose for which they were sold. Therefore, breach of that implied warranty was properly found.

Indiana has adopted the doctrine of strict liability of sellers of products "in a defective condition unreasonably dangerous to the user," as provided in Section 402A of the Restatement of Torts Second. Here the thinness of the lenses made them unreasonably dangerous to users, so that the doctrine of strict liability is applicable. However, defendant argues against strict liability, on the ground that the sunglasses were "unavoidably unsafe products" within the exception of Comment k to Section 402 A. Even assuming arguendo that the state of the art is not capable of producing a shatter-resistant or splinter-free baseball sunglass as defendant claims, Comment k furnishes no shelter from liability in this case. The exception applies only when the product is "accompanied by proper . . . warning," which defendant's product lacked.

Finally, we also agree that defendant was liable for negligence. Defendant knew that these glasses shattered readily, for a hundred were returned daily for lens replacements. At least it had constructive knowledge that the impact of a baseball would shatter these lenses into sharp splinters, for it must anticipate the reasonably foreseeable risks of the use of the product. Moreover, despite the obviously physical stresses to which these glasses would be put, inadequate tests were made concerning their physical properties. Accordingly, even if defendant is not liable for negligence in production and sale of a poorly constructed product, it was properly held liable for its negligent failure to warn users of the danger of its product.

Problem Cases

1. North Pier Company advertised for sale a used "30-ton Railroad Crane." Their ad stated that the crane was in good condition. Capital Equipment, Inc. inquired about the crane and received a letter saying that it is a "30-ton locomotive crane" and that it is "most serviceable." Capital, a dealer in used equipment, arranged a demonstration at which the crane boom was raised and lowered, but no actual lifting was done. At this time the North Pier foreman told the Capital representative that the crane could lift 30 tons and was in very good condition. Capital then bought the crane upon a purchase order which described it as having a 30-ton capacity. When the crane was delivered it was discovered that it could only lift five tons. Can Capital refuse to go through with the sale?

2. Mrs. Carpenter went to the City Drug Store to buy some hair dye. While looking over the more than 20 products that they carried, she was offered assistance by a sales clerk. The clerk stated that she and several of her friends used a particular brand and that their hair came out "very nice" and "very natural." The clerk also told Mrs. Carpenter that "she

would get very fine results." Mrs. Carpenter bought the recommended product and after using it, developed a severe skin reaction. She then filed suit against the drug store for breach of an express warranty. Can she recover for breach of an express warranty?

3. Kruger acquired a 1955 Chevrolet Corvette from Bibi for $2,800. Sometime later Kruger learns that a prior owner had placed a $3,600 lien on the automobile. Does Kruger have any recourse against Bibi?

4. Commerce Poultry Co. purchased several drums of dry sanitizer from Olin Mathieson Chemical Corp., its manufacturer. Although the drums contained no disclaimers of any kind, there were explicit warnings that the product was a powerful oxident and that any contamination with foreign material could result in fire. A janitor at Commerce, who had not read the warnings, placed some of the product in a bucket which formerly contained soap. A fire broke out and totally destroyed Commerce Poultry Company's buildings. Suit was then filed for a breach of an implied warranty of merchantability. Can Commerce Poultry Co. recover for breach of warranty of merchantability?

5. Mrs. Maze purchased three cans of purple hull peas canned by Bush Brothers & Co. at Liberty Cash Grocery. Several days later she opened a can and placed its contents in a saucepan on the stove. While stirring the peas a large green object came to the surface. While at first she believed it to be a stem, upon closer examination she found it to be a green worm. She became nauseated and sick and remained so for several days. She also remained upset over the thought that she had almost served the peas to her children. She then filed suit against Liberty Cash Grocery. Can she recover?

6. Mr. Hochberg, while dining at O'Donnell's Restaurant, ordered a martini. When it arrived it contained an olive. Mr. Hochberg removed the olive and after noticing a hole in one end, bit down on it. He broke his tooth on an olive pit. He then filed suit for a breach of an implied warranty of merchantability by O'Donnell's Restaurant. Can he recover?

7. Mr. Wilson, a farmer engaged in raising squash, inquired of an agent of E-Z Flo Chemical Co., about a pre-emergent herbicide for use on his crops. The agent recommended and sold him a new product, Alanap, distributed by E-Z Flo and manufactured by Uniroyal Chemical. No warnings, either oral or written, were given Mr. Wilson at the time of sale. The product was applied to the soil on the last day of winter. Mr. Wilson used it on his entire crop, except for four rows. The entire crop, but for the four rows, was a total loss. E-Z Flo had received a manual from Uniroyal with the new product which stated that it should not be applied in cold, wet weather. Wilson sued E-Z Flo for breach of an implied warranty of fitness for a particular purpose. E-Z Flo sought indemnification from Uniroyal. Discuss these actions and their possible chances of success.

8. Mr. Williams bought a five-year-old used car from College Dodge, Inc. As part of the sale he was required to fill out a "vehicle buyer's order" form. This was used to apply for a change of title for the car and required a considerable amount of information. On the back of this form, together with still more printing but set in larger type, was this sentence "No implied warranties are made, either of merchantability or fitness for particular purpose." After Williams took the car he began to have serious problems with the engine. After returning it to College Dodge three times, with no results, he rescinded the contract claiming a breach of an implied warranty of merchantability. Is he on sound legal grounds?

9. Mrs. Wilson bought a loaf of bread baked by Ward Baking Co., at her local grocery. She took the bread home and, after making and partially eating a sandwich, noticed a bit of dried grease baked into the bread. She became seriously ill. Upon her recovery she filed suit for a breach of an implied warranty of fitness for a particular purpose. Was there a breach of the warranty of fitness for a particular purpose?

10. Mr. Klimas, an electrician, was testing various fuses with a standard tester. He had not purchased any of the fuses but had been supplied them by his employer. While testing a "Royal Crystal" fuse manufactured by International Telephone and Telegraph Corp., the fuse exploded and injured his eye, blinding him. Upon later examination it was discovered that this fuse had been defective. Mr. Klimas filed an action against IT&T Corp. based on Section 402A of the *Restatement of Torts* (Second) and under Section 2–315 of the Uniform Commercial Code. Discuss the relative merits of each claim. Include any possible defenses available to IT&T.

11. LaGorga, age five, was playing on the premises of a public school near a metal barrel in which refuse was burning. He was wearing a jacket which had been given to him as a Christmas present by his cousin. LaGorga and another child were poking sticks through holes in the barrel. A spark from the fire landed on LaGorga's coat and it burst into flames. The playmate tried to extinguish the burning coat by rubbing dirt on it but failed; she then tried to pull the zipper down but it stuck. LaGorga panicked and ran toward his home. He was noticed by an adult who threw him to the ground and extinguished the fire with considerable difficulty. LaGorga received burns covering 80 percent of his body, but he survived. The jacket was purchased at a Kroger Store. It was not packaged and was displayed on a table in the store with other similar unpackaged jackets. It was not labeled; there was no identity of the fabrics used in its outer shell, interlining or inner lining. There was no warning that it had not been treated with flame retardant. The jacket was designed with a cotton shell, interlining of mill waste comprised of 50 percent acrylic fibers and 50 percent unknown material interspersed with air pockets, and an acetate inner lining. It was established that synthetics of the type used in the jacket tend to melt rather than burn and produce high temperatures; also that when ignited and not immediately extinguished, severe and deep burns are inflicted. LaGorga contends that Kroger is liable for the injuries he received. Is Kroger liable and if so, on what ground?

chapter 35

Performance

Introduction

General Rules. The basic rules relative to the performance of a sales contract do not differ in any material respect from the rules of performance applied to other contracts. Where the contract of sale involves repeated occasions for performance by either party with knowledge of the performance and opportunity for objection to it by the other, any course of performance accepted or acquiesced in without objection shall be relevant to determine the meaning of the agreement. (2–208 [1].)[1]

Course of Dealing and Usage of Trade. In determining the obligations of the parties, the express terms of the agreement and any course of performance, as well as any course of dealing and usage of trade, shall be construed whenever reasonable as consistent with each other; but when such construction is unreasonable, express terms shall control course of performance, and course of performance shall control both course of dealing and usage of trade. (2–208 [2].)

Modification, Rescission, and Waiver. Under the Code, consideration is not required to support a modification or rescission but a signed writing which excludes modification or rescission cannot be modified or rescinded except by a signed writing. Except as between merchants, a modification or rescission of a provision in a form supplied by the merchant must be separately signed by the other party. An inoperative agreement of modification or rescission can operate as a waiver. (2–209.)

A promisee who accepts, without objection, late payments on an installment contract for a substantial period of time will have waived his right to declare a forfeiture for failure of the promisor to make his payments when due. How-

---

[1] The numbers in the parentheses refer to the sections of the Uniform Commercial Code, 1962.

ever, if the promisee gives the promisor reasonable notice that future payments must be made on time he may thereafter declare a forfeiture of the contract for late payment. This concept is made a rule under Section 2–209 (5) of the Code which provides that a party who has made a waiver affecting an executory portion of the contract may retract the waiver by reasonable notification received by the other party that strict performance will be required of any term waived, unless the retraction would be unjust in view of a material change of position in reliance on the waiver.

Assignment and Delegation. The basic principles of the assignment of contracts are discussed in Chapter 13. Some of the rules of law and the standards developed under these basic principles, when applied to sales contracts, do not give desirable and realistic results. Under the Code the basic principles have been retained but there is a liberalization of their application to sales contracts, particularly in regard to the delegation of duties. The courts have generally recognized the right of the promisee in a sales contract to assign his rights but they have been reluctant to recognize the right of either party to delegate his duties.

Under the Code the right of the promisor to delegate his duties is recognized unless the parties agree that the duties shall not be delegated or unless the other party has a substantial interest in having his original promisor perform or control the acts required by the contract. In keeping with basic principles, the promisor cannot relieve himself from his responsibility for the performance of the contract by delegating his duties under it. (2–210 [1].) As an additional protection the promisee may, without prejudicing his rights against the promisor, demand assurance from the assignee. (2–210 [5].)

Unless the circumstances indicate the contrary, a prohibition of assignment of "the contract" is to be construed as barring only the delegation to the assignee of the assignor's performance. (2–210 [3].) An assignment of "the contract" or "of all my rights under the contract" includes a delegation of duties unless otherwise agreed or unless circumstances clearly indicate a contrary intent. (2–210 [4].)

Cooperation Respecting Performance. The leaving of particulars of performance to be specified by one of the parties does not affect the validity of an otherwise enforceable contract. Also, specifications as to assortment of the goods may be left to the option of the buyer and, subject to some limitations, specifications relating to shipment are at the option of the seller. In the performance of a sales contract each party owes a duty to give the other party reasonable cooperation in the performance and each must act in good faith and within the bounds of that which is commercially reasonable. (2–311.)

Summary

The basic rules of contract law relative to the performance of contracts apply to sales contracts. The conduct of the parties, course of dealing, and usage of trade are considered and weighed in determining the duties of performance of the parties to a sales contract. Under the provisions of the Code an agreement to modify or rescind a contract need not be supported by consideration to be valid. A waiver may be retracted if reasonable notice of retraction is given before the other party has changed his position in reliance on the waiver.

The rules relative to the assignment of rights and the delegation of duties under a sales contract have been liberalized by the Code provisions. An assignment of a sales contract, unless otherwise agreed, includes the delegation of duties, and a general prohibition of the assignment of a contract bars only the delegation of duties. The assignor does not relieve himself of his liability for the performance of the contract by the delegation of his duties.

Granting to the buyer and seller options as to performance of a sales contract does not affect the validity of a contract which is otherwise valid. Each party must act in good faith and within the scope of that which is commercially reasonable in exercising his options and must cooperate in a reasonable manner in the performance of the contract.

Associated Hardware Supply Co. v. The Big Wheel Distributing Co.

236 F.Supp. 879 (W.D. Pa. 1965)

This was an action by Associated Hardware Supply Co. (plaintiff) against The Big Wheel Distributing Co. (defendant) to recover a judgment for the unpaid balance of the purchase price of goods sold and delivered. Judgment for Associated Hardware Supply Co.

Associated Hardware Supply Co. (Supply Co.) on February 9, 1962, offered to sell to The Big Wheel Distributing Co. (Distributing Co.) merchandise, subject to a volume of $5,000 per week, at catalogue price (which was based on a 20 percent markup) less 11 percent discount. This offer was not formally accepted but dealings went ahead and between February, 1962, and May, 1964, Supply Co. shipped $800,000 worth of merchandise which Distributing Co. accepted and paid for at the invoice price of 11 percent discount from catalogue price. Distributing Co. refused to pay for $40,185.62 worth of merchandise which had been shipped by Supply Co. and accepted by Distributing Co. When sued for this unpaid balance Distributing Co. set up as a defense that the Supply Co. had agreed to sell it merchandise at cost plus 10 percent and that Supply Co. had been overpaid an amount in excess of the balance in suit, and Distributing Co. filed a counterclaim for overpayment.

DUMBAULT, DISTRICT JUDGE. Section 1–205 (1) says: "A course of dealing is a sequence of previous conduct between the parties to a particular transaction which is in fact fairly to be regarded as establishing a common basis of understanding for interpreting their words and conduct."

Section 1–205 (3) provides: "The parties to a contract are bound by any course of dealing between them."

Section 1–205 (4) (a) declares that "Unless contrary to a mandatory rule of this Act:

(a) A course of dealing . . . gives particular meaning to and supplements or qualifies terms of the agreement."

Section 2–208 provides: "Where the contract for sale involves repeated occasions for performance by either party with knowledge of the nature of the performance and opportunity for objection by the other, any course of performance accepted without objection shall be relevant to determine the meaning of the agreement or to show a waiver or modification of any term inconsistent with such course of performance."

Review of the foregoing Code provisions shows that the Code attaches great weight to the course of dealing of the parties, even in the absence of a written agreement with respect to every term of the contract. Weighing in the light of the Code the conduct of the parties here, it seems clear that the mode of calculating price set forth in Supply Company's letter of February 9, 1962, although not accepted formally by signature of a copy, was adhered to by both parties during an extensive course of dealing, during which Distributing Co. received, accepted, and paid for over $800,000 worth of merchandise. This course of dealing must be held applicable and governing with respect to the remaining merchandise which has been received and accepted but not paid for.

Delivery

General Rules.   Unless otherwise agreed all of the goods called for by a sales contract must be tendered in a single delivery and the buyer owes a duty to accept and pay for the goods if they conform to the contract. Under some circumstances delivery in a single lot may not be practical, and if the circumstances are such that either party has the right to demand or make delivery in lots, the price of each lot may be demanded on delivery if the price can be proportioned and if there is no agreement for the extension of credit. (2–307.)

Unless otherwise agreed the place of delivery is the seller's place of business, or if he has no place of business, then at his house. If the goods are identified and are known by the parties at the time of contracting to be in some place other than the seller's place of business or house, that place is the place of delivery. If the goods are represented by documents of title, such documents may be delivered through banking channels. (2–308.)

Seller's Duties of Delivery.   A seller owes a duty to tender delivery of conforming goods in fulfillment of the sales contract. Tender of delivery requires the seller to put and hold conforming goods at the buyer's disposition and give him any notice reasonably necessary to enable him to take delivery. The tender must be made at a reasonable hour and the goods must be kept available for a time reasonably necessary to enable the buyer to take possession. The buyer, unless otherwise agreed, must furnish facilities reasonably suited for the receipt of the goods. (2–503 [1].) The seller's duties respecting shipment were discussed in Chapter 33.

Where the goods are in the possession of a bailee and the bailee has issued a negotiable warehouse receipt for the goods, the seller must endorse, if required for transfer, and deliver the warehouse receipt to the buyer. In other situations the seller must do that which is necessary to notify the bailee that the goods have been transferred to a buyer and obtain the bailee's consent to hold the goods for the buyer. The goods are at the risk of the seller until the bailee agrees to hold them for the buyer. If the seller is to deliver documents he must tender all necessary documents and they must be in correct form. Documents may be delivered through banking channels. (2–503.)

If the seller is to ship the goods, but not to deliver them at destination, he must put the goods in possession of the carrier, make a reasonable contract of carriage, obtain the usual documents in correct form, and promptly notify the buyer of the shipment. If material delay or loss results from the seller's failure to make a reasonable contract of carriage or to notify the buyer of the shipment, the buyer will have the right to reject the shipment. (2–504.)

If the seller is permitted, under the provisions of the sales contract, to retain a security interest in the goods until accepted and paid for, he may do so by shipping the goods on a negotiable bill of lading drawn to his own order or to the order of a financing agency or to the order of a nominee. A nonnegotiable bill of lading consigning the goods to the seller or his nominee reserves a security interest in the goods; if it consigns the goods to the buyer, it does not. The seller's shipment under reservation of a security interest does not alter the relations of the buyer and seller in any respect other than as to the seller's security interest in the goods.

Shipment under reservation of a security interest by the seller, where it is a breach of the sales contract, constitutes an improper contract of transportation but it impairs neither the rights given to the buyer by shipment and identification of the goods to the contract nor the seller's powers as a holder of a negotiable document. (2–505.)

When the seller tenders delivery of the goods to the buyer, he (the buyer) owes a duty to accept them and, unless otherwise agreed, to pay for them. The buyer's right to retain documents of title or goods is conditioned on his making the payment due. (2–507.)

If a seller tenders nonconforming goods and they are rejected, he may, if time for delivery has not expired or if the seller had had reasonable grounds to believe they would be accepted, notify the buyer of his intention to cure the defect and may, within the time allowed for delivery or within a reasonable time, as the case may be, cure the defect by tendering conforming goods. (2–508.)

Summary

The seller owes a duty to tender conforming goods in fulfillment of the sales contract. Tender must be made at a reasonable time and the buyer must provide reasonable facilities for the acceptance of the goods. If the seller is to ship the goods he must deliver conforming goods to the carrier and make a reasonable contract of transportation. If the sales contract permits, the seller may ship the goods under reservation by shipping them on a negotiable bill of lading drawn to his order or to the order of a financing agency or to a nominee. If he ships the goods on a nonnegotiable bill of lading he can retain a security interest in them by consigning them to himself or a nominee. Where delivery of conforming goods is tendered, the buyer owes a duty to accept and make any payment due. If nonconforming goods are tendered and rejected the seller is given, under limitations stated, the right to cure the defective tender.

Inspection and Payment

Buyer's Right of Inspection.   Unless otherwise agreed, the buyer has the right to inspect the goods before he accepts or pays for them. The time and place of inspection may be determined by the agreement of the parties. In the absence of an agreement, if the seller is to send the goods the inspection may be made after arrival. In other situations the buyer may inspect the goods at any reasonable place and time and in any reasonable manner.

If the goods conform to the contract the buyer must pay the expenses of inspection but if the goods are nonconforming he may recover the expense of inspection from the seller. If the shipping terms are c.o.d. or payment against documents, the buyer must pay before inspection unless the goods are marked "inspection allowed." If the parties have agreed as to time, place, and method of inspection such agreement will control.

Where the contract requires payment before inspection, nonconformity of the goods does not excuse the buyer from payment unless the nonconformity is obvious without inspection. Payment before inspection does not deprive the buyer of any of his remedies against the seller if the goods prove to be nonconforming. (2–512.)

Payment.   The price of the goods may be paid in money, goods, realty, or otherwise. If all or part of the price is payable in realty the transfer of the goods and the seller's obligations in reference to them is subject to the law of sales but the transfer of the interest in the realty and transferor's obligations in connection therewith is subject to real estate law. (2–304.)

Unless the goods are sold on credit the buyer must pay on delivery or tender of the goods after he has inspected. If the goods are shipped under reservation the buyer must pay on arrival of the goods, after inspection. If the terms are c.o.d. or c.i.f. the buyer must pay on arrival of the documents. (2–310.) Unless otherwise agreed documents against which a draft is drawn are to be delivered to the drawee on acceptance of the draft if it is payable more than three days after presentment; otherwise, only on payment. (2–514.)

The buyer may make payment by personal check or any other means current in the ordinary course of business unless the seller demands payment in money and gives any extension of time reasonably necessary to procure it. Payment by check is conditional on the check being paid on presentment. (2–511.)

Summary

In general, the buyer has the right to inspect the goods before acceptance and payment. The place, time, and method of inspection may be fixed by the agreement of the parties. In the absence of agreement, if the goods are to be sent by the seller the place of inspection is the destination of the goods; otherwise at a time, place, and manner reasonable under the circumstances. If the goods are conforming the buyer pays the expense of inspection; if nonconforming, the seller pays the expense.

Unless there is an agreement for credit, payment must be made after inspection of the goods on tender or delivery of the goods or documents of title. Payment may be made by check or any manner current in the ordinary course of business unless the seller demands legal tender.

Acceptance, Revocation, and Rejection

What Constitutes Acceptance. If a buyer, after he has inspected the goods purchased or has been given a reasonable opportunity to inspect them, signifies to the seller that he will take the goods as they are or fails to reject them, he will be held to have accepted them. Furthermore, if a buyer does any act inconsistent with the seller's ownership, such act will constitute an acceptance of the goods. He cannot, however, by such act deprive the seller of rights he has in the goods unless the seller ratifies the buyer's acts. The acceptance of a part of a commercial unit is acceptance of that entire unit. (2–606.)

Effect of Acceptance. If only a part of the goods purchased are accepted by the buyer he must pay for that part at the rate of the contract price. If the buyer accepts nonconforming goods he cannot at a later date reject them unless at the time he accepts them he has reason to believe that the nonconformity will be cured. A buyer does not, by acceptance, forfeit or waive his remedies against a seller for nonconformities in the goods but he must, if he wishes to hold the seller, give him seasonable notice that the goods were nonconforming. The burden is on the buyer to establish any breach with respect to goods accepted.

In the event the buyer is sued for infringement or for breach of warranty under conditions where he would have a right of action over against the seller, the buyer will be barred from such right unless he gives the seller notice of the suit thus providing him (the seller) an opportunity to defend. (2–607.)

Revocation of Acceptance. A buyer may revoke an acceptance of nonconforming goods if such nonconformity substantially impairs the value of the goods and if he has accepted them without discovering the nonconformity and his acceptance was induced either by the difficulty of discovery or by the assurance of the seller.

A buyer must exercise his right to revoke his acceptance within a reasonable time after he discovers or should have discovered the grounds for it and before there has been any substantial change in the goods. Such a revocation is not effective until the buyer notifies the seller. The buyer's rights, after he has revoked his acceptance, are the same as though he had rejected them when delivery was tendered. (2–608.)

Buyer's Rights on Improper Delivery. As a general rule, if goods tendered to the buyer do not conform to the contract he has an election: he may reject all of the goods, accept all, or accept any commercial unit or units and reject the rest, paying for the units accepted at the contract rate. He will not be permitted to accept part of a commercial unit and reject the rest. (2–601.)

However, if the contract is an installment contract in that it requires or authorizes delivery in separate lots to be separately accepted, the buyer's options are more limited. The buyer may reject a nonconforming installment if the nonconformity substantially impairs the value of that installment and cannot be cured; but if the nonconformity is not so great as to substantially impair the value of the whole contract and the seller gives assurance that the nonconformity will be cured, then the buyer must accept that installment. Assurance of cure includes an allowance in price for the nonconformity. (2–612.)

Where the nonconformity or defect in one installment impairs the value of the whole contract, the buyer may treat it as a breach of the whole contract but must proceed carefully so as not to reinstate the remainder of the contract. (2–612.)

Manner of Rejection and Duties after Rejection. A buyer, if he elects to reject the goods, must act within a reasonable time after delivery or tender and must seasonably notify the seller of his rejection. If a buyer has paid part or all of the purchase price of rejected goods he will have a security interest in the rejected goods to the extent of payments made. (2–602.)

A merchant buyer, subject to any security interest he may have in the goods, when the seller has no place of business or agent at the market of rejection, is under a duty, if the goods are in his possession or under his control, to follow any reasonable instructions given by the seller as to the disposition of the goods. If the seller refuses or fails to give instructions and the goods are perishable or threaten to decline in value speedily the buyer owes a duty to make a reasonable effort to sell the goods for the benefit of the seller. The seller, if he gives instructions to the buyer, is bound, if demanded by the buyer, to give indemnity for expenses incurred in carrying out the instructions. (2–603 [1].)

If the buyer sells rejected goods under the circumstances set out above, he is entitled to reimbursement out of the proceeds for expenses incurred and to a commission as is usual in the trade. In making a sale the buyer must act in good faith. (2–603 [2] and [3].)

If the rejected goods are not perishable or if there is no reason to believe they will decline in value speedily, the buyer may store the goods for the seller's account or reship them or resell them for the seller's account and reimburse himself for expenses plus a commission out of the proceeds. (2–604.)

After rejection and notice the buyer has no right to exercise ownership over the goods other than to fulfill his rights and duties as set out above. The buyer must exercise reasonable care in handling rejected goods in his possession and must hold them for a time sufficient to permit the seller to remove them. The buyer has no further obligations with regard to goods rightfully rejected. If the buyer wrongfully rejects goods he is liable to the seller for breach of the sales contract. (2–602 [2] and [3].)

Failure to Particularize. If the buyer, on rejection, fails to state in connection with his rejection a particular defect which is ascertainable by reasonable inspection, he will not be permitted to set up such defect to justify his rejection if the seller could have cured the defect had he been given reasonable notice of it. In a transaction taking place between merchants, the seller has, after rejection, a right to a written statement of all the defects in the goods on which the buyer bases his right to reject and the buyer will not be permitted to set up defects not listed in justification of his rejections. If payment against documents is made without reservation of rights, the buyer cannot recover the payments made if defects in the document are apparent on its face. (2–605.)

Summary

An acceptance of goods occurs when a buyer indicates to the seller, after he (the buyer) has inspected the goods or has had an opportunity to inspect them, that he will keep them in fulfillment of the seller's obligation or when he exercises acts of ownership over them inconsistent with the seller's ownership. Acceptance of any part of a commercial unit is acceptance of the entire unit. The buyer must pay for goods accepted at the contract rate. If the buyer accepts nonconforming goods, he must, if he wishes to hold the seller liable, give him seasonable notice that the goods are nonconforming. If the buyer is sued for infringement or breach of warranty and he has a right over against the seller, the buyer must give the seller notice that the suit has been brought and thus provide him (the seller) an opportunity to defend.

A buyer may revoke an acceptance where he has grounds for revocation if he acts within a reasonable time and if he gives the seller reasonable notice of his revocation.

The buyer, if the contract is an installment contract, has the right to reject any nonconforming installment if the nonconformity substantially impairs the value of the installment and cannot be cured. The seller may cure the defect, but if the defect impairs the value of the whole contract it is a breach of the whole contract.

If nonconforming goods are tendered, the buyer may reject all, accept all, or accept any commercial unit and reject the rest. The buyer has a security interest in rejected goods for any payment made. On rejection, if the goods are in the buyer's possession or control, he owes a duty to use reasonable care to protect the goods. He must hold them for a period sufficient to permit the seller to remove them; if the seller does not have a place of business or agent in the market, the buyer must follow the seller's instructions relative to disposition of the goods and if no instructions are given the buyer must, if the goods are perishable or subject to speedy change in value, sell them for the seller's account. If the goods are not perishable he may store, reship, or sell them for the seller's account. The buyer is entitled to reimbursement for the expenses plus commission. If the buyer wrongfully rejects goods he is liable to the seller for breach of contract.

Rozmus v. Thompson's Lincoln-Mercury Co.

224 A.2d 782 (Super. Ct. Pa. 1966)

This was an action by Rozmus (plaintiff) against Thompson's Lincoln-Mercury (defendant) to recover the sales price of a used automobile that Rozmus had traded in on a new automobile. Judgment for Thompson's Lincoln-Mercury and Rozmus appealed. New trial ordered.

On Saturday, June 22, 1963, Rozmus signed an agreement to purchase a new Mercury. He paid $50 down, traded in the old car, and promised to pay the balance within five days. The contract contained a clause acknowledging Rozmus' acceptance of the new car in good order. While driving the automobile home that evening he noticed smoke coming from the exhaust and that the car made a loud, banging and thumping sound. Rozmus immediately called Thompson's salesman and, as it was Saturday, was told to bring the car in on Monday. In accordance with this request, Rozmus returned the car to Thompson's on Monday. Tuesday evening he called for it but upon driving it ascertained that the loud banging and thumping noise persisted. Rozmus immediately returned the car and sought out Stewart, Thompson's general manager, who confirmed the trouble in a test drive. Stewart and Rozmus then returned to the garage where Stewart instructed a mechanic to place the car upon a rack and to see what was causing the noise. Before the mechanic could correct the source of the trouble, which turned out to be two loose engine mounting bolts allowing a misalignment of the drive shaft to occur, Rozmus told Mr. Stewart he wanted another car or the return of the one he had traded in. His demands not being met, he left without taking the new automobile with him. The Mercury automobile was fully adjusted within a few minutes by Thompson's, but Rozmus never returned for it.

Soon after leaving the new automobile with Thompson's, Rozmus brought an action before a justice of the peace for the sale price of the traded Chevrolet car, $361.50. The question before the appeal court in this case was whether Rozmus had the right to revoke acceptance of the new automobile.

MONTGOMERY, JUSTICE.   The law on the issue before us is found in § 2–608 which provides that a buyer may revoke his acceptance of goods received if its "non-conformity substantially impairs its value to him." There is no doubt that Rozmus accepted this new automobile. He executed the conditional sales contract which provided that he acknowledged the acceptance of the Mercury in good order, and he drove it from the showroom to his home. Section 2–606 provides that acceptance takes force when the buyer either signifies his acceptance to the seller or does an act inconsistent with the seller's ownership.

The reason why "a substantial impairment of value" must take place before a revocation under § 2–608 may take force is to preclude revocation for trivial defects or defects which may be easily corrected.

It seems clear from reading said § 2–608 that revocation of an acceptance of delivery is now permissible only if the conconformity substantially impairs the value of the article which has been accepted either (a) on the reasonable assumption that its nonconformity would be cured and it has not been reasonably cured; or (b), without discovery of such nonconformity the acceptance was reasonably induced either by the difficulty of discovery before acceptance or by the seller's assurances. In the present case, Rozmus did not discover the nonconformity before he accepted the automobile as no opportunity to drive it before acceptance was afforded him, and he accepted on the basis of the usual warranties (assurances) which are part of new car sales.

If we review the evidence in the light most favorable to Thompson's, giving it the benefit of all reasonable inferences therefrom by reason of the original decision of Judge McCarthy being in its favor, we would be justified in concluding that the defect did not substantially impair the value of the automobile. . . . The only evidence in the case concerning the defect or nonconformity is that, due to an improper adjustment of the engine supports the drive shaft was moved out of line, which caused a bumping or thumping noise when the rear seat was fully occupied. When the cause was determined it was remedied within a few minutes by Thompson's mechanic. We find nothing in the record to justify a finding that Thompson's agreed to accept the return of the automobile. The evidence is to the contrary, and indicates that Rozmus abandoned the automobile when he left it in Thompson's repair shop.

Assurance, Repudiation, Breach, and Excuse

Assurance.   If the circumstances are such that either party, tested by commercial standards, is justified in believing that the other party will be unable to perform his obligations under the contract, he may demand assurance of performance. Failure to provide assurance within 30 days after a justified demand is a repudiation of the contract. (6–609.)

Anticipatory Repudiation.   If either party repudiates the contract the aggrieved party may await performance for a commercially reasonable time, or resort to any remedy for breach of the contract. The aggrieved party on repudiation of the contract may suspend further performance on his part or proceed to exercise his right to identify goods to the contract or to salvage unfinished goods. (2–610.)

If a party has repudiated his contract he may withdraw his repudiation provided he gives adequate notice to the aggrieved party and such party has not canceled the contract or materially changed his position. (2–611.)

Excuse.   Under the Code excuse for the failure to perform a sales contract follows closely the general rules of contract law relative to impossibility. Commercial impracticability is substituted for impossibility in most situations. If goods required for the performance of the contract and identified to it are destroyed, the contract is voided. If they are damaged or have deteriorated, the buyer at his option may either treat the contract as voided or accept the goods with due allowance from the purchase price. (2–613.)

If the agreed means of transportation or of payment are not available at the time of performance but a commercially reasonable substitute transportation is available, it must be used and a substituted method of payment may be used provided the seller receives a substantial equivalent. (2–614.)

A seller is excused from delay in delivery or nondelivery in whole or in part if his failure to perform is the result of unforeseen or unforeseeable conditions which make performance impracticable. If only part of the seller's capacity to perform is affected he may allocate his production among his customers. In such a situation the seller owes a duty to notify the buyer seasonably of his allocation. (2–615.) The buyer, on receipt of the notice, may by written notification to the seller as to any delivery concerned, and where the prospective deficiency substantially impairs the value of the whole contract, terminate and discharge any unexecuted portion of the contract or agree to accept his available quota in substitution. If the buyer does not modify his contract within 30 days after receipt of notice from the seller the contract lapses with respect to any deliveries affected. (2–616.)

Summary

If either party to a sales contract deems himself insecure, as tested by commercial standards, he may demand assurance before he proceeds with his performance. If a party repudiates a sales contract, the aggrieved party may wait or he may bring an action for breach of the contract. In event of repudiation the usual remedies for the breach of the sales contract are available to the aggrieved party. If the party who has repudiated a sales contract wishes to withdraw his repudiation he may do so by giving the aggrieved party notice of his withdrawal before such party has canceled the contract or materially changed his position in reliance on the repudiation.

A party to a sales contract is excused from performance if his performance, due to no fault on his part, becomes commercially impracticable. If the impracticability is as to means of transportation or means of payment, substituted means, if available, may be resorted to. If the impracticability causes delay or ability to perform only partially, the seller may allocate performances among his buyers. A buyer may accept his allotment or cancel the contract.

United States v. Wegematic Corp.

360 F.2d 674 (2d Cir. 1966)

This was an action for breach of contract brought by the United States (plaintiff) against Wegematic Corporation (defendant). Judgment for the United States and Wegematic appealed. Affirmed.

In June 1956 the Federal Reserve Board invited electronics manufacturers to submit proposals for an intermediate-type, general purpose electronic digital computing system or systems; the invitation stressed the importance of early delivery as a consideration in determining the Board's choice. Wegematic, a relative newcomer in the field, submitted a proposal for the sale of a new computer designated as the ALWAC 800 which it characterized as "a truly revolutionary system utilizing all of the latest technical advances." In September the Board acted favorably on Wegematic's proposal ordering components of the ALWAC 800 with an aggregate cost of $231,800. Delivery was to be made on June 30, 1957, with liquidated damages of $100 per day for delay. The order also provided that in the event the defendant failed to comply "with any provision" of the agreement, "the Board may procure the services described in the contract from other sources and hold the Contractor responsible for any excess cost occasioned thereby."

After several requests for delays in the delivery time, Wegematic announced in mid-October, 1957, that "due to engineering difficulties it has become impracticable to deliver the ALWAC 800 Computing System at this time"; it requested cancellation of the contract without damages. The Board then procured comparable equipment from IBM and sued Wegematic for the excess cost of the new equipment and the delay costs under the liquidated damages clause. Wegematic sought to defend on the grounds of impossibility.

FRIENDLY, CIRCUIT JUDGE. The principal point of the defense, which is the sole ground of this appeal, is that delivery was made impossible by "basic engineering difficulties" whose correction would have taken between one and two years and would have cost a million to a million and a half dollars, with success likely but not certain. Although the record does not give an entirely clear notion what the difficulties were, two experts suggested that these may have stemmed from the magnetic cores, used instead of transistors to achieve a solid state machine, which did not have sufficient uniformity at this stage of their development. Wegematic contends that under federal law, which both parties concede to govern, the "practical impossibility" of completing the contract excused its defaults in performance.

We find persuasive Wegematic's suggestion of looking to the Uniform Commercial Code as a source for the "federal" law of sales. . . .

We see no basis for thinking that when an electronics system is promoted by its manufacturer as a revolutionary breakthrough, the risk of the revolution's occurrence falls on the purchaser; the reasonable supposition is that it has already occurred or, at least, that the manufacturer is assuring the purchaser that it will be found to have when the machine is assembled. As Judge Graven said: "The Board in its invitation for bids did not request invitations to conduct a development program for it. The Board requested invitations from manufacturers for the furnishing of a computer machine." Acceptance of Wegematic's argument would mean that though a purchaser makes his choice because of the attractiveness of a manufacturer's representation and will be bound by it, the manufacturer is free to express what are only aspirations and gamble on mere probabilities of fulfillment without any risk of liability. In fields of developing technology, the manufacturer would thus enjoy a wide degree of latitude with respect to performance while holding an option to compel the buyer to pay if the gamble should pan out. . . . We do not think this the common understanding—above all as to a contract where the manufacturer expressly agreed to liquidated damages for delay and authorized the purchaser to resort to other sources in the event of non-delivery. If a manufacturer wishes to be relieved of the risk that what looks good on paper may not prove so good in hardware, the appropriate exculpatory language is well known and often used.

Beyond this the evidence of true impracticability was far from compelling. The large sums predicted by Wegematic's witnesses must be appraised in relation not to the single computer ordered by the Federal Reserve Board, evidently for a bargain price, but to the entire ALWAC 800 program as originally contemplated. Although the record gives no idea what this was, even twenty-five machines would gross $10,000,000 if priced at the level of the comparable IBM equipment. While the unanticipated need for expending $1,000,000 or $1,500,000 on redesign might have made such a venture unattractive, as Wegematic's management evidently decided, the sums are thus not so clearly prohibitive as it would have them appear.

Problem Cases

1. Spada, an Oregon corporation, agreed to sell Belson, who operated a business in Chicago, Illinois, two carloads of potatoes at "4.40 per sack, f.o.b. Oregon shipping point." Spada had the potatoes put aboard the railroad cars; however, he did not have floor racks used in the cars under the potatoes as is customary during winter months. As a result there was no warm air circulating and the potatoes were frozen while in transit. Spada claims that his obligations ended with the delivery to the carrier and that the risk of loss was on Belson. What argument would you make for Belson?

2. Perilstein Company knew Mort Company was in financial difficulties so it agreed to sell Mort goods only on a c.o.d. basis. On October 25, 1961, Perilstein delivered the goods to Mort, and it gave its check in payment. On October 27, 1961, Mort was adjudged bankrupt, and the check was not paid because of the filing of the bankruptcy petition even though there were sufficient funds on deposit to pay the check. Perilstein claims this was a cash transaction and it should be entitled to recover the goods. Is this a good claim?

3. Perkins, Inc., placed an order to Acme Co. for certain valves and fittings. The entire order consisted of two 14–inch flanges, two 8–inch valves, two 6–inch valves, one 6–inch gate valve and seven used valves. All of the materials ordered were to be made of steel. Upon delivery, however, it was discovered that the two 14–inch flanges were made of iron. Perkins rejected these, but kept the rest of the order, paying for the goods retained. Acme files suit for the amount owed for the flanges. Can they recover?

4. Mrs. Shea purchased a new Rambler automobile from Menard & Holmberg Rambler, Inc. As part of the deal she traded in her old car. Upon taking delivery her new car continually stalled so she returned it to the dealer who replaced the carburetor. The car continued to stall and would not move in reverse. On the fourth day after delivery she returned the car to the dealer, told him the sale was off and drove off in her old car. He called her and offered to replace the transmission in the new car but she refused. The dealer then instituted an action for the price of the new car and the return of the old car. Can the dealer recover from Mrs. Shea?

5. Mr. Burrough, a service station owner, contacted Larrance Tank Corp. and placed an order for two 10,000 gallon, underground, gasoline storage tanks. The tanks were delivered on March 20, 1963 and installed by Mr. Burroughs. Shortly thereafter Burroughs began to notice that the amount delivered did not correspond to the amount left in the tanks. There was a difference of about 150 gallons a week. In June 1964, Burrough dug up the tanks and discovered that due to an improperly welded seam the gasoline was leaking out. He then filed suit against Larrance Tank Corp. for a breach of an implied warranty of fitness for a particular purpose. Assuming that such a warranty existed and was breached, what will Larrance's defense be? Will it be successful?

6. On March 20, 1968, Boyer Potato Chips purchased a carload of Florida chipping potatoes from A. C. Carpenter Inc. The purchase price was $1,625 and the potatoes were guaranteed to chip at destination. The potatoes arrived on March 27, 1968. Boyer Potato Chips attempted to use some of them on April 2, 1968 but found them unsuitable. Two days later Boyer wrote to Carpenter about the matter. Two days after that, on April 6, 1968 Boyer destroyed the potatoes. Boyer refused to pay for them and Carpenter filed suit. Can Boyer claim that Carpenter breached the sales contract?

7. Berlin & Co., a steel supplier, called Whiting Manufacturing Co. to inform them it was possible for Whiting to obtain the type of steel it normally used at a good price. Whiting said that although they were overstocked at present they would buy the steel provided that it could be stored until they had room for it. On March 15, 1971, Berlin & Co. agreed to store the steel and Whiting ordered 85,000 pounds. On April 25, 1971, one half this amount was delivered and paid for. On May 26, 1971 the balance was delivered but not paid for. On July 29, 1971 Whiting wrote to Berlin & Co. saying the entire shipment was the wrong size, refusing to pay for the second shipment and also demanding return of the payment made. Berlin & Co. sued for payment. Can Berlin & Co. recover?

8. Dade County Dairies purchased a new 1970 Jaguar automobile from Orange Motors, Inc. Almost immediately after delivery Dade had problems with the car. The power steering was stiff, the air conditioner leaked and rattled, the doors did not close properly, and the steering column almost fell off. The car was in the shop for one half of the three months Dade had it. Dade, therefore, filed suit seeking recission of the sale contract. Orange Motors claimed that they should only be required to repair the car. Is Orange Motor's contention correct?

9. Mr. Dewey, a paint store owner, decided to open a toy department for the Christmas trade. He contracted with Hays Merchandise Company to buy toys for $3,500 for an inventory. Several small shipments were made but the number of toys he received fell far below his expectations. He made several calls to Hays to complain and was told that the toys were

back ordered. When less than half the goods that he had ordered had been delivered by December 1, Mr. Dewey called Hays and said that he wanted no more toys and was sending back those that he had received. Hays then filed suit for the entire $3,500. What must Mr. Dewey show in order to win? Will he be successful?

10. Alpirn contracted to purchase from Williams 40,000 feet of ½-inch new steel pipe, "the pipe not to be plugged." Shipment was c.o.d. When the pipe arrived Alpirn's foreman permitted the truck driver to unload about 50 pieces of pipe at which time he discovered that the pipe was plugged. Alpirn refused to accept the pipe. Williams contended that since the shipment was c.o.d. Alpirn was obligated to accept and pay for the pipe. Was Alpirn obligated to accept and pay for the pipe?

11. Whelan ordered fuel oil from Griffith to be delivered at his farm home which was located on a country road. The oil was to be delivered on an agreed c.o.d. basis. Griffith made two attempts to deliver the oil but each time no one was found at home. The morning after a night of heavy snowfall, the heaviest in over 20 years, Griffith equipped the truck with chains and made a third attempt to deliver oil but found on arrival at Whelan's house that the driveway was impassable due to snowdrifts approximately 6 feet high. When the driver drove past the house and attempted to turn around, the truck became stuck in the snow and had to be towed back to the main highway. Whelan ran out of oil and as a result of having no fuel the heating plant froze causing substantial damage to it. Whelan sued Griffith to recover a judgment for the damage to the heating plant claiming its breach of contract to deliver oil was the cause of the loss. Should Griffith be held in breach?

12. On April 15, 1959, Motter purchased farm machinery from Wrightstone on a conditional sales contract which provided: "the buyer is not bound to pay any specific amount each month, provided the total balance is paid within twenty-four months." Motter executed a judgment note for the balance which was renewed from time to time as payments were made. The last renewal was on May 5, 1960, in the amount of $590.40. On June 11, 1960, Wrightstone, Inc., repossessed the machinery and, on June 13, 1960, notified Motter that payment of the balance must be made in full. On June 28, 1960, Wrightstone advised Motter that the machinery had been sold and that he owed a balance of $205.90. Judgment was entered for this amount. Wrightstone based its right to repossess the machinery on the ground that it deemed itself insecure. Motter petitioned to have the judgment opened and the petition was granted. What should Wrightstone have done if it considered itself insecure?

chapter 36

Remedies for Breach

Seller's Remedies

Recovery of Purchase Price. In the usual performance of a sales contract the seller delivers and the buyer accepts conforming goods and the seller is entitled to the agreed purchase price of the goods. If credit has been extended and the purchase price is not paid when due, the seller is entitled to a judgment for the purchase price of the goods. Also, the seller is entitled to the purchase price of conforming goods if the risk of loss has passed to the buyer and goods are lost or damaged within a commercially reasonable time after the risk of loss has passed to the buyer.

If the goods contracted for have been identified to the contract and the buyer refuses to accept and pay for them, the seller is entitled to the purchase price after he has made an honest effort to resell the goods and is unable to do so or if the circumstances reasonably indicate that the goods cannot be resold. If the seller has recovered a judgment for the purchase price of the goods he must hold them and deliver them to the buyer if he pays the judgment. If the seller has an opportunity, however, to sell the goods before the buyer pays the judgment he may do so and credit the amount received on the judgment. If the buyer has wrongfully rejected or revoked acceptance of the goods and the circumstances are such that the seller is not entitled to a judgment for the purchase price, he would be entitled to a judgment for damages. (2–709 [3].)[1]

Recovery of Damages for Breach. The objective of granting a judgment for damages for breach of a contract is to give the injured party a judgment for an amount which will compensate him for the loss suffered which results directly from the breach. Under the provisions of the Code in the event the buyer breaches the contract by nonacceptance of the goods or by repudiating

---

[1] The numbers in the parentheses refer to the sections of the Uniform Commercial Code 1962.

the contract, thus giving the seller a right to damages, the measure of damages is the difference between the market price at the time and place of tender and the unpaid contract price together with the incidental damages but less expenses saved in consequence of the buyer's breach. (2–708 [1].)

Incidental damages include any commercially reasonable charges such as expenses or commissions incurred in stopping delivery or in the transportation of the goods, and the expenses incurred in the care and custody of the goods after the buyer's breach. (2–710.) Expenses saved might be the cost of packaging the goods and of transportation which would be incurred in completing performance of the contract.

If these damages are inadequate to put the seller in as good a position as that he would have occupied had the contract been performed, he would be entitled to recover loss of profits as damages. For example, suppose that the seller is a retail dealer in musical instruments and the buyer contracts to purchase a piano. The seller has or can obtain all the pianos needed to supply his customers. The buyer repudiates the contract and refuses to accept delivery of the piano. The seller would be entitled to a judgment for loss of profit on the piano including reasonable overhead and incidental damages. (2–708 [2].)

Resale as Measure of Damages.   In the event the buyer repudiates the sales contract, the seller has the right to identify to the contract conforming goods which have not already been identified, if at the time of the breach they are in his possession or control, and to resell them. He may also treat as the subject of resale goods which have demonstrably been intended for the particular contract even though the goods are unfinished. If, at the time the buyer repudiates the contract, the goods are in process and have demonstrably been intended for the particular contract, the seller may, in the exercise of reasonable commercial judgment for the purpose of avoiding loss, either complete the manufacture of the goods and wholly identify the goods to the contract or cease manufacture and resell for scrap or salvage value, or he may proceed in any other reasonable manner. This rule permits the seller in such a situation to follow a reasonable course of action to mitigate damages and not be held responsible if the course followed is not as successful as some other course might have been. All that is required of the seller is that he act in good faith and exercise reasonable commercial judgment in determining the course of action to be followed. (2–704.)

On the buyer's breach of the sales contract the seller is not obligated to resell the goods but may bring an action to recover a judgment for damages. However, if the seller elects to resell the goods concerned or the undelivered balance of them, he is entitled to recover as damages the difference between the resale price and the contract price together with any incidental damages provided the resale is made in good faith and in a commercially reasonable manner.

For the protection of the seller rules have been promulgated which, if followed, will ensure the seller that he has made the sale in a "commercially reasonable manner." It does not follow, however, that if he pursues some other course of action he has not made the sale in good faith and in a "commercially reasonable manner." If the parties have agreed as to the manner in which the resale shall be made, the courts will enforce the agreement unless it would be found to be unconscionable. (2–302.) If the parties have not entered into an agreement relative to the resale of the goods, the sale may be at public or private sale, but in all events it must be made in good faith and in a commercially reasonable manner. The resale must be reasonably identified as referring to the broken contract. If the goods are not in existence the resale may be in the form of a contract to sell future goods.

If the goods are resold at private sale the seller must give the buyer reasonable notification of his intention to resell. If the sale is a public sale, and a sale at auction is a public sale, only identified goods may be resold unless there is a future market for such goods. The seller must give the buyer notice of the time and place of the sale unless the goods are perishable or threaten to decline in value rapidly; the sale must be made at a usual place or market for public sales if one is reasonably available; if the goods are not within the view of those attending the sale the notification of the sale must state the place where the goods are located and provide for reasonable inspection by prospective bidders; and the seller may bid at a public sale. (2–706 [3] and [4].)

The purchaser at a public sale who buys in good faith takes free from any rights of the original buyer even though the seller has failed to conduct the sale in compliance with the rules set out in the Code. (2–706 [5].) On a resale the seller is not accountable to the buyer for any profit made on the resale. However, if the sale is in the nature of the foreclosure of a security interest in the goods, the buyer is entitled to any surplus over and above the debt, interest and expenses of the sale. (2–706 [6].)

Seller's Remedies on Discovery of Buyer's Insolvency.   If the seller has not agreed to extend credit to the buyer for the purchase price of the goods, delivery of the goods and payment of the purchase price are concurrent. If the seller tenders delivery of the goods he may withhold delivery unless the agreed payment is made. Where the seller has agreed to extend credit to the buyer for the purchase price of the goods, but discovers before delivery that the buyer is insolvent, the seller may refuse delivery unless the buyer pays cash for the goods together with the unpaid balance for all goods theretofore delivered under the contract. (2–702 [1].)

At common law a seller has the right to rescind a sales contract induced by fraud and recover the goods unless they have been sold to a bona fide purchaser for value. Based on this general legal principle the Code provides that where the seller discovers that the buyer has received goods while insolvent, he may reclaim the goods upon demand made within 10 days after their receipt. This right granted to the seller is based on constructive deceit on the part of the buyer. The receiving of the goods while insolvent is equivalent to a false representation of solvency. To protect his rights all the seller is required to do is to make a demand within the 10-day period; he need not actually repossess the goods.

If the buyer has misrepresented his solvency to this particular seller in writing within three months before the delivery of the goods, the 10-day limitation on his right to reclaim the goods does not apply. However, the seller's right to reclaim the goods is subject to the prior rights of purchasers in the ordinary course of the buyer's business or other good faith purchasers for value or lien creditors. (2–702 [2] and [3].)

Seller's Right to Stop Delivery.   The seller's right to stop delivery of the goods is based either on the insolvency of the buyer or on the buyer's repudiation of the contract or his failure to make payment due before delivery. If the quantity of the goods is less than a carload, truckload, planeload or a large shipment of express or freight, the seller's right to stop delivery by the carrier is based on the insolvency of the buyer, but if the shipment is a carload, truckload, planeload or large express or freight shipment, the seller has the right to stop delivery if the buyer repudiates the sales contract or fails to make a payment due before delivery. (2–705 [1].)

The seller's right to stop delivery terminates when the buyer receives the goods, or when a bailee other than a carrier acknowledges to the buyer that he holds the goods for the buyer, or when the goods are reshipped or the carrier holds the goods for the buyer as a warehouseman, or when any negotiable document of title covering the goods has been negotiated to the buyer. (2–705 [2].)

To stop delivery the seller must notify the carrier or other bailee in time so that by the exercise of reasonable diligence he may prevent the delivery of the goods. After he receives notice to stop delivery the carrier or other bailee owes a duty to hold the goods and deliver them as directed by the seller. The seller is liable to the carrier or other bailee for any expenses incurred or damages resulting from complying with the seller's order to stop delivery. If a negotiable document of title has been issued for the goods, the carrier or other bailee owes no duty to obey a stop-delivery order unless the negotiable document of title is delivered to him. If a carrier has issued a nonnegotiable bill of lading he is not obliged to obey a stop-delivery order issued by any person other than the consignor. (2–705 [3].) Any person, however, in the position of the seller may stop delivery of the goods. A "person in the position of the seller" includes a financing agency which has acquired documents by honoring a letter of credit for the buyer or by discounting a draft issued by the buyer for the seller. (2–707.)

Summary

The seller is entitled to the purchase price of conforming goods delivered to and accepted by the buyer and of conforming goods where the risk of loss has passed to the buyer and the goods are thereafter damaged or destroyed. Also, if the goods have been identified to the contract and the buyer repudiates the sale, the seller is entitled to the purchase price of the goods that cannot, by a reasonable effort on the part of the seller, be resold for a fair price.

The seller is entitled to recover compensatory damages if the buyer breaches the contract and to special damages if such damages were reasonably within the contemplation of the parties. The seller on breach by the buyer is entitled to incidental damages. If necessary to put the seller in the position he would have held had the buyer performed, the seller may be granted loss of profits as damages. The seller is not obligated to resell on the buyer's refusal to accept the goods but if he does resell, in a commercially reasonable manner, he may recover as damages the difference between the sale price and the contract price. A purchaser at a public sale, if he buys in good faith, takes free from any rights of the original buyer.

On the buyer's insolvency the seller may reclaim the goods if he makes the demand within 10 days after receipt. If written misrepresentation of solvency has been made by the buyer to the particular seller within three months, the 10-day period does not apply.

On the buyer's insolvency the seller may stop delivery of the goods by a carrier or other bailee. Delivery of large lots may be stopped on the buyer's repudiation or failure to pay sum due before delivery. Reasonable notice to stop delivery must be given to the carrier or other bailee.

E-Z Roll Hardware Mfg. Co., Inc. v. H & H Products & Finishing Corp.

4 U.C.C. Rep. 1045 (N.Y. Sup. Ct., Nassau Cty., 1968)

This was an action for breach of contract by E-Z Roll Hardware (plaintiff) against H & H Products & Finishing Corporation (defendant). Judgment for E-Z Roll Hardware.

The contract, dated October 31, 1963, was in the form of a letter accepting a blanket order for 10,000 sets of "special folding door hardware." Prices were set forth as follows: 2 feet, 76 cents; 4 feet, $1.47; 5 feet, $1.54; 6 feet, $1.61; 8 feet, $1.75. There was to be a first shipment of 3,000 sets approximately December 15, 1963. The balance of 7,000 sets was to be shipped as needed by the buyer over a period of not later than nine months.

E-Z commenced shipments in January of 1964 which continued until April 7, 1964. A total of 3,010 sets were shipped for an aggregate price of $4,757.90. E-Z testified that on at least five occasions between June, 1964 and January, 1966, H & H was contacted about the balance of the order and each time received excuses for delay or promises that there would be larger orders. Finally, in January 1966, H & H stated there would be no additional orders and this action was brought.

E-Z claimed as damages the sum of $11,101 on the theory that this figure represented the purchase price for the balance of the 7,000 sets computed by treating the price of 3,010 sets actually delivered ($4,757.90) as three-tenths of the full contract price. Judgment for E-Z for $4,002.40.

LYNDE, JUSTICE.   E-Z is entitled to relief, and the question becomes one of measure of damages. E-Z found itself with a large quantity of raw materials on hand which it could not use for any other purpose. Further work would have to be performed before H & H could use the merchandise: metal track would have to be cut to size; plating, assembly and boxing were required. A seller who is in the process of manufacturing goods for the buyer which are not readily saleable when finished and who elects to cease manufacture on repudiation by the buyer does not have an action for the purchase price as such. He does, however, retain his action for damages (U.C.C. § 2–709, sub (3)) which are measured by the difference between costs of performance and contract price and which include losses sustained, such as payments for labor and materials reasonably made in part performance of the contract to the extent that they are wasted if performance is abandoned.

The complicating factor here is that the buyer had the right to control the contract price. The buyer had five alternatives and had the right to demand delivery of the item bearing the lowest price. Its responsibility under the contract would have been fulfilled if it ordered that the balance of the sets (6,990) be delivered in two-foot lengths. In such circumstances the return on the lowest price provides the standard for measuring damages. Assuming completion of the contract on this basis, E-Z would be entitled to $5,312.40 in addition to the amount of $4,757.90 previously received. In order to get that, however, it would have been required to expend an additional $810 in order to identify the material to the contract. H & H may have a credit for that amount plus a credit for $500, the salvage value of the material. The amount, therefore, which is due to E-Z is $4,002.40. This, of course, represents a loss to E-Z but it puts E-Z in the same position as though the contract had been completed. The court cannot remake the contract. Both parties apparently took a business risk when they entered into the agreement. H & H ordered special purpose equipment, hoping that it would have customers for the product and E-Z provided for a loss item in the contract, hoping it would not be a major factor in the entire order.

E-Z's claim for storage is rejected. To qualify for incidental damages as contemplated by U.C.C. § 2–710, there must be compliance with the statutory provisions (U.C.C. §§ 2–709, 2–706) designed to minimize damages. No such action was taken in this case.

Chicago Roller Skate Mfg. Co. v. Sokol Mfg. Co.

177 N.W.2d 25 (Sup. Ct. Neb. 1970)

This was an action by the Chicago Roller Skate Mfg. Co. (plaintiff) against the Sokol Mfg. Co. (defendant) to recover damages for breach of contract. The trial court granted plaintiff judgment for $4,285. Affirmed on appeal.

Defendant purchased from plaintiff truck and wheel assemblies with plates and hangers for use in the manufacture of skate boards. The skate board fad terminated and several weeks later, defendant returned, without plaintiff's consent, a quantity of the merchandise purchased. There was due plaintiff the sum of $12,860. The merchandise was not suitable for other uses and could not be resold. It was held by plaintiff for 7 months. Plaintiff offered a credit of 70 cents per unit which defendant neither accepted nor rejected. Plaintiff then disassembled, cleaned, and rebuilt the units to make them suitable for use on roller skates. The undisputed evidence showed the rebuilt units had a reasonable value of 67 cents and 69 cents. In the salvage operation plaintiff incurred an expense of $3,540.76. Profits lost amounted to an additional $2,572. Plaintiff, disregarding its expense, credited defendant with 70 cents per unit and brought suit for the balance due of $4,285.

NEWTON, JUSTICE.   In accordance with § 2–709, UCC, plaintiff was entitled to hold the merchandise for defendant and recover the full contract price of $12,860. Plaintiff did not elect to enforce this right, but recognizing that there was no market for the goods or resale value and that they were consequently worthless for the purpose for which they were designed, it attempted to mitigate defendant's damages by converting the goods to other uses and credited defendant with the reasonable value of the goods as converted or rebuilt for use in roller skates. In so doing, plaintiff was evidencing good faith and conforming to the general rule requiring one damaged by another's breach of contract to reduce or mitigate damages.

The Uniform Commercial Code contemplates that it shall be supplemented by existing principles of law and equity. It further contemplates that the remedies provided shall be liberally administered to the end that an aggrieved party shall be put in as good a position as it would have been in if the contract had been performed. Here the buyer was demanding of the seller credit for the full contract price for goods that had become worthless. The seller was the aggrieved party and a return of worthless goods did not place it in as good a position as it would have been in had the contract been performed by the buyer paying the contract price. On the other hand, the crediting to defendant of the reasonable value of the rebuilt materials and recovery of the balance of the contract price did reasonably reimburse plaintiff. This procedure appears to be contemplated by § 2–718(4) UCC, which requires that a seller paid in goods credit the buyer with the reasonable value of the goods.

It is the defendant's theory that since the goods were not resold or held for the buyer, the seller cannot maintain an action for the price. We agree with this proposition. We also agree with defendant in its contention that the controlling measure of damages is that set out in § 2–708(2), UCC. This section provides that the measure of damages is the profit which the seller would have made from full performance by the buyer, together with any incidental damages resulting from the breach and costs reasonably incurred. Defendant overlooks the provision for allowance of incidental damages and costs incurred. The loss of profits, together with the additional costs or damage sustained by plaintiff amount to $6,112.76, a sum considerably in excess of that sought and recovered by plaintiff. Although the case was tried by plaintiff and determined on an erroneous theory of damages, the error is without prejudice to defendant. There being no cross-appeal, the judgment of the district court is affirmed.

In re Units, Inc.

3 U.C.C. Rep. 46 (D. Conn. 1965)

This was a reclamation petition filed by Northern Sash & Door Company (plaintiff) against the trustee in bankruptcy of Units, Inc. (defendant). Reclamation petition was denied.

On December 23, 1964, Units, which owed Northern $16,900 and which was legally insolvent at the time, sent a letter to Northern which read in part:

Anticipating your anxiety over the status of our account with your company, we felt it wise to acquaint you with our situation at present.

We are experiencing the typical year end "receivable blues" this coupled with the fact our inventory is extremely heavy and unbalanced has put us in a temporary bind.

Based on the above we are proposing the following payment schedule to help us through this period.

  December—$4,304.77 (check enclosed)
  January   —$4,304.77
  February —$3,856.61
  March   —$3,856.60

At that time the bankrupt had an unfilled order for merchandise amounting to $8,149.09. On January 13, 1965, Northern's sales manager spoke with the bankrupt's treasurer and was allegedly told the January check would be sent if the merchandise was released. Northern sent the merchandise, but the check was never mailed. Northern made no effort to rescind or reclaim until after April 7, 1965, when the petition in bankruptcy was filed.

SEIDMAN, REFEREE.   Connecticut General Statutes § 42a–2–702 is controlling. It provides in part:

(2)   Where the seller discovers that the buyer has received goods on credit while insolvent he may reclaim the goods upon demand made within ten days after the receipt, but if misrepresentation of solvency has been made to the particular seller in writing within three months before delivery, the ten day limitation does not apply. . . .

(3)   The seller's right to reclaim under Subsection (2) is subject to the rights of a buyer in ordinary course . . . or lien creditor under § 42a–2–403. . . .

The reclamation petition alleged a fraudulent misrepresentation of solvency. The trustee pleaded that even if there was a fraudulent misrepresentation the petitioner is not now entitled to reclaim the property since a timely reclamation petition was not made. In reply the petitioner amended its petition by alleging that the bankrupt had made a written misrepresentation of solvency to the petitioner within three months before delivery.

Assuming that a promise that a check would be forthcoming was made, it would be a fraudulent representation that would give the seller a right to reclaim within ten days after delivery. This was not done in the instant case. If the reclaiming creditor is to prevail it is necessary therefore to find there was a misrepresentation of solvency in writing within three months before delivery.

The only evidence of the alleged misrepresentation of solvency is the letter dated December 23, 1964. A careful reading of that letter does not disclose any language which could reasonably be considered a representation of the solvency. The bankrupt in the letter admits that it is unable to pay its bills as they mature and refers to the anxiety which the creditor feels. The letter refers to an unbalanced inventory and a temporary bind. This language might put a reasonably prudent man on further inquiry as to whether or not the debtor is in fact insolvent.

It is impossible for the court to conceive of any reasonable interpretation of the letter of December 23, 1964, to construe it as being a written misrepresentation of solvency. But even assuming that the reclaiming creditor had received a written misrepresentation of solvency within three months before delivery, his right to reclaim is still subject to defeasance. Section 42a–2–703(3) provides the seller's right to reclaim under subsection (2) is subject to the rights of a lien creditor under § 42a–2–403. A lien creditor is defined in § 42a–9–301(3) as a creditor who has acquired a lien on the property involved by attachment, levy or the like and includes a trustee in bankruptcy from the date of the filing of the petition. In the instant case prior to the date of filing, April 7, 1965, the creditor had made no effort to reclaim and his right would have been subject to the lien rights of the trustee in bankruptcy.

Buyer's Remedies

Right to Recover Goods.   The buyer's right to recover the goods which are the subject matter of the sales contract is analogous in many respects to the seller's right to recover the purchase price of goods sold. The forms of action brought by a buyer to recover the goods are specific performance and replevin. The buyer is entitled to the remedy of specific performance only if his remedy at law is inadequate. If the goods are unique or of such a character that other goods of the same or similar characteristics would not be available, the courts may grant the remedy of specific performance. In case a decree of specific performance is granted it may include such terms and conditions as to payment of the price, damages or other relief as the court may deem just. (2–716 [1] and [2].)

The buyer is entitled to the remedy of replevin if the goods have been identified to the contract and after reasonable effort he has been unable to obtain other goods of the same characteristics or the circumstances are such that it is reasonably apparent that a reasonable effort to obtain goods of the same characteristics would be unavailing. Also, if the goods have been shipped under reservation and the buyer has paid or tendered the amount necessary to satisfy the security interest in the goods he can recover the goods in an action of replevin. (2–716 [3].)

Buyer's Right to Damages for Nondelivery.   In the event the seller fails or refuses to deliver the goods or repudiates the contract, the buyer is entitled to recover as damages the difference between the market price at the time the buyer learned of the breach and the contract price plus any incidental and consequential damages. The market price is to be determined as of the place for tender or, in case of rejection after arrival or revocation of acceptance, as of the place of arrival. A tender of delivery of nonconforming goods is a nondelivery as the term is used in the Code. (2–713.)

The buyer has the right to "cover"; that is, purchase in the market goods of the same characteristics as those contracted for. Any "cover" must be made in good faith and without unreasonable delay. If the buyer does purchase or contract to purchase substitute goods under his right to "cover," he can recover from the seller as damages the difference between the cost of cover plus incidental and consequential damages less expenses saved in consequence of the seller's breach. The buyer is not obligated to cover and his failure to do so will not bar him from any other remedy. (2–712.)

Incidental damages include the expenses reasonably incurred by the buyer in inspection, receipt, transportation, and the care and custody of goods rightfully rejected together with any commercially reasonable charges, expenses or commissions in connection with cover and other reasonable expenses incident to the delay or other breach. (2–715 [1].)

The buyer is entitled to recover consequential damages only if the seller at the time of entering into the contract knew or should have known that a failure to perform would result in special damages due to the buyer's general or special requirements or needs and if the damages could not have been prevented by cover. (2–715 [2] [a].)

The seller is liable in damages for injury to person or property resulting from any breach of warranty. (2–715 [2] [b].)

Damages for Defective Goods.   If the buyer accepts defective goods and wishes to hold the seller liable in damages, he must give the seller notice of the breach within a reasonable time after he discovers or should have discovered the breach or he will be barred from any remedy. If the goods are not as warranted and the buyer has given the required notice, he can recover as damages the difference at the time and place of acceptance between the value of the goods accepted and the value they would have had if they had been as warranted, unless special circumstances show proximate damages of a different amount. The buyer may be entitled to incidental or consequential damages including damages to person or property. (2–714.)

The buyer may, on notifying the seller of his intention to do so, deduct all or any part of the damages resulting from any breach of the contract from any part of the price still due under the same contract. (2–717.)

On the buyer's rightful rejection or justifiable revocation of acceptance the buyer has a security interest in the goods in his possession or control for any payment made on their price and any expenses reasonably incurred in their inspection, receipt, transportation, care and custody and may retain possession of the goods until the seller returns the amount paid on the price plus the buyer's incidental expenses. If the seller does not pay the buyer the amount due him, the buyer may sell the goods and deduct from the proceeds the amount due plus the reasonable expenses of the sale. Any surplus must be returned to the seller. (2–711 [3].)

Summary

The buyer may be entitled to the remedy of specific performance if the goods which are the subject matter of the contract are unique or the circumstances warrant the granting of the remedy. The buyer may replevin the goods if they have been identified to the contract and he cannot, with reasonable effort, cover.

The buyer may recover as damages for nondelivery or repudiation on the part of the seller the difference between the market price of the goods and the contract price plus incidental, and under some circumstances consequential, damages. If the buyer covers, the measure of his compensatory damages is the difference between the cost of the cover and the contract price.

In the event the goods are defective and the buyer accepts them, he can, on giving the seller notice of the breach, recover as damages the difference between the value of the goods received and their value had they been conforming goods plus incidental, and under some circumstances consequential, damages.

If the buyer has paid part of the purchase price of the goods and he rejects them or revokes his acceptance, he may retain possession of the goods and claim a security interest in them for the amount paid on the purchase price plus incidental and consequential damages, if any.

Keystone Diesel Engine Co. v. Irwin

191 A.2d 376 (Sup. Ct. Pa. 1963)

This was an action by Keystone Diesel Engine Company (plaintiff) against Floyd T. Irwin (defendant) to recover a judgment for the cost of repairs to an engine, and Irwin filed a counterclaim for damages for breach of warranty and loss of profits. Judgment for Keystone Diesel Engine Company and Irwin appealed. Judgment affirmed.

Keystone Diesel Engine Company (Keystone) was a dealer in diesel engines and Irwin operated tractor-trailers as a contract carrier. Keystone sold Irwin a diesel engine which was subsequently installed in a tractor. The engine did not function properly and Keystone performed certain modifications and repairs to it at its own expense. Subsequent repairs were required and Keystone performed the additional work allegedly based upon an oral contract with Irwin to pay Keystone for the additional work and Keystone brought suit. Irwin filed a counterclaim for loss of profits totalling $5,150.

EAGEN, JUSTICE. The Uniform Commercial Code provisions which are appropriate in the instant case read as follows:

The measure of damages for breach of warranty is the difference at the time and the place of acceptance between the value of the goods accepted and the value they would have had if they had been as warranted, unless *special circumstances* show proximate damages of a different amount.

In a proper case any incidental and consequential damages under the next section may also be recovered.

Consequential damages *resulting from the seller's breach* include (a) any loss resulting from general or particular requirements and needs of which the seller at the time of contracting had reason to know and which could not reasonably be prevented by cover or otherwise.

"Special circumstances" entitling the buyer to damages in excess of the difference between the value as warranted and the value as accepted exist where the buyer has communicated to the seller at the time of entering into the contract sufficient facts to make it apparent that the damages subsequently claimed were within the reasonable contemplation of the parties. The language in *Globe Refining Co. v. Landa Cotton Oil Co.,* gives the rationale of the foregoing rule as follows:

"[O]ne of two contracting parties ought not to be allowed to obtain advantage which he has not paid for. . . . If [a liability for the full profits that might be made by machinery which the defendant was transporting . . .] had been presented to the mind of the ship owner at the time of making the contract, as the basis upon which he was contracting, he would at once have rejected it. . . . The knowledge must be brought home to the party sought to be charged, under such circumstances that he must know that the person he contracts with reasonably believes that he accepts the contract with the special condition attached to it."

In the case at bar, no facts are alleged that would put Keystone on guard to the fact that Irwin would hold Keystone responsible for any loss of profit arising from the inability to use the engine in question. Following Irwin's theory to its logical conclusion, whenever a motor vehicle is sold for use in a profit motivated enterprise and the seller warrants that the vehicle will function properly, the seller will be liable in damages for a breach of warranty to the extent of profits lost on completely unrelated business contracts, where those profits are lost due to the vehicle malfunctioning.

Anticipated profits are not recoverable unless within the contemplation of the parties when the contract was made: *Macchia v. Megow.* Clearly, the claim for loss of profits in the instant case was not within the contemplation of the parties to this contract.

General Rules

Buyer and Seller Agreements as to Damages. The courts will enforce an agreement entered into relative to the nature and amount of damages provided the agreement is not void as an unconscionable contract or clause or is not in violation of other provisions of the Code. (2–302.) An agreement for liquidated damages will be enforced provided the amount is reasonable, that is, not so excessive as to amount to a penalty or so small as to be unconscionable, and provided that in the event of a breach the amount of damages resulting would be difficult of proof and the obtaining of an adequate remedy otherwise would not be convenient or feasible.

If the seller has justifiably withheld delivery of the goods because of the buyer's breach, the buyer is entitled to recover any money or goods he has delivered to the seller over and above the agreed amount of liquidated damages, or if there is no such agreement, the seller will not be permitted to retain an amount in excess of 20 percent of the value of the total performance for which the buyer is obligated under the contract or $500, whichever is the smaller. This right of restitution is subject to the seller's right to recover damages under other provisions of the Code and to the amount of value of benefits received by the buyer directly or indirectly by reason of the contract. (2–718.)

The parties, by agreement, may provide for additional or substituted remedies other than those expressly provided in the Code. For example, the buyer's remedies may be limited to the return of the goods and the repayment of the price or to the replacement or repair of nonconforming goods or parts.

Resort to a remedy as provided is optional unless the agreement expressly states that the remedy is to be exclusive, in which case it will be the sole remedy. However, where the circumstances cause the limited or exclusive remedy to fail of its essential purpose, the parties are entitled to the remedies provided by the Code.

Consequential damages may be limited or excluded unless their limitation or exclusion would be unconscionable. Limitation of consequential damages for injury to the person in case of consumer goods is prima facie unconscionable but limitation of damages where the loss is commercial is not. (2–719.)

Unless a contrary intention appears, expressions of "cancellation" or "rescission" of the contract or the like shall not be construed as a renunciation or discharge of any claim in damages for an antecedent breach. (2–720.)

Proof of Market Price. Where the action based on anticipatory repudiation comes to trial before the time of performance with respect to some or all of the goods, any damage based on market price shall be determined according to the price of such goods prevailing at the time the aggrieved party learns of the repudiation. If such price is not available at the time and place, the court may receive evidence of the price of such goods at a commercially reasonable time before or after the aggrieved party learns of the repudiation and at any other place which in commercial judgment or usage of trade would seem as a reasonable substitute. If market price at any other time or place is to be offered in evidence, the other party must be given reasonable notice of such intent. (2–723.)

Reports of the prevailing price of the goods on an established market are admissible to prove market price. It does not have to be an organized market such as the New York Stock Exchange or the Chicago Board of Trade but must be a recognized market which issues quotations. (2–724.)

Statute of Limitations. The Code provides that any action for breach of a sales contract must be brought within four years after the cause of action accrues. The parties, by agreement, may shorten the period to one year but may not extend it. The cause of action accrues when the breach occurs, whether or not the aggrieved party knows of the breach. The cause of action for breach of warranty accrues when the goods are delivered unless the warranty is as to future performance in which case the cause of action accrues when the buyer should have discovered the breach.

Where suit begun within the four-year period has terminated so as to leave a remedy still available for the same breach, the aggrieved party has six months after the termination of the first action in which to bring another action, provided the first suit was not terminated by voluntary discontinuance or for failure to prosecute. This Code provision does not alter the law on tolling of the statute of limitations. (2–725.)

Summary

As a general rule the courts will enforce an agreement of the parties relative to the damages to which the parties will be entitled provided the agreement is not void as an unconscionable contract or clause. A liquidated damage provision in a contract is enforceable if the amount is reasonable and the damages for the injury suffered by the aggrieved party are not readily provable. The parties by agreement may provide for additional or supplemental damages, and consequential damages may be limited or excluded except damages for injury to the person in case of consumer goods.

In an action for damages for anticipatory breach, damages based on market price shall be determined according to the price of such goods prevailing at the time the aggrieved party learns of the repudiation. If such price is not available the price at a commercially reasonable time before or after the party learns of the repudiation may be used, and if a market price at the place of repudiation is not available a commercially reasonable marketplace may be used. The reported price of the goods on an established market is admissible to prove market price.

The statute of limitations on sales contracts is four years from the time the cause of action accrues. The parties may, by agreement, limit the time to one year but they cannot extend it.

Denkin v. Sterner

1 U.C.C. Rep. 173 (Com. Pleas Pa. 1956)

This was a petition by Denkin and his wife (plaintiffs) against Sterner (defendant) to open a judgment entered under a confession of judgment. Petition granted.

The Denkins contracted to purchase from Sterner certain refrigeration equipment for $35,500. The contract included a confession of judgment whereby, in the event of default by the Denkins, Sterner was given a power of attorney to enter judgment against the Denkins for the full purchase price, $35,500. The Denkins learned later that they could purchase the equipment at a lesser price from another dealer and they canceled the contract with the Sterner who under their power of attorney, took a judgment against the Denkins for $35,500. The Denkins petitioned to have the judgment opened.

ANDERSON, JUSTICE. There is a paucity of decisions under the relatively new Uniform Commercial Code which will no doubt require considerable future court interpretation. We feel that the above sections must be read and interpreted together and as stated in the Comments to the above section, found in § 2–719. . . . "Thus any clause purporting to modify or limit the remedial provisions of this Article in an unconscionable manner is subject to deletion and in that event the remedies made available by this Article are applicable as if the stricken clause had never existed."

While under Section 2–709, we find the following:

The action for the price is now generally limited to those cases where resale of the goods is impracticable except where the buyer has accepted the goods or where they have been destroyed after risk of loss has passed to the buyer. . . . An action for the price under subsection (1) (b) can be sustained only after a "reasonable effort to resell" the goods "at reasonable price" has actually been made or where the circumstances "reasonably indicate" that such an effort will be unavailing.

While there seems little doubt from the depositions taken under the rule issued in this case that Sterner is entitled to damages, for the Denkins admit that they canceled the agreement because they found out after checking that they could buy more equipment for less money elsewhere, yet it also seems evident under all the circumstances that to permit Sterner to recover the full amount of the purchase price without showing what goods, if any, have been identified to the contract, what goods were standard items and readily salable and what goods had actually been specially manufactured prior to the cancellation by the Denkins, as well as what goods have been or can be readily resold, would be in effect "unreasonably large liquidated damages" and, therefore, unconscionable and void.

Problem Cases

1. Mr. Kohn ordered a suit from Meledandi Tailors. A few days later before much work had been completed, Kohn told the tailors that he did not want the suit. They, therefore, stopped its manufacture and filed suit for the entire contract price. Is Kohn liable for the full purchase price?

2. Mrs. Bechtel ordered an alabaster-colored mink coat from Pollack Furs Inc. The coat had been specially made because she required an unusually large size and requested a particular styling. It cost $5,500, of which Mrs. Bechtel paid $250. Several months later she decided that she did not want the coat and canceled it even though the coat had been completed. Pollack Furs then filed suit for the balance of the purchase price. What can Mrs. Bechtel argue in defense? Discuss the merits of this argument.

3. Mr. Schutt, acting as an agent for a Mr. Reed, purchased 180 steers in Arkansas for $27,846. After the steers had been shipped, the seller called Mr. Reed with regard to the bank draft

given him by Mr. Schutt in payment. Mr. Reed refused to pay the draft. The steers were sold upon their arrival at their destination, Kansas City, for $22,663 through a sale barn. The seller then sued Mr. Reed for the difference between the two sale prices. Can he recover this amount?

4. Mrs. Miles sold a dining room table and four chairs to Mr. Lyons for $100. She alleged that the table and chairs were hers but they in reality belonged to her relatives. The value of the set at the time of the sale was $275. After the table and chairs were reclaimed by their rightful owners Mr. Lyons instituted an action against Mrs. Miles. What amount can he claim in damages?

5. Zimmerman Co., a manufacturer of novelty items, contracted with General Mills to provide Plastic Dune Buggies as inpack premiums for one of General Mills's cereals. The production of the cereal was on a very tight schedule so the contract provided that the novelty items must be delivered as of a certain date. When Zimmerman Co. breached the contract and delivered late, General Mills, even though it accepted delivery, was required to find a substitute premium. Because of the shortness of time they were required to pay air freight and overtime labor expenses incurred in getting a substitute. They also destroyed the cartons that they had purchased for the cereal that were imprinted with the Dune Buggy promotion. Discuss these elements as possible damages in a suit by General Mills against Zimmerman Co.

6. Mr. Dennler, an experienced livestock feeder, informed W & W Livestock Enterprises that he was in the market for about 400 good pigs. W & W sold him 408 of what they claimed to be "real good head." A few days after delivery it became evident that some of the pigs were ill. Over time many of the pigs became seriously diseased and 191 of the 408 died before they could be marketed. Mr. Dennler brought an action against W & W Livestock Enterprises claiming as his damages (1) a sum equal to the difference between the value of the pigs at delivery and their value if they had been as warranted, (2) the total sum expended by him on veterinary services and medicines, and (3) the total value of the feed consumed by the pigs that died and the extra feed consumed by the other pigs because of their illness. Are these elements of damages recoverable under the Code?

7. Mr. Myers purchased a new car from Thompson Chrysler-Plymouth Inc. The price he paid included $3,695 for the car, $55.45 sales tax, $88.87 for life insurance, and $574.72 for finance charges, for a total of $4,414.04. From the outset the car was faulty. Many of the car's features malfunctioned or did not work at all. After several return trips to the dealer, all of which failed to remedy the problems, it became evident that Mr. Myers had a valid claim for a breach of an implied warranty. He, therefore, filed an action against the dealer for $4,414.04. The dealer admitted liability but only for $3,695, the cash price of the car. Is the dealer liable for the $4,414.04?

8. On May 16, 1961, Augustine agreed to purchase a heating system from Perry. Assume that the heating system was installed during June of 1961 and the furnace was started in October of that year. In 1965, Perry filed suit to recover the contract price. On July 14, 1965, Augustine filed a counterclaim in which he alleged that Perry had given him a specific warranty that the heating system would "be able to heat at 75° inside at a −20° outside temperature," and further alleged that the furnace did not meet this guarantee as this was discovered after the furnace was started in October. Perry's attorney replied that the breach of warranty claim was barred by Section 2–725. Is the claim barred by Section 2–725?

Part IX

Commercial Paper

chapter 37

Negotiable Instruments

Background

Historical Background. History discloses that every civilization which
engaged to an appreciable extent in commerce used some form of commercial
paper. Probably the oldest type of commercial paper used in the carrying on
of trade was the promissory note. Archaeologists in their excavations found
a promissory note of the approximate date 2100 B.C. made payable to bearer.
The merchants of Europe used commercial paper, which under the law merchant was negotiable, in the 13th and 14th centuries. However, it appears that
such paper was not used in England until about A.D. 1600. In 1896 a Uniform
Negotiable Instruments Law was drafted.

Uniform Commercial Code—Commercial Paper. Today in the United
States the law of commercial paper—drafts, checks, certificates of deposit, and
promissory notes—is embodied in the Uniform Commercial Code's section on
commercial paper. Other negotiable documents, such as investment securities
and documents of title, are treated in other sections of the Code. Essentially,
the Code makes no drastic changes in those basic rules of commercial paper
which have been recognized for centuries, but it has adopted modern terminology and has coordinated, clarified, and simplified the law.

Forms of Commercial Money

Nature of Commercial Paper. All commercial paper is basically a simple
promise to pay money. If the promise is in writing and is so drafted as to fulfill
certain formal requirements, it is given the special characteristics which distinguish commercial paper from simple contracts. Other instruments given char-

acteristics of negotiability by trade usage or by statute are not classed as commercial paper since they are not used currently in trade or are not payable in money. Such instruments as corporate stock, stock warrants, corporate bonds, negotiable bills of lading, and negotiable warehouse receipts are negotiable but are not commercial paper, and money, including bank notes and government notes, is treated as falling in a separate category. Commercial paper must be current in trade if it is to perform the function for which it is intended. Since the basic promise is a promise to pay money, it is a simple matter to determine whether or not the promise has been performed and under our concepts of the assignability of contracts a promise to pay money is generally held to be assignable. These characteristics make the simple contract to pay money peculiarly adaptable to its use to facilitate trade.

Traders need a simple "instrument which can be used in lieu of money." Commercial paper fulfills this need and its use also facilitates the use of credit. Through long usage, commercial paper has acquired certain characteristics not possessed by other types of contracts. A check, draft, certificate of deposit, or promissory note may be termed a contract in shorthand in that if it fulfills the formal requirements for negotiability, trade usage gives to it its full meaning. A signature on commercial paper may bind the signer to a contract composed of several distinct promises.

There are two major classes of commercial paper—orders to pay and promises. Drafts and checks are orders to pay, and certificates of deposit and notes are promises to pay.

Draft.   A draft is a three-party instrument. It is an order by a drawer addressed to a drawee ordering him to pay to a payee a sum certain in money. It has a variety of uses. If B owes A a past-due obligation, A may draw a draft for the amount of the debt naming B as drawee and himself or his bank as payee and send the draft to B's bank for presentment and collection. In freight shipments in which the terms are "cash on delivery" it is a common practice for the seller to ship the goods to the buyer, on an order bill of lading consigned to himself at the place of delivery, endorse the bill of lading, attach a draft naming the buyer drawee, and then send them through banking channels to the buyer's bank where the draft is presented for payment and where on payment the bill of lading is delivered to the buyer. The result: the buyer gets the goods and the seller gets his money. If credit is extended, the same procedure is followed except a time draft is used, that is, a draft payable at some future time. In such a transaction the buyer will "accept" the draft instead of paying it. To accept the draft he writes his name across its face thereby making himself primarily liable on it, or in other words, he obligates himself to pay the amount of the draft when due. If the draft on its face states that it is drawn by the seller of goods on the buyer of goods for the purchase price of the goods, it is known as a "trade acceptance." A "trade acceptance" is given a preferential discount rate by the Federal Reserve Bank.

DRAFT

$ 133.47   July 15   19 74

On sight

the order of   John Doe

One hundred thirty-three and 47/100

WITH EXCHANGE

Pay to

Dollars

Value received and charge the same to account of

To   American National Bank

Chicago, Illinois   60606

Richard Thompson

Check. A check is a draft drawn on a bank and is payable on demand. It is the most widely used of the various forms of commercial paper, and is used in lieu of money. Neither drafts nor checks are drawn on drawees or banks unless there is some relation existing between the drawer and drawee which justifies the drawer in drawing the draft or check. The check plays such an important role in today's society that each state has enacted statutes making the drawing of a check on a bank a crime if the drawer has no credit balance or one insufficient to cover the check when presented for payment. No such statutes have been enacted in regard to drafts. However, the drawer of a draft should know that the drawee will not pay or accept the draft unless he (the drawer) has had business relations with the drawee which warrant the drawing of the draft.

CHECK

No. 1046

CHICAGO,   July 15   19 74

PAY TO THE ORDER OF   Harry J. Johnson $ 298.00

THE SUM ✸✸298 DOL'S 00 CTS   DOLLARS

THE TERMINAL NATIONAL BANK OF CHICAGO

Robert Clark

Certificate of Deposit. The certificate of deposit is a promise to pay. It is an acknowledgment by a bank of receipt of money with an engagement to repay it. Its use is confined to the issuing of the certificate of deposit as evidence of a time deposit with a bank. Usually, it is drawn for a period of six months or a year and draws interest if the money is left on deposit for the time stated.

CERTIFICATE OF DEPOSIT

CERTIFICATE OF DEPOSIT

BLOOMINGTON, IND. _____ March 1 _____ 19 74 No. 18866   71-227/712

THIS IS TO CERTIFY THAT_____ Albert Wells _____ HAS DEPOSITED IN

8 Fee Lane
STREET OR R.F.D.

Spencer, Indiana
CITY & STATE

CITIZENS FIRST NATIONAL BANK
OF BLOOMINGTON
BLOOMINGTON, IND.
47401
ESTABLISHED 1871

$100.00

One hundred and no/100 Dollars

PAYABLE TO _____ Albert Wells _____ OR ORDER _____ Six _____ MONTHS

AFTER DATE WITH INTEREST THEREON AT THE RATE OF _Three_ PER CENT PER ANNUM FROM DATE ON THE RETURN OF THIS CERTIFICATE PROPERLY INDORSED. NO INTEREST WILL BE PAID UPON THIS CERTIFICATE AFTER ITS MATURITY. THE BANK IS PROHIBITED BY FEDERAL LAW FROM PAYING THIS DEPOSIT IN WHOLE OR IN PART BEFORE ITS MATURITY AND FROM PAYING INTEREST AFTER MATURITY. THE RATE OF INTEREST PAYABLE HEREUNDER IS SUBJECT TO CHANGE BY THE BANK TO SUCH EXTENT AS MAY BE NECESSARY TO COMPLY WITH REQUIREMENTS OF THE FEDERAL RESERVE BOARD MADE FROM TIME TO TIME PURSUANT TO THE FEDERAL RESERVE ACT. THE BANK RESERVES THE RIGHT TO REQUIRE THIRTY DAYS NOTICE OF WITHDRAWAL IN WRITING.

DUE _____ August 31, 1974 _____   Richard Roe
CASHIER

NOT SUBJECT TO CHECK

Promissory Note. The promissory note is the simplest form of commercial paper and is very widely used. It is simply a promise to pay. The maker of the note promises to pay the named payee a stated sum of money on demand or at some future date. The note is primarily a credit instrument and is used in a variety of transactions in which credit is extended. If a person purchases an automobile or a home on time, the probability is that the seller will have the buyer execute a promissory note for the unpaid balance, secured by a security interest in the automobile, or by a real estate mortgage, deed of trust or land contract on the home.

PROMISSORY NOTE

$ 460.00 _____ July 15 _____ *19* 74

Sixty days _____ *after date* I *promise to pay to*

the order of _____ James Smith _____

Four hundred sixty and no/100 _____ *Dollars*

at American National Bank, Chicago, Illinois   60606

Value received.

No. 143   Due 9/13/74   *Henry Jenkins*

The terms of payment of the note will correspond with the terms of payment stated in the sales contract on the automobile or the home. Money may be loaned and an unsecured note given which evidences the amount of the loan and the terms of repayment.

Summary

Commercial paper is basically a simple promise to pay money. If the instrument satisfies certain formal requirements, it will be negotiable and will have certain characteristics which will distinguish it from simple contracts. To perform its intended function, commercial paper must be current in trade.

Through long usage commercial paper has acquired certain characteristics not possessed by other types of contracts. A signature on commercial paper may bind the signer to a contract composed of several distinct promises. Drafts and checks are orders to pay and certificates of deposit and notes are promises to pay.

A draft is an order by the drawer addressed to the drawee ordering him to pay the payee a sum certain in money at sight or at some future time. A check is a draft drawn on a bank and payable on demand. It is used in lieu of money to make all types of payments. A certificate of deposit is an acknowledgment by a bank of the receipt of money and an engagement to repay it. It is used by banks in connection with time deposits. The note is the simplest form of commercial paper. It is a promise by the maker to pay a sum certain in money to the payee on demand or at some future time. It is a credit instrument and has a wide variety of uses.

Benefits of Negotiability

Rights of Assignee of Contract. The assignee of a contract acquires no greater rights than his assignor has at the time of the assignment. The assignee cannot know with certainty the nature and scope of the defenses the obligor may have to the assigned contract; consequently, there are certain risks involved in acquiring contract rights as an assignee in addition to the credit risks incident to all contractual obligations. The assignment of contracts was discussed in Chapter 13.

Rights Acquired by Negotiation. The holder of a negotiable instrument acquires certain procedural advantages over the obligee or assignee of a contract. The holder of a negotiable instrument, if he brings suit on the instrument, need not allege and prove consideration. What other procedural advantages he may have will depend upon the procedural statute of the state in which suit is brought.

If the negotiable instrument remains in the hands of the original parties, the advantages of having the promise negotiable in form are mostly procedural, since the original payee holds the instrument subject to all the defenses to the instrument. However, if a negotiable instrument is negotiated to a person who can qualify as a holder in due course,[1] such person takes the instrument free from all defenses to the instrument except defenses which go to the validity of the instrument in its inception.

For example, suppose that Bell, by fraudulent representations, induces Albert to sign a nonnegotiable contract whereby Albert promises to pay Bell $100, and Bell then assigns the contract to Finch, who takes for value and without notice or knowledge of the fraud. When the $100 is due, Finch demands payment, and Albert refuses to pay and Finch brings suit. Albert can set up Bell's fraud as a defense, and the defense is good against Finch. Suppose that Albert, instead of executing a nonnegotiable contract for the $100, issues to Bell his negotiable promissory note, and Bell negotiates the note to Finch, who takes it as a holder in due course. Albert then does not pay the note when due, and Finch sues on the note. The defense that Albert was induced to issue the note by Bell's fraudulent representations would not be a defense to the instrument in the hands of Finch.

If Bell should forge Albert's name to an instrument negotiable in form, and negotiate the instrument to a person who could qualify as a holder in due course, the defense of forgery would be available to Albert in a suit by such holder.

A person taking a negotiable instrument as a holder in due course takes it subject to only two major risks: (1) the ability of the holder to collect from the parties to the instrument and (2) the validity of the instrument in its inception. The assignee of a nonnegotiable contract takes it subject to all oustanding defenses between the parties.

Summary

The assignee of a contract acquires no greater rights than his assignor has.

The holder of a negotiable instrument, if he is an original party to the instrument, acquires technical procedural advantages to which the obligee or assignee of a nonnegotiable contract is not entitled.

If the holder of a negotiable instrument is a holder in due course, he holds the instrument free from personal defenses available to the original parties, but he does not hold the instrument free from real defenses, that is, defenses which go to the validity of the instrument in its inception.

Formal Requirements for Negotiability

Basic Requirements.   An instrument must satisfy certain formal requirements if it is to be negotiable. If the writing does not fulfill these requirements

---

[1] The requirements for a holder in due course are set out in Section 3–302 of the Uniform Commercial Code.

it is a nonnegotiable instrument; it will be a contract which lacks the characteristic of negotiability. The formal requirements for negotiability, as set out in the Code—Commercial Paper, may be stated briefly as follows: (1) The instrument must be in writing and signed by the maker, if it is a certificate of deposit or a note, or by the drawer, if it is a draft or check. (2) It must contain an unconditional promise, if it is a certificate of deposit or note, or an unconditional order, if it is a draft or check, to pay a sum certain in money, and no other promise, order, obligation or power given by the maker or drawer except as authorized by the provisions of the Code—Commercial Paper. (3) It must be payable on demand or at a definite time, and (4) it must be payable to order or bearer. (3–104 [1].)[2]

The details necessary to fulfill the formal requirements are set out in other sections of Article 3 of the Code.

Commercial paper which fulfills the formal requirements for negotiability is a "draft" if it is an order; a "check" if it is a draft drawn on a bank and payable on demand; a "certificate of deposit" if it is an acknowledgment by a bank of receipt of money with an engagement to repay it; and a "note" if it is a promise other than a certificate of deposit. (3–104 [2].) The terms "draft," "check," "certificate of deposit," and "note" may be used to refer to instruments which are not negotiable. (3–104 [3].)

Importance of Form. Whether or not an instrument is so drafted that it satisfies these formal requirements is important for one and only one purpose, and that is for the purpose of determining whether the instrument is negotiable or nonnegotiable. Negotiability should not be confused with validity or collectibility. If the instrument is negotiable, the law of negotiable instruments will control in determining the rights and liabilities of the parties to the instrument. If the instrument is nonnegotiable, the general rules of contract law will control.

An instrument which fulfills all of the formal requirements is a negotiable instrument even though it is void, voidable, unenforceable, or uncollectible. Negotiability is a matter of form and nothing else. If a person gives an instrument in payment of a gambling debt in a state which has a statute declaring that any instrument or promise given in payment of a gambling debt is null and void and of no force and effect, the instrument is a negotiable instrument if it is negotiable in form even though it is absolutely void. Also, an instrument which is negotiable in form is a negotiable instrument even though signed by an infant. The fact that the infant may set up his infancy as a defense if suit is brought to enforce the instrument is immaterial. The instrument is voidable, but it is negotiable.

An instrument which is negotiable in form although void or voidable may give rise to liability on the part of a person who endorses and negotiates it or

---

[2] The numbers in the parentheses refer to the sections of the Uniform Commercial Code, 1962.

transfers it without endorsement whereas if it were nonnegotiable liability to the same extent would not be imposed on an assignor of the instrument.

Language of Negotiable Instrument.   In determining the negotiable character of an instrument the language of the instrument must be carefully analyzed to determine whether or not it satisfies all the requirements for negotiability as set out in the Code—Commercial Paper. There are no technical words which must be used in drafting a negotiable instrument.

For example, the instrument

> I promise to pay Bearer one hundred dollars.
>
> (Signed) Albert Adams

is a negotiable instrument.

This does not follow the phraseology customarily used in the drafting of a promissory note, but it does satisfy all of the requirements of the Code for a negotiable note.

Summary

An instrument, in order to be negotiable, must comply with certain formal requirements which are set out in Section 3–104 of the Code.

The form of the instrument serves only in determining whether the law of negotiable commercial paper or general contract law will control in determining the rights and liabilities of the parties.

No particular technical terms need be used in drafting an instrument which is to be negotiable.

In Writing and Signed

Writing.   Writing is defined in the Code as follows: "Written" or "in writing" includes printing, typewriting or any other intentional reduction to tangible form. (1–201 [46].)

Only something having tangible form can be used as a medium of exchange in the business world. Consequently, if a promise to pay is to be easily transferable, it must be given some tangible form, and a writing evidencing the promise is the most convenient way to satisfy the necessity for tangible form. No particular type of writing is required; no particular material is designated on which the writing shall appear; all that is required is that the instrument be in writing. A person could draw a valid negotiable instrument on a piece of wrapping paper in lead pencil. It would be poor business practice, but it would fulfill the statutory requirement that the instrument be in writing.

Signing.   Signing is defined in Section 1–201 (39) of the Code as follows: "Signed" includes any symbol executed or adopted by a party with present intention to authenticate a writing. If an instrument is to be negotiable it must be signed by the maker or drawer. The common practice is for the maker or drawer to subscribe his name to the instrument but subscription is not required. A typed or rubber stamp signature is sufficient.

As a general rule a commercial paper is signed in the lower, right-hand corner but it need not be signed in any particular place to be negotiable. Under some circumstances, however, the position of a signature on an instrument may be indicative of the capacity in which the person signed. The Code provides, Section 3–402, unless the instrument clearly indicates that a signature is made in some other capacity it is an endorsement.

A certificate of deposit or a note to be negotiable must be signed by the maker and a draft or check to be negotiable must be signed by the drawer. The nature of a certificate of deposit or note is such that there is almost no question as to whether such an instrument has been signed by a maker. However, since the draft or check is a three-party paper there may arise some question whether the instrument bears the signature of the drawer.

A time draft is customarily presented to the drawee for his acceptance. He accepts the draft by signing it on its face. If for some reason a draft should be presented to a drawee and he accepted it by signing his name across the front before it was signed by the drawer, the instrument in that form would not be negotiable since it would not be signed by the drawer.

Summary

To be negotiable, an instrument must be in writing. No particular form of writing is required.

The instrument must be signed by the maker if it is a note or a certificate of deposit or by the drawer if it is a draft or a check. Any mark made on the instrument with the intent of authenticating it is sufficient to satisfy the requirement that the instrument be signed.

Jenkins v. Evans

295 N.Y.S.2d 226 (Sup. Ct. N.Y. 1968)

This was an action brought by Jenkins (plaintiff) against Evans (defendant) to recover the amount of two checks drawn on the account of the Glass Lake House, which was owned by Evans. Both parties moved for summary judgment. The court granted Jenkins' motion and denied Evans' motion. Affirmed on appeal.

Jenkins sued to recover the sum of $295, the face amount of two checks drawn upon the account of the Glass Lake House which were delivered to William Payne as payee by Albert L. Stickler, the managing agent of the Glass Lake House at Averill Park, New York. Thereafter, William Payne endorsed and delivered the checks to Jenkins in payment of an obligation. The checks were subsequently dishonored by the National Exchange Bank of Castleton-on-Hudson, New York.

Jenkins moved for summary judgment upon the ground that he was a holder in due course, since he took the checks for value and in good faith, and without notice of any defenses to them. Evans cross moved for summary judgment upon the grounds that the checks were signed by Albert L. Stickler, individually, and nowhere on the face of the instrument did it indicate that he signed on behalf of the Glass Lake House; that Albert L. Stickler was the maker of the checks, and was personally liable on the checks; that the checks were drawn without the authority of Evans, and that to the best of his knowledge the checks were used for personal obligations of Albert L. Stickler.

STALEY, J.   Evans admits that Albert L. Stickler was authorized to sign checks drawn upon the account of the Glass Lake House, and does not deny that the checks were drawn upon the check forms used by the Glass Lake House. Evans does not deny that Jenkins is a holder in due course.

Evans' contention that he is not liable on the checks, since his signature does not appear thereon, and the words "Glass Lake House" do not appear above the signature line on the checks, is without merit. Any writing to be a negotiable instrument must be signed by the maker or drawer. (Uniform Commercial Code, § 3–104.) No person is liable on an instrument unless his signature appears thereon and a signature may be made by the use of any name. (Uniform Commercial Code, § 3–104.) Evans authorized the use of the name and signature, and nothing upon the face of the check would indicate that it was necessary for Albert L. Stickler to indicate that he was signing in a representative capacity, or that his capacity to sign the checks was limited. It thus appears that Evans' printed name and address at the top of the check establishes he is named in the instrument and that he clothed his agent, Albert L. Stickler, with authority to possess, issue, and sign checks drawn upon his account, and Jenkins took the checks in question without notice of any defense against them. (Uniform Commercial Code, § 3–403.)

Jenkins then is a holder in due course, and took the checks free from any and all defenses on the part of Evans. (Uniform Commercial Code, §§ 3–302, 3–304, 3–305.)

The indication of agency or representation may appear in the body of the instrument as well as in the signature so as to preserve the person signing from individual liability. Thus, an instrument may be regarded as that of a principal although the name of the principal appears, not in the signature or promise, but on the blank or form on which the instrument is written.

Evans is, therefore, bound to the obligation represented by the checks, and summary judgment was properly granted in favor of Jenkins.

Unconditional Promise or Order

Requirement of Promise or Order.   If an instrument is a draft or a check, it must contain an order to pay. The courts have held that a simple request to pay, as a favor, to the drawer of the instrument is not an order to pay; however, if the language used connotes a demand, even though framed in polite language, it is sufficient as an order to pay.

If an instrument is a note, or certificate of deposit, to be negotiable it must contain language which connotes an unconditional promise to pay. A mere acknowledgement of a debt is not sufficient, but an acknowledgment of a debt with words indicating that the debt is to be paid is a sufficient promise to pay. For example, "I owe you $100" has been held not to be a promise to pay, but "Due John Jones or order $100 payable December 1st" has been held to be a promise to pay.

Promise or Order Must Be Unconditional.   If the promise does not bind the promisor to pay in all events, it is a conditional promise, and the instrument is nonnegotiable. Likewise, if the order does not demand the drawee to pay in all events, it is conditional, and the instrument is nonnegotiable. Whether or not a promise or order is unconditional must be determined from an interpretation of the language of the instrument. An instrument, to be negotiable, must be so drafted that, by reading it, the nature and extent of the parties' obligations can be determined. If an instrument is so drafted that it is necessary to read some other document, not a part of the instrument but referred to in it, in order to determine the obligations of the parties to the instrument, such instrument is not negotiable.

For example, an instrument which includes a statement such as "payment to be made subject to the terms of a mortgage of even date herewith" is nonnegotiable; but a statement in an instrument such as "This note is secured by a mortgage of even date herewith" does not affect the negotiable character of the instrument. In determining the rights of the parties to the first instrument, a person would have to read the instrument and the mortgage referred to in the instrument.

The reference to the mortgage in the second instrument merely states a fact—the instrument is secured by a mortgage—and the rights and duties of the parties to the instrument are in no way affected by the terms of the mortgage. In determining the rights of the parties, there would in such a case be no reason to refer to the terms of the mortgage.

Express Conditions.   If the promise or order is expressly conditioned on the happening of some event, the instrument is nonnegotiable. For example, a promise to pay "if I am elected to Congress" is clearly conditional. If the instrument contains a stipulation which, under the accepted rules of contract law, would be interpreted as an express condition, the instrument is nonnegotiable.

Special Provisions of the Code.   The Code sets out certain provisions which may be included in an instrument without affecting the instrument's negotiability. A provision in an instrument stating that it is given in payment for goods to be delivered at some future date does not render the instrument nonnegotiable. Some earlier decisions held that such a provision implied that the promise or order to pay was conditioned on the delivery of the goods. This view is rejected under the Code. (3–105 [1] [*a*].)

A statement of the consideration for which the instrument is given, whether such consideration has been performed or promised, or a statement of the transaction which gave rise to the instrument does not affect its negotiability. A notation on a check or other instrument stating that it was given in payment of last month's rent or next month's rent or a statement that the instrument is given in payment of the purchase price of goods will not render the instrument nonnegotiable. Likewise, a statement in an instrument that it is given for payment as per contract for the purchase of goods of even date, maturity being in conformity with the terms of such contract, does not affect the negotiable character of the instrument. Such a provision does not incorporate the contract by reference. (3–105 [1] [*b*].)

A statement that the instrument is drawn under a letter of credit or that it is secured, whether by mortgage, reservation of title or otherwise, is permissible, but a statement that the instrument is payable according to the terms of the mortgage or other security agreement would incorporate the terms of the security agreements and would render the instrument nonnegotiable. (3–105 [1] [*d*] and [*e*]) and 3–105 [2] [*a*].)

Where an instrument indicates a particular fund to be debited or any other fund or source from which reimbursement is expected, or where an instrument issued by a government or governmental agency or unit contains a provision stating that payment shall be made out of a particular fund or from the proceeds of a particular source, such an indication or provision does not render the instrument nonnegotiable. Such statements on instruments are interpreted as directions for record-keeping purposes and not as conditioning the promise or order. However, a promise or order to *pay out of a fund* will condition the promise or order since the instrument does not carry the general obligation of the maker or drawer; the obligation to pay is, in effect, conditioned on there being a sufficient balance in the fund to cover the instrument, and, since one would have to go outside the instrument to learn whether or not the balance was sufficient, an instrument containing such a provision would not be negotiable even though the fund would be sufficient. (3–105 [1] [*f*] and [*g*]) and (3–105 [2] [*b*].) As noted above, this latter rule does not apply to instruments issued by a government or governmental agency or unit. (3–105 [1] [*g*].)

Summary

A draft or check, to be negotiable, must contain an order to pay and a certificate of deposit or note must contain a promise to pay. The promise or order must be unconditional. Whether a promise or order is or is not unconditional is a matter of the interpretation of the language used and it is the duty of the judge hearing the case to interpret the written instrument.

An instrument is not negotiable if the promise or order to pay is expressly conditioned. Provisions which may be included in an instrument without affecting its negotiable character are set out in the Code. Briefly, they are: implied or constructive conditions; notation of consideration given or the transaction giving rise to the instrument; reference to another agreement for rights of prepayment and acceleration; statement that it is drawn under a letter of credit or that it is secured; notation of account to be debited or out of which reimbursement is to be made; and if issued by government or governmental agency or unit, fund out of which payment is to be made or procured.

A promise or order governed by the terms of another instrument or a promise or order to pay out of a particular fund is not unconditional.

United States v. Farrington

172 F.Supp. 797 (D. Mass. 1959)

This was an action of the United States (plaintiff) against Phillips Farrington (defendant) to recover a judgment on a note. Judgment for the United States.

The note in litigation was given by Davis Aircraft Engineering, Inc., now bankrupt, to a bank as payee. The note contained the following: "having deposited with this obligation as Collateral Security assigned Government Contracts. This note evidences a borrowing made under and is subject to the terms of loan agreement dated Jan. 3, 1952, between the undersigned and the payee thereof and should the market value of the same, in the judgment of the holder or holders hereof decline we promise to furnish satisfactory additional collateral on demand." Farrington signed the note on the back. Farrington contended that the note was not negotiable and that therefore he was not liable on his endorsement. The court held the note was not negotiable but that Farrington was liable as a guarantor.

ALDRICH, DISTRICT JUDGE. Farrington's position is that as a matter of law an instrument is conditional if it incorporates by reference a separate document making it impossible to know whether the obligation is certain or not until that document is examined. The Massachusetts cases upon which Farrington relies, with the possible exception of *Costelo v.* Crowell, all involved separate agreements that in fact imposed contingencies when read into the instrument. Whether the instrument becomes non-negotiable because on its face it is subject to an agreement which may impose contingencies even though in actual fact it does not, is quite a different matter, leading to policy questions of large compass. Although this precise question is often left undiscussed by the cases, there is a considerable body of authority to the effect that if the instrument contains the phrase, "subject to" the terms of another document, or words to that effect, the reference is fatal to negotiability regardless of the actual provisions of the other document.

This principle has apparently been modified in some jurisdictions, particularly with regard to corporate bonds, to the extent of permitting the incorporation of terms of a mortgage or deed of trust designed to secure the obligation of the primary instrument. In such cases it is said that making the note of bond subject to the provisions of what is clearly an agreement regarding collateral security in no way "restricts, or burdens with conditions, the absolute promise to pay" contained in the instrument.

In the case at bar it could be argued from the placement of the handwritten words that the note was described as subject to the loan agreement for the purpose of indicating the circumstances under which it was executed, and setting forth more fully the undertaking with respect to collateral security, and not in order to limit the promise to pay. However, I believe this is not the only and necessary interpretation, and that the ambiguity can be resolved only by examination of the loan agreement. It is true that inspection of this agreement will resolve the ambiguity in favor of the United States, but I rule that that is not enough to make the instrument negotiable.

Sum Certain in Money

Sum Certain.   The promise or order in an instrument must be to pay a sum certain in money. The sum is certain provided it is possible to compute from what is stated in the instrument the amount which will be required to discharge the instrument at any given time. The Code provides that the sum is certain even though it is to be paid with stated interest or in installments; or with different rates of interest before and after default or at a specified date; or with a stated discount or addition if paid before or after the date fixed for payment. A provision providing for the payment with exchange or less exchange, whether at a fixed rate or at the current rate, or a provision for the payment of the costs of collection or an attorney's fee or both on default does not render the instrument nonnegotiable. Although these charges or credits cannot be predetermined, business practice justifies the permission of their inclusion in the instrument without their making the sum payable uncertain. (3–106.)

Payable in Money.   The requirement that, to be negotiable, the instrument must be payable in money distinguishes negotiable instruments from negotiable warehouse receipts, negotiable bills of lading, and similar instruments which have many characteristics of negotiability.

If the holder has the option of accepting something other than money, the negotiability of the instrument is not affected, but if the party obligated to pay the instrument has the option of doing something other than paying money, the instrument is not negotiable.

The Code provides: An instrument is payable in money if the medium of exchange in which it is payable is money at the time the instrument is made. An instrument payable in "currency" or "current funds" is payable in money. (3–107 [1].)

Summary

Under the provisions of the Code a sum is a sum certain if the sum necessary to discharge the instrument at any specific time can be computed from the terms

on the instrument. A provision for the payment of interest, payment in installments, payment of a different rate of interest before and after default or a
specified date, or a discount or allowance for prepayment does not affect the
negotiable character of the instrument. Provisions for the payment of exchange
or collection costs or attorneys' fees are allowable.

An instrument is payable in money if the medium of exchange in which it
is payable is money at the time the instrument is made.

A. Alport & Sons, Inc. v. Hotel Evans, Inc.

317 N.Y.S.2d 937 (Sup. Ct. N.Y. 1970)

This was an action brought by A. Alport & Sons, Inc. (plaintiff) against Hotel Evans,
Inc. (defendant) to recover on two promissory notes. Judgment was granted for the
plaintiff.

The essential facts are given in the opinion.

CASEY, J. The defendants make two claims concerning the form of the instruments.
They claim one note (the note for $1,600.00) contained an indefinite interest rate, and
therefore was not a negotiable instrument. The note contained the notation "with
interest at bank rates." The requirements for a negotiable instrument are set forth in
§ 3–104 (1) of the Uniform Commercial Code, which provides in pertinent part: "Any
writing to be a negotiable instrument within this Article must . . .

(*b*) contain an unconditional promise or order to pay a sum certain in money . . . .

An instrument which recites "interest is payable at the current rate" fails to contain
a promise to pay a sum certain. UCC § 3–106, Official Comment.

Payable on Demand or at Definite Time

Payable on Demand. Instruments payable on demand include those payable at sight or on presentation and those in which no time for payment is stated.
If the instrument is a note it is customary to state specifically that it is payable
on demand. A draft usually states "on sight" or "on presentment" pay to, and
so forth. Since no time of payment is stated in the standard form of a check
it is payable on demand. (3–108.) A cause of action accrues on a demand
instrument upon its date, or, if no date is stated, on the date of issue. (3–122
[1] [*b*].) Unless the instrument provides otherwise, interest runs on a demand
instrument, in the case of a maker, acceptor or other party primarily liable,
at the rate provided by law for a judgment, from the date of demand. (3–122
[4] [*a*].)

Definite Time. From a commercial standpoint the time at which the
payment of an instrument is due should be certain or readily ascertainable. The

provisions in the Code relative to payment at a definite time are intended to provide for reasonable certainty as to such time. An instrument drawn payable on or before a stated date or at a fixed period after a stated date or at a fixed period after sight is payable at a definite time. (3-109 [1] [*a*] and [*b*].) If an instrument is payable at a fixed date, such as July 1, 1975, the obligor would have no right to pay and discharge his obligation before that date. To avoid this result an instrument may be made payable "on or before July 1, 1975." This gives the party primarily liable on the instrument the right to pay at an earlier date and thus stop the running of interest on an interest-bearing obligation.

It is a common practice to make an instrument payable at a specific time after date such as "30 days after date." If the instrument is dated it is payable at a fixed period after a stated date but in case it is not dated the instrument is not payable at a definite time and is not negotiable. The holder may cure this defect, however, by filling in the date before negotiating the instrument. (3–115.) A time draft may be payable at a fixed time after sight which is in effect a provision that it will be paid at a fixed time after the instrument is presented to the drawee for acceptance.

Under the Code provisions permission to accelerate or extend the time of payment of an instrument does not affect its negotiability. The instrument may, by its terms, give the holder the right to accelerate the time of payment at his option or if he deems himself insecure, or it may provide for automatic acceleration on the happening of a stated event. Also, the holder may be given the right to extend the time of payment at his option and the party primarily liable may be given the right to extend the time of payment to a further definite time, or the instrument may provide that the time of payment will be extended automatically upon or after a specified act or event. However, an instrument made payable only upon an act or event uncertain as to time of occurrence is not payable at a definite time even though the act or event has occurred. (3–109 [1] [*c*] and [*d*] and (3–109 [2].)

Summary

An instrument is payable on demand if it is stated to be so payable, or if it is payable at sight or on presentment, or if no time of payment is stated. An instrument is payable at a definite time if it is payable on or before a stated date or at a fixed time after a stated date or at a fixed period after sight. A provision in an instrument giving the parties the right to accelerate the time of payment, or giving the holder the right to extend the time of payment, or giving the party primarily obligated the right to extend the time of payment to a future fixed date does not affect its negotiability. An instrument payable only upon or after the happening of an act or event, the time of occurrence of which is uncertain, is not payable at a definite time.

Liberty Aluminum Products Co. v. Cortis

14 Pa. D. & C.2d 624 (Wash. Co. Pa. 1958)

This was an action by Liberty Aluminum Products Co. (plaintiff) against John Cortis and Julia Cortis (defendants) on a promissory note in which the Cortises petitioned to have a judgment entered against them set aside. Petition refused.

Liberty Aluminum Products Co. took a judgment on a promissory note in the amount of $3,400 against Cortis and his wife. The Cortises made a motion to set the judgment aside basing their motion primarily on two alleged deficiencies: The lack of a maturity date of installments, and the failure to show a default prior to the entry of judgment.

CUMMINS, JUDGE.   The first alleged deficiency is the one which must be explored a little further. Cortises' motion to strike completely overlooks the Uniform Commercial Code § 3–108. This code states categorically that "instruments payable on demand include those payable at sight or on presentation and *those in which no time for payment is stated.*" Under the Commercial Code this instrument is a demand note by virtue of its tenor.

Even if this were not so, the logic of the situation compels this conclusion. The parties have the right to use a blank form and tailor it to their needs. And the failure to include installment payments simply and clearly means that none were intended.

The next question relates to the demand or default necessary prior to the entry of judgment on a demand note. The answer to that is simple: None. The entry of the note itself is sufficient demand for payment.

Payable to Order or Bearer

Necessity of Words of Negotiability.   A basic rule of contract law is that an obligation or risk will not be imposed on a party unless he has voluntarily assumed the obligation or risk. When a person issues a negotiable instrument he assumes obligations and risks which are greater than those assumed on a nonnegotiable instrument. By issuing a negotiable instrument the promisor gives the promisee the power to cut off, by negotiating the instrument to a holder in due course, all personal defenses he (the promisor) might have to the instrument, whereas if the instrument is not negotiable an assignee of the promisee takes subject to all outstanding defenses. The issuer of an instrument indicates that he intends the instrument to be negotiable by drawing it payable to bearer or to the order of a named payee.

"Bearer" and "order" are the words customarily used to indicate the issuer's intent that the instrument be negotiable. Other language, however, which clearly indicates such intent may be used. (3–104 [1] [*d*].)

Payable to Order.   The general rule set out in the Code provides that an instrument is payable to order when by its terms it is payable to the order or assigns of any person therein specified with reasonable certainty, or to him or his order. For example: an instrument drawn payable "to the order of John Jones" or "to John Jones or order" or "to John Jones or assigns" would be payable to order. However, an instrument containing words such as "payable upon return of this instrument properly endorsed" is not payable to order. (3–110 [2].)

An instrument may be payable to the order of the maker or drawer or to the drawee, or to a person who is not maker, drawer, or drawee. If a note is drawn payable to the order of the maker, the maker is in effect promising to pay himself, and before the instrument could be put in the channels of trade the maker would have to endorse the instrument as payee and negotiate it. Drafts are frequently drawn payable to the order of the drawer. The standard form of a trade acceptance is drawn "pay to the order of ourselves," and an instrument so worded is payable to the order of the drawer.

If the customer of a bank owes the bank for money borrowed, he frequently draws a check on the bank as drawee payable to the order of the bank as payee. The effect of giving the bank such a check is to authorize the bank to pay itself out of the drawer's account with the bank. Usually an instrument is made payable to a payee who is not maker, drawer, or drawee. (3–110 [1] [a], [b], and [c].)

An instrument may be drawn payable to the order of two or more payees together or in the alternative. (3–110 [1] [d].) If the instrument is drawn payable to the order of two or more payees together—John Jones *and* Henry Smith—it is payable to all of the named payees and it may be negotiated, discharged or enforced only by all of them. (3–116 [b].) But if it is payable to the order of two or more payees in the alternative—John Jones *or* Henry Smith—it may be negotiated, discharged or enforced by any of them who possesses it. (3–116 [a].)

An instrument may be drawn payable to the order of an estate, trust or fund as, for example, "pay to the order of the estate of William Jones, deceased" or "pay to the order of the Wells Trust." In such case the instrument is payable to the representative of the estate or trust or to his successor. (3–110 [1] [e].)

An instrument may be drawn payable to the order of an office or to an officer by his title. An instrument drawn payable "to the order of the treasurer of Cook County" or "to the order of Henry Smith, treasurer of Cook County" is an order instrument. In case of the latter, the instrument is payable to Henry Smith as principal but the incumbent of the office or his successor may act as if he were the holder. (3–110 [1] [f].)

Under pre-Code law there existed an uncertainty as to the character of an instrument drawn payable to the order of a partnership or unincorporated association. Under the provisions of the Code such an instrument is an order instrument payable to the partnership or association and may be endorsed or transferred by any person authorized to act in behalf of the partnership or association. (3–110 [1] [g].) This provision of the Code is such that instruments drawn payable to the order of a partnership or unincorporated association are comparable in most respects to like instruments drawn payable to the order of a named corporation.

If an instrument is drawn payable both to order and to bearer it is payable to order unless the bearer words are handwritten or typewritten. (3–110 [3].) This rule clears up an ambiguity created when a form instrument is used and the issuer of the instrument fills in either "order" or "bearer" and neglects to cross out the printed "order" or "bearer" on the form with the result that it is drawn payable to both "order" and "bearer." The rule as stated is in keeping with the general rule that written words in a form take priority over printed words.

Payable to Bearer. An instrument drawn "pay to bearer" or "pay to the order of bearer" or "pay to John Jones or bearer" is payable to bearer, but an instrument drawn "pay to bearer John Jones" is not bearer paper and is not a negotiable instrument. The term "pay to bearer John Jones" has been interpreted as authorizing payment to John Jones and no other person; consequently, the issuer of the instrument has indicated that he is not issuing negotiable paper. (3–111 [a] and [b].) An instrument drawn payable to "cash" or to the order of "cash" or any other indication which does not purport to designate a specific payee is bearer paper. Since the instrument is so worded that it indicates that the issuer intends it to be negotiable yet names no payee who can endorse and negotiate it, it is held to be bearer paper which is negotiable without endorsement. (3–111 [c].)

Summary

An instrument is payable to order when by its terms it is payable to the order or assigns of a payee specified therein with reasonable certainty or to him or to his order or when it is conspicuously designated on its face as "exchange" or the like and names a payee.

The instrument may be drawn payable to the order of the maker or drawer or drawee or to a person who is not maker, drawer, or drawee or to two or more payees together or in the alternative. It may be drawn payable to the order of an estate or trust in which case it is payable to the order of the representative of the estate or trust or his successor. An instrument payable to the order of an office or to the holder of an office or to a partnership or unincorporated association is an order instrument. An instrument payable both to order and bearer is an order instrument unless the word "bearer" is written or typewritten.

United States v. First National Bank of Boston

268 F.Supp. 298 (D. Mass. 1967)

This was an action by the United States (plaintiff) to recover payment it had made on a fraudulently issued postal money order to First National Bank (defendant), an endorsee of the postal money order. One question before the court in this case was whether the postal money order was a negotiable instrument within the meaning of the Uniform Commercial Code. The court held that it was not a negotiable instrument.

The face of a blank postal domestic money order, so far as relevant, shows a blank line following the words "PAY TO" to be filled in with the name of the person to whom the money order is payable; three blank lines following the word "FROM" to be filled in with the name and address of the purchaser; a blank for the "initial of issuing employee"; and a blank for the "issuing office stamp." On the back of such an order appears the following:

PAYEE MUST ENDORSE BELOW ON LINE MARKED "PAYEE." OWNERSHIP OF THIS ORDER MAY BE TRANSFERRED TO ANOTHER PERSON OR FIRM IF THE PAYEE WILL WRITE THE NAME OF SUCH PERSON OR FIRM ON THE LINE MARKED "PAY TO" BEFORE WRITING HIS OWN NAME ON THE SECOND LINE. MORE THAN ONE ENDORSEMENT IS PROHIBITED BY LAW. BANK STAMPS ARE NOT REGARDED AS ENDORSEMENTS.

Pay to _____

_____

THIS ORDER BECOMES INVALID AFTER 20 YEARS. THEREAFTER NO CLAIM FOR PAYMENT WILL BE CONSIDERED.

WYZANSKI, CHIEF JUDGE.   First National Bank's broadest contention is that today the postal domestic money order, unlike its pre-1951 prototype, is a negotiable instrument within the meaning of the Uniform Commercial Code and that it is therefore proper to apply to it § 3–418 of the Code which provides that "payment . . . of any instrument is final in favor of a holder in due course, or a person who has in good faith changed his position in reliance on the payment."

There is difficulty in sustaining this broad contention. To be a negotiable instrument within the Uniform Commercial Code and within the laws of the states which have adopted substantially all its provisions, a writing must "be payable to order or to bearer." § 3–104 (1) (d). "An instrument is payable to order when by its terms it is payable to the order or assigns of any person therein specified. . . ." § 3–110 (1). We may assume, without deciding, that a money order though it does not use the word "order" uses equivalent language because the order, going beyond giving a direction to "PAY TO" a specified purchaser, states that "ownership of this order may be transferred to another person or firm if the person will write the name of such person or firm on the line marked 'pay to' before writing his own name on the second line." Compare Comment 5 to § 3–110. However, the money order adds that "More than one endorsement is prohibited by law." Such a restriction is contrary to § 3–301 of the Uniform Commercial Code which provides that "The holder of an instrument whether or not he is the owner may transfer and negotiate it," and is out of harmony with § 3–206 (1) which provides that "No restrictive endorsement prevents further transfer or negotiation of the instrument." Thus it cannot be said that in all respects a postal domestic money order is like the ordinary negotiable instrument covered by modern codes and statutes.

Special Terms

Additional Terms and Omissions. Businessmen and banks use many special forms of commercial paper drafted to serve their particular needs. Such forms may include terms which have no effect on the negotiability of the instrument. Likewise instruments are sometimes drafted which omit terms customarily included in standard forms of the instrument but their omission in no way affects the validity or negotiability of the instrument.

Standard forms of notes and drafts frequently include statements of consideration such as "for value received" or "in payment for goods sold and delivered." The omission of such statements of consideration, however, does not affect the negotiable character of the instrument.

It is also a common practice to state in the instrument the place where the instrument is drawn and/or where it is payable. The place where the instrument is drawn is usually stated together with the date of issue as, for example, Chicago, Ill., Sept. 26, 1970. And the place where it is to be paid is generally noted on the instrument by such a phrase as: "Payable at First Bank of Detroit, Mich." The negotiability of the instrument is not affected, however, by the omission of these details. (3–112 [1] [*a*].)

A statement that collateral has been given to secure obligations either on the instrument or otherwise of an obligor on the instrument, or that in case of default the holder may realize on or dispose of the collateral, or a promise or power to maintain or protect collateral or to give additional collateral does not render the instrument nonnegotiable. (3–112 [1] [*b*] and [*c*].) Under pre-Code law some courts held that such provisions were promises to do something other than pay money and that therefore the instrument was not negotiable.

A term authorizing the confession of judgment on the instrument when due or a term purporting to waive the benefit of any law intended for the advantage or protection of the obligor such as, for instance, appraisement and valuation laws or exemption laws, does not affect the negotiability of the instrument. However, a clause which authorizes confession of judgment prior to the due date of the note and a demand for payment has been held by a number of courts to render the note nonnegotiable.

The negotiability of a draft or check is not affected by a term providing that the payee by endorsing or cashing the draft or check acknowledges full satisfaction of an obligation of the drawer. Such a term is frequently included in a draft or check issued by an insurance company in payment of a loss claim. (3–112 [1] [*f*].)

A seal on an instrument does not affect the negotiable character of the instrument nor does it affect the character of the instrument insofar as the provisions of the article on commercial paper are concerned. The seal may, however, have some effect on rights not covered in the Code. (3–113.)

The negotiability of an instrument is not affected by the fact that it is undated, antedated, or postdated. Where the instrument is antedated or post-dated, the time when it is payable is determined by the stated date if the instrument is payable on demand or at a fixed period after date, and where the instrument or any signature thereon is dated, the date is presumed to be correct. (3–114.)

Ambiguous Terms. The courts have been consistent in their interpretation of certain ambiguous terms sometimes found in commercial paper. Where there is doubt whether the instrument is a note or draft the holder may treat it as either except that a draft drawn on the drawer is treated as a note. In such an instrument the drawer is ordering himself as drawee to pay the draft.

The general rule of interpretation, that handwritten terms control typewritten and printed terms and typewritten terms control printed terms, applies to commercial paper.

If there is a conflict between the amount written on the instrument and the figures, the words control unless the words are ambiguous in which event the figures control.

If an instrument provides for the payment of interest but the rate is not stated, the rate payable is the judgment rate at the place of payment, and the interest is computed from the date of the instrument, or if it is undated from the date of issue.

If two or more persons sign an instrument as maker, acceptor or drawer or endorser as part of the same transaction, they are jointly and severally liable, unless the instrument specifies otherwise, even though the instrument contains such words as "I promise to pay." (3–118.)

Newman v. Manufacturers National Bank

152 N.W.2d 564 (Ct. App. Mich. 1967)

This was an action by Newman (plaintiff) against Manufacturers National Bank (defendant) on the grounds that Manufacturers had improperly paid two of Newman's checks totalling $1,200. Judgment for Manufacturers National Bank and Newman appealed. Affirmed.

In 1955, Newman drew the two checks payable to Belle Epstein but left them undated. There was a printed dateline on the checks which read "Detroit, Mich. _____ 195__" but Newman never filled it in. Newman claimed that over the next four years he had paid all but $400 of the $1,200 debt personally to Epstein and that she told him she had destroyed the two checks. Then on April 17, 1964, the checks were cashed under the endorsement of Belle Epstein. By that time someone had written in the date April 16, 1964 but the original printed figures "195____" remained clearly visible. Newman objected to having his account charged on the grounds the bank had not used ordinary care in paying checks that were stale and altered on their face.

HOLBROOK, JUDGE. The two checks were dated April 16, 1964. It is true that the dates were completed in pen and ink subsequent to the date of issue. However, this was not known by Bank. Bank had a right to rely on the dates appearing on the checks as being correct. Section 3–114 provides in part as follows:

(1) The negotiability of an instrument is not affected by the fact that it is undated, antedated or postdated. . . .
(3) Where the instrument or any signature thereon is dated, the date is presumed to be correct.

Also (3–115) provides in part as follows:

The following rules apply to every instrument: . . .
(b) Handwritten terms control typewritten and printed terms, and typewritten control printed.

. . . Without notice to the contrary, Bank was within its rights to assume that the dates were proper and filled in by Newman or someone authorized by him.

Newman admitted at trial that Bank acted in good faith in honoring the two checks of Newman's in question, and therefore Bank's good faith is not in issue.

* * * * *

In order to determine if defendant bank's action in honoring Newman's two checks under the facts present herein constituted an exercise of proper procedure, we turn to Article 4 of the U.C.C. Section 4–401 provides as follows:

(1) As against its customer, a bank may charge against his account any item which is otherwise properly payable from that account even though the charge creates an overdraft.
(2) A bank which in good faith makes payment to a holder may charge the indicated account of its customer according to
(a) the original tenor of his altered item; or
(b) the tenor of his completed item, even though the bank knows the item has been completed unless the bank has notice that the completion was improper.

Problem Cases

1. Is the following instrument a note, a check, or a draft? Why? If it is not a check, how would you have to change it to make it a check?

   To: *Arthur Adams*   *January 1, 1974*
   TEN DAYS AFTER DATE PAY TO THE ORDER OF: *Bernie Brown*
   THE SUM OF: *Ten and no/100* Dollars.

                                         SIGNED: *Carl Clark*

2. The face of an instrument is as follows:

"AUDITOR CONTROLLER'S GENERAL WARRANT
COUNTY OF LOS ANGELES

The Treasurer of the County of Los Angeles will pay to the order of:

Apr. 1, 1971
Los Angeles, California

[Name and address of payee filled in] $161.00

GENERAL FUND

Approved
Mark H. Bloodgood Auditor-Controller By
[facsimile signature] J. S. Rasmussen"

Would this instrument qualify as a check under the U.C.C.? Why or why not?

3. Jones sells Thomas $6,000 worth of goods. Thomas gives Jones his negotiable note for $3,000 payable in 30 days and Jones agrees to carry the $3,000 balance on open account payable in 30 days. Jones wishes to discount his receivables at the bank. Will the bank discount the negotiable note and the open account at the same discount rate?

4. Wiley, Tate, & Irby, buyers and sellers of used cars, sold several autos to Houston Auto Sales. Houston wrote out the order for payment for each group of cars on the outside of several envelopes. He signed them and they were drawn on his bank, Peoples Bank & Trust Co., to be paid on the demand of Wiley, Tate, & Irby. Houston's bank refused to honor the envelopes as checks and thus returned them unpaid to Wiley, Tate, & Irby. In trying to recover payment against the bank, what will Wiley, et al.'s argument be? Is it a winning argument?

5. Invitations to bid for certain government contracts require bidders to make bid deposits in U.S. currency "or any other form of credit instruments, made payable . . . on demand including first party checks." Surplus Tire submitted a bid and enclosed its check for $500.50 payable to the United States Treasurer. On the face of the check was handprinted the following:

Bid deposit: DSSO Oakland.
Sale 44–8035—Notice: Do not deposit, cash or negotiate this check unless an award and contract is made pursuant to the bid submitted. Otherwise this check will be dishonored.

The government refused to accept the bid, claiming that the check was not a negotiable instrument. Is this contention correct?

6. Is the following a negotiable instrument?
"I.O.U. A. Gay, the sum of seventeen 5/100 dollars for value received.
"John R. Rooke"

7. A note otherwise negotiable contained the following provision: "Title to property described in Sales Contract of even date herewith is retained by the seller or holder of this note until all amounts due hereon are paid in full." Is the instrument negotiable?

8. Is the following instrument negotiable?
"Marshall, Ill., July 18, 1968 No. 112
"The Dulaney National Bank 70–559

"Pay to the order of C. A. Libs $9,200.00
Nine Thousand Two Hundred Dollars
Agent's disbursing account.

"Roy F. Keown"

9. Holliday made a promissory note out to Anderson, leaving the date of payment of the note blank. Anderson filled in the words "on demand" in the blank without Holliday's knowledge. Does this alter the rights or obligations of the parties?

10. An instrument otherwise negotiable contained the following provision: "In case this note is collected by an attorney, either with or without suit, the maker agrees to pay a reasonable attorney's fee." Is the instrument negotiable?

11. A note negotiable in form payable five years after date contained the provision, "due if ranch is sold or mortgaged." Is the note negotiable?

12. Sylvia signed a note dated May 25, 1963, obligating him to pay to Ferri or to her order $3,000 "within ten (10) years after date." Is this a negotiable instrument?

13. A note dated January 20, 1966, and due on July 1, 1966, contained a clause that provided for confession of judgment at any time. Was the note negotiable?

14. Is the following instrument negotiable? Why or why not?

"Winchester, Ky., July 10, 1960

"$2,500

"The Winchester Bank of Winchester, Ky.

"Pay to Arco Refinery Construction Company $2,500.00
Twenty-five hundred and no/100 Dollars.

"Mutual Oil & Refining Co.
"By C. L. Bell, Pres."

15. Nation-Wide Check Corporation sold money orders to drugstores. The money orders contained the statement "Payable to," followed by a blank. Can the money order qualify as a negotiable instrument?

16. Louis Canino signed the following instrument:

"No. 922B. INSTALLMENT NOTE

$27,000.00   March 11, 1970
LOUIS G. CANINO for value received, does promise to pay to the order of CARL MEES the sum of Two Hundred Twenty-Five. . . . . Dollars at Lakewood, Colorado, said principal payable on the first day of each and every month commencing April 1, 1970 with interest at the rate of 8 per cent per annum.

/s/ Louis G. Canino"

When Mees sued Canino on the note, Canino argued that the words "Two Hundred Twenty-Five Dollars" should control the figures "$27,000" and cited U.C.C. Section 3–118 (c). Is this a valid argument?

chapter 38

Negotiation and Holder in Due Course

Negotiation

Nature of Negotiation. A negotiable instrument is intangible personal property and the basic rules of property law apply in determining the rights and liabilities of the parties to the transfer of such an instrument. In the previous chapter the requirements for negotiability were discussed. Certain special rules of law have been developed and these rules are applied in determining the rights acquired by the transferee where the property transferred is negotiable commercial paper.

A "holder" is a person who is in possession of a document of title, or an instrument, or an investment security, drawn, issued or endorsed to him, to his order, to bearer or in blank. (1–201 [20].)[1] Negotiation is the transfer of an instrument in such form that the transferee becomes a holder. The formal requirements for negotiation are very simple and are set out in the Code as follows: If the instrument is payable to order it is negotiated by delivery with any necessary endorsement; if it is payable to bearer it is negotiated by delivery. (3–202 [1].)

Nature of Endorsement. An endorsement of an instrument is made by the writing of the holder's name by him or on his behalf on the instrument or on a paper so firmly affixed thereto as to become a part thereof. (3–202 [2].) If the back of an instrument is written full of endorsements further endorsements should be made on a paper glued firmly to the instrument. Such a paper is called an "allonge."

To be effective as a negotiation an endorsement must convey the entire instrument or any unpaid residue. If it purports to be of less it operates only as a partial assignment. (3–202 [3].) This rule is based on consideration of

[1] The numbers in the parentheses refer to the sections of the Uniform Commercial Code, 1962.

826

practical business policy. One who has issued a negotiable instrument should not be required to make piecemeal payments to several persons. It is not an uncommon practice for a large obligation to be evidenced by a series of notes, thus enabling the holder to negotiate portions of the debt to different persons. Suppose, for instance, that A borrows $10,000 from B. A might instead of giving B a $10,000 note, give him 10, $1,000 notes. B would then be in a position to negotiate a $1,000 note to each of 10 different persons.

Words of assignment, condition, waiver, guarantee, limitation, or disclaimer of liability and the like accompanying an endorsement do not affect its character as an endorsement. (3–202 [4].) If holder A writes on the back of a negotiable instrument, "I hereby sell, assign and set over to B, without warranty, all my rights, title and interest in this instrument," and signs his name, this would operate as an endorsement and the instrument would thereby have been negotiated to B. However, the effect of the form of the endorsement on the rights of A and B is a matter separate and apart from that of endorsement and negotiation of the instrument. (3–119.)

Wrong or Misspelled Name.   In endorsing an instrument the endorser should spell the name in the endorsement the same as it appears in the instrument. If the name is misspelled or is one other than his own the endorser may endorse in that name or his own, but a person who is paying or giving value for the instrument may require the endorser to sign both names. (3–203.)

Transfer of an Instrument.   When an instrument is transferred the transferee has vested in him such rights as the transferor has therein. However, a transferee who has himself been a party to any fraud or illegality affecting the instrument or who as a prior holder has notice of a defense or claim against it cannot improve his position by taking from a later holder in due course. (3–201 [1].) For example, suppose that Axe through fraudulent representations induces Bell to execute a negotiable note payable to Axe, and Axe then negotiates the instrument to Clark, who takes as a holder in due course. If Axe thereafter takes the instrument for value from Clark, Axe cannot acquire Clark's rights as a holder in due course. Axe was a party to the fraud which induced the instrument, and the holder of an instrument cannot improve his position by negotiating such instrument and then reacquiring it.

A transfer of a security interest in an instrument vests the rights of the transferor in the transferee to the extent of the interest transferred. Suppose, for example, that Bell issues his negotiable note in the sum of $5,000 to Axe who then pledges it to First Bank to secure the payment of a $1,000 loan First Bank has made to Axe. First Bank takes as a holder in due course. Suppose then, before this loan which First Bank has made to Axe is due, First Bank is notified that Bell has a defense to the note. First Bank is a holder in due course only to the extent of its interest in the Bell note, that is, as security for the payment of the $1,000 obligation of Axe to First Bank.

Transfer of Order Instrument. If an order instrument is transferred without endorsement, the instrument has not been negotiated and the transferee does not become a holder in due course because he cannot qualify as a holder. However, unless the parties have otherwise agreed, any transfer for value of an instrument not payable to bearer gives the transferee the right to have the unqualified endorsement of the transferor, and should the transferor refuse to endorse the instrument with an unqualified endorsement the transferee would be entitled to a decree ordering the transferor to so endorse the instrument. The negotiation takes effect only when the endorsement is made and until that time there is no presumption that the transferee is the owner. If, subsequent to the transfer of the instrument to him but before he obtains the transferor's endorsement, the transferee learns that the obligor has a defense to the instrument or he learns of other matters which would prevent him from taking as a holder in due course, he could not qualify as a holder in due course. (3–201 [3].)

Summary

Negotiable commercial paper is intangible personal property. Such an instrument may be transferred or negotiated. Only a person to whom a negotiable instrument has been transferred can qualify as a holder in due course. If an instrument is payable to order it is negotiated by delivery with any necessary endorsement; if payable to bearer it is negotiated by delivery. An endorsement is made by the holder signing his name on the instrument or on a paper firmly affixed thereto. An instrument must be negotiated in its entirety. Words of assignment, condition or the like accompanying an endorsement do not affect its character as an endorsement. In endorsing an instrument, if the holder's name is misspelled, the recommended practice is to endorse the name as it appears on the instrument followed by the correct name.

When an instrument is transferred the transferee acquires all the rights his transferor has in the instrument. A person cannot, however, improve his position by reacquiring an instrument. If one takes an instrument as security he acquires in the instrument only the value of his security. The transferee for value of an unendorsed order instrument has the right, unless otherwise agreed, to have the unqualified endorsement of his transferor. His position as a holder in due course is determined as of the time the transferor endorses the instrument.

Watertown Federal Savings & Loan Association v. Spanks

193 N.E.2d 333 (Sup. Jud. Ct. Mass. 1963)

This was an action by Watertown Federal Savings & Loan Association (plaintiff) against Robert W. Spanks and wife (defendants) to recover a judgment on a note.

Judgment for Watertown Federal Savings & Loan Association and the Spankses appealed. Judgment affirmed.

Spanks and wife executed a negotiable note payable to "Greenlaw & Sons Roofing & Siding Co." Greenlaw & Sons Roofing & Siding Co. indorsed the note "Greenlaw & Sons" and negotiated it to Colony Distributors, Inc., and Colony Distributors, Inc., negotiated the note to Watertown Federal Savings & Loan Association. Spanks refused to pay the note when due and set up defective work as a defense. Spanks and wife contended that the note was not properly indorsed and that Watertown Federal Savings & Loan Association is not a holder in due course.

CUTTER, JUSTICE.   The trial judge correctly denied the Spanks' requested ruling as immaterial. It does not appear that Greenlaw & Sons and Greenlaw & Sons Roofing & Siding Co. are not the same company. The indorsement by Greenlaw was not shown to have been in a name other than his own nor is it shown that the name of the payee, as stated in the note, was not a name under which Greenlaw individually did business, identifiably repeated in the indorsement. Section 3–203 purports to give only an indorsee for value, and not the maker of a note, the power to require indorsement in both names in the circumstances stated in the section. No evidence was introduced with respect to the indorsement. It comes within § 3–307 (and see the official comments on that section), which reads in part, "(1) . . . When the effectiveness of a signature is put in issue (a) the burden of establishing it is on the party claiming under the signature; but (b) the signature is presumed to be genuine or authorized [with an exception not here pertinent]. (2) When signatures are . . . established, production of the instrument entitles a holder to recover on it unless the defendant establishes a defense." There was no evidence whatsoever to counter the presumption of the indorsement's regularity existing under § 3–307 (1) (b). Thus the signature of Greenlaw was established under § 3–307 (2), and the bank, as the holder of the note, see § 1–201 (20), is entitled to recover.

Sweedler v. Oboler

8 U.C.C. Rep. Service 724 (Sup. Ct. N.Y. 1971)

This was an action brought by Sweedler (plaintiff) against Oboler (defendant) to require the payment of a number of certified checks and a cashier's check drawn on Oboler. Sweedler moved for summary judgment. Judgment for Sweedler.

At an auction sale conducted by Sweedler, the printed terms of which required payment to be made "only in cash or in certified check of bank acceptable to Auctioneers drawn to the order of the Auctioneers," a purchaser delivered to Sweedler a number of certified checks and a bank cashier's check drawn on Oboler (a bank), all payable to the order of the purchaser, in payment of his bid, receiving $291 in cash from Sweedler for the difference between his bid and the total amount of the certified and cashier's checks. The purchaser took the merchandise away. Sweedler apparently had failed to note that the checks were payable to the order of the purchaser. His endorsement was not obtained and he subsequently refused to affix it, making some claim with regard to the merchandise. In the absence of an endorsement Oboler refused to make payment.

GOLD, JUSTICE. Sweedler has sued the purchaser and the bank. The purchaser has interposed a defense of lack of jurisdiction over his person and Sweedler has made the instant motion only as against defendant bank, giving notice also to the purchaser, who has vaguely referred to some claim on his part.

The bank urges that, in the absence of an endorsement on the checks, there is no presumption that Sweedler is the owner or "holder" thereof (Uniform Commercial Code, § 3–201 [3]) and, therefore, Sweedler cannot establish his right to payment.

The law regards that as done which ought to have been done. There can be no doubt that it was intended that the purchaser endorse the checks given in payment for the merchandise which he took into his possession after his successful bid. The failure to so endorse was either the result of a mutual mistake or mistake on Sweedler's part and fraud on the purchaser's part. Whichever it is, the purchaser has obtained merchandise without paying for it when the known condition was for payment in cash or by certified check. Whatever claim the purchaser might have after taking the merchandise into his possession cannot affect his obligation to have fulfilled the antecedent condition of payment to the auctioneer.

The issuance of a certified or cashier's check by a bank simply means the setting aside of funds to meet payment thereof. The bank, of course, has no interest therein, so long as its depositor cannot hold it liable for releasing such funds in payment of a certified or cashier's check.

A determination by the court that Sweedler is entitled under these circumstances to payment of the certified checks and cashier's check will relieve defendant bank of any responsibility in making such payment and avoid any possibility of liability to its depositor.

The motion is granted.

Endorsements

Effect of Endorsement on Negotiation.   The effect of an endorsement on the further negotiation of the instrument will depend in part on whether it is an order instrument or a bearer instrument and in part on the form of the endorsement. It should be remembered that the form of an endorsement can have no effect on the negotiable character of the instrument; if an instrument is a negotiable instrument when issued, it continues to be a negotiable instrument, irrespective of the form of endorsement on the instrument. However, the form of the endorsement is important in determining the right of the holder to negotiate the instrument and in determining what the holder must do to negotiate the instrument.

A negotiable instrument may be endorsed for two distinct reasons. It may be endorsed because the endorsement is necessary to the negotiation of the instrument, or it may be endorsed for the purpose of adding the obligations of the endorser to those of the party primarily liable. When a person endorses a negotiable instrument, he thereby makes contractual promises to the endorsee and, with some exceptions, to subsequent holders of the instrument. The contractual liability of endorsers will be discussed in the next chapter. We shall confine our present discussion to the effect of the endorsement on the further negotiations of the instrument.

Kinds of Endorsements.   There are five kinds of endorsements recognized by the Code: (1) special, (2) in blank, (3) restrictive, (4) qualified, and (5) unqualified. Either of the first two kinds of endorsements may be combined with (4) and (5). If an instrument is endorsed with a special or in blank endorsement without the addition of qualifying words, the endorsement is unqualified. If an instrument is endorsed either with a special or in blank endorsement and qualifying words such as "without recourse" are added, the endorsement would be a qualified special or a qualified blank endorsement. Only the special, in blank and restrictive endorsements will, when used, have any effect on the further negotiation of the instrument. Whether an instrument is endorsed with a qualified or unqualified endorsement will affect only the contractual liability of the endorser.

Special Endorsement.   A special endorsement specifies the person to whom or to whose order it makes the instrument payable. Any instrument specially endorsed becomes payable to the order of the special endorsee and may be further negotiated only by his endorsement. (3–204 [1].) A special endorsement need not include words of negotiability; "Pay to Hall" is a special endorsement, "Pay any bank, banker or trust company," has been held to be a special endorsement. An order instrument endorsed with a special endorsement continues as an order instrument whereas a bearer instrument endorsed with a special endorsement is converted into an order instrument and must be endorsed by the endorsee before it is further negotiated.

Blank Endorsement.   An instrument endorsed in blank specifies no particular endorsee and may consist of a mere signature. An instrument payable to order and endorsed in blank becomes payable to bearer and may be negotiated by delivery alone until specially endorsed. (3–204 [2].) If an instrument drawn "Pay to the order of Brown" is endorsed "Brown," it is endorsed in blank. Such an instrument then becomes a bearer instrument and thereafter it can be negotiated by delivery alone until it is specially endorsed.

If an instrument is endorsed in blank and delivered to a holder, he may convert the blank endorsement into a special endorsement by writing over the signature of the endorser in blank any contract which will not in any way alter the obligation imposed by the blank endorsement. (3–204 [3].) If a negotiable instrument drawn "Pay to the order of Brown" is endorsed "Brown" and delivered to Finch as endorsee, Finch has the right to write over Brown's endorsement "Pay to Finch," thereby converting the blank endorsement into a special endorsement, and the instrument would then have to be endorsed by Finch before it could be further negotiated.

Restrictive Endorsement.   An endorsement is restrictive which either is conditional or purports to prohibit the further transfer of the instrument. (3–205 [*a*] and [*b*].) Such an endorsement as "pay to Clark if and only if he completes construction of house before November 1, 1966," is conditional, and an endorsement "Pay to Clark only" purports to prohibit the further transfer of the instrument.

Instruments deposited in banks by their customers are frequently endorsed with a restrictive endorsement. An endorsement which includes the words "for collection," "for deposit," "pay any bank," or like terms signifying a purpose of deposit or collection is a restrictive endorsement; and an endorsement which states that it is for the benefit or use of the endorser or of another person such as "Pay to Clark in trust for Drew" is also a restrictive endorsement. (3–205 [*c*] and [*d*].)

Effect of Restrictive Endorsement.   In regard to the effect of a restrictive endorsement a distinction is made between a bank as a restrictive endorsee and a nonbank restrictive endorsee. In general, no restrictive endorsement prevents further transfer or negotiation of the instrument. (3–206 [1].) Under this section of the Code a restrictive endorsement such as "Pay to Clark only," although recognized as a restrictive endorsement, would have no more effect on the further negotiation of the instrument than would an unrestricted endorsement.

In clearing checks and other collection items the standard practice is for the depository bank to send the item through "banking channels." Suppose, for instance, that Clark endorses an item drawn on Y Bank or payable at Y Bank "for deposit" or "for collection" and deposits it at A Bank in which Clark has a commercial account. A Bank will credit the item to Clark's account and send it to M Bank which is a correspondent bank with which A Bank does business. M Bank in turn will send the item on to Y Bank for payment or collection. A Bank is the depository bank, M Bank the intermediary bank, and Y Bank the payor bank. M Bank and Y Bank in handling this item are neither given notice nor otherwise affected by the restrictive endorsement of Clark. (3–206 [2].)

Except for an intermediary bank, any transferee under an endorsement which is conditional or includes the words "for collection," "for deposit," "pay any bank," or like terms must pay or apply any value given by him for or on the security of the instrument consistent with the endorsement and to the extent that he does so he becomes a holder for value.

Suppose that Clark endorses a check payable to his order "for deposit" and deposits it in A Bank in which Clark has a commercial account and A Bank credits Clark's account with the amount of the check. If the check is paid when presented to the drawee bank and remittance is made to A Bank, it will accept the money for the benefit of Clark. However, suppose that A Bank permits Clark to withdraw part or all of the credit created by crediting his account with the amount of the check and the drawer of the check then stops payment on the check. The check will be returned to A Bank marked "payment stopped." A Bank is a holder for value for the amount of the credit created by the deposit of the check which A Bank has permitted Clark to withdraw, and, if it took the check before it was overdue and without notice or knowledge of defenses to it, A Bank can qualify as a holder in due course. (3–206 [3].)

Grounds for Rescission of Endorsement. Negotiation is effective to transfer an instrument although the negotiation is made by an infant, a corporation exceeding its powers, or any other person without capacity; or it is obtained by fraud, duress or mistake of any kind; or is part of an illegal transaction; or is made in breach of duty. A negotiation made under the above circumstances is in an appropriate case subject to rescission, the declaration of a constructive trust or any other remedy permitted by law unless the instrument has subsequent to such endorsement been negotiated to a transferee who can qualify as a holder in due course. (3–207.) The situation discussed above is analogous to a sale of goods where the sale has been induced by fraud or misrepresentation. In such a case the seller may rescind the sale and recover the goods provided he acts before the goods are resold to a bona fide purchaser for value.

Reacquisition. Where an instrument is returned to or reacquired by a prior party he may cancel any endorsement which is not necessary to his title and reissue or further negotiate the instrument, but any intervening party is discharged as against the reacquiring party and subsequent holders not in due course and, if his endorsement has been canceled, is discharged as against subsequent holders in due course as well. For instance, suppose that Axe as maker issues his negotiable note payable to the order of Clark. The note bears the following special endorsements: "Pay Drew, Clark," "Pay Evans, Drew," "Pay Finch, Evans," "Pay Gage, Finch," "Pay Drew, Gage." Drew has reacquired the instrument and may again negotiate it. When Drew reacquires the instrument he is relegated to the position he held when he first acquired the instrument. Consequently Evans, Finch, and Gage are not liable to Drew as prior endorsers and they would not be liable to a transferee of Drew who was not a holder in due course. If Drew, after reacquiring the instrument, canceled the endorsements of Evans, Finch, and Gage or any of them and then negotiated the instrument to a holder in due course, the endorser or endorsers whose endorsement was canceled would not be liable to a holder in due course. (3–208.)

Summary

Under the Code there are five kinds of endorsements: (1) special, (2) in blank, (3) restrictive, (4) qualified, and (5) unqualified. The first three have an effect on the negotiation of the instrument; the last two affect the liability of the parties only.

A special endorsement names a payee, and an instrument specially endorsed must be again endorsed before it is negotiated. A blank endorsement names no endorsee and may be the endorser's signature only. A blank endorsement converts the paper to a bearer instrument.

A restrictive endorsement does not prevent the further negotiation of the instrument but it does impose certain restrictions on the rights of the holder. Special rules relative to the rights of banks to instruments endorsed with words such as "for deposit" are set out in the Code.

If the instrument is endorsed by one not having contractual capacity or authority to endorse or the endorsement is obtained by fraud, duress, or mistake, the endorsement is subject to rescission provided it is rescinded before the instrument is negotiated to a holder in due course.

One who reacquires an instrument does not improve his position. He may renegotiate it and his reacquisition discharges intervening endorsers from their liability to him.

Westerly Hospital v. Higgins

256 A.2d 506 (Sup. Ct. R.I. 1969)

This was an action brought by the Westerly Hospital (plaintiff) against Higgins (defendant) to recover the unpaid balance due on a promissory note made by Higgins on which the Westerly Hospital was the named payee. Judgment for Westerly Hospital. Affirmed on appeal.

On July 13, 1967, Higgins executed a promissory note in the amount of $527.58 payable to the order of the Westerly Hospital. The note was in consideration for services performed by the hospital in connection with the birth of Higgins' child and was payable in 18 monthly installments of $29.31. An agent of the hospital later indorsed the note in blank and negotiated it to the Industrial National Bank at a discount. The indorsement contained an express clause guaranteeing payment of the principal, interest and late charges in the event of default by the maker.

Higgins made three payments, then failed to make any further payments. The provisions of the note made the entire balance immediately due. Industrial returned the note to the hospital pursuant to the indorsement guarantee. Industrial received payment from the hospital and negotiated the note to it by delivery.

The hospital then brought suit against Higgins on the note. Higgins contended, among other things, that Westerly was not the proper person to bring suit on the note.

ROBERTS, CHIEF JUSTICE.   In our opinion, the face of the instrument discloses as a matter of law that Westerly Hospital is the holder of the note in question and, therefore, a proper party to bring this action. The face of the instrument reveals that Westerly Hospital was the payee of the note made by Higgins and his wife as co-makers. It further discloses that an indorsement of guarantee was executed in blank by an authorized representative of plaintiff hospital. The note was then delivered to Industrial. The pertinent provisions of the Uniform Commercial Code provide that where, as in the instant case, there has been a blank indorsement, mere delivery is sufficient to constitute the transferee a holder thereof and is sufficient to make the transfer a valid negotiation. § 6A–3–202; § 6A–3–204. Thereafter when Higgins defaulted, Industrial delivered the note to Westerly in return for the payment of the remaining amount of Higgins' obligation that had been guaranteed by plaintiff hospital.

Higgins argues that this delivery of the note back to Westerly was not sufficient to constitute a valid negotiation. He argues that the attempted special indorsement by Industrial to Westerly Hospital was invalid for the lack of the signature of a duly authorized representative of Industrial and thereby Westerly Hospital was precluded from becoming a holder of the instrument. Thus, according to Higgins, Industrial was the proper party to bring the action on this note. It seems rather obvious that had the transfer of the note from Westerly Hospital to Industrial been other than in blank, this argument would have merit, it being true that an authorized signature of an agent of Industrial would be necessary to negotiate the instrument.

However, § 6A–3–204(2) of the Uniform Commercial Code states, in pertinent part, that "An instrument payable to order and indorsed in blank becomes payable to bearer and may be negotiated by delivery alone until specially indorsed." Here Westerly Hospital as payee of the note caused its indorsement to appear thereon without specifying to whom or to whose order the instrument was payable. Instead, a blank indorsement, one specifying no particular indorsee, was made. The legal effect of such an indorsement and delivery was to authorize Industrial as the transferee and holder of the note to further negotiate the note without indorsement but by mere delivery alone. It is clear that any attempt on its part to achieve negotiation by indorsing the note to Westerly Hospital would have been mere surplusage.

In our opinion, then, the redelivery of the note in question by Industrial to Westerly Hospital accomplished a negotiation of the instrument, and the fact that a purported special indorsement to Westerly Hospital was not legally executed is of no consequence and does not affect Westerly Hospital's status as the holder of the note. It is our conclusion that in these circumstances Higgins' contention that there was a genuine issue as to the identity of the proper party to bring the action on the note in question is without merit.

Holder in Due Course

General Requirements.   In order to be accorded the special position in negotiable instruments law known as a holder in due course, a person must first be a "holder." As was indicated earlier, a "holder" is a person who is in possession of an instrument drawn, issued or endorsed to him, to his order, to bearer or in blank. (1–201 [20].) It is important that all endorsements on the instrument at the time it was order paper be authorized endorsements. A forged endorsement is not effective and prevents anyone from becoming a holder unless and until he obtains a complete chain of authorized endorsements.

To qualify as a holder in due course, the holder must take the instrument (1) for value, (2) in good faith, and (3) without notice that it is overdue or has been dishonored or of any defense against or claim to it by any person. (3–302 [1].) If the holder cannot comply with all these requirements, he is not a holder in due course.

A person who has purchased an instrument at a judicial sale, or has taken it by legal process, or has acquired it by taking over an estate, or has purchased it as part of a bulk transaction not in the regular course of the business of the transferor does not take as a holder in due course. (3–302 [3].) A person taking an instrument under the circumstances set out above has not taken the instrument in the regular course of trade.

Payee as Holder in Due Course.   Section 3–302 (2) expressly provides that a payee *may* be a holder in due course. This provision clears up a conflict which existed under pre-Code law. To become a holder in due course the payee must comply with all the requirements for a holder in due course as set out in Section 3–302 (1) of the Code. Ordinarily, a payee will have notice or knowledge of defenses to the instrument and will know if it is overdue or has been dishonored; consequently, he cannot qualify as a holder in due course. But suppose, for example, that Drew draws a check on First Bank as drawee, payable to the order of Parks but leaves the amount blank. Drew delivers the check to Axe, his agent, and instructs him to fill in $300 as the amount. Axe, instead of filling in $300, fills in $500 as the amount and Parks gives Axe $500 for the check. Axe gives Drew $300 and absconds with the extra $200. In such a case Parks, as payee, is a holder in due course of the check since he has taken it for value, in good faith and without notice of defenses.

Purchases of Limited Interest.   The purchaser of a limited interest in an instrument can be a purchaser in due course only to the extent of the interest purchased. (3–302 [4].) For example, Wells agrees to purchase a note payable to the order of Parks. The note is for the sum of $5,000. Wells pays Parks $1,000 on the negotiation of the note to him (Wells) and agrees to pay the balance of $4,000 in 10 days. Before the payment is due Wells learns that Bell, the maker of the note, has a valid defense to it. Wells is a holder in due course for only $1,000.

Summary

To qualify as a holder in due course the holder must take the instrument for value, in good faith and without notice that it is overdue or has been dishonored or of any defense against or claim to it on the part of any other person. If the holder has not taken the instrument in the regular course of trade, he cannot qualify as a holder in due course. A payee may be a holder in due course.

One who purchases a limited interest in an instrument can be a holder in due course only to the extent of the interest purchased.

Stone & Webster Engineering Corp. v. The First National Bank & Trust Co. of Greenfield

184 N.E.2d 358 (Sup. Jud. Ct. Mass. 1962)

This was an action by Stone & Webster Engineering (plaintiff) against The First National Bank & Trust Company of Greenfield (defendant) to recover a judgment for money paid out on checks on which the payee's endorsement was forged.

Stone & Webster had drawn three checks in the total amount of $64,755.44 on The First National Bank of Boston payable to the order of Westinghouse Electric Corporation. An employee of Stone & Webster obtained possession of the checks, forged Westinghouse's endorsement to them, cashed them at the First National Bank & Trust Company of Greenfield, and put the proceeds to his own use. The first two checks were endorsed in typewriting, "For Deposit Only: Westinghouse Electric Corporation By: Mr. O. D. Costine, Treasury Representative" followed by an ink signature "O. D. Costine." The third check was endorsed in typewriting, "Westinghouse Electric Corporation by: (Sgd.) O. D. Costine, Treasury Representative." When Stone & Webster sued the Greenfield Bank for conversion, one of the issues discussed by the court was the status of the Bank. That portion of the opinion follows.

WILKINS, CHIEF JUSTICE.   In the case at bar the forged endorsements were "wholly inoperative" as the signatures of the payee, Code § § 3–404 (1), 1–201 (43), and equally so both as to the restrictive endorsements for deposits, see § 3–205(c), and as to the endorsement in blank, see § 3–204(2). When the forger transferred the checks to the collecting bank, no negotiation under § 3–202(1) occurred, because there was lacking the necessary endorsement of the payee. For the same reason, the collecting bank could not become a "holder" as defined in § 1–201(20), and so could not become a holder in due course under § 3–202(1).

Waterbury Savings Bank v. Jaroszewski

238 A.2d 446 (Cir. Ct. Conn. 1967)

This was an action by Waterbury Savings Bank (plaintiff) against the Jaroszewskis (defendants) based on a promissory note in the sum of $1,850 payable in twenty-four installments. Judgment for Waterbury Savings Bank.

Execution of the note had been preceded by negotiations between the Jaroszewskis and Merit Food Corporation, a concern which specialized in the sale of food to homeowners on a contract basis and in periodic shipments. The final discussions took place at the home of the Jaroszewskis when two salesmen from Merit were present. At the time, the Jaroszewskis signed a "Purchase and Sales Agreement" covering three deliveries by Merit of frozen foods, for $2,000, and loan of a freezer. The agreement provided for payment of the balance over twenty-four months. At that time, the Merit salesmen exhibited to the Jaroszewskis a four-page form prominently displaying the name of plaintiff bank. The first page was captioned, "Request for personal loan." The second page was a promissory note form. The third page, containing many blanks was entitled "Credit Application." The fourth page provided for an authorization by the Jaroszewskis to Waterbury to pay the proceeds of the loan, $1,850, directly to Merit. Both Jaroszewskis signed the note, as well as the first page of the credit application, which contained details as to their financial status.

The Jaroszewskis contended that the note was signed as a result of fraudulent representations by employees of Merit to the effect that the note was merely a "credit application" and nothing more. The Jaroszewskis further alleged fraud of Merit in that they signed the documents when they were not fully completed, and that the Merit employees misrepresented what would be filled in. The Jaroszewskis attempted to impute knowledge to Waterbury of the claimed fraud, alleging that Waterbury knew, or should have known, of Merit's misconduct, as a result of prior similar transactions financed by Waterbury for Merit customers. Waterbury denied these allegations and relied upon a claim of status as a holder in due course.

LEVINE, JUDGE.   It is now established that Waterbury, as a payee, may be a holder in due course. The court finds, in the instant case, that Waterbury is, in fact, a holder in due course in that it took the note in good faith and under the validating conditions of 3–302. Initially, no representative of Waterbury was present at the meeting at the Jaroszewski home when the documents were signed and there was no testimony that any agent of the bank participated, in any way, in the negotiations leading to execution of the note and contract. There was nothing in the evidence to show that Waterbury was aware of any defenses at the time it discounted the note. The fact that, subsequent to said conference, and after Waterbury had issued its check to Merit, the Jaroszewskis complained to Waterbury regarding Merit's conduct and their status as comakers does not alter the basic conclusion. If Waterbury was a holder in due course at the time it took delivery of the Jaroszewskis' note, notice thereafter to it of Merit's claimed fraud or defective performance would not change its legal position. 3–304(6).

The evidence disclosed that Waterbury had engaged in about five or six hundred similar financing transactions with Merit and its customers and that complaints of defective food service, or related items, had been received by Waterbury in about three to four cases. The complaints, percentagewise, were quite minimal. In any event, it is settled that receipt by a lender of miscellaneous prior complaints regarding a vendor does not prevent the lender from qualifying as a holder in due course, so long as the lender had no notice of a complaint by the particular customer involved, at or before the time it accepted the customer's note. Hence, the Jaroszewskis' attack on Waterbury's status, based on the "prior experience" argument, is without merit.

Failure of Waterbury to inquire as to proper performance by Merit of its underlying contract with the Jaroszewskis does not show a lack of good faith or alter its status under 3–302, 3–304(4), (6).

It is undisputed that Waterbury supplied the forms used by Merit to secure the Jaroszewskis' signatures on the note and credit application. This fact, alone, however, falls short of creating a principal-agent relationship between Waterbury and Merit so as to impute knowledge to Waterbury of Merit's conduct, or make Waterbury responsible for Merit's acts or omissions.

For Value and in Good Faith

Value.   A person, to qualify as a holder in due course of an instrument, must give value therefor. Value includes more than consideration. Under the provisions of the Code a holder takes the instrument for value to the extent that the agreed consideration has been performed or that he acquires a security interest in or a lien on the instrument otherwise than by legal process; or when he takes the instrument in payment of or as security for an antecedent claim against any person whether or not the claim is due; or when he gives a negotiable instrument for it or makes an irrevocable commitment to a third person. (3–303.)

A bank or any person who discounts an instrument in the regular course of trade has given value for it. Likewise, if a loan is made and an instrument is pledged as security for the repayment of the loan, the secured party has given value for the instrument to the extent of the amount of the loan. If Axe owes Bell a past-due debt and he endorses and delivers to Bell an instrument issued to him (Axe) in payment of the debt or as security for its repayment, Bell has given value for the instrument.

Suppose that Axe borrows $1,000 from Bell. Axe gives Bell a note for that amount payable in 30 days and Bell endorses and delivers to Axe a check for $1,000 drawn by Clark and payable to Bell. Axe, in issuing his note for $1,000 to Bell, has given value for the Clark check. Also, suppose that Bell and Clark enter into a contract whereby Clark obligates himself to deliver an automobile to Axe and Bell endorses an instrument issued by Drew and delivers it to Clark in payment for the automobile. Clark has given value for the Drew instrument.

Good Faith.   Good faith is defined in the Code as follows: "Good faith" means honesty in fact in the conduct or transaction concerned. (1–201 [19].) Good faith implies commercial honesty. If negotiable instruments are to serve their purpose of facilitating the carrying-on of trade, they must pass freely in the channels of commerce, and a person must be permitted to take a negotiable instrument without first investigating its origin and the intervening transactions whereby the present holder acquired the instrument.

Good faith always involves a question of fact. The courts have held that the fact that a person takes an instrument under suspicious circumstances is not sufficient to prove bad faith. However, if a person acquires an instrument under circumstances which should have created an inevitable inference that an infirmity existed in the instrument, the person could not have taken such instrument in good faith.

Summary

Value includes the performance of an agreed consideration, the taking of an instrument as security, as payment or security for an antecedent claim whether due or not, or the giving of a negotiable instrument, or the assuming of an irrevocable obligation to a third person. Good faith is honesty in fact.

Korzenik v. Supreme Radio, Inc.

197 N.E.2d 702 (Sup. Jud. Ct. Mass. 1964)

This was an action by Armand A. Korzenik and another (plaintiffs) against Supreme Radio, Inc. (defendant), to recover a judgment on two trade acceptances. Judgment for Supreme Radio, Inc., and Korzenik appealed. Judgment affirmed.

Korzenik and his partner in law took two trade acceptances given by Supreme Radio, Inc. (Supreme), to Southern New England Distributing Corporation (Southern). The trade acceptances were transferred to Korzenik "as a retainer for services to be performed." The two trade acceptances had been obtained by fraud and Supreme set up the fraud as a defense. Korzenik claimed that he was a holder in due course. Korzenik and partner did some work but there was no testimony offered as to the value of the work. Korzenik did not know that the trade acceptances had been obtained by fraud.

WHITTEMORE, JUSTICE.   Decisive of the case, as the Appellate Division held, is the correct ruling that Korzenik and partner are not holders in due course under § 3–302; they have not shown to what extent they took for value under § 3–303. That section provides:

A holder takes the instrument for value (a) to the extent that the agreed consideration has been performed or that he acquires a security interest in or a lien on the instrument otherwise than by legal process; or (b) when he takes the instrument in payment of or as security for an antecedent claim against any person whether or not the claim is due; or (c) when he gives a negotiable instrument for it or makes an irrevocable commitment to a third person.

Under clause (a) of § 3–303 the "agreed consideration" was the performance of legal services. It is often said that a lawyer is "retained" when he is engaged to perform services, and we hold that the judge spoke of "retainer" in this sense. The phrase that the judge used, "retainer *for services*"; shows his meaning as does the finding as to services already performed by Korzenik at the time of the assignments. Even if the retainer had been only a fee to insure the attorney's availability to perform future services, there is no basis in the record for determining the value of this commitment for one week.

The Uniform Laws Comment to § 3–303 points out that in this article "value is divorced from consideration" and that except as provided in paragraph (c) "[*a*]n executory promise to give value is not . . . value. . . . The underlying reason of policy is that when the purchaser learns of a defense . . . he is not required to enforce the instrument, but is free to rescind the transaction for breach of the transferor's warranty."

Section 3–307 (3), provides: "After it is shown that a defense exists a person claiming the rights of a holder in due course has the burden of establishing that he or some person under whom he claims is in all respects a holder in due course." The defense of fraud having been established this section puts the burden on Korzenik and partner and they have failed to show "the extent . . . [to which] the agreed consideration . . . [had] been performed."

The only other possible issue under § 3–303 is whether, because of or in connection with taking the assignments, Korzenik made "an irrevocable commitment to a third person." There is no evidence of such a commitment. The finding as to a payment to counsel shows only that some of the proceeds of other assigned items have been expended by Korzenik.

Pazol v. Citizens National Bank of Sandy Springs

138 S.E.2d 442 (Ct. App. Ga. 1964)

This was an action by Citizens National Bank of Sandy Springs (plaintiff) against Sidney Pazol (defendant). Judgment for Citizens National Bank of Sandy Springs and Pazol appealed. Judgment affirmed.

Pazol issued his check for $49,600 drawn on the National Bank of Atlanta and payable to the order of Edison and Seiden Construction Company, Inc. (Edison). Edison caused the check to be indorsed and deposited in its checking account with the Citizens National Bank of Sandy Springs (Bank). Bank allowed Edison to withdraw all of the credit created by the deposit of the check before it learned that there were defenses to it. When the check was presented for payment it was dishonored. Bank sued Pazol, the drawer of the check, to recover a judgment for the amount of the check. Pazol defended on the ground that Bank was not a holder in due course of the check.

FULTON, CHIEF JUDGE.   An examination of the provisions of the U.C.C. and a comparison of it with the law prior to its passage reveal that the adoption of the U.C.C. has not changed the result under the present alleged factual situation. Bank is at least a holder, as defined by Code Ann. 1–201 (20), i.e., "a person who is in possession of a document of title or an instrument or an investment security drawn, *issued or indorsed* to him or to his order or to bearer or in blank." The petition alleges that the payee delivered the check to Bank and "caused the same to be endorsed for deposit." Even if this is construed to mean that the payee did not personally indorse the instrument, as indeed the copy of the check attached as an exhibit shows to be the case, it was issued to Bank. Code Ann. 3–302 (2) provides that "[a]n indorsement must be written by *or on behalf of* the holder," which holder may be the payee under Code Ann. 302 (2). Code Ann. 4–205 (1) provides as follows: "A depositary bank which has taken an item for collection may supply any indorsement of the customer which is necessary to title unless the item contains the words 'payee's indorsement required' or the like. In the absence of such a requirement a statement placed on the item by the depositary bank to the effect that the item was deposited by a customer or credited to his account is effective as the customer's indorsement." The comment of the National Conference of Commissioners on Uniform State Laws and the American Law Institute pertaining to this particular section explains that this subsection "is designed to speed up collections by eliminating any necessity to return a *non-bank depositor* any items he may have failed to indorse." The phrase "non-bank depositor" means a depositor which is not a bank, rather than one depositing in something other than a bank, as is contended by Pazol. Under the provisions of Code Ann. 3–301, "[t]he holder of an instrument whether or not he is the owner may transfer or negotiate it and, except as otherwise provided in 3–603 on payment or satisfaction, discharge it or *enforce payment in his own name.*"

Furthermore, under the allegations of the petition, Bank was a holder in due course as defined by Code Ann. 3–302 (1), which requires that the holder take the instrument "(a) for value; and (b) in good faith; and (c) without notice that it is overdue or has been dishonored or of any defense against or claim to it on the part of any person." Regarding requirement (a), Code 4–209 provides as follows: "For purposes of determining its status as a holder in due course, the bank has given value *to the extent that it has a security interest in an item* provided that the bank otherwise complies with the requirements of 3–302 on what constitutes a holder in due course." Code Ann. 4–208 (1) provides that "[a] bank has a security interest in an item . . . (a) in case of an item deposited in an account to the extent to which credit given for the item has been withdrawn or applied." Code Ann. 3–303 also provides that a holder takes an instrument for value to the extent that he acquires a security interest in the instrument. Code Ann. 3–205 defines a restrictive indorsement as one which "(c) includes the words 'for collection,' 'for deposit,' 'pay any bank,' or *like terms signifying a purpose of deposit or collection.*" Code Ann. 3–206 (3) provides that the transferee of an instrument with such an indorsement ". . . must pay or apply any value given by him for or on the security of the instrument consistently with the indorsement and to the extent that he does so he becomes a *holder for value.* In addition such transferee is a *holder in due course* if he otherwise complies with the requirements of 3–302 on what constitutes a holder in due course." By causing the check to be indorsed "for deposit," as alleged, the payee signified its purpose of deposit and the plaintiff bank, by applying the value given consistently with this indorsement by crediting the payee-depositor's account with the amount of the check, became a holder for value.

Regarding requirement (b) of a holder in due course, Code Ann. 3–302 (1), there is nothing on the face of the petition to indicate a lack of good faith on the part of the plaintiff in accepting the check. Good faith is presumed until questioned by appropriate pleadings.

Norman v. World Wide Distributors, Inc.

195 A.2d 115 (Super. Ct. Pa. 1963)

This was an action by Clarence W. Norman and wife (plaintiffs) against World Wide Distributors, Inc., and Peoples National Fund, Inc. (defendants), to have a judgment obtained on a note against Norman and wife declared void. Judgment for Norman and wife, and World Wide Distributors, Inc., and Peoples National Fund, Inc., appealed. Judgment affirmed.

Mancen, agent for World Wide Distributors, Inc. (World Wide), called upon the Normans and outlined to them "a program for direct advertising." He represented to them that if they purchased a breakfront, he would pay them $5 for each letter they wrote to a friend requesting an appointment for World Wide's agent to explain the details of a sound advertising program and $20 for each sale made to any such person. Each friend was to be given the same opportunity to supply names. He persuaded the Normans to sign, without reading, a purchase agreement, and attached judgment note in blank and an "Owners Participation Certificate."

After the note was signed and taken from the home of the Normans it was filled in for $1,079.40 and made payable to H. Waldran T/A State Wide Products at the office of Peoples National Fund (Peoples). The note was purchased by Peoples on January 25, 1961, for $831 and judgment was entered thereon February 7, 1961. World Wide was nowhere to be found. Within approximately a year its principals had operated first under the name of Carpet Industries, then under State Wide, and finally under World Wide Distributors. Peoples dealt with all three companies and its officers had knowledge of the referral plan. The referral plan was a fraudulent scheme based on an operation similar to the chain letter racket. Peoples claims that even though World Wide may have been guilty of fraud, it can collect on the note because it was a holder in due course.

WOODSIDE, JUDGE. "A holder in due course is a holder who takes the instrument (a) for value; and (b) in good faith; and (c) without notice that it is overdue or has been dishonored or of any defense against or claim to it on the part of any person." (3–302 [1].)

Section 1–201 (19) of the Code defines "good faith" as meaning "honesty in fact in the conduct or transaction concerned." Thus, to be a holder in due course Peoples must have acted in good faith.

The freedom from the defense of prior equities afforded to a holder in due course is an extraordinary protection, which, although having its origin in the law merchant, is closely akin to similar protection given in other types of cases by courts of equity; and running through all the authorities dealing with holders in due course we find the principle, not always stated, perhaps, that he who seeks the protection given one in that position must have dealt fairly and honestly in acquiring the instrument in controversy and in regard to the rights of all prior parties, this is, the kind of good faith which the law demands, and the principle is closely analogous to the equitable doctrine of clean hands. *Fehr v. Campbell* (1927).

He who seeks protection as a holder in due course must have dealt fairly and honestly in acquiring the instrument as to the rights of prior parties, and where circumstances are such as to justify the conclusion that the failure to make inquiry arose from a suspicion that inquiry would disclose a vice or defect in the title, the person is not a holder in due course.

When the defense of fraud appears to be meritorious as to the payee, the burden of showing it was a holder in due course is on the one claiming to be such.

Peoples here had knowledge of circumstances which should have caused it to inquire concerning the payee's method of obtaining the note. Peoples knew enough about the referral plan to require it to inquire further concerning it. The fact that Peoples' vice-president called the makers of the note and denied any connection with the referral plan, indicates his own suspicion concerning it. The frequency with which the principals changed the name under which they were operating—three times in approximately one year—should have added to his suspicion. Furthermore, the appellant paid $831 for a $1,079.40 note payable three days after date. Under all the circumstances, Peoples was bound to inquire further into the operation of the seller of these notes, and having made no inquiry, it is held as though it had knowledge of all that inquiry would have revealed.

Notice of Defenses

Nature of Notice.   Notice is something less than knowledge and more than mere suspicion. It is knowledge of facts and circumstances which would prompt an honest person to make inquiry to learn the facts. Section 1–201 (25) provides: "A person has 'notice' of a fact when (a) he has actual knowledge of it; or (b) he has received a notice or notification of it; or (c) from all the facts and circumstances known to him at the time in question he has reason to know that it exists." In the cases involving an interpretation of Section 3–302 (1) (*c*) of the Code, "notice" usually involves notice as defined in Section 1–201 (25) (*c*).

Incomplete Paper.   A person cannot take an instrument as a holder in due course if the instrument is, at the time he takes it, blank as to some material term. The courts have held that the fact that the instrument is incomplete in some material respect puts any person taking it on notice that the holder has limited authority to fill in the blanks, and charges the purchaser with knowledge of facts which a reasonable inquiry would disclose. If the instrument contains blanks, the party taking the instrument takes it subject to all defenses available to the original parties irrespective of whether or not there is any relation between the blank terms and the defense.

The courts have held that an instrument is incomplete if it is payable to order and the name of the payee is left blank. An instrument which was drawn payable "——— after date, etc." and one drawn "ten ——— after date, etc." were held to be incomplete. Failure to fill in a pronoun does not make the instrument incomplete, as "——— promise to pay." Likewise, the omission of connective words such as "pay to Brown order" does not make the instrument incomplete. To be material, the omitted term must be one which affects the legal obligations of the parties to the instrument.

Filling in Blanks.   When a paper whose contents at the time of signing show that it is intended to become an instrument is signed while still incomplete in any necessary respect, it cannot be enforced until completed, but when it is completed in accordance with authority given it is effective as completed. (3–115.) Under this provision of the Code a person who takes an instrument which is incomplete in some material respect cannot take as a holder in due course. However, if an incomplete instrument is filled in, a person taking the instrument without notice or knowledge that it was incomplete when delivered or that it was not completed as authorized takes as a holder in due course and can enforce the instrument as completed. (3–407 [3].)

Irregular Paper. The wording of Section 3–304 (1) (*a*) of the Code does not change in any material respect the pre-Code law relative to irregular paper. Anything on the face of an instrument which would put a person on notice that there is something wrong with it makes the instrument irregular on its face. If the instrument is irregular, the person taking it cannot take as a holder in due course. A person taking an instrument which is irregular on its face takes subject to all defenses available to the parties to the instrument, whether or not there is any relation between the irregularity and the defense to the instrument. The existence of the irregularities puts the person taking the instrument on constructive notice of facts which a reasonable inquiry would disclose.

A person is put on notice if one of his experience and training should, in the exercise of reasonable prudence detect the irregularity. Any noticeable alteration makes an instrument irregular on its face, but a clever alteration does not. However, an alteration might be such as would put a bank cashier on notice but might not put on notice a person who was not accustomed to handling negotiable instruments. The courts have held that the following do not make the instrument irregular on its face: (1) postdating, (2) omission of revenue stamps when revenue stamps are required by statute, (3) difference between the handwriting in the body of the instrument and that in the signature, (4) differences in the handwriting in the body of the instrument, and (5) statement of the amount in figures and not in writing. It has also been held that an instrument which is detached from a contract is not irregular paper.

An instrument which is stamped "Paid" or "Payment refused," or one made out to an officer of a corporation and signed by the same officer as agent of the corporation, or an instrument which provides for a usurious rate of interest has been held to be irregular paper. A draft, trade acceptance, or check does not have to be accepted by the drawee to be regular paper.

Summary

A person who takes an instrument which is, at the time he takes it, blank in some material respect, cannot take as a holder in due course.

If a person who can qualify as a holder in due course takes an instrument after the blanks have been filled in, he can enforce the instrument as it is filled in.

Anything on the face of the instrument which would put the holder on notice that there is something wrong with the instrument is an irregularity, and a person taking such an instrument cannot take as a holder in due course.

Matathias v. Bell-Mar Laboratories

2 U.C.C. Rep. 1161 (Sup. Ct. N.Y. 1965)

This was an action by Matathias (plaintiff) against Bell-Mar Laboratories (defendant) on two checks on which Bell-Mar had stopped payment. Matathias moved for summary judgment and the motion was granted.

On September 28, 1964, Bell-Mar Laboratories made two checks for $9,500 payable to the order of J. H. Wember. It dated one of the checks December 29, 1964, and the other January 14, 1965. Prior to those dates Factors and Note Buyers Corporation acquired the checks. In October Factors discounted the checks to Matathias. Matathias duly presented the checks on their due dates but the drawee refused payment on the ground that payment had been stopped. Bell-Mar had stopped payment on November 5, 1964, when it returned the goods that had been sold it by Wember. Matathias then brought suit. Bell-Mar contended that it had a fraud defense that was good against Matathias. It claimed Matathias was not a holder in due course because the instrument was not negotiable and Matathias was on notice of an infirmity or defense since it discounted the checks.

MANGAN, JUSTICE.   Matathias asserts that he is an innocent third-party bona fide holder in due course of the checks and had become the holder, for value, and without notice of any defect or infirmity one month prior to the return of the merchandise November 5. Bell-Mar resists judgment, claiming that Matathias is not a holder in due course. In essence, Bell-Mar argues that the checks issued to Wember during September, 1964, were post-dated; that upon issuance, it was orally agreed that the checks would not be discounted or negotiated, but would be held until the due date by Wember. Moreover, Bell-Mar urges that the fact that the checks were post-dated, and that a discount was given thereon, was notice to Matathias of infirmities in the instrument. Post-dated checks are simply promissory notes,[2] and may be freely negotiated. That subsequent to the negotiation of the instrument a difficulty arose between the parties to the instrument is not sufficient to deprive the holder of its status as a bona fide holder in due course. The fact that the notes were discounted establishes no more than suspicious circumstances as distinguished from facts bringing home to Matathias either knowledge or a duty to make further inquiry. Suspicious circumstances alone do not constitute notice of an infirmity or defect in the instrument sufficient to constitute bad faith and destroy the status of a holder in due course. The discount here does not appear to be so great under the circumstances as to support an inference that Matathias knew the notes had been dishonestly or improperly acquired. Other arguments which Bell-Mar seeks to raise, such as a fraud perpetrated on it by Wember, are not available against Matathias as a holder in due course. It does not appear—nor is it alleged—that Matathias was a party to or knew of the fraud. Accordingly, the motion for summary judgment is granted.

---

[2] The judge appears to be in error on this point since a postdated check is a draft, not a note. This does not, however, affect the negotiability of the instrument.

Voidable Paper and Fiduciaries

Voidable Paper. A holder cannot qualify as a holder in due course if he has notice or knowledge that the obligation of any party is voidable in whole or in part. Notice or knowledge that any signature on the paper was obtained by misrepresentation, fraud, or duress or that the paper was signed by mistake would prevent the holder from qualifying as a holder in due course. If an instrument is paid in full to the holder, all parties are discharged. However, if the party paying an instrument does not take it or have it marked "Paid" or "Canceled" so that it is apparent that it has been discharged, the holder can negotiate it, and any party taking such instrument having no notice can take it as a holder in due course. (3–304 [1] [*b*].)

Negotiation of Fiduciary. Whether or not a purchaser who takes an instrument which has been negotiated to him by a fiduciary takes as a holder in due course will depend on whether such purchaser has notice or knowledge that the fiduciary has negotiated the instrument in violation of his fiduciary duties. The Code provides: The purchaser has notice of a claim against the instrument when he has knowledge that a fiduciary has negotiated the instrument in payment of or as security for his own debt or in any transaction for his own benefit or otherwise in breach of duty. (3–304 [2].)

Summary

A holder cannot qualify as a holder in due course if, at the time he took the paper, he had notice or knowledge that the obligation of any party was voidable in whole or in part or that all parties had been discharged.

A purchaser from a fiduciary cannot take as a holder in due course when he has knowledge that the fiduciary has negotiated the paper for his own benefit or otherwise in breach of duty.

Maber, Inc. v. Factor Cab Corp.

244 N.Y.S.2d 768 (App. Div. N.Y. 1963)

This was an action by Maber, Inc. (plaintiff), against Factor Cab Corp. and others (defendants) to recover a judgment on a note. Judgment for Maber, Inc., for less than full amount of note and it appealed. Judgment affirmed.

Factor Cab Corp. issued a series of notes drawn payable to "the order of Donald E. Richel as attorney for Francisco Silvestry." Twenty-one of the notes were indorsed by Richel and his wife and sold to Maber, Inc. Maber, Inc., in purchasing the notes, made its check payable to Richel in his individual name, without qualification or restriction, in the amount of $5,796.24. In addition, it discharged by payment Richel's personal indebtedness to a bank in the amount of $3,903.75. Richel and his wife indorsed the notes as individuals.

Factor Cab Corp. paid some of Silvestry's hospital bills directly and thereby obtained a counter-claim against the notes. Maber, Inc., contended that it took the notes as a holder in due course and free from the counterclaim.

BREITEL, JUSTICE PRESIDING.   When Maber took the notes from the attorney, by reason of the descriptive qualification of the named payee (i.e., as attorney for Francisco Silvestry), the holder was on notice that the attorney had received the notes as an agent rather than as a principal, and that the funds might be subject to claims in the right of others. This did not mean that the attorney was not entitled to negotiate the notes. On the contrary, he could. (U.C.C. § § 3–117, 3–207, 3–301, 3–304 [4] [e].) He was even empowered to negotiate them for cash, because it may have been within the fiduciary purpose to convert them into cash, provided, of course, there were no other circumstances to put the holder on notice that the instrument was being diverted from a fiduciary purpose. (U.C.C. § 3–304, Comment 5.)

But the case is entirely different when it appears, as it did here, that the notes were negotiated for the benefit or individual purpose of the agent. Under such circumstances the holder is charged with bad faith and notice of any defect or infirmity in the instrument, and is not a holder in due course. (U.C.C. § § 3–302 [1], 3–304 [2]). This includes the absence or failure of consideration whether in whole or in part. (U.C.C. § 3–408.)

Overdue and Dishonored Paper

Paper Payable at Definite Time.   A person must take an instrument before it is overdue if he wishes to take as a holder in due course. The courts have based this rule on the reasoning that as a general rule obligations are performed when performance is due, and if an instrument is not paid when due, the nonpayment of the instrument is a circumstance sufficient to put the purchaser on notice that the party primarily liable has a defense to it, and a person taking an overdue instrument takes with notice of all defenses to such instrument.

The Code provides that the purchaser has notice that an instrument is overdue if he has reason to know that any part of the principal amount is overdue or that there is an uncured default in payment of another instrument of the same series. (3–304 [3] [a].) For example, suppose that Axe borrows $1,000 from Bell and gives Bell 10 notes for $100 each, numbered from 1 to 10 and due serially 1, 2, 3, and so forth, months after date, the 10th note being due 10 months after date. Clark purchases note number five, and at the time he purchases it he has reason to know that notes two and three are past due and unpaid. Clark does not take note number five as a holder in due course.

An instrument payable at a definite date is overdue at the beginning of the day after the due date. An instrument payable at a definite time after date or after sight or presentment is overdue at the beginning of the day after the time stated has elapsed. In counting time, the day the instrument is issued is excluded, but the date of payment is included. For example, if an instrument dated January 2 is payable 30 days after date, January 3 is the first day counted, and the instrument is due on February 1 and overdue at the beginning of February 2. A person taking the instrument on February 2 or thereafter cannot take as a holder in due course. If the date of payment falls on a Sunday or a holiday the instrument is payable on the next succeeding business day.

Instruments Subject to Acceleration. If the holder has the right to accelerate the time of payment of an instrument, the purchaser has notice that the instrument is overdue if he has reason to know that acceleration of the instrument has been made. (3–304 [3] [*b*].)

Demand Paper. If an instrument is drawn payable on demand or on sight or presentment, a person taking the instrument an unreasonable time after its issue cannot take as a holder in due course. The Code provides in Section 1–204 (2): What is a reasonable time for taking any action depends on the nature, purpose, and circumstances of such action, and in Section 3–304 (3) (*c*): A reasonable time for a check drawn and payable within the states and territories of the United States and District of Columbia is presumed to be 30 days. It should be noted that this provision states *is presumed* to be 30 days, not *is* 30 days. The Code further states: "Presumption" or "presumed" means that the trier of fact must find the existence of the fact presumed unless and until evidence is introduced which would support a finding of its nonexistence. (1–201 [31].)

In determining whether a demand instrument is overdue, usage of trade, business practices, the facts and circumstances of the particular case must be considered. In a farming community where the normal period for loans to farmers is six months, a demand note as a general rule can be outstanding a longer period of time before it becomes overdue than could a demand note issued in an industrial community, where the normal period of a loan is 30 to 60 days. In determining when an instrument is overdue, the nature of the transaction in which the instrument is used, the relation of the parties, and all other facts and circumstances must be taken into consideration.

Dishonored Instruments. An instrument has been dishonored when it has been presented for payment or acceptance, and payment or acceptance has been refused. If a demand note has been presented to the maker for payment and payment has been refused, the note has been dishonored. Likewise, if a draft has been presented to the drawee for acceptance or payment, or if a check has been presented to the drawee bank for payment, and acceptance or payment has been refused, the draft or check has been dishonored. Any purchaser taking such note, draft, or check if he has reason to know it has been dishonored cannot take as a holder in due course.

Summary

An instrument payable at a definite time or at a stated time after date is overdue at the beginning of the day following the day on which it is payable. A person taking an instrument when it is overdue cannot take as a holder in due course. A purchaser has notice that an instrument is overdue if he has reason to know that any part of the principal amount is overdue, or that an uncured default exists in the payment of another instrument in the same series, or that the holder of an instrument subject to acceleration has been accelerated.

Demand paper is overdue if it is not paid within a reasonable time after issue, and a reasonable time for the payment of a check drawn and payable in the states or territories of the United States or the District of Columbia is presumed to be 30 days.

Demand paper is dishonored when it is presented for payment or acceptance and payment or acceptance is refused.

Facts Which Are Not Notice

Code Provisions. For the purpose of clarifying uncertainties in the law, situations are set out, knowledge of which does not, standing alone, give a purchaser notice of a defense or claim. Knowledge that an instrument is antedated or postdated or that it was issued or negotiated in return for an executory promise, or that it was accompanied by a separate agreement, does not give the purchaser notice of a defense or claim, unless the purchaser has notice that a defense or claim has arisen from the terms thereof. Also, knowledge that a party signed for accommodation or that an instrument was incomplete when delivered and has been completed, unless the purchaser has notice of an improper completion, or that the instrument was negotiated by a fiduciary or that there has been default in the payment of interest on the instrument or in payment of any other instrument, except one of the same series, does not give the purchaser notice of defenses or claims. (3–304 [4].)

If a purchaser of a negotiable instrument can otherwise qualify as a holder in due course, it is not necessary for him to examine the public records to determine whether there are outstanding defenses or claims to the instrument since the filing or recording of a document does not of itself constitute notice. (3–304 [5].)

Notice, to be effective, must be received at such time and in such manner as to give a reasonable opportunity to act on it. (3–304 [6].)

Rights of Holder in Due Course

Personal Defenses.   The keystone of the law of negotiable commercial paper is the rule that a holder in due course of a negotiable instrument takes it free from "personal defenses" or claims which may exist between the original parties to the instrument. The holder in due course takes free of such defenses as lack or failure of consideration, misrepresentation or fraud in the inducement, setoff or counterclaim, breach of warranty of goods sold for which the instrument was issued, and all other defenses which would be available to a promisor in a suit on a simple contract. (3–305 [1].)

Real Defenses. From the standpoint of public policy there are certain defenses which do go to the validity of the instrument and which are good against a holder in due course of a negotiable instrument. These are the so-called "real defenses." In general a holder in due course takes the instrument free from all defenses of any party to the instrument with whom he has not dealt except the following:

1. Infancy (to the extent that it is a defense to a simple contract).
2. Any other incapacity, or duress, or illegality of the transaction, as renders the obligation of the party a nullity.
3. Such misrepresentation as has induced the party to sign the instrument with neither knowledge nor reasonable opportunity to obtain knowledge of its character or its essential terms.
4. Discharge in insolvency proceedings.
5. Any other discharges of which the holder has notice at the time he takes the instrument. (3–305 [2].)

In regard to infants and others having limited capacity to contract it is basically a matter of social policy whether it is more desirable to protect a holder in due course and thereby facilitate trade or protect the inexperienced and weak from the results of their injudicious acts. As the law has developed the decision has been to protect infants and others having limited contractual capacity. The courts have held that promises made under extreme duress and, usually by statutory enactment, promises made in defined illegal transactions are held to be totally unenforceable. By logical deduction, if the promise in a negotiable instrument is a nullity it is unenforceable, even by a holder in due course of the instrument. The law also protects those persons who have been "tricked" into signing any paper if they have used a reasonable degree of care.

The objective of our bankruptcy laws and other insolvency laws is to relieve the debtor from his debts and give him a new start. In general, the discharge features of these laws are broad enough to discharge the debtor of all his commercial obligations, including debts owing on negotiable instruments held by holders in due course.

Persons Not Holders in Due Course. Negotiable commercial paper is basically a simple contract to pay money. If the holder of such paper is not a holder in due course his rights are no greater than are the rights of any promisee or assignee of a simple contract. Such a holder takes the paper subject to all valid claims on the part of any person and subject to all defenses of any party which would be available in an action on a simple contract. (3–306.)

Procedure. Unless specifically denied, the signatures on a negotiable instrument are admitted. If not admitted, the burden of establishing the signature is on the person claiming under the signature. The signature is presumed to be genuine or authorized except where the action is to enforce the obligation of a purported signer who has died or become incompetent before proof is required.

Production of the instrument entitles the holder to recover if signatures are admitted unless the defendant establishes a defense. For example, if suit is brought by a holder on a negotiable commercial paper and the defendant does appear and defend, all that would be required of the holder would be that he produce the instrument, offer it in evidence and give testimony as to the amount due.

If the party sued on negotiable commercial paper sets up a defense, a person claiming the rights of a holder in due course has the burden of establishing that he or some person under whom he claims is, in all respects, a holder in due course. (3–307.)

Summary

A holder in due course of negotiable commercial paper takes free from personal defenses existing between the parties but takes subject to the real defense of infancy, and other incapacities available as a defense to a simple contract; duress or illegality of the transaction which renders the obligation a nullity; promises induced by "trickery"; discharge in insolvency proceedings; and discharges of which he has notice.

A holder not a holder in due course takes negotiable commercial paper subject to all the defenses which would be available to a promisor on a simple contract to pay money.

Signatures on negotiable commercial paper are admitted unless specifically denied. If denied, the party claiming under the instrument has the burden of establishing it. Production of the instrument entitles the holder to recover unless a defense is established in which event the holder has the burden of proving he holds as a holder in due course.

Reading Trust Co. v. Hutchison

35 Pa. D. & C.2d 790 (Ct. of Common Pleas Pa. 1964)

This was an action by Reading Trust Company (plaintiff) to obtain judgment by confession on a note on which the Hutchisons (defendants) were the makers. Judgment was entered and the Hutchisons moved to open the judgment. Motion to open was denied.

On March 7, 1963, an agent of Gracious Living, Inc., called upon the Hutchisons and identified himself as a "demonstrator" of water softening equipment. It was alleged that upon completion of a demonstration the representative explained the cost of purchasing the equipment and indicated that Gracious Living, Inc., would install it on a four months' trial basis if the Hutchisons would give a list of their friends and neighbors and then permit a demonstration in the Hutchison home. The arrangement also provided for compensation to them if sales resulted from such lists. The Hutchisons maintained that the agent "asked the defendants to sign a form which he could show to his boss to prove that he had made the demonstration and also as a bond to cover the unit while it was on the property of the defendants and until they decided to keep it. Defendant signed both of these forms." The Hutchisons testified that it was not until they received an installment book from Reading on March 27, 1963 that they realized "that they had been tricked into signing a contract and a judgment note." The plaintiff Trust Company clarified that it was not a party to the transaction; that it took the note in the normal course of business and that it had no knowledge of the representations made by the agent of Gracious Living.

KOCH, PRESIDING JUDGE.   At the outset it must be said that the petitioners have not established that Reading Trust had any knowledge of fraudulent business practices. . . .

The Uniform Commercial Code . . . provides as follows:

(1) A holder in due course is a holder who takes the instrument
(a) for value; and
(b) in good faith including observance of the reasonable commercial standards of any business in which the holder may be engaged; and
(c) without notice that it is overdue or has been dishonored or of any defense against or claim to it on the part of any person.

The crux of petitioners' position is that even though the Hutchisons may have had no specific knowledge of the circumstances surrounding the execution of the note, Section 3–305 (2) (c) defeats its rights as a holder in due course. This portion of the Code is as follows:

To the extent that a holder is a holder in due course he takes the instrument free from
(1) . . .
(2) All defenses of any party to the instrument with whom the holder has not dealt except
(c) Such misrepresentation as has induced the party to sign the instrument with neither knowledge nor reasonable opportunity to obtain knowledge of its character or its essential terms.

The Uniform Commercial Code Comment to the foregoing subsection follows:

Paragraph (c) of subsection (2) is new. It follows the great majority of the decisions under the original Act in recognizing the defense of "real" or "essential" fraud, sometimes called fraud in the essence or fraud in the factum, as effective against a holder in due course. The common illustration is that of the maker who is tricked into signing a note in the belief that it is merely a receipt or some other document. The theory of the defense is that his signature on the instrument is ineffective because he did not intend to sign such an instrument at all. Under this provision the defense extends to an instrument signed with knowledge that it is a negotiable instrument, but without knowledge of its essential terms.

The test of the defense here stated is that of excusable ignorance of the contents of the writing signed. The party must not only have been in ignorance, but must also have had no reasonable opportunity to obtain knowledge. In determining what is a reasonable opportunity all relevant factors are to be taken into account, including the age and sex of the party, his intelligence, education and business experience; his ability to read or to understand English, the representations made to him and his reason to rely on them or to have confidence in the person making them; the presence or absence of any third person who might read or explain the instrument to him, or any other possibility of obtaining independent information; and the apparent necessity, or lack of it, for acting without delay.

Unless the misrepresentation meets this test, the defense is cut off by a holder in due course.

We are in accord with the views expressed in this comment. . . . We do not agree with the petitioners' contention that this case presents the classic illustration of a maker who was "tricked" into signing a note in the belief that it was another document. While we do not condone some of the high pressure tactics which were used in this case, nevertheless, a reading of the depositions persuades us that upon taking into consideration the factors of excusable ignorance of the contents of the writing signed the judgment should not be opened.

An analysis of the factors shows that the husband petitioner, age 48, is a high school graduate and is employed as a clerk; the wife, age 51, completed her junior year in high school. In addition to their undoubted ability to read and write the English language and their high degree of intelligence as indicated by their depositions neither of them could establish any basis which would indicate that they had any reason to have confidence in the representations made by the agent for Gracious Living, Inc.

In further analyzing the factors we find that there was a third person present on the occasion of the signing, Mr. Albert Mitchell, an uncle of Mrs. Hutchison. He, too, is a high school graduate, and despite his presence, was not asked by the petitioners for advice.

Problem Cases

1. A purchaser of a prebuilt home paid his general contractor, Lanphear, a check which included in part $11,000 to be paid to the home supplier, Barden. The check was made out to "Lanphear payable to Barden Homes" and Lanphear endorsed both his name and Barden's and deposited the entire amount in his bank to his own account. In a suit against the bank for conversion, Barden charges the bank with cashing a check on a forged indorsement. Is the bank liable to Barden?

2. Bank cashed checks of its customer Dental Supply, Inc., presented to the bank by the customer's agent, Wilson. The checks were endorsed in blank with a rubber stamp of Dental Supply, Inc. Wilson had been stealing the checks by taking cash rather than depositing them to the Dental Supply, Inc.'s account. Dental Supply sues the bank for conversion. Is the bank liable? What could Dental Supply have done to avoid this situation?

3. A check was endorsed: "Pay to the order of any bank, banker, or trust company. All prior endorsements guaranteed." What type of an endorsement is this? What is the effect of this type of endorsement?

4. Freddie Watkins stole a payroll check endorsed in blank from Mrs. Reggie Bluiett and used it to purchase two tires from Western Auto, receiving the balance in cash. Watkins was charged with obtaining money under false pretenses from Western Auto. One element of the crime of obtaining money under false pretenses is that the victim sustains a financial injury. May Watkins be convicted of this crime? (You may want to first consider whether one can be a holder in due course of a stolen instrument.)

5. Williams signed a contract with Peerless and Reynolds whereby Peerless agreed to make certain improvements on the Williams' home and to pay the balance remaining on their automobile. Williams promised to pay $3,200 in monthly installments. Subsequent to the execution of the contract Williams signed a promissory note payable to Reynolds in the amount of $6,399.60 representing principal and interest over a 10-year period. Reynolds negotiated the note to Financial Credit Corporation as part of a purchase of 480 notes. Financial paid $704 for the Williams' note. Financial later sued Williams on the note and Williams sought to impose a fraud defense, claiming that Financial was not a holder in due course. There was testimony at the trial that "every Marylander knew" from the newspapers about Reynold's fraudulent activities. Could Financial qualify as a holder in due course?

6. Horton wrote a check for $20,000 to Axe who in turn endorsed it to Halbert. In return Halbert advanced to Axe $8,000 cash and promised to cancel a $12,000 debt owed him by Axe. The check when presented by Halbert to the bank, was not paid due to insufficient funds. Halbert thus never regarded the debt as canceled. In an action on the check, how much, if anything, can Halbert recover and why?

7. Security Bank took checks for deposit from Park on which Baty was the drawer. The bank's deposit slip covering the checks bore the notation: "All items are credited subject to final payment in cash or solvent credits." In a suit by the bank to recover the amount of the checks against Baty, who had subsequently stopped payment on them, Baty argued that when the bank takes a deposit under such conditions and then pays cash for the checks before collection, it cannot be a holder in due course. Is this a valid argument?

8. Hutcheson held a note made to him by Herron which left blank the rate of interest and date of payment. Hutcheson inserted the interest rate and date of payment they had previously agreed upon. Does this constitute a material alteration so as to discharge Herron's liability on the note?

9. Greenwald brought suit as endorsee of a negotiable promissory note signed by Frank M. and Rose Manzon. The Manzons claimed that the note was incomplete and irregular on its face since the place of payment was not specified in the place provided therefor on the printed form and since the blanks on the printed form appeared to have been filled in by different persons using different colored inks. They also claimed the instrument was irregular because the endorsements on the back were not in the same order as they were signed in. Are these valid claims?

10. Hayworth bought the assets of a mortgage company, including several notes on which Cromwell was the promisor and the mortgage company was the payee. The mortgage company charged usurious interest rates. Hayworth was aware of the excessive interest charged by the mortgage company and had previous dealings with it. The law in this state protects a holder in due course from the defense of usury. Is Hayworth a holder in due course?

11. Kamensky gave a note for $19,000 to his brother. The sum of $1,000 was payable on February 15, 1965, and a like amount on the 15th day of each month for the next 19 months. On January 17, 1967, after it was past due, Kamensky's brother endorsed the note over

to Srochi, who knew it was past due. Srochi brought an action on the note for payment and Kamensky sought to interpose personal defenses. Can they be asserted against Srochi?

12. Delaware Auto Sales was given a check by Hoopes in payment for a car. The next day Hoopes stopped payment on the check due to dissatisfaction with the car. Delaware Auto Sales exchanged the check for a treasurer's check at Hoopes' bank, The Wilmington Trust Co., after the check had been canceled, but before the stop payment notice was processed. Later, when the treasurer's check was presented for payment, notice of the stop payment had gone through and Delaware Auto Sales was refused payment. Delaware Auto Sales sued for the value of the check. Is the bank liable to Delaware Auto Sales?

13. Holder in Due Course of some notes sued Luccarelli, the maker. Luccarelli claimed that the notes were signed by him in blank and delivered to Weiss, an associate of his, at Weiss's request and in reliance on his good faith. He also claimed that he, even though he knew the nature of the instruments, did not know that the notes would be negotiated. Luccarelli was not proficient in English but had been engaged in business for a number of years and knew the nature of negotiable instruments. Luccarelli seeks to use Section 3–305 (2) (c) as a defense against Holder in Due Course. On these facts, has he stated a good defense?

14. Blackburn acquired an automobile from Vanella and gave him a check in payment of it. Vanella endorsed the check and took it to Marine Midland Bank where the bank gave him cash and credit in his account for the check. Blackburn found out that Vanella had misrepresented to him that the automobile was free of liens, and so he stopped payment on the check. Now Marine Midland sues Blackburn as drawer of the check. Even though he admitted Marine Midland was a holder in due course, Blackburn claimed he had a defense of fraud good against even a holder in due course. Does Blackburn have a valid defense?

chapter 39

Liability of Parties and Discharge

Signed

Effect of Signing. The English and American courts have held from the earliest time that any party who has not signed a formal contract cannot be held liable on that contract. A negotiable instrument is classed as a formal contract and consequently this rule has been adopted and applied to negotiable commercial paper. The Code provides that no person is liable on an instrument unless his name appears thereon. (Section 3–401 [1].)[1]

When it is necessary to determine the capacity in which a person has signed an instrument, the position of his signature on such instrument is important but not conclusive. If a signature is placed on the lower right-hand corner of an instrument, the presumption is that he has signed as a maker or drawer. If the named drawee signs across the face of the instrument, it is a clear indication that he has accepted it but his signature on any part of the instrument, front or back, in the absence of credible evidence of an intent to sign in some other capacity, will be held to be an acceptance. A signature on the back of an instrument is presumed to be an endorsement. Unless the instrument clearly indicates that a signature is made in some other capacity it is an endorsement. (3–402.)

Signing by Representative. Negotiable commercial paper may be signed by an authorized agent and, if properly signed, the principal will be bound as he would be had he signed it himself. All negotiable paper issued by a corporation is signed by an agent of the corporation and such agent is usually an officer of the corporation who is authorized to sign negotiable instruments.

No particular form of appointment is necessary to establish the authority to sign negotiable paper as agent. (3–403 [1].)

---

[1] The numbers in the parentheses refer to the sections of the Uniform Commercial Code, 1962.

Since the liability of the parties to a negotiable instrument is determined by what is on the instrument, and parol evidence is admissible only to clear up ambiguities, the manner of signing in a representative capacity is important. An authorized agent is personally liable if he signs the instrument in his own name and neither the name of the principal nor the fact that he is signing in a representative capacity is shown on the instrument. (3–403 [2] [*a*].)

If an authorized representative signs a negotiable instrument in his own name and so signs that he indicates that he has signed in a representative capacity but does not name the person represented, parol evidence would be admissible, as between the immediate parties, to prove that the parties to the instrument intended that the party represented be liable and not the party signing in the representative capacity. For example, if a negotiable instrument is signed, "Axe, agent" and is not negotiated and the payee then sues Axe on the instrument, parol evidence would be admitted to prove that the payee knew that Axe was acting as agent for Parks, his principal, and that the parties intended Parks to be bound and not Axe. But if this instrument were negotiated to a holder in due course, Axe would be personally liable on the instrument. (3–403 [2] [*b*].)

If a negotiable instrument is signed in the name of an organization and the name of the organization is preceded or followed by the name and office of an authorized individual, the organization and not the officer who has signed the instrument in a representative capacity will be bound. (3–403 [3].)

The proper way for a person executing a negotiable instrument in a representative capacity is as follows:

> "Parks Corporation
> "By Axe, Treasurer." or
> "Paul Parks
> "By Leonard Axe, his Agent."

Unauthorized Signature.   If the name of a person is signed to a negotiable instrument by a person who has no authority to so sign the instrument, the signature is wholly inoperative and does not bind the person whose name is signed. Such a signing is a forgery.

Summary

Under the general rule relative to the liability of a party on a formal contract, no one can be held liable whose name does not appear on the contract. A person may use any name or symbol as his signature but if he signs in an ambiguous capacity, he will be presumed to have signed as an endorser.

Commercial paper may be signed by one acting in a representative capacity and no formal authorization is necessary. If one acting as an authorized representative signs only in his own name he is individually liable on the instrument.

If the instrument names the person represented and the representative so signs that he indicates that he has signed in a representative capacity only the person represented will be bound. As between the immediate parties if the person represented is not named but the person signing indicates that he is signing in a representative capacity, parol evidence is admissible to prove the intent of the parties. If the instrument is negotiated to a holder in due course, the representative who has signed will be individually liable to the holder in due course. If an instrument is signed in the name of a corporation and the name of an authorized officer followed by an indication of his office, only the corporation will be bound.

Bell v. Dornan

201 A.2d 324 (Super. Ct. Pa. 1964)

This was an action by James G. Dornan (plaintiff) against Margaret S. Bell, executrix of the estate of William Bell, Jr. (defendant), to have a judgment taken on a judgment note set aside. Judgment for Dornan and Bell appealed. Judgment reversed and judgment reinstated.

In the lifetime of William Bell, Jr., a note signed as follows:

(Corporate Seal)	"Memma M. Good "Chet B. Earl Inc., (Seal) "James G. Dornan (Seal)"

and payable to him was issued. After the death of William Bell, Jr., the executrix of his estate took judgment on the note against James G. Dornan alone and individually.

MONTGOMERY, JUDGE. Under the Uniform Commercial Code § 3–403, it is provided: "(2) An authorized representative who signs his own name to an instrument is also personally obligated unless the instrument names the person represented and shows that the signature is made in a representative capacity. The name of an organization preceded or followed by the name *and office* of an authorized individual is a signature made in a representative capacity."

Mr. Dornan's signature follows the name of the organization but does not show his office. In fact, opposite his name is the word "(SEAL)" as printed on the form of note used, which is in addition to the formal corporate seal imprint which was placed on the note, presumably by the proper custodian. Therefore, we are constrained to hold that under the provision of the code previously set forth he is personally obligated on the instrument. The presence of the corporate seal does not alter our view. The note might very well have been an obligation of the corporation as well as of the appellee.

Pittsburgh National Bank v. Kemilworth Restaurant Co. is readily distinguishable. First, the lower court had admissible depositions and undenied allegations of the petition on which to base its order. In the present case there were neither depositions nor admitted facts. Second, there were allegations of mutual accident and mistake in that case, whereas in the present case the only allegation was that by inadvertence the office was omitted and there was no allegation of accident or mistake or that the inadvertence was mutual. In fact, in the *Pittsburgh National Bank* case both parties to the judgment contended that a mistake had been made in the execution of the instrument.

Pollin v. Mindy Mfg. Co., Inc.

236 A.2d 542 (Sup. Ct. Pa. 1967)

This was an action by Pollin (plaintiff) against Mindy Manufacturing Company and its president, Robert Apfelbaum (defendants), to recover on thirty-six checks drawn in the name of the Company and signed by Apfelbaum. Judgment for Pollin. Apfelbaum appealed. Judgment reversed as to Apfelbaum.

The checks in question had been boldly imprinted at the top with "Mindy Mfg. Co., Inc., 26th & Reed Streets, Philadelphia, Penn., 19146 _____ Payroll Check No. _____" and with "Mindy Mfg. Co., Inc." imprinted above two blank lines appearing at the lower right-hand corner. Under the imprinted name of the corporate defendant on the checks was the signature of Robert Apfelbaum without any designation of office or capacity. Pollin contended that Apfelbaum was liable on the checks since his signature was absolute and unqualified. Apfelbaum claimed he had signed in a representative capacity as president of Mindy Manufacturing and not in his individual capacity.

MONTGOMERY, JUDGE.   Summary judgment against appellant was entered by the lower court on the authority of Section 3–403 of the Uniform Commercial Code which provides, "(2) An authorized representative who signs his (own) name to an instrument. . . . (b) except as otherwise established between the immediate parties, is personally obligated if the instrument names the person represented but does not show that the representative signed in a representative capacity. . . ," and our decisions thereunder.

The issue before us, therefore, is whether a third party to the original transaction, the endorsee in the present case, may recover against one who affixes his name to a check in the place where a maker usually signs without indicating he is signing in a representative capacity, without giving consideration to other parts of the instrument or extrinsic evidence. This appears to be a novel question under the Uniform Commercial Code.

If this were an action brought by the payee, parol evidence would be permitted to establish the capacity of the person affixing his signature under Section 3–403 (b) previously recited and our decisions in *Bell v. Dornan* and *Pittsburgh National Bank v. Kemilworth Restaurant Co.*

However, since this is an action brought by a third party our initial inquiry must be for the purpose of determining whether the instrument indicates the capacity of appellant as a signer. Admittedly, the instrument fails to show the office held by appellant. However, we do not think this is a complete answer to our problem, since the Code imposes liability on the individual only ". . . if the instrument . . . does not show that the representative signed in a representative capacity . . ." This implies that the instrument must be considered in its entirety.

Although Section 3–401 (2) of the Uniform Commercial Code provides that "A signature is made by use of any name, including any trade or assumed name, upon an instrument, or by any word or mark used in lieu of a written signature," which would be broad enough to include the printed name of a corporation, we do not believe that a check showing two lines under the imprinted corporate name indicating the signature of one or more corporate officers would be accepted by any reasonably prudent person as a fully executed check of the corporation. It is common to expect that a corporate name placed upon a negotiable instrument in order to bind the corporation as a maker, especially when printed on the instrument, will be accompanied by the signatures of officers authorized by the by-laws to sign the instrument. While we do not rule out the possibility of a printed name being established as an acceptable signature, we hold that such a situation is uncommon, and against a valid corporate signature. Corporations act through officers.

Next we must give consideration to the distinction between a check and a note. A check is an order of a depositor on a bank in the nature of a draft drawn on the bank and payable on demand. It is revokable until paid or accepted for payment. A note is an irrevocable promise to pay on the part of the maker. The maker of a check impliedly engages not only that it will be paid, but that he will have sufficient funds in the bank to meet it. In the present instance the checks clearly showed that they were payable from a special account set up by the corporate defendant for the purpose of paying its employees. This information disclosed by the instrument of itself would refute any contention that the appellant intended to make the instrument his own order on the named bank to pay money to the payee. The money was payable from the account of the corporation defendant over which appellant as an individual had no control.

Considering the instrument as a whole we conclude that it sufficiently discloses that appellant signed it in a representative capacity.

Acceptance

Acceptance by Drawee. A drawee is not liable on a check or other draft until he accepts it. The drawing of a check or draft on a named drawee is not an assignment of funds in the drawee's hands but is instead an order by the drawer addressed to the drawee ordering him to pay to the payee the sum for which the instrument is drawn. Until the drawee accepts the instrument, there is no contractual relation between the holder of the instrument and the drawee. The drawee may, and usually does, owe a contractual duty to the drawer of the check or draft to pay or accept it and if he dishonors the instrument by his failure or refusal to accept or pay it, he will be liable to the drawer for breach of the drawer-drawee contract. (3–409.)

Nature of Acceptance. An acceptance is the drawee's signed engagement to honor the draft as presented. The acceptance must be written on the draft and it may consist of the drawee's signature alone. The drawee may, however, if he wishes, in addition to his signature, name a particular bank or place in the United States where payment is to be made, unless the acceptance states that the draft is to be paid only at such bank or place. The drawee may accept a draft before it has been signed by the drawer, but such an instrument is not a negotiable instrument until signed by the drawer. (3–104 [1] [a].) Also, the drawee may accept a draft which is incomplete or is overdue or has been dishonored. If the drawee accepts a draft payable at a fixed period after sight and does not date his acceptance, the holder may complete it by supplying a date in good faith. (3–410.)

The holder of a draft has a right to the unqualified acceptance of the draft as drawn and if the drawee's proffered acceptance in any manner varies the draft as presented, the holder may refuse the acceptance and treat the draft as dishonored in which event the drawee, if he has signed the draft, is entitled to have his acceptance canceled. If the holder assents to an acceptance which varies the terms of the draft, each drawer and endorser who does not affirmatively consent is discharged. (3–412.)

Summary

A draft or check is not an assignment of funds in the hands of the drawee and the drawee is not liable on the instrument until he accepts it. The drawee may accept a draft by signing his name on the draft. An acceptance is an engagement to honor the draft as drawn, and the drawee may accept the draft before the drawer has signed it, or while it is incomplete or overdue or after it has been dishonored.

The holder is entitled to the unqualified acceptance of the drawee and if he proffers (offers) anything less the holder can treat the draft as dishonored. If the holder consents to a qualified acceptance, drawers and endorsers are discharged unless they affirmatively assent to the variation.

Parties to Commercial Paper

Primary and Secondary Liability. A party to a negotiable instrument may be either primarily or secondarily liable for the payment of the instrument. The person primarily liable on a negotiable instrument is the person who, by the terms of the instrument, is absolutely required to pay the instrument. For instance, the maker of a note is absolutely required to pay the note and is the person primarily liable.

No person is primarily liable on a draft until it has been accepted by the drawee, after which the drawee becomes the person primarily liable.

Usually, a check is paid when presented to the drawee bank, and no person becomes primarily liable on it. However, the drawee bank may, at the request of the drawer or holder, certify the check, in which case the certification of the check makes the certifying bank absolutely liable for the payment of the check.

All other persons who are liable for the payment of a negotiable instrument are secondarily liable. The drawer of a draft or check and the endorsers on any negotiable instrument are secondarily liable. That is, their liability is collateral, and they will not be required to pay the instrument unless the person primarily liable defaults or unless the instrument is dishonored on its presentment to the drawee.

Nature of Secondary Liability. The liability of the parties secondarily liable on negotiable commercial paper is comparable in most respects to that of a surety on a simple contract. His liability is a contingent liability and does not arise until the party who is primarily liable has defaulted in his performance.

Summary

Parties to negotiable commercial paper are either primarily or secondarily liable for payment of the instrument. Makers of notes and acceptors of drafts or checks are primarily liable; all other parties to such instruments are secondarily liable. In determining the nature and scope of the liability of secondary parties the basic rules relative to the liability of the guarantor of a simple contract apply with some modifications.

Presentment, Notice and Protest

Presentment. Presentment may be for acceptance or for payment. Presentment for acceptance is necessary to charge the drawer or endorsers of a draft in the following three situations: (1) where the draft provides that presentment for acceptance must be made, or (2) where the draft is payable at a place other than the residence or place of business of the drawee, or (3) where the draft is payable at a fixed time after presentment or sight. The holder need not present any other draft for acceptance but if the draft is payable at a stated date he may, at his option, present it for acceptance at any time before its due date. (3–501 [1].) Presentment for payment is necessary to charge any endorser. (3–501 [1] [*b*].)

Time of Presentment. The Code sets out rules as to the time for the presentment for acceptance or payment of an instrument. The basic rule recognizes that an instrument should be presented within a reasonable time.

A reasonable time for presentment for acceptance or payment is determined by the nature of the instrument, by usage of banking or trade, and by the facts of the particular case.

A reasonable time to present a check to charge the drawer is presumed to be 30 days, and to charge an endorsee within 7 days of his endorsement. If due on a day that is not a business day, presentment is made the next day following which is a full business day for both parties.

If the date for presentment falls on a day which is not a full business day presentment is due the next succeeding day which is a full business day for both parties. (3–503 [3].)

Presentment to be sufficient must be made at a reasonable hour, and if presentment is to be made at a bank, during its banking hours. (3–503 [4].)

How Presentment Is Made.   If an instrument is not payable by, through, or at a bank, the collecting bank may, unless otherwise instructed, present the instrument by sending to the party to accept or pay a written notice that the bank holds the instrument for acceptance or payment, as the case may be.

Presentment of instruments not handled by a collecting bank may be made by mail, in which event the time of presentment is determined by the time of the receipt of the mail, or through a clearinghouse. (3–504 [2] [a] and [b].)

If a place of acceptance or payment is specified in the instrument, presentment should be made at that place; if no place of presentment is specified, presentment is made at the place of business or residence of the party to accept or pay.

Rights of Party to Whom Presentment Is Made.   The party to whom presentment is made may, without dishonoring the instrument, require the exhibition of the instrument and reasonable identification of the person making presentment and evidence of his authority to make it if he is making it for another. (3–505 [1] [a] and [b].)

Failure to comply with any of the requirements set out above invalidates the presentment but a person presenting has a reasonable time in which to comply, and the time for acceptance or payment runs from the time of compliance. (3–505 [2].)

Effect of Unexcused Delay in Presentment.   If presentment, without excuse, is delayed beyond the time it is due, any endorser is discharged from liability on the instrument and any drawer or acceptor of a draft payable at a bank or maker of a note payable at a bank who because the drawee or payor bank becomes insolvent during the delay is deprived of funds maintained with the drawee or payor bank to cover the instrument may discharge his liability by written assignment to the holder of his rights against the drawee or payor bank in respect of such funds, but such drawer, acceptor or maker is not otherwise discharged. (3–502 [1].)

Summary

Presentment for acceptance is necessary to charge the drawers and endorsers of a draft (1) if required by the draft, (2) if payable elsewhere than the place of business or residence of the drawee, or (3) if its date of payment depends on such presentment. The holder may at his option present any other draft. Presentment for payment is necessary to charge endorsers. Unless a different time is expressed in the instrument, presentment must be made within a reasonable time.

Presentment may be made by mail or through a clearinghouse or at a place specified or, if none is specified, at the place of business or residence of the party to accept or pay. Presentment may be made to any one of two or more makers, acceptors, drawees or payors or to a person having authority to make or refuse the acceptance or payment. If payable at a bank in the United States, a draft accepted or a note made payable at a bank must be presented at such bank.

Exhibition of the instrument, identity and authority of the party presenting, receipt for payments, and surrender of the instrument on payment in full may be demanded. Failure to present the instrument when due without excuse discharges endorsers and permits the drawer, acceptor of a draft or payor of a note payable at a bank to shift, by assigning funds in writing to holder, any burden resulting from the intervening insolvency of the bank to the holder.

Dluge v. Robinson

204 A.2d 279 (Super. Ct. Pa. 1964)

This was an action by Ethel Dluge and Benjamin Rimm, Executors of the estate of Isaac Dluge, deceased (plaintiffs), against Joseph G. Robinson (defendant) to recover a judgment for the amount of a check. Judgment for Dluge and Robinson appealed. Judgment reversed and judgment for Robinson entered.

Robinson endorsed two checks and negotiated them to Isaac Dluge. When presented for payment the drawee bank refused payment because of insufficient funds. Evidence was offered to prove that the checks were returned to Robinson but there was no evidence offered to prove that a demand was made, and the trial court found that demand was not made until nearly seven months after the dishonor of the checks.

FLOOD, JUDGE.   If Dluge and Rimm were holders in due course, they would have to prove only (1) that Robinson endorsed the checks and delivered them to Dluge, and (2) that they had been presented to the endorser for payment within a reasonable time. Uniform Commercial Code, § 3–501 (1) (b). In the case of an uncertified check this is presumed to be within seven days after the endorsement. U.C.C., § 3–503 (1) (e), § 3–503 (2) (b).

"Presentment is a demand for acceptance or payment . . . by or on behalf of the holder." U.C.C., § 3–504 (1). The only evidence of any demand was the admission by Robinson that he received a letter from Dluge's attorney demanding payment. Robinson did not state when he received this letter. Dluge did not offer the letter in evidence and there is no way to determine from the record when it was sent except that it was presumably sent before the complaint was filed on September 12, 1960, seven months after the checks were dishonored by the drawee bank. Since Robinson denied any demand at the time the checks were returned to him, and the record is otherwise barren of any evidence of demand within seven days, or any reasonable time, after endorsement, the Dluges did not establish any right to recover even if they had been holders in due course.

Dluge's executors are not holders in due course. Dluge gave the checks to Robinson without any demand for payment, so far as the record shows, and was not in possession of them when the suit was brought. Therefore he was not the holder. " 'Holder' means a person who is in possession of a document of title or an instrument or an investment security drawn, issued or indorsed to him or to his order or to bearer or in blank." U.C.C., § 1–201 (20). *A fortiori*, he was not a holder in due course. U.C.C., § 3–302 (1).

Dishonor, Protest, Notice and Waiver

Dishonor. An instrument is dishonored when it has been duly presented and acceptance or payment is refused or cannot be obtained within the prescribed time, or in case of bank collection the instrument is returned by the midnight deadline, or if presentment is excused and the instrument is not duly accepted or paid. (3–507 [1].)

When an instrument has been dishonored, the holder has an immediate right of recourse against the drawers and endorsers provided he has given any necessary notice of dishonor and protest. (3–507 [2].)

Protest. Unless excused, protest of any dishonor is necessary to charge parties secondarily liable on any draft where the draft on its face appears to be drawn or payable outside the states or territories of the United States and the District of Columbia. A holder may at his option make protest of any dishonor. (3–501 [3].)

Protest is a certificate of dishonor made under the hand and seal of a person authorized to certify dishonor by the law of the place where dishonor occurs.

Notice. Notice of dishonor or protest, unless waived, is necessary to charge any endorsers; and, as to any drawer, the acceptor of a draft payable at a bank or the maker of a note payable at bank, notice of any dishonor is necessary, but failure to give notice discharges such drawer, acceptor or maker only as discussed under the heading "Effect of Unexcused Delay in Presentment." (3–502 [2].)

Notice may be given in any reasonable manner. It may be given to any person who may be liable on the instrument by or on behalf of the holder or any party who has himself received notice, or any other party who may be compelled to pay the instrument.

The notice must describe the instrument with reasonable certainty, and sending the instrument bearing a stamp, ticket or writing stating that acceptance or payment has been refused or sending a notice of debit with respect to the instrument is sufficient.

Waiver or Excuse. Delay in presentment, protest or notice of dishonor is excused when the party is without notice that it is due as, for example, when the holder takes an instrument after the time of payment has been accelerated or takes a demand instrument after demand and he has no knowledge of such fact. Delay is excused if the holder makes an honest effort to make presentment and is unsuccessful because of circumstances beyond his control, but he must act with reasonable diligence after the cause of delay ceases. (3–511 [1].)

A waiver of protest includes a waiver of presentment and of notice of dishonor even though protest is not required. (3–511 [2], [3], [4], [5], and [6].)

Summary

An instrument has been dishonored when it has been duly presented and acceptance or payment cannot be obtained within the prescribed time. When an instrument is dishonored and required notices have been given, the holder has a right of recourse against the drawers and endorsers. The usual stamps on the instrument and the records of the dishonor of it are admissible as evidence of presumption of dishonor.

Protest is a certificate of dishonor made under the hand of a person authorized to certify dishonor. The certificate must identify the instrument and certify that due presentment has been made.

Notice of presentment and protest, unless waived, is necessary to charge any endorser. As to any drawer or acceptor of a draft or maker of a note payable at a bank, failure or delay in presentment or giving notice relieves the drawer, acceptor or maker of any liability only as to the loss he suffers as a result thereof. The notice must describe the instrument with reasonable certainty and written notice is effective when sent although not received. Due diligence must be exercised in the giving of notice.

Presentment may be waived by any party and is excused when the party is without notice that the instrument is due or when the party has himself dishonored the instrument or knows that it will not be accepted or paid or when the maker, drawer or drawee is dead or in insolvency proceedings. If dishonored by nonacceptance, it need not be presented for payment unless later accepted. Waiver of protest includes waiver of presentment and notice.

Contract of Parties

Contract in General. The terms of the contract of the parties to negotiable commercial paper are not set out on the face of the instrument but are instead written into the contract by operation of law and are as much a part of the contract as though written out in full. Parol evidence is not admissible to alter, subtract from or add to such terms.

Contract of the Maker, Acceptor, and Drawer.   The maker of a note and the acceptor of a draft are primarily liable on the instrument. Each engages that he will pay the instrument according to its tenor at the time of his engagement or as completed if incomplete, provided it is completed in accordance with authority given. (3–413 [1].) When a drawee accepts a draft he becomes liable on the draft as it reads at the time of his acceptance, and in the hands of a holder in due course such defenses as the alteration of the instrument before he accepted it, forgery of the drawer's signature, lack of authority of the drawer or incapacity of the drawer are not available to him.

The drawer of a draft is secondarily liable on the draft, and he engages that upon dishonor of the draft and the necessary notice of dishonor or protest he will pay the amount of the draft to the holder or to any endorser who takes it up. Since the drawer is secondarily liable on the draft, he may disclaim this liability by drawing without recourse. (3–413 [2].)

By making, drawing or accepting an instrument the party admits as against all subsequent parties including the drawee the existence of the payee and his then capacity to endorse. (3–413 [3].) If an instrument when issued names as payee a nonexistent corporation or an infant or an incompetent person, such fact cannot be set up by the maker, drawer or acceptor of the instrument as a defense to his liability on the instrument.

Contract of Endorsers.   All endorsers are secondarily liable. An endorser may avoid certain liability by qualifying his endorsement, that is, by endorsing without recourse. Unless the endorsement otherwise specifies, every endorser engages that upon dishonor and any necessary notice of dishonor and protest he will pay the instrument according to its tenor at the time of his endorsement to the holder or to any subsequent endorser who takes it up, even though the endorser who takes it up was not obligated to do so. (3–414 [1].)

An endorser who endorses "without recourse" or other qualifying language of similar import is not liable to the holder or endorsers for the nonpayment of the instrument by the party primarily liable. By so endorsing he relieves himself from the contractual liability as a guarantor of the instrument.

Contract of Accommodation Party.   The contract of an accommodation party will depend on the capacity in which he signs the instrument. He is one who signs the instrument in any capacity for the purpose of lending his name to another party to it. The accommodation party may sign as maker, drawer, acceptor or endorser.

As against a holder in due course and without notice of the accommodation, oral proof of the accommodation is not admissible to give the accommodation party the benefit of discharges dependent on his character as such, but in other cases the accommodation character may be shown by oral proof. (3–415 [3].) An endorsement which shows that it is not in the chain of title is notice of its accommodation character. (3–415 [4].)

An accommodation party is not liable to the party accommodated, and if he pays the instrument he has a right of recourse on the instrument against such party. (3–415 [5].)

Summary

The terms of the contract of the parties to negotiable commercial paper are written into the instrument by operation of law. The maker of a note and the acceptor of a draft contract to pay it according to the terms of the instrument. The drawer promises to pay the holder if the instrument is dishonored and he is given notice. Makers, acceptors and drawers admit the existence of the payee and his then capacity to endorse. Endorsers, who do not qualify their endorsements, contract to pay if the instrument, on presentment, is dishonored and they are given notice. Endorsers are presumed to be liable in the order in which they have endorsed.

An accommodation party is liable in the capacity in which he has signed the instrument.

Warranties of Parties

Whether or not a person signs the instrument he may be liable on the basis of certain implied warranties. These warranties are of two types: (1) those imposed on persons who *transfer* instruments and (2) those imposed on persons who *present* instruments *for payment or acceptance.*

Transferor's Warranties.   Any person who transfers an instrument and receives consideration makes five transferor's warranties to his transferee; in addition, if the transfer is by endorsement, they are made to any subsequent holder who takes the instrument in good faith. The five transferor's warranties are:

1. That the transferor has good title to the instrument or is authorized to obtain payment or acceptance on behalf of one who has a good title and that the transfer is otherwise rightful;
2. That all signatures are genuine or authorized;
3. That the instrument has not been materially altered;
4. That the transferor has no knowledge of any defense that is good against him; and
5. That the transferor has no knowledge of any insolvency proceedings instituted with respect to the maker or acceptor or the drawer of an unaccepted instrument. (3–417[2].)

A transferor who endorses with an unqualified endorsement warrants that no defense of any party is good against him, instead of merely warranting that he has no knowledge of defenses as in the case of the transferor without endorsement or the qualified endorser. (3–417 [2] and [3].)

While secondary liability often furnishes a sufficient basis for suing a transferor when the party primarily liable does not pay, warranties are still important. First, they do apply even where the transferor did not endorse. Second, unlike secondary liability, they do not depend on presentment, dishonor, and notice, but may be utilized before presentment has been made or after the time for giving notice has expired. Third, it may be easier to return the instrument to a transferor on the grounds of breach of warranty than to prove one's status as a holder in due course against a maker or drawer.

Presentment Warranties.   Under commercial law, a distinction as to warranties is made between a person who transfers an instrument to another person and a person who presents the instrument for payment or acceptance to a maker or drawee. The person to whom an instrument is presented for acceptance or payment will not normally pay or accept unless he thinks he is legally obligated to pay or is legally entitled to credit or payment from a third party. As a general rule, when payment or acceptance of an instrument is made, it is final in favor of a holder in due course or a person who in good faith changed his position in reliance on the payment. (3–418.) Thus if a drawee bank pays a check without checking to see if the drawer's signature is valid, the drawee cannot later obtain repayment from a holder in due course who presented it for payment if the drawee finds the drawer's signature was forged; likewise, the drawee bank that pays a check out of an insufficient funds account cannot obtain repayment from a holder in due course.

However, the general rule of finality of payment or acceptance is subject to three exceptions which are embodied in the Uniform Commercial Code as warranties made by a party presenting an instrument for payment or acceptance and all prior transferors. These warranties, in general, are:

1.   That the party has good title to the instrument or is authorized to obtain payment or acceptance on behalf of one who has a good title;
2.   That the party has no knowledge that the signature of the maker or the drawer is unauthorized;
3.   That the instrument has not been materially altered. (3–417 [1].)

In certain exceptional cases these warranties do not apply when holders in due course are the presenting parties. For example, a drawer or maker should recognize his own signature and a maker or acceptor should recognize whether the instrument has been materially altered, so they do not get warranties covering these points from a holder in due course.

Summary

The transferor of an instrument warrants title, genuineness of signatures or the authority of one signing, that the instrument has not been materially altered, that no defenses of any party are good against him (if he qualifies his warranty he warrants he has no knowledge of defenses to the instrument) and that he has no knowledge of any insolvency proceedings instituted with respect to the maker or acceptor or the drawer of an unaccepted instrument.

Any person who obtains payment or acceptance and any prior transferor warrants to a person who in good faith accepts or pays the instrument that he has good title or is authorized to act for a person who has good title to the instrument and that the instrument has not been materially altered. A holder in due course acting in good faith does not warrant to a maker or drawer the genuineness of their signatures.

First National City Bank v. Bankers Trust Co.

4 U.C.C. Rep. 324 (N.Y. Sup. Ct., N.Y. Cty. 1967)

This was an action by First National City Bank (plaintiff) against Bankers Trust Company (defendant) to recover for breach of the transferor's warranty that all signatures on the instrument were genuine or authorized. First City National Bank moved for summary judgment and the motion was granted.

MARKEWICH, JUDGE. Plaintiff bank received from defendant bank a purported genuine draft for collection. It was timely presented for payment, which was refused because the instrument was forged, of which fact plaintiff immediately informed defendant, though it had in the interim provisionally settled for the draft's face amount. When the item was forwarded for collection, the signatures were warranted to be genuine or authorized (U.C.C. § 4–207 (2)); this warranty was breached, and defendant is required to repay. The fact that there are other claimants interpleaded by defendant cannot interfere with plaintiff's clear right to recovery on this transaction.

[*The transferor's warranties made by a collecting bank under Section 4–207 (2) are essentially the same as those made by an individual transferee under Section 3–417 (2).*]

Conversion of Instruments

Conversion of Instrument. Conversion of an instrument is an unauthorized assumption and exercise of ownership over it. An instrument is converted by a drawee to whom it is delivered for acceptance if he refuses to return it on demand; or by a person to whom it is delivered for payment and who refuses on demand either to pay or to return it; or by a person who pays on a forged endorsement. (3–419 [1].)

The measure of a drawee's liability who has converted an instrument is the face amount of the instrument; in the other situations set out above, the measure of liability is presumed to be the face amount of the instrument. (3–419 [2].) A special rule applies to banks which handle instruments in the ordinary course of their banking business. (3–419 [3] and [4].)

Harry H. White Lumber Co., Inc., v. Crocker-Citizens National Bank

61 Cal. Rptr. 381 (Ct. App. Cal. 1967)

This was an action by Harry H. White Lumber Company (plaintiff) against Crocker-Citizens National Bank (defendant) to recover for the conversion of a check payable to White Lumber Co. that was paid by Crocker-Citizens Bank on a forged endorsement. White Lumber Company's action was dismissed by the trial court and it appealed. Judgment reversed.

Between December 10, 1964, and January 15, 1965, AIRE-TARE wrote four checks totalling about $4,700 payable to the order of Timberline Roofing Company and Harry H. White Lumber Company and delivered the checks to the joint payee, Timberline Roofing Company. Timberline endorsed its name and then forged the Harry H. White Lumber Company name to each of the checks. Timberline presented them to and received payment for them from Crocker-Citizens National Bank. Harry H. White Lumber claimed it had an interest in the checks, that it was damaged when the bank cashed them for Timberline, and that it was entitled to recover those damages from Crocker National.

McCoy, JUDGE.   The question posed by this appeal is: Does a joint payee of a check have a cause of action against a collecting bank which has paid a check made payable to joint payees bearing an endorsement effected by one joint payee signing his own name and forging that of his joint payee? We hold "yes" under both the Negotiable Instruments Law and the California Commercial Code—Commercial Paper provisions.

The relevant portion of the Commercial Code § 3–116 provides: "An instrument payable to the order of two or more persons . . . (b) if not in the alternative is payable to all of them and may be negotiated, discharged or enforced only by all of them." By the express provisions of § 3–116, subdivision (b) all the joint payees must join not only for negotiation, but also for discharge as well.

*   *   *   *   *

Other pertinent sections of the Commercial Code are: § 3–404: "(1) Any unauthorized signature is wholly inoperative as that of the person whose name is signed unless he ratifies it or is precluded from denying it; but it operates as the signature of the unauthorized signer in favor of any person who in good faith pays the instrument or takes it for value. (2) Any unauthorized signature may be ratified for all purposes of this division. Such ratification does not of itself affect any rights of the person ratifying against the actual signer." Section 1–201, subsection 43: " 'Unauthorized' signature or endorsement means one made without actual, implied or apparent authority and includes a forgery." Section 3–306: "Unless he has the rights of a holder in due course any person takes the instrument subject to. . . . (d) The defense that he or a person through whom he holds the instrument acquired it by theft. . . ." Section 3–419: "(1) An instrument is converted when . . . (c) It is paid on a forged endorsement."

The comments under § § 3–404 and 3–419 indicate that § 3–419 changes the preexisting California law and now gives the payee of a forged check a cause of action for conversion against the drawee (payor) bank. But no change is indicated as to the preexisting California case law permitting the payee to recover from a collecting bank which has paid out on a forged endorsement.

Thus, the plaintiff has a cause of action against the defendant collecting bank on the check governed by the provisions of the Uniform Commercial Code. . . .

Discharge

Discharge by Payment or Tender. Generally all parties to negotiable commercial paper are discharged when the party primarily liable on it pays the amount due in full to the bona fide holder at or after the due date. (3–601 [3].) The liability of any party is discharged to the extent of his payment or satisfaction to the holder. If a third party claims the instrument, payment or satisfaction to the holder will discharge the party making payment even though he is given notice or has knowledge of the claim unless the claimant either supplies indemnity deemed adequate by the party seeking the discharge or enjoins payment or satisfaction by order of a court of competent jurisdiction in an action in which the adverse claimant and the holder arc parties. (3–603 [1].)

A party is not discharged who in bad faith pays or satisfies a holder who acquired the instrument by theft or who (unless having the rights of a holder in due course) holds through one who acquired it by theft. (3–603 [1] [*a*].) Also, a party is not discharged who pays or satisfies a holder of an instrument which has been restrictively endorsed in a manner not consistent with the terms of such restrictive endorsement unless the party paying is an intermediary bank or a payor bank which is not a depository bank. (3–603 [1] [*b*].)

Payment or satisfaction may be made with the consent of the holder by any person, including a stranger to the instrument. If the holder surrenders the instrument to such a person, it gives him the rights of a transferee of the instrument. (3–603 [2].)

A tender of payment does not discharge the liability of the party making the tender *in toto* but any party making tender of full payment to the holder when or after it is due is discharged to the extent of all subsequent liability for interest, costs and attorney fees. (3–604 [1].)

The holder's refusal of a tender wholly discharges any party who has a right of recourse against the party making the tender. (3–604 [2].) For example, suppose that Axe is the maker of a note and Held is the holder, and the note is endorsed by Parks, the payee, and Erwin, endorsee. Axe, at or after the due date, tenders payment in full to Held who refuses the tender. Parks and Erwin will be wholly discharged of their liability as endorsers.

If the instrument is made payable at a bank or other place of payment and the maker or acceptor is able and ready to make payment at any and all such places specified in the instrument when it is due, it is equivalent to tender. (3–604 [3].)

Discharge by Cancellation or Renunciation. The holder of a negotiable instrument may discharge the instrument by cancellation. Any destruction or mutilation of a negotiable instrument is a cancellation if such destruction or mutilation is done with the intent that the instrument will no longer evidence an obligation. (3–605 [1] [a].) However, if such destruction or mutilation is by accident, the instrument will not be discharged. In the event the instrument is lost, destroyed, or mutilated, the original terms of the instrument may be established by parol or secondary evidence. (3–804.)

The holder of negotiable instrument may discharge the instrument by expressly renouncing his rights against the principal debtor. The renunciation, to be effective, must be in writing and must be absolute and unconditional. A renunciation does not affect the rights of a holder in due course without notice. Neither a cancellation nor a renunciation, to be valid, need be supported by consideration. Either is, in effect, a gift of the instrument to the principal debtor. (3–605 [1] [b].) Neither cancellation nor renunciation without surrender of the instrument affects the title thereto. (3–605 [2].)

Discharge by Alteration. Any alteration of an instrument is material which changes the contract of any of the parties thereto in any respect. A change in the number or relation of the parties, or the completing of an incomplete instrument otherwise than as authorized, or the changing of the writing as signed by adding to it or removing any part of it is a material alteration. (3–407 [1].) A change which in no way affects the contract of the parties such as crossing a "t" or dotting an "i" or correcting the grammar in the instrument is not a material alteration.

Against any person other than a subsequent holder in due course, an alteration by the holder which is both fraudulent and material discharges any party whose contract is thereby changed unless the party consents to the change or is precluded from asserting the defense. (3–407 [2] [a].) No other alteration discharges any party and the instrument may be enforced according to its original tenor, or as to incomplete instruments according to the authority given. (3–407 [2] [b].)

A holder in due course who has taken the instrument after it has been altered can enforce it according to its original tenor, and when an incomplete instrument has been completed, he may enforce it as completed. (3–407 [3].)

Discharge by Impairment of Recourse. A holder who discharges any party to an instrument without reserving the rights of others against such party discharges such other persons from liability.

Also, if a party has posted collateral to secure his performance and a holder surrenders the collateral without the consent of parties who would benefit from the collateral, such parties are discharged. (3–606.)

Summary

Payment to a bona fide holder at or after the due date of negotiable commercial paper discharges all parties to the instrument. If a third party makes a claim to the instrument, payment to the holder discharges the party making payment unless the party making the claim supplies indemnity or enjoins payment in a suit in which the adverse claimant and the holder are parties. Payment in bad faith to a thief does not discharge the party.

Tender of full payment to the holder at or after the due date discharges any party who has recourse against the party making the tender and stops the running of interest and costs and attorney fees.

Cancellation must be destruction of the instrument with intent to discharge the parties or by marking it on the face in such a manner that the intent to cancel is apparent. A renunciation must be in writing.

Any material alteration of an instrument by the holder with fraudulent intent discharges any party whose contract is altered thereby, but it does not affect the rights of a holder in due course.

The release of any party or the surrender of collateral discharges any party who has recourse against the discharged party unless all rights are reserved.

Chenowith v. Bank of Dardanelle

419 S.W.2d 792 (Sup. Ct. Ark. 1967)

Action by Bank of Dardanelle (plaintiff) against Chenowith (defendant) to recover on two checks drawn by Chenowith. Judgment for Bank and Chenowith appealed. Reversed.

On January 13, 1966, Chenowith drew two checks in the amounts of $3,800 and $3,000 payable to Parham. Parham deposited the checks on the Bank of Dardanelle, where he had an account. Bank forwarded the checks for payment and then learned that payment had been stopped. It then placed a "hold" on $6,800 in Parham's account pending return of the checks. However, when the checks were returned to Bank, a clerk mistakenly sent them on to Parham. In the meantime another clerk had allowed a $6,800 check written by Parham to clear his account, despite the "hold" order and there were no funds left in the account. Parham and Chenowith, who had a continuing business relationship, settled among themselves for the two checks. Bank then brought suit against Chenowith to obtain payment for the two checks.

HARRIS, CHIEF JUSTICE.   This case is governed by the provisions of the Uniform Commercial Code. Section 3–603 provides as follows:

(1) The liability of any party is discharged to the extent of his payment or satisfaction to the holder even though it is made with knowledge of a claim of another person to the instrument unless prior to such payment or satisfaction by the person making the claim either supplies indemnity deemed adequate by the party seeking the discharge or enjoins payment or satisfaction by order of a court of competent jurisdiction in an action in which the adverse claimant and the holder are parties. This subsection does not, however, result in the discharge of the liability.

(a) of a party who in bad faith pays or satisfies a holder who acquired the instrument by theft or who (unless having the rights of a holder in due course) holds through one who so acquired it;

* * * * *

Appellant contended that his liability was discharged under the provisions of § 3–603 since he fully satisfied the amount of these checks with the holder (Parham). The Circuit Judge, however, denied the motion for directed verdict, because Chenowith was with Parham at the bank when Hamilton (bank's vice-president) advised that the checks were unpaid. This ruling was erroneous. It will be noted that the statute says that the liability of the party is discharged "even though it is made with knowledge of a claim of another person to the instrument," unless the claimant (the bank) supplies indemnity deemed adequate by the party seeking the discharge (Chenowith) or enjoins payment or satisfaction by court order in an action in which the adverse claimant (Chenowith) and the holder (Parham) are parties. No indemnity was supplied, nor did the bank, in filing its suit, seek an injunction as provided by the statute. It is also asserted by appellee that Chenowith and Parham were acting in bad faith, i.e., they knew the checks had not been paid at the time they made this settlement. Appellee, in its brief, asserts that Parham was nothing more than a bailee, and his conduct amounted to a conversion of the checks "to his own use or a larceny by bailee, and accepting them with knowledge of the circumstances, Chenowith participated in the conversion or larceny and was nothing more than an accessory thereto."

Under the statute, Chenowith would not have been discharged from liability if he paid or satisfied a holder "who acquired the instrument by theft or who holds through one who so acquired it," but the commissioners' comment with reference to Subsection (1) makes clear the question of good or bad faith has nothing to do with liability. That comment is as follows:

"Subsection (1) changes the law by eliminating the requirement of the original Section 88 that the payment be made in good faith and without notice that the title of the holder is defective."

Of course, Parham did not steal the check, and it might also be mentioned that the complaint does not charge Chenowith and Parham entered into a conspiracy to defraud the bank.

Appellee also argues, as a matter of supporting its judgment, that Chenowith and Parham had not completely settled their financial transactions with each other (this contention being made on the basis of Parham's testimony), and since they had not fully settled, Chenowith's liability had not been discharged. We disagree. Whether the entire indebtedness between the men had been settled is immaterial here, for it is admitted that the checks had been turned over to Chenowith by Parham, who had become the holder, having been sent the checks by the bank. Thus, Chenowith had settled *this* indebtedness with Parham.

Of course, the checks were sent back to Parham by the bank through error, but, under the quoted section of the Commercial Code, this is of no aid.

Exceptions to General Liability Rules

Normally, a check bearing a forged payee's endorsement is not properly chargeable to a drawer's account nor must a maker pay the note to the current possessor of a note bearing a forged payee's signature. Likewise, the maker or drawer is normally liable for an instrument only according to its tenor at the time he signed it. However, the Uniform Commercial Code makes several exceptions to these general rules of liability.

Imposter Rule. An imposter is a person who misrepresents his identity to another for the purpose of inducing such another to deal with him in the belief that he is the person he represents himself to be. If a negotiable instrument is drawn payable to the order of or is endorsed to the person whom the imposter represents himself to be or to his confederate, an endorsement of the instrument by any person in the name of such payee or endorsee is effective. (3–405 [1] [*a*].) For example, suppose that Axe steals Parks's automobile. Axe finds the certificate of title in the automobile and then representing himself to be Parks sells the automobile to Berger Used Car Company and it draws its check payable to Parks for the agreed purchase price of the automobile and delivers the check to Axe. Any person can negotiate the check by endorsing it in the name of Parks.

Fictitious Payee Rule. Where the person signing as or on behalf of a maker or drawer intends the payee to have no interest in the instrument, or where an agent or employee of the maker or drawer has supplied him with the name of the payee intending the latter to have no interest in the instrument, any person can negotiate the instrument by endorsing it in the name of the named payee. For example, suppose that Axe who is employed by the Moore Corporation as an accountant in charge of accounts payable prepares a false invoice naming Parks, Inc., a supplier of the Moore Corporation, as having supplied Moore Corporation with goods and draws a check payable to Parks, Inc., for the amount of the invoice. He then presents it to Temple, treasurer of Moore Corporation, together with other checks with invoices attached, for Temple's signature, all of which Temple signs and returns to Axe for mailing. Axe then withdraws the check payable to Parks, Inc. Anyone can negotiate the check by endorsing it in the name of Parks, Inc. In such a case an employee of the drawer has supplied the drawer with the name of a payee, intending the named payee to have no interest in the check. (3–405 [1] [*b*] and [*c*].)

Negligence in Signing. If a person is so negligent in the drawing or signing of a negotiable instrument that he in effect invites the alteration or unauthorized signing, such negligent person will be precluded from asserting the alteration or lack of authority against a holder in due course or against a drawee or other payor who pays the instrument in good faith and in accordance with the reasonable commercial standards of the drawee's or payor's business. (3–406.) If a business uses an automatic signing device and leaves this device and blank checks unguarded where they are available to office employees generally, and an employee who is not authorized to issue checks prepares a check and when he has an opportunity signs the check with the signing device, the drawee bank would be protected in cashing the check. Also, if a check or other instrument is drawn for "one dollar" ($1) in such a manner as would easily permit one to alter it to read "One Hundred one dollars" ($101) and it is altered and a person who can qualify as a holder in due course takes the check for $101, the drawer will be held liable for the amount of $101 if under the circumstances the court finds that the negligent manner in which the check was drawn contributed to its alteration.

Summary

Where an imposter has induced a person to issue a negotiable instrument to a named payee whom he intends to have no interest in it, such instrument can be negotiated by an endorsement in the name of the payee made by any person. If the drawer or a person authorized to sign for the drawer makes out a check to a named payee and does not intend that the named payee have any interest in the check, then under the fictitious payee rule any person may sign the name of the named payee and the endorsement will be effective to negotiate the instrument. The drawer of an instrument which is so negligently drawn that it invites alteration or an unauthorized signature and is altered or a forged signature added may be precluded from asserting the alteration or forgery.

Philadelphia Title Insurance Co. v. Fidelity-Philadelphia Trust Co.

212 A.2d 222 (Sup. Ct. Pa. 1965)

This was an action by Philadelphia Title Insurance Company (plaintiff), the drawer of a check, against Fidelity-Philadelphia Trust Company (defendant), the drawee on the check, to have its account recredited. Philadelphia Title argued that one of the payees' signature had been forged so that the check was not properly payable by Fidelity-Philadelphia. Judgment for Fidelity-Philadelphia. Affirmed on appeal.

Mrs. Jezemski was separated from her husband and decided to obtain some money from him by having a mortgage placed on some property her husband held as administrator and heir of his mother's estate and taking the proceeds herself. She went to a lawyer with a gentleman whom she introduced as her husband, and they made out a bond and mortgage on her husband's land. Then she went to a title insurance company which under Philadelphia custom takes care of placing mortgages on property and paying the proceeds to the mortgagor. She told Philadelphia Title's representatives that her husband was too busy to come in that day, but that her husband's signature on the mortgage had been witnessed by her lawyer. Philadelphia Title then placed a mortgage on the property and gave Mrs. Jezemski a check made payable to Edmund and Paula Jezemski and Edmund Jezemski as administrator for his mother's estate. Mrs. Jezemski then forged her husband's signature to the check and negotiated it to a bank. Eventually the check was paid by Fidelity-Philadelphia which then charged the check to Philadelphia Title's account.

COHEN, JUSTICE. The parties do not dispute the proposition that as between payor bank (Fidelity-Philadelphia) and its customer (Title Company), ordinarily, the former must bear the loss occasioned by the forgery of a payee's endorsement (Edmund Jezemski) upon a check drawn by its customer and paid by it, 3–414. The latter provides, inter alia, that "(1) Any unauthorized signature [Edmund Jezemski's] is wholly inoperative as that of the person whose name is signed unless he ratifies it or is precluded from denying it. . . ."

However, the banks argue that this case falls within an exception to the above rule, making the forged indorsement of Edmund Jezemski's name effective so that Fidelity-Philadelphia was entitled to charge the account of its customer, the Title Company, who was the drawer of the check. The exception asserted by the banks is found in § 3–405 (1) (a) of the Uniform Commercial Code—Commercial Paper which provides:

"An indorsement by any person in the name of a named payee is effective if (a) an imposter by the use of the mails or otherwise has induced the maker or drawer to issue the instrument to him or his confederate in the name of the payee; . . ."

The lower court found and the Title Company does not dispute that an imposter appeared before McAllister (attorney) and DiBenefetto (realtor), impersonated Mr. Jezemski, and, in their presence, signed Mr. Jezemski's name to the deed, bond and mortgage; that Mrs. Jezemski was a confederate of the imposter; that the drawer, Title Company, issued the check to Mrs. Jezemski naming her and Mr. Jezemski as payees; and that some person other than Mr. Jezemski indorsed his name on the check. . . .

May Department Stores Co. v. Pittsburgh National Bank

374 F.2d 109 (3rd Cir. 1967)

This was an action by May Department Stores Company (plaintiff) against Pittsburgh National Bank (defendant) for allegedly charging May Department Store's checking account with amounts paid on forged endorsements. Summary judgment for National Bank was affirmed on appeal.

An employee of the May Department Stores fraudulently caused it to draw some checks payable to fictitious suppliers. The wrongdoing employee then forged the endorsements of the fictitious payees, cashed the checks at National Bank, and converted the proceeds. The defendant drawee, National Bank, charged the checks paid against the May Department Store account. May Department Stores sued National Bank, claiming the checks were not properly chargeable to the account since they were paid on forged endorsements.

PER CURIAM. . . . the district court properly concluded that the bank was protected by the following provision of the Uniform Commercial Code as in force in Pennsylvania.

"(1) An indorsement by any person in the name of a named payee is effective if . . .

(a) an agent or employee of the maker or drawer has supplied him with the name of the payee intending the latter to have no such interest." § 3–405(1) (c).

Park State Bank v. Arena Auto Auction, Inc.

207 N.E.2d 158 (App. Ct. Ill. 1956)

This was an action by Park State Bank (plaintiff) against Arena Auto Auction, Inc. (defendant), to recover a judgment on a check. Judgment for Park State Bank and Arena Auto Auction, Inc., appealed. Judgment affirmed.

Arena Auto Auction, Inc. (Arena), drew a check payable to the order of Tom Plunkett of Alabama and mailed it by mistake to Tom Plunkett at Rockford, Illinois. Arena had done business with Tom Plunkett of Rockford and had sent him at least one check in the past. Tom Plunkett of Rockford knew that Arena owed him nothing and that the check was not intended for him, but he endorsed it and cashed it at Park State Bank (Bank) with which he did business. Arena discovered the error and stopped payment on the check. It drew another check payable to Tom Plunkett and repeated the former error and again mailed the check to Tom Plunkett of Rockford. Tom Plunkett presented this check to Bank for payment but since payment was stopped on the first check, it refused to cash the second check. By this time Arena and Bank had discovered the error and Bank requested Tom Plunkett to return the money paid to him in error, but he refused. He had since left Rockford without leaving an address and his whereabouts were unknown. Bank sued Arena to recover the amount paid out on the check.

PETERSON, JUSTICE. Bank relies upon Section 3–406; which, being a new section of our Commercial Code, is as follows:

Any person who by his negligence substantially contributes to a material alteration of the instrument or to the making of an unauthorized signature is precluded from asserting the alteration or lack of authority against a holder in due course or against a drawee or other payor who pays the instrument in good faith in accordance with the reasonable commercial standards of the drawee's or payor's business.

Hence, we may have a case of first impression in construing the latter section of our statutory law.

Without repeating the various errors previously recited, it appears to this Court presumptuous on the part of Arena Auto Auction, Inc., to insist that they did nothing for which they should be held accountable. We point out the interval of lapsed time before they, in their fast-thinking, fast-operating business, decide first to stop payment.

Secondly, bearing in mind the erroneous sending of a second check to the same payee, and considering the custom of the trade as set forth by the testimony of the several gentlemen of the financial world as to the routine handling of checks in banking institutions, it is our considered conclusion that to require the recipient Bank to stop and question persons known to that Bank and presenting checks in routine business and issued by makers likewise known to the Bank, would be placing cogs in the wheels of business, which, in turn, would bring those wheels of the banking business to an astounding and abrupt halt. This, as we see it, was neither the intent nor the purpose of our legislators in passing the section in our Commercial Code to which reference was made.

We, therefore and accordingly, do conclude that the Trial Court was correct in holding that Arena, by their own negligence, substantially assisted in making it possible that an unauthorized person's signature passed title to the funds represented by said check.

Leonard v. National Bank of West Virginia

145 S.E.2d 23 (Sup. Ct. W. Va. 1965)

This was an action by Leonard (plaintiff) against a drawee bank, National Bank of West Virginia (defendant), to recover money paid by Bank on an alleged forged check and charged to Leonard's account. The Supreme Court held that Bank was entitled to a directed verdict in its favor.

On August 3, 1961, Leonard made out a check for $600, signed it as drawer, and also endorsed his signature on the back of the check. He did not date the check nor did he fill in the payee's name. Leonard claimed he gave the check to a man named Santo to whom he owed $600 and that he endorsed the check on the back so that Santo could cash it "at the track." When the check was returned to Leonard by National Bank after it had charged the check to his account, the word "thrity" had been written in front of the "six hundred," the name Martin Mattson had been entered as payee, and the endorsement of Martin Mattson appeared on the back of the check above Leonard's signature. Leonard then sued National Bank to have his account recredited for $3,600.

BERRY, JUSTICE. The general rule with regard to altered or raised checks is that if a bank pays such checks it does so at its peril and can only debit the drawer's account for the amount of the check as originally drawn, but there is an exception in the case of altered or raised checks to the effect that if the altering or raising of the check is because of the carelessness of the maker or depositor, the bank cannot be held liable in such case. . . .

It is clear from the evidence in this case and from the check, which was introduced into evidence as an exhibit, that the name of the payee was left blank, that the amount of the check opposite the dollar sign was left blank and a one and one-half inch space to the left of the words "Six hundred" was left blank, and that Leonard's signature on the back of the check as an endorser left a blank space of one inch from the top of the check. As the check was drawn, the blank space for the payee's name could have been made to "cash," any amount could have been placed in the space for the figure opposite the dollar sign and more than enough room was left for words to be filled in before the words "six hundred" in order to alter or raise this check, and all of such blank spaces were filled up in such manner than they could not easily arouse the suspicions of a careful person. It has been repeatedly held in such cases that the drawer is barred from recovery.

The check in question was drawn in such manner that it could be readily raised or altered and such changes could not be detected by the use of ordinary care. In fact, the carelessness of the drawing of the check in question would amount to gross negligence and Leonard would be estopped from any recovery if his were the only negligence involved because such action on his part would amount to negligence as a matter of law.

However, it has been held that the negligence of a depositor in drawing a check which can be altered does not render him liable if the bank fails to exercise due care in paying such check, but if the maker's carelessness is the proximate cause of the payment of such altered check on the part of the bank, the bank is not liable.

The negligence which the plaintiff endeavors to charge the bank within connection with this transaction is almost entirely based on evidence introduced by the plaintiff to the effect that the bank was negligent in not having the person who presented the check to the defendant bank for payment identified as the named payee and endorser on the check, Martin Mattson. There is no evidence in this case that the person who presented the check was not Martin Mattson, the named payee and also the person who endorsed the check above the endorsement of the plaintiff. . . . It would therefore, appear that the question as to whether the bank was guilty of negligence is not having Martin Mattson identified would be immaterial in this case when it was not proved that the signature was a forgery and further the evidence indicated that the bank did perform some identification procedure in this instance. Leonard also contends that the bank was negligent in not having the person who presented the check endorse it after the endorsement of J. P. Leonard. The signature in question speaks for itself and the more than sufficient space for endorsement of a payee above the name of Leonard's signature on the back of the check would constitute negligence on the part of Leonard for having left such space above his endorsement, and the bank could not be charged with negligence in such instance. Leonard further stated that he endorsed the check on the back in order that it could be cashed at the track which would clearly show his intention that the check could be cashed without difficulty, and the fact that he did endorse the check in blank and it was the last endorsement on the back thus made the check easily cashed without difficulty on the part of any person who presented it because it made the check bearer check payable on delivery. . . .

The only other matter in which the defendant Bank could be charged with negligence in connection with the cashing of the check in question was the word evidently intended as thirty which appeared before the words "Six hundred" in a misspelled form as "Thrity." However, the writing is very similar to the words "Six hundred," which the jury found was in the handwriting of Leonard.

Problem Cases

1. Roberts signed a check which was later dishonored. He alleged that it was signed by him in a representative capacity, but all that was on the check was his signature and the name of the account it was drawn from. Is Roberts liable for the amount of the check?

2. Janota's signature appeared on a note under the name of a corporation, acknowledging a $1,000 debt. No other wording appeared other than Janota's name and the corporate name. The holder of the note sues Janota on the note. What will Janota argue and what will the result be?

3. Defendant, president of a corporation, endorsed a note to plaintiff without including the name of the corporation or his office. On the reverse side of the note he endorsed a guarantee agreement. Now he seeks to present parol evidence that he endorsed the note in his representative capacity. Will this be permitted?

4. If certain checks are drawn by "McCann Industries, Inc., Payroll Account, (signed) J. Y. McCann," and the checks are not paid, who is liable—the individual or the corporation?

5. Phoenix Steel's board of directors adopted a resolution authorizing the Wilmington Bank to honor checks drawn on Phoenix's payroll account which bore facsimile signatures of designated officers. The resolution provided that the bank would be fully protected in acting on such authority. An employee of Phoenix later dishonestly and improperly affixed a facsimile signature of an officer to several blank payroll checks and the bank unknowingly honored them. In an action by Phoenix against the bank for the alleged wrongful negotiation of the checks, will Phoenix prevail?

6. Several promissory notes payable to plaintiff were each signed by Edge and two others. Plaintiff sues only Edge on the nonpayment of the notes. Each note recited the words: "We promise to pay." Defendant Edge argues that the suit must be dismissed since plaintiff must sue all three signers of the notes jointly. Should the suit be dismissed?

7. Adams and Baker entered into a contract of sale. Under its terms Adams was to pay $20,000 to Baker. He then gave Baker a check for this amount. After receiving the check Baker called the bank and was told that Adams' funds there were insufficient to cover the check. Baker refused to go through with the sale and Adams brought an action to enforce the contract. What will Baker argue and will he be successful?

8. Wilson was presented with a check, payable to Jones and Brown, and drawn on Merchant's Bank. The check was endorsed by Brown alone. Wilson accepted the check, endorsed it, and submitted it to Merchant's Bank for payment. Merchant's paid Wilson. Does Merchant's Bank or Wilson bear the liability in the event Jones seeks payment on the check?

9. A check was drawn on First National Bank and made payable to Mr. Howard. It came into the possession of Mr. Carson, who forged Howard's endorsement and cashed it at Merchant's Bank. Merchant's Bank then endorsed it and collected from First National. Assuming that Carson is nowhere to be found, who bears the ultimate liability?

10. Two checks on which the name of another payee had been added to payee line were endorsed by the unauthorized payee and deposited, and the depositary bank, Security Bank, endorsed them "Prior Endorsements Guaranteed" in presenting them to the Riggs Bank, drawee bank for collection. Is the depositary bank liable to the drawee bank?

11. A customer of Franklin National Bank drew a check to the order of a customer of First Israel Bank. The signature of the drawer, however, was a forgery, yet Franklin certified it unknowingly. Then the endorsement of the payee was forged and the check deposited in First Israel Bank to the First Israel's customer's account. First Israel guaranteed all prior endorsements in presenting the check to Franklin National for endorsement. Franklin National sues First Israel Bank for the amount of the check. Is First Israel Bank liable?

12. Frank Mitchell, while assistant treasurer of Travco Corporation, caused two checks, each payable to a fictitious company, to be drawn on his employer's account with the Brown City Savings Bank. The first check was payable to "L. and B. Dist., C/O F. & B. Mitchell." It was endorsed "F. Mitchell" and "B. Mitchell" and was cashed at Citizens Federal Savings & Loan Association. The second check was payable to "L. & B. Distr. Sales, 19704 West Seven Mile Road, Detroit, Michigan 48219." This latter check was endorsed "For deposit only F. Mitchell" and was also cashed at Citizens. Both checks were cleared through normal banking channels and charged against Travco's account with Brown City. Thereafter Travco discovered the embezzlement and demanded that its account be reimbursed. Brown City refused, and Travco initiated suit against Citizens Savings & Loan, and Brown City Bank. Judgment for whom and why?

13. Mrs. Johnson mailed a loan application in her husband's name and without his knowledge to First National Bank. The bank having dealt with her husband before approved the application and mailed a check in the amount requested to Mr. Johnson. Mrs. Johnson then endorsed the check in her husband's name and cashed it at Merchant's Bank. Merchant's Bank endorsed the check and presented it for payment. First National, having discovered the deception, refused to pay. Is First National liable on the check?

14. A construction company's superintendent wrote out several checks to the company's creditors and thereafter converted them to his own use by forging the endorsements of the creditors and cashing the checks at First National Bank. In an action by the company against the Bank for the value of the checks, is the Bank liable?

15. Boulevard Check Cashing, Inc., a check cashing service, cashed checks for Copen with the approval of Copen's employee, X. Copen had told Boulevard that X had the authority to approve the cashing of checks and that Boulevard could rely on X's authority without fear of loss. Several checks proved to be forgeries. Boulevard sues to recover on the checks cashed. Can Boulevard recover?

16. Gordon accepted from an applicant for a loan a note signed by the applicant and one the applicant said was signed by his wife. The "wife" took no part in the negotiations between Gordon and the applicant for the loan. In turn Gordon gave the applicant a check made payable to the applicant and his wife which was endorsed in the name of the applicant and his wife. Later it was found that the wife's signature was a forgery. Gordon sues the drawee bank for the return of the value of the check, claiming that the bank had paid the check on a forged endorsement. Is the drawee bank liable to Gordon?

17. Terry and Jones were partners in a barber shop and had a partnership checking account with National Bank on which both signatures were required. An employee of the barber shop obtained some of the checks and forged Terry's and Jones's names. National Bank honored and cashed the checks. During the four-month period this went on, the employee also intercepted the monthly bank statements and canceled checks, but Terry and Jones never inquired about them. The blank checks were left in an unlocked drawer in the barber shop. The signatures on the checks were skillful forgeries which could not easily be detected as wrongful. In an action to recover the monies paid by the bank from Terry and Jones's account, will Terry and Jones prevail?

18. Franklin National Bank certified two checks drawn by Ricci in the amounts of $8 and $10. Ricci subsequently altered same to $28,600 and $10,000, respectively, since upon certification there were blanks left open. In an action by the payee Brower for $38,600 against the bank for refusal to honor the checks, what theory will Brower use?

19. First National Bank certified Smith's check in the amount of $29. After certification Smith altered the check so that it read $2,900. He then presented the check to a merchant in payment for goods. The merchant then submitted the check to the bank for payment. The bank refused saying that it had only certified the instrument for $29 dollars. Can the merchant recover the $2,900 from the bank?

20. Smith executed a $100,000 promissory note to Jones on a standard note form. Below their signatures they agreed to add that the note was conditioned upon Jones raising an additional $400,000 in capital. Jones took the note and, after cutting off the part containing the condition, pledged it to a bank. The bank then demanded payment on the note from Smith. Is Smith liable to the bank?

chapter 40

Checks and Documents of Title

Checks

Relation between Drawer and Drawee Bank. The use of checks as a method of making payments has become all but universal in the United States. The rights and liabilities of the parties to a check have been discussed in the preceding chapter. Much of the law regarding the rights and liabilities of banks in the handling of checks is not a part of the law of commercial paper. A dual relation exists between the bank and its commercial account customer who draws checks.

When the customer makes a deposit in a bank, the relation created between the customer and the bank is that of debtor and creditor, and if the deposit is a commercial account, the relation is also one of principal and agent. The customer is the principal and the bank is the agent. Under banking law as set out in the Code, the bank as agent owes a duty to the customer as principal to honor all checks properly drawn and payable, provided the customer has a credit balance sufficient to cover the amount of the check. A check is not an assignment of the account (Section 3–409)[1] but is an order to the bank to make payment.

Bank's Duty to Pay. If a bank dishonors a check when the customer has a credit balance in his account sufficient to cover the check, the bank is liable for damages proximately caused by the wrongful dishonor. If the dishonor occurs through a mistake on the part of the bank, its liability is limited to actual damages. However, consequential damages, such as damages for arrest or prosecution, may be recovered if the customer can prove such damages with reasonable certainty. (4–402.)

---

[1] The numbers in parentheses refer to the sections of the Uniform Commercial Code, 1962.

Bank's Right to Charge to Account.   The bank has the right to charge any item, properly payable, to a customer's account even though the charge creates an overdraft. If an overdraft is created, the customer becomes indebted to the bank for the amount of the overdraft, and the bank has the right to charge the next deposit the customer makes with the amount of the overdraft. (4–401 [1].)

If the bank in good faith pays an altered check, it may charge the customer's account with the amount of the check as originally drawn. Also, if an incomplete check of a customer gets into circulation and is completed and presented to the drawee bank for payment and the bank pays the check, it can charge the amount to the drawer—customer's account, even though the bank knows the check has been completed, unless it has notice that the completion was improper. (4–401 [2].)

Stop-Payment Orders.   Since the bank acts as agent of the drawer in the payment of checks, it must follow all reasonable orders of the drawer relative to payments to be made on his behalf. If the drawer draws a check and then before the check is presented for payment or certification requests the bank not to pay the check—issues a stop-payment order—the bank owes a duty to the drawer not to honor the check when presented. To be effective, the stop-payment order must be received by the bank at such time and in such manner as to afford the bank a reasonable opportunity to act on it prior to the time the bank has paid, certified, or committed itself on the check. (4–403 [1].)

The stop-payment order may be oral in which case it is binding on the bank for a period of only 14 days unless confirmed in writing within that time. When confirmed in writing, the stop-payment order is good for six months. The time may be extended, however, by renewing the stop-payment order before the expiration of the six months. (4–402.) The bank is under no obligation to a customer to pay a check, other than a certified check, which is presented more than six months after its date, but may charge its customer's account for payment made thereafter in good faith. (4–404.)

Bank's Liability for Payment after Stop Payment.   The bank is liable to the drawer of a check which it pays while a stop-payment order is in effect for any loss he suffers by reason of such payment, but the drawer has the burden of establishing the amount of the loss. To show a loss the drawer must establish that if the drawee bank had honored the stop-payment order so that the holder of the instrument had to come after the drawer for payment, that the drawer had a valid defense to payment which could have been successfully asserted against that holder of the instrument. To the extent the drawer had such a defense, he has suffered a loss due to the drawer's failure to honor the stop-payment order of the drawer. The bank cannot by agreement disclaim its responsibility for its own lack of good faith or failure to exercise ordinary care nor can it limit the measure of damages for such lack or failure; but the parties may by agreement determine the standards by which such responsibility is to be measured if such standards are not manifestly unreasonable. (4–103 [1].)

If the bank pays a check after it is given a stop-payment order, it acquires the rights of a transferee of the item and acquires, by subrogation, all of the rights of the person to whom it made payment, including his rights based on the transaction on which the check was based.

Certified Check.   Certification of a check is an acceptance by the drawee bank. Unless otherwise agreed, the bank owes no obligation to certify a check. When the bank certifies a check, it debits the amount of the check to the drawer's account and credits the amount to the certified check account. This certified check account, however, is not a trust fund set up for the payment of such checks, and if the certifying bank becomes insolvent before the certified check is presented for payment, the holder is merely a creditor of the bank.

If a check is certified for the drawer, he is secondarily liable on the check, but if it is certified for a holder, the drawer and all prior endorsers are discharged. A bank may certify a check before returning it for lack of proper endorsement, but if it does so, the drawer is discharged. (3–411.)

Death or Incompetence of Customer.   Under the general principles of agency law, the authority of an agent to bind his principal is terminated on the death or incompetence of the principal. This rule has been modified by the provisions of the Code relative to a bank's right to honor checks drawn prior to the death or incompetence of the drawer but presented to the drawee bank for payment thereafter. Under the provisions of the Code, the bank has authority to pay checks drawn by an incompetent customer unless the bank knows of the adjudication of incompetence. Neither death nor incompetence of a customer revokes the bank's authority to pay or certify a check until the bank knows of the fact of death or of an adjudication of incompetence and has a reasonable opportunity to act upon it. Even though the bank has knowledge of the death of the customer, it may, for a period of 10 days after the date of his death, if it elects to do so, pay or certify checks drawn by him on or prior to that date. However, any person claiming an interest in the deceased customer's estate may order the bank to stop payment. (4–405.)

Customer's Duty to Report Forgeries and Alterations.   The canceled checks drawn by a customer together with a statement of account are usually returned by the bank to the customer once a month, or they may be held pursuant to a request or instructions of its customer, or otherwise in a reasonable manner made available to him. The customer, on receiving the checks and statement, owes a duty to examine them to discover if any of his signatures on the checks are forgeries or unauthorized or if any of the checks have been altered. (4–406 [1].)

If the customer fails to examine the checks and statement within a reasonable time, he cannot hold the bank responsible for the payment of checks on which there are forgeries, unauthorized signings or alterations. If a series of forgeries, unauthorized signings or alterations are made by the same wrongdoer on any checks paid in good faith by the bank after the first check which had been forged or signed without authority or altered was available to the customer for a reasonable period not exceeding 14 calendar days and before the bank received notification from the customer of any such forgery, unauthorized signature or alteration, the customer cannot hold the bank responsible for paying the check.

For example, suppose that Axe employs Fell as an accountant and over a period of three months Fell forges Axe's signature to 10 checks and cashes them. One of the forged checks is included in the checks returned to Axe at the end of the first month and within 14 calendar days after the return of these checks Fell forges two more checks and cashes them. Axe does not examine the returned checks until a lapse of three months after the checks which included the first forged check were returned to him. The bank would be responsible for the first forged check and the two checks forged and cashed within the 14-day period after the return of the first statement and checks, but it would not be liable for the seven forged checks cashed after the expiration of the 14-day period. (4–406 [2].)

In other situations the bank will not be held responsible for the honoring of checks on which the customer's signature is forged or unauthorized or which are altered if the customer does not discover and report the forgery, unauthorized signature or alteration within one year from the time the statement and checks are made available or does not within three years of that time discover and report any unauthorized endorsement. (4–406 [4].)

Summary

The relation between a bank and a customer having a commercial account on which checks may be drawn is that of debtor and creditor and principal and agent. In drawing a check the customer as principal authorizes the bank as agent to honor the check. The customer as principal has the right to order the bank to stop payment on a check and if the order to stop payment is received by the bank at such a time and in such form as to give it a reasonable opportunity, the bank owes a duty to refuse payment on an uncertified check. If it pays a check in disregard of a stop-payment order, it is liable to the drawer for any resulting loss.

A bank is not obligated to certify a check, but on certification it becomes primarily liable on the check and, if certified at the request of the holder, the drawer and all prior endorsers are discharged.

A bank may pay checks drawn during a customer's lifetime or while competent and for a period of 10 days after death or adjudication of incompetence.

A customer owes a duty to report to the bank, within a reasonable time after a statement of account and canceled checks are made available, unauthorized signatures and alteration. Failure to do so relieves the bank from responsibility.

Granite Equipment Leasing Corp. v. Hempstead Bank

9 UCC Rep. 1384 (N.Y. 1971)

This was an action brought by Granite Equipment Leasing Corp. (plaintiff) against Hempstead Bank (defendant) to recover the amount of a check charged to Granite's account. Judgment for Hempstead Bank.

Granite Equipment Leasing Corp. kept a checking account with Hempstead Bank. On October 10, 1968 Granite drew a check payable to Overseas Equipment Co., Inc. Five days later, after Overseas advised that the check had not been received, Granite wrote the Bank on October 15, 1968 to stop payment on the check. On that same day Granite authorized the Bank to wire the payee funds in the same amount as the stopped check and the Bank did so. Granite never renewed its stop payment order between October 1968 and November 10, 1969. On November 10, 1969, without notice or inquiry to Granite, the Bank accepted the original check to Overseas which had been stopped the year before, paid the indicated funds to a collecting bank, and charged Granite's account.

Granite then sought to recover from the Bank the amount charged because of the check paid to Overseas in November 1969. The Bank defended on the ground that under UCC § 4-403 the stop payment order had expired for want of renewal, and that acting in good faith it was entitled under UCC § 4-404 to pay the stale check.

HARNETT, JUDGE.   There is no doubt the check is stale. There is no doubt the stop payment order was properly given at the outset, and that it was never renewed. Granite essentially maintains the Bank had a duty to inquire into the circumstances of that stale check, and should not have paid in face of a known lapsed stop order without consulting its depositor.

The Uniform Commercial Code, which became effective in New York on September 27, 1964, provides that:

(1) A customer may by order to his bank stop payment of any item payable for his account . . .
(2) . . . A written [stop] order is effective for only six months unless renewed in writing. UCC § 4-403.

The Official Comment to UCC § 4-403 notes that:

. . . [t]he purpose of the [six-month limit] is, of course, to facilitate stopping payment by clearing the records of the drawee of accumulated unrevoked stop orders, as where the drawer has found a lost instrument or has settled his controversy with the payee, but has failed to notify the drawee. . . .

* * * * *

Granite cannot be permitted to predicate liability on the part of the Bank on its failure to inquire about and find a stop payment order which had become terminated in default of renewal. *Feller v. Manufacturers Trust Co.,* held that a drawee bank was not liable to a drawer for payment of a check two months after expiration of a stop payment order which had not been renewed. See also, *William Savage, Inc. v. Manufacturers Trust Co.,* holding a bank not liable for payment on an eleven month old check after expiration of a stop payment order.

Neither may Granite predicate a claim of liability upon the Bank's payment of a stale check. The legal principles applicable to this circumstance are codified in UCC § 4–404, which provides that:

. . . [a] bank is under no obligation . . . to pay a check, other than a certified check, which is presented more than six months after its date, but it may charge its customer's account for a payment made thereafter in good faith.

. . . There is no obligation under the statute on the Bank to search its records to discover old lapsed stop payment orders. The Bank does not have to pay a stale check, but it may pay one in "good faith." Significantly, UCC § 1–201 (19) defines "good faith" as "honesty in fact in the conduct or transaction concerned." In the absence of any facts which could justify a finding of dishonesty, bad faith, recklessness, or lack of ordinary care, in the face of circumstances actually known, or which should have been known, the Bank is not liable to Granite for its payment of the check drawn to Overseas.

One statute invalidates stop payment orders not renewed within six months. Another statute allows payment in good faith of stale checks. Granite cannot combine the two statutes to reach a synergistic result not contemplated by either separately.

Granite's complete remedy lies in its pending Florida action against Overseas to recover the extra payment.

Jackson v. First National Bank
403 S.W.2d 109 (Ct. App. Tenn. 1966)

This was an action by Jackson (plaintiff) on behalf of Greater St. Matthews Church of which he was senior Trustee against First National Bank (defendant) to have the Church's account recredited for 50 checks which had been forged and charged to the Church's account. Judgment for Jackson was affirmed on appeal.

The Church had opened a checking account in First National Bank in August, 1963, and specified that two signatures, those of Jackson, the Trustee, and Cleve Jordan, the Financial Secretary, were required for withdrawals. The account specified that statements and cancelled checks were to be mailed to Cleve Jordan. The checks involved in this case were drawn between August, 1963, and August, 1964, were payable to Cleve Jordan, and had the signature of Jackson forged on them. The cancelled checks and monthly statements had been sent to Cleve Jordan. The Bank contended that the Church should not be able to recover because of its delay in reporting the forgeries and its negligence.

BEJACH, JUDGE. Under the above quoted statutes (3–405 and 4–406) a drawee bank which pays the check on a forged signature is deemed to have made the payment out of its own funds and not the depositor's, provided the depositor has not been guilty of negligence or fault that misled the bank. In such situation, the burden is upon the bank to show that the loss was due to the negligence of the depositor, rather than to its failure to exercise its legal duty.

In the instant case, the negligence of the depositor relied on by the bank is its failure to examine the checks and report the forgery, thus preventing a repetition thereof. The fallacy of this argument is the checks were mailed to Cleve Jordan, Financial Secretary of the Church, who was the forger. He was an unfaithful servant, and obviously his knowledge and information on the subject would not be reported by him to the Church, nor imputed to it. He had been a faithful and trusted member of the Church and one of its officers for about twenty years, and, consequently, the Church cannot be held guilty of negligence in employing an unfaithful agent. The contention is made, however, that the church officials, other than Cleve Jordan, himself, should have called on Jordan for an accounting from time to time, and that the Church was negligent in its failure to perform this duty. The proof shows that the Church did from time to time call on Cleve Jordan for production of the checks and records of the Church, but that he made excuses, said he forgot to bring them, or made other excuses. Under these circumstances, in view of his previous good record and reputation, we cannot say that the Bank carried the burden of showing negligence on the part of the Church.

Under the Negotiable Instruments Law, no time limit establishing a reasonable period is fixed within which a depositor must examine the canceled checks returned to him, but under the provisions of the Uniform Commercial Code, such limit is fixed at fourteen days. Under the provisions of § 4–406, subsection 2(b), a depositor is precluded by failure to examine the checks within fourteen days from asserting liability against the bank on account of unauthorized signature or alteration of a check paid by the bank in good faith, but subsection (3) of the same Code section provides: "The preclusion under subsection (2) does not apply if the customer establishes lack of ordinary care on the part of the bank in paying the item(s)."

In *Farmers' and Merchants' Bank v. Bank of Rutherford,* the Supreme Court held that, "It is negligence in a drawee bank to pay a forged check drawn on it in the name of its customer, whose signature is well known to it, where the cashier does not examine the signature closely, but relies on the previous endorsements." It is argued on behalf of the Bank that such examination of the signature card, which admittedly was not made in the instant case, is not practical under modern banking methods. Such may be true as a practical matter, but, if so, the Bank, because of that fact, cannot escape the consequences and must, under that decision, be held guilty of negligence.

We think, however, that the Bank must be held to be guilty of negligence in another and much stronger aspect of the instant case. The Bank account here involved was that of a church, which obviously involved trust funds, and the counter signature of Milton Jackson, Trustee, whose signature has been forged, was required on all checks. In the case of *Fidelity and Deposit Co. of Maryland v. Hamilton Nat'l Bank* (1938) this court held that one who takes paper from a trustee importing upon its face its fiduciary character, is bound to inquire of the transferor the right to dispose of it. . . . Any adequate inquiry made in the instant case by the Bank would have disclosed the situation that Cleve Jordan was forging the name of Milton Jackson, Trustee, and would have prevented a repetition of such forgery.

There is another and a stronger reason why the Bank must be held guilty of negligence and held responsible for the result of the forgery here involved. All of the checks, recovery for which was granted in the instant case, were made payable to Cleve Jordan, personally; and many of them bear the endorsement of the Southland Racing Company, which is the corporation operating the dog racing track in Arkansas across the Mississippi River from Memphis. These circumstances, and especially the one that the checks were made payable to Cleve Jordan, personally, should have put the bank on inquiry as to whether or not the funds represented by these checks were being withdrawn for unauthorized purposes. Any inquiry would have disclosed the true situation and prevented further depletion of the Church's bank account. The bank account being a trust fund and the checks withdrawing same being made to one of the authorized signers of checks, was sufficient to put the Bank on notice that the funds were being improperly withdrawn, or should at least have required the bank to make inquiry as to whether or not the withdrawals involved were authorized.

Documents of Title

Introduction. The practice of storing or shipping goods and the giving of a warehouse receipt or bill of lading representing the goods and the transfer of such warehouse receipt or bill of lading as representing the goods is of ancient origin. The warehouseman or the common carrier is a bailee of the goods and he contracts to store or transport the goods and to deliver them to the owner, or to act in accordance with the lawful directions of the owners. The warehouse receipt or the bill of lading may be either negotiable or nonnegotiable. To be negotiable, a warehouse receipt, bill of lading or other document of title must, by its terms, provide that the goods are to be delivered to bearer or to the order of a named person. (7–104 [1].) The primary difference between the law of negotiable commercial paper and that of negotiable documents of title is based on the difference between the obligation to pay money and the obligation to deliver specific goods.

Warehouse Receipts. A warehouse receipt, to be valid, need not be in any particular form, but if it does not embody within its written or printed form each of the following, the warehouseman is liable for damages caused by the omission to a person injured thereby: (*a*) the location of the warehouse where the goods are stored; (*b*) date of issue; (*c*) consecutive number of the receipt; (*d*) whether goods are to be delivered to bearer or to the order of a named person; (*e*) rate of storage and handling charges, except that where goods are stored under a field arrangement, a statement of that fact is sufficient on a nonnegotiable receipt; (*f*) description of the goods or the packages containing them; (*g*) the signature of the warehouseman, which may be made by his agent; (*h*) if the receipt is issued for goods of which the warehouseman is owner, either solely, jointly, or in common with others, such fact of ownership; and (*i*) statement of the amount of advances made and of liabilities incurred for which the warehouseman claims a lien or security interest. Other terms may be inserted. (7–202.)

A warehouseman is liable to a purchaser for value in good faith of a warehouse receipt for nonreceipt or misdescription of goods. The receipt may conspicuously qualify the description by a statement such as "contents, condition and quantity unknown." (7–203.)

Since a warehouseman is a bailee of the goods, he owes to the holder of the warehouse receipt the duties of a mutual benefit bailee. Such duties are set out in Section 7–204 of the Code. The warehouseman may terminate the relation by notification under the conditions and circumstances set out in Section 7–206 of the Code.

Where a blank in a negotiable warehouse receipt has been filled in without authority, a purchaser for value and without notice of the want of authority may treat the insertion as authorized. Any other unauthorized alteration leaves the receipt enforceable against the issuer according to its original tenor. (7–208.) Unless the warehouse receipt otherwise provides, the warehouseman must keep separate the goods covered by each receipt except that different lots of fungible goods may be mingled. (7–207.)

Bills of Lading. In many respects the right and liabilities of the parties to a negotiable bill of lading are the same as those of the parties to a negotiable warehouse receipt. The contract of the issuer of a bill of lading is to transport goods whereas the contract of the issuer of a warehouse receipt is to store goods. Like the issuer of a warehouse receipt, the issuer of a bill of lading is liable for nonreceipt or misdescription of the goods, but he may protect himself from liability where he does not know the contents of packages by marking the bill of lading "contents or condition of contents of packages unknown" or similar language. Such terms are ineffective when the goods are loaded by an issuer who is a common carrier unless the goods are concealed by packages. (7–301.)

A carrier who issues a bill of lading must exercise the same degree of care in relation to the goods as a reasonably careful man would exercise under like circumstances. A liability for damages not caused by the negligence of the carrier may be imposed on it by a special law or rule of law. Under tariff rules a common carrier may limit his liability to a shipper's declaration of value provided the rates are dependent on value. (7–309.)

Negotiation of Document of Title. A negotiable document of title and a negotiable instrument are negotiated in substantially the same manner. If the document of title provides for the delivery of the goods to bearer, it may be negotiated by delivery. If it provides for delivery of the goods to the order of a named person, it must be endorsed by that person and delivered. If an order document of title is endorsed in blank, it may thereafter be negotiated by delivery unless it bears a special endorsement following the blank endorsement, in which event it must be endorsed by the special endorsee and delivered.

A person taking a negotiable document of title takes as a bona fide holder if he takes in good faith and in the regular course of business. The bona fide holder of a negotiable document of title has substantially the same advantages over a holder who is not a bona fide holder or over a holder of nonnegotiable document of title as a holder in due course of a negotiable instrument has over a holder who is not a holder in due course or over the holder of a nonnegotiable instrument.

Rights Acquired by Negotiation. A negotiable document of title is "duly negotiated" when it is negotiated by delivery, if a bearer document, or by endorsement and delivery, if an order document, to a holder who purchases in good faith without notice of any defense against or claim to it on the part of any person and for value, unless it is established that the negotiation is not in the regular course of business or financing or involves receiving the document in settlement of a money obligation. (7–501 [4].) A person who acquires a negotiable document of title by due negotiation acquires (1) title to the document, (2) title to the goods, unless the goods are fungible, (3) the right to the goods delivered to the bailee after the issue of the document, and (4) the direct obligation of the issuer to hold or deliver the goods according to the terms of the document. (7–502 [1].) As to fungible goods, a buyer in the ordinary course of business of fungible goods sold and delivered by a warehouseman who is also in the business of buying and selling such goods takes free of any claim under a warehouse receipt even though it has been duly negotiated. (7–205.)

Under the broad general principle that a person cannot transfer title to goods he does not own, a thief or the owner of goods subject to a valid outstanding security interest cannot, by warehousing or shipping the goods on a negotiable document of title and then negotiating the document of title, transfer to the purchaser of the document of title a better title than such thief or owner has. Under the law of sales, however, if a person can transfer the ownership of goods to a bona fide purchaser for value, he can then warehouse or ship the goods on a negotiable document of title and by negotiating the document of title to a person who takes in due course confer on such person a good title to the goods. (7–503.)

Warranties of Transferor of Document of Title. The transferor of a negotiable document of title warrants to his immediate transferee, in addition to any warranty of goods, only that the document is genuine and that he has no knowledge of any facts that would impair its validity or worth and that his negotiation or transfer is rightful and fully effective with respect to the title to the document and the goods it represents. (7–507.) A collecting bank or intermediary warrants only his good faith and authority. (7–508.)

Summary

The warehouseman or common carrier is a bailee of the goods and he contracts to store or transport them. The warehouse receipt or bill of lading may be either negotiable or nonnegotiable. If the warehouse receipt issued by the warehouseman omits in its written or printed terms the information required under the provisions of the Code, the warehouseman is liable to a purchaser in good faith of a warehouse receipt for failure to describe or for misdescription of the goods. He owes to the holder of a warehouse receipt the duties of a mutual benefit bailee. The common carrier's liability on a negotiable bill of lading is the same in most respects as that of the issuer of a negotiable warehouse receipt. His liability may be increased by special law or rule.

The rules of law relative to the negotiation of a negotiable document of title are the same in most respects as the law relative to the negotiation of negotiable commercial paper.

In general, a holder by due negotiation of a negotiable document of title gets good title to the document and the goods and the contractual rights against the bailee. However, a thief or an owner of goods which are subject to a valid perfected security interest cannot, by warehousing or shipping the goods on a negotiable document of title and negotiating it, pass to such transferee greater rights in the goods than such thief or owner has.

A holder who transfers a negotiable document of title warrants to his immediate transferee that the document is genuine and that he has no knowledge of any facts that would impair its validity or worth and that his transfer is rightful and fully effective.

National Dairy Products Corp. v. Lawrence American Field Warehousing Corp.

255 N.Y.S.2d 788 (App. Div. N.Y. 1965)

This was an action by National Dairy Products Corporation (plaintiff) against Lawrence American Field Warehousing Corporation (defendant) to recover for failure to deliver goods on presentation of warehouse receipts. Summary judgment for National Dairy Products Corporation and Lawrence American Field Warehousing Corporation appealed. Judgment affirmed.

Quantities of soybean oil were delivered to Lawrence American Field Warehousing Corporation (Lawrence) for which nonnegotiable warehouse receipts were issued. National Dairy Products Corporation (National) held warehouse receipts for some of the soybean oil. On presentation of the receipts it was discovered that no soybean oil was in the storage tanks. No satisfactory explanation was given for the disappearance of the soybean oil—95,233,792 pounds. Either the oil had been stolen or the warehouse receipts had been issued without the receipt of soybean oil.

BREITEL, JUSTICE PRESIDING.   Section 7–207 (2) of the Uniform Commercial Code does in some situations change the prior law by giving to certain holders of "overissued" receipts for a portion of a fungible mass the rights of a holder who has made a delivery of existing goods to the warehouseman. Thus the holder of an overissued receipt may obtain a proprietary interest in bailed fungibles of another even though the receipt was not originally issued for the deposit of actual oil. If this provision be applicable, then the holders of overissued receipts for nonexistent oil would be owners of a pro rata share of existing oil and entitled to sue in conversion for the wrongful failure to deliver that share on demand. However, by its own terms this provision of section 7–207 (2) benefits only those holders to whom overissued receipts have been "duly negotiated," and therefore would not seem to apply to nonnegotiable receipts. (U.C.C., § 7–501.)

It is true, as defendants argue, that a bailee is not an insurer. Thus, if despite the exercise of due care, there is an inability to deliver, the bailee is not liable to the one entitled to possession of bailed goods. Consequently, the matter of due care requires consideration before the issues in these cases can be determined.

* * * * *

With the foregoing prefatory comment it is appropriate to consider the obligation of the warehouseman to exercise care. He has not only the obligation to exercise care, but concededly he has the burden of explanation for any loss or disappearance of the property bailed. He is also liable for damages arising from the improper issuance of receipts or documents of title.

From Lawrence's point of view there has not been any showing of sufficient care or explanation to exculpate them from liability. It is not enough to assert that care was taken, describing the practices used, when the disappearance of the oil remains wholly unexplained. This situation is not at all like that of a bailee showing how carefully the property was secured and that nevertheless the thief broke in and removed the property, without fault on the part of the bailee by any reasonable standard. In showing care, the bailee must explain the loss or damage, and not simply point to a mystery for which it has no better explanation than the bailor.

Koreska v. United Cargo Corp.

258 N.Y.S.2d 432 (App. Div. N.Y. 1965)

This was an action by Koreska (plaintiff) against United Cargo Corporation (defendant) to recover a judgment for the value of goods delivered without taking up an order bill of lading. Summary judgment for Koreska granted.

United Cargo Corporation (United) issued a negotiable order bill of lading for goods consisting of four large packages. The goods were consigned to Koreska and the order bill of lading named as Koreska's collecting agent a New York bank. On arrival of the goods United delivered them to Park Whitney, Koreska's customer, without taking up the bill of lading by an oral waiver made by Koreska's agent and also by a binding trade custom or course of dealing. The court found that no agent authorized to act for Koreska had waived the taking up of the bill of lading and that no course of dealing was established.

PER CURIAM.   Even if a factual issue had been raised with respect to Allgemeine's agency, Koreska would be entitled to summary judgment. In the case of an order, or negotiable bill of lading, as opposed to a straight, or nonnegotiable bill, it is ordinarily the consignee or other holder of the negotiable bill, who alone is entitled to authorize a diversion or modification of the delivery term. Even if Allgemeine obtained possession of the bill after authorizing a waiver, as claimed by United, it was never a holder with power to divert, in the absence of an actual indorsement of the bill to it. Moreover the seller-shipper, Koreska, never became a consignee or holder, and therefore did not, under these rules, have the power to divert the goods without the cooperation of its collecting agent-consignee, the New York bank. It follows that its alleged agent, Allgemeine, similarly had no such power.

A further reason why United may not avail itself of the alleged waiver, is that the waiver was oral only, and would modify the express term of the bill that delivery was to be made at the order of the New York bank consignee. One of the conditions printed on the back of the bill provides:

"None of the terms of this bill of lading shall be deemed to have been waived by any person unless by express waiver signed by such person, or his duly authorized agent."

Ordinary prudence, moreover, would dictate that the carrier require that such instructions be noted on the bill itself.

For similar reasons evidence of the course of dealing or trade custom is also without significance. The express term, requiring delivery in accordance with the consignee's order, is controlling, whenever the course of dealing or trade custom is inconsistent with it. (U.C.C., § 1–205 [4].)

Problem Cases

1. Skov sold fish to hotels and restaurants. He acquired his fish under an agreement whereby the supplier stored the fish that Skov had purchased for future delivery and no payment was made until such delivery. Following delivery of one shipment Skov gave his supplier a check drawn on First National Bank. The bank erroneously refused to honor the check and the supplier canceled the agreement. Can Skov recover damages from the bank for the loss of this agreement?

2. Mullinax issued a check payable to Brown for the purchase price of an automobile. Mullinax discovered that the automobile had been stolen and he telephoned Rubin, the vice-president of the Roswell branch of American Bank on which the check was drawn, and told him to stop payment on the check. The stop-payment order was received at 11:05 A.M. and Rubin immediately called other branches of the bank informing them of the stop-payment order. The calls were completed by 11:15 A.M. The check was cashed by the bank at 11:45 A.M. Is the bank liable to Mullinax for cashing the check?

3. Keleher issued a check payable to the order of O'Keefe, who had the check certified. Later, Keleher issued a stop-payment order to the bank before the check was presented for

payment. Keleher has a valid defense if sued on the check. Should the bank pay the check to O'Keefe?

4. Cook had issued a check payable to the order of Light. The next morning, before banking hours, Cook telephoned the bank, talked to the cashier, and ordered payment of the check stopped. Later in the day the bank certified the check and subsequently paid it. When sued, the bank set up as a defense (*a*) that the stop-payment order was not given during banking hours and (*b*) that the stop-payment order was not in writing. Is either of these defenses good?

5. In January of 1970, Mrs. Baker began forging her husband's checks. In June of 1971, Mr. Baker notified the bank that he had not been receiving his checking account statements. The missing statements were then personally delivered to Mr. Baker. Mr. Baker balanced his account statements in February 1973. In March of 1973, he notified the bank that 25 of the checks that they had cashed were forgeries. Does the bank or Mr. Baker bear the liability for the forgeries?

6. An employee of Lawrence Fashions Co. had forged 250 of the company's checks over a period extending from November 1965 to May 1968. The company did not discover the forgeries until May of 1968. It then filed an action against the bank to recover the amount paid on these instruments. Is the bank liable?

7. In 1972, Hirsch Food Co. began storing cases of their pickles in a warehouse owned by Overmyer Co. Later that year Overmyer began shutting down its warehouse operation and reduced the staff to one man, who came to the warehouse only when Hirsch Co. desired to remove some of their pickles. In 1973, when the last of the pickles were removed, 900 cases were missing. Where does the liability lie? Upon what does it depend?

8. Dovax had been shipping goods with Delivery Company for more than a year. On November 1, 1966, Dovax gave Delivery Company goods valued at $1,799.95 for delivery to three different consignees. Delivery Company kept the goods in one of its trucks overnight but the next morning the truck was discovered stolen along with the goods. On the bills of lading given to Dovax was the legend "Liability limited to $50 unless greater value is declared and paid for." Dovax claims he should recover $1,799.95 for the loss; Delivery Company wants to pay only $150. Who is correct?

9. United Elastic Corporation shipped eight cases of yarn by way of a truck line to a consignee mill. The yarn was sent under a freight bill which listed the names of both shipper and consignee. The truck line being unable to deliver the shipment, left it at Pinter Warehouse. Two months later Pinter Warehouse sold the shipment, worth $2,000 for the $25 warehouse charges. Can United Elastic recover from Pinter?

10. On October 15, Young delivered 207 bags of rice to Atteberry's warehouse and received a nonnegotiable receipt. Young then transferred the receipt to Brock for a valuable consideration and on November 3 Brock notified Atteberry of the transfer. However, prior to November 3 Young had procured a negotiable receipt for the rice along with some other rice he had deposited with Atteberry. Now Brock presents his nonnegotiable receipt to Atteberry and demands delivery of the rice. Atteberry contends no rice is held there on Brock's account. Who is correct?

Part X

Credit

chapter 41

Introduction to Security

Introduction

Nature of Security. In the United States today a substantial portion of the business transacted involves the extension of credit. The term "credit" has many meanings. We shall use it, however, as designating a transaction in which goods are sold and delivered, services are rendered, or money is loaned in exchange for the recipient's promise to pay at some future date.

Unsecured Credit. A multitude of transactions are made which are based on unsecured credit. A common example of such credit is the monthly charge account at the local department store, where goods are sold and delivered to the customer, who promises to pay for them at a later date. Such a transaction is usually called an open-book account. The use of the open-book account or other types of unsecured credit is not confined to consumer transactions but is used extensively by jobbers, suppliers of raw materials, and manufacturers.

This type of credit transaction involves the maximum of risk from the standpoint of the creditor. When goods are delivered, services rendered, or money loaned on unsecured credit, the creditor loses all rights in the goods, services, or money and in return has only a claim against the debtor for the agreed price or for whatever he may have promised in return. If the promise is not fulfilled, the creditor's only course of action is to bring a suit and obtain a judgment. He then may have the sheriff levy an execution on any property subject to the execution, or he may garnish wages or other credits due the debtor which may be subject to garnishment. A person may be execution proof; that is, he may not have any property subject to execution, and at the same time he may not have a steady job or credits due him, in which case garnishment would be of no aid in collecting the judgment. A businessman may obtain credit insurance and thereby stabilize his credit risk, even though such action does not reduce it. The credit losses of a business extending unsecured credit is reflected in the price the consumer pays for the goods or services, or in the rate of interest paid by a borrower from such businesses.

Secured Credit.   If the creditor wishes to minimize his credit risk, he can contract for security; that is, he may require his debtor to convey to him a security interest in property, or he may ask that some person promise to be liable in the event the debtor defaults. If a security interest in property is conveyed to the creditor and the debtor defaults in his payments, the creditor will have the right to sell the property and pay the debt out of the proceeds. If the proceeds are not sufficient to pay the debt, he will have, in the absence of a special agreement, an unsecured claim for the unpaid balance.

Development of Security.   Various types of security devices have been developed as social and economic need for them arose. The rights and liabilities of the parties to a secured transaction depend on the nature of the security, that is, whether the security pledged is the promise of another to pay if the debtor does not or whether a security interest in goods, intangibles or real estate is conveyed as security for the payment of a debt or obligation.

If personal credit is pledged, the party may guarantee the payment of the debt, that is, become guarantor, or he may join the debtor in his promise to pay in which case he would become surety for the debt.

The oldest and simplest security device was the pledge. To have a pledge valid against third-person claimants it was necessary that the property used as security be delivered to the pledgee or a pledge holder. On default by the pledgor the pledgee had the right to sell the property and apply the proceeds to the payment of the debt.

Situations arose in which it was desirable to leave the property used as security in the possession of the debtor. To accomplish this objective the debtor would give the creditor a bill of sale to the property, thus passing title to the creditor. The bill of sale would provide that if the debtor performed his promise the bill of sale would become null and void, thus revesting title to the property in the debtor. By this device a secret lien on the goods was created and the early courts held that such a transaction was a fraud on third-party claimants and void as to them. Statutes were enacted providing for the recording or filing of the bill of sale which was later designated as a chattel mortgage. These statutes were not uniform in their provisions. Most of them set up formal requirements for the execution of the chattel mortgage and also stated the effect of recording or filing on the rights of third-party claimants.

To avoid the requirements for the execution and filing of the chattel mortgage, sellers of goods would sell the goods on a contract by the terms of which the seller retained the title to the goods until the purchase price of the goods was paid in full. On default by the buyer the seller could (*a*) repossess the goods or (*b*) pass title and recover a judgment for the unpaid balance of the purchase price. Abuses of this security device gave rise to some regulatory statutes. About one half of the states enacted statutes which provided that the conditional sales contract was void as to third parties unless it was filed or recorded.

No satisfactory device whereby inventory could be used as security was developed. Under the pledge, field warehousing was used and the after-acquired property clause in a chattel mortgage on a stock of goods held for resale partially fulfilled this need. One of the devices which was used was the trust receipt. It was a short-time marketing security arrangement and had its origin in the export-import trade. It was later used extensively as a means of financing retailers of high-unit value consumer goods.

Another method of using inventory as security was that of factoring. The goods involved were delivered to the factor for sale. As a general rule the factor sold the goods in his own name and guaranteed any credit he extended. The factor usually advanced money on the goods, and he had a lien on them for the money advanced and for his charges. Several states enacted factor acts defining the rights and liabilities of the parties involved.

Uniform Commercial Code.   The Uniform Commercial Code, Article 9, Secured Transactions, represents the first comprehensive scheme for the regulation of security interests in personal property and fixtures. It does not include security interests in real estate, nor does it replace existing statutory liens such as the Ship Mortgage Act of 1920, landlords' liens, artisans' liens, equipment trusts covering railroad rolling stock, and other listed special liens. (9–104.)[1] Furthermore, the Uniform Commercial Code makes no change in specific statutes such as those on usury, requirements for disclosure of finance charges, small-loan laws, pawnbrokers' laws, and the like. (9–201.)

One of the objectives of the Uniform Commercial Code is to abolish formal distinctions between security devices and to make distincitons where distinctions are necessary along functional rather than formal lines. The state, on adopting the Uniform Commercial Code, repeals its existing statutes regulating security interests in personal property and fixtures. The Code applies to all types of security interests created by contract and includes all of the familiar devices such as the pledge, chattel mortgages, conditional sales contracts, and trust receipts, regardless of form.

The general effect of the Code is expressed by Professor Coogan as follows:

Article 9 represents neither more nor less than a merger of the previously separate streams of chattel security law—those of pledge, chattel mortgages, conditional sale, assignment of accounts receivable, trust receipt, factor lien acts and the like. The merger has produced a more nearly rational set of rules under which the parties can create, perfect and enforce any of these different kinds of security interests produced under the pre-merger law, ranging from the solid pledge to something little removed, if at all, from a state-created priority. Any lawyer can easily trace practically every important concept, and even every important mechanical device, either to one

---

[1] The numbers in the parentheses refer to the sections of the Uniform Commercial Code, 1962.

or more of the pre-Code bodies of chattel security law of his own state or of a contiguous state. The bringing together of these rules into one statute is the Code's basic contribution to a more orderly chattel security system. Contrary to the impression created by the Official Comments, only minor differences in rules are based on the nature of the collateral.[2]

In discussing security interests in personal property and fixtures, we shall, with few exceptions, be dealing with old friends parading under new names. The drafters of Article 9 of the Code have put old wine into new bottles.

Security Interests in Real Estate.   Three types of contractual security devices have been developed by which real estate may be used as security: (1) the real estate mortgage, (2) the trust deed, and (3) the land contract. In addition to these contract security devices all of the states have enacted statutes granting the right to mechanics' liens on real estate. The real estate mortgage is comparable to the chattel mortgage and the land contract is comparable to the conditional sales contract. The trust deed is used to try to avoid the expense and delay usually accompanying the foreclosure of a mortgage. When it is used the real estate is deeded to a trustee who is empowered to sell it if the debtor does not pay the debt and to apply the proceeds of the sale on the payment of the debt. Under the statutes of some states the trust deed is treated as a real estate mortgage and must be foreclosed as such.

Summary

Credit is a transaction in which goods are sold and delivered, services are rendered, or money is loaned in exchange for the recipient's promise to pay at some future date. When such credit is given on the recipient's unsupported promise to pay, such as, for instance, an open-book account, the credit is unsecured credit. When the credit is supported by the transfer of an interest in property or the supporting promise of a third person to which the creditor can resort for payment if his debtor does not pay, such credit is secured credit.

Various types of security devices have been developed to serve the needs of our economy. The development in this area has been unorganized and the available security devices have been inadequate in many respects. The pledge is the oldest and simplest device. The chattel mortgage was used when it was desirable to leave the goods posted as security in the possession of the debtor. The conditional sales contract could be used only as security for the unpaid balance of the purchase price of the goods. The trust receipt was a short-time marketing device in which high-unit cost goods held as inventory are used as security. Factoring was an inventory security device in which the factor finances the inventory, sells it and repays the money advanced plus his commissions. The Uniform Commercial Code has provided a unified system of using personal property as security.

---

[2] Peter F. Coogan, "The Lay Lawyer's Guide to Secured Transactions under the Code," 60 *Michigan Law Review* 685 (April 1962).

Real estate may be posted as security. The real estate mortgage is comparable to the chattel mortgage, and the land contract is comparable to the conditional sales contract. The deed of trust is used in a limited number of states in lieu of the real estate mortgage.

Common Law and Statutory Liens on Personal Property

Persons Entitled to Common Law Liens. At common law, artisans, innkeepers, and common carriers were entitled to liens to secure the payment of the reasonable value of the services they performed. An artisan, it was reasoned, improved the property of another by his labor and by the addition of his materials, and that improvement became a part of the principal property by accession, and the title of the improved property vested in the owner of the principal property. Therefore the artisan who had enhanced the value of the property was allowed to claim a lien on the property for his reasonable charges.

The innkeeper and the common carrier were bound by law to serve the public. The innkeeper was allowed to claim a lien on his guest's effects for his reasonable charges for food and lodging, and the common carrier was allowed to claim a lien on the goods carried for his reasonable charges for the service. The giving of the common law lien to the innkeeper and common carrier was justified on the ground that since they were obligated to serve the public, they were entitled to the protection of a lien. These common law liens are generally recognized today. Several of the states have incorporated the concept of the common law lien in their statutory liens on personal property, and other states have by statute modified the rights of the common law lienholder.

Characteristics of a Common Law Lien. The common law lien is a possessory lien; it gives the lienholder the right to retain possession of the debtor's property until the debt has been discharged. An artisan is not entitled to a common law lien for his services unless possession of the property has been given to him.

Two essential elements of a common law lien are possession and a debt created by the improvement of the property on which the lien is claimed. If the lien claimant surrenders possession to the debtor voluntarily, the lien is lost, but if the debtor obtains possession by artifice or fraud, the lien is not extinguished. If the debt is paid, the lien is discharged, since the foundation of the right to the lien is the existence of a debt without which a lien right cannot exist. However, the discharge of the lien before the debt is paid does not affect the right to recover on the debt.

Statutory Liens on Personal Property. Statutory liens on personal property are liens created by statutory enactment. Many of these statutes are little more than a codification of existing common law liens. However, these statutes have created many additional liens and, at the same time, have provided a procedure for the foreclosure of the lien. To determine the scope of statutory liens, one must consult the statutes of the several states. Each state has its own lien statutes creating such liens as the needs of the people in the state suggest to the legislators. Carriers' liens and warehousemen's liens are provided for in Article 7, Documents of Title, of the Code.

If the lien created by statute is not recognized at common law, the statute creating the lien is said to be in derogation of the common law. The same is true of a statute providing for a lien which is recognized at common law but which gives to one of the parties rights not recognized under the common law lien. The courts have developed a rule of statutory construction which is generally applied in interpreting and applying such statutes. If the statute is in derogation of the common law, it will be strictly construed; that is, all the provisions of the statute must be complied with before the party can claim benefits under the statute, and the courts will not enlarge the scope of the statute by implication. If one claims a lien on property when he is not entitled to a lien and refuses to surrender possession when demand is made by the owner, he will be liable to the owner either for the conversion of the property or for damages for the unlawful detention.

Foreclosure of Lien. The right of possession of the holder of a common law lien does not give the lienholder the right to sell or claim ownership of the property if his charges are not paid. In the absence of statutes providing for the foreclosure of the lien, the lienholder must bring suit and obtain a judgment for his charges, have the sheriff levy execution on the property, and have the property on which he has a lien sold at execution sale.

Most states have enacted statutes which provide for the sale of the property, after it has been held for a designated period of time, on the giving of notice and on the advertising of the sale by posting or publishing notices of the sale.

Summary

Artisans, innkeepers, and common carriers are entitled to common law liens for their reasonable charges. The common law lien is a possessory lien. An artisan is not entitled to a common law lien on property unless possession of the property on which work is to be done is surrendered to him. The two essential elements of a common law lien are (1) the debt and (2) possession.

Most states have enacted statutes defining the rights to liens on personal property. Many of these statutes are little more than a codification of existing common law liens. However, all states have enlarged, to some extent, the scope of liens on personal property by statutory enactment.

A common law lien gives the lienholder the right of possession of the goods, but if he wishes to foreclose the lien, he must sue the debtor, obtain a judgment, have an execution issued on the judgment and levied on the goods, and have the goods sold at a sheriff's sale. In most states a simplified foreclosure procedure has been provided for by statute.

Beck v. Nutrodynamics, Inc.

186 A.2d 715 (Super. Ct. N.J. 1962)

This was an action in which James S. P. Beck (plaintiff) brought an action in attachment against Nutrodynamics, Inc. (defendant), and attached a quantity of pills. Ivers-Lee intervened, claiming a common-law lien on the pills. The court held that the common-law lien had priority over the attachment and Beck appealed. The Superior Court affirmed the holding.

Prior to the time Beck commenced his suit and attached the pills, Nutrodynamics, Inc., delivered to Ivers-Lee a drug product in completed pill form. Ivers-Lee was to place the pills in foil packages and then in shipping containers suitable for delivery to customers of Nutrodynamics, Inc. The packaged pills were in the possession of Ivers-Lee when Beck instituted his suit by attachment. Approximately 193 cartons of the packaged pills were levied upon and taken into possession by the sheriff. Ivers-Lee claimed an artisan's lien to the goods by virtue of materials, labor and services rendered which had priority over Beck's attachment.

YANCY, JUDGE. A common law lien is the right to retain the possession of personal property until some debt due on or secured by such property is paid or satisfied. This lien is one that arises by implication of law and not from express contract. It is founded on the immemorial recognition of the common law of a right to it in particular cases, or it may result from the established usage of a particular trade or from the mode of dealing between the parties.

The right to this common law lien applies to a bailee, to whom goods have been delivered. To entitle a bailee to a lien on the article bailed, more is necessary than the mere existence of the bailment relationship. The bailee must, by his labor and skill, contribute to the improvement of the article bailed. The bailee having thus performed, the well-settled rule of the common law is that a bailee (artisan) who receives in bailment personal property under an express or implied contract to improve, better, manufacture or repair it for remuneration, and enhances the value of such property by his skill, labor, or materials employed in such undertaking, has a specific lien on such property. This lien may be enforced against the bailor while the property remains in the bailee's possession, and until the reasonable value of his labor, skill, and expenses is paid.

The first question before the court, therefore, is whether the kind of work done by Ivers-Lee is such as to support its assertion to an artisan's lien. The undisputed facts set forth are that Nutrodynamics, Inc. delivered to the claimant a huge quantity of loose, unpackaged capsules so that the same could be rendered salable by having the claimant prepare, mark and package the capsules and place the packages in cardboard mailing containers suitable for delivery to the customers of Nutrodynamics, Inc. The claimant, Ivers-Lee, agreed to render the service and labor and to supply the materials necessary to accomplish the foregoing. The claimant did in fact supply such labor and packaging materials. This work and materials have become assimilated into the final product, and have enhanced the value of the heretofore loose unpackaged pills.

The case of *O'Brien v. Buston* dealt with a lien on goods for personal services rendered and for repairs to the goods. The court stated:

A workman who by his skill and labor has enhanced the value of a chattel, under an employment . . . has a lien on the chattel for his reasonable charge. . . .

The lien arises from the rendering of the service, and if such service be not paid for, there is a right to detain. The court further stated:

. . . It is the natural outcome of the transaction wherein one takes his chattel to another with whom he contracts for the performance by the latter of some service upon it for its betterment.

It is to be concluded from the foregoing that the work done by Ivers-Lee did enhance the value of the product.

Suretyship and Guarantee

Surety and Guarantor.   A surety, in the broad sense, is a person who is liable for the payment of another person's debt or for the performance of another person's duty. A surety joins the principal in making the promise. Both parties make primary promises to the obligee; however, the relation between the promisors is such that if the surety is required to perform, he will be entitled to reimbursement from his principal for any resulting loss.

A guarantor does not join in making a promise. The guarantor's liability arises on the happening of a stipulated event, such as the failure of the principal to perform his obligation, or the insolvency or bankruptcy of the principal. The guarantor's promise is collateral to the primary promise and is unenforceable, under the statute of frauds, unless evidenced by a writing signed by the guarantor or his duly authorized agent.

The rights and liabilities of a surety and of a guarantor are substantially the same, and we shall not attempt to distinguish between the two in our discussion unless the distinction is of basic importance.

Creation of Relation.   The relationship of principal and surety or that of principal and guarantor is created by contract. The rules of contract law apply in determining the existence and nature of the relationship, and the rights and duties of the parties.

As a general rule a corporation does not have the power to bind itself as surety for third persons unless such power is granted to it in its articles of incorporation.

Defenses of Surety.   If the principal has a defense which goes to the merits of the primary contract, the defense is available to the surety. Defenses such as lack or failure of consideration, inducement of the contract by fraud or duress, or material breach on the part of the obligee are available to the surety. Defenses such as infancy, insanity, or bankruptcy of the principal, and other defenses which do not go to the merits of the contract but which are personal to the principal are not available to the surety.

The surety contracts to be responsible for the performance of his principal's obligation. If the principal and the creditor by mutual agreement alter the terms of the primary contract and the surety does not consent thereto, the alteration will operate to relieve the surety of his liability. The surety undertakes to assume the risks incident to the performance of a particular contract, and his obligation cannot be altered without his consent.

Under this rule, if a principal and a creditor enter into an agreement whereby the principal is given an extension of time for the performance of the contract, the surety will be released from his obligation unless he consents thereto. However, mere indulgence on the part of the creditor does not release the surety. If the creditor merely promises the principal that he may have additional time in which to perform, such a promise will not release the surety from his obligation, since it is not a valid agreement to extend the time of performance. The promise to extend the time of performance, if it is to be valid, must be supported by consideration.

Creditor's Duties to Surety.   The creditor owes certain duties to the surety in regard to the risk the surety assumes. If he induces the surety to assume the risk by fraudulent representations as to the nature of the risk, or if he has knowledge of facts which would materially increase the risk and does not disclose such facts to the surety, the surety will be released from liability. If an employer (creditor) knows when he makes application for the bonding of an employee (principal) that such employee has been guilty of fraudulent or criminal misconduct, the employer must disclose this information to the surety. If an employer, after a bonded employee has been guilty of a defalcation covered by the bond, agrees to give the employee another chance and does not report the defalcation to the bonding company (surety), such action will release the bonding company from liability for further defalcations. If the principal has posted security for the performance of his obligation and the creditor surrenders such security without the consent of the surety, the surety will, as a general rule, be released to the extent of the value of the security surrendered. Some states have held, under such circumstances, that the surety is completely discharged.

Subrogation and Contribution.   If the surety is compelled to perform the obligation of his principal, the surety acquires, by operation of law, all the rights the creditor had against the principal. This is known as the surety's "right of subrogation."

If two or more persons become sureties for the same principal on the same obligation and one surety, on the principal's default, pays the obligation in full or pays more than his share of the obligation, he is entitled to reimbursement from his cosureties for the amount paid over and above his share. This is known as a surety's "right of contribution." If one or more of the cosureties is insolvent, the loss will be distributed equally among the solvent sureties. If a surety discharges the obligation for an amount less than the principal sum due, he is entitled to contribution only of the amount actually paid. Cosureties may enter into an express agreement which provides that the risks of the suretyship shall be distributed in unequal portions.

Summary

A surety, in the broad sense, is a person who is liable for the payment of another person's debt. Technically, a surety joins the principal in making the promise to the promisee, whereas a guarantor makes a collateral promise, promising to perform the principal's promise on the happening of a condition precedent.

The relation of surety is created by contract, and the general rules of contract law apply in determining the existence of a contract and in determining the rights and liabilities of the parties. As a general rule, any defense the principal has which goes to the merits of the case is available to the surety. Also, any agreement between the principal and creditor which alters the risks involved in the primary contract will discharge the surety unless he consents thereto or ratifies the agreement, or unless the rights against the surety are reserved.

The creditor owes a duty to use reasonable care in his dealings and not to increase unnecessarily the burden of risk assumed by a surety. If a surety pays his principal's debt, the surety is entitled to all the rights the creditor had against the principal. If there are cosureties and one surety pays more than his share of his principal's debt, he is entitled to contribution from his cosureties.

Mountain States Telephone and Telegraph v. Lee

504 P.2d 807 (Sup. Ct. Idaho 1972)

This was an action brought by Mountain States Telephone and Telegraph (plaintiff) against Ross C. Lee (defendant) to recover on his guarantee of the payment of certain telephone bills. Judgment for Lee. Reversed and remanded on appeal.

In February of 1969, Lee Pontiac, Inc. was doing business as Trans Magic Airlines. On February 10, 1969, Ross C. Lee, president of Lee Pontiac, signed a continuing guarantee contract for payment of the "Trans Magic Airlines" account to Mountain States Telephone.

On March 13, 1970, Trans Magic Airlines Corporation was incorporated with Ross C. Lee being one of many incorporators and only a minority shareholder. The assets of Lee Pontiac were transferred to the new Trans Magic Airlines Corporation on April 10, 1970, in a document signed by Ross C. Lee, president. This transfer was subject to all existing liabilities. In October telephone service to Trans Magic Airlines was discontinued for nonpayment of its account and Mountain States Telephone brought suit against Ross C. Lee on his guarantor contract to recover $2,134, the amount due from Trans Magic Airlines.

McQUADE, CHIEF JUSTICE.   This action relates to the enforceability of a guarantee contract, such type of contract having been held valid in Idaho. A "guarantee contract" is a contract of an assurance by a "guarantor" for payment of a debt, or the performance of a duty, or contract by another person.

* * * * *

Where the principal is a corporation, a mere change in its name, without a change in its business does not discharge the guarantor, especially where such change is participated in by the guarantor as a stockholder. There is more involved in the present case than a mere change in name, however. The change from Lee Pontiac, Inc., dba Trans Magic Airlines to Trans Magic Airlines Corporation involved a basic change in the ownership structure of the business entity. Since there was therefore no unity of ownership and interest, the alter ego doctrine is not applicable in this case.

Respondent Ross Lee did, however, participate in the change of Lee Pontiac, Inc., dba Trans Magic Airlines to Trans Magic Airlines Corporation. Lee, who had been president of Lee Pontiac, Inc., had signed the articles of incorporation of Trans Magic Airlines Corporation and had also become a minority stockholder in the new corporation. His participation in the change of business form of the two business entities estops Lee, as guarantor, from using the cloak of the new corporate entity to deny liability to Mountain States Telephone under the continuing guarantee contract. Estoppel is a bar by which a party is precluded from denying a fact in consequence of his own previous action which has led another party to conduct himself in such a way that the other party would suffer. Lee had actual knowledge of the true facts surrounding the change in business entity, and by failing as guarantor to notify Mountain States Telephone, he in effect concealed a material fact from Mountain States.

* * * * *

As guarantor, Lee should have withdrawn from his guarantee obligation or notified Mountain States of the change of status in Trans Magic Airlines. Since Lee failed to do either of these things until October of 1971, he is liable for the guaranteed debts of "Trans Magic Airlines" which accrued until that time.

Problem Cases

1. Davran accepted delivery of aluminum extrusions from U.S. Extrusion and agreed to fabricate 1,500 finished products and to return both the finished products and the leftover scrap to U.S. Extrusion. Davran had completed and returned 1,127 units on which a charge of $1,608 was due for work performed. Some $2,021 worth of scrap and extrusions remained with Davran. Does Davran have an artisan's lien on the material left in his possession?

2. Maxwell owned the timber on a certain tract of land. He hired Fitzgerald to cut the timber into logs and to put the logs in Maxwell's Mill pond. Fitzgerald had the logs cut and put on the back of the mill pond where they were levied on by a judgment creditor of Maxwell's. Fitzgerald claimed a common law lien on the logs for his labor in cutting and hauling them. Is Fitzgerald entitled to a common law lien on the logs?

3. Bender entered into a contract of guarantee with Richmond Co. whereby Bender guaranteed payment of all obligations owing by Midwest to Richmond Co. The contract provided that "The liability hereby assumed shall not be affected by any forbearance by you, or by the giving of any extension of time or by the acceptance of any settlement or composition offered by Midwest either in liquidation, readjustment, receivership, bankruptcy, or otherwise." It also contained a waiver of notice of default and a promise to pay any bill or bills by Midwest "without question."

   During the period from April 18, 1947, to November 30, 1949, Midwest became indebted to Richmond Co. in the amount of $5,031.03. Thereafter on April 16, 1951, Richmond Co. signed a document entitled "Release pursuant to a general assignment for the benefit of creditors" entered into by Midwest. By this document Richmond Co. agreed to "accept its pro rata and proportionate dividend, if any, under said assignment as an accord and satisfaction of and release, discharge and acquittance of any and all claims and demands, obligations, and liabilities existing in favor of Richmond Co."

   Under the composition agreement Richmond Co. received a dividend of $321.99, leaving a balance of $4,709.04. Richmond Co. sued Bender on the guarantee contract to recover this unpaid balance. Bender claims that since the principal was discharged under the composition the surety is discharged. Was the surety discharged?

chapter 42

Security Interests in Personal Property

Introduction

Security Interests under Article 9 of U.C.C. Today a large portion of our economy involves the extension of credit with the creditor taking a security interest in personal property of the debtor in order to protect his investment. The law pertaining to security interests in personal property has been codified in Article 9 of the Uniform Commercial Code—Secured Transactions. Article 9 applies to situations frequently encountered by consumers and businessmen: for example, the financing of an automobile, the purchase of an appliance on a time-payment plan, or the financing of inventory or business equipment. If the extender of credit wants to retain or attain an interest in the personal property of the debtor to assure the payment of the debt, and wants to be sure that his interest in that personal property will be superior to the claims of other creditors, he must carefully comply with the provisions of Article 9. In the Sales chapters it was pointed out that businessmen often leave out terms in a contract or insert vague terms to be worked out later by mutual agreement of the parties. Such looseness is a luxury that cannot be tolerated when it comes to secured transactions. If a debtor gets into financial difficulties and is unable to meet his financial obligations, it is extremely important from the creditor's standpoint that he have carefully complied with the provisions of Article 9. Even a relatively minor noncompliance can result in the creditor losing his preferred position and finding himself in the same position as an unsecured creditor with little chance of recouping what is owed to him.

Security Interests. Basic to a discussion of secured transactions is the term "security interest" which is broadly defined by the Code to mean "an interest in personal property or fixtures which secures payment or performance of an obligation." [1–201(37.)][1] While it is normal to think of various types of goods

---

[1] The numbers in the parentheses refer to the sections of the Uniform Commercial Code, 1962.

as being used for collateral, the Code actually covers secured interests in a much broader grouping of personal property. The Code breaks personal property down into a number of different classifications which are of importance in determining how a creditor goes about getting an enforceable security interest in a particular type of collateral. These Code classifications are:

1. *Instruments.*   This category includes checks, notes, drafts, stocks, bonds, and other investment securities.
2. *Documents of Title.*   This category includes bills of lading, dock warrants, dock receipts, and warehouse receipts.
3. *Accounts Receivable.*   This category includes rights to payment for goods sold or leased or for services rendered that are not evidenced by instruments or chattel paper but rather are carried on open account.
4. *Contract Rights.*   This category includes rights to payment under a contract which have not yet been earned by performance and which are not evidenced by an instrument or chattel paper.
5. *Chattel Paper.*   This category refers to writings that evidence both a monetary obligation and a security interest in specific goods and includes what is often referred to as a conditional sales contract.
6. *General Intangibles.*   This is a catchall category which includes, among other things, patents, copyrights, literary royalty rights, and franchises.
7. *Goods.*   Goods are divided into several classes; the same item of collateral may fall into different classes at different times, depending on its use.
   a.   *Consumer Goods.*   Goods used or bought for use primarily for personal, family or household use such as automobiles, furniture, and appliances.
   b.   *Equipment.*   Goods used or bought for use primarily in business, including farming or a profession.
   c.   *Farm Products.*   Crops, livestock or supplies used or produced in farming operations as long as they are still in the possession of a debtor engaged in farming.
   d.   *Inventory.*   Goods held for sale or lease or to be used under contracts of service as well as raw materials, work in process, or materials used or consumed in a business.
   e.   *Fixtures.*   Goods which will be so affixed to real property so as to be considered a part of the real property.

Obtaining an Enforceable Security Interest.   Once a creditor determines that the particular collateral offered by a debtor is included within the coverage of the Code, the creditor's next task is to secure a security interest that will be enforceable against the debtor, other creditors of the debtor, and, in some cases, purchasers of the collateral from the debtor. In general, the obtaining of an enforceable security interest is a two-step process consisting of attachment and perfection.

Summary

A security interest is an interest in personal property or fixtures which secures payment or performance of an obligation. The Code sets out rules for obtaining secured interests in instruments, documents of title, accounts receivable, contract rights, chattel paper, general intangibles, and goods. Goods may be consumer goods, equipment, inventory, farm products, or fixtures. To obtain the maximum protection for his security interest the creditor must attach and perfect his security interest.

Attachment of the Security Interest

A security interest is not legally enforceable against the debtor and his property until it attaches to the collateral. In order that it attach there must be an agreement between the debtor and the secured party that it attach, value must be given to the debtor (unless there is a debt there can be no secured interest), and the debtor must have rights in the collateral. (9–204.)

The Security Agreement. As a general rule, the secured party will require that the agreement whereby the debtor grants him a secured interest in the collateral be in writing and signed by the debtor. Such a written agreement is required in all cases except where the collateral is in the possession of the secured party. (9–203.) The security agreement must describe the collateral with reasonable certainty so as to enable it to be identified.

The security agreement usually goes on to spell out the terms of the arrangement between the parties. Thus it will normally contain a promise by the debtor to pay certain amounts of money in a certain way or to perform other obligations and will specify what events will constitute a default. In addition it may contain provisions the secured party deems necessary to protect his interest in the collateral such as requiring the debtor to procure insurance or to periodically report sales of secured inventory goods.

SAMPLE SECURITY AGREEMENT

Mr. and Mrs.
Mrs.
BUYER Miss_____

	Account No.

ADDRESS _____
CITY _____ TEL. NO. _____

	Date

DELIVER TO: _____

SECURITY AGREEMENT
(NAME OF SELLER)

THIS AGREEMENT, executed between (name of Seller), as Secured Party ("Seller"), and Buyer named above, as Debtor ("Buyer"):

Seller agrees to sell and Buyer agrees to purchase, subject to the terms, conditions and agreements herein stated, the goods described below (hereinafter referred to as the "Collateral"), Seller reserving and Buyer granting a purchase money security interest in the Collateral to secure the payment of the balance owed (Item 7) and all other present and future obligations of Buyer to Seller.

DESCRIPTION OF COLLATERAL				TERMS	
Quan.	Article	Unit Price	Total		
				(1) Cash Price	
				(2) Down Payment	
				Trade-in	
				Unpaid Principal (3) Balance Owed	
				(4) Finance Charge	
				Time Balance (5) Owed	
				(6) Sales Tax	
				(7) Balance Owed	

Buyer agrees to pay Seller, without relief from valuation and appraisement laws, the balance owed (Item 7) of $_____ in _____ successive weekly/monthly installments of $_____ each and a final installment of $_____, commencing on _____ ____, 19__, and continuing thereafter on the same day of each week/month, until paid, together with all delinquent charges, costs of repossession, collection, disposition, maintenance and other like charges, allowed by law, and reasonable attorneys' fees.

This sale is made subject to the terms, conditions and agreements stated above and on the reverse side hereof. Buyer hereby represents that the correct name and address of Buyer is as stated above, and that all statements made by Buyer as to financial condition and credit information are true.

Buyer hereby acknowledges delivery by Seller to Buyer of a copy of this agreement.

Buyer warrants and represents that the Collateral will be kept at Buyer's address unless otherwise specified as follows: _____ _____; and will be used or is purchased for use primarily for: (check one) family or household purposes ☐; business use ☐; farming operations ☐. The Collateral will not be affixed to real estate unless checked here ☐. If the Collateral is to be affixed to real estate, a description of the real estate is as follows: _____ _____ _____

and the name of the record owner is _____ _____.

IN WITNESS WHEREOF, the parties hereto have executed this agreement on this _____ day of _____, 19__.

BUYER'S SIGNATURE   (NAME OF SELLER) Seller, (as Secured
                                                                                 Party), Seller's address

_____ By _____
        (as Debtor)

TERMS, CONDITIONS AND AGREEMENTS

1. The security interest of Seller shall extend to all replacements, proceeds (including tort claims and insurance), and accessories, and shall continue until full performance by Buyer of all conditions and obligations hereunder.

2. Buyer shall maintain the Collateral in good repair, pay all taxes and other charges levied upon the Collateral when due, and shall defend the Collateral against any claims. Buyer shall not permit the Collateral to be removed from the place where kept without the prior written consent of Seller. Buyer shall give prompt written notice to Seller of any transfer, pledge, assignment, or any other process or action taken or pending, voluntary or involuntary, whereby a third party is to obtain or is attempting to obtain possession of or any interest in the Collateral. Seller shall have the right to inspect the Collateral at all reasonable times. At its option, but without obligation to Buyer and without relieving Buyer from any default, Seller may discharge any taxes, liens or other emcumbrances levied or placed upon the Collateral for which Buyer agrees to reimburse Seller upon demand.

3. If the Collateral is damaged or destroyed in any manner, the entire balance remaining unpaid under this agreement (hereinafter referred to as the "Agreement Balance") shall immediately become due and payable and Buyer shall first apply any insurance or other receipts compensating for such loss to the Agreement Balance. Buyer shall fully insure the Collateral, for the benefit of both Seller and Buyer, against loss by fire, theft and other casualties by comprehensive extended coverage insurance in an amount equal to the balance owed hereunder.

4. Buyer shall pay all amounts payable hereunder when due at the store of Seller from which this sale is made or at Seller's principal office in _____, Indiana, and upon default shall pay the maximum delinquent charges permitted by law. Upon prepayment of the Agreement Balance, Seller shall allow the minimum discount permitted by law.

5. Time is of the essence of this agreement. Buyer agrees that the following shall constitute an event of default under this Security Agreement: (a) the failure of Buyer to perform any condition or obligation contained herein; (b) when any statement, representation or warranty made herein by Buyer shall be found to have been untrue in any material respect when made; or (c) if Seller in good faith believes that the prospect of payment or performance is impaired. Upon a default, Seller, at its option and without notice or demand to Buyer, shall be entitled to declare the Agreement Balance immediately due and payable, take immediate possession of the Collateral and enter the premises at which the Collateral is located for such purpose or to render the Collateral unusable. Upon request, Buyer shall assemble and make the Collateral available to Seller at a place to be designated by Seller which is reasonably convenient to both parties. Upon repossession, Seller may retain or dispose of any or all of the Collateral in the manner prescribed by the Indiana Uniform Commercial Code and the proceeds of any such disposition shall be first applied in the following order: (a) to the reasonable expenses of retaking, holding, preparing for sale, selling and the like; (b) to the reasonable attorneys' fees and legal expenses incurred by Seller; and (c) to the satisfaction of the indebtedness secured by this security interest. Buyer covenants to release and hold harmless Seller from any and all claims arising out of the repossession of the Collateral. No waiver of any default or any failure or delay to exercise any right or remedy by Seller shall operate as a waiver of any other default or of the same default in the future or as a waiver of any right or remedy with respect to the same or any other occurrence.

6. All rights and remedies of Seller herein specified are cumulative and are in addition to, and shall not exclude, any rights and remedies Seller may have by law.

7. Seller shall not be liable for any damages, including special or consequential damages, for failure to deliver the Collateral or for any delay in delivery of the Collateral to Buyer.

8. Buyer agrees that Seller may carry this agreement, together with any other agreements and accounts, with Buyer in one account upon its records and unless otherwise instructed in writing by Buyer, any payment of less than all amounts then due on all agreements and accounts shall be applied to any accrued delinquent charges, costs of collection and maintenance, and to the balances owing under all agreements or accounts in such order as Seller in its discretion shall determine.

9. Buyer authorizes Seller to execute and file financing statements signed only by Seller covering the Collateral described.

10. Any notice required by this agreement shall be deemed sufficient when mailed to Seller (state Seller's address), or to Buyer at the address at which the Collateral is kept.

11. Buyer shall have the benefit of manufacturers' warranties, if any; however, Seller makes no express warranties (except a warranty of title) and no implied warranties, including any warranty of MERCHANTABILITY or FITNESS. Buyer agrees that there are no promises or agreements between the parties not contained herein. Any modification or rescission of this agreement shall be ineffective unless in writing and signed by both Seller and Buyer.

(Name of Retailer)

Future Advances.   Under the provisions of the Code a security agreement may include a provision covering future advances. (9–204.) Future advances are extensions of credit to be made at some later date by the creditor.

After-Acquired Property.   Under the provisions of the Code a security interest in after-acquired property (future, as opposed to existing assets of the debtor) may be created by a properly worded security agreement. However, the security interest in the after-acquired property cannot attach until the debtor acquires an interest in the collateral. (9–204 [2].) A security interest in after-acquired property may be defeated if the debtor acquires some or all of his new property subject to a purchase money security agreement. Also, the rights of the secured party to property acquired by the debtor within four months of the adjudication of the debtor as a bankrupt are uncertain. Amendment of the Federal Bankruptcy Act is needed to clarify the rights of the secured party to after-acquired property in the event the debtor is adjudged bankrupt.

Proceeds.   The security agreement may provide that the security interest will cover not only the collateral described therein but will attach to the proceeds on the disposal of the collateral by the debtor. To create a security interest in proceeds all that is necessary is to add the word "proceeds" to the description of the collateral in the security agreement. Under the 1972 proposed amendments to Article 9, proceeds would automatically be covered unless the security agreement specifically excluded them. (Revised 9–203 [3].)[2]

The rights of the secured party in proceeds are set out in detail in Section 9–306 of the Code. If the security interest in the collateral is perfected, it continues, as a general rule, in any identifiable proceeds. If the original security agreement does not include proceeds, the secured party has 10 days in which to perfect his security interest in the proceeds. If the debtor becomes insolvent, the secured party with a perfected security interest in proceeds may claim cash proceeds (money, checks and the like) received by the debtor within 10 days of the insolvency subject to the limitations set out in Section 9–306 (4) (*b*), (*c*), (*d*). Subsection 5 of Section 9–306 sets out the rights of the secured party in collateral sold by the debtor and returned to him.

---

[2] In 1972 the National Conference of Commissioners on Uniform State Laws proposed a number of amendments to Article 9 based on the experience with the law over the past decade. The proposed amendments must be adopted by the state legislatures before they become law in any given state. The first state to adopt the new amendments was Illinois which made them effective July 1, 1973.

Assignment. Sales contracts and security agreements for the purchase of consumer goods commonly include a provision that the buyer will not assert against an assignee any claim or defense he may have against the seller. Any buyer who as part of his purchase transaction signs both a negotiable instrument and a security agreement is deemed as a matter of law to have waived such defenses. (9–206 [1].)

Such a waiver clause makes it easier for the retailer to assign his sales contracts/security agreements to a financing institution since the financing institution then knows it can collect from the buyer without being subject to claims and defenses the buyer might have against the retailer. Under the Code, an express or implied waiver is generally valid and enforceable by an assignee who takes his assignment for value, in good faith, and without notice of a claim or defense. (9–206 [1].) There are two exceptions to this rule: (1) the waiver does not hold true as to any type of defense which could be asserted against the holder in due course of negotiable instruments under Article 3, Commercial Paper; (2) the waiver is not effective if a statute or court decision establishes a different rule for buyers of consumer goods. (9–206 [1].)

The waiver of defenses provision in the Code is the subject of complaint by some consumer-oriented groups who argue that it serves to shield unscrupulous retailers and financing institutions that work in concert with them from the legitimate complaints and claims of consumers. The controversy on this issue parallels the controversy on the rights of a holder in due course of a negotiable instrument.

Summary

A security interest is not enforceable until it has been attached to the collateral. To effect this attachment there must be an agreement between the debtor and the secured party that the security interest attach, value must be given to the debtor, and the debtor must have rights in the collateral. A security agreement may cover future advances to be made by the creditor to the debtor. A security agreement may create a security interest in proceeds of the collateral and in after-acquired property of the debtor.

In re Shelton
Gassaway v. Erwin

11 U.C.C. Rep. 1239 (8th Cir. 1973)

This was a turnover petition filed by Gassaway, the Trustee in Bankruptcy, against Ray Erwin, the record lienholder of a 1969 Pontiac, and Robert Shelton, the bankrupt titleholder of the Pontiac, to recover title and possession of the Pontiac automobile. The Referee in Bankruptcy held that Erwin had not complied with UCC 9–203 (1)(b) and thus did not have an enforceable security interest in the automobile. Accordingly, the Referee sustained the Trustee's petition to turn title and possession over to the Trustee. The District Court reversed the decision of the Referee, holding that the original bill of sale between Erwin and Shelton satisfied the Code requirement of a written security agreement. On appeal, the Eighth Circuit Court of Appeals reversed the District Court, holding that while Erwin and Shelton had intended to create a security interest, they had not made the requisite security agreement.

The facts are given in the opinion.

STEPHENSON, CIRCUIT JUDGE.   The question before us in this case is whether a security interest on an automobile was established pursuant to VAMS § 400.9–203 (1)(b) (Uniform Commercial Code § 9–203 (1)(b)).

On August 12, 1970 the bankrupt, Robert Charles Shelton, purchased a 1969 Pontiac from appellee, Raymond Erwin. On that date bankrupt and Erwin executed a bill of sale on the billing stationery of "Ray Erwin Welder Sales." This voucher describes the automobile, sets out the terms of payment and provides that bankrupt shall insure the automobile until he has paid for it in full. Also on August 12, 1970, bankrupt filed an application for Missouri Title showing Erwin as the holder of the first lien and bankrupt as owner. On September 1, 1970 the State of Missouri issued a Certificate of Title showing bankrupt to be the owner of the Pontiac and Erwin the holder of the first lien.

*   *   *   *   *

Appellee Erwin contends that either the bill of sale or the title application or both taken together satisfy the minimal requirements of VAMS § 400.9–203 (1)(b). The necessary requirements of Section 400.9–203 (1)(b) are (1) debtor's signature (2) a "security agreement" and (3) description of the collateral. It is number (2)—the security agreement requirement which is fatal to Erwin. We must look to the Uniform Commercial Code (hereinafter Code) to determine its meaning. In the Code, § 1–201 (3) we find that "agreement" means "the bargain of the parties in fact as found in their language." Section 9–105 (1)(b) defines "security agreement" as "an agreement which creates or provides a security interest." Although no precise words are required in the Code, the definitions given indicate that there must be some language in the agreement actually conveying a security interest. We fail to find such language in the bill of sale or the title application before us. The notation on the title application that a lien in Erwin's favor existed is not sufficient. . . . The Referee found that the title application and subsequent Certificate of Title showing Erwin as lienholder were at best *financing statements.* We agree, as Erwin contends, that these were sufficient to perfect a security interest, if one existed pursuant to the requirements of VAMS § 301.600 (requirements of perfection of liens on automobiles). *In re Jackson. But no interest* existed to be perfected. [Emphasis added.] Although a financing statement conceivably could create a security interest they usually do not contain the necessary grant of an interest § 9–203 (1)(b) requires. . . . The financing statement is merely evidence of the creation of a security interest, not the agreement itself. . . .

Since the Code is not ambiguous on the requirements of the creation of an enforceable security interest, there is no reason to relax those requirements. Although the Code should be liberally construed, UCC § 1–102 (1), the doctrine of equitable mortgages is no longer necessary or useful in a commercial transaction since Article Nine reduces formal requisites to a minimum.

Perfecting the Security Interest

Along with the attachment of the security interest, the secured party is also concerned with obtaining the maximum protection available for the type of collateral involved. This protection against other creditors of the debtor and purchasers of the collateral is obtained through the process of perfecting the security interest. There are three main means of perfection under the Code:

1. *Public filing* of notice of the security interest;
2. The secured party's taking *possession* of the collateral;
3. Perfection by mere *attachment* of the security interest in certain special situations or for certain limited times.

Public Filing. By far the most common method of perfecting a security interest is by filing a financing statement in a public office which then serves as constructive notice to the world that the secured party claims a security interest in collateral belonging to a certain named debtor. The financing statement will usually consist of a multicopy form available from the secretary of state's office although the security agreement may be filed as a financial statement if it contains the required items of information.

The financing statement, to be sufficient, must be signed by the debtor and the secured party, must give an address of the secured party from which information concerning the security interest may be obtained, must give a mailing address of the debtor, and must contain a statement indicating the types or describing the items of collateral. If the financing statement covers crops growing or to be grown or goods which are to become fixtures, the statement must also contain a description of the real estate concerned. (9–402.) The financing statement may be broad in its scope and include all of the debtor's personal property, accounts, contract rights and chattel paper which he owns at the time of its execution or may acquire in the future or it may include a class of property or a few items, or a single item of property.

The requirement as to the place of filing the financing statement is determined by the statutes of the individual state. In all states a security interest in fixtures must be filed in the office where a mortgage on the real estate concerned would be filed or recorded. (9–401 [1] [a].) The secured party acquiring a security interest in property which is a fixture or is to become a fixture, should, in order to obtain maximum security, double file, that is, file as a fixture and as a nonfixture.

UNIFORM COMMERCIAL CODE   **STATE OF INDIANA**   FORM UCC-1
                                          FINANCING STATEMENT

INSTRUCTIONS
1. Please type this form. Fold only along perforation for mailing.
2. Remove Secured Party and Debtor copies and send other three copies with interleaved carbon paper to the filing officer. Enclose filing fee of $1.00 (plus $ .50 if collateral is or to become a fixture).
3. When filing is to be with more than one office, Form UCC-2 may be placed over this set to avoid double typing.
4. If the space provided for any item(s) is inadequate, the item(s) may be continued on additional sheets, preferably 5"x 8" or sizes convenient to secured party in case of long schedules, indentures, etc. Only one sheet is required. Extra names of debtors may be continued below box "1" in space for description of property.
5. If the collateral is crops or goods which are or are to become fixtures, describe the goods and also the real estate with the name of the record owner if he is other than the debtor.
6. Persons filing a security agreement (as distinguished from a financing statement) are urged to complete this form with or without signature and send with security agreement.
7. If collateral is goods which are or are to become fixtures, use Form UCC-1a over this Form to avoid double typing, and enclose regular fee plus $ .50.
8. The filing officer will return the third page of this Form as an acknowledgment. Secured party at a later time may use third page as a Termination Statement by dating and signing the termination legend on that page.

This Financing Statement is presented to Filing Officer for filing pursuant to the UCC: | 3 Maturity Date (if any):

1 Debtor(s) (Last Name First) and Address(es) | 2 Secured Party(ies) and Address(es) | For Filing Officer (Date, Time, Number, and Filing Office)

4 This financing statement covers the following types (or items) of property (also describe realty where collateral is crops or fixtures):

Assignee of Secured Party | This statement is filed without the debtor's signature to perfect a security interest in collateral (check ☒ if so)
                                 | ☐ under a security agreement signed by debtor authorizing secured party to file this statement, or
                                 | ☐ already subject to a security interest in another jurisdiction when it was brought into this state, or
                                 | ☐ which is proceeds of the following described original collateral which was perfected:

Check ☒ if covered: ☐ Proceeds of Collateral are also covered.   ☐ Products of Collateral are also covered. No. of additional Sheets presented:

Filed with: ☐ Secretary of State   ☐ Recorder of_____ County

By:_____   By:_____
        Signature(s) of Debtor(s)   Signature(s) of Secured Party(ies)

(1) Filing Officer Copy—Alphabetical   Approved by: *Charles O. Hendricks*
FORM UCC-1—INDIANA UNIFORM COMMERCIAL CODE   Secretary of State

---

In regard to collateral other than fixtures the state may require only central filing, usually in the office of the secretary of state. However, most states require local filing of those transactions which are local in nature, such as when the collateral is equipment used in farming operations, or is farm products, or accounts, contract rights or general intangibles arising from or relating to the sale of farm products by a farmer or consumer goods. (9–401.)

If no maturity date is stated in the financing statement or if the debt is payable on demand the filing is valid for five years. If a maturity date is stated in the financing statement the filing is valid for the stated period plus 60 days but for a period not to exceed 5 years. (9–403 [2].) This provision would be changed by the 1972 proposed amendments to Article 9 which would make financing statements effective for five years unless a continuation statement has been filed prior to the lapse.

A continuation statement may be filed within 6 months before and 60 days after a stated maturity date of 5 years or less, and otherwise within 6 months prior to the 5-year expiration date. The continuation statement must be signed by the secured party, identify the original statement by file number, and state that the original statement is still effective. Successive continuation statements may be filed. (9–403 [3].)

When all debts and obligations of the debtor secured by a financing statement are completely fulfilled he is entitled to a termination statement signed by the secured party or an assignee of record. Failure to furnish a termination statement after proper demand subjects the affected secured party to a fine of $100 plus damages for any loss caused to the debtor by such failure. (9–404.)

Possession by the Secured Party as Public Notice. Secret liens have been suspect from the earliest times, and in the United States the validity of a lien on personal property left in the possession of the debtor was questionable. The holding of the courts led to the enactment of filing or recording statutes whereby public notice of the lien was given, thereby removing the stigma of a secret lien from the transaction. From the beginning the courts upheld the validity of the lien against the creditors of the debtor if the collateral was delivered to the lender or one who held possession for him.

Under the Code, change of possession of the collateral perfects the security interest of the secured party. (9–302 [1] [a].) Except for the 21-day temporary perfection permitted by 9–304 (4) and (5), possession by the secured party is the only means of perfecting a security interest in instruments. Possession is an alternative and often the most satisfactory means of perfecting a security interest in chattel paper and negotiable documents of title.

Possession is also a possible means for perfecting a security interest in inventory. This is sometimes done through a field warehousing arrangement whereby part of the debtor's inventory is fenced off and withdrawals from it permitted only on the approval of the secured party or his on-the-scene representative.

Possession is usually not a practical means for perfecting a security interest in equipment, farm products, and consumer goods and, of course, is not possible at all with accounts receivable, contract rights or general intangibles.

The person to whom the collateral is delivered holds it as bailee and, as was the law under the pre-Code pledge, he owes the duties of a bailee to the parties in interest. (9–207.)

Perfection by Attachment. Perfection by mere attachment of the security interest, sometimes known as automatic perfection, is the only form of perfection that occurs without the giving of public notice. It occurs automatically when all the requirements of attachment are complete. This form of perfection is limited to certain classes of collateral and in addition may be only a temporary perfection in some situations.

Permanent perfection by attachment of the security interest alone is valid only with respect to purchase money security interests (see 9–107) in consumer goods or in farm equipment having a purchase price not in excess of $2,500. Thus, the retailer who sells a television set on a conditional sales contract to a consumer does not have to file a financing statement but is considered to have perfected his security interest just by virtue of its attachment to the television set now in the hands of the consumer.

There are, however, several important exceptions to this permanent perfection by attachment principle. First, it does not apply to those consumer goods which are or will become fixtures or to motor vehicles if they are required to have a certificate of title under state law. (9–302.) Second, although the retailer who relies on attachment for perfection of his security interest in consumer goods will prevail against other creditors of the debtor, he will not prevail over a buyer from the debtor if the buyer buys the collateral without knowledge of the security interest, for value, and for his own personal, family, or household use. To be protected against such a purchaser from the debtor, the secured party must file a financing statement rather than relying on attachment for perfection. (9–307 [2].)

Temporary perfection without filing or possession is automatically obtained for 21 days after attachment of the security interest in instruments and negotiable documents. (9–304.) To get protection beyond the 21-day period, the secured party must perfect by filing or possession. However, during the 21-day period of temporary perfection, any holder in due course of commercial paper or bona fide purchaser of a security or negotiated document will prevail over the secured party relying on temporary perfection. (9–309.)

Summary

To protect his security interest against other creditors of the debtor and purchasers of the collateral, the secured party must perfect his security interest. Under the Code there are three means of perfection: public filing of a financing statement; the secured party's taking possession of the collateral; and, in some limited cases, mere attachment of the security interest.

A financing statement is filed at either the secretary of state's office or the local recorder's office, depending on the type of collateral it secures. If no maturity date is stated, the filing is good for five years and may be extended for additional five-year periods by filing a continuation statement. A debtor who has fulfilled his obligations is entitled to a termination statement which removes the financing statement from the records.

Industrial Packaging Products Co. v. Fort Pitt Packaging International, Inc.

161 A.2d 19 (Sup. Ct. Pa. 1960)

This was a petition of Robert Mellin, receiver of Fort Pitt Packaging International, Inc. (plaintiff), against Industrial Packaging Products Co. (defendant) to show cause why an assignment made to Industrial Packaging Products Co. should not be declared null and void. The court held that the assignment was valid and Mellin appealed. Judgment affirmed.

JONES, JUSTICE. The Provident Trust Company of Pittsburgh, pursuant to Sec. 9–403 of the Uniform Commercial Code filed the following financing statement in the office of the Prothonotary of Allegheny County on August 18, 1955:

15110 of 1955
Financing Statement

This financing statement is presented to a filing officer for filing pursuant to the Uniform Commercial Code.

1. Debtor (or assignor)—Fort Pitt Packaging Co., Inc., 5615 Butler Street, Pittsburgh 1, Pa.
2. Secured Party (or assignee)—Provident Trust Co., 900 East Ohio St., Pittsburgh 1, Pa.
3. Maturity date of obligation ————.
4. The financing statement covers the following types of property: All present and future accounts receivable submitted.

Fort Pitt Packaging Co., Inc.
Leo A. Levy, Treas.
Provident Trust Company
A. W. Charlton
Executive Vice-Pres.

Under Sec. 9–403 of the Code such a statement remains effective for a period of five years. On August 19, 1955, Provident Trust Company filed a similar statement in the office of the Secretary of the Commonwealth in Harrisburg.

On February 4, 1957, Fort Pitt Packaging International, Inc., entered into a written contract with the United States Government for the maintenance, repair and overhaul of vehicles. On March 26, 1957, Fort Pitt entered into a contract with Empire Commercial Corporation wherein Empire agreed to lend Fort Pitt $140,000 and Fort Pitt agreed to assign to the Provident Trust Company as Empire's agent its contract with the United States Government and any and all payments due or to become due thereunder. On the same day, March 26, Fort Pitt sold and assigned to the Provident Trust Company, the payments due or which may become due under the governmental contract. Notice of the assignment was given to the Contracting Officer of the Department of the Army.

One year later, on March 27, 1958, Fort Pitt was placed in receivership and on May 27, 1958, upon petition of creditors (Industrial was a creditor), Robert Mellin, Esquire, was appointed receiver. On June 10, 1958, the said receiver petitioned the Court of Common Pleas of Allegheny County for a rule upon Empire to show cause why the assignments of the proceeds for Fort Pitt's services performed under the government contracts should not be declared null, void and ineffective as against the receiver. After hearing held and argument, the court below dismissed the receiver's petition. From that order this appeal was taken.

Mellin contends that the filing of the financing statement in 1955 was not sufficient to secure the amounts due under Fort Pitt's contract with the United States Government which was executed in 1957. The filing of the financing statement pursuant to

Sec. 9–403 was entirely proper. The Uniform Commercial Code does not require that the secured party as listed in such statement be a principal creditor and not an agent. The purpose of filing this financing statement is to give notice to potential future creditors of the debtor or purchasers of the collateral. It makes no difference as far as such notice is concerned whether the secured party listed in the filing statement is a principal or an agent, and no provision in the Uniform Commercial Code draws such a distinction.

The financing statement covered "all present and future accounts receivable submitted." Section 9–110 of the Uniform Commercial Code provides that "for the purposes of this Article any description is sufficient whether or not it is specific if it reasonably identifies the thing described." There is no doubt that the description in the financing statement reasonably identifies the collateral security. It is difficult under the circumstances to imagine how the description could be more complete without filing new and amended descriptions each time a new account receivable falls within the purview of the financing statement. Nowhere in the Uniform Commercial Code is such a requirement set forth.

Section 9–204 (3) provides that "except as provided in subsection (4) [which deals with crops and consumer goods] *a security agreement may provide that collateral, whenever acquired, shall secure any* advances made or other *value given at any time* pursuant to the security agreement."

In the 1957 agreement between Fort Pitt and Empire, Fort Pitt agreed to assign to Provident Trust Company all payments to be received as they became due from the United States Government under Fort Pitt's contract on February 4, 1957 with the Government. These amounts due fell within the clause "future accounts receivable submitted" contained in the 1955 financing statement filed by Provident Trust Company. Comment 2 to Sec. 9–303 of the Code states that the "secured party is entitled to have his security interest recognized in insolvency proceedings instituted against the debtor." Therefore, the interest of the secured party, Provident Trust Company, is superior to that of the receiver in bankruptcy and any funds which have been placed in the hands of Provident Trust Company pursuant to the assignment by Fort Pitt need not be turned over to the receiver. These funds are properly being held by the Provident Trust Company for the benefit of its principal, Empire Commercial Corporation.

In re Midas Coin Co., Inc.
264 F.Supp. 193 (D.C. Mo. 1967)

This was a bankruptcy proceeding against the Midas Coin Company. St. John's Community Bank filed a petition to foreclose a collateral note which the Bankruptcy Trustee opposed on the grounds the bank had not filed a financing statement and was required to do so in order to protect its security interest. The Bankruptcy Referee refused to allow the foreclosure petition and St. John's Community Bank appealed. Reversed on appeal with directions to approve the foreclosure petition.

Midas Coin was in the business of buying and selling coins and stamps for profit. On January 14, 1966, Midas executed a promissory note to St. John's Bank for $9,637.58 and pledged as collateral security coins from its inventory having a face value of $9,750.50. The security agreement provided that the collateral was to secure payment of all other liabilities owed to St. John's Bank as well as the note. At the date of bankruptcy, February 7, 1966, St. John's Bank had coins of a face value of $6,432.50 in its possession and was owed some $9,700 by Midas Coin. St. John's Bank claimed it had a perfected security interest in the coins and the trustee claimed that the security interest was unperfected because no financing statement had been filed.

REGAN, DISTRICT JUDGE.   The Referee held that the instant transaction was governed by Article 9 of the Code which pertains to secured transactions. Section 9–102 provides that except as otherwise provided in two designated sections not here involved, Article 9 applies to any transaction which is intended to create a security interest in personal property, "including goods, documents, instruments, general intangibles, chattel paper, accounts or contract rights."

Section 9–302 (1) (a) of Article 9 provides that a financing statement must be filed to perfect all security interests, except a security interest in collateral in possession of the secured party under § 9–305. The latter section authorizes the secured party to perfect a security interest in goods, instruments, negotiable documents or chattel paper (as well as letters of credit and advices of credit) by taking possession of the collateral. It is the Bank's position that having taken possession of the collateral, its security interest has thereby been perfected, so that no financing statement was required to be filed.

The trustee contends, and the Referee held, that § 9–305 is not here applicable, upon the theory that coins are money, and that since money is not one of the kinds of property enumerated in that section, the only method of perfecting a security interest therein is by filing a financing statement.

The trustee does not suggest any possible legislative purpose which would be served by differentiating between the transfer of physical possession of coins (or other money of numismatic value) and any other tangible personal property susceptible to such physical possession. If the coins in question are excluded as subject to pledge simply because they fit the statutory definition of "money," in spite of the fact they constitute part of inventory and in any realistic sense are a commodity, the result would be that without any rhyme or reason they would be the only species of tangible personal property in which a security interest could not be perfected without filing a financing statement. We do not believe such was the legislative intent.

Money as such does not customarily serve as commercial collateral. The coins are so in this case solely because of the numismatic value. We hold, therefore, that the coins which were pledged to the Bank under the security agreement constitute "goods," and therefore, the Bank was not required to file a financing statement in order to perfect its security interest.

In re Nicolosi

4 U.C.C. Rep. 111 (S.D. Ohio 1966)

A trustee in bankruptcy filed a petition to sell a diamond ring in his possession free of liens. Rike-Kumber Company claimed it had enforceable lien on the ring. The court held that Rike-Kumber held a perfected security interest in the ring.

Nicolosi purchased the diamond ring from Rike-Kumber on July 7, 1964, as an engagement present for his fiancée. He executed a purchase money security agreement that was not filed; nor was any financing statement filed.

ANDERSON, REFEREE.   If the diamond ring, purchased as an engagement ring by the bankrupt, cannot be categorized as consumer goods, and therefore exempted from the notice filing requirements of the Uniform Commercial Code as adopted in Ohio, a perfected security interest does not exist. See U.C.C. § 9–302.

No judicial precedents have been cited in the briefs.

Under the commercial code, collateral is divided into tangible, intangible, and documentary categories. Certainly, a diamond ring falls into the tangible category. The classes of tangible goods are distinguished by the primary use intended. Under U.C.C. § 9–109, the four classes are "consumer goods," "equipment," "farm products" and "inventory."

The difficulty is that the code provisions use terms arising in commercial circles which have different semantical values from legal precedents. Does the fact that the purchaser bought the goods as a special gift to another person signify that it was not for his own "personal, family or household purposes"? The trustee urges that these special facts control under the express provisions of the commercial code.

By a process of exclusion, a diamond engagement ring purchased for one's fiancée is not "equipment" bought or used in business, "farm products" used in farming operations, or "inventory" held for sale, lease or service contracts. When the bankrupt purchased the ring, therefore, it could only have been "consumer goods" bought for use "primarily for personal use." There could be no judicial purpose to create a special class of property in derogation of the statutory principles.

Another problem is implicit, although not covered by the briefs.

By the foregoing summary analysis, it is apparent that the diamond ring, when the interest of the bankrupt attached, was consumer goods since it could have been no other class of goods. Unless the fiancée had a special status under the code provision protecting a bona fide buyer, without knowledge, for value, of consumer goods, the failure to file a financing statement is not crucial. No evidence has been adduced pertinent to the scienter question.

Is a promise, as valid contractual consideration, included under the term "value"? In other words, was the ring given to his betrothed in consideration of marriage (promise for a promise)? If so, and "value" has been given, the transferee is a "buyer" under traditional concepts.

The Uniform Commercial Code definition of "value" (because of the code purpose of being so broad as to not derogate from the ideal ubiquitous secured creditor), very definitely covers a promise for a promise. The definition reads that "a person gives 'value' for rights if he acquires them . . . (4) generally, in return for any consideration sufficient to support a simple contract."

It would seem unrealistic, nevertheless, to apply contract law concepts historically developed into the law of marriage relations in the context of new concepts developed for uniform commercial practices. They are not, in reality, the same juristic manifold. The purpose of uniformity of the code should not be defeated by the obsessions of the code drafters to be all inclusive for secured creditors.

Even if the trustee, in behalf of the unsecured creditors, would feel inclined to insert love, romance and morals into commercial law, he is appearing in the wrong era, and possibly the wrong court.

Ordered, that the Rike-Kumber Company holds a perfected security interest in the diamond engagement ring, and the security interest attached to the proceeds realized from the sale of the goods by the trustee in bankruptcy.

Priorities

Because several secured parties may claim an interest in the same collateral of the debtor, the Code establishes a set of rules for determining which of the conflicting security interests has priority. If both security interests are perfected by filing, the first to be filed has priority, whether the security interest attached before or after filing (9–312 [5] [*a*]); if both have not been perfected by filing, the first to perfect has priority, regardless of which security interest attached first, and, in the case of a filed security interest, whether it attached before or after filing (9–312 [5] [*b*]); and, if neither has been perfected, then the first security interest to attach has priority. (9–312 [5] [*c*].)[3]

Thus, if Bank A filed a financing statement covering Retailer's inventory on February 1, 1969, and Bank B filed such a financing statement on March 1, 1969, covering that same inventory, Bank A would have priority over Bank B even though Bank B might have made its loan and attached its security interest to the inventory prior to the time Bank A did so. However, if Bank A neglected to perfect its security interest by filing and Bank B did perfect, then Bank B as the only perfected security interest in the inventory would prevail. And if both neglected to perfect their security interest, then the first security interest that attached would have priority. In connection with the last situation, it is important to note that unperfected secured creditors do not enjoy a preferred position in bankruptcy proceedings, thus giving additional impetus to the desirability of filing or otherwise perfecting a security interest.

To these general rules there are several very important exceptions which are best discussed in the context of hypothetical situations. First, assume that Bank A takes and perfects a security interest in all present and after-acquired inventory of Debtor. Then Debtor acquires some additional inventory from Wholesaler who retains a security interest in the inventory until Debtor pays for it

---

[3] Under the 1972 proposed amendments to Article 9, section 9–312 5 (*a*), (*b*), and (*c*) are revised to provide that priority between conflicting security interests in the same collateral is to be determined as follows:

    (*a*) Conflicting security interests rank according to priority in time of filing or perfection. Priority dates from the time a filing is first made covering the collateral or the time the security interest is first perfected, whichever is earlier, provided that there is no period thereafter when there is neither filing or perfection.

    (*b*) So long as conflicting security interests are unperfected, the first to attach has priority.

The amendments also add new subsections (6) and (7) dealing with priority where proceeds and future advances are involved.

and then Wholesaler perfects this security interest. Wholesaler has a purchase money security interest in inventory goods and will have priority over the prior secured creditor (Bank A) if Wholesaler has perfected the security interest by the time the collateral reaches the Debtor and if Wholesaler sends notice of his purchase money security interest to Bank A. (9–312 [3].)

Second, assume that Bank B takes and perfects a security interest in all the present and after-acquired equipment belonging to Debtor. Then Supplier sells some equipment to Debtor reserving a security interest in the equipment until it is paid for. If Supplier perfects the security interest by filing within 10 days of its attachment he will have priority over Bank B because a purchase money security interest in noninventory collateral prevails over a prior perfected security interest if the purchase money security interest is perfected within 10 days of its attachment. (9–312 [4].)

Finally, a buyer in the ordinary course of business other than a person buying farm products from a person engaged in farming operations takes free from a security interest created by his seller even though the security interest is perfected and even though the buyer knows of its existence. (9–307 [1].) In addition, certain liens arising by operation of law (such as artisan's liens) are given priority over a perfected security interest in the collateral. (9–310.)

Security Interest in Fixtures.   Special treatment for fixtures is provided for under the Code. A security interest which attaches to goods before they become a fixture and which has been perfected takes priority as to the goods over the claims of all persons who have an interest in the real estate.[4] A security interest in goods before they become fixtures where such security interest has attached but has not been perfected and a security interest in goods after they become fixtures do not take priority over a subsequent purchaser for value of an interest in the real estate; or over a creditor with a lien on the real estate subsequently obtained by judicial proceedings; or over a creditor with a prior encumbrance of record on the real estate to the extent he makes subsequent advances.

On default the secured party has the right to remove the collateral from the real estate but he must reimburse any encumbrancer or owner of the real estate who is not the debtor and who has not otherwise agreed for the costs of repairs of any physical injury to the real estate. (9–313 [8].)

National Cash Register Co. v. Firestone & Co., Inc.

191 N.E.2d 471 (Sup. Jud. Ct. Mass. 1963)

This was an action by National Cash Register Company (plaintiff) against Firestone & Co., Inc. (defendant), to recover a tort judgment for conversion of a cash register.

---

[4] In the proposed 1972 amendments to Article 9 the draftsmen define the term "fixture filing" (9–313 [1] [*b*]) and indicate that where such a filing is required it must be indexed in the real estate records in order to afford protection against certain realty interests. (9–403 [7].)

Judgment for National Cash Register Company and Firestone Co., Inc., appealed. Reversed.

On November 18, 1960, Firestone Co., Inc. (Firestone) made a loan to Edmund Carroll doing business as Kozy Kitchen. To secure the loan a security agreement was executed which listed the items of property included and concluded as follows: "together with all property and articles now, and which may hereafter be, used or mixed with, added or attached to, and/or substituted for any of the described property." A financing statement which included all of the items listed in the security agreement was filed with the town clerk on November 18, 1960, and with the Secretary of State on November 22, 1960. There was no reference to a cash register in either the security agreement or the financing statement and there was no after-acquired property provision in the financing statement. On November 25, 1960, National Cash Register Company (National) delivered a cash register to Carroll, on a conditional sales contract. National filed a financing statement on the cash register with the town clerk on December 20, and with the Secretary of State on December 21, 1960. Carroll defaulted in his payments to both Firestone and National. Firestone repossessed all of Carroll's fixtures and equipment covered by its security agreement, including the cash register and sold the same. National claimed that it was the title owner of the cash register and brought suit for its conversion.

WILKINS, CHIEF JUSTICE. Under the Uniform Commercial Code, after-acquired property, such as this cash register, might become subject to Firestone's security agreement when delivered, and likewise its delivery under a conditional sale agreement with retention of title in National would not, in and of itself, affect the rights of Firestone. Although National could have completely protected itself by perfecting its interest before or within ten days of the delivery of the cash register to Carroll, it did not try to do so until more than ten days after delivery. Thus the principal issue is whether Firestone's earlier security interest effectively covers the cash register.

The trial judge gave no reasons for his ruling. The Appellate Division rested its decision upon the mere statement of the omission of Firestone's financing statement to refer to after-acquired property or to the cash register specifically. The Massachusetts Commissioners on Uniform State Laws in their brief as *amici curiae* argue that there need be no reference to after-acquired property in the financing statement. Before we reach that question, however, we must consider several matters raised by National.

First, National argues that the debtor could not have intended to grant security interest to Firestone because the purchase was five months earlier, delivery was about to be made, and the cash register could be repossessed by National for default within the period of twenty-one months provided for instalment payments. It is also urged that, without the cash register, Firestone was well secured for its loan, a fact which cannot be inferred and which, in any event, would not be conclusive. The debtor's intent must be judged by the language of the security agreement.

In § 9–110, it is provided: "For the purposes of this Article any description of personal property or real estate is sufficient whether or not it is specific if it reasonably identifies what is described." In § 9–203 it is provided: (1) . . . . a security interest is not enforceable against the debtor or third parties unless . . . . (b) the debtor has signed a security agreement which contains a description of the collateral. . . ."

Contrary to National's contention, we are of opinion that the security agreement is broad enough to include the cash register, which concededly did not have to be specifically described. The agreement covers "All contents of luncheonette including equipment such as," which we think covers all those contents and does not mean "equipment, to wit." There is a reference to "all property and articles now, and which may hereafter be, used . . . with, [or] added . . . to . . . any of the foregoing described property." We infer that the cash register was used with some of the other equipment even though the case stated does not expressly state that the luncheonette was operated.

The framers of the Uniform Commercial Code, by adopting the "notice filing" system, had the purpose to recommend a method of protecting security interests which at the same time would give subsequent potential creditors and other interested persons information and procedures adequate to enable the ascertainment of the facts they needed to know. In this respect the completed Code reflects a decision of policy reached after several years' study and discussion by experts. We conceive our duty to be the making of an interpretation which will carry out the intention of the framers of uniform legislation which already has been enacted in twenty-five States. That the result of their policy decision may be asserted to favor certain types of creditors as against others or that a different policy could have been decided upon is quite beside the point.

Sterling Acceptance Co. v. Grimes

168 A.2d 600 (Super. Ct. Pa. 1961)

This was an action in replevin by Sterling Acceptance Co. (plaintiff) against Patrick Grimes (defendant) to recover possession of an automobile. Judgment for Grimes and Sterling Acceptance Co. appealed. Judgment affirmed.

Grimes purchased a new Dodge automobile from Homish, a franchised Dodge dealer. The sale was made in the ordinary course of Homish's business and Grimes paid to Homish the purchase price of the automobile at the time of the sale. Homish had borrowed money from Sterling Acceptance Co. (Sterling) and had given it a perfected security interest in all his inventory and in addition had given Sterling a trust receipt covering the Dodge automobile sold to Grimes. A dealer's certificate of title showing the lien in favor of Sterling was issued and was in the possession of Sterling. Homish did not pay Sterling and it replevined the automobile from Grimes.

WOODSIDE, JUDGE.   Article 9 of the Uniform Commercial Code deals with secured transactions including liens on personal property intended to be sold in the ordinary course of business. Section 9–307, provided:

(1) In the case of inventory, and in the case of other goods as to which the secured party files a financing statement in which he claims a security interest in proceeds, a buyer in ordinary course of business takes free of a security interest even though perfected and even though the buyer knows of the terms of the security agreement.

Section 2–403 provides, *inter alia:*

. . . (2) Any entrusting of possession of goods to a merchant who deals in goods of that kind gives him power to transfer all rights of the entruster to a buyer in ordinary course of business.

(3) "Entrusting" includes any delivery and any acquiescence in retention of possession regardless of any condition expressed between the parties to the delivery or acquiescence and regardless of whether the procurement of the entrusting or the possessor's disposition of the goods have been such as to be larcenous under the criminal law.

In the Comment on this section it is said:

The many particular situations in which a buyer in ordinary course of business from a dealer has been protected against reservation of property or other hidden interest are gathered by subsections (2)–(4) into a single principle protecting persons who buy in ordinary course out of inventory. Consignors have no reason to complain, nor have lenders who hold a security interest in the inventory, since the very purpose of goods in inventory is to be turned into cash by sale.

In the recent case of *Weisel v. McBride,* we had occasion to review a sale from inventory of an automobile for which the purchaser was unable to obtain a certificate of title, because the dealer had fraudulently used the certificate to obtain additional financing. Judge Hirt, speaking for this Court: "The instant case presents one of 'the many situations' in which the Commercial Code intends to protect 'persons who buy in ordinary course out of inventory'. . . ."

According to the comment on § 9–307 (Purposes of Changes 2) of the Uniform Commercial Code, "The theory is that when goods are inventory or when proceeds are claimed the secured party contemplates that his debtor will make sales, and so the debtor has effective power to do so, even though his buyers know the goods they buy were subject to the security interest."

Under the provisions of the Uniform Commercial Code, Sterling must look to Homish for repayment of the loan it made to him, and not to the automobile in the possession of Grimes, who paid the full purchase price to Homish.

National Shawmut Bank of Boston v. Jones

236 A.2d 484 (Sup. Ct. N.H. 1967)

This was an action of replevin by National Shawmut Bank of Boston (plaintiff) against Jones (defendant) to recover possession of a 1964 Dart automobile on which National Shawmut claimed to have an enforceable security interest. The case was transferred to the Supreme Court to have several questions of law answered. The questions were answered and the case was remanded.

On February 15, 1965, Robert Wever purchased the Dart from Wentworth Motor Company on a conditional sales contract for personal, family or household use. Wever executed a "Retail Sales Contract" which was assigned by Wentworth to National Shawmut Bank and which was filed with the town clerk pursuant to 9–401. Without National Shawmut's permission Wever sold the automobile to Hanson-Rock, an automobile dealer in the business of selling new and used cars to the public. Then Jones purchased the car from Hanson-Rock on April 8, 1966, for consideration, in good faith and without any actual knowledge of National Shawmut's security interest. Wever did not complete the payments under the installment plan and National Shawmut sought to foreclose its security interest in the automobile.

GRIMES, JUDGE.   Since Wever purchased for personal, family or household purposes, the Dart is classified as consumer goods. (9–109.) National Shawmut's security interest was perfected by filing the financing statement with the town clerk of Hampton where Wever resided (9–401 (1) (a)), and continues when the collateral is sold without its consent as was the case here unless Article 9 provided otherwise. (9–306 (2).) In the case of buyers of goods, Article 9–307 (1) does provide otherwise in certain instances, as follows:

A buyer in ordinary course of business (subsection (9) of Section 1–201) other than a person buying farm products from a person engaged in farming operations takes free of a security interest created by his seller even though the security interest is perfected and even though the buyer knows of its existence

Since Jones purchased in good faith without knowledge that the sale to him was in violation of the security interest of another and bought in the ordinary course from a person in the business of selling automobiles, he was a "buyer in the ordinary course of business." (1–201 (9).) However, § 9–307 (1) permits him to take free only of "a security interest created by his seller." The security interest of National Shawmut was not created by Hanson-Rock, Inc., Jones's seller, but by Wentworth Motor Co., Inc. Jones, therefore, does not take free of National Shawmut's security interest under this section. Neither does he take free of the security interest by reason of the provisions of § 9–307 (2) relating to consumer goods even if he purchased for his own personal, family or household purposes (a fact not agreed upon) because "prior to the purchase, the secured party . . . filed a financing statement. . . ." These are the only two provisions of Article 9 under which a buyer of goods can claim to take free of a security interest where a sale, exchange or other disposition of the collateral was without the consent of the secured party. Jones does not benefit from either one. Article 9–306 (2) gives the court no leeway to create any other exceptions to its dictates and no custom, usage or agreement has been brought to our attention which would permit us to do so. (1–102 (2).)

Corbin Deposit Bank v. King

384 S.W.2d 302 (Ct. App. Ky. 1964)

This was an action by Corbin Deposit Bank (plaintiff) against Thomas L. King (defendant) to determine the rights in the proceeds of the sale of an automobile. Judgment for King and Corbin Deposit Bank appealed. Judgment affirmed.

Corbin Deposit Bank (Bank) had an enforceable security interest in a motor vehicle owned by Floyd Foreman. Foreman, while the Bank's security interest was in full force, had the motor vehicle repaired by King, who was engaged in the business of selling, repairing and furnishing accessories or supplies for motor vehicles. Foreman defaulted on his debt to the Bank and he did not pay King for the repairs. King had possession of the motor vehicle and claimed a lien for repairs which had priority over the security interest of the Bank. The Bank repossessed the motor vehicle under court order and it was sold in accordance with the applicable statute.

DAVIS, COMMISSIONER. The narrow question is whether the first rights to the proceeds inure to the Bank under its perfected security interest or to King under its subsequently acquired statutory lien for services and materials furnished to repair Foreman's vehicle.

Determination of the question requires examination of 9–310, which is as follows:

When a person in the ordinary course of his business furnishes services or materials with respect to goods subject to a security interest, a lien upon goods in the possession of such person given by statute or rule of law for such materials or services takes priority over a perfected security interest unless the lien is statutory and the statute expressly provides otherwise.

In the 1958 text of the Uniform Commercial Code as published by National Conference of Commissioners on Uniform State Laws, American Law Institute, one of the purposes of the just quoted section is said to be:

(1): To provide that liens securing claims arising from work intended to enhance or preserve the value of the collateral take priority over an earlier security interest even though perfected.

It is recognized by the parties that prior to the effective date of Kentucky's Uniform Commercial Code in similar circumstances, this court had adhered to the rule allowing priority to a properly recorded chattel mortgage. The inquiry here is whether the pertinent sections of the Uniform Commercial Code require an opposite result. The trial court found that the provisions of the Commercial Code demand the opposite result, and we agree.

The course for construction of the Uniform Commercial Code was charted in *Lincoln Bank & Trust Co. v. Queenan, Ky.,* in which this court said:

The Code represents an entirely new approach in several areas of commercial law, and especially as to security transactions. Its adoption in this state signifies a legislative policy to join with other states in achieving uniformity. Code 1–102 (2) (c). The realization of this purpose demands that so far as possible the meaning of the law be gathered from the instrument itself, unfettered by anachronisms indigenous to the respective jurisdictions in which it is in force. . . . Accepting that principle, we adopt as a rule of construction that the Code is plenary and exclusive except where the legislature has clearly indicated otherwise.

It is patent that KRS 376.270 contains no provision which may be said to subordinate its statutory lien to an earlier security interest as prescribed in 9–310. Therefore, by the terms of the latter section, the lien of the security interest yields to the statutory mechanic's lien of KRS 376.270, despite the line of cases which had afforded priority to chattel mortgages in similar circumstances.

Default and Foreclosure

Contract Provisions. Within stated limitations the parties may agree as to the rights of the secured party in the event of default on the part of the debtor. In general, an agreement which deprives the debtor of his right to any surplus after sale of the collateral, his right to redeem before sale, his right to notice of the time and place of sale, his right to hold the secured party liable for breach of his duty, or any other basic right vested in the debtor, will not be enforced. (9–501.) The secured party may, if he so elects, reduce his claim to judgment in which event he will not surrender his right in the collateral and the foreclosure will proceed according to the procedure in judicial sales. The secured party may bid at the sale. (9–501 [5].)

Right to Possession.   On default the secured party is entitled to possession of the collateral. If the collateral is in the possession of the debtor and cannot be repossessed without breach of peace he can institute the possessory court action available under the procedural statutes of the state. He may, if the collateral is bulky and difficult to remove, have it rendered useless and sell it on the debtor's premises. (9–503.) If the collateral is intangible, such as, for instance, accounts, contract rights, chattel paper, instruments or documents, and performance has been rendered to the debtor, the secured party may give notice and have payments made or performance rendered to him. (9–502.)

Sale of Collateral.   The secured party may dispose of the collateral by sale or lease or in any manner calculated to produce the greatest benefit to all parties concerned; however, the method of disposal must be commercially reasonable. (9–504.) Notice of the time and place of a public sale must be given to the debtor as must notice of a private sale. The purchaser at a sale is protected against defects in the sale. (9–504 [4].)

Distribution of Proceeds.   Disposition of the proceeds from the liquidation of the collateral follows the standard pattern: expenses of retaking, holding, preparing for sale and the like, and reasonable attorney fees; satisfaction of indebtedness; junior security interests, if written notice of demand is given before distribution; and surplus, if any, to debtor. (9–504 [1].) In the event the amount received on the liquidation is insufficient to satisfy the obligation, the secured party, in the absence of an agreement to the contrary, is entitled to a deficiency judgment. (9–504 [2].)

Consumer Goods.   If the security interest is in consumer goods, the secured party must sell if 60 percent of the purchase price or debt has been paid. If less than 60 percent has been paid or if the security interest is in collateral other than consumer goods, the secured party in possession may propose to retain the collateral in satisfaction of the obligation. If no written objection is made to the proposal within 30 days after written notice of the election to retain the collateral is given, the secured party may retain the collateral in satisfaction of the obligation. (9–505.)

Duties of Secured Party.   The debtor has an absolute right to redeem the collateral at any time before its disposal. (9–506.)

The secured party is liable to injured parties if, in his foreclosure and sale, he has not complied with the provisions of Article 9. (9–507.)

A sale will not be set aside solely on the ground that a better price might have been obtained had the sale been made at a different time or place, or if a different procedure had been followed. (9–507 [2].)

Summary

Within stated limitations the parties may agree as to the rights of the secured party if the debtor defaults. Unless otherwise agreed the secured party has the right to possess the collateral. If it is bulky or hard to remove he may render it useless and sell it where located. He may sell the collateral at public or private sale and he may buy the collateral but he must act in good faith and the sale must be commercially reasonable. The proceeds of the sale are distributed as follows: expenses, reasonable attorney fees, satisfaction of indebtedness, junior creditors, if any, and balance to debtor. If the security interest is in consumer goods the secured party must sell if 60 percent of the debt has been paid. If less than 60 percent has been paid, the secured party may, by agreement, keep the collateral and cancel the debt.

Fort Knox National Bank v. Gustafson

385 S.W.2d 196 (Ct. App. Ky. 1964)

This was an action by Edith M. Gustafson (plaintiff) against Fort Knox National Bank (defendant) to recover a judgment for damages for abuse of process arising out of an action to recover possession of a mobile diner in which the Bank had a security interest. Judgment for Gustafson and Fort Knox National Bank appealed. Reversed.

On October 12, 1960, Arthur and Edith Gustafson borrowed from Fort Knox National Bank (Bank) the sum of $7,380. Arthur and Edith executed their joint promissory note secured by the transfer to the Bank of a security interest in a mobile diner and a lease of the lot on which the diner was located. At first Arthur and Edith operated the restaurant together. In October, 1961, Edith went to Texas to nurse her sick father. In June, 1962, Arthur abandoned the restaurant and went to New York. Edith returned from Texas and attempted to operate the restaurant. On her return she learned that the rent on the lot was $800 in arrears. Arthur was in financial difficulty on other enterprises in which he was engaged. In September, 1962, due to a disturbance and the default in rent payments, the lessor of the lot ordered Edith to remove the diner by October 1, 1962. Edith negotiated with the Bank for a settlement of her financial affairs but no solution was worked out. The Bank brought an action to repossess the mobile diner and Edith refused to surrender possession. There was a technical defect in the repossession bond filed by the Bank in its action. The note included an acceleration provision. The trial court granted Edith a judgment against the Bank of $20,500 actual damages and $15,000 punitive damages.

DAVIS, COMMISSIONER. The note contained an acceleration clause, authorizing the holder to precipitate the maturity date in the event the makers defaulted in any monthly payment. The acceleration clause also provided that the holder of the note could declare it due before maturity if the holder felt insecure. This type of acceleration is permitted by the U.C.C.

Since the acceleration clause was properly invoked, the bank had a right to obtain possession of the collateral by the terms of the security agreement. This right of possession is specifically assured by 9–503, which provides that the secured party may proceed to obtain such possession without judicial process, if this can be accomplished without breach of peace—or by judicial action. Here it is agreed that repossession could not be had peaceably. Thus, we are left to consider whether the judicial action was so defective as to expose appellant bank to the damage claims here asserted.

Upon the authority of *General Motors Acceptance Corp. v. Curry,* we hold that any technical flaw (if indeed there was one sufficient to invalidate the process) in the claim and delivery action did not afford a cause of action to Gustafson for the taking of the diner. We think *Stoll Oil Refining Co. v. Pierce* is compatible with the decision in the *Curry* case, and with our present holding. Although it is true that we approved an award for nominal damages in *Stoll Oil Refining Co. v. Pierce,* we conclude that 9–507 (1) expresses the statutory policy and view of the Uniform Commercial Code that the debtor is confined to recovery of "any loss caused by a failure to comply." In this sense, we construe "loss" to relate to actual compensatory damages—not nominal damages. We think this same concept is implicit in 1–106.

As we have concluded that the bank acted in "good faith," it follows that no issue as to punitive damages was shown. Punitive damages do not flow from "good faith" conduct.

It was incumbent on the bank to comply with the requirements of 9–504 (3), which requires that repossessed collateral be sold or disposed of by the secured party in a commercially reasonable manner. The record before us is voluminous, but it does not contain an adequate account of the disposition of the diner by the bank. The issue as to whether the sale was commercially reasonable was not developed in evidence, nor was it submitted to the jury. Upon another trial, details as to the sale and whether it was commercially reasonable will be developed in evidence, and any appropriate issues reflected in the evidence will be submitted to the jury.

In this connection, it must be noted that 9–507 (1, 2) relate to the measure of damages applicable here. The debtor is entitled to recoup any "loss" caused by failure of the secured party to comply with the Uniform Commercial Code. However, the mere fact that a better price could have been obtained by sale at a different time, or different place or manner is not of itself sufficient to establish that the sale was not commercially reasonable.

Gustafson is not entitled to recover any damage for asserted loss as to the business. We have said that the bank was entitled to the possession of the diner under the terms of the security agreement. Manifestly, taking the diner into possession presupposes terminating the restaurant business conducted in it by the Gustafsons. The consequent disruption of the restaurant business incident to the legal repossession of the diner was a result which the Gustafsons impliedly consented to in the security agreement.

Problem Cases

1. Weiners Men's Apparel, Inc. filed a copy of a financing statement describing property subject to a security agreement given to Dutchess Associates Co. The financing statement included as property covered "inventory, fixtures, improvements, equipment, accounts and accounts receivable." The security agreement itself was much shorter and merely listed "the premises" of the Weiners' store as the collateral. Weiners becomes bankrupt and the trustee seeks to exclude the inventory and accounts receivable from the security agreement. Are the inventory and accounts receivable covered by the security agreement?

2. Mr. Symons, a full-time insurance salesman, bought a set of drums and cymbals from Grinnel Brothers Inc. A security agreement was executed between them but never filed. Mr. Symons purchased the drums to supplement his income by playing with a band. He had done this before and his income from the two jobs was about equal. He also played several other instruments. Mr. Symons became bankrupt and the trustee tried to acquire the drums as part of his bankruptcy estate. Grinnel Brothers tried to enforce their security agreement. What can Grinnel Brothers argue? Will they be successful?

3. Mr. Flynn loaned money to a Mr. Hardin. In return Hardin gave him a valid security agreement stating that it covered "all furniture, fixtures and inventory of the business known as Hardin's Drug Store conducted at 204 Division St., Park Falls, Wisconsin, now owned or hereafter acquired." This agreement was perfected under the Code. The drug store burned down and while the insurance paid most of Flynn's claim there was still a deficiency of $5,000. Hardin opened another Wisconsin store 270 miles away and one year later became insolvent. Mr. Flynn filed a claim for $5,000 on the property of the second store on the basis of his after-acquired property clause. There are other interests in the property. Does Flynn have a valid claim?

4. Root bought a tractor and accessories from Anderson Sales. He signed a conditional sales contract agreeing to make monthly payments and granting Anderson a security interest in the tractor and accessories. The contract also contained a warranty by Anderson that the equipment was "to be free from defects in material or workmanship," and an agreement by Root that:

   "I will settle all claims of any kind against *SELLER* directly with *SELLER*, and if *SELLER* assigns this note I will not use any such claim as a defense, setoff or counterclaim against any effort by the holder to enforce this instrument."

   Anderson assigned the contract to John Deere. Root defaulted in his payments; Deere repossessed the equipment, sold it, and sued Root for the deficiency. Root claims the tractor was defective and that he can assert the breach of warranty against Deere because it has only the assignee's rights on a contract. Deere points to Section 9–206 (1). Would Root or Deere prevail?

5. Thompson & Son, a partnership, owned and operated a service station. On November 19, 1965, they placed an order with National Cash Register Co. for a new cash register. On December 13, 1965 they executed a security agreement with American Bank and Trust which included in part, "all equipment, cash registers, machinery and tools used in the operation of the service station." The agreement also contained an after-acquired property clause. It was perfected by filing on December 27, 1965. On April 20, 1966, National delivered the new register. In return they received a purchase money security interest which was perfected by filing on August 2, 1966. Thompson & Son defaulted to both parties. Who has priority rights to the new register?

6. Mishkin's 125th St. Inc., a drug store, sold its business to Aberdeen Drug Co. As part of the transaction Mishkin's retained a security interest in the store, together with an after-

acquired property clause. This agreement specifically included four cash registers. It was perfected on November 26, 1969. On November 24, 1969 Aberdeen traded the four cash registers to National Cash Register Co. for three new machines. The balance of the price for the new registers was secured by a purchase money security interest in favor of National Cash Register. This statement was filed on December 3, 1969 but the financing statement listed the debtor as Mishkin's Drugs Inc. Aberdeen Drug became insolvent. Who has priority to the new registers?

7. Mr. Laue, as part of a refinancing arrangement with Local Finance Co., received $200 with which to make a down payment on a new car. Local perfected the security agreement given them in return on July 31, 1969. On August 1, 1969 Mr. Laue made the down payment, executed a second agreement with the dealer for the balance of the purchase price and took the car. The dealer perfected its interest on August 2, 1969. Laue became insolvent. Who has the priority interest in the car?

8. Goodyear Tire and Rubber Co. sold two television sets to a Mr. Redding. A valid security agreement was executed for the sets. Mr. Redding then sold the sets to White-Sellies Jewelry Co., a pawnbroker and retail business. The sets were then resold to another party. When Mr. Redding defaulted on his obligation Goodyear filed suit against the jewelry store for conversion. The jewelry store defended, claiming to be a buyer in the ordinary course of business. Can Goodyear recover the value of the television sets from the jeweler?

9. Mr. Kahn applied for a home improvement loan to construct an in-ground swimming pool. Union National Bank approved the loan and construction was begun on Kahn's land. State Bank held a valid mortgage on this land. After the pool was completed Union National gave Kahn the money with which he paid the contractor. Union National then perfected their interest by filing. State Bank later attempted to foreclose on their mortgage. Union National claimed the value of the pool. Is Union National entitled to recover the value of the pool?

10. Galway Funding Corp., loaned $225,000 to Sanray Floor Covering Corp., to build a new store. A mortgage was given and duly recorded. It provided that "fixtures of every kind used in the operation of the building" were included. A similar financing statement was filed by Galway on June 6, 1966. Sanray Corp. purchased $16,000 of air-conditioning equipment from Center Electric Co., to be installed in the store. They gave the electric company a purchase money security interest in this amount. The installation was completed on November 30, 1966. Center Electric perfected on February 27, 1967. Sanray Floor became insolvent. Who has priority and why?

11. Mr. Gibson, a collector of rare old Indian jewelry, took two of his pieces to Mr. Hagberg, a pawnbroker. The two pieces, a silver belt and a silver necklace, were worth $500 each. Mr. Hagberg only loaned $45 on the belt and $50 on the necklace. Mr. Gibson defaulted on both loans and immediately and without notice the belt was sold for $240. A short time later the necklace was sold for $80. At the time of their sale Mr. Gibson owed interest on the loans of $22. What, if anything, can Gibson recover from the pawnbroker?

chapter 43

Security Interests in Real Property

Real Estate Mortgages

Historical Development. The real estate mortgage, as a form of security, was used in England as early as the middle of the 12th century, but our present-day mortgage law developed from the common law mortgage of the 15th century. The common law mortgage was a deed which conveyed the land to the mortgagee, the title to the land to revest in the mortgagor on payment of the debt secured. The mortgagee was given possession of the land during the term of the mortgage, and if the mortgagor defaulted, the mortgagee's title to the land became absolute. The land was forfeited as a penalty for breach of condition, and the forfeiture did not discharge the debt. The mortgagee could sue on the debt, recover a judgment, and collect the debt, in addition to keeping the land.

The early equity courts did not favor the imposition of penalties and would relieve from such forfeitures, provided the mortgagor's default was minor in nature and was due to causes beyond his control. By gradual stages the courts became more lenient in permitting redemptions and allowed the mortgagor to redeem if he tendered performance without unreasonable delay, that is, if he was not guilty of laches. Finally, the courts of equity recognized the mortgagor's right to redeem as an absolute right which would continue until the mortgagee asked the court of equity to decree that the mortgagor's right to redeem be foreclosed and cut off. Our present law relative to the foreclosure of mortgage developed from this practice.

Form, Execution, and Recording. The early real estate mortgage was a deed containing a defeasance clause. In some states the deed with a defeasance clause is still used, but in other states a statutory form of mortgage is used. As a general rule the statutory form of mortgage does not contain words

943

of conveyance but uses "mortgages and warrants" or similar language.

The real estate mortgage is generally recognized as conveying an interest in real property, and it must be executed with the same formality as is a deed. Unless a mortgage is executed as required by the statutes of the state in which the land is located, it is not eligible for recording.

An unrecorded mortgage is not valid against bona fide purchasers or mortgagees for value who have no notice or knowledge of the mortgage, nor is it valid against creditors who acquire a lien on the property. As between the parties the validity of the mortgage does not depend on the fulfillment of the formal requirements. If the transaction is intended as a loan and security for the payment of the loan, the courts will declare it a mortgage, irrespective of the form of the conveyance. The courts jealously guard the mortgagor's right to redeem and will not enforce any contract or agreement cutting off this right. Even though the conveyance is in the form of a warranty deed, the courts will declare it a mortgage if it was given as security.

However, if a deed is given as security for the payment of a loan and the real property is sold by the owner of record (the mortgagee) to an innocent purchaser for value, the innocent purchaser for value acquires good title. The mortgagee will be liable to the mortgagor for any damages the mortgagor has suffered as a result of the sale of the property.

Rights and Liabilities of Mortgagor and Purchasers.   The owner (the mortgagor) may sell the property without the consent of the mortgagee, but such a sale in no way affects the mortgagee's interest in the property or his claim against the mortgagor on the debt. In case there is a default, the mortgagee may foreclose the mortgage and have the mortgaged property sold. If, on foreclosure, sale of the property does not bring enough to pay the costs, interest, and principal, the mortgagee is entitled to a deficiency judgment against the original debtor, the mortgagor, although some courts show reluctance to allow deficiency judgments where real property was used as security for a debt. If the property should sell for more than enough to pay the costs, interest, and principal, the surplus will go to the mortgagor or one who has purchased from him.

The purchaser may buy the mortgaged property "subject to the mortgage," or he may "assume" the mortgage. If he purchases subject to the mortgage and a default and a foreclosure follow, he is not liable for a deficiency; if he assumes the mortgage, he is liable for any deficiency. The property is always liable and may be sold to pay the mortgage debt; and the mortgagor, since he cannot assign his liability, is liable to the mortgagee on the mortgage debt. If the mortgagor sells the mortgaged property to a purchaser who "assumes and agrees to pay the mortgage debt," such purchaser is liable to the mortgagee for the amount of the mortgage debt. In most jurisdictions the mortgagor's liability is that of a surety. If there is a default followed by a foreclosure, the mortgagee in the event of a deficiency may obtain a deficiency judgment against both the mortgagor and the purchaser; and if the mortgagor pays the deficiency, he is entitled to recover the amount paid from the purchaser.

Mortgagee's Right to Assign Mortgage.   The mortgagee may assign his interest in the mortgaged property. To do this, he must assign the debt. If the debt is evidenced by a negotiable note, the assignment is usually made by the negotiation of the note plus an assignment of the mortgage; however, in most jurisdictions the negotiation of the note carries with it the right to the security, and the holder of the note is entitled to the benefits of the mortgage.

Foreclosure of Real Estate Mortgage.   Foreclosure is the process by which all further rights existing in the mortgagor or persons who have acquired the rights of the mortgagor to redeem the mortgaged real property are defeated and lost. Foreclosure proceedings are usually regulated by the statutes of the state in which the real property is located; and in many states, two or more alternative methods of foreclosure are available to the mortgagee or his assignee. The methods in common use today are (1) strict foreclosure, (2) action and sale, and (3) power of sale.

Under a strict foreclosure, all rights of the mortgagor are cut off by the foreclosure proceedings, and title to the mortgaged property is vested in the mortgagee. There is no sale of the property. Strict foreclosure is used extensively in only a few states, and in those states the right to strict foreclosure is generally confined to those cases wherein the debt is equal to or exceeds the value of the security, or where the mortgagor or a person who has acquired a right under the mortgagor has only a technical interest in the mortgaged property.

Foreclosure by action and sale is permitted in all states and is the only method of foreclosure permitted in some states. Although the state statutes are not uniform, they are alike in their basic requirements. In a foreclosure by action and sale, suit is brought in a court having jurisdiction. Any party having a property interest which would be cut off by the foreclosure must be made a party defendant, and if any such party has a defense, he must enter his appearance and set up his defense. The case must be tried in accordance with the established trial procedure of the state, after which a judgment is entered and a sale of the property ordered. The proceeds of the sale are applied to the payment of the mortgage debt, and any surplus is paid over to the mortgagor or such other person or persons who would be entitled thereto. If there is a deficiency, a deficiency judgment is, as a general rule, entered against the mortgagor and such other persons as would be liable on the debt.

The right to foreclose under a power of sale must be expressly conferred on the mortgagee by the terms of the mortgage. If the procedure for the exercise of the power is set out in the mortgage, such procedure must be followed. Several states have enacted statutes which set out the procedure to be followed in the exercise of a power of sale. No court action is required. As a general rule, notice of the sale must be given to the mortgagor, and the sale must be advertised. The sale must be at auction and must be conducted fairly, and an effort must be made to sell the property at the highest price obtainable. The proceeds of the sale are applied to the payment of costs, interest, and the principal of the debt. Any surplus must be paid to the mortgagor or such other persons as may be entitled thereto. If there is a deficiency and the mortgagee wishes to recover a judgment for the deficiency, he must bring suit on the debt.

Right of Redemption.   At common law and under existing statutes the mortgagor or an assignee of the mortgagor has an equity of redemption in the mortgaged real estate; that is, he has the absolute right to discharge the mortgage when due and have title to the mortgaged property restored free and clear of the mortgage debt. Under the statutes of all states the mortgagor or any party having in the mortgaged property an interest which will be cut off by the foreclosure may redeem the property after default and before the mortgagee forecloses the mortgage. In several states by statute the mortgagor or any other party in interest is given what is known as a redemption period (usually of six months or one year and either after the foreclosure proceedings are started or after a foreclosure sale of the mortgaged property is made) in which to pay the mortgaged debt, costs and interest and redeem the property.

As a general rule, if a party in interest wishes to redeem, he must, if the redemption period runs after the foreclosure sale, pay to the purchaser at the foreclosure sale the amount the purchaser has paid plus interest up to the time of redemption. If the redemption period runs before the sale, the party in interest must pay the amount of the debt plus the costs and interest. The person who wishes to redeem from a mortgage foreclosure sale must redeem the entire mortgage interest; he cannot redeem a partial interest by paying a proportionate amount of the debt or by paying a proportionate amount of the price bid at the foreclosure sale.

Summary

At common law the mortgaged property was deeded to the mortgagee who took possession of the property. On default by the mortgagor the mortgaged property was forfeited to the mortgagee as a penalty for the default.

At an early date the courts of equity began to relieve from forfeiture immediately on default, and by gradual evolution the time in which the mortgagor had a right to redeem after default was extended until foreclosure of the mortgage.

Mortgages are executed with the same formalities as are deeds and must be recorded to be valid against third persons. Irrespective of the form of a conveyance, if it is made to secure a debt, the courts will declare it to be a mortgage and will permit the mortgagor the right to redeem.

The mortgagor may convey his interest in the mortgaged property, but the purchaser acquires no greater rights than the mortgagor has. Whether or not the purchaser becomes liable to the mortgagee for the payment of the mortgage debt depends on whether the purchaser has assumed and agreed to pay the mortgage debt as part of the purchase price of the property. The mortgagee may assign the mortgage debt and mortgage.

On default by the mortgagor the mortgagee must foreclose the mortgage to cut off the mortgagor's rights in the property. In foreclosing the mortgage, the statutory procedure of the state in which the land is located must be followed.

In most states the mortgagor and other parties in interest are given a period, usually one year, in which to redeem the property from the foreclosure.

Boysun v. Boysun

368 P.2d 439 (Sup. Ct. Mont. 1962)

This was an action by Mike E. Boysun (plaintiff) against John C. Boysun and Tillie Boysun, his wife (defendants), to quiet title to certain land. Judgment for Mike E. Boysun, and John C. and Tillie Boysun appealed. Judgment affirmed.

John C. and Tillie Boysun owned a farm which was mortgaged for $4,400. They were in default on their payments and delinquent in the payment of their taxes, and the mortgagee was threatening to foreclose.

John was unable to borrow money to pay the mortgage. Mike offered to purchase the land subject to the encumbrances. He stated at the time that it was worth no more than the encumbrances. John and Tillie executed a quitclaim deed conveying the farm to Mike. Mike orally agreed to reconvey the farm to John or to convey it to a purchaser if John found one. Thereafter John and his family moved to another state. Mike worked the farm in 1953 and 1954 and paid the taxes from 1951 through 1958.

In the early part of 1954 John told Mike that he had a purchaser who would pay $11,000 for the farm but Mike wished to keep the farm. Thereafter, Mike sent money to John, and the amount sent plus the amount Mike paid to discharge the encumbrances on the farm amounted to $11,000. John and Tillie claim that the quitclaim deed was to secure a loan and asked the court to hold it to be a mortgage. John claimed that the money Mike sent him was a loan.

HARRISON, CHIEF JUSTICE.   The ultimate question of whether a transaction was intended by the parties to be a mortgage or a sale rests on the intention of the parties at the time of the execution of the instrument, and to establish this intention the courts will examine the surrounding circumstances.

It has been repeatedly held that the evidence to prove that a deed, absolute on its face, was intended to be a mortgage must be clear and convincing. However, this rule is subject to some modification in situations where there is an option to repurchase or a conditional sale. The general rule is that if there is doubt whether a sale or a mortgage was intended, the court will be inclined to resolve the doubt in favor of the mortgage.

John and Tillie in this action rely heavily on the *Murray* case. In that case this court listed a number of facts and circumstances which, if present, tend to confirm the view that the transaction was a mortgage and not a sale. These factors are as follows:

(*a*) The transaction in its inception had for its purpose a loan, not a sale.

(*b*) The grantor was in financial distress at the time of the transaction.

(*c*) The price which the grantee claims he paid for the property appears to have been grossly inadequate.

(*d*) According to grantee's own theory, the transaction did not amount to an absolute sale, but to a conditional sale; that is, a sale with an option to grantor to repurchase.

John and Tillie list the four factors and allege that they are all present in the instant case. We have some difficulty with this assertion. The third principle relied on in the *Murray* case is based on the inadequacy of the price the vendor received for his property. The adequacy of consideration must be tested by conditions existing at the time of the transaction.

In *Titus v. Wallick,* the court held that in order for evidence of a disparity between the consideration for a deed and the value of the land to be of weight, it is essential that there be a satisfactory showing of such disparity.

There is no evidence in the record to support John and Tillie's allegation of a disparity between the purchase price and the value of the land at the time of sale. The only statement as to the value of the land at the time the deed was executed was the testimony of Mike Boysun. He stated the reason he would not loan money against the property was because it was not worth any more than what was against it.

In addition to the above-stated facts here are two elements present in the instant case which were not present in the *Murray* case. A deed, though absolute on its face, will be construed as a mortgage whenever it is shown that the instrument was intended to secure a debt. However, a debt must be shown to exist between the parties, as a mortgage is a mere incident of the debt.

In the *Murray* case there was testimony in the record that the parties intended the money paid to be a loan and that a debt was created between the parties. In the instant case, Mike Boysun testified that the agreement between the parties was that any time John paid the money spent by Mike on the property he was to get the property back. John's testimony supports this theory that he received an option to repurchase. His testimony indicates that he felt no obligation to pay any money back to Mike, but rather he had an option to do so if desired.

John and Tillie place considerable emphasis on the fact that Mike Boysun while testifying stated that John had a year or two to redeem the property. They cite this to show that a mortgage was intended. We feel little weight should be given to such statements made by a layman, especially in a situation such as the present wherein it is evident from the legal tangle of the parties that they knew little, if anything, about the law.

The second factor which is present in the instant case, which is absent from the *Murray* case, is the preponderant and inescapable fact that the option to repurchase was exercised. The testimony of two disinterested witnesses established the fact that in the Spring of 1954, John Boysun exercised his option to repurchase. In addition to exercising his option the testimony in the record establishes that he received his option price.

Trust Deeds and Land Contracts

Trust Deeds. There are three parties to a trust deed transaction: the trustor, who borrows the money; the trustee, who holds legal title to the real property put up as security; and the lender, who is beneficiary of the trust. The purpose of a trust deed transaction is to facilitate the liquidation of the security in the event of default. Most of the states have declared a trust deed to be a mortgage and have required court foreclosure, thereby defeating the purpose of the arrangement.

In a deed-of-trust transaction the borrower deeds to the trustee the real property which is to be put up as security. If the borrower fails to make the required payments on the debt, the trustee is usually given, by the terms of the trust agreement, the power to foreclose or to sell the property. Usually, the trustee does not sell the property until the beneficiary (the lender or his assignee) notifies the trustee that the debtor is in default and demands that the property be sold. The trustee sells the property, usually at public sale, and applies the proceeds to the payment of costs, interest, and principal. If there is a surplus, it is paid over to the trustor. If there is a deficiency and the lender wishes to force collection, he will have to sue on the debt and recover a judgment.

Land Contracts. The land contract, as a security device, is limited in its use to the securing of the payment of the balance of the purchase price of real property. The seller of the property agrees to sell, and the buyer agrees to buy and pay the stipulated purchase price set out in the contract. Usually, the purchaser takes possession of the property, pays all taxes and assessments, keeps the property insured, and assumes all other obligations of an owner. In fact, the purchaser is the equitable owner, but the seller holds the legal title and does not deed the property to the buyer until the purchase price is paid in full. In the event the buyer defaults, the seller has the right to declare a forfeiture and take possession of the property, thereby cutting off all the buyer's rights in the property. The laws of the states vary in regard to the rights of the parties to a land contract.

As a general rule the procedure for declaration of forfeiting and recovery of property sold on land contract is simpler and less time-consuming than the foreclosure of a real estate mortgage by court action. In some states the procedure to be followed in the event of default on a land contract has been set out by statute. In other states the courts of equity have developed the procedure to be followed in the event of default and forfeiture. If the buyer, after default, voluntarily surrenders possession to the seller, no court procedure is necessary; the seller's title will become absolute, and the buyer's equity will be cut off.

Summary

A trust deed may be used in some states in lieu of a mortgage. In the trust deed transaction the borrower (the trustor) conveys the property to a trustee who, after the default of the trustor and at the request of the lender, sells the property and from the proceeds pays the debt.

The owner of real property may sell on land contract. The seller retains title to the property until the purchase price is paid in full. If the buyer defaults, the seller has the right to reclaim the property.

Mechanic's Lien on Real Estate

Nature of Mechanic's Lien on Real Estate.   All rights to a mechanic's lien on real estate must be created by statutory enactment, since the courts have never recognized a common law lien on real property. Consequently, all of the states have enacted statutes pertaining to mechanics' liens on real estate, but the requirements in the various states for obtaining such liens differ so widely and in so many particulars that space does not permit a discussion of these statutes in detail.

Persons Entitled to a Lien.   Some statutes set out in detail the classes of persons who are entitled to a mechanic's lien, whereas others set them out in broad general terms. In general, any person whose labor or material has contributed to the improvement of real estate is entitled to a mechanic's lien.

Rights of Subcontractors and Materialmen.   A general contractor is a person who has contracted with the owner to build, remodel, or improve real property. A subcontractor is a person who has contracted with the general contractor to perform a stipulated portion of the general contract. A materialman is a person who has contracted to furnish certain materials needed to perform a designated general contract.

Two distinct systems are followed by the several states in allowing mechanics' liens on real estate to subcontractors and materialmen: the New York system and the Pennsylvania system.

The New York system is based on the theory of subrogation, and the subcontractors or materialmen cannot recover more than is owing the contractor at the time they file a lien or give notice of a lien to the owner. Under the Pennsylvania system the subcontractors or materialmen have direct liens and are entitled to liens for the value of labor and material furnished, irrespective of the amount due from the owner to the contractor. Under the New York system the failure of the general contractor to perform his contract or his abandonment of the work has a direct effect on the lien rights of subcontractors and materialmen, whereas under the Pennsylvania system, such breach or abandonment by the general contractor does not directly affect the lien rights of subcontractors and materialmen.

Basis for Mechanic's Lien on Real Estate.   In some states, statutes provide that no lien shall be claimed unless the contract for the improvement is in writing and embodies a description of the land on which the improvement is to take place, and of the work to be done, and a statement of the materials to be furnished. Other states permit the contract to be oral, but in no state is a licensee or volunteer entitled to a lien.

No lien can be claimed unless the work is done or the materials are furnished in the performance of a contract to improve specific real property. A sale of materials without reference to the improvement of specific real property does not entitle the person furnishing the material to a lien upon real property which is, in fact, improved by the use of the materials at some time after the sale. Unless the state statute specifically includes submaterialmen, they are not entitled to a lien. For example, if a lumber dealer contracts to furnish the lumber for the erection of a specific building and orders from a sawmill a carload of lumber needed to fulfill the contract, the sawmill will not be entitled to a lien on the building in which the lumber is used unless the state statute expressly provides that submaterialmen are entitled to a lien.

At times the question has arisen as to whether or not materials have been furnished. Some courts have held that the materialmen must prove that the material furnished was actually incorporated into the structure. Under this ruling, if material delivered on the job is diverted by the general contractor or others and not incorporated into the structure, the materialmen will not be entitled to a lien. Other courts have held that the materialman is entitled to a lien if he can furnish proof that the material was delivered on the job under a contract to furnish the material.

Requirements for Obtaining Lien.   The requirements for obtaining a mechanic's lien must be complied with strictly. Although there is no uniformity in the statutes as to the requirements for obtaining a lien, they generally require the filing of a notice of lien with a county official, such as the register of deeds or county clerk, which notice sets forth the amount claimed, the name of the owner, the name of the contractor and claimant, and a description of the property. Frequently, the notice of lien must be verified by an affidavit of the claimant. In some states a copy of the notice must be served on the owner or posted on the property.

The notice of lien must be filed within a stipulated time. The time varies from 30 to 90 days, but the favored time is 60 days after the last work is done or after the last materials are furnished. Some statutes distinguish between labor claims, materialmen's claims, and claims of general contractors as to time of filing. The lien, when filed, must be foreclosed within a specified time, which varies from six months to two years.

Priorities and Foreclosure.   The provisions for priorities vary widely, but most of the statutes provide that a mechanic's lien has priority over all liens attaching after the first work is performed or after the first materials are furnished. This provision in the statute creates a hidden lien on the property, in that a mechanic's lien, filed within the allotted period of time after completion of the work, attaches as of the time the first work is done or the first material is furnished, but no notice of lien need be filed during this period, and if no notice of lien is filed during this period, third persons would have no means of knowing of the existence of a lien. There are no priorities among lien claimants under the majority of statutes.

The procedure followed in the foreclosure of a mechanic's lien on real estate follows closely the procedure followed in a court foreclosure of a real estate mortgage. The rights acquired by the filing of a lien and the extent of property covered by such lien are set out in some of the mechanic's lien statutes. In general, the lien attaches only to the interest the person has in the property which has been improved at the time the notice is filed. Some statutes provide that the lien attaches to the building and city lot on which the building stands, or if the improvement is to farm property, the lien attaches to a specified amount of land.

Waiver of Lien.   The question often arises as to the effect of an express provision in a contract for the improvement of real estate that no lien shall attach to the property for the cost of the improvement. In some states, there are statutes requiring the recording or filing of the contract and making such provision ineffective if the statute is not complied with. In some jurisdictions, it has been held that such a provision is effective against everyone; in other jurisdictions the provision has been held ineffective against all except the contractor; while in still other jurisdictions, such provisions have been held ineffective as to subcontractors, materialmen, and laborers. Whether or not parties have notice of the waiver-of-lien provision plays an important part in several jurisdictions in determining their right to a lien.

Summary

The right to a mechanic's lien on real estate is statutory. The basis of a lien is the improvement of the real estate of one person by the addition of the labor and materials of another.

The persons who are entitled to mechanics' liens on real estate are set out in the statutes, and in this regard the provisions of the statutes vary widely. Under one type of statute the right of a subcontractor or materialman to a mechanic's lien is based on the right of the general contractor, and the total of their claims cannot exceed the amount due the general contractor. Under the other type of statute the subcontractor or materialman is entitled to a direct lien on the improved property for the full value of the work and material furnished. The work and materials must be furnished for the improvement of a particular premise or building. A person is not entitled to a lien for materials sold generally which are not until later incorporated into a building.

To obtain a lien, the lien claimant must comply strictly with the statutory requirements as to the form, content, and time of giving notice of lien, and any other requirements for the obtaining of a lien. As a general rule a lien dates from the time the first labor or materials are furnished and has priority over all subsequent lien claimants.

A lien is foreclosed in the same manner as that followed in a court foreclosure of a real estate mortgage. It attaches to the interest which the person having the improvement made has in the improved property. Under the provisions of some statutes the right to a mechanic's lien may be waived by the insertion of a waiver provision in the contract for the improvement.

Manpower, Inc. v. Phillips

179 N.E.2d 922 (Sup. Ct. Ohio 1962)

This was an action by Manpower, Inc. (plaintiff), against Phillips and Oakley Drive-In Theaters, Inc., and others (defendants) asking for a judgment for labor furnished and the granting of a mechanic's lien. Judgment for Manpower, Inc., and Oakley Drive-In Theaters, Inc., appealed to appellate court where the judgment granting a mechanic's lien was affirmed. Oakley Drive-In Theaters, Inc., appealed to the Supreme Court. Judgment reversed as to mechanic's lien.

Oakley Drive-In Theaters, Inc. (Oakley) engaged Phillips as a general contractor for the construction of an addition to the concession building of Oakley.

Manpower, Inc., had a contract with Phillips to furnish him laborers from time to time. Manpower, Inc., at the request of Phillips, furnished him laborers who worked on the Oakley job and paid the laborers a total of $1,955.45, but Phillips did not pay Manpower, Inc. The trial court granted a judgment against Phillips for $1,955.45 and no appeal was taken from this judgment. It also granted a mechanic's lien on the Oakley building and this appeal was taken from that holding.

GRIFFITH, JUDGE. The question presented in this appeal is whether, under Section 1311.02, Revised Code, a corporation which furnishes laborers to a contractor is entitled to a lien on the property of the owner of real property for labor and work rendered by such laborers, employees of the corporation, in the improvement of such property.

The precise question has never been decided by the courts of this state.

So far as pertinent, Section 1311.02, Revised Code, reads:

Every person or corporation who does work or labor upon, or furnishes machinery, material, or fuel for constructing, altering . . . repairing, or removing a house . . . or other building . . . by virtue of a contract, express or implied, with the owner, part owner, or lessee of any interest in real estate, or his authorized agent, and every person who as a subcontractor, laborer, or materialman, performs any labor, or furnishes machinery, material or fuel, to an original or principal contractor, or any subcontractor, in carrying forward, performing, or completing any such contract, has a lien to secure the payment thereof. . . .

The first part of that section deals with mechanics' liens for persons who deal directly with the owner or the lessee of the real estate; and the second part deals with those persons at least once removed from the owner or lessee who deal with the contractor or subcontractor.

Clearly, Manpower, Inc., did not have any contract, express or implied, with either the lessee or the fee holder.

The next question presented is: Was Manpower, Inc., a "subcontractor" as that term is used in the statute?

"A subcontractor agrees to do something for another, but it is not controlled or subject to the control of the other in the manner or method of accomplishing the result contracted for."

* * * * *

Clearly Manpower does not meet the statutory definition of a "subcontractor," nor does it meet the pronounced judicial description of such.

Problem Cases

1. Davis purchased some real estate by assuming an existing first mortgage on the property and by giving the seller a second mortgage to secure the balance of the purchase price. Stone bought the second mortgage and the accompanying mortgage note of Davis. Davis fell into default on the second mortgage and worked out an agreement with Stone whereby he would not foreclose the mortgage but rather Davis would deed the property to Stone on the understanding it would be deeded back when Davis completed all of the payments on the mortgage note. Stone did not cancel or reduce the indebtedness at the time the deed was transferred and he continued to accept payments from Davis and to record them on the second mortgage note as well as in the payment book. Davis remained in possession of the property for another year at which time he defaulted again. Stone claimed that under the deed he was entitled to the property. Davis contends that the deed should be declared an equitable mortgage. Who should prevail?

2. Hiller owned a farm on which Oakdale Bank held a mortgage. He was in default on his payments and Oakdale Bank was threatening foreclosure. Hiller and Stamberg entered into an agreement whereby Stamberg was to pay Oakdale Bank the amount of the mortgage debt and the farm was to be deeded to Stamberg by absolute deed, and Stamberg was to lease the farm to Hiller for a period of two years with an option to purchase it. This agreement was carried out. Hiller did not exercise his option to purchase the farm within the two-year period, and Stamberg brought an action to recover possession of the farm. Hiller contended that the transaction was a mortgage and that since Stamberg had not foreclosed the mortgage, he was not entitled to possession. Should Stamberg's deed be held to be a mortgage?

3. Plato Dampier owned a parcel of land in Mississippi. He borrowed some money from the Federal Land Bank and in turn granted it a mortgage on his land. One of the terms of the mortgage required him to pay the taxes on the property. Dampier failed to pay the property taxes and the land was sold by the State of Mississippi to recover the taxes due. Dampier repurchased the property at the tax sale. The Federal Land Bank sold and assigned its mortgage on the Dampier property to Polk. Polk seeks to enforce the mortgage against Dampier, and Dampier claims that his repurchase at the tax sale freed the property of the mortgage. Who will prevail?

4. Willie Crisp owned some real property in Oklahoma City which was subject to a first mortgage held by Moore. Effie Crisp, Willie's mother, held a second mortgage on the property. Crisp failed to pay the taxes on the property and the county sold the property at a tax sale to recoup the taxes. Effie Crisp bought the property at the tax sale and obtained a tax deed to the property issued by the county treasurer. Effie Crisp now claims she owns the property free and clear while Moore contends the holder of a junior mortgage cannot obtain title at a tax sale superior to that of a prior mortgagee. Who should prevail?

5. On August 15, 1961, Ward entered into a written contract with Anthony by which Anthony was to supply labor and materials for the alteration of the Ward residence for a total price of $2,250, payable in installments.

   On September 5, 1961, Roofing Co., a materialman, filed with the County Clerk a notice of intention to furnish materials to Anthony, pursuant to the mechanic's lien statute of the state. Between September 5, and September 21, 1961, Roofing Co. furnished Anthony materials having a total value of $742.69. On September 8, 1961, Roofing Co. sent Ward by registered mail a notice of the filing of the notice of intention. A receipt was returned which was signed by Ward which indicated that he received the notice on September 11, 1961. The mechanic's lien statute of the state provides that "notice, in writing, of the filing of such notice of intention shall be given within five days of such filing to the owner of the premises."

   Ward made installment payments to Anthony totaling $2,282.28. The last two of such payments were made on September 7, 1961, ($690) and September 21, 1961, ($92.28). Anthony paid Roofing Co. nothing on account. Was notice of the intent to file a mechanic's lien given within the statutory period?

6. The Florida Mechanic's Lien Law provides in pertinent part that: "an architect or engineer . . . shall have a lien on real property improved for money owed him for his services in preparing plans, specifications or drawings used in connection with improving the real property . . . rendered in accordance with his contract and with the direct contract." Jack Pyms engaged Carson Bennett Wright to architecturally design a residence for Pyms on property he owned. The letter agreement with Wright provided that any engineering services would be exclusive of the architect's fee and would be paid directly by Pyms to the engineer, but that Wright had the right to approve the engineer and to direct his activities. Warshaw, an engineer, began performing engineering services on the residential design for Wright but without having any direct contact or agreement with Pyms as to his fee. There was evidence Pyms knew Warshaw had been asked by Wright to do some work and had given his assent to this action. Warshaw later claimed a mechanic's lien on the property and Pyms contended he was not entitled to a lien under Florida law because he did not have a direct contract with Pyms. Can Warshaw have a valid mechanic's lien?

chapter 44

Bankruptcy

Background

Bankruptcy Laws in the United States. The framers of the Constitution gave the federal government the right to regulate and control bankruptcies. This power was first exercised in 1800, when Congress passed a bankruptcy act. Our present federal Bankruptcy Act is the act of 1898 as amended. The act has been amended many times since it was first enacted, but its general plan has not been changed by the amendments. Congress has restudied our bankruptcy legislation following each major depression, and many new features have been added to the Bankruptcy Act of 1898 since the depression of 1929. The principal additions are the provisions for railroad reorganizations, corporate reorganizations, municipal debt readjustments, agricultural compositions and extensions, and compositions and extensions.

Purpose and Scope of the Bankruptcy Act. The purpose of the Bankruptcy Act is (1) to protect creditors from one another, (2) to protect creditors from their debtors, and (3) to protect the honest debtor from his creditors. To accomplish these objectives, the debtor is required to make a full disclosure of all his property and to surrender it to the trustee. Provisions are made for examination of the debtor and for punishment of the debtor who refuses to make an honest disclosure and surrender of his property. The trustee of the bankrupt's estate administers, liquidates, and distributes the proceeds of the estate to the creditors. Provisions are made for the determination of creditors' rights, the recovery of preferential payments, and the disallowance of preferential liens and encumbrances. If the bankrupt has been honest in his business transactions and in his bankruptcy proceedings, he is granted a discharge.

Bankrupts

Voluntary Bankruptcy.   Under the provisions of our federal Bankruptcy Act a debtor may be adjudged bankrupt on his own petition, in which case he is known as a voluntary bankrupt.

Under the present Bankruptcy Act, any person, partnership, or corporation, with few exceptions, may be adjudged a voluntary bankrupt after filing a petition asking that such judgment be rendered. The person, partnership, or corporation asking to be adjudged bankrupt need not be insolvent at the time of the filing of the petition. Such action must, however, be taken in good faith and not for the purpose of using bankruptcy as a means of perpetrating a fraud. Municipal, railroad, insurance, and banking corporations and building and loan associations are excepted from the operation of the Bankruptcy Act, since other statutes have been enacted which provide for the handling of the affairs of such corporations and associations in the event of their insolvency.

Involuntary Bankrupts.   A debtor may, if he has committed an act of bankruptcy, be adjudged an involuntary bankrupt on the petition of his creditors. Under the provisions of the Bankruptcy Act an involuntary petition may be filed against any natural person, except a wage carner or farmer, and any moneyed, business, or commercial corporation, except a building and loan association, a municipal, railroad, insurance, or banking corporation, owing debts amounting to $1,000 or more and having committed an act of bankruptcy within four months before the filing of the petition. The petition may be filed in the federal district court having jurisdiction over the party involved.

Acts of bankruptcy by a person shall consist of having (1) concealed, removed, or permitted to be concealed or removed any part of his property, with intent to hinder, delay or defraud his creditors or any of them, or made or suffered a transfer of any of his property, fraudulent under section 67 or 70 of the act; or (2) made or suffered a preferential transfer as defined in subdivision of section 60 of the act; or (3) suffered or permitted, while insolvent, any creditor to obtain a lien upon any of his property through legal proceedings or distraint and not having vacated or discharged such lien within 30 days from the date thereof or at least 5 days before the day set for any sale or other disposition of such property; or (4) made a general assignment for the benefit of his creditors; or (5) while insolvent or unable to pay his debts as they matured, procured, permitted, or suffered voluntarily, or involuntarily the appointment of a receiver or trustee to take charge of his property; or (6) admitted in writing his inability to pay his debts and his willingness to be adjudged bankrupt.

An involuntary petition in bankruptcy may be filed against a person by 3 or more creditors who have provable claims not contingent as to liability against a person, amounting in the aggregate to $500 in excess of the value of any security held by them, or, if all the creditors of a person are less than 12 in number, then 1 or more of the creditors, whose claim or claims equal that amount, may file a petition to have him adjudged bankrupt; but the claim or claims if unliquidated shall not be counted in computing the number and aggregate amount of the claims of the creditors joining in the petition, if the court determines that the claim or claims cannot be readily determined or estimated to be sufficient, together with the claims of the other creditors, to aggregate $500, without unduly delaying the decision upon the adjudication.

A creditor is not estopped to act as a petitioning creditor because he participated in a prior matter or judicial proceeding, as, for example, where he consented to a prior receivership proceeding or to a prior assignment for the benefit of creditors, or participated in such proceedings, or accepted dividends therein. However, the courts have held that if a party has brought an action asking for the appointment of a receiver or has participated actively in inducing a debtor to make an assignment for the benefit of creditors, he is estopped from acting as a petitioning creditor.

Summary

A person who is adjudged a bankrupt on his own petition is a voluntary bankrupt. Substantially any person, partnership, or corporation, except a municipal, railroad, insurance, or banking corporation or a building and loan association, may be adjudged a voluntary bankrupt.

Under certain circumstances a debtor may be adjudged bankrupt on the petition of his creditors. Such a debtor is known as an involuntary bankrupt. To be adjudged an involuntary bankrupt, the debtor must have, within four months from the filing of the petition and while insolvent, committed an act of bankruptcy. The Bankruptcy Act sets out what acts are acts of bankruptcy.

Administration of Bankrupt's Estate

Adjudication and Appointment of Trustee.   Petitions for both voluntary and involuntary bankruptcy are filed in the federal district court. After adjudication the estate of the bankrupt is referred to the referee for the purpose of administration.

The referee calls the first meeting of creditors not less than 10 days nor more than 30 days after the adjudication. At the first meeting of creditors the judge or referee presides. The first step in the administration of the estate is the allowance of claims and the election of the trustee. The trustee is elected by a vote of the claims which have been allowed, and the person who receives the majority vote in number and amount is elected. In determining the number of claims voted, claims of $50 or less are not counted, but such claims are counted in computing the amount. The judge or referee is not bound to appoint the person elected by the creditors as trustee. If the person elected is not qualified or for some other reason would not be desirable as trustee, the judge or referee may appoint someone of his own selection.

Examination of Bankrupt. The next step is the public examination of the bankrupt. He is examined by the judge or referee who presides at the meeting and, in addition, may be examined by any creditor. This may be done by the creditor himself or by an attorney whom the creditor has employed to conduct the examination in his behalf. The purpose of the examination of the bankrupt is to bring out all the facts relating to his bankruptcy, to determine whether he has made a full and complete disclosure of all his property, to determine whether he has been guilty of any acts which would bar his discharge, and to clear up any questions arising as to claims, assets, or other matters affecting the bankrupt's estate.

Rights and Duties of Trustee. The trustee, as soon as he has qualified, takes possession of all the property of the bankrupt, inventories it, has it appraised, and sets aside the bankrupt's exemptions. He also examines the claims filed, and objects to any claims which are not allowable or which for any reason are improper. The trustee reduces the estate to money as expeditiously as is compatible with the best interests of the parties.

The trustee represents the creditors in the administration of the estate. Title to the bankrupt's property vests in the trustee, and he has all the rights in such property that the bankrupt had at the time of the adjudication. In addition, the trustee has all the rights against the bankrupt's property that a creditor holding an unsatisfied lien on the property of the bankrupt would have. For example, a creditor who has a security interest in certain property of the bankrupt, but whose security interest has not been perfected by compliance with the recording statutes of the state, has a lien on such property which is valid against a creditor with an unsatisfied execution. In such a situation a trustee in bankruptcy would have all the rights of the creditor with the unsatisfied execution.

To protect the interests of the creditors, the trustee in bankruptcy is given the right to bring suit in any court in which the bankrupt could have brought suit to enforce claims of the bankrupt's estate. Such suits are brought in the name of the trustee. All such suits are brought under the supervision of the court in which the bankruptcy proceedings are pending. Also, the trustee owes a duty to defend all suits brought against the bankrupt estate.

The trustee must keep an accurate account of all the property and money coming into his hands, deposit all money in the authorized depositories, pay by check or draft all dividends within 10 days after they are declared by the referee, and lay before the final meeting of the creditors a detailed statement of the administration of the estate.

Summary

The debtor is adjudged bankrupt by the judge of the federal district court. After adjudication the case is referred to the referee in bankruptcy where, at the first meeting of creditors, a trustee in bankruptcy is elected or appointed. After the election or appointment of the trustee the bankrupt is examined in regard to any matters material to the administration of the estate. The trustee takes possession of all the assets of the bankrupt, collects all claims, sets aside the bankrupt's exemptions, liquidates the assets, and distributes the proceeds among the creditors. Title to the bankrupt's estate vests in the trustee. The trustee must keep accurate accounts and make a final accounting of the administration of the estate.

Debts

Provable Debts.   The debts of a bankrupt, for the purpose of the administration of his estate, are classified as "provable debts," "allowable debts," "debts having priority," and "dischargeable debts." If a debt is provable, it is the basis of its owner's right to share in the estate of the bankrupt.

Provable debts include those founded upon a fixed liability as evidenced by a judgment or an instrument in writing absolutely owing at the time of the filing of the petition by or against him, whether then payable or not, with accrued interest or any rebate of interest due; costs taxable against the bankrupt in a suit by him which the trustee declines to prosecute; taxable costs of creditor incurred in good faith by a creditor; an open account, or a contract express or implied; provable debts reduced to judgment after filing of the petition and before consideration of the bankrupt's discharge; workmen's compensation awards and like awards if the injury occurred prior to adjudication; the right to recover damages in any action for negligence instituted prior to and pending at the time of filing of the petition in bankruptcy; contingent debts and contingent contractual liability; and claims for anticipatory breach of contract, executory in whole or in part, including unexpired leases of personal property or leases not to exceed damages equivalent to one year's rent.

Allowable Debts.   The fact that a debt is classed as a provable debt does not assure its owner's participation in the distribution of the assets. Before a creditor can participate in the bankruptcy proceedings, he must prove his claim, and the claim must be allowed. The proof of claim is a sworn statement of the amount of the claim, the consideration therefor, security held, and so forth; and if it is based on a written instrument, such instrument must be filed with the proof. Claims which are not filed within six months after the first date set for the first meeting of creditors will not be allowed. If the bankrupt has any defense to the debt, such defense will be set up by the trustee, and if established, the claim will not be allowed; or if the defense goes to only part of the claim, the amount of the claim will be reduced. All the defenses which would have been available to the bankrupt will be available to the trustee.

Debts Having Priority.   Certain claims are declared by the Bankruptcy Act to have priority over other classes of claims and should not be confused with those secured. The following claims have priority: Costs and expenses of administration; costs of preserving the estate; filing fees; costs expended by a creditor in the recovery of property which has been transferred or concealed by the bankrupt provided it is recovered for the benefit of the estate; trustee's expenses in opposing the bankrupt's discharge or in his criminal prosecution for violation of the Bankruptcy Act; one reasonable attorney's fee and other professional expenses incurred in connection with a hearing on a voluntary or involuntary petition for the adjudication of bankruptcy if the court adjudges the debtor bankrupt; wages and commissions earned within three months before the commencement of proceedings, due workmen, servants, clerks, or traveling or city salesmen not to exceed $600; and taxes legally owing by the bankrupt to the United States or any state or any subdivision thereof, not to exceed the value of the bankrupt's estate.

Nondischargeable Debts.   Certain debts are not affected by the bankrupt's discharge. Section 17 of the Bankruptcy Act provides that a discharge in bankruptcy shall release a bankrupt from all his provable debts, whether allowable in full or in part, except such as (1) are due as a tax levied by the United States, or any state, county, district, or municipality; or (2) are liabilities for obtaining money or property by false pretense or false representations, or for willful and malicious injuries to the person or property of another, or for alimony due or to become due, or for maintenance or support of wife or child, or for seduction of an unmarried female, or for breach of promise of marriage accompanied by seduction, or for criminal conversation; or (3) having not been duly scheduled in time for proof and an allowance, with the name of the creditor, if known to the bankrupt, unless such creditor had notice or actual knowledge of the proceedings in bankruptcy; or (4) were created by his fraud, embezzlement, misappropriation, or defalcation while acting as an officer or in any fiduciary capacity; or (5) are for wages which have been earned within three months before the date of commencement of the proceedings in bankruptcy due to "workmen, servants, clerks, or traveling or city salesmen" on salary or commission basis, whole or part-time, whether or not selling exclusively for the bankrupt; or (6) are due for moneys of an employee received or retained by his employer to secure the faithful performance by such employee of the terms of a contract of employment.

These debts are provable debts, and the owner of such a debt has the right to participate in the distribution of the bankrupt's estate; but his right to recover the unpaid balance of the debt is not cut off by the bankrupt's discharge. All provable debts except those listed above are dischargeable debts, that is, the right to recover the unpaid balance is cut off by the bankrupt's discharge.

Summary

Provable debts include substantially all claims except unliquidated tort claims. Contingent claims arising on contracts are provable debts. If a debtor wishes to participate in the bankrupt's estate, he must file a proof of claim in the estate within six months of the first meeting of creditors. Certain debts are given priority by the provisions of the Bankruptcy Act. Certain debts, although provable, are not dischargeable.

Preferences, Liens, and Fraudulent Transfers

Preferential Payments.　A preferential payment is a payment made by a debtor (1) while he is insolvent, (2) within four months of the filing of a petition in bankruptcy by or against the debtor, (3) which payment enables the creditor receiving the payment to obtain a greater percentage of his debt than other creditors in the same class, and (4) which creditor, when he received the payment, must have had reasonable grounds to believe that the debtor was insolvent. If a debtor makes a preferential payment, such act is an act of bankruptcy. If a debtor is adjudged bankrupt, the trustee in bankruptcy has the right to recover for the benefit of the estate all preferential payments that have been made by the bankrupt.

One of the purposes of the Bankruptcy Act is to ensure equal treatment for the creditors of an insolvent debtor and to prevent an insolvent debtor from distributing his assets to favored creditors to the detriment of his other creditors. Under the common law, the creditor who first attached or obtained a lien on his debtor's property or who was able to induce a debtor to pay his claim could retain the advantage he had gained, irrespective of the fact that such advantage might deplete the debtor's estate to such a degree that the other creditors could recover nothing. Also, under the common law, if a debtor was solvent but for some reason was temporarily unable to meet his obligations as they matured, one creditor, by starting suit against such debtor, could cause other creditors to rush in and try to salvage as much of their claims as they could, with the result that all persons involved would suffer unnecessary loss due to costs of suit and the inability to realize the full value of assets which would be sold at forced sale. Under the Bankruptcy Act the rights of all persons can be protected.

Even though a debtor is insolvent, he can carry on his business without fear of being adjudged bankrupt if he does not commit an act of bankruptcy. Payments made in the regular course of a business are not preferential payments, and such payments are not acts of bankruptcy. For example, if an insolvent debtor purchases property, paying the purchase price on delivery, such a payment is not a preferential payment. The debtor's estate has been neither increased nor decreased if the property purchased is worth the price paid. Also, the courts have held that if the debtor has purchased goods on credit, the payment of the price of the goods when the account is due is not, under ordinary circumstances, a preferential payment. Such payments are not acts of bankruptcy, and if the debtor is adjudged bankrupt, the trustee in bankruptcy cannot recover such payments even though they have been made while the debtor is insolvent and within four months of the adjudication of bankruptcy.

Preferential Liens. A creditor may attempt to obtain a preference by obtaining a lien on the debtor's property. The lien may be obtained either by legal or equitable process or by contract with the debtor. Any lien which is obtained within four months of the filing of the petition is null and void if the lien is to secure a preexisting debt and if the debtor was insolvent at the time the lien was obtained. A lien which is given as security for present value received is valid against the trustee in bankruptcy.

If an insolvent debtor borrows money or purchases goods and gives a lien on his assets to secure the repayment of the money borrowed or the purchase price of the goods, his assets have not been diminished by the transaction, and the creditor has gained no advantage over existing creditors by the taking of the lien. Such liens are valid against a trustee in bankruptcy of the debtor.

Fraudulent Transfers. Transfers for the purpose of hindering, delaying, or defrauding creditors are null and void. This rule is applied generally throughout the United States. Transfers made by a debtor and every obligation incurred by him within one year of the filing of the petition in bankruptcy are void as to creditors, if made or incurred without fair consideration and while insolvent, or if the transfer or obligation will render him insolvent. If one makes a transfer of property or incurs obligations without fair consideration in contemplation of incurring debts beyond his ability to pay, the transaction is fraudulent to both existing and future creditors. In all the foregoing situations the transfer or obligation may be declared void if made within one year from the date of the filing of the petition in bankruptcy. A transfer made or an obligation incurred within four months of the filing of the petition is fraudulent as to existing and future creditors if made with the intent to use the consideration obtained to effect a preference which is voidable under the act.

In addition to the above, any transfer made or suffered or any obligation incurred by a debtor who has been adjudged a bankrupt, which under any federal or state law applicable thereto is voidable by any creditor having a provable claim, shall be void as against the trustee. Such property remains a part of the bankrupt's estate and passes to the trustee, and the trustee owes a duty to reclaim the property or collect its value for the benefit of the estate.

All these safeguards are set up to prevent the debtor from concealing or disposing of his property in fraud of his creditors or to prevent him from favoring one creditor at the expense of his other creditors; yet they are so framed that the honest but hard-pressed debtor is not unduly handicapped in continuing the operation of his business. If the debtor "plays fair," he is protected; if he does not, the creditors are protected.

Summary

A preferential payment is a payment made to a creditor by an insolvent debtor within four months of his adjudication as a bankrupt, which payment enables the creditor to realize a greater percentage of his claim than other creditors of the same class; such creditor must have reasonable grounds for believing that the debtor is insolvent. A lien given by an insolvent debtor within four months of his adjudication as a bankrupt, to secure a preexisting debt, is void. Any transfer made or obligation incurred without consideration within one year from the debtor's adjudication as a bankrupt is void as to creditors.

Hanes v. Crown Camera Sales, Inc.

468 F.2d 1318 (5th Cir. 1972)

This was an action brought by Hanes, the trustee in bankruptcy for Television Productions International (TPI), (plaintiff) against Crown Camera Sales (defendant) to recover as voidable preferences three payments totaling $10,325.33 paid by the bankrupt, TPI, to Crown Camera Sales. Summary judgment for Hanes. Affirmed per curiam.

The facts are given in the Order of the trial court which was attached as an appendix to the per curiam decision of the Court of Appeals.

ORDER.   The facts are that TPI had the prospect of getting a contract from the Atlanta Hawks basketball team to provide television lighting for games played at the Georgia Tech coliseum. TPI made arrangements to purchase certain lighting fixtures and lamps from defendant in order to fulfill its contract with the Atlanta Hawks. These arrangements were confirmed in a letter dated September 11, 1970 from TPI to defendant which said in part:

This is to confirm in writing the order for fixtures and lamps about which we spoke Thursday, Sept. 10, 1970.

It serves as a definite order, in contract, to purchase through Crown Camera Exchange the following items:

* * * * *

It is agreed that the contract monies received from the Atlanta Hawks basketball office for lighting Alexander Memorial Coliseum will be put in full for payment for these fixtures and lamps.

Defendant delivered the equipment during October and November, and on December 3, 1970 the Board of Directors of TPI passed a resolution authorizing the officers to assign invoice No. 0370 (to be presented to the Atlanta Hawks) to defendant. That same day a formal assignment of the invoice was executed by the president of TPI. On December 15 TPI received $1,800 from the Atlanta Hawks as payment in full for invoice No. 0370 and the following day this sum was paid by TPI to defendant. On February 18, 1971, the president of TPI executed an assignment of invoices No. 0433 (presented to the Atlanta Hawks) and No. 1436 (presented to television station WSMW-TV of Worcester, Massachusetts) to defendant. TPI received the amounts due on these invoices, and on February 26 and March 12 made payments of $2,000 and $6,525.33 to defendant, thereby satisfying the account in full for the fixtures and lamps. TPI filed its petition and was adjudged bankrupt on March 18, 1971.

Section 60 of the Bankruptcy Act provides in part as follows:

(a) (1) A preference is a transfer, as defined in this title, of any of the property of a debtor to or for the benefit of a creditor for or on account of an antecedent debt, made or suffered by such debtor while insolvent and within four months before the filing by or against him of the petition initiating a proceeding under this title, the effect of which transfer will be to enable such creditor to obtain a greater percentage of his debt than some other creditor of the same class.

* * * * *

(b) Any such preference may be avoided by the trustee if the creditor receiving it or to be benefited thereby or his agent acting with reference thereto has, at the time when the transfer is made, reasonable cause to believe that the debtor is insolvent. Where the preference is voidable, the trustee may recover the property. . . . For the purpose of any recovery or avoidance under this section, where plenary proceedings are necessary, any State court which would have had jurisdiction if bankruptcy had not intervened and any court of bankruptcy shall have concurrent jurisdiction.

The parties do not dispute that the three payments made by TPI to defendant were transfers of property by a debtor, while insolvent, made within four months before the filing of a petition in bankruptcy, for the benefit of a creditor, who had reasonable cause to believe that the debtor was insolvent, the effect of which was to prefer that creditor. The only question to be determined by this court is whether the transfers were made "for or on account of an antecedent debt." On this issue defendant contends that the letter of September 11, 1970 was an assignment of the proceeds of the Atlanta Hawks contract and that the transfers to defendant of those proceeds, in consequence, were not "for or on account of an antecedent debt." Plaintiff's position is that the letter was no more than a promise to pay from a particular source, and that the subsequent transfers were payments "for or on account of an antecedent debt," preferential and voidable.

If the letter of September 11, 1970 was a valid assignment, the subsequent three transfers would not be considered preferences because defendant gave fair and present consideration—the fixtures and lamps—for the purported assignment. . . . In such a case the transfers would represent the completion of an exchange of property of equal value rather than payments "for or on account of an antecedent debt.". . . On the other hand, if the letter was not an assignment but merely a promise to pay from a particular source, the transfers would represent payments in satisfaction of a pre-existing debt and would be preferential. . . . The proper construction of the September 11th letter is controlled by Georgia law. . . .

No formal language is necessary under Georgia law to create a legal assignment, and if the language used in a transaction shows the intention of the owner of a right to transfer it instantly so that it becomes the property of the transferee at the time of the transaction, a legal assignment exists. . . . The language of the September 11th letter, however, does not evidence such an intention on the part of TPI. On the contrary, the language shows that TPI intended itself to receive the contract monies from the Atlanta Hawks and then apply such monies as payment for the fixtures and lamps purchased from defendant. It is undisputed that this is exactly what later happened. The court concludes that the September 11th letter did not create a legal assignment.

Discharge

Basis for Granting Discharge. A bankrupt who has not been guilty of serious infractions of the code of business ethics and who has fulfilled his duties as a bankrupt is entitled to a discharge in bankruptcy. The adjudication of any person, except a corporation, shall operate as an application for a discharge. A bankrupt may, however, before the hearing on his application, file a written waiver of his right to discharge. A corporation may, within six months after its adjudication, file an application for a discharge in the court in which the proceedings are pending.

Filing Objections to Discharge. After the statutory filing fees have been paid in full, the court makes an order fixing the time for filing objections to the bankrupt's discharge. The date fixed shall be not less than 30 days after the first date set for the first meeting of creditors. If the examination of the bankrupt has not been completed or will not be completed prior to the time fixed for filing objections, the court, on its own motion or on the motion of the receiver, trustee, creditor, or other party in interest, shall extend the time of filing objections. Notice of the time fixed for filing objections to the discharge is given to all interested parties. If objections have been filed within the time fixed or within any extension of time which may have been granted by the court, the court will hear proofs of the objections at such time as will give the parties a reasonable opportunity to be fully heard. If the court is satisfied that the bankrupt has not committed any of the acts which are a bar to his discharge, the discharge will be granted.

Acts Which Bar Discharge. The acts which are a bar to a bankrupt's discharge are set out in Section 14, Subsection *c,* of the Bankruptcy Act as follows:

The court shall grant the discharge unless satisfied that the bankrupt has (1) committed an offense punishable by imprisonment as provided under title 18, United States Code Section 152; or (2) destroyed, mutilated, falsified, concealed, or failed to keep or preserve books of account or records, from which his financial condition and business transactions might be ascertained, unless the court deems such acts or failure to have been justified under all the circumstances of the case; or (3) while engaged in business as sole proprietor, partnership or as executive of a corporation, obtained for such business money or property on credit or an extension or renewal of credit by making or publishing or causing to be made or published in any manner whatsoever a materially false statement in writing respecting his financial condition or the financial condition of such partnership or corporation; or (4) at any time subsequent to the first day of the twelve months immediately preceding the filing of the petition in bankruptcy, transferred, removed, destroyed, or concealed, or permitted to be removed, destroyed, or concealed, any of his property, with intent to hinder, delay, or defraud his creditors; or (5) in a proceeding under this Act commenced within six years prior to the date of filing the petition in bankruptcy been granted a discharge, or had a composition or arrangement by way of composition or a wage earner's plan by way of composition confirmed under this Act; or (6) in the course of a proceeding under this Act refused to obey any lawful order of, or to answer any material question approved by, the court; or (7) failed to explain satisfactorily any losses of assets or deficiency of assets to meet his liabilities: *Provided,* that if, upon the hearing of an objection to a discharge, the objector shall show to the satisfaction of the court that there are reasonable grounds for believing that the bankrupt has committed any of the acts which, under this subdivision *c,* would prevent his discharge in bankruptcy, then the burden of proving that he has not committed any of such acts shall be upon the bankrupt.

Who May File Objections. The trustee, a creditor, the U.S. attorney, or such other attorney as the Attorney General may designate may file objections to and oppose the discharge of a bankrupt. When requested by the court, it is the duty of the U.S. attorney located in the judicial district in which the bankruptcy proceeding is pending to examine into the acts and conduct of the bankrupt. If satisfied that probable ground exists for the denial of a discharge and that public interest warrants the action, it is his duty to oppose the bankrupt's discharge. Also, if the bankrupt fails to appear at the hearing on his discharge or, having appeared, refuses to submit himself to examination at the first meeting of creditors or at any subsequent meeting called for his examination, he shall be deemed to have waived his right to a discharge.

Summary

A bankrupt is granted a discharge unless he has been guilty of serious infraction of the code of business ethics or has failed to fulfill his duties as a bankrupt. The time for filing the objections to a bankrupt's discharge is fixed at the first meeting of creditors or at a special meeting called for that purpose.

The grounds for denying a bankrupt's discharge are set out in the Bankruptcy Act. The trustee, a creditor, the U.S. attorney, or an attorney designated by the Attorney General may file objections to a bankrupt's discharge.

Charles Edward & Associates v. England
301 F.2d 572 (9th Cir. 1962)

This was an appeal by Charles P. Trafficante and Paul J. Trafficante from an order of the District Court which set aside the individual discharges in bankruptcy granted by the Referee. Judgment affirmed in part.

The Trafficantes filed individual voluntary petitions in bankruptcy and a short time later Charles Edward & Associates, a partnership composed of the two Trafficantes, was adjudged a bankrupt in an involuntary proceeding. The two individual estates and the partnership estate were consolidated for the purposes of administration. The trustee petitioned the Referee for an extension of time for filing objections to the discharge of the individual bankrupts but through error did not include the partnership. The order extending the time was limited to the individuals. The trustee filed objections to the discharge of both the partnership and the individual partners. The objections were based on the individual partners' failure to keep books, the partnership's transfer of property to the individual partners, in fraud of creditors and within one year of the filing of the bankruptcy petition, the individual partners' failure to explain losses in their individual assets amounting to $56,000, and the withdrawal of large amounts of cash within one year of the filing of the petition in bankruptcy and when the partnership was insolvent, with the intent to defraud creditors.

SOLOMON, DISTRICT JUDGE.   The failure to keep or preserve books of account or records from which a bankrupt's financial condition and business transactions might be obtained is a ground for the denial of a discharge in bankruptcy under the Bankruptcy Act (Act), 11 U.S.C.A. ¶ 32, sub. *c* (2).

Specification 1 charges:

1. That said Bankrupt copartnership and each of the bankrupt individual members thereof failed to keep books or records from which the financial condition of said bankrupt copartnership might be ascertained in that they, and each of them, wholly failed and neglected at all times during the existence of said copartnership to maintain books or records relating to the accounts payable of said copartnership.

The Trafficantes contend that this specification charges misconduct against the partnership and not against the individual partners, and they claim that any other construction would disregard the entity theory of partnership.

Although the Bankruptcy Act of 1938 adopted the entity theory for some purposes and the aggregate theory for other purposes, the entity theory is specifically rejected in ¶ 5, sub. *j* of the Act, 11 U.S.C.A. ¶ 23, sub. *j*, which provides that the discharge of a partnership does not discharge the individual partners from partnership debts.

Under either theory, a partner who has engaged in conduct proscribed by the Act, either on behalf of the partnership or on his own behalf, is not entitled to a discharge.

In many cases, as in this one, substantially all of the debts of the individual partners were those of the partnership. The failure of a partner to keep partnership books and records may preclude a creditor or a trustee from ascertaining the true financial condition of a partner.

The Referee's ruling was clearly erroneous, and the District Court was correct in setting it aside.

The transfer of property with intent to hinder, delay or defraud creditors, within twelve months of the filing of a petition in bankruptcy, is also a ground for the denial of a discharge in bankruptcy. 11 U.S.C.A. ¶ 32, sub. *c* (4).

Specification 2 charges:

2. That at times subsequent to the first day of the twelve months immediately preceding the filing of the individual partners' petitions in bankruptcy, and also at items [*sic*] subsequent to

the first day of the twelve months immediately preceding the filing of the petition in bankruptcy against the said bankrupt copartnership, the said partnership, while continually insolvent, the individual members thereof having full knowledge of such partnership insolvency and with intent to defraud the partnership creditors, transferred to the individual members thereof, property of said partnership, to wit, cash in the sum of $22,819.07 or thereabouts.

Specification 4 is similar to 2, but, in addition, charges that the individual partners made cash withdrawals from partnership funds in the amount of approximately $23,-000 and that the partners transferred the money to themselves with intent to defraud partnership creditors.

These two specifications clearly allege improper conduct against the individual partners in personally withdrawing large sums from the partnership with intent to defraud partnership creditors. An individual discharge will be denied a partner who withdraws funds from a partnership with intent to defraud creditors.

Problem Cases

1. An involuntary petition in bankruptcy was filed against Camp Ganeden, Inc. The petition alleged that Camp Ganeden, Inc., was insolvent and that while insolvent and within four months of the filing of the petition it had entered into an agreement to transfer for $25,000 all of its assets, which were of the value of $65,000, to Camp Winslow, Inc. Is the petition sufficient to justify the court in adjudging Camp Ganeden, Inc., bankrupt?

2. An involuntary petition in bankruptcy was filed against Ouellette. The court adjudged Ouellette bankrupt and based its finding of insolvency on the appraisal of an experienced appraiser and all the circumstances of the case. Ouellette's principal asset was the hardware stock of two retail stores which he was operating. Ouellette contended that the basis of determining the value of his assets should be the invoice cost of the stock in the stores and not the appraised value. Is Ouellette's contention correct?

3. Hart was the secretary-treasurer as well as a director and stockholder of the Pacific Oil and Metal Company, a bankrupt corporation. In a corporate reorganization pursuant to the Bankruptcy Act, Hart filed a claim for $1,556.81 for compensation owed him under his contract as secretary-treasurer of the company and contended that he was entitled to a priority payment of $600 as wages earned by a "clerk" within three months prior to commencement of bankruptcy proceedings. A creditor objected to allowance of the priority payment. As a judge how would you rule on the objection?

4. International Marketing was engaged in buying and selling petroleum and gas products under the direction of sole stockholders Davis, Clark, and Wood. Cooper Petroleum was likewise engaged and the two companies were in the practice of conducting as much business as possible with each other. Fagan, who was a dominant figure in the management of Cooper Petroleum, acquired one fourth of International's stock, and subsequently transferred it to the members of his family who also occupied executive positions with Cooper Petroleum. Clark served as vice president and director of both companies. On June 2, 1964, an involuntary bankruptcy petition was filed against International. Records of the companies disclosed that during the four-month period preceding bankruptcy, Cooper Petroleum delivered $45,-000 worth of goods to International on a running open account and was paid a total of $40,154.94 on that account. Creditors of International sought to recover the $40,154.94 from Cooper Petroleum claiming that these were preferential payments. Can Cooper Petroleum avoid the preferential payment rule by claiming that since the payments did not exceed the

value of goods delivered, the net estate of International was thereby enriched by the aggregate transaction and no prejudice resulted to other creditors?

5. Tom Page was employed by Airo Supply Company as its only bookkeeper. Over a three-year period he appropriated $14,775.77 of Airo Supply's money to his own use. Airo Supply discovered the embezzlement and obtained a civil judgment against Page for $14,775.77. Page then filed a voluntary petition in bankruptcy and his discharge was granted. Page obtained new employment and Airo Supply instituted proceedings to garnishee his wages. Page defended on the grounds Airo Supply's judgment had been discharged in bankruptcy. Does Page have a valid defense?

6. Lee Company had obtained a judgment against Carter and had levied an execution on Carter's assets which were sold at execution sale. From the proceeds of the sale, Lee Company's judgment was paid in full. Within four months of the execution sale, Carter was adjudged bankrupt. The court found that Carter was insolvent at the time of the execution sale and that Lee Company knew or should have known that he was insolvent. Carter had concealed assets and was denied a discharge. Lee Company contends that since Carter has been denied a discharge, all creditors have an equal right to recover the full amount of their claims and the trustee in bankruptcy is not entitled to recover from them (Lee Company), as a preferential payment, the amount realized on the execution sale. Is Lee Company's contention correct?

7. On November 2, 1964, Shainman was adjudicated a bankrupt upon the filing of a voluntary petition. In October 1963, Shear's of Affton had loaned Shainman $10,000 secured, at least in part, by inventory. Shear's objected to the discharge of Shainman on the grounds that Shainman had issued a false inventory statement as of January 31, 1964, wherein his inventory was valued at over $800,000 when actual value as established by a physical inventory was less than $175,000. Shear's alleged that this false statement had been relied upon by Receivables Finance Company in extending business loans to Shainman. Should the discharge be denied because of Shear's objections based on false financial statements issued to another creditor?

8. Barnhart had borrowed money from Credit Plan and was in arrears in her payments. She applied for a new loan, with which she intended to pay the existing loan and the interest thereon. At the time of the granting of the new loan, the agent of Credit Plan prepared a financial statement which showed that Barnhart owed $837.50 whereas she owed approximately $1,800. The agent was a schoolmate of Barnhart's and was familiar with her financial affairs. At the time the statement was prepared Barnhart talked to the agent about her other debts. She signed the statement without reading it. Credit Plan filed objections to Barnhart's discharge on the ground that she obtained credit on a materially false credit statement in writing. Should Barnhart be granted a discharge?

Part XI

Economic Relations and the Law

chapter 45

Competitive Torts and the Protection of Ideas

Introduction

Rights Protected. Tort law protecting economic relations from unreasonable interferences developed more recently than did tort law in other areas. However, rights and duties arising out of economic relations now are clearly established in three main categories.

First, business firms are protected against injurious falsehoods or other deceitful practices by competitors which result in diversion of their patronage or otherwise injures their goodwill. Second, protection is given to ideas by the law relating to trade secrets, patents, and copyrights. Third, protection is given against certain unjustifiable interferences with contracts or economic expectations. To an important extent, the rights in these areas now are governed by federal and state statutes creating special procedures, rules, and remedies.

Deceitful Diversion of Patronage

Disparagement. The torts of libel and slander, discussed in Chapter 3, afford remedies against competitors who publish defamatory falsehoods charging other businessmen with personal misconduct. If the falsehood relates to the quality of the product, to the seller's title, or to the type service provided, it is the tort of *disparagement* and proof of actual damage is essential. Although the tort of disparagement originated with cases protecting tangible property rights from injurious falsehoods, protection was later extended to intangible property rights including trademarks, patents, corporate shares, and copyrighted material.

Another form of deceitful diversion of patronage occurs where one firm "palms" its goods off as being those made by a competitor. Although "palming off" is a tort, nearly all actions of this type are now brought under the Lanham Act which affords very extensive protection for trademarks and other product and service identifying marks used by business firms.

Trademarks and Other Marks. A trademark is a distinctive mark, word, design, or picture which is affixed to goods so that purchasers may identify their origin. In general, a trademark must be fanciful, arbitrary, unique, and nondescriptive. Generic terms such as "car" or "ham" and descriptive terms such as "good" or "extra soft" may not be exclusively appropriated as a trademark.

A *trade name* is used as the name under which a firm operates. *Service marks* are used to identify services and need only to be registered. *Certification marks* are used by people who do not own the marks but who have a right to identify the product as being approved or authorized by the owner of the mark. The "Good Housekeeping Seal of Approval" is an example of a certification mark. A *collective mark* is employed by an association or group of people to identify the group as being the source of the product or service. Trade union or trade association marks fall into this category.

Since 1946 the Lanham Act (15 U.S.C. Sections 1050-1127) has greatly expanded the scope of registrability and the protection afforded to trademarks, trade names, service marks, certification marks, and collective marks. Such marks are protected against misuse or infringement by Section 1 of the act which states:

Any person who shall, in commerce, (a) use, without consent of registrant, any reproduction, counterfeit, copy or colorable imitation of any registered mark in connection with the sale, offering for sale, or advertising of any goods or services or in connection with which such use is likely to cause confusion or mistake or to deceive purchasers as to the source of such goods or services shall be . . . [liable for damages and subject to injunction].

Under the Lanham Act there is a Principal Register for the registration of "technical" trademarks (marks which distinguish the goods from those of others); and a Supplemental Register for "all marks capable of distinguishing applicant's goods or services and not registrable on the principal register," including marks which consist of surnames and geographical names and also packages and the configuration of goods.

Registration on the Principal Register carries important presumptions of validity and extends protection beyond that accorded to marks registered on the Supplemental Register. If a firm can establish that any mark has acquired a distinctive secondary meaning identifying its goods, such mark may be registered on the Principal Register. Proof of substantial exclusive continuous use for a period of five years preceding application for registration is prima facie evidence of acquired *secondary meaning*.

Summary

The tort of disparagement protects businessmen from injurious falsehoods relating to the quality of their products, their services, or the title to their property. The Lanham Act now gives extensive protection to registered trademarks, trade names, service marks, certification marks, and collective marks.

Testing Systems, Inc. v. Magnaflux Corp.

251 F. Supp. 286 (E.D. Pa. 1966)

This was an action for product disparagement brought by Testing Systems, Inc. (plaintiff), against Magnaflux Corp. (defendant). Judgment for Testing.

Testing and Magnaflux were competitors making equipment and chemical products. Testing Co. sued Magnaflux for damages for having orally and in writing disparaged Testing Co.'s products. This included statements to Testing Co.'s customers and prospective customers that Testing Co.'s products were "no good" and that the "government is throwing them out." It also included a written report falsely stating that the government had tested Testing Co.'s products and found them to be only 40% as effective as the products of Magnaflux.

LORD, DISTRICT JUDGE. The fine line that separates healthy competitive effort from underhanded business tactics is frequently difficult to determine. Apart from the tradesman's right of free speech, which must be vigorously safeguarded, the public has a genuine interest in learning the relative merits of particular products, however that may come about. To advance these interests the law of the marketplace gives the competitor a wide berth in the conduct of his business. As Mr. Justice Maxcy of the Pennsylvania Supreme Court said in 1932,

He may send out circulars, or give information verbally, to customers of other men, knowing they are bound by contract for a definite term, although acting upon the expectation and with the purpose of getting the trade of such persons for himself.

He may use any mode of persuasion with such a customer . . . . which appeals to his self-interest, reason, or even his prejudices.

He may descant upon the extent of his rival's facilities compared with his own, his rival's means, his insolvency, if it be a fact, and the benefits which will result to the customer in the future from coming to the solicitor rather than remaining where he is. . . . "the law of competition" . . . takes little note of the ordinary rules of good neighborhood or abstract morality.

Nonetheless, there is an outer perimeter to permissible conduct. The tradesman must be assured that his competitors will not be suffered to engage in conduct which falls below the minimum standard of fair dealing.

It is no answer that they can defend themselves by also resorting to disparagement. A self-respecting businessman will not voluntarily adopt, and should not be driven to adopt, a selling method which he regards as undignified, unfair, and repulsive. A competitor should not, by pursuing an unethical practice, force his rival to choose between its adoption and the loss of his trade.

Magnaflux's comments in the case presently before this court do not entitle it to the protection accorded to "unfavorable comparison." There is a readily observable difference between saying that one's product is, in general, better than another's . . . and asserting, as here, that such other's is only 40% as effective as one's own. The former, arguably, merely expresses an opinion, the truth or falsity of which is difficult or impossible of ascertainment. The latter, however, is an assertion of fact, not subject to the same frailties of proof, implying that the party making the statement is fortified with the substantive facts necessary to make it. This distinction has never been seriously questioned. Magnaflux in this case admittedly circulated to Testing's present and prospective customers false statements to the effect that the government had tested both products and found the Magnaflux to be 60% more effective than Testing's. This is not the sort of "comparison" that courts will protect.

Apart from this, there is at least one additional factor which withdraws Magnaflux's comments from the category of unfavorable comparison. Not content with making the admittedly false statements and allowing them to be evaluated independently of any extraneous influence, Magnaflux here gave added authenticity to its assertions by invoking the reputation of a third party, the United States Government. It is unnecessary to speculate on the additional force Magnaflux's remarks must have had when coupled with the purported approval of so highly credible a source. This, of course, is to say nothing of the statements to the effect that Testing had been "thrown out," which by no stretch of the imagination could be termed mere comparison.

Trade Secrets, Patents, and Copyrights

Trade Secrets. Society's interest in free competition is so strong that copying of a competitor's product is lawful unless trademark, trade secret, patent, or copyright rights are infringed. Copying or product simulation is a widespread practice in American business.

A trade secret is any formula, pattern, device, or compilation of special information which gives the firm developing it a differential advantage over competitors. A firm claiming a trade secret must be able to show that the device or formula was protected and treated as a secret within the firm. This usually means only a few people are allowed access to it and that it is never disclosed to anyone except on a confidential basis. Knowledge generally available in the trade cannot form the basis of trade secrets.

Trade secrets are given only limited protection by the law. It is only where competitors discover the secrets by bribery, theft, commercial espionage, or other wrongful means that injunctions and damages may be granted. If a trade secret is disclosed to someone on a confidential basis, any breach of this confidence will constitute a wrongful misappropriation.

Although a trade secret must confer some special competitive advantage, it need not embody the degree of inventiveness required for patentability. Some owners of patentable trade secrets may elect to run the risk of lawful imitation rather than to make the public disclosure of the invention as is required in order to obtain a patent. The legal monopoly conferred by the patent is only good for 17 years and then anyone can copy the invention.

Patents.   A patent may be granted to any person on any new and useful invention of a (1) process, (2) machine, (3) product, (4) composition of matter, (5) new and useful improvement thereof, (6) a growing plant, or (7) a design. The invention must not have been (1) patented or described in any printed publication in this or any foreign country for more than one year prior to application, (2) known or in use by others in this country prior to its invention, and (3) in public use or sale in this country for more than one year prior to application.

Except for design patents, a patentee gets the exclusive right to utilize, make or sell the patented product, machine, or process for a 17-year period. Design patents may be obtained from 3½ to 14 years depending upon the fee paid. The patent monopoly also includes the right to license others, to utilize the patent, and to control the terms and conditions under which such use is made.

The fact that the U.S. Patent Office has issued a patent does not necessarily mean that the patent is valid. About two-thirds of all patents challenged in court are held to be invalid or unenforceable for various technical reasons. Infringement of a valid patent renders the infringer liable to the patentee for any profits earned, and also for damages suffered by the patentee. In addition, injunctive relief is available to the patentee to prevent future acts of infringement.

Copyrights.   A copyright confers on the holder for a period of 28 years the exclusive right to print, publish, copy, sell or perform books, periodicals, lectures, plays, musical compositions, maps, works of art, drawings of a technical nature, photographs, and motion pictures. The Copyright Act does not impair the common law protection given to authors or owners of unpublished works. A copyright is obtained by filing an application with the Register of Copyrights, Copyright Office, Library of Congress, Washington, D.C. It can be renewed for an additional 28-year period provided the application for renewal is filed in the copyright office within one year prior to the expiration of the original term.

In general, any form of reproduction of copyrighted material without the consent of the copyright owner may render the copier liable for any actual damages the copyright owner can prove. The court may award from $250 to $5,000 statutory damages if actual damages cannot be proved. The extensive use of copying machines in the academic and business world creates many questions of possible liability under the Copyright Act. There is, however, an ill-defined "fair use" doctrine which may excuse the highly restricted reproduction and distribution of copyrighted material for nonprofit worthwhile purposes. This "fair use" exception is more likely to apply where the circumstances suggest that the copyright owner could not reasonably expect to receive greater royalties if copying of the type under consideration were to be penalized.

In 1971 Congress enacted legislation (Pub. L. 92–140, 85 Stat. 391) which extends for an "experimental" three-year period, protection to sound recordings fixed, published, and copyrighted after February 15, 1972 and before January 1, 1975. In a 1972 five–four split decision the U.S. Supreme Court upheld a California criminal statute which penalized tape or recording "piracy."[1] The majority opinion seems to hold that each state may enact legislation to regulate the copying of sound recordings.

Summary

In general, in the absence of a patent, copyright, or trade secret the product of others may be imitated or copied. Liability for "palming off" may occur under trademark law if the consumer is being confused. Trade secrets may be duplicated so long as the method of duplication does not involve misappropriation. Patents give a 17-year legal monopoly to the patentee but many patents are held to be invalid. Copyrights confer the exclusive right to reproduce written material for a period of 28 years. Copyright protection has now been extended to sound recordings.

Forest Laboratories, Inc. v. Pillsbury Company

452 F.2d 621 (7th Cir. 1971)

Forest Laboratories (plaintiff), a corporation engaged in producing and packaging effervescent sweetener tablets, sued Pillsbury Company (defendant), alleging that Pillsbury had purloined certain Forest trade secrets. Judgment in the amount of $75,000 for Forest and Pillsbury appealed. Affirmed.

Forest had developed a secret process for packing sweetener tablets so as to extend their shelf life. Forest disclosed this secret in confidence to Tidy House Corporation. Pillsbury then purchased the assets of Tidy House and learned the secret.

CUMMINGS, CIRCUIT JUDGE.   A trade secret is defined in Section 757, comment (b), of the Restatement as follows:

A trade secret may consist of any formula, pattern, device, or compilation of information which is used in one's business, and which gives him an opportunity to obtain an advantage over competitors who do not know or use it. It may be a . . . process of . . . treating or preserving materials. . . .

As stated in an authoritative treatise on this subject:

As distinguished from a patent, a trade secret need not be essentially new, novel or unique; therefore, prior art is a less effective defense in a trade secret case than it is in a patent infringement case. The idea need not be complicated; it may be intrinsically simple and nevertheless qualify as a secret, unless it is in common knowledge and, therefore, within the public domain.

[1] *Goldstein v. California*, 412 U.S. 546 (1972).

Before finally determining that this tablet-tempering step was a trade secret, the district court weighed the six factors prescribed by *Abbott Laboratories,* . . . and the *Restatement.* They are:

1. The extent to which the information is known outside of the claimant's business.
2. The extent to which it is known by employees and others involved in his business.
3. The extent of measures taken by him to guard the secrecy of the information.
4. The value of the information to him and his competitors.
5. The amount of effort or money expended by him in developing the information.
6. The ease or difficulty with which the information could be properly acquired or duplicated by others.

. . . The well settled rule of American jurisdictions, including Wisconsin, is that a corporation which purchases the assets of another corporation does not, by reason of succeeding to the ownership of property, assume the obligations of the transferor corporation.

Exceptions to this rule exist where (a) the purchasing corporation expressly or impliedly agrees to assume the liabilities of the seller, (b) the transaction amounts to a consolidation or merger of the two companies, (c) the purchasing corporation is merely a continuation of the selling corporation, or (d) the transaction is entered into fraudulently to escape liability.

Section 758(b) of the Restatement states:

One who learns another's trade secret from a third person without notice that it is secret and that this person's disclosure is a breach of his duty to the [owner of the trade secret], or who learns the secret through a mistake without notice of the secrecy and the mistake.

* * * * *

(b) is liable to the [owner of the trade secret] for a disclosure or use of the secret after the receipt of such notice unless prior thereto he has in good faith paid value for the secret or has so changed his position that to subject him to liability would be inequitable.

Thus under § 758(b) of the Restatement of Torts, Pillsbury would be liable for its use of the secret after receipt of notice unless prior thereto it had in good faith paid value for the secret.

Sears, Roebuck & Co. v. Stiffel Co.

376 U.S. 225 (U.S. Sup. Ct. 1964)

This was an action for unfair competition brought by Stiffel Co. (plaintiff) against Sears (defendant). Sears appealed from a judgment in favor of Stiffel. Reversed.

Stiffel developed a "pole lamp" which proved to be a commercial success. Sears then brought out a substantially identical lamp at a much lower price and Stiffel sued for unfair competition claiming that Sears had caused confusion in the trade as to the source of the lamps thereby engaging in unfair competition under Illinois law.

MR. JUSTICE BLACK.   Pursuant to . . . constitutional authority, Congress in 1790 enacted the first federal patent and copyright law, 1 Stat. 109, and ever since that time has fixed the conditions upon which patents and copyrights shall be granted. These laws, like other laws of the United States enacted pursuant to constitutional authority, are the supreme law of the land. When state law touches upon the area of these federal statutes, it is "familiar doctrine" that the federal policy "may not be set at naught, or its benefits denied" by the state law. This is true, of course, even if the state law is enacted in the exercise of otherwise undoubted state power.

*   *   *   *   *

Thus the patent system is one in which uniform federal standards are carefully used to promote invention while at the same time preserving free competition. Obviously a State could not, consistently with the Supremacy Clause of the Constitution, extend the life of a patent beyond its expiration date or give a patent on an article which lacked the level of invention required for federal patents. . . .

In the present case, the "pole lamp" sold by Stiffel has been held not to be entitled to the protection of either a mechanical or a design patent. An unpatentable article, like an article on which the patent has expired, is in the public domain and may be made and sold by whoever chooses to do so. What Sears did was to copy Stiffel's design and to sell lamps almost identical to those sold by Stiffel. This it had every right to do under the federal patent laws. That Stiffel originated the pole lamp and made it popular is immaterial. "Sharing in the goodwill of an article unprotected by patent or trade-mark is the exercise of a right possessed by all—and in the free exercise of which the consuming public is deeply interested." To allow a State by use of its law of unfair competition to prevent the copying of an article which represents too slight an advance to be patented would be to permit the State to block off from the public something which federal law has said belongs to the public. . . .

Sears has been held liable here for unfair competition because of a finding of likelihood of confusion based only on the fact that Sears' lamp was copied from Stiffel's unpatented lamp and that consequently the two looked exactly alike. Of course there could be "confusion" as to who had manufactured these nearly identical articles. But mere inability of the public to tell two identical articles apart is not enough to support an injunction against copying or an award of damages for copying that which the federal patent laws permit to be copied. Doubtless a State may, in appropriate circumstances, require that goods, whether patented or unpatented, be labeled or that other precautionary steps be taken to prevent customers from being misled as to the source, just as it may protect businesses in the use of their trademarks, labels, or distinctive dress in the packaging of goods so as to prevent others, by imitating such markings, from misleading purchasers as to the source of the goods. But because of the federal patent laws a State may not, when the article is unpatented and uncopyrighted, prohibit the copying of the article itself or award damages for such copying. . . .[2]

Smith v. Chanel, Inc.
402 F.2d 562 (9th Cir. 1968)

Action by Chanel, Inc. (plaintiff) the owner of trademarked unpatented perfume to enjoin Smith (defendant) from promoting his perfume as equivalent of plaintiff's.

---

[2] The *Goldstein* case, *supra* note 1, apparently modifies this last sentence, at least concerning state laws regulating the copying ("piracy") of sound recordings.

The trial court granted a preliminary injunction and defendant appealed. Reversed and remanded.

Smith, doing business as Ta'Ron, Inc., advertised a fragrance called "Second Chance" as a duplicate of "Chanel No. 5," at a fraction of the latter's price.

The advertisement suggested that a "Blindfold Test" be used "on skeptical prospects," challenging them to detect any difference between a well known fragrance and the Ta'Ron "duplicate." One suggested challenge was, "We dare you to try to detect any difference between Chanel #5 ($25.00) and Ta'Ron's 2nd Chance. $7.00."

In an order blank printed as part of the advertisement each Ta'Ron fragrance was listed with the name of the well known fragrance which it purportedly duplicated immediately beneath. Below "Second Chance" appeared "*(Chanel #5)." The asterisk referred to a statement at the bottom of the form reading "Registered Trade Name of Original Fragrance House."

BROWNING, CIRCUIT JUDGE. The principal question presented on this record is whether one who has copied an unpatented product sold under a trademark may use the trademark in his advertising to identify the product he has copied. We hold that he may, and that such advertising may not be enjoined under either the Lanham Act, 15 U.S.C. § 1125(a) (1964), or the common law of unfair competition, so long as it does not contain misrepresentations or create a reasonable likelihood that purchasers will be confused as to the source, identity, or sponsorship of the advertiser's product.

In *Saxlehner* the copied product was a "bitter water" drawn from certain privately owned natural springs. The plaintiff sold the natural water under the name "Hunyadi Janos," a valid trademark. The defendant was enjoined from using plaintiff's trademark to designate defendant's "artificial" water, but was permitted to use it to identify plaintiff's natural water as the product which defendant was copying.

Justice Holmes wrote:

We see no reason for disturbing the finding of the courts below that there was no unfair competition and no fraud. The real intent of the plaintiff's bill, it seems to us, is to extend the monopoly of such trademark or tradename as she may have to a monopoly of her type of bitter water, by preventing manufacturers from telling the public in a way that will be understood, what they are copying and trying to sell. But the plaintiff has no patent for the water, and the defendants have a right to reproduce it as nearly as they can. *They have a right to tell the public what they are doing, and to get whatever share they can in the popularity of the water by advertising that they are trying to make the same article, and think that they succeed. If they do not convey, but, on the contrary, exclude, the notion that they are selling the plaintiff's goods, it is a strong proposition that when the article has a well-known name they have not the right to explain by that name what they imitate.* By doing so, they are not trying to get the good will of the name, but the good will of the goods.

In *Societe Comptoir de L'Industrie Cotonniere Etablissements Boussac v. Alexander's Dept. Stores, Inc.,* the defendant used plaintiff's registered trademarks "Dior" and "Christian Dior" in defendant's advertising in identifying plaintiff's dresses as the original creation from which defendant's dresses were copied. The district court refused to grant a preliminary injunction.

The appellate court considered plaintiff's rights under both the Lanham Act and common law. Noting that the representation that defendant's dresses were copies of

"Dior" originals was apparently truthful and that there was no evidence of deception or confusion as to the origin or sponsorship of defendant's garments . . . , the court disposed of the claim of right under the Lanham Act as follows:

In any proceeding under the Lanham Act the gist of the proceeding is a "false description or representation," 15 U.S.C.A. § 1125(a), or a use of the mark which "is likely to cause confusion or mistake or to deceive purchasers as to the source of origin of such goods or services," 15 U.S.C.A. § 1114 (1). . . . Registration bestows upon the owner of the mark the limited right to protect his good will from possible harm by those uses of another as may engender a belief in the mind of the public that the product identified by the infringing mark is made or sponsored by the owner of the mark. . . . *The Lanham Act does not prohibit a commercial rival's truthfully denominating his goods a copy of a design in the public domain, though he uses the name of the designer to do so. Indeed it is difficult to see any other means that might be employed to inform the consuming public of the true origin of the design. . . .* [emphasis added.]

The court also rejected the claim of right under common law principles of unfair competition, stating:

Common law unfair competition must be grounded in either deception or appropriation of the exclusive property of the plaintiff. . . .

In the case at bar it is conceded that the "pirating" of the design is lawful and proper. . . . The only property right alleged to have been invaded is the good will embodied in the trademark. But the right of the complainant in his mark is limited to dilution which is brought about by confusion as to source or affiliation. . . .

* * * * *

Anderson's–Black Rock, Inc. v. Pavement Salvage Co., Inc.

396 U.S. 57 (U.S. Sup. Ct. 1969)

Pavement Salvage Co. (plaintiff) brought a patent infringement suit against Anderson's–Black Rock (defendant) and upon losing in the court of appeals, Pavement petitioned the U.S. Supreme Court to review the case. Reversed.

MR. JUSTICE DOUGLAS. Pavement claims that its patent involves a combination of prior art which produces the new and useful result of eliminating the cold joint. Its claim of unobviousness is based largely on the testimony of two individuals who are knowledgeable in the field of asphalt paving, expressing their doubts to the inventor Neville that radiant heat would solve the problem of cold joints. . . .

Each of the elements combined in the patent was known in the prior art. It is urged that the distinctive feature of the patent was the element of a radiant burner. But it seems to be conceded that the burner, by itself, was not patentable. And so we reach the question whether the combination of the old elements created a valid combination patent.

The District Court said: "All that Pavement has done is to construct four elements known in the prior art on one chassis." That is relevant to commercial success, not to invention. The experts tendered by Pavement testified that they had been doubtful that radiant heat would solve the problem of the cold joint. But radiant heat was old in the art. The question of invention must turn on whether the combination supplied the key requirement. We conclude that the combination was reasonably obvious to one with ordinary skill in the art.

There is uncontested evidence that the presence of the radiant burner in the same machine with the other elements is not critical or essential to the functioning of the radiant burner in curing the problem of the cold joint. For it appears that a radiant burner operating in a tandem fashion would work as well. The convenience of putting the burner together with the other elements in one machine, though perhaps a matter of great convenience, did not produce a "new or different function." *Lincoln Co. v. Stewart-Warner Corp. . . . ,* within the test of validity of combination patents.

A combination of elements may result in an effect greater than the sum of the several effects taken separately. No such synergistic result is argued here. It is, however, fervently argued that the combination filled a long felt want and has enjoyed commercial success. But those matters "without invention will not make patentability." . . .

The patent standard is basically constitutional, Article I, § 8 of the Constitution authorizing Congress "To promote the Progress of . . . useful Arts" by allowing inventors monopolies for limited times. We stated in *Graham v. John Deere Co. . . . ,* that under that power Congress may not "enlarge the patent monopoly without regard to the innovation, advancement or social benefit gained thereby. Moreover, Congress may not authorize the issuance of patents whose effects are to remove existent knowledge from the public domain, or to restrict free access to materials already available. Innovation, advancement, and things which add to the sum of useful knowledge are inherent requisites in a patent system which by constitutional command must 'promote the Progress of . . . useful Arts.' This is the *standard* expressed in the Constitution and it may not be ignored."

Gottschalk v. Benson

409 U.S. 63 (U.S. Sup. Ct. 1972)

Petitioner Benson's application for a patent on a particular method of programming was rejected by the U.S. Patent Office, and subsequently by the Board of Appeals of the Patent Office. The decision of the Patent Office was reversed by the U.S. Court of Customs and Patents Appeals, and Gottschalk (respondent) acting Commissioner of Patents, brought the case before the U.S. Supreme Court. Reversed.

Benson developed a method for programming a general-purpose digital computer to convert signals from binary-coded decimal form into pure binary form. A procedure for solving a given type of mathematical problem is known as an "algorithm." The procedures developed by Benson are of that kind; that is to say, they were generalized formulations for programs to solve mathematical problems of converting one form of numerical representation to another. From the generic formulation programs could be developed as specific applications. Benson sought a patent on his method.

MR. JUSTICE DOUGLAS. The Court stated in *Mackay Co. v. Radio Corp.* that ". . . while a scientific truth, or the mathematical expression of it, is not a patentable invention, a novel and useful structure created with the aid of knowledge of scientific truth may be." That statement followed the longstanding rule that "an idea of itself is not patentable." *Rubber-Tip Pencil Co. v. Howard* . . . . "A principle, in the abstract, is a fundamental truth; an original cause; a motive; these cannot be patented, as no one can claim in either of them an exclusive right." . . . Phenomena of nature, though just discovered, mental processes, and abstract intellectual concepts are not patentable, as they are the basic tools of scientific and technological work. As we stated in *Funk Bros. Seed Co. v. Kalo Co.* . . . , "He who discovers a hitherto unknown phenomenon of nature has no claim to a monopoly of it which the law recognizes. If there is to be invention from such a discovery, it must come from the application of the law of nature to a new and useful end." We dealt there with a "product" claim, while the present case deals with a "process" claim. But we think the same principle applies.

It is argued that a process patent must either be tied to a particular machine or apparatus or must operate to change articles or materials to a "different state or thing." We do not hold that no process patent could ever qualify if it did not meet the requirements of our prior precedents. It is said that the decision precludes a patent for any program servicing a computer. We do not so hold. It is said that we have before us a program for a digital computer but extend our holding to programs for analog computers. We have, however, made clear from the start that we deal with a program only for digital computers. It is said we freeze process patents to old technologies, leaving no room for the revelations of the new, onrushing technology. Such is not our purpose.

It is conceded that one may not patent an idea. But in practical effect that would be the result if Benson's formula . . . were patented in this case. The mathematical formula involved here has no substantial practical application except in connection with a digital computer, which means that if the judgment below is affirmed, the patent would wholly pre-empt the mathematical formula and in practical effect would be a patent on the algorithm itself.

Deepsouth Packing Co., Inc. v. Laitram Corp.

406 U.S. 518 (U.S. Sup. Ct. 1972)

Deepsouth Packing Co. (plaintiff) brought suit to establish its patent rights as against Laitram Corp. (defendant). Deepsouth appealed from a judgment ordering it to stop exporting unassembled parts of the patented shrimp deveiner being litigated. Reversed.

Deepsouth and Laitram both hold patents on machines that devein shrimp more cheaply and efficiently than competing machinery or hand labor can do the job. Extensive litigation established that Laitram had the superior claim and that the distribution and use of Deepsouth's machinery in this country should be enjoined to prevent infringement of Laitram's patents. In a related question the trial court held that Deepsouth also was foreclosed by the patent laws from exporting its deveiners, in less than fully assembled form, for use abroad.

MR. JUSTICE WHITE.   Under the common law the inventor had no right to exclude others from making and using his invention. If Laitram has a right to suppress Deepsouth's export trade it must be derived from its patent grant, and thus from the patent statute. . . .

Certainly if Deepsouth's conduct were intended to lead to use of patented deveiners inside the United States its production and sales activity would be subject to injunction as an induced or contributory infringement. But it is established that there can be no contributory infringement without the fact or intention of a direct infringement. "In a word, if there is no direct infringement of a patent there can be no contributory infringer." *Mercoid Corp. v. Mid-Continent Co.* . . .

The statute makes it clear that it is not an infringement to make or use a patented product outside of the United States. . . . Thus, in order to secure the injunction it seeks, Laitram must show a § 271 (a) direct infringement by Deepsouth in the United States, that is, that Deepsouth "makes," "uses," or "sells" the patented product within the bounds of this country.

Laitram does not suggest that Deepsouth "uses" the machines. Its argument that Deepsouth sells the machines—based primarily on Deepsouth's sales rhetoric and related indicia such as price—cannot carry the day unless it can be shown that Deepsouth is selling the "patented invention." The sales question thus resolves itself into the question of manufacture: did Deepsouth "make" (and then sell) something cognizable under the patent law as the patented invention, or did it "make" (and then sell) something that fell short of infringement?

The Court of Appeals, believing that the word "makes" should be accorded "a construction in keeping with the ordinary meaning of that term," . . . held against Deepsouth on the theory that "makes" "means what it ordinarily connotes—the substantial manufacture of the constituent parts of the machine." . . .

We cannot endorse the view that the "substantial manufacture of the constituent parts of [a] machine" constitutes direct infringement when we have so often held that a combination patent protects only against the operable assembly of the whole and not the manufacture of its parts. "For as we pointed out in *Mercoid v. Mid-Continent Investment Co.* . . . , a patent on a combination is a patent on the assembled or functioning whole, not on the separate parts."

*   *   *   *   *

It was this basic tenet of the patent system that led Judge Swan to hold in the leading case, *Radio Corp. of America v. Andrea* . . . , that unassembled export of the elements of an invention did not infringe the patent.

[The] relationship is the essence of the patent.
. . . No wrong is done the patentee until the combination is formed. His monopoly does not cover the manufacture or sale of separate elements capable of being, but never actually, associated to form the invention. Only when such association is made is there a direct infringement of his monopoly, and not even then if it is done outside the territory for which the monopoly was granted."

*   *   *   *   *

Interference with Contract or Economic Expectations

Interference with Contract. In the landmark case *Lumley v. Gye* (1853) a court first ruled that an outsider, who maliciously induced one of the two parties to a contract not to perform the contract, would be liable for damages in tort to the other contracting party who was thereby deprived of the benefits of the contract. The doctrine was later extended to protect all types of business contracts from intentional interferences which were without legal justification. Although the cases are not in complete agreement they seem to make a distinction between those situations where the defendant actively *induced* the breach, and those where the defendant's conduct simply *caused* the breach.

Even where a person induces the breach his conduct might be privileged or justifiable on some ground. For example, it was held that a mother who induced a school to exclude a diseased child from her child's private school was not liable to the parents of the diseased child for having induced the school to breach its contract. Business competition only affords a limited justification for interference with contracts. As Prosser states:

> The courts have held that the sanctity of the existing contract relation takes precedence over any interest in unrestricted competition, and have enforced as law the ethical precept that one competitor must keep his hands off of the contracts of another. This is true of contracts of employment, where workmen are hired away from an employer, as well as competitive business dealings in general; and it has found particular application in cases of offers of better terms to induce the breach of a contract, and of the violation of exclusive agency agreements and the purchase of goods in derogation of a contract limiting their resale.[1]

Interference with Economic Expectations. The early cases of interference with economic expectations usually involved situations where physical violence was employed to drive off customers or workers. Liability was later extended to cover nonviolent malicious interference and then to unjustifiable intentional interference. Where the intent to interfere is present the liability depends upon the motive and purposes of the defendant and upon the means that he utilizes.

Summary

The unjustifiable interference with the contractual relations of others creates tort liability. The cases consider the motive or purpose of the party inducing the breach and make a distinction between actively inducing breach and simply causing breach. Reasonable economic expectations are also protected but the boundaries of this law are ill-defined.

---

[1] William L. Prosser, *Handbook of the Law of Torts,* 4th ed. (St. Paul, Minn.: West Publishing Co., 1971), p. 945.

Carolina Overall Corp. v. East Carolina Linen Supply, Inc.

174 S.E.2d 659 (Ct. App. N.C. 1970)

Carolina Overall Corp. (plaintiff) brought an action against East Carolina Linen Supply, Inc. (defendant) alleging that the latter had wrongfully interfered with one of the plaintiff's employment contracts and also plaintiff's relations with customers. Overall appealed from a judgment for East Carolina. Reversed.

Overall and East Carolina were competitors in the industrial laundry business and East Carolina induced Lowe to breach an employment contract as a route salesman with Overall and to enter the employment of East Carolina. East Carolina, acting through Lowe and other agents, also solicited the business of fourteen of Overall's customers and induced them to breach their contracts with Overall for laundry service.

GRAHAM, JUDGE.   It is well established in this jurisdiction that an action lies against one who, without legal justification, knowingly and intentionally causes or induces one party to a contract to breach that contract and cause damage to the other contracting party.

The elements necessary to establish a cause of action for tortious interference with a contract are summarized in *Childress v. Abeles*. . . . The plaintiff must show: (1) that a contract existed between him and a third person which conferred upon plaintiff some contractual right against the third person; (2) that defendant had knowlege of plaintiff's contract with such third person; (3) that defendant intentionally induced the third person not to perform his contract with plaintiff; (4) that in so doing the defendant acted without justification; and (5) that defendant's acts caused plaintiff actual damages.

East Carolina concedes the general principles but argues that competition is legal justification for interference by a party with a contract between his competitor and a third person.

The following general rule is set forth in the Restatement of the Law of Torts, § 768:

(1) One is privileged purposely to cause a third person not to enter into or continue a business relation with a competitor of the actor if
   (a) the relation concerns a matter involved in the competition between the actor and the competitor, and
   (b) the actor does not employ improper means, and
   (c) the actor does not intend thereby to create or continue an illegal restraint of competition, and
   (d) the actor's purpose is at least in part to advance his interest in his competition with the other.
(2) *The fact that one is a competitor of another for the business of a third person does not create a privilege to cause the third person to commit a breach of contract with the other even under the conditions stated in Subsection (1).* (Emphasis added.)

The theory of the doctrine which permits recovery for the tortious interference with a contract is that the right to the performance of a contract and to reap the profits therefrom are property rights which entitle each party to protection and to seek compensation by action in court for an injury to such contract. . . . We see no valid reason for holding that a competitor is privileged to interfere wrongfully with contractual rights. If contracts otherwise binding are not secure from wrongful interference by competitors, they offer little certainty in business relations, and it is security from competition that often gives them value. It is true that a party to a contract which is breached by another has a cause of action for breach of contract. This, however, affords little remedy where the party breaching the contract is insolvent; or where, as alleged here, numerous contracts involving nominal amounts of money are breached as a result of wrongful inducement by a competitor.

In our opinion the complaint states a cause of action for compensatory damages for tortious interference with plaintiff's contracts.

Problem Cases

1. Baker Realty Company (BRC) filed suit against Jasper T. Baker doing business as Baker Realty Associates (BRA) seeking to enjoin him from transacting business under the name of "Baker Realty Associates." BRC, incorporated in 1964, had established an excellent reputation as a real estate agent and broker. Jasper Baker had incorporated in 1970, and since that time, had actively and openly engaged in, advertised, and solicited business under the name BRA. BRC claimed that BRA's trade name and advertising had misled and deceived the public to the extent that potential clients believed that they were dealing with BRC rather than BRA, to the former's detriment. Jasper Baker declared that not only was he ignorant of BRC when he established his agency as BRA, but that upon discovery of BRC, he had modified his advertising to distinguish the two realties. BRC's suit was premised upon the contention that Jasper Baker's conduct, under the corporate name of BRA, constituted unfair trade, unfair competition, and an encroachment upon its property rights. Should the injunction be granted?

2. After the drowning of Mary Jo Kopechne in Senator Edward Kennedy's car, an inquest was conducted in 1969 to investigate the possibility of criminal activity. Lipman, a freelance court reporter, was hired by the county district attorney to record and transcribe the testimony. Lipman in turn made arrangements to furnish transcript copies to newspapers, wire services, and magazines in return for a fee. Upon discovery that the clerk of the Massachusetts Superior Court was planning to have copies made of the transcript for public sale, Lipman sought an injunction to prevent such action. Is Lipman's claim of a common-law copyright in the transcript of the Chappaquiddick inquest valid?

3. Gibson, Inc. employed three salesmen and sold a sizable volume of coffee, tea, and sundries to restaurants around Omaha. Gibson, founder and president, controlled all but 10 percent of the company stock which was held by Gibson's vice president. Conroy Coffee, Gibson's coffee supplier, informed Gibson that they would give him $30,000 for Gibson, Inc. and that, if he did not accept the offer, they were prepared to take over his salesmen and customers and to go into competition with him on the following Monday. The vice president verified that he and the salesmen were prepared to leave. In view of this, Gibson reluctantly decided to accept the offer. Conroy then said that it had changed its mind and would not offer as much. Gibson sold the company to another firm but the vice president and salesmen went with Conroy. Gibson sued Conroy and the vice president for conspiracy and unfair

competition. Can Conroy successfully defend on the basis that any harm done can be justified by competition?

4. Spring Beverage Company acquired an inventory of bottles, labels, cartons, cases, display pieces, and crowns, all bearing the trademark "Fizz Up." Thereafter, they began advertising and selling in interstate commerce a lemon-lime soft drink beverage under the above trademark name. Seven-Up Company brought this action for an injunction on the basis of trademark infringement. Seven-Up contends that its trademark is registered, that it has made large expenditures in distinctive advertising and that as a result the public has come to recognize Seven-Up as a product sold by the plaintiff. Surveys were introduced showing that not fewer than 25 percent of those interviewed believed that the source and origin of "Fizz Up" was Seven-Up. Should the injunction be granted?

5. Mrs. Galanis, a housewife, sent a letter to Southern Corporation, whose products include several laundry detergents, stating that she had an idea she "would like to sell" and going on to suggest the addition of pulverized blue (bluing) to enhance cleansing power. The corporation responded by letter that it had previously considered the idea but rejected it because the combination product would be limited in use to the laundering of clothes. Later, however, Southern did market a combination product which included blue. Is there a property right in such a suggestion?

6. Atlantic through extensive research developed a more efficient mechanism for processing wool. They treated the new design as confidential and contracted with Lawton, a machine shop owner, to fabricate the new design on the condition that he promise not to reproduce it for anyone else. Norfolk, a competitor, after learning of the general idea of the modifications from a former Atlantic employee, approached Lawton to make a similar mechanism for them; they supplied no detailed specification of their needs. Lawton, who still had Atlantic's blueprints, manufactured the desired machine after consulting a lawyer about his legal position. Can Norfolk defend against Atlantic's suit for misappropriation of a trade secret on the grounds that the essential concepts are already embodied in another well-known machine that performs a similar function?

7. James and Allan jointly purchased a printing business. James became the president of the corporation and took over its day-to-day management while Allan acted as consultant. Some years later James became dissatisfied and Allan bought James's share of the business. Subsequently, James began effectively soliciting old customers of the business on the basis of information, such as names, time of order, and type of printing required, that he had acquired while president. Allan contends that this information constitutes a trade secret and that James is thus engaged in unfair competition. Is Allan correct?

8. Société did business under the names "Dior" and "Christian Dior," which names were registered as trademarks. Alexander, owner of retail discount department stores, used the name of "Dior" and "Christian Dior" extensively to promote the sale of garments copied from original creations designed by the house of Dior. The merchandise was described by Alexander's in newspaper ads and on hang tags attached to the garments as "Original by Christian Dior—Alexander's Exclusive—Paris—Adaptation." Is Alexander in violation of the Lanham Act?

9. Hobart had since 1919 effected a series of registrations of KitchenAid shown always as written without a space between the component words. Cohen had been an "authorized" KitchenAid dealer whose distributorship was terminated. Soon afterward Cohen formed a corporation with the name "Kitchen Aid Service, Inc." which performed no function, but which name Cohen featured in the yellow and white pages of the telephone directory and on his panel truck and on his employees' uniforms. Many KitchenAid owners engaged

his services in the belief that he had Hobart's sponsorship. The repair service performed by Cohen fell far short of the standards expected by Hobart. Can Hobart prevail in a suit for unfair competition in misappropriating its trade name?

10. Electronics Corporation and Honeywell, Inc. were the two leading manufacturers of safety control systems. Honeywell began producing programmers that were adaptable for use in Electronics Corporation's Fireye control system, a product that monitors, supervises, and manages large capacity fuel burners. Honeywell released an advertising brochure, addressed to the retail trade, the cover of which announced, "NOW YOU CAN REPLACE OB-SOLETE . . . FIREYE . . . HONEYWELL Programmers in less than an hour with this new Programmer that plugs right into the old subbase. See inside for other special features." Inside, the brochure had a large cut illustrating Honeywell's programmer being installed in one of Electronics Corporation's boxes. At the trial evidence was introduced showing several misrepresentations in the advertising brochure, one of which was the method of installation of the Honeywell programmer. Is it necessary for Electronics Corporation to show passing off or product disparagement by Honeywell to maintain an unfair competition suit charging deceptive advertising of replacement parts for its Fireye system?

11. Reidl held a copyright on a repair cost service. He induced Bender to give up all other employment to become an exclusive distributor of the service in a multistate territory. The agreement was to continue so long as Bender remained active in the territory and maintained a reasonable number of subscribers. There was no express provision for Reidl's withdrawal. Hearst determined that its competitive service was no longer adequate and after negotiations, purchased Reidl's service. Hearst was familiar with Bender's contract and, as part of the inducement to Reidl, agreed to defend him against any suit by Bender. Hearst was successful in getting Reidl to repudiate the contract. By the terms of their contract with Reidl, Hearst became entitled to receive the profits on subsequent renewals of all outstanding subscriptions, including Bender's. Hearst notified Bender's customers that they were to deal only with Hearst salesmen. Thereafter Bender was not paid for any profits on his renewals which averaged 80 percent of his 3,000 sales and which represented one half of all sales of Reidl's service. Is Hearst liable to Bender for interference with contract?

chapter 46

The Sherman Act

Introduction

Legal History. In the 1800s, several English steamship companies combined for the purpose of controlling competition in the shipping business. They jointly reduced rates below cost in certain ports, gave rebates to shippers dealing exclusively with their association, and refused to haul for any shipper who dealt anywhere with a competing shipping company. Several competing carriers brought a tort action claiming that the defendants had intentionally caused the plaintiffs great harm without any legal justification.

The English court's ruling in favor of the defendants illustrates how few legal constraints there were on monopolistic business practices at common law. The court ruled that the defendants were only pursuing a "war of competition waged in the interest of their own trade;" and the competitive interest justified the harm inflicted.[1]

With the growth of national markets following the Civil War large industrial combines and trusts engaged in monopolistic practices that soon led to a public outcry for regulation. In 1890, Congress enacted the Sherman Act (26 Stat. 209 [1890] as amended, 15 U.S.C. § § 1–7) thereby adopting a public policy calling for the preservation and promotion of free competition within the American economy. Although a number of important exceptions or exemptions have been made, and although additional antitrust laws have been added, this basic competitive policy has been maintained since 1890. The Supreme Court summarized the basis for this belief in competition when it said:

Basic to the faith that a free economy best promotes the public weal is that goods must stand the cold test of competition; that the public, acting through the market's impersonal judgment,

---

[1] *Mogul Steamship Co. Ltd. v. McGregor Gow & Co.,* (1889) 23 Q.B.D. 598, Aff'd. (1892) A.C. 25.

shall allocate the Nation's resources and thus direct the course its economic development will take.[2]

Jurisdiction.   The Sherman Act applies only to restraints which have a significant impact upon commerce, either domestic or foreign. Local activities are subject to the act if the anticompetitive effect on commerce is present. For example, restraints affecting the local distribution of goods originating in another state may be subject to the act even where the local retailer purchased the goods from a local wholesaler. Purely local restraints on competition are subject to state antitrust laws; but state regulation of anticompetitive practices has been highly sporadic and largely ineffective.

Summary

The Sherman Act attempts to promote and protect free competition as the prime regulating mechanism in our economy. The Sherman Act applies only to restraints which have a significant impact on commerce. Purely local restraints are subject to state regulation.

C. A. Page Publishing Co. v. Work

178 F. Supp. 184 (S.D. Cal. 1959)

This was an action for treble damages under Section 1 of the Sherman Act brought by C. A. Page Publishing Co. (plaintiff) against the Los Angeles News Bureau and others (defendants). Judgment for defendants.

Page Publishing Company owned and published the *Commercial News,* a general business newspaper serving the Los Angeles area. Page brought an antitrust action against a number of community newspapers serving small neighborhoods in and around Los Angeles and the Los Angeles Newspaper Service Bureau together with several of its officers. The Bureau was owned substantially by the defendant newspapers and represented them in the solicitation of legal advertising.

Page claimed that collusive and illegal bidding by defendants caused the *Commercial News* to lose printing contracts for the 1951 and 1954 Los Angeles delinquent tax lists.

SOLOMON, DISTRICT JUDGE.   Page argues that a newspaper is by its nature engaged in interstate commerce, and therefore acts which interfere with the normal operation of a newspaper business necessarily affect interstate commerce sufficiently to satisfy the jurisdictional requirements of the Sherman and Clayton Acts.

We may assume that Page and defendant newspapers are engaged in interstate commerce by virtue of (1) their regular purchases of newsprint from sources outside of California, (2) their carriage of some national news and feature items, (3) their carriage of some national advertising, and (4) a few out-of-state subscribers.

However, the test of jurisdiction is not that the acts complained of affect a business engaged in interstate commerce, but that the offensive acts affect the interstate commerce of such business or any business. Furthermore, it is not all economic conse-

---
[2] *Times-Picayune Co. v. U.S.,* 345 U.S. 594, 605 (1953).

quences to interstate commerce which confer jurisdiction but only those anticompetitive consequences which the statutes are designed to prevent.

* * * * *

In *Sears, Roebuck & Company v. Blade,* Sears brought a treble damages action against its former Los Angeles advertising manager and several local engravers, arising out of an alleged kick-back arrangement between the manager and his codefendants in the sale to Sears of engravings and mats.

Ample facts appear to qualify Sears as a business engaged in interstate commerce, and the court so found. Nevertheless, the court dismissed the action on the express ground that the acts complained of were not alleged to have restrained or have tended to restrain these interstate activities in which Sears was engaged.

In every case cited by Page involving news media, a defendant had restrained, or attempted to restrain, competition in the interstate market for national news and advertising.

In each of these cases, newspapers, enjoying dominant positions in local or regional newspaper markets, utilized various methods outlawed by the Sherman Act, to draw advertising from competing news media, in order to drive competitors out of business and to monopolize local markets for interstate news and advertising.

In *Evening News Pub. Co. v. Allied Newspaper Carriers of New Jersey* an association of newspaper carriers utilized its dominant position of the home delivery market to force the Evening News to abandon the use of newsboys in order to restrain and monopolize home deliveries of the News. The court held that the dissemination of national news and advertising was "an essential element of [the newspaper's] being," and that home delivery is "an integral part of the interstate operation."

In the present case, the loss of the delinquent tax list contracts was not alleged to have threatened the normal operation of the *Commercial News*—a newspaper of general circulation neither primarily devoted to, nor economically dependent upon legal advertising. Thus, although the *Commercial News* carried substantial amounts of national news and display advertising, there was no interference with the flow of such news and advertising to *Commercial News* readers.

Page asserts that the defendant newspapers were able to destroy the Journal by the exercise of control over the local legal advertising market. But this control could afford them no leverage to gain control of the interstate markets in newsprint, national news, or national display advertising, no matter how successful their monopoly of the legal advertising market, since the major users of these interstate services and commodities, such as the great metropolitan dailies, are not dependent upon the revenues brought by legal advertising.

Sanctions and Remedies

Criminal and Civil Proceedings. Persons found guilty of violating either Section 1 or 2 of the Sherman Act are subject to criminal prosecution for a misdemeanor and, upon conviction, to a fine not exceeding $50,000, or imprisonment for not more than one year, or both.[3] The Department of Justice also

---

[3] Under the Clayton Act, Section 14, corporate officers participating in a corporate violation are liable for a fine up to $5,000 or one year in prison, or both.

may institute civil proceedings to restrain conduct in violation of the act and ask the court for various remedies including decrees of divorcement, divestiture or, in extreme cases, dissolution.[4]

Any person injured as a result of violations of the act may bring a suit for treble damages against the violators and also recover reasonable attorney's fees. The classic antitrust conviction against General Electric Co. and other electrical equipment manufacturers resulted in the payment of over $200,000,000 in treble damages claims. Criminal fines are not deductible against federal income taxes, but treble damage claims paid may be deducted as business expenses.

A sizable number of the cases brought by the Department of Justice are settled out of court either by consent decrees in civil suits, or pleas of *nolo contendere* in criminal prosecutions. The court decrees are tailored to meet the competitive ills in each situation. On occasion, the defendants may be ordered to license patents on a royalty free basis, file continuing reports showing compliance, or even give aid in the creation of a new competitive firm in the industry.

If a company is adjudged to have violated the Sherman Act this judgment may be used as proof of violation by claimants later filing private treble damage suits. Such claimants would still be required to prove that their losses grew out of the conduct adjudged to be in violation of the act. The fact that the company charged took a consent decree or filed a plea of *nolo contendere* cannot be used as evidence of violation of the Act in subsequent treble damage suits.

Standing under Antitrust.   In order to be able to maintain a private suit for damages or for other remedies under antitrust the person suing must have standing. The test of standing is determined by the directness of injury suffered by the plaintiff. The plaintiff must prove (1) there is a causal connection between an antitrust violation and an injury sufficient to establish the violation as a substantial factor in the occurrence of damage; and (2) that the illegal act is linked to activities of the plaintiff intended to be protected by the antitrust laws.

It has been held that the injury to the particular plaintiffs was too indirect or remote to confer standing in the following cases: a franchisor complaining of an antitrust combination directed at a franchisee; a nonoperating landlord of theaters leased by distributors and exhibitors of films complaining that the lessees were conspiring to limit competition among themselves; a patent owner suing for damages due to restraints directed at his licensees; and stockholders suing for injury directed at their corporation.[5]

In a recent case it has been held that ultimate indirect purchasers (five states) do have standing to sue oil companies for treble damages growing out of an

---

[4] Divorcement means that the company is separated from some operating function. For example, the meat-packers were divorced from owning or controlling retail outlets. A company may be ordered to divest itself of assets or stock. Du Pont was ordered to divest itself of GM stock. Dissolution means that a company must liquidate its assets and go out of business.

[5] *Appraiser Service Co. v. Association of C.&S. Co.,* 382 F.2d 925 (1967). *Calderone Enter. Corp. v. United Theatre Circuit,* 454 F.2d 1292 (1971); *Productive Inventions v. Trico Products,* 224 F.2d 678 (1955); and *Campo v. National Football League,* 334 F. Supp. 1181 (1971).

alleged conspiracy by the latter to fix the prices of liquid asphalt later purchased by the plaintiffs.[6] The defendants argued that since the plaintiffs purchased their asphalt through independent intermediaries, the plaintiffs were not in privity with the defendants and therefore lacked standing. The court rejected this argument stating that privity is not a requirement for standing.

Summary

The Sherman Act provides for both civil and criminal proceedings. Treble damage suits may be brought by private parties suffering losses as a result of conduct prohibited under the act. A very large percentage of all cases brought by the government are settled by consent degrees or pleas of *nolo contendere.*

In order to bring a private suit under the antitrust laws the plaintiff must have "standing." The plaintiff must prove that the alleged illegal acts of the defendant(s) were a substantial factor in the occurrence of damage suffered by the plaintiff and the illegal act is linked to activities of the plaintiff intended to be protected by the antitrust laws.

Section 1

Joint Restraints.   Section 1 of the Sherman Act provides:

Every contract, combination in the form of trust or otherwise, or conspiracy, in restraint of trade or commerce among the several states, or with foreign nations is declared to be illegal.

The "contract" is the agreement to restrain competition. A "combination" occurs when two or more persons join together for the purpose of carrying out united action. A "conspiracy" is a continuing partnership in restraint of trade. At least two persons are required under all of these forms of joint activity. The departments or divisions of a company are viewed as being parts of one company and intracompany conduct not directed against a competitor does not violate Section 1. A principal corporation, however, may be found in violation of Section 1 where it conspires with a subsidiary. As will be discussed later, a single company acting alone may violate Section 2 of the Sherman Act.

Per Se Restraints under Section 1

The Nature of Per Se Restraints.   Justice Black, speaking for the Court in *Northern Pacific Railway Company v. United States,* discussed the doctrine of a per se Sherman Act violation in the following manner:

The Sherman Act was designed to be a comprehensive charter of economic liberty aimed at preserving free and unfettered competition as the rule of trade. It rests on the premise that the unrestrained interaction of competitive forces will yield the best allocation of our economic

---

[6] *Alaska v. Standard Oil of California,* 487 F.2d 191 (9th Cir. 1973).

resources, the lowest prices, the highest quality and the greatest material progress, while at the same time providing an environment conducive to the preservation of our democratic political and social institutions. But even were that premise open to question, the policy unequivocally laid down by the Act is competition. And to this end it prohibits "Every contract, combination . . . or conspiracy, in restraint of trade or commerce among the several States." Although this prohibition is literally all-encompassing, the courts have construed it as precluding only those contracts or combinations which "unreasonably" restrain competition.

However, there are certain agreements or practices which because of their pernicious effect on competition and lack of any redeeming virtue are conclusively presumed to be unreasonable and therefore illegal without elaborate inquiry as to the precise harm they have caused or the business excuse for their use. This principle of *per se* unreasonableness not only makes the type of restraints which are proscribed by the Sherman Act more certain to the benefit of everyone concerned, but it also avoids the necessity for an incredibly complicated and prolonged economic investigation into the entire history of the industry involved, as well as related industries, in an effort to determine at large whether a particular restraint has been unreasonable—an inquiry so often wholly fruitless when undertaken. . . .

Some of the most important restraints of this type include contracts, combinations, or conspiracies to control production, fix or manipulate prices, divide markets or customers, or impose group boycotts.

Restraints on Production.   Under competitive theory, the public is supposed to receive the benefit of an optimum production of goods and services at the lowest possible prices. Joint arrangements among competitors which seek to manipulate production for anticompetitive purposes are per se violations.

Restraints on Pricing.   A majority of the antitrust cases brought by the government under Section 1 involve charges of price fixing. As a general rule, any joint activities fixing or attempting to control prices either horizontally (between competitors) or vertically (between suppliers and distributors) are illegal per se.[7] This prohibition applies regardless of the motive of those fixing, stabilizing, or manipulating prices and applies to setting maximum prices to protect consumers as well as setting minimum prices to protect small firms in a distress industry.

The antitrust agencies often use circumstantial evidence to establish the existence of illegal pricing arrangements. Nor need there be proof of an outright agreement. As the Supreme Court stated in one case:

It is elementary that an unlawful conspiracy may be and often is formed without simultaneous action or agreement on the part of the conspirators. . . . Acceptance by competitors, without previous agreement, of an invitation to participate in a plan, the necessary consequence of which, if carried out, is restraint of interstate commerce, is sufficient to establish an unlawful conspiracy under the Sherman Act. . . .[8]

---

[7] State "Fair Trade" laws may exempt certain types of vertical price fixing arrangements. This exception to competitive policy is discussed subsequently.

[8] *Interstate Circuit Inc. v. U.S.,* 306 U.S. 208, 227 (1939). In dictum in *FTC v. Cement Institute,* 333 U.S. 683, 716 n.17 (1948), the Supreme Court said: "It is enough to warrant a finding of a 'combination' within the meaning of the Sherman Act, if there is evidence that persons, with knowledge that concerted action was contemplated and invited, give adherence to and then participate in a scheme."

On the other hand, the mere fact that competitors may charge the same prices does not of itself prove a violation. In another case, the Supreme Court stated:

> . . . But this Court has never held that proof of parallel business behavior conclusively establishes agreement or, phrased differently, that such behavior itself constitutes a Sherman Act offense. Circumstantial evidence of consciously parallel behavior may have made heavy inroads into the traditional judicial attitude toward conspiracy; but "conscious parallelism" has not yet read conspiracy out of the Sherman Act entirely.[9]

A manufacturer acting unilaterally, is not prohibited from selling to a dealer and *suggesting* a resale price. Such a manufacturer may, subject to supply contract obligations, discontinue selling to any dealer who refuses to abide by the suggested prices. However, if the manufacturer tries to obtain a price maintenance agreement from any dealer or in any way collaborates with other dealers in seeing that the suggested prices are maintained, Section 1 is violated.

Division of Markets or Customers. In one of the earliest antitrust cases, several pipe manufacturers were held guilty of per se violations when they apportioned out their market geographically among themselves.[10] It is likewise illegal per se for competitors to allocate customers and agree not to solicit each other's customers.

A manufacturer or supplier may not impose market area or customer restriction agreements on his distributors who are buying goods for resale. A supplier may, however, designate an area of *primary responsibility* for each distributor and may require that each distributor achieve reasonable market penetration in the designated area.

Group Boycotts. Joint activities by competitors designed to foreclose any competitor's access to a market or to a source of supply are illegal per se. This was held to be true even where dress manufacturers combined to prevent retail stores throughout the nation from dealing with design "pirate" manufacturers who were copying the dress patterns of the "legitimate" dress manufacturers.[11]

Reciprocal Dealing Arrangements. Large firms typically buy large quantities of goods from suppliers. In many cases, these supplying companies have need of goods of the type manufactured by companies which they supply. Under these circumstances, a large firm may find it very advantageous to use its buying power as a means of "encouraging" its suppliers to purchase all or most of their requirements from the large firm. This use of purchasing power to promote sales is called "reciprocity" and may involve serious antitrust consequences.

The case law on reciprocity is very limited. In the 1930s, the FTC found that the coercive use of reciprocity was an unfair method of competition which

---

[9] *Theatre Enterprises Inc. v. Paramount Film Distributing Corp.,* 346 U.S. 537, 540 (1954).

[10] *U.S. v. Addyston Pipe & Steel Co.,* 85 F.271 (6th Cir. 1898), Aff'd. 175 U.S. 211 (1899).

[11] *Fashion Originator's Guild v. FTC,* 312 U.S. 457 (1941).

violated Section 5 of the Federal Trade Commission Act. Reciprocity and even the possibility of reciprocity were important considerations in recent cases brought under the merger prohibitions of the Clayton Act (Section 7).[12]

In *United States v. General Dynamics*[13] the court indicated that either coercive or mutual patronage reciprocity agreements could constitute per se violations of Section 1 of the Sherman Act. The court stated:

the actual or potential implementation of coercive reciprocity, which presupposes the existence of leverage (i.e., large purchases from, and currently small sales to, the prospect), is inimical to a competitive economic society. "Mutual patronage" reciprocity, on the other hand, occurs when both parties stand on equal footing with reference to purchasing power inter se, yet agree to purchase from one another. While the former practice certainly is the more offensive the latter arrangements are equally disruptive of the competitive processes.[14]

Other Per Se Restraints.   Other per se restraints include joint action by competitors to pool profits and losses, refrain from advertising prices, and to refrain from bidding against each other at auctions. Marketing arrangements otherwise legal (i.e., agency distribution or reciprocal dealing) may become illegal per se if a dominant firm exercises coercive control over other firms in creating or operating such arrangements. Also illegal per se are virtually all tying contracts or any activities attempting to extend the antitrust immunities granted in any exceptions or exemptions to the act beyond the strict limitations afforded for such exceptions or exemptions. The exemptions to the antitrust laws are discussed in Chapter 49.

Summary

Section 1 of the act prohibits joint conduct in restraint of competition. Major per se restraints include agreements to: control production; fix or stabilize prices; divide markets or allocate customers; boycott other competitors; and most tying contracts. Where per se restraints are involved no defenses or justifications for the conduct will be permitted.

Esco Corp. v. United States

340 F.2d 1000 (9th Cir. 1965)

Esco and three other distributors of stainless steel pipe were prosecuted for a criminal conspiracy to fix prices under Section 1 of the Sherman Act. The three other defendants filed pleas of *nolo contendere* and only Esco chose to stand trial. Esco appealed from a jury verdict finding Esco guilty. Affirmed.

BARNES, CIRCUIT JUDGE.   While particularly true of price-fixing conspiracies, it is well recognized law that any conspiracy can ordinarily only be proved by inferences drawn from relevant and competent circumstantial evidence, including the conduct of

---

[12] *FTC v. Consolidated Foods,* 380 U.S. 592 (1965).

[13] 258 F. Supp. 36 (S.D. N.Y. 1966).

[14] *Id.* at 59.

the defendants charged. A knowing wink can mean more than words. Let us suppose five competitors meet on several occasions, discuss their problems, and one finally states—"I won't fix prices with any of you, but here is what I am going to do—put the price of my gidget at X dollars; now you all do what you want." He then leaves the meeting. Competitor number two says—"I don't care whether number one does what he says he's going to do or not; nor do I care what the rest of you do, but I am going to price my gidget at X dollars." Number three makes a similar statement—"My price is X dollars." Number four says not one word. All leave and fix "their" prices at "X" dollars.

We do not say the foregoing illustration *compels* an inference in this case that the competitors' conduct constituted a price-fixing conspiracy, *including an agreement to so conspire,* but neither can we say, as a matter of law, that an inference of no agreement is compelled. As in so many other instances, it remains a question for the trier of fact to consider and determine what inference appeals to it (the jury) as most logical and persuasive, after it has heard all the evidence as to what these competitors had done before such meeting, and what actions they took thereafter, or what actions they did not take.

An accidental or incidental price uniformity, or even "pure" conscious parallelism of prices is, standing alone, not unlawful. Nor is an individual competitor's sole decision to follow a price leadership, standing alone, a violation of law. But we do not find that factual situation here.

Esco then adds a definition to "mutual consent," *i.e.,* "an exchange of assurances to take or refrain from a given course of conduct." With this we disagree, if by it Esco means the existence of specific assurances. Written assurances it concedes, are unnecessary. So are oral assurances, if a course of conduct, or a price schedule, once suggested or outlined by a competitor in the presence of other competitors, is followed by all—generally and customarily—and continuously for all practical purposes, even though there be slight variations.

It is not necessary to find an express agreement, either oral or written, in order to find a conspiracy, but it is sufficient that a concert of action be contemplated and that defendants conform to the arrangement. Mutual consent need not be bottomed on express agreement, for any conformance to an agreed or contemplated pattern of conduct will warrant an inference of conspiracy. Thus not only action, but even a lack of action, may be enough from which to infer a combination or conspiracy.

Applying these rules to the facts at hand, the jury came to an opposite conclusion from that which Esco urges, and the fact that Esco's involvement was in but two of ten allegedly conspirational situations does not absolve Esco from participation in the entire conspiracy if its involvement in the two was unlawful and knowingly and purposely performed.

United States v. Container Corporation

393 U.S. 333 (U.S. Sup. Ct. 1969)

This was a civil antitrust action brought by the United States (plaintiff) against Container Corporation and other defendants who were manufacturers of cardboard boxes. The Circuit Court found the defendants not in violation of Section 1 of the Sherman Act and the government appealed. Reversed.

MR. JUSTICE DOUGLAS.   The case as proved is unlike any of other price decisions we have rendered. There was here an exchange of price information but no agreement to adhere to a price schedule as in *Sugar Institute v. United States.* . . . There was here an exchange of information concerning specific sales to identified customers, not a statistical report on the average cost to all members, without identifying the parties to specific transactions, as in *Maple Flooring Mfgs. Assn. v. United States.* . . . While there was present here as in *Cement Manufacturers Protective Assn. v. United States* . . . , an exchange of prices to specific customers, there was absent the controlling circumstances, *viz.,* that cement manufacturers, to protect themselves from delivering to contractors more cement than was needed for a specific job and thus receiving a lower price, exchanged price information as a means of protecting their legal rights from fraudulent inducements to deliver more cement than needed for a specific job.

Here all that was done was a request by each defendant from its competitor for information as to the most recent price charged or quoted, whenever it needed such information and whenever it was not available from another source. Each defendant on receiving that request usually furnished the data with the expectation that he would be furnished reciprocal information when he wanted it. That concerted action is of course sufficient to establish the combination or conspiracy, the initial ingredient of a violation of § 1 of the Sherman Act.

There was of course freedom to withdraw from the agreement. But the fact remains that when a defendant requested and received price information, it was affirming its willingness to furnish such information in return.

The defendants account for about 90% of the shipment of corrugated containers from plants in the southeastern United States. While containers vary as to dimensions, weight, color, and so on, they are substantially identical, no matter who produces them, when made to particular specifications. The prices paid depend on price alternatives. Suppliers when seeking new or additional business or keeping old customers, do not exceed a competitor's price. It is common for purchasers to buy from two or more suppliers concurrently. A defendant supplying a customer with containers would usually quote the same price on additional orders, unless costs had changed. Yet where a competitor was charging a particular price, a defendant would normally quote the same price or even a lower price.

The exchange of price information seemed to have the effect of keeping prices within a fairly narrow ambit. Capacity has exceeded the demand from 1955 to 1963, the period covered by the complaint, and the trend of corrugated container prices has been downward. Yet despite this excess capacity and the downward trend of prices, the industry has expanded in the Southeast from 30 manufacturers with 49 plants to 51 manufacturers with 98 plants. An abundance of raw materials and machinery makes entry into the industry easy with an investment of $50,000 to $75,000.

The result of this reciprocal exchange of prices was to stabilize prices though at a downward level. Knowledge of a competitor's price usually meant matching that price. The continuation of some price competition is not fatal to the Government's case. The limitation or reduction of price competition brings the case within the ban, for as we held in *United States v. Socony Vacuum Oil Co.* . . . , interference with the setting of price by free market forces is unlawful *per se*. Price information exchanged in some markets may have no effect on a truly competitive price. But the corrugated container industry is dominated by relatively few sellers. The product is fungible and the competition for sales is price. The demand is inelastic, as buyers place orders only for immediate, short-run needs. The exchange of price data tends toward price uniformity. For a lower price does not mean a larger share of the available business but a sharing of the existing business at a lower return. Stabilizing prices as well as raising them is within the ban of § 1 of the Sherman Act. As we said in *United States v. Socony Oil Co.* . . . , "in terms of market operations, stabilization is but one form of manipulation." The inferences are irresistible that the exchange of price information has had an anticompetitive effect in the industry, chilling the vigor of price competition. . . .

Price is too critical, too sensitive a control to allow it to be used even in an informal manner to restrain competition.

United States v. Parke, Davis & Co.

362 U.S. 29 (U.S. Sup. Ct. 1960)

The Government (plaintiff) sought an injunction under the Sherman Act against Parke, Davis & Company (defendant) on a complaint alleging that Parke Davis conspired and combined, in violation of Section 1 of the Act, with retail and wholesale druggists in Washington, D.C., and Richmond, Virginia, to maintain the wholesale and retail prices of Parke, Davis pharmaceutical products. The District Court for the District of Columbia dismissed the complaint and the Government appealed. Reversed.

Some time before 1956 Parke Davis announced a resale price maintenance policy in its wholesalers' and retailers' catalogues. The wholesalers' catalogue contained a Net Price Selling Schedule listing suggested minimum resale prices on Parke Davis products sold by wholesalers to retailers. The catalogue stated that it was Parke Davis' continuing policy to deal only with drug wholesalers who observed that schedule and who sold only to drug retailers authorized by law to fill prescriptions. Parke Davis, when selling directly to retailers, quoted the same prices listed in the wholesalers' Net Price Selling Schedule but granted retailers discounts for volume purchases. Wholesalers were not authorized to grant similar discounts. The retailers' catalogue contained a schedule of minimum retail prices applicable in States with Fair Trade Laws and stated that this schedule was suggested for use also in States not having such laws. These suggested minimum retail prices usually provided a 50% mark-up over cost on Parke Davis products purchased by retailers from wholesalers but, because of the volume discount, often in excess of 100% mark-up over cost on products purchased in large quantities directly from Parke Davis.

There are some 260 drugstores in Washington, D.C., and some 100 in Richmond, Virginia. Many of the stores are units of Peoples' Drug Stores, a large retail drug chain. There are five drug wholesalers handling Parke Davis products in the locality who do business with the drug retailers. The wholesalers observed the resale prices suggested by Parke Davis. However, during the spring and early summer of 1956 drug retailers in the two cities advertised and sold several Parke Davis vitamin products at prices substantially below the suggested minimum retail prices; in some instances the prices apparently reflected the volume discounts on direct purchases from Parke Davis since the products sold below the prices listed in the wholesalers' Net Price Selling Schedule. The Baltimore office manager of Parke Davis in charge of the sales district which included the two cities sought advice from his head office how to handle this situation. The Parke Davis attorney advised that the company could legally "enforce an adopted policy arrived at unilaterally" to sell only to customers who observed the suggested minimum resale prices. He further advised that this meant that "we can lawfully say 'we will sell you only so long as you observe such minimum retail prices' but cannot say 'we will sell you only if you agree to observe such minimum retail prices,' since except as permitted by Fair Trade legislation agreements as to resale price maintenance are invalid." Thereafter in July the branch manager put into effect a program for promoting observance of the suggested minimum retail prices by the retailers involved. The program contemplated the participation of the five drug wholesalers. In order to insure that retailers who did not comply would be cut off from sources of supply, representatives of Parke Davis visited the wholesalers and told them, in effect, that not only would Parke Davis refuse to sell to wholesalers who did not adhere to the policy announced in their catalogue, but also that it would refuse to sell to wholesalers who sold Parke Davis products to retailers who did not observe the suggested minimum retail prices. Each wholesaler was interviewed individually but each was informed that his competitors were also being apprised of this. The wholesalers without exception indicated a willingness to go along.

Representatives called contemporaneously upon the retailers involved, individually, and told each that if he did not observe the suggested minimum retail prices, Parke Davis would refuse to deal with him, and that furthermore he would be unable to purchase any Parke Davis products from the wholesalers. Each of the retailers was also told that his competitors were being similarly informed.

Several retailers refused to give any assurances of compliance and continued after these July interviews to advertise and sell Parke Davis products at prices below the suggested minimum retail prices. Their names were furnished by Parke Davis to the wholesalers. Thereafter Parke Davis refused to fill direct orders from such retailers and the wholesalers likewise refused to fill their orders. This ban was not limited to the Parke Davis products being sold below the suggested minimum prices but included all the company's products, even those necessary to fill prescriptions.

The president of Dart Drug Company, one of the retailers cut off, protested to the assistant branch manager of Parke Davis that Parke Davis was discriminating against him because a drugstore across the street, one of the Peoples' Drug chain, had a sign in its window advertising Parke Davis products at cut prices. The retailer was told that if this were so the branch manager "would see Peoples and try to get them in line." The branch manager later talked to Peoples and they did agree to abide by Parke Davis prices.

Five retailers continued selling Parke Davis products at less than the suggested minimum prices from stocks on hand. Within a few weeks Parke Davis modified its program. Its officials believed that the selling at discount prices would be deterred, and the effects minimized of any isolated instances of discount selling which might continue, if all advertising of such prices were discontinued. In August the Parke Davis representatives again called on the retailers individually. When interviewed, the president of Dart Drug Company indicated that he might be willing to stop advertising, although continuing to sell at discount prices, if shipments to him were resumed. Each of the other retailers was then told individually by Parke Davis representatives that Dart was ready to discontinue advertising. Each thereupon said that if Dart stopped advertising he would also. On August 28 Parke Davis reported this reaction to Dart. Thereafter all of the retailers discontinued advertising of Parke Davis vitamins at less than suggested minimum retail prices and Parke Davis and the wholesalers resumed sales of Parke Davis products to them.

MR. JUSTICE BRENNAN.   The Government concedes for the purposes of this case that under the *Colgate* doctrine a manufacturer, having announced a price maintenance policy, may bring about adherence to it by refusing to deal with customers who do not observe that policy. The Government contends, however, that subsequent decisions of this Court compel the holding that what Parke Davis did here by entwining the wholesalers and retailers in a program to promote general compliance with its price maintenance policy went beyond mere customer selection and created combinations or conspiracies to enforce resale price maintenance in violation of Section 1 of the Sherman Act.

In *Beech-Nut* the company had adopted a policy of refusing to sell its products to wholesalers or retailers who did not adhere to a schedule of resale prices. Beech-Nut later implemented this policy by refusing to sell to wholesalers who sold to retailers who would not adhere to the policy. To detect violations the company utilized code numbers on its products and instituted a system of reporting. When an offender was cut off, he would be reinstated upon the giving of assurances that he would maintain prices in the future. The Court construed the Federal Trade Commission Act to authorize the Commission to forbid practices which had a "dangerous tendency unduly to hinder competition or to create monopoly." The Sherman Act was held to be a guide to what constituted an unfair method of competition. The company had urged that its conduct was entirely legal under the Sherman Act as interpreted by *Colgate*. The Court rejected this contention, saying that "The Beech-Nut system goes far beyond the simple refusal to sell goods to persons who will not sell at stated prices, which in the *Colgate* case was held to be within the legal right of the producer." The Court held further that the nonexistence of contracts covering the practices was irrelevant since "the specific facts found show suppression of the freedom of competition by methods in which the company secures the cooperation of its distributors and customers which are quite as effectual as agreements express or implied intended to accomplish the same purpose." . . .

That *Beech-Nut* narrowly limited *Colgate* and announced principles which subject to Sherman Act liability the producer who secures his customers' adherence to his resale prices by methods which go beyond the simple refusal to sell to customers who will not resell at stated prices, was made clear in *United States v. Bausch & Lomb Optical Co.* . . .

Bausch & Lomb, like the instant case, was an action by the United States to restrain alleged violations of Section 1 of the Sherman Act. The Court, relying on *Beech-Nut,* held that a distributor, Soft-Lite Lens Company, Inc., violated the Sherman Act when, as was the case with Parke Davis, the refusal to sell to wholesalers was not used simply to induce acquiescence of the wholesalers in the distributor's published resale price list; the wholesalers "accepted Soft-Lite's proffer of a plan of distribution by cooperating in prices, limitation of sales to and approval of retail licensees. . . . In other words, an unlawful combination is not just such as arises from a price maintenance *agreement,* express or implied; such a combination is also organized if the producer secures adherence to his suggested prices by means which go beyond his mere declination to sell to a customer who will not observe his announced policy.

*   *   *   *   *

The program upon which Parke Davis embarked to promote general compliance with its suggested resale prices plainly exceeded the limitations of the *Colgate* doctrine and under *Beech-Nut* and *Bausch & Lomb* effected arrangements which violated the Sherman Act. Parke Davis did not content itself with announcing its policy regarding retail prices and following this with a simple refusal to have business relations with any retailers who disregarded that policy. Instead Parke Davis used the refusal to deal with the wholesalers in order to elicit their willingness to deny Parke Davis products to retailers and thereby help gain the retailers adherence to its suggested minimum retail prices. The retailers who disregarded the price policy were promptly cut off when Parke Davis supplied the wholesalers with their names. The large retailer who said he would "abide" by the price policy, the multi-unit Peoples' Drug chain, was not cut off. In thus involving the wholesalers to stop the flow of Parke Davis products to the retailers, thereby inducing retailers' adherence to its suggested retail prices. Parke Davis created a combination with the retailers and the wholesalers to maintain retail prices and violated the Sherman Act. . . .

Moreover, Parke Davis also exceeded the "limited dispensation which [*Colgate*] confers," in another way, which demonstrates how far Parke Davis went beyond the limits of the *Colgate* doctrine. With regard to the retailers' suspension of advertising Parke Davis did not rest with the simple announcement to the trade of its policy in that regard followed by a refusal to sell to the retailers who would not observe it. First it discussed the subject with Dart Drug. When Dart indicated willingness to go along the other retailers were approached and Dart's apparent willingness to cooperate was used as the lever to gain their acquiescence in the program. Having secured those acquiescences Parke Davis returned to Dart Drug with the report of that accomplishment. Not until all this was done was the advertising suspended and sales to all the retailers resumed. In this manner Parke Davis sought assurances of compliance and got them, as well as the compliance itself. It was only by actively bringing about substantial unanimity among the competitors that Parke Davis was able to gain adherence to its policy. It must be admitted that a seller's announcement that he will not deal with customers who do not observe his policy may tend to engender confidence in each customer that if he complies his competitors will also. But if a manufacturer is unwilling to rely on individual self-interest to bring about general voluntary acquiescence which has the collateral effect of eliminating price competition, and takes affirmative action to achieve uniform adherence by inducing each customer to adhere to avoid such price competition, the customers' acquiescence is not then a matter of individual free choice prompted alone by the desirability of the product. The product then comes packaged in a competition-free wrapping—a valuable feature in itself—by virtue of concerted action induced by the manufacturer. The manufacturer is thus the organizer of a price-maintenance combination or conspiracy in violation of the Sherman Act.

Siegel v. Chicken Delight, Inc.

448 F.2d 43 (9th Cir. 1971)

Certain franchisees of Chicken Delight (class action plaintiffs) brought a treble damage suit alleging that the franchise arrangements which they had entered into with Chicken Delight (defendant) violated Sec. 1 of the Sherman Act. Chicken Delight appealed from an adverse judgment. Affirmed in part but reversed as to damages.

Chicken Delight franchises required that all franchisees purchase certain essential cooking equipment, dry-mix food items, and trade-mark bearing packaging exclusively from Chicken Delight as a condition of getting a franchise and trade-mark license.

MERRILL, CIRCUIT JUDGE. In order to establish that there exists an unlawful tying arrangement plaintiffs must demonstrate *First,* that the scheme in question involves two distinct items and provides that one (the tying product) may not be obtained unless the other (the tied product) is also purchased. . . . *Second,* that the tying product possesses sufficient economic power appreciably to restrain competition in the tied product market. . . . *Third,* that a "not insubstantial" amount of commerce is affected by the arrangement. . . . Chicken Delight concedes that the third requirement has been satisfied. It disputes the existence of the first two. Further it asserts that, even if plaintiffs should prevail with respect to the first two requirements, there is a *fourth* issue: whether there exists a special justification for the particular tying arrangement in question.

The hallmark of a tie-in is that it denies competitors free access to the tied product market, not because the party imposing the arrangement has a superior product in that market, but because of the power or leverage exerted by the tying product. . . . Rules governing tying arrangements are designed to strike, not at the mere coupling of physically separable objects, but rather at the use of a dominant desired product to compel the purchase of a second, distinct commodity. . . . In effect, the forced purchase of the second, tied product is a price exacted for the purchase of the dominant, tying product. By shutting competitors out of the tied product market, tying arrangements serve hardly any purpose other than the suppression of competition.

Chicken Delight urges us to hold that its trade-mark and franchise licenses are not items separate and distinct from the packaging, mixes, and equipment, which it says are essential components of the franchise system. To treat the combined sale of all these items as a tie-in for antitrust purposes, Chicken Delight maintains, would be like applying the antitrust rules to the sale of a car with its tires or a left shoe with the right. Therefore, concludes Chicken Delight, the lawfulness of the arrangement should not be measured by the rules governing tie-ins. We disagree.

In determining whether an aggregation of separable items should be regarded as one or more items for tie-in purposes in the normal cases of sales of products the courts must look to the function of the aggregation. Consideration is given to such questions as whether the amalgamation of products resulted in cost savings apart from those reductions in sales expenses and the like normally attendant upon any tie-in, and whether the items are normally sold or used as a unit with fixed proportions.

Where one of the products sold as part of an aggregation is a trade-mark or franchise license, new questions are injected. In determining whether the license and the remaining ("tied") items in the aggregation are to be regarded as distinct items which can be traded in distinct markets consideration must be given to the function of trade-marks.

The historical conception of a trade-mark as a strict emblem of source of the product to which it attaches has largely been abandoned. The burgeoning business of franchising has made trade-mark licensing a widespread commercial practice and has resulted in the development of a new rationale for trade-marks as representations of product quality. This is particularly true in the case of a franchise system set up not to distribute the trade-marked goods of the franchisor, but, as here, to conduct a certain business under a common trade-mark or trade name. Under such a type of franchise, the trade-mark simply reflects the goodwill and quality standards of the enterprise which it identifies. As long as the system of operation of the franchisees lives up to those quality standards and remains as represented by the mark so that the public is not misled, neither the protection afforded the trade-mark by law nor the value of the trade-mark to the licensee depends upon the source of the components.

This being so, it is apparent that the goodwill of the Chicken Delight trade-mark does not attach to the multitude of separate articles used in the operation of the licensed system or in the production of its end product. It is not what is used, but how it is used and what results that have given the system and its end product their entitlement to trade-mark protection. It is to the system and the end product that the public looks with the confidence that established goodwill has created.

Chicken Delight's assertions that only a few essential items were involved in the arrangement does not give us cause to reach a different conclusion. The relevant question is not whether the items are essential to the franchise, but whether it is essential to the franchise that the items be purchased from Chicken Delight. This raises not the issue of whether there is a tie-in but rather the issue of whether the tie-in is justifiable. . . .

Under the per se theory of illegality, plaintiffs are required to establish not only the existence of a tying arrangement but also that the tying product possesses sufficient economic power to appreciably restrain free competition in the tied product markets.

The District Court ruled, however, that Chicken Delight's unique registered trade-mark, in combination with its demonstrated power to impose a tie-in, established as matter of law the existence of sufficient market power to bring the case within the Sherman Act.

We agree. In *Fortner Enterprises, Inc. v. United States Steel Corp.* . . . , it is stated:

The standard of "sufficient economic power" does not, as the District Court held, require that the defendant have a monopoly or even a dominant position throughout the market for the tying product. Our tie-in cases have made unmistakably clear that the economic power over the tying product can be sufficient even though the power falls far short of dominance and even though the power exists only with respect to some of the buyers in the market.

Just as the patent or copyright forecloses competitors from offering the distinctive product on the market, so the registered trade-mark presents a legal barrier against competition. It is not the nature of the public interest that has caused the legal barrier to be erected that is the basis for the presumption, but the fact that such a barrier does exist. Accordingly we see no reason why the presumption that exists in the case of the patent and copyright does not equally apply to the trade-mark.

Chicken Delight maintains that, even if its contractual arrangements are held to constitute a tying arrangement, it was not an unreasonable restraint under the Sherman Act. Three different bases for justification are urged.

First, Chicken Delight contends that the arrangement was a reasonable device for measuring and collecting revenue. There is no authority for justifying a tying arrangement on this ground. Unquestionably, there exist feasible alternative methods of compensation for the franchise licenses.

Second, Chicken Delight advances as justification the fact that when it first entered the fast food field in 1952 it was a new business and was then entitled to the protection afforded by *United States v. Jerrold Electronics Corp.* . . . As to the period here involved—1963 to 1970—it contends that transition to a different arrangement would be difficult if not economically impossible.

We find no merit in this contention. Whatever claim Chicken Delight might have had to a new business defense in 1952—a question we need not decide—the defense cannot apply to the 1963–70 period.

The third justification Chicken Delight offers is the "marketing identity" purpose, the franchisor's preservation of the distinctiveness, uniformity and quality of its product.

In the case of a trade-mark this purpose cannot be lightly dismissed. Not only protection of the franchisor's goodwill is involved. The licensor owes an affirmative duty to the public to assure that in the hands of his licensee the trade-mark continues to represent that which it purports to represent. For a licensor, through relaxation of quality control, to permit inferior products to be presented to the public under his licensed mark might well constitute a misuse of the mark. . . .

However, to recognize that such a duty exists is not to say that every means of meeting it is justified. Restraint of trade can be justified only in the absence of less restrictive alternatives. In cases such as this, where the alternative of specification is available, the language used in *Standard Oil Co. v. United States,* in our view states the proper test, applicable in the case of trade-marks as well as in other cases:

. . . the protection of the good will of the manufacturer of the tying device—fails in the usual situation because specification of the type and quality of the product to be used in connection with the tying device is protection enough. . . .

* * * * *

Rule of Reason Restraints

Some Examples.   Other types of activities are found to be illegal only if the purpose or effect of such activities, in light of all of the economic circumstances, is found to be unreasonably restrictive of competition. Activities of this type include: ancillary covenants not to compete found in employment contracts or in contracts for the purchase of a business; price, customer and marketing territory restrictions imposed by a manufacturer in bona fide consignee-agency selling arrangements; various grantback, pooling, marketing restrictions contained in patent licensing contracts; and exclusive dealing and requirement contract arrangements.

Simpson v. Union Oil Co. of California

377 U.S. 13 (U.S. Sup. Ct. 1964)

This was an action for treble damages under Section 1 of the Sherman Act brought by Simpson (plaintiff) against Union Oil (defendant). Judgment for Union Oil and Simpson appealed. Reversed.

Disturbed by price wars, Union Oil required lessees of its retail outlets (including Simpson) to sign product consignment agreements which were one year in duration. The station leases were also for one year. Under the consignment agreement Union retained the title to the gasoline delivered and controlled the retail prices charged. Simpson, however, had the burden of risks, except for acts of God, for gasoline in his possession. Simpson sold some of the gasoline below the price set by Union and Union refused to renew his lease and consignment agreement. Simpson sued claiming that the consignment arrangement was forced on him in violation of Section 1 of the Sherman Act.

MR. JUSTICE DOUGLAS.   We are enlightened on present-day marketing methods by recent congressional investigations. In the automobile field the price is "the manufacturer's suggested retail price," not a price coercively exacted; nor do automobiles go on consignment; they are sold. Resale price maintenance of gasoline through the "consignment" device is increasing. The "consignment" device in the gasoline field is used for resale price maintenance.

Dealers, like Simpson, are independent businessmen; and they have all or most of the indicia of entrepreneurs, except for price fixing. The risk of loss of the gasoline is on them, apart from acts of God. Their return is affected by the rise and fall in the market price, their commissions declining as retail prices drop. Practically the only power they have to be wholly independent businessmen, whose service depends on their own initiative and enterprise, is taken from them by the proviso that they must sell their gasoline at prices fixed by Union Oil. By reason of the lease and "consignment" agreement dealers are coercively laced into an arrangement under which their supplier is able to impose noncompetitive prices on thousands of persons who otherwise might be competitive. The evil of this resale price maintenance program, like that of the requirements contracts held illegal by *Standard Oil Co. of California and Standard Stations v. United States,* is its inexorable potentiality for and even certainty in destroying competition in retail sales of gasoline by these nominal "consignees" who are in reality small struggling competitors seeking retail gas customers.

As we have said, an owner of an article may send it to a dealer who may in turn undertake to sell it only at a price determined by the owner. There is nothing illegal about that arrangement. When, however, a "consignment" device is used to cover a vast gasoline distribution system, fixing prices through many retail outlets, the antitrust laws prevent calling the "consignment" an agency, for then the end result of *United States v. Socony Vacuum Oil Co.* would be avoided merely by clever manipulation of words, not by differences in substance. The present, coercive "consignment" device, if successful against challenge under the anti-trust laws, furnishes a wooden formula for administering prices on a vast scale.

To allow Union Oil to achieve price fixing in this vast distribution system through this "consignment" device would be to make legality for antitrust purposes turn on clever draftsmanship. We refuse to let a matter so vital to a competitive system rest on such easy manipulation.

Hence on the issue of resale price maintenance under the Sherman Act there is nothing left to try, for there was an agreement for resale price maintenance, coercively employed.

United States v. Arnold, Schwinn & Co.

388 U.S. 365 (U.S. Sup. Ct. 1967)

This was a civil action brought by the Government (plaintiff) against Arnold, Schwinn & Co. (defendant) charging that Schwinn violated Section 1 of the Sherman Act. The Government appealed from certain rulings made by the District Court. Reversed.

Over a period of several years Schwinn suffered a decline in its share of the bicycle market dropping from about 22% of the market down to 13% in 1961. To reverse these losses, Schwinn adopted a selective franchising system which included assigning exclusive territories to dealers and distributors. Franchised outlets were obligated not to sell outside of their assigned territories and also obligated not to sell to unfranchised reseller customers within their territories. Other distributors and dealers were put on a consignment plan called the "Schwinn-Plan" with similar territory and customer restrictions imposed. The District Court ruled that the territory restrictions Schwinn imposed on the distributors who bought the bicycles were illegal under Section 1 but refused to order Schwinn to eliminate the customer restrictions. The territory and customer's restrictions were both held valid as to those distributors and dealers operating under the "Schwinn-Plan."

MR. JUSTICE FORTAS. . . . Schwinn has not appealed from the District Court's order, and, accordingly, we have before us only the Government's pleas: (1) that the decree should not be confined to *sale* transactions between Schwinn and wholesalers but should reach territorial restrictions upon distributors whether they are incident to sale and resale transactions or to consignment, agency or Schwinn-Plan relationship between Schwinn and the distributors; (2) that agreements requiring distributors to limit their distribution to only such retailers as are franchised should be enjoined; and (3) that arrangements preventing franchised retailers from supplying non-franchised retailers, including discount stores, should also be forbidden.

As to point (2), the Government argues that it is illogical and inconsistent to forbid territorial limitations on resales by distributors where the distributor owns the goods, having bought them from Schwinn, and, at the same time, to exonerate arrangements which require distributors to confine resales of the goods they have bought to "franchised" retailers. It argues that requiring distributors, once they have purchased the product, to confine sales to franchised retailers is indistinguishable in law and principle from the division of territory which the decree condemns. Both, the Government argues, are in the nature of restraints upon alienation which are beyond the power of the manufacturer to impose upon its vendees and which, since the nature of the transaction includes an agreement combination or understanding, are violations of Section 1 of the Sherman Act. We agree, and upon remand, the decree should be revised to enjoin any limitation upon the freedom of distributors to dispose of the Schwinn products, which they have bought from Schwinn, where and to whomever they choose. The principle is, of course, equally applicable to sales to retailers, and the decree should similarly enjoin the making of any sales to retailers upon any condition, agreement or understanding limiting the retailer's freedom as to where and to whom it will resell the products.

The government vigorously argues that, since this remedy is confined to situations where the distributor and retailer acquire title to the bicycles, it will provide only partial relief; that to prevent the allocation of territories and confinement to franchised retail dealers, the decree can and should be enlarged to forbid these practices, however effected—whether by sale and resale or by agency, consignment, or the Schwinn Plan. But we are dealing here with a vertical restraint embodying the unilateral program of a single manufacturer. We are not dealing with a combination of manufacturers, as in *Klor's*, or of distributors, as in *General Motors*. We are not dealing with a "division" of territory in the sense of an allocation by and among the distributors, or an agreement among distributors to restrict their competition. We are here concerned with a truly vertical arrangement, raising the fundamental question of the degree to which a manufacturer may not only select the customers to whom he will sell, but also allocate territories for resale and confine access to his product to selected, or franchised retailers. We conclude that the proper application of Section 1 of the Sherman Act to this problem requires differentiation between the situation where the manufacturer parts with title, dominion, or risk with respect to the article, and where he completely retains ownership and risk of loss.

As the District Court held, where a manufacturer *sells* products to its distributor subject to territorial restrictions upon resale, a *per se* violation of the Sherman Act results. And, as we have held, the same principle applies to restrictions of outlets with which the distributors may deal and to restraints upon retailers to whom the goods are sold. Under the Sherman Act, it is unreasonable without more for a manufacturer to seek to restrict and confine areas or persons with which an article may be traded after the manufacturer has parted with dominion over it. . . . On the other hand, as indicated in *White Motor,* we are not prepared to introduce the inflexibility which a *per se* rule might bring if it were applied to prohibit all vertical restrictions of territory and all franchising, in the sense of designating specified distributors and retailers as the chosen instruments through which the manufacturer, retaining ownership of the goods, will distribute them to the public. Such a rule might severely hamper smaller enterprises resorting to reasonable methods of meeting the competition of giants and of merchandising through independent dealers, and it might sharply accelerate the trend towards vertical integration of the distribution process. But to allow this freedom where the manufacturer has parted with dominion over the goods—the usual marketing situation—would violate the ancient rule against restraints on alienation and open the door to exclusivity of outlets and limitation of territory further than prudence permits.

On this record, we cannot brand the District Court's finding as clearly erroneous and cannot ourselves conclude that Schwinn's franchising of retailers and its confinement of retail sales to them—so long as it retains all indicia of ownership, including title, dominion, and risk, and so long as the dealings in question are indistinguishable in function from agents or salesmen—constitute an "unreasonable" restraint of trade. Critical in this respect are the facts: (1) that other competitive bicycles are available to distributors and retailers in the marketplace, and there is no showing that they are not in all respects reasonably interchangeable as articles of competitive commerce with the Schwinn product; (2) that Schwinn distributors and retailers handle other brands of bicycles as well as Schwinn's; (3) in the present posture of the case we cannot rule that the vertical restraints are unreasonable because of their intermixture with price fixing; and (4) we cannot disagree with the findings of the trial court that competition made necessary the challenged program; that it was justified by, and went no further than required by, competitive pressures; and that its net effect is to preserve and not to damage competition in the bicycle market. Application of the rule of reason here cannot be confined to intrabrand competition. When we look to the product market as a whole, we cannot conclude that Schwinn's franchise system with respect to products as to which it retains ownership and risk constitutes an unreasonable restraint of trade. This does not, of course, excuse or condone the *per se* violations which, in substance, consist of the control over the resale of Schwinn's products after Schwinn has parted with ownership thereof. Once the manufacturer has parted with title and risk, he has parted with dominion over the product, and his effort thereafter to restrict territory or persons to whom the product may be transferred—whether by explicit agreement or by silent combination or understanding with his vendee—is a *per se* violation of Section 1 of the Sherman Act.

Section 2

Statutory Wording.   Section 2 provides:

Every person who shall monopolize, or attempt to monopolize, or combine or conspire with any other person or persons to monopolize any part of the trade or commerce among the several states, or with foreign nations shall be deemed guilty of a misdemeanor. . . .

A single firm (or person) may monopolize or attempt to monopolize. Two or more firms are required in order to combine or conspire to monopolize.

Monopolizing.   Monopolizing takes place where a firm acting singly, or a group of firms acting together, have the power to control prices or to exclude competitors from a market. This power to monopolize must be coupled with the intent to exercise it.

Illegal power to control prices or to exclude competitors is measured in relation to the relevant market. The relevant market is determined by defining the product line being monopolized and then by fixing the geographic market for the product line as defined. The product line is determined by including those products which are competitive substitutes for the defendant's products. The geographic scope of the market is measured in terms of the area where the products are customarily made available for purchases. A similar determination of the relevant market is made where services are monopolized rather than products. Economically related services are classed as a "cluster" or trade grouping, and then a geographic market is determined.

The mere existence of monopoly power is not of itself illegal, for a firm may have achieved the power by lawful means such as through a patent or through sheer efficiency. However, the existence of monopolizing power acquired, maintained or used in ways from which an *intent* to exercise such power can be inferred creates the basis for a violation. The acts from which the intent may be inferred need not necessarily be illegal. As was stated in the *Alcoa* Case:

Alcoa insists that it never excluded competitors; but we can think of no more effective exclusion than progressively to embrace each new opportunity as it opened, and to face each newcomer with new capacity already geared to a great organization, having the advantage of experience trade connections and an elite of personnel. Only in case we interpret "exclusion" as limited to maneuvers not honestly industrial, but actuated solely by a desire to prevent competition, can such a course, indefatigably pursued, be deemed not exclusionary. So to limit it would in our judgment emasculate the act.[15]

Summary

Section 2 of the act relates to the crime of monopolizing and may involve one or more firms. Monopolizing entails the power to control prices or exclude competitors in relation to the relevant market. The intent to exercise this

---

[15] *U.S. v. Alcoa,* 148 F.2d 416, 431 (2d Cir. 1945).

monopolizing power must also be proven. This intent must be inferred from conduct aimed at either creating or preserving the power.

United States v. Grinnell Corp.

384 U.S. 563 (U.S. Sup. Ct. 1966)

This was a civil suit brought by the United States (plaintiff) against Grinnell Corp. (defendant) under Section 2 of the Sherman Act. The district court held for the Government but both Grinnell and the Government appealed. The Government asked for additional relief. Judgment for the Government affirmed and additional relief granted.

Grinnell manufactures plumbing supplies and fire sprinkler systems. It also owns 76% of the stock of ADT, 89% of the stock of AFA, and 100% of the stock of Holmes. ADT provides both burglary and fire protection services; Holmes provides burglary services alone; AFA supplies only fire protection service. Each offers a central station service under which hazard-detecting devices installed on the protected premises automatically transmit an electric signal to a central station. There are other forms of protective services. But the record shows that subscribers to accredited central station service (i.e., that approved by the insurance underwriters) receive reductions in their insurance premiums that are substantially greater than the reduction received by the users of other kinds of protection service. In 1961 accredited companies in the central station service business grossed $65,000,000. ADT, Holmes, and AFA, all controlled by Grinnell, are the three largest companies in the business in terms of revenue with about 87% of the business.

In 1907 Grinnell entered into a series of agreements with the other defendant companies which allocated the major cities and market for central station alarm services in the United States. Each defendant agreed not to compete outside of the market areas allocated.

Over the years the defendants purchased the stock or assets of 30 companies engaged in the business of providing burglar or fire alarm services. After Grinnell acquired control of the other defendants, the latter continued in their attempts to acquire central station companies—offers being made to at least eight companies between the years 1955 and 1961, including four of the five largest nondefendant companies in the business. When the present suit was filed, each of those defendants had outstanding an offer to purchase one of the four largest nondefendant companies.

ADT over the years reduced its minimum basic rates to meet competition and renewed contracts at substantially increased rates in cities where it had a monopoly of accredited central station service. ADT threatened retaliation against firms that contemplated inaugurating central station service.

MR. JUSTICE DOUGLAS. The offense of monopoly under Section 2 of the Sherman Act has two elements: (1) the possession of monopoly power in the relevant market and (2) the willful acquisition or maintenance of that power as distinguished from growth or development as a consequence of a superior product, business acumen, or historic accident. We shall see that this second ingredient presents no major problem here, as what was done in building the empire was done plainly and explicitly for a single purpose. In *United States v. E. I. Du Pont De Nemours & Co.,* we defined monopoly power as "the power to control prices or exclude competition." The existence of such power ordinarily may be inferred from the predominant share of the market. In *American Tobacco Co. v. United States,* we said that "over two-thirds of the entire domestic field of cigarettes, and . . . over 80% of the field of comparable cigarettes" constituted "a substantial monopoly." In *United States v. Aluminum Co. of America,* 90% of the market constituted monopoly power. In the present case, 87% of the accredited central station service business leaves no doubt that the congeries of these defendants have monopoly power—power which, as our discussion of the record indicates, they did not hesitate to wield—if that business is the relevant market. The only remaining question therefore is, what is the relevant market?

In case of a product it may be of such a character that substitute products must also be considered, as customers may turn to them if there is a slight increase in the price of the main product. That is the teaching of the *du Pont* case, that commodities reasonably interchangeable make up that "part" of trade or commerce which Section 2 protects against monopoly power.

The District Court treated the entire accredited central station service business as a single market and we think it was justified in so doing. Defendants argue that the different central station services offered are so diverse that they cannot under *du Pont* be lumped together to make up the relevant market. For example, burglar alarm services are not interchangeable with fire alarm services. They further urge that *du Pont* requires that protective services other than those of the central station variety be included in the market definition.

But there is here a single use, i.e., the protection of property, through a central station that receives signals. It is that service, accredited, that is unique and that competes with all the other forms of property protection. We see no barrier to combining in a single market a number of different products or services where that combination reflects commercial realities. To repeat, there is here a single basic service—the protection of property through use of a central service station—that must be compared with all other forms of property protection.

There are, to be sure, substitutes for the accredited central station service. But none of them appears to operate on the same level as the central station service so as to meet the interchangeability test of the *du Pont* case.

Defendants earnestly urge that despite these differences, they face competition from these other modes of protection. They seem to us seriously to overstate the degree of competition, but we recognize that (as the District Court found) they "do not have unfettered power to control the price of their services . . . due to the fringe competition of other alarm or watchmen services." What defendants overlook is that the high degree of differentiation between central station protection and the other forms means that for many customers, only central station protection will do.

As the District Court found, the relevant market for determining whether the defendants have monopoly power is not the several local areas which the individual stations serve, but the broader national market that reflects the reality of the way in which they built and conduct their business.

We have said enough about the great hold that the defendants have on this market. The percentage is so high as to justify the finding of monopoly. And, as the facts already related indicate, this monopoly was achieved in large part by unlawful and exclusionary practices. The restrictive agreements that pre-empted for each company a segment of the market where it was free of competition of the others were one device. Pricing practices that contained competitors were another. The acquisition by Grinnell of ADT, AFA, and Holmes were still another. Its control of the three other defendants eliminated any possibility of an outbreak of competition that might have occurred when the 1907 agreements terminated. By those acquisitions it perfected the monopoly power to exclude competitors and fix prices.

[*The court further indicated that the district court should have granted the government relief beyond requiring Grinnell to divest itself of stock in ADT, Holmes and AFA. The monopoly power of ADT in certain cities would have to be broken by divestiture, and the request of the Government for continuing inspection reports, and an injunction was granted.*]

Problem Cases

1. The liquor law of Oregon authorizes licensed wholesalers to sell beer to licensed retail outlets and also, "in quantities of not less than five gallons to any unlicensed organization, lodge, picnic party or private gathering." The law carries an added provision prohibiting the resale of beer purchased by an unlicensed group. Prior to November 1965, it was the practice in Oregon for wholesalers to sell beer in cases and kegs "off the dock," i.e., directly from their premises to the consuming public. Certain of such sales could legally be made as sales to an unlicensed group. However, some of these sales were illegal in that, among other things, certain wholesalers were selling to consumers in quantities less than the five-gallon minimum contained in the "unlicensed organization" exception and were also selling to the consuming public in any quantity.

   The tavern operators became displeased with the competition created by the "off the dock" sales, and, beginning in November 1965, meetings were held between the operators and the wholesalers. At the meetings the wholesalers were told that if they did not cease the practice of "off the dock" selling, the tavern owners would not purchase from them. The antitrust department filed criminal charges against the tavern operators association and certain operators. Were their actions exercises of First Amendment rights and therefore immune?

2. Calderone Enterprises built motion-picture theaters and leased them on a percentage of gross receipts formula. Playhouses, its lessee, was involved with distributors in a scheme which allegedly divided the market among the competitors. Calderone brought a treble damage action against the lessee and distributors claiming that it had been injured by the conspiracy. The defendants claim that there is not a sufficient connection between the conspiracy and Calderone to allow recovery.

   Will Calderone recover?

3. A consumer protection group objects to the President initiating negotiations through his Secretary of State, in which voluntary restrictions upon the import of foreign steel were discussed and approved. Does the President's action give domestic steel producers immunity from the antitrust laws as to their agreements to curtail imports?

4. Webster is a privately owned women's college. It applied to Middle States Assn. for accreditation. Middle States is a nationally recognized accrediting association whose members are those which the organization has accredited. Middle States replied that it only accredited nonprofit institutions and refused to consider the merits of Webster's application. Webster thinks this action is a violation of Sections 1 & 2 of the Sherman Act and asks for an order instructing Middle States to consider the merits of their application ignoring the fact that they are privately owned. Should this order be granted?

5. International is the country's largest producer of salt for industrial uses. It owns patents on machines which dissolve rock salt into a brine and which inject salt tablets into canned products during the canning process. The principal distribution of these machines is under leases which require the lessees to purchase all unpatented salt and salt tablets consumed in the machines from International. International sold $500,000 worth of salt for use in the machines in 1944. International seeks to defend against an antitrust action on the grounds that: (1) an insubstantial amount of the salt business was involved; (2) the leases provided that, if International did not meet a competitor's price, the lessee could buy on the open market; and (3) the machines functioned better with International's high quality salt, thus minimizing the maintenance costs incurred by International under the service requirement of the leases. Are any or all of these defenses adequate?

6. News Syndicate distributes copyrighted and uncopyrighted syndicated features on a national basis. The method used is an exclusive licensing arrangement in which a limited number of newspapers receive the syndicated features within a certain geographical area. The federal government brought an action alleging a violation of Section 1 of the Sherman Act. News Syndicate defends by stating that they can license within any territorial limits they decide because they have an exemption from the antitrust law when dealing with a copyright monopoly. Is News Syndicate correct?

7. County Bar Assn. proposes a floor upon which professional fees should be set. There will be no requirement that the fees actually be in accordance with the schedule. Does this practice violate the antitrust laws?

8. Plaintiffs are a group of franchisees operating retail establishments which sell soft ice cream products. They operate as independent businessmen, but are governed by the provisions of the franchise agreement through which the chain maintains a uniform quality of product, appearance, and operation. The franchisees brought suit alleging that the provisions in the franchise agreement which requires them to sell only the franchiser's products and to purchase a special mix from the franchiser (or his designatees) were invalid as violations of the antitrust laws. Is this correct?

9. The Hardwood Manufacturers' Association instituted an optional activity designated the "Open Competition Plan." Of the 400 association members, 365 were members of the plan. While these members operated only 5 percent of the number of hardwood mills in the country, they produced one third of the total production of the United States. The plan provided for detailed pricing and production reports submitted by each member to be compiled and regularly distributed to the membership. There was no agreement to follow the production and pricing practices of others, but an "expert analyst" was employed to counsel the members and the Association acknowledged that "members do naturally follow their most intelligent competitors." The United States brought suit against the individual manufacturers alleging that the concerted action constituted a combination and conspiracy in restraint of interstate commerce. Should the court enjoin such Association activities.

10. Firestone Tire Company, General Motors, and two of the biggest oil companies—Phillips and Standard Oil of California—agreed to furnish capital to three bus companies—National

City Lines, Pacific City Lines and American City Lines—on the understanding that these latter companies would then look to the former for their requirements of tires, gasoline, and buses. The capital provided by the four companies would be used to purchase financial interests in or outright control of local transport systems in various parts of the United States; these systems too would then become substantially exclusive markets for the four companies. When the Government brought its case, the three affiliated bus companies operated between them 46 transport systems in 16 different states. It was alleged that there were other agreements, such that the National and Pacific companies would not enter into any new contract for supplies from suppliers outside the defendant group without the express permission of the latter, and that they would not dispose of their interest in any bus-operating company without requiring the purchaser to assume the same obligations. Does this conduct by the four companies supplying the capital violate Section 2?

chapter 47

The Clayton Act

Introduction

History. The continued expansion of large firms after the passage of the Sherman Act led critics of the act, mainly supporters of small local businesses, to argue that additional antitrust legislation was needed. Some believed that the prohibitions in the Sherman Act were too general and vague and others felt that court interpretations had weakened the act. Still others argued for prohibitions that would stop monopoly in its incipiency. The Sherman Act could be brought to bear only against accomplished restraints after the "blood was on the ground."

With the passage of the Clayton Act in 1914 (38 Stat. 730 [1914], as amended, 15 U.S.C. §§ 12–27), Congress attempted to strike at specific monopolistic practices in their incipiency. Section 2 of the act made certain forms of price discriminations illegal, but since this section was amended and strengthened with the passage of the Robinson-Patman Act in 1936, price discrimination will be treated when that act is discussed in the next chapter. The major prohibitions in the Clayton Act other than those in Section 2 are found in Section 3 (exclusive dealing, requirement and tying contracts), and Section 7 (antimerger).[1]

---

[1] Section 8 of the Clayton Act provides that . . . "no person at the same time shall be a director in any two or more corporations, any one of which has capital, surplus, and undivided profits aggregating more than $1,000,000 . . . if such corporations are or shall have been theretofore competitors, so that the elimination of competition by agreement between them would constitute a violation of any of the provisions of the antitrust laws." The FTC filed only 13 complaints under this section prior to 1964. Only one cease-and-desist order resulted because in other cases the executives simply resigned. There have been a few court cases. See *U.S. v. Sears, Roebuck and Co.*, 111 F. Supp. 614 (1953).

Section 3

This section makes it unlawful for any person in interstate or foreign commerce, to lease or sell commodities for use, consumption or resale within the United States or its territories, or to fix a price charged therefore:

. . . on condition, agreement, or understanding that the lessee or purchaser thereof shall not use or deal in the goods . . . or other commodities of a competitor or competitors of the lessor or seller, where the effect of such lease, sale or contract for sale or such condition, agreement, or understanding may be to substantially lessen competition or tend to create a monopoly in any line of commerce.

A sizable number of limitations on the application of Section 3 are to be found in the language employed. First, Section 3 applies only to sales of commodities and not to sales of services. An actual sale or leasing arrangement must have been made. The section does not apply to situations where a seller (or lessor) has refused to deal because the buyer (or lessee) was unwilling to accept otherwise illegal tying or exclusive dealing conditions. The section does not apply where goods are shipped by a principal to an agent on consignment since no sale or lease of commodities would be involved. Nor does it apply unless the agreements or understandings involve conditions designed to prevent buyers (or lessees) from dealing with competing sellers (or lessors). Lastly, there must be a *probability* that the agreements or understandings will lessen competition or tend to create a monopoly in a line of commerce (product market).

Summary

The Clayton Act was enacted to strengthen antitrust enforcement and to stop certain anticompetitive practices in their incipiency before harm was done to competition. Section 3 of the act applies to exclusive dealing contracts and to tying contracts.

Tampa Electric Co. v. Nashville Coal Co.
365 U.S. 320 (U.S. Sup. Ct. 1961)

Tampa Electric Co. (plaintiff) brought this action for a declaratory judgment establishing the validity of a contract whereby Tampa agreed to purchase all of its coal requirements for a 20 year period from Nashville Coal Co. (defendant). Tampa appealed from a decision ruling that the contract was illegal under Section 3 of the Clayton Act. Reversed.

Tampa Electric is a public utility serving an area of about 1,800 square miles around Tampa, Florida. Tampa Electric entered a 20 year contract whereby it agreed to buy its total requirements of coal for its Gannon Station from Nashville Coal Co. This purchase obligation also extended to any additional coal using plants Tampa might build at the Gannon Station during the life of the contract. A minimum price for the coal was set with a cost escalation clause. After Tampa had spent approximately

$7,500,000 preparing to burn coal instead of oil, Nashville notified Tampa that it would not perform because the contract violated Section 3 of the Clayton Act.

MR. JUSTICE CLARK.   In practical application, even though a contract is found to be an exclusive-dealing arrangement, it does not violate the section unless the court believes it probable that performance of the contract will foreclose competition in a substantial share of the line of commerce affected. Following the guidelines of earlier decisions, certain considerations must be taken. *First,* the line of commerce, i.e., the type of goods, wares, or merchandise, etc., involved must be determined, where it is in controversy, on the basis of the facts peculiar to the case. *Second,* the area of effective competition in the known line of commerce must be charted by careful selection of the market area in which the seller operates, and to which the purchaser can practicably turn for supplies. In short, the threatened foreclosure of competition must be in relation to the market affected.

To determine substantiality in a given case, it is necessary to weigh the probable effect of the contract on the relevant area of effective competition, taking into account the relative strength of the parties, the proportionate volume of commerce involved in relation to the total volume of commerce in the relevant market area, and the probable immediate and future effects which preemption of that share of the market might have on effective competition therein. It follows that a mere showing that the contract itself involves a substantial number of dollars is ordinarily of little consequence.

In applying these considerations to the facts of the case before us, it appears clear that both the Court of Appeals and the District Court have not given the required effect to a controlling factor in the case—the relevant competitive market area.

Neither the Court of Appeals nor the District Court considered in detail the question of the relevant market. They do seem, however, to have been satisfied with inquiring only as to competition within "Peninsular Florida." By far the bulk of the overwhelming tonnage marketed from the same producing area as serves Tampa is sold outside of Georgia and Florida, and the producers were "eager" to sell more coal in those States. While the relevant competitive market is not ordinarily susceptible to a "metes and bounds" definition, it is of course the area in which respondents and the other 700 producers effectively compete. The record shows that, like the respondents, they sold bituminous coal "suitable for [Tampa's] requirements," mined in parts of Pennsylvania, Virginia, West Virginia, Kentucky, Tennessee, Alabama, Ohio and Illinois. . . . it clearly appears that the proportionate volume of the total relevant coal product as to which the challenged contract pre-empted competition, less than 1 percent, is, conservatively speaking, quite insubstantial. A more accurate figure, even assuming preemption to the extent of the maximum anticipated total requirements, 2,250,000 tons a year, would be .77 percent.

Section 7

Statutory Wording.   As amended in 1950, Section 7 of the Clayton Act prohibits the acquisition by a corporation, in interstate or foreign commerce, unless solely for investment, of:

. . . the whole or any part of the stock . . . or assets of another corporation engaged also in commerce, where in any line of commerce in any section of the country, the effect of such acquisition may be substantially to lessen competition, or to tend to create a monopoly.[2]

Interpretation.   In order to determine the legality of a given acquisition under this section the court first must define the product line (line of commerce) and the relevant market area (section of the country) involved. There need only be a *reasonable probability* that anticompetitive effects will be the result of the merger. The Supreme Court has permitted the FTC to define submarkets within both product and area markets. In the *Brown Shoe* case a merger involving only 5 percent of the shoe industry's sales volume was held illegal where the relevant market was defined to include only sales of men's, women's, and children's shoes in cities of 10,000 or more in population.[3]

An acquisition has been invalidated where there are concentration trends in an industry even though fierce and fragmented competition persisted after the acquisition. A merger might be invalidated because of its effect on *potential* competition; or because a large firm might by a product extension merger, enter a different industry and endanger the existing competitive balance within the industry. The possibility that reciprocal trading exchanges arising out of a merger might foreclose other firms from a significant market might be another factor given weight by the court.

Reports on "conglomerate" mergers dominated the business news during the 1960s. There is some confusion as to definition, but the term conglomerate is usually applied to acquisitions where there is no discernible relationship in the nature of the business between the acquiring and the acquired firms.[4] The possible effect of such mergers on the level of competition depends on the particular circumstances involved. It seems apparent, however, that a large firm will not be permitted to make an acquisition in an already concentrated industry which might confront "existing competitors and such potential competitors as existed with an even more formidable opponent."[5]

Summary

Section 7 of the act can be enforced against all types of mergers and acquisitions. The U.S. Supreme Court has taken the position that any additional concentration in most industries poses a potential threat to the working of our competitive system. Section 7 has been applied to stop acquisitions even in highly fragmented industries provided concentration trends are found to exist.

---

[2] 38 Stat. 731 (1914), as amended 15 U.S.C. Sec. 18 (1952).

[3] *Brown Shoe Co. v. United States,* 370 U.S. 294 (1962).

[4] Sometimes a conglomerate merger is defined as one being neither vertical nor horizontal. See *Antitrust Developments* (Supplement to Report of Attorney General's National Committee to Study the Antitrust Laws, American Bar Association, 1968).

[5] *General Foods v. FTC,* 386 F.2d 936, 944 (3d Cir. 1967).

Ford Motor Company v. United States

405 U.S. 562 (U.S. Sup. Ct. 1972)

The government brought a divestiture action under Sec. 7 of the Celler-Kefauver Anti-merger Act, challenging the acquisition by Ford, the second largest automobile manufacturer of certain assets of Electric Autolite Co., an independent manufacturer of spark plugs and other automotive parts. Ford appealed from a district court finding that Sec. 7 has been violated and an order that Ford divest itself of the Autolite plant and trade name. Affirmed.

Mr. Justice Douglas. Ford, the second leading producer of automobiles, General Motors, and Chrysler together account for 90% of the automobile production in this country. Though Ford makes a substantial portion of its parts, prior to its acquisition of the assets of Autolite, it did not make spark plugs or batteries but purchased those parts from independent companies.

The original equipment of new cars, insofar as spark plugs are concerned, is conveniently referred to as the OE tie. The replacement market is referred to as the *aftermarket.* The independents, including Autolite, furnished the auto manufacturers with OE plugs at cost or less, about six cents a plug, and they continued to sell at that price even when their costs increased threefold. The independents sought to recover their losses on OE sales by profitable sales in the *aftermarket* where the requirement of each vehicle during its lifetime is about five replacement plug sets. By custom and practice among mechanics, the *aftermarket* plug is usually the same brand as the OE plug. . . .

Ford was anxious to participate in this *aftermarket* and after various efforts, not relevant to the present case, concluded that its effective participation in the *aftermarket* required "an established distribution system with a recognized brand name, a full line of high volume service parts, engineering experience in replacement designs, low volume production facilities and experience, and the opportunity to capitalize on an established car population."

Ford concluded it could develop such a division of its own but decided that course would take from five to eight years and be more costly than an acquisition. To make a long story short, it acquired certain assets of Autolite in 1961.

At that time General Motors had entered the spark plug manufacturing field, making the AC brand. The two other major domestic producers were independents —Autolite and Champion. When Ford acquired Autolite, whose share of the domestic spark plug market was about 15%, only one major independent was left and that was Champion whose share of the domestic market declined from just under 50% in 1960 to just under 40% in 1964 and to about 33% in 1966. At the time of the acquisition, General Motors' market share was about 30%. There were other small manufacturers of spark plugs but they had no important share of the market.

The District Court held that the acquisition of Autolite violated § 7 of the Celler-Kefauver Anti-merger Act because its effect "may be substantially to lessen competition." It gave two reasons for its decision.

First, prior to 1961 when Ford acquired Autolite it had a "pervasive impact on the aftermarket," . . . in that it was a moderating influence on Champion and on other companies derivatively. It explained that reason as follows:

An interested firm on the outside has a twofold significance. It may someday go in and set the stage for noticeable deconcentration. While it merely stays near the edge, it is a deterrent to current competitors. . . . This was Ford uniquely, as both a prime candidate to manufacture and the major customer of the dominant member of the oligopoly. Given the chance that Autolite would have been doomed to oblivion by [Ford's] grassroots entry, which also would have destroyed Ford's soothing influence over replacement prices, Ford may well have been more useful as a potential than it would have been as a real producer, regardless how it began fabrication. Had Ford taken the internal-expansion route, there would have been no illegality; not, however, because the result necessarily would have been commendable, but simply because that course has not been proscribed.

Second, the District Court found that the acquisition marked "the foreclosure of Ford as a purchaser of about ten per cent of total industry output.". . .

The District Court added:

In short, Ford's entry into the spark plug market by means of the acquisition of the factory in Fostoria and the trade name "Autolite" had the effect of raising the barriers to entry into that market as well as removing one of the existing restraints upon the actions of those in the business of manufacturing spark plugs.

It will also be noted that the number of competitors in the spark plug manufacturing industry closely parallels the number of competitors in the automobile manufacturing industry and the barriers to entry into the auto industry are virtually insurmountable at present and will remain so for the foreseeable future. Ford's acquisition of the Autolite assets, particularly when viewed in the context of the original equipment (OE) tie and of GM's ownership of AC, has the result of transmitting the rigidity of the oligopolistic structure of the automobile industry to the spark plug industry, thus reducing the chances of future deconcentration of the spark plug market by forces at work within that market.

It is argued, however, that the acquisition had some beneficial effect in making Autolite a more vigorous and effective competitor against Champion and General Motors than Autolite had been as an independent. But what we said in *United States v. Philadelphia National Bank,* disposes of that argument. A merger is not saved from illegality under § 7, we said,

because, on some ultimate reckoning of social or economic debits and credits, it may be deemed beneficial. A value choice of such magnitude is beyond the ordinary limits of judicial competence, and in any event has been made for us already, by Congress when it enacted the amended § 7. Congress determined to preserve our traditionally competitive economy. It therefore proscribed anti-competitive mergers, the benign and the malignant alike, fully aware, we must assume, that some price might have to be paid. . . .

Ford argues that the acquisition left the marketplace with a greater number of competitors. To be sure, after Autolite sold its New Fostoria plant to Ford, it constructed another in Decatur, Alabama, which by 1964 had 1.6% of the domestic business. Prior to the acquisition, however, there were only two major independent producers and only two significant purchasers of original equipment spark plugs. The acquisition thus aggravated an already oligopolistic market.

As we indicated in *Brown Shoe Co. v. United States* . . . :

The primary vice of a vertical merger or other arrangement tying a customer to a supplier is that, by foreclosing the competitors of either party from a segment of the market otherwise open to them, the arrangement may act as a "clog on competition,". . . which "deprive[s] . . . rivals of a fair opportunity to compete.". . . Every extended vertical arrangement by its very nature, for at least a time, denies to competitors of the supplier the opportunity to compete for part or all of the trade of the customer-party to the vertical arrangement.

Moreover, Ford made the acquisition in order to obtain a foothold in the *aftermarket.* Once established, it would have every incentive to perpetuate the OE tie and thus maintain the virtually insurmountable barriers to entry to the *aftermarket.*[6]

FTC v. Procter & Gamble Co.

386 U.S. 568 (U.S. Sup. Ct. 1967)

This was an action brought by the Federal Trade Commission charging that Procter & Gamble Co. had acquired the assets of Clorox Chemical Co. in violation of Section 7 of the Clayton Act. The FTC ordered divestiture but the Court of Appeals reversed and dismissed the action. The FTC appealed. Reversed.

MR. JUSTICE DOUGLAS.   As indicated by the Commission in its painstaking and illuminating report, it does not particularly aid analysis to talk of this merger in conventional terms, namely, horizontal or vertical or conglomerate. This merger may most appropriately be described as a "product-extension merger," as the Commission stated. The facts are not disputed, and a summary will demonstrate the correctness of the Commission's decision.

At the time of the merger, Clorox was the leading manufacturer in the heavily concentrated household liquid bleach industry. It is agreed that household liquid bleach is the relevant line of commerce. The product is used in the home as a germicide and disinfectant, and more importantly, as a whitening agent in washing clothes and fabrics. It is a distinctive product with no close substitutes. Liquid bleach is a low-price, high-turnover consumer product sold mainly through grocery stores and supermarkets. The relevant geographical market is the Nation and a series of regional markets. Because of high shipping costs and low sales price, it is not feasible to ship the product more than 300 miles from its point of manufacture. Most manufacturers are limited

---

[6] The decree of the district court affirmed by the Court—

(1) enjoined Ford for 10 years from manufacturing spark plugs,

(2) ordered Ford for five years to purchase one half of its total annual requirement of spark plugs from the divested plant under the "Autolite" name,

(3) prohibited Ford for the same period from using its own trade names on plugs,

(4) protected New Fostoria, the town where the Autolite plant is located, by requiring Ford to continue for 10 years its policy of selling spark plugs to its dealers at prices no less than its prevailing minimum suggested jobbers' selling price,

(5) protected employees of the New Fostoria plant by ordering Ford to condition its divestiture sale on the purchaser's assuming the existing wage and pension obligations and to offer employment to any employee displaced by a transfer of nonplug operations from the divested plant.

to competition within a single region since they have but one plant. Clorox is the only firm selling nationally; it has 13 plants distributed throughout the Nation. Purex, Clorox's closest competitor in size, does not distribute its bleach in the northeast or middle-Atlantic States; in 1957, Purex's bleach was available in less than 50% of the national market.

At the time of the acquisition, Clorox was the leading manufacturer of household liquid bleach, with 48.8% of the national sales—annual sales of slightly less than $40,000,000. Its market share had been steadily increasing for the five years prior to the merger. The industry is highly concentrated; in 1957, Clorox and Purex accounted for almost 65% of the Nation's household liquid bleach sales, and, together with four other firms, for almost 80%. The remaining 20% was divided among over 200 small producers. Clorox had total assets of $12,000,000; only eight producers had assets in excess of $1,000,000 and very few had assets of more than $75,000.

In light of the territorial limitations on distribution, national figures do not give an accurate picture of Clorox's dominance in the various regions. Thus, Clorox's seven principal competitors did no business in New England, the mid-Atlantic States, or metropolitan New York.

Since all liquid bleach is chemically identical, advertising and sales promotion is vital. In 1957 Clorox spent almost $3,700,000 on advertising, imprinting the value of its bleach in the mind of the consumer. In addition, it spent $1,700,000 for other promotional activities.

Procter is a large, diversified manufacturer of low-price, high-turnover household products sold through grocery, drug and department stores. Prior to its acquisition of Clorox, it did not produce household liquid bleach. Its 1957 sales were in excess of $1,100,000,000 from which it realized profits of more than $67,000,000; its assets were over $500,000,000. Procter has been marked by rapid growth and diversification. It has successfully developed and introduced a number of new products. Its primary activity is in the general area of soaps, detergents, and cleansers; in 1957, of total domestic sales, more than one-half (over $500,000,000) were in this field. Procter was the dominant factor in this area. It accounted for 54.4% of all packaged detergent sales. The industry is heavily concentrated—Procter and its nearest competitors, Colgate-Palmolive and Lever Brothers, account for 80% of the market.

In the marketing of soaps, detergents, and cleansers, as in the marketing of household liquid bleach, advertising and sales promotion are vital. In 1957, Procter was the Nation's largest advertiser, spending more than $80,000,000 on advertising and an additional $47,000,000 on sales promotion. Due to its tremendous volume, Procter receives substantial discounts from the media. As a multi-product producer Procter enjoys substantial advantages in advertising and sales promotion. Thus, it can and does feature several products in its promotions, reducing the printing, mailing, and other costs for each product. It also purchases network programs on behalf of several products, enabling it to give each product network exposure at a fraction of the cost per product that a firm with only one product to advertise would incur.

Prior to the acquisition, Procter was in the course of diversifying into product lines related to its basic detergent-soap-cleanser business. Liquid bleach was a distinct possibility since packaged detergents—Procter's primary product line—and liquid bleach are used complementarily in washing clothes and fabrics, and in general household clothing.

The decision to acquire Clorox was the result of a study conducted by Procter's promotion department designed to determine the advisability of entering the liquid bleach industry. The initial report noted the ascendancy of liquid bleach in the large and expanding household bleach market, and recommended that Procter purchase Clorox rather than enter independently. Since a large investment would be needed to obtain a satisfactory market share, acquisition of the industry's leading firm was attractive.

The Commission found that the acquisition might substantially lessen competition. The findings and reasoning of the Commission need be only briefly summarized. The Commission found that the substitution of Procter with its huge assets and advertising advantages for the already dominant Clorox would dissuade new entrants and discourage active competition from the firms already in the industry due to fear of retaliation by Procter. The Commission thought it relevant that retailers might be induced to give Clorox preferred shelf space since it would be manufactured by Procter, which also produced a number of other products marketed by the retailers. There was also the danger that Procter might underprice Clorox in order to drive out competition, and subsidize the underpricing with revenue from other products. The Commission carefully reviewed the effect of the acquisition on the structure of the industry, noting that "the practical tendency of the . . . merger . . . is to transform the liquid bleach industry into an arena of big business competition only, with the few small firms falling by the wayside, unable to compete with their giant rivals." Further, the merger would seriously diminish potential competition by eliminating Procter as a potential entrant into the industry. Prior to the merger, the Commission found that Procter was the most likely prospective entrant, and absent the merger would have remained on the periphery, restraining Clorox from exercising its market power. If Procter had actually entered, Clorox's dominant position would have been eroded and the concentration of the industry reduced.

Section 7 of the Clayton Act was intended to arrest the anticompetitive effects of market power in their incipiency. The core question is whether a merger may substantially lessen competition, and necessarily requires a prediction of the merger's impact on competition, present and future. And there is certainly no requirement that the anticompetitive power manifest itself in anticompetitive action before § 7 can be called into play. If the enforcement of § 7 turned on the existence of actual anticompetitive practices, the congressional policy of thwarting such practices in their incipiency would be frustrated.

Problem Cases

1. Standard Fashions, a manufacturer of paper patterns for women's clothing, had about 40% of the total industry sales volume. Standard Fashions entered into contracts with retailers under which the retailers, who agreed to buy substantial quantities of patterns and keep a considerable stock, also undertook not to sell or permit to be sold on its premises during

the term of the contract any other make of patterns. Although the contract was dressed up as one of agency, the goods were in fact sold to the retailer. Are these exclusive dealing arrangements legal under Section 3?

2. Window Company issued franchises which required all distributors and dealers of its patented combination storm and screen windows to maintain a sales organization devoted exclusively to the sale of such windows. Distributors and dealers also were required not to offer for sale merchandise competitive with any article manufactured or distributed by the Window Company, and to purchase from Window Company materials necessary for the manufacture of special units. A terminated dealer sued Window Company alleging that this plan caused him losses and that he was terminated for handling competitive goods. Has the dealer stated a valid claim under the antitrust laws?

3. The Standard Oil Company of California is the largest refiner and supplier of petrol in the western states—Arizona, California, Idaho, Nevada, Oregon, Utah, and Washington. The channel of distribution to the consumer is divided between its own service stations and independent filling stations. In 1946, its total sales in the area amounted to 23 percent of all the gasoline sold. Its own filling stations accounted for about 7 percent and its sales to independent filling stations about the same. (The balance of the 23 percent was sold to industrial users.) It has six major competitors who between them supplied about 42 percent of the gasoline sold by retail as against Standard's nearly 14 percent. Seventy other small refiners were also engaged in the business. All the other main companies used the same sort of contracts with their distributors as Standard.

These were exclusive supply contracts. Standard has entered into such contracts with nearly 6,000 Chevron independent filling stations—16 percent of the filling stations in the area—and sold nearly $60 million worth of gasoline through these stations in 1947. Under these exclusive supply contracts the independent dealer undertook to purchase from Standard all his requirements of one or more products; by far the greater number concerned gasoline and other oil products only. Most of the contracts were renewed from year to year, but some were for longer terms. Is this marketing arrangement legal under Section 3?

4. Nelson, a distributor, sought treble damages on the basis of a complaint that Motorola, a manufacturer of communications equipment, refused to renew Nelson's dealer franchise when the latter did not agree to sell Motorola products exclusively. Does this state a cause of action under Section 3?

5. Automatic Radio made car radios which could be installed in new and used cars although none of the car manufacturers used Automatic's products as original equipment. In 1964, Ford redesigned the instrument panel in its cars in such a way that Ford dealers had little choice but to install Ford radios in Ford cars. As a result, Automatic lost a sizable part of its business and brought a treble damage suit alleging that this redesigning in effect created a tying arrangement illegal under Section 3 of the Clayton Act. Is Automatic correct?

6. In 1945, Culligan granted some of its dealers long-term franchises which required these dealers to buy all of their requirements for water-softening services from Culligan. Each dealer was given an exclusive territory in which to sell. The franchise contained standard clauses stipulating that if any part of the franchise was found to be illegal that this should not affect the balance of the contract. In 1956, the FTC issued a complaint against Culligan for violating Section 3 of the Clayton Act (exclusive dealing) and Culligan took a consent decree. Culligan then notified all of its dealers that their old franchises were no longer valid. Culligan sent out new franchises which did not require that the dealer buy all of his requirements from Culligan. In addition, the new franchises were for shorter terms and did not give any dealers exclusive territories. Five filed suit to have their old franchises declared

valid except for the exclusive dealing (requirements) provision. They were canceled by Culligan when they refused to accept the new franchises. Can the dealers win?

7. Pillsbury is a leading producer of flour-base mixes. It was the second largest producer of these products and the third largest producer of bakery flour. In 1951, Pillsbury purchased the assets of Ballard and of Duff, two competing companies in the industry. With the addition of these two companies, Pillsbury increased its manufacturing capacity by as much as 40 percent in certain product lines. The market share of Pillsbury was increased substantially in the southeastern states where Pillsbury moved from fifth to second place in family flour and made other gains. Did this acquisition violate Section 7?

8. American, a cane sugar producer with about 7 percent of total sugar sales in a 10-state area, acquired 23 percent of the stock of Cuban Sugar, a company with about 6 percent of the beet sugar sales in the same area. Cane and beet sugar are highly competitive products. A merger was planned and the resulting company would be the second-largest company in the area. Does this acquisition violate Section 7?

9. In 1958, Pabst, the nation's 10th largest brewer, acquired Blatz, which ranked 18th. The merger made Pabst fifth largest with 4.5 percent of the industry's total sales. By 1961, they ranked third with 5.8 percent of the market. In Wisconsin before the merger Blatz was the leading seller and Pabst ranked fourth. The merger made Pabst first with 24.0 percent and by 1961 this had grown to 27.4 percent. In the three-state area of Wisconsin, Illinois, and Michigan in 1957 Blatz ranked sixth with 5.8 percent of the market and Pabst was seventh with 5.4 percent. The government sued Pabst alleging that the acquisition violated Section 7 of the Clayton Act. The District Court dismissed the government's case on the ground that they failed to show that the effect of the acquisition ". . . may be substantially to lessen competition or to tend to create monopoly in the continental United States, the only relevant geographic market." Should the decision stand on appeal?

chapter 48

The Robinson-Patman Act

Introduction

Objectives. The two primary objectives of the Robinson-Patman Act (49 Stat. 1526, as amended, 15 U.S.C. § 13) are: (1) To prevent suppliers from attempting to gain an unfair advantage over their competitors by discriminating among buyers either in price or in providing allowances or services, and (2) to prevent buyers from using their economic power to gain discriminatory prices from suppliers so as to gain an advantage over their own competitors. The overall objective is to promote equality of economic opportunity for businesses selling and buying goods in the channels of commerce.

History. The Robinson-Patman Act amendment of Section 2 of the Clayton Act was enacted in 1936 because of increasing congressional concern for the plight of small retailers confronted with the growth of chain-store competition. The original Section 2 of the Clayton Act was drafted primarily to prohibit the practice, early used by the Standard Oil Company and others, of employing local and territorial price discrimination to drive out competitors in a given area. However, the complaint of grocers, druggists and other retailers, and the wholesalers who supplied them, was that suppliers discriminated in price between different customers, sometimes charging chain stores even less than they did the wholesalers who sold to the small independent stores. The Clayton Act had been interpreted to require an examination only into the competitive effect at the seller's level—not at the customer's level. Furthermore, it was interpreted to permit a seller to meet the price of a competitor even if the competitor's price itself was discriminatory and to permit different prices for different quantities without regard to the cost savings of the seller.

Concern had been brought to a head in 1934 by the report of a thorough investigation of chain stores conducted by the Federal Trade Commission upon the request of Congress. It publicized not only the fact that chains were buying their goods more cheaply than their smaller competitors but that they also frequently received advertising and promotional allowances, payments in lieu of brokerage and other inducements to buy not available to their competitors and often given secretly.

Price Discrimination

The Statute. Section 2(a) of the amended Clayton Act provides:

That it shall be unlawful for any person engaged in commerce, in the course of such commerce, either directly or indirectly, to discriminate in price between different purchasers of commodities of like grade and quality, where either or any of the purchases involved in such discrimination are in commerce, where such commodities are sold for use, consumption, or resale within the United States or any Territory thereof or the District of Columbia or any insular possession or other place under the jurisdiction of the United States, and where the effect of such discrimination may be substantially to lessen competition or tend to create a monopoly in any line of commerce, or to injure, destroy, or prevent competition with any person who either grants or knowingly receives the benefit of such discrimination, or with customers of either of them: *Provided,* That nothing herein contained shall prevent differentials which make only due allowance for differences in the cost of manufacture, sale, or delivery resulting from the differing methods or quantities in which such commodities are to such purchasers sold or delivered: *Provided, however,* That the Federal Trade Commission may, after due investigation and hearing to all interested parties, fix and establish quantity limits, and revise the same as it finds necessary, as to particular commodities or classes of commodities, where it finds that available purchasers in greater quantities are so few as to render differentials on account thereof unjustly discriminatory or promotive of monopoly in any line of commerce; and the foregoing shall then not be construed to permit differentials based on differences in quantities greater than those so fixed and established: *And provided further,* That nothing herein contained shall prevent persons engaged in selling goods, wares, or merchandise in commerce from selecting their own customers in bona fide transactions and not in restraint of trade: *And provided further,* That nothing herein contained shall prevent price changes from time to time where in response to changing conditions affecting the market for or the marketability of the goods concerned, such as but not limited to actual or imminent deterioration of perishable goods, obsolescence of seasonal goods, distress sales under court process, or sales in good faith in discontinuance of business in the goods concerned.

Commerce. This section requires that the discrimination must occur in "commerce" but, unlike the Sherman Act definition, the courts have interpreted this provision to require that the transaction in question involve two or more states or the District of Columbia and a state. The fact that the customers who are discriminated against are located in the same state as those who are favored does not make the act inapplicable if the goods are shipped in from another state. The act also applies where one of the competing buyers is in another state even though the seller and other buyers are in the same state. However, the act does not apply, for example, to an Indiana manufacturer selling to Indiana customers, although if the Indiana manufacturer is part of an interstate enterprise and uses resources from out of state to finance local price-cutting, a violation may be found.[1] Only domestic commerce involving transactions by American businessmen is covered by the act.

Discrimination in Price. A price discrimination under the act must involve two or more sales to different purchasers at different prices. One who sells to all buyers at a fixed f.o.b. price would clearly not violate Section 2(a) of the act. The price to be considered is the delivered price—that is, the price at the point where the buyer takes the goods. For two or more sales to be treated as discriminatory, they must be fairly close in point of time. How close depends upon the commodity—longer for pianos than meat or corn, which tend to fluctuate rapidly in price due to perishability or rapidly changing supply and demand factors.

Section 2(a) applies only to different prices between different actual purchasers. Merely quoting a discriminatory price or refusing to sell except at a discriminatory price is not a violation under this section. An actual sale at a discriminatory price must occur before the section applies.

Under certain conditions sales will be attributed, for purposes of the act, to a seller which are not made directly by him. For example, sales by a subsidiary will be attributed to the parent if there is a high degree of control exercised by the parent—likewise, a manufacturer who controls the sales of his customer, a wholesaler, by having his own salesmen take the order and referring it to the wholesaler is the seller.

Commodities of Like Grade and Quality. Section 2's prohibition of price discrimination applies only to goods. It does not cover services. Discriminatory pricing practices in selling advertising space or leasing real estate are not prohibited by the act. What goods are of like grade and quality is a more difficult issue. Different prices cannot be justified merely because the labels on the product are different. It has been held that private labeling of merchandise, such as food products and appliances, does not make them different from the same goods carrying the seller's house brand. If a seller can establish that there is an actual physical difference in grade or quality between two products, then he can justify any differential in price between them he wishes. For this reason establishing a lower priced "fighting" brand is not illegal. The differential in price between different grades or qualities of goods need not, under the act, be proportionate to actual differences in the seller's costs. The magnitude of the difference in quality necessary to permit differential pricing is not clear, although courts have tended to require less difference than has the FTC, nor is it clear the extent to which differences in design permit price differentials. Of course, so long as the seller offers all designs, styles, and

---

[1] *Moore v. Mead's Fine Bread Co.,* 348 U.S. 115 (1954).

qualities to all purchasers, he forecloses questions with respect to discrimination when he establishes different prices.

Competitive Effect.   Section 2(a) applies only to discriminations which have the reasonable probability of lessening competition. Such an injury may occur to the competition between the sellers, which is called the *primary* level. A classic case was the early Standard Oil practice of cutting prices in one area to drive out a competitor. It is often claimed that a big national firm can finance this "predatory" price cutting by raising prices elsewhere. In such a case there might be no competition between the customers in the price-cutting market and those in the other areas. Or the injury to competition may be at the buyer or *secondary* level, as between a chain grocery and an independent. Often a price discrimination will cause the requisite injury at both levels. Indeed, a third level or *tertiary* competitive injury may occur, as where the effect is on the competition between customers of customers of the seller granting the lower price.

The act does not specifically deal with functional discounts, that is, discounts granted to a buyer, such as a wholesaler, performing certain functions in the distribution system. Therefore, whether a functional price differential is prohibited depends upon its competitive effect. So long as the distribution system is the same for all of the seller's goods distributed in a given area (for example, a manufacturer sells only to wholesalers who in turn supply the retailers) there is little likelihood of violation. However, where a seller sells to a buyer who serves both as a wholesaler and a retailer, injury to competition at the retail level may occur. A competitive advantage may also arise when a wholesaler customer of the seller sells to retailers at a lower price than the seller himself sells to retailers in the same market. Generally, however, the FTC has not questioned lower prices granted to bona fide wholesalers and jobbers.

Defenses.   There are two primary defenses a seller may use to justify price differentials. The first is to show that a differential can be justified on the basis of differences in cost to the seller in manufacture, sale, or delivery arising from differences in method or quantities involved. The second defense, appearing in Section 2(b), is to show that a price differential was made in good faith to meet a price of a competitor. In addition, the last of the provisos of Section 2(a) specifically permits differentials in price in response to changing market conditions or changes in the marketability of the goods such as the danger of imminent deterioration of perishable goods or of the obsolescence of seasonal goods. The burden of proving a defense is specifically laid by Section 2(b) upon the person claiming the defense.

Cost Justification.   If one buyer purchases the seller's product in reusable containers which may be handled by lift truck and in carload lots at his own warehouse and another buyer requires store door delivery of a few units at a time in small cartons, obviously the cost to the seller will be lower in the first case, although the exact amount of the price differential may be extremely difficult to justify. It is quite unlikely that quantity discounts based upon the annual volume of purchases can be justified on a cost-saving basis. Nor is a seller likely to be able to justify pricing a favored customer on something near to a marginal cost basis because the economies of the additional business would vanish if the other customers were lost. However, the difficulties of cost accounting for a specific product have been recognized and averaging of costs is permitted both by the FTC[2] and the Supreme Court.[3]

Meeting Competition. Section 2(b) states:

> Upon proof being made, at any hearing on a complaint under this section, that there has been discrimination in price or services or facilities furnished, the burden of rebutting the prima facie case thus made by showing justification shall be upon the person charged with a violation of this section, and unless justification shall be affirmatively shown, the Commission is authorized to issue an order terminating the discrimination: *Provided, however,* That nothing herein contained shall prevent a seller rebutting the prima facie case thus made by showing that his lower price or the furnishing of services or facilities to any purchaser or purchasers was made in good faith to meet an equally low price of a competitor, or the services or facilities furnished by a competitor.

Although meeting a competitor's price is an absolute defense, the FTC has taken a very strict view toward it and has been successful in persuading the courts to limit its application. For example, a seller cannot claim the defense if he knows or should know that the competitor's price which he met was itself an unlawful price discrimination. The seller can only meet, not undercut, the lower price of his competitor, and he cannot use the defense to meet a competitor's price for goods of lower quality or in a larger quantity than those involved in the seller's quotation. Nor can he use a price necessary to meet a specific competitive situation to charge systematically lower prices to a certain customer or customers. The FTC has taken the position that the defense is available only to meet a specific competitor's price in order to keep a specific customer and not to gain new customers by meeting the price of a competitor. This view was rejected by the Seventh Circuit Court, however.[4] Although the seller usually cannot prove that a competitor actually did offer the lower price, he must act upon reasonable belief, and merely taking the word of a customer or even one's own salesman may be held not to be sufficient grounds.[5]

Summary

The objectives of the Robinson-Patman Act, amending the Clayton Act, are to prevent discrimination in price or services by sellers which affect competition

---

[2] *Sylvania Electric Products, Inc.,* 51 FTC 282 (1954).
[3] *U.S. v. Borden Co.,* 370 U.S. 460 (1962).
[4] *Sunshine Biscuits, Inc. v. FTC,* 306 F.2d 48 (7th Cir. 1962).
[5] *FTC v. Staley Manufacturing Co.,* 324 U.S. 746 (1945).

among their customers and to prevent discriminatory prices which a seller might use to gain an advantage over his own competitors.

Other discriminatory practices which involve two or more states are covered by the act, either discrimination between buyers located in different states or discrimination by a seller between customers in a state different from the one in which he is located.

A discrimination in price prohibited in Section 2(a) must involve two or more sales to different purchasers at different prices at the point where the buyer takes the goods. Also a discrimination in price must involve goods of like grade and quality. Different brand names alone have been held insufficient to permit a different price. The discrimination in price must also have an adverse effect on competition among the sellers, their customers or customers further along in the channels of distribution in order to be covered by the act.

A seller has two defenses to justify differences in price between customers—(1) that the difference in price reflects differences in cost to the seller in manufacture, sale or delivery and (2) that the discriminatory price merely meets a nondiscriminatory price of a competitor for goods of the same quantity and quality.

Utah Pie Co. v. Continental Baking Co.

386 U.S. 685 (U.S. Sup. Ct. 1967)

Suit for treble damages and injunction brought by Utah Pie Company (plaintiff) against Continental Baking Company, Carnation Company and Pet Milk Company (defendants) charging conspiracy under the Sherman Act and price discrimination under the Robinson-Patman Act. The jury found for Utah Pie on the price discrimination charge. The circuit court reversed on appeal. Reversed.

Utah Pie had been baking pies in its plant in Salt Lake City and selling them in the surrounding area for 30 years. It had entered the frozen pie business in late 1957 and it was immediately successful. It was a small company having 18 employees at the time of the trial. The defendant companies were large and each was a major factor in the frozen pie market in one or more regions of the country. All three entered the Utah frozen pie market before Utah Pie did. None of them had a plant in Utah and most of their pies were shipped in from California. This gave Utah Pie a natural advantage.

The number of frozen pies sold in the Salt Lake market during the time covered by the suit—1958 through the first eight months of 1961—increased nearly five-fold. Utah Pie's share of the market in those years was 66.5%, 34.3%, 45.5% and 45.3%, and its net worth increased from $31,651 on October 31, 1957 to $68,802 on October 31, 1961.

For most of the period covered by the suit Utah's prices were the lowest in the market, but this was challenged by each of the defendant competitors at one time or another for varying periods. The level of prices for frozen pies in the market dropped during this period of intense competition, with Utah's prices falling from $4.15 per dozen to $2.75 per dozen. Each of the defendant competitors sold frozen pies in the Salt Lake City market during parts of this period at prices lower than they were selling comparable pies in other markets considerably closer to their plants.

MR. JUSTICE WHITE.   We disagree with the Court of Appeals in several respects. First, there was evidence from which the jury could have found considerably more price discrimination by Pet with respect to "Pet-Ritz" and "Swiss Miss" pies than was considered by the Court of Appeals. In addition to the seven months during which Pet's prices in Salt Lake were lower than prices in the California markets, there was evidence from which the jury could reasonably have found that in 10 additional months the Salt Lake City prices for "Pet-Ritz" pies were discriminatory as compared with sales in western markets other than California. Likewise, with respect to "Swiss Miss" pies, there was evidence in the record from which the jury could have found that in 5 of the 13 months during which the "Swiss Miss" pies were sold prior to the filing of this suit, prices in Salt Lake City were lower than those charged by Pet in either California or some other western market.

*   *   *   *   *

. . . (T)he Court of Appeals almost entirely ignored other evidence which provides material support for the jury's conclusion that Pet's behavior satisfied the statutory test regarding competitive injury. This evidence bore on the issue of Pet's predatory intent to injure Utah Pie. As an initial matter, the jury could have concluded that Pet's discriminatory pricing was aimed at Utah Pie; Pet's own management, as early as 1959, identified Utah Pie as an "unfavorable factor," one which "d(u)g holes in our operation" and posed a constant "check" on Pet's performance in the Salt Lake City market. Moreover, Pet candidly admitted that during the period when it was establishing its relationship with Safeway, it sent into Utah Pie's plant an industrial spy to seek information that would be of use to Pet in convincing Safeway that Utah Pie was not worthy of its custom. Pet denied that it ever in fact used what it had learned against Utah Pie in competing for Safeway's business. The parties, however, are not the ultimate judges of credibility. But even giving Pet's view of the incident a measure of weight does not mean the jury was foreclosed from considering the predatory intent underlying Pet's mode of competition. Finally, Pet does not deny that the evidence showed it suffered substantial losses on its frozen pie sales during the greater part of the time involved in this suit. . . .

Utah Pies' case against Continental is not complicated. Continental was a substantial factor in the market in 1957. But its sales of frozen 22-ounce dessert pies, sold under the "Morton" brand amounted to only 1.3% of the market in 1958, 2.9% in 1959, and 1.8% in 1960. . . . Then in June 1961, it took the steps which are the heart of Utah Pie's complaint against it. Effective for the last two weeks of June it offered its 22-ounce frozen apple pies in the Utah area at $3.85 per dozen. It was then selling the same pies at substantially higher prices in other markets. The Salt Lake City price was less than its direct cost plus an allocation for overhead. Utah's going price at the time for its 24-ounce "Frost 'N' Flame" apple pie sold to Associated Grocers was $3.10 per dozen, and for its "Utah" brand $3.40 per dozen.

* * * * *

We need not dwell long upon the case against Carnation. . . . After Carnation's temporary setback in 1959 it instituted a new pricing policy to regain business in the Salt Lake City market. The new policy involved a slash in price of 60¢ per dozen pies, which brought Carnation's price to a level admittedly well below its costs, and well below the other prices prevailing in the market. The impact of the move was felt immediately, and the two other major sellers in the market reduced their prices. Carnation's banner year, 1960, in the end involved eight months during which the prices in Salt Lake City were lower than prices charged in other markets.

Section 2(a) does not forbid price competition which will probably injure or lessen competition by eliminating competitors, discouraging entry into the market or enhancing the market shares of the dominant sellers. But Congress has established some ground rules for the game. Sellers may not sell like goods to different purchasers at different prices if the result may be to injure competition in either the sellers' or the buyers' market unless such discriminations are justified as permitted by the Act. This case concerns the sellers market. In this context, the Court of Appeals placed heavy emphasis on the fact that Utah Pie constantly increased its sales volume and continued to make a profit. But we disagree with its apparent view that there is no reasonably possible injury to competition as long as the volume of sales in a particular market is expanding and at least some of the competitors in the market continue to operate at a profit. Nor do we think that the Act only comes into play to regulate the conduct of price discriminators when their discriminatory prices consistently undercut other competitors. . . . Courts and commentators alike have noted that the existence of predatory intent might bear on the likelihood of injury to competition. In this case there was some evidence of predatory intent with respect to each of these respondents. There was also other evidence upon which the jury could rationally find the requisite injury to competition. The frozen pie market in Salt Lake City was highly competitive. At times Utah Pie was a leader in moving the general level of prices down, and at other times each of the respondents also bore responsibility for the downward pressure on the price structure. We believe that the Act reaches price discrimination that erodes competition as much as it does price discrimination that is intended to have immediate destructive impact. In this case, the evidence shows a drastically declining price structure which the jury could rationally attribute to continued or sporadic price discrimination. The jury was entitled to conclude that "the effect of such discrimination," by each of the respondents, "may be substantially to lessen competition . . . or to injure, destroy, or prevent competition with any person who either grants or knowingly receives the benefit of such discrimination. . . ." The statutory test is one that necessarily looks forward on the basis of proven conduct in the past. Proper application of that standard here requires reversal of the judgment of the Court of Appeals.

MR. JUSTICE STEWART (DISSENTING).   There is only one issue in this case in its present posture: . . . did the respondents' actions have the anticompetitive effect required by the statute as an element of a cause of action?

The Court's own description of the Salt Lake City frozen pie market from 1958 through 1961, shows that the answer to that question must be no. In 1958 Utah Pie had a quasi-monopolistic 66.5% of the market. In 1961—after the alleged predations of the respondents—Utah Pie still had a commanding 45.3%, Pet had 29.4%, and the remainder of the market was divided almost equally between Continental, Carnation, and other small local bakers. . . . Thus, if we assume that the price discrimination proven against the respondents had any effect on competition, that effect must have been beneficent.

. . . [T]he Court has fallen into the error of reading the Robinson-Patman Act as protecting competitors, instead of competition. . . . [L]ower prices are the hallmark of intensified competition.

Brokerage Payments

Unlawful Brokerage.   Section 2(c) establishes a per se violation of the act in that any type of dummy brokerage payment is prohibited, whether or not paid directly to the buyer. Unlike Section 2(a), no effect on competition need be shown to prove the violation. The section was aimed at price discrimination granted by means of brokerage payments to the buyer or his nominee. To accomplish this objective some courts have, by their interpretation of the section, eliminated the words "except for services rendered," and this is the position which has been taken by the FTC.[6] Even when a buyer's broker renders a service such as warehousing or breaking bulk, payment to him as been held to be a violation.[7] Therefore, any commission or allowance to a person directly or indirectly controlled by the buyer is prohibited whether or not any of the payment ever reaches the buyer. It has also been held to be a violation of Section 2(c) if a seller's broker accepts a lower commission and passes the savings to the buyer. Independent grocers' buying cooperatives have found this subsection an obstacle to their operations although it was aimed at their major competitors, the large food chains.

Discriminatory Payments and Services

Introduction.   Sellers and their customers both benefit from merchandising activities carried on by the customer to promote the sale of the goods. These would include such activities as advertising, displays of the goods, demonstrations and distribution of samples or premiums. Section 2(d) applies primarily to payments made by the seller to his customers to encourage such activities

---

[6] *Cf. Southgate Brokerage Co. v. FTC,* 150 F.2d 607 (4th Cir. 1945) with *Thomasville Chair Co. v. FTC,* 306 F.2d 541 (5th Cir. 1962).

[7] *FTC v. Henry Broch & Company,* 368 U.S. 360 (1962).

by them. Section 2(e) applies primarily to furnishing such services to the customer by the seller. These sections make either the payment for or the furnishing of a service illegal unless it is made available to all competing customers on proportionately equal terms. Many more enforcement actions have been brought under these sections than under Section 2(a).

Section 2(d) states:

> That it shall be unlawful for any person engaged in commerce to pay or contract for the payment of anything of value to or for the benefit of a customer of such person in the course of such commerce as compensation or in consideration for any services or facilities furnished by or through such customer in connection with the processing, handling, sale or offering for sale of any products or commodities manufactured, sold, or offered for sale by such person, unless such payment or consideration is available on proportionally equal terms to all other customers competing in the distribution of such products or commodities.

Section 2(e) declares:

> That it shall be unlawful for any person to discriminate in favor of one purchaser against another purchaser or purchasers of a commodity bought for resale, without or with processing, by contracting to furnish or furnishing, or by contributing to the furnishing of, any services or facilities connected with the processing, handling, sale, or offering for sale of such commodity so purchased upon terms not accorded to all purchasers on proportionally equal terms.

Both sections define per se violations. That is, whether the discriminatory allowance or service has the effect of injuring competition is immaterial. However, Section 2(b) of the act specifically includes the furnishing of services as part of the meeting competition defense, and this has been interpreted to apply to the payment of allowances under Section 2(d).

Competing Customers. It will be noted that the language of the two sections differs in some respects but they have been interpreted as having substantially the same meaning. For example, the requirement that the customers be competing in Section 2(d) has been read into 2(e).[8]

One may be considered a customer under the act although not buying directly from the seller offering services or payments. A buyer such as a food market who buys for resale from a wholesaler is treated as a customer of the manufacturer or processer selling to the wholesaler.

Available. The requirement of availability demands of the seller offering promotional payments or services more than merely not denying the request of a customer to be given a similar payment or service. For example, a seller of coffee who wants to offer a cooperative advertising contract to a grocery customer to encourage the customer to include the seller's branded product in his or her weekly newspaper advertising must actually make known to other customers who are in competition with that customer that the seller will make promotional payments to them on a proportional basis.

To be available the service must be something appropriate to the customer.

---

[8]*FTC v. Simplicity Pattern Co.,* 360 U.S. 55 (1959).

It is not enough for a seller of coffee to make a payment available only to customers who advertise in newspapers. The cooperative advertising plan must be flexible enough to permit all competing customers to participate—with handbills or other types of advertising or perhaps even other kinds of promotional devices such as window or counter displays.

On Proportionately Equal Terms. The most common method of proportionalizing is relating payments or services to the quantity of goods purchased. An example would be a payment of 50 cents per case of coffee or for each $5 worth of merchandise purchased. It has been suggested that payments or services, such as furnishing a display case, could be proportionalized by furnishing one case for each of the buyer's stores or payments could be related to the square feet of window space devoted to a display of the seller's product. The fact that it is impracticable to furnish a cosmetics demonstrator for one hour to a small drug store when one is furnished for a full day to a store selling eight times as much of the cosmetics firm's products does not excuse the offering of a proportional service. However, it need not be the same service; it might be quite a different sort of promotional device, such as a demonstration kit.

The seller who makes payments for customer's merchandising services has, according to the FTC, a duty to ensure that the payments are actually used for that purpose.

Summary

Section 2(d) prohibits payments by a seller to a customer for furnishing any service or facility unless such payments are made available on proportionately equal terms to all competing customers. Section 2(e) prohibits the seller from himself furnishing services or facilities which are not available on a proportionalized basis. "Competing customers" has been held to include those buying for resale from a seller's customer such as a wholesaler. The requirement of availability requires that the seller actually make known the offer of the payment of service.

FTC v. Fred Meyer, Inc.

390 U.S. 341 (U.S. Sup. Ct. 1968)

This was a proceeding on petition of Fred Meyer, Inc. (petitioner), to review and set aside an order of the Federal Trade Commission (respondent) requiring Meyer to cease and desist from inducing certain suppliers to engage in discriminatory sales promotional activities prohibited by Section 2(d) of the Clayton Act as amended by the Robinson-Patman Act. The Court of Appeals for the Ninth Circuit disagreed in part with the Commission's interpretation of Section 2(d) and directed it to modify the order. Reversed and remanded to the FTC.

Fred Meyer, Inc., operating a chain of 13 supermarkets in the Portland, Oregon, area and making one fourth of the retail food sales in the area, conducted a four week promotional campaign each year. The promotion involved the distribution of a 72-page coupon book to its customers, each coupon good for a special price, often a one-third reduction from the regular price on a specified item carried in the Meyer stores. The coupon book was sold by Meyer to consumers for 10 cents and, in addition, Meyer charged each supplier joining in the promotion $3.50 for each coupon page. The suppliers usually underwrote the promotion further by redeeming coupons for cash or replacing without charge some proportion of the goods sold by Meyer during the promotion.

The proceeding before the commission involved Tri-Valley Packing Association and Idaho Canning Co. as suppliers who, it was alleged, had violated Section 2(d) in participating in the 1957 promotion. Both paid Meyer $3.50 for the coupon and each agreed to replace for Meyer every third can sold under the offer. Both suppliers also sold to two wholesalers, Hudson House and Wadhams, who resold to a number of Meyer's retail competitors. No comparable promotional allowances had been accorded either of the wholesalers.

Meyer argued that there had been no violation of Section 2(d) because Meyer was not competing with the wholesalers and that the retailers who were competing with Meyer were not customers of Tri-Valley and Idaho Canning but were customers of the wholesalers. The FTC took the view that Meyer's retail competitors buying through the wholesalers were indirect customers of Tri-Valley and Idaho Canning. The FTC ruled that Section 2(d) prohibits a supplier from granting promotional allowances to a direct-buying retailer, such as Meyer, unless the allowances are also made available to wholesalers who purchase from the supplier and resell to retailers who compete with the direct buyer.

MR. CHIEF JUSTICE WARREN.   We agree with the Commission that the proscription of Section 2(d) reaches the kind of discriminatory promotional allowances granted Meyer by Tri-Valley and Idaho Canning. Therefore, we reverse the judgment of the Court of Appeals on this point. However, because we have concluded that Meyer's retail competitors, rather than the two wholesalers, were competing customers under the statute, we also remand the case to the Commission for appropriate modification of its order.

For reasons stated below, we agree with Meyer that, on the facts of this case, Section 2(d) reaches only discrimination between customers competing for resales at the same functional level and, therefore, does not mandate proportional equality between Meyer and the two wholesalers.

Of course, neither the Committee Report nor other parts of the legislative history in so many words defines "customer" to include retailers who purchase through wholesalers and compete with direct buyers in resales. But a narrower reading of Section 2(d) would lead to the following anomalous result. On the one hand, direct-buying retailers like Meyer, who resell large quantities of their suppliers' products and therefore find it feasible to undertake the traditional wholesaling functions for themselves, would be protected by the provision from the granting of discriminatory promotional allowances to their direct-buying competitors. On the other hand, smaller retailers whose only access to suppliers is through independent wholesalers would not be entitled to this protection. Such a result would be diametrically opposed to Congress' clearly stated intent to improve the competitive position of small retailers by eliminating what was regarded as an abusive form of discrimination. If we were to read "customer" as excluding retailers who buy through wholesalers and compete with direct buyers, we would frustrate the purpose of Section 2(d). We effectuate it by holding that the section includes such competing retailers within the protected class.

Given these findings, it was unnecessary for the Commission to resort to the indirect customer doctrine. Whether suppliers deal directly with disfavored competitors or not, they can, and here did, afford a direct buyer the kind of competitive advantage which Section 2(d) was intended to eliminate. In light of our holding that "customer" in Section 2(d) includes retailers who buy through wholesalers and compete with a direct buyer in the resale of the supplier's product, the requirement of direct dealing between the supplier and disfavored competitors imposed by the Court of Appeals rests on too narrow a reading of the statute.

Although we approach the Commission's ruling with the deference due the agency charged with day-to-day administration of the Act, we hold that, at least on the facts before us, Section 2(d) does not require proportional equality between Meyer and the two wholesalers.

The Commission believed it found support for its position in the language of Section 2(d) itself, which requires that promotional allowances be accorded on proportionally equal terms to "customers competing in the distribution" of a supplier's product, rather than merely to customers competing in resales. The majority reasoned that Hudson House and Wadhams, when they resold to Meyer's retail competitors, were competing with Meyer in the distribution of Tri-Valley and Idaho Canning products because the two wholesalers were "seeking exactly the same consumer dollars that respondents are after." While it cannot be doubted that Congress reasonably could have employed such a broad concept of competition in Section 2(d), we do not believe that the use of the word "distribution" rather than "resale" is a clear indication that it did, and what discussion there was of the promotional allowance provision during the congressional hearings indicates that the section was meant to impose proportional equality only where buyers competed on the same functional level.

We recognize that it would be both inappropriate and unwise to attempt to formulate an all-embracing rule applying the elusive language of the section to every system of distribution a supplier might devise for getting his product to the consumer. But, on the concrete facts here presented, it is clear that the direct impact of Meyer's receiving discriminatory promotional allowances is felt by the disfavored retailers with whom Meyer competes in resales. We cannot assume without a clear indication from Congress that Section 2(d) was intended to compel the supplier to pay the allowances to a reseller further up the distributive chain who might or might not pass them on to the level where the impact would be felt directly. We conclude that the most reasonable construction of Section 2(d) is one which places on the supplier the responsibility for making promotional allowances available to those resellers who compete directly with the favored buyer.

The Commission argues here that the view we take of Section 2(d) is impracticable because suppliers will not always find it feasible to bypass their wholesalers and grant promotional allowance directly to their numerous retail outlets. Our decision does not necessitate such bypassing. We hold only that, when a supplier gives allowances to a direct-buying retailer, he must also make them available on comparable terms to those who buy his products through wholesalers and compete with the direct buyer in resales. Nothing we have said bars a supplier, consistently with other provisions of the anti-trust laws, from utilizing his wholesalers to distribute payments or administer a promotional program, so long as the supplier takes responsibility, under rules and guides promulgated by the Commission for the regulation of such practices, for seeing that the allowances are made available to all who compete in the resale of his product.

Vanity Fair Paper Mills v. FTC

311 F.2d 480 (2d Cir. 1962)

This was a petition by Vanity Fair Paper Mills, Inc. (plaintiff), to review an order of the Federal Trade Commission (defendant) directing Vanity Fair to cease and desist from making payments to a customer for advertising or other services or facilities unless such payments were made available to other customers on proportionately equal terms. Commission's order enforced with modification.

Vanity Fair, a manufacturer of household paper products in New York, sold its products to retail and wholesale grocers and druggists in Texas, Louisiana and other states. In 1958 it used a standard Cooperative Advertising Agreement in the Texas-Louisiana area. In addition, because Vanity Fair did not have funds available for extensive advertising, it occasionally participated in special promotions conducted by its customers which featured its products along with other suppliers.

Weingarten, a retail grocery chain operating in Texas and Louisiana and one of Vanity Fair's customers, requested Vanity Fair to participate in its 57th Anniversary Sale in February 1958. It offered Vanity Fair a schedule of promotional services combining an advertisement of Vanity Fair's products in Weingarten's newspaper advertising and special product displays and the "personal enthusiasm" of Weingarten store personnel in one or more of the geographical areas covered by Weingarten stores. The cost of participation, according to the schedule, ranged from $56.05 to $3,995.90. Vanity Fair chose the $215 item which gave it the promotional service in all of Weingarten's Texas and Louisiana stores plus 1/16 page in the newspapers in Houston, Freeport, Baytown and Texas City. Vanity Fair also participated in October 1958, in Weingarten's 20th Texas and Louisiana Products Sale.

Childs Big Chain was the only other customer of Vanity Fair which competed with Weingarten in southeastern Texas and southwestern Louisiana which received a special promotional allowance in 1958. None of the other customers requested such an allowance. The combined payments from the standard cooperative advertising contract and the special promotional allowances gave Weingarten 3.4% and Childs 2.2% on Vanity Fair's gross sales to them. The other customers who received no special allowance received allowances ranging from 1.9% to zero.

The Commission found that the special allowances to Weingarten violated Section 2(d) of the Robinson-Patman Act.

FRIENDLY, CIRCUIT JUDGE.   It is not disputed that Weingarten received from Vanity Fair something of value for services or facilities furnished in the sale of Vanity Fair's products which was not received by "other customers competing in the distribution of such products or commodities." The issue is whether the Commission was warranted in finding that the "payment or consideration" given to Weingarten was not "available" to all the non-recipients "on proportionally equal terms."

Determination of what a seller must do in order that payments of the sort described in § 2(d) should be "available" to all customers has not been easy. . . .

. . . A promotional allowance is not "available" to all customers if it has been "denied" to some. *Corn Products Refining Co. v. FTC* (1945). Neither is it "available" if steps have been taken to conceal it. On the other hand, the legislative history argues against a construction that would require the seller to make an actual "offer" to all customers, including many who might not be interested. Between these polar positions the Commission has shifted uneasily. For some years it tended toward an ever stronger attitude coming perilously close to requiring an offer, as can be seen by comparing earlier cases where the complaint emphasized secrecy and concealment, e.g., *N. Erlanger, Blumgart & Co.,* with the increasingly severe requirements of affirmative and specific notification set forth in *Kay Windsor Frocks, Inc.* Then it made a slight retreat toward a more generalized notification requirement in its 1960 Guides for Advertising Allowances and Other Merchandising Payments and Services, which say:

> The seller should take some action to inform all his customers competing with any participating customer that the plan is available. He can do this by any means he chooses, including letter, telegram, notice on invoices, salesmen, brokers, etc. However, if a seller wants to be able to show later that he did make an offer to a certain customer, he is in a better position to do so if he made it in writing.

Unsatisfactory as the 1960 formulation may be, perhaps it is as much as can be expected when Congress has spoken in such Delphic terms.

A showing here not only that Vanity Fair's sales representatives had been "advised" of its policies with respect to special promotional allowances and "instructed to inform respondent's customers thereof," but also that they had carried out such instructions, would have met the Commission's definition of the statutory standard. However, the stipulation was altogether silent on the latter score. The Commission was entitled to deem the silence significant and to conclude, as it did, that the information had not been generally passed on.

*   *   *   *   *

We also sustain the Commission's alternative position that even if respondent's special promotional allowances were "available" to all customers, they were not available "on proportionally equal terms." . . . Little as the stipulation here tells us of Vanity Fair's "policy," it tells enough to show that the requirement of proportional equality was not satisfied. Even as to identically situated customers, the policy left Vanity Fair free to discriminate both in the quantum of promotional services it would support and in the degree to which it would support them. Altogether consistently with its policy, Vanity Fair could have paid Weingarten as much as $3,995.90 and an identically situated competitor, offering it the same choices as Weingarten, as little as $56.05. It is true that since Weingarten would have had to furnish more newspaper advertising than its competitor, Vanity Fair would have derived greater benefit from the larger payment, although perhaps not proportionally greater, since both customers would have been furnishing the same displays and "personnel enthusiasm." But Weingarten would have received an enormously greater benefit from Vanity Fair than the equally entitled competitor. Also, even if Vanity Fair chose to support the same advertising space for identical customers, the policy did not require it to pay a uniform proportion of the cost but only "an amount reasonably related" thereto; if the stipulation meant "equal to" or "the same percentage of" the cost, it did not say so. Neither did the policy make any attempt to relate the amount of support accorded different customers to their respective volumes of purchases. To be sure, it was not established that Vanity Fair in fact applied its policy in a discriminatory fashion. But a seller who has paid a special promotional allowance to some customers and not to others does not avoid the proscription of § 2(d) merely because payment *might have been* "available on proportionally equal terms to all other customers competing in the distribution of such products or commodities"; he avoids it only if such payment "is" available. Whatever the statute does or does not require with respect to proportionality, it is not satisfied by a policy as loose as Vanity Fair's.

Buyer Inducement of Discrimination

Inducements Prohibited.   Section 2(f) is directed at the buyer and makes it illegal for him to induce or receive knowingly a discrimination in price prohibited by Section 2(a). It states:

> That it shall be unlawful for any person engaged in commerce, in the course of such commerce, knowingly to induce or receive a discrimination in price which is prohibited by this section.

It does not apply to promotional payments or services prohibited by Sections 2(d) and 2(e). A violation occurs only when the buyer knows that the price he receives is lower than that which the seller charges other customers. However, he need not have knowledge that the discrimination actually violates Section 2(a). For example, to be in violation of Section 2(f) the buyer need not be aware of the injury to competition necessary for a violation of Section 2(a).

Enforcement

Types of Proceedings.   The various provisions of Section 2 of the Clayton Act as amended by the Robinson-Patman Act may be enforced by four types of proceedings. First, the FTC on its own motion or upon the application of a private party, may make an investigation and issue a complaint which may result in a cease and desist order after proceedings before the Commission. Second, the Attorney General of the United States may bring an injunction suit in a U.S. District Court. Third, an individual or corporation may seek an injunction. Fourth, any individual or corporation who is injured by a violation may bring a suit for treble damages. A substantial number of such treble damage suits have been successful and courts have been relatively liberal in their requirements for proof of damages.

In addition, Section 3 of the Robinson-Patman Act makes it a crime to participate in general price discriminations, in geographical price discriminations seeking to eliminate a competitor in a certain area, and in selling at unreasonably low prices for the purpose of destroying competition or eliminating a competitor. There have been few impositions of criminal penalties under this section.

Problem Cases

1. The Kraft Foods Division of National Dairy Products Corporation had by 1961 become the largest producer of fruit spreads in the United States and was the only nationwide seller of a full line of variously flavored spreads. It heavily advertised these spreads on network TV, in consumer magazines, and in local newspapers during 1959–61. In 1960, Kraft was dissatisfied with its sale of fruit spreads in the Washington, D.C. area, which included Baltimore, Norfolk and Richmond. Its survey showed that in terms of shelf facing or display space (which is thought to be closely related to volume) three regional packers of fruit spreads, Old Virginia, Theresa Friedman, and Polaner, exceeded Kraft in shelf space. Welch, offering only grape spreads, and two house brands of chain stores also were ahead of Kraft.

    Kraft decided on a promotion running from January 16 to February 10, 1961, which would give an additional case of fruit spread with each one purchased at regular list price by any customer, the free goods to be delivered after February 10. The net price (half price) was substantially below the manufacturing cost without taking into account delivery cost. All customers were notified of the promotion, which included heavy local TV and regional *Life* Magazine advertising plus newspaper coupon offers of a free jar of fruit spread with the purchase of one jar of a different flavor and a cooperative advertising in connection with floor or table displays during the period February 27 to April 28. A repeat of the display agreement was scheduled for May 29 through July 28. Prices were not changed and a comparable promotion was not adopted in other market areas.

    The response of the trade to the program was massive and many customers took advantage of the opportunity to buy the high quality, heavily advertised product at half price to the full extent of their financial ability and warehouse capacity. As a result Kraft canceled the planned additional promotional activities but continued the free case offer as announced, except that, to avoid glutting the market, it paid cash in lieu of delivering 61 percent of the unbilled goods. The cost of the promotion to Kraft was $1,346,000. Sales of Old Virginia for the first six months of 1961 declined 23 percent in Washington, D.C., and by 41 percent in Richmond, with the other cities falling in between. Other competitors suffered comparable declines.

The FTC found territorial price discrimination in violation of Section 2(a) of the Robinson-Patman Act. National Dairy Products filed a petition to set aside the order on the ground that the evidence of an adverse effect on competition was insufficient. Should the FTC be upheld?

2.   D. L. & Edwin Ingram were partners serving as a jobber for Phillips Petroleum, and they were assigned a territory in New Mexico surrounding the town of Clovis. Helton was Phillips' wholesaler in an area near Farwell, Texas, which is nine miles east of Clovis. Helton also did business in Texico, New Mexico, which was distinguishable from Farwell only because of the state border. For a long time prior to February 1965, Helton had purchased gasoline in Farwell from Phillips for one-half cent per gallon less than paid by the Ingrams in Clovis. In early 1965, Phillips made certain price changes in Farwell with the result that the differential favoring Helton increased to 1.8 cents per gallon. Most of the Ingrams' business was with service stations, with about 25 percent to consumers, such as farmers, buying at wholesale.

The service stations in Clovis had been engaged in an almost continuous price war for three years. The Ingrams suffered no loss of service station accounts or reduction in their volume of sales. They had urged their farm customers not to change suppliers until after their suit had been adjudicated and only three or four of these accounts had been lost.

The Ingrams sued Phillips to enjoin price discrimination which they allege violates Section 2(a) of the Robinson-Patman Act. Should the injunction be granted?

3.   In 1959, United Biscuit Co. divided its customers in the Midwest into two categories: independents (those operating only one store) and chains (more than one store). United used graduated monthly discount schedules which allowed discounts up to 6 percent based on the volume of purchases made by each retail store customer. The discount was calculated on the basis of the aggregated purchases of the store operated by the customer. The larger chains received larger discounts than did the independents. The FTC ordered United to cease and desist violating Section 2(a) of the Robinson-Patman Act by its discount practices. Its case against United was based upon purchases made and discounts earned during two separate three-month periods of 1959 by 13 independent stores and by a few chain store outlets located in portions of three communities served by the Sawyer Division—Gary, Indiana; South Bend, Indiana; and Burlington, Wisconsin. Most of the major retail grocery stores and a few of the large independents received a 6 percent volume discount. Other stores received discounts varying from 1½ percent to 5 percent. Some received no discount. The Commission found that as a result of the differences in the volume discounts, United charged some customers a higher price for like goods than it charged a competing customer or competing customers.

United petitioned the court to review the cease and desist order claiming there was no injury to competition. Should the order be affirmed?

4.   In the past, Ackerman Sales Company had acted as the factory representative for the Mohawk Cabinet Company in the New York area. Mohawk paid the Ackerman Sales Company a 4 percent commission on all sales of Mohawk products to distributors within this prescribed area. One of these distributors was Ackerman Distributors, Inc. Both the Ackerman Sales Company and Ackerman Distributors, Inc. are owned solely by the same individual, Mr. Morton L. Ackerman. The dispute arose when Mohawk informed Ackerman Sales that it would no longer pay commissions on sales to Ackerman Distributors. For a time thereafter, business continued as usual with Mohawk paying Ackerman Sales a 4 percent commission on all sales except those to Ackerman Distributors. Finally Ackerman Sales brought suit against Mohawk for the commissions it claimed were due on its sales to

Ackerman Distributors. Does the Mohawk Cabinet Company have a good defense under the Robinson-Patman Act?

5. Clairol was reimbursing certain large beauty salon chains for sums spent on advertising. The advertising was not directed at salon customers of Clairol, but at the public—the potential customers of the salon—and promoted both the advertiser and the Clairol products it offered. Its aim was to persuade the reader to go to the salon for service and to ask for Clairol products in connection with that service. The FTC ordered Clairol to cease and desist from discrimination between competing customers in violation of Section 2(d) of the Robinson-Patman Act. Clairol contends that Section 2(d) is not applicable since its beauty salon customers do not distribute Clairol products; that "distribution" as used in Section 2(d) means "resale"; that beauty salons do not sell Clairol products but themselves consume them in connection with the service they perform for their customers. Clairol emphasizes that a salon patron pays no separate charge for the Clairol product used and that generally, the cost of the Clairol product is minimal. Should Clairol prevail in its defense?

6. Simplicity, one of the nation's largest manufacturers of patterns for ladies dresses, sold to about 12,300 retailers with approximately 17,200 outlets. These customers were of two types: department stores and variety stores, which constituted 18 percent of the number of customers but 70 percent of sales volume and small yard-goods fabric stores which represented 82 percent of Simplicity's customers but only 30 percent of its sales volume. Retail prices of the patterns were uniform, as were Simplicity's prices at 60 percent of retail price. However, variety stores were furnished monthly with Simplicity's current catalog and also with steel cabinets in which to store the patterns. Furthermore, the variety stores were furnished their stock of patterns on a consignment basis and transportation costs were paid by Simplicity, while fabric stores were required to pay cash and to bear the transportation cost. In 1954, four major variety chains were furnished catalogs and cabinets which would have been priced at approximately $649,000 to fabric stores and their inventory of patterns held on consignment was valued at $1,775,000. While in variety stores patterns had to compete for space on the basis of their profitability, fabric stores carried the patterns and sold them at a loss for the convenience of their yard-goods customers.

   The FTC ordered Simplicity to cease and desist from violating Section 2(e) of the Robinson-Patman Act. In seeking judicial review, Simplicity argues that there was an absence of competitive injury to the fabric stores, since their main concern was selling fabric, and that it should have been permitted to show that its extra facilities and services for variety stores were justified by its lower costs in selling them. Should the FTC order be affirmed?

7. The Centex Corporation is a Chicago area builder and developer of homes. From 1968 to August 1969, it purchased lumber from the Hines Lumber Company to resell as part of completed houses. Centex has brought suit against Hines alleging that the lumber company from May 1968 to August 1969 had engaged in a continuous course of discrimination against them by consistently delivering lumber to them behind contractual schedules while delivering lumber to their competitors in preference to them. Rather than attempting to justify its more prompt lumber deliveries to other builders, Hines rests its defense on the contention that Section 2(e) of the Robinson-Patman Act does not apply to consistent, preferential differences in the timeliness of delivery services because (1) these are not promotional services, and (2) they are not connected with the sale of lumber by Centex. Is Hines defense a good one under Section 2(e)?

8. Kroger decided to offer a line of private label dairy products and indicated to suppliers that it expected to do an annual volume of approximately $2 million per year. When the Beatrice

Foods representative indicated to the Kroger purchasing agent that it intended to enter a bid for the business at approximately 15 percent off its list prices, he was told, "Forget it, I've already got one at 20 percent," which was a discount unheard of in the market area at that time. After numerous negotiations Beatrice met the prices Kroger informed it that a competitor, Broughton, had offered. In fact, the prices offered by Broughton were higher than the Beatrice prices that were accepted by Kroger.

The FTC issued a cease and desist order against Kroger for violating Section 2(f) and absolved Beatrice from violating Section 2(a) of the Robinson-Patman Act. Kroger seeks judicial review contending that, as a matter of law, the discharge of Beatrice requires the acquittal of Kroger because there can be no violation of Section 2(f) by the buyer without a violation of 2(a) by the seller. Does Kroger have a good defense?

chapter 49

The Federal Trade Commission Act and Other Acts and Law Relating to Competition

The Federal Trade Commission Act

The Federal Trade Commission Act (38 Stat. 717 [1914] as amended, 15 U.S.C. § § 41–58) like the Clayton Act was enacted because its proponents felt that the Sherman Act had not sufficiently curtailed certain monopolistic practices and tendencies in the American economy. The act created a special bipartisan administrative agency charged with giving expert and continuing enforcement of antitrust policies. Under Section 5 of the act the FTC is given very broad powers to police "unfair methods of competition in commerce, and unfair or deceptive acts or practices in commerce."

While the Federal Trade Commission Act is not technically a part of the antitrust laws and private treble damage actions cannot be brought under Section 5, the act overlaps the Sherman Act in that it also makes illegal as "unfair methods of competition," any of the restraints of trade which are illegal under the Sherman Act. In addition, the powers of the FTC reach incipient anticompetitive practices, false advertising, and other deceptive practices which are not reached by the Sherman Act. The FTC has concurrent jurisdiction with the Department of Justice to enforce the Clayton Act. In practice, the FTC alone has brought the cases under the Robinson-Patman Act amendments to the Clayton Act. The FTC also has jurisdiction in regard to various other acts including: the Webb-Pomerene Act; Wool Products Labeling Act; Federal Drug and Cosmetic Act; Fur Products Labeling Act; Flammable Fabric Act; Lanham Trade-Mark Act; and the Fair Packaging and Labeling Act.

The FTC issues "cease and desist" orders against violations of the act which become final unless appealed to the courts. Businesses which violate these orders are subject to $5,000 fines for each day of continuing violation.

Summary

The FTC has broad powers to stop anticompetitive and deceptive practices. The Commission issues cease and desist orders and also has the power to levy fines. Private treble damage suits are not permitted for violations of the FTC Act.

Firestone Tire & Rubber Co. v. FTC

481 F. 2d 246 (6th Cir. 1973)

Firestone (defendant) sought a review of a Federal Trade Commission cease and desist order which was issued after the FTC found Firestone guilty of unfair and deceptive advertising practices in violation of the Federal Trade Commission Act. Order of FTC affirmed and enforcements ordered.

The FTC order was issued in regard to two particular ads, one called the "Safe Tire" ad, and the other the "Stop 25% Quicker" ad.

I. The "Safe Tire" Ad

As to this series of advertisements, the parties stipulated as follows:
1. *Duration of Advertising Program*

1. Beginning on December 25, 1967, and continuing through May 18, 1968, the following text, or a text substantially similar to it, was used in certain Firestone advertisements:

THE SAFE TIRE. *FIRESTONE*

When you buy a Firestone tire—no matter how much or how little you pay—you get a safe tire. Firestone tires are custom-built one by one. By skilled craftsmen. And they're personally inspected for an extra margin of safety. If these tires don't pass all of the exacting Firestone inspections, they don't get out.

Every new Firestone design goes through rugged tests of safety and strength far exceeding any driving condition you'll ever encounter. We prove them in our test lab. On our test track. And in rigorous day-to-day driving conditions. All Firestone tires meet or exceed the new Federal Government testing requirements. (They have for some time.)

Firestone—The Safe Tire. At 60,000 Firestone Safe Tire Centers. At no more cost than ordinary tires.

II. The "Stops 25% Quicker" Ad

The Firestone "Stops 25% Quicker" ad reads:

. . . Like the original Super Sports Wide Oval Tire. It came straight out of Firestone racing research. It's built lower, wider. Nearly two inches wider than regular tires. To corner better, run cooler, stop 25% quicker.

EDWARDS, CIRCUIT JUDGE.   In approaching decision on this issue, this court is limited by statute and case law as to its proper function. The statute which provides for our review also provides that "the findings of the Commission as to the facts if supported by evidence, shall be conclusive." . . . This court has described such findings as "entitled to be given great weight," and has noted that "the Commission is permitted to draw reasonable inferences from the evidence. . . ."

Employing these standards, we affirm the findings of the FTC on the "Safe Tire" issue and enforce its order.

There is, of course, no question but that the ad indulges in some puffing. The statement, "When you buy a Firestone Tire . . . you get a safe tire," contains no use qualifications as to inflation, load and speed, and is measured against no comparative performance.

We deal, of course, with a statutory ban on "unfair or deceptive acts or practices." If no one were misled, we might reexamine our own conclusions vis-a-vis the Commission's inferences about this ad in considerably more detail. Here, however, Firestone's own consumer survey demonstrated that 15.3% of a scientifically selected sample of tire purchasers thought the "Safe Tire" ad meant:

(d) "Every Firestone tire is absolutely safe no matter how it is used and regardless of the tire inflation pressure and load of the car;" or "Every single Firestone tire will be absolutely free from any defects."

We find it hard to overturn the deception findings of the Commission if the ad thus misled 15% (or 10%) of the buying public.[1]

We find no overbreadth or deficiency in the remedial order of the Commission, and as to it we affirm and grant enforcement.

. . . Firestone argues that its "Stops 25% Quicker" ad (1) . . . did not impliedly assert that the "stops 25% quicker" language was based on scientific testing and that the Commission made no explicit finding to that effect; (2) that in any event, its own series of tests on wet, slippery pavement did represent adequate scientific proof of its assertion, or if not that, such proof could reasonably be extrapolated from that test, and (3) that the cease and desist order was unreasonably broad and restrictive in requiring scientific proof as to *any* safety or performance characteristic advertised.

As to the first of these issues, we believe the Commission did find that the "Stops 25% Quicker" ad implied scientific testing. It said:

In the circumstances of *this* case, we believe that consumers could reasonably have expected Firestone's performance and safety claims to have been substantiated by scientific tests.

In addition, we think such an implication is entirely reasonable from the comparison and percentage language employed.

As to Firestone's second argument above, we note at the outset that Firestone presented no witnesses at all in this proceeding. It relied entirely upon data provided by a comparison of two tires (both Firestone products) in ten runs on the same day on the same wet, smooth concrete surface at 15 m.p.h. with the same tire pressure and

---

[1] As to the issue the Commission's opinion stated:

We conclude that Firestone's absolute representation that its tires are "safe" is false and deceptive on its own admission that tires cannot under today's technology be assured of being free of defects. In view of this technological impossibility, it is an unfair and deceptive act and practice for defendant to make the unqualified assertion of safety which it made in this case.

load. These ten runs showed an average stopping distance of 29.8% less for the Firestone Super Sports Wide Oval tire as compared to a Firestone Super Sports tire of standard tread width.

The Commission makes no comment derogatory to the scientific nature or the accuracy of the test upon which Firestone relies. Rather, it attacks the adequacy of one set of tests on one surface (we would be tempted to add, at one speed) to support the "stops 25% quicker" generalization. Of course, we note that the Commission's own expert witness, Dr. Brenner, seemed to concede that a tire which stopped quicker on a wet surface would, under similar conditions, as to surface, speed, etc., stop still more quickly on a dry surface. What Dr. Brenner would not concede was that testing on any one surface was adequate to represent driving conditions nationwide. . . .

We are by no means sure that the Firestone Wide Oval tire does not "stop 25% quicker." But that is not our question. We have to deal with the record that has been submitted in this case. On this record we conclude that the Commission's finding (that Firestone's "broad stopping claim" was "unfair and deceptive to consumers" because it was "without substantial scientific test data to support it") was supported by the evidence in this record and by the fair inferences which the Commission was entitled to draw therefrom. . . .

FTC v. Texaco, Inc.

393 U.S. 223 (U.S. Sup. Ct. 1968)

The FTC brought this proceeding against Texaco under Section 5 of the FTC Act charging that Texaco's sales commission plan with its dealers constituted an unfair method of competition. The Circuit Court set aside a cease and desist order issued by the Commission and the Commission appealed. Reversed.

MR. JUSTICE BLACK.   The question presented by this case is whether the FTC was warranted in finding that it was an unfair method of competition in violation of § 5 of the Federal Trade Commission Act for respondent Texaco to undertake to induce its service station dealers to purchase Goodrich tires, batteries, and accessories (hereafter referred to as TBA) in return for a commission paid by Goodrich to Texaco.

The Commission and Texaco agree that the Texaco-Goodrich arrangement for marketing TBA will fall under the rationale of our *Atlantic* decision if the Commission was correct in its three ultimate conclusions that (1) Texaco has dominant economic power over its dealers; (2) that Texaco exercises that power over its dealers in fulfilling its agreement to promote and sponsor Goodrich products; and (3) that anticompetitive effects result from the exercise of that power.

That Texaco holds dominant economic power over its dealers is clearly shown by the record in this case. In fact, Texaco does not contest the conclusion of the Court of Appeals below and the Fifth Circuit Court of Appeals in *Shell* that such power is "inherent in the structure and economics of the petroleum distribution system." Nearly 40% of the Texaco dealers lease their stations from Texaco. These dealers typically hold a one-year lease on their stations, and these leases are subject to termination at the end of any year on 10 days' notice. At any time during the year a man's lease on his service station may be immediately terminated by Texaco without advance notice if in Texaco's judgment any of the "house-keeping" provisions of the lease, relating to the use and appearance of the station, are not fulfilled. The contract under which Texaco dealers receive their vital supply of gasoline and other petroleum products also runs from year to year and is terminable on 30 days' notice under Texaco's standard form contract. The average dealer is a man of limited means who has what is for him a sizable investment in his station. He stands to lose much if he incurs the ill will of Texaco. As Judge Wisdom wrote in *Shell,* "A man operating a gas station is bound to be overawed by the great corporation that is his supplier, his banker, and his landlord."

It is against the background of this dominant economic power over the dealers that the sales commission arrangement must be viewed. The Texaco-Goodrich agreement provides that Goodrich will pay Texaco a commission of 10% on all purchases by Texaco service station dealers of Goodrich TBA. In return, Texaco agrees to "promote the sale of Goodrich products" to Texaco dealers. During the five-year period studied by the Commission (1952–1956) $245,000,000 of the Goodrich and Firestone TBA sponsored by Texaco was purchased by Texaco dealers, for which Texaco received almost $22,000,000 in commissions. Evidence before the Commission showed that Texaco carried out its agreement to promote Goodrich products through constantly reminding its dealers of Texaco's desire that they stock and sell the sponsored Goodrich TBA. Texaco emphasizes the importance of TBA and the recommended brands as early as its initial interview with a prospective dealer and repeats it recommendation through a steady flow of campaign materials utilizing Goodrich products. Texaco salesmen, the primary link between Texaco and the dealers, promote Goodrich products in their day-to-day contact with the Texaco dealers. The evaluation of a dealer's station by the Texaco salesman is often an important factor in determining whether a dealer's contract or lease with Texaco will be renewed. Thus the Texaco salesmen, whose favorable opinion is so important to every dealer, are the key men in the promotion of Goodrich products, and on occasion accompany the Goodrich salesmen in their calls on the dealers. Finally, Texaco receives regular reports on the amount of sponsored TBA purchased by each dealer. Texaco contends, however, that these reports are used only for maintaining its accounts with Goodrich and not for policing dealer purchases.

The sales commission system for marketing TBA is inherently coercive. A service station dealer whose very livelihood depends upon the continuing good favor of a major oil company is constantly aware of the oil company's desire that he stock and sell the recommended brand of TBA.

We are similarly convinced that the Commission was correct in determining that this arrangement has an adverse effect on competition in the marketing of TBA. Service stations play an increasingly important role in the marketing of tires, batteries, and other automotive accessories. With five major companies supplying virtually all of the tires that come with new cars, only in the replacement market can the smaller companies hope to compete. Ideally, each service station dealer would stock the brands of TBA that in his judgment were most favored by customers for price and quality. To the extent that dealers are induced to select the sponsored brand in order to maintain the good favor of the oil company upon which they are dependent, to that extent the operation of the competitive market is adversely affected. The nonsponsored brands do not compete on the even terms of price and quality competition; they must overcome, in addition, the influence of the dominant oil company that has been paid to induce its dealers to buy the recommended brand. While the success of this arrangement in foreclosing competitors from the TBA market has not matched that of the direct coercion employed by Atlantic, we feel that the anticompetitive tendencies of such a system are clear, and that the Commission was properly fulfilling the task that Congress assigned it in halting this practice in its incipiency. The Commission is not required to show that a practice it condemns has totally eliminated competition in the relevant market.

The Commission was justified in concluding that more than an insubstantial amount of commerce was involved. Texaco is one of the nation's largest petroleum companies. It sells it products to approximately 30,000 service stations, or about 16.5% of all service stations in the United States. The volume of sponsored TBA purchased by Texaco dealers in the five-year period 1952–1956 was $245,000,000, five times the amount involved in the *Atlantic* case.

Other Acts and Law Relating to Competition

Exceptions and Exemptions to Antitrust. The 1914 Clayton Act created a broad exemption to the antitrust laws so as to permit the formation of agricultural cooperatives. A similar exemption was created for those engaged in commercial fishing in 1934.

The Clayton Act likewise attempted to exempt the activities of labor unions from the antitrust law but restrictive court interpretations left the unions subject to the laws until the exemption was reinterpreted after the passage of the Norris-LaGuardia Act in 1932.[2] Union activities are now exempt except where unions combine with businesses for the purpose of fixing prices or imposing other illegal restraints on competition.

The Webb-Pomerene Act exempts the activity of exporters engaged in foreign trade provided such activity does not "artificially or intentionally enhance or depress prices within the United States." It is argued that this exemption is necessary so that American firms can compete on an even foot with the many cartels operating in foreign markets.

Many industries are classed as "affected with the public interest" and are subject to varying degrees of regulation by state and federal agencies. Some of these industries including insurance, banking, electric power, airline, telephone, radio and television broadcasting, railroad, pipeline, stock exchange, and ocean shipping are permitted to compete within the varying limits set by

---

[2] The landmark case exempting unions for most purposes was *U.S. v. Hutchenson,* 312 U.S. 219 (1941).

the various regulatory commissions; but in general, regulation rather than competition is relied upon to protect the public interest.[3]

Fair-Trade Laws. One of the most controversial exemptions to the antitrust laws was created in 1937 with the passage of the Miller-Tydings Act. This statute permits states to enact so-called "fair-trade" laws exempting otherwise illegal vertical price-fixing arrangements from the antitrust laws. The exemption applies only to the sale of trademarked goods which are in "free and open competition with goods of the same general class."

Fair trade permits sellers who are trademark proprietors to contract with their buyers that their trademarked goods will not be resold at less than a specified minimum price. In addition, if the buyer is also a dealer he frequently must agree not to sell to a subvendee unless the latter assents to a similar restriction, namely, vertical price fixing. A more far-reaching provision of most state fair-trade laws is that the buyers not a party to such contracts are bound by law to refrain from knowingly and willfully advertising, offering for sale, or selling goods subject to such an agreement at a price below that set in any fair-trade contract in force within that state. These provisions, known as "nonsigner laws," make possible statewide price schedules without individual consent.

Although seemingly designed to validate all provisions of state fair-trade laws as applied to goods in the interstate commerce, the Miller-Tydings Act did not expressly exempt nonsigner provisions from the antitrust laws. Subsequently, the McGuire Act was passed which specifically validated nonsigner provisions of state fair-trade law.

The passage of the McGuire Act enabled the state to establish fair-trade systems, including nonsigner provisions, without fear of federal sanction. Yet since 1950, state courts have increasingly invalidated their own fair-trade laws, particularly the vital nonsigner provisions, as violative of their state constitutions. Such decisions are frequently grounded on denial of due process and unlawful delegation of legislative power. These courts have evinced a willingness to pass upon matters of substantive economic policy and have held that the law operates not to protect the trademark owner's goodwill, but to benefit the retail merchant by protecting him from the rigors of price competition. Finding no substantial basis for the latter, they have invalidated the law as an unreasonable deprivation of the buyer's property right to sell his goods at whatever price he desires and as an unlawful delegation to private parties of the legislature's power to fix prices. On the other hand, those courts upholding the constitutionality of their fair-trade laws have expressed reluctance to review

---

[3] The doctrine of *"primary jurisdiction"* often requires that the appropriate regulatory agency pass on public policy questions relating to competition in regulated industries before such issues can be presented in the courts.

or interfere with a matter of state substantive economic policy and have deferred to their legislatures.

Fair-trade laws originally existed in 46 states but by 1964, 23 states had reduced the effectiveness of such laws by decisions that either threw them out entirely or nullified the nonsigner clause. An even more serious blow was dealt fair trade in cases holding that price cutters are able to avoid state fair-trade laws by shipping goods in from areas where such laws are not in force. As a consequence, price maintenance was publicly abandoned by the leading manufacturers of electrical appliances and other costly consumer goods.

State Unfair Practice Acts. Thirty-one states have enacted "unfair practices" acts aimed at preventing sales below cost "for the purpose of injuring competitors or destroying competition." The acts usually attempt to define cost so as to include all costs including all overhead expenses. Some statutes require a definite percentage markup—such as 12 percent over the invoice or replacement cost and provide that any sale below such a figure is *prima facie* a sale below cost.

These statutes have been successfully challenged on constitutional grounds in a number of states. On the whole they have been rarely enforced and are of little importance.

Noerr and *Parker* **Doctrines.** In the *Noerr* case (1961) the Supreme Court held that "the Sherman Act does not prohibit two or more persons from associating together in an attempt to persuade the legislature or the executive to take particular action with respect to a law that would produce a restraint on a monopoly." As has generally been true of other sweeping pronouncements made by the Court, the later cases begin to define limits and to make exceptions to this broad rule.[4]

In the *Trucking Unlimited* case several large trucking companies joined a conspiracy for the purpose of blocking the granting or transfer of the certificates of public convenience and necessity to all potential competitions. One or more of the members of the group would appear before the state regulatory commission and oppose each new application with or without cause and regardless of its merits and continue to do so throughout all stages of appeal. The Supreme Court ruled that this conduct violated the Sherman Act saying that it fell within the "sham exception" to the *Noerr* case. The Court stated:

A combination of entrepreneurs to harass and deter their competitors from having "free and unlimited access" to the agencies and courts, to defeat that right by massive, concerted and purposeful activities of the group are ways of building up one empire and destroying another. As stated in the concurring opinion, that is the essence of those parts of the complaint to which we refer. If these facts are proved, a violation of the antitrust laws has been established. If the end result is unlawful, it matters not that the means used in violation may be lawful.[5]

---

[4] *Eastern R.R. President's Conference v. Noerr Motor Freight, Inc.,* 365 U.S. 127 (1961).
[5] *California Transport Co. v. Trucking Unlimited,* 404 U.S. 508 (1972).

Under the *Parker* doctrine "state actions" are exempt from the antitrust laws.[6] In order to find shelter under this exemption the acts must be those of state officials acting under authority of state law, or those of private individuals acting under the "active supervision of authorized state officials."

Summary

There are numerous major exceptions or exemptions to the application of the antitrust laws including: most union activities; agricultural cooperatives; exporters; public utilities and other regulated business; and vertical price fixing under fair-trade laws. Fair-trade, or resale price maintenance, laws are under heavy attack and are now fully effective in only about one half of the states. Closely related to fair-trade laws are the state unfair practices acts, which prohibit sales below cost. On the whole unfair practice acts have been of little importance.

The *Noerr-Pennington* doctrine gives a broad antitrust immunity to political activities aimed at influencing the legislative branches of government even where the purpose and effect of such activities is to lessen competition. The *Parker* doctrine permits the states to replace competition with state regulation under an antitrust immunity given to "state action." There is a "sham" exception to these immunities where attempts are made to subvert the functions of the courts or the functions of regulatory agencies.

Mine Workers v. Pennington

381 U.S. 657 (U.S. Sup. Ct. 1964)

The United Mine Workers of America (plaintiff) sued the Pennington partners (defendants) for royalty payments under the National Bituminous Coal Wage Agreement of 1950. Pennington filed a cross claim for damages under the antitrust laws. The Court of Appeals affirmed a trial court ruling in favor of Pennington. UMW appealed. Affirmed except as to the amount of damages awarded Pennington.

In its cross claim Pennington alleged that the UMW and certain large coal operators had conspired to restrain and monopolize commerce in violation of §§ 1 and 2 of the Sherman Act. It was alleged that, to eradicate overproduction in the coal industry, the UMW and large operators agreed to eliminate the smaller companies, by imposing the terms of the 1950 Agreement on all companies regardless of ability to pay, by increasing royalties due the welfare fund, by excluding the marketing, production and sale of nonunion coal, by refusing to lease coal lands to nonunion operators and refusing to buy or sell coal mined by such operators, by obtaining from the Secretary of Labor the establishment of a minimum wage under the Walsh-Healey Act higher than that in other industries, by urging TVA to curtail spot market purchases which were exempt

---

[6] *Parker v. Brown,* 317 U.S. 341 (1943).

from the Walsh-Healey order, and by waging a price-cutting campaign to drive small companies out of the spot market.

MR. JUSTICE WHITE.   The question presented . . . is whether in the circumstances of this case the union is exempt from liability under the antitrust laws. We think the answer is clearly in the negative and that the union's motions were correctly denied.

The antitrust laws do not bar the existence and operation of labor unions as such. Moreover, § 20 of the Clayton Act, 38 Stat. 738, and § 4 of the Norris-LaGuardia Act, 47 Stat. 70, permit a union, acting alone, to engage in the conduct therein specified without violating the Sherman Act. *United States v. Hutcheson.* . . .

But neither § 20 nor § 4 expressly deals with arrangements or agreements between unions and employers. Neither section tells us whether any or all such arrangements or agreements are barred or permitted by the antitrust laws. Thus *Hutcheson* itself stated:

So long as a union acts in its self-interest *and does not combine with non-labor groups,* the licit and the illicit under § 20 are not to be distinguished by any judgment regarding the wisdom or unwisdom, the rightness or wrongness, the selfishness or unselfishness of the end of which the particular union activities are the means. . . . (Emphasis added.)

And in *Allen Bradley Co. v. Union* . . . this Court made explicit what had been merely a qualifying expression in *Hutcheson* and held that "when the unions participated with a combination of business men who had complete power to eliminate all competition among themselves and to prevent all competition from others, a situation was created not included within the exemptions of the Clayton and Norris-LaGuardia Acts." . . . Subsequent cases have applied the *Allen Bradley* doctrine to such combinations without regard to whether they found expression in a collective bargaining agreement, and even though the mechanism for effectuating the purpose of the combination was an agreement on wages.

* * * * *

It is true that wages lie at the very heart of those subjects about which employers and unions must bargain and the law contemplates agreements on wages not only between individual employers and a union but agreements between the union and employers in a multi-employer bargaining unit. . . . The union benefit from the wage scale agreed upon is direct and concrete and the effect on the product market, though clearly present, results from the elimination of competition based on wages among the employers in the bargaining unit, which is not the kind of restraint Congress intended the Sherman Act to proscribe. . . . We think it beyond question that a union may conclude a wage agreement with the multi-employer bargaining unit without violating the antitrust laws and that it may as a matter of its own policy, and not by agreement with all or part of the employers of that unit, seek the same wages from other employers.

* * * * *

But we think a union forfeits its exemption from the antitrust laws when it is clearly shown that it has agreed with one set of employers to impose a certain wage scale on other bargaining units.

* * * * *

We agree with the UMW that both the Court of Appeals and the trial court failed to take proper account of the *Noerr* case. In approving the instructions of the trial court with regard to the approaches of the union and the operators to the Secretary of Labor and to the TVA officials, the Court of Appeals considered *Noerr* as applying only to conduct "unaccompanied by a purpose or intent to further a conspiracy to violate a statute. It is the illegal purpose or intent inherent in the conduct which vitiates the conduct which would otherwise be legal." . . . *Noerr* shields from the Sherman Act a concerted effort to influence public officials regardless of intent or purpose.

. . . It is clear under *Noerr* that Pennington could not collect any damages under the Sherman Act for any injury which it suffered from the action of the Secretary of Labor. The conduct of the union and the operators did not violate the Act, the action taken to set a minimum wage for government purchases of coal was the act of a public official who is not claimed to be a co-conspirator, and the jury should have been instructed, as UMW requested, to exclude any damages which *Pennington* may have suffered as a result of the Secretary's Walsh-Healey determinations.[7]

Otter Tail Power Co. v. United States

410 U.S. 366 (U.S. Sup. Ct. 1973)

A Sherman Act suit was brought by the Government (plaintiff) against Otter Tail Power Co. (defendant), and the District Court enjoined as violative of Sec. 2 of the Sherman Act certain practices of the defendant. Otter Tail appealed. Affirmed in part and reversed and remanded in part.

MR. JUSTICE DOUGLAS. In this civil antitrust suit brought by appellee against Otter Tail Power Company (Otter Tail), an electric utility company, the District Court found that Otter Tail had attempted to monopolize and had monopolized the retail distribution of electric power in its service area in violation of § 2 of the Sherman Act, 15 U. S. C. § 2. The District Court found that Otter Tail had attempted to prevent communities in which its retail distribution franchise had expired from replacing it with a municipal distribution system. The principal means employed were (1) refusals to sell power at wholesale to proposed municipal systems in the communities where it had been retailing power; (2) refusals to "wheel" power to such systems, that is to say to transfer, by direct transmission or displacement, electric power from one utility to another over the facilities of an intermediate utility; (3) the institution and support of litigation designed to prevent or delay establishment of those systems; and (4) the invocation of provisions in its transmission contracts with several other power suppliers for the purpose of denying the municipal systems access to other suppliers by means of Otter Tail's transmission.

Otter Tail contends that by reason of the Federal Power Act it is not subject to antitrust regulation with respect to its refusal to deal. We disagree with that position.

"Repeals of the antitrust laws by implication from a regulatory statute are strongly

---

[7] The case was remanded to have the damages in the amount of $270,000 awarded Pennington scaled downward in accordance with the *Noerr* Doctrine.

disfavored, and have only been found in cases of plain repugnancy between the antitrust and regulatory provisions." . . . Activities which come under the jurisdiction of a regulatory agency nevertheless may be subject to scrutiny under the antitrust laws.

In *California v. Federal Power Commission* . . . the Court held that approval of an acquisition of the assets of a natural gas company by the Federal Power Commission pursuant to § 7 of the Natural Gas Act "would be no bar to [an] antitrust suit." Under § 7 the standard for approving such acquisitions is "public convenience and necessity." Although the impact on competition is relevant to the Commission's determination, the Court noted that there was "no 'pervasive regulatory scheme' including the antitrust laws that had been entrusted to the Commission." . . .

The record makes abundantly clear that Otter Tail used its monopoly power in the cities in its service area to foreclose competition or gain a competitive advantage, or to destroy a competitor, all in violation of the antitrust laws. . . . The District Court determined that Otter Tail has "a strategic dominance in the transmission of power in most of its service area" and that it used this dominance to foreclose potential entrants into the retail arena from obtaining electric power from outside sources of supply. Use of monopoly power "to destroy threatened competition" is a violation of the "attempt to monopolize" clause of § 2 of the Sherman Act. . . . So are agreements not to compete, with the aim of preserving or extending a monopoly. . . . In *Associated Press v. United States* . . . a cooperative news association had bylaws that permitted member newspapers to bar competitors from joining the association. We held that that practice violated the Sherman Act, even though the transgressor "had not yet achieved a complete monopoly." . . .

. . . There were no engineering factors that prevented Otter Tail from selling power at wholesale to those towns that wanted municipal plants nor of wheeling the power. The District Court found—and its findings are supported—that Otter Tail's refusals to sell at wholesale or to wheel were solely to prevent municipal power systems from eroding its monopolistic position.

Otter Tail relies on its "wheeling" contracts with the Bureau of Reclamation and with cooperatives which it says relieves it of any duty to wheel power to municipalities served at retail by Otter Tail at the time the contracts were made. The District Court held that these restrictive provisions were "in reality, territorial allocation schemes" . . . and were *per se* violations of the Sherman Act, citing *Northern Pacific R. Co.* v. *United States*. . . . Like covenants were there held to "deny defendant's competitors access to the fenced-off market in the same terms as the defendant." . . . The fact that some of the restrictive provisions were contained in a contract with the Bureau of Reclamation is not material to our problem, for as the Solicitor General says, "government contracting officers do not have the power to grant immunity from the Sherman Act."

The District Court found that the litigation sponsored by Otter Tail had the purpose of delaying and preventing the establishment of municipal electric systems "with the expectation that this would preserve its predominant position in the sale and transmission of electric power in the area." . . . The District Court in discussing *Eastern Railroad Conference v. Noerr Motor Freight, Inc.,* . . . explained that it was applicable "only to efforts aimed at influencing the legislative and executive branches of the government." . . . That was written before we decided *California Motor Transport Co.*

v. Trucking Unlimited . . . where we held that the principle of *Noerr* may also apply to the use of administrative or judicial processes where the purpose is to suppress competition evidenced by repetitive lawsuits carrying the hallmark of insubstantial claims and thus within the "mere sham" exception announced in *Noerr*. . . . On that phase of the order we vacate and remand for consideration in light of our intervening decision in *California Motor Transport Co.*

Otter Tail argues that, without the weapons which it used, more and more municipalities will turn to public power and Otter Tail will go downhill. The argument is a familiar one. It was made in *United States v. Arnold, Schwinn & Co.* . . . We said: "The promotion of self-interest alone does not invoke the rule of reason to immunize otherwise illegal conduct." . . .

The same may properly be said of § 2 cases under the Sherman Act. That Act assumes that an enterprise will protect itself against loss by operating with superior service, lower costs, and improved efficiency. Otter Tail's theory collides with the Sherman Act as it sought to substitute for competition anticompetitive uses of its dominant economic power.

Black & Decker Mfg. Co. v. Ann & Hope, Inc. of Danvers

277 N.E. 2d 687 (Sup. Ct. Mass. 1972)

Black & Decker (plaintiff) brought this action against Ann & Hope, Inc. (defendant) for an injunction and damages under the state Fair Trade Laws. Judgment for Ann & Hope and Black & Decker appealed. Affirmed.

Black & Decker, which manufactures and sells power tools which are identified by a brand name and trade mark, entered into "fair trade contracts," all in the same form, with Massachusetts retailers. In these contracts retailers agreed that they would not advertise, offer for sale or sell products of Black & Decker at less than the prices set forth in an attached price list.

Each price list included the following language: "The products listed above shall not be sold by Retailers at less than said fair trade retail price. Unless otherwise prohibited by law, a bona fide cash discount may be given by a Retailer in an amount not exceeding three per cent (3%) of the minimum retail selling price only under the following terms and conditions: (1) The discount must be in the form of cash, trading stamps, coupons, cash register receipts or analogous form. (2) The discount must be given as a matter of the Retailer's general policy and not on Black & Decker products alone. (3) Black & Decker products must continue to be advertised and offered for sale at the minimum retail price as set out in this Schedule. (4) The discount shall not be given solely for the purpose of selling trademarked Black & Decker products below the established minimum retail price." Ann & Hope did not sign a fair trade contract but was notified by Black & Decker that such contracts were in effect with other dealers in Massachusetts.

QUIRICO, JUSTICE. The Fair Trade Law, first enacted in 1937, appears by its terms to have had two objectives. One was to eliminate any question about the validity of price fixing contracts between the producer, distributor or vendor of certain commodities bearing the trade mark, brand or name of the producer or owner, and the purchaser, who is usually a retailer. These contracts generally relate to the price at which the retailer is required to resell the commodity. The other objective was to permit the enforcement of such price fixing contracts not only against the immediate parties thereto but against any person "wilfully and knowingly advertising, offering for sale or selling any commodity at less than the price stipulated in any contract . . . [fixing such price] *whether the person so advertising, offering for sale or selling is or is not a party to such contract"* (emphasis supplied). . . . This represented a radical departure from the common law which permitted the enforcement of such contracts against the parties thereto. . . . Because the Fair Trade Law represents such a departure as to nonsigners, and because it creates an exception to the general public policy of protecting the consuming public by prohibiting monopolies and requiring free and open price competition in the sale of commodities which are neither harmful nor critical in supply, it will be strictly interpreted and narrowly circumscribed.

The Fair Trade Law appears to have evolved from a number of bills filed in the Legislature in 1937 for the purpose of taking advantage of the then recently enacted Miller-Tydings Act, amending § 1 of the Sherman Antitrust Act. Some of the bills would have permitted contracts requiring that commodities would not be resold "at less than the minimum price stipulated by the vendor." Others would have permitted contracts requiring that commodities be sold "at the price stipulated by the vendor." Ultimately the Legislature enacted G.L. c. 93, §§ 14A–14D, and in so doing elected to validate and permit enforcement of contracts providing "that the buyer will not resell such commodity except at *the price stipulated* by the vendor" (emphasis supplied). We conclude from this that the Legislature intended to authorize the fixing by contract of a specific fair trade price, not a variable price, and not a maximum nor a minimum price.

Black & Decker argues that the Fair Trade Law should be construed to require only that the price fixing agreement specify a minimum price, and not a specific invariable price.

. . . We do not agree with the interpretation urged on us by Black & Decker. We hold that because Black & Decker's fair trade contracts with persons other than the defendant do not fix a specific invariable price for the commodities which it sells, it is not entitled to enforce such contracts and prices against the defendant who is not a party thereto. The benefits of the enforcement provisions of G.L. c. 93, § 14B, as to nonsigners of fair trade contracts, are available only on contracts complying with the strict requirement of § 14A for a fixed and invariable resale price. Black & Decker's contract does not comply because it authorizes each retailer, at his sole option, to vary, by as much as three per cent, the price of any article covered by Black & Decker's fair price lists.

Although the constitutionality of our Fair Trade Law as applied to noncontracting third parties has not been placed in issue in this case, it may not be inappropriate to comment thereon. The law was initially held constitutional by us in this respect in 1956 in *General Elec. Co. v. Kimball Jewelers,* . . . where we observed: "Where the question has been presented it has been decided in the great majority of cases that State fair trade statutes are valid and not contrary to the State or Federal Constitution," citing numerous cases. However, only eleven years later, in our decision in *Shulton, Inc. v. Consumer Value Stores, Inc.,* . . . we observed: "Massachusetts is one of the minority jurisdictions which hold the Fair Trade Law to be valid." Indeed, at this point in time one source reports that out of the forty States which presently have such legislation, twenty-three have declared their acts unconstitutional as applied to noncontracting third parties, fifteen have declared theirs to be constitutional in this respect and two have not ruled on the question. Beyond this review of the trend of the decisions, we intimate no opinion on this question at this time. . . .

Problem Cases

1. Paint Company advertised and sold paint with a policy that, with the purchase of a gallon or quart of paint, each customer received an equivalent size can free. Evidence disclosed that Paint Company had no history of selling single cans of paint, but that with rare exception always sold two cans of paint at the advertised price. However, there was no evidence of the company inflating or discounting the single can price. The Commission enjoined Paint Company's practice essentially on the grounds that, since the company recovers the cost of the second can in the price of the first, the customer "pays" for the second can with the first; and, therefore, the second can is not free. Should the Commission's finding be reversed on appeal?

2. Carter Products, Inc., in advertising "Rise," its shaving cream, on television sought to convince the viewer that its cream remained moist on the skin longer than other creams. For this purpose it used "mockups." To depict ordinary aerated lathers it used "ultra-wet 60L" which came out of an aerosol can with a puff and dried almost immediately. Its own product appeared to remain moist and creamy. A man was shown in great discomfort shaving with what was purported to be a competitor's product in contrast to enjoying a shave with "Rise." The announcer declared, "Instead of drying out on your face . . . Rise wetter lather puts more moisture into whiskers . . . keeps them wet and soft . . . all through your shave. Guards against Razor scratch. . . ."

    The FTC charged Carter under Section 5 of the Federal Trade Commission Act with having falsely represented that shaving creams competing with "Rise" dry out in the course of a shave when, in fact, some of the competing products were made under license from Carter and did not dry out any faster than "Rise." The Commission ordered Carter to cease and desist from disparaging competing products through false and misleading pictures and from representing that pictures depict the superiority of its products when the depiction is not a genuine or accurate comparison. Should the order be enforced?

3. Sav-U Chain Store advertised several products showing "manufacturer's list prices" and then offering the products at substantial discounts. The FTC prosecuted the manufacturer under Section 5 of the Federal Trade Commission Act for engaging in unfair or deceptive list price practices. The FTC proved that the products advertised rarely, if ever, were sold to consumers at the prices shown as "manufacturer's list prices." Was the manufacturer subject to a fine and cease and desist order?

4. Motion Picture Advertising produced and distributed advertising films. Many of its contracts with exhibitors relating to the showing of these films contained a provision that the theatre-owner would not show any advertising films produced by other companies. M.P.A., the biggest company in the industry, had exclusive contracts of this type with about 40 percent of the theatres in its area of operation. The contracts ran for varying periods up to five years,

though the normal period was one year only. A case was brought under Section 5 of the Federal Trade Commission Act, and the Commission found that the exclusive contracts were unduly restrictive so as to amount to an "unfair method of competition." The Commission ordered that no contract of more than one year's duration should be entered into. Is this a valid order by the Commission?

5. Whitten and the three affiliated corporations of Paddock are competitors specializing in the manufacture of pipeless swimming pools for sale primarily to public agencies. Paddock is by far the largest supplier of pipeless pools. Whitten brought a civil antitrust suit charging that Paddock's selling efforts violated Sections 1 and 2 of the Sherman Act by conspiring to require the use of the Paddock specifications in the public swimming pool industry with the intent to exclude the competition of Whitten. The district court granted summary judgment dismissing Whitten's complaint basing its ruling on *Parker v. Brown* and the *Noerr-Pennington* doctrine. Should this ruling be reversed on appeal?

6. Yellow Cab is having difficulties with its labor union which it believes is the result of its competitor's conspiracy with the union. Yellow Cab brings an action alleging restraint of trade pursuant to Sections 1 and 2 of the Sherman Act. The union claims that there is no federal jurisdiction because only 0.5 percent of Yellow Cab's gross revenues are from interstate commerce. Will the union's defense prevail?

7. In 1959, Ohio enacted a new Fair Trade Act and Eli Lilly Co., a manufacturer of products bearing its trademark, notified all Ohio retailers that in accordance with that act, it intended to establish minimum retail resale prices of its products and to invite retailers to enter into fair-trade contracts. Hudson Co., a retail drug chain, refused to enter into any such agreement, ignored the specified minimum resale price, and filed a petition declaring the Ohio Fair Trade Act unconstitutional because its application (including its nonsigner provision) would violate the Sherman Act. Eli Lilly contends that the McGuire Act granted state fair-trade laws an exception from the prohibitions of the Sherman Act.

8. Corning manufactures a prestige line of cookware which is fair-traded in every state where lawful. Corning sells its products through distributors who are required to sell only to retailers who sign fair-trade agreements. Vornado, a large retail merchandiser, signed a fair-trade agreement and began purchasing Corning Ware. Vornado operates a trading stamp program whereby its stamps are issued on food sales and are redeemable for merchandise at its stores. Vornado commenced a merchandising sale using Corning Ware as a "loss leader" by selling $29.95 Corning sets for one book of stamps plus $15.75. The stamps were advertised by Vornado as being worth $2.25 per book; the disclosure is contrary to normal trading stamp company policy. Corning telegramed Vornado to stop its campaign, and when they refused, terminated their franchise. Vornado sued Corning alleging an illegal fair-trade program. Corning does sell to trading stamp companies whose stamps normally require $120 to $150 in purchase to fill a book. Corning does not require these companies to sign fair-trade agreements nor do they require them to abide by Corning's suggested valuations. Should Vornado prevail in their action?

9. In a Sherman Act complaint, plaintiffs, joint ventures desiring to participate in the ownership of a professional football team that would play its games in the District of Columbia, charged that the 30-year lease of the Robert F. Kennedy Stadium to the Washington Redskins constituted a contract in unreasonable restraint of professional football in the District of Columbia. The Washington Redskins and the District of Columbia Armory Board moved for summary judgment on the ground that the approving board was a governmental agency and that the lease is therefore not under the scope of the antitrust laws. Is this a valid argument?

Appendixes

THE UNIFORM COMMERCIAL CODE (1962 TEXT)

The Uniform Commercial Code

ARTICLE 1. General Provisions

§ 1–101. Short Title.

This Act shall be known and may be cited as Uniform Commercial Code.

§ 1–102. Purposes; Rules of Construction; Variation by Agreement.

(1) This Act shall be liberally construed and applied to promote its underlying purposes and policies.

(2) Underlying purposes and policies of this Act are

    (a) to simplify, clarify and modernize the law governing commercial transactions;

    (b) to permit the continued expansion of commercial practices through custom, usage and agreement of the parties;

    (c) to make uniform the law among the various jurisdictions.

(3) The effect of provisions of this Act may be varied by agreement, except as otherwise provided in this Act and except that the obligations of good faith, diligence, reasonableness and care prescribed by this Act may not be disclaimed by agreement but the parties may by agreement determine the standards by which the performance of such obligations is to be measured if such standards are not manifestly unreasonable.

(4) The presence in certain provisions of this Act of the words "unless otherwise agreed" or words of similar import does not imply that the effect of other provisions may not be varied by agreement under subsection (3).

(5) In this Act unless the context otherwise requires

    (a) words in the singular number include the plural, and in the plural include the singular;

    (b) words of the masculine gender include the feminine and the neuter, and when the sense so indicates words of the neuter gender may refer to any gender.

§ 1–103. Supplementary General Principles of Law Applicable.

Unless displaced by the particular provisions of this Act, the principles of law and equity, including the law merchant and the law relative to capacity to contract, principal and agent, estoppel, fraud, misrepresentation, duress, coercion, mistake, bankruptcy, or other validating cause shall supplement its provisions.

Note: *Sections of the code affected by amendments made in 1972 are indicated by *; Article 9 was substantially revised by these changes but as of Jan. 1, 1974, the amendments had been adopted only by Illinois. Sections of the Code affected by minor revisions made in 1966 are indicated by †.*

§ 1–104. Construction Against Implicit Repeal.

This Act being a general act intended as a unified coverage of its subject matter, no part of it shall be deemed to be impliedly repealed by subsequent legislation if such construction can reasonably be avoided.

§ 1–105. Territorial Application of the Act; Parties' Power to Choose Applicable Law.

(1) Except as provided hereafter in this section, when a transaction bears a reasonable relation to this state and also to another state or nation the parties may agree that the law either of this state or of such other state or nation shall govern their rights and duties. Failing such agreement this Act applies to transactions bearing an appropriate relation to this state.

(2) Where one of the following provisions of this Act specifies the applicable law, that provision governs and a contrary agreement is effective only to the extent permitted by the law (including the conflict of laws rules) so specified:

Rights of creditors against sold goods. Section 2–402.

Applicability of the Article on Bank Deposits and Collections. Section 4–102.

Bulk transfers subject to the Article on Bulk Transfers. Section 6–102.

Applicability of the Article on Investment Securities. Section 8–106.

Policy and scope of the Article on Secured Transactions. Sections 9–102 and 9–103.*

§ 1–106. Remedies to Be Liberally Administered.

(1) The remedies provided by this Act shall be liberally administered to the end that the aggrieved party may be put in as good a position as if the other party had fully performed but neither consequential or special nor penal damages may be had except as specifically provided in this Act or by other rule of law.

(2) Any right or obligation declared by this Act is enforceable by action unless the provision declaring it specifies a different and limited effect.

§ 1–107. Waiver or Renunciation of Claim or Right After Breach.

Any claim or right arising out of an alleged breach can be discharged in whole or in part without consideration by a written waiver or renunciation signed and delivered by the aggrieved party.

§ 1–108. Severability.

If any provision or clause of this Act or application thereof to any person or circumstances is held invalid, such invalidity shall not affect other provisions or applications of the Act which can be given effect without the invalid provision or application, and to this end the provisions of this Act are declared to be severable.

§ 1–109. Section Captions.

Section captions are parts of this Act.

PART 2
GENERAL DEFINITIONS AND PRINCIPLES OF INTERPRETATION

§ 1–201. General Definitions.

Subject to additional definitions contained in the subsequent Articles of this Act which are applicable to specific Articles or Parts thereof, and unless the context otherwise requires, in this Act:

(1) "Action" in the sense of a judicial proceeding includes recoupment, counterclaim, set-off, suit in equity and any other proceedings in which rights are determined.

(2) "Aggrieved party" means a party entitled to resort to a remedy.

(3) "Agreement" means the bargain of the parties in fact as found in their language or by implication from other circumstances including course of dealing or usage of trade or course of performance as provided in this Act (Sections 1–205 and 2–208). Whether an agreement

has legal consequences is determined by the provisions of this Act, if applicable; otherwise by the law of contracts (Section 1–103). (Compare "Contract".)

(4) "Bank" means any person engaged in the business of banking.

(5) "Bearer" means the person in possession of an instrument, document of title, or security payable to bearer or indorsed in blank.

(6) "Bill of lading" means a document evidencing the receipt of goods for shipment issued by a person engaged in the business of transporting or forwarding goods, and includes an airbill. "Airbill" means a document serving for air transportation as a bill of lading does for marine or rail transportation, and includes an air consignment note or air waybill.

(7) "Branch" includes a separately incorporated foreign branch of a bank.

(8) "Burden of establishing" a fact means the burden of persuading the triers of fact that the existence of the fact is more probable than its non-existence.

(9) "Buyer in ordinary course of business" means a person who in good faith and without knowledge that the sale to him is in violation of the ownership rights or security interest of a third party in the goods buys in ordinary course from a person in the business of selling goods of that kind but does not include a pawnbroker. "Buying" may be for cash or by exchange of other property or on secured or unsecured credit and includes receiving goods or documents of title under a pre-existing contract for sale but does not include a transfer in bulk or as security for or in total or partial satisfaction of a money debt.*

(10) "Conspicuous": A term or clause is conspicuous when it is so written that a reasonable person against whom it is to operate ought to have noticed it. A printed heading in capitals as: (NON-NEGOTIABLE BILL OF LADING) is conspicuous. Language in the body of a form is "conspicuous" if it is in larger or other contrasting type or color. But in a telegram any stated term is "conspicuous". Whether a term or clause is "conspicuous" or not is for decision by the court.

(11) "Contract" means the total legal obligation which results from the parties' agreement as affected by this Act and any other applicable rules of law. (Compare "Agreement".)

(12) "Creditor" includes a general creditor, a secured creditor, a lien creditor and any representative of creditors, including an assignee for the benefit of creditors, a trustee in bankruptcy, a receiver in equity and an executor or administrator of an insolvent debtor's assignor's estate.

(13) "Defendant" includes a person in the position of defendant in a cross-action or counterclaim.

(14) "Delivery" with respect to instruments, documents of title, chattel paper or securities means voluntary transfer of possession.

(15) "Document of title" includes bill of lading, dock warrant, dock receipt, warehouse receipt or order for the delivery of goods, and also any other document which in the regular course of business or financing is treated as adequately evidencing that the person in possession of it is entitled to receive, hold and dispose of the document and the goods it covers. To be a document of title a document must purport to be issued by or addressed to a bailee and purport to cover goods in the bailee's possession which are either identified or are fungible portions of an identified mass.

(16) "Fault" means wrongful act, omission or breach.

(17) "Fungible" with respect to goods or securities means goods or securities of which any unit is, by nature or usage of trade, the equivalent of any other like unit. Goods which are not fungible shall be deemed fungible for the purposes of this Act to the extent that under a particular agreement or document unlike units are treated as equivalents.

(18) "Genuine" means free of forgery or counterfeiting.

(19) "Good faith" means honesty in fact in the conduct or transaction concerned.

(20) "Holder" means a person who is in possession of a document of title or an instrument or an investment security drawn, issued or indorsed to him or to his order or to bearer or in blank.

(21) To "honor" is to pay or to accept and pay, or where a credit so engages to purchase or discount a draft complying with the terms of the credit.

(22) "Insolvency proceedings includes any assignment for the benefit of creditors or other proceedings intended to liquidate or rehabilitate the estate of the person involved.

(23) A person is "insolvent who either has ceased to pay his debts in the ordinary course of business or cannot pay his debts as they become due or is insolvent within the meaning of the federal bankruptcy law.

(24) "Money means a medium of exchange authorized or adopted by a domestic or foreign government as a part of its currency.

(25) A person has "notice" of a fact when

(a) he has actual knowledge of it; or

(b) he has received a notice or notification of it; or

(c) from all the facts and circumstances known to him at the time in question he has reason to know that it exists.

A person "knows" or has "knowledge" of a fact when he has actual knowledge of it. "Discover" or "learn" or a word or phrase of similar import refers to knowledge rather than to reason to know. The time and circumstances under which a notice or notification may cease to be effective are not determined by this Act.

(26) A person "notifies" or "gives" a notice or notification to another by taking such steps as may be reasonably required to inform the other in ordinary course whether or not such other actually comes to know of it. A person "receives" a notice or notification when

(a) it comes to his attention; or

(b) it is duly delivered at the place of business through which the contract was made or at any other place held out by him as the place for receipt of such communications.

(27) Notice, knowledge or a notice or notification received by an organization is effective for a particular transaction from the time when it is brought to the attention of the individual conducting that transaction, and in any event from the time when it would have been brought to his attention if the organization had exercised due diligence. An organization exercises due diligence if it maintains reasonable routines for communicating significant information to the person conducting the transaction and there is reasonable compliance with the routines. Due diligence does not require an individual acting for the organization to communicate information unless such communication is part of his regular duties or unless he has reason to know of the transaction and that the transaction would be materially affected by the information.

(28) "Organization" includes a corporation, government or governmental subdivision or agency, business trust, estate, trust, partnership or association, two or more persons having a joint or common interest, or any other legal or commercial entity.

(29) "Party," as distinct from "third party," means a person who has engaged in a transaction or made an agreement within this Act.

(30) "Person" includes an individual or an organization (See Section 1–102).

(31) "Presumption" or "presumed" means that the trier of fact must find the existence of the fact presumed unless and until evidence is introduced which would support a finding of its nonexistence.

(32) "Purchase" includes taking by sale, discount, negotiation, mortgage, pledge, lien, issue or re-issue, gift or any other voluntary transaction creating an interest in property.

(33) "Purchaser" means a person who takes by purchase.

(34) "Remedy" means any remedial right to which an aggrieved party is entitled with or without resort to a tribunal.

(35) "Representative" includes an agent, an officer of a corporation or association, and a trustee, executor or administrator of an estate, or any other person empowered to act for another.

(36) "Rights" includes remedies.

(37) "Security interest" means an interest in personal property or fixtures which secures payment or performance of an obligation. The retention or reservation of title by a seller of goods notwithstanding shipment or delivery to the buyer (Section 2–401) is limited in effect to a reservation of a "security interest." The term also includes any interest of a buyer of accounts, chattel paper, or contract rights which is subject to Article 9. The special property

interest of a buyer of goods on identification of such goods to a contract for sale under Section 2–401 is not a "security interest," but a buyer may also acquire a "security interest" by complying with Article 9. Unless a lease or consignment is intended as security, reservation of title thereunder is not a "security interest" but a consignment is in any event subject to the provisions on consignment sales (Section 2–326). Whether a lease is intended as security is to be determined by the facts of each case; however, (a) the inclusion of an option to purchase does not of itself make the lease one intended for security, and (b) an agreement that upon compliance with the terms of the lease the lessee shall become or has the option to become the owner of the property for no additional consideration or for a nominal consideration does make the lease one intended for security.*

(38) "Send" in connection with any writing or notice means to deposit in the mail or deliver for transmission by any other usual means of communication with postage or cost of transmission provided for and properly addressed and in the case of an instrument to an address specified thereon or otherwise agreed, or if there be none to any address reasonable under the circumstances. The receipt of any writing or notice within the time at which it would have arrived if properly sent has the effect of a proper sending.

(39) "Signed" includes any symbol executed or adopted by a party with present intention to authenticate a writing.

(40) "Surety" includes guarantor.

(41) "Telegram" includes a message transmitted by radio, teletype, cable, any mechanical method of transmission, or the like.

(42) "Term" means that portion of an agreement which relates to a particular matter.

(43) "Unauthorized" signature or indorsement means one made without actual, implied or apparent authority and includes a forgery.

(44) "Value." Except as otherwise provided with respect to negotiable instruments and bank collections (Sections 3–303, 4–208 and 4–209) a person gives "value" for rights if he acquires them

   (a) in return for a binding commitment to extend credit or for the extension of immediately available credit whether or not drawn upon and whether or not a charge-back is provided for in the event of difficulties in collection; or

   (b) as security for or in total or partial satisfaction of a pre-existing claim; or

   (c) by accepting delivery pursuant to a pre-existing contract for purchase; or

   (d) generally, in return for any consideration sufficient to support a simple contract.

(45) "Warehouse receipt" means a receipt issued by a person engaged in the business of storing goods for hire.

(46) "Written" or "writing" includes printing, typewriting or any other intentional reduction to tangible form.

§ 1–202. Prima Facie Evidence by Third Party Documents.

A document in due form purporting to be a bill of lading, policy or certificate of insurance, official weigher's or inspector's certificate, consular invoice, or any other document authorized or required by the contract to be issued by a third party shall be prima facie evidence of its own authenticity and genuineness and of the facts stated in the document by the third party.

§ 1–203. Obligation of Good Faith.

Every contract or duty within this Act imposes an obligation of good faith in its performance or enforcement.

§ 1–204. Time; Reasonable Time; "Seasonably."

(1) Whenever this Act requires any action to be taken within a reasonable time, any time which is not manifestly unreasonable may be fixed by agreement.

(2) What is a reasonable time for taking any action depends on the nature, purpose and circumstances of such action.

(3) An action is taken "seasonably" when it is taken at or within the time agreed or if no time is agreed at or within a reasonable time.

§ 1–205. **Course of Dealing and Usage of Trade.**

(1) A course of dealing is a sequence of previous conduct between the parties to a particular transaction which is fairly to be regarded as establishing a common basis of understanding for interpreting their expressions and other conduct.

(2) A usage of trade is any practice or method of dealing having such regularity of observance in a place, vocation or trade as to justify an expectation that it will be observed with respect to the transaction in question. The existence and scope of such a usage are to be proved as facts. If it is established that such a usage is embodied in a written trade code or similar writing the interpretation of the writing is for the court.

(3) A course of dealing between parties and any usage of trade in the vocation or trade in which they are engaged or of which they are or should be aware give particular meaning to and supplement or qualify terms of an agreement.

(4) The express terms of an agreement and an applicable course of dealing or usage of trade shall be construed wherever reasonable as consistent with each other; but when such construction is unreasonable express terms control both course of dealing and usage of trade and course of dealing controls usage of trade.

(5) An applicable usage of trade in the place where any part of performance is to occur shall be used in interpreting the agreement as to that part of the performance.

(6) Evidence of a relevant usage of trade offered by one party is not admissible unless and until he has given the other party such notice as the court finds sufficient to prevent unfair surprise to the latter.

§ 1–206. **Statute of Frauds for Kinds of Personal Property Not Otherwise Covered.**

(1) Except in the cases described in subsection (2) of this section a contract for the sale of personal property is not enforceable by way of action or defense beyond five thousand dollars in amount or value of remedy unless there is some writing which indicates that a contract for sale has been made between the parties at a defined or stated price, reasonably identifies the subject matter, and is signed by the party against whom enforcement is sought or by his authorized agent.

(2) Subsection (1) of this section does not apply to contracts for the sale of goods (Section 2–201) nor of securities (Section 8–319) nor to security agreements (Section 9–203).

§ 1–207. **Performance or Acceptance Under Reservation of Rights.**

A party who with explicit reservation of rights performs or promises performance or assents to performance in a manner demanded or offered by the other party does not thereby prejudice the rights reserved. Such words as "without prejudice," "under protest" or the like are sufficient.

§ 1–208. **Option to Accelerate at Will.**

A term providing that one party or his successor in interest may accelerate payment or performance or require collateral or additional collateral "at will" or "when he deems himself insecure" or in words of similar import shall be construed to mean that he shall have power to do so only if he in good faith believes that the prospect of payment or performance is impaired. The burden of establishing lack of good faith is on the party against whom the power has been exercised.

ARTICLE 2. Sales

PART 1
SHORT TITLE, CONSTRUCTION AND SUBJECT MATTER

§ 2–101. **Short Title.**

This Article shall be known and may be cited as Uniform Commercial Code—Sales.

§ 2–102. Scope; Certain Security and Other Transactions Excluded From This Article.

Unless the context otherwise requires, this Article applies to transactions in goods; it does not apply to any transaction which although in the form of an unconditional contract to sell or present sale is intended to operate only as a security transaction nor does this Article impair or repeal any statute regulating sales to consumers, farmers or other specified classes of buyers.

§ 2–103. Definitions and Index of Definitions.

(1) In this Article unless the context otherwise requires

    (a) "Buyer" means a person who buys or contracts to buy goods.

    (b) "Good faith" in the case of a merchant means honesty in fact and the observance of reasonable commercial standards of fair dealing in the trade.

    (c) "Receipts" of goods means taking physical possession of them.

    (d) "Seller" means a person who sells or contracts to sell goods.

(2) Other definitions applying to this Article or to specified Parts thereof, and the sections in which they appear are:

"Acceptance." Section 2–606.

"Banker's credit." Section 2–325.

"Between merchants." Section 2–104.

"Cancellation." Section 2–106(4).

"Commercial unit." Section 2–105.

"Confirmed credit." Section 2–325.

"Conforming to contract." Section 2–106.

"Contract for sale." Section 2–106.

"Cover." Section 2–712.

"Entrusting." Section 2–403.

"Financing agency." Section 2–104.

"Future goods." Section 2–105.

"Goods." Section 2–105.

"Identification." Section 2–501.

"Installment contract." Section 2–612.

"Letter of Credit." Section 2–325.

"Lot." Section 2–105.

"Merchant." Section 2–104.

"Overseas." Section 2–323.

"Person in position of seller." Section 2–707.

"Present sale." Section 2–106.

"Sale." Section 2–106.

"Sale on approval." Section 2–326.

"Sale or return." Section 2–326.

"Termination." Section 2–106.

(3) The following definitions in other Articles apply to this Article:

"Check." Section 3–104.

"Consignee." Section 7–102.

"Consignor." Section 7–102.

"Consumer goods." Section 9–109.

"Dishonor." Section 3–507.

"Draft." Section 3–104.

(4) In addition Article 1 contains general definitions and principles of construction and interpretation applicable throughout this Article.

§ 2–104. Definitions: "Merchant"; "Between Merchants"; "Financing Agency."

(1) "Merchant" means a person who deals in goods of the kind or otherwise by his occupation holds himself out as having knowledge or skill peculiar to the practices or goods involved in the transaction or to whom such knowledge or skill may be attributed by his employment

of an agent or broker or other intermediary who by his occupation holds himself out as having such knowledge or skill.

(2) "Financing agency" means a bank, finance company or other person who in the ordinary course of business makes advances against goods or documents of title or who by arrangement with either the seller or the buyer intervenes in ordinary course to make or collect payment due or claimed under the contract for sale, as by purchasing or paying the seller's draft or making advances against it or by merely taking it for collection whether or not documents of title accompany the draft. "Financing agency" includes also a bank or other person who similarly intervenes between persons who are in the position of seller and buyer in respect to the goods (Section 2–707).

(3) "Between merchants" means in any transaction with respect to which both parties are chargeable with the knowledge or skill of merchants.

§ 2–105. Definitions: Transferability; "Goods"; "Future" Goods; "Lot"; "Commercial Unit."

(1) "Goods" means all things (including specially manufactured goods) which are movable at the time of identification to the contract for sale other than the money in which the price is to be paid, investment securities (Article 8) and things in action. "Goods" also includes the unborn young of animals and growing crops and other identified things attached to realty as described in the section on goods to be severed from realty (Section 2–107).

(2) Goods must be both existing and identified before any interest in them can pass. Goods which are not both existing and identified are "future" goods. A purported present sale of future goods or of any interest therein operates as a contract to sell.

(3) There may be a sale of a part interest in existing identified goods.

(4) An undivided share in an identified bulk of fungible goods is sufficiently identified to be sold although the quantity of the bulk is not determined. Any agreed proportion of such a bulk or any quantity thereof agreed upon by number, weight or other measure may to the extent of the seller's interest in the bulk be sold to the buyer who then becomes an owner in common.

(5) "Lot" means a parcel or a single article which is the subject matter of a separate sale or delivery, whether or not it is sufficient to perform the contract.

(6) "Commercial unit" means such a unit of goods as by commercial usage is a single whole for purposes of sale and division of which materially impairs its character or value on the market or in use. A commercial unit may be a single article (as a machine) or a set of articles (as a suite of furniture or an assortment of sizes) or a quantity (as a bale, gross, or carload) or any other unit treated in use or in the relevant market as a single whole.

§ 2–106. Definitions: "Contract"; "Agreement"; "Contract for Sale"; "Sale"; "Present Sale"; "Conforming" to Contract; "Termination"; "Cancellation."

(1) In this Article unless the context otherwise requires "contract" and "agreement" are limited to those relating to the present or future sale of goods. "Contract for sale" includes both a present sale of goods and a contract to sell goods at a future time. A "sale" consists in the passing of title from the seller to the buyer for a price (Section 2–401). A "present sale" means a sale which is accomplished by the making of the contract.

(2) Goods or conduct including any part of a performance are "conforming" or conform to the contract when they are in accordance with the obligations under the contract.

(3) "Termination" occurs when either party pursuant to a power created by agreement or law puts an end to the contract otherwise than for its breach. On "termination" all obligations which are still executory on both sides are discharged but any right based on prior breach or performance survives.

(4) "Cancellation" occurs when either party puts an end to the contract for breach by the other and its effect is the same as that of "termination" except that the cancelling party also retains any remedy for breach of the whole contract or any unperformed balance.

§ 2–107. Goods to Be Severed From Realty: Recording.*

(1) A contract for the sale of timber, minerals or the like or a structure or its materials to be removed from realty is a contract for the sale of goods within this Article if they are to

be severed by the seller but until severance a purported present sale thereof which is not effective as a transfer of an interest in land is effective only as a contract to sell.

(2) A contract for the sale apart from the land of growing crops or other things attached to realty and capable of severance without material harm thereto but not described in subsection (1) is a contract for the sale of goods within this Article whether the subject matter is to be severed by the buyer or by the seller even though it forms part of the realty at the time of contracting, and the parties can by identification effect a present sale before severance.

(3) The provisions of this section are subject to any third party rights provided by the law relating to realty records, and the contract for sale may be executed and recorded as a document transferring an interest in land and shall then constitute notice to third parties of the buyer's rights under the contract for sale.

PART 2
FORM, FORMATION AND READJUSTMENT OF CONTRACT

§ 2–201. Formal Requirements; Statute of Frauds.

(1) Except as otherwise provided in this section a contract for the sale of goods for the price of $500 or more is not enforceable by way of action or defense unless there is some writing sufficient to indicate that a contract for sale has been made between the parties and signed by the party against whom enforcement is sought or by his authorized agent or broker. A writing is not insufficient because it omits or incorrectly states a term agreed upon but the contract is not enforceable under this paragraph beyond the quantity of goods shown in such writing.

(2) Between merchants if within a reasonable time a writing in confirmation of the contract and sufficient against the sender is received and the party receiving it has reason to know its contents, it satisfies the requirements of subsection (1) against such party unless written notice of objection to its contents is given ten days after it is received.

(3) A contract which does not satisfy the requirements of subsection (1) but which is valid in other respects is enforceable
   (a) if the goods are to be specially manufactured for the buyer and are not suitable for sale to others in the ordinary course of the seller's business and the seller, before notice of repudiation is received and under circumstances which reasonably indicate that the goods are for the buyer, has made either a substantial beginning of their manufacture or commitments for their procurement; or
   (b) if the party against whom enforcement is sought admits in his pleading, testimony or otherwise in court that a contract for sale was made, but the contract is not enforceable under this provision beyond the quantity of goods admitted; or
   (c) with respect to goods for which payment has been made and accepted or which have been received and accepted (Sec. 2–606).

§ 2–202. Final Written Expression: Parol or Extrinsic Evidence.

Terms with respect to which the confirmatory memoranda of the parties agree or which are otherwise set forth in a writing intended by the parties as a final expression of their agreement with respect to such terms as are included therein may not be contradicted by evidence of any prior agreement or of a contemporaneous oral agreement but may be explained or supplemented
   (a) by course of dealing or usage of trade (Section 1–205) or by course of performance (Section 2–208); and
   (b) by evidence of consistent additional terms unless the court finds the writing to have been intended also as a complete and exclusive statement of the terms of the agreement.

§ 2–203. Seals Inoperative.

The affixing of a seal to a writing evidencing a contract for sale or an offer to buy or sell goods does not constitute the writing a sealed instrument and the law with respect to sealed instruments does not apply to such a contract or offer.

§ 2–204. Formation in General.

(1) A contract for sale of goods may be made in any manner sufficient to show agreement, including conduct by both parties which recognizes the existence of such a contract.

(2) An agreement sufficient to constitute a contract for sale may be found even though the moment of its making is undetermined.

(3) Even though one or more terms are left open a contract for sale does not fail for indefiniteness if the parties have intended to make a contract and there is a reasonably certain basis for giving an appropriate remedy.

§ 2–205. Firm Offers.

An offer by a merchant to buy or sell goods in a signed writing which by its terms gives assurance that it will be held open is not revocable, for lack of consideration, during the time stated or if no time is stated for a reasonable time, but in no event may such period of irrevocability exceed three months; but any such term of assurance on a form supplied by the offeree must be separately signed by the offeror.

§ 2–206. Offer and Acceptance in Formation of Contract.

(1) Unless otherwise unambiguously indicated by the language or circumstances
    (a) an offer to make a contract shall be construed as inviting acceptance in any manner and by any medium reasonable in the circumstances;
    (b) an order or other offer to buy goods for prompt or current shipment shall be construed as inviting acceptance either by a prompt promise to ship or by the prompt or current shipment of conforming or nonconforming goods, but such a shipment of non-conforming goods does not constitute an acceptance if the seller seasonably notifies the buyer that the shipment is offered only as an accommodation to the buyer.

(2) Where the beginning of a requested performance is a reasonable mode of acceptance an offeror who is not notified of acceptance within a reasonable time may treat the offer as having lapsed before acceptance.

§ 2–207. Additional Terms in Acceptance or Confirmation.

(1) A definite and seasonable expression of acceptance or a written confirmation which is sent within a reasonable time operates as an acceptance even though it states terms additional to or different from those offered or agreed upon, unless acceptance is expressly made conditional on assent to the additional or different terms.

(2) The additional terms are to be construed as proposals for addition to the contract. Between merchants such terms become part of the contract unless:
    (a) the offer expressly limits acceptance to the terms of the offer;
    (b) they materially alter it; or
    (c) notification of objection to them has already been given or is given within a reasonable time after notice of them is received.

(3) Conduct by both parties which recognizes the existence of a contract is sufficient to establish a contract for sale although the writings of the parties do not otherwise establish a contract. In such case the terms of the particular contract consist of those terms on which the writings of the parties agree, together with any supplementary terms incorporated under any other provisions of this Act.

§ 2–208. Course of Performance or Practical Construction.

(1) Where the contract for sale involves repeated occasions for performance by either party with knowledge of the nature of the performance and opportunity for objection to it by the other, any course of performance accepted or acquiesced in without objection shall be relevant to determine the meaning of the agreement.

(2) The express terms of the agreement and any such course of performance, as well as any course of dealing and usage of trade, shall be construed whenever reasonable as consistent with

each other; but when such construction is unreasonable, express terms shall control course of performance and course of performance shall control both course of dealing and usage of trade (Section 1–205).

(3) Subject to the provisions of the next section on modification and waiver, such course of performance shall be relevant to show a waiver or modification of any term inconsistent with such course of performance.

§ 2–209. Modification, Rescission and Waiver.

(1) An agreement modifying a contract within this Article needs no consideration to be binding.

(2) A signed agreement which excludes modification or rescission except by a signed writing cannot be otherwise modified or rescinded, but except as between merchants such a requirement on a form supplied by the merchant must be separately signed by the other party.

(3) The requirements of the statute of frauds section of this Article (Section 2–201) must be satisfied if the contract as modified is within its provisions.

(4) Although an attempt at modification or rescission does not satisfy the requirements of subsection (2) or (3) it can operate as a waiver.

(5) A party who has made a waiver affecting an executory portion of the contract may retract the waiver by reasonable notification received by the other party that strict performance will be required of any term waived, unless the retraction would be unjust in view of a material change of position in reliance on the waiver.

§ 2–210. Delegation of Performance; Assignment of Rights.

(1) A party may perform his duty through a delegate unless otherwise agreed or unless the other party has a substantial interest in having his original promisor perform or control the acts required by the contract. No delegation of performance relieves the party delegating of any duty to perform or any liability for breach.

(2) Unless otherwise agreed all rights of either seller or buyer can be assigned except where the assignment would materially change the duty of the other party, or increase materially the burden or risk imposed on him by his contract, or impair materially his chance of obtaining return performance. A right to damages for breach of the whole contract or a right arising out of the assignor's due performance of his entire obligation can be assigned despite agreement otherwise.

(3) Unless the circumstances indicate the contrary a prohibition of assignment of "the contract" is to be construed as barring only the delegation to the assignee of the assignor's performance.

(4) An assignment of "the contract" or of "all my rights under the contract" or an assignment in similar general terms is an assignment of rights and unless the language or the circumstances (as in an assignment for security) indicate the contrary, it is a delegation of performance of the duties of the assignor and its acceptance by the assignee constitutes a promise by him to perform those duties. This promise is enforceable by either the assignor or the other party to the original contract.

(5) The other party may treat any assignment which delegates performance as creating reasonable grounds for insecurity and may without prejudice to his rights against the assignor demand assurances from the assignee (Section 2–609).

PART 3
GENERAL OBLIGATION AND CONSTRUCTION OF CONTRACT

§ 2–301. General Obligations of Parties.

The obligation of the seller is to transfer and deliver and that of the buyer is to accept and pay in accordance with the contract.

§ 2–302. Unconscionable Contract or Clause.

(1) If the court as a matter of law finds the contract or any clause of the contract to have been unconscionable at the time it was made the court may refuse to enforce the contract, or

it may enforce the remainder of the contract without the unconscionable clause, or it may so limit the application of any unconscionable clause as to avoid any unconscionable result.

(2) When it is claimed or appears to the court that the contract or any clause thereof may be unconscionable the parties shall be afforded a reasonable opportunity to present evidence as to its commercial setting, purpose and effect to aid the court in making the determination.

§ 2–303. Allocation or Division of Risks.

Where this Article allocates a risk or a burden as between the parties "unless otherwise agreed," the agreement may not only shift the allocation but may also divide the risk or burden.

§ 2–304. Price Payable in Money, Goods, Realty, or Otherwise.

(1) The price can be made payable in money or otherwise. If it is payable in whole or in part in goods each party is a seller of the goods which he is to transfer.

(2) Even though all or part of the price is payable in an interest in realty the transfer of the goods and the seller's obligations with reference to them are subject to this Article, but not the transfer of the interest in realty or the transferor's obligations in connection therewith.

§ 2–305. Open Price Term.

(1) The parties if they so intend can conclude a contract for sale even though the price is not settled. In such a case the price is a reasonable price at the time for delivery if

(a) nothing is said as to price; or

(b) the price is left to be agreed by the parties and they fail to agree; or

(c) the price is to be fixed in terms of some agreed market or other standard as set or recorded by a third person or agency and it is not so set or recorded.

(2) A price to be fixed by the seller or by the buyer means a price for him to fix in good faith.

(3) When a price left to be fixed otherwise than by agreement of the parties fails to be fixed through fault of one party the other may at his option treat the contract as cancelled or himself fix a reasonable price.

(4) Where, however, the parties intend not to be bound unless the price be fixed or agreed and it is not fixed or agreed there is no contract. In such a case the buyer must return any goods already received or if unable so to do must pay their reasonable value at the time of delivery and the seller must return any portion of the price paid on account.

§ 2–306. Output, Requirements and Exclusive Dealings.

(1) A term which measures the quantity by the output of the seller or the requirements of the buyer means such actual output or requirements as may occur in good faith, except that no quantity unreasonably disproportionate to any stated estimate or in the absence of a stated estimate to any normal or otherwise comparable prior output or requirements may be tendered or demanded.

(2) A lawful agreement by either the seller or the buyer for exclusive dealing in the kind of goods concerned imposes unless otherwise agreed an obligation by the seller to use best efforts to supply the goods and by the buyer to use best efforts to promote their sale.

§ 2–307. Delivery in Single Lot or Several Lots.

Unless otherwise agreed all goods called for by a contract for sale must be tendered in a single delivery and payment is due only on such tender but where the circumstances give either party the right to make or demand delivery in lots the price if it can be apportioned may be demanded for each lot.

§ 2–308. Absence of Specified Place for Delivery.

Unless otherwise agreed

(a) the place for delivery of goods is the seller's place of business or if he has none his residence; but

(b) in a contract for sale of identified goods which to the knowledge of the parties at the time of contracting are in some other place, that place is the place for their delivery; and

(c) documents of title may be delivered through customary banking channels.

§ 2–309. Absence of Specific Time Provisions; Notice of Termination.

(1) The time for shipment or delivery or any other action under a contract if not provided in this Article or agreed upon shall be a reasonable time.

(2) Where the contract provides for successive performances but is indefinite in duration it is valid for a reasonable time but unless otherwise agreed may be terminated at any time by either party.

(3) Termination of a contract by one party except on the happening of an agreed event requires that reasonable notification be received by the other party and an agreement dispensing with notification is invalid if its operation would be unconscionable.

§ 2–310. Open Time for Payment or Running of Credit; Authority to Ship Under Reservation.

Unless otherwise agreed

(a) payment is due at the time and place at which the buyer is to receive the goods even though the place of shipment is the place of delivery; and

(b) if the seller is authorized to send the goods he may ship them under reservation, and may tender the documents of title, but the buyer may inspect the goods after their arrival before payment is due unless such inspection is inconsistent with the terms of the contract (Section 2–513); and

(c) if delivery is authorized and made by way of documents of title otherwise than by subsection (b) then payment is due at the time and place at which the buyer is to receive the documents regardless of where the goods are to be received; and

(d) where the seller is required or authorized to ship the goods on credit the credit period runs from the time of shipment but post-dating the invoice or delaying its dispatch will correspondingly delay the starting of the credit period.

§ 2–311. Options and Cooperation Respecting Performance.

(1) An agreement for sale which is otherwise sufficiently definite (subsection (3) of Section 2–204) to be a contract is not made invalid by the fact that it leaves particulars of performance to be specified by one of the parties. Any such specification must be made in good faith and within limits set by commercial reasonableness.

(2) Unless otherwise agreed specifications relating to assortment of the goods are at the buyer's option and except as otherwise provided in subsections (1) (c) and (3) of Section 2–319 specifications or arrangements relating to shipment are at the seller's option.

(3) Where such specification would materially affect the other party's performance but is not seasonably made or where one party's cooperation is necessary to the agreed performance of the other but is not seasonably forthcoming, the other party in addition to all other remedies

(a) is excused for any resulting delay in his own performance; and

(b) may also either proceed to perform in any reasonable manner or after the time for a material part of his own performance treat the failure to specify or to cooperate as a breach by failure to deliver or accept the goods.

§ 2–312. Warranty of Title and Against Infringement; Buyer's Obligation Against Infringement.

(1) Subject to subsection (2) there is in a contract for sale a warranty by the seller that

(a) the title conveyed shall be good, and its transfer rightful; and

(b) the goods shall be delivered free from any security interest or other lien or encumbrance of which the buyer at the time of contracting has no knowledge.

(2) A warranty under subsection (1) will be excluded or modified only by specific language or by circumstances which give the buyer reason to know that the person selling does not claim title in himself or that he is purporting to sell only such right or title as he or a third person may have.

(3) Unless otherwise agreed a seller who is a merchant regularly dealing in goods of the kind warrants that the goods shall be delivered free of the rightful claim of any third person by way of infringement or the like but a buyer who furnishes specifications to the seller must hold the seller harmless against any such claim which arises out of compliance with the specifications.

§ 2–313. Express Warranties by Affirmation, Promise, Description, Sample.

(1) Express warranties by the seller are created as follows:

    (a) Any affirmation of fact or promise made by the seller to the buyer which relates to the goods and becomes part of the basis of the bargain creates an express warranty that the goods shall conform to the affirmation or promise.

    (b) Any description of the goods which is made part of the basis of the bargain creates an express warranty that the goods shall conform to the description.

    (c) Any sample or model which is made part of the basis of the bargain creates an express warranty that the whole of the goods shall conform to the sample or model.

(2) It is not necessary to the creation of an express warranty that the seller use formal words such as "warrant" or "guarantee" or that he have a specific intention to make a warranty, but an affirmation merely of the value of the goods or a statement purporting to be merely the seller's opinion or commendation of the goods does not create a warranty.

§ 2–314. Implied Warranty: Merchantability; Usage of Trade.

(1) Unless excluded or modified (Section 2–316), a warranty that the goods shall be merchantable is implied in a contract for their sale if the seller is a merchant with respect to goods of that kind. Under this section the serving for value of food or drink to be consumed either on the premises or elsewhere is a sale.

(2) Goods to be merchantable must be at least such as

    (a) pass without objection in the trade under the contract description; and

    (b) in the case of fungible goods, are of fair average quality within the description; and

    (c) are fit for the ordinary purposes for which such goods are used; and

    (d) run, within the variations permitted by the agreement, of even kind, quality and quantity within each unit and among all units involved; and

    (e) are adequately contained, packaged, and labeled as the agreement may require; and

    (f) conform to the promises or affirmations of fact made on the container or label if any.

(3) Unless excluded or modified (Section 2–316) other implied warranties may arise from course of dealing or usage of trade.

§ 2–315. Implied Warranty: Fitness for Particular Purpose.

Where the seller at the time of contracting has reason to know any particular purpose for which the goods are required and that the buyer is relying on the seller's skill or judgment to select or furnish suitable goods, there is unless excluded or modified under the next section an implied warranty that the goods shall be fit for such purpose.

§ 2–316. Exclusion or Modification of Warranties.

(1) Words or conduct relevant to the creation of an express warranty and words or conduct tending to negate or limit warranty shall be construed wherever reasonable as consistent with each other; but subject to the provisions of this Article on parol or extrinsic evidence (Section 2–202) negation or limitation is inoperative to the extent that such construction is unreasonable.

(2) Subject to subsection (3), to exclude or modify the implied warranty of merchantability or any part of it the language must mention merchantability and in case of a writing must be conspicuous, and to exclude or modify any implied warranty of fitness the exclusion must be by a writing and conspicuous. Language to exclude all implied warranties of fitness is sufficient if it states, for example, that "There are no warranties which extend beyond the description on the face hereof."

(3) Notwithstanding subsection (2)

    (a) unless the circumstances indicate otherwise, all implied warranties are excluded by expressions like "as is," "with all faults" or other language which in common understanding calls the buyer's attention to the exclusion of warranties and makes plain that there is no implied warranty; and

    (b) when the buyer before entering into the contract has examined the goods or the sample or model as fully as he desired or has refused to examine the goods there is no implied warranty with regard to defects which an examination ought in the circumstances to have revealed to him; and

    (c) an implied warranty can also be excluded or modified by course of dealing or course of performance or usage of trade.

(4) Remedies for breach of warranty can be limited in accordance with the provisions of this Article on liquidation or limitation of damages and on contractual modification of remedy (Sections 2–718 and 2–719).

§ 2–317. Cumulation and Conflict of Warranties Express or Implied.

Warranties whether express or implied shall be construed as consistent with each other and as cumulative, but if such construction is unreasonable the intention of the parties shall determine which warranty is dominant. In ascertaining that intention the following rules apply:

    (a) Exact or technical specifications displace an inconsistent sample or model or general language of description.

    (b) A sample from an existing bulk displaces inconsistent general language of description.

    (c) Express warranties displace inconsistent implied warranties other than an implied warranty of fitness for a particular purpose.

§ 2–318. Third Party Beneficiaries of Warranties Express or Implied.†

A seller's warranty whether express or implied extends to any natural person who is in the family or household of his buyer or who is a guest in his home if it is reasonable to expect that such person may use, consume or be affected by the goods and who is injured in person by breach of the warranty. A seller may not exclude or limit the operation of this section.

§ 2–319. F.O.B. and F.A.S Terms

(1) Unless otherwise agreed the term F.O.B. (which means "free on board") at a named place, even though used only in connection with the stated price, is a delivery term under which

    (a) when the term is F.O.B. the place of shipment, the seller must at that place ship the goods in the manner provided in this Article (Section 2–504) and bear the expense and risk of putting them into the possession of the carrier; or

    (b) when the term is F.O.B. the place of destination, the seller must at his own expense and risk transport the goods to that place and there tender delivery of them in the manner provided in this Article (Section 2–503);

    (c) when under either (a) or (b) the term is also F.O.B. vessel, car or other vehicle, the seller must in addition at his own expense and risk load the goods on board. If the term is F.O.B. vessel the buyer must name the vessel and in an appropriate case the seller must comply with the provisions of this Article on the form of bill of lading (Section 2–323).

(2) Unless otherwise agreed the term F.A.S. vessel (which means "free alongside") at a named port, even though used only in connection with the stated price, is a delivery term under which the seller must

    (a) at his own expense and risk deliver the goods alongside the vessel in the manner usual in that port or on a dock designated and provided by the buyer; and

    (b) obtain and tender a receipt for the goods in exchange for which the carrier is under a duty to issue a bill of lading.

(3) Unless otherwise agreed in any case falling within subsection (1) (a) or (c) or subsection (2) the buyer must seasonably give any needed instructions for making delivery, including when the term is F.A.S. or F.O.B. the loading berth of the vessel and in an appropriate

case its name and sailing date. The seller may treat the failure of needed instructions as a failure of cooperation under this Article (Section 2–311). He may also at his option move the goods in any reasonable manner preparatory to delivery or shipment.

(4) Under the term F.O.B. vessel or F.A.S. unless otherwise agreed the buyer must make payment against tender of the required documents and the seller may not tender nor the buyer demand delivery of the goods in substitution for the documents.

§ 2–320 C.I.F. and C. & F. Terms.

(1) The term C.I.F. means that the price includes in a lump sum the cost of the goods and the insurance and freight to the named destination. The term C. & F. or C.F. means that the price so includes cost and freight to the named destination.

(2) Unless otherwise agreed and even though used only in connection with the stated price and destination, the term C.I.F. destination or its equivalent requires the seller at his own expense and risk to

> (a) put the goods into the possession of a carrier at the port for shipment and obtain a negotiable bill or bills of lading covering the entire transportation to the named destination; and
>
> (b) load the goods and obtain a receipt from the carrier (which may be contained in the bill of lading) showing that the freight has been paid or provided for; and
>
> (c) obtain a policy or certificate of insurance, including any war risk insurance, of a kind and on terms then current at the port of shipment in the usual amount, in the currency of the contract, shown to cover the same goods covered by the bill of lading and providing for payment of loss to the order of the buyer or for the account of whom it may concern; but the seller may add to the price the amount of the premium for any such war risk insurance; and
>
> (d) prepare an invoice of the goods and procure any other documents required to effect shipment or to comply with the contract; and
>
> (e) forward and tender with commercial promptness all the documents in due form and with any indorsement necessary to perfect the buyer's rights.

(3) Unless otherwise agreed the term C. & F. or its equivalent has the same effect and imposes upon the seller the same obligations and risks as a C.I.F. term except the obligation as to insurance.

(4) Under the term C.I.F. or C. & F. unless otherwise agreed the buyer must make payment against tender of the required documents and the seller may not tender nor the buyer demand delivery of the goods in substitution for the documents.

§ 2–321. C.I.F. or C. & F.: "Net Landed Weights"; "Payment on Arrival"; Warranty of Condition on Arrival.

Under a contract containing a term C.I.F. or C. & F.

(1) Where the price is based on or is to be adjusted according to "net landed weights," "delivered weights," "out turn" quantity or quality or the like, unless otherwise agreed the seller must reasonably estimate the price. The payment due on tender of the documents called for by the contract is the amount so estimated, but after final adjustment of the price a settlement must be made with commercial promptness.

(2) An agreement described in subsection (1) or any warranty of quality or condition of the goods on arrival places upon the seller the risk of ordinary deterioration, shrinkage and the like in transportation but has no effect on the place or time of identification to the contract for sale or delivery or on the passing of the risk of loss.

(3) Unless otherwise agreed where the contract provides for payment on or after arrival of the goods the seller must before payment allow such preliminary inspection as is feasible; but if the goods are lost delivery of the documents and payment are due when the goods should have arrived.

§ 2–322. Delivery "Ex-Ship."

(1) Unless otherwise agreed a term for delivery of goods "ex-ship" (which means from the carrying vessel) or in equivalent language is not restricted to a particular ship and requires

delivery from a ship which has reached a place at the named port of destination where goods of the kind are usually discharged.

(2) Under such a term unless otherwise agreed

    (a) the seller must discharge all liens arising out of the carriage and furnish the buyer with a direction which puts the carrier under a duty to deliver the goods; and

    (b) the risk of loss does not pass to the buyer until the goods leave the ship's tackle or are otherwise properly unloaded.

§ 2–323. Form of Bill of Lading Required in Overseas Shipment; "Overseas."

(1) Where the contract contemplates overseas shipment and contains a term C.I.F. or C. & F. or F.O.B. vessel, the seller unless otherwise agreed must obtain a negotiable bill of lading stating that the goods have been loaded on board or, in the case of a term C.I.F. or C. & F., received for shipment.

(2) Where in a case within subsection (1) a bill of lading has been issued in a set of parts, unless otherwise agreed if the documents are not to be sent from abroad the buyer may demand tender of the full set; otherwise only one part of the bill of lading need be tendered. Even if the agreement expressly requires a full set

    (a) due tender of a single part is acceptable within the provisions of this Article on cure of improper delivery (subsection (1) of Section 2–508); and

    (b) even though the full set is demanded, if the documents are sent from abroad the person tendering an incomplete set may nevertheless require payment upon furnishing an indemnity which the buyer in good faith deems adequate.

(3) A shipment by water or by air or a contract contemplating such shipment is "overseas" insofar as by usage of trade or agreement it is subject to the commercial, financing or shipping practices characteristic of international deep water commerce.

§ 2–324. "No Arrival, No Sale" Term.

Under a term "no arrival, no sale" or terms of like meaning, unless otherwise agreed,

    (a) the seller must properly ship conforming goods and if they arrive by any means he must tender them on arrival but he assumes no obligation that the goods will arrive unless he has caused the non-arrival; and

    (b) where without fault of the seller the goods are in part lost or have so deteriorated as no longer to conform to the contract or arrive after the contract time, the buyer may proceed as if there had been casualty to identified goods (Section 2–613).

§ 2–325. "Letter of Credit" Term; "Confirmed Credit."

(1) Failure of the buyer seasonably to furnish an agreed letter of credit is a breach of the contract for sale.

(2) The delivery to seller of a proper letter of credit suspends the buyer's obligation to pay. If the letter of credit is dishonored, the seller may on seasonable notification to the buyer require payment directly from him.

(3) Unless otherwise agreed the term "letter of credit" or "banker's credit" in a contract for sale means an irrevocable credit issued by a financing agency of good repute and, where the shipment is overseas, of good international repute. The term "confirmed credit" means that the credit must also carry the direct obligation of such an agency which does business in the seller's financial market.

§ 2–326. Sale on Approval and Sale or Return; Consignment Sales and Rights of Creditors.

(1) Unless otherwise agreed, if delivered goods may be returned by the buyer even though they conform to the contract, the transaction is

    (a) a "sale on approval" if the goods are delivered primarily for use, and

    (b) a "sale or return" if the goods are delivered primarily for resale.

(2) Except as provided in subsection (3), goods held on approval are not subject to the claims of the buyer's creditors until acceptance; goods held on sale or return are subject to such claims while in the buyer's possession.

(3) Where goods are delivered to a person for sale and such person maintains a place of business at which he deals in goods of the kind involved, under a name other than the name of the person making delivery, then with respect to claims of creditors of the person conducting the business the goods are deemed to be on sale or return. The provisions of this subsection are applicable even though an agreement purports to reserve title to the person making delivery until payment or resale or uses such words as "on consignment" or "on memorandum." However, this subsection is not applicable if the person making delivery

  (a) complies with an applicable law providing for a consignor's interest or the like to be evidenced by a sign, or
  (b) establishes that the person conducting the business is generally known by his creditors to be substantially engaged in selling the goods of others, or
  (c) complies with the filing provisions of the Article on Secured Transactions (Article 9).

(4) Any "or return" term of a contract for sale is to be treated as a separate contract for sale within the statute of frauds section of this Article (Section 2–201) and as contradicting the sale aspect of the contract within the provisions of this Article on parol or extrinsic evidence (Section 2–202).

§ 2–327. Special Incidents of Sale on Approval and Sale or Return.

(1) Under a sale on approval unless otherwise agreed

  (a) although the goods are identified to the contract the risk of loss and the title do not pass to the buyer until acceptance; and
  (b) use of the goods consistent with the purpose of trial is not acceptance but failure seasonably to notify the seller of election to return the goods is acceptance, and if the goods conform to the contract acceptance of any part is acceptance of the whole; and
  (c) after due notification of election to return, the return is at the seller's risk and expense but a merchant buyer must follow any reasonable instructions.

(2) Under a sale or return unless otherwise agreed

  (a) the option to return extends to the whole or any commercial unit of the goods while in substantially their original condition, but must be exercised seasonably; and
  (b) the return is at the buyer's risk and expense.

§ 2–328. Sale by Auction.

(1) In a sale by auction if goods are put up in lots each lot is the subject of a separate sale.

(2) A sale by auction is complete when the auctioneer so announces by the fall of the hammer or in other customary manner. Where a bid is made while the hammer is falling in acceptance of a prior bid the auctioneer may in his discretion reopen the bidding or declare the goods sold under the bid on which the hammer was falling.

(3) Such a sale is with reserve unless the goods are in explicit terms put up without reserve. In an auction with reserve the auctioneer may withdraw the goods at any time until he announces completion of the sale. In an auction without reserve, after the auctioneer calls for bids on an article or lot, that article or lot cannot be withdrawn unless no bid is made within a reasonable time. In either case a bidder may retract his bid until the auctioneer's announcement of completion of the sale, but a bidder's retraction does not revive any previous bid.

(4) If the auctioneer knowingly receives a bid on the seller's behalf or the seller makes or procures such a bid, and notice has not been given that liberty for such bidding is reserved, the buyer may at his option avoid the sale or take the goods at the price of the last good faith bid prior to the completion of the sale.

PART 4
TITLE, CREDITORS AND GOOD FAITH PURCHASERS

§ 2–401. Passing of Title; Reservation for Security; Limited Application of This Section.

Each provision of this Article with regard to the rights, obligations and remedies of the seller, the buyer, purchasers or other third parties applies irrespective of title to the goods except where the provision refers to such title. Insofar as situations are not covered by the other provisions of this Article and matters concerning title became material the following rules apply:

(1) Title to goods cannot pass under a contract for sale prior to their identification to the contract (Section 2–501), and unless otherwise explicitly agreed the buyer acquires by their identification a special property as limited by this Act. Any retention or reservation by the seller of the title (property) in goods shipped or delivered to the buyer is limited in effect to a reservation of a security interest. Subject to these provisions and to the provisions of the Article on Secured Transactions (Article 9), title to goods passes from the seller to the buyer in any manner and on any conditions explicitly agreed on by the parties.

(2) Unless otherwise explicitly agreed title passes to the buyer at the time and place at which the seller completes his performance with reference to the physical delivery of the goods, despite any reservation of a security interest and even though a document of title is to be delivered at a different time or place; and in particular and despite any reservation of a security interest by the bill of lading.

    (a) if the contract requires or authorizes the seller to send the goods to the buyer but does not require him to deliver them at destination, title passes to the buyer at the time and place of shipment; but

    (b) if the contract requires delivery at destination, title passes on tender there.

(3) Unless otherwise explicitly agreed where delivery is to be made without moving the goods,

    (a) if the seller is to deliver a document of title, title passes at the time when and the place where he delivers such documents; or

    (b) if the goods are at the time of contracting already identified and no documents are to be delivered, title passes at the time and place of contracting.

(4) A rejection or other refusal by the buyer to receive or retain the goods, whether or not justified, or a justified revocation of acceptance revests title to the goods in the seller. Such revesting occurs by operation of law and is not a "sale."

§ 2–402. Rights of Seller's Creditors Against Sold Goods.

(1) Except as provided in subsections (2) and (3), rights of unsecured creditors of the seller with respect to goods which have been identified to a contract for sale are subject to the buyer's rights to recover the goods under this Article (Sections 2–502 and 2–716).

(2) A creditor of the seller may treat a sale or an identification of goods to a contract for sale as void if as against him a retention of possession by the seller is fraudulent under any rule of law of the state where the goods are situated, except that retention of possession in good faith and current course of trade by a merchant-seller for a commercially reasonable time after a sale or identification is not fraudulent.

(3) Nothing in this Article shall be deemed to impair the rights of creditors of the seller

    (a) under the provisions of the Article on Secured Transactions (Article 9); or

    (b) where identification to the contract or delivery is made not in current course of trade but in satisfaction of or as security for a pre-existing claim for money, security or the like and is made under circumstances which under any rule of law of the state where the goods are situated would apart from this Article constitute the transaction a fraudulent transfer or voidable preference.

§ 2–403. Power to Transfer; Good Faith Purchase of Goods; "Entrusting."

(1) A purchaser of goods acquires all title which his transferor had or had power to transfer except that a purchaser of a limited interest acquires rights only to the extent of the interest purchased. A person with voidable title has power to transfer a good title to a good faith purchaser for value. When goods have been delivered under a transaction of purchase the purchaser has such power even though

    (a) the transferor was deceived as to the identity of the purchaser, or

    (b) the delivery was in exchange for a check which is later dishonored, or

    (c) it was agreed that the transaction was to be a "cash sale," or

(d) the delivery was procured through fraud punishable as larcenous under the criminal law.

(2) Any entrusting of possession of goods to a merchant who deals in goods of that kind gives him power to transfer all rights of the entruster to a buyer in ordinary course of business.

(3) "Entrusting" includes any delivery and any acquiescence in retention of possession regardless of any condition expressed between the parties to the delivery or acquiescence and regardless of whether the procurement of the entrusting or the possessor's disposition of the goods have been such as to be larcenous under the criminal law.

(4) The rights of other purchasers of goods and of lien creditors are governed by the Articles on Secured Transactions (Article 9), Bulk Transfers (Article 6) and Documents of Title (Article 7).

PART 5
PERFORMANCE

§ 2–501. Insurable Interest in Goods; Manner of Identification of Goods.

(1) The buyer obtains a special property and an insurable interest in goods by identification of existing goods as goods to which the contract refers even though the goods so identified are non-conforming and he has an option to return or reject them. Such identification can be made at any time and in any manner explicitly agreed to by the parties. In the absence of explicit agreement identification occurs

(a) when the contract is made if it is for the sale of goods already existing and identified;

(b) if the contract is for the sale of future goods other than those described in paragraph (c), when goods are shipped, marked or otherwise designated by the seller as goods to which the contract refers;

(c) when the crops are planted or otherwise become growing crops or the young are conceived if the contract is for the sale of unborn young to be born within twelve months after contracting or for the sale of crops to be harvested within twelve months or the next normal harvest season after contracting whichever is longer.

(2) The seller retains an insurable interest in goods so long as title to or any security interest in the goods remains in him and where the identification is by the seller alone he may until default or insolvency or notification to the buyer that the identification is final substitute other goods for those identified.

(3) Nothing in this section impairs any insurable interest recognized under any other statute or rule of law.

§ 2–502. Buyer's Right to Goods on Seller's Insolvency.

(1) Subject to subsection (2) and even though the goods have not been shipped a buyer who has paid a part or all of the price of goods in which he has a special property under the provisions of the immediately preceding section may on making and keeping good a tender of any unpaid portion of their price recover them from the seller if the seller becomes insolvent within ten days after receipt of the first installment on their price.

(2) If the identification creating his special property has been made by the buyer he acquires the right to recover the goods only if they conform to the contract for sale.

§ 2–503. Manner of Seller's Tender of Delivery.

(1) Tender of delivery requires that the seller put and hold conforming goods at the buyer's disposition and give the buyer any notification reasonably necessary to enable him to take delivery. The manner, time and place for tender are determined by the agreement and this Article, and in particular

(a) tender must be at a reasonable hour, and if it is of goods they must be kept available for the period reasonably necessary to enable the buyer to take possession; but

(b) unless otherwise agreed the buyer must furnish facilities reasonably suited to the receipt of the goods.

(2) Where the case is within the next section respecting shipment tender requires that the seller comply with its provisions.

(3) Where the seller is required to deliver at a particular destination tender requires that he comply with subsection (1) and also in any appropriate case tender documents as described in subsections (4) and (5) of this section.

(4) Where goods are in the possession of a bailee and are to be delivered without being moved

(a) tender requires that the seller either tender a negotiable document of title covering such goods or procure acknowledgment by the bailee of the buyer's right to possession of the goods; but

(b) tender to the buyer of a non-negotiable document of title or of a written direction to the bailee to deliver is sufficient tender unless the buyer seasonably objects, and receipt by the bailee of notification of the buyer's rights fixes those rights as against the bailee and all third persons; but risk of loss of the goods and of any failure by the bailee to honor the non-negotiable document of title or to obey the direction remains on the seller until the buyer has had a reasonable time to present the document or direction, and a refusal by the bailee to honor the document or to obey the direction defeats the tender.

(5) Where the contract requires the seller to deliver documents

(a) he must tender all such documents in correct form, except as provided in this Article with respect to bills of lading in a set (subsection (2) of Section 2–323); and

(b) tender through customary banking channels is sufficient and dishonor of a draft accompanying the documents constitutes non-acceptance or rejection.

§ 2–504. Shipment by Seller.

Where the seller is required or authorized to send the goods to the buyer and the contract does not require him to deliver them at a particular destination, then unless otherwise agreed he must

(a) put the goods in the possession of such a carrier and make such a contract for their transportation as may be reasonable having regard to the nature of the goods and other circumstances of the case; and

(b) obtain and promptly deliver or tender in due form any document necessary to enable the buyer to obtain possession of the goods or otherwise required by the agreement or by usage of trade; and

(c) promptly notify the buyer of the shipment.

Failure to notify the buyer under paragraph (c) or to make a proper contract under paragraph (a) is a ground for rejection only if material delay or loss ensues.

§ 2–505. Seller's Shipment Under Reservation.

(1) Where the seller has identified goods to the contract by or before shipment:

(a) his procurement of a negotiable bill of lading to his own order or otherwise reserves in him a security interest in the goods. His procurement of the bill to the order of a financing agency or of the buyer indicates in addition only the seller's expectation of transferring that interest to the person named.

(b) a non-negotiable bill of lading to himself or his nominee reserves possession of the goods as security but except in a case of conditional delivery (subsection (2) of Section 2–507) a non-negotiable bill of lading naming the buyer as consignee reserves no security interest even though the seller retains possession of the bill of lading.

(2) When shipment by the seller with reservation of a security interest is in violation of the contract for sale it constitutes an improper contract for transportation within the preceding section but impairs neither the rights given to the buyer by shipment and identification of the goods to the contract nor the seller's powers as a holder of a negotiable document.

§ 2–506. Rights of Financing Agency.

(1) A financing agency by paying or purchasing for value a draft which relates to a ship-
rights under the draft and any document of title securing it any rights of the shipper in the
goods including the right to stop delivery and the shipper's right to have the draft honored by
ment of goods acquires to the extent of the payment or purchase and in addition to its own
the buyer.

(2) The right to reimbursement of a financing agency which has in good faith honored or
purchased the draft under commitment to or authority from the buyer is not impaired by subsequent discovery of defects with reference to any relevant document which was apparently
regular on its face.

§ 2–507. Effect of Seller's Tender; Delivery on Condition.

(1) Tender of delivery is a condition to the buyer's duty to accept the goods and, unless
otherwise agreed, to his duty to pay for them. Tender entitles the seller to acceptance of the
goods and to payment according to the contract.

(2) Where payment is due and demanded on the delivery to the buyer of goods or documents of title, his right as against the seller to retain or dispose of them is conditional upon
his making the payment due.

§ 2–508. Cure by Seller of Improper Tender or Delivery; Replacement.

(1) Where any tender or delivery by the seller is rejected because non-conforming and the
time for performance has not yet expired, the seller may seasonably notify the buyer of his
intention to cure and may then within the contract time make a conforming delivery.

(2) Where the buyer rejects a non-conforming tender which the seller had reasonable
grounds to believe would be acceptable with or without money allowance the seller may if he
seasonably notifies the buyer have a further reasonable time to substitute a conforming tender.

§ 2–509. Risk of Loss in the Absence of Breach.

(1) Where the contract requires or authorizes the seller to ship the goods by carrier

    (a) if it does not require him to deliver them at a particular destination, the risk of loss
        passes to the buyer when the goods are duly delivered to the carrier even though
        the shipment is under reservation (Section 2-505); but

    (b) if it does require him to deliver them at a particular destination and the goods are
        there duly tendered while in the possession of the carrier, the risk of loss passes to
        the buyer when the goods are there duly so tendered as to enable the buyer to take
        delivery.

(2) Where the goods are held by a bailee to be delivered without being moved, the risk of
loss passes to the buyer

    (a) on his receipt of a negotiable document of title covering the goods; or

    (b) on acknowledgment by the bailee of the buyer's right to possession of the goods; or

    (c) after his receipt of a non-negotiable document of title or other written direction to
        deliver, as provided in subsection (4) (b) of Section 2–503.

(3) In any case not within subsection (1) or (2), the risk of loss passes to the buyer on
his receipt of the goods if the seller is a merchant; otherwise the risk passes to the buyer on
tender of delivery.

(4) The provisions of this section are subject to contrary agreement of the parties and to
the provisions of this Article on sale on approval (Section 2–327) and on effect of breach on
risk of loss (Section 2–510).

§ 2–510. Effect of Breach on Risk of Loss.

(1) Where a tender or delivery of goods so fails to conform to the contract as to give a
right of rejection the risk of their loss remains on the seller until cure or acceptance.

(2) Where the buyer rightfully revokes acceptance he may to the extent of any deficiency

in his effective insurance coverage treat the risk of loss as having rested on the seller from the beginning.

(3) Where the buyer as to conforming goods already identified to the contract for sale repudiates or is otherwise in breach before risk of their loss has passed to him, the seller may to the extent of any deficiency in his effective insurance coverage treat the risk of loss as resting on the buyer for a commercially reasonable time.

§ 2–511. Tender of Payment by Buyer; Payment by Check.

(1) Unless otherwise agreed tender of payment is a condition to the seller's duty to tender and complete any delivery.

(2) Tender of payment is sufficient when made by any means or in any manner current in the ordinary course of business unless the seller demands payment in legal tender and gives any extension of time reasonably necessary to procure it.

(3) Subject to the provisions of this Act on the effect of an instrument on an obligation (Section 3–802), payment by check is conditional and is defeated as between the parties by dishonor of the check on due presentment.

§ 2–512. Payment by Buyer Before Inspection.

(1) Where the contract requires payment before inspection non-conformity of the goods does not excuse the buyer from so making payment unless
    (a) the non-conformity appears without inspection; or
    (b) despite tender of the required documents the circumstances would justify injunction against honor under the provisions of this Act (Section 5–114).

(2) Payment pursuant to subsection (1) does not constitute an acceptance of goods or impair the buyer's right to inspect or any of his remedies.

§ 2–513. Buyer's Right to Inspection of Goods.

(1) Unless otherwise agreed and subject to subsection (3), where goods are tendered or delivered or identified to the contract for sale, the buyer has a right before payment or acceptance to inspect them at any reasonable place and time and in any reasonable manner. When the seller is required or authorized to send the goods to the buyer, the inspection may be after their arrival.

(2) Expenses of inspection must be borne by the buyer but may be recovered from the seller if the goods do not conform and are rejected.

(3) Unless otherwise agreed and subject to the provisions of this Article on C.I.F. contracts (subsection (3) of Section 2–321), the buyer is not entitled to inspect the goods before payment of the price when the contract provides
    (a) for delivery "C.O.D." or on other like terms; or
    (b) for payment against documents of title, except where such payment is due only after the goods are to become available for inspection.

(4) A place or method of inspection fixed by the parties is presumed to be exclusive but unless otherwise expressly agreed it does not postpone identification or shift the place for delivery or for passing the risk of loss. If compliance becomes impossible, inspection shall be as provided in this section unless the place or method fixed was clearly intended as an indispensable condition failure of which avoids the contract.

§ 2–514. When Documents Deliverable on Acceptance; When on Payment.

Unless otherwise agreed documents against which a draft is drawn are to be delivered to the drawee on acceptance of the draft if it is payable more than three days after presentment; otherwise, only on payment.

§ 2–515. Preserving Evidence of Goods in Dispute.

In furtherance of the adjustment of any claim or dispute
    (a) either party on reasonable notification to the other and for the purpose of ascer-

taining evidence has the right to inspect, test and sample the goods including such of them as may be in the possession or control of the other; and

(b) the parties may agree to a third party inspection or survey to determine the conformity or condition of the goods and may agree that the findings shall be binding upon them in any subsequent litigation or adjustment.

PART 6
BREACH, REPUDIATION AND EXCUSE

§ 2–601. Buyer's Rights on Improper Delivery.

Subject to the provisions of this Article on breach in installment contracts (Section 2–612) and unless otherwise agreed under the sections on contractual limitations of remedy (Sections 2–718 and 2–719), if the goods or the tender of delivery fail in any respect to conform to the contract, the buyer may

(a) reject the whole; or

(b) accept the whole; or

(c) accept any commercial unit or units and reject the rest.

§ 2–602. Manner and Effect of Rightful Rejection.

(1) Rejection of goods must be within a reasonable time after their delivery or tender. It is ineffective unless the buyer seasonably notifies the seller.

(2) Subject to the provisions of the two following sections on rejected goods (Sections 2–603 and 2–604),

(a) after rejection any exercise of ownership by the buyer with respect to any commercial unit is wrongful as against the seller; and

(b) if the buyer has before rejection taken physical possession of goods in which he does not have a security interest under the provisions of this Article (subsection (3) of Section 2–711), he is under a duty after rejection to hold them with reasonable care at the seller's disposition for a time sufficient to permit the seller to remove them; but

(c) the buyer has no further obligations with regard to goods rightfully rejected.

(3) The seller's rights with respect to goods wrongfully rejected are governed by the provisions of this Article on seller's remedies in general (Section 2–703).

§ 2–603. Merchant Buyer's Duties as to Rightfully Rejected Goods.

(1) Subject to any security interest in the buyer (subsection (3) of Section 2–711), when the seller has no agent or place of business at the market of rejection a merchant buyer is under a duty after rejection of goods in his possession or control to follow any reasonable instructions received from the seller with respect to the goods and in the absence of such instructions to make reasonable efforts to sell them for the seller's account if they are perishable or threaten to decline in value speedily. Instructions are not reasonable if on demand indemnity for expenses is not forthcoming.

(2) When the buyer sells goods under subsection (1), he is entitled to reimbursement from the seller or out of the proceeds for reasonable expenses of caring for and selling them, and if the expenses include no selling commission then to such commission as is usual in the trade or if there is none to a reasonable sum not exceeding ten per cent on the gross proceeds.

(3) In complying with this section the buyer is held only to good faith and good faith conduct hereunder is neither acceptance nor conversion nor the basis of an action for damages.

§ 2–604. Buyer's Options as to Salvage of Rightfully Rejected Goods.

Subject to the provisions of the immediately preceding section on perishables if the seller gives no instructions within a reasonable time after notification of rejection the buyer may store the rejected goods for the seller's account or reship them to him or resell them for the seller's account with reimbursement as provided in the preceding section. Such action is not acceptance or conversion.

§ 2–605. Waiver of Buyer's Objections by Failure to Particularize.

(1) The buyer's failure to state in connection with rejection a particular defect which is ascertainable by reasonable inspection precludes him from relying on the unstated defect to justify rejection or to establish breach

    (a) where the seller could have cured it if stated seasonably; or

    (b) between merchants when the seller has after rejection made a request in writing for a full and final written statement of all defects on which the buyer proposes to rely.

(2) Payment against documents made without reservation of rights precludes recovery of the payment for defects apparent on the face of the documents.

§ 2–606. What Constitutes Acceptance of Goods.

(1) Acceptance of goods occurs when the buyer

    (a) after a reasonable opportunity to inspect the goods signifies to the seller that the goods are conforming or that he will take or retain them inspite of their nonconformity; or

    (b) fails to make an effective rejection (subsection (1) of Section 2–602), but such acceptance does not occur until the buyer has had a reasonable opportunity to inspect them; or

    (c) does any act inconsistent with the seller's ownership; but if such act is wrongful as against the seller it is an acceptance only if ratified by him.

(2) Acceptance of a part of any commercial unit is acceptance of that entire unit.

§ 2–607. Effect of Acceptance; Notice of Breach; Burden of Establishing Breach After Acceptance; Notice of Claim or Litigation to Person Answerable Over.

(1) The buyer must pay at the contract rate for any goods accepted.

(2) Acceptance of goods by the buyer precludes rejection of the goods accepted and if made with knowledge of a non-conformity cannot be revoked because of it unless the acceptance was on the reasonable assumption that the non-conformity would be seasonably cured but acceptance does not of itself impair any other remedy provided by this Article for nonconformity.

(3) Where a tender has been accepted.

    (a) the buyer must within a reasonable time after he discovers or should have discovered any breach notify the seller of breach or be barred from any remedy; and

    (b) if the claim is one for infringement or the like (subsection (3) of Section 2–312) and the buyer is sued as a result of such a breach he must so notify the seller within a reasonable time after he receives notice of the litigation or be barred from any remedy over for liability established by the litigation.

(4) The burden is on the buyer to establish any breach with respect to the goods accepted.

(5) Where the buyer is sued for breach of a warranty or other obligation for which his seller is answerable over

    (a) he may give his seller written notice of the litigation. If the notice states that the seller may come in and defend and that if the seller does not do so he will be bound in any action against him by his buyer by any determination of fact common to the two litigations, then unless the seller after seasonable receipt of the notice does come in and defend he is so bound.

    (b) if the claim is one for infringement or the like (subsection (3) of Section 2–312) the original seller may demand in writing that his buyer turn over to him control of the litigation including settlement or else be barred from any remedy over and if he also agrees to bear all expense and to satisfy any adverse judgment, then unless the buyer after seasonable receipt of the demand does turn over control the buyer is so barred.

(6) The provisions of subsections (3), (4) and (5) apply to any obligation of a buyer to hold the seller harmless against infringement or the like (subsection (3) of Section 2–312).

§ 2–608. Revocation of Acceptance in Whole or in Part.

(1) The buyer may revoke his acceptance of a lot or commercial unit whose non-conformity substantially impairs its value to him if he has accepted it

    (a) on the reasonable assumption that its non-conformity would be cured and it has not been seasonably cured; or

    (b) without discovery of such non-conformity if his acceptance was reasonably induced either by the difficulty of discovery before acceptance or by the seller's assurances.

(2) Revocation of acceptance must occur within a reasonable time after the buyer discovers or should have discovered the ground for it and before any substantial change in condition of the goods which is not caused by their own defects. It is not effective until the buyer notifies the seller of it.

(3) A buyer who so revokes has the same rights and duties with regard to the goods involved as if he had rejected them.

§ 2–609. Right to Adequate Assurance of Performance.

(1) A contract for sale imposes an obligation on each party that the other's expectation of receiving due performance will not be impaired. When reasonable grounds for insecurity arise with respect to the performance of either party the other may in writing demand adequate assurance of due performance and until he receives such assurance may if commercially reasonable suspend any performance for which he has not already received the agreed return.

(2) Between merchants the reasonableness of grounds for insecurity and the adequacy of any assurance offered shall be determined according to commercial standards.

(3) Acceptance of any improper delivery or payment does not prejudice the aggrieved party's right to demand adequate assurance of future performance.

(4) After receipt of a justified demand failure to provide within a reasonable time not exceeding thirty days such assurance of due performance as is adequate under the circumstances of the particular case is a repudiation of the contract.

§ 2–610. Anticipatory Repudiation.

When either party repudiates the contract with respect to a performance not yet due the loss of which will substantially impair the value of the contract to the other, the aggrieved party may

    (a) for a commercially reasonable time await performance by the repudiating party; or

    (b) resort to any remedy for breach (Section 2–703 or Section 2–711), even though he has notified the repudiating party that he would await the latter's performance and has urged retraction; and

    (c) in either case suspend his own performance or proceed in accordance with the provisions of this Article on the seller's right to identify goods to the contract notwithstanding breach or to salvage unfinished goods. (Section 2–704).

§ 2–611. Retraction of Anticipatory Repudiation.

(1) Until the repudiating party's next performance is due he can retract his repudiation unless the aggrieved party has since the repudiation cancelled or materially changed his position or otherwise indicated that he considers the repudiation final.

(2) Retraction may be by any method which clearly indicates to the aggrieved party that the repudiating party intends to perform, but must include any assurance justifiably demanded under the provisions of this Article (Section 2–609).

(3) Retraction reinstates the repudiating party's rights under the contract with due excuse and allowance to the aggrieved party for any delay occasioned by the repudiation.

§ 2–612. "Installment Contract"; Breach.

(1) An "installment contract" is one which requires or authorizes the delivery of goods in separate lots to be separately accepted, even though the contract contains a clause "each delivery is a separate contract" or its equivalent.

(2) The buyer may reject any installment which is non-conforming if the non-conformity substantially impairs the value of that installment and cannot be cured or if the non-conformity is a defect in the required documents; but if the non-conformity does not fall within subsection (3) and the seller gives adequate assurance of its cure the buyer must accept that installment.

(3) Whenever non-conformity or default with respect to one or more installments substantially impairs the value of the whole contract there is a breach of the whole. But the aggrieved party reinstates the contract if he accepts a non-conforming installment without seasonably notifying of cancellation or if he brings an action with respect only to past installments or demands performance as to future installments.

§ 2–613. Casualty to Identified Goods.

Where the contract requires for its performance goods identified when the contract is made, and the goods suffer casualty without fault of either party before the risk of loss passes to the buyer, or in a proper case under a "no arrival, no sale" term (Section 2–324) then
  (a) if the loss is total the contract is avoided; and
  (b) if the loss is partial or the goods have so deteriorated as no longer to conform to the contract the buyer may nevertheless demand inspection and at his option either treat the contract as avoided or accept the goods with due allowance from the contract price for the deterioration or the deficiency in quantity but without further right against the seller.

§ 2–614. Substituted Performance.

(1) Where without fault of either party the agreed berthing, loading, or unloading facilities fail or an agreed type of carrier becomes unavailable or the agreed manner of delivery otherwise becomes commercially impracticable but a commercially reasonable substitute is available, such substitute performance must be tendered and accepted.

(2) If the agreed means or manner of payment fails because of domestic or foreign government regulation, the seller may withhold or stop delivery unless the buyer provides a means or manner of payment which is commercially a substantial equivalent. If delivery has already been taken, payment by the means or in the manner provided by the regulation discharges the buyer's obligation unless the regulation is discriminatory, oppressive or predatory.

§ 2–615. Excuse by Failure of Presupposed Conditions.

Except so far as a seller may have assumed a greater obligation and subject to the preceding section on substituted performance:
  (a) Delay in delivery or non-delivery in whole or in part by a seller who complies with paragraphs (b) and (c) is not a breach of his duty under a contract for sale if performance as agreed has been made impracticable by the occurrence of a contingency the non-occurrence of which was a basic assumption on which the contract was made or by compliance in good faith with any applicable foreign or domestic governmental regulation or order whether or not it later proves to be invalid.
  (b) Where the causes mentioned in paragraph (a) affect only a part of the seller's capacity to perform, he must allocate production and deliveries among his customers but may at his option include regular customers not then under contract as well as his own requirements for further manufacture. He may so allocate in any manner which is fair and reasonable.
  (c) The seller must notify the buyer seasonably that there will be delay or non-delivery and, when allocation is required under paragraph (b), of the estimated quota thus made available for the buyer.

§ 2–616. Procedure on Notice Claiming Excuse.

(1) Where the buyer receives notification of a material or indefinite delay or an allocation justified under the preceding section he may by written notification to the seller as to any delivery concerned, and where the prospective deficiency substantially impairs the value of the

whole contract under the provisions of this Article relating to breach of installment contracts (Section 2–612), then also as to the whole,

(a) terminate and thereby discharge any unexecuted portion of the contract; or

(b) modify the contract by agreeing to take his available quota in substitution.

(2) If after receipt of such notification from the seller the buyer fails so to modify the contract within a reasonable time not exceeding thirty days the contract lapses with respect to any deliveries affected.

(3) The provisions of this section may not be negated by agreement except in so far as the seller has assumed a greater obligation under the preceding section.

PART 7
REMEDIES

§ 2–701. Remedies for Breach of Collateral Contracts Not Impaired.

Remedies for breach of any obligation or promise collateral or ancillary to a contract for sale are not impaired by the provisions of this Article.

§ 2–702. Seller's Remedies on Discovery of Buyer's Insolvency.

(1) Where the seller discovers the buyer to be insolvent he may refuse delivery except for cash including payment for all goods theretofore delivered under the contract, and stop delivery under this Article (Section 2–705).

(2) Where the seller discovers that the buyer has received goods on credit while insolvent he may reclaim the goods upon demand made within ten days after the receipt, but if misrepresentation of solvency has been made to the particular seller in writing within three months before delivery the ten day limitation does not apply. Except as provided in this subsection the seller may not base a right to reclaim goods on the buyer's fraudulent or innocent misrepresentation of solvency or of intent to pay.

(3) The seller's right to reclaim under subsection (2) is subject to the rights of a buyer in ordinary course or other good faith purchaser or lien creditor under this Article (Section 2–403). Successful reclamation of goods excludes all other remedies with respect to them.†

§ 2–703. Seller's Remedies in General.

Where the buyer wrongfully rejects or revokes acceptance of goods or fails to make a payment due on or before delivery or repudiates with respect to a part or the whole, then with respect to any goods directly affected and, if the breach is of the whole contract (Section 2–612), then also with respect to the whole undelivered balance, the aggrieved seller may

(a) withhold delivery of such goods;

(b) stop delivery by any bailee as hereafter provided (Section 2–705);

(c) proceed under the next section respecting goods still unidentified to the contract;

(d) resell and recover damages as hereafter provided (Section 2–706);

(e) recover damages for non-acceptance (Section 2–708) or in a proper case the price (Section 2–709);

(f) cancel.

§ 2–704. Seller's Right to Identify Goods to the Contract Notwithstanding Breach or to Salvage Unfinished Goods.

(1) An aggrieved seller under the preceding section may

(a) identify to the contract conforming goods not already identified if at the time he learned of the breach they are in his possession or control;

(b) treat as the subject of resale goods which have demonstrably been intended for the particular contract even though those goods are unfinished.

(2) Where the goods are unfinished an aggrieved seller may in the exercise of reasonable commercial judgment for the purposes of avoiding loss and of effective realization either complete the manufacture and wholly identify the goods to the contract or cease manufacture and resell for scrap or salvage value or proceed in any other reasonable manner.

§ 2–705. Seller's Stoppage of Delivery in Transit or Otherwise.

(1) The seller may stop delivery of goods in the possession of a carrier or other bailee when he discovers the buyer to be insolvent (Section 2–702) and may stop delivery of carload, truckload, planeload or larger shipments of express or freight when the buyer repudiates or fails to make a payment due before delivery or if for any other reason the seller has a right to withhold or reclaim the goods.

(2) As against such buyer the seller may stop delivery until

    (a) receipt of the goods by the buyer; or

    (b) acknowledgment to the buyer by any bailee of the goods except a carrier that the bailee holds the goods for the buyer; or

    (c) such acknowledgment to the buyer by a carrier by reshipment or as warehouseman; or

    (d) negotiation to the buyer of any negotiable document of title covering the goods.

(3) (a) To stop delivery the seller must so notify as to enable the bailee by reasonable diligence to prevent delivery of the goods.

    (b) After such notification the bailee must hold and deliver the goods according to the directions of the seller but the seller is liable to the bailee for any ensuing charges or damages.

    (c) If a negotiable document of title has been issued for goods the bailee is not obliged to obey a notification to stop until surrender of the document.

    (d) A carrier who has issued a non-negotiable bill of lading is not obliged to obey a notification to stop received from a person other than the consignor.

§ 2–706. Seller's Resale Including Contract for Resale.

(1) Under the conditions stated in Section 2–703 on seller's remedies, the seller may resell the goods concerned or the undelivered balance thereof. Where the resale is made in good faith and in a commercially reasonable manner the seller may recover the difference between the resale price and the contract price together with any incidental damages allowed under the provisions of this Article (Section 2–710), but less expenses saved in consequence of the buyer's breach.

(2) Except as otherwise provided in subsection (3) or unless otherwise agreed resale may be at public or private sale including sale by way of one or more contracts to sell or of identification to an existing contract of the seller. Sale may be as a unit or in parcels and at any time and place and on any terms but every aspect of the sale including the method, manner, time, place and terms must be commercially reasonable. The resale must be reasonably identified as referring to the broken contract, but it is not necessary that the goods be in existence or that any or all of them have been identified to the contract before the breach.

(3) Where the resale is at private sale the seller must give the buyer reasonable notification of his intention to resell.

(4) Where the resale is at public sale

    (a) only identified goods can be sold except where there is a recognized market for a public sale of futures in goods of the kind; and

    (b) it must be made at a usual place or market for public sale if one is reasonably available and except in the case of goods which are perishable or threaten to decline in value speedily the seller must give the buyer reasonable notice of the time and place of the resale; and

    (c) if the goods are not to be within the view of those attending the sale the notification of sale must state the place where the goods are located and provide for their reasonable inspection by prospective bidders; and

    (d) the seller may buy.

(5) A purchaser who buys in good faith at a resale takes the goods free of any rights of the original buyer even though the seller fails to comply with one or more of the requirements of this section.

(6) The seller is not accountable to the buyer for any profit made on any resale. A person

in the position of a seller (Section 2–707) or a buyer who has rightfully rejected or justifiably revoked acceptance must account for any excess over the amount of his security interest, as hereinafter defined (subsection (3) of Section 2–711).

§ 2–707. "Person in the Position of a Seller."

(1) A "person in the position of a seller" includes as against a principal an agent who has paid or become responsible for the price of goods on behalf of his principal or anyone who otherwise holds a security interest or other right in goods similar to that of a seller.

(2) A person in the position of a seller may as provided in this Article withhold or stop delivery (Section 2–705) and resell (Section 2–706) and recover incidental damages (Section 2–710).

§ 2–708. Seller's Damages for Non-acceptance or Repudiation.

(1) Subject to subsection (2) and to the provisions of this Article with respect to proof of market price (Section 2–723), the measure of damages for non-acceptance or repudiation by the buyer is the difference between the market price at the time and place for tender and the unpaid contract price together with any incidental damages provided in this Article (Section 2–710), but less expenses saved in consequence of the buyer's breach.

(2) If the measure of damages provided in subsection (1) is inadequate to put the seller in as good a position as performance would have done then the measure of damages is the profit (including reasonable overhead) which the seller would have made from full performance by the buyer, together with any incidental damages provided in this Article (Section 2–710), due allowance for costs reasonably incurred and due credit for payments or proceeds of resale.

§ 2–709. Action for the Price.

(1) When the buyer fails to pay the price as it becomes due the seller may recover, together with any incidental damages under the next section, the price
  (a) of goods accepted or of conforming goods lost or damaged within a commerically reasonable time after risk of their loss has passed to the buyer; and
  (b) of goods identified to the contract if the seller is unable after reasonable effort to resell them at a reasonable price or the circumstances reasonably indicate that such effort will be unavailing.

(2) Where the seller sues for the price he must hold for the buyer any goods which have been identified to the contract and are still in his control except that if resale becomes possible he may resell them at any time prior to the collection of the judgment. The net proceeds of any such resale must be credited to the buyer and payment of the judgment entitles him to any goods not resold.

(3) After the buyer has wrongfully rejected or revoked acceptance of the goods or has failed to make a payment due or has repudiated (Section 2–610), a seller who is held not entitled to the price under this section shall nevertheless be awarded damages for non-acceptance under the preceding section.

§ 2–710. Seller's Incidental Damages.

Incidental damages to an aggrieved seller include any commercially reasonable charges, expenses or commissions incurred in stopping delivery, in the transportation, care and custody of goods after the buyer's breach, in connection with return or resale of the goods or otherwise resulting from the breach.

§ 2–711 Buyer's Remedies in General; Buyer's Security Interest in Rejected Goods.

(1) Where the seller fails to make delivery or repudiates or the buyer rightfully rejects or justifiably revokes acceptance then with respect to any goods involved, and with respect to the whole if the breach goes to the whole contract (Section 2–612), the buyer may cancel and whether or not he has done so may in addition to recovering so much of the price as has been paid

(a) "cover" and have damages under the next section as to all the goods affected whether or not they have been identified to the contract; or

(b) recover damages for non-delivery as provided in this Article (Section 2–713).

(2) Where the seller fails to deliver or repudiates the buyer may also

(a) if the goods have been identified recover them as provided in this Article (Section 2–502); or

(b) in a proper case obtain specific performance or replevy the goods as provided in this Article (Section 2–716).

(3) On rightful rejection or justifiable revocation of acceptance a buyer has a security interest in goods in his possession or control for any payments made on their price and any expenses reasonably incurred in their inspection, receipt, transportation, care and custody and may hold such goods and resell them in like manner as an aggrieved seller (Section 2–706).

§ 2–712. "Covert"; Buyer's Procurement of Substitute Goods.

(1) After a breach within the preceding section the buyer may "cover" by making in good faith and without unreasonable delay any reasonable purchase of or contract to purchase goods in substitution for those due from the seller.

(2) The buyer may recover from the seller as damages the difference between the cost of cover and the contract price together with any incidental or consequential damages as hereinafter defined (Section 2–715), but less expenses saved in consequence of the seller's breach.

(3) Failure of the buyer to effect cover within this section does not bar him from any other remedy.

§ 2–713. Buyer's Damages for Non-Delivery or Repudiation.

(1) Subject to the provisions of this Article with respect to proof of market price (Section 2–723), the measure of damages for non-delivery or repudiation by the seller is the difference between the market price at the time when the buyer learned of the breach and the contract price together with any incidental and consequential damages provided in this Article (Section 2–715), but less expenses saved in consequence of the seller's breach.

(2) Market price is to be determined as of the place for tender or, in cases of rejection after arrival or revocation of acceptance, as of the place of arrival.

§ 2–714. Buyer's Damages for Breach in Regard to Accepted Goods.

(1) Where the buyer has accepted goods and given notification (subsection (3) of Section 2–607) he may recover as damages for any non-conformity of tender the loss resulting in the ordinary course of events from the seller's breach as determined in any manner which is reasonable.

(2) The measure of damages for breach of warranty is the difference at the time and place of acceptance between the value of the goods accepted and the value they would have had if they had been as warranted, unless special circumstances show proximate damages of a different amount.

(3) In a proper case any incidental and consequential damages under the next section may also be recovered.

§ 2–715. Buyer's Incidental and Consequential Damages.

(1) Incidental damages resulting from the seller's breach include expenses reasonably incurred in inspection, receipt, transportation and care and custody of goods rightfully rejected, any commercially reasonable charges, expenses or commissions in connection with effecting cover and any other reasonable expense incident to the delay or other breach.

(2) Consequential damages resulting from the seller's breach include

(a) any loss resulting from general or particular requirements and needs of which the seller at the time of contracting had reason to know and which could not reasonably be prevented by cover or otherwise; and

(b) injury to person or property proximately resulting from any breach of warranty.

§ 2–716. Buyer's Right to Specific Performance or Replevin.

(1) Specific performance may be decreed where the goods are unique or in other proper circumstances.

(2) The decree for specific performance may include such terms and conditions as to payment of the price, damages, or other relief as the court may deem just.

(3) The buyer has a right of replevin for goods identified to the contract if after reasonable effort he is unable to effect cover for such goods or the circumstances reasonably indicate that such effort will be unavailing or if the goods have been shipped under reservation and satisfaction of the security interest in them has been made or tendered.

§ 2–717. Deduction of Damages From the Price.

The buyer on notifying the seller of his intention to do so may deduct all or any part of the damages resulting from any breach of the contract from any part of the price still due under the same contract.

§ 2–718. Liquidation or Limitation of Damages; Deposits.

(1) Damages for breach by either party may be liquidated in the agreement but only at an amount which is reasonable in the light of the anticipated or actual harm caused by the breach, the difficulties of proof of loss, and the inconvenience or nonfeasibility of otherwise obtaining an adequate remedy. A term fixing unreasonably large liquidated damages is void as a penalty.

(2) Where the seller justifiably withholds delivery of goods because of the buyer's breach, the buyer is entitled to restitution of any amount by which the sum of his payments exceeds

    (a) the amount to which the seller is entitled by virtue of terms liquidating the seller's damages in accordance with subsection (1), or

    (b) in the absence of such terms, twenty per cent of the value of the total performance for which the buyer is obligated under the contract or $500, whichever is smaller.

(3) The buyer's right to restitution under subsection (2) is subject to offset to the extent that the seller establishes

    (a) a right to recover damages under the provisions of this Article other than subsection (1), and

    (b) the amount or value of any benefits received by the buyer directly or indirectly by reason of the contract.

(4) Where a seller has received payment in goods their reasonable value or the proceeds of their resale shall be treated as payments for the purposes of subsection (2); but if the seller has notice of the buyer's breach before reselling goods received in part performance, his resale is subject to the conditions laid down in this Article on resale by an aggrieved seller (Section 2–706).

§ 2–719. Contractual Modification or Limitation of Remedy.

(1) Subject to the provisions of subsections (2) and (3) of this section and the preceding section on liquidation and limitation of damages,

    (a) the agreement may provide for remedies in addition to or in substitution for those provided in this Article and may limit or alter the measure of damages recoverable under this Article, as by limiting the buyer's remedies to return of the goods and repayment of the price or to repair and replacement of non-conforming goods or parts; and

    (b) resort to a remedy as provided is optional unless the remedy is expressly agreed to be exclusive, in which case it is the sole remedy.

(2) Where circumstances cause an exclusive or limited remedy to fail of its essential purpose, remedy may be had as provided in this Act.

(3) Consequential damages may be limited or excluded unless the limitation or exclusion is unconscionable. Limitation of consequential damages for injury to the person in the case of consumer goods is prima facie unconscionable but limitation of damages where the loss is commercial is not.

§ 2–720. Effect of "Cancellation" or "Rescission" on Claims for Antecedent Breach.

Unless the contrary intention clearly appears, expressions of "cancellation" or "rescission" of the contract or the like shall not be construed as a renunciation or discharge of any claim in damages for an antecedent breach.

§ 2–721. Remedies for Fraud.

Remedies for material misrepresentation or fraud include all remedies available under this Article for non-fraudulent breach. Neither rescission or a claim for rescission of the contract for sale nor rejection or return of the goods shall bar or be deemed inconsistent with a claim for damages or other remedy.

§ 2–722. Who Can Sue Third Parties for Injury to Goods.

Where a third party so deals with goods which have been identified to a contract for sale as to cause actionable injury to a party to that contract

  (a) a right of action against the third party is in either party to the contract for sale who has title to or a security interest or a special property or an insurable interest in the goods; and if the goods have been destroyed or converted a right of action is also in the party who either bore the risk of loss under the contract for sale or has since the injury assumed that risk as against the other;

  (b) if at the time of the injury the party plaintiff did not bear the risk of loss as against the other party to the contract for sale and there is no arrangement between them for disposition of the recovery, his suit or settlement is, subject to his own interest, as a fiduciary for the other party to the contract;

  (c) either party may with the consent of the other sue for the benefit of whom it may concern.

§ 2–723. Proof of Market Price: Time and Place.

(1) If an action based on anticipatory repudiation comes to trial before the time for performance with respect to some or all of the goods, any damages based on market price (Section 2–708 or Section 2–713) shall be determined according to the price of such goods prevailing at the time when the aggrieved party learned of the repudiation.

(2) If evidence of a price prevailing at the times or places described in this Article is not readily available the price prevailing within any reasonable time before or after the time described or at any other place which in commercial judgment or under usage of trade would serve as a reasonable substitute for the one described may be used, making any proper allowance for the cost of transporting the goods to or from such other place.

(3) Evidence of a relevant price prevailing at a time or place other than the one described in this Article offered by one party is not admissible unless and until he has given the other party such notice as the court finds sufficient to prevent unfair surprise.

§ 2–724. Admissibility of Market Quotations.

Whenever the prevailing price or value of any goods regularly bought and sold in any established commodity market is in issue, reports in official publications or trade journals or in newspapers or periodicals of general circulation published as the reports of such market shall be admissible in evidence. The circumstances of the preparation of such a report may be shown to affect its weight but not its admissibility.

§ 2–725. Statute of Limitations in Contracts for Sale.

(1) An action for breach of any contract for sale must be commenced within four years after the cause of action has accrued. By the original agreement the parties may reduce the period of limitation to not less than one year but may not extend it.

(2) A cause of action accrues when the breach occurs, regardless of the aggrieved party's lack of knowledge of the breach. A breach of warranty occurs when tender of delivery is

made, except that where a warranty explicitly extends to future performance of the goods and discovery of the breach must await the time of such performance the cause of action accrues when the breach is or should have been discovered.

(3) Where an action commenced within the time limited by subsection (1) is so terminated as to leave available a remedy by another action for the same breach such other action may be commenced after the expiration of the time limited and within six months after the termination of the first action unless the termination resulted from voluntary discontinuance or from dismissal for failure or neglect to prosecute.

(4) This section does not alter the law on tolling of the statute of limitations nor does it apply to causes of action which have accrued before this Act becomes effective.

ARTICLE 3. Commercial Paper

PART 1
SHORT TITLE, FORM AND INTERPRETATION

§ 3–101. Short Title.

This Article shall be known and may be cited as Uniform Commercial Code—Commercial Paper.

§ 3–102. Definitions and Index of Definitions.

(1) In this Article unless the context otherwise requires
  (a) "Issue" means the first delivery of an instrument to a holder or a remitter.
  (b) An "order" is a direction to pay and must be more than an authorization or request. It must identify the person to pay with reasonable certainty. It may be addressed to one or more such persons jointly or in the alternative but not in succession.
  (c) A "promise" is an undertaking to pay and must be more than an acknowledgment of an obligation.
  (d) "Secondary party" means a drawer or endorser.
  (e) "Instrument" means a negotiable instrument.
(2) Other definitions applying to this Article and the sections in which they appear are:
"Acceptance." Section 3–410.
"Accommodation party." Section 3–415.
"Alteration." Section 3–407.
"Certificate of deposit." Section 3–104.
"Certification." Section 3–411.
"Check." Section 3–104.
"Definite time." Section 3–109.
"Dishonor." Section 3–507.
"Draft." Section 3–104.
"Holder in due course." Section 3–302.
"Negotiation." Section 3–202.
"Note." Section 3–104.
"Notice of dishonor." Section 3–508.
"On demand." Section 3–108.
"Presentment." Section 3–504.
"Protest." Section 3–509.
"Restrictive Indorsement." Section 3–205.
"Signature." Section 3–401.
(3) The following definitions in other Articles apply to this Article:
"Account." Section 4–104.
"Banking Day." Section 4–104.
"Clearing house." Section 4–104.

"Collecting bank." Section 4–105.
"Customer." Section 4–104.
"Depositary Bank." Section 4–105.
"Documentary Draft." Section 4–104.
"Intermediary Bank." Section 4–105.
"Item." Section 4–104.
"Midnight deadline." Section 4–104.
"Payor bank." Section 4–105.

(4) In addition Article 1 contains general definitions and principles of construction and interpretation applicable throughout this Article.

§ 3–103. Limitations on Scope of Article.

(1) This Article does not apply to money, documents of title or investment securities.

(2) The provisions of this Article are subject to the provisions of the Article on Bank Deposits and Collections (Article 4) and Secured Transactions (Article 9).

§ 3–104. Form of Negotiable Instruments; "Draft"; "Check"; "Certificate of Deposit"; "Note."

(1) Any writing to be a negotiable instrument within this Article must
   (a) be signed by the maker or drawer; and
   (b) contain an unconditional promise or order to pay a sum certain in money and no other promise, order, obligation or power given by the maker or drawer except as authorized by this Article; and
   (c) be payable on demand or at a definite time; and
   (d) be payable to order or to bearer.

(2) A writing which complies with the requirements of this section is
   (a) a "draft" ("bill of exchange") if it is an order;
   (b) a "check" if it is a draft drawn on a bank and payable on demand;
   (c) a "certificate of deposit" if it is an acknowledgment by a bank of receipt of money with an engagement to repay it;
   (d) a "note" if it is a promise other than a certificate of deposit.

(3) As used in other Articles of this Act, and as the context may require, the terms "draft," "check," "certificate of deposit" and "note" may refer to instruments which are not negotiable within this Article as well as to instruments which are so negotiable.

§ 3–105. When Promise or Order Unconditional.

(1) A promise or order otherwise unconditional is not made conditional by the fact that the instrument
   (a) is subject to implied or constructive conditions; or
   (b) states its consideration, whether performed or promised, or the transaction which gave rise to the instrument, or that the promise or order is made or the instrument matures in accordance with or "as per" such transaction; or
   (c) refers to or states that it arises out of a separate agreement or refers to a separate agreement for rights as to prepayment or acceleration; or
   (d) states that it is drawn under a letter of credit; or
   (e) states that it is secured, whether by mortgage, reservation of title or otherwise; or
   (f) indicates a particular account to be debited or any other fund or source from which reimbursement is expected; or
   (g) is limited to payment out of a particular fund or the proceeds of a particular source, if the instrument is issued by a government or governmental agency or unit; or
   (h) is limited to payment out of the entire assets of a partnership, unincorporated association, trust or estate by or on behalf of which the instrument is issued.

(2) A promise or order is not unconditional if the instrument
   (a) states that it is subject to or governed by any other agreement; or
   (b) states that it is to be paid only out of a particular fund or source except as provided in this section.

§ 3–106. Sum Certain.

(1) The sum payable is a sum certain even though it is to be paid

    (a) with stated interest or by stated installments; or

    (b) with stated different rates of interest before and after default or a specified date; or

    (c) with a stated discount or addition if paid before or after the date fixed for payment; or

    (d) with exchange or less exchange, whether at a fixed rate or at the current rate; or

    (e) with costs of collection or an attorney's fee or both upon default.

(2) Nothing in this section shall validate any term which is otherwise illegal.

§ 3–107. Money.

(1) An instrument is payable in money if the medium of exchange in which it is payable is money at the time the instrument is made. An instrument payable in "currency" or "current funds" is payable in money.

(2) A promise or order to pay a sum stated in a foreign currency is for a sum certain in money and, unless a different medium of payment is specified in the instrument, may be satisfied by payment of that number of dollars which the stated foreign currency will purchase at the buying sight rate for that currency on the day on which the instrument is payable or, if payable on demand, on the day of demand. If such an instrument specifies a foreign currency as the medium of payment the instrument is payable in that currency.

§ 3–108. Payable on Demand.

Instruments payable on demand include those payable at sight or on presentation and those in which no time for payment is stated.

§ 3–109. Definite Time.

(1) An instrument is payable at a definite time if by its terms it is payable

    (a) on or before a stated date or at a fixed period after a stated date; or

    (b) at a fixed period after sight; or

    (c) at a definite time subject to any acceleration; or

    (d) at a definite time subject to extension at the option of the holder, or to extension to a further definite time at the option of the maker or acceptor or automatically upon or after a specified act or event.

(2) An instrument which by its terms is otherwise payable only upon an act or event uncertain as to time of occurrence is not payable at a definite time even though the act or event has occurred.

§ 3–110. Payable to Order.

(1) An instrument is payable to order when by its terms it is payable to the order or assigns of any person therein specified with reasonable certainty, or to him or his order, or when it is conspicuously designated on its face as "exchange" or the like and names a payee. It may be payable to the order of

    (a) the maker or drawer; or

    (b) the drawee; or

    (c) a payee who is not maker, drawer or drawee; or

    (d) two or more payees together or in the alternative; or

    (e) an estate, trust or fund, in which case it is payable to the order of the representative of such estate, trust or fund or his successors; or

    (f) an office, or an officer by his title as such in which case it is payable to the principal but the incumbent of the office or his successors may act as if he or they were the holder; or

    (g) a partnership or unincorporated association, in which case it is payable to the partnership or association and may be indorsed or transferred by any person thereto authorized.

(2) An instrument not payable to order is not made so payable by such words as "payable upon return of this instrument properly indorsed."

(3) An instrument made payable both to order and to bearer is payable to order unless the bearer words are handwritten or typewritten.

§ 3–111. Payable to Bearer.

An instrument is payable to bearer when by its terms it is payable to
  (a) bearer or the order of bearer; or
  (b) a specified person or bearer; or
  (c) "cash" or the order of "cash," or any other indication which does not purport to designate a specific payee.

§ 3–112. Terms and Omissions Not Affecting Negotiability.

(1) The negotiability of an instrument is not affected by
  (a) the omission of a statement of any consideration or of the place where the instrument is drawn or payable; or
  (b) a statement that collateral has been given to secure obligations either on the instrument or otherwise of an obligor on the instrument or that in case of default on those obligations the holder may realize on or dispose of the collateral; or
  (c) a promise or power to maintain or protect collateral or to give additional collateral; or
  (d) a term authorizing a confession of judgment on the instrument if it is not paid when due; or
  (e) a term purporting to waive the benefit of any law intended for the advantage or protection of any obligor; or
  (f) a term in a draft providing that the payee by indorsing or cashing it acknowledges full satisfaction of an obligation of the drawer; or
  (g) a statement in a draft drawn in a set of parts (Section 3–801) to the effect that the order is effective only if no other part has been honored.
(2) Nothing in this section shall validate any term which is otherwise illegal.

§ 3–113. Seal.

An instrument otherwise negotiable is within this Article even though it is under a seal.

§ 3–114. Date, Antedating, Postdating.

(1) The negotiability of an instrument is not affected by the fact that it is undated, antedated or postdated.

(2) Where an instrument is antedated or postdated the time when it is payable is determined by the stated date if the instrument is payable on demand or at a fixed period after date.

(3) Where the instrument or any signature thereon is dated, the date is presumed to be correct.

§ 3–115. Incomplete Instruments.

(1) When a paper whose contents at the time of signing show that it is intended to become an instrument is signed while still incomplete in any necessary respect it cannot be enforced until completed, but when it is completed in accordance with authority given it is effective as completed.

(2) If the completion is unauthorized the rules as to material alteration apply (Section 3–407), even though the paper was not delivered by the maker or drawer; but the burden of establishing that any completion is unauthorized is on the party so asserting.

§ 3–116. Instruments Payable to Two or More Persons.

An instrument payable to the order of two or more persons
  (a) if in the alternative is payable to any one of them and may be negotiated, discharged or enforced by any of them who has possession of it;

(b) if not in the alternative is payable to all of them and may be negotiated, discharged or enforced only by all of them.

§ 3–117. Instruments Payable With Words of Description.

An instrument made payable to a named person with the addition of words describing him
   (a) as agent or officer of a specified person is payable to his principal but the agent or officer may act as if he were the holder;
   (b) as any other fiduciary for a specified person or purpose is payable to the payee and may be negotiated, discharged or enforced by him;
   (a) in any other manner is payable to the payee unconditionally and the additional words are without effect on subsequent parties.

§ 3–118. Ambiguous Terms and Rules of Construction.

The following rules apply to every instrument:
   (a) Where there is doubt whether the instrument is a draft or a note the holder may treat it as either. A draft drawn on the drawer is effective as a note.
   (b) Handwritten terms control typewritten and printed terms, and typewritten control printed.
   (c) Words control figures except that if the words are ambiguous figures control.
   (d) Unless otherwise specified a provision for interest means interest at the judgment rate at the place of payment from the date of the instrument, or if it is undated from the date of issue.
   (e) Unless the instrument otherwise specifies two or more persons who sign as maker, acceptor or drawer or indorser and as a part of the same transaction are jointly and severally liable even though the instrument contains such words as "I promise to pay."
   (f) Unless otherwise specified consent to extension authorizes a single extension for not longer than the original period. A consent to extension, expressed in the instrument, is binding on secondary parties and accommodation makers. A holder may not exercise his option to extend an instrument over the objection of a maker or acceptor or other party who in accordance with Section 3–604 tenders full payment when the instrument is due.

§ 3–119. Other Writings Affecting Instrument.

(1) As between the obligor and his immediate obligee or any transferee the terms of an instrument may be modified or affected by any other written agreement executed as a part of the same transaction, except that a holder in due course is not affected by any limitation of his rights arising out of the separate written agreement if he had no notice of the limitation when he took the instrument.

(2) A separate agreement does not affect the negotiability of an instrument.

§ 3–120. Instruments "Payable Through" Bank.

An instrument which states that it is "payable through" a bank or the like designates that bank as a collecting bank to make presentment but does not of itself authorize the bank to pay the instrument.

§ 3–121. Instruments Payable at Bank.

Note: *If this Act is introduced in the Congress of the United States this section should be omitted. (States to select either alternative)*

Alternative A—A note or acceptance which states that it is payable at a bank is the equivalent of a draft drawn on the bank payable when it falls due out of any funds of the maker or acceptor in current account or otherwise available for such payment.

Alternative B—A note or acceptance which states that it is payable at a bank is not of itself an order or authorization to the bank to pay it.

§ 3–122. Accrual of Cause of Action.

(1) A cause of action against a maker or an acceptor accrues
(a) in the case of a time instrument on the day after maturity;
(b) in the case of a demand instrument upon its date or, if no date is stated, on the date of issue.

(2) A cause of action against the obligor of a demand or time certificate of deposit accrues upon demand, but demand on a time certificate may not be made until on or after the date of maturity.

(3) A cause of action against a drawer of a draft or an indorser of any instrument accrues upon demand following dishonor of the instrument. Notice of dishonor is a demand.

(4) Unless an instrument provides otherwise, interest runs at the rate provided by law for a judgment
(a) in the case of a maker, acceptor or other primary obligor of a demand instrument, from the date of demand;
(b) in all other cases from the date of accrual of the cause of action.

PART 2
TRANSFER AND NEGOTIATION

§ 3–201. Transfer: Right to Indorsement.

(1) Transfer of an instrument vests in the transferee such rights as the transferor has therein, except that a transferee who has himself been a party to any fraud or illegality affecting the instrument or who as a prior holder had notice of a defense or claim against it cannot improve his position by taking from a later holder in due course.

(2) A transfer of a security interest in an instrument vests the foregoing rights in the transferee to the extent of the interest transferred.

(3) Unless otherwise agreed any transfer for value of an instrument not then payable to bearer gives the transferee the specifically enforceable right to have the unqualified indorsement of the transferor. Negotiation takes effect only when the indorsement is made and until that time there is no presumption that the transferee is the owner.

§ 3–202. Negotiation.

(1) Negotiation is the transfer of an instrument in such form that the transferee becomes a holder. If the instrument is payable to order it is negotiated by delivery with any necessary indorsement; if payable to bearer it is negotiated by delivery.

(2) An indorsement must be written by or on behalf of the holder and on the instrument or on a paper so firmly affixed thereto as to become a part thereof.

(3) An indorsement is effective for negotiation only when it conveys the entire instrument or any unpaid residue. If it purports to be of less it operates only as a partial assignment.

(4) Words of assignment, condition, waiver, guaranty, limitation or disclaimer of liability and the like accompanying an indorsement do not affect its character as an indorsement.

§ 3–203. Wrong or Misspelled Name.

Where an instrument is made payable to a person under a misspelled name or one other than his own he may indorse in that name or his own or both but signature in both names may be required by a person paying or giving value for the instrument.

§ 3–204. Special Indorsement; Blank Indorsement.

(1) A special indorsement specifies the person to whom or to whose order it makes the instrument payable. Any instrument specially indorsed becomes payable to the order of the special indorsee and may be further negotiated only by his indorsement.

(2) An indorsement in blank specifies no particular indorsee and may consist of a mere signature. An instrument payable to order and indorsed in blank becomes payable to bearer and may be negotiated by delivery alone until specially indorsed.

(3) The holder may convert a blank indorsement into a special indorsement by writing over the signature of the indorser in blank any contract consistent with the character of the indorsement.

§ 3–205. Restrictive Indorsements.

An indorsement is restrictive which either

  (a) is conditional; or
  (b) purports to prohibit further transfer of the instrument; or
  (c) includes the words "for collection," "for deposit," "pay any bank," or like terms signifying a purpose of deposit or collection; or
  (d) otherwise states that it is for the benefit or use of the indorser or of another person.

§ 3–206. Effect of Restrictive Indorsement.

(1) No restrictive indorsement prevents further transfer or negotiation of the instrument.

(2) An intermediary bank, or a payor bank which is not the depositary bank, is neither given notice nor otherwise affected by a restrictive indorsement of any person except the bank's immediate transferor or the person presenting for payment.

(3) Except for an intermediary bank, any transferee under an indorsement which is conditional or includes the words "for collection," "for deposit," "pay any bank," or like terms (subparagraphs (a) and (c) of Section 3–205) must pay or apply any value given by him for or on the security of the instrument consistently with the indorsement and to the extent that he does so he becomes a holder for value. In addition such transferee is a holder in due course if he otherwise complies with the requirements of Section 3–302 on what constitutes a holder in due course.

(4) The first taker under an indorsement for the benefit of the indorser or another person (subparagraph (d) of Section 3–205) must pay or apply any value given by him for or on the security of the instrument consistently with the indorsement and to the extent that he does so he becomes a holder for value. In addition such taker is a holder in due course if he otherwise complies with the requirements of Section 3–302 on what constitutes a holder in due course. A later holder for value is neither given notice nor otherwise affected by such restrictive indorsement unless he has knowledge that a fiduciary or other person has negotiated the instrument in any transaction for his own benefit or otherwise in breach of duty (subsection (2) of Section 3–304).

§ 3–207. Negotiation Effective Although It May Be Rescinded.

(1) Negotiation is effective to transfer the instrument although the negotiation is

  (a) made by an infant, a corporation exceeding its powers, or any other person without capacity; or
  (b) obtained by fraud, duress or mistake of any kind; or
  (c) part of an illegal transaction; or
  (d) made in breach of duty.

(2) Except as against a subsequent holder in due course such negotiation is in an appropriate case subject to rescission, the declaration of a constructive trust or any other remedy permitted by law.

§ 3–208. Reacquisition.

Where an instrument is returned to or reacquired by a prior party he may cancel any indorsement which is not necessary to his title and reissue or further negotiate the instrument, but any intervening party is discharged as against the reacquiring party and subsequent holders not in due course and if his indorsement has been cancelled is discharged as against subsequent holders in due course as well.

PART 3
RIGHTS OF A HOLDER

§ 3–301. Rights of a Holder.

The holder of an instrument whether or not he is the owner may transfer or negotiate it and, except as otherwise provided in Section 3–603 on payment or satisfaction, discharge it or enforce payment in his own name.

§ 3–302. Holder in Due Course.

(1) A holder in due course is a holder who takes the instrument
    (a) for value; and
    (b) in good faith; and
    (c) without notice that it is overdue or has been dishonored or of any defense against or claim to it on the part of any person.

(2) A payee may be a holder in due course.

(3) A holder does not become a holder in due course of an instrument:
    (a) by purchase of it at judicial sale or by taking it under legal process; or
    (b) by acquiring it in taking over an estate; or
    (c) by purchasing it as part of a bulk transaction not in regular course of business of the transferor.

(4) A purchaser of a limited interest can be a holder in due course only to the extent of the interest purchased.

§ 3–303. Taking for Value.

A holder takes the instrument for value
    (a) to the extent that the agreed consideration has been performed or that he acquires a security interest in or a lien on the instrument otherwise than by legal process; or
    (b) when he takes the instrument in payment of or as security for an antecedent claim against any person whether or not the claim is due; or
    (c) when he gives a negotiable instrument for it or makes an irrevocable commitment to a third person.

§ 3–304. Notice to Purchaser.

(1) The purchaser has notice of a claim or defense if
    (a) the instrument is so incomplete, bears such visible evidence of forgery or alteration, or is otherwise so irregular as to call into question its validity, terms of ownership or to create an ambiguity as to the party to pay; or
    (b) the purchaser has notice that the obligation of any party is voidable in whole or in part, or that all parties have been discharged.

(2) The purchaser has notice of a claim against the instrument when he has knowledge that a fiduciary has negotiated the instrument in payment of or as security for his own debt or in any transaction for his own benefit or otherwise in breach of duty.

(3) The purchaser has notice that an instrument is overdue if he has reason to know
    (a) that any part of the principal amount is overdue or that there is an uncured default in payment of another instrument of the same series; or
    (b) that acceleration of the instrument has been made; or
    (c) that he is taking a demand instrument after demand has been made or more than a reasonable length of time after its issue. A reasonable time for a check drawn and payable within the states and territories of the United States and the District of Columbia is presumed to be thirty days.

(4) Knowledge of the following facts does not of itself give the purchaser notice of a defense or claim
    (a) that the instrument is antedated or postdated;
    (b) that it was issued or negotiated in return for an executory promise or accompanied by a separate agreement, unless the purchaser has notice that a defense or claim has arisen from the terms thereof;
    (c) that any party has signed for accommodation;
    (d) that an incomplete instrument has been completed, unless the purchaser has notice of any improper completion;
    (e) that any person negotiating the instrument is or was a fiduciary;

(f) that there has been default in payment of interest on the instrument or in payment of any other instrument, except one of the same series.

(5) The filing or recording of a document does not of itself constitute notice within the provisions of this Article to a person who would otherwise be a holder in due course.

(6) To be effective notice must be received at such time and in such manner as to give a reasonable opportunity to act on it.

§ 3–305. Rights of a Holder in Due Course.

To the extent that a holder is a holder in due course he takes the instrument free from
(1) all claims to it on the part of any person; and
(2) all defenses of any party to the instrument with whom the holder has not dealt except
    (a) infancy, to the extent that it is a defense to a simple contract; and
    (b) such other incapacity, or duress, or illegality of the transaction, as renders the obligation of the party a nullity; and
    (c) such misrepresentation as has induced the party to sign the instrument with neither knowledge nor reasonable opportunity to obtain knowledge of its character or its essential terms; and
    (d) discharge in insolvency proceedings; and
    (e) any other discharge of which the holder has notice when he takes the instrument.

§ 3–306. Rights of One Not Holder in Due Course.

Unless he has the rights of a holder in due course any person takes the instrument subject to
    (a) all valid claims to it on the part of any person; and
    (b) all defenses of any party which would be available in an action on a simple contract; and
    (c) the defenses of want or failure of consideration, nonperformance of any condition precedent, non-delivery, or delivery for a special purpose (Section 3–408); and
    (d) the defense that he or a person through whom he holds the instrument acquired it by theft, or that payment or satisfaction to such holder would be inconsistent with the terms of a restrictive indorsement. The claim of any third person to the instrument is not otherwise available as a defense to any party liable thereon unless the third person himself defends the action for such party.

§ 3–307. Burden of Establishing Signatures, Defenses and Due Course.

(1) Unless specifically denied in the pleadings each signature on an instrument is admitted. When the effectiveness of a signature is put in issue
    (a) the burden of establishing it is on the party claiming under the signature; but
    (b) the signature is presumed to be genuine or authorized except where the action is to enforce the obligation of a purported signer who has died or become incompetent before proof is required.

(2) When signatures are admitted or established, production of the instrument entitles a holder to recover on it unless the defendant establishes a defense.

(3) After it is shown that a defense exists a person claiming the rights of a holder in due course has the burden of establishing that he or some person under whom he claims is in all respects a holder in due course.

PART 4
LIABILITY OF PARTIES

§ 3–401. Signature.

(1) No person is liable on an instrument unless his signature appears thereon.

(2) A signature is made by use of any name, including any trade or assumed name, upon an instrument, or by any word or mark used in lieu of a written signature.

§ 3–402. Signature in Ambiguous Capacity.

Unless the instrument clearly indicates that a signature is made in some other capacity it is an indorsement.

§ 3–403. Signature by Authorized Representative.

(1) A signature may be made by an agent or other representative, and his authority to make it may be established as in other cases of representation. No particular form of appointment is necessary to establish such authority.

(2) An authorized representative who signs his own name to an instrument

    (a) is personally obligated if the instrument neither names the person represented nor shows that the representative signed in a representative capacity;

    (b) except as otherwise established between the immediate parties, is personally obligated if the instrument names the person represented but does not show that the representative signed in a representative capacity, or if the instrument does not name the person represented but does show that the representative signed in a representative capacity.

(3) Except as otherwise established the name of an organization preceded or followed by the name and office of an authorized individual is a signature made in a representative capacity.

§ 3–404. Unauthorized Signatures.

(1) Any unauthorized signature is wholly inoperative as that of the person whose name is signed unless he ratifies it or is precluded from denying it but it operates as the signature of the unauthorized signer in favor of any person who in good faith pays the instrument or takes it for value.

(2) Any unauthorized signature may be ratified for all purposes of this Article. Such ratification does not of itself affect any rights of the person ratifying against the actual signer.

§ 3–405. Imposters; Signature in Name of Payee.

(1) An indorsement by any person in the name of a named payee is effective if

    (a) an imposter by use of the mails or otherwise has induced the maker or drawer to issue the instrument to him or his confederate in the name of the payee; or

    (b) a person signing as or on behalf of a maker or drawer intends the payee to have no interest in the instrument; or

    (c) an agent or employee of the maker or drawer has supplied him with the name of the payee intending the latter to have no such interest.

(2) Nothing in this section shall affect the criminal or civil liability of the person so indorsing.

§ 3–406. Negligence Contributing to Alteration or Unauthorized Signature.

Any person who by his negligence substantially contributes to a material alteration of the instrument or to the making of an unauthorized signature is precluded from asserting the alteration or lack of authority against a holder in due course or against a drawee or other payor who pays the instrument in good faith and in accordance with the reasonable commercial standards of the drawee's or payor's business.

§ 3–407. Alteration.

(1) Any alteration of an instrument is material which changes the contract of any party thereto in any respect, including any such change in

    (a) the number or relations of the parties; or

    (b) an incomplete instrument, by completing it otherwise than as authorized; or

    (c) the writing as signed, by adding to it or by removing any part of it.

(2) As against any person other than a subsequent holder in due course

    (a) alteration by the holder which is both fraudulent and material discharges any party whose contract is thereby changed unless that party assents or is precluded from asserting the defense;

(b) no other alteration discharges any party and the instrument may be enforced according to its original tenor, or as to incomplete instruments according to the authority given.

(3) A subsequent holder in due course may in all cases enforce the instrument according to its original tenor, and when an incomplete instrument has been completed, he may enforce it as completed.

§ 3–408. Consideration.

Want or failure of consideration is a defense as against any person not having the rights of a holder in due course (Section 3–305), except that no consideration is necessary for an instrument or obligation thereon given in payment of or as security for an antecedent obligation of any kind. Nothing in this section shall be taken to displace any statute outside this Act under which a promise is enforceable notwithstanding lack or failure of consideration. Partial failure of consideration is a defense pro tanto whether or not the failure is in an ascertained or liquidated amount.

§ 3–409. Draft Not an Assignment.

(1) A check or other draft does not of itself operate as an assignment of any funds in the hands of the drawee available for its payment, and the drawee is not liable on the instrument until he accepts it.

(2) Nothing in this section shall affect any liability in contract, tort or otherwise arising from any letter of credit or other obligation or representation which is not an acceptance.

§ 3–410. Definition and Operation of Acceptance.

(1) Acceptance is the drawee's signed engagement to honor the draft as presented. It must be written on the draft, and may consist of his signature alone. It becomes operative when completed by delivery or notification.

(2) A draft may be accepted although it has not been signed by the drawer or is otherwise incomplete or is overdue or has been dishonored.

(3) Where the draft is payable at a fixed period after sight and the acceptor fails to date his acceptance the holder may complete it by supplying a date in good faith.

§ 3–411. Certification of a Check.

(1) Certification of a check is acceptance. Where a holder procures certification the drawer and all prior indorsers are discharged.

(2) Unless otherwise agreed a bank has no obligation to certify a check.

(3) A bank may certify a check before returning it for lack of proper indorsement. If it does so the drawer is discharged.

§ 3–412. Acceptance Varying Draft.

(1) Where the drawee's proferred acceptance in any manner varies the draft as presented the holder may refuse the acceptance and treat the draft as dishonored in which case the drawee is entitled to have his acceptance cancelled.

(2) The terms of the draft are not varied by an acceptance to pay at any particular bank or place in the United States, unless the acceptance states that the draft is to be paid only at such bank or place.

(3) Where the holder assents to an acceptance varying the terms of the draft each drawer and indorser who does not affirmatively assent is discharged.

§ 3–413. Contract of Maker, Drawer and Acceptor.

(1) The maker or acceptor engages that he will pay the instrument according to its tenor at the time of his engagement or as completed pursuant to Section 3–115 on incomplete instruments.

(2) The drawer engages that upon dishonor of the draft and any necessary notice of dishonor or protest he will pay the amount of the draft to the holder or to any indorser who takes it up. The drawer may disclaim this liability by drawing without recourse.

(3) By making, drawing or accepting the party admits as against all subsequent parties including the drawee the existence of the payee and his then capacity to indorse.

§ 3–414. Contract of Indorser; Order of Liability.

(1) Unless the indorsement otherwise specifies (as by such words as "without recourse") every indorser engages that upon dishonor and any necessary notice of dishonor and protest he will pay the instrument according to its tenor at the time of his indorsement to the holder or to any subsequent indorser who takes it up, even though the indorser who takes it up was not obligated to do so.

(2) Unless they otherwise agree indorsers are liable to one another in the order in which they indorse, which is presumed to be the order in which their signatures appear on the instrument.

§ 3–415. Contract of Accommodation Party.

(1) An accommodation party is one who signs the instrument in any capacity for the purpose of lending his name to another party to it.

(2) When the instrument has been taken for value before it is due the accommodation party is liable in the capacity in which he has signed even though the taker knows of the accommodation.

(3) As against a holder in due course and without notice of the accommodation oral proof of the accommodation is not admissible to give the accommodation party the benefit of discharges dependent on his character as such. In other cases the accommodation character may be shown by oral proof.

(4) An indorsement which shows that it is not in the chain of title is notice of its accommodation character.

(5) An accommodation party is not liable to the party accommodated, and if he pays the instrument has a right of recourse on the instrument against such party.

§ 3–416. Contract of Guarantor.

(1) "Payment guaranteed" or equivalent words added to a signature mean that the signer engages that if the instrument is not paid when due he will pay it according to its tenor without resort by the holder to any other party.

(2) "Collection guaranteed" or equivalent words added to a signature mean that the signer engages that if the instrument is not paid when due he will pay it according to its tenor, but only after the holder has reduced his claim against the maker or acceptor to judgment and execution has been returned unsatisfied, or after the maker or acceptor has become insolvent or it is otherwise apparent that it is useless to proceed against him.

(3) Words of guaranty which do not otherwise specify guarantee payment.

(4) No words of guaranty added to the signature of a sole maker or acceptor affect his liability on the instrument. Such words added to the signature of one of two or more makers or acceptors create a presumption that the signature is for the accommodation of the others.

(5) When words of guaranty are used presentment, notice of dishonor and protest are not necessary to charge the user.

(6) Any guaranty written on the instrument is enforcible not withstanding any statute of frauds.

§ 3–417. Warranties on Presentment and Transfer.

(1) Any person who obtains payment or acceptance and any prior transferor warrants to a person who in good faith pays or accepts that

    (a) he has a good title to the instrument or is authorized to obtain payment or acceptance on behalf of one who has a good title; and

    (b) he has no knowledge that the signature of the maker or drawer is unauthorized, except that this warranty is not given by a holder in due course acting in good faith

(i) to a maker with respect to the maker's own signature; or

(ii) to a drawer with respect to the drawer's own signature, whether or not the drawer is also the drawee; or

(iii) to an acceptor of a draft if the holder in due course took the draft after the acceptance or obtained the acceptance without knowledge that the drawer's signature was unauthorized; and

(c) the instrument has not been materially altered, except that this warranty is not given by a holder in due course acting in good faith

(i) to the maker of a note or

(ii) to the drawer of a draft whether or not the drawer is also the drawee or

(iii) to the acceptor of a draft with respect to an alteration made prior to the acceptance if the holder in due course took the draft after the acceptance, even though the acceptance provided "payable as originally drawn" or equivalent terms; or

(iv) to the acceptor of a draft with respect to an alteration made after the acceptance.

(2) Any person who transfers an instrument and receives consideration warrants to his transferee and if the transfer is by indorsement to any subsequent holder who takes the instrument in good faith that

(a) he has a good title to the instrument or is authorized to obtain payment or acceptance on behalf of one who has a good title and the transfer is otherwise rightful; and

(b) all signatures are genuine or authorized; and

(c) the instrument has not been materially altered; and

(d) no defense of any party is good against him; and

(e) he has no knowledge of any insolvency proceeding instituted with respect to the maker or acceptor or the drawer of an unaccepted instrument.

(3) By transferring "without recourse" the transferor limits the obligation stated in subsection (2) (d) to a warranty that he has no knowledge of such a defense.

(4) A selling agent or broker who does not disclose the fact that he is acting only as such gives the warranties provided in this section, but if he makes such disclosure warrants only his good faith and authority.

§ 3–418. Finality of Payment or Acceptance.

Except for recovery of bank payments as provided in the Article on Bank Deposits and Collections (Article 4) and except for liability for breach of warranty on presentment under the preceding section, payment or acceptance of any instrument is final in favor of a holder in due course, or a person who has in good faith changed his position in reliance on the payment.

§ 3–419. Conversion of Instrument; Innocent Representative.

(1) An instrument is converted when

(a) a drawee to whom it is delivered for acceptance refuses to return it on demand or

(b) any person to whom it is delivered for payment refuses on demand either to pay or to return it; or

(c) it is paid on a forged indorsement.

(2) In an action against a drawee under subsection (1) the measure of the drawee's liability is the face amount of the instrument. In any other action under subsection (1) the measure of liability is presumed to be the face amount of the instrument.

(3) Subject to the provisions of this Act concerning restrictive indorsements a representative, including a depositary or collecting bank, who has in good faith and in accordance with the reasonable commercial standards applicable to the business of such representative dealt with an instrument or its proceeds on behalf of one who was not the true owner is not liable in conversion or otherwise to the true owner beyond the amount of any proceeds remaining in his hands.

(4) An intermediary bank or payor bank which is not a depositary bank is not liable in conversion solely by reason of the fact that proceeds of an item indorsed restrictively (Sections 3–205 and 3–206) are not paid or applied consistently with the restrictive indorsement of an indorser other than its immediate transferor.

PART 5
PRESENTMENT, NOTICE OF DISHONOR AND PROTEST

§ 3–501. When Presentment, Notice of Dishonor, and Protest Necessary or Permissible.

(1) Unless excused (Section 3–511) presentment is necessary to charge secondary parties as follows:

    (a) presentment for acceptance is necessary to charge the drawer and indorsers of a draft where the draft so provides, or is payable elsewhere than at the residence or place of business of the drawee, or its date of payment depends upon such presentment. The holder may at his option present for acceptance any other draft payable at a stated date;

    (b) presentment for payment is necessary to charge any indorser;

    (c) in the case of any drawer, the acceptor of a draft payable at a bank or the maker of a note payable at a bank, presentment for payment is necessary, but failure to make presentment discharges such drawer, acceptor or maker only as stated in Section 3–502(1) (b).

(2) Unless excused (Section 3–511)

    (a) notice of any dishonor is necessary to charge any indorser;

    (b) in the case of any drawer, the acceptor of a draft payable at a bank or the maker of a note payable at a bank, notice of any dishonor is necessary, but failure to give such notice discharges such drawer, acceptor or maker only as stated in Section 3–502(1) (b).

(3) Unless excused (Section 3–511) protest of any dishonor is necessary to charge the drawer and indorsers of any draft which on its face appears to be drawn or payable outside of the states and territories of the United States and the District of Columbia. The holder may at his option make protest of any dishonor of any other instrument and in the case of a foreign draft may on insolvency of the acceptor before maturity make protest for better security.†

(4) Notwithstanding any provision of this section, neither presentment nor notice of dishonor nor protest is necessary to charge an indorser who has indorsed an instrument after maturity.

§ 3–502. Unexcused Delay; Discharge.

(1) Where without excuse any necessary presentment or notice of dishonor is delayed beyond the time when it is due

    (a) any indorser is discharged; and

    (b) any drawer or the acceptor of a draft payable at a bank or the maker of a note payable at a bank who because the drawee or payor bank becomes insolvent during the delay is deprived of funds maintained with the drawee or payor bank to cover the instrument may discharge his liability by written assignment to the holder of his rights against the drawee or payor bank in respect of such funds, but such drawer, acceptor or maker is not otherwise discharged.

(2) Where without excuse a necessary protest is delayed beyond the time when it is due any drawer or indorser is discharged.

§ 3–503. Time of Presentment.

(1) Unless a different time is expressed in the instrument the time for any presentment is determined as follows:

    (a) where an instrument is payable at or a fixed period after a stated date any presentment for acceptance must be made on or before the date it is payable;

    (b) where an instrument is payable after sight it must either be presented for acceptance or negotiated within a reasonable time after date or issue whichever is later;

    (c) where an instrument shows the date on which it is payable presentment for payment is due on that date;

    (d) where an instrument is accelerated presentment for payment is due within a reasonable time after the acceleration;

    (e) with respect to the liability of any secondary party presentment for acceptance or payment of any other instrument is due within a reasonable time after such party becomes liable thereon.

(2) A reasonable time for presentment is determined by the nature of the instrument, any usage of banking or trade and the facts of the particular case. In the case of an uncertified check which is drawn and payable within the United States and which is not a draft drawn by a bank the following are presumed to be reasonable periods within which to present for payment or to initiate bank collection:

    (a) with respect to the liability of the drawer, thirty days after date or issue whichever is later; and

    (b) with respect to the liability of an indorser, seven days after his indorsement.

(3) Where any presentment is due on a day which is not a full business day for either the person making presentment or the party to pay or accept, presentment is due on the next following day which is a full business day for both parties.

(4) Presentment to be sufficient must be made at a reasonable hour, and if at a bank during its banking day.

§ 3–504. How Presentment Made.

(1) Presentment is a demand for acceptance or payment made upon the maker, acceptor, drawee or other payor by or on behalf of the holder.

(2) Presentment may be made

    (a) by mail, in which event the time of presentment is determined by the time of receipt of the mail; or

    (b) through a clearing house; or

    (c) at the place of acceptance or payment specified in the instrument or if there be none at the place of business or residence of the party to accept or pay. If neither the party to accept or pay nor anyone authorized to act for him is present or accessible at such place presentment is excused.

(3) It may be made

    (a) to any one of two or more makers, acceptors, drawees or other payors; or

    (b) to any person who has authority to make or refuse the acceptance or payment.

(4) A draft accepted or a note made payable at a bank in the United States must be presented at such bank.

(5) In the cases described in Section 4–210 presentment may be made in the manner and with the result stated in that section.

§ 3–505. Rights of Party to Whom Presentment Is Made.

(1) The party to whom presentment is made may without dishonor require

    (a) exhibition of the instrument; and

    (b) reasonable identification of the person making presentment and evidence of his authority to make it if made for another; and

    (c) that the instrument be produced for acceptance or payment at a place specified in it, or if there be none at any place reasonable in the circumstances; and

    (d) a signed receipt on the instrument for any partial or full payment and its surrender upon full payment.

(2) Failure to comply with any such requirement invalidates the presentment but the person presenting has a reasonable time in which to comply and the time for acceptance or payment runs from the time of compliance.

§ 3–506. Time Allowed for Acceptance or Payment.

(1) Acceptance may be deferred without dishonor until the close of the next business day following presentment. The holder may also in a good faith effort to obtain acceptance and without either dishonor of the instrument or discharge of secondary parties allow postponement of acceptance for an additional business day.

(2) Except as a longer time is allowed in the case of documentary drafts drawn under a letter of credit, and unless an earlier time is agreed to by the party to pay, payment of an instrument may be deferred without dishonor pending reasonable examination to determine whether it is properly payable, but payment must be made in any event before the close of business on the day of presentment.

§ 3–507. Dishonor; Holder's Right of Recourse; Term Allowing Re-Presentment.

(1) An instrument is dishonored when

   (a) a necessary or optional presentment is duly made and due acceptance or payment is refused or cannot be obtained within the prescribed time or in case of bank collections the instrument is seasonably returned by the midnight deadline (Section 4–301); or

   (b) presentment is excused and the instrument is not duly accepted or paid.

(2) Subject to any necessary notice of dishonor and protest, the holder has upon dishonor an immediate right of recourse against the drawers and indorsers.

(3) Return of an instrument for lack of proper indorsement is not dishonor.

(4) A term in a draft or an indorsement thereof allowing a stated time for re-presentment in the event of any dishonor of the draft by nonacceptance if a time draft or by nonpayment if a sight draft gives the holder as against any secondary party bound by the term an option to waive the dishonor without affecting the liability of the secondary party and he may present again up to the end of the stated time.

§ 3–508. Notice of Dishonor.

(1) Notice of dishonor may be given to any person who may be liable on the instrument by or on behalf of the holder or any party who has himself received notice, or any other party who can be compelled to pay the instrument. In addition an agent or bank in whose hands the instrument is dishonored may give notice to his principal or customer or to another agent or bank from which the instrument was received.

(2) Any necessary notice must be given by a bank before its midnight deadline and by any other person before midnight of the third business day after dishonor or receipt of notice of dishonor.

(3) Notice may be given in any reasonable manner. It may be oral or written and in any terms which identify the instrument and state that it has been dishonored. A misdescription which does not mislead the party notified does not vitiate the notice. Sending the instrument bearing a stamp, ticket or writing stating that acceptance or payment has been refused or sending a notice of debit with respect to the instrument is sufficient.

(4) Written notice is given when sent although it is not received.

(5) Notice to one partner is notice to each although the firm has been dissolved.

(6) When any party is in insolvency proceedings instituted after the issue of the instrument notice may be given either to the party or to the representative of his estate.

(7) When any party is dead or incompetent notice may be sent to his last known address or given to his personal representative.

(8) Notice operates for the benefit of all parties who have rights on the instrument against the party notified.

§ 3–509. Protest; Noting for Protest.

(1) A protest is a certificate of dishonor made under the hand and seal of a United States consul or vice consul or a notary public or other person authorized to certify dishonor by the

law of the place where dishonor occurs. It may be made upon information satisfactory to such person.

(2) The protest must identify the instrument and certify either that due presentment has been made or the reason why it is excused and that the instrument has been dishonored by nonacceptance or nonpayment.

(3) The protest may also certify that notice of dishonor has been given to all parties or to specified parties.

(4) Subject to subsection (5) any necessary protest is due by the time that notice of dishonor is due.

(5) If, before protest is due, an instrument has been noted for protest by the officer to make protest, the protest may be made at any time thereafter as of the date of the noting.

§ 3–510. Evidence of Dishonor and Notice of Dishonor.

The following are admissible as evidence and create a presumption of dishonor and of any notice of dishonor therein shown:

(a) a document regular in form as provided in the preceding section which purports to be a protest;

(b) the purported stamp or writing of the drawee, payor bank or presenting bank on the instrument or accompanying it stating that acceptance or payment has been refused for reasons consistent with dishonor;

(c) any book or record of the drawee, payor bank, or any collecting bank kept in the usual course of business which shows dishonor, even though there is no evidence of who made the entry.

§ 3–511. Waived or Excused Presentment, Protest or Notice of Dishonor or Delay Therein.

(1) Delay in presentment, protest or notice of dishonor is excused when the party is without notice that it is due or when the delay is caused by circumstances beyond his control and he exercises reasonable diligence after the cause of the delay ceases to operate.

(2) Presentment or notice or protest as the case may be is entirely excused when

(a) the party to be charged has waived it expressly or by implication either before or after it is due; or

(b) such party has himself dishonored the instrument or has countermanded payment or otherwise has no reason to expect or right to require that the instrument be accepted or paid; or

(c) by reasonable diligence the presentment or protest cannot be made or the notice given.

(3) Presentment is also entirely excused when

(a) the maker, acceptor or drawee of any instrument except a documentary draft is dead or in insolvency proceedings instituted after the issue of the instrument; or

(b) acceptance or payment is refused but not for want of proper presentment.

(4) Where a draft has been dishonored by nonacceptance a later presentment for payment and any notice of dishonor and protest for nonpayment are excused unless in the meantime the instrument has been accepted.

(5) A waiver of protest is also a waiver of presentment and of notice of dishonor even though protest is not required.

(6) Where a waiver of presentment or notice or protest is embodied in the instrument itself it is binding upon all parties; but where it is written above the signature of an indorser it binds him only.

PART 6
DISCHARGE

§ 3–601. Discharge of Parties.

(1) The extent of the discharge of any party from liability on an instrument is governed by the sections on

(a) payment or satisfaction (Section 3–603); or

(b) tender of payment (Section 3–604); or

(c) cancellation or renunciation (Section 3–605); or

(d) impairment of right of recourse or of collateral (Section 3–606); or

(e) reacquisition of the instrument by a prior party (Section 3–208); or

(f) fraudulent and material alteration (Section 3–407); or

(g) certification of a check (Section 3–411); or

(h) acceptance varying a draft (Section 3–412); or

(i) unexcused delay in presentment or notice of dishonor or protest (Section 3–502).

(2) Any party is also discharged from his liability on an instrument to another party by any other act or agreement with such party which would discharge his simple contract for the payment of money.

(3) The liability of all parties is discharged when any party who has himself no right of action or recourse on the instrument

(a) reacquires the instrument in his own right; or

(b) is discharged under any provision of this Article, except as otherwise provided with respect to discharge for impairment of recourse or of collateral (Section 3–606).

§ 3–602.) Effect of Discharge Against Holder in Due Course.

No discharge of any party provided by this Article is effective against a subsequent holder in due course unless he has notice thereof when he takes the instrument.

§ 3–603. Payment or Satisfaction.

(1) The liability of any party is discharged to the extent of his payment or satisfaction to the holder even though it is made with knowledge of a claim of another person to the instrument unless prior to such payment or satisfaction the person making the claim either supplies indemnity deemed adequate by the party seeking the discharge or enjoins payment or satisfaction by order of a court of competent jurisdiction in an action in which the adverse claimant and the holder are parties. This subsection does not, however, result in the discharge of the liability

(a) of a party who in bad faith pays or satisfies a holder who acquired the instrument by theft or who (unless having the rights of a holder in due course) holds through one who so acquired it; or

(b) of a party (other than an intermediary bank or a payor bank which is not a depositary bank) who pays or satisfies the holder of an instrument which has been restrictively indorsed in a manner not consistent with the terms of such restrictive indorsement.

(2) Payment or satisfaction may be made with the consent of the holder by any person including a stranger to the instrument. Surrender of the instrument to such a person gives him the rights of a transferee (Section 3–201).

§ 3–604. Tender of Payment.

(1) An party making tender of full payment to a holder when or after it is due is discharged to the extent of all subsequent liability for interest, costs and attorney's fees.

(2) The holder's refusal of such tender wholly discharges any party who has a right of recourse against the party making the tender.

(3) Where the maker or acceptor of an instrument payable otherwise than on demand is able and ready to pay at every place of payment specified in the instrument when it is due, it is equivalent to tender.

§ 3–605. Cancellation and Renunciation.

(1) The holder of an instrument may even without consideration discharge any party

(a) in any manner apparent on the face of the instrument or the indorsement, as by intentionally cancelling the instrument or the party's signature by destruction or mutilation, or by striking out the party's signature; or

(b) by renouncing his rights by a writing signed and delivered or by surrender of the instrument to the party to be discharged.

(2) Neither cancellation nor renunciation without surrender of the instrument affects the title thereto.

§ 3–606. Impairment of Recourse or of Collateral.

(1) The holder discharges any party to the instrument to the extent that without such party's consent the holder

(a) without express reservation of rights releases or agrees not to sue any person against whom the party has to the knowledge of the holder a right of recourse or agrees to suspend the right to enforce against such person the instrument or collateral or otherwise discharges such person, except that failure or delay in effecting any required presentment, protest or notice of dishonor with respect to any such person does not discharge any party as to whom presentment, protest or notice of dishonor is effective or unnecessary; or

(b) unjustifiably impairs any collateral for the instrument given by or on behalf of the party or any person against whom he has a right of recourse.

(2) By express reservation of rights against a party with a right of recourse the holder preserves

(a) all his rights against such party as of the time when the instrument was originally due; and

(b) the right of the party to pay the instrument as of that time; and

(c) all rights of such party to recourse against others.

PART 7
ADVICE OF INTERNATIONAL SIGHT DRAFT

§ 3–701. Letter of Advice of International Sight Draft.

(1) A "letter of advice" is a drawer's communication to the drawee that a described draft has been drawn.

(2) Unless otherwise agreed when a bank receives from another bank a letter of advice of an international sight draft the drawee bank may immediately debit the drawer's account and stop the running of interest pro tanto. Such a debit and any resulting credit to any account covering outstanding drafts leaves in the drawer full power to stop payment or otherwise dispose of the amount and creates no trust or interest in favor of the holder.

(3) Unless otherwise agreed and except where a draft is drawn under a credit issued by the drawee, the drawee of an international sight draft owes the drawer no duty to pay an unadvised draft but if it does so and the draft is genuine, may appropriately debit the drawer's account.

PART 8
MISCELLANEOUS

§ 3–801. Drafts in a Set.

(1) Where a draft is drawn in a set of parts, each of which is numbered and expressed to be an order only if no other part has been honored, the whole of the parts constitutes one draft but a taker of any part may become a holder in due course of the draft.

(2) Any person who negotiates, indorses or accepts a single part of a draft drawn in a set thereby becomes liable to any holder in due course of that part as if it were the whole set, but as between different holders in due course to whom different parts have been negotiated the holder whose title first accrues has all rights to the draft and its proceeds.

(3) As against the drawee the first presented part of a draft drawn in a set is the part entitled to payment, or if a time draft to acceptance and payment. Acceptance of any subsequently presented part renders the drawee liable thereon under subsection (2). With respect both to a holder and to the drawer payment of a subsequently presented part of a draft payable

at sight has the same effect as payment of a check notwithstanding an effective stop order (Section 4–407).

(4) Except as otherwise provided in this section, where any part of a draft in a set is discharged by payment or otherwise the whole draft is discharged.

§ 3–802. Effect of Instrument on Obligation for Which It Is Given.

(1) Unless otherwise agreed where an instrument is taken for an underlying obligation

    (a) the obligation is pro tanto discharged if a bank is drawer, maker or acceptor of the instrument and there is no recourse on the instrument against the underlying obligor; and

    (b) in any other case the obligation is suspended pro tanto until the instrument is due or if it is payable on demand until its presentment. If the instrument is dishonored action may be maintained on either the instrument or the obligation; discharge of the underlying obligor on the instrument also discharges him on the obligation.

(2) The taking in good faith of a check which is not postdated does not of itself so extend the time on the original obligation as to discharge a surety.

§ 3–803. Notice to Third Party.

Where a defendant is sued for breach of an obligation for which a third person is answerable over under this Article he may give the third person written notice of the litigation, and the person notified may then give similar notice to any other person who is answerable over to him under this Article. If the notice states that the person notified may come in and defend and that if the person notified does not do so he will in any action against him by the person giving the notice be bound by any determination of fact common to the two litigations, then unless after seasonable receipt of the notice the person notified does come in and defend he is so bound.

§ 3–804. Lost, Destroyed or Stolen Instruments.

The owner of an instrument which is lost, whether by destruction, theft or otherwise, may maintain an action in his own name and recover from any party liable thereon upon due proof of his ownership, the facts which prevent his production of the instrument and its terms. The court may require security indemnifying the defendant against loss by reason of further claims on the instrument.

§ 3–805. Instruments Not Payable to Order or to Bearer.

This Article applies to any instrument whose terms do not preclude transfer and which is otherwise negotiable within this Article but which is not payable to order or to bearer, except that there can be no holder in due course of such an instrument.

ARTICLE 4. Bank Deposits and Collections

PART 1
GENERAL PROVISIONS AND DEFINITIONS

§ 4–101. Short Title.

This Article shall be known and may be cited as Uniform Commercial Code—Bank Deposits and Collections.

§ 4–102. Applicability.

(1) To the extent that items within this Article are also within the scope of Articles 3 and 8, they are subject to the provisions of those Articles. In the event of conflict the provisions of this Article govern those of Article 3 but the provisions of Article 8 govern those of this Article.

(2) The liability of a bank for action or non-action with respect to any item handled by it

for purposes of presentment, payment or collection is governed by the law of the place where the bank is located. In the case of action or non-action by or at a branch or separate office of a bank, its liability is governed by the law of the place where the branch or separate office is located.

§ 4–103. Variation by Agreement; Measure of Damages; Certain Action Constituting Ordinary Care.

(1) The effect of the provisions of this Article may be varied by agreement except that no agreement can disclaim a bank's responsibility for its own lack of good faith or failure to exercise ordinary care or can limit the measure of damages for such lack or failure; but the parties may by agreement determine the standards by which such responsibility is to be measured if such standards are not manifestly unreasonable.

(2) Federal Reserve regulations and operating letters, clearing house rules, and the like, have the effect of agreements under subsection (1), whether or not specifically assented to by all parties interested in items handled.

(3) Action or non-action approved by this Article or pursuant to Federal Reserve regulations or operating letters constitutes the exercise of ordinary care and, in the absence of special instructions, action or non-action consistent with clearing house rules and the like or with a general banking usage not disapproved by this Article, prima facie constitutes the exercise of ordinary care.

(4) The specification or approval of certain procedures by this Article does not constitute disapproval of other procedures which may be reasonable under the circumstances.

(5) The measure of damages for failure to exercise ordinary care in handling an item is the amount of the item reduced by an amount which could not have been realized by the use of ordinary care, and where there is bad faith it includes other damages, if any, suffered by the party as a proximate consequence.

§ 4–104. Definitions and Index of Definitions.

(1) In this Article unless the context otherwise requires
    (a) "Account" means any account with a bank and includes a checking, time, interest or savings account;
    (b) "Afternoon" means the period of a day between noon and midnight;
    (c) "Banking day" means that part of any day on which a bank is open to the public for carrying on substantially all of its banking functions;
    (d) "Clearing house" means any association of banks or other payors regularly clearing items;
    (e) "Customer" means any person having an account with a bank or for whom a bank has agreed to collect items and includes a bank carrying an account with another bank;
    (f) "Documentary draft" means any negotiable or nonnegotiable draft with accompanying documents, securities or other papers to be delivered against honor of the draft;
    (g) "Item" means any instrument for the payment of money even though it is not negotiable but does not include money;
    (h) "Midnight deadline" with respect to a bank is midnight on its next banking day following the banking day on which it receives the relevant item or notice or from which the time for taking action commences to run, whichever is later;
    (i) "Properly payable" includes the availability of funds for payment at the time of decision to pay or dishonor;
    (j) "Settle" means to pay in cash, by clearing house settlement, in a charge or credit or by remittance, or otherwise as instructed. A settlement may be either provisional or final;
    (k) "Suspends payments" with respect to a bank means that it has been closed by order of the supervisory authorities, that a public officer has been appointed to take it over or that it ceases or refuses to make payments in the ordinary course of business.
(2) Other definitions apply to this Article and the sections in which they appear are:

"Collecting bank"	Section 4–105
"Depository bank"	Section 4–105
"Intermediary bank"	Section 4–105
"Payor bank"	Section 4–105
"Presenting bank"	Section 4–105
"Remitting bank"	Section 4–105

(3) The following definitions in other Articles apply to this Article:

"Acceptance"	Section 3–410
"Certificate of deposit"	Section 3–104
"Certification"	Section 3–411
"Check"	Section 3–104
"Draft"	Section 3–104
"Holder in due course"	Section 3–302
"Notice of dishonor"	Section 3–508
"Presentment"	Section 3–504
"Protest"	Section 3–509
"Secondary party"	Section 3–102

(4) In addition Article 1 contains general definitions and principles of construction and interpretation applicable throughout this Article.

§ 4–105. "Depository Bank"; "Intermediary Bank"; "Collecting Bank"; "Payor Bank"; "Presenting Bank"; "Remitting Bank."

In this Article unless the context otherwise requires:

(a) "Depository bank" means the first bank to which an item is transferred for collection even though it is also the payor bank;

(b) "Payor bank" means a bank by which an item is payable as drawn or accepted;

(c) "Intermediary bank" means any bank to which an item is transferred in course of collection except the depository or payor bank;

(d) "Collecting bank" means any bank handling the item for collection except the payor bank;

(e) "Presenting bank" means any bank presenting an item except a payor bank;

(f) "Remitting bank" means any payor or intermediary bank remitting for an item.

§ 4–106. Separate Office of a Bank.

A branch or separate office of a bank [maintaining its own deposit ledgers] is a separate bank for the purpose of computing the time within which and determining the place at or to which action may be taken or notices or orders shall be given under this Article and under Article 3.

Note: *The brackets are to make it optional with the several states whether to require a branch to maintain its own deposit ledgers in order to be considered to be a separate bank for certain purposes under Article 4. In some states "maintaining its own deposit ledgers" is a satisfactory test. In others branch banking practices are such that this test would not be suitable.*

§ 4–107. Time of Receipt of Items.

(1) For the purpose of allowing time to process items, prove balances and make the necessary entries on its books to determine its position for the day, a bank may fix an afternoon hour of two P.M. or later as a cut-off hour for the handling of money and items and the making of entries on its books.

(2) Any item or deposit of money received on any day after a cut-off hour so fixed or after the close of the banking day may be treated as being received at the opening of the next banking day.

§ 4–108. Delays.

(1) Unless otherwise instructed, a collecting bank in a good faith effort to secure payment may, in the case of specific items and with or without the approval of any person involved,

waive, modify or extend time limits imposed or permitted by this Act for a period not in excess of an additional banking day without discharge of secondary parties and without liability to its transferor or any prior party.

(2) Delay by a collecting bank or payor bank beyond time limits prescribed or permitted by this Act or by instructions is excused if caused by interruption of communication facilities, suspension of payments by another bank, war, emergency conditions or other circumstances beyond the control of the bank provided it exercises such diligence as the circumstances require.

§ 4–109. Process of Posting.

The "process of posting" means the usual procedure followed by a payor bank in determining to pay an item and in recording the payment including one or more of the following or other steps as determined by the bank:

    (a) verification of any signature;

    (b) ascertaining that sufficient funds are available;

    (c) affixing a "paid" or other stamp;

    (d) entering a charge or entry to a customer's account;

    (e) correcting or reversing an entry or erroneous action with respect to the item.

PART 2
COLLECTION OF ITEMS: DEPOSITORY AND COLLECTING BANKS

§ 4–201. Presumption and Duration of Agency Status of Collecting Banks and Provisional Status of Credits; Applicability of Article; Item Indorsed "Pay Any Bank."

(1) Unless a contrary intent clearly appears and prior to the time that a settlement given by a collecting bank for an item is or becomes final (subsection (3) of Section 4–211 and Section 4–212 and 4–213) the bank is an agent or sub-agent of the owner of the item and any settlement given for the item is provisional. This provision applies regardless of the form of indorsement or lack of indorsement and even though credit given for the item is subject to immediate withdrawal as of right or is in fact withdrawn; but the continuance of ownership of an item by its owner and any rights of the owner to proceeds of the item are subject to rights of a collecting bank such as those resulting from outstanding advances on the item and valid rights of setoff. When an item is handled by banks for purposes of presentment, payment and collection, the relevant provisions of this Article apply even though action of parties clearly establishes that a particular bank has purchased the item and is the owner of it.

(2) After an item has been indorsed with the words "pay any bank" or the like, only a bank may acquire the rights of a holder

    (a) until the item has been returned to the customer initiating collection; or

    (b) until the item has been specially indorsed by a bank to a person who is not a bank.

§ 4–202. Responsibility for Collection; When Action Seasonable.

(1) A collecting bank must use ordinary care in

    (a) presenting an item or sending it for presentment; and

    (b) sending notice of dishonor or non-payment or returning an item other than a documentary draft to the bank's transferor [or directly to the depositary bank under subsection (2) of Section 4–212] *(see note to Section 4–212)* after learning that the item has not been paid or accepted as the case may be; and

    (c) settling for an item when the bank receives final settlement; and

    (d) making or providing for any necessary protest; and

    (e) notifying its transferor of any loss or delay in transit within a reasonable time after discovery thereof.

(2) A collecting bank taking proper action before its midnight deadline following receipt of an item, notice or payment acts seasonably; taking proper action within a reasonably longer time may be seasonable but the bank has the burden of so establishing.

(3) Subject to subsection (1) (a), a bank is not liable for the insolvency, neglect, misconduct, mistake or default of another bank or person or for loss or destruction of an item in transit or in the possession of others.

§ 4–203. Effect of Instructions.

Subject to the provisions of Article 3 concerning conversion of instruments (Section 3–419) and the provisions of both Article 3 and this Article concerning restrictive indorsements only a collecting bank's transferor can give instructions which affect the bank or constitute notice to it and a collecting bank is not liable to prior parties for any action taken pursuant to such instructions or in accordance with any agreement with its transferor.

§ 4–204. Methods of Sending and Presenting; Sending Direct to Payor Bank.

(1) A collecting bank must send items by reasonably prompt method taking into consideration any relevant instructions, the nature of the item, the number of such items on hand, and the cost of collection involved and the method generally used by it or others to present such items.

(2) A collecting bank may send
   (a) any item direct to the payor bank;
   (b) any item to any non-bank payor if authorized by its transferor; and
   (c) any item other than documentary drafts to any non-bank payor, if authorized by Federal Reserve regulation or operating letter, clearing house rule or the like.

(3) Presentment may be made by a presenting bank at a place where the payor bank has requested that presentment be made.

§ 4–205. Supplying Missing Indorsement; No Notice from Prior Indorsement.

(1) A depositary bank which has taken an item for collection may supply any indorsement of the customer which is necessary to title unless the item contains the words "payee's indorsement required" or the like. In the absence of such a requirement a statement placed on the item by the depositary bank to the effect that the item was deposited by a customer or credited to his account is effective as the customer's indorsement.

(2) An intermediary bank, or payor bank which is not a depositary bank, is neither given notice nor otherwise affected by a restrictive indorsement of any person except the bank's immediate transferor.

§ 4–206. Transfer Between Banks.

Any agreed method which identifies the transferor bank is sufficient for the item's further transfer to another bank.

§ 4–207. Warranties of Customer and Collecting Bank on Transfer or Presentment of Items; Time for Claims.

(1) Each customer or collecting bank who obtains payment or acceptance of an item and each prior customer and collecting bank warrants to the payor bank or other payor who in good faith pays or accepts the item that
   (a) he has a good title to the item or is authorized to obtain payment or acceptance on behalf of one who has a good title; and
   (b) he has no knowledge that the signature of the maker or drawer is unauthorized, except that this warranty is not given by any customer or collecting bank that is a holder in due course and acts in good faith
      (i) to a maker with respect to the maker's own signature; or
      (ii) to a drawer with respect to the drawer's own signature, whether or not the drawer is also the drawee; or
      (iii) to an acceptor of an item if the holder in due course took the item after the acceptance or obtained the acceptance without knowledge that the drawer's signature was unauthorized; and
   (c) the item has not been materially altered, except that this warranty is not given by any customer or collecting bank that is a holder in due course and acts in good faith
      (i) to the maker of a note; or
      (ii) to the drawer of a draft whether or not the drawer is also the drawee; or

(iii) to the acceptor of an item with respect to an alteration made prior to the acceptance if the holder in due course took the item after the acceptance, even though the acceptance provided "payable as originally drawn" or equivalent terms; or

(iv) to the acceptor of an item with respect to an alteration made after the acceptance.

(2) Each customer and collecting bank who transfers an item and receives a settlement or other consideration for it warrants to his transferee and to any subsequent collecting bank who takes the item in good faith that

(a) he has a good title to the item or is authorized to obtain payment or acceptance on behalf of one who has a good title and the transfer is otherwise rightful; and

(b) all signatures are genuine or authorized; and

(c) the item has not been materially altered; and

(d) no defense of any party is good against him; and

(e) he has no knowledge of any insolvency proceeding instituted with respect to the maker or acceptor or the drawer of an unaccepted item.

In addition each customer and collecting bank so transferring an item and receiving a settlement or other consideration engages that upon dishonor and any necessary notice of dishonor and protest he will take up the item.

(3) The warranties and the engagement to honor set forth in the two preceding subsections arise notwithstanding the absence of indorsement or words of guaranty or warranty in the transfer or presentment and a collecting bank remains liable for their breach despite remittance to its transferor. Damages for breach of such warranties or engagement to honor shall not exceed the consideration received by the customer or collecting bank responsible plus finance charges and expenses related to the item, if any.

(4) Unless a claim for breach of warranty under this section is made within a reasonable time after the person claiming learns of the breach, the person liable is discharged to the extent of any loss caused by the delay in making claim.

§ 4–208. Security Interest of Collecting Bank in Items, Accompanying Documents and Proceeds.

(1) A bank has a security interest in an item and any accompanying documents or the proceeds of either

(a) in case of an item deposited in an account to the extent to which credit given for the item has been withdrawn or applied;

(b) in case of an item for which it has given credit available for withdrawal as of right, to the extent of the credit given whether or not the credit is drawn upon and whether or not there is a right of charge-back; or

(c) if it makes an advance on or against the item.

(2) When credit which has been given for several items received at one time or pursuant to a single agreement is withdrawn or applied in part the security interest remains upon all the items, any accompanying documents or the proceeds of either. For the purpose of this section, credits first given are first withdrawn.

(3) Receipt by a collecting bank of a final settlement for an item is a realization on its security interest in the item, accompanying documents and proceeds. To the extent and so long as the bank does not receive final settlement for the item or give up possession of the item or accompanying documents for purposes other than collection, the security interest continues and is subject to the provisions of Article 9 except that

(a) no security agreement is necessary to make the security interest enforceable (subsection (1) (b) of Section 9–203); and

(b) no filing is required to perfect the security interest; and

(c) the security interest has priority over conflicting perfected security interests in the item, accompanying documents or proceeds.

§ 4–209. When Bank Gives Value for Purposes of Holder in Due Course.

For purposes of determining its status as a holder in due course, the bank has given value to the extent that it has a security interest in an item provided that the bank otherwise complies with the requirements of Section 3–302 on what constitutes a holder in due course.

§ 4–210. Presentment by Notice of Item Not Payable by, Through or at a Bank; Liability of Secondary Parties.

(1) Unless otherwise instructed, a collecting bank may present an item not payable by, through or at a bank by sending to the party to accept or pay a written notice that the bank holds the item for acceptance or payment. The notice must be sent in time to be received on or before the day when presentment is due and the bank must meet any requirement of the party to accept or pay under Section 3–505 by the close of the bank's next banking day after it knows of the requirement.

(2) Where presentment is made by notice and neither honor nor request for compliance with a requirement under Section 3–505 is received by the close of business on the day after maturity or in the case of demand items by the close of business on the third banking day after notice was sent, the presenting bank may treat the item as dishonored and charge any secondary party by sending him notice of the facts.

§ 4–211. Media of Remittance; Provisional and Final Settlement in Remittance Cases.

(1) A collecting bank may take in settlement of an item

    (a) a check of the remitting bank or of another bank on any bank except the remitting bank; or

    (b) a cashier's check or similar primary obligation of a remitting bank which is a member of or clears through a member of the same clearing house or group as the collecting bank; or

    (c) appropriate authority to charge an account of the remitting bank or of another bank with the collecting bank; or

    (d) if the item is drawn upon or payable by a person other than a bank, a cashier's check, certified check or other bank check or obligation.

(2) If before its midnight deadline the collecting bank properly dishonors a remittance check or authorization to charge on itself or presents or forwards for collection a remittance instrument of or on another bank which is of a kind approved by subsection (1) or has not been authorized by it, the collecting bank is not liable to prior parties in the event of the dishonor of such check, instrument or authorization.

(3) A settlement for an item by means of a remittance instrument or authorization to charge is or becomes a final settlement as to both the person making and the person receiving the settlement

    (a) if the remittance instrument or authorization to charge is of a kind approved by subsection (1) or has not been authorized by the person receiving the settlement and in either case the person receiving the settlement acts seasonably before its midnight deadline in presenting, forwarding for collection or paying the instrument or authorization,—at the time the remittance instrument or authorization is finally paid by the payor by which it is payable;

    (b) if the person receiving the settlement has authorized remittance by a non-bank check or obligation or by a cashier's check or similar primary obligation of or a check upon the payor or other remitting bank which is not of a kind approved by subsection (1) (b),—at the time of the receipt of such remittance check or obligation; or

    (c) if in a case not covered by sub-paragraphs (a) or (b) the person receiving the settlement fails to seasonably present, forward for collection, pay or return a remittance instrument or authorization to it to charge before its midnight deadline,—at such midnight deadline.

§ 4–212. Right of Charge-Back or Refund.

(1) If a collecting bank has made provisional settlement with its customer for an item and itself fails by reason of dishonor, suspension of payments by a bank or otherwise to receive a settlement for the item which is or becomes final, the bank may revoke the settlement given by it, charge back the amount of any credit given for the item to its customer's account

or obtain refund from its customer whether or not it is able to return the items if by its midnight deadline or within a longer reasonable time after it learns the facts it returns the item or sends notification of the facts. These rights to revoke, charge-back and obtain refund terminate if and when a settlement for the item received by the bank is or becomes final (subsection (3) of Section 4-211 and subsections (2) and (3) of Section 4-213).

[(2) Within the time and manner prescribed by this section and Section 4-301, an intermediary or payor bank, as the case may be, may return an unpaid item directly to the despositary bank and may send for collection a draft on the depositary bank and obtain reimbursement. In such case, if the depositary bank has received provisional settlement for the item, it must reimburse the bank drawing the draft and any provisional credits for the item between banks shall become and remain final.]

Note: *Direct returns is recognized as an innovation that is not yet established bank practice, and therefore, Paragraph 2 has been bracketed. Some lawyers have doubts whether it should be included in legislation or left to development by agreement.*

(3) A depositary bank which is also the payor may charge-back the amount of an item to its customer's account or obtain refund in accordance with the section governing return of an item received by a payor bank for credit on its books (Section 4-301).

(4) The right to charge-back is not affected by

    (a) prior use of the credit given for the item; or

    (b) failure by any bank to exercise ordinary care with respect to the item but any bank so failing remains liable.

(5) A failure to charge-back or claim refund does not affect other rights of the bank against the customer or any other party.

(6) If credit is given in dollars as the equivalent of the value of an item payable in a foreign currency the dollar amount of any charge-back or refund shall be calculated on the basis of the buying sight rate for the foreign currency prevailing on the day when the person entitled to the charge-back or refund learns that it will not receive payment in ordinary course.

§ 4-213. Final Payment of Item by Payor Bank; When Provisional Debits and Credits Become Final; When Certain Credits Become Available for Withdrawal.

(1) An item is finally paid by a payor bank when the bank has done any of the following, whichever happens first:

    (a) paid the item in cash; or

    (b) settled for the item without reserving a right to revoke the settlement and without having such right under statute, clearing house rule or agreement; or

    (c) completed the process of posting the item to the indicated account of the drawer, maker or other person to be charged therewith; or

    (d) made a provisional settlement for the item and failed to revoke the settlement in the time and manner permitted by statute, clearing house rule or agreement.

Upon a final payment under subparagraphs (b), (c) or (d) the payor bank shall be accountable for the amount of the item.

(2) If provisional settlement for an item between the presenting and payor banks is made through a clearing house or by debits or credits in an account between them, then to the extent that provisional debits or credits for the item are entered in accounts between the presenting and payor banks or between the presenting and successive prior collecting banks seriatim, they become final upon final payment of the item by the payor bank.

(3) If a collecting bank receives a settlement for an item which is or becomes final (subsection (3) of Section 4-211, subsection (2) of Section 4-213) the bank is accountable to its customer for the amount of the item and any provisional credit given for the item in an account with its customer becomes final.

(4) Subject to any right of the bank to apply the credit to an obligation of the customer, credit given by a bank for an item in an account with its customer becomes available for withdrawal as of right

(a) in any case where the bank has received a provisional settlement for the item,—when such settlement becomes final and the bank has had a reasonable time to learn that the settlement is final;

(b) in any case where the bank is both a depositary bank and a payor bank and the item is finally paid,—at the opening of the bank's second banking day following receipt of the item.

(5) A deposit of money in a bank is final when made but, subject to any right of the bank to apply the deposit to an obligation of the customer, the deposit becomes available for withdrawal as of right at the opening of the bank's next banking day following receipt of the deposit.

§ 4–214. Insolvency and Preference.

(1) Any item in or coming into the possession of a payor or collecting bank which suspends payment and which item is not finally paid shall be returned by the receiver, trustee or agent in charge of the closed bank to the presenting bank or the closed bank's customer.

(2) If a payor bank finally pays an item and suspends payments without making a settlement for the item with its customer or the presenting bank which settlement is or becomes final, the owner of the item has a preferred claim against the payor bank.

(3) If a payor bank gives or a collecting bank gives or receives a provisional settlement for an item and thereafter suspends payments, the suspension does not prevent or interfere with the settlement becoming final if such finality occurs automatically upon the lapse of certain time or the happening of certain events (subsection (3) of Section 4–211, subsections (1) (d), (2) and (3) of Section 4–213).

(4) If a collecting bank receives from subsequent parties settlement for an item which settlement is or becomes final and suspends payments without making a settlement for the item with its customer which is or becomes final, the owner of the item has a preferred claim against such collecting bank.

PART 3
COLLECTION OF ITEMS: PAYOR BANKS

§ 4–301. Deferred Posting; Recovery of Payment by Return of Items; Time of Dishonor.

(1) Where an authorized settlement for a demand item (other than a documentary draft) received by a payor bank otherwise than for immediate payment over the counter has been made before midnight of the banking day of receipt the payor bank may revoke the settlement and recover any payment if before it has made final payment (subsection (1) of Section 4–213) and before its midnight deadline it

(a) returns the item; or

(b) sends written notice of dishonor or nonpayment if the item is held for protest or is otherwise unavailable for return.

(2) If a demand item is received by a payor bank for credit on its books it may return such item or send notice of dishonor and may revoke any credit given or recover the amount thereof withdrawn by its customer, if it acts within the time limit and in the manner specified in the preceding subsection.

(3) Unless previous notice of dishonor has been sent an item is dishonored at the time when for purposes of dishonor it is returned or notice sent in accordance with this section.

(4) An item is returned:

(a) as to an item received through a clearing house, when it is delivered to the presenting or last collecting bank or to the clearing house or is sent or delivered in accordance with its rules; or

(b) in all other cases, when it is sent or delivered to the bank's customer or transferor or pursuant to his instructions.

§ 4–302. Payor Bank's Responsibility for Late Return of Item.

In the absence of a valid defense such as breach of a presentment warranty (subsection (1) of Section 4–207), settlement effected or the like, if an item is presented on and received by a payor bank the bank is accountable for the amount of

(a) a demand item other than a documentary draft whether properly payable or not if the bank, in any case where it is not also the depositary bank, retains the item beyond midnight of the banking day of receipt without settling for it or, regardless of whether it is also the depositary bank, does not pay or return the item or send notice of dishonor until after its midnight deadline; or

(b) any other properly payable item unless within the time allowed for acceptance or payment of that item the bank either accepts or pays the item or returns it and accompanying documents.

§ 4–303. When Items Subject to Notice, Stop-Order, Legal Process or Setoff; Order in Which Items May Be Charged or Certified.

(1) Any knowledge, notice or stop-order received by, legal process served upon or setoff exercised by a payor bank, whether or not effective under other rules of law to terminate, suspend or modify the bank's right or duty to pay an item or to charge its customer's account for the item, comes too late to so terminate, suspend or modify such right or duty if the knowledge, notice, stop-order or legal process is received or served and a reasonable time for the bank to act thereon expires or the setoff is exercised after the bank has done any of the following:

(a) accepted or certified the item;

(b) paid the item in cash;

(c) settled for the item without reserving a right to revoke the settlement and without having such right under statute, clearing house rule or agreement;

(d) completed the process of posting the item to the indicated account of the drawer, maker or other person to be charged therewith or otherwise has evidenced by examination of such indicated account and by action its decision to pay the item; or

(e) become accountable for the amount of the item under subsection (1) (d) of Section 4–213 and Section 4–302 dealing with the payor bank's responsibility for late return of items.

(2) Subject to the provisions of subsection (1) items may be accepted, paid, certified or charged to the indicated account of its customer in any order convenient to the bank.

PART 4
RELATIONSHIP BETWEEN PAYOR BANK AND ITS CUSTOMER

§ 4–401. When Bank May Charge Customer's Account.

(1) As against its customer, a bank may charge against his account any item which is otherwise properly payable from that account even though the charge creates an overdraft.

(2) A bank which in good faith makes payment to a holder may charge the indicated account of its customer according to

(a) the original tenor of his altered item; or

(b) the tenor of his completed item, even though the bank knows the item has been completed unless the bank has notice that the completion was improper.

§ 4–402. Bank's Liability to Customer for Wrongful Dishonor.

A payor bank is liable to its customer for damages proximately caused by the wrongful dishonor of an item. When the dishonor occurs through mistake liability is limited to actual damages proved. If so proximately caused and proved damages may include damages for an arrest or prosecution of the customer or other consequential damages. Whether any consequential damages are proximately caused by the wrongful dishonor is a question of fact to be determined in each case.

§ 4–403. Customer's Right to Stop Payment; Burden of Proof of Loss.

(1) A customer may by order to his bank stop payment of any item payable for his account but the order must be received at such time and in such manner as to afford the bank a reason-

able opportunity to act on it prior to any action by the bank with respect to the item described in Section 4–303.

(2) An oral order is binding upon the bank only for fourteen calendar days unless confirmed in writing within that period. A written order is effective for only six months unless renewed in writing.

(3) The burden of establishing the fact and amount of loss resulting from the payment of an item contrary to a binding stop payment order is on the customer.

§ 4–404. Bank Not Obligated to Pay Check More Than Six Months Old.

A bank is under no obligation to a customer having a checking account to pay a check, other than a certified check, which is presented more than six months after its date, but it may charge its customer's account for a payment made thereafter in good faith.

§ 4–405. Death or Incompetence of Customer.

(1) A payor or collecting bank's authority to accept, pay or collect an item or to account for proceeds of its collection if otherwise effective is not rendered ineffective by incompetence of a customer of either bank existing at the time the item is issued or its collection is undertaken if the bank does not know of an adjudication of incompetence. Neither death nor incompetence of a customer revokes such authority to accept, pay, collect or account until the bank knows of the fact of death or of an adjudication of incompetence and has reasonable opportunity to act on it.

(2) Even with knowledge a bank may for ten days after the date of death pay or certify checks drawn on or prior to that date unless ordered to stop payment by a person claiming an interest in the account.

§ 4–406. Customer's Duty to Discover and Report Unauthorized Signature or Alteration.

(1) When a bank sends to its customer a statement of account accompanied by items paid in good faith in support of the debit entries or holds the statement and items pursuant to a request or instructions of its customer or otherwise in a reasonable manner makes the statement and items available to the customer, the customer must exercise reasonable care and promptness to examine the statement and items to discover his unauthorized signature or any alteration on an item and must notify the bank promptly after discovery thereof.

(2) If the bank establishes that the customer failed with respect to an item to comply with the duties imposed on the customer by subsection (1) the customer is precluded from asserting against the bank

> (a) his unauthorized signature or any alteration on the item if the bank also establishes that it suffered a loss by reason of such failure; and
>
> (b) an authorized signature or alteration by the same wrongdoer on any other item paid in good faith by the bank after the first item and statement was available to the customer for a reasonable period not exceeding fourteen calendar days and before the bank receives notification from the customer of any such unauthorized signature or alteration.

(3) The preclusion under subsection (2) does not apply if the customer establishes lack of ordinary care on the part of the bank in paying the item(s).

(4) Without regard to care or lack of care of either the customer or the bank a customer who does not within one year from the time the statement and items are made available to the customer (subsection (1)) discover and report his unauthorized signature or any alteration on the face or back of the item or does not within three years from that time discover and report any unauthorized indorsement is precluded from asserting against the bank such unauthorized signature or indorsement or such alteration.

(5) If under this section a payor bank has a valid defense against a claim of a customer upon or resulting from payment of an item and waives or fails upon request to assert the defense the bank may not assert against any collecting bank or other prior party presenting or transferring the item a claim based upon the unauthorized signature or alteration giving rise to the customer's claim.

§ 4–407. Payor Bank's Right to Subrogation on Improper Payment.

If a payor bank has paid an item over the stop payment order of the drawer or maker or otherwise under circumstances giving a basis for objection by the drawer or maker, to prevent unjust enrichment and only to the extent necessary to prevent loss to the bank by reason of its payment of the item, the payor bank shall be subrogated to the rights

    (a) of any holder in due course on the item against the drawer or maker; and

    (b) of the payee or any other holder of the item against the drawer or maker either on the item or under the transaction out of which the item arose; and

    (c) of the drawer or maker against the payee or any other holder of the item with respect to the transaction out of which the item arose.

PART 5
COLLECTION OF DOCUMENTARY DRAFTS

§ 4–501. Handling of Documentary Drafts; Duty to Send for Presentment and to Notify Customer of Dishonor.

A bank which takes a documentary draft for collection must present or send the draft and accompanying documents for presentment and upon learning that the draft has not been paid or accepted in due course must seasonably notify its customer of such fact even though it may have discounted or bought the draft or extended credit available for withdrawal as of right.

§ 4–502. Presentment of "On Arrival" Drafts.

When a draft or the relevant instructions require presentment "on arrival," "when goods arrive" or the like, the collecting bank need not present until in its judgment a reasonable time for arrival of the goods has expired. Refusal to pay or accept because the goods have not arrived is not dishonor; the bank must notify its transferor of such refusal but need not present the draft again until it is instructed to do so or learns of the arrival of the goods.

§ 4–503. Responsibility of Presenting Bank for Documents and Goods; Report of Reasons for Dishonor; Referee in Case of Need.

Unless otherwise instructed and except as provided in Article 5 a bank presenting a documentary draft

    (a) must deliver the documents to the drawee on acceptance of the draft if it is payable more than three days after presentment; otherwise, only on payment; and

    (b) upon dishonor, either in the case of presentment for acceptance or presentment for payment, may seek and follow instructions from any referee in case of need designated in the draft or if the presenting bank does not choose to utilize his services it must use diligence and good faith to ascertain the reason for dishonor, must notify its transferor of the dishonor and of the results of its effort to ascertain the reasons therefor and must request instructions.

But the presenting bank is under no obligation with respect to goods represented by the documents except to follow any reasonable instructions seasonably received; it has a right to reimbursement for any expense incurred in following instructions and to prepayment of or indemnity for such expenses.

§ 4–504. Privilege of Presenting Bank to Deal With Goods; Security Interest for Expenses.

(1) A presenting bank which, following the dishonor of a documentary draft, has seasonably requested instructions but does not receive them within a reasonable time may store, sell, or otherwise deal with the goods in any reasonable manner.

(2) For its reasonable expenses incurred by action under subsection (1) the presenting bank has a lien upon the goods or their proceeds, which may be foreclosed in the same manner as an unpaid seller's lien.

ARTICLE 5. Letters of Credit

(omitted)

ARTICLE 6. Bulk Transfers

§ 6–101. Short Title.

This Article shall be known and may be cited as Uniform Commercial Code—Bulk Transfers.

§ 6–102. "Bulk Transfer"; Transfers of Equipment; Enterprises Subject to This Article; Bulk Transfers Subject to This Article.

(1) A "bulk transfer" is any transfer in bulk and not in the ordinary course of the transferor's business of a major part of the materials, supplies, merchandise or other inventory (Section 9–109) of an enterprise subject to this Article.

(2) A transfer of a substantial part of the equipment (Section 9–109) of such an enterprise is a bulk transfer if it is made in connection with a bulk transfer of inventory, but not otherwise.

(3) The enterprises subject to this Article are all those whose principal business is the sale of merchandise from stock, including those who manufacture what they sell.

(4) Except as limited by the following section all bulk transfers of goods located within this state are subject to this Article.

§ 6–103. Transfers Excepted From This Article.

The following transfers are not subject to this Article:

(1) Those made to give security for the performance of an obligation;

(2) General assignments for the benefit of all the creditors of the transferor, and subsequent transfers by the assignee thereunder;

(3) Transfers in settlement or realization of a lien or other security interest;

(4) Sales by executors, administrators, receivers, trustees in bankruptcy, or any public officer under judicial process;

(5) Sales made in the course of judicial or administrative proceedings for the dissolution or reorganization of a corporation and of which notice is sent to the creditors of the corporation pursuant to order of the court or administrative agency;

(6) Transfers to a person maintaining a known place of business in this State who becomes

bound to pay the debts of the transferor in full and gives public notice of that fact, and who is solvent after becoming so bound;

(7) A transfer to a new business enterprise organized to take over and continue the business, if public notice of the transaction is given and the new enterprise assumes the debts of the transferor and he receives nothing from the transaction except an interest in the new enterprise junior to the claims of creditors;

(8) Transfers of property which is exempt from execution.

Public notice under subsection (6) or subsection (7) may be given by publishing once a week for two consecutive weeks in a newspaper of general circulation where the transferor had its principal place of business in this state an advertisement including the names and addresses of the transferor and transferee and the effective date of the transfer.

§ 6–104. Schedule of Property, List of Creditors.

(1) Except as provided with respect to auction sales (Section 6–108), a bulk transfer subject to this Article is ineffective against any creditor of the transferor unless:

(a) The transferee requires the transferor to furnish a list of his existing creditors prepared as stated in this section; and

(b) The parties prepare a schedule of the property transferred sufficient to identify it; and

(c) The transferee preserves the list and schedule for six months next following the transfer and permits inspection of either or both and copying therefrom at all reasonable hours by any creditor of the transferor, or files the list and schedule in (*a public office to be here identified*).

(2) The list of creditors must be signed and sworn to or affirmed by the transferor or his agent. It must contain the names and business addresses of all creditors of the transferor, with the amounts when known, and also the names of all persons who are known to the transferor to assert claims against him even though such claims are disputed. If the transferor is the obligor of an outstanding issue of bonds, debentures or the like as to which there is an indenture trustee, the list of creditors need include only the name and address of the indenture trustee and the aggregate outstanding principal amount of the issue.

(3) Responsibility for the completeness and accuracy of the list of creditors rests on the transferor, and the transfer is not rendered ineffective by errors or omissions therein unless the transferee is shown to have had knowledge.

§ 6–105. Notice to Creditors.

In addition to the requirements of the preceding section, any bulk transfer subject to this Article except one made by auction sale (Section 6–108) is ineffective against any creditor of the transferor unless at least ten days before he takes possession of the goods or pays for them, whichever happens first, the transferee gives notice of the transfer in the manner and to the persons hereafter provided (Section 6–107).

[§ 6–106. Application of the Proceeds.

In addition to the requirements of the two preceding sections:

(1) Upon every bulk transfer subject to this Article for which new consideration becomes payable except those made by sale at auction it is the duty of the transferee to assure that such consideration is applied so far as necessary to pay those debts of the transferor which are either shown on the list furnished by the transferor (Section 6–104) or filed in writing in the place stated in the notice (Section 6–107) within thirty days after the mailing of such notice. This duty of the transferee runs to all the holders of such debts, and may be enforced by any of them for the benefit of all.

(2) If any of said debts are in dispute the necessary sum may be withheld from distribution until the dispute is settled or adjudicated.

(3) If the consideration payable is not enough to pay all of the said debts in full distribution shall be made pro rata.]

Note: *This section is bracketed to indicate division of opinion as to whether or not it is a wise provision, and to suggest that this is a point on which State enactments may differ without serious damage to the principle of uniformity.*

In any State where this section is omitted, the following parts of sections, also bracketed in the text, should also be omitted, namely:

> Section 6–107(2) (e).
>> 6–108(3) (c)
>> 6–109(2).

In any State where this section is enacted, these other provisions should be also.

Optional Subsection (4)

[(4) The transferee may within ten days after he takes possession of the goods pay the consideration into the *(specify court)* in the county where the transferor had its principal place of business in this state and thereafter may discharge his duty under this section by giving notice by registered or certified mail to all the persons to whom the duty runs that the consideration has been paid into that court and that they should file their claims there. On motion of any interested party, the court may order the distribution of the consideration to the persons entitled to it.]

Note: *Optional subsection (4) is recommended for those states which do not have a general statute providing for payment of money into court.*

§ 6–107. The Notice.

(1) The notice to creditors (Section 6–105) shall state:

  (a) that a bulk transfer is about to be made; and
  (b) the names and business addresses of the transferor and transferee, and all other business names and addresses used by the transferor within three years last past so far as known to the transferee; and
  (c) whether or not all the debts of the transferor are to be paid in full as they fall due as a result of the transaction, and if so, the address to which creditors should send their bills.

(2) If the debts of the transferor are not to be paid in full as they fall due or if the transferee is in doubt on that point then the notice shall state further:

  (a) the location and general description of the property to be transferred and the estimated total of the transferor's debts;
  (b) the address where the schedule of property and list of creditors (Section 6–104) may be inspected;
  (c) whether the transfer is to pay existing debts and if so the amount of such debts and to whom owing;
  (d) whether the transfer is for new consideration and if so the amount of such consideration and the time and place of payment; [and]
  [(e) if for new consideration the time and place where creditors of the transferor are to file their claims.]

(3) The notice in any case shall be delivered personally or sent by registered or certified mail to all the persons shown on the list of creditors furnished by the transferor (Section 6–104) and to all other persons who are known to the transferee to hold or assert claims against the transferor.

§ 6–108. Auction Sales; "Auctioneer."

(1) A bulk transfer is subject to this Article even though it is by sale at auction, but only in the manner and with the results stated in this section.

(2) The transferor shall furnish a list of his creditors and assist in the preparation of a schedule of the property to be sold, both prepared as before stated (Section 6–104).

(3) The person or persons other than the transferor who direct, control or are responsible for the auction are collectively called the "auctioneer." The auctioneer shall:

(a) receive and retain the list of creditors and prepare and retain the schedule of property for the period stated in this Article (Section 6–104);

(b) give notice of the auction personally or by registered or certified mail at least ten days before it occurs to all persons shown on the list of creditors and to all other persons who are known to him to hold or assert claims against the transferor; [and]

[(c) assure that the net proceeds of the auction are applied as provided in this Article (Section 6–106).]

(4) Failure of the auctioneer to perform any of these duties does not affect the validity of the sale or the title of the purchasers, but if the auctioneer knows that the auction constitutes a bulk transfer such failure renders the auctioneer liable to the creditors of the transferor as a class for the sums owing to them from the transferor up to but not exceeding the net proceeds of the auction. If the auctioneer consists of several persons their liability is joint and several.

§ 6–109. What Creditors Protected; [Credit for Payment to Particular Creditors].

(1) The creditors of the transferor mentioned in this Article are those holding claims based on transactions or events occurring before the bulk transfer, but creditors who become such after notice to creditors is given (Sections 6–105 and 6–107) are not entitled to notice.

[(2) Against the aggregate obligation imposed by the provisions of this Article concerning the application of the proceeds (Section 6–106 and subsection (3) (c) of 6–108) the transferee or auctioneer is entitled to credit for sums paid to particular creditors of the transferor, not exceeding the sums believed in good faith at the time of the payment to be properly payable to such creditors.]

§ 6–110. Subsequent Transfers.

When the title of a transferee to property is subject to a defect by reason of his non-compliance with the requirements of this Article, then:

(1) a purchaser of any of such property from such transferee who pays no value or who takes with notice of such non-compliance takes subject to such defect, but

(2) a purchaser for value in good faith and without such notice takes free of such defect.

§ 6–111. Limitation of Actions and Levies.

No action under this Article shall be brought nor levy made more than six months after the date on which the transferee took possession of the goods unless the transfer has been concealed. If the transfer has been concealed, actions may be brought or levies made within six months after its discovery.

Note to Article 6: *Section 6–106 is bracketed to indicate division of opinion as to whether or not it is a wise provision, and to suggest that this is a point on which State enactments may differ without serious damage to the principle of uniformity.*

In any State where Section 6–106 is not enacted, the following parts of sections, also bracketed in the text, should also be omitted, namely:

Section 6–107(2) (e).

6–108(3) (c)

6–109(2).

In any State where Section 6–106 is enacted, these other provisions should be also.

ARTICLE 7. Warehouse Receipts, Bills of Lading and Other Documents of Title

PART 1
GENERAL

§ 7–101. Short Title.

This Article shall be known and may be cited as Uniform Code—Documents of Title.

§ 7–102. Definitions and Index of Definitions.

(1) In this Article, unless the context otherwise requires:

(a) "Bailee" means the person who by a warehouse receipt, bill of lading or other document of title acknowledges possession of goods and contracts to deliver them.

(b) "Consignee" means the person named in a bill to whom or to whose order the bill promises delivery.

(c) "Consignor" means the person named in a bill as the person from whom the goods have been received for shipment.

(d) "Delivery order" means a written order to deliver goods directed to a warehouseman, carrier or other person who in the ordinary course of business issues warehouse receipts or bills of lading.

(e) "Document" means document of title as defined in the general definitions in Article 1 (Section 1–201).

(f) "Goods" means all things which are treated as movable for the purposes of a contract of storage or transportation.

(g) "Issuer" means a bailee who issues a document except that in relation to an unaccepted delivery order it means the person who orders the possessor of goods to deliver. Issuer includes any person for whom an agent or employee purports to act in issuing a document if the agent or employee has real or apparent authority to issue documents, notwithstanding that the issuer received no goods or that the goods were misdescribed or that in any other respect the agent or employee violated his instructions.

(h) "Warehouseman" is a person engaged in the business of storing goods for hire.

(2) Other definitions applying to this Article or to specified Parts thereof, and the sections in which they appear are:

"Duly negotiate." Section 7–501.

"Person entitled under the document." Section 7–403(4).

(3) Definitions in other Articles applying to this Article and the sections in which they appear are:

"Contract for sale." Section 2–106.

"Overseas." Section 2–323.

"Receipt" of goods. Section 2–103.

(4) In addition Article 1 contains general definitions and principles of construction and interpretation applicable throughout this Article.

§ 7–103. Relation of Article to Treaty, Statute, Tariff, Classification or Regulation.

To the extent that any treaty or statute of the United States, regulatory statute of this State or tariff, classification or regulation filed or issued pursuant thereto is applicable, the provisions of this Article are subject thereto.

§ 7–104. Negotiable and Non-Negotiable Warehouse Receipt, Bill of Lading or Other Document of Title.

(1) A warehouse receipt, bill of lading or other document of title is negotiable

(a) if by its terms the goods are to be delivered to bearer or to the order of a named person; or

(b) where recognized in overseas trade, if it runs to a named person or assigns.

(2) Any other document is non-negotiable. A bill of lading in which it is stated that the goods are consigned to a named person is not made negotiable by a provision that the goods are to be delivered only against a written order signed by the same or another named person.

§ 7–105. Construction Against Negative Implication.

The omission from either Part 2 or Part 3 of this Article of a provision corresponding to a provision made in the other Part does not imply that a corresponding rule of law is not applicable.

PART 2
WAREHOUSE RECEIPTS: SPECIAL PROVISIONS

§ 7–201. Who May Issue a Warehouse Receipt; Storage Under Government Bond.

(1) A warehouse receipt may be issued by any warehouseman.

(2) Where goods including distilled spirits and agricultural commodities are stored under a statute requiring a bond against withdrawal or a license for the issuance of receipts in the nature of warehouse receipts, a receipt issued for the goods has like effect as a warehouse receipt even though issued by a person who is the owner of the goods and is not a warehouseman.

§ 7–202. Form of Warehouse Receipt; Essential Terms; Optional Terms.

(1) A warehouse receipt need not be in any particular form.

(2) Unless a warehouse receipt embodies within its written or printed terms each of the following, the warehouseman is liable for damages caused by the omission to a person injured thereby:

(a) the location of the warehouse where the goods are stored;

(b) the date of issue of the receipt;

(c) the consecutive number of the receipt;

(d) a statement whether the goods received will be delivered to the bearer, to a specified person, or to a specified person or his order;

(e) the rate of storage and handling charges, except that where goods are stored under a field warehousing arrangement a statement of that fact is sufficient on a non-negotiable receipt;

(f) a description of the goods or of the packages containing them;

(g) the signature of the warehouseman, which may be made by his authorized agent;

(h) if the receipt is issued for goods of which the warehouseman is owner, either solely or jointly or in common with others, the fact of such ownership; and

(i) a statement of the amount of advances made and of liabilities incurred for which the warehouseman claims a lien or security interest (Section 7–209). If the precise amount of such advances made or of such liabilities incurred is, at the time of the issue of the receipt, unknown to the warehouseman or to his agent who issues it, a statement of the fact that advances have been made or liabilities incurred and the purpose thereof is sufficient.

(3) A warehouseman may insert in his receipt any other terms which are not contrary to the provisions of this Act and do not impair his obligation of delivery (Section 7–403) or his duty of care (Section 7–204). Any contrary provisions shall be ineffective.

§ 7–203. Liability for Non-Receipt or Misdescription.

A party to or purchaser for value in good faith of a document of title other than a bill of lading relying in either case upon the description therein of the goods may recover from the issuer damages caused by the non-receipt or misdescription of the goods, except to the extent that the document conspicuously indicates that the issuer does not know whether any part or all of the goods in fact were received or conform to the description, as where the description is in terms of marks or labels or kind, quantity or condition, or the receipt or description is qualified by "contents, condition and quality unknown," "said to contain" or the like, if such indication be true, or the party or purchaser otherwise has notice.

§ 7–204. Duty of Care; Contractual Limitation of Warehouseman's Liability.

(1) A warehouseman is liable for damages for loss of or injury to the goods caused by his failure to exercise such care in regard to them as a reasonably careful man would exercise under like circumstances but unless otherwise agreed he is not liable for damages which could not have been avoided by the exercise of such care.

(2) Damages may be limited by a term in the warehouse receipt or storage agreement limiting the amount of liability in case of loss or damage, and setting forth a specific liability per

article or item, or value per unit of weight, beyond which the warehouseman shall not be liable; provided, however, that such liability may on written request of the bailor at the time of signing such storage agreement or within a reasonable time after receipt of the warehouse receipt be increased on part or all of the goods thereunder, in which event increased rates may be charged based on such increased valuation, but that no such increase shall be permitted contrary to a lawful limitation of liability contained in the warehouseman's tariff, if any. No such limitation is effective with respect to the warehouseman's liability for conversion to his own use.

(3) Reasonable provisions as to the time and manner of presenting claims and instituting actions based on the bailment may be included in the warehouse receipt or tariff.

(4) This section does not impair or repeal . . .

Note: *Insert in subsection (4) a reference to any statute which imposes a higher responsibility upon the warehouseman or invalidates contractual limitations which would be permissible under this Article.*

§ 7–205. Title Under Warehouse Receipt Defeated in Certain Cases.

A buyer in the ordinary course of business of fungible goods sold and delivered by a warehouseman who is also in the business of buying and selling such goods takes free of any claim under a warehouse receipt even though it has been duly negotiated.

§ 7–206. Termination of Storage at Warehouseman's Option.

(1) A warehouseman may on notifying the person on whose account the goods are held and any other person known to claim an interest in the goods require payment of any charges and removal of the goods from the warehouse at the termination of the period of storage fixed by the document, or, if no period is fixed, within a stated period not less than thirty days after the notification. If the goods are not removed before the date specified in the notification, the warehouseman may sell them in accordance with the provisions of the section on enforcement of a warehouseman's lien (Section 7–210).

(2) If a warehouseman in good faith believes that the goods are about to deteriorate or decline in value to less than the amount of his lien within the time prescribed in subsection (1) for notification, advertisement and sale, the warehouseman may specify in the notification any reasonable shorter time for removal of the goods and in case the goods are not removed, may sell them at public sale held not less than one week after a single advertisement or posting.

(3) If as a result of a quality or condition of the goods of which the warehouseman had no notice at the time of deposit the goods are a hazard to other property or to the warehouse or to persons, the warehouseman may sell the goods at public or private sale without advertisement on reasonable notification to all persons known to claim an interest in the goods. If the warehouseman after a reasonable effort is unable to sell the goods he may dispose of them in any lawful manner and shall incure no liability by reason of such disposition.

(4) The warehouseman must deliver the goods to any person entitled to them under this Article upon due demand made at any time prior to sale or other disposition under this section.

(5) The warehouseman may satisfy his lien from the proceeds of any sale or disposition under this section but must hold the balance for delivery on the demand of any person to whom he would have been bound to deliver the goods.

§ 7–207. Goods Must Be Kept Separate; Fungible Goods.

(1) Unless the warehouse receipt otherwise provides, a warehouseman must keep separate the goods covered by each receipt so as to permit at all times identification and delivery of those goods except that different lots of fungible goods may be commingled.

(2) Fungible goods so commingled are owned in common by the persons entitled thereto and the warehouseman is severally liable to each owner for that owner's share. Where because of overissue a mass of fungible goods is insufficient to meet all the receipts which the warehouseman has issued against it, the persons entitled include all holders to whom overissued receipts have been duly negotiated.

§ 7–208. Altered Warehouse Receipts.

Where a blank in a negotiable warehouse receipt has been filled in without authority, a purchaser for value and without notice of the want of authority may treat the insertion as authorized. Any other unauthorized alteration leaves any receipt enforceable against the issuer according to its original tenor.

§ 7–209. Lien of Warehouseman.

(1) A warehouseman has a lien against the bailor on the goods covered by a warehouse receipt or on the proceeds thereof in his possession for charges for storage or transportation (including demurrage and terminal charges), insurance, labor, or charges present or future in relation to the goods, and for expenses necessary for preservation of the goods or reasonably incurred in their sale pursuant to law. If the person on whose account the goods are held is liable for like charges or expenses in relation to other goods whenever deposited and it is stated in the receipt that a lien is claimed for charges and expenses in relation to other goods, the warehouseman also has a lien against him for such charges and expenses whether or not the other goods have been delivered by the warehouseman. But against a person to whom a negotiable warehouse receipt is duly negotiated a warehouseman's lien is limited to charges in an amount or at a rate specified on the receipt or if no charges are so specified then to a reasonable charge for storage of the goods covered by the receipt subsequent to the date of the receipt.

(2) The warehouseman may also reserve a security interest against the bailor for a maximum amount specified on the receipt for charges other than those specified in subsection (1), such as for money advanced and interest. Such a security interest is governed by the Article on Secured Transactions (Article 9).

(3) A warehouseman's lien for charges and expenses under subsection (1) or a security interest under subsection (2) is also effective against any person who so entrusted the bailor with possession of the goods that a pledge of them by him to a good faith purchaser for value would have been valid but is not effective against a person as to whom the document confers no right in the goods covered by it under Section 7–503.†

(4) A warehouseman loses his lien on any goods which he voluntarily delivers or which he unjustifiably refuses to deliver.

§ 7–210. Enforcement of Warehouseman's Lien.

(1) Except as provided in subsection (2), a warehouseman's lien may be enforced by public or private sale of the goods in bloc or in parcels, at any time or place and on any terms which are commercially reasonable, after notifying all persons known to claim an interest in the goods. Such notification must include a statement of the amount due, the nature of the proposed sale and the time and place of any public sale. The fact that a better price could have been obtained by a sale at a different time or in a different method from that selected by the warehouseman is not of itself sufficient to establish that the sale was not made in a commercially reasonable manner. If the warehouseman either sells the goods in the usual manner in any recognized market therefor, or if he sells at the price current in such market at the time of his sale, or if he has otherwise sold in conformity with commercially reasonable practices among dealers in the type of goods sold, he has sold in a commercially reasonable manner. A sale of more goods than apparently necessary to be offered to insure satisfaction of the obligation is not commercially reasonable except in cases covered by the preceding sentence.

(2) A warehouseman's lien on goods other than goods stored by a merchant in the course of his business may be enforced only as follows:

    (a) All persons known to claim an interest in the goods must be notified.

    (b) The notification must be delivered in person or sent by registered or certified letter to the last known address of any person to be notified.

    (c) The notification must include an itemized statement of the claim, a description of the goods to the lien, a demand for payment within a specified time not less than ten days after receipt of the notification, and a conspicuous statement that unless the claim is paid within the time the goods will be advertised for sale and sold by auction at a specified time and place.

(d) The sale must conform to the terms of the notification.

(e) The sale must be held at the nearest suitable place to that where the goods are held or stored.

(f) After the expiration of the time given in the notification, an advertisement of the sale must be published once a week for two weeks consecutively in a newspaper of general circulation where the sale is to be held. The advertisement must include a description of the goods, the name of the person on whose account they are being held, and the time and place of the sale. The sale must take place at least fifteen days after the first publication. If there is no newspaper of general circulation where the sale is to be held, the advertisement must be posted at least ten days before the sale in not less than six conspicuous places in the neighborhood of the proposed sale.

(3) Before any sale pursuant to this section any person claiming a right in the goods may pay the amount necessary to satisfy the lien and the reasonable expenses incurred under this section. In that event the goods must not be sold, but must be retained by the warehouseman subject to the terms of the receipt and this Article.

(4) The warehouseman may buy at any public sale pursuant to this section.

(5) A purchaser in good faith of goods sold to enforce a warehouseman's lien takes the goods free of any rights of persons against whom the lien was valid, despite noncompliance by the warehouseman with the requirements of this section.

(6) The warehouseman may satisfy his lien from the proceeds of any sale pursuant to this section but must hold the balance, if any, for delivery on demand to any person to whom he would have been bound to deliver the goods.

(7) The rights provided by this section shall be in addition to all other rights allowed by law to a creditor against his debtor.

(8) Where a lien is on goods stored by a merchant in the course of his business the lien may be enforced in accordance with either subsection (1) or (2).

(9) The warehouseman is liable for damages caused by failure to comply with the requirements for sale under this section and in case of willful violation is liable for conversion.

PART 3
BILLS OF LADING: SPECIAL PROVISIONS

§ 7-301. Liability for Non-Receipt or Misdescription; "Said to Contain"; "Shipper's Load and Count"; Improper Handling.

(1) A consignee of a non-negotiable bill who has given value in good faith or a holder to whom a negotiable bill has been duly negotiated relying in either case upon the description therein of the goods, or upon the date therein shown, may recover from the issuer damages caused by the misdating of the bill or the non-receipt or misdescription of the goods, except to the extent that the document indicates that the issuer does not know whether any part or all of the goods in fact were received or conform to the description, as where the description is in terms of marks or labels or kind, quantity, or condition or the receipt or description is qualified by "contents or condition of contents of packages unknown," "said to contain," "shipper's weight, load and count" or the like, if such indication be true.

(2) When goods are loaded by an issuer who is a common carrier, the issuer must count the packages of goods if package freight and ascertain the kind and quantity if bulk freight. In such cases "shipper's weight, load and count" or other words indicating that the description was made by the shipper are ineffective except as to freight concealed by packages.

(3) When bulk freight is loaded by a shipper who makes available to the issuer adequate facilities for weighing such freight, an issuer who is a common carrier must ascertain the kind and quantity within a reasonable time after receiving the written request of the shipper to do so. In such cases "shipper's weight" or other words of like purport are ineffective.

(4) The issuer may by inserting in the bill the words "shipper's weight, load and count"

or other words of like purport indicate that the goods were loaded by the shipper; and if such statement be true the issuer shall not be liable for damages caused by the improper loading. But their omission does not imply liability for such damages.

(5) The shipper shall be deemed to have guaranteed to the issuer the accuracy at the time of shipment of the description, marks, labels, number, kind, quantity, condition and weight, as furnished by him; and the shipper shall indemnify the issuer against damage caused by inaccuracies in such particulars. The right of the issuer to such indemnity shall in no way limit his responsibility and liability under the contract of carriage to any person other than the shipper.

§ 7–302. Through Bills of Lading and Similar Documents.

(1) The issuer of a through bill of lading or other document embodying an undertaking to be performed in part by persons acting as its agents or by connecting carriers is liable to anyone entitled to recover on the document for any breach by such other persons or by a connecting carrier of its obligation under the document but to the extent that the bill covers an undertaking to be performed overseas or in territory not contiguous to the continental United States or an undertaking including matters other than transportation this liability may be varied by agreement of the parties.

(2) Where goods covered by a through bill of lading or other document embodying an undertaking to be performed in part by persons other than the issuer are received by any such person, he is subject with respect to his own performance while the goods are in his possession to the obligation of the issuer. His obligation is discharged by delivery of the goods to another such person pursuant to the document, and does not include liability for breach by any other such persons or by the issuer.

(3) The issuer of such through bill of lading or other document shall be entitled to recover from the connecting carrier or such other person in possession of the goods when the breach of the obligation under the document occurred, the amount it may be required to pay to anyone entitled to recover on the document therefor, as may be evidenced by any receipt, judgment, or transcript thereof, and the amount of any expense reasonably incurred by it in defending any action brought by anyone entitled to recover on the document therefor.

§ 7–303. Diversion; Reconsignment; Change of Instructions.

(1) Unless the bill of lading otherwise provides, the carrier may deliver the goods to a person or destination other than that stated in the bill or may otherwise dispose of the goods on instructions from

- (a) the holder of a negotiable bill; or
- (b) the consignor on a non-negotiable bill notwithstanding contrary instructions from the consignee; or
- (c) the consignee on a non-negotiable bill in the absence of contrary instructions from the consignor, if the goods have arrived at the billed destination or if the consignee is in possession of the bill; or
- (d) the consignee on a non-negotiable bill if he is entitled as against the consignor to dispose of them.

(2) Unless such instructions are noted on a negotiable bill of lading, a person to whom the bill is duly negotiated can hold the bailee according to the original terms.

§ 7–304. Bills of Lading in a Set.

(1) Except where customary in overseas transportation, a bill of lading must not be issued in a set of parts. The issuer is liable for damages caused by violation of this subsection.

(2) Where a bill of lading is lawfully drawn in a set of parts, each of which is numbered and expressed to be valid only if the goods have not been delivered against any other part, the whole of the parts constitute one bill.

(3) Where a bill of lading is lawfully issued in a set of parts and different parts are negotiated to different persons, the title of the holder to whom the first due negotiation is made prevails as to both the document and the goods even though any later holder may have re-

ceived the goods from the carrier in good faith and discharged the carrier's obligation by surrender of his part.

(4) Any person who negotiates or transfers a single part of a bill of lading drawn in a set is liable to holders of that part as if it were the whole set.

(5) The bailee is obliged to deliver in accordance with Part 4 of this Article against the first presented part of a bill of lading lawfully drawn in a set. Such delivery discharges the bailee's obligation on the whole bill.

§ 7–305. Destination Bills.

(1) Instead of issuing a bill of lading to the consignor at the place of shipment a carrier may at the request of the consignor procure the bill to be issued at destination or at any other place designated in the request.

(2) Upon request of anyone entitled as against the carrier to control the goods while in transit and on surrender of any outstanding bill of lading or other receipt covering such goods, the issuer may procure a substitute bill to be issued at any place designated in the request.

§ 7–306. Altered Bills of Lading.

An unauthorized alteration or filling in of a blank in a bill of lading leaves the bill enforceable according to its original tenor.

§ 7–307. Lien of Carrier.

(1) A carrier has a lien on the goods covered by a bill of lading for charges subsequent to the date of its receipt of the goods for storage or transportation (including demurrage and terminal charges) and for expenses necessary for preservation of the goods incident to their transportation or reasonably incurred in their sale pursuant to law. But against a purchaser for value of a negotiable bill of lading a carrier's lien is limited to charges stated in the bill or the applicable tariffs, or if no charges are stated then to a reasonable charge.

(2) A lien for charges and expenses under subsection (1) on goods which the carrier was required by law to receive for transportation is effective against the consignor or any person entitled to the goods unless the carrier had notice that the consignor lacked authority to subject the goods to such charges and expenses. Any other lien under subsection (1) is effective against the consignor and any person who permitted the bailor to have control or possession of the goods unless the carrier had notice that the bailor lacked such authority.

(3) A carrier loses his lien on any goods which he voluntarily delivers or which he unjustifiably refuses to deliver.

§ 7–308. Enforcement of Carrier's Lien.

(1) A carrier's lien may be enforced by public or private sale of the goods, in bloc or in parcels, at any time or place and on any terms which are commercially reasonable, after notifying all persons known to claim an interest in the goods. Such notification must include a statement of the amount due, the nature of the proposed sale and the time and place of any public sale. The fact that a better price could have been obtained by a sale at a different time or in a different method from that selected by the carrier is not of itself sufficient to establish that the sale was not made in a commercially reasonable manner. If the carrier either sells the goods in the usual manner in any recognized market therefor or if he sells at the price current in such market at the time of his sale or if he has otherwise sold in conformity with commercially reasonable practices among dealers in the type of goods he has sold in a commercially reasonable manner. A sale of more goods than apparently necessary to be offered to ensure satisfaction of the obligation is not commercially reasonable except in cases covered by the preceding sentence.

(2) Before any sale pursuant to this section any person claiming a right in the goods may pay the amount necessary to satisfy the lien and the reasonable expenses incurred under this section. In that event the goods must not be sold, but must be retained by the carrier subject to the terms of the bill and this Article.

(3) The carrier may buy at any public sale pursuant to this section.

(4) A purchaser in good faith of goods sold to enforce a carrier's lien takes the goods free of any rights of persons against whom the lien was valid, despite noncompliance by the carrier with the requirements of this section.

(5) The carrier may satisfy his lien from the proceeds of any sale pursuant to this section but must hold the balance, if any, for delivery on demand to any person to whom he would have been bound to deliver the goods.

(6) The rights provided by this section shall be in addition to all other rights allowed by law to a creditor against his debtor.

(7) A carrier's lien may be enforced in accordance with either subsection (1) or the procedure set forth in subsection (2) of Section 7–210.

(8) The carrier is liable for damages caused by failure to comply with the requirements for sale under this section and in case of willful violation is liable for conversion.

§ 7–309. Duty of Care; Contractual Limitation of Carrier's Liability.

(1) A carrier who issues a bill of lading whether negotiable or non-negotiable must exercise the degree of care in relation to the goods which a reasonably careful man would exercise under like circumstances. This subsection does not repeal or change any law or rule of law which imposes liability upon a common carrier for damages not caused by its negligence.

(2) Damages may be limited by a provision that the carrier's liability shall not exceed a value stated in the document if the carrier's rates are dependent upon value and the consignor by the carrier's tariff is afforded an opportunity to declare a higher value or a value as lawfully provided in the tariff, or where no tariff is filed he is otherwise advised of such opportunity; but no such limitation is effective with respect to the carrier's liability for conversion to its own use.

(3) Reasonable provisions as to the time and manner of presenting claims and instituting actions based on the shipment may be included in a bill of lading or tariff.

PART 4
WAREHOUSE RECEIPTS AND BILLS OF LADING: GENERAL OBLIGATIONS

§ 7–401. Irregularities in Issue of Receipt or Bill or Conduct of Issuer.

The obligations imposed by this Article on an issuer apply to a document of title regardless of the fact that

 (a) the document may not comply with the requirements of this Article or of any other law or regulation regarding its issue, form or content; or

 (b) the issuer may have violated laws regulating the conduct of his business; or

 (c) the goods covered by the document were owned by the bailee at the time the document was issued; or

 (d) the person issuing the document does not come within the definition of warehouseman if it purports to be a warehouse receipt.

§ 7–402. Duplicate Receipt or Bill; Overissue.

Neither a duplicate nor any other document of title purporting to cover goods already represented by an outstanding document of the same issuer confers any right in the goods, except as provided in the case of bills in a set, overissue of documents for fungible goods and substitutes for lost, stolen or destroyed documents. But the issuer is liable for damages caused by his overissue or failure to identify a duplicate document as such by conspicuous notation on its face.

§ 7–403. Obligation of Warehouseman or Carrier to Deliver; Excuse.

(1) The bailee must deliver the goods to a person entitled under the document who complies with subsections (2) and (3), unless and to the extent that the bailee establishes any of the following:

(a) delivery of the goods to a person whose receipt was rightful as against the claimant;

(b) damage to or delay, loss or destruction of the goods for which the bailee is not liable [but the burden of establishing negligence in such cases is on the person entitled under the document];

Note: *The brackets in (1) (b) indicate that State enactments may differ on this point without serious damage to the principle of uniformity.*

(c) previous sale or other disposition of the goods in lawful enforcement of a lien or on warehouseman's lawful termination of storage;

(d) the exercise by a seller of his right to stop delivery pursuant to the provisions of the Article on Sales (Section 2–705);

(e) a diversion, reconsignment or other disposition pursuant to the provisions of this Article (Section 7–303) or tariff regulating such right;

(f) release, satisfaction or any other fact affording a personal defense against the claimant;

(g) any other lawful excuse.

(2) A person claiming goods covered by a document of title must satisfy the bailee's lien where the bailee so requests or where the bailee is prohibited by law from delivering the goods until the charges are paid.

(3) Unless the person claiming is one against whom the document confers no right under Section 7–503(1), he must surrender for cancellation or notation of partial deliveries any outstanding negotiable document covering the goods, and the bailee must cancel the document or conspicuously note the partial delivery thereon or be liable to any person to whom the document is duly negotiated.

(4) "Person entitled under the document" means holder in the case of a negotiable document, or the person to whom delivery is to be made by the terms of or pursuant to written instructions under a non-negotiable document.

§ 7–404. No Liability for Good Faith Delivery Pursuant to Receipt or Bill.

A bailee who in good faith including observance of reasonable commercial standards has received goods and delivered or otherwise disposed of them according to the terms of the document of title or pursuant to this Article is not liable therefor. This rule applies even though the person from whom he received the goods had no authority to procure the document or to dispose of the goods and even though the person to whom he delivered the goods had no authority to receive them.

PART 5
WAREHOUSE RECEIPTS AND BILLS OF LADING: NEGOTIATION AND TRANSFER

§ 7–501. Form of Negotiation and Requirements of "Due Negotiation."

(1) A negotiable document of title running to the order of a named person is negotiated by his indorsement and delivery. After his indorsement in blank or to bearer any person can negotiate it by delivery alone.

(2) (a) A negotiable document of title is also negotiated by delivery alone when by its original terms it runs to bearer.

(b) When a document running to the order of a named person is delivered to him the effect is the same as if the document had been negotiated.

(3) Negotiation of a negotiable document of title after it has been indorsed to a specified person requires indorsement by the special indorsee as well as delivery.

(4) A negotiable document of title is "duly negotiated" when it is negotiated in the manner stated in this section to a holder who purchases it in good faith without notice of any defense against or claim to it on the part of any person and for value, unless it is established that the negotiation is not in the regular course of business or financing or involves receiving the document in settlement or payment of a money obligation.

(5) Indorsement of a non-negotiable document neither makes it negotiable nor adds to the transferee's rights.

(6) The naming in a negotiable bill of a person to be notified of the arrival of the goods does not limit the negotiability of the bill nor constitute notice to a purchaser thereof of any interest of such person in the goods.

§ 7–502. Rights Acquired by Due Negotiation.

(1) Subject to the following section and to the provisions of Section 7–205 on fungible goods, a holder to whom a negotiable document of title has been duly negotiated acquires thereby:

    (a) title to the document;

    (b) title to the goods;

    (c) all rights accruing under the law of agency or estoppel, including rights to goods delivered to the bailee after the document was issued; and

    (d) the direct obligation of the issuer to hold or deliver the goods according to the terms of the document free of any defense or claim by him except those arising under the terms of the document or under this Article. In the case of a delivery order the bailee's obligation accrues only upon acceptance and the obligation acquired by the holder is that the issuer and any indorser will procure the acceptance of the bailee.

(2) Subject to the following section, title and rights so acquired are not defeated by any stoppage of the goods represented by the document or by surrender of such goods by the bailee, and are not impaired even though the negotiation or any prior negotiation constituted a breach of duty or even though any person has been deprived of possession of the document by misrepresentation, fraud, accident, mistake, duress, loss, theft or conversion, or even though a previous sale or other transfer of the goods or document has been made to a third person.

§ 7–503. Document of Title to Goods Defeated in Certain Cases.

(1) A document of title confers no right in goods against a person who before issuance of the document had a legal interest or a perfected security interest in them and who neither

    (a) delivered or entrusted them or any document of title covering them to the bailor or his nominee with actual or apparent authority to ship, store or sell or with power to obtain delivery under this Article (Section 7–403) or with power of disposition under this Act (Sections 2–403 and 9–307) or other statute or rule of law; nor

    (b) acquiesced in the procurement by the bailor or his nominee of any document of title.

(2) Title to goods based upon an unaccepted delivery order is subject to the rights of anyone to whom a negotiable warehouse receipt or bill of lading covering the goods has been duly negotiated. Such a title may be defeated under the next section to the same extent as the rights of the issuer or a transferee from the issuer.

(3) Title to goods based upon a bill of lading issued to a freight forwarder is subject to the rights of anyone to whom a bill issued by the freight forwarder is duly negotiated; but delivery by the carrier in accordance with Part 4 of this Article pursuant to its own bill of lading discharges the carrier's obligation to deliver.

§ 7–504. Rights Acquired in the Absence of Due Negotiation; Effect of Diversion; Seller's Stoppage of Delivery.

(1) A transferee of a document, whether negotiable or nonnegotiable, to whom the document has been delivered but not duly negotiated, acquires the title and rights which his transferor had or had actual authority to convey.

(2) In the case of a non-negotiable document, until but not after the bailee receives notification of the tansfer, the rights of the transferee may be defeated.

    (a) by those creditors of the transferor who could treat the sale as void under Section 2–402; or

    (b) by a buyer from the transferor in ordinary course of business if the bailee has delivered the goods to the buyer or received notification of his rights; or

(c) as against the bailee by good faith dealings of the bailee with the transferor.

(3) A diversion or other change of shipping instructions by the consignor in a non-negotiable bill of lading which causes the bailee not the deliver to the consignee defeats the consignee's title to the goods if they have been delivered to a buyer in ordinary course of business and in any event defeats the consignee's rights against the bailee.

(4) Delivery pursuant to a non-negotiable document may be stopped by a seller under Section 2–705, and subject to the requirement of due notification there provided. A bailee honoring the seller's instructions is entitled to be indemnified by the seller against any resulting loss or expense.

§ 7–505. Indorser Not a Guarantor for Other Parties.

The indorsement of a document of title issued by a bailee does not make the indorser liable for any default by the bailee or by previous indorsers.

§ 7–506. Delivery Without Indorsement: Right to Compel Indorsement.

The transferee of a negotiable document of title has a specifically enforceable right to have his transferor supply any necessary indorsement but the transfer becomes a negotiation only as of the time the indorsement is supplied.

§ 7–507. Warranties on Negotiation or Transfer of Receipt or Bill.

Where a person negotiates or transfers a document of title for value otherwise than as a mere intermediary under the next following section, then unless otherwise agreed he warrants to his immediate purchaser only in addition to any warranty made in selling the goods
   (a) that the document is genuine; and
   (b) that he has no knowledge of any fact which would impair its validity or worth; and
   (c) that his negotiation or transfer is rightful and fully effective with respect to the title to the document and the goods it represents.

§ 7–508. Warranties of Collecting Bank as to Documents.

A collecting bank or other intermediary known to be entrusted with documents on behalf of another or with collection of a draft or other claim against delivery of documents warrants by such delivery of the documents only its own good faith and authority. This rule applies even though the intermediary has purchased or made advances against the claim or draft to be collected.

§ 7–509. Receipt or Bill: When Adequate Compliance With Commercial Contract.

The question whether a document is adequate to fulfill the obligations of a contract for sale or the conditions of a credit is governed by the Articles on Sales (Article 2) and on Letters of Credit (Article 5).

PART 6
WAREHOUSE RECEIPTS AND BILLS OF LADING: MISCELLANEOUS PROVISIONS

§ 7–601. Lost and Missing Documents.

(1) If a document has been lost, stolen or destroyed, a court may order delivery of the goods or issuance of a substitute document and the bailee may without liability to any person comply with such order. If the document was negotiable the claimant must post security approved by the court to indemnify any person who may suffer loss as a result of non-surrender of the document. If the document was not negotiable, such security may be required at the discretion of the court. The court may also in its discretion order payment of the bailee's reasonable costs and counsel fees.

(2) A bailee who without court order delivers goods to a person claiming under a missing negotiable document is liable to any person injured thereby, and if the delivery is not in good faith becomes liable for conversion. Delivery in good faith is not conversion if made in accordance with a filed classification or tariff or, where no classification or tariff is filed,

if the claimant posts security with the bailee in an amount at least double the value of the goods at the time of posting to indemnify any person injured by the delivery who files a notice of claim within one year after the delivery.

§ 7–602. Attachment of Goods Covered by a Negotiable Document.

Except where the document was originally issued upon delivery of the goods by a person who had no power to dispose of them, no lien attaches by virtue of any judicial process to goods in the possession of a bailee for which a negotiable document of title is outstanding unless the document be first surrendered to the bailee or its negotiation enjoined, and the bailee shall not be compelled to deliver the goods pursuant to process until the document is surrendered to him or impounded by the court. One who purchases the document for value without notice of the process or injunction takes free of the lien imposed by judicial process.

§ 7–603. Conflicting Claims; Interpleader.

If more than one person claims title or possession of the goods, the bailee is excused from delivery until he has had a reasonable time to ascertain the validity of the adverse claims or to bring an action to compel all claimants to interplead and may compel such interpleader, either in defending an action for non-delivery of the goods, or by original action, whichever is appropriate.

ARTICLE 8. Investment Securities

PART 1
SHORT TITLE AND GENERAL MATTERS

§ 8–101. Short Title.

This Article shall be known and may be cited as Uniform Commercial Code—Investment Securities.

§ 8–102. Definitions and Index of Definitions.

(1) In this Article unless the context otherwise requires
    (a) A "security" is an instrument which
        (i) is issued in bearer or registered form; and
        (ii) is of a type commonly dealt in upon securities exchanges or markets or commonly recognized in any area in which it is issued or dealt in as a medium for investment; and
        (iii) is either one of a class or series or by its terms is divisible into a class or series of instruments; and
        (iv) evidences a share, participation or other interest in property or in an enterprise or evidences an obligation of the issuer.
    (b) A writing which is a security is governed by this Article and not by Uniform Commercial Code–Commercial Paper even though it also meets the requirements of that Article. This Article does not apply to money.
    (c) A security is in "registered form" when it specifies a person entitled to the security or to the rights it evidences and when its transfer may be registered upon books maintained for that purpose by or on behalf of an issuer or the security so states.
    (d) A security is in "bearer form" when it runs to bearer according to its terms and not by reason of any indorsement.
(2) A "subsequent purchaser" is a person who takes other than by original issue.
(3) A "clearing corporation" is a corporation all of the capital stock of which is held by or for a national securities exchange or association registered under a statute of the United States such as the Securities Exchange Act of 1934.

(4) A "custodian bank" is any bank or trust company which is supervised and examined by state or federal authority having supervision over banks and which is acting as custodian for a clearing corporation.

(5) Other definitions applying to this Article or to specified Parts thereof and the sections in which they appear are:

"Adverse claim"	Section 8–301
"Bona fide purchaser"	Section 8–302
"Broker"	Section 8–303
"Guarantee of the signature"	Section 8–402
"Intermediary Bank"	Section 4–105
"Issuer"	Section 8–201
"Overissue"	Section 8–104

(6) In addition Article 1 contains general definitions and principles of construction and interpretation applicable throughout this Article.

§ 8–103 Issuer's Lien.

A lien upon a security in favor of an issuer thereof is valid against a purchaser only if the right of the issuer to such lien is noted conspicuously on the security.

§ 8–104 Effect of Overissue; "Overissue."

(1) The provisions of this Article which validate a security or compel its issue or reissue do not apply to the extent that validation, issue or reissue would result in overissue; but

    (a) if an identical security which does not constitute an overissue is reasonably available for purchase, the person entitled to issue or validation may compel the issuer to purchase and deliver such a security to him against surrender of the security, if any, which he holds; or

    (b) if a security is not so available for purchase, the person entitled to issue or validation may recover from the issuer the price he or the last purchaser for value paid for it with interest from the date of his demand.

(2) "Overissue" means the issue of securities in excess of the amount which the issuer has corporate power to issue.

§ 8–105. Securities Negotiable; Presumptions.

(1) Securities governed by this Article are negotiable instruments.

(2) In any action on a security

    (a) unless specifically denied in the pleadings, each signature on the security or in a necessary indorsement is admitted;

    (b) when the effectiveness of a signature is put in issue the burden of establishing it is on the party claiming under the signature but the signature is presumed to be genuine or authorized;

    (c) when signatures are admitted or established production of the instrument entitles a holder to recover on it unless the defendant establishes a defense or a defect going to the validity of the security; and

    (d) after it is shown that a defense or defect exists the plaintiff has the burden of establishing that he or some person under whom he claims is a person against whom the defense or defect is ineffective (Section 8–202).

§ 8–106. Applicability.

The validity of a security and the rights and duties of the issuer with respect to registration of transfer are governed by the law (including the conflict of laws rules) of the jurisdiction of organization of the issuer.

§ 8–107. Securities Deliverable; Action for Price.

(1) Unless otherwise agreed and subject to any applicable law or regulation respecting short sales, a person obligated to deliver securities may deliver any security of the specified issue in bearer form or registered in the name of the transferee or indorsed to him or in blank.

(2) When the buyer fails to pay the price as it comes due under a contract of sale the seller may recover the price
  (a) of securities accepted by the buyer; and
  (b) of other securities if efforts at their resale would be unduly burdensome or if there is no readily available market for their resale.

PART 2
ISSUE—ISSUER

§ 8–201. "Issuer."

(1) With respect to obligations on or defenses to a security "issuer" includes a person whom
  (a) places or authorizes the placing of his name on a security (otherwise than as authenticating trustee, registrar, transfer agent or the like) to evidence that it represents a share, participation or other interest in his property or in an enterprise or to evidence his duty to perform an obligation evidenced by the security; or
  (b) directly or indirecting creates fractional interests in his rights or property which fractional interests are evidenced by securities; or
  (c) becomes responsible for or in place of any other person described as an issuer in this section.

(2) With respect to obligations on or defenses to a security a guarantor is an issuer to the extent of his guaranty whether or not his obligation is noted on the security.

(3) With respect to registration of transfer (Part 4 of this Article) "issuer" means a person on whose behalf transfer books are maintained.

§ 8–202. Issuer's Responsibility and Defenses; Notice of Defect or Defense.

(1) Even against a purchaser for value and without notice, the terms of a security include those stated on the security and those made part of the security by reference to another instrument, indenture or document or to a constitution, statute, ordinance, rule, regulation, order or the like to the extent that the terms so referred to do no conflict with the stated terms. Such a reference does not of itself charge a purchaser for value with notice of a defect going to the validity of the security even though the security expressly states that a person accepting it admits such notice.

(2) (a) A security other than one issued by a government or governmental agency or unit even though issued with a defect going to its validity is valid in the hands of a purchaser for value and without notice of the particular defect unless the defect involves a violation of constitutional provisions in which case the security is valid in the hands of a subsequent purchaser for value and without notice of the defect.

  (b) The rule of subparagraph (a) applies to an issuer which is a government or governmental agency or unit only if either there has been substantial compliance with the legal requirements governing the issue or the issuer has received a substantial consideration for the issue as a whole or for the particular security and a stated purpose of the issue is one for which the issuer has power to borrow money or issue the security.

(3) Except as otherwise provided in the case of certain unauthorized signatures on issue (Section 8–205), lack of genuineness of a security is a complete defense even against a purchaser for value and without notice.

(4) All other defenses of the issuer including nondelivery and conditional delivery of the security are ineffective against a purchaser for value who has taken without notice of the particular defense.

(5) Nothing in this section shall be construed to affect the right of a party to a "when, as and if issued" or a "when distributed" contract to cancel the contract in the event of a material change in the character of the security which is the subject of the contract or in the plan or arrangement pursuant to which such security is to be issued or distributed.

§ 8–203. Staleness as Notice of Defects or Defenses.

(1) After an act or event which creates a right to immediate performance of the principal

obligation evidenced by the security or which sets a date on or after which the security is to be presented or surrendered for redemption or exchange, a purchaser is charged with notice of any defect in its issue or defense of the issuer

    (a) if the act or event is one requiring the payment of money or the delivery of securities or both on presentation or surrender of the security and such funds or securities are available on the date set for payment or exchange and he takes the security more than one year after that date; and

    (b) if the act or event is not covered by paragraph (a) and he takes the security more than two years after the date set for surrender or presentation or the date on which such performance became due.

(2) A call which has been revoked is not within subsection (1).

§ 8–204. Effect of Issuer's Restrictions on Transfer.

Unless noted conspicuously on the security a restriction on transfer imposed by the issuer even though otherwise lawful is ineffective except against a person with actual knowledge of it.

§ 8–205. Effect of Unauthorized Signature on Issue.

An unauthorized signature placed on a security prior to or in the course of issue is ineffective except that the signature is effective in favor of a purchaser for value and without notice of the lack of authority if the signing has been done by

    (a) an authenticating trustee, registrar, transfer agent or other person entrusted by the issuer with the signing of the security or of similar securities or their immediate preparation for signing; or

    (b) an employee of the issuer or of any of the foregoing entrusted with responsible handling of the security.

§ 8–206. Completion or Alteration of Instrument.

(1) Where a security contains the signatures necessary to its issue or transfer but is incomplete in any other respect

    (a) any person may complete it by filling in the blanks as authorized; and

    (b) even though the blanks are incorrectly filled in, the security as completed is enforceable by a purchaser who took it for value and without notice of such incorrectness.

(2) A complete security which has been improperly altered even though fraudulently remains enforceable but only according to its original terms.

§ 8–207. Rights of Issuer With Respect to Registered Owners.

(1) Prior to due presentment for registration of transfer of a security in registered form the issuer or indenture trustee may treat the registered owner as the person exclusively entitled to vote, to receive notifications and otherwise to exercise all the rights and powers of an owner.

(2) Nothing in this Article shall be construed to affect the liability of the registered owner of a security for calls, assessments or the like.

§ 8–208. Effect of Signature of Authenticating Trustee, Registrar or Transfer Agent.

(1) A person placing his signature upon a security as authenticating trustee, registrar, transfer agent or the like warrants to a purchaser for value without notice of the particular defect that

    (a) the security is genuine; and

    (b) his own participation in the issue of the security is within his capacity and within the scope of the authorization received by him from the issuer; and

    (c) he has reasonable grounds to believe that the security is in the form and within the amount the issuer is authorized to issue.

(2) Unless otherwise agreed, a person by so placing his signature does not assume responsibility for the validity of the security in other respects.

PART 3

PURCHASE

§ 8–301. Rights Acquired by Purchaser; "Adverse Claim"; Title Acquired by Bona Fide Purchaser.

(1) Upon delivery of a security the purchaser acquires the rights in the security which his transferor had or had actual authority to convey except that a purchaser who has himself been a party to any fraud or illegality affecting the security or who as a prior holder had notice of an adverse claim cannot improve his position by taking from a later bona fide purchaser. "Adverse claim" includes a claim that a transfer was or would be wrongful or that a particular adverse person is the owner of or has an interest in the security.

(2) A bona fide purchaser in addition to acquiring the rights of a purchaser also acquires the security free of any adverse claim.

(3) A purchaser of a limited interest acquires rights only to the extent of the interest purchased.

§ 8–302. "Bona Fide Purchaser."

A "bona fide purchaser" is a purchaser for value in good faith and without notice of any adverse claim who takes delivery of a security in bearer form or of one in registered form issued to him or indorsed to him or in blank.

§ 8–303. "Broker."

"Broker" means a person engaged for all or part of his time in the business of buying and selling securities, who in the transaction concerned acts for, or buys a security from or sells a security to a customer. Nothing in this Article determines the capacity in which a person acts for purposes of any other statute or rule to which such person is subject.

§ 8–304. Notice to Purchaser of Adverse Claims.

(1) A purchaser (including a broker for the seller or buyer but excluding an intermediary bank) of a security is charged with notice of adverse claims if

    (a) the security whether in bearer or registered form has been indorsed "for collection" or "for surrender" or for some other purpose not involving transfer; or

    (b) the security is in bearer form and has on it an unambiguous statement that it is the property of a person other than the transferor. The mere writing of a name on a security is not such a statement.

(2) The fact that the purchaser (including a broker for the seller or buyer) has notice that the security is held for a third person or is registered in the name of or indorsed by a fiduciary does not create a duty of inquiry into the rightfulness of the transfer or constitute notice of adverse claims. If, however, the purchaser (excluding an intermediary bank) has knowledge that the proceeds are being used or that the transaction is for the individual benefit of the fiduciary or otherwise in breach of duty, the purchaser is charged with notice of adverse claims.

§ 8–305. Staleness as Notice of Adverse Claims.

An act or event which creates a right to immediate performance of the principal obligation evidenced by the security or which sets a date on or after which the security is to be presented or surrendered for redemption or exchange does not of itself constitute any notice of adverse claims except in the case of a purchase

    (a) after one year from any date set for such presentment or surrender for redemption or exchange; or

    (b) after six months from any date set for payment of money against presentation or surrender of the security if funds are available for payment on that date.

§ 8–306. Warranties on Presentment and Transfer.

(1) A person who presents a security for registration of transfer or for payment or exchange warrants to the issuer that he is entitled to the registration, payment or exchange. But a pur-

chaser for value without notice of adverse claims who receives a new, reissued or re-registered security on registration of transfer warrants only that he has no knowledge of any unauthorized signature (Section 8–311) in a necessary indorsement.

(2) A person by transferring a security to a purchaser for value warrants only that

(a) his transfer is effective and rightful; and

(b) the security is genuine and has not been materially altered; and

(c) he knows no fact which might impair the validity of the security.

(3) Where a security is delivered by an intermediary known to be entrusted with delivery of the security on behalf of another or with collection of a draft or other claim against such delivery, the intermediary by such delivery warrants only his own good faith and authority even though he has purchased or made advances against the claim to be collected against the delivery.

(4) A pledgee or other holder for security who redelivers the security received, or after payment and on order of the debtor delivers that security to a third person makes only the warranties of an intermediary under subsection (3).

(5) A broker gives to his customer and to the issuer and a purchaser the warranties provided in this section and has the rights and privileges of a purchaser under this section. The warranties of and in favor of the broker acting as an agent are in addition to applicable warranties given by and in favor of his customer.

§ 8–307. Effect of Delivery Without Indorsement; Right to Compel Indorsement.

Where a security in registered form has been delivered to a purchaser without a necessary indorsement he may become a bona fide purchaser only as of the time the indorsement is supplied, but against the transferor the transfer is complete upon delivery and the purchaser has a specifically enforceable right to have any necessary indorsement supplied.

§ 8–308. Indorsement, How Made; Special Indorsement; Indorser Not a Guarantor; Partial Assignment.

(1) An indorsement of a security in registered form is made when an appropriate person signs on it or on a separate document an assignment or transfer of the security or a power to assign or transfer it or when the signature of such person is written without more upon the back of the security.

(2) An indorsement in blank includes an indorsement to bearer. A special indorsement specifies the person to whom the security is to be transferred, or who has power to transfer it. A holder may convert a blank indorsement into a special indorsement.

(3) "An appropriate person" in subsection (1) means

(a) the person specified by the security or by special indorsement to be entitled to the security; or

(b) where the person so specified is described as a fiduciary but is no longer serving in the described capacity,—either that person or his successor; or

(c) where the security or indorsement so specifies more than one person as fiduciaries and one or more are no longer serving in the described capacity,—the remaining fiduciary or fiduciaries, whether or not a successor has been appointed or qualified; or

(d) where the person so specified is an individual and is without capacity to act by virtue of death, incompetence, infancy or otherwise,—his executor, administrator, guardian or like fiduciary; or

(e) where the security or indorsement so specifies more than one person as tenants by the entirety or with right of survivorship and by reason of death all cannot sign,—the survivor or survivors; or

(f) a person having power to sign under applicable law or controlling instrument; or

(g) to the extent that any of the foregoing persons may act through an agent,—his authorized agent.

(4) Unless otherwise agreed the indorser by his indorsement assumes no obligation that the security will be honored by the issuer.

(5) An indorsement purporting to be only of part of a security representing units intended by the issuer to be separately transferable is effective to the extent of the indorsement.

(6) Whether the person signing is appropriate is determined as of the date of signing and an indorsement by such a person does not become unauthorized for the purposes of this Article by virtue of any subsequent change of circumstances.

(7) Failure of a fiduciary to comply with a controlling instrument or with the law of the state having jurisdiction of the fiduciary relationship, including any law requiring the fiduciary to obtain court approval of the transfer, does not render his indorsement unauthorized for the purposes of this Article.

§ 8–309. Effect of Indorsement Without Delivery.

An indorsement of a security whether special or in blank does not constitute a transfer until delivery of the security on which it appears or if the indorsement is on a separate document until delivery of both the document and the security.

§ 8–310. Indorsement of Security in Bearer Form.

An indorsement of a security in bearer form may give notice of adverse claims (Section 8–304) but does not otherwise affect any right to registration the holder may possess.

§ 8–311. Effect of Unauthorized Indorsement.

Unless the owner has ratfiied an unauthorized indorsement or is otherwise precluded from asserting its ineffectiveness
   (a) he may assert its ineffectiveness against the issuer or any purchaser other than a purchaser for value and without notice of adverse claims who has in good faith received a new, re-issued or re-registered security on registration of transfer; and
   (b) an issuer who registers the transfer of a security upon the unauthorized indorsement is subject to liability for improper registration (Section 8–404).

§ 8–312. Effect of Guaranteeing Signature or Indorsement.

(1) Any person guaranteeing a signature of an indorser of a security warrants that at the time of signing
   (a) the signature was genuine; and
   (b) the signer was an appropriate person to indorse (Section 8–308); and
   (c) the signer had legal capacity to sign.
But the guarantor does not otherwise warrant the rightfulness of the particular transfer.

(2) Any person may guarantee an indorsement of a security and by so doing warrants not only the signature (subsection 1) but also the rightfulness of the particular transfer in all respects. But no issuer may require a guarantee of indorsement as a condition to registration of transfer.

(3) The foregoing warranties are made to any person taking or dealing with the security in reliance on the guarantee and the guarantor is liable to such person for any loss resulting from breach of the warranties.

§ 8–313. When Delivery to the Purchaser Occurs; Purchaser's Broker as Holder.

(1) Delivery to a purchaser occurs when
   (a) he or a person designated by him acquires possession of a security; or
   (b) his broker acquires possession of a security specially indorsed to or issued in the name of the purchaser; or
   (c) his broker sends him confirmation of the purchase and also by book entry or otherwise identifies a specific security in the broker's possession as belonging to the purchaser; or
   (d) with respect to an identified security to be delivered while still in the possession of a third person when that person acknowledges that he holds for the purchaser.
   (e) appropriate entries on the books of a clearing corporation are made under Section 8–320.

(2) The purchaser is the owner of a security held for him by his broker, but is not the holder except as specified in subparagraphs (b), (c) and (e) of subsection (1). Where a security is part of a fungible bulk the purchaser is the owner of a proportionate property interest in the fungible bulk.

(3) Notice of an adverse claim received by the broker or by the purchaser after the broker takes delivery as a holder for value is not effective either as to the broker or as to the purchaser. However, as between the broker and the purchaser the purchaser may demand delivery of an equivalent security as to which no notice of an adverse claim has been received.

§ 8–314. Duty to Deliver, When Completed.

(1) Unless otherwise agreed where a sale of a security is made on an exchange or otherwise through brokers
- (a) the selling customer fulfills his duty to deliver when he places such a security in the possession of the selling broker or of a person designated by the broker or if requested causes an acknowledgment to be made to the selling broker that it is held for him; and
- (b) the selling broker including a correspondent broker acting for a selling customer fulfills his duty to deliver by placing the security or a like security in the possession of the buying broker or a person designated by him or by effecting clearance of the sale in accordance with the rules of the exchange on which the transaction took place.

(2) Except as otherwise provided in this section and unless otherwise agreed, a transferor's duty to deliver a security under a contract of purchase is not fulfilled until he places the security in form to be negotiated by the purchaser in the possession of the purchaser or of a person designated by him or at the purchaser's request causes an acknowledgment to be made to the purchaser that it is held for him. Unless made on an exchange a sale to a broker purchasing for his own account is within this subsection and not within subsection (1).

§ 8–315. Action Against Purchaser Based Upon Wrongful Transfer.

(1) Any person against whom the transfer of a security is wrongful for any reason, including his incapacity, may against any one except a bona fide purchaser reclaim possession of the security or obtain possession of any new security evidencing all or part of the same rights or have damages.

(2) If the transfer is wrongful because of an unauthorized indorsement, the owner may also reclaim or obtain possession of the security or new security even from a bona fide purchaser if the ineffectiveness of the purported indorsement can be asserted against him under the provisions of this Article on unauthorized indorsements (Section 8–311).

(3) The right to obtain or reclaim possession of a security may be specifically enforced and its transfer enjoined and the security impounded pending the litigation.

§ 8–316. Purchaser's Right to Requisites for Registration of Transfer on Books.

Unless otherwise agreed the transferor must on due demand supply his purchaser with any proof of his authority to transfer or with any other requisite which may be necessary to obtain registration of the transfer of the security but if the transfer is not for value a transferor need not do so unless the purchaser furnishes the necessary expenses. Failure to comply with a demand made within a reasonable time gives the purchaser the right to reject or rescind the transfer.

§ 8–317. Attachment or Levy Upon Security.

(1) No attachment or levy upon a security or any share or other interest evidenced thereby which is outstanding shall be valid until the security is actually seized by the officer making the attachment or levy but a security which has been surrendered to the issuer may be attached or levied upon at the source.

(2) A creditor whose debtor is the owner of a security shall be entitled to such aid from courts of appropriate jurisdiction, by injunction or otherwise, in reaching such security or in

satisfying the claim by means thereof as is allowed at law or in equity in regard to property which cannot readily be attached or levied upon by ordinary legal process.

§ 8–318. No Conversion by Good Faith Delivery.

An agent or bailee who in good faith (including observance of reasonable commercial standards if he is in the business of buying, selling or otherwise dealing with securities) has received securities and sold, pledged or delivered them according to the instructions of his principal is not liable for conversion or for participation in breach of fiduciary duty although the principal had no right to dispose of them.

§ 8–319. Statute of Frauds.

A contract for the sale of securities is not enforceable by way of action or defense unless
  (a) there is some writing signed by the party against whom enforcement is sought or by his authorized agent or broker sufficient to indicate that a contract has been made for sale of a stated quantity of described securities at a defined or stated price; or
  (b) delivery of the security has been accepted or payment has been made but the contract is enforceable under this provision only to the extent of such delivery or payment; or
  (c) within a reasonable time a writing in confirmation of the sale or purchase and sufficient against the sender under paragraph (a) has been received by the party against whom enforcement is sought and he has failed to send written objection to its contents within ten days after its receipt; or
  (d) the party against whom enforcement is sought admits in his pleading, testimony or otherwise in court that a contract was made for sale of a stated quantity of described securities at a defined or stated price.

§ 8–320. Transfer or Pledge within a Central Depository System.

  (1) If a security
    (a) is in the custody of a clearing corporation or of a custodian bank or a nominee of either subject to the instructions of the clearing corporation; and
    (b) is in bearer form or indorsed in blank by an appropriate person or registered in the name of the clearing corporation or custodian bank or a nominee of either; and
    (c) is shown on the account of a transferor or pledgor on the books of the clearing corporation;
then, in addition to other methods, a transfer or pledge of the security or any interest therein may be effected by the making of appropriate entries on the books of the clearing corporation reducing the account of the transferor or pledgor and increasing the account of the transferee or pledgee by the amount of the obligation or the number of shares or rights transferred or pledged.

  (2) Under this section entries may be with respect to like securities or interests therein as a part of a fungible bulk and may refer merely to a quantity of a particular security without reference to the name of the registered owner, certificate or bond number or the like and, in appropriate cases, may be on a net basis taking into account other transfers or pledges of the same security.

  (3) A transfer or pledge under this section has the effect of a delivery of a security in bearer form or duly indorsed in blank (Section 8–301) representing the amount of the obligation or the number of shares or rights transferred or pledged. If a pledge or the creation of a security interest is intended, the making of entries has the effect of a taking of delivery by the pledgee or a secured party (Sections 9–304 and 9–305). A transferee or pledgee under this section is a holder.

  (4) A transfer or pledge under this section does not constitute a registration of transfer under Part 4 of this Article.

  (5) That entries made on the books of the clearing corporation as provided in subsection (1) are not appropriate does not affect the validity or effect of the entries nor the liabilities or obligations of the clearing corporation to any person adversely affected thereby.

PART 4
REGISTRATION

§ 8–401. Duty of Issuer to Register Transfer.

(1) Where a security in registered form is presented to the issuer with a request to register transfer, the issuer is under a duty to register the transfer as requested if

    (a) the security is indorsed by the appropriate person or persons (Section 8–308); and

    (b) reasonable assurance is given that those indorsements are genuine and effective (Section 8–402); and

    (c) the issuer has no duty to inquire into adverse claims or has discharged any such duty (Section 8–403); and

    (d) any applicable law relating to the collection of taxes has been complied with; and

    (e) the transfer is in fact rightful or is to a bona fide purchaser.

(2) Where an issuer is under a duty to register a transfer of a security the issuer is also liable to the person presenting it for registration or his principal for loss resulting from any unreasonable delay in registration or from failure or refusal to register the transfer.

§ 8–402. Assurance that Indorsements are Effective.

(1) The issuer may require the following assurance that each necessary indorsement (Section 8–308) is genuine and effective

    (a) in all cases, a guarantee of the signature (subsection (1) of Section 8–312) of the person indorsing; and

    (b) where the indorsement is by an agent, appropriate assurance of authority to sign;

    (c) where the indorsement is by a fiduciary, appropriate evidence of appointment or incumbency;

    (d) where there is more than one fiduciary, reasonable assurance that all who are required to sign have done so;

    (e) where the indorsement is by a person not covered by any of the foregoing, assurance appropriate to the case corresponding as nearly as may be to the foregoing.

(2) A "guarantee of the signature" in subsection (1) means a guarantee signed by or on behalf of a person reasonably believed by the issuer to be responsible. The issuer may adopt standards with respect to responsibility provided such standards are not manifestly unreasonable.

(3) "Appropriate evidence of appointment or incumbency" in subsection (1) means

    (a) in the case of a fiduciary appointed or qualified by a court, a certificate issued by or under the direction or supervision of that court or an officer thereof and dated within sixty days before the date of presentation for transfer; or

    (b) in any other case, a copy of a document showing the appointment or a certificate issued by or on behalf of a person reasonably believed by the issuer to be responsible or, in the absence of such a document or certificate, other evidence reasonably deemed by the issuer to be appropriate. The issuer may adopt standards with respect to such evidence provided such standards are not manifestly unreasonable. The issuer is not charged with notice of the contents of any document obtained pursuant to this paragraph (b) except to the extent that the contents relate directly to the appointment or incumbency.

(4) The issuer may elect to require reasonable assurance beyond that specified in this section but if it does so and for a purpose other than that specified in subsection 3(b) both requires and obtains a copy of a will, trust, indenture, articles of co-partnership, by-laws or other controlling instrument it is charged with notice of all matters contained therein affecting the transfer.

§ 8–403. Limited Duty of Inquiry.

(1) An issuer to whom a security is presented for registration is under a duty to inquire into adverse claims if

    (a) a written notification of an adverse claim is received at a time and in a manner which affords the issuer a reasonable opportunity to act on it prior to the issuance of a new, reissued or re-registered security and the notification identifies the claimant, the registered owner and the issue of which the security is a part and provides an address for communications directed to the claimant; or

(b) the issuer is charged with notice of an adverse claim from a controlling instrument which it has elected to require under subsection (4) of Section 8–402.

(2) The issuer may discharge any duty of inquiry by any reasonable means, including notifying an adverse claimant by registered or certified mail at the address furnished by him or if there be no such address at his residency or regular place of business that the security has been presented for registration of transfer by a named person, and that the transfer will be registered unless within thirty days from the date of mailing the notification, either

(a) an appropriate restraining order, injunction or other process issues from a court of competent jurisdiction; or

(b) an indemnity bond sufficient in the issuer's judgment to protect the issuer and any transfer agent, registrar or other agent of the issuer involved, from any loss which it or they may suffer by complying with the adverse claim is filed with the issuer.

(3) Unless an issuer is charged with notice of an adverse claim from a controlling instrument which it has elected to require under subsection (4) of Section 8–402 or receives notification of an adverse claim under subsection (1) of this section, where a security presented for registration is indorsed by the appropriate person or persons the issuer is under no duty to inquire into adverse claims. In particular

(a) an issuer registering a security in the name of a person who is a fiduciary or who is described as a fiduciary is not bound to inquire into the existence, extent, or correct description of the fiduciary relationship and thereafter the issuer may assume without inquiry that the newly registered owner continues to be the fiduciary until the issuer receives written notice that the fiduciary is no longer acting as such with respect to the particular security;

(b) an issuer registering transfer on an indorsement by a fiduciary is not bound to inquire whether the transfer is made in compliance with a controlling instrument or with the law of the state having jurisdiction of the fiduciary relationship, including any law requiring the fiduciary to obtain court approval of the transfer; and

(c) the issuer is not charged with notice of the contents of any court record or file or other recorded or unrecorded document even though the document is in its possession and even though the transfer is made on the indorsement of a fiduciary to the fiduciary himself or to his nominee.

§ 8–404. Liability and Non-Liability for Registration.

(1) Except as otherwise provided in any law relating to the collection of taxes, the issuer is not liable to the owner or any other person suffering loss as a result of the registration of a transfer of a security if

(a) there were on or with the security the necessary indorsements (Section 8–308); and

(b) the issuer had no duty to inquire into adverse claims or has discharged any such duty (Section 8–403).

(2) Where an issuer has registered a transfer of a security to a person not entitled to it the issuer on demand must deliver a like security to the true owner unless

(a) the registration was pursuant to subsection (1); or

(b) the owner is precluded from asserting any claim for registering the transfer under subsection (1) of the following section; or

(c) such delivery would result in overissue, in which case the issuer's liability is governed by Section 8–104.

§ 8–405. Lost, Destroyed and Stolen Securities.

(1) Where a security has been lost, apparently destroyed or wrongfully taken and the owner fails to notify the issuer of that fact within a reasonable time after he has notice of it and the issuer registers a transfer of the security before receiving such a notification, the owner is pre-

cluded from asserting against the issuer any claim for registering the transfer under the preceding section or any claim to a new security under this section.

(2) Where the owner of a security claims that the security has been lost, destroyed or wrongfully taken, the issuer must issue a new security in place of the original security if the owner

    (a) so requests before the issuer has notice that the security has been acquired by a bona fide purchaser; and

    (b) files with the issuer a sufficient indemnity bond; and

    (c) satisfies any other reasonable requirements imposed by the issuer.

(3) If, after the issue of the new security, a bona fide purchaser of the original security presents it for registration of transfer, the insurer must register the transfer unless registration would result in overissue, in which event the issuer's liability is governed by Section 8–104. In addition to any rights on the indemnity bond, the issuer may recover the new security from the person to whom it was issued or any person taking under him except a bona fide purchaser.

§ 8–406. Duty of Authenticating Trustee, Transfer Agent or Registrar.

(1) Where a person acts as authenticating trustee, transfer agent, registrar, or other agent for an issuer in the registration of transfers of its securities or in the issue of new securities or in the cancellation of surrendered securities

    (a) he is under a duty to the issuer to exercise good faith and due diligence in performing his functions; and

    (b) he has with regard to the particular functions he performs the same obligation to the holder or owner of the security and has the same rights and privileges as the issuer has in regard to those functions.

(2) Notice to an authenticating trustee, transfer agent, registrar or other such agent is notice to the issuer with respect to the functions performed by the agent.

ARTICLE 9. Secured Transactions; Sales of Accounts, Contract Rights and Chattel Paper

PART 1
SHORT TITLE, APPLICABILITY AND DEFINITIONS

§ 9–101. Short Title.

This Article shall be known and may be cited as Uniform Commercial Code—Secured Transactions.

§ 9–102. Policy and Scope of Article.*

(1) Except as otherwise provided in Section 9–103 on multiple state transactions and in Section 9–104 on excluded transactions, this Article applies so far as concerns any personal property and fixtures within the jurisdiction of this state

    (a) to any transaction (regardless of its form) which is intended to create a security interest in personal property or fixtures including goods, documents, instruments, general intangibles, chattel paper, accounts or contract rights; and also

    (b) to any sale of accounts, contract rights or chattel paper.

(2) This Article applies to security interests created by contract including pledge, assignment, chattel mortgage, chattel trust, trust deed, factor's lien, equipment trust, conditional sale, trust receipt, other lien or title retention contract and lease or consignment intended as security. This Article does not apply to statutory liens except as provided in Section 9–310.

(3) The application of this Article to a security interest in a secured obligation is not affected by the fact that the obligation is itself secured by a transaction or interest to which this Article does not apply.

Note: *The adoption of this Article should be accompanied by the repeal of existing statutes dealing with conditional sales, trust receipts, factor's liens where the factor is given a non-possessory lien, chattel mortgages, crop mortgages, mortgages on railroad equipment, assignment of accounts and generally statutes regulating security interests in personal property.*

Where the state has a retail installment selling act or small loan act, that legislation should be carefully examined to determine what changes in those acts are needed to conform them to this Article. This Article primarily sets out rules defining rights of a secured-party against persons dealing with the debtor; it does not prescribe regulations and controls which may be necessary to curb abuses arising in the small loan business or in the financing of consumer purchases on credit. Accordingly, there is no intention to repeal existing regulatory acts in those fields. See Section 9–203(2) and the Note thereto.

§ 9–103. Accounts, Contract Rights, General Intangibles and Equipment Relating to Another Jurisdiction; and Incoming Goods Already Subject to a Security Interest.*

(1) If the office where the assignor of accounts or contract rights keeps his records concerning them is in this state, the validity and perfection of a security interest therein and the possibility and effect of proper filing is governed by this Article; otherwise by the law (including the conflict of laws rules) of the jurisdiction where such office is located.

(2) If the chief place of business of a debtor is in this state, this Article governs the validity and perfection of a security interest and the possibility and effect of proper filing with regard to general intangibles or with regard to goods of a type which are normally used in more than one jurisdiction (such as automotive equipment, rolling stock, airplanes, road building equipment, commercial harvesting equipment, construction machinery and the like) if such goods are classified as equipment or classified as inventory by reason of their being leased by the debtor to others. Otherwise, the law (including the conflict of laws rules) of the jurisdiction where such chief place of business is located shall govern. If the chief place of business is located in a jurisdiction which does not provide for perfection of the security interest by filing or recording in that jurisdiction, then the security interest may be perfected by filing in this state. [For the purpose of determining the validity and perfection of a security interest in an airplane, the chief place of business of a debtor who is a foreign air carrier under the Federal Aviation Act of 1958, as amended, is the designated office of the agent upon whom service of process may be made on behalf of the debtor.]

(3) If personal property other than that governed by subsections (1) and (2) is already subject to a security interest when it is brought into this state, the validity of the security interest in this state is to be determined by the law (including the conflict of laws rules) of the jurisdiction where the property was when the security interest attached. However, if the parties to the transaction understood at the time that the security interest attached that the property would be kept in this state and it was brought into this state within 30 days after the security interest attached for purposes other than transportation through this state, then the validity of the security interest in this state is to be determined by the law of this state. If the security interest was already perfected under the law of the jurisdiction where the property was when the security interest attached and before being brought into this state, the security interest continues perfected in this state for four months and also thereafter if within the four month period it is perfected in this state. The security interest may also be perfected in this state after the expiration of the four month period; in such case perfection dates from the time of perfection in this state. If the security interest was not perfected under the law of the jurisdiction where the property was when the security interest attached and before being brought into this state, it may be perfected in this state; in such case perfection dates from the time of perfection in this state.

(4) Notwithstanding subsections (2) and (3), if personal property is covered by a certificate of title issued under a statute of this state or any other jurisdiction which requires indication on a certificate of title of any security interest in the property as a condition of perfection, then the perfection is governed by the law of the jurisdiction which issued the certificate.

[(5) Notwithstanding subsection (1) and Section 9–302, if the office where the assignor of accounts or contract rights keeps his records concerning them is not located in a jurisdiction which is a part of the United States, its territories or possessions, and the accounts or contract rights are within the jurisdiction of this state or the transaction which creates the security interest otherwise bears an appropriate relation to this state, this Article governs the validity and perfection of the security interest and the security interest may only be perfected by notification to the account debtor.]

Note: *The last sentence of subsection (2) and subsection (5) are bracketed to indicate optional enactment. In states engaging in financing of airplanes of foreign carriers and of international open accounts receivable bracketed language will be of value. In other states not engaging in financing of this type, the bracketed language may not be considered necessary.*

§ 9–104. Transactions Excluded From Article.*

This Article does not apply
   (a) to a security interest subject to any statute of the United States such as the Ship Mortgage Act, 1920, to the extent that such statute governs the rights of parties to and third parties affected by transactions in particular types of property; or
   (b) to a landlord's lien; or
   (c) to a lien given by statute or other rule of law for services or materials except as provided in section 9–310 on priority of such liens; or
   (d) to a transfer of a claim for wages, salary or other compensation of an employee; or
   (e) to an equipment trust covering railway rolling stock; or
   (f) to a sale of accounts, contract rights or chattel paper as part of a sale of the business out of which they arose, or an assignment of accounts, contract rights or chattel paper which is for the purpose of collection only, or a transfer of a contract right to an assignee who is also to do the performance under the contract; or
   (g) to a transfer of an interest or claim in or under any policy of insurance; or
   (h) to a right represented by a judgment; or
   (i) to any right of setoff; or
   (j) except to the extent that provision is made for fixtures in Section 9–313, to the creation or transfer of an interest in or lien on real estate, including a lease or rents thereunder; or
   (k) to a transfer in whole or in part of any of the following: any claim arising out of tort; any deposit, savings, passbook or like account maintained with a bank, savings and loan association, credit union or like organization.

§ 9–105. Definitions and Index of Definitions.* †

   (1) In this Article unless the context otherwise requires:
   (a) "Account debtor" means the person who is obligated on an account, chattel paper, contract right or general intangible;
   (b) "Chattel paper" means a writing or writings which evidence both a monetary obligation and a security interest in or a lease of specific goods. When a transaction is evidenced both by such a security agreement or a lease and by an instrument or a series of instruments, the group of writings taken together constitutes chattel paper;
   (c) "Collateral" means the property subject to a security interest, and includes accounts, contract rights and chattel paper which have been sold;
   (d) "Debtor" means the person who owes payment or other performance of the obligation secured, whether or not he owns or has rights in the collateral, and includes the seller of accounts, contract rights or chattel paper. Where the debtor and the owner of the collateral are not the same person, the term "debtor" means the owner of the collateral in any provision of the Article dealing with the collateral, the obligor in any provision dealing with the obligation, and may include both where the context so requires;
   (e) "Document" means document of title as defined in the general definitions of Article 1 (Section 1–201);
   (f) "Goods" includes all things which are movable at the time the security interest attaches or which are fixtures (Section 9–313), but does not include money, docu-

ments, instruments, accounts, chattel paper, general intangibles, contract rights and other things in action. "Goods" also include the unborn young of animals and growing crops;

   (g) "Instrument" means a negotiable instrument (defined in Section 3–104), or a security (defined in Section 8–102) or any other writing which evidences a right to the payment of money and is not itself a security agreement or lease and is of a type which is in ordinary course of business transferred by delivery with any necessary indorsement or assignment;

   (h) "Security agreement" means an agreement which creates or provides for a security interest;

   (i) "Secured party" means a lender, seller or other person in whose favor there is a security interest, including a person to whom accounts, contract rights or chattel paper have been sold. When the holders of obligations issued under an indenture of trust, equipment trust agreement or the like are represented by a trustee or other person, the representative is the secured party.

(2) Other definitions applying to this Article and the sections in which they appear are:

"Account"	Section 9–106
"Consumer goods"	Section 9–109 (1)
"Contract right"	Section 9–106
"Equipment"	Section 9–109 (2)
"Farm products"	Section 9–109 (3)
"General intangibles"	Section 9–106
"Inventory"	Section 9–109 (4)
"Lien creditor"	Section 9–301 (3)
"Proceeds"	Section 9–306 (1)
"Purchase money security interest"	Section 9–107

(3) The following definitions in other Articles apply to this Article:

"Check"	Section 3–104
"Contract for sale"	Section 2–106
"Holder in due course"	Section 3–302
"Note"	Section 3–104
"Sale"	Section 2–106

(4) In addition Article 1 contains general definitions and principles of construction and interpretation applicable throughout this Article.

§ 9–106. Definitions: "Account"; "Contract Right"; "General Intangibles."* †

"Account" means any right to payment for goods sold or leased or for services rendered which is not evidenced by an instrument or chattel paper. "Contract right" means any right to payment under a contract not yet earned by performance and not evidenced by an instrument or chattel paper. "General intangibles" means any personal property (including things in action) other than goods, accounts, contract rights, chattel paper, documents and instruments.

§ 9–107. Definitions: "Purchase Money Security Interest."

A security interest is a "purchase money security interest" to the extent that it is

   (a) taken or retained by the seller of the collateral to secure all or part of its price; or

   (b) taken by a person who by making advances or incurring an obligation gives value to enable the debtor to acquire rights in or the use of collateral if such value is in fact so used.

§ 9–108. When After-Acquired Collateral Not Security for Antecedent Debt.

Where a secured party makes an advance, incurs an obligation, releases a perfected security interest, or otherwise gives new value which is to be secured in whole or in part by after-acquired property his security interest in the after-acquired collateral shall be deemed to be taken for new value and not as security for an antecedent debt if the debtor acquires his rights in such collateral either in the ordinary course of his business or under a contract of purchase made pursuant to the security agreement within a reasonable time after new value is given.

§ 9–109. Classification of Goods; "Consumer Goods"; "Equipment"; "Farm Products"; "Inventory."

Goods are

(1) "consumer goods" if they are used or bought for use primarily for personal, family or household purposes;

(2) "equipment" if they are used or bought for use primarily in business (including farming or a profession) or by a debtor who is a non-profit organization or a governmental subdivision or agency or if the goods are not included in the definitions of inventory, farm products or consumer goods;

(3) "farm products" if they are crops or livestock or supplies used or produced in farming operations or if they are products of crops or livestock in their unmanufactured states (such as ginned cotton, wool-clip, maple syrup, milk and eggs), and if they are in the possession of a debtor engaged in raising, fattening, grazing or other farming operations. If goods are farm products they are neither equipment nor inventory.

(4) "inventory" if they are held by a person who holds them for sale or lease or to be furnished under contracts of service or if he has so furnished them, or if they are raw materials, work in process or materials used or consumed in a business. Inventory of a person is not to be classified as his equipment.

§ 9–110. Sufficiency of Description.

For the purposes of this Article any description of personal property or real estate is sufficient whether or not it is specific if it reasonably identifies what is described.

§ 9–111. Applicability of Bulk Transfer Laws.

The creation of a security interest is not a bulk transfer under Article 6(see Section 6–103).

§ 9–112. Where Collateral Is Not Owned by Debtor.

Unless otherwise agreed, when a secured party knows that collateral is owned by a person who is not the debtor, the owner of the collateral is entitled to receive from the secured party any surplus under Section 9–502(2) or under Section 9–504(1), and is not liable for the debt or for any deficiency after resale, and he has the same right as the debtor

    (a) to receive statements under Section 9–208;

    (b) to receive notice of and to object to a secured party's proposal to retain the collateral in satisfaction of the indebtedness under Section 9–505;

    (c) to redeem the collateral under Section 9–506;

    (d) to obtain injunctive or other relief under Section 9–507(1); and

    (e) to recover losses caused to him under Section 9–208(2).

§ 9–113. Security Interests Arising Under Article on Sales.

A security interest arising solely under the Article on Sales (Article 2) is subject to the provisions of this Article except that to the extent that and so long as the debtor does not have or does not lawfully obtain possession of the goods

    (a) no security agreement is necessary to make the security interest enforceable; and

    (b) no filing is required to perfect the security interest; and

    (c) the rights of the secured party on default by the debtor are governed by the Article on Sales (Article 2).

PART 2
VALIDITY OF SECURITY AGREEMENT AND RIGHTS OF PARTIES THERETO

§ 9–201. General Validity of Security Agreement.

Except as otherwise provided by this Act a security agreement is effective according to its terms between the parties, against purchasers of the collateral and against creditors. Nothing in this **Article** validates any charge or practice illegal under any statute or regulation thereunder governing usury, small loans, retail installment sales, or the like, or extends the application of any such statute or regulation to any transaction not otherwise subject thereto.

§ 9–202. Title to Collateral Immaterial.

Each provision of this Article with regard to rights, obligations and remedies applies whether title to collateral is in the secured party or in the debtor.

§ 9–203. Enforceability of Security Interest; Proceeds, Formal Requisites.*

Subject to the provisions of Section 4–208 on the security interest of a collecting bank and Section 9–113 on a security interest arising under the Article on Sales, a security interest is not enforceable against the debtor or third parties unless

   (a) the collateral is in the possession of the secured party; or
   (b) the debtor has signed a security agreement which contains a description of the collateral and in addition, when the security interest covers crops or oil, gas or minerals to be extracted or timber to be cut, a description of the land concerned. In describing collateral, the word "proceeds" is sufficient without further description to cover proceeds of any character.

(2) A transaction, although subject to this Article, is also subject to —————‡, and in the case of conflict between the provisions of this Article and any such statute, the provisions of such statute control. Failure to comply with any applicable statute has only the effect which is specified therein.

Note: *At ‡ in subsection (2) insert reference to any local statute regulating small loans, retail installment sales and the like.*

The foregoing subsection (2) is designed to make it clear that certain transactions, although subject to this Article, must also comply with other applicable legislation.

This Article is designed to regulate all the "security" aspects of transactions within its scope. There is, however, much regulatory legislation, particularly in the consumer field, which supplements this Article and should not be repealed by its enactment. Examples are small loan acts, retail installment selling acts and the like. Such acts may provide for licensing and rate regulation and may prescribe particular forms of contract. Such provisions should remain in force despite the enactment of this Article. On the other hand if a Retail Installment Selling Act contains provisions on filing, rights on default, etc., such provisions should be repealed as inconsistent with this Article.

§ 9–204. When Security Interest Attaches; After-Acquired Property; Future Advances.*

(1) A security interest cannot attach until there is agreement (subsection (3) of Section 1–201) that it attach and value is given and the debtor has rights in the collateral. It attaches as soon as all of the events in the preceding sentence have taken place unless explicit agreement postpones the time of attaching.

(2) For the purposes of this section the debtor has no rights
   (a) in crops until they are planted or otherwise become growing crops, in the young of livestock until they are conceived;
   (b) in fish until caught, in oil, gas or minerals until they are extracted, in timber until it is cut;
   (c) in a contract right until the contract has been made;
   (d) in an account until it comes into existence.

(3) Except as provided in subsection (4) a security agreement may provide that collateral whenever acquired, shall secure all obligations covered by the security agreement.

(4) No security interest attaches under an after-acquired property clause
   (a) to crops which become such more than one year after the security agreement is executed except that a security interest in crops which is given in conjunction with a lease or a land purchase or improvement transaction evidenced by a contract, mortgage or deed of trust may if so agreed attach to crops to be grown on the land concerned during the period of such real estate transaction;

(b) to consumer goods other than accessions (Section 9–314) when given as additional security unless the debtor acquires rights in them within ten days after the secured party gives value.

(5) Obligations covered by a security agreement may include future advances or other value whether or not the advances or value are given pursuant to commitment.

§ 9–205. Use or Disposition of Collateral Without Accounting Permissible.*

A security interest is not invalid or fraudulent against creditors by reason of liberty in the debtor to use, commingle or dispose of all or part of the collateral (including returned or repossessed goods) or to collect or compromise accounts, contract rights or chattel paper, or to accept the return of goods or make repossessions, or to use, commingle or dispose of proceeds, or by reason of the failure of the secured party to require the debtor to account for proceeds or replace collateral. This section does not relax the requirements of possession where perfection of a security interest depends upon possession of the collateral by the secured or by a bailee.

§ 9–206. Agreement Not to Assert Defenses Against Assignee; Modification of Sales Warranties Where Security Agreement Exists.

(1) Subject to any statute or decision which establishes a different rule for buyers or lessees of consumer goods, an agreement by a buyer or lessee that he will not assert against an assignee any claim or defense which he may have against the seller or lessor is enforceable by an assignee who takes his assignment for value, in good faith and without notice of a claim or defense, except as to defenses of a type which may be asserted against a holder in due course of a negotiable instrument under the Article on Commercial Paper (Article 3). A buyer who as part of one transaction signs both a negotiable instrument and a security agreement makes such an agreement.

(2) When a seller retains a purchase money security interest in goods the Article on Sales (Article 2) governs the sale and any disclaimer, limitation or modification of the seller's warranties.

§ 9–207. Rights and Duties When Collateral Is in Secured Party's Possession.

(1) A secured party must use reasonable care in the custody and preservation of collateral in his possession. In the case of an instrument or chattel paper reasonable care includes taking necessary steps to preserve rights against prior parties unless otherwise agreed.

(2) Unless otherwise agreed, when collateral is in the secured party's possession
   (a) reasonable expenses (including the cost of any insurance and payment of taxes or other charges) incurred in the custody, preservation, use or operation of the collateral are chargeable to the debtor and are secured by the collateral;
   (b) the risk of accidental loss or damage is on the debtor to the extent of any deficiency in any effective insurance coverage;
   (c) the secured party may hold as additional security any increase or profits (except money) received from the collateral, but money so received, unless remitted to the debtor, shall be applied in reduction of the secured obligation;
   (d) the secured party must keep the collateral identifiable but fungible collateral may be commingled;
   (e) the secured party may repledge the collateral upon terms which do not impair the debtor's right to redeem it.

(3) A secured party is liable for any loss caused by his failure to meet any obligation imposed by the preceding subsections but does not lose his security interest.

(4) A secured party may use or operate the collateral for the purpose of preserving the collateral or its value or pursuant to the order of a court of appropriate jurisdiction or, except in the case of consumer goods, in the manner and to the extent provided in the security agreement.

§ 9–208. Request for Statement of Account or List of Collateral.

(1) A debtor may sign a statement indicating what he believes to be the aggregate amount of unpaid indebtedness as of a specified date and may send it to the secured party with a request

that the statement be approved or corrected and returned to the debtor. When the security agreement or any other record kept by the secured party identifies the collateral a debtor may similarly request the secured party to approve or correct a list of the collateral.

(2) The secured party must comply with such a request within two weeks after receipt by sending a written correction or approval. If the secured party claims a security interest in all of a particular type of collateral owned by the debtor he may indicate that fact in his reply and need not approve or correct an itemized list of such collateral. If the secured party without reasonable excuse fails to comply he is liable for any loss caused to the debtor thereby; and if the debtor has properly included in his request a good faith statement of the obligation or a list of the collateral or both the secured party may claim a security interest only as shown in the statement against persons misled by his failure to comply. If he no longer has an interest in the obligation or collateral at the time the request is received he must disclose the name and address of any successor in interest known to him and he is liable for any loss caused to the debtor as a result of failure to disclose. A successor in interest is not subject to this section until a request is received by him.

(3) A debtor is entitled to such a statement once every six months without charge. The secured party may require payment of a charge not exceeding $10 for each additional statement furnished.

PART 3
RIGHTS OF THIRD PARTIES; PERFECTED AND UNPERFECTED SECURITY INTERESTS; RULES OF PRIORITY

§ 9–301. Persons Who Take Priority Over Unperfected Security Interests; "Lien Creditor." *

(1) Except as otherwise provided in subsection (2), an unperfected security interest is subordinate to the rights of

    (a) persons entitled to priority under Section 9–312;

    (b) a person who becomes a lien creditor without knowledge of the security interest and before it is perfected;

    (c) in the case of goods, instruments, documents, and chattel paper, a person who is not a secured party and who is a transferee in bulk or other buyer not in ordinary course of business to the extent that he gives value and receives delivery of the collateral without knowledge of the security interest and before it is perfected;

    (d) in the case of accounts, contract rights, and general intangibles, a person who is not a secured party and who is a transferee to the extent that he gives value without knowledge of the security interest and before it is perfected.

(2) If the secured party files with respect to a purchase money security interest before or within ten days after the collateral comes into possession of the debtor, he takes priority over the rights of a transferee in bulk or of a lien creditor which arise between the time the security interest attaches and the time of filing.

(3) A "lien creditor" means a creditor who has acquired a lien on the property involved by attachment, levy or the like and includes an assignee for benefit of creditors from the time of assignment, and a trustee in bankruptcy from the date of the filing of the petition or a receiver in equity from the time of appointment. Unless all the creditors represented had knowledge of the security interest such a representative of creditors is a lien creditor without knowledge even though he personally has knowledge of the security interest.

§ 9–302. When Filing Is Required to Perfect Security Interest; Security Interests to Which Filing Provisions of This Article Do Not Apply. *

(1) A financing statement must be filed to perfect all security interests except the following:

    (a) a security interest in collateral in possession of the secured party under Section 9–305;

    (b) a security interest temporarily perfected in instruments or documents without delivery under Section 9–304 or in proceeds for a 10 day period under Section 9–306;

    (c) a purchase money security interest in farm equipment having a purchase price not in excess of $2500; but filing is required for a fixture under Section 9–313 or for a motor vehicle required to be licensed;

(d) a purchase money security interest in consumer goods; but filing is required for a fixture under Section 9–313 or for a motor vehicle required to be licensed;

(e) an assignment of accounts or contract rights which does not alone or in conjunction with other assignments to the same assignee transfer a significant part of the outstanding accounts or contract rights of the assignor;

(f) a security interest of a collecting bank (Section 4–208) or arising under the Article on Sales (see Section 9–313) or covered in subsection (3) of this section.

(2) If a secured party assigns a perfected security interest, no filing under this Article is required in order to continue the perfected status of the security interest against creditors of and transferees from the original debtor.

(3) The filing provisions of this Article do not apply to a security interest in property subject to a statute

(a) of the United States which provides for a national registration or filing of all security interests in such property; or

Note: *States to select either Alternative A or Alternative B.*
Alternative A—
(b) of this state which provides for central filing of, or which requires indication on a certificate of title of, such security interests in such property.
Alternative B—
(b) of this state which provides for central filing of security interests in such property, or in a motor vehicle which is not inventory held for sale for which a certificate of title is required under the statutes of this state if a notation of such a security interest can be indicated by a public official on a certificate or a duplicate thereof.

(4) A security interest in property covered by a statute described in subsection (3) can be perfected only by registration or filing under that statute or by indication of the security interest on a cerificate of title or a duplicate thereof by a public official.

§ 9–303. When Security Interest Is Perfected; Continuity of Perfection.

(1) A security interest is perfected when it has attached and when all of the applicable steps required for perfection have been taken. Such steps are specified in Sections 9–302, 9–304, 9–305 and 9–306. If such steps are taken before the security interest attaches, it is perfected at the time when it attaches.

(2) If a security interest is originally perfected in any way permitted under this Article and is subsequently perfected in some other way under this Article, without an intermediate period when it was unperfected, the security interest shall be deemed to be perfected continuously for the purposes of this Article.

§ 9–304. Perfection of Security Interest in Instruments, Documents, and Goods Covered by Documents; Perfection by Permissive Filing; Temporary Perfection Without Filing or Transfer of Possession.*

(1) A security interest in chattel paper or negotiable documents may be perfected by filing. A security interest in instruments (other than instruments which constitute part of chattel paper) can be perfected only by the secured party's taking possession, except as provided in subsections (4) and (5).

(2) During the period that goods are in the possession of the issuer of a negotiable document therefor, a security interest in the goods is perfected by perfecting a security interest in the document, and any security interest in the goods otherwise perfected during such period is subject thereto.

(3) A security interest in goods in the possession of a bailee other than one who has issued a negotiable document therefor is perfected by issuance of a document in the name of the secured party or by the bailee's receipt of notification of the secured party's interest or by filing as to the goods.

(4) A security interest in instruments or negotiable documents is perfected without filing or the taking of possession for a period of 21 days from the time it attaches to the extent that it arises for new value given under a written security agreement.

(5) A security interest remains perfected for a period of 21 days without filing where a secured party having a perfected security interest in an instrument, a negotiable document or goods in possession of a bailee other than one who has issued a negotiable document therefor

(a) makes available to the debtor the goods or documents representing the goods for the purpose of ultimate sale or exchange or for the purpose of loading, unloading, storing, shipping, transshipping, manufacturing, processing or otherwise dealing with them in a manner preliminary to their sale or exchange; or

(b) delivers the instrument to the debtor for the purpose of ultimate sale or exchange or of presentation, collection, renewal or registration of transfer.

(6) After the 21 day period in subsections (4) and (5) perfection depends upon compliance with applicable provisions of this Article.

§ 9–305. When Possession by Secured Party Perfects Security Interest Without Filing.*

A security interest in letters of credit and advices of credit (subsection (2) (a) of Section 5–116), goods, instruments, negotiable documents or chattel paper may be perfected by the secured party's taking possession of the collateral. If such collateral other than goods covered by a negotiable document is held by a bailee, the secured party is deemed to have possession from the time the bailee receives notification of the secured party's interest. A security interest is perfected by possession from the time possession is taken without relation back and continues only so long as possession is retained, unless otherwise specified in this Article. The security interest may be otherwise perfected as provided in this Article before or after the period of possession by the secured party.

§ 9–306. "Proceeds"; Secured Party's Rights on Disposition of Collateral.*

(1) "Proceeds" includes whatever is received when collateral or proceeds is sold, exchanged, collected or otherwise disposed of. The term also includes the account arising when the right to payment is earned under a contract right. Money, checks and the like are "cash proceeds." All other proceeds are "non-cash proceeds."

(2) Except where this Article otherwise provides, a security interest continues in collateral notwithstanding sale, exchange or other disposition thereof by the debtor unless his action was authorized by the secured party in the security agreement or otherwise, and also continues in any identifiable proceeds including collections received by the debtor.

(3) The security interest in proceeds is a continuously perfected security interest if the interest in the original collateral was perfected but it ceases to be a perfected security interest and becomes unperfected ten days after receipt of the proceeds by the debtor unless

(a) a filed financing statement covering the original collateral also covers proceeds; or

(b) the security interest in the proceeds is perfected before the expiration of the ten day period.

(4) In the event of insolvency proceedings instituted by or against a debtor, a secured party with a perfected security interest in proceeds has a perfected security interest

(a) in identifiable non-cash proceeds;

(b) in identifiable cash proceeds in the form of money which is not commingled with other money or deposited in a bank account prior to the insolvency proceedings;

(c) in identifiable cash proceeds in the form of checks and the like which are not deposited in a bank account prior to the insolvency proceedings; and

(d) in all cash and bank accounts of the debtor, if other cash proceeds have been commingled or deposited in a bank account, but the perfected security interest under this paragraph (d) is

(i) subject to any right of setoff; and

(ii) limited to an amount not greater than the amount of any cash proceeds received by the debtor within ten days before the institution of the insolvency proceedings and commingled or deposited in a bank account prior to the insolvency proceedings less the amount of cash proceeds received by the debtor and paid over to the secured party during the ten day period.

(5) If a sale of goods results in an account or chattel paper which is transferred by the seller to a secured party, and if the goods are returned to or are repossessed by the seller or the secured party, the following rules determine priorities:

(a) If the goods were collateral at the time of sale for an indebtedness of the seller which is still unpaid, the original security interest attaches again to the goods and continues as a perfected security interest if it was perfected at the time when the goods were sold. If the security interest was originally perfected by a filing which is still effective, nothing further is required to continue the perfected status; in any other case, the secured party must take possession of the returned or repossessed goods or must file.

(b) An unpaid transferee of the chattel paper has a security interest in the goods against the transferor. Such security interest is prior to a security interest asserted under paragraph (a) to the extent that the transferee of the chattel paper was entitled to priority under Section 9–308.

(c) An unpaid transferee of the account has a security interest in the goods against the transferor. Such security interest is subordinate to a security interest asserted under paragraph (a).

(d) A security interest of an unpaid transferee asserted under paragraph (b) or (c) must be perfected for protection against creditors of the transferor and purchasers of the returned or repossessed goods.

§ 9–307. Protection of Buyers of Goods.*

(1) A buyer in ordinary course of business (subsection (9) of Section 1–201) other than a person buying farm products from a person engaged in farming operations takes free of a security interest created by his seller even though the security interest is perfected and even though the buyer knows of its existence.

(2) In the case of consumer goods and in the case of farm equipment having an original purchase price not in excess of $2500 (other than fixtures, see Section 9–313), a buyer takes free of a security interest even though perfected if he buys without knowledge of the security interest, for value and for his own personal, family or household purposes or his own farming operations unless prior to the purchase the secured party has filed a financing statement covering such goods.

§ 9–308. Purchase of Chattel Paper and Non-Negotiable Instruments.*

A purchaser of chattel paper or a non-negotiable instrument who gives new value and takes possession of it in the ordinary course of his business and without knowledge that the specific paper or instrument is subject to a security interest has priority over a security interest which is perfected under Section 9–304 (permissive filing and temporary perfection). A purchaser of chattel paper who gives new value and takes possession of it in the ordinary course of his business has priority over a security interest in chattel paper which is claimed merely as proceeds of inventory subject to a security interest (Section 9–306), even though he knows that the specific paper is subject to the security interest.

§ 9–309. Protection of Purchasers of Instruments and Documents.

Nothing in this Article limits the rights of a holder in due course of a negotiable instrument (Section 3–302) or a holder to whom a negotiable document of title has been duly negotiated (Section 7–501) or a bona fide purchaser of a security (Section 8–301) and such holders or purchasers take priority over an earlier security interest even though perfected. Filing under this Article does not constitute notice of the security interest to such holders or purchasers.

§ 9–310. Priority of Certain Liens Arising by Operation of Law.

When a person in the ordinary course of his business furnishes services or materials with respect to goods subject to a security interest, a lien upon goods in the possession of such person given by statute or rule of law for such materials or services takes priority over a perfected security interest unless the lien is statutory and the statute expressly provides otherwise.

§ 9–311. Alienability of Debtor's Rights: Judicial Process.

The debtor's rights in collateral may be voluntarily or involuntarily transferred (by way of sale, creation of a security interest, attachment, levy, garnishment or other judicial process) notwithstanding a provision in the security agreement prohibiting any transfer or making the transfer constitute a default.

§ 9–312. Priorities Among Conflicting Security Interests in the Same Collateral.*

(1) The rules of priority stated in the following sections shall govern where applicable; Section 4–208 with respect to the security interest of collecting banks in items being collected, accompanying documents and proceeds; Section 9–301 on certain priorities; Section 9–304 on goods covered by documents; Section 9–306 on proceeds and repossessions; Section 9–307 on buyers of goods; Section 9–308 on possessory against nonpossessory interests in chattel paper or non-negotiable instruments; Section 9–309 on security interests in negotiable instruments, documents or securities; Section 9–310 on priorities between perfected security interests and liens by operation of law; Section 9–313 on security interests in fixtures as against interests in real estate; Section 9–314 on security interests in accessions as against interest in goods; Section 9–315 on conflicting security interests where goods lose their identity or become part of a product; and Section 9–316 on contractual subordination.

(2) A perfected security interest in crops for new value given to enable the debtor to produce the crops during the production season and given not more than three months before the crops become growing crops by planting or otherwise takes priority over an earlier perfected security interest to the extent that such earlier interest secures obligations due more than six months before the crops become growing crops by planting or otherwise, even though the person giving new value had knowledge of the earlier security interest.

(3) A purchase money security interest in inventory collateral has priority over a conflicting security interest in the same collateral if

    (a) the purchase money security interest is perfected at the time the debtor receives possession of the collateral; and

    (b) any secured party whose security interest is known to the holder of the purchase money security interest or who, prior to the date of the filing made by the holder of the purchase money security interest, had filed a financing statement covering the same items or type of inventory, has received notification of the purchase money security interest before the debtor receives possession of the collateral covered by the purchase money security interest; and

    (c) such notification states that the person giving the notice has or expects to acquire a purchase money security interest in inventory of the debtor, describing such inventory by item or type.

(4) A purchase money security interest in collateral other than inventory has priority over a conflicting security interest in the same collateral if the purchase money security interest is perfected at the time the debtor receives possession of the collateral or within ten days thereafter.

(5) In all cases not governed by other rules stated in this section (including cases of purchase money security interests which do not qualify for the special priorities set forth in subsections (3) and (4) of this section), priority between conflicting security interests in the same collateral shall be determined as follows:

    (a) in the order of filing if both are perfected by filing, regardless of which security interest attached first under Section 9–204(1) and whether it attached before or after filing;

    (b) in the order of perfection unless both are perfected by filing, regardless of which security interest attached first under Section 9–204(1) and, in the case of a filed security interest, whether it attached before or after filing; and

(c) in the order of attachment under Section 9–204(1) so long as neither is perfected.

(6) For the purpose of the priority rules of the immediately preceding subsection, a continuously perfected security interest shall be treated at all times as if perfected by filing if it was originally so perfected and it shall be treated at all times as if perfected otherwise than by filing if it was originally perfected otherwise than by filing.

§ 9–313. Priority of Security Interests in Fixtures.*

(1) The rules of this section do not apply to goods incorporated into a structure in the manner of lumber, bricks, tile, cement, glass, metal work and the like and no security interest in them exists under this Article unless the structure remains personal property under applicable law. The law of this state other than this Act determines whether and when other goods become fixtures. This Act does not prevent creation of an encumbrance upon fixtures or real estate pursuant to the law applicable to real estate.

(2) A security interest which attaches to goods before they become fixtures takes priority as to the goods over the claims of all persons who have an interest in the real estate except as stated in subsection (4).

(3) A security interest which attaches to goods after they become fixtures is valid against all persons subsequently acquiring interests in the real estate except as stated in subsection (4) but is invalid against any person with an interest in the real estate at the time the security interest attaches to the goods who has not in writing consented to the security interest or disclaimed an interest in the goods as fixtures.

(4) The security interests described in subsections (2) and (3) do not take priority over
  (a) a subsequent purchaser for value of any interest in the real estate; or
  (b) a creditor with a lien on the real estate subsequently obtained by judicial proceedings; or
  (c) a creditor with a prior encumbrance of record on the real estate to the extent that he makes subsequent advances

if the subsequent purchase is made, the lien by judicial proceedings is obtained, or the subsequent advance under the prior encumbrance is made or contracted for without knowledge of the security interest and before it is perfected. A purchaser of the real estate at a foreclosure sale other than an encumbrancer purchasing at his own foreclosure sale is a subsequent purchaser within this section.

(5) When under subsections (2) or (3) and (4) a secured party has priority over the claims of all persons who have interests in the real estate, he may, on default, subject to the provisions of Part 5, remove his collateral from the real estate but he must reimburse any encumbrancer or owner of the real estate who is not the debtor and who has not otherwise agreed for the cost of repair of any physical injury, but not for any diminution in value of the real estate caused by the absence of the goods removed or by any necessity for replacing them. A person entitled to reimbursement may refuse permission to remove until the secured party gives adequate security for the performance of this obligation.

§ 9–314. Accessions.

(1) A security interest in goods which attaches before they are installed in or affixed to other goods takes priority as to the goods installed or affixed (called in this section "accessions") over the claims of all persons to the whole except as stated in subsection (3) and subject to Section 9–315(1).

(2) A security interest which attaches to goods after they become part of a whole is valid against all persons subsequently acquiring interests in the whole except as stated in subsection (3) but is invalid against any person with an interest in the whole at the time the security interest attaches to the goods who has not in writing consented to the security interest or disclaimed an interest in the goods as part of the whole.

(3) The security interests described in subsections (1) and (2) do not take priority over
  (a) a subsequent purchaser for value of any interest in the whole; or
  (b) a creditor with a lien on the whole subsequently obtained by judicial proceedings; or
  (c) a creditor with a prior perfected security interest in the whole to the extent that he makes subsequent advances

if the subsequent purchase is made, the lien by judicial proceedings obtained or the subsequent advance under the prior perfected security interest is made or contracted for without knowledge of the security interest and before it is perfected. A purchaser of the whole at a foreclosure sale other than the holder of a perfected security interest purchasing at his own foreclosure sale is a subsequent purchaser within this section.

(4) When under subsections (1) or (2) and (3) a secured party has an interest in accessions which has priority over the claims of all persons who have interests in the whole, he may on default subject to the provisions of Part 5 remove his collateral from the whole but he must reimburse any encumbrancer or owner of the whole who is not the debtor and who has not otherwise agreed for the cost of repair of any physical injury but not for any diminution in value of the whole caused by the absence of the goods removed or by any necessity for re-placing them. A person entitled to reimbursement may refuse permission to remove until the secured party gives adequate security for the performance of this obligation.

§ 9–315. Priority When Goods Are Commingled or Processed.

(1) If a security interest in goods was perfected and subsequently the goods or a part thereof have become part of a product or mass, the security interest continues in the product or mass if

    (a) the goods are so manufactured, processed, assembled or commingled that their identity is lost in the product or mass; or

    (b) a financing statement covering the original goods also covers the product into which the goods have been manufactured, processed or assembled.

In a case to which paragraph (b) applies, no separate security interest in that part of the original goods which has been manufactured, processed or assembled into the product may be claimed under Section 9–314.

(2) When under subsection (1) more than one security interest attaches to the product or mass, they rank equally according to the ratio that the cost of the goods to which each interest originally attached bears to the cost of the total product or mass.

§ 9–316. Priority Subject to Subordination.

Nothing in this Article prevents subordination by agreement by any person entitled to priority.

§ 9–317. Secured Party Not Obligated on Contract of Debtor.

The mere existence of a security interest or authority given to the debtor to dispose of or use collateral does not impose contract or tort liability upon the secured party for the debtor's acts or omissions.

§ 9–318. Defenses Against Assignee; Modification of Contract After Notification of Assignment Ineffective; Identification and Proof of Assignment.*

(1) Unless an account debtor has made an enforceable agreement not to assert defenses or claims arising out of a sale as provided in Section 9–206 the rights of an assignee are subject to

    (a) all the terms of the contract between the account debtor and assignor and any defense or claim arising therefrom; and

    (b) any other defense or claim of the account debtor against the assignor which accrues before the account debtor receives notification of the assignment.

(2) So far as the right to payment under an assigned contract right has not already become an account, and notwithstanding notification of the assignment, any modification of or substitution for the contract made in good faith and in accordance with reasonable commercial standards is effective against an assignee unless the account debtor has otherwise agreed but the assignee acquires corresponding rights under the modified or substituted contract. The assignment may provide that such modification or substitution is a breach by the assignor.

(3) The account debtor is authorized to pay the assignor until the account debtor receives notification that the account has been assigned and that payment is to be made to the assignee. A notification which does not reasonably identify the rights assigned is ineffective. If requested

by the account debtor, the assignee must seasonably furnish reasonable proof that the assignment has been made and unless he does so the account debtor may pay the assignor.

(4) A term in any contract between an account debtor and an assignor which prohibits assignment of an account or contract right to which they are parties is ineffective.

PART 4
FILING

§ 9–401. Place of Filing; Erroneous Filing; Removal of Collateral.*

First Alternative Subsection (1)

(1) The proper place to file in order to perfect a security interest is as follows:

(a) when the collateral is goods which at the time the security interest attaches are or are to become fixtures, then in the office where a mortgage on the real estate concerned would be filed or recorded;

(b) in all other cases, in the office of the [Secretary of State].

Second Alternative Subsection (1)

(1) The proper place to file in order to perfect a security interest is as follows:

(a) when the collateral is equipment used in farming operations, or farm products, or accounts, contract rights or general intangibles arising from or relating to the sale of farm products by a farmer, or consumer goods, then in the office of the _____ in the county of the debtor's residence or if the debtor is not a resident of this state then the office of the _____ in the county where the goods are kept, and in addition when the collateral is crops in the office of the _____ in the county where the land on which the crops are growing or to be grown is located;

(b) when the collateral is goods which at the time the security interest attaches are or are to become fixtures, then in the office where a mortgage on the real estate concerned would be filed or recorded;

(c) in all other cases, in the office of the [Secretary of State].

Third Alternative Subsection (1)

(1) The proper place to file in order to perfect a security interest is as follows:

(a) when the collateral is equipment used in farming operations, or farm products, or accounts, contract rights or general intangibles arising from or relating to the sale of farm products by a farmer, or consumer goods, then in the office of the _____ in the county of the debtor's residence or if the debtor is not a resident of this state then in the office of the _____ in the county where the goods are kept, and in addition when the collateral is crops in the office of the _____ in the county where the land on which the crops are growing or to be grown is located;

(b) when the collateral is goods which at the time the security interest attaches are or are to become fixtures, then in the office where a mortgage on the real estate concerned would be filed or recorded;

(c) in all other cases, in the office of the [Secretary of State] and in addition, if the debtor has a place of business in only one county of this state, also in the office of _____ of such county, or, if the debtor has no place of business in this state, but resides in the state, also in the office of _____ of the county in which he resides.

Note: *One of the three alternatives should be selected as subsection (1).*

(2) A filing which is made in good faith in an improper place or not in all of the places required by this section is nevertheless effective with regard to any collateral as to which the filing complied with the requirements of this Article and is also effective with regard to collateral covered by the financing statement against any person who has knowledge of the contents of such financing statement.

(3) A filing which is made in the proper place in this state continues effective even though the debtor's residence or place of business or the location of the collateral or its use, whichever controlled the original filing, is thereafter changed.

Alternative Subsection (3)

[(3) A filing which is made in the proper county continues effective for four months after a change to another county of the debtor's residence or place of business or the location of the collateral, whichever controlled the original filing. It becomes ineffective thereafter unless a copy of the financing statement signed by the secured party is filed in the new county within said period. The security interest may also be perfected in the new county after the expiration of the four-month period, in such case perfection dates from the time of perfection in the new county. A change in the use of the collateral does not impair the effectiveness of the original filing.]

(4) If collateral is brought into this state from another jurisdiction, the rules stated in Section 9–103 determine whether filing is necessary in this state.

§ 9–402. Formal Requisites of Financing Statement; Amendments.*

(1) A financing statement is sufficient if it is signed by the debtor and the secured party, gives an address of the secured party from which information concerning the security interest may be obtained, gives a mailing address of the debtor and contains a statement indicating the types, or describing the items, of collateral. A financing statement may be filed before a security agreement is made or a security interest otherwise attaches. When the financing statement covers crops growing or to be grown or goods which are or are to become fixtures, the statement must also contain a description of the real estate concerned. A copy of the security agreement is sufficient as a financing statement if it contains the above information and is signed by both parties.

(2) A financing statement which otherwise complies with subsection (1) is sufficient although it is signed only by the secured party when it is filed to perfect a security interest in

   (a) collateral already subject to a security interest in another jurisdiction when it is brought into this state. Such a financing statement must state that the collateral was brought into this state under such circumstances.

   (b) proceeds under Section 9–30 if the security interest in the original collateral was perfected. Such a financing statement must describe the original collateral.

(3) A form substantially as follows is sufficient to comply with subsection (1):

Name of debtor (or assignor) _____

Address _____

Name of secured party (or assignee) _____

Address _____

1. This financing statement covers the following types (or items) of property:
   (Describe) _____

2. (If collateral is crops) The above described crops are growing or are to be grown on:
   (Describe Real Estate) _____

3. (If collateral is goods which are or to become fixtures) The above described goods are affixed or to be affixed to:
   (Describe Real Estate) _____

4. (If proceeds or products of collateral are claimed) Proceeds—Products of the collateral are also covered.
   Signature of Debtor (or Assignor) _____
   Signature of Secured Party (or Assignee) _____

(4) The term "financing statement" as used in this Article means the original financing statement and any amendments but if any amendment adds collateral, it is effective as to the added collateral only from the filing date of the amendment.

(5) A financing statement substantially complying with the requirements of this section is effective even though it contains minor errors which are not seriously misleading.

§ 9–403. What Constitutes Filing; Duration of Filing; Effect of Lapsed Filing; Duties of Filing Officer.*

(1) Presentation for filing of a financing statement and tender of the filing fee or acceptance of the statement by the filing officer constitutes filing under this Article.

(2) A filed financing statement which states a maturity date of the obligation secured of five years or less is effective until such maturity date and thereafter for a period of sixty days. Any other filed financing statement is effective for a period of five years from the date of filing. The effectiveness of a filed financing statement lapses on the expiration of such sixty day period after a stated maturity date or on the expiration of such five year period, as the case may be, unless a continuation statement is filed prior to the lapse. Upon such lapse the security interest becomes unperfected. A filed financing statement which states that the obligation secured is payable on demand is effective for five years from the date of filing.

(3) A continuation statement may be filed by the secured party (i) within six months before and sixty days after a stated maturity date of five years or less, and (ii) otherwise within six months prior to the expiration of the five year period specified in subsection (2). Any such continuation statement must be signed by the secured party, identify the original statement by file number and state that the original statement is still effective. Upon timely filing of the continuation statement, the effectiveness of the original statement is continued for five years after the last date to which the filing was effective whereupon it lapses in the same manner as provided in subsection (2) unless another continuation statement is filed prior to such lapse. Succeeding continuation statements may be filed in the same manner to continue the effectiveness of the original statement. Unless a statute on disposition of public records provides otherwise, the filing officer may remove a lapsed statement from the files and destroy it.

(4) A filing officer shall mark each statement with a consecutive file number and with the date and hour of filing and shall hold the statement for public inspection. In addition the filing officer shall index the statements according to the name of the debtor and shall note in the index the file number and the address of the debtor given in the statement.

(5) The uniform fee for filing, indexing and furnishing filing data for an original or a continuation statement shall be $_____.

§ 9–404. Termination Statement.*

(1) Whenever there is no outstanding secured obligation and no commitment to make advances, incur obligations or otherwise give value, the secured party must on written demand by the debtor send the debtor a statement that he no longer claims a security interest under the financing statement, which shall be identified by file number. A termination statement signed by a person other than the secured party of record must include or be accompanied by the assignment or a statement by the secured party of record that he has assigned the security interest to the signer of the termination statement. The uniform fee for filing and indexing such an assignment or statement thereof shall be $_____. If the affected secured party fails to send such a termination statement within ten days after proper demand therefor he shall be liable to the debtor for one hundred dollars, and in addition for any loss caused to the debtor by such failure.

(2) On presentation to the filing officer of such a termination statement he must note it in the index. The filing officer shall remove from the files, mark "terminated" and send or deliver to the secured party the financing statement and any continuation statement, statement of assignment or statement of release pertaining thereto.

(3) The uniform fee for filing and indexing a termination statement including sending or delivering the financing statement shall be $_____.

§ 9–405. Assignment of Security Interest; Duties of Filing Officer; Fees.*

(1) A financing statement may disclose an assignment of a security interest in the collateral described in the statement by indication in the statement of the name and address of the assignee or by an assignment itself or a copy thereof on the face or back of the statement. Either the original secured party or the assignee may sign this statement as the secured party. On presentation to the filing officer of such a financing statement the filing officer shall mark the same as provided in Section 9–403(4). The uniform fee for filing, indexing and furnishing filing data for a financing statement so indicating an assignment shall be $_____.

(2) A secured party may assign of record all or a part of his rights under a financing state-

ment by the filing of a separate written statement of assignment signed by the secured party of record and setting forth the name of the secured party of record and the debtor, the file number and the date of filing of the financing statement and the name and address of the assignee and containing a description of the collateral assigned. A copy of the assignment is sufficient as a separate statement if it complies with the preceding sentence. On presentation to the filing officer of such a separate statement, the filing officer shall mark such separate statement with the date and hour of the filing. He shall note the assignment on the index of the financing statement. The uniform fee for filing, indexing and furnishing filing data about such a separate statement of assignment shall be $_____.

(3) After the disclosure or filing of an assignment under this section, the assignee is the secured party of record.

§ 9–406. Release of Collateral; Duties of Filing Officer; Fees.*

A secured party of record may by his signed statement release all or a part of any collateral described in a filed financing statement. The statement of release is sufficient if it contains a description of the collateral being released, the name and address of the debtor, the name and address of the secured party, and the file number of the financing statement. Upon presentation of such a statement to the filing officer he shall mark the statement with the hour and date of filing and shall note the same upon the margin of the index of the filing of the financing statement. The uniform fee for filing and noting such a statement of release shall be $_____.

§ 9–407. Information From Filing Officer.*

[(1) If the person filing any financing statement, termination statement, statement of assignment, or statement of release, furnishes the filing officer a copy thereof, the filing officer shall upon request note upon the copy the file number and date and hour of the filing of the original and deliver or send the copy to such person.

(2) Upon request of any person, the filing officer shall issue his certificate showing whether there is on file on the date and hour stated therein, any presently effective financing statement naming a particular debtor and any statement of assignment thereof and if there is, giving the date and hour of filing of each such statement and the names and addresses of each secured party therein. The uniform fee for such a certificate shall be $_____ plus $_____ for each financing statement and for each statement of assignment reported therein. Upon request the filing officer shall furnish a copy of any filed financing statement or statement of assignment for a uniform fee of $_____ per page.]

Note: *This new section is proposed as an optional provision to require filing officers to furnish certificates. Local law and practices should be consulted with regard to the advisability of adoption.*

PART 5
DEFAULT

§ 9–501. Default; Procedure When Security Agreement Covers Both Real and Personal Property.

(1) When a debtor is in default under a security agreement, a secured party has the rights and remedies provided in this Part and except as limited by subsection (3) those provided in the security agreement. He may reduce his claim to judgment, foreclose or otherwise enforce the security interest by any available judicial procedure. If the collateral is documents the secured party may proceed either as to the documents or as to the goods covered thereby. A secured party in possession has the rights, remedies and duties provided in Section 9–207. The rights and remedies referred to in this subsection are cumulative.

(2) After default, the debtor has the rights and remedies provided in this Part, those provided in the security agreement and those provided in Section 9–207.

(3) To the extent that they give rights to the debtor and impose duties on the secured party, the rules stated in the subsections referred to below may not be waived or varied except

as provided with respect to compulsory disposition of collateral (subsection (1) of Section 9–505) and with respect to redemption of collateral (Section 9–506) but the parties may by agreement determine the standards by which the fulfillment of these rights and duties is to be measured if such standards are not manifestly unreasonable:*

(a) subsection (2) of Section 9–502 and subsection (2) of Section 9–504 insofar as they require accounting for surplus proceeds of collateral;

(b) subsection (3) of Section 9–504 and subsection (1) of Section 9–505 which deal with disposition of collateral;

(c) subsection (2) of Section 9–505 which deals with acceptance of collateral as discharge of obligation;

(d) Section 9–506 which deals with redemption of collateral; and

(e) subsection (1) of Section 9–507 which deals with the secured party's liability for failure to comply with this Part.

(4) If the security agreement covers both real and personal property, the secured party may proceed under this Part as to the personal property or he may proceed as to both the real and the personal property in accordance with his rights and remedies in respect of the real property in which case the provisions of this Part do not apply.

(5) When a secured party has reduced his claim to judgment the lien of any levy which may be made upon his collateral by virtue of any execution based upon the judgment shall relate back to the date of the perfection of the security interest in such collateral. A judicial sale, pursuant to such execution, is a foreclosure of the security interest by judicial procedure within the meaning of this section, and the secured party may purchase at the sale and thereafter hold the collateral free of any other requirements of this Article.

§ 9–502. Collection Rights of Secured Party.*

(1) When so agreed and in any event on default the secured party is entitled to notify an account debtor or the obligor on an instrument to make payment to him whether or not the assignor was theretofore making collections on the collateral, and also to take control of any proceeds to which he is entitled under Section 9–306.

(2) A secured party who by agreement is entitled to charge back uncollected collateral or otherwise to full or limited recourse against the debtor and who undertakes to collect from the account debtors or obligors must proceed in a commercially reasonable manner and may deduct his reasonable expenses of realization from the collections. If the security agreement secures an indebtedness, the secured party must account to the debtor for any surplus, and unless otherwise agreed, the debtor is liable for any deficiency. But, if the underlying transaction was a sale of accounts, contract rights, or chattel paper, the debtor is entitled to any surplus or is liable for any deficiency only if the security agreement so provides.

§ 9–503. Secured Party's Right to Take Possesssion After Default.

Unless otherwise agreed a secured party has on default the right to take possession of the collateral. In taking possession a secured party may proceed without judicial process if this can be done without breach of the peace or may proceed by action. If the security agreement so provides the secured party may require the debtor to assemble the collateral and make it available to the secured party at a place to be designated by the secured party which is reasonably convenient to both parties. Without removal a secured party may render equipment unusable, and may dispose of collateral on the debtor's premises under Section 9–504.

§ 9–504. Secured Party's Right to Dispose of Collateral After Default; Effect of Disposition.*

(1) A secured party after default may sell, lease or otherwise dispose of any or all of the collateral in its then condition or following any commercially reasonable preparation or processing. Any sale of goods is subject to the Article on Sales (Article 2). The proceeds of disposition shall be applied in the order following to

(a) the reasonable expenses of retaking, holding, preparing for sale, selling and the like and, to the extent provided for in the agreement and not prohibited by law, the reasonable attorneys' fees and legal expenses incurred by the secured party;

(b) the satisfaction of indebtedness secured by the security interest under which the disposition is made;

(c) the satisfaction of indebtedness secured by any subordinate security interest in the collateral if written notification of demand therefor is received before distribution of the proceeds is completed. If requested by the secured party, the holder of a subordinate security interest must seasonably furnish reasonable proof of his interest, and unless he does so, the secured party need not comply with his demand.

(2) If the security interest secures an indebtedness, the secured party must account to the debtor for any surplus, and, unless otherwise agreed, the debtor is liable for any deficiency. But if the underlying transaction was a sale of accounts, contract rights, or chattel paper, the debtor is entitled to any surplus or is liable for any deficiency only if the security agreement so provides.

(3) Disposition of the collateral may be by public or private proceedings and may be made by way of one or more contracts. Sale or other disposition may be as a unit or in parcels and at any time and place and on any terms but every aspect of the disposition including the method, manner, time, place and terms must be commercially reasonable. Unless collateral is perishable or threatens to decline speedily in value or is of a type customarily sold on a recognized market, reasonable notification of the time and place of any public sale or reasonable notification of the time after which any private sale or other intended disposition is to be made shall be sent by the secured party to the debtor, and except in the case of consumer goods to any other person who has a security interest in the collateral and who has duly filed a financing statement indexed in the name of the debtor in this state or who is known by the secured party to have a security interest in the collateral. The secured party may buy at any public sale and if the collateral is of a type customarily sold in a recognized market or is of a type which is the subject of widely distributed standard price quotations he may buy at private sale.

(4) When collateral is disposed of by a secured party after default, the disposition transfers to a purchaser for value all of the debtor's rights therein, discharges the security interest under which it is made and any security interest or lien subordinate thereto. The purchaser takes free of all such rights and interests even though the secured party fails to comply with the requirements of this Part or of any judicial proceedings

(a) in the case of a public sale, if the purchaser has no knowledge of any defects in the sale and if he does not buy in collusion with the secured party, other bidders or the person conducting the sale; or

(b) in any other case, if the purchaser acts in good faith.

(5) A person who is liable to a secured party under a guaranty, indorsement, repurchase agreement or the like and who receives a transfer of collateral from the secured party or is subrogated to his rights has thereafter the rights and duties of the secured party. Such a transfer of collateral is not a sale or disposition of the collateral under this Article.

§ 9–505. Compulsory Disposition of Collateral; Acceptance of the Collateral as Discharge of Obligation.

(1) If the debtor has paid sixty per cent of the cash price in the case of a purchase money security interest in consumer goods or sixty per cent of the loan in the case of another security interest in consumer goods, and has not signed after default a statement renouncing or modifying his rights under this Part a secured party who has taken possession of collateral must dispose of its under Section 9–504 and if he fails to do so within ninety days after he takes possession the debtor at his option may recover in conversion or under Section 9–507(1) on secured party's liability.

(2) In any other case involving consumer goods or any other collateral a secured party in possession may, after default, propose to retain the collateral in satisfaction of the obligation. Written notice of such proposal shall be sent to the debtor and except in the case of consumer goods to any other secured party who has a security interest in the collateral and who has duly filed a financing statement indexed in the name of the debtor in this state or is known by the secured party in possession to have a security interest in it. If the debtor or other person entitled to receive notification objects in writing within thirty days from the receipt of the notification or

if any other secured party objects in writing within thirty days after the secured party obtains possession the secured party must dispose of the collateral under Section 9–504. In the absence of such written objection the secured party may retain the collateral in satisfaction of the debtor's obligation.*

§ 9–506. Debtor's Right to Redeem Collateral.

At any time before the secured party has disposed of collateral or entered into a contract for its disposition under Section 9–504 or before the obligation has been discharged under Section 9–505(2) the debtor or any other secured party may unless otherwise agreed in writing after default redeem the collateral by tendering fulfillment of all obligations secured by the collateral as well as the expenses reasonably incurred by the secured party in retaking, holding and preparing the collateral for disposition, in arranging for the sale, and to the extent provided in the agreement and not prohibited by law, his reasonable attorneys' fees and legal expenses.

§ 9–507. Secured Party's Liability for Failure to Comply With This Part.

(1) If it is established that the secured party is not proceeding in accordance with the provisions of this Part disposition may be ordered or restrained on appropriate terms and conditions. If the disposition has occurred the debtor or any person entitled to notification or whose security interest has been made known to the secured party prior to the disposition has a right to recover from the secured party any loss caused by a failure to comply with the provision of this Part. If the collateral is consumer goods, the debtor has a right to recover in any event an amount not less than the credit service charge plus ten per cent of the principal amount of the debt or the time price differential plus ten per cent of the cash price.

(2) The fact that a better price could have been obtained by a sale at a different time or in a different method from that selected by the secured party is not of itself sufficient to establish that the sale was not made in a commercially reasonable manner. If the secured party either sells the collateral in the usual manner in any recognized market therefor or if he sells at the price current in such market at the time of his sale or if he has otherwise sold in conformity with reasonable commercial practices among dealers in the type of property sold he has sold in a commercially reasonable manner. The principles stated in the two preceding sentences with respect to sales also apply as may be appropriate to other types of disposition. A disposition which has been approved in any judicial proceeding or by any bona fide creditors' committee or representative of creditors shall conclusively be deemed to be commercially reasonable, but this sentence does not indicate that any such approval must be obtained in any case nor does it indicate that any disposition not so approved is not commercially reasonable.

ARTICLE 10. Effective Date and Repealer

(omitted)

Uniform Partnership Act

PART I

PRELIMINARY PROVISIONS

Sec. 1. (Name of Act.) This act may be cited as Uniform Partnership Act.

Sec. 2. (Definition of Terms.) In this act, "Court" includes every court and judge having jurisdiction in the case.

"Business" includes every trade, occupation, or profession.

"Person" includes individuals, partnerships, corporations, and other associations.

"Bankrupt" includes bankrupt under the Federal Bankruptcy Act or insolvent under any state insolvent act.

"Conveyance" includes every assignment, lease, mortgage, or encumbrance.

"Real property" includes land and any interest or estate in land.

Sec. 3. (Interpretation of Knowledge and Notice.) (1) A person has "knowledge" of a fact within the meaning of this act not only when he has actual knowledge thereof, but also when he has knowledge of such other facts as in the circumstances shows bad faith.

(2) A person has "notice" of a fact within the meaning of this act when the person who claims the benefit of the notice

(a) States the fact to such person, or

(b) Delivers through the mail, or by other means of communication, a written statement of the fact to such person or to a proper person at his place of business or residence.

Sec. 4. (Rules of Construction.) (1) The rule that statutes in derogation of the common law are to be strictly construed shall have no application to this act.

(2) The law of estoppel shall apply under this act.

(3) The law of agency shall apply under this act.

(4) This act shall be so interpreted and construed as to effect its general purpose to make uniform the law of those states which enact it.

(5) This act shall not be construed so as to impair the obligations of any contract existing when the act goes into effect, nor to affect any action or proceedings begun or right accrued before this act takes effect.

Sec. 5. (Rules for Cases Not Provided for in this Act.) In any case not provided for in this act the rules of law and equity, including the law merchant, shall govern.

PART II

NATURE OF PARTNERSHIP

Sec. 6. (Partnership Defined.) (1) A partnership is an association of two or more persons to carry on as co-owners a business for profit.

(2) But any association formed under any other statute of this state, or any statute adopted by authority, other than the authority of this state, is not a partnership under this act, unless such association would have been a partnership in this state prior to the adopion of this act; but this act shall apply to limited partnerships except in so far as the statutes relating to such partnerships are inconsistent herewith.

Sec. 7. (Rules for Determining the Existence of a Partnership.) In determining whether a partnership exists, these rules shall apply:

(1) Except as provided by Section 16 persons who are not partners as to each other are not partners as to third persons.

(2) Joint tenancy, tenancy in common, tenancy by the entireties, joint property, common property, or part ownership does not of itself establish a partnership, whether such co-owners do or do not share any profits made by the use of the property.

(3) The sharing of gross returns does not of itself establish a partnership, whether or not the persons sharing them have a joint or common right or interest in any property from which the returns are derived.

(4) The receipt by a person of a share of the profits of a business is prima facie evidence that he is a partner in the business, but no such inference shall be drawn if such profits were received in payment:

    (a) As a debt by installments or otherwise,

    (b) As wages of an employee or rent to a landlord,

    (c) As an annuity to a widow or representative of a deceased partner,

    (d) As interest on a loan, though the amount of payment vary with the profits of the business,

    (e) As the consideration for the sale of a good-will of a business or other property by installments or otherwise.

Sec. 8. (Partnership Property.) (1) All property originally brought into the partnership stock or subsequently acquired by purchase or otherwise, on account of the partnership, is partnership property.

(2) Unless the contrary intention appears, property acquired with partnership funds is partnership property.

(3) Any estate in real property may be acquired in the partnership name. Title so acquired can be conveyed only in the partnership name.

(4) A conveyance to a partnership in the partnership name, though without words of inheritance, passes the entire estate of the grantor unless a contrary intent appears.

PART III

RELATIONS OF PARTNERS TO PERSONS DEALING
WITH THE PARTNERSHIP

Sec. 9. (Partner Agent of Partnership as to Partnership Business.) (1) Every partner is an agent of the partnership for the purpose of its business, and the act of every partner, including the execution in the partnership name of any instrument, for apparently carrying on in the usual way the business of the partnership of which he is a member binds the partnership, unless the partner so acting has in fact no authority to act for the partnership in the particular matter, and the person with whom he is dealing has knowledge of the fact that he has no such authority.

(2) An act of a partner which is not apparently for the carrying on of the business of the

partnership in the usual way does not bind the partnership unless authorized by the other partners.

(3) Unless authorized by the other partners or unless they have abandoned the business, one or more but less than all the partners have no authority to:

    (a) Assign the partnership property in trust for creditors or on the assignee's promise to pay the debts of the partnership,

    (b) Dispose of the good-will of the business,

    (c) Do any other act which would make it impossible to carry on the ordinary business of a partnership,

    (d) Confess a judgment,

    (e) Submit a partnership claim or liability to arbitration or reference.

(4) No act of a partner in contravention of a restriction on authority shall bind the partnership to persons having knowledge of the restriction.

Sec. 10. (Conveyance of Real Property of the Partnership.) (1) Where title to real property is in the partnership name, any partner may convey title to such property by a conveyance executed in the partnership name; but the partnership may recover such property unless the partner's act binds the partnership under the provisions of paragraph (1) of section 9 or unless such property has been conveyed by the grantee or a person claiming through such grantee to a holder for value without knowledge that the partner, in making the conveyance, has exceeded his authority.

(2) Where title to real property is in the name of the partnership, a conveyance executed by a partner, in his own name, passes the equitable interest of the partnership, provided the act is one within the authority of the partner under the provisions of paragraph (1) of section 9.

(3) Where title to real property is in the name of one or more but not all the partners, and the record does not disclose the right of the partnership, the partners in whose name the title stands may convey title to such property, but the partnership may recover such property if the partners' act does not bind the partnership under the provisions of paragraph (1) of section 9, unless the purchaser or his assignee, is a holder for value, without knowledge.

(4) Where the title to real property is in the name of one or more or all the partners, or in a third person in trust for the partnership, a conveyance executed by a partner in the partnership name, or in his own name, passes the equitable interest of the partnership, provided the act is one within the authority of the partner under the provisions of paragraph (1) of section 9.

(5) Where the title to real property is in the names of all the partners a conveyance executed by all the partners passes all their rights in such property.

Sec. 11. (Partnership Bound by Admission of Partner.) An admission or representation made by any partner concerning partnership affairs within the scope of his authority as conferred by this act is evidence against the partnership.

Sec. 12. (Partnership Charged with Knowledge of or Notice to Partner.) Notice to any partner of any matter relating to partnership affairs, and the knowledge of the partner acting in the particular matter, acquired while a partner or then present to his mind, and the knowledge of any other partner who reasonably could and should have communicated it to the acting partner, operate as notice to or knowledge of the partnership, except in the case of a fraud on the partnership committed by or with the consent of that partner.

Sec. 13. (Partnership Bound by Partner's Wrongful Act.) Where, by any wrongful act or omission of any partner acting in the ordinary course of the business of the partnership or with the authority of his co-partners, loss or injury is caused to any person, not being a partner in the partnership, or any penalty is incurred, the partnership is liable therefor to the same extent as the partner so acting or omitting to act.

Sec. 14. (Partnership Bound by Partner's Breach of Trust.) The partnership is bound to make good the loss:

    (a) Where one partner acting within the scope of his apparent authority receives money or property of a third person and misapplies it; and

(b) Where the partnership in the course of its business receives money or property of a third person and the money or property so received is misapplied by any partner while it is in the custody of the partnership.

Sec. 15. (Nature of Partner's Liability.) All partners are liable:
(a) Jointly and severally for everything chargeable to the partnership under sections 13 and 14,
(b) Jointly for all other debts and obligations of the partnership; but any partner may enter into a separate obligation to perform a partnership contract.

Sec. 16. (Partner by Estoppel.) (1) When a person, by words spoken or written or by conduct, represents himself, or consents to another representing him to any one, as a partner in an existing partnership or with one or more persons not actual partners, he is liable to any such person to whom such representation has been made, who has, on the faith of such representation, given credit to the actual or apparent partnership, and if he has made such representation or consented to its being made in a public manner he is liable to such person, whether the representation has or has not been made or communicated to such person so giving credit by or with the knowledge of the apparent partner making the representation or consenting to its being made.
(a) When a partnership liability results, he is liable as though he were an actual member of the partnership.
(b) When no partnership liability results, he is liable jointly with the other persons, if any, so consenting to the contract or representation as to incur liability, otherwise separately.

(2) When a person has been thus represented to be a partner in an existing partnership, or with one or more persons not actual partners, he is an agent of the persons consenting to such representation to bind them to the same extent and in the same manner as though he were a partner in fact, with respect to persons who rely upon the representation. Where all the members of the existing partnership consent to the representation, a partnership act or obligation results; but in all other cases it is the joint act or obligation of the person acting and the persons consenting to the representation.

Sec. 17. (Liability of Incoming Partner.) A person admitted as a partner into an existing partnership is liable for all the obligations of the partnership arising before his admission as though he had been a partner when such obligations were incurred, except that this liability shall be satisfied only out of partnership property.

PART IV

RELATIONS OF PARTNERS TO ONE ANOTHER

Sec. 18. (Rules Determining Rights and Duties of Partners.) The rights and duties of the partners in relation to the partnership shall be determined, subject to any agreement between them, by the following rules:
(a) Each partner shall be repaid his contributions, whether by way of capital or advances to the partnership property and share equally in the profits and surplus remaining after all liabilities, including those to partners, are satisfied; and must contribute towards the losses, whether of capital or otherwise, sustained by the partnership according to his share in the profits.
(b) The partnership must indemnify every partner in respect of payments made and personal liabilities reasonably incurred by him in the ordinary and proper conduct of its business, or for the preservation of its business or property.
(c) A partner, who in aid of the partnership makes any payment or advance beyond the amount of capital which he agreed to contribute, shall be paid interest from the date of the payment or advance.
(d) A partner shall receive interest on the capital contributed by him only from the date when repayment should be made.

(e) All partners have equal rights in the management and conduct of the partnership business.

(f) No partner is entitled to remuneration for acting in the partnership business, except that a surviving partner is entitled to reasonable compensation for his services in winding up the partnership affairs.

(g) No person can become a member of a partnership without the consent of all the partners.

(h) Any difference arising as to ordinary matters connected with the partnership business may be decided by a majority of the partners; but no act in contravention of any agreement between the partners may be done rightfully without the consent of all the partners.

Sec. 19. (Partnership Books.) The partnership books shall be kept, subject to any agreement between the partners, at the principal place of business of the partnership, and every partner shall at all times have access to and may inspect and copy any of them.

Sec. 20. (Duty of Partners to Render Information.) Partners shall render on demand true and full information of all things affecting the partnership to any partner or the legal representative of any deceased partner or partner under legal disability.

Sec. 21. (Partner Accountable as a Fiduciary.) (1) Every partner must account to the partnership for any benefit, and hold as trustee for it any profits derived by him without the consent of the other partners from any transaction connected with the formation, conduct, or liquidation of the partnership or from any use by him of its property.

(2) This section applies also to the representatives of a deceased partner engaged in the liquidation of the affairs of the partnership as the personal representatives of the last surviving partner.

Sec. 22. (Right to an Account.) Any partner shall have the right to a formal account as to partnership affairs:

(a) If he is wrongfully excluded from the partnership business or possession of its property by his co-partners,

(b) If the right exists under the terms of any agreement,

(c) As provided by section 21,

(d) Whenever other circumstances render it just and reasonable.

Sec. 23. (Continuation of Partnership Beyond Fixed Term.) (1) When a partnership for a fixed term or particular undertaking is continued after the termination of such term or particular undertaking without any express agreement, the rights and duties of the partners remain the same as they were at such termination, so far as is consistent with a partnership at will.

(2) A continuation of the business by the partners or such of them as habitually acted therein during the term, without any settlement or liquidation of the partnership affairs, is prima facie evidence of a continuation of the partnership.

PART V

PROPERTY RIGHTS OF A PARTNER

Sec. 24. (Extent of Property Rights of a Partner.) The property rights of a partner are (1) his rights in specific partnership property, (2) his interest in the partnership, and (3) his right to participate in the management.

Sec. 25. (Nature of a Partner's Right in Specific Partnership Property.) (1) A partner is co-owner with his partners of specific partnership property holding as a tenant in partnership.

(2) The incidents of this tenancy are such that:

(a) A partner, subject to the provisions of this act and to any agreement between the partners, has an equal right with his partners to possess specific partnership property for partnership purposes; but he has no right to possess such property for any other purpose without the consent of his partners.

(b) A partner's right in specific partnership property is not assignable except in connection with the assignment of rights of all the partners in the same property.

(c) A partner's right in specific partnership property is not subject to attachment or execution, except on a claim against the partnership. When partnership property is attached for a partnership debt the partners, or any of them, or the representatives of a deceased partner, cannot claim any right under the homestead or exemption laws.

(d) On the death of a partner his right in specific partnership property vests in the surviving partner or partners, except where the deceased was the last surviving partner, when his right in such property vests in his legal representative. Such surviving partner or partners, or the legal representative of the last surviving partner, has no right to possess the partnership property for any but a partnership purpose.

(e) A partner's right in specific partnership property is not subject to dower, curtesy, or allowances to widows, heirs, or next of kin.

Sec. 26. (Nature of Partner's Interest in the Partnership.) A partner's interest in the partnership is his share of the profits and surplus, and the same is personal property.

Sec. 27. (Assignment of Partner's Interest.) (1) A conveyance by a partner of his interest in the partnership does not of itself dissolve the partnership, nor, as against the other partners in the absence of agreement, entitle the assignee, during the continuance of the partnership to interfere in the management or administration of the partnership business or affairs, or to require any information or account of partnership transactions, or to inspect the partnership books; but it merely entitles the assignee to receive in accordance with his contract the profits to which the assigning partner would otherwise be entitled.

(2) In case of a dissolution of the partnership, the assignee is entitled to receive his assignor's interest and may require an account from the date only of the last account agreed to by all the partners.

Sec. 28. (Partner's Interest Subject to Charging Order.) (1) On due application to a competent court by any judgment creditor of a partner, the court which entered the judgment, order, or decree, or any other court, may charge the interest of the debtor partner with payment of the unsatisfied amount of such judgment debt with interest thereon; and may then or later appoint a receiver of his share of the profits, and of any other money due or to fall due to him in respect of the partnership, and make all other orders, directions, accounts and inquiries which the debtor partner might have made, or which the circumstances of the case may require.

(2) The interest charged may be redeemed at any time before foreclosure, or in case of a sale being directed by the court may be purchased without thereby causing a dissolution:

(a) With separate property, by any one or more of the partners, or

(b) With partnership property, by any one or more of the partners with the consent of all the partners whose interests are not so charged or sold.

(3) Nothing in this act shall be held to deprive a partner of his right, if any, under the exemption laws, as regards his interest in the partnership.

PART VI

DISSOLUTION AND WINDING UP

Sec. 29. (Dissolution Defined.) The dissolution of a partnership is the change in the relation of the partners caused by any partner ceasing to be associated in the carrying on as distinguished from the winding up of the business.

Sec. 30. (Partnership Not Terminated by Dissolution.) On dissolution the partnership is not terminated, but continues until the winding up of partnership affairs is completed.

Sec. 31. (Causes of Dissolution.) Dissolution is caused: (1) Without voliation of the agreement between the partners,

(a) By the termination of the definite term or particular undertaking specified in the agreement,

(b) By the express will of any partner when no definite term or particular undertaking is specified,

(c) By the express will of all the partners who have not assigned their interest or suffered them to be charged for their separate debts, either before or after the termination of any specified term or particular undertaking,

(d) By the expulsion of any partner from the business bona fide in accordance with such a power conferred by the agreement between the partners;

(2) In contravention of the agreement between the partners, where the circumstances do not permit a dissolution under any other provision of this section, by the express will of any partner at any time;

(3) By any event which makes it unlawful for the business of the partnership to be carried on or for the members to carry it on in partnership;

(4) By the death of any partner;

(5) By the bankruptcy of any partner or the partnership;

(6) By decree of court under section 32.

Sec. 32. (Dissolution by Decree of Court.) (1) On application by or for a partner the court shall decree a dissolution whenever:

(a) A partner has been declared a lunatic in any judicial proceeding or is shown to be of unsound mind,

(b) A partner becomes in any other way incapable of performing his part of the partnership contract,

(c) A partner has been guilty of such conduct as tends to affect prejudicially the carrying on of the business,

(d) A partner wilfully or persistently commits a breach of the partnership agreement, or otherwise so conducts himself in matters relating to the partnership business that it is not reasonably practicable to carry on the business in partnership with him,

(e) The business of the partnership can only be carried on at a loss,

(f) Other circumstances render a dissolution equitable.

(2) On the application of the purchaser of a partner's interest under sections 27 or 28:

(a) After the termination of the specified term or particular undertaking,

(b) At any time if the partnership was a partnership at will when the interest was assigned or when the charging order was issued.

Sec. 33. (General Effect of Dissolution on Authority of Partner.) Except so far as may be necessary to wind up partnership affairs or to complete transactions begun but not then finished, dissolution terminates all authority of any partner to act for the partnership,

(1) With respect to the partners,

(a) When the dissolution is not by the act, bankruptcy or death of a partner; or

(b) When the dissolution is by such act, bankruptcy or death of a partner, in cases where section 34 so requires.

(2) With respect to persons not partners, as declared in section 35.

Sec. 34. (Right of Partner to Contribution From Copartners After Dissolution.) Where the dissolution is caused by the act, death or bankruptcy of a partner, each partner is liable to his copartners for his share of any liability created by any partner acting for the partnership as if the partnership had not been dissolved unless:

(a) The dissolution being by act of any partner, the partner acting for the partnership had knowledge of the dissolution, or

(b) The dissolution being by the death or bankruptcy of a partner, the partner acting for the partnership had knowledge or notice of the death or bankruptcy.

Sec. 35. (Power of Partner to Bind Partnership to Third Persons After Dissolution.) (1) After dissolution a partner can bind the partnership except as provided in Paragraph (3):

(a) By any act appropriate for winding up partnership affairs or completing transactions unfinished at dissolution;

(b) By any transaction which would bind the partnership if dissolution had not taken place, provided the other party to the transaction:

    (I) Had extended credit to the partnership prior to dissolution and had no knowledge or notice of the dissolution; or

    (II) Though he had not so extended credit, had nevertheless known of the partnership prior to dissolution, and, having no knowledge or notice of dissolution, the fact of dissolution had not been advertised in a newspaper of general circulation in the place (or in each place if more than one) at which the partnership business was regularly carried on.

(2) The liability of a partner under paragraph (1b) shall be satisfied out of partnership assets alone when such partner had been prior to dissolution:

    (a) Unknown as a partner to the person with whom the contract is made; and

    (b) So far unknown and inactive in partnership affairs that the business reputation of the partnership could not be said to have been in any degree due to his connection with it.

(3) The partnership is in no case bound by any act of a partner after dissolution:

    (a) Where the partnership is dissolved because it is unlawful to carry on the business, unless the act is appropriate for winding up partnership affairs; or

    (b) Where the partner has become bankrupt; or

    (c) Where the partner has no authority to wind up partnership affairs; except by a transaction with one who:

        (I) Had extended credit to the partnership prior to dissolution and had no knowledge or notice of his want of authority; or

        (II) Had not extended credit to the partnership prior to dissolution, and, having no knowledge or notice of his want of authority, the fact of his want of authority has not been advertised in the manner provided for advertising the fact of dissolution in paragraph (1bII).

(4) Nothing in this section shall affect the liability under section 16 of any person who after dissolution represents himself or consents to another representing him as a partner in a partnership engaged in carrying on business.

Sec. 36. (Effect of Dissolution on Partner's Existing Liability.) (1) The dissolution of the partnership does not of itself discharge the existing liability of any partner.

(2) A partner is discharged from any existing liability upon dissolution of the partnership by an agreement to that effect between himself, the partnership creditor and the person or partnership continuing the business; and such agreement may be inferred from the course of dealing between the creditor having knowledge of the dissolution and the person or partnership continuing the business.

(3) Where a person agrees to assume the existing obligations of a dissolved partnership, the partners whose obligations have been assumed shall be discharged from any liability to any creditor of the partnership who, knowing of the agreement, consents to a material alteration in the nature or time of payment of such obligations.

(4) The individual property of a deceased partner shall be liable for all obligations of the partnership incurred while he was a partner but subject to the prior payment of his separate debts.

Sec. 37. (Right to Wind Up.) Unless otherwise agreed the partners who have not wrongfully dissolved the partnership or the legal representative of the last surviving partner, not bankrupt, has the right to wind up the partnership affairs; provided, however, that any partner, his legal representative or his assignee, upon cause shown, may obtain winding up by the court.

Sec. 38. (Rights of Partners to Application of Partnership Property.) (1) When dissolution is caused in any way, except in contravention of the partnership agreement, each partner as against his co-partners and all persons claiming through them in respect of their interests in the partnership, unless otherwise agreed, may have the partnership property applied to discharge its liabilities, and the surplus applied to pay in cash the net amount owing to the respective partners.

But if dissolution is caused by expulsion of a partner, bona fide under the partnership agreement and if the expelled partner is discharged from all partnership liabilities, either by payment or agreement under section 36(2), he shall receive in cash only the net amount due him from the partnership.

(2) When dissolution is caused in contravention of the partnership agreement the rights of the partners shall be as follows:

(a) Each partner who has not caused dissolution wrongfully shall have:

(I) All the rights specified in paragraph (1) of this section, and

(II) The right, as against each partner who has caused the dissolution wrongfully, to damages for breach of the agreement.

(b) The partners who have not caused the dissolution wrongfully, if they all desire to continue the business in the same name, either by themselves or jointly with others, may do so, during the agreed term for the partnership and for that purpose may possess the partnership property, provided they secure the payment by bond approved by the court, or pay to any partner who has caused the dissolution wrongfully, the value of his interest in the partnership at the dissolution, less any damages recoverable under clause (2aII) of the section, and in like manner indemnify him against all present or future partnership liabilities.

(c) A partner who has caused the dissolution wrongfully shall have:

(I) If the business is not continued under the provisions of paragraph (2b) all the rights of a partner under paragraph (1), subject to clause (2aII), of this section.

(II) If the business is continued under paragraph (2b) of this section the right as against his co-partners and all claiming through them in respect of their interests in the partnership, to have the value of his interest in the partnership, less any damages caused to his co-partners by the dissolution, ascertained and paid to him in cash, or the payment secured by bond approved by the court, and to be released from all existing liabilities of the partnership; but in ascertaining the value of the partner's interest the value of the good-will of the business shall not be considered.

Sec. 39. (Rights Where Partnership is Dissolved for Fraud or Misrepresentation.) Where a partnership contract is rescinded on the ground of the fraud or misrepresentation of one of the parties thereto, the party entitled to rescind is, without prejudice to any other right, entitled,

(a) To a lien on, or right of retention of, the surplus of the partnership property after satisfying the partnership liabilities to third persons for any sum of money paid by him for the purchase of an interest in the partnership and for any capital or advances contributed by him; and

(b) To stand, after all liabilities to third persons have been satisfied, in the place of the creditors of the partnership for any payments made by him in respect of the partnership liabilities; and

(c) To be indemnified by the person guilty of the fraud or making the representation against all debts and liabilities of the partnership.

Sec. 40. (Rules for Distribution.) In settling accounts between the partners after dissolution, the following rules shall be observed, subject to any agreement to the contrary:

(a) The assets of the partnership are:

(I) The partnership property,

(II) The contributions of the partners necessary for the payment of all the liabilities specified in clause (b) of this paragraph.

(b) The liabilities of the partnership shall rank in order of payment, as follows:

(I) Those owing to creditors other than partners,

(II) Those owing to partners other than for capital and profits,

(III) Those owing to partners in respect of capital,

(IV) Those owing to partners in respect of profits.

(c) The assets shall be applied in the order of their declaration in clause (a) of this paragraph to the satisfaction of the liabilities.

(d) The partners shall contribute, as provided by section 18(a) the amount necessary to satisfy the liabilities; but if any, but not all, of the partners are insolvent, or, not being subject to process, refuse to contribute, the other parties shall contribute their share of the liabilities, and, in the relative proportions in which they share the profits, the additional amount necessary to pay the liabilities.

(e) An assignee for the benefit of creditors or any person appointed by the court shall have the right to enforce the contributions specified in clause (d) of this paragraph.

(f) Any partner or his legal representative shall have the right to enforce the contributions specified in clause (d) of this paragraph, to the extent of the amount which he has paid in excess of his share of the liability.

(g) The individual property of a deceased partner shall be liable for the contributions specified in clause (d) of this paragraph.

(h) When partnership property and the individual properties of the partners are in possession of a court for distribution, partnership creditors shall have priority on partnership property and separate creditors on individual property saving the rights of lien or secured creditors as heretofore.

(i) Where a partner has become bankrupt or his estate is insolvent the claims against his separate property shall rank in the following order:

(I) Those owing to separate creditors,

(II) Those owing to partnership creditors,

(III) Those owing to partners by way of contribution.

Sec. 41. (Liability of Persons Continuing the Business in Certain Cases.) (1) When any new partner is admitted into an existing partnership, or when any partner retires and assigns (or the representative of the deceased partner assigns) his rights in partnership property to two or more of the partners, or to one or more of the partners and one or more third persons, if the business is continued without liquidation of the partnership affairs, creditors of the first or dissolved partnership are also creditors of the partnership so continuing the business.

(2) When all but one partner retire and assign (or the representative of a deceased partner assigns) their rights in partnership property to the remaining partner, who continues the business without liquidation of partnership affairs, either alone or with others, creditors of the dissolved partnership are also creditors of the person or partnership so continuing the business.

(3) When any partner retires or dies and the business of the dissolved partnership is continued as set forth in paragraphs (1) and (2) of this section, with the consent of the retired partners or the representative of the deceased partner, but without any assignment of his right in partnership property, rights of creditors of the dissolved partnership and of the creditors of the person or partnership continuing the business shall be as if such assignment had been made.

(4) When all the partners or their representatives assign their rights in partnership property to one or more third persons who promise to pay the debts and who continue the business of the dissolved partnership, creditors of the dissolved partnership are also creditors of the person or partnership continuing the business.

(5) When any partner wrongfully causes a dissolution and the remaining partners continue the business under the provisions of section 38(2b), either alone or with others, and without liquidation of the partnership affairs, creditors of the dissolved partnership are also creditors of the person or partnership continuing the business.

(6) When a partner is expelled and the remaining partners continue the business either alone or with others, without liquidation of the partnership affairs, creditors of the dissolved partnership are also creditors of the person or partnership continuing the business.

(7) The liability of a third person becoming a partner in the partnership continuing the business, under this section, to the creditors of the dissolved partnership shall be satisfied out of partnership property only.

(8) When the business of a partnership after dissolution is continued under any conditions set forth in this section the creditors of the dissolved partnership, as against the separate creditors of the retiring or deceased partner or the representative of the deceased partner, have a prior right to any claim of the retired partner or the representative of the deceased partner against the person or partnership continuing the business, on account of the retired or deceased partner's

interest in the dissolved partnership or on account of any consideration promised for such interest or for his right in partnership property.

(9) Nothing in this section shall be held to modify any right of creditors to set aside any assignment on the ground of fraud.

(10) The use by the person or partnership continuing the business of the partnership name, or the name of a deceased partner as part thereof, shall not of itself make the individual property of the deceased partner liable for any debts contracted by such person or partnership.

Sec. 42. (Rights of Retiring or Estate of Deceased Partner When the Business is Continued.) When any partner retires or dies, and the business is continued under any of the conditions set forth in section 41(1, 2, 3, 5, 6), or section 38(2b), without any settlement of accounts as between him or his estate and the person or partnership continuing the business, unless otherwise agreed, he or his legal representative as against such persons or partnership may have the value of his interest at the date of dissolution ascertained, and shall receive as an ordinary creditor an amount equal to the value of his interest in the dissolved partnership with interest, or, at his option or at the option of his legal representative, in lieu of interest, the profits attributable to the use of his right in the property of the dissolved partnership; provided that the creditors of the dissolved partnership as against the separate creditors, or the representative of the retired or deceased partner, shall have priority on any claim arising under this section, as provided by section 41(8) of this act.

Sec. 43. (Accrual of Actions.) The right to an account of his interest shall accrue to any partner, or his legal representative, as against the winding up partners or the surviving partners or the person or partnership continuing the business, at the date of dissolution, in the absence of any agreement to the contrary.

PART VII

MISCELLANEOUS PROVISIONS

Sec. 44. (When Act Takes Effect.) This act shall take effect on the _____ day of _____ one thousand nine hundred and _____.

Sec. 45. (Legislation Repealed.) All acts or parts of acts inconsistent with this act are hereby repealed.

Model Business Corporation Act

§ 1. Short Title

This Act shall be known and may be cited as ". . . . . .* Business Corporation Act."

§ 2. Definitions

As used in this Act, unless the context otherwise requires, the term:

(a) "Corporation" or "domestic corporation" means a corporation for profit subject to the provisions of this Act, except a foreign corporation.

(b) "Foreign corporation" means a corporation for profit organized under laws other than the laws of this State for a purpose or purposes for which a corporation may be organized under this Act.

(c) "Articles of incorporation" means the original or restated articles of incorporation or articles of consolidation and all amendments thereto including articles of merger.

(d) "Shares" means the units into which the proprietary interests in a corporation are divided.

(e) "Subscriber" means one who subscribes for shares in a corporation, whether before or after incorporation.

(f) "Shareholder" means one who is a holder of record of shares in a corporation.

(g) "Authorized shares" means the shares of all classes which the corporation is authorized to issue.

(h) "Treasury shares" means shares of a corporation which have been issued, have been subsequently acquired by and belong to the corporation, and have not, either by reason of the acquisition or thereafter, been cancelled or restored to the status of authorized but unissued shares. Treasury shares shall be deemed to be "issued" shares, but not "outstanding" shares.

(i) "Net assets" means the amount by which the total assets of a corporation exceed the total debts of the corporation.

(j) "Stated capital" means, at any particular time, the sum of (1) the par value of all shares of the corporation having a par value that have been issued, (2) the amount of the consideration received by the corporation for all shares of the corporation without par value that have been issued, except such part of the consideration therefor as may have been allocated to capital surplus in a manner permitted by law, and (3) such amounts not included in clauses (1) and (2) of this paragraph as have been transferred to stated capital of the corporation, whether upon

---

*Supply name of state.

the issue of shares as a share dividend or otherwise, minus all reductions from such sum as have been effected in a manner permitted by law. Irrespective of the manner of designation thereof by the laws under which a foreign corporation is organized, the stated capital of a foreign corporation shall be determined on the same basis and in the same manner as the stated capital of a domestic corporation, for the purpose of computing fees, franchise taxes and other charges imposed by this Act.

(k) "Surplus" means the excess of the net assets of a corporation over its stated capital.

(l) "Earned surplus" means the portion of the surplus of a corporation equal to the balance of its net profits, income, gains and losses from the date of incorporation, or from the latest date when a deficit was eliminated by an application of its capital surplus or stated capital or otherwise, after deducting subsequent distributions to shareholders and transfers to stated capital and capital surplus to the extent such distributions and transfers are made out of earned surplus. Earned surplus shall include also any portion of surplus allocated to earned surplus in mergers, consolidations or acquisitions of all or substantially all of the outstanding shares or of the property and assets of another corporation, domestic or foreign.

(m) "Capital surplus" means the entire surplus of a corporation other than its earned surplus.

(n) "Insolvent" means inability of a corporation to pay its debts as they become due in the usual course of its business.

(o) "Employee" includes officers but not directors. A director may accept duties which make him also an employee.

§ 3. Purposes

Corporations may be organized under this Act for any lawful purpose or purposes, except for the purpose of banking or insurance.

§ 4. General Powers

Each corporation shall have power:

(a) To have perpetual succession by its corporate name unless a limited period of duration is stated in its articles of incorporation.

(b) To sue and be sued, complain and defend, in its corporate name.

(c) To have a corporate seal which may be altered at pleasure, and to use the same by causing it, or a facsimile thereof, to be impressed or affixed or in any other manner reproduced.

(d) To purchase, take, receive, lease, or otherwise acquire, own, hold, improve, use and otherwise deal in and with, real or personal property, or any interest therein, wherever situated.

(e) To sell, convey, mortgage, pledge, lease, exchange, transfer and otherwise dispose of all or any part of its property and assets.

(f) To lend money and use its credit to assist its employees.

(g) To purchase, take, receive, subscribe for, or otherwise acquire, own, hold, vote, use, employ, sell, mortgage, lend, pledge, or otherwise dispose of, and otherwise use and deal in and with, shares or other interests in, or obligations of, other domestic or foreign corporations, associations, partnerships or individuals, or direct or indirect obligations of the United States or of any other government, state, territory, governmental district or municipality or of any instrumentality thereof.

(h) To make contracts and guarantees and incur liabilities, borrow money at such rates of interest as the corporation may determine, issue its notes, bonds, and other obligations, and secure any of its obligations by mortgage or pledge of all or any of its property, franchises and income.

(i) To lend money for its corporate purposes, invest and reinvest its funds, and take and hold real and personal property as security for the payment of funds so loaned or invested.

(j) To conduct its business, carry on its operations and have offices and exercise the powers granted by this Act, within or without this State.

(k) To elect or appoint officers and agents of the corporation, and define their duties and fix their compensation.

(l) To make and alter by-laws, not inconsistent with its articles of incorporation or with the laws of this State, for the administration and regulation of the affairs of the corporation.

(m) To make donations for the public welfare or for charitable, scientific or educational purposes.

(n) To transact any lawful business which the board of directors shall find will be in aid of governmental policy.

(o) To pay pensions and establish pension plans, pension trusts, profit sharing plans, stock bonus plans, stock option plans and other incentive plans for any or all of its directors, officers and employees.

(p) To be a promoter, partner, member, associate, or manager of any partnership, joint venture, trust or other enterprise.

(q) To have and exercise all powers necessary or convenient to effect its purposes.

§ 5. Indemnification of Officers, Directors, Employees and Agents

(a) A corporation shall have power to indemnify any person who was or is a party or is threatened to be made a party to any threatened, pending or completed action, suit or proceeding, whether civil, criminal, administrative or investigative (other than an action by or in the right of the corporation) by reason of the fact that he is or was a director, officer, employee or agent of the corporation, or is or was serving at the request of the corporation as a director, officer, employee or agent of another corporation, partnership, joint venture, trust or other enterprise, against expenses (including attorneys' fees), judgments, fines and amounts paid in settlement actually and reasonably incurred by him in connection with such action, suit or proceeding if he acted in good faith and in a manner he reasonably believed to be in or not opposed to the best interests of the corporation, and, with respect to any criminal action or proceeding, had no reasonable cause to believe his conduct was unlawful. The termination of any action, suit or proceeding by judgment, order, settlement, conviction, or upon a plea of nolo contendere or its equivalent, shall not, of itself, create a presumption that the person did not act in good faith and in a manner which he reasonably believed to be in or not opposed to the best interests of the corporation, and, with respect to any criminal action or proceeding, had reasonable cause to believe that his conduct was unlawful.

(b) A corporation shall have power to indemnify any person who was or is a party or is threatened to be made a party to any threatened, pending or completed action or suit by or in the right of the corporation to procure a judgment in its favor by reason of the fact that he is or was a director, officer, employee or agent of the corporation, or is or was serving at the request of the corporation as a director, officer, employee or agent of another corporation, partnership, joint venture, trust or other enterprise against expenses (including attorneys' fees) actually and reasonably incurred by him in connection with the defense or settlement of such action or suit if he acted in good faith and in a manner he reasonably believed to be in or not opposed to the best interests of the corporation and except that no indemnification shall be made in respect of any claim, issue or matter as to which such person shall have been adjudged to be liable for negligence or misconduct in the performance of his duty to the corporation unless and only to the extent that the court in which such action or suit was brought shall determine upon application that, despite the adjudication of liability but in view of all circumstances of the case, such person is fairly and reasonably entitled to indemnity for such expenses which such court shall deem proper.

(c) To the extent that a director, officer, employee or agent of a corporation has been successful on the merits or otherwise in defense of any action, suit or proceeding referred to in subsections (a) or (b), or in defense of any claim, issue or matter therein, he shall be indemnified against expenses (including attorneys' fees) actually and reasonably incurred by him in connection therewith.

(d) Any indemnification under subsections (a) or (b) (unless ordered by a court) shall be made by the corporation only as authorized in the specific case upon a determination that indemnification of the director, officer, employee or agent is proper in the circumstances because he has met the applicable standard of conduct set forth in subsections (a) or (b). Such determination shall be made (1) by the board of directors by a majority vote of a quorum consisting of directors who were not parties to such action, suit or proceeding, or (2) if such a quorum is not obtainable, or, even if obtainable a quorum of disinterested directors so directs, by independent legal counsel in a written opinion, or (3) by the shareholders.

(e) Expenses (including attorneys' fees) incurred in defending a civil or criminal action, suit or proceeding may be paid by the corporation in advance of the final disposition of such action, suit or proceeding as authorized in the manner provided in subsection (d) upon receipt of an undertaking by or on behalf of the director, officer, employee or agent to repay such amount unless it shall ultimately be determined that he is entitled to be indemnified by the corporation as authorized in this section.

(f) The indemnification provided by this section shall not be deemed exclusive of any other rights to which those indemnified may be entitled under any by-law, agreement, vote of shareholders or disinterested directors or otherwise, both as to action in his official capacity and as to action in another capacity while holding such office, and shall continue as to a person who has ceased to be a director, officer, employee or agent and shall inure to the benefit of the heirs, executors and administrators of such a person.

(g) A corporation shall have power to purchase and maintain insurance on behalf of any person who is or was a director, officer, employee or agent of the corporation, or is or was serving at the request of the corporation as a director, officer, employee or agent of another corporation, partnership, joint venture, trust or other enterprise against any liability asserted against him and incurred by him in any such capacity or arising out of his status as such, whether or not the corporation would have the power to indemnify him against such liability under the provisions of this section.

§ 6. Right of Corporation to Acquire and Dispose of Its Own Shares

A corporation shall have the right to purchase, take, receive or otherwise acquire, hold, own, pledge, transfer or otherwise dispose of its own shares, but purchases of its own shares, whether direct or indirect, shall be made only to the extent of unreserved and unrestricted earned surplus available therefor, and, if the articles of incorporation so permit or with the affirmative vote of the holders of a majority of all shares entitled to vote thereon, to the extent of unreserved and unrestricted capital surplus available therefor.

To the extent that earned surplus or capital surplus is used as the measure of the corporation's right to purchase its own shares, such surplus shall be restricted so long as such shares are held as treasury shares, and upon the disposition or cancellation of any such shares the restriction shall be removed pro tanto.

Notwithstanding the foregoing limitation, a corporation may purchase or otherwise acquire its own shares for the purpose of:

(a) Eliminating fractional shares.

(b) Collecting or compromising indebtedness to the corporation.

(c) Paying dissenting shareholders entitled to payment for their shares under the provisions of this Act.

(d) Effecting, subject to the other provisions of this Act, the retirement of its redeemable shares by redemption or by purchase at not to exceed the redemption price.

No purchase of or payment for its own shares shall be made at a time when the corporation is insolvent or when such purchase or payment would make it insolvent.

§ 7. Defense of Ultra Vires

No act of a corporation and no conveyance or transfer of real or personal property to or by a corporation shall be invalid by reason of the fact that the corporation was without capacity or power to do such act or to make or receive such conveyance or transfer, but such lack of capacity or power may be asserted:

(a) In a proceeding by a shareholder against the corporation to enjoin the doing of any act or the transfer of real or personal property by or to the corporation. If the unauthorized act or transfer sought to be enjoined is being, or is to be, performed or made pursuant to a contract to which the corporation is a party, the court may, if all of the parties to the contract are parties to the proceeding and if it deems the same to be equitable, set aside and enjoin the performance of such contract, and in so doing may allow to the corporation or to the other parties to the contract, as the case may be, compensation for the loss or damage sustained by either of them which may result from the action of the court in setting aside and enjoining the performance of such contract, but anticipated profits to be derived from the performance of the contract shall not be awarded by the court as a loss or damage sustained.

(b) In a proceeding by the corporation, whether acting directly or through a receiver, trustee, or other legal representative, or through shareholders in a representative suit, against the incumbent or former officers or directors of the corporation.

(c) In a proceeding by the Attorney General, as provided in this Act, to dissolve the corporation, or in a proceeding by the Attorney General to enjoin the corporation from the transaction of unauthorized business.

§ 8. Corporate Name

The corporate name:

(a) Shall contain the word "corporation," "company," "incorporated" or "limited," or shall contain an abbreviation of one of such words.

(b) Shall not contain any word or phrase which indicates or implies that it is organized for any purpose other than one or more of the purposes contained in its articles of incorporation.

(c) Shall not be the same as, or deceptively similar to, the name of any domestic corporation existing under the laws of this State or any foreign corporation authorized to transact business in this State, or a name the exclusive right to which is, at the time, reserved in the manner provided in this Act, or the name of a corporation which has in effect a registration of its corporate name as provided in this Act, except that this provision shall not apply if the applicant files with the Secretary of State either of the following: (1) the written consent of such other corporation or holder of a reserved or registered name to use the same or deceptively similar name and one or more words are added to make such name distinguishable from such other name, or (2) a certified copy of a final decree of a court of competent jurisdiction establishing the prior right of the applicant to the use of such name in this State.

A corporation with which another corporation, domestic or foreign, is merged, or which is formed by the reorganization or consolidation of one or more domestic or foreign corporations or upon a sale, lease or other disposition to or exchange with, a domestic corporation of all or substantially all the assets of another corporation, domestic or foreign, including its name, may have the same name as that used in this State by any of such corporations if such other corporation was organized under the laws of, or is authorized to transact business in, this State.

§ 9. Reserved Name

The exclusive right to the use of a corporate name may be reserved by:

(a) Any person intending to organize a corporation under this Act.

(b) Any domestic corporation intending to change its name.

(c) Any foreign corporation intending to make application for a certificate of authority to transact business in this State.

(d) Any foreign corporation authorized to transact business in this State and intending to change its name.

(e) Any person intending to organize a foreign corporation and intending to have such corporation make application for a certificate of authority to transact business in this State.

The reservation shall be made by filing with the Secretary of State an application to reserve a specified corporate name, executed by the applicant. If the Secretary of State finds that the name is available for corporate use, he shall reserve the same for the exclusive use of the applicant for a period of one hundred and twenty days.

The right to the exclusive use of a specified corporate name so reserved may be transferred to any other person or corporation by filing in the office of the Secretary of State a notice of such transfer, executed by the applicant for whom the name was reserved, and specifying the name and address of the transferee.

§ 10. Registered Name

Any corporation organized and existing under the laws of any state or territory of the United States may register its corporate name under this Act, provided its corporate name is not the same as, or deceptively similar to, the name of any domestic corporation existing under the laws of this State, or the name of any foreign corporation authorized to transact business in this State, or any corporate name reserved or registered under this Act.

Such registration shall be made by:

(a) Filing with the Secretary of State (1) an application for registration executed by the corporation by an officer thereof, setting forth the name of the corporation, the state or territory under the laws of which it is incorporated, the date of its incorporation, a statement that it is carrying on or doing business, and a brief statement of the business in which it is engaged, and (2) a certificate setting forth that such corporation is in good standing under the laws of the state or territory wherein it is organized, executed by the Secretary of State of such state or territory or by such other official as may have custody of the records pertaining to corporations, and

(b) Paying to the Secretary of State a registration fee in the amount of . . . . for each month, or fraction thereof, between the date of filing such application and December 31st of the calendar year in which such application is filed.

Such registration shall be effective until the close of the calendar year in which the application for registration is filed.

§ 11. Renewal of Registered Name

A corporation which has in effect a registration of its corporate name, may renew such registration from year to year by annually filing an application for renewal setting forth the facts required to be set forth in an original application for registration and a certificate of good standing as required for the original registration and by paying a fee of . . . . A renewal application may be filed between the first day of October and the thirty-first day of December in each year, and shall extend the registration for the following calendar year.

§ 12. Registered Office and Registered Agent

Each corporation shall have and continuously maintain in this State:

(a) A registered office which may be, but need not be, the same as its place of business.

(b) A registered agent, which agent may be either an individual resident in this State whose business office is identical with such registered office, or a domestic corporation, or a foreign corporation authorized to transact business in this State, having a business office identical with such registered office.

§ 13.   Change of Registered Office or Registered Agent

A corporation may change its registered office or change its registered agent, or both, upon filing in the office of the Secretary of State a statement setting forth:

(a) The name of the corporation.

(b) The address of its then registered office.

(c) If the address of its registered office is to be changed, the address to which the registered office is to be changed.

(d) The name of its then registered agent.

(e) If its registered agent is to be changed, the name of its successor registered agent.

(f) That the address of its registered office and the address of the business office of its registered agent, as changed, will be identical.

(g) That such change was authorized by resolution duly adopted by its board of directors.

Such statement shall be executed by the corporation by its president, or a vice president, and verified by him, and delivered to the Secretary of State. If the Secretary of State finds that such statement conforms to the provisions of this Act, he shall file such statement in his office, and upon such filing the change of address of the registered office, or the appointment of a new registered agent, or both, as the case may be, shall become effective.

Any registered agent of a corporation may resign as such agent upon filing a written notice thereof, executed in duplicate, with the Secretary of State, who shall forthwith mail a copy thereof to the corporation at its registered office. The appointment of such agent shall terminate upon the expiration of thirty days after receipt of such notice by the Secretary of State.

If a registered agent changes his or its business address to another place within the same . . . .*, he or it may change such address and the address of the registered office of any corporation of which he or it is registered agent by filing a statement as required above except that it need be signed only by the registered agent and need not be responsive to (e) or (g) and must recite that a copy of the statement has been mailed to the corporation.

§ 14.   Service of Process on Corporation

The registered agent so appointed by a corporation shall be an agent of such corporation upon whom any process, notice or demand required or permitted by law to be served upon the corporation may be served.

Whenever a corporation shall fail to appoint or maintain a registered agent in this State, or whenever its registered agent cannot with reasonable diligence be found at the registered office, then the Secretary of State shall be an agent of such corporation upon whom any such process, notice, or demand may be served. Service on the Secretary of State of any such process, notice, or demand shall be made by delivering to and leaving with him, or with any clerk having charge of the corporation department of his office, duplicate copies of such process, notice or demand. In the event any such process, notice or demand is served on the Secretary of State, he shall immediately cause one of the copies thereof to be forwarded by registered mail, addressed to the corporation at its registered office. Any service so had on the Secretary of State shall be returnable in not less than thirty days.

The Secretary of State shall keep a record of all processes, notices and demands served upon

---

* Supply designation of jurisdiction, such as county, etc., in accordance with local practice.

him under this section, and shall record therein the time of such service and his action with reference thereto.

Nothing herein contained shall limit or affect the right to serve any process, notice or demand required or permitted by law to be served upon a corporation in any other manner now or hereafter permitted by law.

§ 15. Authorized Shares

Each corporation shall have power to create and issue the number of shares stated in its articles of incorporation. Such shares may be divided into one or more classes, any or all of which classes may consist of shares with par value or shares without par value, with such designations, preferences, limitations, and relative rights as shall be stated in the articles of incorporation. The articles of incorporation may limit or deny the voting rights of or provide special voting rights for the shares of any class to the extent not inconsistent with the provisions of this Act.

Without limiting the authority herein contained, a corporation, when so provided in its articles of incorporation, may issue shares of preferred or special classes:

(a) Subject to the right of the corporation to redeem any of such shares at the price fixed by the articles of incorporation for the redemption thereof.

(b) Entitling the holders thereof to cumulative, noncumulative or partially cumulative dividends.

(c) Having preference over any other class or classes of shares as to the payment of dividends.

(d) Having preference in the assets of the corporation over any other class or classes of shares upon the voluntary or involuntary liquidation of the corporation.

(e) Convertible into shares of any other class or into shares of any series of the same or any other class, except a class having prior or superior rights and preferences as to dividends or distribution of assets upon liquidation, but shares without par value shall not be converted into shares with par value unless that part of the stated capital of the corporation represented by such shares without par value is, at the time of conversion, at least equal to the aggregate par value of the shares into which the shares without par value are to be converted or the amount of any such deficiency is transferred from surplus to stated capital.

§ 16. Issuance of Shares of Preferred or Special Classes in Series

If the articles of incorporation so provide, the shares of any preferred or special class may be divided into and issued in series. If the shares of any such class are to be issued in series, then each series shall be so designated as to distinguish the shares thereof from the shares of all other series and classes. Any or all of the series of any such class and the variations in the relative rights and preferences as between different series may be fixed and determined by the articles of incorporation, but all shares of the same class shall be identical except as to the following relative rights and preferences, as to which there may be variations between different series:

(A) The rate of dividend.

(B) Whether shares may be redeemed and, if so, the redemption price and the terms and conditions of redemption.

(C) The amount payable upon shares in event of voluntary and involuntary liquidation.

(D) Sinking fund provisions, if any, for the redemption or purchase of shares.

(E) The terms and conditions, if any, on which shares may be converted.

(F) Voting rights, if any.

If the articles of incorporation shall expressly vest authority in the board of directors, then, to the extent that the articles of incorporation shall not have established series and fixed and determined the variations in the relative rights and preferences as between series, the board of directors shall have authority to divide any or all of such classes into series and, within the limitations set forth in this section and in the articles of incorporation, fix and determine the relative rights and preferences of the shares of any series so established.

In order for the board of directors to establish a series, where authority so to do is contained in the articles of incorporation, the board of directors shall adopt a resolution setting forth the designation of the series and fixing and determining the relative rights and preferences thereof, or so much thereof as shall not be fixed and determined by the articles of incorporation.

Prior to the issue of any shares of a series established by resolution adopted by the board of directors, the corporation shall file in the office of the Secretary of State a statement setting forth:

(a) The name of the corporation.

(b) A copy of the resolution establishing and designating the series, and fixing and determining the relative rights and preferences thereof.

(c) The date of adoption of such resolution.

(d) That such resolution was duly adopted by the board of directors.

Such statement shall be executed in duplicate by the corporation by its president or a vice president and by its secretary or an assistant secretary, and verified by one of the officers signing such statement, and shall be delivered to the Secretary of State. If the Secretary of State finds that such statement conforms to law, he shall, when all franchise taxes and fees have been paid as in this Act prescribed:

(1) Endorse on each of such duplicate originals the word "Filed," and the month, day, and year of the filing thereof.

(2) File one of such duplicate originals in his office.

(3) Return the other duplicate original to the corporation or its representative.

Upon the filing of such statement by the Secretary of State, the resolution establishing and designating the series and fixing and determining the relative rights and preferences thereof shall become effective and shall constitute an amendment of the articles of incorporation.

§ 17. Subscriptions for Shares

A subscription for shares of a corporation to be organized shall be irrevocable for a period of six months, unless otherwise provided by the terms of the subscription agreement or unless all of the subscribers consent to the revocation of such subscription.

Unless otherwise provided in the subscription agreement, subscriptions for shares, whether made before or after the organization of a corporation, shall be paid in full at such time, or in such installments and at such times, as shall be determined by the board of directors. Any call made by the board of directors for payment on subscriptions shall be uniform as to all shares of the same class or as to all shares of the same series, as the case may be. In case of default in the payment of any installment or call when such payment is due, the corporation may proceed to collect the amount due in the same manner as any debt due the corporation. The by-laws may prescribe other penalities for failure to pay installments or calls that may become due, but no penalty working a forfeiture of a subscription, or of the amounts paid thereon, shall be declared as against any subscriber unless the amount due thereon shall remain unpaid for a period of twenty days after written demand has been made therefor. If mailed, such written demand shall be deemed to be made when deposited in the United States mail in a sealed envelope addressed to the subscriber at his last post-office address known to the corporation, with postage thereon prepaid. In the event of the sale of any shares by reason of any forfeiture, the excess of proceeds realized over the amount due and unpaid on such shares shall be paid to the delinquent subscriber or to his legal representative.

§ 18. Consideration for Shares

Shares having a par value may be issued for such consideration expressed in dollars, not less than the par value thereof, as shall be fixed from time to time by the board of directors.

Shares without par value may be issued for such consideration expressed in dollars as may be fixed from time to time by the board of directors unless the articles of incorporation reserve to the shareholders the right to fix the consideration. In the event that such right be reserved as to any shares, the shareholders shall, prior to the issuance of such shares, fix the consideration to be received for such shares, by a vote of the holders of a majority of all shares entitled to vote thereon.

Treasury shares may be disposed of by the corporation for such consideration expressed in dollars as may be fixed from time to time by the board of directors.

That part of the surplus of a corporation which is transferred to stated capital upon the issuance of shares as a share dividend shall be deemed to be the consideration for the issuance of such shares.

In the event of the issuance of shares upon the conversion or exchange of indebtedness or shares, the consideration for the shares so issued shall be (1) the principal sum of, and accrued interest on, the indebtedness so exchanged or converted, or the stated capital then represented by the shares so exchanged or converted, and (2) that part of surplus, if any, transferred to stated capital upon the issuance of shares for the shares so exchanged or converted, and (3) any additional consideration paid to the corporation upon the issuance of shares for the indebtedness or shares so exchanged or converted.

§ 19. Payment for Shares

The consideration for the issuance of shares may be paid, in whole or in part, in money, in other property, tangible or intangible, or in labor or services actually performed for the corporation. When payment of the consideration for which shares are to be issued shall have been received by the corporation, such shares shall be deemed to be fully paid and nonassessable.

Neither promissory notes nor future services shall constitute payment or part payment for the issuance of shares of a corporation.

In the absence of fraud in the transaction, the judgment of the board of directors or the shareholders, as the case may be, as to the value of the consideration received for shares shall be conclusive.

§ 20. Stock Rights and Options

Subject to any provisions in respect thereof set forth in its articles of incorporation, a corporation may create and issue, whether or not in connection with the issuance and sale of any of its shares or other securities, rights or options entitling the holders thereof to purchase from the corporation shares of any class or classes. Such rights or options shall be evidenced in such manner as the board of directors shall approve and, subject to the provisions of the articles of incorporation, shall set forth the terms upon which, the time or times within which and the price or prices at which such shares may be purchased from the corporation upon the exercise of any such right or option. If such rights or options are to be issued to directors, officers or employees as such of the corporation or of any subsidiary thereof, and not to the shareholders generally, their issuance shall be approved by the affirmative vote of the holders of a majority of the shares entitled to vote thereon or shall be authorized by and consistent with a plan approved or ratified by such a vote of shareholders. In the absence of fraud in the transaction, the judgment of the board of directors as to the adequacy of the consideration received for such rights or options shall be conclusive. The price or prices to be received for any shares having a par value, other than treasury shares to be issued upon the exercise of such rights or options, shall not be less than the par value thereof.

§ 21.   Determination of Amount of Stated Capital

In case of the issuance by a corporation of shares having a par value, the consideration received therefor shall constitute stated capital to the extent of the par value of such shares, and the excess, if any, of such consideration shall constitute capital surplus.

In case of the issuance by a corporation of shares without par value, the entire consideration received therefor shall constitute stated capital unless the corporation shall determine as provided in this section that only a part thereof shall be stated capital. Within a period of sixty days after the issuance of any shares without par value, the board of directors may allocate to capital surplus any portion of the consideration received for the issuance of such shares. No such allocation shall be made of any portion of the consideration received for shares without par value having a preference in the assets of the corporation in the event of involuntary liquidation except the amount, if any, of such consideration in excess of such preference.

If shares have been or shall be issued by a corporation in merger or consolidation or in acquisition of all or substantially all of the outstanding shares or of the property and assets of another corporation, whether domestic or foreign, any amount that would otherwise constitute capital surplus under the foregoing provisions of this section may instead be allocated to earned surplus by the board of directors of the issuing corporation except that its aggregate earned surplus shall not exceed the sum of the earned surpluses as defined in this Act of the issuing corporation and of all other corporations, domestic or foreign, that were merged or consolidated or of which the shares or assets were acquired.

The stated capital of a corporation may be increased from time to time by resolution of the board of directors directing that all or a part of the surplus of the corporation be transferred to stated capital. The board of directors may direct that the amount of the surplus so transferred shall be deemed to be stated capital in respect of any designated class of shares.

§ 22.   Expenses of Organization, Reorganization and Financing

The reasonable charges and expenses of organization or reorganization of a corporation, and the reasonable expenses of and compensation for the sale or underwriting of its shares, may be paid or allowed by such corporation out of the consideration received by it in payment for its shares without thereby rendering such shares not fully paid or assessable.

§ 23.   Certificates Representing Shares

The shares of a corporation shall be represented by certificates signed by the president or a vice president and the secretary or an assistant secretary of the corporation, and may be sealed with the seal of the corporation or a facsimile thereof. The signatures of the president or vice president and the secretary or assistant secretary upon a certificate may be facsimiles if the certificate is manually signed on behalf of a transfer agent or a registrar, other than the corporation itself or an employee of the corporation. In case any officer who has signed or whose facsimile signature has been placed upon such certificate shall have ceased to be such officer before such certificate is issued, it may be issued by the corporation with the same effect as if he were such officer at the date of its issue.

Every certificate representing shares issued by a corporation which is authorized to issue shares of more than one class shall set forth upon the face or back of the certificate, or shall state that the corporation will furnish to any shareholder upon request and without charge, a full statement of the designations, preferences, limitations, and relative rights of the shares of each class authorized to be issued, and if the corporation is authorized to issue any preferred or special class in series, the variations in the relative rights and preferences between the shares of each such series so far as the same have been fixed and determined and the authority of the board of directors to fix and determine the relative rights and preferences of subsequent series.

Each certificate representing shares shall state upon the face thereof:

(a) That the corporation is organized under the laws of this State.

(b) The name of the person to whom issued.

(c) The number and class of shares, and the designation of the series, if any, which such certificate represents.

(d) The par value of each share represented by such certificate, or a statement that the shares are without par value.

No certificate shall be issued for any share until such share is fully paid.

§ 24.   Fractional Shares

A corporation may (1) issue fractions of a share, (2) arrange for the disposition of fractional interests by those entitled thereto, (3) pay in cash the fair value of fractions of a share as of the time when those entitled to receive such fractions are determined, or (4) issue scrip in registered or bearer form which shall entitle the holder to receive a certificate for a full share upon the surrender of such scrip aggregating a full share. A certificate for a fractional share shall, but scrip shall not unless otherwise provided therein, entitle the holder to exercise voting rights, to receive dividends thereon, and to participate in any of the assets of the corporation in the event of liquidation. The board of directors may cause scrip to be issued subject to the condition that it shall become void if not exchanged for certificates representing full shares before a specified date, or subject to the condition that the shares for which scrip is exchangeable may be sold by the corporation and the proceeds thereof distributed to the holders of scrip, or subject to any other conditions which the board of directors may deem advisable.

§ 25.   Liability of Subscribers and Shareholders

A holder of or subscriber to shares of a corporation shall be under no obligation to the corporation or its creditors with respect to such shares other than the obligation to pay to the corporation the full consideration for which such shares were issued or to be issued.

Any person becoming an assignee or transferee of shares or of a subscription for shares in good faith and without knowledge or notice that the full consideration therefor has not been paid shall not be personally liable to the corporation or its creditors for any unpaid portion of such consideration.

An executor, administrator, conservator, guardian, trustee, assignee for the benefit of creditors, or receiver shall not be personally liable to the corporation as a holder of or subscriber to shares of a corporation but the estate and funds in his hands shall be so liable.

No pledgee or other holder of shares as collateral security shall be personally liable as a shareholder.

§ 26.   Shareholders' Preemptive Rights

The shareholders of a corporation shall have no preemptive right to acquire unissued or treasury shares of the corporation, or securities of the corporation convertible into or carrying a right to subscribe to or acquire shares, except to the extent, if any, that such right is provided in the articles of incorporation.

§ 26A.   Shareholders' Preemptive Rights [Alternative]

Except to the extent limited or denied by this section or by the articles of incorporation, shareholders shall have a preemptive right to acquire unissued or treasury shares or securities convertible into such shares or carrying a right to subscribe to or acquire shares.

Unless otherwise provided in the articles of incorporation,

(a) No preemptive right shall exist

(1) to acquire any shares issued to directors, officers or employees pursuant to approval by the affirmative vote of the holders of a majority of the shares entitled to vote thereon or when authorized by and consistent with a plan theretofore approved by such a vote of shareholders; or

(2) to acquire any shares sold otherwise than for cash.

(b) Holders of shares of any class that is preferred or limited as to dividends or assets shall not be entitled to any preemptive right.

(c) Holders of shares of common stock shall not be entitled to any preemptive right to shares of any class that is preferred or limited as to dividends or assets or to any obligations, unless convertible into shares of common stock or carrying a right to subscribe to or acquire shares of common stock.

(d) Holders of common stock without voting power shall have no preemptive right to shares of common stock with voting power.

(e) The preemptive right shall be only an opportunity to acquire shares or other securities under such terms and conditions as the board of directors may fix for the purpose of providing a fair and reasonable opportunity for the exercise of such right.

§ 27. By-Laws

The initial by-laws of a corporation shall be adopted by its board of directors. The power to alter, amend or repeal the by-laws or adopt new by-laws, subject to repeal or change by action of the shareholders, shall be vested in the board of directors unless reserved to the shareholders by the articles of incorporation. The by-laws may contain any provisions for the regulation and management of the affairs of the corporation not inconsistent with law or the articles of incorporation.

§ 27A. By-Laws and Other Powers in Emergency [Optional]

The board of directors of any corporation may adopt emergency by-laws, subject to repeal or change by action of the shareholders, which shall, notwithstanding any different provision elsewhere in this Act or in the articles of incorporation or by-laws, be operative during any emergency in the conduct of the business of the corporation resulting from an attack on the United States or any nuclear or atomic disaster. The emergency by-laws may make any provision that may be practical and necessary for the circumstances of the emergency, including provisions that:

(a) A meeting of the board of directors may be called by any officer or director in such manner and under such conditions as shall be prescribed in the emergency by-laws;

(b) The director or directors in attendance at the meeting, or any greater number fixed by the emergency by-laws, shall constitute a quorum; and

(c) The officers or other persons designated on a list approved by the board of directors before the emergency, all in such order of priority and subject to such conditions, and for such period of time (not longer than reasonably necessary after the termination of the emergency) as may be provided in the emergency by-laws or in the resolution approving the list shall, to the extent required to provide a quorum at any meeting of the board of directors, be deemed directors for such meeting.

The board of directors, either before or during any such emergency, may provide, and from time to time modify, lines of succession in the event that during such an emergency any or all officers or agents of the corporation shall for any reason be rendered incapable of discharging their duties.

The board of directors, either before or during any such emergency, may, effective in the emergency, change the head office or designate several alternative head offices or regional offices, or authorize the officers so to do.

To the extent not inconsistent with any emergency by-laws so adopted, the by-laws of the corporation shall remain in effect during any such emergency and upon its termination the emergency by-laws shall cease to be operative.

Unless otherwise provided in emergency by-laws, notice of any meeting of the board of directors during any such emergency may be given only to such of the directors as it may be feasible to reach at the time and by such means as may be feasible at the time, including publication or radio.

To the extent required to constitute a quorum at any meeting of the board of directors during any such emergency, the officers of the corporation who are present shall, unless otherwise provided in emergency by-laws, be deemed, in order of rank and within the same rank in order of seniority, directors for such meeting.

No officer, director or employee acting in accordance with any emergency by-laws shall be liable except for willful misconduct. No officer, director or employee shall be liable for any action taken by him in good faith in such an emergency in furtherance of the ordinary business affairs of the corporation even though not authorized by the by-laws then in effect.

§ 28.   Meetings of Shareholders

Meetings of shareholders may be held at such place within or without this State as may be stated in or fixed in accordance with the by-laws. If no other place is stated or so fixed, meetings shall be held at the registered office of the corporation.

An annual meeting of the shareholders shall be held at such time as may be stated in or fixed in accordance with the by-laws. If the annual meeting is not held within any thirteen-month period the Court of . . . . may, on the application of any shareholder, summarily order a meeting to be held.

Special meetings of the shareholders may be called by the board of directors, the holders of not less than one-tenth of all the shares entitled to vote at the meeting, or such other persons as may be authorized in the articles of incorporation or the by-laws.

§ 29.   Notice of Shareholders' Meetings

Written notice stating the place, day and hour of the meeting and, in case of a special meeting, the purpose or purposes for which the meeting is called, shall be delivered not less than ten nor more than fifty days before the date of the meeting, either personally or by mail, by or at the direction of the president, the secretary, or the officer or persons calling the meeting, to each shareholder of record entitled to vote at such meeting. If mailed, such notice shall be deemed to be delivered when deposited in the United States mail addressed to the shareholder at his address as it appears on the stock transfer books of the corporation, with postage thereon prepaid.

§ 30.   Closing of Transfer Books and Fixing Record Date

For the purpose of determining shareholders entitled to notice of or to vote at any meeting of shareholders or any adjournment thereof, or entitled to receive payment of any dividend, or in order to make a determination of shareholders for any other proper purpose, the board of directors of a corporation may provide that the stock transfer books shall be closed for a stated period but not to exceed, in any case, fifty days. If the stock transfer books shall be closed for the purpose of determining shareholders entitled to notice of or to vote at a meeting of shareholders, such books shall be closed for at least ten days immediately preceding such meeting. In lieu of closing the stock transfer books, the by-laws, or in the absence of an applicable by-law the board of directors, may fix in advance a date as the record date for any such determination of shareholders, such date in any case to be not more than fifty days and, in case of a meeting of shareholders, not less than ten days prior to the date on which the particular action, requiring such determination of shareholders, is to be taken. If the stock transfer books are not closed and no record date is fixed for the determination of shareholders entitled to notice of or to vote at a meeting of shareholders, or shareholders entitled to receive a payment of a dividend, the date on which notice of the meeting is mailed or the date on which the resolution of the board of directors declaring such dividend is adopted, as the case may be, shall be the record date for such determination of shareholders. When a determination of shareholders entitled to vote at any meeting of shareholders has been made as provided in this section, such determination shall apply to any adjournment thereof.

§ 31. Voting Record

The officer or agent having charge of the stock transfer books for shares of a corporation shall make a complete record of the shareholders entitled to vote at such meeting or any adjournment thereof, arranged in alphabetical order, with the address of and the number of shares held by each. Such record shall be produced and kept open at the time and place of the meeting and shall be subject to the inspection of any shareholder during the whole time of the meeting for the purposes thereof.

Failure to comply with the requirements of this section shall not affect the validity of any action taken at such meeting.

An officer or agent having charge of the stock transfer books who shall fail to prepare the record of shareholders, or produce and keep it open for inspection at the meeting, as provided in this section, shall be liable to any shareholder suffering damage on account of such failure, to the extent of such damage.

§ 32. Quorum of Shareholders

Unless otherwise provided in the articles of incorporation, a majority of the shares entitled to vote, represented in person or by proxy, shall constitute a quorum at a meeting of shareholders, but in no event shall a quorum consist of less than one-third of the shares entitled to vote at the meeting. If a quorum is present, the affirmative vote of the majority of the shares represented at the meeting and entitled to vote on the subject matter shall be the act of the shareholders, unless the vote of a greater number or voting by classes is required by this Act or the articles of incorporation or by-laws.

§ 33. Voting of Shares

Each outstanding share, regardless of class, shall be entitled to one vote on each matter submitted to a vote at a meeting of shareholders, except as may be otherwise provided in the articles of incorporation. If the articles of incorporation provide for more or less than one vote for any share, on any matter, every reference in this Act to a majority or other proportion of shares shall refer to such a majority or other proportion of votes entitled to be cast.

Neither treasury shares, nor shares held by another corporation if a majority of the shares entitled to vote for the election of directors of such other corporation is held by the corporation, shall be voted at any meeting or counted in determining the total number of outstanding shares at any given time.

A shareholder may vote either in person or by proxy executed in writing by the shareholder or by his duly authorized attorney-in-fact. No proxy shall be valid after eleven months from the date of its execution, unless otherwise provided in the proxy.

[Either of the following prefatory phrases may be inserted here: "The articles of incorporation may provide that" or "Unless the articles of incorporation otherwise provide"] . . . at each election for directors every shareholder entitled to vote at such election shall have the right to vote, in person or by proxy, the number of shares owned by him for as many persons as there are directors to be elected and for whose election he has a right to vote, or to cumulate his votes by giving one candidate as many votes as the number of such directors multiplied by the number of his shares shall equal, or by distributing such votes on the same principle among any number of such candidates.

Shares standing in the name of another corporation, domestic or foreign, may be voted by such officer, agent or proxy as the by-laws of such other corporation may prescribe, or, in the absence of such provision, as the board of directors of such other corporation may determine.

Shares held by an administrator, executor, guardian or conservator may be voted by him, either in person or by proxy, without a transfer of such shares into his name. Shares standing in the name of a trustee may be voted by him, either in person or by proxy, but no trustee shall be entitled to vote shares held by him without a transfer of such shares into his name.

Shares standing in the name of a receiver may be voted by such receiver, and shares held by or under the control of a receiver may be voted by such receiver without the transfer thereof into his name if authority so to do be contained in an appropriate order of the court by which such receiver was appointed.

A shareholder whose shares are pledged shall be entitled to vote such shares until the shares have been transferred into the name of the pledgee, and thereafter the pledgee shall be entitled to vote the shares so transferred.

On and after the date on which written notice of redemption of redeemable shares has been mailed to the holders thereof and a sum sufficient to redeem such shares has been deposited with a bank or trust company with irrevocable instruction and authority to pay the redemption price to the holders thereof upon surrender of certificates therefor, such shares shall not be entitled to vote on any matter and shall not be deemed to be outstanding shares.

§ 34. Voting Trusts and Agreements Among Shareholders

Any number of shareholders of a corporation may create a voting trust for the purpose of conferring upon a trustee or trustees the right to vote or otherwise represent their shares, for a period of not to exceed ten years, by entering into a written voting trust agreement specifying the terms and conditions of the voting trust, by depositing a counterpart of the agreement with the corporation at its registered office, and by transferring their shares to such trustee or trustees for the purposes of the agreement. Such trustee or trustees shall keep a record of the holders of voting trust certificates evidencing a beneficial interest in the voting trust, giving the names and addresses of all such holders and the number and class of the shares in respect of which the voting trust certificates held by each are issued, and shall deposit a copy of such record with the corporation at its registered office. The counterpart of the voting trust agreement and the copy of such record so deposited with the corporation shall be subject to the same right of examination by a shareholder of the corporation, in person or by agent or attorney, as are the books and records of the corporation, and such counterpart and such copy of such record shall be subject to examination by any holder of record of voting trust certificates, either in person or by agent or attorney, at any reasonable time for any proper purpose.

Agreements among shareholders regarding the voting of their shares shall be valid and enforceable in accordance with their terms. Such agreements shall not be subject to the provisions of this section regarding voting trusts.

§ 35. Board of Directors

The business and affairs of a corporation shall be managed by a board of directors except as may be otherwise provided in the articles of incorporation. If any such provision is made in the articles of incorporation, the powers and duties conferred or imposed upon the board of directors by this Act shall be exercised or performed to such extent and by such person or persons as shall be provided in the articles of incorporation. Directors need not be residents of this State or shareholders of the corporation unless the articles of incorporation or by-laws so require. The articles of incorporation or by-laws may prescribe other qualifications for directors. The board of directors shall have authority to fix the compensation of directors unless otherwise provided in the articles of incorporation.

§ 36. Number and Election of Directors

The board of directors of a corporation shall consist of one or more members. The number of directors shall be fixed by, or in the manner provided in, the articles of incorporation or the by-laws, except as to the number constituting the initial board of directors, which number shall be fixed by the articles of incorporation. The number of directors may be increased or decreased from time to time by amendment to, or in the manner provided in, the articles of incorporation or the by-laws, but no decrease shall have the effect of shortening the term of any incumbent director. In the absence of a by-law providing for the number of directors, the number shall be the same as that provided for in the articles of incorporation. The names and addresses of the members of the first board of directors shall be stated in the articles of incorporation. Such persons shall hold office until the first annual meeting of shareholders, and until their successors shall have been elected and qualified. At the first annual meeting of shareholders and at each annual meeting thereafter the shareholders shall elect directors to hold office until the next succeeding annual meeting, except in case of the classification of directors as permitted by this Act. Each director shall hold office for the term for which he is elected and until his successor shall have been elected and qualified.

§ 37. Classification of Directors

When the board of directors shall consist of nine or more members, in lieu of electing the whole number of directors annually, the articles of incorporation may provide that the directors be divided into either two or three classes, each class to be as nearly equal in number as possible, the term of office of directors of the first class to expire at the first annual meeting of shareholders after their election, that of the second class to expire at the second annual meeting after their election, and that of the third class, if any, to expire at the third annual meeting after their election. At each annual meeting after such classification the number of directors equal to the number of the class whose term expires at the time of such meeting shall be elected to hold office until the second succeeding annual meeting, if there be two classes, or until the third succeeding annual meeting, if there be three classes. No classification of directors shall be effective prior to the first annual meeting of shareholders.

§ 38. Vacancies

Any vacancy occurring in the board of directors may be filled by the affirmative vote of a majority of the remaining directors though less than a quorum of the board of directors. A director elected to fill a vacancy shall be elected for the unexpired term of his predecessor in office. Any directorship to be filled by reason of an increase in the number of directors may be filled by the board of directors for a term of office continuing only until the next election of directors by the shareholders.

§ 39. Removal of Directors

At a meeting of shareholders called expressly for that purpose, directors may be removed in the manner provided in this section. Any director or the entire board of directors may be removed, with or without cause, by a vote of the holders of a majority of the shares then entitled to vote at an election of directors.

In the case of a corporation having cumulative voting, if less than the entire board is to be removed, no one of the directors may be removed if the votes cast against his removal would be sufficient to elect him if then cumulatively voted at an election of the entire board of directors, or, if there be classes of directors, at an election of the class of directors of which he is a part.

Whenever the holders of the shares of any class are entitled to elect one or more directors by the provisions of the articles of incorporation, the provisions of this section shall apply, in respect to the removal of a director or directors so elected, to the vote of the holders of the outstanding shares of that class and not to the vote of the outstanding shares as a whole.

§ 40. Quorum of Directors

A majority of the number of directors fixed by or in the manner provided in the by-laws or in the absence of a by-law fixing or providing for the number of directors, then of the number stated in the articles of incorporation, shall constitute a quorum for the transaction of business unless a greater number is required by the articles of incorporation or the by-laws. The act of the majority of the directors present at a meeting at which a quorum is present shall be the act of the board of directors, unless the act of a greater number is required by the articles of incorporation or the by-laws.

§ 41. Director Conflicts of Interest

No contract or other transaction between a corporation and one or more of its directors or any other corporation, firm, association or entity in which one or more of its directors are directors or officers or are financially interested, shall be either void or voidable because of such relationship or interest or because such director or directors are present at the meeting of the board of directors or a committee thereof which authorizes, approves or ratifies such contract or transaction or because his or their votes are counted for such purpose, if:

(a) the fact of such relationship or interest is disclosed or known to the board of directors or committee which authorizes, approves or ratifies the contract or transaction by a vote or consent sufficient for the purpose without counting the votes or consents of such interested directors; or

(b) the fact of such relationship or interest is disclosed or known to the shareholders entitled to vote and they authorize, approve or ratify such contract or transaction by vote or written consent; or

(c) the contract or transaction is fair and reasonable to the corporation.

Common or interested directors may be counted in determining the presence of a quorum at a meeting of the board of directors or a committee thereof which authorizes, approves or ratifies such contract or transaction.

§ 42. Executive and Other Committees

If the articles of incorporation or the by-laws so provide, the board of directors, by resolution adopted by a majority of the full board of directors, may designate from among its members an executive committee and one or more other committees each of which, to the extent provided in such resolution or in the articles of incorporation or the by-laws of the corporation, shall have and may exercise all the authority of the board of directors, but no such committee shall have the authority of the board of directors in reference to amending the articles of incorporation, adopting a plan of merger or consolidation, recommending to the shareholders the sale, lease, exchange or other disposition of all or substantially all the property and assets of the corporation otherwise than in the usual and regular course of its business, recommending to the shareholders a voluntary dissolution of the corporation or a revocation thereof, or amending the by-laws of the corporation. The designation of any such committee and the delegation thereto of authority shall not operate to relieve the board of directors, or any member thereof, of any responsibility imposed by law.

§ 43. Place and Notice of Directors' Meetings

Meetings of the board of directors, regular or special, may be held either within or without this State.

Regular meetings of the board of directors may be held with or without notice as prescribed in the by-laws. Special meetings of the board of directors shall be held upon such notice as is prescribed in the by-laws. Attendance of a director at a meeting shall constitute a waiver of notice of such meeting, except where a director attends a meeting for the express purpose of objecting to the transaction of any business because the meeting is not lawfully called or convened. Neither the business to be transacted at, nor the purpose of, any regular or special meeting of the board of directors need be specified in the notice or waiver of notice of such meeting unless required by the by-laws.

§ 44. Action by Directors Without a Meeting

Unless otherwise provided by the articles of incorporation or by-laws, any action required by this Act to be taken at a meeting of the directors of a corporation, or any action which may be taken at a meeting of the directors or of a committee, may be taken without a meeting if a consent in writing, setting forth the action so taken, shall be signed by all of the directors, or all of the members of the committee, as the case may be. Such consent shall have the same effect as a unanimous vote.

§ 45. Dividends

The board of directors of a corporation may, from time to time, declare and the corporation may pay dividends in cash, property, or its own shares, except when the corporation is insolvent or when the payment thereof would render the corporation insolvent or when the declaration or payment thereof would be contrary to any restriction contained in the articles of incorporation, subject to the following provisions:

(a) Dividends may be declared and paid in cash or property only out of the unreserved and unrestricted earned surplus of the corporation, except as otherwise provided in this section.

[Alternative] (a) Dividends may be declared and paid in cash or property only out of the unreserved and unrestricted earned surplus of the corporation, or out of the unreserved and unrestricted net earnings of the current fiscal year and the next preceding fiscal year taken as a single period, except as otherwise provided in this section.

(b) If the articles of incorporation of a corporation engaged in the business of exploiting natural resources so provide, dividends may be declared and paid in cash out of the depletion reserves, but each such dividend shall be identified as a distribution of such reserves and the amount per share paid from such reserves shall be disclosed to the shareholders receiving the same concurrently with the distribution thereof.

(c) Dividends may be declared and paid in its own treasury shares.

(d) Dividends may be declared and paid in its own authorized but unissued shares out of any unreserved and unrestricted surplus of the corporation upon the following conditions:

(1) If a dividend is payable in its own shares having a par value, such shares shall be issued at not less than the par value thereof and there shall be transferred to stated capital at the time such dividend is paid an amount of surplus equal to the aggregate par value of the shares to be issued as a dividend.

(2) If a dividend is payable in its own shares without par value, such shares shall be issued at such stated value as shall be fixed by the board of directors by resolution adopted at the time such dividend is declared, and there shall be transferred to stated capital at the time such dividend is paid an amount of surplus equal to the aggregate stated value so fixed in respect of such shares; and the amount per share so transferred to stated capital shall be disclosed to the shareholders receiving such dividend concurrently with the payment thereof.

(e) No dividend payable in shares of any class shall be paid to the holders of shares of any other class unless the articles of incorporation so provide or such payment is authorized by the affirmative vote or the written consent of the holders of at least a majority of the outstanding shares of the class in which the payment is to be made.

A split-up or division of the issued shares of any class into a greater number of shares of the same class without increasing the stated capital of the corporation shall not be construed to be a share dividend within the meaning of this section.

§ 46. Distributions from Capital Surplus

The board of directors of a corporation may, from time to time, distribute to its shareholders out of capital surplus of the corporation a portion of its assets, in cash or property, subject to the following provisions:

(a) No such distribution shall be made at a time when the corporation is insolvent or when such distribution would render the corporation insolvent.

(b) No such distribution shall be made unless the articles of incorporation so provide or such distribution is authorized by the affirmative vote of the holders of a majority of the outstanding shares of each class whether or not entitled to vote thereon by the provisions of the articles of incorporation of the corporation.

(c) No such distribution shall be made to the holders of any class of shares unless all cumulative dividends accrued on all preferred or special classes of shares entitled to preferential dividends shall have been fully paid.

(d) No such distribution shall be made to the holders of any class of shares which would reduce the remaining net assets of the corporation below the aggregate preferential amount payable in event of involuntary liquidation to the holders of shares having preferential rights to the assets of the corporation in the event of liquidation.

(e) Each such distribution, when made, shall be identified as a distribution from capital surplus and the amount per share disclosed to the shareholders receiving the same concurrently with the distribution thereof.

The board of directors of a corporation may also, from time to time, distribute to the holders of its outstanding shares having a cumulative preferential right to receive dividends, in discharge of their cumulative dividend rights, dividends payable in cash out of the capital surplus of the corporation, if at the time the corporation has no earned surplus and is not insolvent and would not thereby be rendered insolvent. Each such distribution when made, shall be identified as a payment of cumulative dividends out of capital surplus.

§ 47. Loans to Employees and Directors

A corporation shall not lend money to or use its credit to assist its directors without authorization in the particular case by its shareholders, but may lend money to and use its credit to assist any employee of the corporation or of a subsidiary, including any such employee who is a director of the corporation, if the board of directors decides that such loan or assistance may benefit the corporation.

§ 48. Liability of Directors in Certain Cases

In addition to any other liabilities imposed by law upon directors of a corporation:

(a) Directors of a corporation who vote for or assent to the declaration of any dividend or other distribution of the assets of a corporation to its shareholders contrary to the provisions of this Act or contrary to any restrictions contained in the articles of incorporation, shall be jointly and severally liable to the corporation for the amount of such dividend which is paid or the value of such assets which are distributed in excess of the amount of such dividend or distribution which could have been paid or distributed without a violation of the provisions of this Act or the restrictions in the articles of incorporation.

(b) Directors of a corporation who vote for or assent to the purchase of its own shares contrary to the provisions of this Act shall be jointly and severally liable to the corporation for the amount of consideration paid for such shares which is in excess of the maximum amount which could have been paid therefor without a violation of the provisions of this Act.

(c) The directors of a corporation who vote for or assent to any distribution of assets of a corporation to its shareholders during the liquidation of the corporation without the payment and discharge of, or making adequate provision for, all known debts, obligations, and liabilities of the corporation shall be jointly and severally liable to the corporation for the value of such assets which are distributed, to the extent that such debts, obligations and liabilities of the corporation are not thereafter paid and discharged.

A director of a corporation who is present at a meeting of its board of directors at which action on any corporate matter is taken shall be presumed to have assented to the action taken unless his dissent shall be entered in the minutes of the meeting or unless he shall file his written dissent to such action with the secretary of the meeting before the adjournment thereof or shall forward such dissent by registered mail to the secretary of the corporation immediately after the adjournment of the meeting. Such right to dissent shall not apply to a director who voted in favor of such action.

A director shall not be liable under (a), (b) or (c) of this section if he relied and acted in good faith upon financial statements of the corporation represented to him to be correct by the president or the officer of such corporation having charge of its books of account, or stated in a written report by an independent public or certified public accountant or firm of such accountants fairly to reflect the financial condition of such corporation, nor shall he be so liable if in good faith in determining the amount available for any such dividend or distribution he considered the assets to be of their book value.

Any director against whom a claim shall be asserted under or pursuant to this section for the payment of a dividend or other distribution of assets of a corporation and who shall be held liable thereon, shall be entitled to contribution from the shareholders who accepted or received any such dividend or assets, knowing such dividend or distribution to have been made in violation of this Act, in proportion to the amounts received by them.

Any director against whom a claim shall be asserted under or pursuant to this section shall be entitled to contribution from the other directors who voted for or assented to the action upon which the claim is asserted.

§ 49. Provisions Relating to Actions by Shareholders

No action shall be brought in this State by a shareholder in the right of a domestic or foreign corporation unless the plaintiff was a holder of record of shares or of voting trust certificates therefor at the time of the transaction of which he complains, or his shares or voting trust certificates thereafter devolved upon him by operation of law from a person who was a holder of record at such time.

In any action hereafter instituted in the right of any domestic or foreign corporation by the holder or holders of record of shares of such corporation or of voting trust certificates therefor, the court having jurisdiction, upon final judgment and a finding that the action was brought without reasonable cause, may require the plaintiff or plaintiffs to pay to the parties named as defendant the reasonable expenses, including fees of attorneys, incurred by them in the defense of such action.

In any action now pending or hereafter instituted or maintained in the right of any domestic or foreign corporation by the holder or holders of record of less than five per cent of the outstanding shares of any class of such corporation or of voting trust certificates therefor, unless the shares or voting trust certificates so held have a market value in excess of twenty-five thousand dollars, the corporation in whose right such action is brought shall be entitled at any time before final judgment to require the plaintiff or plaintiffs to give security for the reasonable expenses, including fees of attorneys, that may be incurred by it in connection with such action or may be incurred by other parties named as defendant for which it may become legally liable. Market value shall be determined as of the date that the plaintiff institutes the action or, in the case of an intervenor, as of the date that he becomes a party to the action. The amount of such security may from time to time be increased or decreased, in the discretion of the court, upon showing that the security provided has or may become inadequate or is excessive. The corporation shall have recourse to such security in such amount as the court having jurisdiction shall determine upon the termination of such action, whether or not the court finds the action was brought without reasonable cause.

§ 50.   Officers

The officers of a corporation shall consist of a president, one or more vice presidents as may be prescribed by the by-laws, a secretary, and a treasurer, each of whom shall be elected by the board of directors at such time and in such manner as may be prescribed by the by-laws. Such other officers and assistant officers and agents as may be deemed necessary may be elected or appointed by the board of directors or chosen in such other manner as may be prescribed by the by-laws. Any two or more offices may be held by the same person, except the offices of president and secretary.

All officers and agents of the corporation, as between themselves and the corporation, shall have such authority and perform such duties in the management of the corporation as may be provided in the by-laws, or as may be determined by resolution of the board of directors not inconsistent with the by-laws.

§ 51.   Removal of Officers

Any officer or agent may be removed by the board of directors whenever in its judgment the best interests of the corporation will be served thereby, but such removal shall be without prejudice to the contract rights, if any, of the person so removed. Election or appointment of an officer or agent shall not of itself create contract rights.

§ 52.   Books and Records

Each corporation shall keep correct and complete books and records of account and shall keep minutes of the proceedings of its shareholders and board of directors and shall keep at its registered office or principal place of business, or at the office of its transfer agent or registrar, a record of its shareholders, giving the names and addresses of all shareholders and the number and class of the shares held by each. Any books, records and minutes may be in written form or in any other form capable of being converted into written form within a reasonable time.

Any person who shall have been a holder of record of shares or of voting trust certificates therefor at least six months immediately preceding his demand or shall be the holder of record of, or the holder of record of voting trust certificates for, at least five per cent of all the outstanding shares of the corporation, upon written demand stating the purpose thereof, shall have the right to examine, in person, or by agent or attorney, at any reasonable time or times, for any proper purpose its relevant books and records of account, minutes, and record of shareholders and to make extracts therefrom.

Any officer or agent who, or a corporation which, shall refuse to allow any such shareholder or holder of voting trust certificates, or his agent or attorney, so to examine and make extracts from its books and records of account, minutes, and record of shareholders, for any proper purpose, shall be liable to such shareholder or holder of voting trust certificates in a penalty of ten per cent of the value of the shares owned by such shareholder, or in respect of which such voting trust certificates are issued, in addition to any other damages or remedy afforded him by law. It shall be a defense to any action for penalties under this section that the person suing therefor has within two years sold or offered for sale any list of shareholders or of holders of voting trust certificates for shares of such corporation or any other corporation or has aided or abetted any person in procuring any list of shareholders or of holders of voting trust certificates for any such purpose, or has improperly used any information secured through any prior examination of the books and records of account, or minutes, or record of shareholders or of holders of voting trust certificates for shares of such corporation or any other corporation, or was not acting in good faith or for a proper purpose in making his demand.

Nothing herein contained shall impair the power of any court of competent jurisdiction, upon proof by a shareholder or holder of voting trust certificates of proper purpose, irrespective of the period of time during which such shareholder or holder of voting trust certificates shall have been a shareholder of record or a holder of record of voting trust certificates, and irrespective of the number of shares held by him or represented by voting trust certificates held by him, to compel the production for examination by such shareholder or holder of voting trust certificates of the books and records of account, minutes and record of shareholders of a corporation.

Upon the written request of any shareholder or holder of voting trust certificates for shares of a corporation, the corporation shall mail to such shareholder or holder of voting trust certificates its most recent financial statements showing in reasonable detail its assets and liabilities and the results of its operations.

§ 53. Incorporators

One or more persons, or a domestic or foreign corporation, may act as incorporator or incorporators of a corporation by signing and delivering in duplicate to the Secretary of State articles of incorporation for such corporation.

§ 54. Articles of Incorporation

The articles of incorporation shall set forth:

(a) The name of the corporation.

(b) The period of duration, which may be perpetual.

(c) The purpose or purposes for which the corporation is organized which may be stated to be, or to include, the transaction of any or all lawful business for which corporations may be incorporated under this Act.

(d) The aggregate number of shares which the corporation shall have authority to issue; if such shares are to consist of one class only, the par value of each of such shares, or a statement that all of such shares are without par value; or, if such shares are to be divided into classes, the number of shares of each class, and a statement of the par value of the shares of each such class or that such shares are to be without par value.

(e) If the shares are to be divided into classes, the designation of each class and a statement of the preferences, limitations and relative rights in respect of the shares of each class.

(f) If the corporation is to issue the shares of any preferred or special class in series, then the designation of each series and a statement of the variations in the relative rights and preferences as between series insofar as the same are to be fixed in the articles of incorporation, and a statement of any authority to be vested in the board of directors to establish series and fix and determine the variations in the relative rights and preferences as between series.

(g) If any preemptive right is to be granted to shareholders, the provisions therefor.

(h) Any provision, not inconsistent with law, which the incorporators elect to set forth in the articles of incorporation for the regulation of the internal affairs of the corporation, including any provision restricting the transfer of shares and any provision which under this Act is required or permitted to be set forth in the by-laws.

(i) The address of its initial registered office, and the name of its initial registered agent at such address.

(j) The number of directors constituting the initial board of directors and the names and addresses of the persons who are to serve as directors until the first annual meeting of shareholders or until their successors be elected and qualify.

(k) The name and address of each incorporator.

It shall not be necessary to set forth in the articles of incorporation any of the corporate powers enumerated in this Act.

§ 55. Filing of Articles of Incorporation

Duplicate originals of the articles of incorporation shall be delivered to the Secretary of State. If the Secretary of State finds that the articles of incorporation conform to law, he shall, when all fees have been paid as in this Act prescribed:

(a) Endorse on each of such duplicate originals the word "Filed," and the month, day and year of the filing thereof.

(b) File one of such duplicate originals in his office.

(c) Issue a certificate of incorporation to which he shall affix the other duplicate original.

The certificate of incorporation, together with the duplicate original of the articles of incorporation affixed thereto by the Secretary of State, shall be returned to the incorporators or their representative.

§ 56. Effect of Issuance of Certificate of Incorporation

Upon the issuance of the certificate of incorporation, the corporate existence shall begin, and such certificate of incorporation shall be conclusive evidence that all conditions precedent required to be performed by the incorporators have been complied with and that the corporation has been incorporated under this Act, except as against this State in a proceeding to cancel or revoke the certificate of incorporation or for involuntary dissolution of the corporation.

§ 57. Organization Meeting of Directors

After the issuance of the certificate of incorporation an organization meeting of the board of directors named in the articles of incorporation shall be held, either within or without this State, at the call of a majority of the directors named in the articles of incorporation, for the purpose of adopting by-laws, electing officers and transacting such other business as may come before the meeting. The directors calling the meeting shall give at least three days' notice thereof by mail to each director so named, stating the time and place of the meeting.

§ 58. Right to Amend Articles of Incorporation

A corporation may amend its articles of incorporation, from time to time, in any and as many respects as may be desired, so long as its articles of incorporation as amended contain only such provisions as might be lawfully contained in original articles of incorporation at the time of making such amendment, and, if a change in shares or the rights of shareholders, or an exchange, reclassification or cancellation of shares or rights of shareholders is to be made, such provisions as may be necessary to effect such change, exchange, reclassification or cancellation.

In particular, and without limitation upon such general power of amendment, a corporation may amend its articles of incorporation, from time to time, so as:

(a) To change its corporate name.

(b) To change its period of duration.

(c) To change, enlarge or diminish its corporate purposes.

(d) To increase or decrease the aggregate number of shares, or shares of any class, which the corporation has authority to issue.

(e) To increase or decrease the par value of the authorized shares of any class having a par value, whether issued or unissued.

(f) To exchange, classify, reclassify or cancel all or any part of its shares, whether issued or unissued.

(g) To change the designation of all or any part of its shares, whether issued or unissued, and to change the preferences, limitations, and the relative rights in respect of all or any part of its shares, whether issued or unissued.

(h) To change shares having the par value, whether issued or unissued, into the same or a different number of shares without par value, and to change shares without par value, whether issued or unissued, into the same or a different number of shares having a par value.

(i) To change the shares of any class, whether issued or unissued and whether with or without par value, into a different number of shares of the same class or into the same or a different number of shares, either with or without par value, of other classes.

(j) To create new classes of shares having rights and preferences either prior and superior or subordinate and inferior to the shares of any class then authorized, whether issued or unissued.

(k) To cancel or otherwise affect the right of the holders of the shares of any class to receive dividends which have accrued but have not been declared.

(l) To divide any preferred or special class of shares, whether issued or unissued, into series and fix and determine the designations of such series and the variations in the relative rights and preferences as between the shares of such series.

(m) To authorize the board of directors to establish, out of authorized but unissued shares, series of any preferred or special class of shares and fix and determine the relative rights and preferences of the shares of any series so established.

(n) To authorize the board of directors to fix and determine the relative rights and preferences of the authorized but unissued shares of series theretofore established in respect of which either the relative rights and preferences have not been fixed and determined or the relative rights and preferences theretofore fixed and determined are to be changed.

(o) To revoke, diminish, or enlarge the authority of the board of directors to establish series out of authorized but unissued shares of any preferred or special class and fix and determine the relative rights and preferences of the shares of any series so established.

(p) To limit, deny or grant to shareholders of any class the preemptive right to acquire additional or treasury shares of the corporation, whether then or thereafter authorized.

§ 59. Procedure to Amend Articles of Incorporation

Amendments to the articles of incorporation shall be made in the following manner:

(a) The board of directors shall adopt a resolution setting forth the proposed amendment and, if shares have been issued, directing that it be submitted to a vote at a meeting of shareholders, which may be either the annual or a special meeting. If no shares have been issued, the amendment shall be adopted by resolution of the board of directors and the provisions for adoption by shareholders shall not apply. The resolution may incorporate the proposed amendment in restated articles of incorporation which contain a statement that except for the designated amendment the restated articles of incorporation correctly set forth without change the corresponding provisions of the articles of incorporation as theretofore amended, and that the restated articles of incorporation together with the designated amendment supersede the original articles of incorporation and all amendments thereto.

(b) Written notice setting forth the proposed amendment or a summary of the changes to be effected thereby shall be given to each shareholder of record entitled to vote thereon within the time and in the manner provided in this Act for the giving of notice of meetings of shareholders. If the meeting be an annual meeting, the proposed amendment of such summary may be included in the notice of such annual meeting.

(c) At such meeting a vote of the shareholders entitled to vote thereon shall be taken on the proposed amendment. The proposed amendment shall be adopted upon receiving the affirmative vote of the holders of a majority of the shares entitled to vote thereon, unless any class of shares is entitled to vote thereon as a class, in which event the proposed amendment shall be adopted upon receiving the affirmative vote of the holders of a majority of the shares of each class of shares entitled to vote thereon as a class and of the total shares entitled to vote thereon.

Any number of amendments may be submitted to the shareholders, and voted upon by them, at one meeting.

§ 60. Class Voting on Amendments

The holders of the outstanding shares of a class shall be entitled to vote as a class upon a proposed amendment, whether or not entitled to vote thereon by the provisions of the articles of incorporation, if the amendment would:

(a) Increase or decrease the aggregate number of authorized shares of such class.

(b) Increase or decrease the par value of the shares of such class.

(c) Effect an exchange, reclassification or cancellation of all or part of the shares of such class.

(d) Effect an exchange, or create a right of exchange, of all or any part of the shares of another class into the shares of such class.

(e) Change the designations, preferences, limitations or relative rights of the shares of such class.

(f) Change the shares of such class, whether with or without par value, into the same or a different number of shares, either with or without par value, of the same class or another class or classes.

(g) Create a new class of shares having rights and preferences prior and superior to the shares of such class, or increase the rights and preferences or the number of authorized shares, of any class having rights and preferences prior or superior to the shares of such class.

(h) In the case of a preferred or special class of shares, divide the shares of such class into series and fix and determine the designation of such series and the variations in the relative rights and preferences between the shares of such series, or authorize the board of directors to do so.

(i) Limit or deny any existing preemptive rights of the shares of such class.

(j) Cancel or otherwise affect dividends on the shares of such class which have accrued but have not been declared.

§ 61. Articles of Amendment

The articles of amendment shall be executed in duplicate by the corporation by its president or a vice president and by its secretary or an assistant secretary, and verified by one of the officers signing such articles, and shall set forth:

(a) The name of the corporation.

(b) The amendments so adopted.

(c) The date of the adoption of the amendment by the shareholders, or by the board of directors where no shares have been issued.

(d) The number of shares outstanding, and the number of shares entitled to vote thereon, and if the shares of any class are entitled to vote thereon as a class, the designation and number of outstanding shares entitled to vote thereon of each such class.

(e) The number of shares voted for and against such amendment, respectively, and, if the shares of any class are entitled to vote thereon as a class, the number of shares of each such class voted for and against such amendment, respectively, or if no shares have been issued, a statement to that effect.

(f) If such amendment provides for an exchange, reclassification or cancellation of issued shares, and if the manner in which the same shall be effected is not set forth in the amendment, then a statement of the manner in which the same shall be effected.

(g) If such amendment effects a change in the amount of stated capital, then a statement of the manner in which the same is effected and a statement, expressed in dollars, of the amount of stated capital as changed by such amendment.

§ 62. Filing of Articles of Amendment

Duplicate originals of the articles of amendment shall be delivered to the Secretary of State. If the Secretary of State finds that the articles of amendment conform to law, he shall, when all fees and franchise taxes have been paid as in this Act prescribed:

(a) Endorse on each of such duplicate originals the word "Filed," and the month, day and year of the filing thereof.

(b) File one of such duplicate originals in his office.

(c) Issue a certificate of amendment to which he shall affix the other duplicate original.

The certificate of amendment, together with the duplicate original of the articles of amendment affixed thereto by the Secretary of State, shall be returned to the corporation or its representative.

§ 63. Effect of Certificate of Amendment

Upon the issuance of the certificate of amendment by the Secretary of State, the amendment shall become effective and the articles of incorporation shall be deemed to be amended accordingly.

No amendment shall affect any existing cause of action in favor of or against such corporation, or any pending suit to which such corporation shall be a party, or the existing rights of persons other than shareholders; and, in the event the corporate name shall be changed by amendment, no suit brought by or against such corporation under its former name shall abate for that reason.

§ 64. Restated Articles of Incorporation

A domestic corporation may at any time restate its articles of incorporation as theretofore amended, by a resolution adopted by the board of directors.

Upon the adoption of such resolution, restated articles of incorporation shall be executed in duplicate by the corporation by its president or a vice president and by its secretary or assistant secretary and verified by one of the officers signing such articles and shall set forth all of the operative provisions of the articles of incorporation as theretofore amended together with a statement that the restated articles of incorporation correctly set forth without change the corresponding provisions of the articles of incorporation as theretofore amended and that the restated articles of incorporation supersede the original articles of incorporation and all amendments thereto.

Duplicate originals of the restated articles of incorporation shall be delivered to the Secretary of State. If the Secretary of State finds that such restated articles of incorporation conform to law, he shall, when all fees and franchise taxes have been paid as in this Act prescribed:

(1) Endorse on each of such duplicate originals the word "Filed," and the month, day and year of the filing thereof.

(2) File one of such duplicate originals in his office.

(3) Issue a restated certificate of incorporation, to which he shall affix the other duplicate original.

The restated certificate of incorporation, together with the duplicate original of the restated articles of incorporation affixed thereto by the Secretary of State, shall be returned to the corporation or its representative.

Upon the issuance of the restated certificate of incorporation by the Secretary of State, the restated articles of incorporation shall become effective and shall supersede the original articles of incorporation and all amendments thereto.

§ 65.   Amendment of Articles of Incorporation in Reorganization Proceedings

Whenever a plan of reorganization of a corporation has been confirmed by decree or order of a court of competent jurisdiction in proceedings for the reorganization of such corporation, pursuant to the provisions of any applicable statute of the United States relating to reorganizations of corporations, the articles of incorporation of the corporation may be amended, in the manner provided in this section, in as many respects as may be necessary to carry out the plan and put it into effect, so long as the articles of incorporation as amended contain only such provisions as might be lawfully contained in original articles of incorporation at the time of making such amendment.

In particular and without limitation upon such general power of amendment, the articles of incorporation may be amended for such purpose so as to:

(A) Change the corporate name, period of duration or corporate purposes of the corporation;

(B) Repeal, alter or amend the by-laws of the corporation;

(C) Change the aggregate number of shares or shares of any class, which the corporation has authority to issue;

(D) Change the preferences, limitations and relative rights in respect of all or any part of the shares of the corporation, and classify, reclassify or cancel all or any part thereof, whether issued or unissued;

(E) Authorize the issuance of bonds, debentures or other obligations of the corporation, whether or not convertible into shares of any class or bearing warrants or other evidences of optional rights to purchase or subscribe for shares of any class, and fix the terms and conditions thereof; and

(F) Constitute or reconstitute and classify or reclassify the board of directors of the corporation, and appoint directors and officers in place of or in addition to all or any of the directors or officers then in office.

Amendments to the articles of incorporation pursuant to this section shall be made in the following manner:

(a) Articles of amendment approved by decree or order of such court shall be executed and verified in duplicate by such person or persons as the court shall designate or appoint for the purpose, and shall set forth the name of the corporation, the amendments of the articles of incorporation approved by the court, the date of the decree or order approving the articles of amendment, the title of the proceedings in which the decree or order was entered, and a statement that such decree or order was entered by a court having jurisdiction of the proceedings for the reorganization of the corporation pursuant to the provisions of an applicable statute of the United States.

(b) Duplicate originals of the articles of amendment shall be delivered to the Secretary of State. If the Secretary of State finds that the articles of amendment conform to law, he shall, when all fees and franchise taxes have been paid as in this Act prescribed:

(1) Endorse on each of such duplicate originals the word "Filed," and the month, day and year of the filing thereof.

(2) File one of such duplicate originals in his office.

(3) Issue a certificate of amendment to which he shall affix the other duplicate original.

The certificate of amendment, together with the duplicate original of the articles of amendment affixed thereto by the Secretary of State, shall be returned to the corporation or its representative.

Upon the issuance of the certificate of amendment by the Secretary of State, the amendment shall become effective and the articles of incorporation shall be deemed to be amended accordingly, without any action thereon by the directors or shareholders of the corporation and with the same effect as if the amendments had been adopted by unanimous action of the directors and shareholders of the corporation.

§ 66. Restriction on Redemption or Purchase of Redeemable Shares

No redemption or purchase of redeemable shares shall be made by a corporation when it is insolvent or when such redemption or purchase would render it insolvent, or which would reduce the net assets below the aggregate amount payable to the holders of shares having prior or equal rights to the assets of the corporation upon involuntary dissolution.

§ 67. Cancellation of Redeemable Shares by Redemption or Purchase

When redeemable shares of a corporation are redeemed or purchased by the corporation, the redemption or purchase shall effect a cancellation of such shares, and a statement of cancellation shall be filed as provided in this section. Thereupon such shares shall be restored to the status of authorized but unissued shares, unless the articles of incorporation provide that such shares when redeemed or purchased shall not be reissued, in which case the filing of the statement of cancellation shall constitute an amendment to the articles of incorporation and shall reduce the number of shares of the class so cancelled which the corporation is authorized to issue by the number of shares so cancelled.

The statement of cancellation shall be executed in duplicate by the corporation by its president or a vice president and by its secretary or an assistant secretary, and verified by one of the officers signing such statement, and shall set forth:

(a) The name of the corporation.

(b) The number of redeemable shares cancelled through redemption or purchase, itemized by classes and series.

(c) The aggregate number of issued shares, itemized by classes and series, after giving effect to such cancellation.

(d) The amount, expressed in dollars, of the stated capital of the corporation after giving effect to such cancellation.

(e) If the articles of incorporation provide that the cancelled shares shall not be reissued, the number of shares which the corporation will have authority to issue itemized by classes and series, after giving effect to such cancellation.

Duplicate originals of such statement shall be delivered to the Secretary of State. If the Secretary of State finds that such statement conforms to law, he shall, when all fees and franchise taxes have been paid as in this Act prescribed:

(1) Endorse on each of such duplicate originals the word "Filed," and the month, day and year of the filing thereof.

(2) File one of such duplicate originals in his office.

(3) Return the other duplicate original to the corporation or its representative.

Upon the filing of such statement of cancellation, the stated capital of the corporation shall be deemed to be reduced by that part of the stated capital which was, at the time of such cancellation, represented by the shares so cancelled.

Nothing contained in this section shall be construed to forbid a cancellation of shares or a reduction of stated capital in any other manner permitted by this Act.

§ 68. Cancellation of Other Reacquired Shares

A corporation may at any time, by resolution of its board of directors, cancel all or any part of the shares of the corporation of any class reacquired by it, other than redeemable shares redeemed or purchased, and in such event a statement of cancellation shall be filed as provided in this section.

The statement of cancellation shall be executed in duplicate by the corporation by its president or a vice president and by its secretary or an assistant secretary, and verified by one of the officers signing such statement, and shall set forth:

(a) The name of the corporation.

(b) The number of reacquired shares cancelled by resolution duly adopted by the board of directors, itemized by classes and series, and the date of its adoption.

(c) The aggregate number of issued shares, itemized by classes and series, after giving effect to such cancellation.

(d) The amount, expressed in dollars, of the stated capital of the corporation after giving effect to such cancellation.

Duplicate originals of such statement shall be delivered to the Secretary of State. If the Secretary of State finds that such statement conforms to law, he shall, when all fees and franchise taxes have been paid as in this Act prescribed:

(1) Endorse on each of such duplicate originals the word "Filed," and the month, day and year of the filing thereof.

(2) File one of such duplicate originals in his office.

(3) Return the other duplicate original to the corporation or its representative.

Upon the filing of such statement of cancellation, the stated capital of the corporation shall be deemed to be reduced by that part of the stated capital which was, at the time of such cancellation, represented by the shares so cancelled, and the shares so cancelled shall be restored to the status of authorized but unissued shares.

Nothing contained in this section shall be construed to forbid a cancellation of shares or a reduction of stated capital in any other manner permitted by this Act.

§ 69. Reduction of Stated Capital in Certain Cases

A reduction of the stated capital of a corporation, where such reduction is not accompanied by any action requiring an amendment of the articles of incorporation and not accompanied by a cancellation of shares, may be made in the following manner:

(A) The board of directors shall adopt a resolution setting forth the amount of the proposed reduction and the manner in which the reduction shall be effected, and directing that the question of such reduction be submitted to a vote at a meeting of shareholders, which may be either an annual or a special meeting.

(B) Written notice, stating that the purpose or one of the purposes of such meeting is to consider the question of reducing the stated capital of the corporation in the amount and manner proposed by the board of directors, shall be given to each shareholder of record entitled to vote thereon within the time and in the manner provided in this Act for the giving of notice of meetings of shareholders.

(C) At such meeting a vote of the shareholders entitled to vote thereon shall be taken on the question of approving the proposed reduction of stated capital, which shall require for its adoption the affirmative vote of the holders of a majority of the shares entitled to vote thereon.

When a reduction of the stated capital of a corporation has been approved as provided in this section, a statement shall be executed in duplicate by the corporation by its president or a vice president and by its secretary or an assistant secretary, and verified by one of the officers signing such statement, and shall set forth:

(a) The name of the corporation.

(b) A copy of the resolution of the shareholders approving such reduction, and the date of its adoption.

(c) The number of shares outstanding, and the number of shares entitled to vote thereon.

(d) The number of shares voted for and against such reduction, respectively.

(e) A statement of the manner in which such reduction is effected, and a statement, expressed in dollars, of the amount of stated capital of the corporation after giving effect to such reduction.

Duplicate originals of such statement shall be delivered to the Secretary of State. If the Secretary of State finds that such statement conforms to law, he shall, when all fees and franchise taxes have been paid as in this Act prescribed:

(1) Endorse on each of such duplicate originals the word "Filed," and the month, day and year of the filing thereof.

(2) File one of such duplicate originals in his office.

(3) Return the other duplicate original to the corporation or its representative.

Upon the filing of such statement, the stated capital of the corporation shall be reduced as therein set forth.

No reduction of stated capital shall be made under the provisions of this section which would reduce the amount of the aggregate stated capital of the corporation to an amount equal to or less than the aggregate preferential amounts payable upon all issued shares having a preferential right in the assets of the corporation in the event of involuntary liquidation, plus the aggregate par value of all issued shares having a par value but no preferential right in the assets of the corporation in the event of involuntary liquidation.

§ 70. Special Provisions Relating to Surplus and Reserves

The surplus, if any, created by or arising out of a reduction of the stated capital of a corporation shall be capital surplus.

The capital surplus of a corporation may be increased from time to time by resolution of the board of directors directing that all or a part of the earned surplus of the corporation be transferred to capital surplus.

A corporation may, by resolution of its board of directors, apply any part or all of its capital surplus to the reduction or elimination of any deficit arising from losses, however incurred, but only after first eliminating the earned surplus, if any, of the corporation by applying such losses against earned surplus and only to the extent that such losses exceed the earned surplus, if any. Each such application of capital surplus shall, to the extent thereof, effect a reduction of capital surplus.

A corporation may, by resolution of its board of directors, create a reserve or reserves out of its earned surplus for any proper purpose or purposes, and may abolish any such reserve in the same manner. Earned surplus of the corporation to the extent so reserved shall not be available for the payment of dividends or other distributions by the corporation except as expressly permitted by this Act.

§ 71. Procedure for Merger

Any two or more domestic corporations may merge into one of such corporations pursuant to a plan of merger approved in the manner provided in this Act.

The board of directors of each corporation shall, by resolution adopted by each such board, approve a plan of merger setting forth:

(a) The names of the corporations proposing to merge, and the name of the corporation into which they propose to merge, which is hereinafter designated as the surviving corporation.

(b) The terms and conditions of the proposed merger.

(c) The manner and basis of converting the shares of each corporation into shares, obligations or other securities of the surviving corporation or of any other corporation or, in whole or in part, into cash or other property.

(d) A statement of any changes in the articles of incorporation of the surviving corporation to be effected by such merger.

(e) Such other provisions with respect to the proposed merger as are deemed necessary or desirable.

§ 72. Procedure for Consolidation

Any two or more domestic corporations may consolidate into a new corporation pursuant to a plan of consolidation approved in the manner provided in this Act.

The board of directors of each corporation shall, by a resolution adopted by each such board, approve a plan of consolidation setting forth:

(a) The names of the corporations proposing to consolidate, and the name of the new corporation into which they propose to consolidate, which is hereinafter designated as the new corporation.

(b) The terms and conditions of the proposed consolidation.

(c) The manner and basis of converting the shares of each corporation into shares, obligations or other securities of the new corporation or of any other corporation or, in whole or in part, into cash or other property.

(d) With respect to the new corporation, all of the statements required to be set forth in articles of incorporation for corporations organized under this Act.

(e) Such other provisions with respect to the proposed consolidation as are deemed necessary or desirable.

§ 73. Approval by Shareholders

The board of directors of each corporation, upon approving such plan of merger or plan of consolidation, shall, by resolution, direct that the plan be submitted to a vote at a meeting of shareholders, which may be either an annual or a special meeting. Written notice shall be given to each shareholder of record, whether or not entitled to vote at such meeting, not less than twenty days before such meeting, in the manner provided in this Act for the giving of notice of meetings of shareholders, and, whether the meeting be an annual or a special meeting, shall state that the purpose or one of the purposes is to consider the proposed plan of merger or consolidation. A copy or a summary of the plan of merger or plan of consolidation, as the case may be, shall be included in or enclosed with such notice.

At each such meeting, a vote of the shareholders shall be taken on the proposed plan of merger or consolidation. The plan of merger or consolidation shall be approved upon receiving the affirmative vote of the holders of a majority of the shares entitled to vote thereon of each such corporation, unless any class of shares of any such corporation is entitled to vote thereon as a class, in which event, as to such corporation, the plan of merger, or consolidation shall be approved upon receiving the affirmative vote of the holders of a majority of the shares of each class of shares entitled to vote thereon as a class and of the total shares entitled to vote thereon. Any class of shares of any such corporation shall be entitled to vote as a class if the plan of merger or consolidation, as the case may be, contains any provision which, if contained in a proposed amendment to articles of incorporation, would entitle such class of shares to vote as a class.

After such approval by a vote of the shareholders of each corporation, and at any time prior to the filing of the articles of merger or consolidation, the merger or consolidation may be abandoned pursuant to provisions therefor, if any, set forth in the plan of merger or consolidation.

§ 74. Articles of Merger or Consolidation

Upon such approval, articles of merger or articles of consolidation shall be executed in duplicate by each corporation by its president or a vice president and by its secretary or an assistant secretary, and verified by one of the officers of each corporation signing such articles, and shall set forth:

(a) The plan of merger or the plan of consolidation.

(b) As to each corporation, the number of shares outstanding, and, if the shares of any class are entitled to vote as a class, the designation and number of outstanding shares of each such class.

(c) As to each corporation, the number of shares voted for and against such plan, respectively, and, if the shares of any class are entitled to vote as a class, the number of shares of each such class voted for and against such plan, respectively.

Duplicate originals of the articles of merger or articles of consolidation shall be delivered to the Secretary of State. If the Secretary of State finds that such articles conform to law, he shall, when all fees and franchise taxes have been paid as in this Act prescribed:

(1) Endorse on each of such duplicate originals the word "Filed," and the month, day and year of the filing thereof.

(2) File one of such duplicate originals in his office.

(3) Issue a certificate of merger or a certificate of consolidation to which he shall affix the other duplicate original.

The certificate of merger or certificate of consolidation, together with the duplicate original of the articles of merger or articles of consolidation affixed thereto by the Secretary of State, shall be returned to the surviving or new corporation, as the case may be, or its representative.

§ 75. Merger of Subsidiary Corporation

Any corporation owning at least ninety percent of the outstanding shares of each class of another corporation may merge such other corporation into itself without approval by a vote of the shareholders of either corporation. Its board of directors shall, by resolution, approve a plan of merger setting forth:

(A) The name of the subsidiary corporation and the name of the corporation owning at least ninety per cent of its shares, which is hereinafter designated as the surviving corporation.

(B) The manner and basis of converting the shares of the subsidiary corporation into shares, obligations or other securities of the surviving corporation or of any other corporation or, in whole or in part, into cash or other property.

A copy of such plan of merger shall be mailed to each shareholder of record of the subsidiary corporation.

Articles of merger shall be executed in duplicate by the surviving corporation by its president or a vice president and by its secretary or an assistant secretary, and verified by one of its officers signing such articles, and shall set forth:

(a) The plan of merger;

(b) The number of outstanding shares of each class of the subsidiary corporation and the number of such shares of each class owned by the surviving corporation; and

(c) The date of the mailing to shareholders of the subsidiary corporation of a copy of the plan of merger.

On and after the thirtieth day after the mailing of a copy of the plan of merger to shareholders of the subsidiary corporation or upon the waiver thereof by the holders of all outstanding shares duplicate originals of the articles of merger shall be delivered to the Secretary of State. If the Secretary of State finds that such articles conform to law, he shall, when all fees and franchise taxes have been paid as in this Act prescribed:

(1) Endorse on each of such duplicate originals the word "Filed," and the month, day and year of the filing thereof,

(2) File one of such duplicate originals in his office, and

(3) Issue a certificate of merger to which he shall affix the other duplicate original.

The certificate of merger, together with the duplicate original of the articles of merger affixed thereto by the Secretary of State shall be returned to the surviving corporation or its representative.

§ 76.   Effect of Merger or Consolidation

Upon the issuance of the certificate of merger or the certificate of consolidation by the Secretary of State, the merger or consolidation shall be effected.

When such merger or consolidation has been effected:

(a) The several corporations parties to the plan of merger or consolidation shall be a single corporation, which, in the case of a merger, shall be that corporation designated in the plan of merger as the surviving corporation, and, in the case of a consolidation, shall be the new corporation provided for in the plan of consolidation.

(b) The separate existence of all corporations parties to the plan of merger or consolidation, except the surviving or new corporation, shall cease.

(c) Such surviving or new corporation shall have all the rights, privileges, immunities and powers and shall be subject to all the duties and liabilities of a corporation organized under this Act.

(d) Such surviving or new corporation shall thereupon and thereafter possess all the rights, privileges, immunities, and franchises, of a public as well as of a private nature, of each of the merging or consolidating corporations; and all property, real, personal and mixed, and all debts due on whatever account, including subscriptions to shares, and all other choses in action, and all and every other interest of or belonging to or due to each of the corporations so merged or consolidated, shall be taken and deemed to be transferred to and vested in such single corporation without further act or deed; and the title to any real estate, or any interest therein, vested in any of such corporations shall not revert or be in any way impaired by reason of such merger or consolidation.

(e) Such surviving or new corporation shall thenceforth be responsible and liable for all the liabilities and obligations of each of the corporations so merged or consolidated; and any claim existing or action or proceeding pending by or against any of such corporations may be prosecuted as if such merger or consolidation had not taken place, or such surviving or new corporation may be substituted in its place. Neither the rights of creditors nor any liens upon the property of any such corporation shall be impaired by such merger or consolidation.

(f) In the case of a merger, the articles of incorporation of the surviving corporation shall be deemed to be amended to the extent, if any, that changes in its articles of incorporation are stated in the plan of merger; and, in the case of a consolidation, the statements set forth in the articles of consolidation and which are required or permitted to be set forth in the articles of incorporation of corporations organized under this Act shall be deemed to be the original articles of incorporation of the new corporation.

§ 77. Merger or Consolidation of Domestic and Foreign Corporations

One or more foreign corporations and one or more domestic corporations may be merged or consolidated in the following manner, if such merger or consolidation is permitted by the laws of the state under which each such foreign corporation is organized:

(a) Each domestic corporation shall comply with the provisions of this Act with respect to the merger or consolidation, as the case may be, of domestic corporations and each foreign corporation shall comply with the applicable provisions of the laws of the state under which it is organized.

(b) If the surviving or new corporation, as the case may be, is to be governed by the laws of any state other than this State, it shall comply with the provisions of this Act with respect to foreign corporations if it is to transact business in this State, and in every case it shall file with the Secretary of State of this State:

(1) An agreement that it may be served with process in this State in any proceeding for the enforcement of any obligation of any domestic corporation which is a party to such merger or consolidation and in any proceeding for the enforcement of the rights of a dissenting shareholder of any such domestic corporation against the surviving or new corporation;

(2) An irrevocable appointment of the Secretary of State of this State as its agent to accept service of process in any such proceeding; and

(3) An agreement that it will promptly pay to the dissenting shareholders of any such domestic corporation the amount, if any, to which they shall be entitled under the provisions of this Act with respect to the rights of dissenting shareholders.

The effect of such merger or consolidation shall be the same as in the case of the merger or consolidation of domestic corporations, if the surviving or new corporation is to be governed by the laws of this State. If the surviving or new corporation is to be governed by the laws of any state other than this State, the effect of such merger or consolidation shall be the same as in the case of the merger or consolidation of domestic corporations except insofar as the laws of such other state provide otherwise.

At any time prior to the filing of the articles of merger or consolidation, the merger or consolidation may be abandoned pursuant to provisions therefor, if any, set forth in the plan of merger or consolidation.

§ 78. Sale of Assets in Regular Course of Business and Mortgage or Pledge of Assets

The sale, lease, exchange, or other disposition of all, or substantially all, the property and assets of a corporation in the usual and regular course of its business and the mortgage or pledge of any or all property and assets of a corporation whether or not in the usual and regular course of business may be made upon such terms and conditions and for such consideration, which may consist in whole or in part of cash or other property, including shares, obligations or other securities of any other corporation, domestic or foreign, as shall be authorized by its board of directors; and in any such case no authorization or consent of the shareholders shall be required.

§ 79. Sale of Assets Other Than in Regular Course of Business

A sale, lease, exchange, or other disposition of all, or substantially all, the property and assets, with or without the good will, of a corporation, if not in the usual and regular course of its business, may be made upon such terms and conditions and for such consideration, which may consist in whole or in part of cash or other property, including shares, obligations or other securities of any other corporation, domestic or foreign, as may be authorized in the following manner:

(a) The board of directors shall adopt a resolution recommending such sale, lease, exchange, or other disposition and directing the submission thereof to a vote at a meeting of shareholders, which may be either an annual or a special meeting.

(b) Written notice shall be given to each shareholder of record, whether or not entitled to vote at such meeting, not less than twenty days before such meeting, in the manner provided in this Act for the giving of notice of meetings of shareholders, and, whether the meeting be an annual or a special meeting, shall state that the purpose, or one of the purposes is to consider the proposed sale, lease, exchange, or other disposition.

(c) At such meeting the shareholders may authorize such sale, lease, exchange, or other disposition and may fix, or may authorize the board of directors to fix, any or all of the terms and conditions thereof and the consideration to be received by the corporation therefor. Such authorization shall require the affirmative vote of the holders of a majority of the shares of the corporation entitled to vote thereon, unless any class of shares is entitled to vote thereon as a class, in which event such authorization shall require the affirmative vote of the holders of a majority of the shares of each class of shares entitled to vote as a class thereon and of the total shares entitled to vote thereon.

(d) After such authorization by a vote of shareholders, the board of directors nevertheless, in its discretion, may abandon such sale, lease, exchange, or other disposition of assets, subject to the rights of third parties under any contracts relating thereto, without further action or approval by shareholders.

§ 80. Right of Shareholders to Dissent

Any shareholder of a corporation shall have the right to dissent from any of the following corporate actions:

(a) Any plan of merger or consolidation to which the corporation is a party; or

(b) Any sale or exchange of all or substantially all of the property and assets of the corporation not made in the usual and regular course of its business, including a sale in dissolution, but not including a sale pursuant to an order of a court having jurisdiction in the premises or a sale for cash on terms requiring that all or substantially all of the net proceeds of sale be distributed to the shareholders in accordance with their respective interests within one year after the date of sale.

A shareholder may dissent as to less than all of the shares registered in his name. In that event, his rights shall be determined as if the shares as to which he has dissented and his other shares were registered in the names of different shareholders.

This section shall not apply to the shareholders of the surviving corporation in a merger if a vote of the shareholders of such corporation is not necessary to authorize such merger. Nor shall it apply to the holders of shares of any class or series if the shares of such class or series were registered on a national securities exchange on the date fixed to determine the shareholders entitled to vote at the meeting of shareholders at which a plan of merger or consolidation or a proposed sale or exchange of property and assets is to be acted upon unless the articles of incorporation of the corporation shall otherwise provide.

§ 81. Rights of Dissenting Shareholders

Any shareholder electing to exercise such right of dissent shall file with the corporation, prior to or at the meeting of shareholders at which such proposed corporate action is submitted to a vote, a written objection to such proposed corporate action. If such proposed corporate action be approved by the required vote and such shareholder shall not have voted in favor thereof, such shareholder may, within ten days after the date on which the vote was taken or if a corporation is to be merged without a vote of its shareholders into another corporation, any of its shareholders may, within fifteen days after the plan of such merger shall have been mailed to such shareholders, make written demand on the corporation, or, in the case of a merger or consolidation, on the surviving or new corporation, domestic or foreign, for payment of the fair value of such shareholder's shares, and, if such proposed corporate action is effected, such corporation shall pay to such shareholder, upon surrender of the certificate or certificates representing such shares, the fair value thereof as of the day prior to the date on which the vote was taken approving the proposed corporate action, excluding any appreciation or depreciation in anticipation of such corporate action. Any shareholder failing to make demand within the applicable ten-day or fifteen-day period shall be bound by the terms of the proposed corporate action. Any shareholder making such demand shall thereafter be entitled only to payment as in this section provided and shall not be entitled to vote or to exercise any other rights of a shareholder.

No such demand may be withdrawn unless the corporation shall consent thereto. If, however, such demand shall be withdrawn upon consent, or if the proposed corporate action shall be abandoned or rescinded or the shareholders shall revoke the authority to effect such action, or if, in the case of a merger, on the date of the filing of the articles of merger the surviving corporation is the owner of all the outstanding shares of the other corporations, domestic and foreign, that are parties to the merger, or if no demand or petition for the determination of fair value by a court shall have been made or filed within the time provided in this section, or if a court of competent jurisdiction shall determine that such shareholder is not entitled to the relief provided by this section, then the right of such shareholder to be paid the fair value of his shares shall cease and his status as a shareholder shall be restored, without prejudice to any corporate proceedings which may have been taken during the interim.

Within ten days after such corporate action is effected, the corporation, or, in the case of a merger or consolidation, the surviving or new corporation, domestic or foreign, shall give written notice thereof to each dissenting shareholder who has made demand as herein provided, and shall make a written offer to each such shareholder to pay for such shares at a specified price deemed by such corporation to be the fair value thereof. Such notice and offer shall be accompanied by a balance sheet of the corporation the shares of which the dissenting shareholder holds, as of the latest available date and not more than twelve months prior to the making of such offer, and a profit and loss statement of such corporation for the twelve months' period ended on the date of such balance sheet.

If within thirty days after the date on which such corporate action was effected the fair value of such shares is agreed upon between any such dissenting shareholder and the corporation, payment therefor shall be made within ninety days after the date on which such corporate action was effected, upon surrender of the certificate or certificates representing such shares. Upon payment of the agreed value the dissenting shareholder shall cease to have any interest in such shares.

If within such period of thirty days a dissenting shareholder and the corporation do not so agree, then the corporation, within thirty days after receipt of written demand from any dissenting shareholder given within sixty days after the date on which such corporate action was effected, shall, or at its election at any time within such period of sixty days may, file a petition in any court of competent jurisdiction in the county in this State where the registered office of the corporation is located requesting that the fair value of such shares be found and determined. If, in the case of a merger or consolidation, the surviving or new corporation is a foreign corporation without a registered office in this State, such petition shall be filed in the county where the registered office of the domestic corporation was last located. If the corporation shall fail to institute the proceeding as herein provided, any dissenting shareholder may do so in the name of the corporation. All dissenting shareholders, wherever residing, shall be made parties to the proceeding as an action against their shares quasi in rem. A copy of the petition shall be served on each dissenting shareholder who is a resident of this State and shall be served by registered or certified mail on each dissenting shareholder who is a nonresident. Service on nonresidents shall also be made by publication as provided by law. The jurisdiction of the court shall be plenary and exclusive. All shareholders who are parties to the proceeding shall be entitled to judgment against the corporation for the amount of the fair value of their shares. The court may, if it so elects, appoint one or more persons as appraisers to receive evidence and recommend a decision on the question of fair value. The appraisers shall have such power and authority as shall be specified in the order of their appointment or an amendment thereof. The judgment shall be payable only upon and concurrently with the surrender to the corporation of the certificate or certificates representing such shares. Upon payment of the judgment, the dissenting shareholder shall cease to have any interest in such shares.

The judgment shall include an allowance for interest at such rate as the court may find to be fair and equitable in all the circumstances, from the date on which the vote was taken on the proposed corporate action to the date of payment.

The costs and expenses of any such proceeding shall be determined by the court and shall be assessed against the corporation, but all or any part of such costs and expenses may be apportioned and assessed as the court may deem equitable against any or all of the dissenting shareholders who are parties to the proceeding to whom the corporation shall have made an offer to pay for the shares if the court shall find that the action of such shareholders in failing to accept such offer was arbitrary or vexatious or not in good faith. Such expenses shall include reasonable compensation for and reasonable expenses of the appraisers, but shall exclude the fees and expenses of counsel for and experts employed by any party; but if the fair value of the shares as determined materially exceeds the amount which the corporation offered to pay therefor, or if no offer was made, the court in its discretion may award to any shareholder who is a party to the proceeding such sum as the court may determine to be reasonable compensation to any expert or experts employed by the shareholder in the proceeding.

Within twenty days after demanding payment for his shares, each shareholder demanding payment shall submit the certificate or certificates representing his shares to the corporation for notation thereon that such demand has been made. His failure to do so shall, at the option of the corporation, terminate his rights under this section unless a court of competent jurisdiction, for good and sufficient cause shown, shall otherwise direct. If shares represented by a certificate on which notation has been so made shall be transferred, each new certificate issued therefor shall bear similar notation, together with the name of the original dissenting holder of such shares, and a transferee of such shares shall acquire by such transfer no rights in the corporation other than those which the original dissenting shareholder had after making demand for payment of the fair value thereof.

Shares acquired by a corporation pursuant to payment of the agreed value therefor or to payment of the judgment entered therefor, as in this section provided, may be held and disposed of by such corporation as in the case of other treasury shares, except that, in the case of a merger or consolidation, they may be held and disposed of as the plan of merger or consolidation may otherwise provide.

§ 82.   Voluntary Dissolution by Incorporators

A corporation which has not commenced business and which has not issued any shares, may be voluntarily dissolved by its incorporators at any time in the following manner:

(a) Articles of dissolution shall be executed in duplicate by a majority of the incorporators, and verified by them, and shall set forth:

(1) The name of the corporation.

(2) The date of issuance of its certificate of incorporation.

(3) That none of its shares has been issued.

(4) That the corporation has not commenced business.

(5) That the amount, if any, actually paid in on subscriptions for its shares, less any part thereof disbursed for necessary expenses, has been returned to those entitled thereto.

(6) That no debts of the corporation remain unpaid.

(7) That a majority of the incorporators elect that the corporation be dissolved.

(b) Duplicate originals of the articles of dissolution shall be delivered to the Secretary of State. If the Secretary of State finds that the articles of dissolution conform to law, he shall, when all fees and franchise taxes have been paid as in this Act prescribed:

(1) Endorse on each of such duplicate originals the word "Filed," and the month, day and year of the filing thereof.

(2) File one of such duplicate originals in his office.

(3) Issue a certificate of dissolution to which he shall affix the other duplicate original.

The certificate of dissolution, together with the duplicate original of the articles of dissolution affixed thereto by the Secretary of State, shall be returned to the incorporators or their representative. Upon the issuance of such certificate of dissolution by the Secretary of State, the existence of the corporation shall cease.

§ 83. Voluntary Dissolution by Consent of Shareholders

A corporation may be voluntarily dissolved by the written consent of all of its shareholders.

Upon the execution of such written consent, a statement of intent to dissolve shall be executed in duplicate by the corporation by its president or a vice president and by its secretary or an assistant secretary, and verified by one of the officers signing such statement, which statement shall set forth:

(a) The name of the corporation.

(b) The names and respective addresses of its officers.

(c) The names and respective addresses of its directors.

(d) A copy of the written consent signed by all shareholders of the corporation.

(e) A statement that such written consent has been signed by all shareholders of the corporation or signed in their names by their attorneys thereunto duly authorized.

§ 84. Voluntary Dissolution by Act of Corporation

A corporation may be dissolved by the act of the corporation, when authorized in the following manner:

(a) The board of directors shall adopt a resolution recommending that the corporation be dissolved, and directing that the question of such dissolution be submitted to a vote at a meeting of shareholders, which may be either an annual or a special meeting.

(b) Written notice shall be given to each shareholder of record entitled to vote at such meeting within the time and in the manner provided in this Act for the giving of notice of meetings of shareholders, and, whether the meeting be an annual or special meeting, shall state that the purpose, or one of the purposes, of such meeting is to consider the advisability of dissolving the corporation.

(c) At such meeting a vote of shareholders entitled to vote thereat shall be taken on a resolution to dissolve the corporation. Such resolution shall be adopted upon receiving the affirmative vote of the holders of a majority of the shares of the corporation entitled to vote thereon, unless any class of shares is entitled to vote thereon as a class, in which event the resolution shall be adopted upon receiving the affirmative vote of the holders of a majority of the shares of each class of shares entitled to vote thereon as a class and of the total shares entitled to vote thereon.

(d) Upon the adoption of such resolution, a statement of intent to dissolve shall be executed in duplicate by the corporation by its president or a vice president and by its secretary or an assistant secretary, and verified by one of the officers signing such statement, which statement shall set forth:

(1) The name of the corporation.

(2) The names and respective addresses of its officers.

(3) The names and respective addresses of its directors.

(4) A copy of the resolution adopted by the shareholders authorizing the dissolution of the corporation.

(5) The number of shares outstanding, and, if the shares of any class are entitled to vote as a class, the designation and number of outstanding shares of each such class.

(6) The number of shares voted for and against the resolution, respectively, and, if the shares of any class are entitled to vote as a class, the number of shares of each such class voted for and against the resolution, respectively.

§ 85.   Filing of Statement of Intent to Dissolve

Duplicate originals of the statement of intent to dissolve, whether by consent of shareholders or by act of the corporation, shall be delivered to the Secretary of State. If the Secretary of State finds that such statement conforms to law, he shall, when all fees and franchise taxes have been paid as in this Act prescribed:

(a) Endorse on each of such duplicate originals the word "Filed," and the month, day and year of the filing thereof.

(b) File one of such duplicate originals in his office.

(c) Return the other duplicate original to the corporation or its representative.

§ 86.   Effect of Statement of Intent to Dissolve

Upon the filing by the Secretary of State of a statement of intent to dissolve, whether by consent of shareholders or by act of the corporation, the corporation shall cease to carry on its business, except insofar as may be necessary for the winding up thereof, but its corporate existence shall continue until a certificate of dissolution has been issued by the Secretary of State or until a decree dissolving the corporation has been entered by a court of competent jurisdiction as in this Act provided.

§ 87.   Procedure after Filing of Statement of Intent to Dissolve

After the filing by the Secretary of State of a statement of intent to dissolve:

(a) The corporation shall immediately cause notice thereof to be mailed to each known creditor of the corporation.

(b) The corporation shall proceed to collect its assets, convey and dispose of such of its properties as are not to be distributed in kind to its shareholders, pay, satisfy and discharge its liabilities and obligations and do all other acts required to liquidate its business and affairs, and, after paying or adequately providing for the payment of all its obligations, distribute the remainder of its assets, either in cash or in kind, among its shareholders according to their respective rights and interests.

(c) The corporation, at any time during the liquidation of its business and affairs, may make application to a court of competent jurisdiction within the state and judicial subdivision in which the registered office or principal place of business of the corporation is situated, to have the liquidation continued under the supervision of the court as provided in this Act.

§ 88. Revocation of Voluntary Dissolution Proceedings by Consent of Shareholders

By the written consent of all of its shareholders, a corporation may, at any time prior to the issuance of a certificate of dissolution by the Secretary of State, revoke voluntary dissolution proceedings theretofore taken, in the following manner:

Upon the execution of such written consent, a statement of revocation of voluntary dissolution proceedings shall be executed in duplicate by the corporation by its president or a vice president and by its secretary or an assistant secretary, and verified by one of the officers signing such statement, which statement shall set forth:

(a) The name of the corporation.

(b) The names and respective addresses of its officers.

(c) The names and respective addresses of its directors.

(d) A copy of the written consent signed by all shareholders of the corporation revoking such voluntary dissolution proceedings.

(e) That such written consent has been signed by all shareholders of the corporation or signed in their names by their attorneys thereunto duly authorized.

§ 89. Revocation of Voluntary Dissolution Proceedings by Act of Corporation

By the act of the corporation, a corporation may, at any time prior to the issuance of a certificate of dissolution by the Secretary of State, revoke voluntary dissolution proceedings theretofore taken, in the following manner:

(a) The board of directors shall adopt a resolution recommending that the voluntary dissolution proceedings be revoked, and directing that the question of such revocation be submitted to a vote at a special meeting of shareholders.

(b) Written notice, stating that the purpose or one of the purposes of such meeting is to consider the advisability of revoking the voluntary dissolution proceedings, shall be given to each shareholder of record entitled to vote at such meeting within the time and in the manner provided in this Act for the giving of notice of special meetings of shareholders.

(c) At such meeting a vote of the shareholders entitled to vote thereat shall be taken on a resolution to revoke the voluntary dissolution proceedings, which shall require for its adoption the affirmative vote of the holders of a majority of the shares entitled to vote thereon.

(d) Upon the adoption of such resolution, a statement of revocation of voluntary dissolution proceedings shall be executed in duplicate by the corporation by its president or a vice president and by its secretary or an assistant secretary, and verified by one of the officers signing such statement, which statement shall set forth:

(1) The name of the corporation.

(2) The names and respective addresses of its officers.

(3) The names and respective addresses of its directors.

(4) A copy of the resolution adopted by the shareholders revoking the voluntary dissolution proceedings.

(5) The number of shares outstanding.

(6) The number of shares voted for and against the resolution, respectively.

§ 90. Filing of Statement of Revocation of Voluntary Dissolution Proceedings

Duplicate originals of the statement of revocation of voluntary dissolution proceedings, whether by consent of shareholders or by act of the corporation, shall be delivered to the Secretary of State. If the Secretary of State finds that such statement conforms to law, he shall, when all fees and franchise taxes have been paid as in this Act prescribed:

(a) Endorse on each of such duplicate originals the word "Filed," and the month, day and year of the filing thereof.

(b) File one of such duplicate originals in his office.

(c) Return the other duplicate original to the corporation or its representative.

§ 91. Effect of Statement of Revocation of Voluntary Dissolution Proceedings

Upon the filing by the Secretary of State of a statement of revocation of voluntary dissolution proceedings, whether by consent of shareholders or by act of the corporation, the revocation of the voluntary dissolution proceedings shall become effective and the corporation may again carry on its business.

§ 92. Articles of Dissolution

If voluntary dissolution proceedings have not been revoked, then when all debts, liabilities and obligations of the corporation have been paid and discharged, or adequate provision has been made therefor, and all of the remaining property and assets of the corporation have been distributed to its shareholders, articles of dissolution shall be executed in duplicate by the corporation by its president or a vice president and by its secretary or an assistant secretary, and verified by one of the officers signing such statement, which statement shall set forth:

(a) The name of the corporation.

(b) That the Secretary of State has theretofore filed a statement of intent to dissolve the corporation, and the date on which such statement was filed.

(c) That all debts, obligations and liabilities of the corporation have been paid and discharged or that adequate provision has been made therefor.

(d) That all the remaining property and assets of the corporation have been distributed among its shareholders in accordance with their respective rights and interests.

(e) That there are no suits pending against the corporation in any court, or that adequate provision has been made for the satisfaction of any judgment, order or decree which may be entered against it in any pending suit.

§ 93. Filing of Articles of Dissolution

Duplicate originals of such articles of dissolution shall be delivered to the Secretary of State. If the Secretary of State finds that such articles of dissolution conform to law, he shall, when all fees and franchise taxes have been paid as in this Act prescribed:

(a) Endorse on each of such duplicate originals the word "Filed," and the month, day and year of the filing thereof.

(b) File one of such duplicate originals in his office.

(c) Issue a certificate of dissolution to which he shall affix the other duplicate original.

The certificate of dissolution, together with the duplicate original of the articles of dissolution affixed thereto by the Secretary of State, shall be returned to the representative of the dissolved corporation. Upon the issuance of such certificate of dissolution the existence of the corporation shall cease, except for the purpose of suits, other proceedings and appropriate corporate action by shareholders, directors and officers as provided in this Act.

§ 94. Involuntary Dissolution

A corporation may be dissolved involuntarily by a decree of the . . . . court in an action filed by the Attorney General when it is established that:

(a) The corporation has failed to file its annual report within the time required by this Act, or has failed to pay its franchise tax on or before the first day of August of the year in which such franchise tax becomes due and payable; or

(b) The corporation procured its articles of incorporation through fraud; or

(c) The corporation has continued to exceed or abuse the authority conferred upon it by law; or

(d) The corporation has failed for thirty days to appoint and maintain a registered agent in this State; or

(e) The corporation has failed for thirty days after change of its registered office or registered agent to file in the office of the Secretary of State a statement of such change.

§ 95. Notification to Attorney General

The Secretary of State, on or before the last day of December of each year, shall certify to the Attorney General the names of all corporations which have failed to file their annual reports or to pay franchise taxes in accordance with the provisions of this Act, together with the facts pertinent thereto. He shall also certify, from time to time, the names of all corporations which have given other cause for dissolution as provided in this Act, together with the facts pertinent thereto. Whenever the Secretary of State shall certify the name of a corporation to the Attorney General as having given any cause for dissolution, the Secretary of State shall concurrently mail to the corporation at its registered office a notice that such certification has been made. Upon the receipt of such certification, the Attorney General shall file an action in the name of the State against such corporation for its dissolution. Every such certificate from the Secretary of State to the Attorney General pertaining to the failure of a corporation to file an annual report or pay a franchise tax shall be taken and received in all courts as prima facie evidence of the facts therein stated. If, before action is filed, the corporation shall file its annual report or pay its franchise tax, together with all penalties thereon, or shall appoint or maintain a registered agent as provided in this Act, or shall file with the Secretary of State the required statement of change of registered office or registered agent, such fact shall be forthwith certified by the Secretary of State to the Attorney General and he shall not file an action against such corporation for such cause. If, after action is filed, the corporation shall file its annual report or pay its franchise tax, together with all penalties thereon, or shall appoint or maintain a registered agent as provided in this Act, or shall file with the Secretary of State the required statement of change of registered office or registered agent, and shall pay the costs of such action, the action for such cause shall abate.

§ 96. Venue and Process

Every action for the involuntary dissolution of a corporation shall be commenced by the Attorney General either in the . . . . court of the county in which the registered office of the corporation is situated, or in the . . . . court of . . . . county. Summons shall issue and be served as in other civil actions. If process is returned not found, the Attorney General shall cause publication to be made as in other civil cases in some newspaper published in the county where the registered office of the corporation is situated, containing a notice of the pendency of such action, the title of the court, the title of the action, and the date on or after which default may be entered. The Attorney General may include in one notice the names of any number of corporations against which actions are then pending in the same court. The Attorney General shall cause a copy of such notice to be mailed to the corporation at its registered office within ten days after the first publication thereof. The certificate of the Attorney General of the mailing of such notice shall be prima facie evidence thereof. Such notice shall be published at least once each week for two successive weeks, and the first publication thereof may begin at any time after the summons has been returned. Unless a corporation shall have been served with summons, no default shall be taken against it earlier than thirty days after the first publication of such notice.

§ 97. Jurisdiction of Court to Liquidate Assets and Business of Corporation

The . . . . courts shall have full power to liquidate the assets and business of a corporation:

(a) In an action by a shareholder when it is established:

(1) That the directors are deadlocked in the management of the corporate affairs and the shareholders are unable to break the deadlock, and that irreparable injury to the corporation is being suffered or is threatened by reason thereof; or

(2) That the acts of the directors or those in control of the corporation are illegal, oppressive or fraudulent; or

(3) That the shareholders are deadlocked in voting power, and have failed, for a period which includes at least two consecutive annual meeting dates, to elect successors to directors whose terms have expired or would have expired upon the election of their successors; or

(4) That the corporate assets are being misapplied or wasted.

(b) In an action by a creditor:

(1) When the claim of the creditor has been reduced to judgment and an execution thereon returned unsatisfied and it is established that the corporation is insolvent; or

(2) When the corporation has admitted in writing that the claim of the creditor is due and owing and it is established that the corporation is insolvent.

(c) Upon application by a corporation which has filed a statement of intent to dissolve, as provided in this Act, to have its liquidation continued under the supervision of the court.

(d) When an action has been filed by the Attorney General to dissolve a corporation and it is established that liquidation of its business and affairs should precede the entry of a decree of dissolution.

Proceedings under clause (a), (b) or (c) of this section shall be brought in the county in which the registered office or the principal office of the corporation is situated.

It shall not be necessary to make shareholders parties to any such action or proceeding unless relief is sought against them personally.

§ 98. Procedure in Liquidation of Corporation by Court

In proceedings to liquidate the assets and business of a corporation the court shall have power to issue injunctions, to appoint a receiver or receivers pendente lite, with such powers and duties as the court, from time to time, may direct, and to take such other proceedings as may be requisite to preserve the corporate assets wherever situated, and carry on the business of the corporation until a full hearing can be had.

After a hearing had upon such notice as the court may direct to be given to all parties to the proceedings and to any other parties in interest designated by the court, the court may appoint a liquidating receiver or receivers with authority to collect the assets of the corporation, including all amounts owing to the corporation by subscribers on account of any unpaid portion of the consideration for the issuance of shares. Such liquidating receiver or receivers shall have authority, subject to the order of the court, to sell, convey and dispose of all or any part of the assets of the corporation wherever situated, either at public or private sale. The assets of the corporation or the proceeds resulting from a sale, conveyance or other disposition thereof shall be applied to the expenses of such liquidation and to the payment of the liabilities and obligations of the corporation, and any remaining assets or proceeds shall be distributed among its shareholders according to their respective rights and interests. The order appointing such liquidating receiver or receivers shall state their powers and duties. Such powers and duties may be increased or diminished at any time during the proceedings.

The court shall have power to allow from time to time as expenses of the liquidation compensation to the receiver or receivers and to attorneys in the proceeding, and to direct the payment thereof out of the assets of the corporation or the proceeds of any sale or disposition of such assets.

A receiver of a corporation appointed under the provisions of this section shall have authority to sue and defend in all courts in his own name as receiver of such corporation. The court appointing such receiver shall have exclusive jurisdiction of the corporation and its property, wherever situated.

§ 99. Qualifications of Receivers

A receiver shall in all cases be a natural person or a corporation authorized to act as receiver, which corporation may be a domestic corporation or a foreign corporation authorized to transact business in this State, and shall in all cases give such bond as the court may direct with such sureties as the court may require.

§ 100. Filing of Claims in Liquidation Proceedings

In proceedings to liquidate the assets and business of a corporation the court may require all creditors of the corporation to file with the clerk of the court or with the receiver, in such form as the court may prescribe, proofs under oath of their respective claims. If the court requires the filing of claims it shall fix a date, which shall be not less than four months from the date of the order, as the last day for the filing of claims, and shall prescribe the notice that shall be given to creditors and claimants of the date so fixed. Prior to the date so fixed, the court may extend the time for the filing of claims. Creditors and claimants failing to file proofs of claim on or before the date so fixed may be barred, by order of court, from participating in the distribution of the assets of the corporation.

§ 101. Discontinuance of Liquidation Proceedings

The liquidation of the assets and business of a corporation may be discontinued at any time during the liquidation proceedings when it is established that cause for liquidation no longer exists. In such event the court shall dismiss the proceedings and direct the receiver to redeliver to the corporation all its remaining property and assets.

§ 102. Decree of Involuntary Dissolution

In proceedings to liquidate the assets and business of a corporation, when the costs and expenses of such proceedings and all debts, obligations and liabilities of the corporation shall have been paid and discharged and all of its remaining property and assets distributed to its shareholders, or in case its property and assets are not sufficient to satisfy and discharge such costs, expenses, debts and obligations, all the property and assets have been applied so far as they will go to their payment, the court shall enter a decree dissolving the corporation, whereupon the existence of the corporation shall cease.

§ 103. Filing of Decree of Dissolution

In case the court shall enter a decree dissolving a corporation, it shall be the duty of the clerk of such court to cause a certified copy of the decree to be filed with the Secretary of State. No fee shall be charged by the Secretary of State for the filing thereof.

§ 104. Deposit with State Treasurer of Amount Due Certain Shareholders

Upon the voluntary or involuntary dissolution of a corporation, the portion of the assets distributable to a creditor or shareholder who is unknown or cannot be found, or who is under disability and there is no person legally competent to receive such distributive portion, shall be reduced to cash and deposited with the State Treasurer and shall be paid over to such creditor or shareholder or to his legal representative upon proof satisfactory to the State Treasurer of his right thereto.

§ 105. Survival of Remedy after Dissolution

The dissolution of a corporation either (1) by the issuance of a certificate of dissolution by the Secretary of State, or (2) by a decree of court when the court has not liquidated the assets and business of the corporation as provided in this Act, or (3) by expiration of its period of duration, shall not take away or impair any remedy available to or against such corporation, its directors, officers, or shareholders, for any right or claim existing, or any liability incurred, prior to such dissolution if action or other proceeding thereon is commenced within two years after the date of such dissolution. Any such action or proceeding by or against the corporation may be prosecuted or defended by the corporation in its corporate name. The shareholders, directors and officers shall have power to take such corporate or other action as shall be appropriate to protect such remedy, right or claim. If such corporation was dissolved by the expiration of its period of duration, such corporation may amend its articles of incorporation at any time during such period of two years so as to extend its period of duration.

§ 106. Admission of Foreign Corporation

No foreign corporation shall have the right to transact business in this State until it shall have procured a certificate of authority so to do from the Secretary of State. No foreign corporation shall be entitled to procure a certificate of authority under this Act to transact in this State any business which a corporation organized under this Act is not permitted to transact. A foreign corporation shall not be denied a certificate of authority by reason of the fact that the laws of the state or country under which such corporation is organized governing its organization and internal affairs differ from the laws of this State, and nothing in this Act contained shall be construed to authorize this State to regulate the organization or the internal affairs of such corporation.

Without excluding other activities which may not constitute transacting business in this State, a foreign corporation shall not be considered to be transacting business in this State, for the purposes of this Act, by reason of carrying on in this State any one or more of the following activities:

(a) Maintaining or defending any action or suit or any administrative or arbitration proceeding, or effecting the settlement thereof or the settlement of claims or disputes.

(b) Holding meetings of its directors or shareholders or carrying on other activities concerning its internal affairs.

(c) Maintaining bank accounts.

(d) Maintaining offices or agencies for the transfer, exchange and registration of its securities, or appointing and maintaining trustees or depositaries with relation to its securities.

(e) Effecting sales through independent contractors.

(f) Soliciting or procuring orders, whether by mail or through employees or agents or otherwise, where such orders require acceptance without this State before becoming binding contracts.

(g) Creating evidences of debt, mortgages or liens on real or personal property.

(h) Securing or collecting debts or enforcing any rights in property securing the same.

(i) Transacting any business in interstate commerce.

(j) Conducting an isolated transaction completed within a period of thirty days and not in the course of a number of repeated transactions of like nature.

§ 107. Powers of Foreign Corporation

A foreign corporation which shall have received a certificate of authority under this Act shall, until a certificate of revocation or of withdrawal shall have been issued as provided in this Act, enjoy the same, but no greater, rights and privileges as a domestic corporation organized for the purposes set forth in the application pursuant to which such certificate of authority is issued; and, except as in this Act otherwise provided, shall be subject to the same duties, restrictions, penalties and liabilities now or hereafter imposed upon a domestic corporation of like character.

§ 108. Corporate Name of Foreign Corporation

No certificate of authority shall be issued to a foreign corporation unless the corporate name of such corporation:

(a) Shall contain the word "corporation," "company," "incorporated," or "limited," or shall contain an abbreviation of one of such words, or such corporation shall, for use in this State, add at the end of its name one of such words or an abbreviation thereof.

(b) Shall not contain any word or phrase which indicates or implies that it is organized for any purpose other than one or more of the purposes contained in its articles of incorporation or that it is authorized or empowered to conduct the business of banking or insurance.

(c) Shall not be the same as, or deceptively similar to, the name of any domestic corporation existing under the laws of this State or any foreign corporation authorized to transact business in this State, or a name the exclusive right to which is, at the time, reserved in the manner provided in this Act, or the name of a corporation which has in effect a registration of its name as provided in this Act, except that this provision shall not apply if the foreign corporation applying for a certificate of authority files with the Secretary of State any one of the following:

(1) a resolution of its board of directors adopting a fictitious name for use in transacting business in this State which fictitious name is not deceptively similar to the name of any domestic corporation or of any foreign corporation authorized to transact business in this State or to any name reserved or registered as provided in this Act, or

(2) the written consent of such other corporation or holder of a reserved or registered name to use the same or deceptively similar name and one or more words are added to make such name distinguishable from such other name, or

(3) a certified copy of a final decree of a court of competent jurisdiction establishing the prior right of such foreign corporation to the use of such name in this State.

§ 109. Change of Name by Foreign Corporation

Whenever a foreign corporation which is authorized to transact business in this State shall change its name to one under which a certificate of authority would not be granted to it on application therefor, the certificate of authority of such corporation shall be suspended and it shall not thereafter transact any business in this State until it has changed its name to a name which is available to it under the laws of this State or has otherwise complied with the provisions of this Act.

§ 110. Application for Certificate of Authority

A foreign corporation, in order to procure a certificate of authority to transact business in this State, shall make application therefor to the Secretary of State, which application shall set forth:

(a) The name of the corporation and the state or country under the laws of which it is incorporated.

(b) If the name of the corporation does not contain the word "corporation," "company," "incorporated," or "limited," or does not contain an abbreviation of one of such words, then the name of the corporation with the word or abbreviation which it elects to add thereto for use in this State.

(c) The date of incorporation and the period of duration of the corporation.

(d) The address of the principal office of the corporation in the state or country under the laws of which it is incorporated.

(e) The address of the proposed registered office of the corporation in this State, and the name of its proposed registered agent in this State at such address.

(f) The purpose or purposes of the corporation which it proposes to pursue in the transaction of business in this State.

(g) The names and respective addresses of the directors and officers of the corporation.

(h) A statement of the aggregate number of shares which the corporation has authority to issue, itemized by classes, par value of shares, shares without par value, and series, if any, within a class.

(i) A statement of the aggregate number of issued shares itemized by classes, par value of shares, shares without par value, and series, if any, within a class.

(j) A statement, expressed in dollars, of the amount of stated capital of the corporation, as defined in this Act.

(k) An estimate, expressed in dollars, of the value of all property to be owned by the corporation for the following year, wherever located, and an estimate of the value of the property of the corporation to be located within this State during such year, and an estimate, expressed in dollars, of the gross amount of business which will be transacted by the corporation during such year, and an estimate of the gross amount thereof which will be transacted by the corporation at or from places of business in this State during such year.

(l) Such additional information as may be necessary or appropriate in order to enable the Secretary of State to determine whether such corporation is entitled to a certificate of authority to transact business in this State and to determine and assess the fees and franchise taxes payable as in this Act prescribed.

Such application shall be made on forms prescribed and furnished by the Secretary of State and shall be executed in duplicate by the corporation by its president or a vice president and by its secretary or an assistant secretary, and verified by one of the officers signing such application.

§ 111. Filing of Application for Certificate of Authority

Duplicate originals of the application of the corporation for a certificate of authority shall be delivered to the Secretary of State, together with a copy of its articles of incorporation and all amendments thereto, duly authenticated by the proper officer of the state or country under the laws of which it is incorporated.

If the Secretary of State finds that such application conforms to law, he shall, when all fees and franchise taxes have been paid as in this Act prescribed:

(a) Endorse on each of such documents the word "Filed," and the month, day and year of the filing thereof.

(b) File in his office one of such duplicate originals of the application and the copy of the articles of incorporation and amendments thereto.

(c) Issue a certificate of authority to transact business in this State to which he shall affix the other duplicate original application.

The certificate of authority, together with the duplicate original of the application affixed thereto by the Secretary of State, shall be returned to the corporation or its representative.

§ 112. Effect of Certificate of Authority

Upon the issuance of a certificate of authority by the Secretary of State, the corporation shall be authorized to transact business in this State for those purposes set forth in its application, subject, however, to the right of this State to suspend or to revoke such authority as provided in this Act.

§ 113. Registered Office and Registered Agent of Foreign Corporation

Each foreign corporation authorized to transact business in this State shall have and continuously maintain in this State:

(a) A registered office which may be, but need not be, the same as its place of business in this State.

(b) A registered agent, which agent may be either an individual resident in this State whose business office is identical with such registered office, or a domestic corporation, or a foreign corporation authorized to transact business in this State, having a business office identical with such registered office.

§ 114. Change of Registered Office or Registered Agent of Foreign Corporation [Text Omitted]

§ 115. Service of Process on Foreign Corporation

The registered agent so appointed by a foreign corporation authorized to transact business in this State shall be an agent of such corporation upon whom any process, notice or demand required or permitted by law to be served upon the corporation may be served.

Whenever a foreign corporation authorized to transact business in this State shall fail to appoint or maintain a registered agent in this State, or whenever any such registered agent cannot with reasonable diligence be found at the registered office, or whenever the certificate of authority of a foreign corporation shall be suspended or revoked, then the Secretary of State shall be an agent of such corporation upon whom any such process, notice, or demand may be served. Service on the Secretary of State of any such process, notice or demand shall be made by delivering to and leaving with him, or with any clerk having charge of the corporation department of his office, duplicate copies of such process, notice or demand. In the event any such process, notice or demand is served on the Secretary of State, he shall immediately cause one of such copies thereof to be forwarded by registered mail, addressed to the corporation at its principal office in the state or country under the laws of which it is incorporated. Any service so had on the Secretary of State shall be returnable in not less than thirty days.

The Secretary of State shall keep a record of all processes, notices and demands served upon him under this section, and shall record therein the time of such service and his action with reference thereto.

Nothing herein contained shall limit or affect the right to serve any process, notice or demand, required or permitted by law to be served upon a foreign corporation in any other manner now or hereafter permitted by law.

§ 116. Amendment to Articles of Incorporation of Foreign Corporation [Text Omitted]

§ 117. Merger of Foreign Corporation Authorized to Transact Business in This State [Text Omitted]

§ 118. Amended Certificate of Authority [Text Omitted]

§ 119.   **Withdrawal of Foreign Corporation** [Text Omitted]

§ 120.   **Filing of Application for Withdrawal** [Text Omitted]

§ 121.   **Revocation of Certificate of Authority** [Text Omitted]

§ 122.   **Issuance of Certificate of Revocation** [Text Omitted]

§ 123.   **Application to Corporations Heretofore Authorized to Transact Business in This State** [Text Omitted]

§ 124.   **Transacting Business Without Certificate of Authority**

No foreign corporation transacting business in this State without a certificate of authority shall be permitted to maintain any action, suit or proceeding in any court of this State, until such corporation shall have obtained a certificate of authority. Nor shall any action, suit or proceeding be maintained in any court of this State by any successor or assignee of such corporation on any right, claim or demand arising out of the transaction of business by such corporation in this State, until a certificate of authority shall have been obtained by such corporation or by a corporation which has acquired all or substantially all of its assets.

The failure of a foreign corporation to obtain a certificate of authority to transact business in this State shall not impair the validity of any contract or act of such corporation, and shall not prevent such corporation from defending any action, suit or proceeding in any court of this State.

A foreign corporation which transacts business in this State without a certificate of authority shall be liable to this State, for the years or parts thereof during which it transacted business in this State without a certificate of authority, in an amount equal to all fees and franchise taxes which would have been imposed by this Act upon such corporation had it duly applied for and received a certificate of authority to transact business in this State as required by this Act and thereafter filed all reports required by this Act, plus all penalties imposed by this Act for failure to pay such fees and franchise taxes. The Attorney General shall bring proceedings to recover all amounts due this State under the provisions of this Section.

§ 125.   **Annual Report of Domestic and Foreign Corporations**

Each domestic corporation, and each foreign corporation authorized to transact business in this State, shall file, within the time prescribed by this Act, an annual report setting forth:

(a) The name of the corporation and the state or country under the laws of which it is incorporated.

(b) The address of the registered office of the corporation in this State, and the name of its registered agent in this State at such address, and, in case of a foreign corporation, the address of its principal office in the state or country under the laws of which it is incorporated.

(c) A brief statement of the character of the business in which the corporation is actually engaged in this State.

(d) The names and respective addresses of the directors and officers of the corporation.

(e) A statement of the aggregate number of shares which the corporation has authority to issue, itemized by classes, par value of shares, shares without par value, and series, if any, within a class.

(f) A statement of the aggregate number of issued shares, itemized by classes, par value of shares, shares without par value, and series, if any, within a class.

(g) A statement, expressed in dollars, of the amount of stated capital of the corporation, as defined in this Act.

(h) A statement, expressed in dollars, of the value of all the property owned by the corporation, wherever located, and the value of the property of the corporation located within this State, and a statement, expressed in dollars, of the gross amount of business transacted by the corporation for the twelve months ended on the thirty-first day of December preceding the date herein provided for the filing of such report and the gross amount thereof transacted by the corporation at or from places of business in this State. If, on the thirty-first day of December preceding the time herein provided for the filing of such report, the corporation had not been in existence for a period of twelve months, or in the case of a foreign corporation had not been authorized to transact business in this State for a period of twelve months, the statement with respect to business transacted shall be furnished for the period between the date of incorporation or the date of its authorization to transact business in this State, as the case may be, and such thirty-first day of December. If all the property of the corporation is located in this State and all of its business is transacted at or from places of business in this State, or if the corporation elects to pay the annual franchise tax on the basis of its entire stated capital, then the information required by this subparagraph need not be set forth in such report.

(i) Such additional information as may be necessary or appropriate in order to enable the Secretary of State to determine and assess the proper amount of franchise taxes payable by such corporation.

Such annual report shall be made on forms prescribed and furnished by the Secretary of State, and the information therein contained shall be given as of the date of the execution of the report, except as to the information required by subparagraphs (g), (h) and (i) which shall be given as of the close of business on the thirty-first day of December next preceding the date herein provided for the filing of such report. It shall be executed by the corporation by its president, a vice president, secretary, an assistant secretary, or treasurer, and verified by the officer executing the report, or, if the corporation is in the hands of a receiver or trustee, it shall be executed on behalf of the corporation and verified by such receiver or trustee.

§ 126.   Filing of Annual Report of Domestic and Foreign Corporations [Text Omitted]

§ 127.   Fees, Franchise Taxes and Charges to Be Collected by Secretary of State [Text Omitted]

§ 128.   Fees for Filing Documents and Issuing Certificates [Text Omitted]

§ 129.   Miscellaneous Charges [Text Omitted]

§ 130.   License Fees Payable by Domestic Corporations [Text Omitted]

§ 131.   License Fees Payable by Foreign Corporations [Text Omitted]

§ 132.   Franchise Taxes Payable by Domestic Corporations [Text Omitted]

§ 133.   Franchise Taxes Payable by Foreign Corporations [Text Omitted]

§ 134.   Assessment and Collection of Annual Franchise Taxes [Text Omitted]

§ 135.   Penalties Imposed upon Corporations

Each corporation, domestic or foreign, that fails or refuses to file its annual report for any year within the time prescribed by this Act shall be subject to a penalty of ten per cent of the amount of the franchise tax assessed against it for the period beginning July 1 of the year in which such report should have been filed. Such penalty shall be assessed by the Secretary of State at the time of the assessment of the franchise tax. If the amount of the franchise tax as originally assessed against such corporation be thereafter adjusted in accordance with the provisions of this Act, the amount of the penalty shall be likewise adjusted to ten per cent of the amount of the adjusted franchise tax. The amount of the franchise tax and the amount of the penalty shall be separately stated in any notice to the corporation with respect thereto.

If the franchise tax assessed in accordance with the provisions of this Act shall not be paid on or before the thirty-first day of July, it shall be deemed to be delinquent, and there shall be added a penalty of one per cent for each month or part of month that the same is delinquent, commencing with the month of August.

Each corporation, domestic or foreign, that fails or refuses to answer truthfully and fully within the time prescribed by this Act interrogatories propounded by the Secretary of State in accordance with the provisions of this Act, shall be deemed to be guilty of a misdemeanor and upon conviction thereof may be fined in any amount not exceeding five hundred dollars.

§ 136. Penalties Imposed upon Officers and Directors

Each officer and director of a corporation, domestic or foreign, who fails or refuses within the time prescribed by this Act to answer truthfully and fully interrogatories propounded to him by the Secretary of State in accordance with the provisions of this Act, or who signs any articles, statement, report, application or other document filed with the Secretary of State which is known to such officer or director to be false in any material respect, shall be deemed to be guilty of a misdemeanor, and upon conviction thereof may be fined in any amount not exceeding . . . . dollars.

§ 137. Interrogatories by Secretary of State

The Secretary of State may propound to any corporation, domestic or foreign, subject to the provisions of this Act, and to any officer or director thereof, such interrogatories as may be reasonably necessary and proper to enable him to ascertain whether such corporation has complied with all the provisions of this Act applicable to such corporation. Such interrogatories shall be answered within thirty days after the mailing thereof, or within such additional time as shall be fixed by the Secretary of State, and the answers thereto shall be full and complete and shall be made in writing and under oath. If such interrogatories be directed to an individual they shall be answered by him, and if directed to a corporation they shall be answered by the president, vice president, secretary or assistant secretary thereof. The Secretary of State need not file any document to which such interrogatories relate until such interrogatories be answered as herein provided, and not then if the answers thereto disclose that such document is not in conformity with the provisions of this Act. The Secretary of State shall certify to the Attorney General, for such action as the Attorney General may deem appropriate, all interrogatories and answers thereto which disclose a violation of any of the provisions of this Act.

§ 138. Information Disclosed by Interrogatories

Interrogatories propounded by the Secretary of State and the answers thereto shall not be open to public inspection nor shall the Secretary of State disclose any facts or information obtained therefrom except insofar as his official duty may require the same to be made public or in the event such interrogatories or the answers thereto are required for evidence in any criminal proceedings or in any other action by this State.

§ 139. Powers of Secretary of State

The Secretary of State shall have the power and authority reasonably necessary to enable him to administer this Act efficiently and to perform the duties therein imposed upon him.

§ 140. Appeal from Secretary of State [Text Omitted]

§ 141. Certificates and Certified Copies to Be Received in Evidence [Text Omitted]

§ 142. Forms to Be Furnished by Secretary of State [Text Omitted]

§ 143. Greater Voting Requirements

Whenever, with respect to any action to be taken by the shareholders of a corporation, the articles of incorporation require the vote or concurrence of the holders of a greater proportion of the shares, or of any class or series thereof, than required by this Act with respect to such action, the provisions of the articles of incorporation shall control.

§ 144. Waiver of Notice

Whenever any notice is required to be given to any shareholder or director of a corporation under the provisions of this Act or under the provisions of the articles of incorporation or bylaws of the corporation, a waiver thereof in writing signed by the person or persons entitled to such notice, whether before or after the time stated therein, shall be equivalent to the giving of such notice.

§ 145. Action by Shareholders Without a Meeting

Any action required by this Act to be taken at a meeting of the shareholders of a corporation, or any action which may be taken at a meeting of the shareholders, may be taken without a meeting if a consent in writing, setting forth the action so taken, shall be signed by all of the shareholders entitled to vote with respect to the subject matter thereof.

Such consent shall have the same effect as a unanimous vote of shareholders, and may be stated as such in any articles or document filed with the Secretary of State under this Act.

§ 146. Unauthorized Assumption of Corporate Powers

All persons who assume to act as a corporation without authority so to do shall be jointly and severally liable for all debts and liabilities incurred or arising as a result thereof.

§ 147. Application to Existing Corporations [Text Omitted]

§ 148. Application to Foreign and Interstate Commerce [Text Omitted]

§ 149. Reservation of Power [Text Omitted]

§ 150. Effect of Repeal of Prior Acts [Text Omitted]

§ 151. Effect of Invalidity of Part of This Act [Text Omitted]

§ 152. Repeal of Prior Acts

(Insert appropriate provisions) . . . .

Glossary of Legal Terms and Definitions

abatement of nuisance. Removal of a nuisance by court action.

ab initio. From the beginning. A contract which is void ab initio is void from its inception.

absque injuria. Without violation of a legal right.

abstract of title. A summary of the conveyances, transfers, and other facts relied on as evidence of title, together with all such facts appearing of record which may impair its validity. It should contain a brief but complete history of the title.

abutting owners. Those owners whose lands touch.

acceleration. The shortening of the time for the performance of a contract or the payment of a note by the operation of some provision in the contract or note itself.

acceptance. The actual or implied receipt and retention of that which is tendered or offered. The acceptance of an offer is the assent to an offer which is requisite to the formation of a contract. It is either express or evidenced by circumstances from which such assent may be implied.

accession. In its legal meaning it is generally used to signify the acquisition of property by its incorporation or union with other property.

accommodation paper. A negotiable instrument signed without consideration by a party as acceptor, drawer, or endorser for the purpose of enabling the payee to obtain credit.

accord and satisfaction. The adjustment of a disagreement as to what is due from one person to another, and the payment of the agreed amount.

account stated. An account which has been rendered by one to another and which purports to state the true balance due and which balance is either expressly or impliedly admitted to be due by the debtor.

acknowledgment. A form for authenticating instruments conveying property or otherwise conferring rights. It is a public declaration by the grantor that the act evidenced by the instrument is his act and deed. Also an admission or confirmation.

acquit. To set free or judicially to discharge from an accusation; to release from a debt, duty, obligation, charge or suspicion of guilt.

act of God. An occurrence resulting exclusively from natural forces which could not have been prevented or whose effects could not have been avoided by care or foresight.

actionable. Remedial by an action at law.

action ex contractu. An action arising out of the breach of a contract.

action ex delicto. An action arising out of the violation of a duty or obligation created by positive law independent of contract. An action in tort.

ad litem. During the pendency of the action or proceeding.

adjudge. To give judgment; to decide; to sentence.

adjudicate. To adjudge; to settle by judicial

decree; to hear or try and determine, as a court.

administrator. A person appointed by a probate court to settle the estate of a deceased person. His duties are customarily defined by statute. If a woman is appointed she is called the administratrix.

adverse possession. Open and notorious possession of real property over a given length of time which denies ownership in any other claimant.

advisement. When a court takes a case under advisement it delays its decision until it has examined and considered the questions involved.

affidavit. A statement or declaration reduced to writing and sworn or affirmed to before an officer who has authority to administer an oath or affirmation.

affirm. To confirm a former judgment or order of a court. Also to declare solemnly instead of making a sworn statement.

agent. An agent is the substitute or representative of his principal and derives his authority from him.

aggrieved. One whose legal rights have been invaded by the act of another is said to be aggrieved. Also one whose pecuniary interest is directly affected by a judgment, or whose right of property may be divested thereby, is to be considered a party aggrieved.

alienation. The voluntary act or acts by which one person transfers his own property to another.

aliquot. Strictly, forming an exact proper divisor, but treated as meaning fractional when applied to trusts, etc.

allegation. A declaration, a formal averment or statement of a party to an action in a declaration or pleading of what he intends to prove.

allege. To make a statement of fact; to plead.

amortize. In modern usage the word means to provide for the payment of a debt by creating a sinking fund or paying in installments.

ancillary. Auxiliary to. An ancillary receiver is a receiver who has been appointed in aid of, and in subordination to, the primary receiver.

answer. The pleading of a defendant in which he may deny any or all the facts set out in the plaintiff's declaration or complaint.

anticipatory breach. The doctrine of the law of contracts that when the promisor has repudiated the contract before the time of performance has arrived the promisee may sue forthwith.

appearance. The first act of the defendant in court.

appellant. A person who files an appeal.

appellate jurisdiction. Jurisdiction to revise or correct the work of a subordinate court.

appellee. A party against whom a cause is appealed from a lower court to a higher court. He is called the "respondent" in some jurisdictions.

applicant. A petitioner; one who files a petition or application.

appurtenances. An accessory; something that belongs to another thing; e.g., buildings are appurtenant to the land and a bar would be appurtenant to a tavern.

arbitrate. To submit some disputed matter to selected persons and to accept their decision or award as a substitute for the decision of a judicial tribunal.

argument. The discussion by counsel for the respective parties of their contentions on the law and the facts of the case being tried in order to aid the jury in arriving at a correct and just conclusion.

as per. Commonly used and understood to mean in accordance with, or in accordance with the terms of, or as by the contract authorized. The term is not susceptible of literal translation.

assent. To give or express one's concurrence or approval of something done. Assent does not include consent.

assignable. Capable of being lawfully assigned or transferred; transferable; negotiable. Also capable of being specified or pointed out as an assignable error.

assignee. A person to whom an assignment is made.

assignment. A transfer or setting over of property or some right or interest therein, from one person to another. In its ordinary application the word is limited to the transfer of choses in action, e.g., the assignment of a contract.

assignor. The maker of an assignment.

assumpsit. An action at common law to recover damages for breach of contract.

attachment. Taking property into the legal custody of an officer by virtue of the directions contained in a writ of attachment. A seizure under a writ of a debtor's property.

attest. To bear witness to; to affirm; to be true or genuine.

attorney-in-fact. A person who is authorized by his principal, either for some particular purpose, or to do a particular act, not of a legal character.

authentication. Such official attestation of a written instrument as will render it legally admissible in evidence.

authority. Judicial or legislative precedent; delegated power; warrant.

averment. A positive statement of fact made in a pleading.

avoidable. Capable of being nullified or made void.

bad faith. The term imparts a person's actual intent to mislead or deceive another; an intent to take an unfair and unethical advantage of another.

bail. The release of a person from custody upon the undertaking of one or more persons for him and also upon his own recognizance, that he shall appear to answer the charge against him at the time appointed; the delivery or bailment of a person to his sureties, so that he is placed in their friendly custody instead of remaining in prison.

bailee. The person to whom a bailment is made.

bailment. A delivery of personal property by one person to another in trust for a specific purpose, with a contract, express or implied, that the trust shall be faithfully executed and the property returned or duly accounted for when the special purpose is accomplished, or kept until the bailor reclaims it.

bailor. The maker of a bailment; one who delivers personal property to another to be held in bailment.

banc. A bench; a meeting of all the judges of a court.

bankruptcy. The state of a person who is unable to pay his debts without respect to time; one whose liabilities exceed his assets.

bar. As a collective noun it is used to include those persons who are admitted to practice law, members of the bar. The court itself. A plea or peremptory exception of a defendant sufficient to destroy the plaintiff's action.

barratry. The habitual stirring up of quarrels and suits; a single act would not constitute the offense.

barter. To exchange one commodity for another; to negotiate for the acquisition of a thing.

bearer. The designation of the bearer as the payee of a negotiable instrument signifies that the instrument is payable to the person who seems to be the holder.

bench. A court; the judges of a court; the seat upon which the judges of a court are accustomed to sit while the court is in session.

beneficiary. The person for whose benefit an insurance policy, trust, will, or contract is established but not the promisee. In the case of a contract, the beneficiary is called a *third-party beneficiary.* A *donee beneficiary* is one who is not a party to a contract but who receives the promised performance as a gift. A *creditor beneficiary* is one who is not a party to a contract but receives the performance in discharge of a debt owed by the promisee to him.

bequeath. Commonly used to denote a testamentary gift of real estate; synonymous to "to devise."

bid. To make an offer at an auction or at a judicial sale. As a noun it means an offer.

bilateral contract. A contract in which the promise of one of the parties forms the consideration for the promise of the other; a contract formed by an offer requiring a reciprocal promise.

bill of exchange. An unconditional order in writing by one person to another, signed by the person giving it, requiring the person to whom it is addressed to pay on demand or at a fixed or determinable future time a sum certain in money to order or to bearer.

bill of lading. A written acknowledgment of the receipt of goods to be transported to a designated place and delivery to a named person or to his order.

bill of sale. A written agreement by which one person assigns or transfers his interests or rights in personal property to another.

binder. Also called a binding slip—a brief memorandum or agreement issued by an insurer as a temporary policy for the convenience of all the parties, constituting a present insurance in the amount specified, to continue in force until the execution of a formal policy.

blacklist. A document whereby, either voluntarily or in pursuance of a previous arrangement, one person communicates to another or other persons information about a third person which is likely to prevent them from entering into business relations with that third person.

"blue sky" laws. A popular name for statutes regulating the sale of securities and intended to protect investors against fraudulent and visionary schemes.

bona fide. Good faith.

bond. A promise under seal to pay money.

breaking bulk. The division or separation of the contents of a package or container.

brief. A statement of a party's case; usually an abridgment of either the plaintiff's or defendant's case prepared by his attorneys for use of counsel on a trial at law. Also an abridgment of a reported case.

broker. An agent who bargains or carries on negotiations in behalf of his principal as an intermediary between the latter and third persons in transacting business relative to the acquisition of contractual rights, or to the sale or purchase of property the custody of which is not intrusted to him for the purpose of discharging his agency.

bulk transfer. The sale or transfer of a major part of the stock of goods of a merchant at one time and not in the ordinary course of business.

burden of proof. The necessity or obligation of affirmatively proving the fact or facts in dispute on an issue raised in a suit in court.

bylaw. A rule or law of a corporation for its government. It includes all self-made regulations of a corporation affecting its business and members which do not operate on third persons, or in any way affect their rights.

c.i.f. An abbreviation for cost, freight, and insurance, used in mercantile transactions, especially in import transactions.

c.o.d. "Cash on delivery." When goods are delivered to a carrier for a cash on delivery shipment the carrier must not deliver without receiving payment of the amount due.

call. A notice of a meeting to be held by the stockholders or board of directors of a cor-

poration. Also a demand for payment. In securities trading, a negotiable option contract granting the bearer the right to buy a certain quantity of a particular security at the agreed price on or before the agreed date.

cancellation. The act of crossing out a writing. The operation of destroying a written instrument.

caption. The heading or title of a document.

carte blanche. A signed blank instrument intended by the signer to be filled in and used by another person without restriction.

case law. The law as laid down in the decisions of the courts. The law extracted from decided cases.

cashier's check. A bill of exchange, drawn by a bank upon itself, and accepted by the act of issuance.

cause of action. A right of action at law arises from the existence of a primary right in the plaintiff, and an invasion of that right by some delict on the part of the defendant, and that the facts which establish the existence of that right and that delict constitute the cause of action.

caveat emptor. Let the buyer beware. This maxim expresses the general idea that the buyer purchases at his peril, and that there are no warranties, either express or implied, made by the seller.

caveat venditor. Let the seller beware. It is not accepted as a rule of law in the law of sales.

certification. The return of a writ; a formal attestation of a matter of fact; the appropriate marking of a certified check.

certified check. A check which has been "accepted" by the drawee bank and has been so marked or certified that it indicates such acceptance.

cestui que trust. The person for whose benefit property is held in trust by a trustee.

champerty. The purchase of an interest in a matter in dispute so as to take part in the litigation.

chancellor. A judge of a court of chancery.

chancery. Equity or a court of equity.

charge. To charge a jury is to instruct the jury as to the essential law of the case. The first step in the prosecution of a crime is to formally accuse the offender or charge him with the crime.

charter. An instrument or authority from the

sovereign power bestowing the right or power to do business under the corporate form of organization. Also the organic law of a city or town, and representing a portion of the statute law of the state.

chattel interest. Any interest in land of a less dignity than a freehold estate.

chattel mortgage. An instrument whereby the owner of chattels transfers the title to such property to another as security for the performance of an obligation subject to be defeated on the performance of the obligation. Under the U.C.C. called merely a security interest.

chattel real. Interests in real estate less than a freehold, such as an estate for years.

chattels. Goods both movable and immovable except such as are in the nature of freehold or a part of a freehold.

check. A written order on a bank or banker payable on demand to the person named or his order or bearer and drawn by virtue of credits due the drawer from the bank created by money deposited with the bank.

chose in action. A personal right not reduced to possession but recoverable by a suit at law.

citation. A writ issued out of a court of competent jurisdiction, commanding the person therein named to appear on a day named to do something therein mentioned.

citation of authorities. The reference to legal authorities such as reported cases or treatises to support propositions advanced.

civil action. An action brought to enforce a civil right; in contrast to a criminal action.

claimant. One who makes a claim. A voluntary applicant for justice.

class action. An action brought on behalf of other persons similarly situated.

clause. A sentence or paragraph in a written instrument. One of the subdivisions of a written or printed document.

close corporation. A corporation wherein a major part of the persons to whom the corporate powers have been granted have the right to fill vacancies occurring in their ranks. Also used to refer to any corporation whose stock is not freely traded and whose shareholders are personally known to each other.

code. A system of law; a systematic and complete body of law.

codicil. Some addition to or qualification of one's last will and testament.

cognovit. To acknowledge an action. A cognovit note is a promissory note which contains an acknowledgment clause.

collateral attack. An attempt to impeach a decree, a judgment or other official act in a proceeding which has not been instituted for the express purpose of correcting or annulling or modifying the decree, judgment or official act.

comaker. A person who with another or others signs a negotiable instrument on its face and thereby becomes primarily liable for its payment.

commercial law. The law which relates to the rights of property and persons engaged in trade or commerce.

commission merchant. A person who sells goods in his own name at his own store, and on commission, from sample. Also one who buys and sells goods for a principal in his own name and without disclosing his principal.

common carrier. One who undertakes, for hire or reward, to transport the goods of such of the public as choose to employ him.

compensatory damages. Damages which will compensate a party for an injury suffered and nothing more.

complaint. A form of legal process which usually consists of a formal allegation or charge against a party, made or presented to the appropriate court or officer. The technical name of a bill in chancery by which the complainant sets out his cause of action.

composition with creditors. An agreement between creditors and their common debtor and between themselves whereby the creditors agree to accept the sum or security stipulated in full payment of their claims.

concurrent. Running with, simultaneous with. The word is used in different senses. In contracts concurrent conditions are conditions which must be performed simultaneously by the mutual acts required by each of the parties.

condemn. To appropriate land for public use. To adjudge a person guilty; to pass sentence upon a person convicted of a crime.

condition. A provision or clause in a contract which operates to suspend or rescind the principal obligation. A qualification or restriction annexed to a conveyance of lands, whereby it is provided that in the case a particular event does or does not happen, or in case the grantor or grantees do or omit to do a particular act, an estate shall commence, be enlarged or be defeated.

condition precedent. A condition which must happen before either party is bound by the principal obligation of a contract; e.g., one agrees to purchase goods if they are delivered before a stated day. Delivery before the stated day is a condition precedent to one's obligation to purchase.

condition subsequent. A condition which operates to relieve or discharge one from his obligation under a contract.

conditional acceptance. An acceptance of a bill of exchange containing some qualification limiting or altering the acceptor's liability on the bill.

conditional sale. The term is most frequently applied to a sale wherein the seller reserves the title to the goods, though the possession is delivered to the buyer, until the purchase price is paid in full.

confession of judgment. An entry of judgment upon the admission or confession of the debtor without the formality, time, or expense involved in an ordinary proceeding.

conservator (of an insane person). A person appointed by a court to take care of and oversee the person and estate of an idiot or other incompetent person.

consignee. A person to whom goods are consigned, shipped, or otherwise transmitted, either for sale or for safekeeping.

consignment. A bailment for sale. The consignee does not undertake the absolute obligation to sell or pay for the goods.

consignor. One who sends goods to another on consignment; a shipper or transmitter of goods.

construe. To read a statute or document for the purpose of ascertaining its meaning and effect but in doing so the law must be regarded.

contempt. Conduct in the presence of a legislative or judicial body tending to disturb its proceedings, or impair the respect due to its authority or a disobedience to the rules or orders of such a body which interferes with the due administration of law.

contra. Otherwise; disagreeing with; contrary to.

contra bonos moris. Contrary to good morals.

contribution. A payment made by each, or by any, of several having a common interest or liability of his share in the loss suffered, or in the money necessarily paid by one of the parties in behalf of the others.

conversion. Any distinct act of dominion wrongfully exerted over another's personal property in denial of or inconsistent with his rights therein. That tort which is committed by a person who deals with chattels not belonging to him in a manner which is inconsistent with the ownership of the lawful owner.

conveyance. In its common use it refers to a written instrument transferring the title to land or some interest therein from one person to another. It is sometimes applied to the transfer of the property in personalty.

copartnership. A partnership.

corporation. An artificial being, invisible, intangible and existing only in contemplation of law. It is exclusively the work of the law, and the best evidence of its existence is the grant of corporate powers by the commonwealth.

corporeal. Possessing physical substance; tangible; perceptible to the senses.

counterclaim. A claim which, if established, will defeat or in some way qualify a judgment to which the plaintiff is otherwise entitled.

counter-offer. A cross offer made by the offeree to the offeror.

covenant. The word is used in its popular sense as synonymous to contract. In its specific sense it ordinarily imparts an agreement reduced to writing, and executed by a sealing and delivery.

covenantor. A person who covenants; the maker of a covenant.

coverture. The condition of a married woman.

credible. As applied to a witness the word means competent.

culpable. Censurable, also sometimes used to mean criminal.

cumulative voting. A method of voting by which an elector entitled to vote for several candidates for the same office may cast more than one vote for the same candidate, distributing among the candidates as he chooses a number of votes equal to the number of candidates to be elected.

curtesy. Under the early English land law if a man married a woman who had an interest in real estate, and issue was born, the man was entitled to a life estate in his wife's real estate. This life estate was known as curtesy.

custody. The bare control or care of a thing as distinguished from the possession of it.

d/b/a/. Doing business as; indicates the use of a trade name.

damages. Indemnity to the person who suffers loss or harm from an injury; a sum recoverable as amends for a wrong. An adequate compensation for the loss suffered or the injury sustained.

   consequential. Damages which are not produced without the concurrence of some other event attributable to the same origin or cause.

   liquidated. Damages made certain by the prior agreement of the parties.

   nominal. Damages which are recoverable where a legal right is to be vindicated against an invasion which has produced no actual present loss.

date of issue. As the term is applied to notes, bonds, etc., of a series, it usually means the arbitrary date fixed as the beginning of the term for which they run, without reference to the precise time when convenience or the state of the market may permit of their sale or delivery.

deal. To engage in mutual intercourse or transactions of any kind.

debenture. A written acknowledgment of a debt; specifically an instrument under seal for the repayment of money lent.

debtor. A person who owes another anything, or who is under obligation, arising from express agreement, implication of law, or from the principles of natural justice, to render and pay a sum of money to another.

deceit. A specie of fraud; actual fraud consisting of any false representations or contrivance whereby one person overreaches and misleads another to his hurt.

decide. To weigh the reasons for and against and see which preponderates and to be governed by that preponderance.

decision. A decision is the judgment of a court, while the opinion represents merely the reasons for that judgment.

declaration. The pleadings by which a plaintiff in an action at law sets out his cause of action. An admission or statement subsequently used as evidence in the trial of an action.

declaratory. Explanatory affirmative; tending to remove doubt.

declaratory judgment. One which expresses the opinion of a court on a question of law without ordering anything to be done.

decree. An order or sentence of a court of equity determining some right or adjudicating some matter affecting the merits of the cause.

deed. A writing, sealed and delivered by the parties; an instrument conveying real property.

de facto. In fact as distinguished from "de jure," by right.

de jure. By right; complying with the law in all respects.

de minimis non curat lex. The law is not concerned with trifles. The maxim has been applied to exclude the recovery of nominal damages where no unlawful intent or disturbance of a right of possession is shown, and where all possible damage is expressly disproved.

de novo, trial. Anew; over again; a second time. A trial de novo is a new trial in which the entire case is retried in all its detail.

defalcation. The word includes both embezzlement and misappropriation and is a broader term than either.

default. Fault; neglect; omission; the failure of a party to an action to appear when properly served with process; the failure to perform a duty or obligation; the failure of a person to pay money when due or when lawfully demanded.

defeasible (of title to property). Capable of being defeated. A title to property which is open to attack or which may be defeated by the performance of some act.

defend. To oppose a claim or action; to plead in defense of an action; to contest an action suit or proceeding.

defendant. A party sued in a personal action.

defendant in error. Any of the parties in whose favor a judgment was rendered which the losing party seeks to have reversed or modified by writ of error and whom he names as adverse parties.

deficiency. That part of a debt which a mortgage was made to secure, not realized by the liquidation of the mortgaged property. Something which is lacking.

defraud. To deprive another of a right by deception or artifice. To cheat; to wrong another by fraud.

dehors. Outside of; disconnected with; unrelated to.

del credere agent. An agent who guarantees his principal against the default of those with whom contracts are made.

deliver. To surrender property to another person.

demand. A claim; a legal obligation; a request to perform an alleged obligation; a written statement of a claim.

demurrage. A compensation for the delay of a vessel beyond the time allowed for loading, unloading, or sailing. It is also applied to the compensation for the similar delay of a railroad car.

demurrer. An objection made by one party to his opponents pleading, alleging that he ought not to answer it, for some defect in law in the pleading.

dependent covenants. Covenants made by two parties to a deed or agreement which are such that the thing covenanted or promised to be done on each part enters into the whole consideration for the covenant or promise on the part of the other, or such covenants as are concurrent, and to be performed at the same time. Neither party to such a covenant can maintain an action against the other without averring and proving performance on his part.

deposition. An affidavit; an oath; the written testimony of a witness given in the course of a judicial proceeding, either at law or in equity, in response to interrogatories either oral or written, and where an opportunity is given for cross-examination.

deputy. A person subordinate to a public officer whose business and object is to perform the duties of the principal.

derivative action. A suit by a shareholder to enforce a corporate cause of action.

descent. Hereditary succession. It is the title whereby a man on the death of his ancestor acquires his estate by right of representation as his heir at law, an heir being one upon whom the law casts the estate immediately at the death of the ancestor, the estate so descending being the inheritance.

detinue. A common-law action, now seldom used, which lies where a party claims the specific recovery of goods and chattels unlawfully detained from him.

detriment. A detriment is any act or forebearance by a promisee. A loss or harm suffered in person or property.

dictum. The opinion of a judge which does not embody the resolution or determination of the court and is made without argument, or full consideration of the point, and is not the professed deliberation of the judge himself.

directed verdict. A verdict which the jury returns as directed by the court. The court may thus withdraw the case from the jury whenever there is no competent, relevant and material evidence to support the issue.

discharge in bankruptcy. An order or decree rendered by a court in bankruptcy proceedings, the effect of which is to satisfy all debts provable against the estate of the bankrupt as of the time when the bankruptcy proceedings were initiated.

discount. A loan upon an evidence of debt, where the compensation for the use of the money until the maturity of the debt is deducted from the principal and retained by the lender at the time of making the loan.

dismiss. To discontinue; to order a cause, motion, or prosecution to be discontinued or quashed.

diverse citizenship. A term of frequent use in the interpretation of the federal constitutional provision for the jurisdiction of the federal courts which extends it to controversies between citizens of different states.

divided court. A court is so described when there has been a division of opinion between its members on a matter which has been submitted to it for decision.

dividend. A gain or profit. A fund which a corporation sets apart from its profits to be divided among its members.

domain. The ownership of land; immediate or absolute ownership. The public lands of a state are frequently termed the public domain.

domicile. A place where a person lives or has his home; in a strict legal sense, the place where he has his true, fixed, permanent home and principal establishment, and to which place he has whenever he is absent, the intention of returning.

dominion (property). The rights of dominion or property are those rights which a man may acquire in and to such external things as are unconnected with his body.

donee. A person to whom a gift is made.

donor. A person who makes a gift.

dower. The legal right or interest which his wife acquires by marriage in the real estate of her husband.

draft. A written order drawn upon one person by another, requesting him to pay money to a designated third person. A bill of exchange payable on demand.

drawee. A person upon whom a draft or bill of exchange is drawn by the drawer.

drawer. The maker of a draft or bill of exchange.

due bill. An acknowledgment of a debt in writing, not made payable to order.

dummy. One posing or represented as acting for himself, but in reality acting for another. A tool or straw man for the real parties in interest.

duress. Overpowering of the will of a person by force or fear.

earnest. Something given as part of the purchase price to bind the bargain.

easement. A liberty, privilege or advantage in land without profit, existing distinct from the ownership of the soil; the right which one person has to use the land of another for a specific purpose.

edict. A command or prohibition promulgated by a sovereign and having the effect of law.

effects. As used in wills, the word is held equivalent to personal property. It denotes property in a more extensive sense than goods and includes all kinds of personal property but will be held not to include real property, unless the context discloses an intention on the part of the testator to dispose of his realty by the use of the word.

e.g. An abbreviation for "exempli gratia," meaning for or by the way of example.

ejectment. By statute in some states, it is an action to recover the immediate possession of real property. At common law, it was a purely possessory action, and as modified by statute, though based upon title, it is still essentially a possessory action.

eleemosynary corporation. A corporation created for a charitable purpose or for charitable purposes, such as are constituted for the perpetual distribution of free alms to such purposes as their founders and supporters have directed.

emancipate. To release; to set free. Where a father expressly or impliedly by his conduct waives his right generally to the services of his minor child, the child is said to be emancipated and he may sue on contracts made by him for his services.

embezzlement. A statutory offense consisting of the fraudulent conversion of another's personal property by one to whom it has been intrusted, with the intention of depriving the owner thereof, the gist of the offense being usually the violation of relations of fiduciary character.

encumbrance. An encumbrance on land is a right in a third person in the land to the diminuition of the value of the land, though consistent with the passing of the fee by the deed of conveyance.

endorsement. Writing on the back of an instrument; the contract whereby the holder of a bill or note transfers to another person his right to such instrument and incurs the liabilities incident to the transfer.

entry. Recordation; noting in a record; going upon land; taking actual possession of land. Literally, the act of going into a place after a breach has been effected.

eo nominee. By or in that name or designation.

equity. That which in human transactions is founded in natural justice, in honesty and right, and which arises in equity and good conscience; that portion of remedial justice which is exclusively administered by a court of equity, as counterdistinguished from that portion of remedial justice which is exclusively administered by a court of common law.

error. A mistake of law or fact; a mistake of the court in the trial of an action.

escheat. The revision of land to the state in the event there is no person competent to inherit it.

estate. Technically the word refers only to an interest in land.

estate at will. A lease of lands or tenements to be held at the will of the lessor. Such can be determined by either party.

estate for a term. An estate less than a freehold which is in fact a contract for the possession of land or tenements for some determinate period.

estate for life. An estate created by deed or grant conveying land or tenements to a person to hold for the term of his own life or for the life of any other person or for more lives than one.

estate in fee simple. An absolute inheritance, clear of any conditions, limitations or restrictions to particular heirs. It is the highest estate known to the law and necessarily implies absolute dominion over the land.

estate per autre vie. An estate which is to endure for the life of another person than the grantee, or for the lives of more than one, in either of which cases the grantee is called the tenant for life.

estoppel. That state of affairs which arises when one is forbidden by law from alleging or denying a fact because of his previous action or inaction.

et al. An abbreviation for the Latin "et alius" meaning, and another; also of "et alii" meaning, and others.

et ux. An abbreviation for the Latin "et uxor" meaning, and his wife.

eviction. Originally, as applied to tenants, the word meant depriving the tenant of the possession of the demised premises, but technically, it is the disturbance of his possession, depriving him of the enjoyment of the premises demised or any portion thereof by title paramount or by entry and act of the landlord.

evidence. That which makes clear or ascertains the truth of the fact or point in issue either on the one side or the other; those rules of law whereby we determine what testimony is to be admitted and what rejected in each case and what is the weight to be given to the testimony admitted.

exception. An objection; a reservation; a contradiction.

ex contractu. From or out of a contract.

ex delicto. From or out of a wrongful act; tortious; tortiously.

executed. When applied to written instruments the word is sometimes used as synonymous with the word "signed" and means no more than that, but more frequently it imports that everything has been done to complete the transaction; that is that the instrument has been signed, sealed, and delivered. An executed contract is one in which the object of the contract is performed.

execution. A remedy in the form of a writ or process afforded by law for the enforcement of a judgment. The final consummation of a contract of sale, including only those acts which are necessary to the full completion of an instrument, such as the signature of the seller, the affixing of his seal and its delivery to the buyer.

executor. A person who is designated in a will

as one who is to administer the estate of the testator.

executory. Not yet executed; not yet fully performed, completed, fulfilled or carried out; to be performed wholly or in part.

executrix. Feminine of executor.

exemption. A release from some burden, duty or obligation; a grace; a favor; an immunity; taken out from under the general rule, not to be like others who are not exempt.

exhibit. A copy of a written instrument on which a pleading is founded, annexed to the pleading and by reference made a part of it. Any paper or thing offered in evidence and marked for identification.

f.a.s. An abbreviation for the expression "free alongside steamer."

f.o.b. An abbreviation of "free on board."

face value. The nominal or par value of an instrument as expressed on its face; in the case of a bond this is the amount really due, including interest.

factor. An agent who is employed to sell goods for a principal, usually in his own name, and who is given possession of the goods.

fee simple absolute. Same as fee simple. See estate in fee simple.

felony. As a general rule all crimes punishable by death or by imprisonment in a state prison are felonies.

feme covert. A married woman.

feme sole. An unmarried woman.

fiction. An assumption made by the law that something is true which is or may be false.

fiduciary. One who holds goods in trust for another or one who holds a position of trust and confidence.

fieri facias. You cause to be made—an ordinary writ of execution whereby the officer is commanded to levy and sell and to "make," if he can, the amount of the judgment creditors demand.

fixture. A thing which was originally a personal chattel and which has been actually or constructively affixed to the soil itself or to some structure legally a part of such soil; an article which was once a chattel, but which by being physically annexed or affixed to the realty has become accessory to it and part and parcel of it.

forwarder. A person who, having no interest in goods and no ownership or interest in the means of their carriage, undertakes, for hire, to forward them by a safe carrier to their destination.

franchise. A special privilege conferred by government upon individuals, and which does not belong to the citizens of a country generally, of common right. Also a contractual relationship establishing a means of marketing goods or services giving certain elements of control to the supplier (franchiser) in return for the right of the franchisee to use the supplier's tradename or trademark, usually in a specific marketing area.

fungible goods. Goods any unit of which is from its nature or by mercantile custom treated as the equivalent of any other unit.

futures. Contracts for the sale and future delivery of stocks or commodities, wherein either party may waive delivery, and receive or pay, as the case may be, the difference in market price at the time set for delivery.

garnishee. As a noun, the term signifies the person upon whom a garnishment is served, usually a debtor of the defendant in the action. Used as a verb, the word means to institute garnishment proceedings; to cause a garnishment to be levied on the garnishee.

garnishment. The term denotes a proceeding whereby property, money, or credits of a debtor in possession of another, the garnishee, are applied to the payment of the debts by means of process against the debtor and the garnishee. It is a statutory proceeding based upon contract relations, and can only be resorted to where it is authorized by statute.

general issue. A plea of the defendant amounting to a denial of every material allegation of fact in the plaintiff's complaint or declaration.

going business. An establishment which is still continuing to transact its ordinary business, though it may be insolvent.

good faith. An honest intention to abstain from taking an unfair advantage of another.

grantee. A person to whom a grant is made.

grantor. A person who makes a grant.

gravamen. Gist, essence; substance. The grievance complained of; the substantial cause of the action.

guarantor. A person who promises to answer for the debt, default or miscarriage of another.

guaranty. An undertaking by one person to be answerable for the payment of some debt, or the due performance of some contract or duty by another person, who himself remains liable to pay or perform the same.

guardian. A person (in some rare cases a corporation) to whom the law has entrusted the custody and control of the person, or estate, or both, of an infant, lunatic or incompetent person.

habeas corpus. Any of several common-law writs having as their object to bring a party before the court or judge. The only issue it presents is whether the prisoner is restrained of his liberty by due process.

habendum. The second part of a deed or conveyance following that part which names the grantee. It describes the estate conveyed and to what use. It is no longer essential and if included in a modern deed is a mere useless form.

hearing. The supporting of one's contentions by argument and if need be by proof. It is an absolute right and if denied to a contestant it would amount to the denial of one of his constitutional rights.

hedging. A market transaction wherein a party buys a certain quantity of a given commodity at the price current on the date of the purchase and sells an equal quantity of the same commodity for future delivery, thereby protecting himself against loss due to fluctuation in the market; for if the price goes down he gains on futures and if the price advances he loses on futures, but, in either event, he is secure in the profit he has gained on the price of the commodity at the time he purchased it.

heirs. Those persons appointed by law to succeed to the real estate of a decedent, in case of intestacy.

hereditaments. A larger and more comprehensive word than either "land" or "tenements," and meaning anything capable of being inherited, whether it be corporeal, incorporeal, real, personal, or mixed.

holder in due course. A holder who has taken a negotiable instrument under the following conditions:

(1) That it is complete and regular on its face; (2) that he became the holder of it before it was overdue, and without notice that it had been previously dishonored, if such was the fact; (3) that he took it in

good faith and for value; (4) that at the time it was negotiated to him he had no notice of any infirmity in the instrument or defect in the title of the person negotiating it.

holding company. A corporation the purpose of which is in many instances to circumvent antitrust laws and, by which, combination among competing corporations is sought to be effected through the absolute transfer of the stocks of the constituent companies to the central "holding" company. This plan is executed by organizing a corporation, often under the laws of a foreign state, to hold the shares of the stock of the constituent companies, their shareholders receiving, upon an agreed basis of value, shares in the holding corporation in exchange therefor.

homestead. In a legal sense the word means the real estate occupied as a home and also the right to have it exempt from levy and forced sale. It is the land, not exceeding the prescribed amount, upon which the dwelling house, or residence, or habitation, or abode of the owner thereof and his family resides, and includes the dwelling house as an indispensable part.

illusory. Deceiving or intending to deceive, as by false appearances; fallacious. An illusory promise is a promise which appears to be binding but which in fact does not bind the promisor.

immunity. A personal favor granted by law, contrary to the general rule.

impanel. To place the names of the jurors on a panel; to make a list of the names of those persons who have been selected for jury duty; to go through the process of selecting a jury which is to try a cause.

implied warranty. An implied warranty arises by operation of law and exists without any intention of the seller to create it. It is a conclusion or inference of law, pronounced by the court, on facts admitted or proved before the jury.

inalienable. Incapable of being alienated, transferred, or conveyed; nontransferrable.

in banc. With all the judges of the court sitting.

in camera. In the judge's chambers; in private.

in pari delicto. Equally at fault in tort or crime; in equal fault or guilt.

in personam. Against the person.

in re. In the matter; in the transaction.

in rem. Against a thing and not against a person; concerning the condition or status of a thing.

in statu quo. In the situation in which he was.

in toto. In the whole, altogether; wholly.

in transitu. On the journey. Goods are as a rule considered as in transitu while they are in the possession of a carrier, whether by land or water, until they arrive at the ultimate place of their destination and are delivered into the actual possession of the buyer, whether or not the carrier has been named or designated by the buyer.

incapacity. In its legal meaning it applies to one's legal disability, such as infancy, want of authority, or other personal incapacity to alter legal relationship.

inception. Initial stage. The word does not refer to a state of actual existence but to a condition of things or circumstances from which the thing may develop; as the beginning of work on a building.

inchoate. Imperfect; incipient; not completely formed.

incorporeal. Having no body or substances; intangible; without physical existence.

indemnify. To hold harmless against loss or damage.

indemnity. An obligation or duty resting on one person to make good any loss or damage another has incurred while acting at his request or for his benefit. By a contract of indemnity one may agree to save another from a legal consequence of the conduct of one of the parties or of some other person.

indenture. Indentures were deeds which originally were made in two parts formed by cutting or tearing a single sheet across the middle in a jagged or indented line, so that the two parts might be subsequently matched; and they were executed by both grantor and grantee. Later the indenting of the deed was discontinued, yet the term came to be applied to all deeds which were executed by both parties.

independent contractor. One who, exercising an independent employment, contracts to do a piece of work according to his own methods, and without being subject to the control of his employer except as to the result of his work; one who contracts to perform the work at his own risk and cost, the workmen being his servants, and he being liable for their misconduct.

indictment. An accusation founded on legal testimony of a direct and positive character, and the concurring judgment of at least 12 of the grand jurors that upon the evidence presented to them the defendant is guilty.

indorsement. See endorsement.

information. A written accusation of crime preferred by a public prosecuting officer without the intervention of a grand jury.

injunction. A restraining order issued by a court of equity; a prohibitory writ restraining a person from committing or doing an act, other than a criminal act, which appears to be against equity and conscience. There is also the mandatory injunction which commands an act to be done or undone and compels the performance of some affirmative act.

insolvency. The word has two distinct meanings. It may be used to denote the insufficiency of the entire property and assets of an individual to pay his debts, which is its general meaning and its meaning as used in the National Bankruptcy Act; but in a more restricted sense, it expresses the inability of a party to pay his debts as they become due in the regular course of his business, and it is so used when traders and merchants are said to be insolvent.

instrument. In its broadest sense, the term includes formal or legal documents in writing, such as contracts, deeds, wills, bonds, leases, and mortgages. In the law of evidence it has still a wider meaning and includes not merely documents, but witnesses and things animate and inanimate which may be presented for inspection.

insurable interest. Any interest in property the owner of which interest derives a benefit from the existence of the property or would suffer a loss from its destruction. It is not necessary, to constitute an insurable interest, that the interest is such that the event insured against would necessarily subject the insured to loss; it is sufficient that it might do so.

inter alia. Among other things or matters.

interlocutory. Something not final but deciding only some subsidiary matter raised while a law suit is pending.

interpleader. An equitable remedy which lies when two or more persons severally claim the same thing under different titles or in separate interests from another, who, not claiming any title or interest therein himself, and not knowing to which of the claimants he ought in right to render the debt or duty claimed or to deliver the property in his custody, is either molested in an action or actions brought against him, or fears that he may suffer injury from the conflicting claims of the parties.

intervention. A proceeding by which one not originally made a party to an action or suit is permitted, on his own application, to appear therein and join one of the original parties in maintaining his cause of action or defense, or to assert some cause of action against some or all of the parties to the proceeding as originally instituted.

intestate. A person who has died without leaving a valid will disposing of his property and estate.

ipso facto. By the fact itself; by the very fact; by the act itself.

irreparable injury. As applied to the law of injunctions, the term means that which cannot be repaired, restored, or adequately compensated for in money or where the compensation cannot be safely measured.

joint bank account. A bank account of two persons so fixed that they shall be joint owners thereof during their mutual lives, and the survivor shall take the whole on the death of other.

jointly. Acting together or in concert or cooperating; holding in common or interdependently, not separately. Persons are "jointly bound" in a bond or note when both or all must be sued in one action for its enforcement, not either one at the election of the creditor.

jointly and severally. Persons who find themselves "jointly and severally" in a bond or note may all be sued together for its enforcement, or the creditor may select any one or more as the object of his suit.

joint tenancy. An estate held by two or more jointly, with an equal right in all to share in the enjoyments of the land during their lives. Four requisites must exist to constitute a joint tenancy, viz: the tenants must have one and the same interest; the interest must accrue by one and the same conveyance; they must commence at one and the same time; and the property must be held by one and the same undivided possession. If any one of these four elements is lacking, the estate will not be one of joint tenancy. An incident of joint tenancy is the right of survivorship.

judgment. The sentence of the law upon the record; the application of the law to the facts and pleadings. The last word in the judicial controversy; the final consideration and determination of a court of competent jurisdiction upon matters submitted to it in an action or proceeding.

judgment lien. The statutory lien upon the real property of a judgment debtor which is created by the judgment itself. At common law a judgment imposes no lien upon the real property of the judgment debtor, and to subject the property of the debtor to the judgment it was necessary to take out a writ called an elegit.

judgment n.o.v. (judgment non obstante veredicto). Judgment notwithstanding the verdict. Under certain circumstances the judge has the power to enter a judgment which is contrary to the verdict of the jury. Such a judgment is a judgment non obstante veredicto.

jurisdiction. The right to adjudicate concerning the subject matter in a given case. The modern tendency is to make the word include not only the power to hear and determine, but also the power to render the particular judgment in the particular case.

jury. A body of laymen, selected by lot, or by some other fair and impartial means, to ascertain, under the guidance of the judge, the truth in questions of fact arising either in civil litigation or a criminal process.

kite. To secure the temporary use of money by issuing or negotiating worthless paper and then redeeming such paper with the proceeds of similar paper. The word is also used as a noun, meaning the worthless paper thus employed.

laches. The established doctrine of equity that, apart from any question of statutory limitation, its courts will discourage delay and sloth in the enforcement of rights. Equity demands conscience, good faith, and reasonable diligence.

law merchant. The custom of merchants, or lex mercatorio, which grew out of the necessity and convenience of business, and which, although different from the general rules of the common law, was engrafted into it and became a part of it. It was founded on the custom and usage of merchants and it is today the combined result of reason and experience slowly modified by the necessities and changes in commercial affairs.

leading case. A case often referred to by the courts and by counsel as having finally settled and determined a point of law.

leading questions. Those questions which suggest to the witness the answer desired, those which assume a fact to be proved which is not proved, or which, embodying a material fact, admit of an answer by a simple negative or affirmative.

lease. A contract for the possession and use of land on one side, and a recompense of rent or other income on the other; a conveyance to a person for life, or years, or at will in consideration of a return of rent or other recompense.

legacy. A bequest; a testamentary gift of personal property. Sometimes incorrectly applied to a testamentary gift of real property.

legal. According to the principles of law; according to the method required by statute; by means of judicial proceedings; not equitable.

legitimacy. A person's status embracing his right to inherit from his ancestors, to be inherited from, and to bear the name and enjoy the support of his father.

letter of attorney. A power of attorney; a formal document authorizing some act which shall have a binding effect upon the person who grants the authority. It is usually under seal, and while the want of a seal might not invalidate the instrument as a power of attorney, it is not true that every paper conferring authority upon another is a letter of attorney.

letter of credit. An instrument containing a request (general or special) to pay to the bearer or person named money, or sell him some commodity on credit or give him something of value and look to the drawer of the letter for recompense. It partakes of the nature of a negotiable instrument, but the rules governing bills of exchange and promissory notes are always the same, while letters of credit are to be construed with reference to the particular and often varying terms in which they may be expressed, the circumstances and intention of the parties to them, and the usage of the particular trade or business contemplated.

levy. At common law a levy on goods consisted of an officer's entering the premises where they were and either leaving an assistant in charge of them or removing them after taking an inventory. Today courts differ as to what is a valid levy, but by the weight of authority there must be an actual or constructive seizure of the goods. In most states, a levy on land must be made by some unequivocal act of the officer indicating his intention of singling out certain real estate for the satisfaction of the debt.

license. A personal privilege to do some act or series of acts upon the land of another, without possessing any estate therein. A permit or authorization to do what, without a license, would be unlawful.

lien. In its most extensive meaning it is a charge upon property for the payment or discharge of a debt or duty; a qualified right; a proprietary interest which, in a given case, may be exercised over the property of another.

life estate. See estate for life.

lis pendens. A pending suit. As applied to the doctrine of lis pendens it is the jurisdiction, power, or control which courts acquire over property involved in a suit, pending the continuance of the action, and until its final judgment therein.

listing contract. A so-called contract whereby an owner of real property employs a broker to procure a purchaser without giving the broker exclusive right to sell. Under such an agreement, it is generally held that the employment may be terminated by the owner at will, and that a sale of the property by the owner terminates the employment.

litigant. A party to a lawsuit.

livery. Delivery. The act of delivering legal possession of property, as of lands or tenements.

long arm statute. A statute subjecting a foreign corporation to jurisdiction although it may have committed only a single act within the state.

magistrate. A word commonly applied to the lower judicial officers, such as justices of the peace, police judges, town recorders, and other local judicial functionaries. In a broader sense, a magistrate is a public civil officer invested with some part of the legislative, executive, or judicial power given by the Constitution. The President of the United States is the chief magistrate of the nation.

maker. A person who makes or executes an instrument, the signer of an instrument.

mala fides. Bad faith.

malfeasance. The doing of an act which a person ought not to do at all. It is to be distinguished from misfeasance, which is the improper doing of an act which a person might lawfully do.

malum in se. Evil in and of itself. An offense or act which is naturally evil as adjudged by the senses of a civilized community. Acts malum in se are usually criminal acts, but not necessarily so.

malum prohibitum. An act which is wrong because it is made so by statute.

mandamus. We command. It is a command issuing from a competent jurisdiction, in the name of the state or sovereign, directed to some inferior court, officer, corporation, or person, requiring the performance of a particular duty therein specified, which duty results from the official station of the party to whom it is directed, or from operation of law.

margin. A deposit by a buyer in stocks with a seller or a stockbroker, as security to cover fluctuations in the market in reference to stocks which the buyer has purchased, but for which he has not paid. Commodities are also traded on margin.

marshals. Ministerial officers belonging to the executive department of the federal government, who with their deputies have the same powers of executing the laws of the United States in each state as the sheriffs and their deputies in such state may have in executing the laws of that state.

mechanic's lien. A claim created by law for the purpose of securing a priority of payment of the price or value of work performed and materials furnished in erecting or repairing a building or other structure; as such it attaches to the land as well as to the buildings erected therein.

mens rea. A guilty mind, criminal intent.

merchantable. Of good quality and salable, but not necessarily the best. As applied to articles sold, the word requires that the article shall be such as is usually sold in the market, of medium quality and bringing the average price.

minor. A person who has not reached the age at which the law recognizes a general contractual capacity, formerly 21 years; recently changed to 18 by some states.

misdemeanor. Any crime which is punishable neither by death nor by imprisonment in a state prison.

mistrial. An invalid trial due to lack of jurisdiction, error in selection of jurors or some other fundamental requirement.

mitigation of damages. A term relating only to exemplary damages and their reduction by extenuating circumstances such as provocation or malice. The theory of such mitigation is based on the regard of the law for the frailty of human passions, since it looks with some indulgence upon violations of good order which are committed in a moment of irritation and excitement.

moiety. One half.

mortgage. A conveyance of property to secure the performance of some obligation, the conveyance to be void on the due performance thereof.

motive. The cause or reason that induced a person to commit a crime.

movables. A word derived from the civil law and usually understood to signify the utensils which are to furnish or ornament a house, but it would seem to comprehend personal property generally.

mutuality. Reciprocal obligations of the parties required to make a contract binding on either party.

necessaries. With reference to an infant, the word includes whatever is reasonably necessary for his proper and suitable maintenance, in view of his means and prospects, and the customs of the social circle in which he moves and is likely to move.

negligence. The word has been defined as the omission to do something which a reasonable man, guided by those considerations which ordinarily regulate human affairs, would do, or doing something which a prudent and reasonable man would not do.

negotiability. A technical term derived from the usage of merchants and bankers in transferring, primarily, bills of exchange and, af-

terward, promissory notes. At common law no contract was assignable, so as to give to an assignee a right to enforce it by suit in his own name. To this rule, bills of exchange and promissory notes, payable to order or bearer, have been admitted exceptions, made such by the adoption of the law merchant.

negotiable instrument. An instrument which may be transferred or negotiated, so that the holder may maintain an action thereon in his own name.

no arrival, no sale. A sale of goods "to arrive" or "on arrival," per or ex a certain ship, has been construed to be a sale subject to a double condition precedent, namely, that the ship arrives in port and that when she arrives the goods are on board, and if either of these conditions fails, the contract becomes nugatory.

no-par value stock. Stock of a corporation having no face or par value.

nolo contendere. A plea in a criminal action which has the same effect as a guilty plea except that it does not bind the defendant in a civil suit on the same wrong.

nominal damages. Damages which are recoverable where a legal right is to be vindicated against an invasion that has produced no actual present loss of any kind, or where there has been a breach of a contract and no actual damages whatever have been or can be shown, or where, under like conditions, there has been a breach of legal duty.

non compos mentis. Totally and positively incompetent. The term denotes a person entirely destitute or bereft of his memory or understanding.

nonfeasance. In the law of agency, it is the total omission or failure of an agent to enter upon the performance of some distinct duty or undertaking which he has agreed with his principal to do. It is not every omission or failure to perform a duty that will constitute a nonfeasance, but only an omission to perform such distinct duties as he owes to his principal, as distinguished from those which he owes to third persons or to the public in general, as a member of society.

non obstante veredicto. See judgment non obstante veredicto.

nonsuit. A judgment given against the plaintiff when he is unable to prove a case, or when he refuses or neglects to proceed to the trial of the cause after it has been put at issue without determining such issue.

noting protest. The act of making a memorandum on a bill or note at the time of, and embracing the principal facts attending, its dishonor. The object is to have a record from which the instrument of protest may be written, so that a notary need not rely on his memory for the fact.

novation. Under the civil law, a mode of extinguishing one obligation by another. Under common law, it was at first a transaction whereby a debtor was discharged from his liability to his original creditor by contracting a new obligation in favor of a new creditor by the order of the original creditor. In modern law, it is a mutual agreement, between all parties concerned, for the discharge of a valid existing obligation by the substitution of a new valid obligation on the part of the debtor or another, or a like agreement for the discharge of a debtor to his creditor by the substitution of a new creditor.

nudum pactum. A naked promise, a promise for which there is no consideration.

nuisance. In legal parlance, the word extends to everything that endangers life or health, gives offense to the senses, violates the laws of decency, or obstructs the reasonable and comfortable use of property.

oath. Any form of attestation by which a person signifies that he is bound in conscience to perform an act faithfully and truthfully. It involves the idea of calling on God to witness what is averred as truth, and it is supposed to be accompanied with an invocation of His vengeance, or a renunciation of His favor, in the event of falsehood.

obiter dictum. That which is said in passing; a rule of law set forth in a court's opinion, but not involved in the case; what is said by the court outside the record or on a point not necessarily involved therein.

objection. In the trial of a case it is the formal remonstrance made by counsel to something which has been said or done, in order to obtain the court's ruling thereon; and when the court has ruled, the alleged error is preserved by the objector's exception to the ruling, which exception is noted in the record.

obligee. A person to whom another is bound by a promise or other obligation; a promisee.

obligor. A person who is bound by a promise or other obligation; a promisor.

offer. A proposal by one person to another which is intended of itself to create legal relations on acceptance by the person to whom it is made.

offeree. A person to whom an offer is made.

offeror. A person who makes an offer.

opinion. The opinion of the court represents merely the reasons for its judgment, while the decision of the court is the judgment itself.

option. A contract whereby the owner of property agrees with another person that he shall have the right to buy the property at a fixed price within a certain time. There are two elements in an option contract: First, the offer to sell, which does not become a contract until accepted; second, the completed contract to leave the offer open for a specified time. These elements are wholly independent and cannot be treated together without great liability to confusion and error. The offer must be considered wholly independent of the contract to leave it open in determining whether or not it had itself ripened into a contract, and the question whether or not there was a valid contract to leave the offer open is wholly immaterial if the offer was in fact accepted before it was withdrawn.

oral. By word of mouth; verbal; spoken as opposed to written.

ordinance. A legislative enactment of a county or an incorporated city or town.

ostensible authority. Such authority as a principal, either intentionally or by want of ordinary care, causes or allows a third person to believe the agent to possess. If a principal by his acts has led others to believe that he has conferred authority upon his agent, he cannot be heard to assert, as against third persons who have relied thereon, in good faith, that he did not intend such power.

ostensible partners. Members of a partnership whose names are made known and appear to the world as partners.

overdraft. The withdrawal from a bank by a depositor of money in excess of the amount of money he has on deposit there.

overdraw. A depositor overdraws his account at a bank when he obtains on his check or checks from the bank more money than he deposited in the account.

overplus. That which remains; a balance left over.

owner's risk. A term employed by common carriers in bills of lading and shipping receipts to signify that the carrier does not assume responsibility for the safety of the goods.

oyer. To hear. To demand oyer or to crave oyer was a demand as of right to hear an instrument read. The modern practice is usually to demand the privilege of inspecting the document or to demand a copy of it.

par. Par means equal, and par value means a value equal to the face of a bond or a stock certificate. A sale of bonds at par is a sale at the rate of one dollar in money for one dollar in bonds.

parol. Oral; verbal; by word of mouth; spoken as opposed to written.

parties. All persons who are interested in the subject matter of an action and who have a right to make defense, control the proceedings, examine and cross-examine witnesses, and appeal from the judgment.

partition. A proceeding the object of which is to enable those who own property as joint tenants or tenants in common, to put an end to the tenancy so as to vest in each a sole estate in specific property or an allotment of the lands and tenements. If a division of the estate is impracticable the estate ought to be sold, and the proceeds divided.

partners. Those persons who contribute property, money, or services to carry on a joint business for their common benefit, and who own and share the profits thereof in certain proportions; the members of a partnership.

patent. A patent for land is a conveyance of title to government lands by the government; a patent of an invention is the right of monopoly secured by statute to those who invent or discover new and useful devices and processes.

pawn. A pledge; a bailment of personal property as security for some debt or engagement, redeemable on certain terms, and with an implied power of sale on default.

payee. A person to whom a payment is made or is made payable.

pecuniary. Financial; pertaining or relating to money; capable of being estimated, computed, or measured by money value.

penal. The words "penal" and "penalty" have many different meanings. Strictly and primarily, they denote punishment, whether corporeal or pecuniary, imposed and enforced by the state for a crime or offense against its laws. But they are also commonly used as including an extraordinary liability to which the law subjects a wrongdoer in favor of the person wronged, not limited to the damages suffered. They are also applied to cases of private contract as when one speaks of the "penal sum" or "penalty" of a bond.

penalty. A word which when used in a contract is sometimes construed as meaning liquidated damages, as where the sum named is reasonable, and the actual damages are uncertain in amount and difficult of proof. If, however, it is called a penalty in the contract, it will be held to be a penalty if there is nothing in the nature of the contract to show a contrary intent. An exaction in the nature of a punishment for the nonperformance of an act, or the performance of an unlawful act, and involving the idea of punishment, whether enforced by a civil or criminal action or proceeding.

per curiam. By the court; by the court as a whole.

per se. The expression means by or through itself; simply, as such; in its own relations.

peremptory challenge. A challenge to a proposed juror which a defendant in a criminal case may make as an absolute right, and which cannot be questioned by either opposing counsel or the court.

performance. As the word implies, it is such a thorough fulfillment of a duty as puts an end to obligations by leaving nothing to be done. The chief requisite of performance is that it shall be exact.

perjury. The willful and corrupt false swearing or affirming, after an oath lawfully administered, in the course of a judicial or quasi judicial proceeding as to some matter material to the issue or point in question.

petition. In equity pleading, a petition is in the nature of a pleading (at least when filed by a stranger to the suit) and forms a basis for independent action.

plaintiff. A person who brings a suit, action, bill, or complaint.

plaintiff in error. The unsuccessful party to the action who prosecutes a writ of error in a higher court.

plea. A plea is an answer to a declaration or complaint or any material allegation of fact therein which if untrue would defeat the action. In criminal procedure, a plea is the matter which the accused, on his arraignment, alleges in answer to the charge against him.

pledge. A pawn; a bailment of personal property as security for some debt or engagement, redeemable on certain terms, and with an implied power of sale on default.

pledgee. A person to whom personal property is pledged by a pledgor.

pledgor. A person who makes a pledge of personal property to a pledgee.

positive law. Laws actually and specifically enacted or adopted by proper authority for the government of a jural society as distinguished from principles of morality or laws of honor.

possession. Respecting real property, possession involves exclusive dominion and control such as owners of like property usually exercise over it. The existence of such possession is largely a question of fact dependent on the nature of the property and the surrounding circumstances.

power of attorney. A written authorization to an agent to perform specified acts in behalf of his principal. The writing by which the authority is evidenced is termed a letter of attorney and is dictated by the convenience and certainty of business.

precedent. A previous decision relied upon as authority. The doctrine of stare decisis, commonly called the doctrine of precedents, has been firmly established in the law. It means that we should adhere to decided cases and settled principles, and not disturb matters which have been established by judicial determination.

preference. The act of a debtor in paying or securing one or more of his creditors in a manner more favorable to them than to other creditors or to the exclusion of such other creditors. In the absence of statute, a preference is perfectly good, but to be legal it must be bona fide, and not a mere subterfuge of the debtor to secure a future benefit to himself or to prevent the application of his property to his debts.

prerogative. A special power, privilege, or immunity, usually used in reference to an official or his office.

presumption. A term used to signify that which may be assumed without proof, or taken for granted. It is asserted as a self-evident result of human reason and experience.

prima facie. At first view or appearance of the business, as a holder of a bill of exchange, endorsed in blank, is prima facie its owner. Prima facie evidence of fact is in law sufficient to establish the fact, unless rebutted.

privies. Persons connected together or having mutual interests in the same action or thing by some relation other than actual contract between them.

privilege. A right peculiar to an individual or body.

privity. A mutual or successive relationship as, for example, between the parties to a contract.

pro rata. According to the rate, proportion, or allowance. A creditor of an insolvent estate is to be paid pro rata with creditors of the same class. According to a certain rule or proportion.

pro tanto. For so much; to such an extent.

probate. The word originally meant merely "relating to proof," and later "relating to the proof of wills," but in American law it is now a general name or term used to include all matters of which probate courts have jurisdiction which in many states are the estates of deceased persons and of persons under guardianship.

process. In law, generally the summons or notice of beginning of suit.

proffer. To offer for acceptance or to make a tender of.

promisee. The person to whom a promise is made.

promisor. A person who makes a promise to another; a person who promises.

promoters. The persons who bring about the incorporation and organization of a corporation.

prospectus. An introductory proposal for a contract in which the representations may or may not form the basis of the contract actually made; it may contain promises which are to be treated as a sort of floating obligation to take effect when appropriated by persons to whom they are addressed, and amount to a contract when assented to by any person who invests his money on the faith of them.

proximate cause. That cause of an injury

which, in natural and continuous sequence, unbroken by any efficient intervening cause, produces the injury, and without which the injury would not have occurred.

qualified acceptance. A conditional or modified acceptance. In order to create a contract an acceptance must accept the offer substantially as made; hence a qualified acceptance is no acceptance at all, is treated by the courts as a rejection of the offer made, and is in effect an offer by the offeree, which the offeror may, if he chooses, accept and thus create a contract.

quantum meruit. As much as is deserved. A part of a common law action in assumpsit for the value of services rendered.

quash. To vacate or make void.

quasi contract. Sometimes called a contract implied in law, but more properly known as a quasi contract or constructive contract. It is a contract in the sense that it is remediable by the contractual remedy of assumpsit. The promise is purely fictitious and is implied in order to fit the actual cause of action to the remedy. The liability under it exists from an implication of law that arises from the facts and circumstances independent of agreement or presumed intention.

quasi judicial. The acts of an officer which are executive or administrative in their character and which call for the exercise of that officer's judgment and discretion are not ministerial acts, and his authority to perform such acts is quasi judicial.

quitclaim deed. A deed conveying only the right, title, and interest of the grantor in the property described, as distinguished from a deed conveying the property itself.

quo warranto. By what authority. The name of a writ (and also of the whole pleading) by which the government commences an action to recover an office or franchise from the person or corporation in possession of it.

quorum. That number of persons, shares represented, or officers who may lawfully transact the business of a meeting called for that purpose.

ratification. The adoption by one in whose name an unauthorized act has been performed by another upon the assumption of authority to act as his agent, even though without any precedent authority whatever, which adoption or ratification relates back, supplies the original authority to do the act, binding the principal so adopting or ratifying to the same extent as if the act had been done in the first instance—by his previous authority. The act of an infant upon reaching his majority affirming a voidable contract made by him during his infancy and giving it the same force and effect as if it had been valid from the beginning.

rebuttal. Testimony addressed to evidence produced by the opposite party; rebutting evidence.

receiver. An indifferent person between the parties to a cause, appointed by the court to receive and preserve the property or funds in litigation, and receive its rents, issues, and profits, and apply or dispose of them at the direction of the court, when it does not seem reasonable that either party should hold them.

recognizance. At common law, an obligation entered into before some court of record or magistrate duly authorized, with a condition to do some particular act, usually to appear and answer to a criminal accusation. Being taken in open court and entered upon the order book, it was valid without the signature or seal of any of the obligors.

recorder. A public officer of a town or county charged with the duty of keeping the record books required by law to be kept in his office and of receiving and causing to be copied in such books such instruments as by law are entitled to be recorded.

recoupment. The doctrine under which in an action for breach of contract the defendant may show that the plaintiff has not performed the same contract on his part, and may recoup his damages for such breach in the same action, whether liquidated or not.

redemption. The buying back of one's property after it has been sold. The right to redeem property sold under an order or decree of court is purely a privilege conferred by, and does not exist independently of, statute.

redress. Remedy; indemnity; reparation.

release. The giving up or abandoning of a claim or right to a person against whom the claim exists or the right is to be enforced or exercised. It is the discharge of a debt by the act of the party in distinction from an extinguishment which is a discharge by operation of law.

remainderman. One who is entitled to the remainder of the estate after a particular estate carved out of it has expired.

remand. An action of an appellate court returning a case to the trial court to take further action.

remedy. The appropriate legal form of relief by which a remediable right may be enforced.

remittitur. The certificate of reversal issued by an appellate court upon reversing the order or judgment appealed from.

replevin. A common-law action by which the owner recovers possession of his own goods.

res. The thing; the subject matter of a suit; the property involved in the litigation; a matter; property; the business; the affair; the transaction.

res adjudicata. A matter which has been adjudicated; that which is definitely settled by a judicial decision.

rescind. As the word is applied to contracts, to rescind in some cases means to terminate the contract as to future transactions, while in others it means to annul the contract from the beginning.

residue. All that portion of the estate of a testator of which no effectual disposition has been made by his will otherwise than in the residuary clause.

respondent. The defendant in an action; a party adverse to an appellant in an action which is appealed to a higher court. The person against whom a bill in equity was exhibited.

restitution. Indemnification.

reversion. The residue of a fee simple remaining in the grantor, to commence in possession after the determination of some particular estate granted out by him. The estate of a landlord during the existence of the outstanding leasehold estate.

reversioner. A person who is entitled to a reversion.

right. When we speak of a person having a right, we must necessarily refer to a civil right as distinguished from the elemental idea of a right absolute. We must have in mind a right given and protected by law, and a person's enjoyment thereof is regulated entirely by the law which creates it.

riparian. From the Latin word "riparius," of or belonging to the bank of a river, in turn derived from "ripa," a bank, and defined as "pertaining to or situated on the bank of a river"; the word has reference to the bank and not to the bed of the stream.

sanction. The part of a law which signifies the evil or penalty which will be incurred by the wrongdoer for his breach of it.

satisfaction. A performance of the terms of an accord. If such terms require a payment of a sum of money, then "satisfaction" means that such payment has been made.

scienter. In cases of fraud and deceit, the word means knowledge on the part of the person making the representations, at the time when they are made, that they are false. In an action for deceit it is generally held that scienter must be proved.

scintilla of evidence. The least particle of evidence. A slight amount of evidence supporting a material issue.

seal. At common law, a seal is an impression on wax or some other tenacious material, but in modern practice the letters "l.s." (locus sigilli) or the word "seal" enclosed in a scroll, either written, or printed, and acknowledged in the body of the instrument to be a seal, are often used as substitutes.

security. That which makes the enforcement of a promise more certain than the mere personal obligation of the debtor or promisor, whatever may be his possessions or financial standing. It may be a pledge of property or an additional personal obligation; but it means more than the mere promise of the debtor with property liable to general execution.

security agreement. An agreement which creates or provides a security interest or lien on personal property. A term used in the U.C.C. including a wide range of transactions in the nature of chattel mortgages, conditional sales, etc.

seizin. In a legal sense, the word means possession of premises with the intention of asserting a claim to a freehold estate therein; it is practically the same thing as ownership; it is a possession of a freehold estate, such as by the common law is created by livery of seizin.

service. As applied to a process of courts, the word ordinarily implies something in the nature of an act or proceeding adverse to the party served, or of a notice to him.

setoff. A setoff both at law and in equity is that right which exists between two parties, each of whom, under an independent contract, owes an ascertained amount to the other, to set off their respective debts by way of mutual deduction, so that, in any action brought for the larger debt, the residue only, after such deduction, shall be recovered.

severable contract. A contract which is not entire or indivisible. If the consideration is single, the contract is entire; but if it is expressly or by necessary implication apportioned, the contract is severable. The question is ordinarily determined by inquiring whether the contract embraces one or more subject matters, whether the obligation is due at the same time to the same person, and whether the consideration is entire or apportioned.

shareholder. It is generally held that one who holds shares on the books of the corporation is a shareholder and that one who merely holds a stock certificate is not. Shareholders may become such either by original subscription, by direct purchase from the corporation, or by subsequent transfer from the original holder.

share of stock. The right which its owner has in the management, profits and ultimate assets of the corporation. The tangible property of a corporation and the shares of stock therein are separate and distinct kinds of property and belong to different owners, the first being the property of an artificial person—the corporation—the latter the property of the individual owner.

sight. A term signifying the date of the acceptance or that of protest for the nonacceptance of a bill of exchange; for example, 10 days after sight.

sinking fund. A fund accumulated by an issuer to redeem corporate securities.

situs. Location; local position; the place where a person or thing is, is his situs. Intangible property has no actual situs, but it may have a legal situs, and for the purpose of taxation its legal situs is at the place where it is owned and not at the place where it is owed.

specific performance. The actual accomplishment of a contract by the party bound to fulfill it; the name of an equitable remedy of very ancient origin the object of which is to secure a decree to compel the defendant specifically to perform his contract, which is nothing more or less than a means of compelling a party to do precisely what he ought

to have done without being coerced by a court.

stare decisis. The doctrine or principle that the decisions of the court should stand as precedents for future guidance.

stated capital. Defined specifically in the Model Business Corporation Act; generally, the amount received by a corporation upon issuance of its shares except that assigned to capital surplus.

stipulation. An agreement between opposing counsel in a pending action, usually required to be made in open court and entered on the minutes of the court, or else to be in writing and filed in the action, ordinarily entered into for the purpose of avoiding delay, trouble, or expense in the conduct of the action.

stockholder. See shareholder.

stoppage in transitu. A right which the vendor of goods on credit has to recall them, or retake them, on the discovery of the insolvency of the vendee. It continues so long as the carrier remains in the possession and control of the goods or until there has been an actual or constructive delivery to the vendee, or some third person has acquired a bona fide right in them.

subpoena. A process the purpose of which is to compel the attendance of a person whom it is desired to use as a witness.

subrogation. The substitution of one person in the place of another with reference to a lawful claim or right, frequently referred to as the doctrine of substitution. It is a device adopted or invented by equity to compel the ultimate discharge of a debt or obligation by him who in good conscience ought to pay it. It is the machinery by which the equity of one man is worked out through the legal rights of another.

sui generis. Of its own kind; peculiar to itself.

summary judgment. A decision of a trial court without hearing evidence.

summary proceedings. Proceedings, usually statutory, in the course of which many formalities are dispensed with. But such proceedings are not concluded without proper investigation of the facts, or without notice, or an opportunity to be heard by the person alleged to have committed the act, or whose property is sought to be affected.

summons. A writ or process issued and served upon a defendant in a civil action for the purpose of securing his appearance in the action.

supra. Above; above mentioned; in addition to.

surety. One who by accessory agreement called a contract of suretyship binds himself with another, called the principal, for the performance of an obligation in respect to which such other person is already bound and primarily liable for such performance.

tacking. The adding together of successive periods of adverse possession of persons in privity with each other, in order to constitute one continuous adverse possession for the time required by the statute, to establish title.

tangible. Capable of being possessed or realized; readily apprehensible by the mind; real; substantial; evident.

tenancy. A tenancy exists when one has let real estate to another to hold of him as landlord. When duly created and the tenant put into possession, he is the owner of an estate for the time being, and has all the usual rights and remedies to defend his possession.

tender. An unconditional offer of payment, consisting in the actual production in money or legal tender of a sum not less than the amount due.

tender offer. An offer to security holders to acquire their securities in exchange for money or other securities.

tenement. A word commonly used in deeds which passes not only lands and other inheritances but also offices, rents, commons, and profits arising from lands. Usually it is applied exclusively to land, or what is ordinarily denominated real property.

tenor. The tenor of an instrument is an exact copy of the instrument. Under the rule that an indictment for forgery must set out in the instrument according to its "tenor," the word means an exact copy—that the instrument is set forth in the very words and figures.

tenure. In its technical sense, the word means the manner whereby lands or tenements are holden, or the service that the tenant owes his lord. In the latter case there can be no tenure without some service, because the service makes the tenure. The word is also used as signifying the estate in land. The most common tenure by which lands are held in the United States is "fee simple."

testament. Redfield, in his work on wills, defined a last will and testament as the disposition of one's property to take effect after death.

testator. A deceased person who died leaving a will.

testatrix. Feminine of testator.

testimony. In some contexts the word bears the same import as the word "evidence," but in most connections it has a much narrower meaning. Testimony is the words heard from the witness in court, and evidence is what the jury considers it worth.

tort. An injury or wrong committed, either with or without force, to the person or property of another. Such injury may arise by nonfeasance, or by the malfeasance or the misfeasance of the wrongdoer.

tort-feasor. A person who commits a tort; a wrongdoer.

tortious. Partaking of the nature of a tort; wrongful; injurious.

trade fixtures. Articles of personal property which have been annexed to the freehold and which are necessary to the carrying on of a trade.

transcript. A copy of a writing.

transferee. A person to whom a transfer is made.

transferor. A person who makes a transfer.

treasury shares. Shares of stock of a corporation which have been issued as fully paid to shareholders and subsequently acquired by the corporation.

treble damages. Three times provable damages, as may be granted to private parties bringing an action under the antitrust laws.

trespass. Every unauthorized entry on another's property is a trespass and any person who makes such an entry is a trespasser. In its widest signification, trespass means any violation of law. In its most restricted sense, it signifies an injury intentionally inflicted by force either on the person or property of another.

trial. An examination before a competent tribunal, according to the law of the land, of the facts or law put in issue in a cause, for the purpose of determining such issue. When the court hears and determines any issue of fact or law for the purpose of determining the rights of the parties, it may be considered a trial.

trover. A common-law action for damages due to a conversion of personal property.

trust. A confidence reposed in one person, who

is termed trustee, for the benefit of another, who is called the cestui que trust, respecting property, which is held by the trustee for the benefit of the cestui que trust. As the word is used in the law pertaining to unlawful combinations and monopolies, a trust in its original and typical form is a combination formed by an agreement among the shareholders in a number of competing corporations to transfer their shares to an unincorporated board of trustees, and to receive in exchange trust certificates in some agreed proportion to their shareholdings.

trustee. A person in whom property is vested in trust for another.

trustee in bankruptcy. The federal bankruptcy act defines the term as an officer, and he is an officer of the courts in a certain restricted sense, but not in any such sense as a receiver. He takes the legal title to the property of the bankrupt and in respect to suits stands in the same general position as a trustee of an express trust or an executor. His duties are fixed by statute. He is to collect and reduce to money the property of the estate of the bankrupt.

ultra vires act. An act of a corporation which is beyond the powers conferred upon the corporation.

unilateral contract. A contract formed by an offer or a promise on one side for an act to be done on the other, and a doing of the act by the other by way of acceptance of the offer or promise; that is, a contract wherein the only acceptance of the offer that is necessary is the performance of the act.

usury. The taking more than the law allows upon a loan or for forbearance of a debt. Illegal interest; interest in excess of the rate allowed by law.

utter. As applied to counterfeiting, to utter and publish is to declare or assert, directly or indirectly, by words or actions, that the money or note is good. Thus to offer it in payment is an uttering or publishing. To utter and publish a document is to offer directly or indirectly, by words or actions, such document as good and valid. There need be no acceptance by the offeree to constitute an uttering.

valid. Effective; operative; not void; subsisting; sufficient in law.

vendee. A purchaser of property. The word is more commonly applied to a purchaser of real property, the word "buyer" being more commonly applied to the purchaser of personal property.

vendor. A person who sells property to a vendee. The words "vendor" and "vendee" are more commonly applied to the seller and purchaser of real estate, and the words "seller" and "buyer" are more commonly applied to the seller and purchaser of personal property.

vendue. A sale; a sale at auction.

venire. The name of a writ by which a jury is summoned.

venue. The word originally was employed to indicate the county from which the jurors were to come who were to try a case, but in modern times it refers to the county in which a case is to be tried.

verdict. The answer of a jury given to the court concerning the matters of fact committed to their trial and examination; it makes no precedent, and settles nothing but the present controversy to which it relates. It is the decision made by the jury and reported to the court, and as such it is an elemental entity which cannot be divided by the judge.

verification. The affidavit of a party annexed to his pleadings which states that the pleading is true of his own knowledge except as to matters which are therein stated on his information or belief, and as to those matters, that he believes it to be true. A sworn statement of the truth of the facts stated in the instrument verified.

versus. Against. Versus, vs., and v. have become ingrafted upon the English language; their meaning is as well understood and their use quite as appropriate as the word "against" could be.

vest. To give an immediate fixed right of present or future enjoyment.

void. That which is entirely null. A void act is one which is not binding on either party, and which is not susceptible of ratification.

voidable. Capable of being made void; not utterly null, but annullable, and hence that may be either voided or confirmed.

waive. To throw away; to relinquish voluntarily, as a right which one may enforce, if he chooses.

waiver. The intentional relinquishment of a known right. It is a voluntary act and implies an election by the party to dispense with something of value, or to forego some advantage which he might at his option have demanded and insisted on.

warrant. An order authorizing a payment of money by another person to a third person. Also an option to purchase a security. As a verb, the word means to defend; to guarantee; to enter into an obligation of warranty.

warrant of arrest. A legal process issued by competent authority, usually directed to regular officers of the law, but occasionally issued to private persons named in it, directing the arrest of a person or persons upon grounds stated therein.

warranty. In the sale of a commodity, an undertaking by the seller to answer for the defects therein is construed as a warranty. In a contract of insurance, as a general rule, any statement or description, or any undertaking on the part of the insured on the face of the policy or in another instrument properly incorporated in the policy, which relates to the risk, is a warranty.

waste. The destruction or material alteration of any part of a tenement by a tenant for life or years, to the injury of the person entitled to the inheritance; an unlawful act or omission of duty on the part of the tenant which results in permanent injury to the inheritance; any spoil or destruction done or permitted with respect to land, houses, gardens, trees or other corporeal hereditaments, by the tenant thereof, to the prejudice of him in reversion or remainder, or, in other words to the lasting injury of the inheritance.

watered stock. Stock issued by a corporation as fully paid up, when in fact it is not fully paid up.

writ. A mandatory precept, issued by the authority and in the name of the sovereigns or the state, for the purpose of compelling the defendant to do something therein mentioned. It is issued by a court or other competent jurisdiction and is returnable to the same. It is to be under seal and tested by the proper officer and is directed to the sheriff or other officer lawfully authorized to execute the same.

zone. To designate the uses to which areas of land may be put.

Indexes

Case Index

General Index

This book has been set in 11 point, 10 point, and 9 point Times Roman, leaded 2 points. Part numbers are 24 point, part titles are 16 point, chapter numbers and titles are 18 point, all set in Helvetica Medium. The size of the type page is 30 by 47 picas.